'Magnificent. . . It is no small compliment to say that in its attention to detail, its eye for pattern, and its ear for the apposite phrase, this biography is worthy of its subject.'
Times Literary Supplement

'An impressive biography of a remarkable man. . . It deserves to be widely read.'
BBC History Magazine

'Biographies don't come better than *Nikolaus Pevsner*.'
Evening Standard, Books of the Year

'The book's very fitting scale and tirelessness are more than matched by its wit, subtlety and human understanding.'
Alan Hollinghurst, *Guardian*, Books of the Year

'A biographical masterpiece. . . Harries's book is of infinite value.'
New Statesman

'Impressive and comprehensive.'
Spectator

Also by Susie Harries (with Meirion Harries)

The Academy of St Martin in the Fields
The War Artists
Opera Today
Sheathing the Sword: the Demilitarisation of Japan 1945–53
A Pilgrim Soul: the Life and Work of Elisabeth Lutyens
Soldiers of the Sun: the Imperial Japanese Army 1868–1945
The Last Days of Innocence: America and the First World War

NIKOLAUS PEVSNER

The Life

SUSIE HARRIES

PIMLICO

Published by Pimlico 2013

2 4 6 8 10 9 7 5 3 1

First published in Great Britain in 2011 by
Chatto & Windus

Pimlico
Random House, 20 Vauxhall Bridge Road,
London SW1V 2SA

www.vintage-books.co.uk

Addresses for companies within The Random House Group Limited can be found at:
www.randomhouse.co.uk/offices.htm

The Random House Group Limited Reg. No. 954009

A CIP catalogue record for this book
is available from the British Library

ISBN 9780712668392

The Random House Group Limited supports the Forest Stewardship Council® (FSC®),
the leading international forest-certification organisation. Our books carrying the FSC label are
printed on FSC®-certified paper. FSC is the only forest-certification scheme supported by the leading
environmental organisations, including Greenpeace. Our paper procurement policy can be found
at www.randomhouse.co.uk/environment

Typeset by Palimpsest Book Production Ltd, Falkirk, Stirlingshire
Printed in Great Britain by Clays Ltd, St Ives plc

FOR M.E.H.

Contents

List of Illustrations

Roundel illustrations on part-title pages reproduced by permission of *The Buildings of England*, Yale University Press.

Acknowledgements

This biography has been over twenty years in the writing. It is far longer than either I or the publishers anticipated. Both of these facts owe a great deal to the richness of the primary source material – extraordinary and, in the beginning, unsuspected. The professional correspondence, covering half a century of an exceptionally busy life at the centre of the world of art history, is the tip of an immense iceberg. I was given exclusive access to personal letters that no one besides their original recipients had read and diaries that no one had opened except Pevsner himself – a remarkable opportunity, not likely to be repeated, but also a responsibility.

To do justice to a figure who is known but not notorious, and whose life has not been fully described before, calls for an examination in depth – appropriate for a man with an inexhaustible appetite for detail. Pevsner's career is a prism through which to view the world of art history as it developed in England in the middle of the twentieth century: his achievement can only be gauged by filling in at least some of this background. His unassuming description of himself as a 'General Practitioner' cloaks the fact that he was active and influential across a prodigiously wide spectrum. He has always had different audiences with separate interests – architecture, design, modernism, Englishness, art education, conservation, town planning, garden history. I have aimed to provide enough information to satisfy these specialist constituencies without losing sight of the general picture of the man.

Long as it is, the book could easily have been three times longer. For those looking for even more detail, there is my Pevsner website – www.pevsner.info.

This biography is not 'official', 'authorised' or 'approved', but it could never have been written without the help of Pevsner's family – Dieter and Florence Pevsner, Uta and the late Ian Hodgson, and Tom and Inge Pevsner. They gave me access to the private man through hours of honest and affecting conversation about their father, and by giving me the private papers that I did not know were there, without ever seeking to influence the use I have made of the material. They have my wholehearted thanks for their faith, generosity and encouragement, and not least for their extraordinary patience in waiting for me to finish the book.

Another person who played a key part in the writing was Rose Knowles, who pored with me over the enigmas of Pevsner's handwriting, not to mention his own personal shorthand. She provided the translations of letters and diary entries without which I could not possibly have covered the ground, and illumined Pevsner's background from her own knowledge and experience.

Several people have read the entire manuscript at different stages, some of them more than once. They all offered comments, queries, corrections, cuts and insertions which were invaluable. Emily Lane and the late Ian Sutton were the first to take on what was originally an even longer manuscript. They helped me to make it presentable: this should have been a painful process, but, in their friendly and expert hands, it was quite the reverse. From the Pevsner Guides, Bridget Cherry, Simon Bradley and Charles O'Brien all read the manuscript. Apart from providing the insiders' insight into *The Buildings of England* – and, in Bridget's case, the years of working with Pevsner – they have saved me from many mistakes. (It goes without saying that any which remain are my responsibility.) Simon Bradley also helped in the task of tightening the text and waging war on the wanton footnote. Gavin Stamp, Paul Crossley, Alan Powers and Molly Marriner read the text from different standpoints and helped in different ways but all with the same effect of cheering and encouraging me. Professor Sir Brian Harrison read long sections of the book and made shrewd and constructive suggestions. Nicholas Taylor served Pevsner once again by studying the manuscript in depth and at speed, tidying inaccuracies, supplying enlightening details and providing crucial perspective. I owe them all a great deal.

I am very grateful to the Arts Council, the Winston Churchill Memorial Trust and the Getty Research Institute, all of whom made grants towards the research expenses of the book.

I should also like to thank the staff of the various archives and libraries where the most significant collections of Pevsner material are kept: the Getty Research Institute, Los Angeles; the BBC Written Archives at Caversham; the Penguin Archive in Bristol; the archive of the *Times Literary Supplement;* the archives of the Victorian Society in Bedford Park and the London Metropolitan Archives; the Design Council archive at Brighton University; the National Archives of the UK in Kew; the archives of the Society for the Protection of Science and Learning in the Bodleian Library, Oxford; and the RIBA archives at the Victoria and Albert Museum.

The people listed below helped me in a variety of ways: with reminiscences, references and introductions; with access to research materials and guidance through the labyrinths; with the loan of books, cuttings and photographs; and with permission to quote from published or unpublished materials. Very many thanks to: the late Athalie Abraham; Mathew Aitchison; the late Camilla Bagg; Winnie Bailey; Jo Ballingal; Stephen Bayley; Peter Beacham; Mary Beagles; Geoffrey Beard; Professor Geoffrey Best; the late Ralph Beyer; Enid Bloomfield; the late Sir Hermann Bondi; Laura Boorman; David Boswell; Nikolaus Boulting; Professor Pat Boyde; Professor Charmian Brinson; Russell Burlingham; Ian Buruma; Professor John Carey; the late Freddy Charles; Mary Charles; Margaret Chester; Ian Chown; Margaret Clark; Peter Alexander Clarke; Giles Clotworthy; Jeanette Clough; Alan Crawford; Alan Crookham; the late Joseph Darracott; the late Patric Dickinson; Ellen Dreesen; the late Elsie Duncan-Jones; Dr Ian Dungavell; Dr Erdem Erten; the late Viscount Esher (Lionel Brett); Hazel Evinson and the late Denis Evinson; the late Michael Farr; Jane Fawcett; Alan Fern; the late Peter Ferriday; the late Leonie Findlay (Cohn); Adi Foksheneanu; Mary Fox; Helen Fraser; David Fraser Jenkins; Professor Gunther Gillessen; Dr Silvana Giordani; Dr Mark Girouard; Godfrey Golzen; the late Sir Ernst Gombrich; Susan Gomme (Koechlin); Professor Lionel Gossman; Tim Graham; the late Ian Grant; the late Bertschy Grigson; Caroline Grigson; Sophie Grigson; Paul Grinke; Professor Marlite Halbertsma; Michael Hall; Professor Robert Harbison; Steve Hare; Colin Harris; John Harris; Rachel Hassall; Robin Healey; Marc Heine; the late Wolfgang Herrmann; Bevis Hillier; Hugh Honour; Lady Elizabeth Horder; Peter Howell; Jack Hubbard; Alan Irvine; the late Dr Christian Adolf Isermeyer; Dame Jennifer Jenkins; Sir Simon Jenkins; Celia Joicey; Dr R. Brinley Jones; Jessica Kelly; J.M. Kent; the late Eunice Kerr (Frost); James Semple Kerr; Perilla Kinchin; Bruce Kirby; Valentin Kockel; Sophie Kullmann; Emily Lane; the late Lady Lane; the late Dr Susi Lang; the late Sir Denys Lasdun; the late Professor Peter Lasko; David Lee; Ray Leigh; David Lowenthal; Hannah Lowery; Sutherland Lyall; Candida Lycett Green; Sir Neville and Lady Marriner; the late Sir Leslie Martin; Gerda Mayer; Nick Mays; the late Colin McWilliam; the late Mary Mouat; Trilokesh Mukherjee; the late Linda and Professor Peter Murray; Michael Murray; Roger and Steve Musgrave; Gerald Nason; John Newman; the late Ian Norrie; Eric Norris; Louise North; Dr Anna Nyburg; the late Iris Omer-Cooper; Julian Orbach; Robert Organ; Diana Parikian; Steve Parnell; Michael Phipps; Michael Pick; Heinrich Israel Pollack; Jack Press; the late Rosalind Priestman; Isabel Quigly; Professor Anthony Quiney; the late Roger Radford; Colin Ransom; Reg Read; the late Sir J.M. Richards; Biddy Ridley; Elizabeth Robinson; Birgit Rohowsky;

Ruth Rosenberg; Professor Alistair Rowan; Marian Russell (Pepler); Professor Andrew Saint; Sally Salvesen; Tanya Schmoller; Tracey Schuster; the late Joan Schwitzer; Jill Seddon; Rufus Segar; Sophie Sheldrake; Charmian Shenton; Ben Smith; Alan Spain; Professor Frances Spalding; Dr Margaret Sparks; Kevin Spencer; Edith Standen; David B. Stewart; Emma Stower; Professor Neil Stratford; the late Sir John Summerson; the late Ian Sutton; Michael Taylor; the late Tom Tatham; Anne Thomas; Robert Thorne; Professor Lisa Tickner; Margaret Tims; Edward Towne; Kathleen Traini; Professor William Vaughan; Suzanne Vennix; Christopher Wade; Professor David Walker; Dr Lynne Walker; Dr Lesley Whitworth; Dan Wild; Elizabeth Williamson; Arnold Wilson; Fred Wolsey; Christopher Woodward; the late Giles Worsley; Peter Worth; the late Professor George Zarnecki.

Chatto & Windus waited a very long time for Pevsner, for which I am exceedingly grateful. I should like to thank Juliet Brooke, Parisa Ebrahimi and, most particularly, Clara Farmer for all their advice, encouragement, help and hard work in getting the job done at last. Mandy Greenfield, Myra Jones, Ilsa Yardley and Alison Worthington were the immaculate copy-editor, proof-readers and indexer. Above all, my gratitude to Penelope Hoare, who is the editor that all writers dream of having: calm, funny, sympathetic and skilful.

A full bibliography of all books, articles, reviews and broadcasts by Nikolaus Pevsner can be found on my website at www.pevsner.info

Susie Harries, London
June 2011

NIKOLAUS PEVSNER

PART ONE

LEIPZIG YOUTH

1902–1921

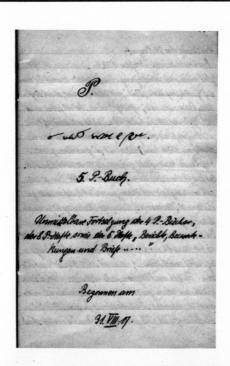

Dated at the foot of the page, 31.VIII.17: From Pevsner's *Heftchen* – the diaries
that he kept in ruled blue notebooks from the age of fourteen until a few months
before his death. He sometimes used a secret shorthand of his own devising.

CHAPTER 1

'This is how I am'

'This is how I am, this is my background,' confided Nikolaus Pevsner to his diary in November 1918. 'And this is what I love in people – everything I am not.'[1] At sixteen, he was a gangling figure in a high-waisted Norfolk jacket and serge knickerbockers, acutely conscious of bitten nails and beaky nose, an uneasy combination of intellectual arrogance and emotional misgivings, shutting himself away from his mother and older brother in his Leipzig bedroom to record the thoughts that he felt set him apart.

The family flat at Schwägrichenstrasse 11 was a comfortable setting for self-examination, twelve rooms laid out round a huge central dining room. It occupied the entire first floor of a substantial grey stone block of flats. Designed by Otto Brückwald, the architect who oversaw construction of the Bayreuth Festspielhaus, and built between 1894 and 1896, the block stood in a row of others like it on a wide street running north–south through the 'music quarter' of Leipzig, within walking distance of the Gewandhaus concert hall, ten minutes from the university and five minutes from the Johannapark. Number 11 had a painted neo-Renaissance façade with Ionic columns, and a magnificent entrance hall with a double staircase leading to the individual apartments, whose tenants were a rich sample of Leipzig's cultured middle classes, including a music publisher, the writer Elsa Asenjieff[2] and, on the ground floor, Brückwald himself. Over the entrance was inscribed the legend (an Old Testament quotation from the book of Hebrews) 'Every house is prepared by someone. All are prepared by God.'[3]

Inside the Pevsner flat, all was taste and comfort: Louis Quinze in the music room and Art Nouveau in the corner bedroom, beautiful rugs piled one on top of another, a fine majolica stove and a Renaissance-style desk from which Frau Pevsner handled the household accounts and ran her societies. Nikolaus's bedroom was in the most advanced modern style. As he wrote, he could look with some pride at the Deutsche Werkstätten bookcases, bought from Wertheim in Berlin in 1913, and at the library of art books growing on the shelves.

The young Nikolaus's diary was a small blue ruled notebook, the kind used by every German grammar-school pupil as a vocabulary book.

By the age of sixteen he was already on to the thirty-second volume in a series which he had begun two years before and which he would continue for another sixty, until he was no longer able to control the pen well enough within the narrow lines. There would be whole years when he would enter very little; and he would ultimately destroy dozens of the little blue books – his *Heftchen* – as part of a promise he had made to his wife. But the *Heftchen* that remain are an extraordinary record of a personality, revealing not only in what they say but in their tone and intensity and the prodigious determination that has gone into their writing. Astonishingly detailed and yet incomplete, both authoritative and inconsistent, pedantic and passionate, analytical and unreasonable, they anticipate by some thirty years the other remarkable series of writings by which Pevsner is most usually judged.

The boy labouring over the blue books had a clear picture of his ideal. 'I really belong in a strict civil service family,' he wrote. He longed to be ordinary, simple, disciplined, Prussian and respectable – and felt himself to fail on all counts. His family was exotic, opulent and artistic, where he wanted it to be solid and austere; and he himself was too complex, too knowing, too dark. 'The image that I have of myself in later life,' he wrote gloomily, 'is very vague and not at all good.'

Even his name was wrong, in his eyes. At birth it was not Nikolaus (a good German name) but the Russian Nikolai – invariably shortened by family and friends to 'Nika' – and not Pevsner but Pewsner, both derived from 'Posener', the label of the Posen Jew. 'The fundamental fact you must keep in mind,' he would write to his children forty years later, 'is that you are, to put it in the Nazi way, 75% Jewish.'[4]

'Leipzig,' wrote Richard Wagner, 'is a Jewish metropolis.' He was talking about the world of music, and locating Leipzig (his own birth-place) at its centre, but the city contained, indeed, one of the largest Jewish communities in Germany, embedded in a predominantly Prot-estant population. At the turn of the century it was a busy, intelligent, practical place, growing fast, with a strong tradition of concern for the rights of the working man and a thriving middle-class culture. Standing on a featureless plain in the centre of Germany, with no sizeable river or hill to distinguish it, and ringed with large manufac-turing plants, Leipzig was not exquisite like its regal Saxon neighbour Dresden, or glamorous like Berlin. But it had variety and a taste for superlatives – the biggest railway station in the world, the most modern telephone network in Europe – and a great deal of energy, physical and mental.

4

The university was long-established, founded in 1409; Goethe and Schiller had both been students there. The library was famous, and the city was the centre of the German book trade, home to hundreds of printers, binders, illustrators, engravers and publishers, with a book fair dating back to the seventeenth century. Its musical tradition was equally strong. At the start of the twentieth century the orchestra of the Leipzig Gewandhaus was enjoying a second heyday with Arthur Nikisch as its principal conductor, and the Gewandhaus itself had become a favourite rendezvous for polite society.*

The city's main strength lay in commerce. Lying at the junction of major trade routes, Leipzig had been holding trade fairs since the Middle Ages, and by the eighteenth century had become a hub of commerce in furs, cloth, tobacco, glass, porcelain, books and other goods – 'the market place of Europe'.

Fur traders in particular used the city as a base and trans-shipment centre, moving raw materials and finished pelts – ermine, mink, sable, silver fox, marten, polecat – between Russia, Poland, the Urals, America, Scandinavia and the rest of Europe. Along with Ritterstrasse, Reichsstrasse and Nikolaistrasse, the focus was the Brühl, a wide thoroughfare in the north of the old city, lined with showrooms, shops and storehouses. The street itself was used as a market place, crowded with dealers and agents talking business, negotiating and socialising, giving way only grudgingly to the traffic and the weather.

Half of this trade was transacted by Jews, the majority from Eastern Europe – Galicia, Russia, Austria and Poland. From the early nineteenth century Jewish migrants had been permitted to settle in Saxony, and had rapidly become crucial to the fur trade there, as wholesalers and retailers as well as pedlars.

Among the firms doing business on the Brühl at the turn of the century was the house of Emil Barban, a medium-sized concern that employed a quiet, uncomplicated man named Hugo Pevsner. Brühl 69, Nikolaus recalled, was nondescript, 'the staircases and the offices humble. It always smelt of furs and their preservatives against moth, and was full of trading, gossiping and arguing Jewish businessmen.' Hugo Pevsner had become a broker for the firm in 1895, and was often away, travelling to Irbit in the Urals in the winter and the great fair at Nizhni Novgorod in the summer; he thrilled his children with

---

*Arthur Nikisch (1855–1922), a charismatic Hungarian, was considered one of the founders of modern conducting. He moved to Leipzig in 1878 and became principal conductor of both the Leipzig Gewandhausorchester and the Berlin Philharmonic in 1895.

tales of sledge rides pursued by wolves and adventures on the Trans-Siberian Railway. At a time when it was not uncommon for the Russian authorities to refuse permanent passports to Russian Jews living outside Russia, Hugo did not emphasise his religion and was not, in any case, orthodox in his faith.* His roots, however, lay in Russia and in Judaism.

In 1954, Nikolaus investigated his family tree and recorded the results for his children. Hugo, he informed them, was descended from generations of learned men, probably rabbis, in Russia. Both his grandfather, Gershen Tanchum Posnen, and his father, Schmuel Schmelkin Posnjak ('all names from the ghetto'), were scholars by inclination, but they married into merchant families and were persuaded into the fur trade. Schmuel then took the name of Pewsner or Pevsner from a friend, apparently as a means of avoiding military service.†
Schmuel's son, accordingly, was born Gilel (or Hillel) Pewsner, in the town of Shklov, north-east of Minsk, on 30 January 1869. When he was about eighteen, he was sent to learn the fur trade in the offices of a customer in Leipzig, and it was at that point that he chose to adopt the more German-sounding name of Hugo.

'My father,' Nikolaus remembered, 'was a man with a heart of gold. I don't think my mother thought he was a great success at his business.'⁵ Hugo was dark, with brown skin, dark-brown eyes, dark hair, a little black moustache twisted up at the ends and very big ears. He had a naturally loud voice, but often stayed silent in company, a consequence partly of chronic lung disease that worsened with the years, partly of diffidence about his faulty German which he spoke with a heavy Russian accent. He was a warm, straightforward man, ready to play interminable board games with visiting children and never likely to tease or deliberately embarrass them, though with adults he could be tactless. His tastes were modest and his pleasures simple. Tea was a passion, drunk Russian-style from a glass in an enamelled container, black and with sugar, which had to be absolutely pure. He loved to swim: as a child he had nearly drowned in the Volga, after diving from the bank and coming up underneath a moored raft. Not a reader – again, perhaps through uncertainty in his adopted language

---

*For the problems experienced by Russian Jews living, for example, in America, see the *New York Times*, 7/7/1904, 'President's Criticism May Offend Russia: His Comments on Jewish Passport Issue Amaze Diplomats'.
†Where one brother from a family had already served, the younger brother was not required to do so. Schmuel's brother was not fit for service, which left Schmuel liable to call-up, whereas his friend Pewsner was exempt, his brother having already discharged the family duty.

– he much preferred to play cards, usually Skat (a rather lower-middle-class game, in the adolescent Nika's opinion) or bridge.

Why he married Annie Perlmann their children were never quite sure. 'Whether intellectually or emotionally, they had no common ground,' remarked Nikolaus dispassionately some sixty years later.[6] Annie was sharp, clever, intense, very attractive, with artistic leanings and intellectual ambitions, which she was rarely able to achieve at first hand. Her enthusiasms – art, poetry, music, literature, psychology and philosophy, teetotalism, pacifism, social work – meant little to Hugo, and her acquaintances intimidated him. 'When they were newly married,' wrote Nikolaus sadly, 'their friends had been rather gay and more unsophisticated, and my father would perhaps have liked better to go on with that circle.' As it was, on the rare occasions when he had Russian friends round to smoke and play cards, Annie was nowhere to be seen, and she never visited the stuffy rooms at Brühl 69. For his part, Hugo faded into the background at home when confronted with poets and university professors. 'We were all of us cruel to him,' concluded Nikolaus. 'He must have been puzzled by many things in the house.'

Annie's family, the Perlmanns, were also originally from Russia, from the Baltic provinces, though they had been settled for some time in Prussian Silesia. They were also Jewish, though in their case the process of assimilation was further advanced. (Her grandfather and his wife had indeed been 'declared dead' by their local Jewish community, so firmly had they carved their niche in Gentile society.) Annie, born in 1876, was one of the eight children of Saveli Maximovich Perlmann. Like the Pewsners, the Perlmanns combined learning with commercial acumen, but Saveli was a better scholar than trader and in 1901 his Leipzig fur business folded. Leaving Annie and the other older children to look after the younger ones, Saveli and his wife Jeanette embarked on travels that would keep them out of Germany for ten years, settling in China and then, less exotically, at 66 Solent Road, West Hampstead. ('One of those innumerable little red brick houses . . . in terraces', wrote Nikolaus later, unimpressed.)

Saveli spent most of his time in London in the British Museum, emerging at intervals to publish a variety of idiosyncratic theories. A paper in *The Zoologist* of 1908 established beyond debate – had there been any – that an animal mentioned in the books of Exodus and Ezekiel was not a zebra, but on the contrary the newly discovered okapi. In *The Jews in China* (1909), he argued that in that country Jews have developed Mongol features without any racial admixture, and he followed this with a radically new interpretation of *Hamlet*.

7

When he died, Jeanette moved back to Germany to live with her family – first her daughter Ida in Berlin, then her son Georg, and finally Annie and Hugo in Leipzig. She was a stout old lady, who did little to add to the gaiety of nations, Nikolaus remembered: 'Grandmother was more lethargic . . . Mother said if there were any crises, she went to bed.' Crises were quite common. Annie and Hugo were effectively supporting the other Perlmann children – Paula, Sonya, Else, Georg, Bernhard, Waldemar and Ida – some of whom lived with them at various times. Paula, a lively and amiable girl to whom Hugo was also much attracted, had followed her parents to China and London, where she ultimately settled. Sonya had done the same, but only after a disastrous marriage to a smart Berlin doctor who gambled, womanised and deserted her; after a spell at the Central School of Arts and Crafts in London, she came back to Leipzig. Georg became a ship's doctor on routes between India and East Africa; when his wife left him, he settled in Kabul. Else was engaged to a morphine addict, and herself died young of blood poisoning. Bernhard, another gambler, contracted venereal disease and killed himself in China.

In the midst of these dramas, Hugo's stolidity may have been a major part of his charm for Annie. Their early married life at least seems to have been happy, with some parties, a little travel to Paris and St Moritz, and a circle of undemanding friends with whom to go to the operetta, the races and the theatre. Hugo bought Annie good jewellery and she was chic; she learned to paint, to sing and to amuse herself on the piano: 'Italian opera to negro stuff and the cake walk'. But in her heart she aimed higher. From her father, Nikolaus reckoned, she had inherited 'the intelligence, the longing, and the constant interest in certain topics'. Saveli had sent her to the Latzelschen höheren Privat-töchterschule in Leipzig, where she had been given the best education available, but not for long enough to satisfy her. In later life she would go back and try to educate herself, even to take her *Abitur*, the demanding final examination that was the only gateway to university in the German educational system. But in the early years of her marriage her aspirations were unfulfilled.

Annie's pleasures, in the end, were largely vicarious. She gathered round her a salon of people distinguished in all the accomplishments she would have liked for herself – poets, philosophers, artists, academics and musicians, a mixture of Christians and liberal Jews, in what one habitué described as 'a cosmopolitan, genial atmosphere', wreathed in the smoke of Russian cigarettes. She remained one of the best-dressed women in Leipzig and drew many eyes in café society. A short story by Franz Adam Beyerlein, found among Nikolaus's papers after his death, shows all the signs of being a *roman à clef* with Annie as its (anti-)heroine.* 'Like a Feather in the Wind' documents the passion of young violinist Leopold Waltram for the 'special, refined, piquant coquetry' of the one-time singer 'Alice Pahlmann' – mature, chilly, desirable, married, in love with the glamour of art and the intellect.

This was the backdrop to Nikolaus's memories of his adolescence: parties after concerts at the Gewandhaus, when eighty people would sit down in the Pevsner flat to eat crab suppers and wait for Nikisch and the other artistes to arrive, and then the poker sessions in which Nikisch was a key player. But the children of Hugo and Annie had been born in a rather different setting.

Elsterstrasse, where Nika was born Nikolai Bernhard Leon Pewsner on 31 January 1902, lay in the Waldstrassenviertel.† This remained one of Leipzig's most strongly Jewish districts until 1939. One-fifth of all Leipzig's Jews lived there, in an area of tall tenement houses, corner shops, stables, factories and lawyers' offices, with the occasional grand merchant's house: very far from squalid, but crowded and by no means smart. When the Pewsner family moved to the Konzertviertel (the music quarter) in 1904, it was a step up the social ladder, in keeping with Annie's quest for self-improvement.

Ferdinand-Rhode-Strasse ran south from the Johannapark, just south-west of the old centre of Leipzig, intersecting Beethovenstrasse where the University Library and Gewandhaus lay. Number 41 was where Nika spent his first ten years, his main company a nursemaid and a brilliant, self-destructive brother. Heinz (born Heinrich Wolfgang) was two years older in age, but, in Nika's eyes, immeasurably more mature. In family photographs he has an alien appearance – a slight, self-possessed figure, neater and more compact than Nika, with dark hair and bright, challenging eyes. Schoolmates remembered him as a magnetic personality, far ahead of them in the sharpness of his mind and the sophistication of his attitudes. He seemed to share none of Nika's timidity or uncertainty; in their walks through the park to the canal, it was Heinz who would launch himself without looking from the parapet of the bridge into the long grass at its foot, while Nika

---

*Franz Beyerlein (1871–1949), a German lawyer, novelist and playwright, also wrote a monograph on the Leipzig Literary Society.
†Pevsner erroneously believed himself to have been born at 27 Fregestrasse, also in the Waldstrassenviertel, where the family lived for a year in 1903.

weighed the pros and cons and wavered. Heinz was a leading actor in his brother's games – but only in Nika's imagination.

Nika devised a game which he would rehearse endlessly in his brain while walking to his piano lesson. He himself was always a prisoner, enticed by a faceless enemy on to a seat at the top of a very high pole, swaying dangerously from side to side. From this predicament he would be rescued by Heinz aboard Kerminsky, a mechanical horse with astonishing powers. As the game evolved, Kerminsky grew ever more miraculous, with the ability to pass through walls and travel at 600 kph. His stomach housed a platform where the brothers could ride together, one keeping watch at the front, the other tucked up in a sleeping berth at the back. Every night, almost without fail, Nika would lie in bed and rerun the adventures of the Kerminsky riders, and then summarise their progress in a little nonsense rhyme, a mantra before sleeping:

> *Ich liege im Kerminsky Bauch*
> *Und denke 'Will, will, tun, tun.*
> *Heute war ein schöner / schlechter Tag.*
> *Ubifalaralara.'*

> I lie in Kerminsky's belly and think,
> 'Want, want, do, do.
> Today was a good / bad day.
> Ubifalaralara.'

Nika, as he reflected later, was 'a collector by nature'. With care, if not exactly fanaticism, he accumulated actors' photographs, hotel brochures, stamps and autographs, taking advantage of his mother's distinguished guests. 'To dear little Nika Pevsner', wrote Nikisch in the autograph book on 20 October 1912, accompanying his signature with the opening bars of Beethoven's Fifth Symphony and the tag '*So pocht das Schicksal an unsere Pforte*' / 'Thus fate knocks at the door'. (He would later give Nika his cigarette case as a souvenir.) Ignacy Jan Paderewski preferred a snatch of the *Andante* from his own Symphony 'Polonia', Op. 24 – 'to my little friend Nikolai Pevsner'. Nika also took advantage of a chance encounter at Bayreuth, as he told Ernst Gombrich sixty years later: 'My mother pointed out to me two people in a Biergarten whom I should ask for their autographs. They were Isadora Duncan and Melchior Lechter.'*

---

*Isadora Duncan (1877–1927), the American dancer. Melchior Lechter (1865–1937), a Westphalian artist and designer best known for his work with glass.

He constructed elaborate landscapes for his train set and collection of cars, and devised dialogues for a pair of hand puppets – Neffe Adolf and Affe Nedolf (Nephew Adolf and Nedolf the Chimp). By the age of seven he was writing full-scale dramas for adult humans. The first, 'Danton's Death', 'had a childish, disjointed plot, verses dictated by the rhyme, and not a single more profound thought', as he later commented severely. A few scenes from 'Macdonald' (completed in 1912, when he was ten) attained greater depth, but were still guilty of 'totally unmotivated characters. None had ever heard the word "psychology".' Each visit to the theatre produced a corresponding opus – 'Coriolan', 'The Shrew', 'Gottfried vom Bledow'. 'Scipio Tiberius' was a political thriller in iambic verse; Nika originally set it in the Republican era in Rome and it was very moral, but with the onset of adolescence he lowered the tone to make room for lurid Imperial detail and the eventual triumph of evil. Under the sway of Conan Doyle, he produced a clutch of detective stories and a novel that reached 200 pages without ever finding a denouement. He was also inspired to produce a short piece in the style of Thomas Mann: 'a testimony to my admiration for the author . . . but quite worthless'.

In the 'Prince Game' he showed altogether more mastery. From a small-scale fantasy he developed a complete geography of countries and continents, with their mountain ranges, rivers, cities and inland seas. His power base was a capital of eight million people, whose way of life grew progressively more organised. Not content with drafting constitutions, laws, brochures for all the principal institutions and prospectuses for major companies, he composed a body of historical writing to give his princedom an ancestry, and regulated its daily workings with railway timetables. He could walk through its streets in his mind. Every building had a floor plan and elevation, with a written description attached; the plan of the whole city unrolled to five and a half metres. For seven years, from the age of seven to fourteen, he spent much of his time dispensing stern but fair rule, with the occasional lapse into bloody excess on bad days.

Naïve in some ways, he was thoroughly precocious in others. 'I was in the nursery,' he remembered, 'and Muo [his name for his mother] had Professor Spranger to tea. She asked me what I was reading, and I said "Goethe für Jungens / Goethe for Young People". I am still ashamed of this story.' Initially, Nika was educated largely at home by tutors – a Russian governess, briefly, a series of French teachers, and one Dr Kohn, with a large black beard and a habit of dropping asleep in mid-sentence, who came in to give the two boys lessons in reading in Hebrew. Later he went to the Höhere

Bürgerschule (middle school) round the corner from Ferdinand-Rhode-Strasse. He was, in his own words, something of a boaster as a child. 'I did quite well, but when the teacher said to me that I could do better (I must have been ten), I said: "Yes, I would indeed do better in the Gymnasium [upper school] . . . because there'd be some point in the work there."' He was interested in underlying patterns and fundamental principles, in how things worked and fitted together, and at twelve he briefly cherished an ambition to be a geologist or palae-ontologist.

All through these early years Nika's material needs, and many of his emotional ones, were met by his nurse Anna Lucke, a barber's daughter, calm and cheerful. Anna cared for the boys as babies, fed them, dressed them in their heavy dark-blue sailor suits and *Ringel-socken* (long socks with coloured bands at the top), took them for long, dull walks in the park, and up the escalator in Polich's department store, opposite the Deutsche Bank, to the refreshment room on the top floor for a *Mohrenkopf* or Moor's Head, a type of chocolate éclair.

Anna ordered their daily lives, and came with them on holidays. As children they went most often to spa towns in the mountains of Germany and Austria, such as Bad Reichenhall south of Salzburg. But Nika also remembered an early visit to the Vierwaldstätter See (Lake Lucerne), where he was taken to a performance of Schiller's *William Tell* in the memorial theatre and had to be removed, frightened to tears by the ferocity of the actor playing the Friar. He spent much of another family holiday wandering on the banks of the River Nahe, fascinated by nearby saltworks with a high wall of twigs, down which the salt water trickled sluggishly and evaporated in the sun. During a trip to Bayreuth, he divided his time between trying to identify Wagnerian wave motifs played to him on the piano and marshalling his car collection, less uplifting but more fun. In 1913, the summer he was eleven, he went to visit his maternal grandparents in England, in the 'little red brick terrace house' at 66 Solent Road. He brought away with him a memory of having been deeply impressed by nineteenth-century kitsch in the Tate Gallery, but more significantly by his first experience of the lift in Hampstead Underground station.

Anna Lucke was a constant, reassuring presence. She provided support, amusement and the kind of warmth and responsiveness that the two boys sought in vain from their mother. When they were both still small, Annie Pevsner had begun to suffer from depression, and around the end of 1908 she had a bad nervous breakdown, 'a kind of emotional indisposition with a deep melancholy . . . caused perhaps by lack of occupation adequate to her intellectual capabilities, perhaps by dissatisfaction in other ways'. Nika remembered finding, tucked between two bookcases, a book on sexual frigidity, which would have provided a convenient explanation for Annie's unhappiness, but he always suspected that the real cause was a chronically anxious temperament and frustrated ambition.

Annie turned in her distress to a Swiss psychiatrist, Auguste Forel, author of *Die Sexuelle Frage (Sexual Problems)*, fanatical teetotaller, socialist and authority on the behaviour of the ant. She visited him at his clinic in the village of Yvorne next to Aigle, in the wine area at the eastern end of Lake Geneva. So dependent did she become on him that she persuaded Hugo to let her buy a cottage near Forel's house, 'La Fourmilière', and took the children with her on holiday visits. Nika remembered Yvorne with a mixture of fear and fascination: 'The whole cure was wrapped in secrecy . . . The room, the techniques of suggestion and hypnosis – we had no way of knowing about them.' Hugo rarely, if ever, accompanied his wife.

Annie was there in January 1910, when Forel was visited by 'a mad young painter'. Oskar Kokoschka had been brought to Switzerland by the Moravian architect Adolf Loos, whose plan was for him to paint portraits of titled consumptives and other wealthy individuals seeking cures in Swiss clinics. Kokoschka arrived at Yvorne with a glowing letter of introduction, but Forel was not enthusiastic, and agreed to sit for him only on condition that he be allowed to carry on working. Every evening he would carefully weigh out the nuts and apple peel that were his staple diet and eat them before taking up his pose.

Forel liked Annie's earnest young son, and named an ant after him;* but from Nika's point of view, the psychiatrist was horribly threatening. At Annie's instigation, Forel informed the beloved nursemaid Anna Lucke that she was too emotionally tied to the boys and should distance herself. Anna regarded Forel 'as the devil, bent as he was on destroying what was her real life', and for a time there was a danger that she would leave. It was the only serious threat to Nika's happiness in those early days, and caused him great misery.

---

*Stephen Games, *Pevsner: The Early Life: Germany and Art* (Continuum, 2010), p.28, records the ant's full title as *Crematogaster distans r. Pevsnerae*, a Venezuelan species with a head 'as long as it is broad'.

But for Annie Pevsner, Forel offered a new life. Firing her with some of his own enthusiasms, he steered her in the direction of social work and a means of reinventing herself. By 1912 Annie was running a teetotal restaurant in Leipzig. Every Christmas Eve, before the present-giving ceremony, the family would eat there together – a full meal for no more than seventy pfennigs. She discovered unsuspected administrative skills and an aptitude for business. With her confidence bolstered, Annie extended her social circle to include academics. Always a reader of philosophy, she now embarked on a translation of Jean-Marie Guyau's treatise on English utilitarian ethics, published in Leipzig in 1914.

Annie would never be free of her anxieties, and in 1913 the firm of Emil Barban suffered some kind of financial crisis. Nika remembered being woken up by Heinz in a state of high excitement: 'He was very upset. We would have to be errand boys.' But somehow the immediate threat receded, and by this time the Pevsner family had moved into the elegant flat on Schwägrichenstrasse. Annie's salon was developing. Gone were 'the negro stuff and the cake walk', the days at the races and the frivolous outings. Annie had no interest in other people's money or titles, but she was deeply impressed by the aristocracy of intellect and talent, and now her friends were mostly drawn from the artists and academics who populated the 'Konzertviertel'. Writers came to Annie's drawing room to read their latest work. The poet Theodor Däubler stayed on for 'weeks if not months, rather to our despair'. Musicians called in after concerts; there were rumours of affairs for Annie, perhaps even one with Nikisch himself. She built up an excellent library, bought some fine prints by Rembrandt and Claude Lorrain, and developed an informed interest in Expressionist painting.

These were tastes she passed on to her children. She was lavish with books and prints, music lessons, visits to the theatre. 'Extremely opulent presents at Christmas and birthdays – that is how I built my library,' Nikolaus remembered, though he bitterly resented her efforts to make him arrange his books according to subject rather than size: 'I wept.' Annie and Hugo had a box at the Gewandhaus, looking sideways over the orchestra. Nika, however, took himself to task in a *Heftchen* entry in 1918, writing loftily and in the third person of his younger self: 'When P[evsner] was eleven or twelve and went to the Gewandhaus, his whole reaction was a fake. He had to fight back the yawns, and counted the lamps and bulbs and the organ pipes in the hall.' But a holiday encounter with an automatic piano fired him with the urge to take lessons. Annie found him a teacher, Lis Knauth, a woman in her twenties who would become one of the family's staunchest friends. Nika found her inspiring and, for two or three years at least, strove mightily: 'I used to practise on the grand piano – fervently, for two hours on end, and in a roaring fury, because I was so totally devoid of talent . . . No rhythm, no singing voice, no anything.' Lis's lessons did leave him with a genuine love of music as a listener; he was soon finding both pleasure and comfort in concerts. 'When P hears a symphony he knows very well . . . it gives him more intense pleasure than anything else in the world.' But his own performances were never anything but a torment to the whole household. Annie, he noted, bore the cacophony and the accompanying shrieks and curses with great patience.

Much later in his life Nikolaus would be able to see and admit how much he owed to his mother's encouragement. But at the time there was nothing about his upbringing that he liked. With the help of several servants, whom she controlled strictly, Annie must have been quite competent in looking after her home and her children in the practical sense. One of the most curious features of the *Heftchen* is the almost complete absence of detail about the First World War. 'I didn't notice the war years much,' wrote Nikolaus later, testimony to the smooth running of a household cushioned by money from many hardships.

His father was away from home for much of the war. Hugo's position was precarious: although he had long been seeking naturalisation as a German citizen, he remained a Russian national. He had made his first application for citizenship in 1896, and had been rejected. He waited sixteen years and then applied again in 1912, this time for both his sons as well. 'The applicant is one of the best renowned tradesmen of the Bruehl in Leipzig and has the lively desire to belong completely to the municipality . . . Particularly he would like to mediate to his two sons an affiliation to Germany, in which he, his wife and children have completely immersed.' He was rejected once more in April 1913 on the grounds that his petition was not particularly pressing. This time Hugo was not prepared to submit so tamely. There was, in fact, a degree of urgency in his application on behalf of the boys, which was to ensure that, if war came, they would be eligible as German citizens for call-up into the Saxon armed forces rather than the Russian army. He complained to the Saxon Minister of the Interior and applied again, with a list of the works of art he had given to Leipzig's Grassi Museum, a letter of recommendation from the charitable foundation where his wife did social work, and a testimonial from a Lutheran prison chaplain.[7]

The machinery for naturalisation was set in motion. But when Germany declared war on Russia on 1 August 1914, Hugo was still a Russian citizen, and was actually in Russia on a buying trip. With irregularities in his passport, from the Russian point of view, he was now obliged to keep moving, unable to find out whether his citizenship had come through (it had arrived, in fact, on 7 August) and, if not, what the implications were. By Christmas he was in Haparanda, a small coastal town on the border between Finland and Sweden, and he appears to have spent most of the rest of the war in Stockholm, working for a Scandinavian fur company and struggling to save his own business. He was effectively stateless, and his movements were mysterious even to his family; Nikolaus noted later, 'Once when he came [home] he was arrested, but released with many apologies.'

In Hugo's absence, Annie had to make all the decisions for the household as best she could. 'How she coped, what she thought about it, remains mysterious.' She discussed very little of her life with her sons and, in Nika's view, involved herself too little in theirs, beyond their material needs. As he grew older, he longed for a confidante and a guide and got instead a detached observer. 'What should an education be like – if one assumes that mine was wrong?' he wrote at sixteen. 'With a little more interest in educating me, Muo could have made something quite different out of me. Educated in a more circumspect way, I could still be a happy child.'

Her crime, as he saw it, was to have brought him – or got others to bring him – too far, too fast. 'My ideal education would try to preserve childhood as long as possible . . . a prolonged childhood, without reading, without drama' (and here he cited Rousseau's dictum from *Émile*, that no child should be given a book until he is sixteen). Instead, Annie had treated him 'as a kind of *wunderkind*', handing him over to an accelerated education which placed all its stress on the intensive acquisition of knowledge and none on the maturing of personality. Had the term 'emotional literacy' been invented, Nika would undoubtedly have used it to describe what he had been denied. He felt that, left to their mother's sole care, both he and Heinz had endured 'the same kind of education and early blossoming, then a coldness, and a particular attitude to women'.

Sixteen is a censorious age and Nika's reflections on his education might have been different had he written them ten years later. Certainly one would not guess at his feelings about his education from his school reports. In 1912 he had started as a pupil at the prestigious

Thomasschule, a distinguished example of the *Gymnasium* type of secondary school for which Saxony and Prussia were particularly famous. The *Gymnasium* was comparable in structure with the English grammar school, but it had a remarkably thoroughgoing curriculum, which was both broad and deep, ranging over classics and moderns alike, embracing new scientific discoveries alongside religion and philosophy. It aimed at producing what Germans call *Bildung*, a cultivation which was both intellectual and moral, and a mark of the highest respectability.

Bildung was rooted in a vision of learning as 'personal self-fulfilment through interpretative interaction with venerated texts', and its acquisition was as much a process of character formation as an accumulation of knowledge.[8] *Bildung* encompassed an individual view of the world – *Weltanschauung* – and it was developed through diligent use of personal insight and sharp critical faculties. An education of this sort, in the historian Michael Ignatieff's phrase, 'laid down a layer of cultural and artistic references' that English contemporaries would have found startling.[9] The works of Strindberg, Daudet, Cicero, Dickens, Cervantes and Shakespeare, not to mention Forel's *Ants of South America*, sat on Nika's bookcase in Schwägrichenstrasse alongside Schiller, Goethe, the score of Weber's *Der Freischütz* and Georg Dehio's *Handbook of German Architectural Monuments*.

Nika excelled at German, Latin, Greek, French, mathematics and history, and acquitted himself more than adequately in English and geography. His conduct was 'satisfactory in every way'. Only in physics was his grade simply 'Good', and he did at one point sign up for remedial gymnastics. By the end of his school career he was 'Primus', top of his year. But the price was high. The Thomasschule at this time was run by Franz Emil Jungmann, Rector since 1881. Jungmann liked to say that he conducted himself as a teacher in accordance with four conjugations – '*amo-amare*', to love; '*doceo-docere*', to teach, or to learn; '*rego-regere*', to rule; '*punio-punire*', to punish. Writer and poet Stefan Zweig, some twenty years older than Nika, wrote with venom about the *Gymnasium* education. 'We were constantly filled with a feeling of inadequacy,' he complained. 'No teacher asked us even once what we personally wished to learn, and that encouraging stimulus, for which every young person secretly longs, was totally lacking . . . We can look into the records of the psycho-analysts to see how many "inferiority complexes" this absurd method of teaching brought about.'[10] At one point in his mid-teens, Nika remembered, 'I felt an almost hysterical anxiety about school. I remember soaking my feet in cold water at night and leaving them to dry in bed, simply because

I wanted to get ill and be allowed to miss school . . . Few people can have suffered as much from school as I did.'

Looking back from the lofty heights of nineteen, he castigated his pubescent self. 'P was lazy, stayed in bed till lunchtime, vacillated in his tastes, only finished one of the plays he had sketched out, didn't know the meaning of work, had no willpower, no idea of his future.' 'Fond of warmth, sitting by the stove, hot water bottles.' He read large numbers of novels, inclining towards gloomy Scandinavian sagas of mental and spiritual anguish, and took some interest in the genre of the *Entwicklungsroman*, the sensitive and detailed account (usually heavily autobiographical) of a young man's emotional coming-of-age.

He identified especially closely with Thomas Mann's novella *Tonio Kröger*. Published in 1903, it both laments and celebrates the isolation of the artist and the pleasures and pains of unrequited love. Tonio – dark, sophisticated, burdened with knowledge and the creative temperament – is infatuated with the fair, the naïve, the popular, the straightforward. In his hearty, philistine schoolfriend Hans Hansen, and the blonde, artless Ingeborg Holm, he sees an openness to simple delight that he can never share. These people are *harmlos*, 'harm-less', innocent of the awareness of the world and human nature which is so damaging to any chance of contentment. He feels himself both superior and hopelessly worse off. 'To feel stirring within you the wonderful and melancholy play of strange forces and to be aware that those others you yearn for are blithely inaccessible to all that moves you – what a pain is this.' Moving south in search of warmth and light and sensual pleasure, then north again for the reassurance of bourgeois solidity and the values of the mind, Tonio finds himself at home nowhere. Standing on the verandah of a Danish seaside hotel, a perpetual outsider, peering from the darkness into a lighted room, he sees another pair of 'belongers' – blond, blue-eyed, radiant with banal happiness, the reincarnation of Hans and Inge. 'To be like you! To begin again, to grow up . . . simple and normal and cheerful . . . to live free from the curse of knowledge and the torment of creation . . .'

Tonio Kröger resonated with Nika as with many another German adolescent of the time. Already he was beginning to hope that he too might have the gifts and temperament of an artist. He may also have been reacting to the homosexual undertones in the story. As a schoolboy, Mann had written love poems to a schoolfriend, Armin Martens, who was at least in part the model for Hans Hansen.

Nika had had one or two vaguely homosexual brushes with schoolfriends, rather in a spirit of enquiry. He had also sought such heterosexual titillation as he could glean from nude statuary and his mother's volumes of Krafft-Ebing. But his views on girls were embryonic, idealised and not a little priggish. Heinz seemed immeasurably more worldly. He had lost his virginity when barely seventeen, and now added constantly to a string of sexual conquests. 'He isn't at all attracted by "nice" young ladies – he feels much more at home with actresses.' Nika attributed his brother's tastes to a fundamental heartlessness, inherited from Annie. 'When one discovers that a brother who is not yet nineteen has already had six affairs and three violent passions [in eighteen months] . . . this is a person who doesn't know love . . . Not a word about tenderness.' There is a note of envy in Nika's voice.

CHAPTER 2

'A talent for misery'

The winter of 1916–17 was extraordinarily hard, with temperatures in February 1917 of –24°C. Many families like the Pevsners were protected by their wealth from the hardships that earned this the name of 'the turnip winter', when turnips formed the staple diet of the poor, but no one could escape the cold. A tightening of the Allied blockade created shortages of food and fuel. Ersatz substitutes could be found for many foodstuffs, but, as the freeze stretched into months, the demands on fuel for civilian heating became greater than the over-strained economy could bear. Schools were ordered to close their doors, and pupils were sent away to shiver at home.

The pupils of the Thomasschule mostly headed for the parks, where all the ponds were frozen and skating was in full swing. Nika went with them, more for the company than for the activity itself, being, in his own words, 'thin and long and bad at sports'. He cut an unimpressive figure, according to his future sister-in-law. 'We teased him terribly, as he skated very badly. He was completely unathletic, had disastrously long monkey arms which he flailed around . . . and a white turtleneck jumper, which we hated.' Nervous and self-conscious, he felt every wounding remark keenly, and found it something of a relief when at last the ice began to thaw. Soon it was no longer safe to skate, but the schools remained closed, and he was pleased to be invited to the house of a younger boy with whom he had formed a tentative friendship.

Dieter Kurlbaum was twelve, an open, friendly child who lived not far from the Pevsners with his parents and two sisters – one older, one younger – in the bottom two floors of a solid, sprawling house on Sebastian-Bach-Strasse, less smart than the flat in Schwägrichenstrasse, but with an air of comfortable, intelligent respectability about it. It was the older sister who had already caught Nika's eye on the ice. Carola Kurlbaum, always known as 'Lola', was fourteen when they first met in January 1917, and seemed even younger. She was a tiny, vital figure with long hair streaming childishly over her shoulders, and Nika found her impulsiveness and candour irresistible. Here was *die Harmlose* embodied.

Within weeks he was writing passionate poetry in her honour, no less affecting for being very bad. 'In praise of ApoLLO' (thoughtfully annotated in the margin 'A-L-L-O – <u>LOLA</u>', lest the reader miss the point) was an ode in the style of Friedrich Hölderlin, labouring to convey the combination of intellectual, spiritual and physical beauty that Lola, like her Olympian anagram, possessed:

> Let me see her whose name strikes sound from you, whose name
>   is yours . . .
> O the stockings that embrace the bare slimness of her leg!
> Let my glances brush her brown-blonde hair, my hand caress her
>   white feet . . .
> Show her to me with her school bag under the trees
> Or with her satchel on her back in the corridor of the train.

Her profile enchanted him, 'this rather cheeky, curious outline which mocks any classical feature, the brownish colour of her skin, the soft lines of her face, the curve of her cheek', and her combination of naïvety, honesty and vivacity – qualities he felt, at the advanced age of fifteen, he had already lost or had never had.

Happiness, Thomas Mann once wrote, lay not in being loved, but in loving and in snatching fugitive glimpses of the object of one's love. Living so near, Nika could count on random sightings; he often saw Lola coming home from school, dashing along like a child, with her head down, sometimes even bowling a hoop, and there were occasional meetings with Dieter. But he found he could not leave these encounters to chance. In April he made himself a small sketch map of the streets between her house and his, and carefully marked on it the routes she was most likely to take. He made detours on his own way to school, and paced the streets around Sebastian-Bach-Strasse, finding pretexts for waiting on strategic corners, braving the mockery of rude street children who saw through the feigned casualness and guessed precisely what he was doing.

These brief, painful glimpses were enough to fuel his infatuation, and by May he was beginning to feel he was making some headway with Lola. Some years later he came upon a passage in Arnold Zweig's novel *Aufzeichnungen über eine Familie Klopfer* (*Notes on the Klopfer Family*) which reminded him forcefully of his feelings. 'You stood at a distance, adored her, and trembled lest she see you. You behaved as if you were enjoying the pain. You deceived everyone – but never yourself . . . She preferred the blond, the bright ones – and when you were with her, or on the promenade path or playing croquet, then you fell silent, rather gauche with excitement.'

'There was only one danger for you,' Zweig wrote of his hero, 'that she should ever hear about it!!' It was 20 May 1917 – a day ever afterwards ringed with black circles and exclamation marks in the *Heftchen* – when disaster struck for Nika. A schoolfriend, either out of malice or simple human interest, told Lola that Pevsner loved her. 'It embarrassed her immensely, she showed [her embarrassment] to me, I gave up all hope at once and disappeared from their circle in great misery.'

He could not, of course, disappear very far, but the patrolling of streets came to an end, and he tracked her only in his thoughts. As the weeks passed he even began to find a kind of satisfaction and pride in his own anguish, as a mark of character. 'He noticed with pleasure that inwardly he was excited,' he wrote at the start of an unfinished novella some time later. 'His own heartbeat pleased him, powered by anticipation, hope, even fear . . . He loved these patent indications of his own feeling.' Suffering, he reflected sagely, or 'the echo of suffering', played a part in happiness.

He certainly had no intention of relinquishing his love for Lola. It was, at the very least, an excellent subject for the *Heftchen*, which over the next two years stretched to remarkable length and minute detail, two or more long entries a day, with whole volumes covering no more than a single week. 'The intimacy is at an end, but the analysis is not.' Some of the passages are carefully worked, as consciously 'poetic' as the Apollonian ode:

February 14, 1918. P goes to the Gewandhaus; he dresses up rather more *à la bohème* . . . He brings his score, takes his seat . . . He waits for the beginning of *Leonora III*, hears the first notes, glances for a moment to his left and, while the music swells, catches sight of a shadowed brow with a lock of dark hair falling over it. A violent shock runs through him – Lola! Lola! . . . His heart pounds throughout the overture, he listens with every sense keyed up. He has few conscious thoughts – only that she hasn't seen him yet . . . How can he contrive it? . . . During the Gluck, quite charming, he sits leaning forward slightly to see her, especially her hair, which has been dressed very carefully for the evening, gleaming with a water wave, against the light it looks almost black . . . Her dress, the steel-blue silk with the thin white bands of lace at neck and elbow . . . He sees the bow in her hair and the wide fall of ribbon, and her lovely forearms and the little hand with which she tries to tidy her hair . . . The second half . . . While Brahms comes to a grandiose conclusion, he works out how he can talk to her and what he can say . . . Lola leaves the hall with her chaperone . . . Now they exchange a couple of words.

'Marvellous', says P. 'Wonderful', says L . . . She leaves and he watches the little black hat and long nut-brown raincoat disappear . . . He goes home and gives way to his joy. It was a beautiful evening . . .

Early in March he arrived in the classroom to find 'Lola and Nikolai' chalked on the board: 'P blushes deeply and darkly and then cracks a lot of jokes.' Lola, however, was oblivious, or at least unmoved. She was far more interested in an older boy, Joachim Thiess, the son of an ear-nose-and-throat specialist with a clinic in a smart area of Leipzig. Thiess was strapping, conventional and confident, and Lola had grown close to him during the summer of 1917, while Nika was wrapped in embarrassment and paralysed by self-awareness. But at the start of 1918 Thiess had rather brutally dropped her, and in her humiliation she may have been sufficiently responsive to keep Nika's hopes alive. As she drew near to her sixteenth birthday in April 1918, he spurred himself on with reflections drawn from his reading. 'In Balzac, they often have their first night of love at this stage,' he mused optimistically. Now, he felt, was the time 'to step out from this secret love into something more open, something that can be accepted or rejected'.

But he could not bring himself to do it. 'It's a sickening, disfiguring fear, a chronic anxiety not to be pushy, which makes P reticent, self-effacing, even brusque – and unlikeable as a result.' Lola monopolised his dreams, to the point where he woke disappointed if he had dreamed of anything else. He met her, in his sleep, in forests, city streets, hotel corridors, lifts, railway carriages and trams, schoolrooms, the Gewand-haus, on river banks, skating, cycling, swimming, walking down endless parallel paths two metres apart. But he hung back from declaring his feelings, and as the summer holidays approached, he found himself doubting their sincerity. With so little to nourish it, his interest in romantic love was faltering and being overtaken, at least temporarily, by a growing interest in sex.

'Inexperienced but perturbed' was how Nika later summed up his attitude at sixteen. His information was now derived from the graffiti in public lavatories, Boccaccio's *Decameron,* and holiday conversations with Nikisch's son Mitya, a fund of obscene jokes.* He had been briefed on the theory and practice of masturbation by a solemn and well-meaning schoolfriend, and had given passing thought to the possibility

---

*Mitya Nikisch (1899–1936) trained as a classical pianist and performed as a soloist under Furtwängler and Henry Wood. However, he was best known as the leader of a successful jazz band during the Weimar Republic; after it was disbanded as a result of the Nazi ascendancy, he committed suicide in Venice in 1936.

that he might be homosexual, but he had not been much troubled by lust for the opposite sex; part of Lola's attraction for him lay precisely in her innocence.

Then in August 1918 he accompanied his mother to a rural health resort, where she was undergoing treatment for her nerves. 'Thelma Q' was the niece of another patient, 'Fräulein W'. Thelma was well-bred and reasonably attractive – 'a bit plump', Nika noted, with features that were pretty, 'if not exactly animated' – and he put up little resistance to Fräulein W's arch manoeuvrings to throw the young people together. On the second evening she left them sitting together on a sofa and embarked on a fictitious errand: 'Anyone who is still sitting there nicely when she comes back will get a kiss, but they must already have *given* one – and hand kisses don't count . . .' Dutifully they set to, propelled largely by bravado. By the following evening, when Fräulein W's charade was repeated, Nika was warming to his task. At the same time, he was aware of a certain intellectual detachment from the job in hand: 'He is always a little cooler than he had expected . . . Although she responds very readily to his kisses, somehow he finds a lot about her off-putting – the noises her stomach makes.' He worried, too, about his hands being clammy, but 'is rather impressed with his performance . . . Surely it's rare for it to go so well first time?'

As the end of the holiday approached, Nika invited Thelma to join an overnight excursion. He booked her a separate room at the hotel, but made careful preparations in his own, setting up a little lamp, arranging the divan, ordering a bottle of wine with two glasses. He became too pressing. 'P calms her down . . . He could probably have had her, but . . . he doesn't want to, he is afraid of the consequences. And of course he fears failing, fears he might do it wrong, fears such a lot . . . He goes away, wondering what Heinz would have done.'

Boredom was threatening now. Nika was losing interest in 'repeat performances' on the sofa – 'a bit monotonous' – and Thelma's laugh was beginning to grate. He predicted with some gloom the kind of letters she would write him once they had parted, and one evening went to bed without the usual fond farewells. The following morning Fräulein W informed him reproachfully that she had found Thelma sobbing on the doorstep in her nightdress. 'P is really rather proud of this.' Nika had already pigeonholed the encounter as an educational experience, and his dominant emotions on parting were relief and a certain complacency.*

---

*The relationship, as he had anticipated, did not survive separation; when he met Thelma again the following year at the same resort, he noted only, 'She has got fatter', and neither of them mentioned the previous summer.

He was, however, aware that he had not behaved well, and when he heard that Lola had also been heavily embroiled with Thiess, he was inclined to view it as a punishment. Lola saw Nika, a friend informed him, as someone who was 'very clever but didn't understand things', and her relationship with the less-complicated Thiess had gone further than he had ever suspected. 'Thiess has defiled Lola's pure lips with his kisses. Although it is quite normal and not particularly surprising in a girl of her age, P is appalled.' Conscious of how he had used Thelma, he tortured himself with the thought that Lola was being used in the same way.

He made a manful attempt to rise above his jealousy and shame, striving to fix his thoughts on Tolstoy, Christian ethics, paintings, the theatre, the cut and thrust of intellectual debate, but for all his rationalising, the next year was a period of miserable and unproductive introspection. All around him, in the months leading up to and immediately following the Armistice, adults were struggling to come to terms with the despair and disillusion of military defeat and its chaotic social consequences. Nika's battles were all with himself. He peered long and hard at his own image and despised it.

'Thin legs, flat feet,' he wrote. 'Thin miserable arms – hands white, red to blue, bitten nails; a tendency to get spots on arms and wrists – intolerable – and the veins protrude. Ears – dirty, with hair. Hair – long, curly, greasy, with dandruff. Skin – bad, with spots and freckles. Face – seriously flawed: irregular teeth and an impossible nose – big, crooked, Jewish . . . He rarely washes, and then only cursorily.' His figure was passable as long as he was standing still; he was over six foot now, with a high waist, and carried his belted, buckled tweed suits with a certain air. But in motion he was clumsy and, in his own eyes, ridiculous. Once, on his way home from school, he was confronted by a group of boys who jeered and called him stuck-up. To demonstrate his mateyness, he moved forward to jump the wire fence between them. 'Desperate to cut a dash, he falls awkwardly, rolling over and over, covered with dirt. Gets up and tries to talk coolly, but it is gibberish. By the time he has recovered himself, they have all gone. P walks home calmly enough, but inside he is seething. He rips papers to bits, wants to shoot himself.' 'This miserable specimen,' he raged to the *Heftchen*, 'intellectually very gifted – can he ever be a lover, can he ever sire children? Does everybody else know what it's like to be loved except me?'

One of the *Harmlose*, of course, would have cleared the fence with ease, but Nika was becoming ever more acutely aware of the contrast between his ideal and his actual persona. It was his brother, with his taste for the *esprit* of the French, the passion of the Southerner, who should have been given the flamboyant name of Nikolai. Nika himself would have been better suited to the solid German 'Heinz', a more fitting label for a colder Nordic temperament. Repressed, solitary, cautious, incapable of spontaneity – he sketched the darkest possible picture of himself. 'Because he is always calculating the consequences, P never really enjoys the present . . . I have a talent for misery.'

Meanwhile, he had taken the first tentative steps towards worldly success. In January 1918 he had had his first drink with a gang of boys from school – 'all rather loud-mouthed and crude' – and told his first dirty stories. He had even begun to brave his mother's drawing room and bohemian friends:

> Now and again P does not stalk off to bed ostentatiously. People come to play skat late into the night, and he stays up and joins the party. He gets positively witty . . . one quip after another . . . Given half a chance, P can amuse people, young ladies, wonderfully, and is popular, people even notice if he is not there. The bride of an operetta tenor – P entertains her for hours. When P's brother flirts with her, P huddles up on the sofa with both of them . . . Even Heinz admires the way in which P can say outrageous things and get away with it.

Even at the time, though, Nika could feel that badinage did not come naturally, and he scorned this cheap success. Now he vowed to put it all behind him and be truer to his own nature. He turned first, instinctively, to reading to reinforce his mood, and devised a downbeat programme of Schopenhauer, Nietzsche and Dostoevsky. Happiness, he declared, was a logical impossibility for one of his temperament. To aspire to art was to aspire to knowledge – and knowledge was misery. The only truly 'happy' life was a vegetable existence, untroubled by thought, feeling, aspiration or responsibility. In Dostoevsky's words, 'To love people as they are is quite impossible. And yet one should try . . . Hold your nose, shut your eyes . . .' 'I love Dostoevsky,' wrote Nika, 'he is pitiless, remorseless.'

His reading, he was well aware, was a vehicle for self-analysis. Dostoevsky, Mann, Strindberg, Wedekind all provided mirrors in front of which to strike attitudes. But he was never so far gone in introspection as to lose perspective on himself. 'In the theatre and at concerts . . . P considers it very impressive to get up in the middle of an act, stretch and walk out stony-faced. Likewise, he is given to showing disapproval of the performers by a gentle smile or shake of the head.' Even in his unhappiness over Lola, he could see an element of theatre. 'He paces from room to room, shakes his fists, covers his eyes with his hands or allows his arms to fall limply to his sides, runs his hands through his hair, lies stretched out, eyes closed, on the floor, lunges menacingly, talks with jutting jaw – and takes pleasure in all this, without actually wanting to look like a poseur.'

But at a time of shifting values, social disorder and political confusion, Nika's personal insecurity was real enough. 'I can't cheer myself up with my hopes for the future,' he wrote, 'because I don't have any.' Lola's uncle lived next door to Thomas Mann in Munich. Tenuous as the link was, it encouraged Nika in a fantasy of meeting, courting and marrying Mann's eldest daughter, Erika, and thus becoming an intimate of the great man.*

For a time he attempted to convince himself that salvation might lie in writing, and, in the last months of 1918, set out to mine his limited emotional experience. At the start of 'Nora', a fifteen-year-old schoolboy flings down his satchel with its dog-eared cardboard files and hurries to the park in the hope of catching sight of his love. Nora is a shadowy figure, but the circumstantial details of the lover's behaviour – setting his watch by the clock tower, tying his laces, searching his pockets for a pencil stub with which to make unnecessary notes – have all the power of direct and painful experience.

The heroine of 'Kurmusik' (written under the name of Nikolai Allo) begins to have the suspicion of a personality, albeit one straight out of Thomas Mann. *Kurmusik* is the music played in the pavilion at a spa, where invalids have come to take the cure (*Kur*). As the narrative opens, the writer is sitting in an uncomfortable deckchair on the promenade of a small spa town in Thuringia. He has come to the town to be near the girl whom he loves. As he gazes at the pine woods on the slopes above the town, he is briefly transported by the meretricious melodies, but is plagued by the suspicion that she and her brother, sitting further back in the audience, are laughing at him. Must he always be excluded, cut off from the ordinary and lovable by his own sensitivity? 'He crossed several squares, through brightly lit pavilions, to his nondescript hotel room, feeling sick and old. He could not work on his novella that evening.'

Nika applied himself to 'Kurmusik' at odd hours of the day and night over a period of six months. He was wounded, but not entirely

---

*Erika Mann was in fact a lesbian, who entered into a marriage of convenience with W.H. Auden in 1935.

surprised, when it was briskly rejected by the Berlin publisher to whom
he had sent it. He was doomed, he reflected, to be that sad phenomenon, a *Künstler ohne Talent* – a soul with the temperament of an
artist, but none of the necessary gifts – and his world-view grew
increasingly sombre. 'Die Letzte Stunde' ('The Final Hour'), begun in
September 1918, followed the stream of consciousness of a seventeen-
year-old boy in the hour leading up to the moment at which he has
resolved to shoot himself. Tormented by an unhappy love affair, he
has already made one botched attempt at drowning; now he reviews
the pros and cons of life. 'Die Letzte Stunde' is a virtual transcription
of the *Heftchen* account of Nika's developing love for Lola, with
'literary' trimmings. She becomes 'Nora' once again, and the author's
love for her grows out of a deliberate attempt to insinuate himself
into the charmed circle of the *Harmlose*. The author, Nora tells her
brother, is 'a darned clever fellow', but not at all attractive; he is
reduced to trailing her furtively in a 'sickly-sweet fever' of longing,
anxiety and shame. The hated Joachim Thiess becomes 'Jürgen Laass'
– confident, relaxed, lecherous – and Laass's casual successes with
Nora drive the writer to the verge of suicide. With the revolver in his
shaking hands, he hears the clock strike the hour – and in the nick of
time an image flashes into his mind. He remembers a girl he met on
holiday (probably not the fleshly Thelma) and recalls the happiness of
which he was capable then. 'The blue and white bathing suit, and the
tendrils of hair peeping from the bathing cap . . . the tree with her
initials . . . the joy of the Brahms C minor sonata.' He lays down the
gun, resolves to keep his love at a distance and find his fulfilment in
Die Walküre and Mozart's 'Jupiter' symphony. Weighing up the arguments for and against death, he is simply unable to reach a conclusion,
rather like the novella.

At low moments, Nika toyed with the idea of suicide outside the
confines of his novel. 'He re-enacts this little charade,' he wrote,
'whenever he feels unhappy in himself. Once he even cuts his right
wrist near the pulse point – but not *too* near.' His grim reading schedule
deepened his depression and confusion. Schopenhauer, he noted, characterised suicide as the pursuit of the greatest happiness. 'There should
be a revolver in every house,' he declared at the end of October. 'Only
now, because of the revolution, you can't buy them – and anyway I
haven't got the money. Yesterday I started a full-scale savings campaign,
to be able to buy one when I might need it more, when I have definitely decided that I am unfit to live.'

As ever, he was aware of an element of melodrama. 'A very private
comment – am I perhaps talking myself into these ideas of suicide

– convincing myself that I owe it to my *Heftchen* to do it?' But there was more to his fascination with the subject than simple adolescent attitudinising. Suicide was something real to him, something well within the bounds of his understanding. On 1 November, one of his school-mates – 'Herbert Lukas, a nice, naughty, little boy, one of the cheek-iest in the school, a *Harmlose*' – had been caught at the school noticeboard trying to rub out the record of his absences and had been threatened with relegation to the class below. Petrified by the probable reaction of his father, a wealthy factory owner, the child had not dared to go home. 'He roamed about aimlessly,' Nika recorded in his diary, 'and then towards evening, in a suburb of the town, threw himself in front of a train and was killed.'

Closer to home, Nika may have been aware of the suicide of his uncle Bernhard, and whether or not he recognised its severity, he had felt the repercussions of his mother's recurrent depression. In later life he came to feel he had inherited her predisposition; but in 1918 he could not share with her his thoughts on this or any other subject. With friends and acquaintances Annie was immediately friendly, helpful, charming; with her family she alternated between ridicule and ill-temper. 'My mother has been spreading discomfort around her for more than a year – not in public, of course . . . I think it is very sad that at such a young age I see all my parent's failings so clearly.'

Much later, Nika acknowledged that Annie was by no means entirely to blame. They were, he could already see, too alike to be comfortable together – 'He has her tendency to moodiness, an almost neurotic sensitivity, and horror of criticism' – but he made far too few allowances for her nervous state. 'I was unjust and cruel to her in those years,' he wrote after her death. She gave him books, paid for the piano lessons, filled the house with artists, writers, scholars; unquestionably she approved of the direction that his interests were taking – and yet they could not talk about it. 'The reading programme – Schopenhauer and Dostoevsky – the description of it all is in the *Heftchen*. But is there the slightest hint of any discussion of this kind of thing with Muo? I read and read and wrote and wrote and hated her.'

Annie found an outlet for her nervous energy in the social work to which Forel had introduced her: work on the rehabilitation of prisoners, on public sanitation and the recycling of rubbish, on the National Women's Service and the Women's Art Association. Hugo was still largely abroad, based in Stockholm and travelling in Europe for his

Swedish employers, simultaneously struggling to shore up his Leipzig business. Nika was absorbed in self-examination – 'a kind of piety towards oneself', his brother called it. No one in the family appeared to notice that, in its midst, Heinz was foundering.

To Nika, his brother had always appeared smooth, hard and cold, with a slightly tawdry social polish and flashes of intellectual brilliance. Heinz, he concluded, did not need friends. Although he occasionally showed a strong streak of Russian sentimentality, Heinz had inherited Annie's lack of feeling, particularly obvious in his treatment of the string of girls – women – whom he had no trouble in attracting. For Heinz's nineteenth birthday Nika wrote an ode, an alphabet of girls with names like Carli, Deli, Finny, Hansi, Kitty, Moruschka. He had been greatly tempted by Heinz's offer to take him to a nightclub, the Intime Bar, and introduce him to exotica of this kind, though in the end his nerve seems to have failed. In spite of himself, he was impressed by his brother's prowess. But the poem also betrays unease at some of the risks Heinz was taking:

> *Andrea wollt' nicht von Dir lassen,*
> *Obwohl sie bald Dir war zu viel . . .*
> *Die Ella, von semit'scher Rasse,*
> *In einem Harem passt sie gut . .*
> *Der Nora Feuer Stars nur schaffen,*
> *Du hast sie nur mit Pausen gern. . . .*
> *Frau Pewsner weiss von Deinen Sünden.*
> *Ist sie entsetzt? Ist sie gerührt?. . .*
> *Was würde wohl der Vati denken,*
> *Kennt' er Dein folgenreiches Tun? . .*
> *Wird Deine Zukunft weiter glücklich?*
> *Ich weiss natürlich nichts davon.*

> Andrea did not want to let you go,
> Although soon she was a bit much for you . . .
> Jewish Ella would suit a harem . . .
> Only stars light Nora's fire . . .
> You can only enjoy her now and then . . .
> Frau Pewsner knows all about your vices.
> Is she horrified? Or is she touched . . .
> What would Vati [Daddy] think
> About your goings-on these days – and their consequences? . . .
> Will your future [Zukunft] be happy? I have no idea.[1]

At the bottom Nika added a greeting: 'Success for evermore! Masses of money, and laughter and joy for ever – and of course no more swinish debt.' Heinz was mixing with people who had far more money than he did. He had originally intended to study history and economics, but after the financial crisis of 1913 in his father's business he had agreed that he would eventually go in with Hugo and, without much enthusiasm, had become apprenticed when he left school in the summer of 1918. Only weeks later he had been drafted into the army, despite his passionate dislike of German nationalism and professed support of the English cause. He never got to the Front, and was exposed only to the so-called 'stab in the back' – the military's betrayal, as they saw it, by the civilian authorities, which led to the humiliations of the peace.

In the months following the Armistice, disillusioned and aimless, Heinz became further and further embroiled with fast friends, drink, gambling and prostitutes. He may well have been suffering from venereal disease even before he joined the army, and a letter of May 1919 to a specialist in dermatology and urology suggests that the condition persisted.* He apparently borrowed money – a lot of money, 1,500 marks – from the urologist in May[2] and then took cash from one of his mother's hiding places. Hugo was still away, and Heinz (who, like Nika, found it difficult to talk to Annie) had no idea how he might extricate himself. With nowhere else to turn, during June 1919 he seems to have dropped hints of his despair to his brother. Almost sixty years later, making notes for an autobiography, Nikolaus still found the memory of his own reaction shaming and painful:

> Heinz talked to nobody about his troubles – a curse in our family – but I should have guessed . . . But I was blind or too young . . . He had got into bad company and took some money . . . The next thing I knew was that he had tried to drown himself. Somehow I knew where he was – Lampe Street? Grassi Street? – and went to see him. He was in bed. Did he tell me about the money? How else would I have known? Anyway, I ought to have gone to my mother to explain, and I didn't. I even dimly remember joking with him about the drowning effort. He must have felt deserted. He moved

---

*So great was public paranoia about the risk of venereal disease after demobilisation that the government had issued a decree in mid-December 1918 imposing a penalty of up to three years in prison for those who had sex while knowing themselves to be infected.

into the Park Hotel opposite the station and there shot himself [on 30 June 1919]. (The hotel still stands – I saw it the other day.) Could I have saved his life, if I had been less of a child? As it was, I must have joked and left him alone to shoot himself . . . I still hold myself at least partly responsible for his death.

His reactions at the time were more confused. Among them, to his distress, were a strong sense of relief from a presence he had often found disturbing and distasteful, and the selfish fear that he would now have to go into business to take Heinz's place. These were mixed with guilt at his own self-righteousness and lack of understanding. Heinz, he felt, had perhaps been trying to get closer to him, but he had turned his back. He had refused consciously to acknowledge the signs that something was terribly wrong – but had he been aware of them at a deeper level? How, for instance, had he come to write in *The Final Hour*, only weeks earlier, about a failed drowning that was to be the prelude to a suicide by shooting?

In the weeks after Heinz's death, Nika was left to himself. Hugo had come home from Sweden, too late. 'His coming was probably the worst of all the things in Muo's life.' Gripped by guilt as well as grief, his parents seemed to Nika to wear a mask at all times. In his harsh judgement, they seemed as much embarrassed by the circumstances of their son's dying as bereft by his loss. They refused to look at the events leading up to Heinz's death, whereas Nika found it hard to think of anything else. Had Heinz been driven to his death by 'sexual excitement and confusion'? By fear of his creditors – 'When he took his life, there was a dreadful hunt at his heels' – or terror of incurable illness? 'Did Heinz make meat of himself in uncontrollable *rage*?'

He turned once again to the idea of writing a novel as a means of finding some of the answers. 'Two Brothers', a study of their relationship, was to explore the sharp contrasts between them in outlook and aspirations, and perhaps show how they could have been reconciled.[3] It was never finished.

Nika, with his thoughts running on self-obliteration, also produced his first piece of art criticism, a short article on Van Gogh which was more an obituary for the man than an assessment of the work. Suicide for Van Gogh, he argued, was a sign of strength, not weakness, a rational and responsible decision not to outlive his capacity to produce his greatest work. It was not a view of self-destruction that Nika could sustain for long, as the reality of Heinz's death sank in: within a year he was dismissing the article as silly.

Annie could not be consoled for the loss of the son she had thought so brilliant and so promising, and Nika does not seem to have tried to draw closer to her. But Heinz's death had another, completely unexpected effect. Out of the blue, as a gesture of sympathy and comfort, came an invitation to visit the Kurlbaums: a chance to see Lola again after months of estrangement. A somewhat stilted tea party in Sebastian-Bach-Strasse – 'She is coquettish, sits on the table, waves her hands about' – was followed by an invitation to the Kurlbaums' holiday house. Suddenly Nika was being offered the easy familiarity with her, and with her family, that he had wanted for so long.

CHAPTER 3

'Castles in the air'

The holiday house stood on a terrace of vines just outside the old town of Naumburg on the River Saale. Its core was one of the vineyard towers, originally used for storing tools and equipment, with a single large room on top for shelter and the occasional overnight stay. Around this tower had been built a house in the Biedermeier style, homely and charming rather than elegant, with a delight in the minutiae of ordinary life, like a Dutch seventeenth-century interior. Downstairs the main entrance was built into the rock, with kitchen and dining room on either side. Hanging by the door was a huge tin horn, which was used to call the children in for lunch. An outside staircase led to the first floor – living room, children's bedrooms, and a wine cellar with a spiral staircase to the attic rooms above. The furniture was polished fruitwood or white lacquer, the bell pulls were mother-of-pearl with flowers on them, and the curtains were gathered with brass or tin rosettes. In front of the house was a broad terrace. Vines and fruit trees stretched down to the road, beyond which was an apple orchard and then the river. Above the house, a wide wooden staircase led upwards to the higher terraces through a tangle of cherries, gooseberries and currants. Nothing was luxurious – there was no running water, and the well water for drinking had to be lugged up seventy-six steps from the vineyard entrance – but there was no pretence, no affectation, no attempt at sophistication, and Nika revelled in it.

When he arrived at the house for the first time in September 1919, Lola was concentrating on her maths homework in the dining room. She looked up briefly, welcomed him and went on working. Her manner, in this setting, was completely natural, and for almost the first time since he had met her, certainly for the first time since the 'catastrophe' of May 1917, Nika was able to relax in her presence. They talked endlessly during his stay. Lola offered him what comfort she could for Heinz's death. He, in his turn, found himself able to console her for the misery of the unhappy liaison with Joachim Thiess and for the loss of her mother, who had died of cancer the previous summer. He had found in Lola the confidante he had so badly wanted.

He had also found a setting in which he could feel truly at home. The Kurlbaums, as Lola liked to remark in later life, were a 'good' Prussian family which could document its history back into the seventeenth century. Nika teased her for the snobbery – 'The Kurlbaums are quite ready to keep Charlemagne up their sleeves for conversations with other family-conscious folk' – but he envied her the attributes that came with the status. Lola's grandfather, Karl Dietrich Adolf Kurlbaum, came from a line of civic-minded merchants who had gradually transformed themselves into a dynasty of public servants. Karl Dietrich was an eminent lawyer, and Alfred, Lola's father, followed him into the law. However, his friends were, by his family's standards, somewhat unorthodox. Alfred, in Nika's words, 'was altogether so often and so clearly attracted by Jews that his family called him "the Jew" for fun'. His closest friend was a Jewish medical student called Max Neisser, from a family that had already been eminent in medicine for two generations and included the discoverer of the bacterium that causes gonorrhoea. Max himself would eventually be one of the most distinguished bacteriologists in Europe, an authority on public hygiene and the inventor of the Neisser stain for diagnosing and treating diphtheria.

Alfred and Max kept in touch while their careers developed in parallel. By 1897 Alfred was in practice as a lawyer in Berlin and courting a young woman named Augusta Koslowska. A year after their marriage, during Augusta's first pregnancy, she died suddenly, in the middle of a breakfast-time conversation with Alfred. Four years later, in 1901, he married Max's sister Paula, a calm, capable girl rather younger than himself. The couple set up home in Potsdam, where Alfred was now an advocate in the district court, and here, in 1902, Lola was born in a house overlooking the River Havel. In 1906 Alfred was promoted to the Supreme Court in Leipzig, a prestigious appointment at the relatively young age of thirty-eight, and he moved his family, which now included the two-year-old Dieter, to the maisonette at 7 Sebastian-Bach-Strasse.

It was a household which Nika found irresistible, with its atmosphere 'of a cultured, disciplined Prussian family of far-back-reaching traditions . . . Here there is both closeness and firmness, old-fashioned values but also happiness and consideration.' The area round Sebastian-Bach-Strasse itself seemed to Nika to proclaim these values, its leafy streets lined with houses that were less stately-smart than those of Schwägrichenstrasse, but thoroughly secure and reassuring, with their shutters and geranium-filled balconies.

Alfred had a personality to which Nika immediately responded: 'a very remarkable and a very lovable character, warm, wise, wide of interests in all directions, endowed with an exceptional memory, lively, *charmeur*, and distinctly impetuous. What added so much to his charm was a naïveté which he never lost, that is an ability to look at things and people for himself, to wonder, and to make comments regardless of what might be expected of him.'* He had served in the Great War, albeit as a rather elderly lieutenant working first in a prisoner-of-war camp and then in a telegraph office near Wittenberg. He had a very close relationship with his children; his only vices in their eyes were to repeat his funny stories, and to sing in the road when relaxing on holiday.

Alfred read widely – English novels, Roman history, music and art criticism, theology and philosophy – and wrote poetry in the Horatian metre. Meanwhile the household ran smoothly around him. Paula had been a good organiser and a devoted mother, with progressive ideas on child-rearing which involved quantities of milk, vegetables and fresh air. After Paula died, Lola, who had been rather in awe of her mother, tried to maintain the same standards and took as much responsibility as she could for Dieter, now fifteen, and Marianne, who was twelve.

Back in the Pevsner household, Hugo Pevsner was at home more often now, and Nika was made constantly aware of his father's lack of refinement. 'He is not very cultured – and there is the bad German . . . P thinks a lot of his father's human qualities, in fact he rates them more highly than his mother's intellectual distinction, but these characteristics are less obvious than the lack of polish.' Hugo snored, his jokes were often crude, he stumbled over literary names and confused his mythological references. He had a sister who looked like an anarchist, with her long black hair centre-parted and swept back into a tight bun, and she gabbled in Russian.

Meanwhile his mother continued to fill the Schwägrichenstrasse flat with people Nika decided he could no longer abide. 'The artists, Spartacist types, expressionists – I can't bear them. The intellectuals, too – fair enough, but they are too democratic and unpatriotic. Their conversation is full of opinions which are radically different from mine.' In their midst Annie cut a dashing figure of which Nika wholeheartedly disapproved. 'She is dressed too elegantly and too youthfully . . . Her high, artificial coiffure is suited to a woman of forty. [She was in fact forty-two when he wrote this.] How can she go around in little silk slippers, or smoke so much, or wear such thin stockings at her age? . . . It's a

---

*On one occasion, Nika would later remember, a client was in the middle of explaining his case when Alfred called out, 'Stop, stop – I want to act for the other side.' Ian Sutton, 'Reminiscences of Nikolaus Pevsner', unpublished memoir, 1992.

revolting sight – the skat-playing cigarette-smoking woman shouting "Schuss!"' He cast his mind back to what he remembered of the Kurlbaum household under Paula's rule. 'There's a mother who has all the qualities of a *Hausfrau*. She surely manages to get off her chaise-longue – if she even has such a thing – at some point during the day. My mother, on the other hand, spends most of her time there.' He later annotated this diary entry, 'How unreasonable and sour!', realising that Annie's languor had much to do with the state of her nerves; but at the time he felt she was letting him down.

A more serious irritant than the denier of Annie's stockings was the cast of her politics. While in London, her father Saveli had sympathised strongly with English liberalism and he had done much to shape her views. All through the war she had expressed pacifist opinions, worked for pacifist causes and supported Heinz in his anti-patriotic sentiments. 'We had "Tipperary" amongst the files of music,' Nika remembered, and he lived in dread that she would sing it in public. She and Heinz were prone to remark to the rest of the family that an English victory would be a good thing. After the revolution of 1918 she worked with Heinz for the newly founded Democratic Party. Nika had little time for her radical tendencies: 'She shows warm sympathy for communism and things like that – a bit incongruous, with her mouth full of . . . good Schnitzel.'

He attributed her wilder statements to her nerves – 'I always tell myself it is virtually a disease' – but he never failed to rise to the bait:

> She accuses the Kaiser of being solely responsible for the war . . . She says of the German people's sufferings, 'They deserve it, it doesn't matter' . . . She compares the Germans to the Conquistadores . . . Good enough reason for me to get out of this house . . . I pointed out the behaviour of the French in occupied territory, and the behaviour of the black troops [regiments from the French colonies, which had been accused during the war of widespread rape and looting]. She agreed this was bad – but said that anyway the blacks had behaved better than the Germans. She doesn't believe this rubbish, of course – but it makes any dealings with her impossible. I have to get away from her, I have *had* it.

Nika's own position by 1919 was a vague brand of conservatism stimulated largely by Thomas Mann's *Betrachtungen eines Unpolitischen (Reflections of a Non-political Man)*. Mann had been prompted early in the war to defend German militarism as the legitimate self-assertion of a nation grown too powerful to submit to a European status quo formulated at a time when Germany was weak. Germans, he argued, were driven by soul and *Kultur*, stimuli more compelling than the reason and good breeding of 'less profound peoples'. Actions rooted in German *Kultur* must override the imperatives of the world of politics.

Nika was fired to write to his hero to defend the merits of reason. *Sachlichkeit*, or objectivity, was very much part of the current German cultural climate, and to deny its significance was surely outmoded. Could Mann not write another book 'similar to *Betrachtungen*', but more even-handed in its treatment of soul and intellect? Mann took the trouble to reply to his fan in a brief but courteous note.[1] The idea that 'the identification of intellect and politics is impossible in the land of Luther and Goethe' was, he said, 'in no way antiquated or outdated'.

In fact, Nika's own beliefs, however he may have rationalised them, derived their energy more from emotion than intellect, and more from a reflexive love of country than any interest in ideology. He too now found that he despised politics as an activity and looked down upon the lack of intellectual rigour in most political manifestos. But even in his own eyes his personal philosophy did not bear much examination, being a jumble of ideas drawn largely from literature and religion, with a fine disregard for consistency.

He had the true Leipziger's concern for the working man: 'I know that war is terrible, dreadful, ghastly – but mines, child exploitation, chemical factories, the machine rooms of ships are dreadful too. I reject the sort of pacifism that combats war and yet permits the rest . . . Who worries about our tubercular workers?' At the same time he was much struck by the anti-democratic ideas put into the mouth of the Grand Inquisitor by Dostoevsky in *The Brothers Karamazov*. These he took to mean that since responsibility entailed knowledge, and knowledge meant misery, the only truly happy man was he who lacked all responsibility, political or otherwise, and left government in the hands of the few. 'Muo once told me,' he wrote later, 'that a democratic friend . . . pitied her for having such a son.'

The only constant in Nika's thinking was the kind of patriotism that stems from a desire to belong. The Kurlbaums belonged, and were Germans in the truest sense, as longtime servants of the state. They were bound even more tightly into the fabric of the nation by their religion. Alfred may have been drawn to Jews, but he was not a Jew himself. He and his children were devout Lutherans, and part of the Christian community in the area. The Pevsners, on the other hand, belonged to neither orthodox Jewish nor Gentile society.

'The non-religious Jew,' writes publisher Marion Berghahn, 'finds himself in a cultural vacuum. He is not a Jew proper any more, but purely defined as such by his enemies.'² The Hebrew lessons Nika had taken as a child had been with a view to becoming a *Bar Mitzvah*. He never completed the course and, like the rest of the family, was not a practising Jew. He was, however, acutely sensitive to signs of anti-Semitism among his schoolfriends and their parents. He remembered having gone once to a *Tanzstunde* or formal dance at the house of a friend and then never again: 'It was probably anti-Semitism – did I know?' He was certainly aware that the mother of one friend was unwilling to receive another of his classmates in her house. 'Someone got cross and said, "*Judenbengel* (Jewboy)". That's nasty . . . It's hurtful, and makes P gauche and uncertain of himself.' 'Why don't I find my own acquaintances?' he wrote miserably at eighteen. 'Because I am solitary, I abhor people impinging too much, and I fear anti-Semitism.'

In 1910, two-thirds of the Jewish population of Leipzig were *Ostjuden*, from the East, and large numbers were not yet naturalised. To Jews who had already been successfully assimilated – as bankers, lawyers, doctors, engineers, academics – these people represented a threat. 'Assimilation,' wrote the political theorist Hannah Arendt, 'is only possible if one assimilates oneself to anti-semitism.'³ The older Jewish population of Leipzig was substantially middle-class, having acquired the two distinguishing marks of the German bourgeoisie: property and *Bildung*. People who had worked hard, whose parents and grandparents had worked hard, to be inconspicuously absorbed into the community now faced a challenge. These newcomers, with whom they might be associated in the minds of Gentiles by virtue of their race, were alien in their language and their dress, many of them still Yiddish-speakers, at best speaking German with a thick accent, and wearing the distinctive clothes of the orthodox Jew. They were less well-off, most of them, less educated, less cultured, and association with them could only impede the process of becoming true Germans.

Nika looked for anti-Semitism in others because he was aware of its existence in himself. He did not feel Jewish, nor did he wish to be a Jew. His admiration for the blond and blue-eyed Hans and Inge in *Tonio Kröger* was at least in part a rejection of Jewishness. He disliked the intellectuals who surrounded his mother because so many of them were Jews as well as socialists. 'Dostoevsky believes that the destructive elements of Russian and German socialism are particularly unwestern. I think this must be right, because so many of the leaders are in fact Jews, and the Jews are the most non-western element.' 'I am . . . a strong anti-Semite and can only get over this by becoming a christened non-Jew, amongst other non-Jewish Jews. Once I can ignore the solidarity that is being forced on me, then perhaps this anti-Semitism will become less raw and aggressive.'

At eighteen, Nika believed that he had two routes to happiness, to finding his place in the world. One was his relationship with Lola, whom he loved not just for herself – her naïvety, naturalness, intelligence and candour – but also for her setting. 'This is what he will get – a family of Christians, but sufficiently influenced by Jewishness not to be anti-Semitic – terribly nice people, well-educated, Prussians, servants of the state.'

The other route was the dawning realisation that there was one unfailing release from the torments of his own temperament. In work – hard work – he could always find oblivion, and he was beginning to feel more certain of what that work should be. In the spring of 1918, preoccupied with his hopes of winning Lola back, he could not see the way ahead. 'I suppose I will end up in my father's business – a joyless career.' Six months later, in the depths of depression over Lola's love for Thiess, he was casting around for another source of stability. 'What profession would make me happy? . . . Trade? There I would always secretly feel that I had misapplied my talents . . . There is always the secret dream of becoming an artist – not very likely . . . Art history? . . . I don't think I have many of the qualities I would need – and again, no real enthusiasm.'

Reason, however, and his mother's promptings, recommended art history to him. Slowly he began to construct a sense of vocation for himself. In a rare conversation with Heinz and Annie that he had had towards the end of 1918 (recorded, equally unusually, in the first person):

I mentioned, rather provocatively, that I liked people who weren't interested in making money – and got the reply I was perhaps hoping for: Mother asked what I wanted to be. I . . . described the dream I had been cherishing for some time: to see myself as a professor of art history, in a small house of my own, with the lady wife and a child, teaching, going about my business, maybe now and again writing – a German idyll which Heinz sneers at . . . If my interest in art . . . were more than just an experiment, I could very well have the makings of a German professor.

Having taken the decision, he clung to it with increasing determination. 'P's fascination with suicide has diminished,' he reported in January 1919, 'since he decided to become a university teacher and art historian. Now he builds castles in the air . . . which look like a route to happiness, and banish despair.'

CHAPTER 4

Entwicklungsroman

The brief stay with the Kurlbaums in Naumburg in September 1919 turned a shadow relationship into a real one. Nika made himself the confidant that Lola needed, not only for the death of her mother, but for the potential loss of her father. Alfred, she told Nika, was 'unable to be alone'. Every Sunday morning he took Lola and Marianne to tend their mother's grave. On the way back from the cemetery he fell into the habit of calling upon an acquaintance, the novelist Margarete Siebert, at the Henriette-Goldschmidt-Haus for feminist women. Margarete, Nika recalled, was 'a rather masculine, intellectual, strong-boned and badly dressed woman, who had a reputation as a writer of historical and other novels with a respectful if not enthusiastic reception.' She was cultured, clever and determined, with a bohemian air that intrigued Alfred, and before long he had proposed.

Marianne ('Ma') would later claim that her father tried to get out of this ill-advised marriage.[1] He asked Margarete to release him just before the wedding, but she was unable to face the embarrassment and he was too honourable to shame her. Marianne, of course, was far from being an impartial observer. Margarete combined progressive ideas on education with a Prussian sense of duty, which made her a most uncomfortable step-parent. She dressed Marianne in hideous 'Reform' clothing of her own design, a shapeless tunic made out of stiff striped material, and locked her dolls away at night to stop her becoming emotionally dependent upon them. She took Ma for interminable walks to improve her posture, made her read the whole of *Ben-Hur* out loud to remove any trace of a Saxon accent, and fed her on salt herring and boiled potato, keeping any delicacies for her own foster-daughter Lotte Johne, who also became part of the Kurlbaum household. The money that Margarete saved, she used to buy up antiques which elderly gentlefolk were obliged to sell during the years of the inflation.

Margarete was jealous and suspicious of Lola's devotion to Alfred, and accused her stepdaughter of being perpetually moody and lazy. Lola was too old to be moulded. She had assumed the running of the household after her mother's death, and now she sensed that her stepmother would be pleased to have her out of the way.

* * *

In May 1920 Nika agonised over a tea party he had organised to introduce Alfred, Margarete, Lola and Dieter to his entire family, including a grandmother, who had, he recorded guiltily, an 'astonishingly strong Yiddish accent'. What would Alfred make of Hugo, 'whose accent is sometimes the butt of jokes by Germans'? What would Lola, with her childish dress and hair and candour, make of Annie, 'artistic' and sharp-tongued and, to Nika's eyes, shamefully smart at a time when the Kurlbaums were suffering quite severely amidst the post-war austerity?

Lola survived the encounter perfectly well, and a couple of weeks later Nika felt able to unburden himself to her. 'P tells her about his Hebraic relations,' he informed the *Heftchen* on 20 June 1920, 'I have been brought up within the German culture, grown up with it. I feel much more like a German than a Jew. I can be baptised and married, have German children and grandchildren. I tell myself that I am a German – it is very painful to be constantly reminded by these Ostliche of the unGerman in me. If only I could, I would break away – get away from all this, make my own friends, all completely German.'* Lola sympathised with Nika's repudiation of Jewishness, which did nothing to broaden his mind.

Gradually the casual meetings, telephone calls and walks in the Johannapark became a courtship. Lola, he confided to the *Heftchen*, was his ideal: 'vivacious, an Inge [in the *Tonio Kröger* sense], childlike, but not so childish that she does not speak his language. He began to love her by chance, having this ideal in mind – and now he knows her, he loves her all the more. Amazing good luck!' They talked about everything, from the most banal to the most bizarre subjects, well outside the range of conventional conversation, 'almost as if they were married'. He learned her likes (white narcissi, bitter chocolate, potatoes with pepper, sea bathing, strong winds, mandarin oranges, punctuality) and dislikes (beer, fish) and her inability to remain neutral. 'I either adore people or I can't stand them,' she told him, 'there is nothing in between.'

Once committed, it was not in her nature to hold back, and almost as soon as she recognised her feelings for him, she considered herself as good as engaged. 'To be honest, I did not,' he wrote later, 'but when I saw her attitude, nothing better could happen to me.' They pledged their love and felt themselves bound by a secret betrothal,

---

*It had become fashionable to distinguish the old *deutsche Stämme*, German 'strains' or 'tribes' – Hessians, Franconians, Saxonians, Holsteiners, Prussians, etc. – and many assimilated German Jews liked to speak of themselves as the *deutsche jüdische Stamm*. Professor Günther Gillessen to the author, February 2002.

which Nika documented meticulously in the *Heftchen*. Now the *Heftchen* took on the complexion of a literary memoir, his own *Entwicklungsroman*, his romantic testament – albeit with an index and the occasional footnote.

From July 1920 onwards, when they exchanged their first kisses, much of the writing has to do with physical love. Lola was inexperienced, for all Nika's anxieties about Joachim Thiess, and she approached their modest lovemaking with a frank enjoyment that delighted him. This was the summer of long evenings in the Johannapark, wandering down the sandy avenues of lime trees with all the other couples, stopping discreetly in the twilight to kiss under a tree or in the shadow of the humpbacked bridges over the pond. 'Her cool neck and cheek move him profoundly,' he wrote, and he noted with astonishment that she did not seem to mind his bitten nails and the occasional boil on the back of his neck.

By the end of the year, their relationship was accepted by both families. On New Year's Eve Annie asked about his intentions, and proposed a toast to their engagement in 1921. 'When you have finished studying, and if her parents give her something, it would work financially,' she told him, 'provided the Kurlbaums agree. Anyway, I'll promote it.' Nika was aghast – 'No, don't!' – but he realised that Margarete too had her reasons for wishing the relationship well, to remove Lola from her home.

Nika was completing his preparations for his *Abitur* that summer. To go on to higher education it was essential to pass these final examinations; failure in the *Abitur*, it was said, effectively barred you from the middle class. He passed top of his year, and was chosen for the honour of giving the leaving address to the whole school. Much to his mother's mortification, he seized the opportunity to deliver a denunciation of revolutionary democracy, which owed a good deal to the *Reflections of a Non-political Man*.

He was already going to lectures on art history – Leipzig sixth-formers quite frequently attended seminars at the university. Art history as an academic discipline, after all, was a quintessentially German phenomenon. The phrase had first been used in Germany in 1764 and for more than a century the study of art history had been seen as an independent subject with aims and techniques of its own.* Understanding a country's art was crucial to understanding its thought and life and soul, but it

---

*The first professorship in art history had been established in 1813, at Göttingen.

was also valid as an end in itself. Georg Dehio, the most senior living German art historian, was just about to complete his *History of German Art* – an achievement that would not only illuminate Germans' understanding of their own culture but would also enhance the prestige of art history as a discipline.*

Some historians saw art history as the history of aesthetic properties alone, a study of form and style and other visual facts purely for their own sake. Others saw it as their task to relate the art of an age to its social and intellectual context. Art for them did not arise in abstraction from life, but was an expression of the temper of the times, and should be used to interpret those times. It was the art historian's job to look beyond the image itself to the meaning of the image. Nika studied these different approaches carefully to see which had the most resonance for his own intellect and temperament.

His progress was accelerated dramatically by his mother's intervention. Discreetly and with discernment, she made sure that art historians were well represented in her salons. For once, he was grateful. Nika was able to ask for practical advice, rehearse his theories and test his sense of vocation. 'Meeting went on till two in the morning,' he informed his diary late in November 1920:

> Got interested at about 11.30. Dr Ackerman, Hoffmann's friend, asked me something very theoretical about the meaning and purpose of art history and then argued against everything I said. Long, long debate. It was fascinating – but then came the misery of trying to make sense of it. I had to concentrate like hell, and later in bed I was too wound up to sleep. I feel the same today – I'm just realising how fearsome it's going to be.

Having been assured of his intellectual superiority throughout a conventional school career, he was now conscious of a profound ignorance of his new subject. He needed a different kind of intuition and analysis, needed to learn how to look, *really* look, at a painting, a sculpture or a building. 'I must learn *how to learn*,' he wrote. 'Is there enough talent there? Do I lack natural visual appreciation? It takes me so long to really get into a picture – none of the musing and analysing and judging comes naturally, so I get little real enjoyment. I have so little confidence in my own talent for academic work. I am

---

*Georg Gottlieb Dehio (1850–1932), an art and architectural historian, conservationist and author of the *Handbuch der deutschen Kunstdenkmäler*. See Chapter 25.

so prone to make mistakes of judgement – I can hardly judge the quality of anything instinctively, except perhaps colour.'

The German university system allowed students to move from university to university, from teacher to teacher in pursuit of their chosen courses, spending a year here, a semester there, wherever the demands of their subjects took them. Staying in Leipzig, Nika felt, was not an option, despite its strong tradition of art history; he must get away from home. But should he try first for Munich, where he could study with Heinrich Wölfflin, the elder statesman of German art history? Or Vienna, where Max Dvořák held court? Or should he go to Adolph Goldschmidt, reputedly the most impressive lecturer of all, in Berlin? This would have the advantage of bringing him closer to Lola, who spent holidays there with her grandmother, Julie Sabersky, the widow of a wealthy distiller. Going to Berlin for the galleries and, ostensibly, to get the feel of the university, Nika paid frequent visits to the comfortable flat in Genthiner Strasse, where Julie lived with her brother Heinrich, an eminent philologist with a forked white beard, author of several Langenscheidt dictionaries of English and Italian. 'Quick courting hour in the library after lunch . . . Onkel Heinrich, courteous and embarrassed, knocked at his own door before entering.'

The relationship was, in fact, still essentially innocent; Nika recorded with some confusion the occasion on which he inadvertently discovered that Lola was not wearing a corset. He continued to dream constantly of her, the settings detailed to reflect holiday travels and new preoccupations: a castle near Stockholm, a forest near Marienbad, a winter-sport hotel, sand dunes at Ostend, the Caspar David Friedrich room in the Berlin National Gallery. They exchanged presents – Mann's *Buddenbrooks*, the folk-poem collection *Des Knaben Wunderhorn*, a Greek sketchbook, a slim folio of Holbein drawings, porcelain by Villeroy & Boch, a cyclamen in a pot, and flowers pressed between the pages of books: pansies, edelweiss and a four-leaved clover.

In deference to Lola's nervous father, they were supposed to be concentrating on their studies. Nika disguised some of his frequent letters to her by adopting the old-fashioned Gothic script, which he normally never used, and signing himself as 'Margot', her closest friend from school. But in the time they snatched together they were planning their future, illustrating it with little sketches of the ideal home and lists of furniture they might need; and when it was finally time to choose his first course of study, Nika plumped for Berlin and Goldschmidt. On intellectual considerations alone, his first choice had been Wölfflin in Munich, but he had been persuaded otherwise by flattering conversations with art historians in Berlin and by heavy pressure from

Lola, who was destined for a finishing school in Kassel. With his doubts resolved, he took another decision. On his way to Berlin, he would spend some weeks in Potsdam with a Lutheran pastor by the name of Theodor Krummacher, preparing for confirmation into the Protestant faith.

His conversion was less a matter of religious conviction than emotional inclination. To become a Protestant was, for Nika, a statement of Germanness. 'The act,' he remembered later, 'was of course done for me to be normal German.' He had other motives as well. In terms of his future career, conversion would probably open doors that would have remained closed to a Jew; the best way of getting up the academic ladder was to convert. It was a step that very many Jews had been taking over the last thirty years, as an 1896 cartoon in the satirical magazine *Simplicissimus* testified: 'How come you've been baptised a Catholic?' 'Well, you know, there are just too many Jews for me among the Protestants.' The gesture would also please Lola and her family. And his own parents? 'My parents cannot have objected,' he wrote thirty years later, 'or I would have remembered. But I think now that it must have hurt my father . . . He was much too good to insist on anything.' Nika loved his father, but would have liked him to be different.

At the start of April 1921, Lola saw Nika off from the station in Leipzig. Her ring was on a chain round his neck, and she kissed him goodbye on the platform, holding hands through the train window, waving her handkerchief as the train pulled out.

The weeks in Potsdam were a dream-like interlude. The town was pretty and full of spring flowers, and he strolled in shirtsleeves through the formal gardens of the Marmorpalais. He visited Lola's birthplace, and made excursions to churches and galleries nearby. On one of these expeditions the railway station at Potsdam lacked its usual bustle. 'I found the platform very empty . . . and there, walking straight towards me were Hindenburg and Ludendorff.' Germany's wartime leaders were, it transpired, going to the funeral of the former Empress.

Pastor Krummacher – besides having married Alfred and Paula Kurlbaum – had close connections with the imperial family, which disconcerted Nika.* '[Krummacher] doesn't baptise anything lowlier than a Wartenburg or von Bülow,' he observed. 'I feel like a cuckoo in the nest.' The pastor had been a protégé of the Empress, and his

---

*Theodor Krummacher (1867–1945) was the grandson of the evangelical theologian Friedrich William Krummacher (1796–1868). Chaplain to the Empress, he left a memoir of his career that read like a *Who's Who* of the German Empire.

47

plans were thrown into confusion by her sudden death. He now proposed condensing the preparation period for confirmation.

Nika was on balance relieved. However mixed his motives, conversion was a significant step for him, not merely a practical expedient, and he worked hard, reading from the Bible, learning his catechism, thinking broadly about the beliefs he proposed to embrace. 'A marvellous conversation about fundamentals,' he reported after one meeting with Krummacher. 'K spoke very well and earnestly. Given my own sincere intent, it was profoundly affecting.' But he was never without some doubts, and he remained aware that there were dimensions to Christian faith that he was not wholeheartedly sharing. 'I read my Gospels faithfully – no, conscientiously; for certain things I could not believe.' He realised that his responses were often as much to do with aesthetics as with faith. 'Fantastic building,' he wrote of one church he attended, 'gets one into the right Baroque mood. The organ was playing, people praying, mostly little old women. Makes one feel quite a villain – this unquestioning piety . . . I have thoughts of giving up. At some point I will have to prove that I mean it.'

On 20 April 1921 he was baptised, and almost at once set off for university. By this time, his choice had changed. Goldschmidt, it seemed, was due for extended leave from Berlin, and Nika's rationale for starting his studies there was gone. In haste, he had drawn on Margarete Kurlbaum's close friendship with the eminent historian Ricarda Huch to find him a place at Munich instead.

PART TWO

ACADEMIC ON THE RISE

1921–1933

Roundel for the cover of the 1963
edition of *The Buildings of England: Herefordshire*

CHAPTER 5

'It takes . . . diligence to make a genius'

Nika's first base as a university student in the summer of 1921 was the Pension Korn at 3 Augustusstrasse, Munich. 'Perfectly adequate,' he wrote. 'Trams to and fro below – room opens to the front, but that doesn't matter. What does matter is the lack of a desk lamp.'

He wanted Lola to be able to visualise him in his new setting, and he sent her a plan of the room: divan, wardrobe with compartments for books and food, washstand, stove, bag for laundry, and so forth, with a reproduction of a Boucher above the bed ('The landlady's taste!') and Corot, Greuze and Moritz von Schwindt on the other walls. His neighbours he had heard but not seen: 'The gentleman next door sings and practises, and the lady next door whistles.'

With his books neatly ranged on the shelves, he spent the early summer days before the start of term setting up his new life – registering at the police station, collecting coupons for those foods that were still on the ration as a result of the Allies' wartime blockade of Germany, filling in the forms and making the payments that the university demanded. 'I've got my student card and my wallet is swelling – cards for library, bicycle shed, place in college, registration, passport, seminars – awful.' He marked Wölfflin's house on the map, and included it in the promenades round the town that were his evening entertainment.

The system that allowed students to move freely and construct their own curriculum – *Lernfreiheit* – loaded a good deal of responsibility on their shoulders. It was for the student to get hold of the list of lectures and register for the courses he wanted to take. He then drew up his 'student-book', a roster of the lectures and seminars he wished to attend. 'Nobody felt responsible for the intellectual and spiritual welfare of the students,' wrote Ernst Gombrich of his own experience of university life in the 1920s, 'least of all the academic staff, because this milling mass of youngsters who were free to attend lectures in any faculty or subject had rarely any contact with the high and mighty professors.'[1]

Nika spent his first weeks picking his way through a wide curriculum, sampling lectures on psychology, mythology, bibliography and the French Revolution as well as his prescribed lectures on art, hurrying from class to class and library to library, thrilled by the atmosphere

51

of concentrated effort and the universes of knowledge opening out before him. 'This kind of life doesn't tire me – on the contrary, it's very pleasant. All the work places are close together.' He revelled in the rich variety of personality and mannerisms displayed by the lecturers: 'blond, accent Prussian, somewhere between diplomat and general', 'a typical Professor out of *Fliegende Blätter* [a German equivalent of *Punch*] – waistcoat buttoned wrongly, cravat awry, stooped, full red beard – very courteous and very gauche'; 'a tall parson type, looking like a Catholic and talking the most common Bavarian'. Their academic performance, however, did not always meet his demanding standards. One, he remarked severely, 'defended Impressionism well, but did not give a very clear outline at the beginning – slapdash.'

Even the great Wölfflin was not above criticism. Nika had rather hoped to be singled out to attend his seminars, but was soon disabused. Forty-three years later, reviewing Wölfflin's work for the *Times Literary Supplement*, he recalled his humiliation. 'The professor was nearing sixty,' he wrote:

[He] was a law-giver . . . Tall, quietly and rather formally dressed (blue pinstripe, double breasted) and frighteningly aloof. His first words to the freshman were, 'In what way can I be of service to you?' The poor freshman dried up entirely and was not, of course, admitted to Wölfflin's seminar . . . So he went only to the lectures.[2]

For all his zeal in registering, Nika was still number 379 on the list for the lecture series on Renaissance art. The hall, the second-largest space in the university, was packed. 'I sat there, glasses on my nose. I looked towards the door, and there he was – tall, thin, greying short hair, small goatee and rather receding chin, a little bit Swiss-Deutsch, otherwise well turned-out.' The professor, Nika observed, 'talks a good deal about himself. Clearly aware of being a VIP (which of course he is).' But the lectures contained nothing that was not in his books, and were 'to the exacting freshman, rather a bore'.

Wölfflin's approach to art history was by this time beginning to go out of fashion. He was a champion of the analysis of art in aesthetic terms, abstracting the structural unity of a type or period of painting or sculpture from a multitude of examples, examining familiar works in minute detail to demonstrate the aesthetic principles that lay behind them. The history of art was for him the history of *seeing*. It was the visual data that were paramount, not any associations which they might have with people or ideas, purposes or social trends. He quoted his master Jacob Burckhardt: 'The connection between art and general culture can only be taken loosely and lightly; art has its own life and its own history.'

Nika wanted to learn Wölfflin's techniques of formal analysis, but he wanted them as a means to an end. Temperamentally, he was becoming drawn to the grand theories of *Kulturgeschichte* or cultural history that had begun to evolve in Germany towards the end of the eighteenth century. These theories saw art developing according to detectable laws, rather like a biological process, as part of the organic whole that was 'culture', in which all human activity – aesthetic, intellectual, literary, political, economic, social – was bound together. It was part of the art historian's job to trace the patterns in human existence, to see where art expressed the thoughts and emotions of the time, where it reflected social or political trends. Nika was becoming interested in the teachings of Max Dvořák and others on *Geistesgeschichte*, an untranslatable term which means literally 'the history of spirit' and refers to the currents lying below the physical manifestations of cultural development – perhaps best rendered loosely as 'the history of ideas'. He was keen now to study the spirit of a nation or an era as expressed in its art, and the way in which art evolved alongside developments in religion and philosophy. But he was aware that to do this required a solid basis of knowledge and minutely detailed understanding of the art itself. 'The jump into social history,' he wrote later, 'history of religion, the history of ideas, can only be made after the work of art and the building too have been analysed and compared with others strictly formally.'

Painstakingly, Nika laid the foundations of a career in art history, attending lectures, visiting churches and galleries, scouring libraries, gutting and annotating books, accumulating sketches, diagrams and photographs of the works he was adding to his mental collection. Little by little he was developing the compendious work method that would last him the rest of his life. Sixty years later, working in the Getty Collection of historical manuscripts, art historian Wolfgang Herrmann saw Nika's notes. 'I realised then what I was supposed to have learnt at university. I must have heard the same lectures, the same seminars, but I don't remember much about them, whereas he – pages and pages and pages of notes. He can't have taken them on the spot; he must have gone home and sat down and written these notes, using the lectures. Quite extraordinary – I don't think I was unusually lazy.'[3]

Nika was learning languages too, Herrmann remembered: English from a teacher and Italian from a book:

For the Italian he used the Toussaint-Langenscheidt method – a parallel text with German on the bottom and Italian on the top. You cut out a cardboard grid with which you covered up the foreign language and read the German and said what you thought the foreign words should be. But you didn't just say 'table' or 'go', you said all the cases and conjugated the verbs, every time, working through it to get it into your brain – incredibly laborious. He is really the only person I know who did the whole Toussaint-Langenscheidt method from beginning to end . . . To get through it required unbelievable perseverance. There were other methods; this was a very dry one.

Nika could be sociable when he wanted to be, and coped easily with small talk over lunch in his *pension*, but it was on the whole a spartan and single-minded existence. He could hear 'life' going on in neighbouring rooms, but left himself little time to relax, which would have been time stolen either from his work or from thoughts of Lola. Every morning, sitting up in bed under the Boucher, and every evening before going to sleep, he wrote to her, forming a habit that lasted until her death. These letters had the briefest of salutations, no formal shape and no regard for style; they were a one-sided conversation carried on, with breaks, for days at a time, posted only when they became unwieldy or when Nika had something particularly momentous to communicate. They brought her his anxieties and his love (often in that order), and the details of his everyday life, and were to some extent written for his benefit as much as hers. 'Without you,' he wrote, 'I think I would develop into the most dreadful troll – cold and moody . . . My hermit life is self-imposed. You think it is dangerous – and perhaps it is . . . Without you the very best has been torn out of me, the only bit that is not just egotism.'

As the summer grew warmer, he changed to his lightweight green knickerbockers, put his bicycle on the train and took himself on expeditions into the surrounding countryside, always with the ultimate objective of a great house or church or gallery. For these trips he sustained himself with bread smeared thinly with lard – good practice, he told Lola, for lean times ahead as an ill-paid academic; some days his wrist ached for hours after the labour of cutting and spreading. The expeditions, too, were tiring, as he laboured to improve his powers of observation and analysis. Something in his nature made him feel that nothing should be easy – 'the only things worth having take effort' – but from time to time he was near despair. The 'careful looking and memorising', which were a crucial part of the art historian's armoury, were still 'hopeless . . . nothing like good enough', and he seriously questioned his natural ability in his chosen subject:

> Pathetic – P lacks a feeling for space and, with that, all sense of the distinctive characteristics of buildings. I can hardly believe this is something that can be learnt. What is more, he has a very under-developed memory for form and colour – can't remember a thing, so he is always quite incapable of drawing comparisons . . . Am I deceiving myself to think myself gifted? Am I to be no more than a lowly sweeper-up of other men's ideas? Do I actually have a sense of form, just waiting to develop? Or will I develop panache without real skill? Will I become pleasant, urbane, witty, stimulating, good at engaging people's interest – and yet basically superficial and second-rate? I can imagine making a quick success and reasonable career like that . . . I shall never know objectively what I am really capable of.

Objectively, he was advancing rapidly. In that autumn of 1921, he finally made contact with Adolph Goldschmidt in Berlin, where he studied for the best part of a term. His notes range from Greek philosophy to Kant, Renaissance iconography to French religious painting, Shakespeare to Spengler. It was here that he was introduced to Italian baroque painting, by Werner Weisbach, a pupil of Robert Vischer and friend of Wölfflin and one of the first scholars to write an analysis of Italian Mannerism. He spent further hours at home in Leipzig in the offices of E.A. Seemann, a leading art publisher, pains-takingly extracting references and illustrations from tottering piles of art magazines. He somehow found time to attend lectures on literature and make copious notes on Byron, Casanova, the Brothers Grimm and Plautus. He helped to put together conference programmes and was carrying out small research jobs for professors – a sure sign of a favoured pupil. The leap forward, however, came at the start of 1922, when he found himself a mentor, the most potent influence of his intellectual life.

Studying at home in Leipzig, before he ever left for university, Nika had cast an eye over the academics working in his subject like a race-goer assessing the field, and fastened on one as a potential front runner: 'Wilhelm Pinder – he looks as if he will be the coming man'.* In early 1922 Pinder was forty-three, son of the director of the museum at Kassel, educated at Göttingen, Munich and Berlin, with a doctorate taken under August Schmarsow in Leipzig.† After positions in Würzburg, Darmstadt and Breslau, specialising in medieval German sculpture, he had been called up and spent the last two years of the war as an officer in the Imperial German Army. Since 1920 he had been in Leipzig, having moved into Schmarsow's position as head of the art history department. At Nika's urgent request, Annie had gone to take notes at a public lecture that Pinder was giving on Oswald Spengler and *The Decline of the West*. The subject, she found, was uninspiring – Pinder was dismissive of Spengler as pompous and platitudinous – but she was deeply impressed by the attacking delivery, as rapid as gunfire, 'unbelievable speed, hardly giving himself time to breathe'.

Pinder was in fact one of the most successful of all pre-televisual popularisers of art. His books on German cathedrals in the *Blauen Bücher* series sold millions, his public lectures were both cultural and social highlights, and he became one of the best-known chairmen of the German Association of Art Historians. What Nika saw in him was a public speaker of genius, with an emotional but disciplined response to art that he was able to convey to a wide audience. Being thrilled by beauty was not enough: communicating that thrill was everything. Pinder, writes his biographer Marlite Halbertsma, 'combined the very un-German characteristics of being a prophet and a stand-up comedian'.[4] He was a sensitive, cultivated man, a good pianist who played chamber music with a wide circle of acquaintances, and a discerning art collector. By the time Nika met him, he had left a first wife and child to marry one of his students.

Pinder attracted a large number of pupils, and supervised over a hundred doctoral dissertations, but he never set up a 'school' with disciples and a formal body of teaching, as other art historians did.‡

---

*Games, op. cit., p.76, notes that Nika had heard Pinder lecture the previous winter on 'Attitudes to Art in Different Periods' and had been so excited that he sent him flowers.

†August Schmarsow (1853–1936), specialist in Renaissance and Northern European art and architecture, was the first art historian to consider space as an architectural element.

‡'If anyone ever asks me what my method is, what's your school, what's your direction, I start to get embarrassed,' Pinder confessed in a filmed interview in 1943. 'Dehio said to me one day: "School? I have no school. Direction? I have no direction."' Quoted by Games, op. cit., p.98.

His central ideas, however, were well known, rooted in his guiding faith in art, history and Germany. He subscribed to the theory of *Kunstgeschichte als Geistesgeschichte*, 'the history of art as the history of ideas': art history as the history of the psyche of the age. Art was not simply a reflection of men's sense perceptions, but an expression of their psychological insights. The art historian's goal must be to identify the *Weltanschauung* or world-view underlying the work of art.

Pinder had his own tools for analysing the style and spirit of a nation's art at any particular point in time. During those first years of his professorship in Leipzig, he was evolving a theory that he eventually published as *Das Problem der Generationen in der Kunstgeschichte Europas* in 1924. It made sense, he felt, to map the development of art within a nation or era in terms of 'generations' of artists. Every thirty years or so, a new generation would arise. The artists of that generation, whilst displaying some individual characteristics, would also have common stylistic traits, and would be jointly preoccupied with one problem above all others: painting in one generation, perhaps; architecture in the next. Being born into a particular generation would inevitably colour an artist's ideas.

Any era in a nation's art history would have different generations working next to one another: the *Zeitgeist*, or spirit of the age, was a polyphony of voices from different generations. Each generation would be serving its own style, but would also be influenced by the overarching style of the era, and all would be linked by the *Zeitfarbe* or colour of the age, with key factors – nationhood, race – remaining constant underneath. It was the job of the art historian to identify the rhythmic impulse of the generations, identify the problem engrossing each, and decipher the pattern that was made by their interweaving. To analyse a nation's art at any particular point in time was to drop a plumb line through the different layers of simultaneous activity.

Pinder's other guiding principle as an art historian was less abstruse. He was a passionate and effective champion of German art. The context was the growth of German nationalism. At the start of the nineteenth century Germany was still a cluster of independent states. Alongside the campaign for political unification would run a quest for the nature of 'Germanness'. Herder evolved the semi-mystical idea of the German nation (*Volk*) as a cultural entity, with its own characteristic *Geist*, an essence displayed in its language and its values, evolving over time. Schiller explained the artist's responsibility for conveying the history of the *Volksgeist* by projecting a sense of a lost past, with critical reflection on the present and hopes for a future restoration. Lacking focus and continuity in their cultural development, Germans had often submitted to the dominance of French culture and the influence of antiquity. Now the *Volk* should preserve, celebrate and cultivate its own distinct culture. Fichte called for the German people to reassert the purity of their own language – the 'mother tongue' that gave birth to the 'fatherland' – and the German Romantics sought a national literature rooted in folklore (*Des Knaben Wunderhorn*, say, and the tales of the Brothers Grimm), Germanic myths and epic poems such as the *Nibelungenlied*.

In painting, sculpture and architecture, too, there was a corresponding art that was quintessentially German, and art historians such as Heinrich Thode had already fiercely challenged the notion that it was in any way inferior to that of any other nation. Thode's particular target was French Impressionism, which had achieved such critical dominance at the end of the nineteenth century. New German art, he maintained, should display technical mastery, realism and the German spirit, and it should be art for the people, not just for the bourgeoisie. Georg Dehio had already begun the task of telling the story of German art, which he likewise believed was determined by national characteristics. The First World War had prevented the publication of a monograph in which he explored the connections between the history of Germany's art and its social, political and economic history, but the first volume of his *Geschichte der deutschen Kunst* had come out in 1919.

Pinder, then, was not unique as a champion of a 'national' art, but he was particularly explicit and eloquent in his framing of the theory. He saw German art as lying at the heart of European art, combining abstract northern tendencies with southern naturalism, just as Germany lay geographically at the heart of Europe. German art was essentially spiritual in character, and demanded intellectual and emotional engagement; each work – painting, building, sculpture – must be constantly reinterpreted by the critic and historian, much as a piece of music is created anew by each performer. There were certain phases of history in which the essence of Germanness was concentrated: the early Middle Ages, for example, and, interestingly, the present; the Bauhaus, for Pinder, expressed the spirit of Germany in a pure and complete form.

On 4 January 1922, Nika emerged from an hour's conversation with Pinder in Leipzig confident that he was going to be accepted for the great man's seminar – not, to his chagrin, for his outstanding ability, but largely on the strength of his connections. He saw Annie's hand in this, but his resentment was outweighed by his relief at having found a teacher who was both congenial and up to date. In Pinder and his teaching he had found a role model as a lecturer, and a subject that was to inspire him for the rest of his life.

Pinder had been introduced to the greatness of German medieval sculpture as a pupil of Schmarsow, who had done much to 'discover' and introduce early sculpture to a wider public in Germany. Schmarsow's work centred on the magnificent thirteenth-century statues from the cathedral in Naumburg, statues not of saints but of the founders of the cathedral, knights and their ladies. The statues stood in the west choir and were the work of a group of sculptors trained in Reims, who had moved to Naumburg around 1250. All around the figures, which stood against the shafts running up the walls between the windows of the west choir, were scenes of the judgement to come, surrounded by exquisite foliage. So the founders – Margrave Eckhart and his wife Uta, Margrave Hermann and his wife Reglindis, and companion knights – both embodied human chivalry and set it in the context of the will of God.

Pinder was working on Naumburg, along with the cathedrals at Bamberg and Strassburg, and persuaded Nika that these were the finest works of art of their time in Europe. In Eckhart, Uta, Hermann, Reglindis and the others, Nika saw the embodiment of his own view of the German spirit: intense emotion expressed with strict formal control. He found in them what he found in Lutheranism: spiritual fervour contained within a framework of responsibility and self-discipline. Like the works of Bach, they were for him the perfect synthesis of form and content, mind and soul, and they contained within them the dualities he found intriguing in himself – austerity and sensuality, masculinity and femininity, duty and instinct at war. He was particularly enraptured by the figure of Uta, 'the stony miracle', gazing into the far distance over the high upturned collar of her robe – offered to generations of little girls as the archetype of German femininity. 'Naumburg' became a code word for all the qualities and values he admired, not only the qualities expressed in the actual sculptures, but also the values embodied in their making. 'The most affecting thing is the unity between art and life,' he wrote. 'Art was at one with its own time and life then in the most beautiful way . . . The architects and sculptors were craftsmen, nothing more – and yet they were the greatest artists of Western culture.'

Nika seems to have worked in Leipzig throughout the spring and summer of 1922, both inspired and intimidated by Pinder's apparently effortless brilliance, beside which he felt himself pedestrian and laboured. 'My admiration for Pinder may be excessive,' he noted, but it had served to give direction to his own natural drive. He had a clear picture of himself during his university years: 'austere, proper, pedantic, diligent, serious-minded, indifferent to comfort, preferring to have a goal to strive towards'. The austerity was in part a reaction against his background and all that his parents had done to make things easy – 'I find any kind of luxury embarrassing, in dress as well as living conditions' – but it was also part of his temperament, something he could not help. Diligence, on the other hand, he saw as a positive virtue to be cultivated, the engine of his future success.

Carefully he copied into the *Heftchen* a pronouncement of Theodor Fontane. 'Gifts – who hasn't got them? Talents – children's playthings. It takes earnestness to make a man and diligence to make a genius.' The idea became a manifesto for his career in art history. 'Hasn't Goethe said somewhere that man achieves what he sets out to achieve?' he wrote. 'That is my motto. I am going to achieve what I want to. To fall short would just be a failure of will.' All his reflections on life led him to the same conclusion: 'I must just carry on working, with no pleasures – gloomy, but the truth, because my whole vision of the future depends on success in my work.' This vision was reinforced by a new essay by Thomas Mann, *Von deutscher Republik* (1922), in which Nika found everything he would demand of himself: the qualities of the good citizen – perseverance, restraint, high-mindedness, social responsibility. 'Here,' he wrote solemnly at the age of twenty, 'one can see man's path towards happiness in marriage and parenthood. This stands as the synthesis for which P is striving – love, marriage, and a joyous fully accepted *Bürgerlichkeit*. This meets the demands of conscience and grows out of a sense of duty, a work ethic which rejects the simple pursuit of pleasure.'

Before the war, Nika might have been confident that his talents and capacity for hard work would secure him the kind of job he wanted. By the end of 1922, with recession and inflation looming, times were more uncertain, and he set out his plans with some hesitancy. Next year, he thought, would see him formally engaged to Lola. He would do his Finals at Easter 1924, and then they would get married, and probably live in the back of the family flat in Leipzig, where he would, with any luck, be working on his doctorate under Pinder. Who knows, he might be Pinder's seminar assistant. One way or another, he would dearly like to see himself as Pinder's successor – and he drew a tentative line of descent from Schmarsow to Pinder to Pevsner. 'If nothing comes of me,' he noted in the margin, 'then this diagram is just a delusion of grandeur. But if I come to something, then I could perhaps boast this ancestry. I *must* become something. *Ich muss werden.*'

CHAPTER 6

'Coupled to a tender heart'

'As long as you don't become jealous of my work,' Nika told Lola, 'nothing matters.' He was asking a lot of her. Gradually his studies were squeezing her from the forefront of his mind. Now that his intellectual energies were fully engaged in the history of art, the *Heftchen* had become a purely emotional record – and the entries were becoming less frequent.

'Do you remember when you sat next to me in my room as I worked?' he had written to her just before setting out for Munich. 'That is how it will be later. I can't think of anything more beautiful.' Lola was loyally supportive of him, to the point where she was prepared to give up studying mathematics, her favourite subject, and take up art history instead, and this despite what Nika sensed to be her 'subdued feeling that history of art was not a real subject'. But she had too much energy to be content simply to sit and watch him work, while at the same time she lacked confidence in her own ability to do anything more.

She had a good brain, and had been well educated at the private school next door in Sebastian-Bach-Strasse. Private tutors had prepared her for her *Abitur* and, for all her dark forebodings, she had dealt efficiently with a variety of probing questions ('The bow only shows its strength when bent: discuss', 'What picture of the British people do you get from the book *The Fishermen of Ireland*?'), to emerge with a creditable 2:B grade. She signed up for courses at Leipzig University at the same time as Nika, at the end of April 1922.* But constant comparison of herself with him – his breadth of reading, his powers of reasoning and concentration, his formidable memory – had made her feel ignorant, lazy, flighty, easily distracted. An outstanding student such as Nika, a future professor without a doubt, surely demanded a level of intellectual companionship that was beyond her.

Her fears had been confirmed early that year on a visit to Berlin by an acutely uncomfortable evening in the company of a female student with whom Nika had had the occasional high-minded literary discussion. The girl had something of a lingering crush on him and

---

*Games, op. cit., p.85, notes that Lola took four courses in Leipzig in 1922–3, including the beginner's course in art history with Pinder that Nika also took.

no doubt contrived to exclude Lola, reducing her to a state of speechless, twitching misery, near to tears. 'The twitches,' Nika recorded
guiltily, 'I might once have thought were put on, but now recognise
as a spontaneous reaction which, as a candid person, she doesn't try
to conceal.'

His guilt was compounded by his own sneaking suspicion, which
he knew to be unworthy, that she might not be able to keep up with
him. Her letters were childish, and in some ways he liked that: 'I think
you write very good letters . . . I am always annoyed by how dry and
cold *my* writing is. Your letter is almost like having you here. I, phlegmatic and cool, feel very impoverished in comparison – and I'm afraid
that won't change . . . Watch out – by the time I am thirty, I will be
dry as a skeleton, married only to my subject, like Tesman [in Ibsen's
Hedda Gabler].' But he was bitterly disappointed when she was bored
by Mann's *Reflections of a Non-political Man*, unwilling to look up
all the foreign expressions: 'P finds that embarrassing and depressing.'
Anxious for common bonds, she had begged him to fill out her education while she was working for her *Abitur* and, somewhat self-
consciously, he had made lists of works they could read together
– Shaw, Shakespeare, Strindberg – as well as lists for private study
(Mann, Gorky, Dostoevsky). They pored over books of architectural
pictures, and he was delighted when she produced the correct technical
terms.

But Lola was not an intellectual. She was less interested in the
abstract than the concrete, the theoretical than the practical, and she
was driven by a temperament that was very different from Nika's. She
ran on nervous energy, as he did, but at the same time she was direct,
unsophisticated, impulsive where he was oblique, subtle, cautious. She
had a loud voice – 'the sign of a naturalness, even childishness' – and
she used it to express her feelings and beliefs without reserve or
qualification. Germany was for her a living entity, 'an organism to
which she herself belongs', to which she attributed many of the characteristics of her own family. Germany to her was essentially Prussian,
and at this stage of her life she was intolerant of the elements that did
not conform to that ideal: socialists, Jews, pacifists.

'L thinks that patriotism and conservatism are inseparable from
character,' Nika noted with awe. 'She would in fact inform on a socialist
to the police and would be quite able to kill someone like that.' Lola's
feelings were no doubt inflamed by memories of the day in 1920, during
the Kapp putsch (an attempt to unseat the new government of the
Weimar Republic), when the house in Sebastian-Bach-Strasse had found
itself in the path of a mob and the Kurlbaums had been forced to escape

over the garden wall.* Irritated by the immoderation of her outbursts, Nika nevertheless had some sympathy with the underlying sentiment. 'P dreams of a most romantic duel with a socialist. Engels is there, aware that he is about to die. The house burns. Lola looks into the blaze, and P sees the flames reflected in her eyes.'

Lola was half-Jewish through her mother Paula, but rarely acknowledged it. To her, to be a Jew was to be correspondingly less of a German. Early in their relationship she made this clear with unconscious brutality. 'P has just condemned patriotism as heightened egotism. Lola's answer is, "But you're not a German".'

The vehemence, the spontaneity, the lack of compromise were all part of the formula for *die Harmlose*, and in theory Nika loved them, but in practice they were sometimes hard to live with. When Lola was with him, he found it impossible to satisfy her emotional demands as well as meeting his own exacting standards in his work. He was aware that he was overtaxing his energies: running for a train, he had frightened himself by blacking out on the platform. After a working day in the library, anywhere from eight to ten hours, what he wanted from Lola was relaxation and reassurance, and what he often got was an outpouring of the day's accumulated anxieties and resentments. 'One thing I really do demand of her,' he wrote in exasperation, 'is some kind of restraint – she has to learn how to control her evil moods. But what if her strained nerves aren't up to it? . . . She is shy, insecure, and so completely undisciplined.' Work, which would be his own panacea throughout life, might, he thought, bring her comfort and stability, and he suggested buckling down; to Lola this must have seemed like adding insult to injury.

He could see that the balance of their relationship was changing. Originally he had been the suitor, trying to enter a family and an environment that were more secure and fulfilling than his own. Now Lola was uncertain, and needed him perhaps more than he needed her. 'What else has she got? She has not really got a very happy home, she has no money, she dislikes Margarete . . . There is not a single day when she does completely what she wants.' More painful than any of this was the acute misery of a rift with her father, who had started an affair. This time she could neither ignore it nor forgive him.

---

*The putsch itself took place in Berlin on 13 March 1920. The Weimar government called on all workers to defeat the uprising by means of a general strike. It was probably clashes between strikers and supporters of the putsch that forced the Kurlbaums from their house in Leipzig.

Lotte Johne, Margarete Siebert's foster-daughter, was living with them in Sebastian-Bach-Strasse. The daughter of a miller, she was attractive and highly intelligent, and Margarete had seen it as her civic duty to give Lotte the chance of a good education by sending her to university to study medicine. The two younger Kurlbaum children found Lotte fascinating and formed long-lasting friendships with her; Lola, subconsciously aware of the threat she posed, hated her from the start. Nika had been startled by the violence of her feelings: 'When P tries to defend Fraulein J and says she is very nice, Lola stops dead in the middle of the road and shows her dislike so openly that P is secretly disconcerted. This is not quite what it seems – Lola is not telling him everything.'

Unwilling as he was to believe the worst of his father-in-law, Nika was forced to recognise that Lola's suspicions were justified: Alfred was having an affair with Lotte. Lola 'raged to me, expressing her hatred of him whom she loved more than anyone else'. Nika understood and sympathised with her pain and disillusionment, but she distracted him from his work. 'The spirit of Naumburg,' he wrote sadly, 'is remote from her.'

They began to have destructive arguments. Lola 'knew what she believed was right and what was wrong, and she felt it her duty to say it. And more often than not, her right was right and wrong wrong, and quite often too that right was an unfashionable right. But the way she expressed her opinions was awkward, naïve, unsubtle and only too easily assailable.' He used his own particular weapons, logic and detachment, to assail her, sometimes on his own account, sometimes as a devil's advocate, attacking her cherished beliefs in a cool, reasonable way, which hurt and infuriated her. 'It ends as it always does,' he wrote after one argument about Dostoevsky and Christian ethics: 'She is overcome with such hatred that she hits me. I am completely horrified – it's ridiculous, ridiculous. So I get into a rage and without stopping to think, shout, "You disgusting animal!", and lash out with both fists. I am sorry at once, and she is filled with devotion. I cry, and have a dreadful conscience.'

Lola was chilled by Nika's capacity to defend the indefensible for the sake of argument. He was envious of her instinctive and natural qualities, but often irritated and disturbed by them in action. On Christmas Eve 1922, on the way home after a party, his conversation was frosty. She had been dancing at the party; her naïve lack of inhibition had embarrassed him, and as they walked along he told her so:

Quite unexpectedly she hits me . . . a really nasty box on the ears.
I don't know what to do, I'm defeated by this. She is immediately
full of shame and regret – but what's the use? . . . I love her very
much, that hasn't changed . . . but I still worry about our future
happiness. I tell myself it will be all right when we are married and
by ourselves – and then it comes back to me: I have been hit in
public . . . It is the dark side of her principal virtue: openness and
spontaneity simply can't go that far without jeopardising our chances
of a happy life together.

The tension between them was at least partly physical. Long periods
apart and watchful parents had limited their lovemaking; but as the
months passed, when opportunities arose, they became ever bolder.
For Nika, this was a source of joy and anxiety in about equal proportions. His misgivings about his appearance and his ability to perform
sexually had not vanished with adolescence. He had solemnly copied
out a muscle-building regimen – 'Dr Michaelis's exercises' – and strove
to stick to it, but was not sanguine about the results: 'P . . . knows
his body is repulsive . . . People like us, the half-humans, the mis-
shapen, should really stay in our cells instead of trying to make a deal
with happiness.' When Lola playfully conjectured that the dark hair
on his forearms covered his whole body – 'just like a monkey' – he
was filled with apprehension for his wedding night.

He was clumsy at sports, where Lola was neat and quick; here, he
reflected later, he 'felt the same pangs of inferiority which Lola so
often felt in other ways'. He loved swimming, but preferred it as a
solitary exercise. Lola would set off for the pool, leaving him in his
room: 'P has stayed behind because he is afraid that, with his short
sight, he will look as if he is peering at people . . . If I come out of
my monastic cell to be with people who are gayer, happier, freer –
dancing, shrieking with pleasure, splashing in the water – I feel damned,
cut off, even cast out.'

Sensuality was an integral part of the 'Naumburg spirit', in the
service of spirituality, and Nika longed to unlock it in himself, reading
with a mixture of envy and hope the writings of Stefan George, Gerhart
Hauptmann and Franz Wedekind on the liberating power of sexual
expression. 'How wonderful it would be if gradually I could come to
feel this behaviour natural for me.'

Lola, as Nika realised, had made an enduring commitment to him
with their secret 'betrothal' two years before. She was far from sophisticated about sex, but she was generous and brave, and regarded sexual
love as part of the compact she had made with him. During the times

of resentment and animosity in their relationship during 1922, they used lovemaking to patch over the rifts; but by the spring of 1923 it had become an end in itself. The *Heftchen* became a record of exploration and discovery. Amidst the physical and emotional turmoil, he sometimes forgot now to date the diary entries; but it is clear that by the beginning of April they were sleeping together.

'All fear of marriage is gone,' he wrote. 'Lola, Lola, I am so grateful.' He was grateful to her not only for banishing his fears of impotence, but also for her understanding of what the experience meant to him. For the first time he had let her read the *Heftchen* – or, rather, persuaded her to do so. Up till then they had been a private record, which he had intended her to see only after his death, for fear that she would be shocked and contemptuous. Now he felt it would be artificial to keep anything from her. 'You will find lots of shocking, crude things, frighteningly repulsive things,' he told her. 'I am the one whom the *Heftchen* reveal in his nakedness. But I feel duty bound to let you – whom I love, and who loves me – know everything about me . . . This is the highest proof of my trust in you.'

In time, Lola would come to hate the *Heftchen*. In April 1923 she was simply astonished by them as a record of emotional and physical evolution. 'She finds a lot of things puzzling. P is dreadfully ashamed – as ashamed as when *Die Letzte Stunde* [his suicide novel] went to the publishers.' She asked that Nika burn them after her death, for they were a record of her development too, as intensely personal in some ways about her as about him. But for the present she accepted with dignity and understanding what he had written about their love and their sexual initiation. 'I was never more thankful to her . . . It would hardly be an exaggeration to say that I had fallen in love today . . . It is more precious than ever to be coupled to a tender heart – and not alone.'

CHAPTER 7

'Germany's present ruin'

Suddenly, it seemed to Nika, they were planning for marriage. The Kurlbaums were now willing for them to marry in the autumn of 1923, and what had been vague sketches of the floor-plan and furnishings for their ideal home had crystallised into wedding lists and invitations. The plan for a formal engagement to sustain their relationship while he finished his Finals had apparently been abandoned. Something had overridden not only the reservations of both sets of parents but also Nika's own practical anxieties. 'Think of the material aspect of the future,' he had written in October 1922. 'Just think of Germany's present ruin . . . Will I be able to earn the money to support a family? . . . Why do I have to live in times like these? How easy life, marriage, bringing up children all were in earlier times! Better times for Germany must be on the way – but the crisis hasn't come yet, it's still coming. Does this revolution look as if it's over? My profession does depend on a certain measure of national prosperity.'

The revolution, as he must have realised, was far from over, and Germany during the Weimar Republic was a most insecure setting for an attempt to make a career in art history. Topical references are few in the *Heftchen*, but where they occur, they give glimpses of the political uncertainty that had followed the creation of the new republic in 1918. This was the first democracy in German history, a period of wildly vacillating political fortunes. The ruling party – a coalition of social democrats, liberals and the Catholic 'centre party' – found itself constantly vulnerable to rebellion from both ends of the political spectrum: in January 1919 from the communists and Spartacists whom Nika had found so unacceptable in his mother's drawing room, and then a year later from the right-wing leaders of the Kapp putsch which had disturbed the peace of Sebastian-Bach-Strasse.

Nika gave his first lecture, a discourse on Tintoretto. He began English lessons, in December 1922. He helped to put together a seminar whose guest speakers included Walter Gropius, by whom he was much impressed. He also spent a term in Frankfurt in the winter of 1922, studying baroque architecture with Rudolph Kautzsch, carrying out small research assignments there for Pinder and for other senior scholars. But by the spring of 1923 he was back in Leipzig working with Pinder on his dissertation.

Pinder had done much to isolate German Baroque as a style; now Nika was to narrow the focus and concentrate on 'Leipzig Baroque', with a study of the magnificent early eighteenth-century arcaded merchants' houses that were the visible symbols of the city's prosperity. At a time when architects further north, in Dresden and beyond, had been turning towards French classicism, the burghers of Leipzig had not been interested in restraint and still demanded lavish ornamentation from their builders. Their houses had energy and flamboyance. Many, however, had already been destroyed or spoiled in the restructuring of the inner city some twenty years earlier. Shop fronts had been crudely glued on to elegant façades. Gateways and entrances had been defaced by advertisements and more permanently ruined by hoardings which channelled water behind them and lifted the stucco or brought down the beautifully moulded ceilings inside. Some buildings had simply been demolished, to make more space for the Trade Fair, and their contents removed to museums. Nika had no sentimental attachment to the occupants of these houses, as he freely admitted later.[1] He 'totally neglected' the buildings' social history to concentrate on their stylistic analysis and their conservation as a record of Leipzig's heyday as a cultured, bourgeois trading city.*

The city archive had materials that enabled him to date individual buildings with confidence and to trace their stylistic development, closely examining plans and elevations, minutely describing façades, castigating what he saw as a 'lack of tectonic conscience' among builders who had exuberantly obscured function with the extravagant decoration that at the same time delighted him. There are in his writing on Leipzig Baroque the first signs of the style Nika was to make his own – a combination of meticulous description and formal analysis with highly idiosyncratic interpretation rooted in emotion and a personal philosophy of meaning and purpose. He was, for example, unafraid to cross-refer the excessive and quirky character of Leipzig's baroque buildings to the 'split' temperament of the Saxon people – an early outcropping of the beliefs he had inherited from Pinder on the 'geography of art' and the influence of place and nation on culture.[2]

He was on course to write a most successful thesis, but in the meantime he had no income at all. And Lola was pregnant. By mid-1923

---

*In his foreword to John Barr's bibliography of his works (in W. O'Neal, (ed.) *Papers of the American Association of Architectural Bibliographers*, Vol. VII, University Press of Virginia, 1970), Pevsner would regret having ignored 'the peculiar, indeed unique, function of the high merchants' houses', both as residences and as exhibition premises for the Leipzig trade fairs.

she was in a state of high anxiety about the fact that the marriage date was not yet certain, and about her own probable inadequacies as a home-maker. 'But equally,' complained Nika to his diary, 'if we were to live with my parents to start with' (as he had originally planned), 'she is worried that she will not get on with my mother.'

He was torn between his work and his emotions: 'P can hardly sit down, moves around all the time, picks at his nails, mutters in the street . . . He is rather noisy, immodest, intolerant, clumsy.' He was resentful at the prospect of having to take money from his father to keep Lola in the style to which he imagined she was accustomed. He could have got by on his own, because he was quite prepared to live meanly, but he could not impose the same restraint on Lola. Nevertheless, he felt diminished by his financial dependence. 'However much my parents might like to clothe Lola, this is not my way of doing things . . . I am not entitled to live more opulently than I can on what the state pays me for my job – or will in future be prepared to pay. Only then will I be able to call myself a citizen – and the trader on whose money I am living will have no place in this set-up.' Fortunately 'the trader' was oblivious to his son's scruples; Hugo effectively paid for the writing of Nika's thesis and would underwrite his career for at least ten more years.

On 23 July 1923, the awkward wait was over, and the wedding took place, a curious hybrid affair, as fellow-student Wolfgang Herrmann remembered it. He had been surprised to be invited to act as a witness to the ceremony, as he had not considered himself to be a particularly close friend. Many years later it occurred to him that his main qualification might have been his own mixed background as a Jew-become-Lutheran, converted at birth for pragmatic reasons. The ceremony was held neither in church nor in synagogue, but in the Pevsners' flat. It was conducted by a clergyman, there were a pleasing number of Christian guests, and it was made known that any children would be baptised and have names acceptable to the Lutheran Church – but, Herrmann noted, the Pevsner parents were 'obviously Jewish, talking in broken German'. The clerk who wrote the civil marriage certificate first wrote 'Pewsner', then crossed it out neatly and substituted 'Pevsner'.[3]

As man and wife, the young Pevsners spent their honeymoon riding round Bavaria on bicycles looking at baroque churches. Years later Lola told friends that Nika had been thoroughly miserable until she suggested that he did some work – whereupon, deeply relieved, he produced thick folders from the bottom of the suitcase where he had hidden them. Lola, on the other hand, was exhausted by the pace. As they arrived at each new church she would get off her bicycle, lie on the ground in the churchyard and go to sleep, while Nika inspected the building; his studies complete, he would wake her up and they would set off again.[4]

They saw a doctor in Munich about Lola's pregnancy. 'Asked whether a fausse couche were to be done,' wrote Nika.* 'Of course he said no.' The enquiry may have been prompted by his mother's attitude. Annie's mental state remained precarious and Nika's relationship with her was as uncomfortable as ever. When he and Lola set up their first home in Leipzig it was not, in the event, in the back rooms of the family apartment, but in a small flat on Dittrichring in the centre of the city. It was not very far from his parents' home, three minutes from the Thomaskirche, where Bach had worked as cantor, and, given their financial state, it was perfectly adequate. But life there was far from the cushioned bourgeois existence of Schwägrichenstrasse.

By 1923 the German government was wrestling with inflation on a colossal scale. The wartime policy of financing the fighting with loans had led to a vast increase in the amount of money in circulation and the devaluation of the German currency on the international market. This was exacerbated by the Allies' imposition of punitive reparations.

Within a few months, the currency had spectacularly collapsed. In January 1914, there were 4.2 marks to the US dollar. With war and its aftermath, this rate had declined to 76.7 by July 1921. Suddenly, in January 1923, the rate ballooned to a grotesque 17,972 marks to the dollar. By July it was 353,412, by August 4,620,455, by September 98,860,000, by October 25,260,208,000. In November 1923 there were 4,200,000,000,000 marks to the dollar. 'For millions of Germans, these figures created a lunatic world . . . in which the simplest of objects were invested by alchemy with monstrous value – the humble kohlrabi shamefacedly wearing a price tag of 50 millions,' wrote Gordon Craig in *Germany 1866–1946*.[5] By the end of the year the government was running 1,783 presses twenty-four hours a day to print notes which had to be transported to banks in large crates by armies of porters.

Lola went daily to the bank to collect their allowance, to spend it before noon when the new dollar exchange rate was published. She was skimping her own studies now, struggling to cope with her new role as wife and housekeeper. Her father's life was in turmoil, as his marriage to Margarete Siebert finally disintegrated, and in the same

---

* 'Fausse couche' usually means 'miscarriage'; Pevsner almost certainly meant 'abortion'.

period Lola the daughter became Lola the mother, with the birth on 12 March 1924 of Uta, named after 'the miracle in stone' decorating their beloved Naumburg cathedral. Lola was deeply wounded by Annie's refusal to come to the christening. 'What must have been going through her mind?' wrote Nika. 'After all, I was still her son.' He, meanwhile, was sailing through his dissertation. He submitted his manuscript on 10 May 1924; by the end of the month he had passed his oral examinations with distinction, and Pinder formally recommended the granting of the doctorate at the beginning of June. 'Nothing,' wrote Nika, 'disturbed my study.'

Within weeks, *Die Baukunst der Barockzeit in Leipzig* had earned the young Doktor Pevsner his first job. Following the conventional path for successful doctoral students in the history of art, he offered his services as an unpaid assistant to the director of one of Germany's most important art collections, and was taken on in August 1924 as a *Volontär* at the Gemäldegalerie in Dresden.[6]

If he were lucky, a *Volontär* might eventually move into a permanent position in the same museum or gallery; in any event he would receive an indispensable training in the classification, cataloguing and exhibiting of art works – provided he could support himself through the long learning period without pay. Nika had chosen well. 'Bring the map of Dresden,' he wrote home to Leipzig. 'We won't be able to manage without it.' The Gemäldegalerie was housed in a handsome building, designed by Gottfried Semper around 1860 to form one side of the magnificent Zwinger complex in the heart of the city. Dresden's liberal political tradition also made it a good forum for the modern arts. There was plenty to see for an art historian in the making.

During the three years the young couple stayed in the city, their accommodation was miscellaneous. The first stop was two rooms on the second floor of a house overlooking the Opera, with space for a pram in the hall and a place to hang the baby's washing; here they lived as paying guests, alongside 'a Swedish gentleman' and an Armenian major. They moved later – and presumably with relief – to a self-contained flat with a hall big enough to accommodate a richly coloured copy of Titian's *Sacred and Profane Love*. At around this time, Lola drew a room plan which, if it was not of this flat, still gives a clear impression of the way in which she wanted them to live. The main bedroom had a pleasant glassed-in balcony, big enough for sitting out, but it was the study that was most carefully planned, for both working and relaxing. In one corner Nika's desk was within strategic reach of the bookcase. On the other side of the room, by the corner seats flanking the big window, Lola had her sewing table and writing desk.

Behind the daybed, to be used for after-lunch rests, stood a Meissen vase on a stand. On her 'wish-list' Lola noted that the room needed a grandfather clock, and she wanted a gas boiler and patent washing-up table for the kitchen. It was a comfortable domestic picture, filled out now not only by the infant Uta but also the dog Ello. Nika was devoted to the somewhat shapeless Ello: 'Three times in nine days I have cleared up little sausages with my own hands – heroic.'

The Gemäldegalerie collection was rich in both Old and New Masters. Its core was the remarkable collection of Italian Renaissance and baroque paintings that Elector Augustus III had bought from the Dukes of Modena, the Wallenstein collections and the Imperial Gallery in Prague. It was also strong in German painting of the nineteenth century, with fine works by Caspar David Friedrich and other Romantics, and good examples of the leading Impressionists – Liebermann, Corinth and Slevogt – alongside their French counterparts.

Since 1913, with the arrival of a new director, the gallery had done more buying. Hans Posse, only thirty-four when he took office, was a vigorous and innovative curator with clear ideas on how the collection should be augmented, catalogued and hung, and he carried the young *Volontär* along in his wake.* For several years Posse had been working on a catalogue of the Italian, French and Spanish collections, pioneering a method of 'scientific editing', providing a critical apparatus detailing the size, date, canvas type and acquisition history of each painting. Nika was deeply impressed, and flattered to be involved. He also took note of Posse's radical new ideas on hanging. The overall visual effect of a room must be pleasing; ceiling lights should be lower and canvases displayed against a background of woven material rather than wallpaper. But the viewer must also be able to study individual works for them to have their full educational effect, and so paintings were hung further apart rather than virtually frame to frame in the eighteenth-century mode.

This lavishness with wall space caused the art collection to overflow its quarters in the Semper building. Early German and French paintings migrated into two of the Zwinger pavilions, and the larger of the Italian baroque canvases were displayed on the main stairway

*Hans Posse (1879–1942) had a chequered career. In these early years he vigorously opposed the Nazi view of modern art and acquired paintings that would later be categorised as 'degenerate', which briefly cost him his Dresden job in 1933. Reinstated in 1939, he would be appointed by Hitler to take charge of the looting of art from Jewish collectors – see Chapter 18 below.

of the Royal Palace. Nika was involved in the reshuffle, and became familiar with major works by Giordano, Reni, Ribera and Spada. He also observed at close quarters Posse's additions to the Italian sixteenth- and seventeenth-century collections, an affordable alternative to the great eighteenth-century Dutch and German paintings, which were beyond Dresden's purse.*

Gradually, as his knowledge and his confidence increased, Nika began to take independent steps. He gave occasional lectures on the Italian collection to the Friends of the Gallery,† and regularly wrote about exhibitions of contemporary art for the *Dresdner Anzeiger*, starting a career as a reviewer that would span half a century. These Dresden reviews revealed as much about his own character as about their ostensible subjects. They were well informed, diverse, independent of fashion, sympathetic to the new; but above all they were serious, framed in terms of morality, aspirations and ideals, insistent that art and the artist did not exist in a vacuum. To some extent this gravity was a reaction to the turmoil of the times, but it was also a continuation of the philosophical reflections and self-examination of the *Heftchen*.

'Pevsner', as he now sometimes signed himself, was not above making topical, even political, references. He bemoaned the conversion of the Galerie Arnold from an innovative exhibition space to a simple sale-room, and saw in it the general decline of Dresden as a cultural centre; Berlin, he felt, was swallowing or diminishing Germany's other cultural institutions. He used his review of an exhibition commemorating a thousand years of the Rhineland to air one or two patriotic prejudices. How poignant it was, he pointed out, to be celebrating a geographical entity which the French were currently scheming to separate from Germany; and how much more development there might have been here in recent times – in modern architecture, say – 'if everything was not cramped by the Treaty of Versailles, by sanctions and occupation!'‡

His aversion to France and things French was more than simple post-war political point-scoring. Quoting a disparaging reference to

---

*Pevsner also offered his services as a *Volontär* in the Dresden Print Room (Kupferstich-Kabinett). Under Kurt Zoege von Manteuffel (1881–1941) the collection became particularly strong in contemporary German works.

†He also took conducted tours of the gallery on Sundays, before opening hours, for groups including the Workers' Education Committee of the ruling Social Democrat administration. Games, op.cit., p.119.

‡The Rhineland was effectively placed under French and Belgian military authority after the Treaty of Versailles.

Paris as 'the largest "small town" in the world', he detected in French art an inability to engage with the big issues. With some honourable exceptions, recent French painters were precise, lifeless or superficial. For all their beauty, the works of the major French Impressionists lacked meaning and 'spiritual richness'; they were simply 'art for art's sake', they had in the end no positive contribution to make to society. This insistence on the social responsibility of the artist was a theme that would dominate much of Pevsner's writing for the next fifteen years (and, in the view of some of his critics, would disfigure it to the end of his career).

He found the same deliberate failure to connect in Picasso during his early Cubist years. And Kandinsky's abstracts, he wrote, appealed only to the eye and the brain, not to the soul. Kandinsky intellectualised the forms of objects without conveying their atmosphere or emotional impact. He *may* have been trying to use clear line and pure colour as an expression of spiritual impulses, in which case it was an expression that only a few would be able to read.

Against the chill of abstraction and the inconsequentiality of French Impressionism, Pevsner set Germanness and the ardour of the German Expressionists. 'With the art of our epoch,' he wrote, 'has come a new world-view and a new appreciation of what German art *ought* to mean – a new acknowledgement of *personality* as well as technical skill.' 'Germanness' meant moral seriousness, respect for nature, passion and struggle. He found these qualities in a variety of artists, not all of them strictly German: Dürer, the creators of the Naumburg sculptures, Goethe in his later years, but also in the Norwegian Edvard Munch, who for these purposes was adopted as an honorary German, one of the leading painters 'of the Germanic races'. Munch, he wrote, was engaged in the task of portraying the age-old problems of conception, birth, love, death, and could convey a sense of the significance of human existence while at the same time brilliantly evoking the alienation of 'modern psychic life'.

Given what Pevsner would write later about expressionism in architecture, the warmth of his response to Expressionist painters is interesting. Expressionism, he argued, was 'the art of the ugly', 'an heroic stylisation of the hideous'. In the hands of an artist such as Max Beckmann, ugliness was ennobled by earnestness, by the battling, immature sincerity of his philosophical essays in paint on biblical or mythological themes. In Emil Nolde, too, Pevsner perceived spiritual energy in action, particularly in his use of colour, 'colour with the breath of the soul on it'. Works that ten years later would be condemned by the Nazis as 'painted witchspittle . . . carved pamphlets issued by psychopathic hooligans and turned to a profit by industrious Jews as a revelation of German religiosity', Pevsner described as 'timeless like the deeds of the Nordic heroes: timeless like the words of the Old Covenant: timeless like the figures of the great masters of the Middle Ages . . . Here, if it is still possible anywhere today, one feels the living aura of holiness round one.'

Oskar Kokoschka was another favourite, despite the shaven head, the sensational private life, and the ego which prompted him at the age of thirty-four to tell his father, 'I believe, in all seriousness, that I am now the best painter on earth.' Pevsner remembered the family link with 'Crazy Kokoschka' from the days in Yvorne with Auguste Forel, and was pleased by the coincidence of his having been a teacher at the Dresden Kunstakademie between 1919 and 1922. He may have been suspicious of Kokoschka the man: Lola later maintained that he had prevented Kokoschka from painting her portrait, because he was afraid that the 'Art Thug' (George Grosz's phrase) would seduce her. But the works had all the qualities that he valued: directness, vitality, richness of colour, joy in paint, and a warmth that atoned for the self-regard.

Pevsner was even able to find redeeming features in the work of Otto Dix. Dix roused him to his greatest eloquence, even if it was the eloquence of disgust:

> Here speaks an artist who couldn't do without the gruesome and the decadent . . . He is not interested in nakedness itself, only in old, emaciated or inordinately fat bodies, or pus, or wounds. Only after he has succeeded in inspiring a thorough horror of sexuality does one realise that he takes sensual pleasure in these deviations.

'To sense the revolting, make it visible, and then revel in it – what a relationship of the artist to the world and to his own work!' Often, Pevsner felt, these were 'ethically damaging' works of art. Yet the commitment to social themes was to be respected and made Dix an artist whom he could not dismiss as he dismissed, say, Paul Klee, for being no more than 'a witty arts and crafts artist', dealing in 'ghostlike fantasies, mentally sick'. Dix was an important figure on the German art scene, both for his involvement in controversial issues and for his exaggerated expressiveness, 'a very typically German – especially central or North German – perversion, more deeply rooted in the essentially German artistic character than many will allow'.

The significance Pevsner attached to Expressionist painting explains the prominence he gave to German art in his reporting of the International

Exhibition of Modern Art in 1926. This was the first international exhibition in Germany since before the war, and an indication of the nation's post-war advance into the vanguard of modern art. Hans Posse was the exhibition organiser, and Pevsner, as his assistant, was deeply embroiled.* He was able now to pronounce with confidence on Soviet art ('nothing much from the Bolsheviks'), on the Italian Futurists whom he saw as an important link between Impressionists and Expressionists, and on England as a 'culturally significant nation' though not one that really valued the visual arts. The exhibition was an important social event in Dresden life; Lola's father visited at least once, with her sister Marianne, and bought, among other works, two by Emil Nolde and another by Karl Schmidt-Rottluff.

This brief immersion in the contemporary art of the 1920s altered the way in which Pevsner approached the history of art. As a pupil (albeit temporary) of Wölfflin, he had concentrated largely on formal analysis. Even though he had declared these techniques to be merely a first step, a tool for achieving a richer understanding of art in its social context, too often in practice they became an end in themselves – as in the case of his thesis, where he had contented himself with stylistic analysis of the Leipzig merchants' houses at the expense of any extended investigation of their owners' lives and motives.

Now, alongside his studies of the art of the past, Pevsner was encountering a variety of artists of the present, and was increasingly reflecting on the position and role of the artist in society. It was very important, he felt, for the scholar to be connected with contemporary needs, 'in a century of Liberalism declining, and Absolutism returning, of Collectivism with widely accepted ideologies in the ascendancy and Individualism with patient unbiased research on the downturn'.

A study of the relationship between the artist and society, rooted in historical detail, was his rather narrow definition of the 'social history of art'. It did not include any economic or political theory, and it eschewed what he described as the 'barren pale generalisations' of *Kunstsoziologie* or 'art sociology'. He was interested in the specifics of the artist's education and his relationship with the public; the ways in which public tastes changed and were reflected in methods of collecting, dealing, exhibiting and criticising art. He was intrigued by the way in which particular art forms or types of building reflected

---

*He would also work as an assistant on the Exhibition of Modern German Prints staged by the Deutscher Künstlerbund (Association of German Artists) in Dresden in 1927.

the social conditions in which they were created, and he saw this engagement with their context as a precondition of success. It was this moral conviction that would in the end play a major part in focusing his attention on architecture – 'because architecture is both art and service'.

CHAPTER 8

'Now the climb can begin'

Pevsner's reaction against Otto Dix was a symptom of a wider unease, a profound dislike of the atmosphere and values of the Weimar Republic. 'The overwhelming menace of our time,' he wrote in a review of a Max Beckmann exhibition, 'has gained true artistic expression . . . Beckmann belongs to those painterly personalities of today who feel very strongly the unhealthy and despicable sides, the misery and hopelessness of the 20th-century world.'

The years of the Weimar Republic were a period of fervid creative activity. 'Everything felt new because of the caesura of war.'[1] Modern movements began to work their way into popular culture, and the ideas of Marx, Freud and Nietzsche appeared on the stage, on the concert platform and in the novel. The arts became contentious and politicised, with riots at theatre premieres and demonstrations at operatic first nights. It was the world of George Grosz, Kurt Weill and Bertolt Brecht, *The Rise and Fall of the City of Mahagonny* and *The Cabinet of Dr Caligari*, jazz cellars and strippers, drugs and mutilated beggars.

Pevsner would have agreed with Herman Hesse's description of Weimar Germany (in a letter of 1931 to his own old hero Thomas Mann) as 'this spineless and mindless state'. Mann himself had written in *Disorder and Early Sorrow* (1925), 'History professors . . . hate a revolution like the present one because they feel it is lawless, incoherent, irrelevant – in a word, unhistoric', and for these purposes Pevsner could be seen as a history professor. He found Weimar disorienting, disturbing and infinitely frustrating. 'You cannot conceive,' he explained later, 'how weary we were with governments that did nothing. Everything was paralysed by party strife, and the corruption in public life was appalling.'[2] He disliked the squalor, the inconvenience and the sense that society's values were eroding, apparently with no one to stop them.

In fact, alongside and partly in reaction to this ferment, new values were emerging. Many people felt the need for a coherent identity, both national and individual. They felt the need for a return to basics, for simplicity, health and the rediscovery of nature and the spirit. Organisations mushroomed to supply these needs: naturist clubs catering to the cult of the body, youth organisations preaching the gospel of the outdoor life and, on the political level, associations offering to point the way to a new sense of German uniqueness and strength. In 1919 a small nationalist group – the anti-capitalist, anti-Bolshevik, anti-Versailles, anti-Semitic *Nationalsozialistische Deutsche Arbeiterpartei* – recruited an Austrian corporal named Adolf Hitler, and developed a twenty-five-point plan. By 1923 this 'Nazi' Party had attempted a coup against the Bavarian provincial government – the Munich beer-hall putsch – and Hitler was sentenced to five years in prison, during which time he wrote *Mein Kampf.*

It was against this background that Pevsner began to evolve his own political philosophy, such as it was. The single most significant influence here, as in his academic life, was very probably Wilhelm Pinder, who was a 'modern nationalist' rather than primarily a National Socialist.[3] Just as he believed German art to be the cultural core of Western civilisation, so he wanted to see Germany as the political hub of Europe. He longed to see German society regenerated, and looked forward to a new Golden Age whose ethos, shaped by the ideals of the Middle Ages, would grow most naturally out of a non-democratic community. These objectives, Pinder thought, could be achieved through the Nazis.

Pinder had little interest in politics for their own sake; like many conservative academics, he felt superior to the crudities of party politics. He was not by nature anti-Semitic: when pressure was applied to his Jewish pupils, he helped them to obtain their qualifications and secure employment while there was still time. ('I can't forget the truly close relationship which has bound us,' he wrote to his pupil Ruth Rosenberg in 1931. 'I hold you in my heart as I did before, and this is something you ought to realise.'[4]) Nor was he in sympathy with repressive Nazi policies towards art; he did not want to see art regulated, and he made a spirited defence of particular trends in modern painting and architecture in the teeth of Nazi disapproval. But Pinder was prepared to tolerate many highly objectionable features of Nazi policy in order to achieve his own ends. 'My destiny and my duty drive me into the front line,' he told Ruth Rosenberg.

It would have been natural for Pevsner, sharing many of Pinder's beliefs about art, to have looked with interest, even respect, at the political philosophy that his mentor appeared to be supporting. Further than that, one can only speculate.

Pevsner's political views were still far from explicit in the 1920s. The most he ever said was that, as a 'non-liberal', he felt an outsider under the Weimar regime. There were elements in his thinking – as in the thinking of many other German intellectuals – that could without much difficulty be perverted into some of the tenets of Nazism: his veneration of the 'Naumburg spirit' and the essence of German-ness; his dislike of materialism; his exaltation of communal priorities over individual desires; his admiration of the blond and innocent *Harmlose* as opposed to the dark and complicated 'outsider'; his vague adolescent musings on the nature of leadership as expounded by Nietzsche, Dostoevsky and Spengler (with whom he had corresponded briefly in 1923). But these quasi-political reflections were far from the forefront of his mind in Dresden. His priorities, as he had explained while he was still a student, were 'work, quietness, objectivity. I would have to give up my profession if I had any intention of taking part in politics.'

Pevsner's attention was focused on his work and his family – now enlarged by the birth of a second child, Thomas, on 2 October 1926. His relationship with his parents, which had never been easy, also demanded increasing care. 'It might have been jealousy of the Kurl-baums,' he suggested later. 'I was so taken with them . . . We didn't often get together. Lola didn't want holidays with Muo [Pevsner's mother]. She criticised a lot and wasn't good for the children. There were quarrels. But Lola went on visiting her, and that must have been good for her. She did need warmth, and didn't get it from me. Very often she said I didn't care for her, that none of us cared for her.'

To others, Annie Pevsner remained a glamorous and fascinating figure. Her grandchildren remembered her as exciting to be around; the Kurlbaum family always suspected that she had had, and continued to have, affairs. Pevsner's attitude was a complicated mixture of crit-icism and impatient pity. 'There's an element of self-destruction in it,' he concluded. 'When did she cease to take pleasure in herself and the detail of everyday life? . . . When did she give up the two front-row seats at the Gewandhaus? After Nikisch's death [in 1926] she rarely went . . . What on earth did she do in later years? How did she fill those years 1923–33? She said she was reading . . . She gradually began to feel herself very alone.'

She endured frequent mental breakdowns. Her husband Hugo's lung disease progressively worsened. He had to spend one winter in Montreux, because Annie was so concerned for him, and then in the summer of 1926, on one of his visits to Sweden, he caught influenza, which rapidly developed into pneumonia. Nika hurried to Helsinki and from there to Stockholm. By the time he arrived the doctors had despaired of his father's life. Dr Salzmann (whose ancestor, Pevsner noted, had been gardener to Frederick the Great) was giving him four injections of camphor a day, plus digitalis. But the crisis passed, and Pevsner took the opportunity to have a short holiday, buying himself a brightly coloured shirt and bow tie, and admiring the local girls. 'It's full of Lolas here,' he wrote to his own Lola, 'you know what I mean . . . The simplest girls serving in a shop – wonderful, reserved, upright – no make-up, no forwardness.' But he, like Annie, would continue to be anxious about his father.

In part, the anxiety was about money. The firm of Emil Barban had suffered along with the rest of the fur trade from the effects of the war. These conditions worsened with the onset of the Russian Revolution, after which the fur trade became a state monopoly. Then came the German inflation. Pevsner watched his father's financial position slowly deteriorate along with his health.

He himself was earning nothing at the Gemäldegalerie, very little from his reviews, and he supplemented this meagre income by teaching history of art at a girls' finishing school. 'It must have been sad for [my father] to see me develop into such an out-of-the-way and financially unpromising career,' he reflected later, 'but he never protested, and went on paying for my life.'

Granted, it was not a very extravagant life. Pevsner travelled around Dresden on his bicycle and rarely went out, though during a quiet patch at work in August 1925, while Lola was on holiday in Naumburg, he did take dancing lessons. 'I'm like a boy,' he reported to her, 'pleased by every word of praise and cast into the abyss by every false step. I can't tell whether I'm a simply awful learner – that's what it feels like . . . Dance tunes run through my head in my sleep, about 170 of them.' He used to arrive early, before the girls, and, to keep his nerves at bay, sat reading Pirandello at the side of the dance floor.

He spent some time with members of his extended family; his cousin Heinrich Israel Pollack remembered him as tall, thin and consistently kind, a resourceful, knowledgeable and protective companion on excursions. He had a few close friends, perhaps the closest of whom was Ernst Michalski. A *Privatdozent*, or assistant lecturer, under Wilhelm Pinder, Michalski had become a *Volontär* at the Gemäldegalerie six weeks after Pevsner. He was rich, dark, very good-looking and, in Ruth Rosenberg's view, almost certainly homosexual. He was a brilliant and original scholar, one of the earliest to value Art Nouveau and take it seriously.

But as ever, Pevsner's most significant relationship was with Lola, and here too he was experiencing problems. He never stopped loving or needing Lola; this much is obvious from the *Heftchen*, and from the stream of letters that he wrote to her whenever they were apart. But he was more critical, more capable of detached observation than he had been during their courtship: 'L gets tired and he can suddenly see what she will be like as an elderly lady. Everything is more pointed, fox-like.' Sometimes his letters have a nagging tone, and his close attention must often have been oppressive. But Lola's answers do not survive, so there is no corrective to the picture that Pevsner paints of his behaviour in these early years of marriage. It may be unduly severe, as he was always his own sternest critic; but what is clear is that on a summer holiday to Bordighera in about 1926, he succumbed to the first of a series of infatuations that remained on his conscience to the end of his life.

In notes for an autobiography that he made in 1977, Pevsner divided his life into three categories: professional, domestic and secret. His infatuations – 'my ill-fated escapades' – were in the 'secret' category.

In 1918, in the interlude of his exile from Lola's circle, he had been much taken with another 'blonde *Harmlose*' whom he had seen at the Gewandhaus. He used to stand by the window daily to catch a glimpse of her, and muse on her while listening to Mahler. He had had similarly disloyal thoughts in 1921, about a very young friend of the family: 'Faust and Mephisto – there she comes – is she not simply beautiful, more beautiful than Lola? – graceful, slim, tall, well-made.' These were teenage crushes, and Pevsner might have been forgiven for passing over them in silence. But the habit persisted.

'No sooner had we been married,' he confessed thirty years later, 'than I began to watch for girls outside (successless). I taught for additional money in a finishing school, but there, as far as I remember, I fell for no one and was in fact undisturbed. But I also remember stopping on my bicycle on the way home from the gallery to watch schoolgirls at play.'

The object of his attentions in Bordighera was Lola's closest friend Margot, the girl whose handwriting he had imitated in order to deceive Lola's parents. She was bolder and less *harmlos* than the rest of Lola's circle, a striking girl with 'curly African hair, but red', and he had first been smitten with her no more than a few months after his marriage. Now he manipulated his time during this Italian holiday to be with her. Kept well within bounds by Pevsner's timidity, this was a very far from torrid relationship. 'Cowardly,' he admitted later, 'cowardly when I learn to drive, cowardly when I am in love with a girl and neither tell her nor go into action.' But it was a betrayal nonetheless, and both he and Lola were deeply shaken by it.

'This should have shown Lola my inadequacy,' he wrote later, 'should have shown *me* my inadequacy.' Technically he was never unfaithful to his wife, but he thought about it and he wanted to be; he just never dared make the attempt. 'I longed and urged and got nowhere.' To him, the Margot affair detracted not at all from his feelings for Lola. It was largely a matter of physical attraction, combined with the thrill of the chase; but he knew Lola could not comprehend this. 'What she could not and could never understand is that such a love of mine could be hot and corrosive and all-embracing and yet not meant to be for ever . . . I really was "strictly dishonourable" . . . It would not make honest sense to Lola . . . Our first kiss meant engagement. Another kiss would be another engagement. Cupidity with any other scope would be evil . . . Sex in married life – yes, any pattern, any artifice. Outside married life – nothing.'

'I never had pity on her when the urges pinched me,' he admitted in his 1954 memoir, and he knew that he did damage. 'To Lola I lied easily and concealed early. The shock of discovering that she never quite lived down . . . How successless these seven-year-itches were is my business. To have the will was as bad as the deed.' He wrote to her after that Bordighera summer while she was still by the sea and he was back in Dresden: 'You are right – it *is* very bad, and I am deeply, truly ashamed . . . If I think of what I confronted you with . . . You bore with me so patiently, until it simply went too far . . . Please believe in my love and see it all just as a bad case of confusion. She was so beautiful . . . I am running through Dresden mask-like, with constant jolts of shock as I chew over the last ten days. I will hold a proper Day of Judgement.'

The picture that emerges from the letters is blurred, but there may have been another episode with a girl from the dancing class, early in 1927, and Lola seems to have gone back to Leipzig to stay with her father for a while. Alfred Kurlbaum was now very eminent, and had used some of his prosperity to commission the Dresden architect Arnulf Schelcher to build one of the first modern houses in Leipzig at Mainzerstrasse 11. Pevsner pinned his hopes for forgiveness on his father-in-law. 'It all feels so long ago, in a dream,' he wrote to Lola in March 1927:

Only now, in the last few days, looking at it clearly, have I been able to see how I have gambled a good, rich, enjoyed life for the sake of a dancing-lesson fling. Please come back – your house and husband are waiting for you. Our happiness was growing day by day – do believe how I long for it and for you. Do talk to Vati – it can only be cured if other people are aware what chaos lies beneath our respectability. If you aren't ready to come, then stay – but not with hatred in your heart. I shall be at the station to meet the four o'clock train, by the engine.

Vati urged composure on Lola, and persuaded her to persevere, and by July 1927 the young couple were reconciled. 'I was so much in love the day before yesterday in Leipzig,' Pevsner rejoiced, 'and I'm loyal again now, aren't I? . . . You have given me a male heir, and I have given you bitter days in the spring . . . It will not happen again next year.'

By this time, now aged twenty-five, he was deep in preparations for his *Habilitation*, an extended piece of original research that was essential for any young German academic seeking entry into tenure; only those with *Habilitation* were permitted to supervise doctoral candidates, the first step towards admission to the faculty. The subject he had chosen was Italian Mannerist painting of the sixteenth and early seventeenth centuries, from Michelangelo and Pontormo to Tintoretto and Caravaggio – its origins, its character and its influence.

'Mannerism' was a style that a small group of art historians sought to insert between the Renaissance and the Baroque. The contrast between these two styles had long been clear – the Renaissance static, compact, idealised, the Baroque dynamic, expansive, and over-expressive. But now scholars such as Walter Friedländer and Max Dvorák were pointing to a period of transition between the two, starting around 1520 and running to the end of the century, with distinctive characteristics of its own. 'Mannerist' art was artificial, stylised, with expressionist intentions. In Mannerist paintings, forms were tortuous, compositions tangled and confusing, gestures excessive. Human figures were elongated and arranged in unnatural positions, with insignificant characters in the foreground and the protagonists behind them, and the action was frequently off-centre. There was often a 'funnel' effect of space receding. The architectural settings were fantastic or mysterious. The atmosphere was one of restlessness, instability, unreality, airlessness – 'no space, no logic, no ease'.

To Pevsner in his present mood, the subject had immediate appeal. It had the automatic advantage of having been endorsed by his professor. Pinder always emphasised the importance of transitional periods, and was particularly intrigued by the psychological characteristics of this one; he liked revaluating previously neglected topics, and had given a series of lectures on Mannerism in Leipzig in 1924. Pevsner's privileged position at the Gemäldegalerie, with its outstanding collection of Italian painting, also helped to weight the scales. But most importantly, Mannerism made emotional sense to him at this point in his life.

'I tend towards decadent scepticism,' he had declared boldly as a student. 'I like the brilliant, mannered, later stages of things.' Pontormo, Tintoretto, Caravaggio were, in his view, putting on to canvas the deep tensions of a period of profound change encompassing both malign decay and the promise of regeneration – tensions that he felt all around him in Weimar Germany. Everything he wrote about Mannerist art, he could equally have written about the work of, say, Otto Dix. It was extremist and uncomfortable, 'rife with potential disturbance everywhere'. It was 'highly artificial, intellectually interesting and of a peculiar cold sensuality . . . Mannerism invented pornography.'

This was 'the first Western style of the troubled conscience', he wrote, with his own conscience only newly quietened. In its unease and contradictions, Mannerism was a vivid expression of the sixteenth-century *Zeitgeist*. The Counter-Reformation in Italy, in his eyes, was a time of polarities and excess – of both fanaticism and doubt. This spirit was to be found not only in the paintings of the period, but also in its music and literature, its science, its law and politics.

'No artist can live against his century,' Pevsner wrote. 'The *Zeitgeist* must come out.' Truly great art was only produced when genius and nationality came together with 'the style demanded by the century'. The goal of the historian was to pierce to the essence of an age; the art historian's task was to analyse how that essence was expressed in its art.

The notion of *Zeitgeist* had long been embedded in the language and logic of German history and art criticism. Hegel had declared early in the nineteenth century that all the social phenomena of a period were related as expressions of a single hidden 'spirit'. He placed emphasis on the cultural unity which this 'spirit' produced within individual nations. Others were more interested in the bonds that a particular time and its characteristic ethos could create across national boundaries. The Austrian art historian Alois Riegl, for example, wrote of 'a deep change in the temper of the times which compels artists to choose particular styles to achieve particular aims which they share with others of their era'. The *Zeitgeist* was conceived as an active, almost tangible force: 'The air about us is not dead, is not empty,' wrote Stefan Zweig, 'it carries in itself the vibration and the rhythm of the hour, it presses them unknowingly into our blood and directs them deep into our heart and brain.'[5] Pevsner was not out of the ordinary in treating the *Zeitgeist* as a reality. 'It was like saying that the earth is round,' comments Ernst Gombrich. 'These were unreflective ideas – Pevsner had inherited them, he just applied them.'

For Pevsner, the notion of the *Zeitgeist* was a useful analytical tool, a way of imposing structure and meaning on multiplicity. 'Fixed terms for styles of ages are there to keep a host of data in reasonable order,' he wrote. He was aware that there were objections to the *Zeitgeist* theory, not least that the connections and correspondences in which it traded were intellectual short cuts. For the sake of clarity, champions of the *Zeitgeist* ran the risk of systematically ignoring differences between individual artists and cultural phenomena that could be far more revealing than any similarities. Pevsner could not resist it. He revelled in finding links and analogies within his ever-increasing knowledge of artists and their works; he loved pattern and order, and he loved to locate himself, his ideas and his experience within an overall framework. In the *Zeitgeist* he found the means to do this.

He had first written about Mannerism as a distinct style in 1925, in an article for the journal *Repertorium für Kunstwissenschaft*, and he would eventually encapsulate his ideas in a 1946 article on Mannerism in architecture.[6] The bulk of his Dresden research on the Italian Mannerists was intended for his *Habilitation* thesis; but long before the thesis was complete, Pevsner had received an invitation that would give it far wider exposure, from the editors of a prestigious series of art encyclopaedias entitled *Handbuch der Kunstwissenschaft* (roughly, *A Guide to Art*). He had offered, and been accepted, to write a volume on Italian baroque painting (*Barockmalerei in den romanischen Ländern. Teil 1: Die italienische Malerei vom Ende der Renaissance bis zum ausgehenden Rokoko*).* He would be standing shoulder to shoulder with some of the most distinguished art historians in Germany, including Paul Frankl from Halle, Georg Graf Vitzthum from Göttingen, Otto Grautoff from Berlin (who would be writing the companion volume on baroque painting in Spain and France), and his old mentor, Wilhelm Pinder, who was now Professor of Art History in Munich.

---

*Pevsner's volume was scheduled to appear in instalments from the end of 1925; it was finally published entire three years later.

For this grander project he needed to confront his subject matter far more directly, and what had been occasional, relatively spontaneous study trips to Italy now became lengthy research tours, with careful itineraries, every summer. Travel for Pevsner had never been relaxed. He had a poor sense of direction, an uncertain digestion, and sensitivity to both draughts and high temperatures. 'Covered in heat lumps,' he wrote from Palermo, 'but great souls have to suffer.' He endured agonies of anxiety about missing trains and buses, invariably arriving at stations and depots with hours to wait.

He was ruffled by disorder, dirt and minor dishonesties. 'I can't get rid of the feeling that I am being conned,' he complained a few days into his first visit to Venice. He was overwhelmed by the beauty on all sides and by the astonishing quantity and quality of the Venetian painting that he had admired for so long from photographs. But his room was tiny, decrepit and full of mosquitoes, opening into a shared bathroom with no lock. By far his best option was to retreat to his bed – he loved Venetian beds, 'just as Carpaccio painted them, unbelievable, so high and flat' – drawing the curtains round it to conceal the squalor: 'One doesn't see the miserable walls and the dirty alley and houses opposite, a metre away. One is in one's own little realm.' But it was not a realm in which one could expect to sleep, as the neighbours owned a lapdog prey to night-long bad dreams, and he emerged every morning with what he described as a 'hangover of tiredness'.

Setting off hopefully, he was soon reduced to sweating, footsore confusion: 'I always end up zigzagging backwards and forwards, as you do in a particular kind of dream . . . My socks are in holes.' The average gondola, he declared, was 'like a coffin – one is half lying down, rocked about. And very expensive.' Smart little motor boats serving the grand *palazzi* seemed like a taunt, and he was affronted by the stark contrast between the elegance of the Venetian rich and the filth of so much of their setting. Everywhere he turned, he detected the smell of disinfectant, and Thomas Mann and *Death in Venice* were much in his mind.

Even Venetians complained about Naples, which epitomised all that Pevsner disliked about the south. He made his first visit there in August 1928. 'A uniquely beautiful situation and a town which doesn't deserve it,' he commented tartly. 'Mussolini's Europeanisation doesn't seem to have got this far . . . They are too wild for me, barbarian. Women breast-feeding in the street, their children in one-piece clothing and that often in rags. I could feel the fleas hopping all over me.' He hated the constant haggling, the pickpockets and the exaggerated mimes of disgust and disappointment at tips considered paltry.

'Naples has nothing for me,' he wrote. Pompeii turned out to be shut and, although the sky was overcast every morning with clouds of ash from Vesuvius, the volcano itself was a disappointment. Pevsner embarked on a purgatorial trek up to the summit, folded uncomfortably on to a small and bony horse, only to find that the crater shown on all the postcards had actually collapsed some twenty years before and was now invisible from the slopes below. 'Imagine your husband on horseback,' he wrote to Lola, 'first trotting and then even a gallop. Madness to go in for such strenuous exercise on a study tour.'

As his visits to Italy became more frequent, he became more resigned. 'I'm back in the same room I stayed in three years ago,' he wrote from Gambaro, west of Parma. 'If only the lavatory had been repaired.'

On the bright side, he took pleasure in Italian coffee and the elegance of men's clothes. Seriously tempted by a pair of white sailcloth trousers, he was held back from buying them by the reflection that he possessed nothing but black leather shoes: 'We Germans are not a fashion-conscious race.' In Rome he was disadvantaged by an acute lack of summer neckwear, having apparently brought with him nothing but his full collection of thirty-six bow ties, 'including those for the tailcoat and one for funerals'.

'Impressions attack one like a hurricane,' he wrote dazedly from Venice. In Naples, despite all impediments, he managed to inspect fifty-five churches in nine days, but not without cost. He took almost as a personal affront the Italian churches' habit of closing for lunch; and many a watertight viewing schedule was holed by the sudden and unexpected appearance of the *Chiuso* sign on palace or museum. In Florence in 1928, in order to be sure of packing in everything of importance, he had to go about with an aged but meticulous guidebook dating from 1804. 'Now I really know what is above every altar in every church in Florence,' he reflected with satisfaction.

By the time he had completed his studies in Italy he was on the way to being considered something of an authority on Italian Mannerism. His *Habilitation,* which he took with ease in 1927, the publication of his volume of the *Handbuch der Kunstwissenschaft* in 1928, and the series of articles that he would draw from the same material – on Crespi, Tiepolo, Caravaggio – would all help to establish him as an extremely promising young academic. He could look forward to ascending the next stages of the conventional academic ladder, towards a position as a lecturer, and the eventual goal of a professorship. 'Now the climb can begin.'

CHAPTER 9

'The satisfaction of getting there'

The next step up the ladder was not long in coming: an appointment as a *Privatdozent*, or assistant lecturer, in art history at the University of Göttingen, less than 160 kilometres to the west of Leipzig, in Lower Saxony.

The invitation came through Georg Graf Vitzthum von Eckstädt, a fellow contributor to the *Handbuch der Kunstwissenschaft*, who had been the Professor of Art History in Göttingen since 1920. Like Pinder, another former pupil of August Schmarsow in Leipzig, Vitzthum was a specialist in medieval art and, in Pevsner's words, 'the sweetest of men', combining aristocratic dignity with personal modesty, 'but alas in a very precarious mental state'. He was 'a European in the best sense of the word', someone who loved and appreciated the continent's cultural heritage as a unity; Germany's wartime bombing and shelling of Reims with all its medieval treasures had been a shock and a grief from which his nerves had never recovered. He also lived in a state of constant concern about the stability of the Weimar Republic, and increasingly found his environment threatening and distasteful.

Politically, Vitzthum had liberal sympathies; Göttingen in 1929 did not. It was a small, steep-roofed town of 50,000 people, studded with medieval towers and belfries, its streets lined with plum and cherry trees, in a picturesque setting on the River Weser south-west of the Harz Mountains. According to Heinrich Heine, Göttingen was 'famous for its sausage and its university'. The university was not one of the German 'big four' – Berlin, Bonn, Leipzig and Munich – but it had a pronounced identity, with a strong tradition of attracting the sons of the wealthy and well placed. Elite alumni included Schopenhauer and Bismarck, as well as Heine himself. When it first opened in 1737 in its classical buildings on Wilhelms-platz, it had earned a reputation as the first 'modern' university for its liberal views on freedom of instruction. But over the years, Göttingen and its professors had become increasingly conservative – Prussian, Protestant and nationalist – and by the time Pevsner arrived in 1929, many teachers and students were already showing signs of sympathy with the new creed of National Socialism.

To many it seemed that the Weimar Republic was continuing the work of destruction which the war had begun. Militarisation had done violence to the economy; defeat and loss had wounded the national spirit, and the provisions of the Treaty of Versailles had been a gross affront to German pride. Then the Weimar regime, with its factions and feuds, had highlighted divisions of class, religion and party. People longed to revive traditional values and craved a sense of belonging. 'It is not freedom they are out to find,' protested Hugo von Hofmannsthal in a lecture in Munich in 1927, 'but communal bonds.'

Some of the key tenets of Nazism were shared by respectable conservatives. It borrowed its symbols from existing sources of deep feeling – the Church, the army, the youth movement, Fascism in other guises and in other countries – and welded them together into a creed of regeneration, order and good health. It used the language of idealism rather than materialism, and in doing so spoke directly to many academics. As a body, German professors were conservative, anti-democratic and chauvinist. They were also extremely jealous of their own power and influence, which they felt now to be under threat. They looked back longingly to a pre-war society that had shown due respect for their own humanist values and had protected their privileged position. Education had been the principal means of defining social class, and academics had enjoyed status, a respectable income and the comforts of a cultured existence.

Now a modern materialist society appeared to be discounting and devaluing their way of life. Inflation – which they attributed to the Republic's economic policies – had made foreign travel and library purchases into luxuries, and the cost of printing was restricting the publication of academic books. New men were wielding power in government, in politics, in the bureaucracies, in the professions, even within the universities themselves – men who were 'proletarian', 'progressive' and, increasingly, Jewish. In the minds of many conservative academics, Jews were associated with materialism, liberalism, internationalism, pacifism and Marxism. Jews were taking a disproportionate and ever-increasing number of teaching jobs.*

From a position of assumed superiority, many German academics felt able to ignore those aspects of Nazi philosophy which they found disquieting, while giving their tacit support to the strands that reinforced their own prejudices or advanced their own aims. Few involved

---

*Although few Jews were reaching professorial levels, by the late 1920s they occupied about 12 per cent of university posts, while representing no more than 1 per cent of the population, with another 19 per cent of jobs held by converted Jews.

themselves actively in Nazi politics, but equally the majority declined to challenge, intervene or protest.

Students too were surprisingly unenthusiastic about the new intellectual, political and moral freedoms of the Weimar Republic. A large proportion came from the middle-class civil service and academic families which had been hardest hit by inflation, and they found themselves struggling to survive financially, with a diminishing number of jobs open to them on graduation. There was a yearning for young, strong, decisive leaders; but where political radicalism existed, it was likely to be right-inclined and tinged with anti-Semitism. As early as 1919 there had been attacks in German universities on Jewish students, and demonstrations against Jewish professors – against Einstein, for instance, in Berlin in 1919–20. In 1926, the National Socialist Students' Association had been founded with the charismatic Baldur von Schirach as its first leader, strongly supported in the student fraternities of the older universities. In 1927, 77 per cent of Prussian students had voted in support of the so-called 'Aryan paragraph', which excluded Jews from the ruling bodies of academic self-government in Prussian universities. Students wielded great influence through their capacity for boycotting lectures and, potentially, closing universities – and Göttingen in 1929 was among the more politically active institutions, with Nazi support rising very fast in student union elections.

There is little indication that the young Doktor Pevsner was conscious of much of this. Vitzthum had qualms about the political climate in Göttingen, but Pevsner's only known reservations about the university were that it was very small and largely science-focused. He originally thought it would be 'death to be stuck there'. But, characteristically, once he had arrived, he threw himself with vigour into the business of becoming a don.

Pevsner's defining feature was his industriousness – though it no longer held the same glamour for him as when he had copied out Fontane's pronouncement: 'It takes earnestness to make a man and diligence to make a genius.' Now it was the words of Goethe that he echoed: 'I think it's a great advantage not to mind being called a pedant.'

He was, as usual, being unfair on himself, although he unquestionably possessed some of the hallmarks of pedantry. 'When I see how Pinder is inspired,' he had written five years earlier, 'I am intimidated – I am not like that. Everything I do takes me a lot of work.' This was, however, partly the result of a temperamental preference, a constitutional suspicion of short cuts. Some years later he would write with irritation of a plan to build a railway to the top of a Swiss mountain: 'It is all very well for people who only want a nice view, but the very devil for those of us who want the satisfaction of getting there.'

'Getting there', in terms of his work, involved reading, note-taking, observation and memorising of fact and image, all on a prodigious scale. A second catalogue of his library, made around this time, revealed an ever more voracious appetite for books: Wedekind's *Spring Awakening* next to Forel's *Ants of the Argentine*, Margarete Siebert's *Maria Stuart in Schottland* alongside *Westward Ho!* and *Ivanhoe*. Shakespeare, Swift and Shaw sat beside Dickens and Conan Doyle, Dumas and Corneille in French, Tacitus in Latin, Dante in Italian. The topographical guidebooks of Georg Dehio and much-thumbed works by Pevsner's scholarly 'ancestors', Schmarsow and Pinder, were joined now by more contemporary writings by modernists Bruno Taut, Sigfried Giedion and Walter Gropius.

Sometimes, however, it seemed as if books and ideas did not truly exist for Pevsner unless and until they had their corresponding wad of notes, crowded on to A4 paper folded into quarters to fit more readily into the note-taker's palm. For paintings and sculpture, on the other hand, he was confident in keeping purely mental archives, committing works to memory, piling one image on another, compiling and comparing his impressions, object after object, gallery after gallery, day after day, often to the point of nervous exhaustion, but with astonishing accuracy. Almost fifty years later, a friend who had accompanied him to a private house in Berkshire for the *Buildings of England* saw him notice a small bronze on a column. 'He said, "I remember this . . . I used to dust it, when I had my first job as an assistant in a gallery in Dresden."'

'The historian must let facts speak,' he would say much later, 'but it would be sad if it were his only frame of mind all day and every day.' He had, and would always have, a penchant for tracing the patterns into which facts could be arranged, for grand theories and 'lusty generalisations'. Art history for him was an arena for engagement with moral and social questions, but that engagement did not have to be solemn or worthy, or even fair or reasonable. There were contradictions in his ideas, and he freely admitted to personal prejudices. Classical art and architecture failed to excite him, nor did he care much for France or the French.*

---

*These were, of course, biases shared by many German scholars in the nineteenth-century tradition, but he may have been following more directly behind Thomas Mann, who had declared after the French occupation of the Rhineland in 1923 that they were 'a ghastly nation, ghastly, ghastly – cruel, sentimental, hypocritical'.

Certainly his Göttingen students did not perceive him as pedantic. Previously he had done no more than deliver isolated lectures to different audiences. Now he was called upon to design proper courses, on Italian Mannerism, naturally, but also on German medieval sculpture, German engravings, Impressionism and Expressionism in painting, and architecture 'from Romanticism to the Avant Garde'.

In addition to his existing passions he added subjects that he would continue to explore for the rest of his life. He now began to develop more systematically his ideas about the social role of art and the artist. Why was the contemporary artist dislocated from society? And why was modern art not 'popular' in the literal sense? Pevsner was inclined to blame the ways in which artists had been educated in preceding centuries, and to look for salvation to new German art schools like the Bauhaus. He tried out some of these notions in a short article entitled 'Kunst-akademien und Kunstgeschichte' ('Art Schools and the History of Art'), and started tentatively assembling more material, as he realised how little had been done to collect data for a social history of this kind. His interest was extending to the social role of the architect, too. When did the 'architect', as such, appear? Were not the stonemasons of the twelfth century the original 'architects'? And what did this mean for the notion of individual creativity in architecture? He began to analyse building types, speculating about the affinities between particular social activities and the architectural styles of the buildings that housed them, and focusing in particular on the building types created or reconsidered by nineteenth-century architects. He was revealing for the first time an enthusiasm for the buildings of the nineteenth century – responding to the challenge of 'a dark age' – which in 1929 was considered wildly eccentric.

Once established as a lecturer, he began to collect his own circle of postgraduates. 'Half an hour ago,' he reported to Lola with pride, 'I had my first student, Herr Lehmann . . . He wants a subject from me – Middle Ages, art and sociology, the kind of thing I've been working on with Schramm.'* Another pupil, Christian Adolf Isermeyer, was specialising in Giotto.†

Pevsner was only some six or seven years older than his students, and he felt comfortable with them. He now began to take pleasure in

---

*Pevsner would seem to have been working with Percy Ernst Schramm (1894–1970), the recently appointed Professor of History at Göttingen.
†Members of the group would eventually end up in universities throughout Europe, among them Hans Gronau in London, Wolfgang Schöne in Hamburg, Horst Gerson in The Hague. Others – Eberhard Wiegand, Heinz Heinrichs, Eckhardt von Wersebe – were killed in the Second World War.

a relaxed social life that he had rarely experienced during his own undergraduate years or his angst-ridden adolescence. After evening seminars he would invite the participants back to his home.

Once again, Nika and Lola were living in considerable style in the tradition of the Pevsner family flat on Schwägrichenstrasse. Christian Isermeyer remembered going to a turn-of-the-century house on Friedländerweg, a street in the best part of Göttingen, and entering a very large apartment through a huge hall crowned with a Murano chandelier. Lola had her own saloon, there was a separate dining room on the street side, and Doktor Pevsner received them in a study of generous proportions. The entertainment was simple – orange juice, biscuits, and the chance to compare different recordings of symphonies and operas on the wind-up gramophone – but the informality was sufficiently unusual in a German academic of the period to make the evenings memorable, and Pevsner's pupils were fond of him. When he turned thirty, they made him a mock-*Festschrift*, a presentation volume of essays. He joined their picnics and expeditions to the swimming pool, went home with them to dine with their families and took them further afield on expeditions to museums, galleries and churches across the country and beyond. There survives a postcard that was sent from Venice in 1931 to Lola, signed by Pevsner and half a dozen of the entourage.

Lola had not looked forward to coming to Göttingen, predicting – accurately – that she would feel inadequate in aggressively intellectual circles, and would be frustrated by the snobberies and petty restrictions of academic life. She might have had fun with the students, but Pevsner kept her in check. 'I may well have been very wrong,' he admitted later, 'crushing her impulses for fear, at Göttingen, as a junior lecturer, of offending staid professors.' She was all the more grateful to strike up a new friendship, through her children, with other 'foreigners' in the university – an English teacher called Pallister Barkas and his young family.

Born in 1898 in Newcastle, Barkas had served in the war and then gone on to do a degree in philosophy, only to find himself quite unable to get a job in England. He had married a Newcastle girl called Muriel Wilson and, desperate to secure some kind of living, offered his services as a teacher of English to twelve different German universities. Göttingen was the only one to respond, and he brought his wife and young daughters Rosalind and Enid to Germany in 1924.

It was in some ways an ill-assorted friendship. Muriel Barkas came from an oppressive background in a strict Plymouth Brethren household, and suffered from chronic ill-health, whereas Lola was a very young and energetic mother, as Rosalind Barkas remembered enviously – always rushing off to go swimming with the children or take them skating on a flooded and frozen tennis court nearby. Pallister was talkative, dogmatic and emotional, but he, like Pevsner, enjoyed the company of his students, and they shared a distaste for Weimar liberalism, though Barkas's romantic conservatism was more pronounced and eloquent than any of Pevsner's views.

Lola, for all the swimming and skating, took her responsibilities as a mother seriously. She was ambitious for Uta, now at primary school, and very strict with her about lessons and homework. Rosalind, less envious now, remembered an outing to a performance of Schiller's *Don Carlos*, intended as a treat, but planned like a military campaign, with weeks of preparation of the text. Pevsner was a loving father, but preoccupied with students, seminars, lectures and his own research. As she had done while he was still a student, Lola resented his priorities; this was to become glaringly obvious when he decided to embark on the longest study trip he had ever undertaken.

CHAPTER 10

'Englishness of course is the purpose of my journey': England 1930

Pevsner's last visit to England had been in 1913, at the age of eleven. Now he suddenly found he had a reason to return. Since 1917 the Prussian Ministry of Science, Art and Public Education had been promoting a programme of *Förderung der Auslandsstudien* or 'world political training', to educate German youth to understand the outside world. This entailed universities specialising in particular foreign cultures, allocated to them by Culture Minister von Trott zu Solz according to existing strengths and interests. As a Hanoverian foundation, the University of Göttingen had long had an affiliation with England. As a result, English culture became its specialism. In addition, the university expected all its lecturers to offer at least one course outside their specialist subjects. So it was that Pevsner found himself called upon in the summer of 1930 to prepare four series of lectures on English art and architecture as background for an English Studies course scheduled for the following academic year. Staged in collaboration with the Anglo-American Cultural Association, the lectures were to cover English architecture up to the end of the Middle Ages; the painting and sculpture of the Middle Ages; the art of the sixteenth and seventeenth centuries; and art from the Romantic era to the twentieth century.

Pevsner took this as an invitation to explore the idea of Englishness as manifested in art and architecture, to provide a counterpoint to the peculiarly 'English' qualities that the students would discover in the language, history and literature they were studying. To do this, he first had to be convinced that he knew himself what those qualities were, and he decided to dedicate his summer to research in the field, with a two-month tour of England under the aegis of the German government. 'Englishness of course is the purpose of my journey,' he told Lola, 'the focus of my present work just as the Saxon was my focus at the time of my work in Leipzig.' He would saturate himself once more with impressions of climate, landscape, people and their artefacts, as he had done so often in Italy, in an attempt to distil the essence of the nation's character. 'In the daytime I have to collect all kinds of details . . . generalisations are a luxury for the evenings.'

In July 1930, Pevsner watched the white cliffs of Dover take shape on the horizon. 'A precise but unromantic beginning,' he observed. As the train carried him north through Kent, he noted with interest – but not excitement – innumerable examples of *das englische Haus*, the neo-vernacular suburban detached dwelling with its plain façade, sash windows and neat front garden, which he believed had been so influential in Germany at the turn of the century.* Only when he reached London did his pulse quicken. After the placidity of Göttingen, he was stunned by the scale and pace of the city, 'the noise of the traffic which rages all over town, without interruption, and the smell of petrol, and the constant need to be careful when crossing the road . . . It really wears you out . . . You can't imagine the crowds here, in these gigantic lifts and on the escalators and stairs. If you dropped a pin, no one would have room to pick it up.'

He retreated with relief to his hotel, an establishment one step up from a boarding house in a quiet square in Bloomsbury. His bedroom was clean, if bare, and he could always seek sanctuary in the communal parlour, with its full-length windows, Pre-Raphaelite prints, flowers, antimacassars and a neat fire burning in the grate. 'This whole area is well-crafted,' he wrote, 'a pleasure to the eye with its trees and squares, the product of centuries of a very self-aware bourgeoisie . . . The groups of squares are not very organic – accumulation without a focal point – but they are most agreeable to look at.' All the more unfortunate that so many of their central gardens were fenced and locked: 'very anti-social'.

Pevsner pushed out from his Bloomsbury base in ever larger circles, tramping huge distances on foot and gradually coming to grips with London's public transport. One mystery tour, prompted by catching an open-top bus on impulse at Marble Arch, took him to the Crystal Palace on the top of Sydenham Hill, 'an adventurous journey being shaken about for an hour for 7d', past little estates scattered higgledy-piggledy, through parks on either side of the road as the bus climbed the hill and offered 'tremendous unexpected views over the whole of unforgettable London – St Paul's, Parliament, everything there and all enormous, like Paris from Sacré Coeur'.

He cast a professional curatorial eye over English exhibition

---

*Largely through the publication of Hermann Muthesius's detailed and affectionate three-volume study of British domestic architecture in the last forty years of the nineteenth century, *Das englische Haus*, published by Wasmuth in Berlin in 1904–5.

techniques and museum catalogues – 'so cursedly practical' – and was faintly irritated to find that they often compared favourably with those he had known in Germany. In the British Museum he was impressed by an innovative kind of popularising: 'reconstructions, photos, all the things which people in Germany are only just beginning to try'. 'I especially admire the technical aspects of exhibitions,' he wrote after a day in the Victoria and Albert Museum. 'There were a good fifty stools scattered about where one could rest – one could carry them away from the main hall. Also magnifying glasses hung up in the miniature and manuscript galleries. Catalogues hanging up all over the place for reference. As a German museum man I can copy a lot of this.'

At Hampton Court he found paintings guaranteed to stir his blood – works by Caravaggio, Tintoretto, Holbein, Dürer – and waited six hours for the rain to stop, so that he could see them in a good light. Kenwood House, he noted, had 'only 65 works in all, but barely five or ten which are not first rate . . . A late Rembrandt self-portrait, something to make your heart pound . . . A Vermeer, and the best of the English 18th century.' As for the modern European works in the Tate, 'They've only been collecting for the last few years, but in this damn prosperous land the collection is already so rich, even in major works. A Renoir better than any I've ever seen, Van Goghs, whatever you could want.'

To Lola, he wrote mostly of what had surprised him: the arresting hideousness of High Victorian architecture at its highest – 'the Hotel Russell should be photographed,' he remarked, with no compliment intended – and the dearth of anything resembling modernism.

What puzzled him was the apparent unwillingness of British architects and their clients to embrace European ideas, and their determination to cling to the ponderous neoclassicism of Empire. 'From Regent Street and Kingsway,' he wrote, 'I have now seen something of the monumental architecture of today. I think it's mostly dreadful. In Berlin everything is modern and almost always good and satisfying – in London I haven't seen a single building that we would regard as giving a modern effect . . . The city simply doesn't subscribe to the artistic styles of the international leaders . . . What is being built is enormous – Caracalla and Diocletian, with an awful lot of glass in between.'

London, he was beginning to find, could be lonely. He had professional contacts with the Finnish scholar Tancred Borenius and the drawings specialist Jim Byam Shaw, and they in their turn had given him references outside the capital, but he had no real friends, and nowhere really to relax.* He was working to a tight budget and was grateful for the full English breakfast, which often had to see him through the day. He rarely braved pubs, though on the occasion when he was driven into a medieval-type hostelry south of the river, complete with 'wenches', he owned to enjoying himself very much. As for the Bloomsbury parlour, it was beginning to irk: 'How am I supposed to write?!' he exploded. 'An elderly English spinster is singing sentimental German songs to the piano – German songs! In German! Now she's playing Mahler's *Kindertotenlieder* – I really can't write any more.'

He pursued his family connections now, with more tolerance than he had shown as a teenager. Solent Road was 'middle middle class . . . I like it very much there – very quiet and homely and comfortable.' He visited the grave of his Perlmann grandparents, and found it 'in a better state than I had expected. The administrator of the cemetery is conscientious . . . The whole Rothschild clan are buried here too – called van Rijn, just like Rembrandt.' His aunt Paula had settled in London, and was living in Manson Place, a small lane off Queen's Gate, behind the Cromwell Road in South Kensington. Here she had a nice modern room, he reported, with a sofa bed. She had once run a small milliner's establishment – 'Madame Pervi' – but now had a job in the hat department of Marshall & Snelgrove. 'She works very hard for not much money, paints herself very liberally, but eats simply and hardly ever goes out . . . Don't let Muo know that Paula is just a saleswoman,' he cautioned. 'Muo can't understand that the small salary is no reason to pity her.'

Pevsner liked Paula, finding her frank and natural and comfortable. He enjoyed some of her more flamboyant gestures and her stories of rich friends. 'She has a colourful life. One might sometimes think she is simply showing off and letting her imagination run riot, were she not able to provide evidence for her claims – the signed photo of the car in which she went at 180 kph.' He was less at ease with the oppressive gentility of his cousin Anne-Marie, who had married an Englishman and was living in the Midlands. Anne-Marie (who now called herself 'Joan' and would not speak German with him) had apparently sealed off her past in order to protect a rather bourgeois marriage and a lower-middle-class existence blighted by lack of money. 'They are little people in their outward appearance as well. Their

---

*Tancred Borenius (1885–1948), an expert on medieval wall-paintings and specialist in Italian Renaissance art whom Pevsner had previously invited to speak in Göttingen. James Byam Shaw (1903–92), an expert on the drawings of Guardi and Tiepolo, assistant to W.G. Constable at the Courtauld Institute, and a dealer and later director of the firm of P. & D. Colnaghi.

clothes and their furniture, their house is one among thousands the same, and there is no maid – which may be the norm here. But the children – they say "kiddies" – are sweet.'

Systematically he planned an itinerary that would take him as far as Hadrian's Wall in the north, Stonehenge and Snowdon in the south and west. These travels exposed him for the first time to the best and, more frequently, the worst that the English bed-and-breakfast had to offer. They were also achieved in the teeth of the English transport system:

> You need the phlegm of the Englishman . . . There are . . . four different railway companies – green, red, brown and chocolate-and-vanilla. On the borders between the different companies, every place has two or more stations, even tiny places. You may notice this in the railway guide – or you may not. In which case, you toddle with your heavy luggage through the most uninteresting nooks for ten or fifteen minutes as the stations are mostly on the outskirts . . . The buses never conceive of the notion that they might start from the railway stations.

'The Baedeker,' remarked Pevsner disapprovingly, 'is not at all good.' Chester was a disappointment ('famous as the best preserved medieval town in England, but you couldn't compare it with Württemberg'), but Fountains Abbey was a breathtaking combination of picturesque ruin with the essence of the English country idyll: 'The light, in the mist, over these lush meadows – marvellous.' At Chatsworth there was 'material for a whole book' in its collection of Italian paintings, 'all unpublished', alongside 'the most beautiful private collection of drawings in existence'. In the Yorkshire countryside around Richmond he found the landscape that moved him most, reminding him of walking holidays at home: 'I need forest for a landscape to satisfy me.'

Port Sunlight provided a spot of light relief. 'The picture gallery is enough to make you laugh your head off,' he informed Lola, 'one long leg-pull . . . Mr Hesketh Lever, otherwise known as the 1st Viscount Leverhulme – a title he probably bought – donated it as a monument to his late wife, a very respectable lady of humble origins who now hangs in a white ball gown in the main hall at the centre of this Art Palace.' Its thirty rooms were crammed with 'the worst 19th-century painting imaginable; one can have enough of the Pre-Raphaelites and their successors, who are worse. In between – armour, bits of furniture, all sorts of miscellanea, some genuine, some repro, and some certainly fake – tremendously comic.' But Pevsner sobered up fast enough when he reached Liverpool, which he described as a hilly, sooty city with an interesting layout and a starkly defined gap between rich and poor, between neoclassical public buildings and crumbling tenements and factories.

In a country which on the whole had the appearance of being 'damn prosperous', he was disturbed by the numbers of drunks in the city streets, some of them women, and tinkers and tramps on the roads – well built, incredibly scruffy, pushing belongings in prams or carrying large numbers of filthy children in horse-drawn carts, shouting 'Penny, sir?' 'Altogether the country is rich,' he reported, 'but the poor areas are dirty and the people filthy to a degree that is rare in Germany. I believe that upper-class intellectual interests are confined to the economically privileged.' He wrote disapprovingly:

> This land has had no class revolution – no '89, no '30, no '48 – and so it is still somehow rooted in feudalism. In every corner the Middle Ages still peep out – not just in the wigs of mayors and the college system at the universities, but probably also in the legal system, with its judges without a code. I'm talking about the large estates, the very generous rich people, the famous hospitality towards the visitor, the culture of Form – and also the lack of concern for social deprivation, and the dirt of the beggars.

In Durham he reached the high point of his journey, and a building that would always be one of his favourites. 'A dream,' he told Lola breathlessly:

> I'm bowled over . . . Imagine a river valley cut into the landscape with wooded sides. The river bends, and in the bend, on the hillside, lies the old town – first the residential town, then separate from it, and higher up, the castle – and then, out on its own, in the midst of tall trees, the enormous cathedral with its twin end towers. From the bridge it is a Romantic dream . . . The first thing that has made my heart pound . . . The cathedral in itself, just like the Matterhorn in itself – gigantic, grey, on its own.*

---

*According to Geoffrey Grigson, *Recollections: Mainly of Writers and Artists* (Chatto & Windus, 1984), Pevsner was entertained in Durham by John Meade Falkner, the poet, arms manufacturer, collector and author of *Moonfleet*, but there is no mention of this encounter in his letters to Lola.

'The good Lord was surely in a temper when he created this climate,' he complained from Wales. His aim was to reach the summit of Snowdon, but he found himself the only person on the wet and wind-swept platform at Llanberis for the 10 a.m. departure, which was promptly cancelled. Perseverance took him to the top on the midday train, and he lost no time in writing a letter of triumph to Lola the moment he got back to the hotel:

> It was a great adventure. Although I am a little damp, I wouldn't have missed it. The mountain top was in a gale, a constant thick veil of fine rain swathing it – one could hardly stand upright on the top and most of the people on the 12 o'clock train went straight to the refreshment kiosk and stayed there – it had heating and coffee. One could only see the landscape piecemeal on the journey up – slopes with outcrops of rock, fields, farms, heather, everything drip-ping with water, brooks and waterfalls – really Ossian. And some of it not entirely unthreatening – after our train, they wouldn't let any more run; and we had to go down very slowly with the side windows open to stop the rain forming a curtain. At some high points they were even worried about landslides.

In Exeter his room smelled powerfully of stout, while Bath was both a disappointment and perhaps a secret comfort. 'Very generous layout, narrow high terraces of houses, circles and semi-circles – but now it's all blackened and with the rheumaticky patients every-where, looks rather *triste* . . . I suppose the English can't really build a spa where one feels at home' – evidence at last of clear German superiority.

'Oh, to be back in Italy!' he exclaimed after a hurried route-march through Wilton House, escorted by an impatient clerk. 'From the point of view of serious research, this kind of castle [*sic*] visit is totally meaningless . . . If only I had used the introduction which Byam Shaw gave me . . .' Introductions were of no avail at Blenheim, for the Duke was away, and Pevsner was refused entry. He contained his disappoint-ment with ease, as he told Lola, because he did not much care for English Baroque houses, and this one looked 'very rich and fantastic, but badly neglected . . . Not my cup of tea'. Only at Longleat did he have a chance to look and absorb and make notes, under the charge of a puzzled but tolerant maid.

At Nuneham Park he was received as a guest rather than a tourist, thanks to his introduction, and now he was exposed for the first time in practice, rather than theory, to the English aristocracy in full cry.

His reaction was a mixture of amusement, disapproval and awe. 'Quite unforgettable,' he wrote:

> just like a play, and I bless my good education. One of the Oxford colleges has a motto – 'Manners Makyth Man' . . . A butler and three servants served six of us a modest lunch of fried goose liver with fried egg, in tiny individual dishes; duck with champignons and other trimmings; cold ham, tongue and a very diverting choice of rice salads; cheese, fruit, coffee. Three wines, lemonade and port . . . But all the presentation and proclamation of each dish for every guest . . . The announcing by the butler of every guest – 'Dr Pevsner!' – and in one steps with ceremony.

These proceedings were interrupted only by the entry of another flunkey to enquire discreetly whether the hostess would care to send a wreath for Lord Birkenhead, who had passed away. 'Just like the films, and I'm in the midst of it. I have to be very careful not to make any *faux pas*.'

The fried goose liver was in stark contrast to Pevsner's normal English diet. Although, as he pointed out himself, he was much more concerned with hygiene than cuisine – 'My standard for food is maybe two or three times lower than my standards for accommodation' – he was startled by the vileness of what English catering had to offer. 'The meals are big enough, but they are disgusting, quite tasteless. Every day the same beans, the same Yorkshire pudding, a ghastly floury gravy and the same tough beef or mutton . . . Even the sandwiches are in uniform; in no tea rooms is there anything but ham and tongue, cheese is apparently "inappropriate", and you need binoculars to see the butter.'

'I find that I look rather shabby,' he wrote dismally during the second month. His sponge bag had been left in Market Harborough and he could no longer execute a satisfactory *toilette*: 'I've no sponge and only a nailbrush – you can imagine what it's like trying to scrub my corpus with that.' He had run out of clean shirts and socks, and starched collars were a distant memory. His shoes were leaking, and the uppers were 'nasty': 'I shall have to run around London in patent leather.' The belt for his trousers had broken, and he was forced to experiment with knickerbockers and long socks girt with elastic. 'Rescue me with a rubber garter, I implore you. I am held together with safety pins.'

'I am a bit conspicuous,' he wrote, 'with sketchbook, opera glasses and books under my arm, and I can't deny it gets me down at times. An Englishman doesn't stand and stare – but I am constantly getting amazed glances for a fraction of a second. So what is it? The hat? the socks? the horn-rimmed glasses? I simply don't know. Here men's clothes are very odd; but they can sense the foreigner – I don't know how.' The patent-leather shoes and knickerbockers might have been a clue. Nor would his forays into English have helped him to melt into the background. Although he had learned the language thoroughly and read it well, he had had little opportunity to practise speaking, and he was afraid of the kind of grammatical lapses or laughable mispronunciations perpetrated by his fellow-foreigners in the Bloomsbury hotel. 'I blush in sympathy when I think I might sound like that . . . I often become too anxious, in the effort to join in.' Frequently it was easier to retreat into German novels and magazines sent to him by his mother:

> I can't help it – I am enjoying Vicki Baum.* It would be better for me to buy English papers, but they are not sufficiently enticing . . . As soon as there's a pause from work, there is a void, however beautiful the day's impressions have been. Only when I lie in bed and read am I back in my own world and at peace . . . There isn't a day when, for a second, deep down, I don't wonder why on earth I'm in England. For a moment the whole thing strikes me as quite unbelievable.

He had begun to devise a method for processing the information that had threatened to swamp him. He had learned to be less ambitious in what he attempted to compress into a day. 'An hour and a quarter in the cathedral,' he wrote despairingly in Hereford. 'Such a hurry, with heart pounding, and I'm afraid not much sticks in the memory. It's much better to cancel some things and look at others quietly and in detail.' Travel, with its long hiatuses, gave him a chance to digest. 'I am making a great effort, going over and over them in my mind, to keep all the different cathedrals and castles apart. The rail journeys in comfortable and mostly empty compartments are very good for this.' But, to make doubly sure, he spent a significant proportion of his small budget on black-and-white picture postcards as *aides-mémoires*, and developed the habit of sitting up at night in his uncomfortable bedrooms, drawing together what he had seen.

Small differences in daily life struck him forcibly. There were more lavatories to be found in England, and no graffiti in them, just as there were more policemen on the streets and a multitude of signposts. The Underground system in London was enviable – 'We have a long way to

---

*Hedwig ('Vicki') Baum (1888–1960), one of the first modern best-seller writers. Her 1929 novel *Menschen im Hotel* was made into the Hollywood film *Grand Hotel*.

catch up' – and yet after one o'clock in the morning nothing ran and nothing was open, 'in the largest city in the world – incredible', and the sepulchral silence that was the norm on public transport made him nervous.

'Rolled-up sleeves, bare knees, open collars and rucksacks abound in towns and cathedrals, as many as at home' – but there were also familiar English stereotypes: the maiden lady of a certain age, agog for culture ('One knows them from abroad, and trips over them everywhere here') and the eccentric English cleric. In the aisles of Wells Cathedral he encountered 'a very friendly old man . . . tall and emaciated, with flowing white hair and clacking dentures', who was intrigued by Pevsner's opera glasses and invited him in for a drink. 'That's England again! His rooms were 14th-century but clothed with *noblesse* and elegance. What kind of salary must he get? – most unProtestant luxury!' His host, who turned out to be the Dean of the cathedral, let slip that he had climbed the Matterhorn. 'All English priests are good mountaineers,' Pevsner concluded sagely.

Not all churchmen were obliging. 'Why are the museum attendants so nice and helpful and the servers in churches so discourteous?' he fumed after a visit to St Paul's Cathedral. 'People – foreigners, I suppose – were leaning on pillars and not taking their seats, perhaps just because they were shy. But that is not allowed. And it's the way in which they say it – "Kindly sit down or leave!" I suppose they have to protect the good Lord from social *faux pas*. Good Lord, I prefer the bicycles in Italian churches. How pleased I am when I hear Italian spoken here . . .'

He noted more fathers pushing prams, women smoking in public and older women in pubs, more boys in caps and blazers with crests, 'a striking number of girls with glasses', poorer children out on the streets late at night with no coats. ('I belong to those draught-conscious Germans,' he conceded.) Even the dogs were different: no dachshunds or fox-hounds, but innumerable terriers and Pekinese. 'You have no idea how much national diversity appears in such details,' he wrote, and yet still he felt that the national character eluded him.

CHAPTER 11

'Culture-politics'

By the early 1930s Pevsner's academic career was progressing precisely as he had always imagined it would.* But other areas of his life were by no means so well ordered.

He had become perhaps a trifle complacent in his relationship with Lola. 'All the pleasure I have in seeing things has only been mine since I have been with you, my darling,' he told her, sincerely. But he over-estimated the pleasurableness of the second-hand experience. 'I'm afraid you're not at all interested in all the detail I give you,' he had once written huffily from Italy. 'There's never a word about all my effort.' He was even able to fancy himself ill-used when she failed to respond promptly to his letters: 'Look, dear Lolchen, you're enjoying yourself at the moment, nothing but fun, while things are getting harder and harder for me here. I really haven't got it easy. Please spare some time from your relaxing to answer me . . . You are, and remain, an abso-lutely rotten egotist. The excuse – that you are too happy – leaves rather a bad taste.'

With two small children and another one coming now, Lola was rarely able to see for herself any of the things to which she had opened his eyes. She loved travelling, but when Pevsner returned from his study trips, he wanted to enjoy the comforts of home life and was reluctant to stir. When his journeys coincided with school holidays and she was able to go away herself, especially to her favourite retreat, the village of Sils Maria in the Swiss Alps, the contrast between their two lives was less stark. He wrote her a brief ode that year:

> *Käse, Bohnerwachs, Heringe*
> *Stehst Du unter dem Eh'ringe.*
> *Lätzchen, Cakes, Kinderkragen,*
> *Fährst Du im Eisenbahnwagen.*
> *Schwimmdress, Couleur, Apfelsine*
> *Bad'st Du im Engadine.*

---

*Games, op. cit., p.162, quotes a letter written jointly by Count Vitzthum and Hans Hecht, chair of Göttingen's Anglo-American Society, praising Pevsner's work in making Göttingen the only place in Prussia where English art history could be studied profes-sionally, and recommending him for a salaried post.

Cheese, floor polish, herrings –
That's what's on your mind when you're a wife.
Bibs, rusks, children's collars –
That's what fills your brain in the railway carriage.
But swimming costume, colour – orange –
That's what you need when you're bathing in the
    Engadine!

But back in Göttingen, Lola was not always 'too happy'. She worked extremely hard to run a clean and disciplined household, which was disrupted at regular intervals by the need to move house. To her frugal mind, it had always seemed a wilful extravagance to pay rent for apartments that stood empty during the summer holidays, when Pevsner was abroad and she took the children to Sils or to Naumburg, and so, with little help, every summer since 1925 she had packed up their possessions, put them into store, found a new flat and reinstalled the family in the autumn.

Tired by housework, anxious about Uta's French verbs and Thomas's bitten nails, tied to the house (even more so after the birth of their third child, Dieter, on 2 August 1932), Lola may well have resented the paternal enquiries Pevsner made from abroad. 'I am a little suspicious because you don't give me regular reports on the children,' he wrote. 'Sometimes I think you have things to hide – that with all the beauty around you, you haven't looked after the little ones, and they've become a bit sloppy in their dressing and washing.' Her replies to his English letters do not survive, but it is a safe bet that they contrasted his foreign jaunts, and his 'something beautiful every day', with her domestic drudgery. 'Would it have been better if I had been miserable here?' he burst out angrily.

Lola, now thirty, had always been prey to her moods. She was troubled by the engagement of her sister Marianne to Carl Walter Kockel, a young lecturer in metallurgy at the University of Marburg. 'C.W.', who would later play an extremely important part in the Pevsners' life, was at that stage 'not one of them' – by which Lola really meant 'not one of the Kurlbaums' kind'. He came from a more academic background; the Kockels, in short, made her feel inadequate. She disliked the shape of his glasses. 'Ma[rianne] looks as if she could take on the world,' Pevsner wrote to Lola's father that summer, 'in contrast to Lola, who occasionally looks at the end of her tether, at least in our marriage.'

Alfred Kurlbaum was well aware of some of the reasons for Lola's edginess and discontent and, as someone who had shown himself susceptible to attractive young women, he may have had some sympathy with his son-in-law. Pevsner combined highly romantic notions of love with realism about his own physical needs. 'Oh, my nature!' he wrote, after six weeks away from Lola in England. 'I'm sure that other people aren't as racked with sexual desire . . . It's high time I got back.' Even nude statues, however classical, had the power to distract him: 'I loathe this hyper-sensitivity that long abstinence produces – it ruins my work. This afternoon in Dulwich I had to give up on the gallery. It confuses me very much, and I really can't afford that.'

'If I am faithful to you in weeks like this,' he continued, 'it is because of the language problem, which makes any kind of ingratiating approach impossible . . . and the lack of skill, and the serious temperament . . . You may think it's just as well – but it doesn't do me any good in the Lord's eyes, for there the wish counts for as much as the deed.' Sometimes he was inclined to attribute his restraint to noble reasons rather than simple cowardice. 'I am a romantic. That's one of the reasons I hold on to fidelity. I simply couldn't just absorb a casual experience as others do. With me it would have to come from the heart.' But he added a note of warning: 'That's the very thing that makes it doubly bad when it comes.'

Pevsner made his bouts of amorous longing, which would recur throughout his life, sound like visitations from above, beyond his control. At intervals, strongly attracted by girls usually rather younger than himself, he would veer uneasily between the two poles of physical desire and idealised romantic devotion, creating for himself a most uncomfortable synthesis that resembled nothing so much as an adolescent crush, perpetually unfulfilled, but nonetheless painful and embarrassing for all concerned – for Lola, for the objects of his infatuation and for himself. In the autumn of 1930 one of these interludes was on the horizon, and Lola's unease was well founded.

Meanwhile his parents too were facing disquieting changes. Hugo's financial position was becoming ever more precarious. Fur firms worldwide had lost huge amounts of capital in the American financial crash of 1929. The centre of the remaining business now lay in retail, not broking, and in London, not Leipzig. Other misfortunes for the firm of Emil Barban remain shrouded in mystery, hinted at only in fragmentary notes made by Pevsner near the end of his life:

'Then the accountant ?Goya cheated him. The young ?partner was incapable.* Then came the other firm's takeover . . . Schapiro got the lead on us.' 'Father never spoke much of it,' Pevsner wrote in his 1950s memoir. 'In his own way he was very reserved, and maybe he was afraid of Mother's contempt. But gradually he could no longer afford to give her the life she had enjoyed before.'

In 1931 his parents gave up the lease on their Leipzig apartment and moved into rooms in the Hotel Kaiserhof. 'We always assumed that they were comfortably off,' wrote Pevsner's Aunt Em, one of Hugo's many dependants, 'but ever since they moved to the hotel this has changed, and I feel awful that they have to worry about their day-to-day existence. I had heard that they had assets in Sweden – but now I wonder . . .'

Day-to-day existence in 1931 was in fact changing in ways that Nika shows little sign of having recognised. Germany was struggling to combat the effects of the Depression that had followed the economic disasters of 1929 – recession, unemployment, protective tariffs imposed in the US and elsewhere, a decline in exports and an end to foreign loans – long before the nation had had a chance to recover from the impact of war and reparations. 'The moral and political disorientation that had affected Germany since the war,' the historian Richard Grunberger has written, 'made the Depression assume a significance far beyond the purely economic one it had elsewhere; there was a mood of living in an "Endsituation" . . . which presaged either chaos or an "ineluctable transformation".'[1]

There were signs everywhere of the shape that this 'ineluctable transformation' might take. That June the university in Munich had been closed by protests directed at Jewish teachers, during which students broke down the door of a lecture room used by a Jewish lecturer in international law. In the elections to the Reichstag, or German parliament, that September, there was a huge increase in support for the Nazi Party, which received 6.5 million votes and 107 seats.

'O amiable Göttingen,' Pevsner would write later, 'where one feels further from Berlin than in Birmingham.' Throughout his years at Göttingen, he continued to display what one historian has charitably called 'the political naïvety that was the price of the traditional aloofness of the German *Dichter* and *Denker* [poet and thinker] from

---

* This may refer to Heinrich Barban, son of the firm's founder, Emil Barban. He had been brought in to the firm as a limited partner in 1923 when his father left; a lawyer, he may have had limited aptitude for the business.

practical affairs.'[2] Emotionally he retained the somewhat inchoate elitist conservatism of his youth – anti-communist, anti-proletarian – without, as far as we know, giving much thought to the practical implications of his instincts. He had a tendency to use 'liberal' as a term of disparagement, while at the same time displaying the key liberal quality of tolerance and revering the liberal humanism of his father-in-law. In as much as his political views could be said to be 'shaped' at all, they were shaped by his ideas on the subjects that were genuinely close to his heart: on art, on literature and on culture in general. His political *Weltanschauung* or 'world-view', such as it was, grew out of his aesthetic and intellectual theories, and not vice versa.

There was much in Nazi attitudes to art and art history that Pevsner was always likely to find attractive, drawn as he was both temperamentally and intellectually to the twin concepts of German-ness and the medieval ideal which he had found so perfectly combined in Naumburg. He believed that the maker of a painting or sculpture should find joy in the making, and that the artist should subordinate his individuality to the communal goal, should be to some extent a servant of the state, as the medieval craftsman had been a servant of the guild. Art, in this sense, could be seen as an instrument of nationhood – German art as a legitimate expression of the German nation.

Locked as we are today within the confines of hindsight, it is hard to free these ideas of the taint of Nazi doctrine. All the more impor-tant, then, to acknowledge that, just as 'Germanness' had been a reputable subject for study in Germany for almost a century, so theo-ries of national characteristics in art were currently fashionable in wider art historical circles in Europe.* 'The individuality of race is stronger than that of genius,' wrote Sir Reginald Blomfield in 1934. Blomfield was an archetypal Edwardian architect, former President of the RIBA and a devout exponent of the virtues of Englishness; stead-fastness, restraint, modesty, gravity, thoroughness, refinement – all, he thought, were the 'expression of permanent racial characteristics' inherent in the Englishman.† The belief in national character in art was neither anti-Semitic nor chauvinist by definition – the Jewish historian Hans Jaffé, for example, would attempt an exposition of

---

*Marlite Halbertsma, letter to author, 2/4/97. The 12th International Congress of Art History in Stockholm in 1933 would be devoted to the subject of national character-istics.
†Quoted in D. Watkin, *The Rise of Architectural History* (Architectural Press, 1980), p.97.

Jewishness in Jewish art – and the immediate association of the theory with Nazi doctrine is too glib.*

Notions of 'Germanness' and 'service to society' could actually be used to defend art that might otherwise have been condemned as subversive. This may have been in Pevsner's mind when he wrote a review of the collected works of Le Corbusier in 1931, strongly refuting the claim that Le Corbusier was the leading figure in the Modern Movement in architecture and that therefore the Modern Movement was French (more precisely, Swiss) in origin. The Modern Movement, Pevsner wrote, was in its essence German.[3]

Pevsner acknowledged Le Corbusier as a genius, 'perhaps the greatest artist of all', but had little respect for him as a man.[†] Le Corbusier 'had neither wisdom nor equitableness nor was he guided by ethics'. No one so committed to the supremacy of the 'artistic' individual – 'I want to create poetry, not prose,' he had proclaimed – could be considered a pioneer of the Modern Movement. The real pioneers, Pevsner intimated, were committed to the ideal of community.

He elaborated this theme in a long article entitled 'Social Ideals amongst Creative Artists',[4] prefacing it with the statement that tracing an intellectual or ideological thread could be more revealing for the history of art than plotting purely aesthetic continuities of line, colour and composition. The thread he had chosen was the subordination of individual artistic ego to the cause of collectivity, and he picked it up with the group known as the Nazarenes, a nineteenth-century 'brotherhood' of students in Vienna who formed themselves into a community along medieval guild lines, working jointly to paint large frescoes on spiritual subjects, as disciples of loyalty, truth and mutual responsibility. The thread then led naturally on to another 'brotherhood', the English Pre-Raphaelites, who even more forcefully proclaimed the moral purpose of art.

Most influential of all in articulating and passing on these social ideals was William Morris, with his insistence that artists must work alongside craftsmen in a community whose joy in making would have the power to redeem and transform an industrialising society. And finally the far end of the thread was held by Walter Gropius, who acknowledged Morris as a spiritual ancestor and was putting his ideals into practice, perhaps more effectively than Morris himself ever did,

---

*Hans Jaffé (1915–84), born Hans Ludwig Cohn, was an admirer of Pinder's work. He made his career in Amsterdam as the leading scholar of De Stijl and one of the first university professors of modern art.
†See p.216.

in the Bauhaus school of arts, crafts and architecture in its new home in Dessau.

Pevsner returned to the theme of social ideals in modern architecture two years later in a lengthy review of the proceedings of the 3rd International Congress of New Building, which had taken place in 1930 in Brussels.[5] Under the title 'Rational Developments in Building', he argued that truly 'modern' building had a style that was unintentional, in the sense that it grew less from any deliberate artistic manifesto than from the architects' focus on function, 'the purely purpose-directed collectivist frame of mind of its creators'. The aim of the modern architect engaged in social housing was to meet the modest needs of the many, rather than to gratify the whims of the wealthy few.* In this context, detached houses were a luxury; Gropius was praised for his plans for ten-storey blocks of flats in a setting of grass and trees, Le Corbusier less warmly commended for more romantic but less practical towers, with corridors opening on to a hundred or more flats at a time.

The articles of 1931 are studded with 'should' and 'ought', even 'must'; they present an idealised vision of a new society, symptomatic of a widely shared revulsion against the decaying Weimar democracy.[6] Pevsner does not seem to have pushed his argument to its logical conclusion in determining what should be done with those artists who were *not* willing or able to repress their individuality in the service of the common weal. There was plenty of evidence, however, that the Nazis had no such inhibitions and were already dealing in the 'should not' and 'must not' in art.

In 1927 Alfred Rosenberg had founded a National Socialist Society for German Culture, to raise the German nation's consciousness of itself as a *Volk* and to instruct the *Volk* on 'the connections between race, art, science and moral and military virtues'.† By 1929 the Nazi architect Paul Schultze-Naumburg, author of the book *Kunst und Rasse* (*Art and Race*), had been appointed Director of the Weimar Kunstgewerbeschule and in 1930 he personally supervised the painting-over of a mural by Oskar Schlemmer in one of the buildings that had been used by the Bauhaus.

Schultze-Naumburg went on to remove from view selected works by Paul Klee and Wassily Kandinsky. Pevsner admired neither Klee

---

*Pevsner's interest in the provision of decent social housing for the working classes – past, present and future – would remain constant from the German *Siedlungshäuser* of the 1920s to the LCC estates of the 1950s.

†The society was renamed in 1929 as the League for the Defence of German Culture, *Kampfbund für deutsche Kultur.*

nor Kandinsky – both, in his view, were guilty of making 'art-for-art's-sake' – but his solution was a less crude and more cerebral one. Artists should be persuaded to relinquish their individuality out of *conviction*, as the Nazarenes and Pre-Raphaelites had done, and they would probably be moved to do so under the influence of the spirit of the age. The vulgar and direct Nazi notions of compulsion, such as banning, burning or shredding, were outside Pevsner's frame of reference.

During 1931 Pevsner was distracted by personal confusion of a familiar sort – one reason, perhaps, for his lack of sensitivity to the political upheavals around him. He had gradually become infatuated with one of his students, Lise Weissenborn. The *Heftchen* covering this period of his life no longer survive, but in all probability Lola recognised the symptoms and reacted with a combination of misery, irritation and understanding. She went back once again to stay with her father – 'to give me explicitly a free hand to see where I could get', Pevsner confessed later.

By now Alfred Kurlbaum was extremely eminent in the field of jurisprudence, and his income had survived the slump; increasingly he took over from Hugo Pevsner the charge of the young Pevsner family. After Marianne's marriage to Carl Walter Kockel, he found himself lonely. He formed a relationship with Marta Vidor, a highly successful Hungarian pianist who would later find a second career as a psychiatrist, and took some comfort in it. But he was possibly mindful of his own emotional tribulations since his first wife's death when he advised Lola, quite brusquely, to master her wounded feelings and persevere with her marriage.

Lola and Pevsner were always able to talk about his entanglements: she was, in a curious way, his only reliable counsellor. Of one prickly telephone call during this time, Pevsner wrote: 'It's normal, and just underlines the basic solidity of our marriage. Neither of us backs down easily, you especially.' She contented herself with suggesting that he put more distance between himself and his students, and she treated his behaviour more as self-indulgence than as a deliberate effort to hurt her. By July 1932 he had 'disciplined himself', in her phrase – and in any case there was the possibility that Lise would not be coming back in the autumn term, so 'in a single stroke the burden could be removed from you'.

With one part of his mind he desired this solution, but could not shake himself entirely free. 'In all our goings-on, everything has come out all right in the end, hasn't it?' he wrote awkwardly in November. 'Don't be too gloomy about the other thing – we've muddled through much worse.' But it was he who had some kind of nervous collapse by the end of the year. Alfred paid for him to go for a period of convalescence to a spa hotel in Oberhof, a forest retreat in the mountains of Thuringia, all carved woodwork, peasant furniture and dark red and green painted walls. 'Good soap,' Pevsner commented, and described the menu at some length to Lola. 'You can walk for four hours in the pines and not meet a soul. Your mind takes a complete rest, just listening to the footfalls and looking at the constantly changing views.'

Beside the pressure of his strained relationship with Lola, he may also have been reduced to breakdown by the weight of work, and he may at last have woken up to increasingly ominous changes in the political climate by the end of 1932: 'things that make one really afraid', he admitted in November. It was becoming more difficult to get news and views from abroad. Listening to foreign radio stations was considered suspect. Their English friends, the Barkases, received the *Manchester Guardian* by post, and other people from the university used to drop in to read it, but on days when it was critical of Germany, the paper failed to arrive. Posters were beginning to appear on the walls in Göttingen – 'Where two Jews meet together, they plot against their country' – and the Pevsners were occasionally taken by surprise by disparaging or spiteful remarks from neighbours or landladies. A few people – the 'Germanist Neumann', for example – cut them dead.*

There was a constant sense of unreality in this for Pevsner. He and Lola had decided not to tell the children that they were Jewish. As Christians, they would have been completely out of place in Jewish schools, their parents felt, having little in common with Orthodox or even liberal practising Jews. Uta spent time with Enid Barkas tearing down anti-Semitic posters in innocence of any personal implication. 'It wasn't really an issue,' she remembered much later. 'We wouldn't have been able to understand how you could be Jewish when you were Lutherans, christened, confirmed and married in church.'

Better not to advertise one's Jewishness, in any event, at this point in an academic career. In 1931, 60 per cent of the national student union had supported the Nazis, a balance reflected in Göttingen. Members of the union were invited to report back to headquarters on

---

*Almost certainly Germanist Friedrich Neumann (1889–1978), who joined the Nazi Party on 1 May 1933, at which point he also became the Rector of the University.

'suspect' teachers and there were anti-Semitic riots in universities in Berlin, Munich, Cologne and Halle.

When it was announced that Hitler was coming to Göttingen on 21 July, for an open-air rally in the Kaiser Wilhelm Park, Pevsner persuaded his students to make up a party for the occasion. 'We took it as an entertainment,' he later recalled – but by the time Hitler arrived, he had lost enthusiasm. 'The brown flood has broken out here,' he wrote with an air of distaste on the day of the rally. 'The whole town has been putting out flags. Cars and coaches from all over the place, six special trains . . . Will it be a circus? Or end in cater-wauling? Everyone is too excited to work. But I am forcing myself to it . . . I could do with the hours I have to devote to Hitler.'

Pevsner would never be a political activist. 'I think in the end the Left will be the correct path,' he wrote in July 1932, 'if National Socialism doesn't follow a decisive socialist course . . . But . . . the way it's going in Russia – no, that I won't have, the kind of *cold* revolution that solves nothing.' He did not lack opinions, but scarcely held them with passion. They rarely appear in his letters, hardly ever in his adult diaries, and he never translated them into action. There is, for example, no evidence that he ever joined a political party of any persuasion.

But the correspondences between Nazi philosophy and his own ideas on the role of the artist remained, and he continued to worry away at them. 'As for politics,' he wrote, 'Tschah! I am involved in culture-politics.' He may have been referring to a pair of articles he wrote early in 1933 on the teaching of art history in secondary schools. One was printed in a paper with Nazi sympathies, the other in a more neutral publication aimed at education professionals.[7] Both focused on the virtues of art history as a means for enriching the teaching of German history and language – arguing, for instance, for the use of the passionate, exalted realism of Dürer's engravings to illustrate lectures on the German Renaissance as an era when man was coming to terms with his own individuality. Art historians, Pevsner suggested, should not only think in terms of lecturing to art students, but also to teachers in other subjects, preparing them to use art as a tool for illuminating their own disciplines.

This practical application of art history was not a new suggestion. Pevsner's motives in reviving the idea were perfectly obvious. He believed implicitly in the power of art history to make cultural connections and deepen understanding of both the historical and the creative process – it would be one of his articles of faith some thirty years later, as a member of the Coldstream Committee reviewing the curriculum in British art schools and colleges – and he saw an opportunity to argue the case more strongly, with the prospect of a ministry under the Nazis devoted to putting art to work in the service of the nation.

In the article for the education magazine, though not the Nazi publication, he criticised the 'narrowly party political' teaching of history, but he was aware that he was taking a risk. 'How one has got to be on the alert!' he wrote to Lola. 'I don't doubt that, for our university as well, the time will come when one has to weigh one's words.' He may have been temporising in this way when he wrote an article entitled 'Art of the Present and Art of the Future'. This piece, apparently never published, contains ideas that are already familiar from his early writings, but are expressed here in new and sometimes disturbing terms, and his motives are hard to divine.

Pevsner introduced himself in this article as a historian of the 'reformist' rather than 'liberal individualist' type, hinting at an underlying ethical agenda. His mission was to examine the art and architecture of the past hundred years in search of lessons for the future – both dire warnings and positive pointers – and then position the art of the present day on the continuum between the two. He first returned to the charge against Impressionism that he had launched as a young critic in Dresden. Solipsistic and devoid of deeper meaning, bourgeois in its subject matter and elitist in its appeal, accessible (like fine wine and dainty porcelain) only to the effete few, Impressionism had the stamp of the selfish and individualistic all over it. In its building, too, the nineteenth century had often shown a complete disdain for social well-being, throwing together a jumble of showy and vacuous forms from the scrapbook of previous centuries' styles.

Looking to the future, Pevsner forecast a time when housing would be simple, uniform, disciplined, in a shared style that was accessible to all, 'not . . . a single little turret for each single little soul', and there would be 'no soft forms or lazy adherence to the past for the sake of beauty'. The artist would be a servant of the state, from instinct and a sense of duty, and art would be 'propaganda' in the best sense of conveying important truths from which all would benefit. In this sense, it would be both 'national' and 'socialist', 'the two parts of the term separated for once, giving each equal weight and definition'*. Some forms of painting would 'recede' for a while, as their subjects

---

* Lionel Gossmann, in a close analysis of Pevsner's 'Art of the Present and Art of the Future'/*Kunst der Gegenwart und Kunst der Zukunft*, makes the important point that views very like Pevsner's were shared by many on the Left as well as on the Right in the inter-war years. Professor Gossmann's extended examination of Pevsner's politics (which also scrutinises Pevsner's article 'Kunst and Staat' – see p.165 below) will appear in his forthcoming monograph on the German archaeologist Max von Oppenheim.

were 'inessential' – landscapes, portraits, still life – and more than likely there would be some lowering of standards of taste, even an element of kitsch. But both these sacrifices must be considered necessary in the greater cause of art gaining in content, and once the new philosophy of art was established, higher standards would doubtless reassert themselves. 'It is better to have a painting that is kitsch but designed to serve the state,' wrote Pevsner, 'than a good painting that serves nothing and no one but the egotism of the painter.'

It was through this prism of humanity and national purpose that one should view German art and architecture of the present, he declared. Abstract art, self-referential and inaccessible, might seem to fall naturally into the same category as Impressionism, but Expressionist painting surely could be seen as presaging the art of the future, because of its capacity to express moral ideas and social messages. Realistic, harsh, angry, in tune with the revolutionary spirit of its age, it used straightforward shapes and strong warm colours to communicate with the ordinary man. The buildings of the Modern Movement, too, he argued, had demonstrable links with the future, through their social ideals and community spirit – and, of course, their German origins. Indeed, it was Germany alone that truly manifested modern trends: 'Unrelenting radicalism is what Germany contributes in the fields of politics, philosophy and art history in general.'

The views Pevsner expressed in this article were clearly recognisable as views he had always held, but they were couched for the first time in language that now has an unpleasant taint of Nazism about it. He referred to 'international types' and 'foreign influences', and used the terms 'health' and 'degeneracy' in the context of culture, as the Nazis would do. He spoke of a 'sociological necessity' to serve the state, and predicted an architecture that would be characterised by 'strict rhythm', extending across the horizon 'with discipline, and common purpose, moving proudly in step like innumerable marching columns'. His forecast of the visual art of the future accurately described, and might have appeared to defend, a significant section of Nazi painting – social realist kitsch, laden with the 'truths' of the Nazi philosophy – and yet at the same time what he wrote about the Expressionists ran directly counter to their programme for destroying 'degenerate art'.

Pevsner's motives are certainly not clear to us now, and may not have been entirely clear to him then.* Putting the worst possible

---

*His intentions might be clearer if it were possible to give 'Art of the Past and Art of the Future' an exact date, but there is no indication on the manuscript, which can only be dated to around 1933–4 from oblique references in his correspondence with Lola.

construction on what he wrote, he may have been attempting to ingratiate himself with the Nazi art establishment. More likely is the theory that he was trying to use Nazi vocabulary and concepts to reinforce his own arguments and promote his own cherished causes by lodging them in a Nazi context. Late in his career it was put to him by an Italian historian apparently eager to recruit him as an anti-Fascist hero that, in his earlier article on Le Corbusier, he had been trying to project the Modern Movement as quintessentially German in order to endear it to, or at least protect it from, the Nazi art establishment. As he had done consistently throughout his life, Pevsner flatly rejected the idea of political motivation in anything he had written; he was, he maintained, a historian pure and simple. But it is still tempting to detect an attempt of this sort in 'Art of the Past and Art of the Future'.*

Pevsner embraced few of the Nazis' notions of their spiritual mission, and none of their irrationalism. He wrote much later, 'I used to say "It's a pity the Nazis call themselves National Socialists. If they didn't, I would call myself a National Socialist: National meaning *Europe des Nations*, and Socialist meaning socialist"', revealing the naïvety of his political perceptions in the early 1930s. He was, as he claimed, dabbling in 'culture-politics' rather than party politics, but by 1933 the distinction was beginning to be somewhat artificial.

---

*It is interesting to note Pevsner's comments on attempts of this sort by Italian art critics to ingratiate modern architecture with Mussolini. In an article on the Italian critic Edoardo Persico in the *Architectural Review* (*AR*), February 1966, he wrote: 'There were those who thought that if they could convince Mussolini that modern, rationalist architecture . . . was somehow Fascist, all might still be well.'

CHAPTER 12

'Ante-chambering'

At the end of January 1933, Hitler became Chancellor of Germany. Before he had even taken the oath of office, he had managed to get the Reichstag dissolved and new elections called for March, leaving him scope to govern independently through administrative decree, arrests and an increasing level of harassment and violence. Within a fortnight he had taken control of the police force. A presidential decree of 4 February authorised the prohibition of newspapers or public meetings that 'abused' or 'endangered' the interests of the state; radio was already under state control.

On the evening of 27 February, the Reichstag building, the seat of parliament, was set on fire and gutted. Hitler immediately attributed the blaze to communist saboteurs and used the threat of a communist revolution to persuade President Hindenburg to sign a decree suspending all individual rights of the citizen for the duration of the 'emergency'. This decree, which enabled the regime to make arbitrary arrests on suspicion and hold detainees indefinitely without trial, would form the basis of Nazi repression until their fall.

On 5 March, the Nazi Party won a clear majority of seats in the Reichstag. Before the other parties could mobilise an effective or united opposition, Hitler demanded an Enabling Act that for four years would allow the government to ignore constitutional forms and limitations, in order to solve Germany's problems. The Act's passage on 23 March 1933 made him dictator. The party system and state governments were effectively abolished, and the way was clear for Hitler's regime to embark on a formal process of *Gleichschaltung* or 'bringing into line'.

Some elements, of course, could never find a place within the lines drawn by the Nazi state. On 13 March, Josef Goebbels had become Minister of Propaganda and People's Education, declaring that cultural and intellectual life must be put into the same gear; there must be harmony between artistic expression and the political ideology of the state. Two days later, he issued the first official black list in the fine arts. On 21 March, Kurt Weill left Germany after his opera *Silbersee* was removed from the repertoire of the Leipzig Opera; in Dresden, Fritz Busch had already been forced to resign from the Sächsische Staatskapelle. In Leipzig again, a concert that was to have been conducted by Bruno Walter was cancelled. 'I suppose we'll get a less good conductor,' Marianne wrote to Lola, 'but a true German.' For some of those less 'true Germans', the concentration camp at Dachau had been set up on 22 March.

During this extraordinary month, Pevsner was in Berlin. He was, he complained to Lola, doing a great deal of 'ante-chambering', hanging around and awaiting the pleasure of officials who were ominously grudging of their time and attention. He was almost certainly doing some research on academies of art and the education of the artist – he described to Lola a guided tour that had been arranged for him around workshops, master ateliers and schools – with a view to turning his accumulating material into a book.

At the same time, however, it would seem from cryptic comments made to Lola in these Berlin letters that he was in search of information of a more dangerous and personal kind. He may have been looking for documentary evidence of his descent or, more positively, his conversion to Lutheranism, trying perhaps to find ways round the development that he feared most: the request that he stop teaching at Göttingen, at the behest of students who refused to be lectured by a Jew. 'Berlin is very quiet – outwardly at least, completely Hitlerised,' he wrote on 5 March, the day of the elections. 'Special police, *Hakenkreuz* [swastika] flags and torchlight processions . . . You can't really think of getting close to anyone now – they're all afraid of being arrested at any moment . . . Nowadays one doesn't know what's happening from one day to the next.' This was a remark that may have had a double edge. Though the infatuation with Lise Weissenborn was over, his relationship with Lola was still strained, and he wrote home bitterly from Berlin, 'I don't even know if you want post from me . . . You don't think I'm even worth a signature . . . Don't let the silence artificially harden again.'

By 1 April, Jewish shops were being boycotted in many cities, and signs in windows announced: 'Jews are parasites and gravediggers of German craftsmen.' Artists who were either Jewish or 'subversive' in other ways were already losing their jobs; Otto Dix had been removed from his teaching job at the Dresden Academy of Fine Arts, Max Beckmann from the Städelschule. Then, on 7 April, Hitler promulgated an Act for the Restoration of a Professional Civil Service (the *Berufsbeamtengesetz*). This abolished tenure and removed all other protection from civil service officials, including university teachers, who could be dismissed if they failed to meet their superiors' standards of 'suitability' or could not prove their political soundness or pure Aryan descent. (All state officials had already completed official forms that included full details of their parentage and faith.) Almost all Jewish officials would eventually lose their jobs under this law, and the lesser consequences began to be felt at once.

In Göttingen the world-famous science faculties began to suffer immediately. James Franck, one of the university's twenty-six Nobel laureates, resigned his chair as a protest against the Civil Service Act and was promptly condemned in a circular letter signed by thirty-three other Göttingen professors, who regarded his gesture as an act of sabotage against the new Germany: 'We hope that the government will speed up the requisite cleansing measures.' The 'cleansing' would cost the university the rest of its renowned circle of quantum physicists, whose arrival in the United States considerably accelerated the development of the American atom bomb.

It did not take long for the blow to fall on Pevsner. He was not dismissed from his post, but some time in the days after 7 April he was, in the current phrase, 'asked not to lecture', and he began to consider his options.* To Lola's irritation, these did not include looking for other kinds of work. He could more easily contemplate moving out of his native land than out of his chosen field, and he began to explore the possibilities of art-historical jobs outside Germany. She would later accuse him of putting job and status before nationality – to which he replied, with some bitterness, 'You, of course, have never wanted to be a bourgeois pedant.' But arguably he was being prudent rather than prestige-conscious. Fellow academic Victor Klemperer, a lecturer in Romance Studies in Dresden, summed up the feelings of many Jewish academics: 'For the moment I am still safe. But as someone on the gallows who has the rope around his neck is safe. At any moment a new "law" can kick away the steps on which I'm standing and then I'm hanging.'[1]

On 11 April, the Bauhaus (which had moved the previous year from Dessau to Berlin) was closed. Some time during this month it was decreed that the Gothic script was to be used only by 'pure' Germans: 'The Jew can only think in a Jewish way. If he writes German, he is lying.' Jewish writing was to be printed in Hebrew, or labelled 'translation'. On 25 April, a law was passed against 'the over-crowding of German Schools and Institutes of Higher Learning' by non-Aryan students. On the following day, Göring merged the political and intelligence units of the former Prussian secret police to create the Gestapo.

---

*Games, op. cit., p.191, reports Vitzthum writing on 17 May 1933, 'Both my *Privatdozenten* [Pevsner and Stechow] have had their lectures put on hold until their legal position is clear, that is, both of them, for the whole semester.'

On 11 April, the *Wolffsche Telegraphenbüro* had published an exchange of letters between Goebbels and Wilhelm Furtwängler, the chief conductor of the Berlin Philharmonic Orchestra. Furtwängler had protested against the treatment of Jewish musicians under the Nazis. His language was circumspect but his message was plain: 'Quality in music is not simply an ideal, it is necessary for its survival . . . So we must state loud and clear that men like [Bruno] Walter, [Otto] Klemperer, [Fritz] Reinhardt etc. must be allowed to practise their art in Germany in future.'

Goebbels was swift to respond. Quality, he argued, was *not* the only criterion in artistic life, or even the most important one. National spirit determined what was appropriate in art. Artists should aim to be close to the *Volk*, the German people, and share in the task of moulding the *Volk* to take up their destiny. So those who did not share full German nationality – who were not 'true Germans', in Marianne's phrase – were not entitled to take a full part in German artistic life, let alone dominate it as they had done in the past. It was, in Goebbels's view, unreasonable for Furtwängler to protest at people like Bruno Walter having to cancel a few concerts, when for years genuine German artists had been silenced by the predominance of Jews on the German music scene. 'Art must not only be good, it must be . . . conditioned by its origins. Art which finds its roots in nationality, that is the only good art – art with meaning for the people for whom it has been created.'

'Art with meaning for the people for whom it has been created' – it was a phrase that might have been written by William Morris, and an idea in which Pevsner most deeply believed. Once more he seems to have felt obliged to locate and promote his own intellectual position somewhere within the framework of the new regime, and he wrote a long and detailed critique of the Goebbels–Furtwängler correspondence, largely endorsing Goebbels's position, but trying to find accommodation within it for some of his own causes. *Art pour l'art*, he agreed, was an outdated nineteenth-century philosophy, and skill was no longer an excuse for a lack of the right attitude. The twentieth century believed in the supremacy of the state, and art must reflect this ideal of the collective good. The artist should serve the state, and should be willing to accept the control of the state.

Pevsner's sticking point, however, was on the nature and inflexibility of this control. Goebbels had claimed that for the first time the state had set up institutions which were capable of furthering ideas about art and seeing that the right developments were encouraged. Pevsner seemed to accept this claim, and even concede the state's right to suppress some art, but he insisted that it should be done with very great care, for fear of destroying the good (and by this he meant the aesthetically superior) along with the dangerous and meretricious. The criteria should be clear, but they must not be too narrow or too rigid, and artistic quality should be one of them.

Art, Goebbels had said, should be 'close to the people'. But to define this term, one must fully understand the nature both of German art and of the German character, and these could take many forms. To Goebbels, for example, the German art that was 'led by the driving forces of the age' was didactic art – social criticism in painting, the novel as reportage, political films, the youth movement in music. One might equally, however, bring in under this heading the representatives of the *Neue Sachlichkeit* or 'New Objectivity', who had been some of the most vital forces in the art and architecture of the last thirty years – and thus Pevsner made room once again for the Bauhaus. These forces, he seemed to be arguing, were worthy of preservation, regardless of nationality or of race.

There was no need for Pevsner to intervene in this debate, and his motives are unclear. He will have known that no gesture of support for Goebbels's arguments could have counterbalanced the evidence of his descent and redeemed his position at the university. Equally, this was hardly a passionate statement in defence of Jewish artists: nowhere in his article is the word 'Jew' to be found. He may simply have taken the opportunity to prolong public discussion of the current debate around the social role of the artist, a subject that he found perennially interesting.* Whatever his reasons, his intervention makes it no easier to gauge the strength or significance of his sympathies with the regime.

At the beginning of May 1933, Pevsner met a woman who would change the course of his life. Francesca Wilson was Muriel Barkas's sister, a woman of extraordinary and unconventional energy, and her imagination was fired by Pevsner's predicament. She had escaped as a girl from the oppressive atmosphere of her Plymouth Brethren family home in Newcastle by means of a history degree from Cambridge and a job teaching within the progressive framework of Bedales. But it was the war that finally set her loose, by bringing her into Quaker relief work for refugees – in Corsica with Serbs in 1917, in North Africa

---

*Games, op. cit., p.195, quotes a letter Pevsner wrote to publisher Eugen Diederichs during this period, offering him one of his articles on art and the state: 'You know as well as I do that nothing intelligent is currently being published in the field of art and politics – at least, nothing that will last.'

with the disabled, in Serbia itself, in Austria with Russian Jews fleeing the pogroms after the Russian Revolution, and in Russia engaged on famine relief. She also appeared in Vienna in 1920 to organise aid for displaced children. Before long, she was involved in organising the first major exhibition of children's art in Britain.

She came back to Britain in 1922, now in her thirties. By 1925 she was earning her keep by teaching history at the Edgbaston Church of England College for Girls in Birmingham. She was also, however, the secretary of the Birmingham Slavonic Society, and she kept her interest in refugees very much alive with sporadic articles for the *Manchester Guardian* and then a book entitled *They Came As Strangers: the Story of Refugees to Great Britain*. She took a house at 35 Duchess Road, Edgbaston, behind the Oratory, in a street whose other residents included J.R.R. Tolkien and his mother, and she filled it, in the acid phrase of a Birmingham contemporary, with 'deserving foreigners of an interesting kind'. Her aim, she wrote modestly, was 'to brighten up home life and give myself an ersatz family'. But she was an intellectual by temperament, and saw the refugee scheme as an extension of the tradition of wandering scholars, so her 'ersatz family' included a remarkable collection of powerful and original thinkers. She rejoiced in having had Freud to supper in Paris, and gloried in bringing intellects together. 'To have had such wonderful minds discoursing around your fire!' she enthused later to her friend and amanuensis, Fred Wolsey.

In the 1920s most of the beneficiaries of her generosity were Russian. She owned a tiny flat in Paris and installed a starving Russian lodger in it, paid for a Russian girl to prepare for Oxford, and eventually adopted a small Russian boy, whom she sent to school in Birmingham. But by the 1930s she had turned her attention to the consequences of anti-Semitism. She was on her way home from a tour of observation in Austria when she met Pevsner.

Francesca Wilson's German was excellent, and they had long conversations, which she reported in the *Manchester Guardian* as interviews with an unnamed scholar. 'Tall and blonde,' she commented:

Only a German with his sixth sense for a Jew would have known that he wasn't Aryan – dignified and refined, not only in appearance but in cast of mind . . . He told us of his bewilderment. He had no Jewish affinities. He had been brought up as a German in German culture. He had thought of himself as on the high road to a university professorship. His world had crumbled . . . 'I love Germany', he said. 'It is my country. I am a Nationalist, and in spite of the way I am treated I want this movement to succeed. There is no alternative but chaos, and I cannot want my country to be plunged in civil war. There are things worse than Hitlerism; I think your Press in England does not realise that . . . If there had been no reparations, no invasion of the Ruhr and the Rhineland, there would have been no Hitler . . . No wonder that Hitler appeals to our youth when he tells them to believe in themselves again . . . And there is much idealism in the movement. There are many things in it which I greet with enthusiasm and which I myself have preached in my writings . . . There is much that is Puritan and moral.'

There was also much that was frightening. On May Day 1933, processions had filled the narrow streets of Göttingen, pushing along under the avenues of plum blossom: the SS in black; the *Stahlhelm*, a paramilitary veterans' organisation, in field grey; students in the colours of their fraternities, some with duelling scars (now legitimate again); postmasters and other minor functionaries all proudly in uniform with their marks of office. Nine days later, at Goebbels's instigation, the National Socialist Student Union in Berlin collected 2,000 books – among them the works of Freud, Marx, Erich Maria Remarque, and Heinrich Mann – and burned them. 'The period of Jewish intellectual imperialism is over,' Goebbels declared for the newsreels. 'From its ashes a new spirit will arise.'

By June 1933, Pevsner was looking in earnest for a job outside Germany. On 5 July, he wrote on the advice of Pallister Barkas to the newly formed Academic Assistance Council in England. The AAC (later renamed as the Society for the Protection of Science and Learning) had been founded by Sir William Beveridge, the Director of the London School of Economics, specifically to help the German academics who were losing their jobs for political or racial reasons. From its offices at the top of Burlington House, in the rooms of the Royal Society, the Council assessed hundreds of applications, researched job vacancies and gave grants to buy time for foreign scholars to learn English, make contacts and even establish means of continuing their research, while looking for employment in England. Only those who seemed most likely to find such employment were given money, a significant proportion of which was subscribed by British university teachers contributing a percentage of their salaries.

The success of the scheme – 'a rescue operation of scholars by scholars' – depended on existing academic networks. While the AAC would provide modest fellowships to successful applicants, the host universities had to provide library facilities or bench space, and many offers of work or research came through invitations from individual British academics. Most were temporary appointments, the idea being that the newcomers would not compete for permanent jobs, but would supply expertise in new fields or occupy short-term posts in existing fields. 'I would be willing to go to any part of Europe, America or the British Dominions,' wrote Pevsner, 'in which I could find suitable employment. Besides I consider that I would be able to act as German Lektor in any University in the world . . . If your Council can take my case into consideration I shall be profoundly grateful.'* In support of his application, he submitted glowing references from Wilhelm Pinder, Tancred Borenius, and Ernst Schramm, the Göttingen history professor with whom he had been working on art and sociology in the Middle Ages. At this point the Council does not seem to have considered – or perhaps researched – political affiliations: both Pinder and Schramm were, or would become, members of the Nazi Party.

With a few scattered contacts among English curators and academics, and the possibility of building on his 1930 visit, it was natural that Pevsner should have considered England as a possible source of short-term employment, but it was not the most natural destination for an art historian in the 1930s, and it was to Italy that he travelled first to begin the search for work in person.† In his letters home, from Florence, Rome, Bologna, Ferrara, Padua, Orvieto, Milan, a picture emerges of this summer of 1933 as a period of fear, exhaustion, sickness and depression – the beginning of exile. Pevsner had made progress with his book on academies of art, and was now writing the foreword and afterword for it, as well as several articles and reviews for German papers, but his main purpose was job-seeking, and he saw little prospect of success.

---

*Papers of the Society for the Protection of Science and Learning (SPSL) in the Bodleian Library, Oxford, SPSL 191/2, 54. In a later questionnaire Pevsner identified the countries he would prefer to go to as England, the Dominions, USA, Italy. Asked 'Would you go to: Tropical Countries? The Far East? USSR? South America?', he replied Yes. The list of 'Countries you are not willing to go to' contained only one entry: France.

†This was not the first time he had applied for positions in Italy. Research by Bernhard Maaz into the correspondence between Hans Posse, Pevsner's employer at the Dresden Gemäldegalerie, and Wilhelm von Bode, director of the Kaiser Friedrich-Museum in Berlin, refers to an application by Pevsner for a scholarship at the Kunsthistorisches Institut in Florence in 1927. Bode, who opposed what he called the *Verjüdelung* (increasing Jewishness) of German society, wrote to Posse: 'I have one serious reservation about your candidate [Pevsner], which I have indeed already expressed openly to you: his race.' *The Art Newspaper*, No. 220, January 2011.

In purely personal terms, this separation from Lola could not have come at a more sensitive moment, when her faith in Pevsner had been severely shaken and she was critical of his apparent readiness to leave Germany. 'I can't look to you for any encouragement if it doesn't work, I know that,' he wrote to her bitterly. 'Perhaps Vati [Lola's father] would be more understanding . . . I would advise you to make use of the time that you have to yourself at the moment to think hard about whether or not you want to stay with me. Because whatever happens, it is going to be a difficult time.'

He had once more failed to pack the clothes he would need, and found himself in Rome without long trousers, confined to a permanent uniform of shorts and ankle socks. He trailed around town listlessly, disoriented by the rash of demolitions and new building, or sat leafing idly through the works of George Bernard Shaw borrowed from the library in his *pensione*, 'then dragged myself around the Pincio park, and tea with sentimental music, then back to the post office'. 'I am terribly restless,' he wrote. 'Only from a distance do I gradually begin to realise what I am losing.' He was subsisting on toast and tea. 'Today I had a real little crisis,' he confessed to Lola, 'misery, lethargy, diar-rhoea and depression . . . Midday, sitting on my bed, I began to blubber, for God's sake. That hasn't happened to me for years. It started quite suddenly, out of the blue – damn it, **damn it!** . . . How much older I've got . . . The duty of keeping all of you is, after all, quite new to me – it has only just become real now. I desperately hope to be up to it – not for myself, but as a good *paterfamilias*.'

Earning a living in Italy, however, was going to be far from easy. There was stiff competition for curating, cataloguing, translation and administrative jobs in organisations such as the National Art Institute and the German-Italian Institute, both from native Italians and from an increasingly large number of other German émigrés. He had already encountered several of them – Cassirer, Heinemann, Salomon, Stenzel – all beating paths to the same doors.

'He is anything but benevolent and trustworthy,' Pevsner complained of one official in Padua, 'although we are all very buddy-buddy.' He had always been irritated by Italian inefficiency and slovenliness – 'I've never seen so clearly what I have against this country' – but now he was also beginning to perceive the rather more sinister draw-backs of 'Mussolini's Europeanisation'. He was writing a few articles for German papers, and among them was a review of the blockbuster Exhibition of the Fascist Revolution, which had opened in Rome the previous year. Pevsner was stunned by the overall impact of the show, but never lost sight of the techniques that had been used to create the effects – photomontages, slogans, over-life-sized statues and other devices that he identified as having first been used in Soviet film, propaganda and theatre*. 'Even as a foreigner one's heart beats faster,' he wrote. 'Imagine the effect it must have on an Italian . . . One can imagine the enjoyment with which Dr Goebbels has gone through this exhibition.' 'Doubtless there is a lot to learn here,' he continued, '[and] tempting prospects for cultural politics', but the degree of manipulation and the level of aggression unsettled and perturbed him.

He was increasingly dismayed by his lack of success in finding even the humblest and least tempting of jobs, and the need to move was becoming ever more pressing. On 6 June, Lola had sent on to him a number of 'long questionnaires' from the authorities, apparently concerning his racial origin. A week later he was expressing 'dark forebodings' about the fact that several parcels he had been expecting from Germany seemed to be being held at the border. 'In three weeks I'll surely be back,' he wrote early in July, 'but Göttingen frightens me too . . . There is nothing about Germany in the papers here . . . Do write if anything is happening.'

There was a great deal that Lola could have told him. On 5 June, Toscanini had refused to conduct at Bayreuth, and had been replaced by Richard Strauss. Jews were no longer permitted to work in opera houses or orchestras and had been expelled from the German Chess Organisation. Students were being encouraged to report to the headquarters of the National Socialist Student Union if their professors were insufficiently 'national' in their lectures.

In July, Pevsner's comments on the Furtwängler–Goebbels correspondence were published in the *Zeitwende* newspaper. Within six weeks, on Hitler's instructions, Goebbels would create the Reichskulturkammer or Reich Chamber of Culture, a central organisation to control the artistic life of the nation. The RKK's aim was to regulate the economic and social affairs of the cultural professions, and all who practised these professions were obliged to belong to it – unless they were Jewish, in which case they were explicitly excluded and, by implication, prevented from following their vocations.

At last, in September 1933, Pevsner was officially dismissed from his post as *Privatdozent* in Göttingen and 'encouraged to resign' from all professional bodies and associations in Germany. Italy had yielded nothing. Now he made the decision to try his luck in England.

---

*Alan Irvine, himself a renowned exhibition designer, points out that Pevsner was one of very few to recognise the originality of the design techniques used in Rome.

From a cold station platform in Cologne at the end of October 1933, he wrote:

Oh Lola, how perverse to have to go away . . . Your unhappy face is with me all the time, and Uta's tears. Even I have been crying, if you can credit it – now sadness is a permanent lead weight within me all the time . . . The Rhine is gone now. I'm sitting on a bench in the middle of the station, to avoid paying for the waiting room . . . I'm terribly tempted just to turn round and come back . . . Instead I just go on and on, further away . . . If only I could count off the days, like I did on other journeys – but this time there is no end in sight.

PART THREE

CHANGING TRACKS: ENGLAND

1933–1939

Roundel for the cover of the 1960
edition of *The Buildings of England: Buckinghamshire*

CHAPTER 13

'If a German – why this one?'

Pevsner passed the journey to England in a daze, too anxious to sleep and unsettled by 'many dark thoughts, some looking back, some forward'. He could not help comparing his new existence with the life he was leaving behind – a life where Lola would be beginning her Göttingen weekend with housework 'as usual', pausing for a hearty lunch of macaroni followed by a rest, then time with the children in the evening, reading and helping Uta with her grammar. Her father would, if necessary, guarantee Lola's financial security. Meanwhile Pevsner sat in limbo on the deck of the ferry to Dover, unable to afford a first-class cabin and reluctant to brave the public lounge: 'The second-class is almost entirely occupied by non-Aryans. Dreadful, dreadful – to think that's where I belong.'

Little in his future was certain. He had made his move, it would seem, guided by Francesca Wilson and influenced by the offer of some lectures at the Courtauld Institute early in 1934. But he had been given a permit to reside in England for only five months, until the end of March 1934, after which his capacity to earn an independent living would be reassessed.

The Academic Assistance Council had given him a grant of £250, a figure on which they considered it was possible to live 'very carefully' for a year. But Pevsner's goal was to make enough to bring Lola and the children over to join him, an objective that he reckoned could not be achieved for less than £700 per year, a high figure probably designed to enable them to maintain something resembling their former standard of living. In addition to the AAC grant, he had a small income coming from Germany, apparently from a source related to his father's business; but to achieve the target of £700, he would obviously have to secure a permanent job.

He knew, of course, his immediate destination. He was to stay with John Fletcher, one of Francesca Wilson's Quaker contacts, who was currently Albert Schweitzer's secretary in England. Fletcher met him at Waterloo and – symbolic welcome – took him at once to the station buffet for a cup of tea. Back at their house, Pevsner took stock of his hosts: 'He is tall, with a grey pointed beard and the kind of cravat which is pulled through a gold ring. He speaks very slowly and rather magisterially . . . Mrs Fletcher is dark-haired, thin and more lively, past middle age. Before I saw her, I was a bit depressed – the whole winter alone with him . . .' In the end, her vivacity would irritate him, while he came to find John Fletcher charming and wise.

The Fletchers' house, 4a Maurice Walk, NW11, in the heart of Hampstead Garden Suburb, appealed to him for its reminiscences of the pretty garden city of Hellerau outside Dresden, but it was borne in on him almost at once that he was going to have to modify his expectations of a bourgeois lifestyle. The house was very small, by his lights – only two bedrooms and two living rooms – and his room, for which he would be paying £8 10s a month, was unaccustomedly cramped. 'There's a sofa-bed and a little stool instead of a bedside table – no other table . . . A chest of drawers – barely big enough for my underwear. A bookshelf, almost full already. Where am I going to put my work things? . . . Washing upstairs in the bathroom – but no room for my sponge bag, which stands on my chest of drawers. I clean my shoes myself.' He solved the problems of his *toilette* by finding a basin which he supported on the little stool, tucking his sponge bag between its legs, but work – a priority as ever – was harder to accommodate. When he wanted to type, he found he had to repossess the stool, turn it upside down and rest one volume of the *Handbuch der Kunstwissenschaft* on the cross-bars to form a makeshift desk over which to bend his tall frame. A sharp wind gusted around the tiny windows, and he soon became adept at building small wood fires in the large empty grate.

'How spoilt we have been!' he wrote to Lola. 'Please keep telling yourself that you are much better off than me – with Germany, with the children, and with central heating.' Like many Europeans, he found England's housing absurdly ill adapted to its climate. ('An average English house,' wrote George Mikes, 'combines all the curses of civilisation with the vicissitudes of life in the open.') 'This is a very modest country, satisfied with very little,' Pevsner observed. 'All morning one can see one's breath indoors . . . To look at it positively, I suppose people are closer to nature . . . They sit next to an open fire, just like the Middle Ages, and freeze everywhere else.' He turned with gratitude to the 'ghastly' woollen underwear he had brought with him.

'London swallows me completely,' he wrote. 'I think I'm walking about 10 km a day, to save on fares.' He had been dismayed to discover that on his tight budget he was expected to find his own midday meal, and he ate most lunches in acute discomfort out of a paper bag on a bench in a foggy Regent's Park. Entertainment in the evening usually consisted of conversation around the fire downstairs, exploring politics and art with the Fletchers and their Hampstead friends. '10.45 p.m.

I'm dead tired. This talking English is very strenuous.' England was a hard place in which to learn a language – an island with no shared borders, where class divisions were defined by speech, foreigners were considered comic or sinister and there had long been a particular aversion to the accents of *Mitteleuropa*.[1] Pevsner was determined to progress beyond his tourist's English, copying down twenty new words every day from his reading, vocabulary constantly revolving in his brain to a degree that disturbed his sleep; but it was a struggle. 'The style somehow comes more naturally in Italian. I can't distinguish what is really good English – I don't fully understand what matters . . . When people speak very fast, I hardly catch half of it – sit there stupidly, trying to make a good impression in silence.'

'I am getting old,' he wrote disconsolately, two weeks after his arrival. 'I can see it, with amazement, when I look in the mirror. The white hairs are increasing – Mrs Fletcher thought I was 35.' (He was thirty-one.) On bad days he suffered from palpitations, nosebleeds and neuralgia: 'I've never known such pain – except in love.' As consolation, he treated himself occasionally in small Italian restaurants to spaghetti and memories of warmer, happier times, and he chose an expensive laundry service that could starch his collars. 'I'm very glad to be properly dressed at last,' he confided. 'The brown hat has got a new ribbon, and the grey is getting one. The narrow ribbon really looked too much like a gigolo. The dark grey suit had to be invisibly mended.' As time went by, he would consult Lola on whether he should add grey flannels and a brown tweed jacket to his wardrobe.

'If only I didn't feel so alone inside,' he wrote. 'It doesn't go away, not for a moment . . . It's the human side that is missing . . . There is no medicine for the English Sunday.' The Fletchers were kind, generous and well-meaning. 'They are so nice to me, and really I don't like them very much,' he confessed guiltily.

Francesca Wilson was in Birmingham, and the Quaker office in London claimed never to have heard of him. He turned, of course, to his German relations, but here too he was often uncomfortable. His aunt Paula was now married to Captain Eric Graddon – 'a somewhat shady Irishman', Pevsner remembered later, 'rather dissipated, a bit like an old actor . . . full of improbable stories and a great liar. I have still a scrawly letter of abuse addressed to me headed "Pevsner!" because I had asked him for the return of a small loan.' The Graddons had done a moonlight flit from the flat in Manson Place and now lived in a basement ('stuffy and depressing') off Cadogan Street, opposite the Catholic church – Paula had converted to Rome – with her sister Sonja, Pevsner's 'Aunt So'.

It was, Pevsner reported, 'a rather outlandish household, but a loving one'. Eric, like many infirm ex-officers, had no regular employment, and the couple were living off Paula's savings and earnings. He had had a job with Electrolux, selling vacuum cleaners, and was now attempting to do the same with water softeners, but spent much of his time around the house, doing chores and discoursing. 'He is a typical Irishman,' observed Pevsner, 'loud, sentimental, overwhelmingly affectionate – and drinks a lot, I'm afraid. His convictions are rather typical and embarrassing – *Stahlhelm*, we'd call them. He's an ex-officer, with great respect for the German army and the Emperor and days gone by – hopeless . . . He was gassed in the war and it has done something to his breathing. Also the cigarettes, of course, and the ale and port.' Pevsner spent one remarkable evening with Eric at the Gargoyle Club, and another in a gathering of what appeared to be ultra-rightists of an affable and disorganised kind, but it was not a friendship made in heaven.

He would perhaps have been better able to handle the loneliness had he been more confident of Lola's love. 'I did something idiotic on the Underground,' he wrote to her in November. 'I was stupid enough to read through my whole diary from mid-November of last year . . . I saw at once what was at stake at that point, how futile it all was . . . You have behaved unbelievably well.' 'I promise you that I will help you with everything in England,' he wrote; but he could not be sure how much she really wanted to come over. 'The children have to have a father again at some point,' he wrote wearily in December 1933. 'But I do see it's all very painful – and understandably you prefer Germany without me to England with me. It could hardly be otherwise.'

The children had written to him only once in six weeks, and he was desperately concerned about their future in Germany. Uta was experiencing 'unpleasantness' at school, and the time was surely coming when she must be told in full about her Jewish heritage. Pevsner was still fiercely attached to the homeland where he had always seen himself as an assimilated German. 'What is good so far,' he wrote, 'is that I am treated [here] entirely as a German and not as a Jew.' He was in consequence extremely homesick.

Restrictions on travel between England and Germany were years in the future, and Pevsner had always planned to go home briefly for Christmas. 'In another month I will again be among Germans . . . I am looking forward beyond all reason to seeing you, just sitting peacefully beside you, and to the children and to the Gewandhaus, and to the German-speaking and the warmth.' He summed up his feelings in one heartfelt cry: 'Why can't we live in peace, at home? (*Warum leben wir nicht friedlich, in der Heimat?*)'

On his arrival at the offices of the Academic Assistance Council in Burlington House, Pevsner discovered that what they were envisaging for him in the longer term was 'something in adult education': they suggested, for example, that he might act as an examiner to senior civil servants in their German language training.* In the immediate future, however, there was the short series of lectures at the recently founded Courtauld Institute, secured for him through Tancred Borenius, who had written on his behalf to the new director. Pevsner was to speak in February 1934, starting with a talk on the subject of 'English art – how it strikes a foreigner'. It was a toe in the door to the field of English art history.

Pevsner was well aware that here he would find himself on largely unfamiliar ground. In Germany, art history was accorded the status of an academic pursuit, tackled with the same analytical and philosophical tools as the other branches of the humanities. It was expected to yield general aesthetic theories with appropriate terminologies and stylistic typologies. English art history was for the most part far more positivist and descriptive, and less concerned with theory and interpretation. 'England distrusts generalisations,' Pevsner would write later.[2] 'The tendency is to treat each case on its own merit and leave the perfection of codes of law to more logical and less practical nations . . . Plenty of antiquarian and archaeological work going on, but little that reaches broad conclusions as to the characteristic style of a man or a nation or an age.'

English art historians, some felt, were more concerned to authenticate an object than to place it in its context – 'at its worst, an activity a bit like stamp collecting,' Ernst Gombrich once concluded, 'but in some senses very useful. After all, every collector and every museum wants to know what to put on the label.' In this respect, 'art history' in England was nearer to connoisseurship than to an academic discipline, closer to the auction house and the art market than to the lecture room or study. It was centred less on universities, though by 1933 university posts did exist, and more on museums, whose keepers – men

---

*This would seem to have been partly due to Tancred Borenius, who had responded to an enquiry from the Council in July 1933: 'Although [Pevsner] could admirably fill any University post involving the teaching of art history, I fear the provision of any such post for him in England is not a matter of practical politics.' SPSL 191/2, 60.

such as Campbell Dodgson at the British Museum, and Kenneth Clark and Ellis Waterhouse at the National Gallery – had commonly taken degrees in other subjects and gone as civil servants into their museums, libraries and galleries, where they trained on the job.

German methods of *Kunstgeschichte* were treated with reserve. 'Ellis Waterhouse and others,' Ernst Gombrich remembered, 'distanced themselves from the Germanic way', or even openly mocked it. 'A word did the rounds – "Forschen" – astounding, because it doesn't exist. *Kunstforschung* means "art research", and they found the sound of the word "Kunstforscher" funny, and so they pronounced it in a certain way: "I must do Forschen". It was partly banter, but not all banter.'

The appreciation of art had a distinctly refined ethos, as Pevsner would observe when he was taken to dinner at the Portman Square house of art grandee Sir Robert Witt, and on to a reception at the Burlington Fine Arts Club: 'Everything in evening dress – tails or dinner jacket. Among them all, your great man – thank goodness, self-assured and in good form. So I am not depressed now, but irritated and amused by all this money which surrounds England's art.'

He was less amused by the air of nonchalance and effortless superiority which the 'experts' brought to their job, and by their apparent lack of reverence or commitment to their subject, and he began to have qualms about his ability to adapt:

I observe with astonishment and some real fear how different art history lectures are here . . . There are, for example, the lectures by Kenneth Clark, new director of the National Gallery, about Leonardo. I detect a lot of work on the originals – but the tenor of it is an arrogance for which I could box his ears. 'Leonardo shouldn't have done this', 'That was a waste of time', and then rather *blasé* jokes in between to make the students laugh. Just like the young man I heard talking on Mannerism, talking with condescension and without any real respect. This gang just want their own tastes, their own style at any price, and put this before the work of art. There isn't the real passion of our scholars . . . Will they accept the way I do it? I certainly shan't change it. Time and time again, it just seems obvious – our way is better.

Pevsner would not have been alone in his suspicion that some of the more urbane English gentleman-scholars were bluffing their way, through charm of manner and a glittering but shallow field of reference. Kenneth Clark himself wrote later of his 'hedonist, or at best epicurean, position' with regard to art, his 'almost insane self-confidence', and concluded: 'I had much better never have given a lecture at all. The lecture form encouraged all the evasions and half-truths that I had learnt to practise in my weekly essays at Oxford . . . The practice of lecturing . . . ended my ambition to be a scholar.'³ He also showed himself to be aware of the public manner that had so annoyed Pevsner: 'Whether from shyness or from a lack of human warmth in my upbringing, I evidently had what the French call *un abord horriblement froid* and appeared to be conceited.'⁴

Somehow, Pevsner had to find himself a niche in this alien environment. 'A lot of things are changing,' he wrote, 'and one might slip in somehow.' The Courtauld Institute had been founded as part of the University of London in 1931, and had started taking its first students the following year – the first establishment in Britain to offer the study of art history as an independent discipline and to award an honours degree in the history of art and architecture.* When Pevsner arrived, the Courtauld had recently appointed its first Director, William George Constable, formerly Assistant Director of the National Gallery (described unflatteringly by Kenneth Clark as 'an industrious official'). Pevsner had no illusions: 'The Courtauld doesn't give much impression of a serious German-style approach. All girls, and they can present themselves for examination after one year. The courses are all far too short and not very thorough.' In the words of a later critic, the Courtauld in its early days sometimes appeared to offer little more than 'occupational therapy for the upper classes who wanted to get to grips with the iconography of their family portraits'.⁵ It was, however, the nearest approximation in England to an art academy. Whatever Constable's limitations, he was inviting a remarkable roster of leading figures in British and continental art history to appear as guest lecturers.

Pevsner was anxious to speak directly to Constable, 'whom I've got to grease with all available soft soap'. In the meantime his approach to the Courtauld was roundabout. He went every day to the large house at 20 Portman Square to sit and be seen and make himself known, while reading Wölfflin in translation to improve his technical vocabulary. 'At least it's somewhere to work, near an electric fire.' 'The library is quite large,' wrote Pevsner, 'full of girls reading – some Jewish, some heavily made-up. Very few men.' By November he could note, 'I am making myself useful in the library – oh Lord!', and towards the end of the month, 'I have been moved from the students' reading

*In, for example, Manchester and Edinburgh, art history was taught only in joint degrees, while at University College London lectures on art history were offered just to supplement the education of art students at the Slade School.

room into the professors' common room. It may be an honour, but it's not as warm. Still, I pass the time of day with one or two people and hope that in case other plans come to nothing, I might become part of the furniture here and slide into a kind of job.'

Elsewhere in the University of London he had got a small job lined up for January 1934 as an external examiner in the history of art at University College, examining a thesis on the followers of Goya at a fee of £5. Once again, Pevsner owed this appointment to Tancred Borenius.* Borenius was Professor of Art History at the Slade School of Art within University College, London, and a regular and valued contributor to the art periodical *The Burlington Magazine*. 'His first word of advice,' Pevsner told Lola, 'is also his last word – PATIENCE.'

Part of Pevsner's long-range strategy was to develop a new and appropriate persona. Now, he told Lola, he must somehow make himself visible but not conspicuous, must be effectual without being pushy in the manner of the Teuton, lively but not overexcitable in the manner of the Jew. He must 'impersonate the cheerful, successful and charming young man', and play the game by English rules, establishing the correct form of address for each new acquaintance, learning to recognise ironic understatement, bowling slow underarm deliveries to the children of a promising contact.

This kind of 'passing' had its risks. At first, Pevsner seems to have given the impression of being somewhat cautious and wooden: 'manners very, very careful, very anxious to take on the English style', according to a Birmingham acquaintance. He was, in his own words, striving towards 'the English *sang froid*, which in me is limited to experiments with a poker face'. He was perhaps right to be reticent; five years later, when the influx of refugees to England was at its height, the German Jewish Advisory Committee would warn foreign Jews against making themselves conspicuous in public places. They should, for instance, avoid dressing loudly: 'The Englishman attaches very great importance to modesty, understatement and quietness of dress and manner. He values good manners far more than he values the evidence of wealth.'

---

*Himself a protégé of Roger Fry, Borenius moved in elevated social circles, and would have been a strong contender for the post of Keeper of the King's Pictures later in the 1930s, had he not been known, in Kenneth Clark's words, 'to have followed the continental practice . . . of taking payment for certificates of authenticity – and what was worse, quite small payments (known as "smackers under the table")'. Kenneth Clark, *Another Part of the Wood* (Coronet, 1974), p.208. It has recently been suggested that Borenius was an agent for MI6, responsible for luring Rudolf Hess to Britain in 1941 – see John Harris, *Rudolf Hess: The British Illusion of Peace* (Jema Publications, 2010).

Some hurdles Pevsner would never overcome. Sending Lola a copy of *Punch*, he grieved: 'I realise all over again – I don't understand English jokes.' But without transforming himself into a humorist, he began to develop the techniques, and the linguistic facility, to fit in. Whether he ever felt that he had left his true self behind him in Germany is hard to assess; he certainly put enormous effort into moulding a new demeanour as a tool for building a new career.

His plan of attack alternated between London – his preferred target – and Birmingham, where his prospects were perhaps brighter, because of the contacts that the indispensable Francesca Wilson could provide. He moved between Hampstead Garden Suburb and 35 Duchess Road, Edgbaston, making his availability known. Telephone calls, telegrams, half a dozen letters a day all made heavy demands on his energy and his English.

In the meantime, he took odds and ends of work where he could find them. Starting with little 'socials' at the Fletchers' house, he began addressing amateur societies on art-historical subjects, and received invitations to speak to groups of working men through the Workers' Educational Association. 'I feel like a pocket Pinder,' he commented wryly. He looked forward with 'pathetic satisfaction' to the Goya examinee at University College, his first postgraduate student outside Germany; in the meantime he had acquired two rich culture-seeking American girls for private coaching, inheriting them from his Dresden friend Ernst Michalski, now living and working in England.

In the end, however, his first foray as a teacher in his new life took the form of Italian lessons administered to three students at the Courtauld, twenty hours a week at five shillings an hour. It was a hard-earned five pounds, requiring him to translate from German to Italian to ask the questions, then translate the questions out of Italian into English if the students were unable to answer them. 'Thank goodness none of them knows anything at all,' he blurted. 'The first lesson went badly. I felt like crying over the English girl. Two foreign languages at once! – but the girl is nice. The lessons take place in the lovely 1770s house belonging to the Courtauld Institute, in a bathroom with marble walls and alabaster pillars. The built-in bath tub is still in place and in view, not covered. Oh England . . .'

Eric Graddon got him an interview with the Foreign Editor of the *Morning Post*, 'a conservative, chauvinist, rather anti-German paper'. Delighted to have found an opening on a national paper so quickly, Pevsner planned to write them a version of his German articles on art schools – 'very sober, pure facts' – but his first effort at journalism in

English was chastening. 'Donkey work, and it feels like writer's block. What if this happens with my lectures?' he worried. Francesca Wilson, with years of newspaper writing behind her, went over it for him. She meant it as a kindness, but he was mortified. 'She's changed so much, and now I notice myself that it's very lame and boring, very heavy – which is how the German way of writing strikes English people anyway, but worse because of writing in a foreign language. A blow to my pride – I'm dreadfully embarrassed.'

Among Miss Wilson's many lodgers was Constance Braithwaite, an assistant lecturer in social economics in the Department of Commerce at the university in Birmingham.* 'A rather peculiar person, a masculine woman,' commented Pevsner, but on one of his visits to Duchess Road it was she who introduced him in November 1933 to Philip Sargant Florence, at that point Birmingham's Professor of Commerce. The son of a musician and a mural painter, some twelve years older than Pevsner, Florence had been educated at Rugby and Caius College, Cambridge, before travelling to Columbia University in New York to study for his doctorate in economics and sociology. While in America, he married Lella Faye Secor, painter, pacifist, women's rights campaigner and champion of birth control. Returning to England, he became a lecturer in economics at Cambridge before taking the chair at Birmingham in 1929.

Like his wife, Florence was politically liberal.[†] An authority on industrial relations and the relationship of industry with society, he was a vigorous promoter of Taylorian 'scientific management', the point of which was to improve efficiency and therefore productivity, but not simply for its own sake or purely for profit. The aim was, by making mass-produced goods more freely available to the labouring classes, to raise the general standard of living and thereby promote content and social harmony.[‡]

Florence's concern was to analyse, define and evaluate the

---

*Birmingham's Department of Commerce, established in 1902, was the first in Britain. Constance Braithwaite (1904–85), a Quaker, was an expert on the social issues surrounding conscientious objection and author of *The Voluntary Citizen: An Enquiry into the Place of Philanthropy in the Community* (Methuen, 1938).
[†]His sister Alix was married to James Strachey, psychoanalyst and translator of Freud.
[‡]F.W. Taylor (1865–1915) wrote *The Principles of Scientific Management* in 1911. It was a major influence on industrialists, social planners and architects (such as Le Corbusier) in the early twentieth century. His vision of a new social order achievable through 'rationalisation' was one of the beliefs underpinning the Modern Movement. A reference in the *Heftchen* during November 1918 to the 'Taylorian system' suggests that Pevsner had been interested in Taylor's ideas since his teens, which would have commended him to Florence and vice versa.

contribution made by each of the participants in the industrial process to its overall efficiency – and at the end of 1933 he was looking for someone to carry out a piece of research on the role of design and the designer in industry. 'With the relative decay of the basic industries such as coal, iron and steel and textile spinning,' he wrote, 'the future of British industry lies with the finishing processes, hence the importance of design pleasing to the ultimate consumer.'[6]

As a liberal intellectual, Florence was well aware of the circumstances in which men like Pevsner found themselves. 'Many of my colleagues and I regarded as our international duty the job of caring for refugees from German and Austrian universities fleeing from Nazi persecution,' he wrote.[7] With the assurance of matching funds from the Academic Assistance Council, he offered Pevsner a fellowship of £120 per year. It was a far more substantial prospect than anything else that had yet come into view. But design? industry? commerce? – it was not, in Pevsner's view, a job in art history. If he was going to have to work in Birmingham, he would greatly have preferred the new art history department which was in the process of being founded and might have fellowships to offer. He was also very reluctant to leave London and risk losing touch with its art circles.

He struggled to keep an open mind, accepted provisionally and continued to look around for better offers. A lectureship in the history of art had just been filled at Manchester, and the whisper of an opening in Liverpool came to nothing. Summoning all his newly cultivated sangfroid, he travelled to Oxford to build on a tenuous contact he had established with the Rector of Lincoln College, archaeologist and historian Dr John Arthur Ruskin Munro, through his daughter Katharine. But from the first moment he could sense that Oxford, a tightly self-contained system, was not for him. 'Not doing too well,' he reported to Lola:

It's not just that I've only got my black suit and no dinner jacket . . . It's the whole atmosphere . . . where it's inconceivable to have financial worries, or to be in a hurry . . . Without a doubt we don't belong here. In Oxford I feel more German than I do anywhere else – like an elephant in a china shop. There is a way of talking here, fast and very informal, with innumerable Oxford allusions, a lot of irony and very little solid seriousness – quite hopeless. You know how uneasy you felt in the Nikisch circle? – that is what it is like for me here . . . A ghastly miasma of humanism . . . 'Great fun', one says in English – that is, attractive, amusing, cheerful. I mean, a manservant has laid everything out, even the cufflinks for my shirt

. . . Perhaps it wouldn't be so much like this among the students, where the 20th century might be knocking at the door . . . The town itself is incomparably beautiful in the moonlight, between these old grey college walls and courts. But it's all the past. I think you would be miserable here. The middle-range universities seem a better bet, more natural, more human.

As 1933 drew to an end, his mood was volatile. A visit to the cinema with Miss Wilson reduced him to misery, perhaps through its unfortunate choice of film, 'a war story with spies, set in Belgium, very English but fair and good. When *"Deutschland Über Alles"* was played, I was quite kaput – not just a few tears but like that time in Rome – oh hell.' 'It's just a bad dream,' he found himself thinking. 'I can't be going to live here for ever – too silly.'

'Everything is little and ugly,' he wrote, 'but I mustn't get depressed and I mustn't give up . . . What a wobbly man I am – if I'm laid low, I do bob back up.' Although a significant number of the Jewish exiles of April 1933 did go back to Germany in 1934 to stay, Pevsner appears never to have considered it. His return home over Christmas and the New Year was only temporary, and even this was enough to frighten him badly by jeopardising his émigré status in Britain. On his re-entry he was stopped at Harwich and given only one month's permit to remain in the country, leaving him liable (in theory at least) to be deported in mid-February, before he had finished his Courtauld lectures.

In universities throughout Germany teachers were now required to perform the 'Heil Hitler!' salute on entering their classrooms; in Dresden, Victor Klemperer, who refused to do it, was living in fear that one of his students would betray him. Back in Hampstead, the Fletchers had been expecting a Christmas visit from a young German girl and were concerned by her non-appearance. 'They have immediately started worrying about concentration camps,' Pevsner commented sardonically.

As for his own children, he longed to know how they were reacting. Did they miss him? Did they suspect that this was something different from the usual study trips? What did they make of the fact that they had had to move flats again? That they were having extra English lessons? And, on a more personal note, what new words had the two-year-old Dieter learned to say? They must all be reunited soon – and yet to bring them over before he could adequately support them would surely be damaging to the family, and particularly to the marriage.

Lola, it seemed, was refusing to engage in discussions about when and how to move to England, and he was aware of lingering resentments and hostility which must be factors in any decisions they reached. 'Our marriage is, for you, still very fragile,' he wrote to her in February 1934. 'If you feel that a longer separation will force us further apart, then of course we must act fast – let's make the move.' Once she was in England, she would need him, and that would reinforce the relationship – provided, of course, he could give her enough time. He needed freedom to operate: 'I have to keep up my connections with the professors and important people and nurse these relationships, be a "pleasant young man" and cuddle up.' She might well find herself often on her own and neglected, and whilst she might be feeling that she was in precisely that situation already, at least in Göttingen she was in familiar surroundings. 'It must always be painful for you how much I experience and how little you do. But would you actually enjoy all this variety and bustle? No, my love – you stay in peace and quiet with the small circle of people whom you love and who love you, and let me notch up the experiences.'

Irritating as these sentiments may well have been to Lola, constrained by domesticity, she must have realised that he was also making a sacrifice in refraining from asking her to join him. He was lonely. 'Nobody loves me, not even you, in the spring fever sense, and I am so hungry – not so much for passion, but for a little bit of fun and tenderness.' Passion, in fact, was also a problem, if he were to be honest. For several years he had sensed that Lola found him too eager sexually, and that she had little sympathy with the frustration he felt when they were apart. 'I feel like a lion who hasn't eaten anything for 34 days,' he had written to her in December 1933. 'I hope you can at least read this with the kind of understanding one offers to the experience of characters in novels . . . Poor victim! Marriage certainly has its embarrassments.' Occasionally, he was attacked by doubts: 'What if you were unfaithful to me? It seems quite unbelievable that you can live like this, calm and untroubled physically for so long a time. We are not that old. Surely you must have desires at least occasionally?'

Pevsner noted nervously in the spring of 1934 that the 'German run' was now well under way, which would crowd the academic field and compromise his own chances of success. He had made enough headway, however, to venture upon a few general conclusions about the country to which he had come. In February, the German weekly *Deutsche Zukunft: Wochenzeitung für Politik, Wirtschaft und Kultur* published his review of an exhibition of nine centuries of British art at the Royal Academy, entitled 'What is English in English art'.[8] Pevsner was engaging once more with racial characteristics in art.

In this German article he launched the suggestion that painting was not the most natural form of expression for the English, an essentially reserved, unemotional and utilitarian race. Why in the sixteenth and seventeenth centuries were there no English counterparts to Michelangelo, Titian, Rubens, Rembrandt, Velàzquez? Why did English painting achieve greatness only with Reynolds and Gainsborough, Constable and Turner? Because, he argued, England does not produce fervour and fantasy, romanticism and passionate engagement, but objectivity, pragmatism and a genius for close observation. The portrait is a genre of immediately obvious utility; the landscape demands powers of description, not expression. The English prefer to draw a sharp line between 'the closely observed world of fact' and 'the distant aesthetic dream world'. Rarely do they attempt to combine the two worlds as the painters of other nations do, pouring their individual personalities, emotions, ideals and imaginations into the representation of real life. 'We have no truly English expressionism – the term does not even exist.' When they do try to combine objective with subjective, they fail – like the Pre-Raphaelites, in using the vocabulary of strict naturalism to express spiritual messages. 'The bright, sweet colours are hopeless. Lack of artistic sensitivity prevents the realisation of the great concept.'

In his concluding paragraph Pevsner appeared to be suggesting that this lack of 'a freely-developed sensitivity' would leave the English incapable even of appreciating, let alone creating, the masterworks of other more emotionally responsive nations. 'How can the English react to Bamberg, to Grünewald, to the great Baroque architecture of Germany, to Caspar David Friedrich, to Nolde? Simply to pose the question is to prove how necessary it is to engage in the politics of culture, the serious, truthful interpretation of national character in the art of the peoples of the western world.'*

In *Deutsche Zukunft* Pevsner was addressing a German audience. He may well have been more tentative in his generalisations about English inadequacies when he gave the first of his Courtauld lectures early in February 1934 on 'English Art – How It Strikes a Foreigner'. He had been unusually nervous, asking Lola weeks in advance to send him bromide capsules on his customary prescription, to calm his nerves. 'The stupid thing takes me eight times more work than

---

*His own 'serious truthful interpretation' of Englishness in his Reith Lectures is discussed in Chapter 31.

usual,' he had written in November 1933. 'It's enough to make one spit. Every tiny joke has to be typed out word for word – you can imagine what it will be like, being nailed together like this.'* In the event, the lecture was delivered without disaster, but the Courtauld audience 'sat there cold and stony', and left him with a leaden sense of anticlimax. Borenius offered a practical explanation of the audience's seeming detachment. '[He] praised everything highly but said "You were too quiet" – the last thing I thought about and something I could easily have cured . . . Perhaps it was because it was off by heart that I had no proper contact . . . Or the fault may lie with this stupid country – maybe they just don't go in for rapturous applause.' The occasion also passed with very little public notice: 'No reviews for a while – and then one in *The Times*, as obtuse as it could possibly be.'

Pevsner went on to give a further series of talks at the Courtauld later in February on Italian Mannerist and baroque painting, straightforward narrative accounts with little allusion to the theoretical underpinnings of *Zeitgeist*, but, in a quiet way, invaluable as a detailed and accurate map of territory that had not yet been thoroughly explored in Britain. He also made his first excursion into the world of the Bloomsbury Group by taking up a chance introduction to Roger Fry, whom he went to see for tea shortly before Fry's death. 'Nothing practical to be gained from him,' Pevsner wrote resignedly to Lola, 'but we had long talks – arguments even – about Tintoretto, whom he finds cheap and operatic. I don't know whether I held my own. The house and studio were rather messy, though the bathroom had all mod cons.'

That February he delivered a lecture at a Workers' Educational Association in Birmingham, and reported:

> One thing did rather grate on the nerves. They had a kind of song book from which they sang to start the proceedings – 19th-century anthems for the working class, with suitable texts but miscellaneous tunes – and what do you think the first tune was? *'Deutschland, Deutschland Über Alles'*! So there I was, engulfed in undignified emotion, singing the national hymn without anyone noticing. You can't imagine how lonely I felt in this badly heated hall in an English suburb.

---

*The reading of lectures from a script would become anathema at the Courtauld, according to Anthony Blunt, who claimed to have been responsible for entrenching this attitude. ('The Courtauld Institute of Art, 1932–45', *Courtauld Institute News*, 2, 2007.)

At every turn he encountered the unfamiliar and disconcerting. 'I'm sitting in the British Museum – astonishing types here in the Reading Room – Negroes with hats on, women with hair all over the place, men in brown overalls – no one seems to worry here.' 'I feel, in a foreign land, perpetually like a grey, made-up actor . . . My grey hairs increase viciously . . . I often feel so old, and then so young and unjustly robbed of so much, like life in Göttingen.' In the confidential questionnaire he filled out for the Academic Assistance Council in March 1934 he answered the question 'Have you definitely "emigrated" from Germany?' with a flat 'No'.

To consort with other Germans making their way in the English art world was, he found, not much help, either personally or professionally. 'Voss, from Berlin' was intolerable, he told Lola, and Edgar Wind (who would eventually rise to the chair of art history in Oxford) was spurious and flashy. The largest gathering of German and Austrian art historians was to be found within the Warburg Institute, at this point an independent library and research organisation situated in a large office building on Millbank. Originating in Hamburg late in the nineteenth century as the private collection of Aby Warburg, eldest son of the Jewish banking family, the library had been given academic respectability and turned into a research institute by Viennese art historian Fritz Saxl. Its focus was the study of the classical tradition and its influence on European culture, primarily but not exclusively in the Renaissance, tracing the relationships between the art of the period and its intellectual and social background, and reflecting Warburg's personal interest in mythology, astrology and magic.

In 1933 it had become apparent that the Institute must leave Germany. Kenneth Clark has described how Lord Lee of Fareham promptly engineered its removal to London as a personal loan to himself, pending its possible adoption by the Courtauld.[9] The Warburg community, which included Ernst Gombrich and Rudolf Wittkower, revolved around an extraordinary establishment in Dulwich run by Saxl, now the Institute's director, and its librarian, Saxl's partner Gertrud Bing. It was known in the émigré world as 'the elastic house, because there was always room for still another refugee'.[10] Pevsner was not a member. He shared few of the Institute's interests – the classical tradition, mythology, iconography – and was not at that point convinced of its intellectual standing. After tea with Fritz Saxl in January 1934 he remarked, 'He is very nice – although I have my doubts about him from the academic point of view.' Pevsner may also have felt distanced from what was largely a Jewish and strongly anti-Nazi society, though it is important not to exaggerate this point. Ernst

Gombrich flatly denied ever having been aware of political or religious tensions of this sort, and pointed out that few of the Warburg community were practising Jews at this time.[11]

Pevsner did not see himself as a refugee – the degree of personal threat to him did not justify the term, in his view – and he acknowledged that he stood further to the right than the majority of the Institute's staff. Largely removed from first-hand experience of developments in Germany, he had seen no reason to waver in his political sympathies since leaving home. Both elements in his particular brand of 'National Socialist' ideas – nationalism and socialism – were exacerbated by the circumstances in which he now found himself. He was aware of his national loyalties intensifying in the face of perceived slights and open criticism of Germany; and every fresh encounter with the English class system predisposed him to look favourably on any doctrine that could conceivably lay claim to the title of socialism. 'We're all Socialists, we Germans, since the war,' he would claim expansively.

Setting off for a concert to be conducted in London by Furtwängler in January 1934, he had written impatiently, 'I hope there won't be any disturbances. The Labour press has created an atmosphere against him – unbelievable.' A couple of weeks later he burst out, 'Lolchen, I can't help it – I must defend Germany, even if it costs me prospects.' He borrowed and read books on National Socialism, and was perfectly prepared to discuss in public what he had read. The previous October he had been taken by the Fletchers to tea with a young couple named Abbatt, founders of the well-known toy manufacturing company. 'Very amusing and enlightening,' he commented. '"Marxist"-ish but openminded, and very ready to be converted by me towards Hitler-ism.'* Now, after a long conversation with Philip Sargant Florence and his wife early in March, he reported: 'I think they're both members of the Labour party, but they listened to my explanations of National Socialism with interest and even acknowledged some of the things I said.'

He may perhaps have been unaware that Bruno Taut, a modernist architect he much admired, had recently been dismissed from the Prussian Academy of Arts, and that in February Goebbels had pronounced Jews 'unfit to be entrusted with German cultural assets'. It is hard to believe that he can still have expected the Nazis to pursue the more enlightened and inclusive policies that he had advocated in his 1933

*There is absolutely no evidence that the Abbatts' response to Pevsner's views was anything other than good manners.

articles on 'culture-politics', although the appointment of his successor in Göttingen, a Doktor Pätz, raised his hopes: 'I am honestly pleased. It means that there is still room for an honest, worthy, competent scholar.' A matter of days later, early in March 1934, his friend and colleague Wolfgang Stechow was sacked, and Pevsner's unease was growing. 'I am almost ashamed to escape all this – through no fault of my own.'*

That month he came closest to the kind of academic post he wanted. The previous December, Borenius had urged him to apply for a newly vacant professorship in the history of art and architecture at the University of Edinburgh. The chair had previously been given over largely to archaeology, but promised now to lay more emphasis on art history, and the salary was good. 'I will mount my campaign as effectively as I can,' Pevsner wrote optimistically, 'sending in my collected works, and the certificates from Pinder and Vitzthum.' To his delight, he was shortlisted, and Edinburgh approached his referees – W.G. Constable and Jim Byam Shaw. Pevsner's feelings towards Shaw were a little ambivalent: 'You've no idea how relatively well-to-do people are here,' he grumbled to Lola. 'When I see Byam Shaw strutting off to his lunch, I feel distinctly communistic urges.' But he valued his opinion, and was depressed when Shaw informed him that his qualifications were not ideal. He had hoped that his opposition in Edinburgh might be 'indifferent Scots', and was crestfallen to hear that he had serious English competition. There was bound to be some prejudice against foreigners: 'I expect they will also ask, "If a German – why this one?"'

As soon as he arrived in Edinburgh for interview at the beginning of March 1934, he knew how badly he wanted the job:

This town is really beautiful, even if it is misty and the rain began first thing. The university looks like a university . . . Everything is somehow more familiar than London, much more what I am used to . . . The picture gallery is good too . . . only twelve rooms, but what things they've got! . . . The whole scene has style and culture – in contrast to Birmingham . . . To have seen this town and then to have to say 'Adieu' to it . . . Everything just as one would want it – blast!

---

*Stechow, as a veteran of the First World War and one with only a single Jewish grandparent, had survived as an associate professor in Göttingen for six months longer than Pevsner.

The interview appeared to go well. 'All very dignified people, friendly questioning, nothing political,' he mused. 'They asked if I would bring in a lot of very modern stuff. Prudently, I held back, and said that the course was too short for that, it might be just a matter for one's own personal enthusiasms, but one could do a lot privately with interested students.' He had reached the last two, he was told – but then the blow fell. 'I know who's got it – he's nice, very good-looking, and knows all about Byzantium.' David Talbot Rice, an archetypal Eton and Oxford man (OUDS, Hypocrites Club, friend of Robert Byron and Evelyn Waugh) had not read art history, but archaeology and anthropology, after which he had put in two years at the Sorbonne. He had a considerable private income and lived the life of a country gentleman.[12]

'Hell! – it irks me terribly,' confessed poor Pevsner. 'We get so far – and then it's the same thing all over again – "a foreigner" . . . I'm stiff with melancholy and despair' – and he was afraid that in addition, by applying for Edinburgh, he might well have alienated his former allies, Constable and Byam Shaw. Constable in particular might see his bid for so prestigious a job as 'a bit thrusting'. His friends tried to console him: Borenius regarded the appointment as 'a scandal' and Herbert Read, a new acquaintance, assured him that Talbot Rice would not like the work and would soon depart.* But nothing could alter the fact that, after almost six months of effort in England, Pevsner's only prospect of permanent employment lay in research into industrial design, and in Birmingham.

---

*Talbot Rice held the chair in Edinburgh for thirty-eight years until his death in 1972.

CHAPTER 14

'More than just an episode'

During the spring of 1934, Pevsner made the journey to Birmingham with increasing regularity. He went with the greatest reluctance. 'The town is awful. The moment you come off the four or five main streets, you are amidst two-storey houses in grubby brick, indescribably dreary and sooty. It gets you down.' 'Chimneys to right of us, chimneys to left of us,' wrote Louis MacNeice, another Birmingham resident, 'someone had blundered.'[1] The city may have been bigger than Leipzig, Pevsner complained, but in comparison it was deeply provincial, a place of 'little cultural importance'. 'To the newcomer,' Miss Wilson conceded, 'society in the residential quarters of Birmingham seems cold and un-enterprising.'[2] She herself found life there akin to living in the country, with little to do except read and think and see one's friends. Reading was initially a problem for Pevsner: 'This town of 600,000 inhabitants has practically no art books,' he wrote incredulously, sending Lola complicated instructions for the shipping of large parts of his own library. And he had few friends in Birmingham, though before long he would make valuable acquaintances in Austin Duncan-Jones, a young lecturer in the faculty of moral sciences at the university, and his wife Elsie.*

At 35 Duchess Road, Edgbaston, Miss Wilson had once again turned her large terraced house into a refuge, keeping only a small flat for herself and giving the other rooms over to a motley collection of lodgers, mostly now German Jews. She was not the only benefactress in the street – Mrs Simmons at 2 Duchess Road, herself from Frankfurt, presided over a similar household – and she saw her generosity as a source of pleasure primarily to herself. When she eventually left the house, she gave it to her charlady with the remark, 'I could never have had the happiness of all these people without you, Mrs V.'

Pevsner's rent was nominal, the location was convenient and he met new people – 'rather strange bohemian types . . . amusing, not at all like English stiffs'[3] – but he was not sure that he had done the

---

*As Elsie Phare, she was a graduate of Newnham College, Cambridge, and author of the first book on Gerard Manley Hopkins.

right thing in turning down the alternative and more conventional offers of hospitality that he had received in Birmingham. He and his hostess had not yet got each other's measure. 'Though I really like Miss Wilson very much,' he told Lola in March, 'there is something like Lis about her. Not to put too fine a point on it, I'm afraid of a repressed passion there. I'm sure it would stay repressed, but it seems a bit unholy nonetheless . . . What do I want with these virgin ladies?'*

As for Francesca, her first impressions of her guest were muted:

I'm not sure if he has any originality at all. He's well-informed and has well-trained taste – has he more? He has an iron core of determination. He certainly will get on. I believe he's a loyal fellow. It was nice of him to tell Mrs Barrow he couldn't stay with her because he would be staying with me. If he had only an eye to the main chance he wouldn't do that, as Walter Barrow is pro-Chancellor.† He has a lot of simple virtues – devotion to wife and children, conscientiousness, hard work, dignity in trouble.

He had, in fact, all the basic qualifications to win her favour. According to Elsie Duncan-Jones, Miss Wilson preferred men, certainly brilliant and preferably foreign – 'It was rather a matter of luck if Francesca liked you much if you were English' – and she was soon showing more enthusiasm:

I have begun suddenly to like him much more. Why? It's true that he is water rather than wine, but good water, pleasant to have every day. He is much more interesting because of his disasters. I don't mean only to me but objectively speaking. They have brought out the latent energy of his character: whereas success would have made rather a complacent and commonplace professor out of him, hardship has showed him up well. I admire every day the admirable dignity with which he bears his ridiculous situation and accomplishes his rather tiresome tasks.

He had, she added, a delightful sense of humour 'absent in other Germans'. She was mortified to discover after some weeks together

<hr/>

*'Lis' was Lis Knauth, the young Nika's unfortunate piano teacher, who would in fact be a lifelong friend.
†Walter Barrow (1867–1954) was a Birmingham philanthropist related to the Cadbury family.

that she had been mispronouncing his name as 'Peyvsner'. It would become a standing joke, and she would use it as a nickname for him, out of affection.

On his first visits to Duchess Road she had put him up in her own flat. 'Terribly untidy,' he informed Lola in dismay. 'Thick dust on all the books – the kind I've only ever seen on books seven years old in bookshops . . . You have made me orderly – so now I am suffering in this household.' Elsie Duncan-Jones felt the squalor was almost deliberate, a refusal to conform to other people's standards. 'The food was abundant, but there was always a bottle of sour milk around, turning into yogurt . . . Francesca smoked, but very frugally, so there would always be cork-tipped cigarettes around, cut down – she'd take three or four puffs, then cut the cigarette off.' There was also a good deal of animal hair: 'I don't like being cuddled by cats,' Pevsner remarked austerely, but they did at least keep the mice down. A fat, slovenly housekeeper made little impact on the general grime. Pevsner noted with disapproval that there were holes in her dress, 'but there are holes in Miss Wilson's as well'.

He soon moved, with relief, into one of the upstairs rooms:

It . . . always reminds me of a Paris studio somehow – a window seven feet wide divided into six little panes at the top . . . with a view on to and across the roofs, with a lot of chimney pots. Do you remember the first act of *Bohème* we saw in Dresden, the bit when Mimi sings down from the window, and Rodolfo tells Marcello '*Ich bin nicht allein – wir sind ein paarchen*' ('I'm not alone – there are two of us') – oh really, it's enough to make one bawl.

During that first chilly spring in Birmingham he had to spend scarce shillings on the gas fire. (Later he would come to suspect Miss Wilson of feeding his meter on the sly.) 'In the end one endures the cold as one does a chronic illness.' The slot he had been allocated in the lone bathroom was 7.30 until 8 a.m., and if he missed his appointment with the ancient Ascot heater, he had to wait until 9.30. 'My room is next to the bathroom and I can hear all the maiden ladies splashing about,' he complained. 'It really is miserable living with all these middle-aged people.'

When Miss Wilson took him to her club in April, he was appalled: 'An international and peace affair . . . Noisy debate, loud humanitarian ladies, committee, conferences, vote-taking – I can't stand it.' He was more comfortable talking to the debating society at the girls' grammar school where she taught history, and listening to her pupils reciting

German verse for an exam. He was also aware that her attitudes and way of life had grown out of a difficult background, and his admiration for her increased after a visit to her Christian fundamentalist family in Newcastle. 'What an inner struggle it must have cost Miss Wilson and Frau Barkas to find their way to the Quakers and freedom from this milieu,' he wrote to Lola twenty-four hours into his stay. The atmosphere was thick with biblical quotations, and Francesca's mother, a devout member of the Plymouth Brethren, was fond of applying them to every situation. '"England won the First World War because she was kind to the Jews" – and then she presents one with a coloured picture of the Vision of Nebuchadnezzar and points out where his prophecies have come true . . . Talk about the meaning of life, talk of all kinds, ends in hopeless platitudes. Lolchen, you often think you are very average – but here you would feel like a cynical, bold, independent philosopher.'

Francesca's own emotional life, in contrast, he found intriguing. She was at this time absorbed by Nikolai Bakhtin – White Russian turned communist, linguistics scholar and expert in modern Greek, continental traveller, Paris intellectual, elder brother of the philosopher Mikhail Bakhtin, and the man to whom Wittgenstein first read his *Philosophical Investigations* out loud. Having served in the White Guard in the aftermath of the First World War and suffered terrible hardships in the retreat over the Caucasus, Bakhtin had gone into exile from Russia and turned to service in the Foreign Legion, attracted by what he perceived to be its asceticism, only to be invalided out with a wounded hand. Miss Wilson had been much smitten by this romantic figure, but the affair had now settled down into a stable if unorthodox friendship.

Having lectured briefly in classics at Southampton, Bakhtin was now a Reader in Linguistics in Birmingham, Miss Wilson's initial efforts to get him a chair at Cambridge having failed. He was 'given to extremes of passion and an uncontrolled exuberance of feeling and expression', a friend remembered. 'He always seemed on the verge of erupting, like a volcano.'[4] Pevsner passed an evening drinking Chianti with him:

A very strange person, very Russian in his accent and his looks . . . Doesn't read a paper, is quite without a clue about the 101 usual intellectual subjects that come up in this house . . . Something astonishingly naïve about him. Most of the time he is silent and then suddenly comes to life and is very amusing. Miss W bosses him about – he is part of her property, she tells him 'We shall do this, buy that' and he goes and does her shopping. An extraordinary relationship.

'Bakhtin and P make a good blend,' Miss Wilson noted, gratified. 'B finds P's smooth and easy urbanity very soothing: nothing insolent about him, no corners.' Pevsner spent time with him in Cambridge later in the year, when he went to give a lecture on Dürer to the German Society there, and Bakhtin was able to offer him a camp bed in Caius. 'Very proletarian with Bakhtin,' he told Lola, 'but extremely close and friendly. He does all the cooking himself . . . He has a couple of plates, a few sticks of furniture . . . I'm afraid he has given me all his rugs to make the camp bed and air mattress reasonably warm. I suppose he is naturally hard-wearing, having been in the Foreign Legion.'

Back in Duchess Road, with his residence permit extended for a year on the recommendation of the Academic Assistance Council, Pevsner was finding it easier to relax, spending hours reading in the garden as the weather grew warmer. 'At the back of the house . . . there is a whole island,' Miss Wilson had written. 'The prevailing wind drives away the smoke, and it is possible to sit in the garden without being drowned in smuts or pick flowers without becoming black from head to foot.' Pevsner may even have enjoyed one side-benefit of Birmingham's industrial atmosphere. 'When the wind blew from the South,' observed Louis MacNeice, 'the air would thicken with chocolate' from the nearby Cadbury works.

He was beginning to take himself off on modest jaunts. In May 1934, putting behind him his 1930 ordeal on the slopes of Snowdon, he ventured back into Wales with a walking holiday from Builth Wells. Hotels, it seemed, had not improved in four years. 'No running water, one of the towel-rails had a leg missing, and there is broken china in the corridor.' He was reduced to flicking through magazines in the hotel lounge: 'English sporting life in pictures, all ladies and golf parties and dogs.' But the walks themselves lifted his spirits. 'I am apparently the only person in Britain who does this kind of thing,' he informed Lola. 'No signposts, because nobody walks here. In thirty years it will be different, of course, but in the meantime one gets lost all the time.' Setting out southwards in the direction of Brecon, he was rapidly blown off course:

Soon missed the path and just kept going, wet through, with my glasses blurred, into a strong wind . . . Bare mountains can already be seen . . . I am looking forward to them – prettiness only makes me sad. The landscape helps me to reach resolutions – the same one every time: to be able to give you a more comfortable life . . . The afternoon was just what I had hoped – by myself across those bare mountains, deserts of fallen brown firs – and always sheep jumping away in fright before me . . . The aim was to look at a church. I've taken some notes on it – good boy!

Pevsner's art-historical ambitions in Birmingham were still very much alive, and he kept a weather eye on the developing art history department at the university, but his main effort in these early months was to make sense of the brief he had received from Philip Sargant Florence – to enquire into the role of the designer in industry. Were designers widely used in British industry? Where did they come from? What was their impact in terms of artistic standards, sales and general social benefit?

'*Sachenvoll, nicht wortgelehrt*', roughly translatable in this context as 'based on experience of real things, not learned from books' – this was the quote from Herder that Pevsner would eventually use as a tag to introduce the first part of his report, and he repeated the idea elsewhere: 'What we want more than anything in discussion on industrial art is facts.'[5] He never had anything against facts, but in this case did not relish the manner in which he had to acquire them. The methodology for the project, as design historian Pauline Madge has argued convincingly, was dictated by Florence, and Pevsner never felt comfortable with it.[6]

Florence distrusted abstract theorising in economics, and asked his researcher to conduct an empirical survey of industrial practice in pursuit of hard statistics. Pevsner may have been happy to view finished products in design exhibitions, but he knew little about the practical activities that lay behind their manufacture, neither the mechanical processes nor the roles of such people as the factory proprietor, the buyer or the retailer. 'How can I get down to brass tacks?' he wrote despairingly to Lola. 'Where can I get the figures and evidence? I am slithering about terribly . . . How does one establish whether sales figures have anything to do with design?. . . I should work out a set of questions for factory owners, as a basis to show people what I really want to know in every case. If only I knew that myself.' 'I know people feel sorry for me having to work on something so far from my real subject,' he would write later. 'The moment I think of the art and industry thing, I feel such lead in my bones that I would like to run away.'

Contrary to all his natural instincts, he had to plunge straight into his investigations without a long period of preparatory reading. He did as much as he could manage in the time available, familiarising himself with the contemporary crafts scene, memorising the names of designers, digesting the recent history of the Design and Industries Association (DIA), poring over Herbert Read's *Art in Industry*, which came out in 1934. He toiled to catch up, but critics have pointed out that there is no sign of him having consulted even the studies on local industries – glass, jewellery, nails – that were already sitting in Florence's own Department of Commerce.

He was of course attempting to read documents, some of them highly technical, in the intervals between field trips. In a period of some fifteen months he visited 149 manufacturers, fifteen retailers and a large number of art schools, designers and architects in the Birmingham area. Making the contacts and gaining an entrée was a struggle in itself. Some introductions were made for him by Robert Dudley Best, successful lighting designer and manufacturer and recent head of the Birmingham branch of the DIA, who was part of a circle of cultured businessmen in Edgbaston. Pevsner did not really enjoy relying on this kind of patronage – 'I feel like a beggar' – but where he had no personal recommendations, he often found it hard to get a foot in the door at all. Approximately one in six firms, mostly smaller ones, turned him down outright.

Gradually he assembled a schedule of visits in the industries of his choice, categorised into 'large home equipment' – such as furniture, carpets, wallpapers, electric and gas fittings and fires; 'small home furnishings' – pottery, glass, silver, plastics, textiles; personal wear – leather and jewellery; and a select sample of cars. He built up lists of stock questions for manufacturers: What is the state of your trade – boom or decline? What proportion of your work is carried out by machine? How is design generally handled within your trade? How is it handled in your firm – is there a special department, or a trained head of design? Where do you get your designers? What do you pay them? Is anyone else involved in the design process – managers, salesmen or workmen? Do you ever use artists or architects? Do you consult popular taste? Or as Miss Wilson succinctly paraphrased it some years later, 'He went round asking manufacturers (as tactfully as possible) why they went in for such hideous designs.'

Perhaps unsurprisingly, his welcome was not always warm and there was rarely a meeting of minds. When he came to review his patron Robert Best's memoir *Brass Chandelier*, he remarked with undisguised astonishment that it was 'a document of culture, tact and well-informed documentation – the reverse of what one would expect from a biography of a Birmingham manufacturer by a Birmingham manufacturer'.[7] On occasion he faced considerable embarrassment. In at least one firm in the Potteries he came across the suspicion that he was a foreign spy, which he attributed to the director of one of the Birmingham museums 'going round saying I'm in the employ of a German firm. Marvellous – but Florence and Best both say he's barmy.' Barmy or not, it caused several manufacturers to complain to 'the man who makes the most important and valuable introductions, so he has backed off in the most embarrassing manner. I am compromised with a number of firms and perhaps also the Dean of the Department of Commerce. Florence was nice about it, but it has cost me some sleep.'

At the other end of the product development chain, Pevsner visited the managers of shops and department stores to establish how big a part design might play in their purchasing decisions. It was also an opportunity to write to designers, artists and architects for their views – a note in the finished report thanks Gropius, Marcel Breuer and Mies van der Rohe for their 'kind help' in the matter of tubular steel chairs – though this interesting correspondence formed a regrettably small part of his work.* Far more characteristic were 'visits to ludicrous art schools in small industrial towns, between 7.30 and 8.30 p.m., an awful time. It means eating supper at 9.30. And the conditions in the schools are pre-1879 – unbelievable – and those towns in the gloomy evening light . . .' He was unfair to some of these schools, which he was visiting in order to find out whether they held courses in industrial design. The larger ones were already awake to the special requirements of machine production, and he found much to admire in their efforts to supply designers to industry. The Royal College of Art, on the other hand, was in 'excessively urgent' need of reform, having been for decades 'a school for the training of drawing masters'.

Gradually Pevsner began to make progress. He made his first formal report to Florence at Highfield, the professor's huge and rambling house in Selly Park with grounds large enough to accommodate a lake with a boat, and cottages rented to deserving cases, including Louis MacNeice.† Florence was cordial, but, for a project supervisor, did not seem impatient to hear the results of Pevsner's labours. After a leisurely lunch – 'grapefruit, filled omelette, stewed pears' – Pevsner was sent

---

*Pevsner had been in contact with Gropius previously, while writing his article on Le Corbusier in 1930. They met at least once in Berlin, and corresponded subsequently. Gropius, pleased by Pevsner's highlighting of the German origins of modernism, ordered a dozen copies of the article. W. Gropius/NP, 23/9/31. GP Series 1, Box 2.
†Highfield, 128 Selly Park Road, was built in the 1860s and demolished in 1984. Southbourne Close now sits on the site.

for a stroll through the grounds and was then left to his own devices for most of the afternoon, reading a book in the garden, before being invited to say a word to the professor about what he had been doing. 'All on a perfectly ordinary week day,' he reported to Lola, bemused. 'I suppose they do a little more in term time.'

Only to Lola could he reveal his true feelings about his Birmingham project. 'I go round to my art schools and factories, quite dead inside,' he wrote bleakly. Coming back from a factory visit at the end of April 1934, he got into the wrong end of a train that divided at an interchange and found himself stranded at midnight at a little station outside Birmingham. Sitting in the stationmaster's office, he took the opportunity, as usual, to compose a letter to Lola. 'Trains are running through the night – I can hear the whistling and shunting, incessant, melancholy,' he wrote:

> I am totally alone, in the whole of England. Nobody knows where I am, and my mind is full of thoughts of Germany and of the future . . . Where will I be able to look after you? . . . and in all this am I not betraying Germany? . . . I think of our life . . . We have travelled half our course already – are we ready for the end? I'm not – I still feel very much at the beginning. The thought of the children is still always . . . an incentive to act. For them there must be money and some social status.

Unable to do anything to secure his emotional future, he kept his eyes fixed firmly on business and the short term. He had made a new friend and ally in London in the person of Alec Clifton-Taylor, a young man – 'charming and nice, not too elegant' – who had come up to him after one of his lectures at the Courtauld Institute earlier in the year and paid him diffident compliments. But, to Pevsner's chagrin, a proposed lecture series at Morley College on the study of art history withered on the vine when too few students signed up for the course. His series of lectures at University College on Venetian painting did materialise, however, arranged and chaired by Tancred Borenius. The first of the series was billed as a 'special university lecture in fine art'. Pevsner was very nervous beforehand. Every lecture in London was a chance to shine which he could not afford to waste. He confided to Lola that he felt like 'that singer in Göttingen who was always convinced that tonight the director of the Vienna Court Opera would be in the stalls', and he was anxious to dazzle with his brilliance.

He started smoothly by complimenting University College on the atmosphere of its buildings – 'so familiar, its seriousness, soberness and, I might even say, homeliness. All that reminds me of the atmosphere I left in the German University where I was teaching' – and went on to pay lavish tribute to Borenius. Soon, however, he felt himself stumbling and gabbling. 'When I had got through more than half of the slides, I glanced at my watch – 5.15. Cold sweat – by 5.30 the material would be finished, and that would be a disaster of quite exceptional magnitude. I had to stretch it out somehow . . . so with my knees knocking, I extemporised . . . said the same thing X times, varying it as best I could with my limited vocabulary, and then picked up speed again – and it was *still* 5.15. Thank heaven, my watch had stopped.' After the second lecture, he did at least get questions – 'All sorts of people – a German-speaking Russian lady singer, an old auntie from Hamburg, an elegant young painted Englishwoman, all very funny' – but it was hardly what he was used to. He burst out impatiently to Lola, 'These silly lectures in London – just gibberish, for money. Nothing, nothing! . . . In my own eyes, Lolchen, I am nothing, less than nothing. I have to prove myself, push on, which needs energy . . . But today everything looks so very grey.'

He was miserably upset by the arrival of his cherished library. One chest had gone astray and eventually turned up damaged, with dozens of key reference works missing. Other books had apparently had nails driven into them by the packers, and were covered in stains and smears; a manuscript was crumpled, photographs were torn, and his papers were sufficiently disordered to make him wonder uneasily whether the chest had been opened and interfered with by the German authorities. 'When I looked over the chaos . . . I felt like a very poor refugee for the first time.' 'The wobbly man looks as if he isn't going to bob up this time,' he wrote in June. 'I'd like to lie down and howl.' He took his setbacks stoically – perhaps too stoically. 'I wish I could explode sometimes,' he wrote, 'then at least I'd get over these things quicker. At the moment they're buried in my stomach, undigested, acid.'

The bleakness of his English existence had been thrown into the sharpest possible relief earlier in May by the visit to London of Walter Gropius. Pevsner attended a discussion meeting at the Design and Industries Association at which Gropius spoke on 'The Formal and Technical Problems of Modern Architecture and Planning'. He was both inspired and disturbed by this contact with his hero. '10.15 on Euston Station,' he wrote to Lola:

I'm still so stirred up, I'm sitting in the waiting room, waiting for the midnight train back to Birmingham, filling up this scrap of paper just to let off steam. I have such a wild veneration for this man – the way he holds himself, what he has achieved, and his manner of speaking . . . Someone who really belongs to your 'Deutschland', with the very greatest creative gifts as well. My head whirls with it. Everything else seems so petty – the worries, the prospects, every-thing.*

The contrast with his own situation seemed ludicrous, and reduced him to near-incoherence:

I'm 32 and I've done nothing that will last, and I'm pretty certain I won't, because I'm just not in that league. If I were already a professor, I would have money and status, damn it. There was Gro [sic] and all the others round him – Mendelsohn, Read et al – and there was I, the small fry.

He wanted a job that would, in his words, be at the centre of his life, and not just a means of scraping a living, but he could see no way of achieving it. Around this time a professor of German in Birmingham expressed surprise that Pevsner had not been given a helping hand by 'rich Jews'. 'I said that was only for people of the Jewish religion, but he didn't want to believe it. And all the time there was this feeling in the background, though nothing strictly personal – no English money for foreigners.'

It was a revealing conversation, but the reference to religion was not particularly characteristic. Pevsner's religious beliefs were not gener-ally a factor either in how people treated him or in how he viewed his own situation. He was reading the Bible quite regularly during these early months in Birmingham, and found some comfort in the Gospel messages on endurance in adversity, but, outwardly at least, showed more interest in the literary than the spiritual qualities of the Old Testament. 'How incredible,' he wrote, 'that this *Volksbuch* [book of legends] should be seen as the verbatim word of God . . . Fables and creation-myth all muddled up together.'

---

*cf. Maxwell Fry's description of Gropius's talk in his *Autobiographical Sketches* (Elek, 1975), pp.145–6. 'He spoke haltingly but in a voice rich with emotion, and from time to time held us with a level and commanding glance . . . Listening to this man speaking awkwardly in a language he had yet to adopt we realised that the task he set us would last our lifetime, that we were concerned now not with architecture alone, but with society and that he had filled us with a fervour as moral as it was aesthetic.'

His first experience of a service in the Church of England made him feel distinctly Protestant. 'Very strange, very Catholic,' he wrote, revealing an aversion to the trappings of religion which he would elaborate later in his comments on German baroque churches and religious monuments: 'The Protestant is led to direct and unaided intercourse with God . . . There is something taciturn and solitary in the Protestant attitude', chiming closely with his own present feelings. But even Protestantism could not help him now. 'If only I had real faith in God,' he wrote near the end of June 1934. 'But I don't. I trust to my own strength, and even that fails me at times.'

The industrial design project was his subsistence, but in July he was given advance warning from the Academic Assistance Council that it was not going to be able to renew its grant to him on its expiry, and he set about trying to stitch together a patchwork of other 'real' jobs. The art history department at Birmingham looked less and less promising; the vacancy, it now seemed, was not going to be a lectureship, which might have been within his reach, but the loftier post of Director. An application to Harvard – and, apparently, another to the University of Louisville, Kentucky* – got nowhere, and prospective employers in Berne rejected him on the grounds that they wanted a Swiss. He had been given some external examining for the Courtauld Institute, and guarded it jealously, afraid that 'other proved Germans' might turn up and poach the work. It was the status and the connections he prized, however, as travelling to London cost him more than he could earn while he was there.

'To stick it out and not lose heart, not lose my grip . . . to keep on the ball, a pleasant, competent man – not to lose patience or one's edge, not to miss a trick.' To the outside observer, as Miss Wilson testified, he successfully projected the image of a charming young man, urbane, suave, keen to make himself agreeable. But underneath the smooth exterior he was edgy, aware of constant compromise and dissembling. 'This damned hypocrisy is becoming harder and harder.' Lola had reproached him for adapting too easily to English ways, a charge he angrily rejected. He only wanted to succeed in England in order that they might live as much like *Germans* as they wanted. Sitting outside on a July evening, reading the Gospels, he was pierced with anguish when a fellow-lodger put on a record of Beethoven's

---

*A letter from the General Secretary of the AAC to Pevsner on 21/7/34 asks for his consent to submit his name to Louisville as a candidate. The job – teacher of the History of Art and Culture – would have lasted for two years in the first instance, at a salary of $2000 a year. (SPSL 191/2-3, 70.)

Fifth Symphony to accompany her supper. 'There it was again suddenly – memories of Nikisch and the Gewandhaus. Surely this can't be true – that all of that should be the past and that Birmingham should be the present, and more than just an episode?'

He was not simply lonely, but nostalgic for a social structure where he would feel at ease. England, he felt, was riddled with class consciousness, and divided by inequalities. This had been brought home to him by a visit to a public swimming pool:

> Oh heavens, how English! . . . It is for the lower classes, I suppose
> . . . A large pool between good trees – long, deep, good for swim-
> ming. But no grass verge, in this land of grass and lawns, just wooden
> duckboards and antediluvian changing cubicles – about 100 for men
> and 30 for women – none of our wonderful changing cabins. And
> hardly more than 100 people there, despite the marvellous weather
> . . . and this is *the* pool . . . I'd like to know who on earth among
> the upper classes would ever use this pool. Repulsive, really – is this
> the country I want to come to?

Was he unaware that the majority of German swimming pools had been closed to Jews, rich or poor, since 1933?

30 June 1934 saw the 'Night of the Long Knives' ('*Nacht der langen Messer*'), when Hitler used SS troops to eliminate Ernst Röhm, the insubordinate commander of the special *Sturmabteilung* forces, together with dozens of other SA leaders and several other senior figures whom he considered a threat. 'My first reaction,' wrote Pevsner, 'was admiration for the incredibly direct and rather brave intervention of Hitler himself.' He was perhaps echoing the German Defence Minister, General Werner von Blomberg, who on 1 July had spoken of Hitler's 'soldierly decision and exemplary courage' in stamping out 'mutineers and traitors'. But on reflection Pevsner concluded, 'The new developments have really jolted me.' A quick visit to Germany confirmed his disquiet. On his way home from Naumburg he stopped in Cologne, and saw the Rhine bridge flanked with SS troopers to escort Hitler on his way to Koblenz. 'A final dreadful indicator of the change in people's mood,' he noted. 'Would it have been possible at Easter?' By August, Hindenburg had died and Hitler had amalgamated the office of President with his existing post of Chancellor, to become *Führer und Reichskanzler*, and Supreme Commander of the German *Wehrmacht*.

In private, Pevsner was troubled. 'What on earth will come of all this?' he questioned Lola anxiously. But back in England his inchoate and confused attitudes to German politics were hardened by slighting remarks made to him in everyday conversation, and constant unfavourable comment on German affairs in English newspapers. He found it hard to get news, he told Lola, 'among all the gossip and rumour'. Why did she not write more about politics? He was having to read Nazi papers for information.

'Everyone here sees what he wants to see,' wrote Pevsner, unwittingly summing up his own position. He had clearly not lost the sense that Germany was his home and the place where he should be working, and those professional and intellectual roots, rather than any political theory, were the source of what, as late as October 1934, he was still describing as 'my National Socialist feelings'. 'Dear God!' he had exclaimed a few months earlier. 'How productive I could be if only I were in the right place!', and there was no doubt where he believed that to be. He had fantasies of giving up the struggle and going home to Germany, and had made Lola go through the motions of applying on his behalf to the department within the Reichserziehungsministerium (Ministry of Science, Education and Culture) that handled teaching. 'As soon as the Aryan business fades out, I'm back home,' he declared in September 1934. 'I could do so much now. Everything I read is just the kind of thing I would like to do myself. Should I have hung on, despite all the bad prognoses, and forced myself on them?'

Just how he might have fitted in back at home is illustrated by an article entitled '*Kunst und Staat*' ('Art and the State'), which he had written in March 1934 for a leading Nazi magazine.* *Der Türmer*, founded in 1898, had started as a Protestant monthly journal of the arts, which gradually became associated with the promotion of the cultural concept of *Heimatkunst*, literally 'regional art' or 'homeland art' – rural rather than urban culture, native rather than cosmopolitan. After 1918 the magazine's interpretation of *Heimatkunst* became increasingly conservative and nationalistic. By 1929 the editorship was in the hands of Friedrich Castelle, an early member of the Nazi Party, and *Der Türmer* was rapidly becoming a vehicle for blatant *Blut-und-Boden*/ 'Blood and Soil' propaganda. It greeted Hitler's seizure of power in 1933 with enthusiasm.

In his article Pevsner once again argued for the existence of a contract between artist and state – a contract all the more inevitable now that an authoritarian state was in the process of being formed in Germany.

---

*There is an interesting discussion of '*Kunst und Staat*', with extended extracts from it, in Erdem Erten, 'Shaping "The Second Half-Century": *The Architectural Review* 1947–71', PhD thesis, MIT, 2004, pp.179–82.

Expressionist painting could be seen as a turning-away from self-absorption towards a concern with social themes. The evolution, too, of a uniform contemporary building style aimed at putting the needs of the many before the egos of the few. Both these trends could be viewed as being in the same line of descent as the militant state art of this era of authoritarianism. 'Message' painting and poetry, poster art, the novel as reportage – all directly served the needs of the state in moulding public opinion, and if the state were to push this kind of art, it would eventually form a uniform style like that of the Middle Ages or the France of Louis XIV. Kitsch would be a constant hazard, but, argued Pevsner, 'Hasn't the ethically positive painter of topical kitsch the vital advantage over the most gifted of esoteric Cubists of actually meeting a demand?'

'This recognition of the vital importance of being in touch with demand is perhaps the most important product of the Expressionist decades, as far as the history of art is concerned,' wrote Pevsner. 'Art is once again to be functional, as it was throughout the Middle Ages and the Baroque era.' But whereas the function of art in the Middle Ages was to convey religious ideas, in the present day it was not religious but political ideas – giving 'political' its widest meaning – that were to the forefront, and the consequences for the arts were irrefutable: the new state would demand the devotion and the service of every artist.

In return for loyal service, the state should support the drive within the arts towards 'social recovery' – by which Pevsner meant the reforms in art education that had been implemented by the Bauhaus. 'The art schools have for some time been engaged in combining fine and applied art once again . . . These endeavours will not, one hopes, be hindered by uncertainties over personnel. For the new state should recognise clearly that the change of direction away from Art for Art's sake towards an acceptance of functional art is a turning towards service, and therefore in the final analysis a turning towards the state.' In addition, 'the creative genius should be allowed as much freedom as he needs for his development . . . The paragraphs of a programme can easily so smother the creative spirit that it withers away. It is one of the duties of the state here to show generosity and understanding, for it must win the help of the arts and the artist.'

Can he possibly still have believed either that the Nazi art establishment would moderate its repressive policies or that there could be a place for him within it? His views on the artist as a servant of the state may have been in line with official thinking, but common sense, and increasingly ominous news from home, should surely have warned him that in every other way his hopes were pipe-dreams. His children, Lola told him, were worrying now about people 'not consorting with them'; Uta's teacher Fräulein Feierbach had made 'some odious remarks'. He himself suspected that some of his German correspond-ence had been intercepted – and yet he apparently continued to cling to a belief of sorts in the Nazi regime.

What exactly did Pevsner's political views amount to in the 1930s? There was unquestionably still an element of defiant reaction against his mother's liberalism; he would refer later to his *perverse* interest in National Socialism', which embarrassed Annie to the point where she did not want to show her face among her husband's business associates. There was also a thin strand of the kind of anti-Semitism that was more common among assimilated Jews than is often acknow-ledged. In a fascinating study of the attitudes of German-Jewish refu-gees in England, *Continental Britons*, Marion Berghahn quotes a 'Mr I': 'My father once said to me, "Thank God, you were born Jewish, because you would have made a vicious Antisemite". I am one of the Jewish Antisemites . . . I find what is a typical Jew repulsive . . . I know, it is unforgivable.'[8]

Pevsner was never vicious, but he told Lola that he much disliked 'the typical emigrant atmosphere, which I usually try to avoid', and, in spite of himself, he felt a strong antipathy towards some character-istics that he considered to be distinctively Jewish. Among Miss Wilson's other lodgers was a young Jewish boy whom he found intolerably bumptious and familiar, 'rather *Berliner* . . . an immature anti-Nazi . . . Such pushiness and such a thick skin . . . A horror . . . a living advertisement for anti-Semitism.' He confided to Lola, 'When I'm with [him], I feel like Streicher – physically repelled.' These feelings were never translated into behaviour (in practice, Pevsner was kind and patient with the boy) and they are worlds away from support for official Nazi policies of persecution; but, holding these views, Pevsner would have felt it hypocritical to disassociate himself from National Socialism solely on grounds of its dislike of Jewishness.

He seems to have been aware that he was known, in parts of the German-speaking community at least, for holding National Socialist views, and realised the need for caution. But he desperately needed to believe that he still had a place in Germany. He had not seen enough of Nazi ideology in action there to appreciate how the articles of his own personal credo would be tarnished by association – how the Uta figure that had moved him so deeply in Naumburg would be exploited in official propaganda as the archetype of Aryan womanhood, and Naumburg itself become a place of pilgrimage for the Party.

He was also far from ready to embrace Englishness. 'One can smell the dogs in all the rooms, but of course that doesn't worry anyone in England,' he snapped. The English were 'untidy, unexacting and unreliable in individual workmanship and personal services'. Worse, they appeared to mistrust and resent anyone who tried to do things properly. 'The English don't like people to work too hard.' Nor, apparently, did they like people to know a lot, unless this expertise was modestly concealed, or to speak foreign languages with any degree of panache. ('A little French is permissible,' commented George Mikes, 'but only with an atrocious accent.')

Pevsner was not yet able to make light of these foibles. 'You really can't say that I have ever appreciated the English attitude to the expert,' he burst out. 'It is contrary to my nature, like everything else here.' It also neutralised the only advantages he currently possessed. Superiority of knowledge – the wide and systematic knowledge conferred by a thorough German education – somehow did not count, or at least could not be made to pay off. 'It's a misery to have so much to say, trying to be content to be so much in the background.'

'Every sentence, every lecture, every book, every conversation here means something quite different from what it would mean at home,' he wrote after his first bruising experience with Oxford insularity. 'The words mean something different, the brain itself is wound differently.' A year later he was still baffled. 'This cursed tactful secretiveness in England! It drives one mad – you're guessing all the time.' ('People on the Continent either tell you the truth or lie,' observed George Mikes. 'In England they hardly ever lie, but they would not dream of telling you the truth.')

This made it impossible for Pevsner to gauge the impression he was making. Was he causing offence in some indefinably German way? Writing a stream of business letters, he worried constantly about 'perhaps not writing in the style of this goddamned country'. He was fairly confident that his English was coming on well; a lecture on William Morris was, he felt, 'very nearly as free as it would have been in German. I make fewer mistakes in lectures than in quick conversations.' Even in conversation he was making progress: 'Thank God for this gift with languages! Almost everyone I meet speaks with more accent than I do' – but then perhaps it was possible, as a foreigner, to speak English *too* correctly? George Bernard Shaw certainly thought so, and Pevsner cut out and kept the relevant article, 'Spoken English and Broken English', that Shaw had written for the Linguaphon-Institut in 1927. 'Do not try to speak English perfectly,' G.B.S. commanded, 'because if you do, no one will understand you . . . The first thing you have to do is to speak with a strong foreign accent and speak broken English . . . Then every English person to whom you speak will at once know that you are a foreigner and try to understand you and be ready to help you.'

Many émigrés wrote of their fear of being considered 'pushing Jew or workaholic German' when they first came to England, and Pevsner feared the consequences of trying too hard to find a way in. The art history department in Birmingham was a case in point. 'I have to put up my defences,' Pevsner told Lola in October 1934. 'The first names of applicants for the chair here are filtering through – so far, not one with any reputation. I think I could do just as well – and yet I mustn't let on, but must be quiet as a mouse.' Similarly, he was going to have to be discreet when reviewing a large exhibition at the Birmingham Art Gallery of pictures – 'British Art Treasures' – drawn from private collections in the Midlands. Several of the attributions, he felt, owed a good deal to the optimism or ambition of their owners, but he should be careful in saying so: 'It's not worth making the Director here my enemy.'

He was about to find out the hard way that his caution was amply justified. The art world in the 1930s was, in the words of Kenneth Clark, 'like a battlefield at nightfall. The principal combatants were exhausted and had retired to their own quarters, surrounded by their attendants; but their enmities continued unabated.'[9] One of the hottest spots in the combat zone was the Courtauld Institute. Its staff guarded their status and exclusivity fiercely, and were particularly suspicious of arrivistes. In the autumn of 1934, Pevsner became convinced that he had somehow blotted his copybook there. With a little help from Borenius, he had been reinvited to act as an external examiner. 'I'm afraid in [Constable's] eyes this is another piece of domineering by Borenius on my behalf. But I don't know how far all this was really caused by my clumsiness – I think it's probably more the bare fact of the Edinburgh application and the position here in Birmingham . . . This is where Constable has got the idea of me as someone who will thrust himself in by force.'

Pevsner's diagnosis was accurate. A note in the files of the Academic Assistance Council for 4 May 1934 reads 'Professor Constable said to W.A. [Walter Adams, Secretary to the Council] that this grant [to Pevsner] was a bad mistake by AAC. There are very many more distinguished and deserving art historians' – a remark that may have contributed to the Council's decision not to renew the grant in July.[10]

Equally, the AAC might by now have realised that at least one of Pevsner's three referees – Wilhelm Pinder – was a member of the Nazi Party.* There is no hard evidence to suggest that the Council's decision was made in the end on anything other than financial grounds, but Constable's hostile comment can hardly have helped.

Constable was reputed to be less than generous to professional colleagues – Lord Lee, the Courtauld Institute's founder, would later describe him as 'consumed with personal ambition [which] swelled and festered into an almost insane jealousy of anyone who held any other comparable post' – but the reason for his particular animus here is not clear. It is possible that the harder Pevsner tried to appear competent and confident, the less sympathy Constable would have had for him. Pevsner would always be perceived as having good connections and not hesitating to use them, on his own or others' behalf; to the ill-disposed this might have been construed as 'thrusting'.† Again, the situation at the Courtauld may have been one where a recommendation from Tancred Borenius was a drawback rather than an advantage.

Alternatively, Constable may, as Pevsner suspected, simply have resented his presumption in going for British jobs and, what was more, expecting Constable to act as a referee for him against the claims of British scholars. (Constable was willing to recommend Pevsner to the more distant University of Louisville, although even then he pointed out that Pevsner appeared to have some private means and was therefore less deserving of help than some other potential candidates.) 'Ach – "blast it all",' wrote Pevsner mutinously to Lola, trying out a newly acquired English expression. 'I'm not sorry. What use would Constable's sympathy be if I hadn't got my salary here?' But he could not help concluding, 'I'm ashamed, because it is quite clearly a real failure.'

He had perhaps reached his lowest point, and not just in professional terms. His social life was severely limited. Miss Wilson's household could on occasion feel claustrophobic, and in the Florences' more relaxed and luxurious setting, he felt himself to be stiff, cautious and out of place. As someone who avowedly found one young English girl's 'lack of knowledge of the accusative and dative . . . rather shattering', he was, not surprisingly, ill at ease amidst a group of dashing

---

*A second referee, Percy Ernst Schramm, would join the *Wehrmacht* in 1939 and become its official historian in 1943. It is not clear that in 1934 he was already a member of the Party.

†In 1941 the Artists' Refugee Committee would express surprise that Pevsner should be finding it hard to get a job, 'as he knows so many influential people'. (Helen Roeder/Esther Simpson, 4/1/41. SPSL 191/2, 171.)

young people, familiar and first-naming, keen on cards, party games, horses and shows. No coincidence, perhaps, that he had strong fellow-feelings for a reserved and formal German exile from the previous century. 'The Coburg prince interests me,' he told Lola, while halfway through reading Lytton Strachey's life of Queen Victoria. 'So very German in England – hard-working, punctual, pedantic, conscientious, bourgeois and driven to despair by the English lack of system. He was an important figure for the arts, and I would like to spend more time on him.'

He did take himself out sometimes in the evening – to a lecture and organ recital, for example, by Albert Schweitzer, just back from missionary work in the Congo. Schweitzer he found simple and without pomposity, and he also managed a few words with a Huxley (whether Aldous or Julian is not clear), who looked, he added cryptically, 'as one would expect'. More commonly, Pevsner's idea of a good day in London was an extended visit to the National Gallery, followed by Lyons Corner House for steak and – a particular treat – orangeade with ice; he celebrated Lola's thirty-second birthday sitting in an armchair in his room, reading a book *for pleasure*, eating biscuits and drinking half a bottle of cider. He was, he told Lola sadly, keen to help with the washing- and drying-up when visiting the Fletchers in Hampstead: 'I seize on anything that gets me together with people.'

He had made few close academic friends: 'Relationships aren't developing here,' he wrote about the university in Birmingham, 'it's not in their nature . . . Real life here takes place away from the job.' But what little domestic or family life he had in England was often too 'real' for comfort. His aunt Paula was ill with diabetes, and racked by money worries. The landlord of her flat was pressing for payment, but when she decided to sublet a room and put up a 'For Rent' sign in the window, her husband smashed it in a passion. Eric Graddon, Pevsner reported grimly, was liable to bring home at any time a 'witches' sabbath' of unsuitable friends, Mosley Fascists among them.

'On alien soil, one's self-respect tends to diminish,' wrote fellow-exile Stefan Zweig. Pevsner was certainly feeling older, iller and less prepossessing. 'There's a mirror over my sham fireplace,' he informed Lola. 'I find I'm getting uglier, partly in the Jewish direction.' He had to make an effort not to retreat to bed too early, and woke to anxieties on all sides: 'I wake quite regularly at 6 and lie here and hear all the first noises from the street and people going to work. I think of the job, of politics, of Germany, of you, and other troubling things. At 7 the letters fall through the door and I get my post.' 'Let's suppose – and it's improbable but not impossible – that my nerves suddenly let me down and I succumb to a breakdown. A nervous disposition does run in the family, after all – I know it can happen.'

What was clear to him was what he had lost. Jakob Grimm had outlined the position neatly a century earlier. Exiles, he claimed, lose three things when they lose *Heimat* or homeland: 'securitas', their personal standing within the order and legal framework of a community; 'dexteritas', their adaptability and confidence to move around and communicate with others whom they trust; and a common culture. Pevsner had been forced to abandon a relatively comfortable, secure and promising life in Göttingen – a good job and clearly demarcated research area in a profession with social prestige; an extended family and network of friends, colleagues and contacts; a desirable place to live, in an upper-middle-class area; a suitable wife and handsome young family; a cultural milieu in which he moved with ease. He was now living alone and from hand to mouth, in a single room in an ill-favoured city in what he described in a low moment as 'this tedious, puritanical, drab land'.

For Tom's eighth birthday, Pevsner sent him a postcard of a German airship: 'If I really had the Graf Zeppelin at my disposal, I should fly to Germany tomorrow, to Göttingen, and land in the fields behind Dahlmannstrasse and invite you on a little birthday trip.' He was determined not to bring his family over until he could look after them properly – he had visited an émigré family whose living conditions, with babies' nappies draped everywhere, had shocked him. But he was afraid of the price he might have to pay for prolonging the separation from Lola.

'I think of you a lot, my love, and not just during the evening jitters – tenderness as well, your cheeks, your hair. Strange, after more than ten years – that's a good thing, isn't it, after all this living apart.' But sometimes his confidence gave out. In the same month he queried: 'I wonder if you really believe in me and my eventual success? . . . What thoughts of me and of our marriage are you keeping to yourself? Perhaps you feel you can manage quite well without a man about the house? Do you sometimes feel afraid of living together again? . . . I often long for your quiet breathing when you're already asleep and I'm still awake.' 'Do you think we'll ever climb the Matterhorn as a happy couple?' he asked. 'When will we sit weeping in the Dresden Opera again? . . . Strange how everything in my life is the wrong way round from the norm – first marriage, and then the sixth-form crushes; first the comfortable married life, and then the search for money and position.'

'How long ago it seems since I was peacefully preparing, reading, working through books,' he wrote. 'I do believe that if I had a bit of peace, all my suppressed productivity would burst out.' Again and again he repeated the plea for 'peace in a little work', unconscious of its resonance with another phrase – '*Arbeit macht frei*' – the motto emblazoned over at least one of the fifteen concentration camps opened in Germany that year.

CHAPTER 15

'Amor fati'

The first months of 1935 found Pevsner still without a permanent post. Birmingham University had now appointed the head of its art history department and had gone for Thomas Bodkin, previously Director of the National Gallery of Ireland in Dublin. Pevsner found him personally congenial – '48 years old. A white pointed beard, very witty and amusing . . . Half an hour of pleasant conversation' – but was startled by the apparent superficiality of his knowledge, by the standards of German scholarship: 'A shocking ignorance of all sorts of areas which happen not to be his hobby . . . He can't read architecture in German or Italian, and ordinary books only with difficulty.' Bodkin later became a highly influential figure in the English art establishment, invited to become the first director of the Arts Council; but in 1935 Pevsner viewed him as one more well-connected amateur, and the appointment made his own lack of an official teaching position the more galling.*

One job, however, was a source of real pleasure. Some time in 1934 he had received a request for private lessons from a young Oxford graduate named Denis Mahon. Mahon had become interested in the Italian Baroque through Kenneth Clark, then Director of the Ashmolean, and studied with Clark at the museum for a year. In October 1933 he began studying for an Academic Diploma at the Courtauld. During the following year he attended Pevsner's lectures on Mannerist painting, and now he asked to become a pupil.

Mahon, who was heir to the Guinness Mahon banking fortune, was also looking for guidance as a collector, having already laid the foundations of an impressive collection of Italian Baroque art. Pevsner suggested concentrating on the works of Guercino (Giovanni Francesco Barbieri) – a tip that would become highly profitable, when 'the Squinter' became less unfashionable in English art-historical circles. In 1936, acting on Pevsner's advice, Mahon bought the very important *Elijah fed by Ravens* relatively cheaply; he offered it to the National

---

*Another attempt to secure an academic post – ironically, at the National Gallery in Dublin – was unsuccessful, though Pevsner was again shortlisted.

Gallery, but Kenneth Clark declined it, on the grounds that he could never get it past the Trustees.*

But in these early days it was Pevsner who was indebted to Mahon. On Valentine's Day in 1935, he had what he described as a 'most marvellous' evening. In a reversal of his situation as a young teacher in Göttingen, when he had invited his seminar students back for orange juice and biscuits, he had gone after an evening tutorial to his pupil's home, to listen to records till midnight. 'Lola, you can't imagine, about 1000 records, complete operas, like *Chenier*. We played part of that, then a lot of *Forza*, and then *Otello*. Dear God, this is where one can *really* envy his money. Of course he listened to everything with piano score in hand. "Any time", he said.'

Pevsner went to concerts as often as time and money allowed, and was able to report confidently of a programme conducted by Sir Thomas Beecham (Rossini, Delius and Mozart) that it was 'marvellous – perhaps the best to be heard in England. Beecham, of course, I knew from having met him at the Munros [in Oxford] – a terrific chap. True, he dances around like nobody's business, but he has charm, rhythm, and a marvellous *piano*.' The Spanish mezzo-soprano Conchita Supervia, on the other hand, failed to amuse. 'A scandal,' he wrote severely. 'Good voice, but Spanish songs in three different costumes, and flowers all over her, fat with red hair – impossible, pure music hall.'

He was reading Spengler and the Epistle to the Romans, but in January 1935 he told his children, 'The papers for the last few days have been full of something which we will surely also get soon – the Television . . . You will be able to see films and acrobats and sport and all manner of things.'† He preferred his films in the cinema, and would occasionally take Miss Wilson with him. 'Last night to a disappointing Garbo film,' he told Lola. 'Sometimes she is just beautiful and nothing else, and her partner did nothing for me, because he looked rather like Gropius.'‡ Long walks were his main exercise, as his growing collection of walkers' guides testified, but he could on

---

*It is now one of four Guercinos in the extremely valuable collection of Italian Baroque paintings on loan to the National Gallery from Sir Denis: he himself would be a Trustee of the Gallery in 1957–64 and 1966–73.
†The BBC's public service had existed for three years, but sets cost some £100, the price of a small car, and there were fewer than 2,000 in operation. The breakthrough, presumably being forecast when Pevsner wrote, was the replacement of a mechanical service by an electronic one, making television affordable for a wider audience.
‡This was probably *Anna Karenina*. Garbo's Vronsky was Fredric March, who did indeed resemble Gropius.

occasion be persuaded to dance. He attended a 'Commerce Ball' in Birmingham with the Florences. 'No chance to fall in love,' he remarked, 'so could join in everything comfortably.' He won an elimination dance with one of the German girls – '"Any gentleman wearing something from Woolworths, sit down", or wearing glasses, or that kind of thing' and took the opportunity to relax, for once, in the company of students: 'Very childish, but one would like to have children like that.' At 5 a.m., with the party still going strong, he had a raw egg in the kitchen and went to bed.

He could not help being aware that, for all his growing ease and lengthening list of contacts, he remained on the fringes of the art history establishment. To make his way to the centre, he decided, he needed to make his mark with published books. He had, in fact, finished the first draft of a piece entitled *Academies of Art Past and Present* before he left Germany, hoping to have it published there in 1933, and he laboured on it intermittently during his first spring in Birmingham, adding new footnotes gleaned from his visits to English art schools and trying to 'Anglicise' the content of the preface and epilogue and make a translation of the original German text.

Academies chronicled the changing relationship between artist and society, through the prism of education. It was, he wrote, 'a straight-forward description of four centuries of artists' education, linked up with certain political, social and aesthetic data . . . the history of art academies through the Italian Cinquecento, the *siècle de* Louis XIV, the time of Goethe and the Romantic Movement, and the century of Liberalism'. In his argument he was working forwards from Naumburg and backwards from the Bauhaus – his two emotional and philo-sophical centres – on a thesis that was crucial to his whole ideology of art: the artist should not be separated from his community, and should also be a craftsman, dedicating his gifts to the service of that community's practical and spiritual needs.

The theme of *Academies* was in Pevsner's eyes still more of a German subject than an English one, and the style and level of scholarship were better suited to a German audience. 'My heart bleeds that it should have to come out in England. It isn't really something for them – it *must* be German. But who will read it now at home?' He started looking for a translator to speed the process of producing an English text, and turned to friends – Katharine Munro and Francesca Wilson – to read and improve the draft. He also sent a copy to Kenneth Clark, who returned it with a 'nice and flattering' letter, and offered to give him references to a publisher. It was, however, through Katharine Munro's father that he eventually approached Oxford University Press.

There an editor agreed to put it on the OUP list, but there was no definite promise to publish and, for the time being, *Academies* would remain a manuscript.

Pevsner was proud of *Academies*, which had been carried out by the methods of research and analysis that he preferred, at a level of scholarship where he felt happy, originally written in his first language. The English version would be a logical continuation of his previous career, rooted in his former life and personality. But, paradoxically, he would prosper far more in his new existence from the other piece of writing that preoccupied him – something with no pretensions to erudition, produced by the job he despised.

By the middle of 1935 he was beginning to draft his report on design in industry for Professor Florence. He was uncomfortable with the scrappy, subjective, unverifiable nature of his raw material – a mixture of disparate factual information, sales talk, opinion and his own extempore observations – and painfully aware of gaps and inaccuracies where he had been unable to gain access to particular firms. He was also struggling to write at length in English for the first time.

He planned the structure of the report in German, but then had to clothe the bones. He was learning or revising 300 words of vocabulary a day, and his spoken English was coming on fast, but on paper he was over-conscious of the mechanics of grammar and style, and unconfident of reproducing an authentically English voice. He was aware that transposing literally from German would not do. Much later he would write, 'The German language allows freedoms that the English does not, and while the meaning in good German writing . . . always penetrates the creative fog of heaped-on words and fragmentary sentences, no other language can imitate it without becoming ridiculous.'[1] Deprived of his 'creative fog', Pevsner found his own English writing style 'rather hard, concise . . . I feel it is very different from my German style – almost unbelievably simpler.'

He was not too proud to ask for help with 'this Goddamn language' from his friends, particularly Austin and Elsie Duncan-Jones, and would eventually offer generous thanks to those who 'helped to improve the foreigner's dry and insipid style'. He would also thank his mother, who typed the English manuscript up for him at long range, a chapter at a time; for more than a year he would keep her supplied with his handwritten drafts as he produced them, and, postal services and customs authorities permitting, she returned a mounting pile of immaculate typescript.

In spite of himself, Pevsner had been drawn more often than not into the detail of design, manufacturing and marketing, and he had amassed the facts he had been asked for: data on door handles, cushion covers, radiators and radios, production rates for patent sprung chairs, sales figures for aluminium 'beauty boxes' and leather match-cases, comparative fees for designing furnishing fabrics and dress materials, the relative popularity of 'College Views' and 'Rustic Floral' patterns on dinner plates, the cost of the tools for manufacturing a small undecorated ashtray in beetle ('made from urea and formaldehyde'), the processes for pressing plate glass, tufting Axminster carpets, jolleying china cups and manufacturing linoleum.

At the same time, long before the fact-finding was finished, value judgement had crept in – if, indeed, it had not always been implicit in the original premise – and his report went far beyond the original topic. He had slipped effortlessly from 'how are designers used?' to 'how *should* designers be used?' and 'why does design matter?', and straight into the realms of politics, economics, sociology and ethics.

'90% of British industrial art,' Pevsner declared, 'is devoid of any aesthetic merit.' Aware that this might seem a little bald, he hurried on, 'It may be less insulting than it sounds at first,' and added placatingly, 'I do not know of any modern country where the majority of industrial products is not deplorably bad in design.' His job as he saw it was to explain why this should be so.

'I have tried not to mistake the modern for the beautiful,' he insisted, acknowledging the risk; but, without ever attempting to define beauty of design, he made it clear that his touchstone for assessing it was contemporary and continental. It was not, he explained, that he failed to appreciate the products of the past; he just felt that the manufacturers of the day should not be copying them, but should instead be making objects in the spirit of their own age – and this was the spirit of modernism. 'It seems as if today nothing of vital energy and beauty can be created unless it be fit for its purpose, in harmony with the material and the process of production, clean, straightforward and simple.' The prospects looked gloomy for flamboyance and fantasy, elaboration and embellishment in design; but he sought to lay fears to rest. 'I do not think it is good policy to be as orthodox as some of the best English critics are at the moment. To abuse or ridicule any nostalgia for ornamentation can only deter people from studying the modern style and from trying to appreciate it . . . If it is decent in shape and decent in decoration, let us allow it a place among the sheep and not relegate it to the goats.'

Methodically, trade by trade, he lined up his livestock and labelled them. His 'sheep' were easiest to find among the products of industries that were started in the twentieth century – wireless and gramophone cabinets, refrigerators, electric fires, wristwatches. Cars, for example, were manifestly associated with modernity and progress – 'Speed is one of the leading motives of our age' – and the association with speed made it perfectly reasonable to employ the fashionable device of stream-lining, in which Pevsner took a slightly guilty pleasure. Streamlining did not really *add* speed, he noted conscientiously, but it was curiously expressive of the era – provided it was not taken to extremes. 'I once saw something in a shop window,' he remarked witheringly, 'which was called a streamlined lipstick.'

For someone who never enjoyed driving, Pevsner displayed an endearing enthusiasm for cars, detailing the virtues of the mid-priced Alvis, Riley and Rover ('very dignified and satisfactory appearance', price £298) and becoming positively lyrical about the Rolls-Royce Phantom III Sports Saloon ('almost perfect balance and beauty', £3,000). 'Changes in [cars'] appearance are discussed everywhere and seem to concern everybody . . . The ambition to recognise the various makes of car in the streets has infected all boys between four and seventy . . . All this creates an extremely adventurous and cheerful atmosphere in the motor works' – and such an attitude was bound to foster creative design, provided it was tempered by native caution. 'The scepticism and steadiness that characterise English politics and English cultural life have saved the motor-cars of this country from most of the excesses of modernity to be seen on the Continent.' Car manufacturers, Pevsner wrote slightly wistfully, 'know what a risk means and that it is only the taking of risks which makes life worth living. Why should they be afraid of a genuinely modern shape?' To be modern, a shape must be clean and clear. Some table glassware, for example, particularly that produced by designer Keith Murray, had 'the simplicity and dignity, the straight-forwardness and precision of the modern style in architecture', achieved by eschewing the 'death by a thousand cuts' of traditional English crystal. Steel window frames, too, won praise that in hind-sight seems improbably warm – 'almost perfect in proportion and clearness of expression'.

Pevsner was an admirer of British tweeds, particularly commending the way in which a tradition of exquisite hand-weaving had been successfully transferred to the factory. He was also complimentary about furniture from the Gordon Russell workshops, which seemed to him to strike a perfect balance between high aesthetic standards and the demands of mass production. But, if the truth be told, the most entertaining parts of Pevsner's report are the passages where the apparent apathy, irresponsibility or sheer philistinism of manufacturers incensed him and he allowed himself some literary leeway in describing his dislikes.

He noted 'the atrocities of modernistic "jazz" patterns', for example, in the most improbable places – in geometric door knobs, pseudo-futurist chandeliers and 'antique copper' hearth furniture with jagged ornaments. While expensive carpets were prone to period imitation, cheap ones more often fell into 'a deplorably misunderstood Continental cubism, the prevailing colours being a brown, a blatant orange and, in more recent years, a grass-green no less blatant'. It was, Pevsner thundered, an 'abyss of vulgarity', and the manufacture of such loathsome articles was 'a serious indictment of contemporary civilisation', all the more lamentable for being, quite often, deliberate. Manufacturers knew how nasty their wares were, and made them anyway. One 'said in a forlorn way: "I wish you could tell me who the people are who buy my stuff. I have never been in a house with carpets like that." There was also a . . . director whose expressions in front of his products varied between "hideous", "horrible", "beastly" and "nasty", and a fifth who seemed to get a perverse joy and self-tormenting pride out of displaying his worst best-sellers. I still remember the sound of his: "Now look at this, isn't it a brute?"'

Having delivered himself of his views on the current miserable state of English design, Pevsner moved on in the second section of the report to explain it. The size and structure of a firm, he decided, were not relevant. A big company might have the money to make innovations, but prefer the easier rewards of routine mass production; a small firm controlled by a single personality might in theory have the focus and agility to experiment, but in practice be 'too much concerned with securing orders and keeping afloat to recognise their social duties'.

Far more to the point was the degree to which a product's design was purely functional; where there was a deliberate element of decoration, taste deteriorated sharply. 'In many industries,' he wrote sombrely, 'it was alarming to see that the more art is applied to an article the worse its appearance becomes.' This he attributed, typically enough, to the character of the modern age, which he felt was not an age of decoration. 'Most modern architects feel at sea as soon as they are asked to create for decoration, for adornment only', and designers of all types were equally ill at ease. '[The reason] is the "Zeitgeist" of our age, the age of steel, of speed, of work, or whatever one may call it, that does not allow for much play and much carefree enjoyment. One may regret living in such an age, but one cannot alter it.'

Equally depressing was his reluctant conclusion that popular taste did have an influence on design, and not for the better. Standards of design 'for the masses' were significantly lower than those of more expensive items made for a middle-class market – and this he found mystifying. Was it really the case that there was no demand for modern design among the lower classes? Pevsner found it hard to reach a conclusion. Sales techniques skewed the evidence. The shopkeeper, he wrote, 'unconsciously pushes what he likes and conceals in dark corners what seems to him unattractive. He may also kill articles by bad and overcrowded display . . . As to buyers and travellers, they are usually not in the best position for energetic action in favour of anything new. A traveller paid commission on sales transacted, a buyer in a store entirely dependent on turnover, these men can less afford to take risks.'

And yet he had also to confront the evidence that, when offered showy, vulgar, sentimental and meretricious objects, people simply did not 'dislike them as thoroughly as one would wish them to'. 'A certain admiration for elaborate craftsmanship . . . is a natural outcome of a simple, unsophisticated mind,' he wrote solemnly, desperately trying to find reasons why anyone would make, or spend a lot of money on buying, an electric fire with a flickering coal effect. '[The engineer] is just as proud of his ingenious gadgets as was the patient 16th-century craftsman of the skill of his hand when he carved a crucifixion with 52 attendants out of a cherry stone. Both achievements have nothing to do with aesthetics.'

Pevsner looked hard for extenuating circumstances. 'There are several excuses for the humble consumer,' he wrote, 'excuses derived from the social conditions in which he is compelled to live' – cramped, uncomfortable and joyless in the extreme. 'No wonder that in such conditions no sense of beauty and hardly a sense of tidiness can be developed.' 'A cardboard travelling-case made to imitate alligator skin . . . a bakelite hair-brush made to imitate enamel . . . a machine-made coal-scuttle trying to look hand-beaten' – these faked effects were dishonest to the point of immorality, and yet the longing for them should be understood and condoned as an attempt to escape from hardships imposed, ultimately, by the exploitation of the labouring classes in the Industrial Revolution.

The question of who actually carried out the design of a product was, in Pevsner's view, a critical one. In his researches, he had discovered that the use of staff designers was far from universal. In some trades – pottery, for example – a similar function was performed by a 'decoration manager': 'He may have attended evening classes in an art school, or he may not.' Elsewhere, designs could equally be produced by the manufacturer himself or by the worker on the shop floor. Little good, in Pevsner's view, could come from any of these sources as a rule. By far the best solution, he argued unsurprisingly, was to employ an artist or architect as designer, uniting art once more with handcraft and bringing the most finely developed sensibilities to bear on design.

The artist should, perhaps, be a commercial artist, in order to put manufacturers at their ease. Ordinary artists, they say, are hard to deal with 'because they are unbusinesslike and touchy. This is so, I am afraid, partly because, being artists, they must be like that and partly because, having been brought up with the idea of the great message of free and independent art, they want to be like that.'

Better still would be to employ architects as designers. (Pevsner would never budge from this Bauhaus-bred view; twenty years later, when professional designers were far better established, he still maintained the superiority of the architect.) Architects were the principal experts on design in the community, thanks to their practical abilities in engineering and business management, their understanding of materials and processes, their comprehensive training. They were, he argued, engaged in 'never-ending mediation between imagination and production, between art as an aesthetic and art as a social phenomenon'. Examples of their contribution to the best design were all around – the steel-framed windows he had so much admired, designed by a council of architects; the fabrics of C.F.A. Voysey and the bentwood furniture of Alvar Aalto; the Ekco radio cabinets of Serge Chermayeff and Wells Coates.

But the most important factor of all in explaining the current dismal state of British industrial design was, in Pevsner's view, human nature and individual failings. More specifically, individual producers were failing to acknowledge their duty to society – 'the overwhelming moral responsibility of any manufacturer whose products act on the taste of such an immense multitude of his fellow-countrymen' – and it was in this area that the weight of his recommendations would fall.

Publicity and 'art propaganda' would be one practical way of raising standards – a Museum of Modern Design, perhaps, in London, and an annual design exhibition on the lines of the Ideal Home Exhibition or the Motor Show. The BBC could help more than it did; and railway, bus and tram companies should follow the example of London Underground in bringing good design to the travelling public in their posters, their tickets, their signs and the style of their stations.

Most of his suggestions, however, were rooted in the systems of modern art education that he had discussed in *Academies of Art*. Specialist art schools should devote more time to practical training and less to theory, and seek to cooperate more closely with technical schools. Only in a few art schools 'in the centres of cultural life' should the study of painting and sculpture be encouraged, as opposed to the training of designers:

> Demand for pictures and sculpture is small, much smaller than it was before the industrial revolution which, by the invention of photography and colour reproduction, has so greatly affected the social conditions of art . . . It is wrong, sociologically and morally wrong, to base the organisation of art schools on provision for future painters and sculptors. It helps to create an art proletariat without really furthering the genius, who is nowadays the only artist that matters, and who cannot be materially furthered by any organised training.

All would come to naught, however, unless individual manufacturers were prepared to employ the designers coming out of this reformed educational system, which would require a major shift in their priorities. 'It would be absurd,' Pevsner admitted, 'to suggest to the producer that he ought to ruin himself for the community, but what one is justified in asking is that he should consider carefully and conscientiously how he can best obtain a balance between his business and his public duties.' Striving for a better personal understanding of design, the manufacturer 'must realise the seriousness of the problem, must train his appreciation and deepen his consciousness of beauty in his house, in his office, in the articles of his personal wear and use'.

Educating the masses was the moral duty of the manufacturer. Popular taste might currently be doubtful: unlike John Betjeman, whose *Ghastly Good Taste* had appeared in 1933, Pevsner believed that it could be changed. If poorer and less-educated people were offered better design that was within their means, they could, and almost certainly would, learn to want it. Other classes in society shared the responsibility for disseminating finer discernment. The rich, for example, should realise that 'buying reproduction work means fleeing from contemporary life' and set an example. 'Snobbery could be a great help to the growing Modern Movement in England, if only more members of the upper class would give up Chippendale for modern furniture of equally high craftsmanship and perfect design.' The Royal Family itself should help by introducing a 'decidedly modern and well-advised buying policy'.* But in the end it was the enlightened manufacturer – men like Gordon Russell or Sir James Morton of Edinburgh Weavers – who could make the most difference to standards of design by shouldering their moral responsibilities.

Pevsner had travelled a remarkable distance from a simple narrative of teapots and bedsteads, handbags and hollow-ware, and towards the end of his report an underlying message began to emerge. Improving design in Britain, improving public taste, mattered, not just for its own sake, but as a facet of improving social conditions generally. 'Design in daily life is not a detached question,' he wrote. 'It is an integral part of *the* social question of our time.' He would write later, responding to a critic, 'Taste, as I understand it . . . is but an expression of inner harmony, dignity, cleanliness.' Logically, then, poor taste was somehow a reflection of inner disharmony, indignity, grime, the indicator of a damaging and undesirable way of life and an ailing society – and so the fight to improve it through good design became a battle to improve the general condition of one's fellow-men.

For the quality of life to be genuinely affected, of course, it would not be enough simply to tinker with the design of suitcases and hair-brushes. 'No conclusive improvements can be made in design unless social improvements are achieved before and alongside them,' wrote Pevsner. 'The distance between the wealthy and the poor is larger in England than in Central Europe . . . Unless a further levelling of social differences takes place in this country, no steady development towards the aims of the Modern Movement is possible . . . The battle has to be fought on all fronts.' This holistic approach, linking innovation in design to political, social and moral reform, was not at all uncommon among English modernists in the 1930s. But was *An Enquiry into Industrial Art in England* (the title under which the report was eventually published) really characteristic of Pevsner himself?

A close interest in the subject was not. For a period of about ten years the *Enquiry* would make Pevsner something of an authority on design, in other people's minds at least, but he was the most reluctant of gurus. For as long as he needed to do so, he would keep broadly abreast of developments in industrial design, but he would give up the attempt with relief as soon as alternative methods of making a living presented themselves.

---

*Pevsner's predictions for a royal influence on public taste may not have been entirely serious. Certainly by 1944 he was treating the subject with some levity; in a letter to designer Sadie Speight he remarked, 'I must say that Princess Elizabeth's hats make me rather doubtful.' (NP/Speight, 19/4/44, in the Circle papers of Sir Leslie Martin, RIBA Archive at the Victoria and Albert Museum.)

The style of the report was at once typical of Pevsner, in its mixture of ideological statements slung within an empirical framework, and unusual in the occasional violence of its tone.* He would never again write quite as aggressively about 'the unbearable oversupply of artists whom nobody wants and whose private feelings are totally uninteresting in a century such as this . . . If the painter is not so great as to express with the utmost intensity and vitality the essence of his time, let him starve, unless he is willing to find the way back to serving the community.'

Nor would he always espouse the somewhat austere modernism which he appeared to be preaching at this time. In an article entitled 'Design for Mass Production' written a little later for the *DIA News*, he explored the consequences of mass production, taking them to their logical conclusion with apparent equanimity. 'We may have good furniture, but it will be uniformed furniture. We may have well-designed glass and pottery etc – but they will all be pressed in the same moulds . . . The theatre has already been uniformed all over the country – we all see the same films. Music has followed. All of us hear what a few radio stations transmit. Thought on everyday matters is shaped by less than a dozen newspapers. What is the good of resisting this development?' We have to live at the end of a civilisation and in a mechanised society, and must strive to find the makings of a new civilisation within the possibilities of the century. 'We require this *amor fati* more than anything.'

Amor fati (literally 'love of fate', or 'embracing one's destiny') was hardly characteristic of Pevsner's state of mind when he wrote the *Enquiry*, and there was much about this particular piece of work that surprised him when he looked back on it. 'How could I find the courage in 1935 to [distribute prizes and reprimands] . . . unhesitatingly?' he queried in 1953, apparently recanting some of his more puritanical remarks. 'The style of the straight line and the annihilated ornament is not the whole modern style of design . . . The many want something livelier, and have a right to it.'

One might also ask what prompted him to make what are the most overtly political statements to be found anywhere in his work. 'A sweeping change of social conditions, such as the establishment of some kind of State Socialism, might lead to a sweeping change in the appearance of industrial products,' he wrote, without necessarily

---

*Josiah Wedgwood, reviewing the *Enquiry* for *The Economic Journal* (47/188, December 1937), commented: 'It is an ethical, not an economic standpoint; and the book, written throughout with the care and precision of a scholar, is animated throughout by the zeal of a second Ruskin.'

stipulating when, where or by whom this sweeping change should be instituted. He referred elsewhere to 'public enterprise', presumably the form of government instituted by 'State Socialism', which would enforce better design by somehow compelling industrialists to acknowledge their responsibilities. 'The manufacturer and the retailer who say that they are proud of not having any taste . . . and that educating the public is no business of theirs, must be called public enemies plainly and bluntly. They must change their outlook, or sooner or later public enterprise will interfere and make life rather unpleasant for them.' Again, this was probably intended more as prophecy than threat, but he was on shaky ground and, venturing even further into the morass, he hazarded a tentative generalisation about the political temper of the twentieth century: 'If there is any relation between the modern style and that shrinkage of private wealth which may well characterise our century, it can only be due to a deep-rooted "Zeitgeist" expressing itself in art as well as in economics.'

This perfunctory sortie into the field of economics and politics had little weight of conviction behind it, and it is very tempting to accept the suggestion that the ideological subtext of the *Enquiry* was drawn not from Pevsner's own views, but from those of Philip Sargant Florence. The most obvious clue that Pevsner was familiar with Florence's political sentiments is his quotation in the *Enquiry* from a report compiled by Florence's wife Lella Secor Florence and M.W. McIver on 'Birmingham's Black Spots', to the effect that 28,000 houses needed slum clearance and immediate replacement. But, more obliquely, he may also have inherited some of Florence's attitudes to the British class structure and its supposed inhibiting effect on industrial design.

In works such as *The Logic of Industrial Organisation* (1933), Florence had argued that industry in Britain was shaped internally by a conspiracy of manufacturers to divide markets according to income and class, rather than creating a single 'rational' and egalitarian system of production and distribution. The public, Florence maintained, would be better served by a rational system – and would almost certainly accept better design than was currently being offered. There is no direct evidence of a specific brief from Florence to collect empirical data to prove these assertions; but there are echoes of these themes throughout Pevsner's text – and occasionally beyond. The suggestion, for example, that England's class structure was one of the reasons for its failure to take up modernism would become an important element in Pevsner's account of the evolution of the Modern Movement in Europe. 'As soon as the problem began to embrace the people as a whole, other nations took the lead, nations that . . . did not accept or did not know England's educational and social contrasts between the privileged classes and those in the suburbs and slums.'*

The energies that powered the research and writing of Pevsner's *Enquiry* were surely less political than personal and emotional. His description there of the spirit of the present age was perhaps revealing: 'our age, the age of steel, of speed, of work . . . *that does not allow for much play and much carefree enjoyment*' (my italics). For Pevsner, this was a time of very little enjoyment at all. He had few friends, little money, effectively neither wife nor family, no time for relaxation or his real interests. He was operating in an environment that was physically uncomfortable, visually unattractive and socially awkward, and writing in a foreign language that led him into some crudities of expression and a perhaps unintentional severity of tone. Nevertheless, the *Enquiry* was the work with which he would make his first mark in his adopted country.

---

*The quotation comes from Pevsner's *Pioneers of the Modern Movement*, published in 1936.

CHAPTER 16

'Little man, what now?'

Long before he had finished writing up the *Enquiry*, Pevsner had started worrying about his next source of paid work. The Birmingham research grant had expired in April 1935, the AAC grant having already gone, and by the end of the year the small amount of money that had been coming from his father's business would also have stopped.* He had applied to the Carnegie Corporation for a three-year fellowship 'in the colonies', but had not yet had a response.† He had offered to do more research for Florence, but had heard nothing. 'I can't imagine leaving someone in limbo for such a long time,' he complained. 'I keep thinking, "He doesn't want me".'‡ However, Pevsner was far from sure that he wanted what Florence, or England, had to offer.

Were his struggles to break into the sphere of English art history really worth the effort? 'I can't say I'm stirred intellectually by this,' he wrote of a lecture he was to give in Birmingham on the methods and principles of art history. 'It's just as well that standards are not as high as in Germany . . . I've produced a silly little effort . . . The audience is composed of university teachers in a country where there is no history of fine art.' He had not yet found much in English university life to counter the disagreeable impression left by the common rooms of Oxford. Cambridge appeared to be equally hard to infiltrate – 'It is quite impossible to talk on a personal level to anybody who is anybody' – and a long gossip with a professor of French, one of Miss Wilson's Russian friends, persuaded him that Manchester would be even less welcoming:

---

*He informed the AAC that this was 'owing to his [father] leaving his firm, partly on account of political reasons too'. ('Confidential Information' supplied to AAC, 9/10/34. SPSL 191/2–3, 19.)

†The Carnegie Corporation funded Fellowships in Commonwealth universities willing to employ 'displaced' scholars, provided they believed the scholars had a chance of establishing themselves independently after two years. The AAC circulated scholars' credentials to likely universities, who then applied to the Carnegie. Pevsner's details went to Toronto, Montreal, Cape Town, Melbourne and Adelaide, where he had contact with individual academics.

‡Pevsner may not have known how much he owed to Florence, who had provided not only the *Enquiry* research, but also 'a valuable and confidential opinion' supplied to the AAC in December 1934, which will have helped to secure their continuing support. (SPLS 191/2, 73.)

He has told me all sorts of stories, enough to make you leave this country at once – all cases of colleagues who had somehow acted 'immorally' and were ruined quite mercilessly . . . 200% cant and hypocrisy – enough to make you spit . . . I couldn't possibly do any of the things I used to do in Göttingen. In one case, the person was totally innocent but too proud to correct the rumours. Although this goes back twenty years, he is still compromised today and not allowed to sit at High Table. Breathtaking!

The previous Christmas he had found himself unwilling to buy the children the tin soldiers he had promised them. 'All I'd get would be Tommies,' he wrote bitterly. Events in Germany in the spring of 1935 had all served to play on his chauvinism. In January a plebiscite had been held among the populace of the Saarland to decide whether or not the area should be returned to Germany by France. The vote was 91 per cent in favour of a return, and Pevsner rejoiced over a decision 'after our own hearts'. He saw it as a gesture towards national unity and strength; but Victor Klemperer, a shrewder political observer and one who was on the spot, had no hesitation in identifying it as a party political issue – 'really not only a vote for Germany, but literally for Hitler's Germany . . . There was no lack of information, counter-propaganda, free ballot . . . In the Reich too 90% want the Führer and servitude and the death of scholarship, of thought, of the spirit, of the Jews.'

Eighteen months earlier, on 14 October 1933, Hitler had announced Germany's withdrawal from the Geneva Disarmament Conference. By February 1935 England and France had cobbled together a plan promising Germany equality in armaments in return for a variety of collective security agreements; but the offer came too late. On 8 March 1935, Hitler revealed that Germany already had a new military air force, and a week later announced that the German government was no longer prepared to abide by the military clauses of the Treaty of Versailles, and was planning to expand the army from the treaty strength of 100,000 to some 550,000 men. In his conversations with English people, Pevsner was very defensive about this unilateral repudi-ation. It should not, he argued, be seen as a 'warlike' gesture, merely a righting of the balance. Germany had been the only nation to disarm properly after the war – 'while France – ach!' – and should now be allowed to recoup some of her strength without being accused of being confrontational. 'It's all such a muddle here, all misunderstandings and unreason. Nobody thinks of Germany's situation since 1918.' His view, he conceded in a revealing phrase, was not one that was shared by 'proper emigrants': 'Maybe the proper emigrants, at home and abroad, will regard this as direct preparation for war.'

Pevsner did not see himself as an emigrant or a refugee or an outcast in England because he was not yet able to see himself as *anything* in England. He was still able to make brief visits home, and his place, in his own eyes, was still in Germany. On 16 March 1935, conscription was introduced, and it is entirely indicative of his frame of mind, and his detachment from the realities of life in Germany, that he briefly cherished fantasies of being called up into the new German army. 'I wouldn't mind such an adventure if it came my way,' he announced to Lola. 'An interruption of my efforts here would be painful, of course, but I can't deny that I would welcome a compulsory training, even if it were hard . . . Perhaps it would be the last chance to do something energetic for this worthy cause . . . I don't believe there would be any unpleasant treatment because of the Aryan thing, not with the military – but maybe in the end it will be different.'

Victor Klemperer was assured by a Gentile friend later that year that it was still possible to be a Nazi for idealistic reasons without being a criminal or an idiot. It was still also possible to be a Jew and not acknowledge what was happening. 'If you looked neither to left nor right, above nor below,' wrote Rolf Kralovitz, one of only four Leipzig Jews to emerge alive from Buchenwald, 'it was possible at this time to live a near-normal life.' You could live in your own home, go to the cinema, use trains and trams – but if you opened your eyes you saw chests and trunks on the street, with the labels 'Leipzig–Tel Aviv', 'Leipzig–Buenos Aires', 'Leipzig–New York'.[1] 'It must be the aim of every German Jew,' a Jewish agency declared in 1935, 'to become a refugee.'

Pevsner was finding it increasingly difficult to ignore the implications of the 'Aryan thing'. This most recent wave of anti-Semitism, it was becoming obvious, was not a simple matter of social discomfort or professional disadvantage. To be Jewish now was to live under permanent political (and possibly even physical) threat, and he and Lola had to decide once more whether or not to conceal this threat from their children. 'We will have to tell Uta soon,' Pevsner argued in February 1935. 'Please think of a form of words, in case the need arises suddenly. Oma and Opa [Annie and Hugo Pevsner] are to be the scapegoats – that's what we arranged and I think we should stick to that. Or shall we wait?' After much agonising, they appear to have opted for keeping the secret as long as possible. There was pressure now on Uta, who was eleven, to join the Hitler Youth, and the fact of her Jewishness would have been the simplest possible way of gaining exemption for her. Providentially, Pevsner decided not to play that card: 'If I can prove myself soon, perhaps we won't have to enlighten them.'

His motives for the deception would appear to have been purely pragmatic; he did not wish his children to live in anxiety if they did not have to. There is no sense that he was ashamed of their descent. He would write to Lola on 19 May 1935:

> 18 years ago today I came to Naumburg for the first time. You were wearing a dress in a large lilac and white check, with your hair down and – amazing – ankle socks. Your mother was there, and we had coffee under a huge umbrella on the terrace. What an expanse of years lies in between that time and now – and in three years Uta will have reached the time when perhaps a tall, thin boy will turn up and possibly lose his heart to her. I wonder what race he will belong to?

He may, of course, have been considering the possibility, even the likelihood, that Uta's suitor, whether he were Jew or Gentile, would be English, and considering it with slightly more equanimity. There were aspects of the British character that, rather against his will, he would always find attractive – sangfroid, for example, and the capacity to rise to a crisis. That April he had caught himself thoroughly enjoying Henry Hathaway's film *The Lives of a Bengal Lancer*. ('1,750 to 1!' shouted the trailer. 'Always out-numbered! Never out-fought! These are the Bengal Lancers . . . heroes all . . . guarding each other's lives, sharing each other's tortures, fighting each other's battles.') It was, he thought, a picture of British imperialism at its best (albeit one constructed by an American director, with three American Lancers: Gary Cooper, Franchot Tone and Richard Cromwell), 'very tendentious but fabulous all the same'. The following month, going to see a patriotic film in honour of George V's Silver Jubilee, made overtly as a celebration of national government, he pronounced it 'amazingly good':

> [It] impressed on me once again the profound superiority of the English gentleman. They take pride in not going on about their heroism, just making a joke of it. No other nation could have made this kind of film. All the gloomy things of the reign are reported calmly and with dignity – Scott, the Titanic, the suffragettes, the war, the General Strike. No gesture against the German. All the gruesome business of the war – so much that one refuses to believe that anything like it could happen again. At the moment of the Armistice, the soldier shoots into the air and says, 'The blooming

war is over' – so anti-heroic and yet so completely honourable. That is the point where I am most sympathetic to the English character. It's an attitude we Germans never manage to achieve. Just think of our illustrated books about the period after Versailles – full of reproach, hatred etc. I'm also thinking of my own dislike of liberalism. It must all seem very undignified from the pedestal on which the educated Englishman finds himself.

Jubilee Day itself, 6 May, he had been dreading as a foreigner, and he accompanied his fellow-lodgers to a nearby Edgbaston park without enthusiasm, drawn largely by the prospect of fireworks – 'I have a passion for them and my heart warmed.' In the midst of a tightly packed crowd he found himself next to a small boy, and lifted him up at intervals to watch the bagpipe bands and passing processions – not without thoughts, presumably, of his own three-year-old son at home. He had written sadly a few weeks before that he did not envy young men with sex appeal as much as parents with children of Dieter's age; like a father at the Front, he must accept that he was losing his children's childhood for ever.

Looking back, Pevsner would describe himself as having been seduced by certain English qualities – the constitutional tendency towards understatement, the poker face and stiff upper lip, the urbanity, the ability to keep cool and treat every case on its own merit – 'and as I fell in love with these English qualities, I was destined not to be a bird of passage here, and not to end in the bustle of America'. Remembering his early revulsion from the hauteur he sometimes detected in English acquaintances, it is difficult not to feel that he was speaking here in rose-coloured hindsight. But there were friends in whom he also found warmth: in his journal for 3 May 1935, Alec Clifton-Taylor noted: 'NP takes me out to lunch. The chairs at our table are of uneven height and he motions me into the lower, which is also the more comfortable. "Now," he says, "your conversation will be De Profundis".'[2] And Pevsner was undoubtedly becoming less fixed in his sympathies and loyalties.

His analysis of the British character and of British politics was hardly sophisticated, and one should perhaps see his analysis of German politics at this time in the same light. He was certainly no longer as confident in confronting his hosts with his political views. 'We Germans are putting ourselves in an indefensible position,' he wrote, 'vis-à-vis foreigners who take a superficial view.' 'Are you thinking about war as much as people here?' he asked Lola. 'It is ghastly to look on, unable to do anything. What is there in our character which excites the world, united, against us again and again? . . . I am constantly asked about details and in answering them I feel ashamed for Germany.'

It would seem that 1935 saw a virtual end to Pevsner's overt expressions of sympathy for National Socialism. He had applied to join the Reichsschriftskammer, or state literary organisation, to enable him to work as a writer and critic in Germany, and now found himself rejected outright. 'Perhaps it's good for one if once again one is struck by the icy blast,' he admitted. 'Otherwise here, far from events, I am all too inclined to see the theory of National Socialism favourably.' He seems to have accepted that he would no longer manage to be sympathetic if he were on the spot. Lola kept him informed of the fate of his former academic colleagues. 'I find the news from Göttingen extremely painful,' he wrote at the end of April. 'Is there no end to it?'

The prospects for the academics now leaving Germany were, he conceded, even grimmer than his own. Job opportunities were limited, and he was incensed when one of the best openings – a series of twelve lectures in Cambridge, for £500, a sum that would have brought him near his annual target of £700 – was filled by W.G. Constable, who was hardly in need of the work. All around him other people were being offered jobs that he would have liked. Meanwhile, away from the mainstream, he continued to flounder in the shallows of art history. 'My time is taken up with trivia.'

'Little man, what now?' he wrote. He was quoting the title of a 1920s novel by *Neue Sachlichkeit* author Hans Fallada, which had recently been turned into a sentimental Hollywood film about the trials of a young couple moving from the German countryside to Berlin and struggling to face the realities of post-war life. Lola was not in particularly good health, suffering from some kind of stomach trouble that gave her a good deal of pain, and the regular house moves that economy dictated were a drain on her energy and her courage. Pevsner wrote in distress, 'It cuts me to the heart that you now only have one room for living and dining. I'm ashamed because I can't offer you anything better.' And every time the family moved, they were dependent anew on the goodwill and discretion of their non-Jewish neighbours. 'What's the landlady like about our cloven hoof?' he wrote bitterly in February 1935.

Lola found it a strain to have sole responsibility for the children's manners and education, and for his part Pevsner worried that she would take out some of her frustrations on them. He was constantly urging her to be softer and more patient with them – 'Bear in mind that objectively they have really turned out rather well' – and to encourage as well as discipline them. Don't spoil Dieter, he urged, and remember to cuddle Tom as well, and praise Uta for her drawings, which were really very good: 'If fate is with us, it would be very nice if she could go in for something like this in the future – but in Germany, of course.' From the heart he wrote, 'Please talk to the children about me and praise me, so that I don't vanish from their field of vision.'

Under all these pressures, Lola would appear to have been letting her impatience show, and urging Pevsner to do whatever it took to secure a regular income, even if this meant looking further afield, perhaps even outside art history. The implied condemnation hurt him:

> Sweetheart, we can't change each other. I have certainly never asked *you* to start a salon . . . It must be a constant misery in Göttingen that you can't but be ashamed of your husband, in comparison with those who have found something. But don't forget that our getting married young was also a difficulty, so I haven't made as much progress as others who are now professors . . . I don't see what else I can do, unless you are thinking of me giving up my calling for something completely different. I still feel the same about that – it's not just bare existence that we are thinking about. If it is still possible to live within my vocation, then that is worth doing – I am not going to abandon it prematurely for the sake of the children. You must see that. It is you who somehow forces me to pick up work where I can.

Pevsner's sense of vocation was recharged by a further encounter with Walter Gropius, visiting the Florences in connection with a building project in Birmingham. Philip Sargant Florence owned a plot of land on Kensington Road in Selly Oak, and there was a proposal that Gropius should be engaged to build a block of flats on it – 'Isokon 4' – for the English furniture manufacturer and champion of modernism Jack Pritchard.* The plan would eventually be thwarted by local opposition, but in the meantime it provided Pevsner with another opportunity to meet his hero. 'I had a longer conversation with him!' he reported breathlessly. 'And then the evening ended, as if everything had evaporated . . . Stirred up, like the last time – and what's behind it is just vanity. I'm still nothing. It doesn't mean that I could be a Gropius, but heaven knows I could be more than I am now.'

---

* While an engineering student at Cambridge, Pritchard had attended Florence's lectures on economics and scientific management. ('Architecture in England during the 1930s' in D. Sharp (ed.), *Planning and Architecture: Essays presented to Arthur Korn by the Architectural Association*, Barrie & Rockliff, 1967).

He had hoped that writing books would be the route to recognition in his true profession. *Academies* and the *Enquiry* were completed in manuscript, and he had been doing a good deal of preparatory work on another subject: what he described as 'this 1890–1900 hobby'. But he could see now that he could not wait for any of these writing projects to bear fruit, driven as he was by his duty as a provider. He himself was finding the constant lack of money oppressive – 'I have reached the point where I simply must be able to pass a shop and think "I can buy that"' – and he was beginning to be afraid that his marriage would not survive the stresses of their situation.

'Are you still in love with me?' he asked Lola in April. 'How will it turn out when we are together again? I can't picture what it will be like . . . Can you still remember what I look like? Try to think suddenly.' He could still make jokes. Miss Wilson had just taken some photographs of him:

> I hardly dare look at them, and even fear that a visage like this might be damaging my job prospects – and of course I believe that appearance and character are related, so I am more and more worried. Apparently I behave quite like a gentleman – so how come my looks are becoming vaguer and more indistinct? I have glasses and my turn-ups dangle . . . When you come, though, I will try to manage without my specs and look like a well-presented husband.

'I hope you have got over the trouble of 1932–33,' he had written nervously at the beginning of the year. 'Or have you? I don't know you well enough after all.' Rereading diary entries for the period, detailing his infatuation with Lise and his nervous collapse at the end of 1932, he was mortified:

> I'm by no means an objective judge, but one thing is clear – if ever anyone else sees it, you will shine out of it as the overwhelmingly honest and upright figure in it all. I show myself as a dreadful shit. And to set against your record I have nothing but my praise for National Socialism, redundancy and unemployment . . . I could sink into the ground for shame . . . I was fighting for very narrow objectives and you for your whole life . . . Muster all your resources, in a single act of faith, and don't give up on me.

Like Lola, Pevsner seemed to be spending most of his time either doing chores or waiting, in a deadly combination of tedium and tension, his only escape half an hour's reading before bedtime with old copies of the *Frankfurter Zeitung,* 'for happy and undepressed sleep'. He suffered from giddiness and palpitations, and was constantly hoarse. He wrote to ask for fresh supplies of his old tranquillisers, in the face of the kind of moods that had made his mother take to her bed.

And then, without warning, opportunities began to open out. Two universities in Australia had been expressing tentative interest in employing Pevsner. First Adelaide, then Melbourne approached the Carnegie Corporation, and by the end of May Melbourne would appear to have applied for two years' funding for a lectureship for him in the history of art. Writing to the Home Office on 1 June 1935 for an extension of Pevsner's residence permit, the General Secretary of the Academic Assistance Council commented, 'It is almost certain that he has secured a position in Australia and he is waiting in Birmingham until the negotiations are complete.'[3] In the meantime, however, came a counter-offer, which forced him to resolve his priorities. The furniture manufacturer Gordon Russell, whose products Pevsner had singled out for praise in the *Enquiry,* was in the audience at a lecture that he gave about his research in industrial design to the Design and Industries Association. 'He showed such a comprehensive grasp of the subject,' wrote Russell later, 'that I went over to Birmingham the next day and asked him if he would like to buy textiles, rugs, glass and so on for us.'

The firm of Gordon Russell personified all that Pevsner considered to be best in modern furniture and interior design. It made frequent use of architects to work with its designers, and its work was 'entirely contemporary, never mannered and never showy'. Russell himself was a craftsman who, frustrated by his own practical limitations, had turned himself into a designer and businessman. His first productions as a teenager had been furniture for the bedrooms at the Lygon Arms in Broadway, an historic Cotswold pub that his father Sidney Russell had turned into an upmarket country inn in 1903 to cater to the new motor trade. A repair shop had been set up for the original antique furnishings, but this was gradually transformed into a workshop for the manufacture of new furniture, and among the designs used were several by Gordon. After service in the trenches during the First World War, he became a partner in the firm and did more designing, calling on the craft traditions that flourished nearby in the colonies of William Morris disciples at Sapperton, under Ernest Gimson, and in Chipping Campden, around C.R. Ashbee. His early pieces – including his own marriage bed – were accordingly made from natural English woods, eschewing decoration; but it was not long before he had begun to look forward rather than sideways.

At a time when furniture production was dominated either by neo-Georgian imitations or pseudo-Parisian jazz, Russell's manifesto of 1923 entitled *Honesty and the Crafts* proclaimed the need for a new craft idiom that would represent the true essence of the current age. While respecting the integrity of Morris's work and the simple strengths of the Arts and Crafts movement, Russell could not share their repudiation of industry and machine production. He felt their distaste for business was hypocritical, given that several of them actually lived off industrial profits, and he rejected their socialist ideals. He himself held conservative political views and saw in capitalist manufacturing the chance to create fine objects on a large scale; machinery was just another tool, which could be used to serve the craftsman rather than replacing him. In 1929 he opened a London shop at 28 Wigmore Street to supply good modern fabrics and decorative furnishings to go with the furniture, and by the following year, in Pevsner's view, the firm of Gordon Russell had hit its stride. In 1930 its furniture could truly be described as modern, with its flush surfaces, square legs, exact angles and seemingly effortless simplicity.

Russell wanted to make this modern style more accepted and more widely available, though for financial rather than ideological reasons. He was not, in the opinion of his sister-in-law, the textile designer Marian Pepler, a true modernist either in his aesthetic tastes or in his social outlook. Visually, he preferred the softer Scandinavian modernism to its harder-line German counterparts, and politically he had very little interest in the lot of the working man. At the end of the 1920s his 'modern' furniture was still primarily handmade. He had to shift further towards the techniques of mass production if he was either to advance beyond luxury furniture into a larger middle-class market or move into work for schools, hotels, public buildings and office suites. He also had to do it quickly, if his firm was to survive. The Depression had all but destroyed the luxury market and had hit the tourist trade for antiques at the Lygon Arms, and the Gordon Russell company badly needed a secure source of income.

Thus he was already thinking in terms of mass production when he was approached in 1930 by the manufacturer Frank Murphy and asked to make wireless cabinets for him. Later publicity for Murphy radios would claim that 'We neither "give the public what it wants" nor what we think it ought to want. We try to clothe our sets sensibly and decently and pleasantly.' Be that as it may, the first Gordon Russell model of 1931 was known as the 'Dartmoor special' because of the bars running across the front, while a later model was known as the 'commode'. But the line as a whole was successful and popular enough to make it necessary for Russell to build a factory in Park Royal in 1935.

By this time, though the firm was still delivering some expensive handmade items, the bulk of its production was machine-made furniture. It was in order to provide a showcase for these suites that Russell planned to open new premises at the end of 1935. The shop at 28 Wigmore Street had failed to survive the Depression, but six doors down the road a warehouse formerly belonging to Debenham & Freebody provided him with new premises, 'neither as small as a decorator's nor as large as a furnishing store's, but sufficiently reminiscent of both to be attractive to either type of customer'.

The job that Pevsner was being offered was that of a buyer of products outside the Gordon Russell range: modern textiles, glass, china and other wares that would enhance the Russell furniture, generate income and improve overall public taste. Marian Pepler, who had previously been doing this buying as a sideline, commented that Russell really offered Pevsner the job to help him out of his difficulties. In one sense, it did precisely that; paying £500 per year, it enabled him at last to consider bringing his family over to England. He notified the Academic Assistance Council that he would not be taking the Melbourne lectureship.

Three decades later, the architectural historian David Walker was in Glasgow, visiting some of its principal buildings with Pevsner.* 'When we passed by Mathieson's General Post Office in George Square,' David Walker remembered, 'he said he wanted to go inside for a few moments, I assumed to buy stamps or send a telegram, but he just stood in silence in the then unaltered counter hall, and became visibly moved. After I suppose about three or four minutes, he turned, smiled and said, "You are wondering what this is all about, aren't you? Thirty-three years ago I sent a telegram from this room to Lola. It said, 'Bring the children'. I had got a job."'†

---

* David Walker was the co-author, with Andor Gomme, of *The Architecture of Glasgow*, published by Lund Humphries in 1968 with a foreword by Pevsner. Professor Walker was later Chief Inspector of Historic Buildings in Scotland and a contributing author to the *Buildings of Scotland*.
† Letter to the author, 9/7/92. Pevsner's remark might refer, as David Walker suggests, to discussions he had been having with Sir James Morton about possible employment with Morton Sundour Fabrics; he could have had an offer from Morton that subsequently fell through. Or he could have been in Glasgow when he received formal confirmation of the offer from Gordon Russell.

The new job was a lifeline, but it also condemned Pevsner to a further stretch of operating in the alien, or at best peripheral, territory of design, and brought him nearer than he would ever otherwise get to the business career he had once feared so much.* He liked his immediate boss, Ted Ould, very much – a generous, unfussy, amusing man – and was always fond of Gordon Russell, though many found him something of a bully. (The tone of some of the firm's advertising perhaps reflected the attitudes of its director: 'You have to take our word for it that only the best hair and springs are used for our upholstery. It is so.') But Pevsner made the decision to accept Russell's job with a heavy heart.

He had wanted a job that, in his words, would be 'at the core of his existence', and he knew that this came nowhere near. 'Forgive the bitterness,' he wrote to Lola. 'I am 33 now, when the second half of your life is supposed to begin, and it starts with failure in my own profession, for which I have been trained for so long and at such expense . . . I have fight left in me, as much as on the very first day, and I feel my wings clipped.' He felt that he had sacrificed all hope of romance and a wider view. He was, besides, losing social status in his own eyes. 'I can't see it as a great compliment when a firm, even a very good one, wants to give me a job in a rather lowly position. There are 1000 people who might succeed in this job. In my own subject I was convinced I could become more than that.'

Even before Gordon Russell made his offer, Pevsner had already relinquished the other cause he had felt himself to be serving. 'The idea of returning to Germany one day is out,' he wrote at the end of April 1935. 'The idea of being considered to have served Germany is a forlorn hope.' Hitler's first successes in foreign affairs had spurred the party faithful on to new attacks on Jewish property and civil rights. Petty displays of spite – signs on lawns in public parks reading 'Jews not wanted here' – would by September 1935 have culminated in the Nuremberg Race Laws: the 'Law for the protection of Blood and German Honour', prohibiting sexual intercourse with Jews and the keeping by Jews of non-Jewish domestic servants; and the citizenship laws which ruled that only those of Aryan blood could be citizens. Henceforward German Jews were 'subjects'. 'I am condemned to stay in England,' wrote Pevsner. 'England remains alien to me and, despite all my admiration for it, somehow hateful.'

---

* Asked in an AAC questionnaire in 1934, 'Would you be willing to accept an Industrial or Commercial Position?', Pevsner had replied guardedly, 'I doubt, if my training would make me fit to an Industrial position [sic]. May be, that my work I am doing at Birmingham . . . is of a certain value in that line.' (SPSL 191/2–3, 21.)

Some years after being exiled from Austria, the Viennese writer Stefan Zweig described his feelings. 'I ceased to feel as if I quite belonged to myself. A part of the natural identity with my original and essential ego was destroyed for ever.'⁴ Victor Klemperer experienced much the same sensations without leaving Germany. 'My inner sense of belonging is gone . . . Contempt and disgust and deepest mistrust with respect to Germany can never leave me now. And yet in 1933 I was so convinced of my Germanness . . . How unbelievably I have deceived myself to belong to Germany, and how completely homeless I am.'⁵ Pevsner would never write explicitly in this way or speak much in later life about his feelings for Germany, and yet the sense of desolation, disjunction and loss of identity must have been very similar.

In order to start his new job, he had to leave Francesca Wilson's house. They had become close friends, she generously sharing her acquaintances as well as her home with him, he escorting her to the cinema and helping her to spend the proceeds of her *Manchester Guardian* articles on making over some of the shabbier areas of 35 Duchess Road – new walls and a sink for the pantry, two Aalto chairs for upstairs. 'Under my influence her living room has changed quite considerably,' he boasted to Lola. 'A new carpet, a new lamp, new cushions, a new day-bed – under electric light, it looks almost gay and modern.' He tried to sum up his gratitude to Miss Wilson in a leaving letter whose English was halting, but this time from emotion:

I feel I ought to thank you once more, and more thoroughly, for what you have done for me all this time . . . I owe such a lot to you. Just try to imagine what I should have felt like during all those crises and troubles and struggles if I had lived in digs with goodness know whom. I don't think I should have survived it. Instead of that, I had – well, I'm afraid I mustn't, you don't like it. But may I say at least that all the nice people of Birmingham I met, I met through you . . . Goodbye. Don't regard me as a callous villain because I don't say more.

CHAPTER 17

'This 1890–1900 hobby':
Pioneers of the Modern Movement

Pevsner's working papers include pamphlets with titles such as 'The Romance of Rayon', 'The Use of Rubber Furniture' and 'Kapok and its Uses'. From the moment he took up the job at 40 Wigmore Street, he started buying fine German papers and textiles, branching out quickly into the best British furnishing tweeds. Shop manager L.J. Smith 'thought it absurd that a fellow of Pevsner's knowledge and horizons should be restricted to fabrics', and soon he was ordering Thonet bentwood chairs from Czechoslovakia, billiard tables, record cabinets and folding beds. His 1936 promotion for 'Christmas present ideas' included a Swedish decanter, a Bakelite tray and a gunmetal vase, and he managed to import into the Gordon Russell shop some of Jack Pritchard's Isokon furniture, including a Marcel Breuer chaise-longue.

He immersed himself with predictable conscientiousness in bulletins on stocks and sales, and the details of lines and materials, writing, for example, in his Daily Report to 'Mr Gordon' on 23 April 1936: 'For a cheap bedroom I thought of stained Birch in case we use the Walnut for the cheap dining room. The bedroom should not sell at more than £25 . . . the English public as a rule considers Oak to be superior to other cheap woods . . . Whether Bird's Eye Maple has been used too much in a certain London trade of rather meretricious taste I do not know.'[1] He predicted turnover, and offered advice on how to improve it. The firm could, he suggested, increase the number of staff in the Drawing Office, to generate a less monolithic style and prompt a more inventive approach: 'At present we feel we are lacking in enterprise as to timbers.'[2] He studied the psychology of advertising, and recommended taking less space in magazines, more in newspapers: *The Times* (his own paper of choice) would be best for Gordon Russell's clientele.

Echoing some of his more lenient pronouncements on 'decent decoration' in the *Enquiry into Industrial Art*, he occasionally urged 'the achievement of more decorative effect in modern design':

> The introduction of effects such as inlaid lines or inlaid edges might be considered . . . Another suggestion might be to make more frequent use of glass. I have seen . . . sideboards with doors on the

left and the right, and the whole centre as a row of drawers entirely done in glass. It had a very fascinating effect . . . We might consider trying some . . . light 'boudoir' furniture in metal if our smithy could do this.[3]

(Gordon Russell himself might well have sympathised with these ornamental flourishes: 'I find we've gone too far,' he once wrote, 'in just using nothing but straight legs in furniture. My wife has a very good pair of legs and I observed them for many years before I thought I might as well do a bit of experimenting in legs put on to furniture.')

Pevsner did a good job for Gordon Russell. The shop was popular with the émigré community (many of whom were music-lovers who frequented the nearby Wigmore Hall), and it enjoyed some success in fashionable circles, with actors including Robert Donat and Charles Laughton on its books. Pevsner's own interest in interiors increased to the point where, in 1938, he was to be found actually preparing and submitting designs himself for the entrance hall and staircase of Gribloch House, a country residence built by the young architect Basil Spence the previous year.[4] For the staircase he proposed a baluster constructed from panels of armour-plated glass set between vertical rails in a dark-rose colour, with a handrail of the same colour; the back wall of the entrance hall was to contain semicircular openings to the dining and living rooms, and niches lined with the kind of exotic timber with which he was becoming increasingly familiar at Gordon Russell. Sadly, his sketches were not accepted and the world was denied a unique Pevsner creation.

But Gordon Russell Ltd could never really be more than a method of earning a living. 'Real life here,' he wrote, 'takes place away from the job . . . It is not time I lack so much as peace . . . I am really longing for the peace that comes with academic work . . . When I get into my own work, I am enveloped in stillness and fulfilment which I can simply not find anywhere else.' Out of business hours, somehow, he managed to make time for 'real life' and real work. Alec Clifton-Taylor had helped with the translation of *Academies* into good English, but it was still seeking a publisher. The *Enquiry*, however, was beginning to reach an audience in the form of illustrated articles. Over the course of the year the *Architectural Review* featured several chapters separately – 'Carpets' in April, 'Furnishing fabrics' in June, 'Gas and electrical fittings' in July, 'Architectural metalwork' in September, 'New materials and new processes' in October, and Pevsner's thoughts on 'The role of the architect' in November.

These articles aroused some interest; but Pevsner's main chance to make his mark came from a completely different piece of work. Since his Göttingen lectures on British art in 1930, and over the long recent months in England, he had been pulling together material and ideas on the nineteenth-century origins, in Britain and Germany, of the Modern Movement in architecture and design. This research reflected the real Pevsner: a scholar who was a historian rather than a philosopher, and yet someone who wanted to write with moral seriousness about the social responsibility of art and the artist. For once, he was drawing on his own interests and his own resources.

In Germany he would by no means have considered himself an expert on the Modern Movement, as compared, for instance, with his friend Wolfgang Herrmann, who had given him a brief guided tour of contemporary building in Berlin in the mid-1920s; but he had kept *au courant* with new ideas, and had ventured into print with his review of the works of Le Corbusier and his 1933 essay on 'Rational Developments in Building'. From his experiences during the research for the *Enquiry* he had perceived that it did not take much to make you an expert in Britain on continental ideas, and he had felt free to express 'conscientiously considered judgements' on British design as one who had tried to follow 'the ways of the Modern Movement . . . on the Continent'. But he had used the vocabulary and the canons of the theory without expressly saying what 'the ways of the Modern Movement' were. In *Pioneers of the Modern Movement – from William Morris to Walter Gropius*, he moved nearer to a description.*

For Pevsner, 'modern' buildings and smaller objects alike had clean lines, whether straight or curved, and a general lack of ornament; roofs were flat, composition asymmetrical, walls smooth, unbroken and frequently white, windows free of mouldings. They were true to their materials: plastic did not pretend to be wood, and walls could display their bare brick or concrete proudly, without paint or plaster.† Nor was their construction disguised; the frame of a building was obvious or even visible, and each of a structure's components had a distinct visual identity. Most importantly, buildings and objects directly expressed the purpose for which they had been made; their form grew out of their function.

This style, Pevsner argued, had been produced by three different

---

Pioneers' dedication is cryptic and interesting; it reads 'To T.B., T.B., W.B., W.A.C., W.G.C., J.P. *and* D.F., P.S.F., P. *and* E.G., H.R., F.M.W., *the* A.A.C., *the* C.I. *in gratitude*'. The most likely attributions are Tancred Borenius, Thomas Bodkin, Walter Barrow, W.A. Cadbury, W.G. Constable, John and Dorothy Fletcher, Philip Sargant Florence, Paula and Eric Graddon, Herbert Read, Francesca Wilson, the Academic Assistance Council and the Courtauld Institute.

†Gavin Stamp points out that in fact it was not unknown for 'pioneer' buildings to have brick walls clad with white render pretending to be concrete.

forces: political and social changes, aesthetic currents and technical developments. Modernism was to some extent a revolt against the social consequences of the Industrial Revolution – dirt, clutter, ugliness and inequity – and had at its core commitment to a better society. This rebellion had its aesthetic counterpart: revulsion against the sheer ugliness of machine goods made at high speed in appalling conditions by uneducated manufacturers led to the creation of new visual symbols, shapes and images. At the same time it was the new technologies of the Industrial Revolution that enabled the pioneers of modernism to realise their vision of lightness and space in practical terms – to alternate solids with space more flexibly and with greater transparency, to create horizontal bands of windows or large areas of undivided glass.

To this extent, the style was an outgrowth of nineteenth-century history, but in some less mechanistic, more metaphysical ways it was also an expression of the spirit of the twentieth century. 'Architecture,' Mies van der Rohe had written in 1923, 'is the will of an epoch translated into space: living, changing, new. Not yesterday, not tomorrow, only today can be given form.'[5] In giving form to today, Pevsner believed, modern architects and designers would have to operate within the particular range of qualities that characterised the modern age; their work, like the times, would have to be hard, direct, efficient, taut, rational, economical and, to some degree, icy.

The English architect Maxwell Fry once remarked, 'Modern architecture is an attitude to life as much as to materials,' and without doubt the attitude of the Modern Movement was a moralistic one.[6] Every made object – cup, car, kitchen, factory, housing estate – had a job to do in its social context, and the duty of the maker was to ensure that it did this job as well as possible, to improve the material and spiritual quality of life. 'I don't regard it as especially Protestant or especially Puritan to believe that the architect has a responsibility to his fellow beings,' Pevsner would write much later. 'Once this is agreed, the result is that functionalism is not one of a variety of attitudes, but the only wholly acceptable one.'[7] This moral imperative, he felt, was especially clear in the world of the 1930s. 'In today's circumstances,' he had written in 1931, 'for all European countries after the world war, social questions have become burning issues that the builder must face. Practical problems are more important in this situation than artistic questions.'[8]

'In today's circumstances' – Pevsner would be stubbornly attached to the doctrines of the Modern Movement all his life. This was not simply a cerebral attachment. He was attracted to them in the first place for reasons that were more emotional and personal than intellectual or political. There may have been in his passion for rationality,

space and light a straightforward reaction against all that had made his childhood uncomfortable: his mother's unreason, the crowded luxury of the flat in Schwägrichenstrasse, the grim greyness of school. As a student, he had been drawn to art theory at least in part by the hope of finding stability in universal principles and solutions, being without a settled religious faith and having found ethics and politics wanting. Then, as an insecure young man, in the shifting, uneasy world of the 1920s, he had used work as a refuge from the pressures of life with his family and the emotional turmoil of his love for Lola.

Surrounded by a different kind of uncertainty and discomfort in England, he clung to the doctrines of the Modern Movement with even more ardour and some homesickness. These were the discussions of his student days. This generation of thinkers was his generation; the Modern Movement was somewhere he felt at home. Tracking paths, establishing patterns of influence and intellectual interchange, especially between his native habitat and his present setting, must have given him some sense of order, perhaps even a vicarious sensation of belonging. In attempting to characterise the age of which the Modern Movement style was an expression, he was trying to define a context and locate himself within it.

It was, he wrote, 'a world of . . . speed and danger, of hard struggles and no personal security', 'hard and ruthless . . . adventurous and unsafe' – and it is impossible not to see in these descriptions a reflection of his own immediate situation.[9] This was not necessarily how he wanted the world to be – he felt the twentieth century to be in many ways 'less humane and less joyful' than, say, the eighteenth – but this was how it was, and one must accept it in order to make the most out of it. *Pioneers* might be seen as an attempt by Pevsner to develop *amor fati* – rationalising his feelings of alienation, and giving some kind of point to his present experiences. To be himself, and feel rooted again, were things he desperately craved as he researched and wrote *Pioneers*.

One of the more endearing qualities of *Pioneers* is its conversational, almost familiar tone, perfectly suited to what is a gallery of people rather than a catalogue of ideas. Pevsner was not in the least objective in his reactions to personalities and sometimes seems to have been drawn into writing *Pioneers* largely by his personal attraction to the two powerful individuals of his subtitle, Walter Gropius and William Morris.

'I know I am a square man who likes things square,' Pevsner would write in his sixties.[10] In Gropius he had found all the qualities of balance, measure and rectitude that 'squareness' implies. He was much struck by Gropius's physical presence. When he met him in 1930 in Berlin, he found him formidable: 'He wore a fringe, which was slightly disconcerting.'[11] But it was the strength of character that really mesmerised Pevsner. 'Discipline and integrity – I have never in my life met these two qualities united in one man so powerfully, so intensively as they are in Walter Gropius.'[12] He was, Pevsner would eventually conclude, 'a moral force working towards aims which the century badly needed and still needs', working with a burning sense of social responsibility and yet with the prized qualities of precision and restraint.[13] Pevsner's admiration amounted almost to infatuation. In March 1935, writing to Lola as he looked forward to a dinner where he might meet Gropius again, he felt 'the excitement of someone in love, anticipating it'.

His emotions did not blind him, however, to the fact that Gropius was partially responsible for some of the dourer formulations of Modern Movement thought – the kind of tight-lipped fastidiousness that had prompted a cartoon in 1928 by the satirist Th.Th. Heine with the caption '*New Style*. In his fight against superfluous ornaments, a Dessau architect cuts off his own and his family's ears.'[14] Pevsner was well aware that there were other strands in Modern Movement philosophy, and he appreciated them. 'Romance and poetry mustn't be forgotten. Or, in the end, we'll have a mechanised and sterilised Utopia without anything imaginative, playful – in short, without anything human.'[15]

It was the human element that attracted him so powerfully to the other of his two key 'pioneers' – William Morris, whose writings he would draw on throughout his life, using them 'like a Gideon Bible'. 'Not the greatest artist of the 19th century,' Pevsner concluded, 'but the greatest man.' He sympathised deeply with the stress Morris placed on 'the responsibility of man towards man', his passionate concern for the happiness of the greatest number, and his vision of architecture as 'moulding and altering to human needs the face of the earth'. Nevertheless, for all these elevated ideals, Morris the man was very much of this world, and highly complex. 'I don't want to be an accomplice in establishing Morris as a nothing-but-pioneer,' Pevsner wrote. He was interested in him in the round, and the portrait he drew of him – boisterous, grubby, emotional, contrary – is affectionate and revealing. 'Morris was much too lively a character to be consistent. His writing and his life are full of contradictions and one can only get a full understanding if one looks at him that way.'[16] Pevsner loved Morris's childish gusto in pleasures, his practical jokes and fondness for the funny passages in Dickens. He forgave the fact that Morris was fidgety and hot-tempered, and was fascinated by the idea that he once bit the rim of a table during an argument. (It was hardly how Pevsner would have behaved himself, but how one imagines he often felt, especially during his Birmingham days.)

There were other affinities: a middle-class background; an early yearning to be an artistic creator oneself, rather than a commentator or designer for other people; energy and industry. 'Love isn't enough in itself; love and work, yes!' Morris proclaimed. 'Work and love, that's the life of a man' – a sentiment that Pevsner echoed. 'Work filled him out,' he wrote in a lecture on Morris, quoting the words of Wilfrid Blunt. '[Work] gave him self-confidence and conveyed that self-confidence to others.' He could have been describing his own slow progress towards self-possession in the 1930s.

Pevsner was not blind to Morris's failings and, as with a real Gideon Bible, left many sections of the Collected Works untouched. He was not interested, for example, in Morris's socialist politics, considering them at best unconvincing, at worst unbecoming in one who was living off the profits of his father's mines, and who ultimately found his customers not among the workers, but, in Morris's own words, 'serving the swinish luxury of the rich'. Morris was, Pevsner felt, an artist-designer first and a political thinker last – one who had, after all, confessed, 'I have tried to understand Marx's theory but political economy is not my line and much of it appears to me dreary rubbish.' Even in art, Morris was not a revolutionary, favouring Gothic forms in architecture and medievalism in his literary romances. It was as a social reformer that, like Gropius, he reached into the future.

Inspired by these two dynamic personalities, who in some ways were better company than the flesh-and-blood figures who surrounded him in England, Pevsner determined to alert the British public to the importance of their ideas and the chain of connections and influences that stretched between them. It was, he realised, an uphill task.

He had recently been exposed to the worst in British design, and he had been conscious since his first visit to England five years ago of the backwardness of British architecture. Buildings were, of course, being put up all over Britain in an extremely wide range of styles in the early 1930s, all of them 'modern' in the sense of 'new' – neoclassical, neo-Gothic, neo-Swedish or neo-Dutch, pseudo-Tudor, Moderne – but there were, it was true, very few buildings executed wholeheartedly in the Modern Movement style.[17] One could point (and Pevsner himself would later do so) to buildings by English architects which displayed some of the features that he had identified as being 'modern': the Crawford Building in Holborn (1929), for example, by Frederick Etchells, or Joseph Emberton's Royal Corinthian Yacht Club in Burnham-on-Crouch (1930). But where one did find truly 'contemporary' work, it had largely been created by foreign architects.* Wells Coates, for example, born in Japan of Canadian parents, was responsible for the 'Isokon' (Isometric Unit Construction) flats in Lawn Road, Hampstead (1933–4). Modular units were laid out along cantilevered approach galleries connected at one end by zigzag stairs. They contained all the aids to modern living that 'people of moderate means' (in this context, Hampstead intellectuals) could possibly need. Jack Pritchard, by whom the block had been commissioned, saw it as 'an aesthetically satisfying machine to live in', using Le Corbusier's famous but unhelpful description of the house as a *machine à habiter*.

However modest Britain's efforts at contemporary building might have been, they provoked much suspicion. Sir Robert Tasker, DL, JP, MP, called 66 Frognal (by New Zealanders Amyas Connell and Basil Ward) 'one of the greatest pieces of vandalism ever perpetrated in London'. A London vicar was reported as claiming that 'flat roofs and terraces stood for nudity', while Gilbert Jenkins, Principal of the Architectural Association, maintained that no one but a 'vegetarian bacteriologist' would choose to live in houses of the Le Corbusier style. *Country Life*, going further, remarked in August 1934, 'There is something to be said for Herr Hitler's objection to the "international" style.'[18]

Nevertheless, the foundations for future Modern Movement buildings had to some extent been laid on paper. Frederick Etchells had translated Le Corbusier's hugely influential tract *Vers une architecture* in 1927, and architectural journalists were travelling to examine new buildings in Europe and reporting on the innovations they had seen, prompting English architects to go and look for themselves. 'By 1930 the traffic in architects to Sweden was only rivalled by the traffic in old horses to Antwerp,' remarked the architectural historian John Summerson drily. In 1933 came the formation of the MARS (Modern Architectural ReSearch) Group to promote in Britain the ideas of the

---

* For example, 'New Ways' in Northamptonshire (1926) by the German Peter Behrens; the De la Warr Pavilion in Bexhill-on-Sea (1933–5) by Erich Mendelsohn from Prussia and Serge Chermayeff, an old Harrovian, but born in Grozny; the Penguin Pool at London Zoo (1934) and the Highpoint 1 flats in Highgate (1936), both by the firm of Tecton, dominated in its early years by Berthold Lubetkin, also from Russia.

Swiss propagandist study group Congrès Internationaux d'Architecture Moderne (CIAM). The members of the MARS Group were mostly young architects or critics, undeniably middle-class with leftish social ideals, some home-grown (Summerson, Maxwell Fry and, curiously, John Betjeman), others more or less recent arrivals from abroad, such as Chermayeff, Lubetkin, Mendelsohn and Marcel Breuer.[19] The group's objective was to link architecture with social and technological considerations. MARS members, Summerson declared, wanted 'programmes aimed at some reasonable standard of life, education and work which could be seen as setting a standard in a socialist future'.[20] Without directly producing many actual buildings, the MARS Group provided a badly needed focus for the exchange of ideas.

One of the most significant contributions to this debate came from Philip Morton Shand. Shand (always 'P. Morton', not Philip) was, in Maxwell Fry's words, 'an enthusiast heavily disguised as a diplomat, trilingual and exceedingly cultivated'. The son of a sociologist and a psychiatrist, an Etonian graduate of both King's, Cambridge and the Sorbonne, he had lived for some time in France. Back in England, he bred and grew rare species of apples, and during the 1920s wrote several books on wine and food. 'He led the way,' John Betjeman remembered, 'to my own generation in the appreciation of good wine, food and architecture', and contributed an article to the *Architects' Journal* entitled 'Wine-cellar design in the Private House'. He was also one of the most passionate propagandists for the Modern Movement in Britain.

Shand, like Pevsner, was interested in establishing a British genealogy for international ideas. In 1934 he had written for the *Architectural Review* a series of six articles entitled 'Scenario for a Human Drama' in which he set out to trace the British antecedents of Modern Movement theories of house-building. His plan, stated in the first article, was to work backwards from modern functionalism to what he considered to be its origins in Georgian architecture. In the event, he ran out of time and space before he was even halfway back to Sir John Soane.

Nevertheless, the idea of British roots for international modernism, albeit Georgian rather than Victorian, had quite recently been mooted in England. What Pevsner was doing in *Pioneers* was reiterating, elucidating, illustrating and extending already-established ideas – his own, and those of other people – on how modern art, design and architecture had evolved. The thesis of the book was simple: 'The phase between Morris and Gropius is an historical unit. Morris laid the foundation of the modern style; with Gropius its character was ultimately determined.'

Pevsner was offering one path through the thicket of developments in art and architecture, one line of evolution, one canon of key names acting as handholds to help the student of art history swing through the jungle of ideas and images. Notwithstanding all his previous attacks on the cult of individualism, he couched *Pioneers* essentially in terms of individual artists.* It achieves much of its immediacy and intelligibility through its constant use of concrete examples. It creates a web of significant ideas, but anchors these ideas by reference to specific people.

Pevsner was perfectly aware that there were other threads of nineteenth-century art history that he could have picked up instead. He had already suggested, in fact, in *Social Ideals amongst Creative Artists* in 1931, that he had selected his particular route largely in reaction to critical genealogies that were designed to culminate not in the Modern Movement but in Impressionism. 'The history of the 19th-century art that is relevant to our time has not yet been written,' he had declared then. In *Pioneers* he sought to remedy that lack.

He had, of course, been collecting materials relating to his 'hobby' for several years. He now supplemented his researches with direct contacts with his 'pioneers'. He met C.R. Ashbee, then in his seventies, 'for a chat' in the London Library in St James's Square during the summer of 1934, and they later corresponded in some detail over an article that Pevsner had written for a German journal, entitled 'William Morris, C.R. Ashbee and the Twentieth Century'.[21] (Ashbee was pleased with the piece – he wrote to his wife, taking pleasure in 'that most interesting essay of the learned German telling me how famous I appear to be!' – and he offered to introduce Pevsner to surviving members of his Guild and School of Handicraft.)

The venue for the meetings with C.F.A. Voysey was the Arts Club in Dover Street, where Voysey impressed Pevsner as a 'dear old gentleman with [a] shrewd and kindly face . . . a little figure, somewhat lonely and somewhat pathetic . . . in his large armchair', with 'a gentle voice, growing irritable only when talked to admiringly about his work'. Voysey, however, was not at all fragile in his pursuit of some photographs that he had lent Pevsner. In a series of increasingly stern

---

*He always acknowledged the need to reconcile the claims of individual genius with those of the character of a nation or spirit of an age as an explanation of a work of art. In the foreword to his Reith Lectures on 'The Englishness of English Art' (printed in the *Radio Times* on 14/10/55) he wrote, 'Ultimately it is of course personal genius that creates worthwhile art or architecture and neither the abstraction of an age nor the abstraction of a period'; but he added that harmony with the spirit of the age was often key to an artist's greatness.

postcards (which would amuse Pevsner's own students, pursued later with similar enquiries by NP himself), Voysey demanded their return. (His anxieties were not unfounded; to Pevsner's mortification, one of the photographs was badly damaged while in the publisher's keeping.)*

Voysey did, however, put him in touch with Arthur Heygate Mackmurdo, a sweet-natured man of extraordinarily diverse interests whom Pevsner would always regard as an inspiration. 'I tracked Mackmurdo down to a cottage in Essex,' he told the *Architects' Journal,* and found 'a man of 81 with long white hair and glittering light blue eyes wearing a blouse of butcher blue – the kind of blue blouse which William Morris wore. He no longer practised architecture, but was passionately engaged on social and economic research which led him to advocate a system of State socialism with wages and pensions fixed by the State and a monetary system founded on food values.' On his retirement from architecture in 1904, Mackmurdo had built himself a large house in the village of Wickham Bishops, near Colchester, which he had discovered 'by scientific means' to be the healthiest place in England. 'Unfortunately, shortly after his retirement he invested most of his money in a speculation to get salt from the sea – and lost it. He then had to move to a tiny cottage . . . in which I found him, but he seemed equally happy living with his devoted wife in two tiny rooms: one a bedroom where he used to rest in a scarlet dressing gown (scarlet was good for the health), and one living room, enriched by an original Alfred Stevens mantelpiece and pictures by Brangwyn.'[22] Mackmurdo was delighted by what Pevsner wrote about him, in *Pioneers* and a later article in 1937, and wrote to him in characteristic fashion: 'I do congratulate you upon your literary style and your good English . . . But you have seen me through rose-coloured spectacles. My friends are very pleased with you . . . I hope one day to hear that your labours are rewarded by a position upon the staff of the Courtauld Institute.'[23]

Research on Charles Rennie Mackintosh took Pevsner to Glasgow in 1935, and he met the Belgian architect Henry van de Velde the

---

*Voysey, then nearly eighty, could be crusty. Pevsner kept a letter of October 1941 from the actor Robert Donat (married to Voysey's niece) about his abortive plans to commission a building. 'Alas, the Voysey house did not materialise . . . Actually the old gentleman was not very happy about the design, because I had very modern ideas about a play room running the length and breadth of the house in the roof, and he did not approve of it at all! The result was not a very happy compromise.' GP Series II, Box 16.

same year during a summer holiday in Germany.* He also arranged an interview with Gropius, seeking confirmation of *Pioneers'* main thesis. 'I showed him a photograph [of William Morris] – that splendid photograph with the high, broad forehead and the flowing hair and beard which Emery Walker took – every inch a Viking. "So that is Morris," said Gropius, "I have never seen a picture of him. And yet I owe him so very much."'[24]

In *Pioneers of the Modern Movement* Pevsner presented his argument in two strands, tracing the evolution of modern design as a background to the evolution of modern architecture. In dealing with design, he was effectively filling in the historical context for *An Enquiry into Industrial Art in England*, describing the reaction against what he called 'historicism'– the revival of elements of styles from the past – and outlining the various steps in the reuniting of industry and art.[†] 'It is essential,' he argued, 'ultimately to understand the style of the 20th century as a synthesis of the Morris Movement, the development of steel building, and Art Nouveau.'[25] In other words, the changes that created modern design were rooted in a new philosophy, new materials and new visual forms.

In expounding the new philosophy, Pevsner actually went back beyond the first 'pioneer' of his subtitle to trace the influence on Morris of John Ruskin. Art, Ruskin had declared, was not set apart in an aesthetic vacuum, but intimately related to morality, politics and the workings of daily life. Morris echoed his alarm at the erosion of the social foundations of art. Art, he wrote, must be 'by the people for the people, a joy to the maker and the user . . . What business have we with art at all unless all can share it?' To be available to all, and an integral and useful part of life, art must be allied with craft; artists must be craftsmen, and craftsmen artists. The Arts and Crafts movement that developed round this notion was influential less in its artistic ideas, which relied heavily on the revival of earlier traditions of simplicity and honesty in design, than in its social idealism.

'The Arts and Crafts,' Pevsner would declare later, 'are a moral matter; Art Nouveau is an aesthetic matter' – and it was from Art

---

*Alan Crawford points out that, though Pevsner made the trip to Glasgow, he appears to have overlooked a good deal of the material that had become available since Mackintosh's death seven years before.

†Pevsner's use of the term 'historicism' was idiosyncratic, differing sharply from the definition being evolved at roughly the same time by Karl Popper. See Chapter 36.

Nouveau that new visual forms would emerge for a new century. This short-lived style, flourishing from around 1895 to around 1910, had a curious fascination for Pevsner, possibly due to the influence of his Leipzig fellow-student Ernst Michalski. Pevsner was intrigued by the strange mixture of abstract and natural forms in the book illustrations of Aubrey Beardsley, the ironwork of Victor Horta and Hector Guimard, the glass of Louis Comfort Tiffany, and the architecture – 'amazing, fascinating, horrible and inimitable' – of Antoni Gaudí. He wrote almost lyrically of the leitmotif of Art Nouveau: 'the long sensitive curve, reminiscent of the lily's stem, an insect's feeler, the filament of a blossom, or occasionally a slender flame, the curve undulating, flowing and interplaying with others, sprouting from corners and covering asymmetrically all available surfaces'. His description of Edvard Munch's lithograph *Madonna* (1895) neatly encapsulated his attitude to the whole movement: 'original and striking in appearance, independent of tradition, but questionable as to its sanity and vital value'. The middle term here – independent – is the important one. Art Nouveau had no social conscience at all; it was frequently decadent and seemingly anti-rational – and yet it was crucially important in introducing new forms to the history of art. This was, declared Pevsner, the first set of forms since the Rococo period to be independent of classical tradition. In itself, it led nowhere (especially not, as some critics pointed out, to the Modern Movement); but in breaking through the boundaries of past styles, it left room for other path-finders to advance.

The designers of Art Nouveau were also receptive to the third of Pevsner's catalysts of change – the new materials produced by the engineers of the nineteenth century, which made it possible to translate modern design ideas into reality. Pevsner would always be excited by both the look and the power of iron – as in the Clifton Suspension Bridge: 'an architecture without weight, the age-old contrast of passive resistance and active will neutralised, pure functional energy swinging out in a glorious curve to conquer the 700 feet between the two banks of the deep valley'. When iron became steel, and the steel skeleton replaced the load-bearing wall as the primary structural component of large buildings, and reinforced glass and Portland cement were developed to clothe the skeleton, the main building blocks of the Modern Movement style were in place.

One of the trickiest leaps Pevsner had to make was that from art as handcraft to the art of industrial design – from the 'intellectual Ludditism' of Morris, who expressed a powerful distaste for the machine, to Gropius's 'new unity' of 'Art and Technics'. In his search for stepping stones, Pevsner lit on C.R. Ashbee, taking his modest acknowledgement that 'Modern civilisation rests on machinery' to imply that machine production was not antipathetic to art, but could indeed serve it. To find a genuinely wholehearted celebration of machine art at the appropriate time, however, he had to look over to the continent and the United States, to the Austrian Otto Wagner, the Belgian Henry van de Velde and, most vociferous of all, the American Frank Lloyd Wright.

Once it had been accepted that the craftsman could and should design for machine production, one consequence, Pevsner felt, was inevitable: 'the theory of designing for the machine . . . was bound to lead to the condemnation of unnecessary ornament'. This condemnation was expressed most vehemently by Adolf Loos in an article to which he gave the title 'Ornament and Crime'.[26] 'To find beauty in form,' Loos argued, 'instead of making it depend on ornament is the goal towards which humanity is aspiring.'[27] This notion of 'form' was not confined to 'shape': it also incorporated 'the degree to which [the work] attains utility' – in other words, the degree to which it fulfilled its function.[28]

Pevsner then pointed to the way in which these two features of modernity – lack of ornament and respect for function – were neatly and explicitly linked in the concept of *Sachlichkeit* [literally, 'thing-ish-ness'] as articulated by Hermann Muthesius, the man who in Pevsner's view acted most clearly as 'a connecting link between the English style of the nineties and Germany'. The word *Sachlich*, Pevsner acknowledged, though it became a catchword of the Modern Movement, was virtually untranslatable, 'meaning at the same time pertinent, matter-of-fact, and objective'. In terms of buildings or objects, the best examples were to be found in railway stations, exhibition halls, bridges, steamships and other products of the Machine Age. 'Here,' Muthesius argued, 'we are faced with a severe and almost scientific *Sachlichkeit*, with abstinence from all outward decoration, and with shapes completely dictated by the purposes which they are meant to serve.'[29]

Muthesius was primarily a civil servant, critic and theorist. What was also needed was a practical demonstration of what *Sachlichkeit* might produce when applied to design. The architect Peter Behrens had the perfect opportunity, around 1907–11, as 'visual dictator' of the electrical engineering giant AEG. Besides building two of its factories, he addressed the appearance of every aspect of the organisation – from the lamps, kettles and telephones that it manufactured for sale to its publicity materials and the furnishings of its workers' quarters. By seeking to develop an aesthetic for machine production, Behrens did much to define and validate the role of the designer in industry, as well as establishing the notion of the architect as universal designer.

The style of the Modern Movement was formed in embryo, but it required incubation, which began rapidly to take place in art schools throughout Germany as its advocates were installed as principals and teachers. Muthesius, as Superintendent of the Prussian Board of Trade for Schools of Arts and Crafts, contrived the appointment of Behrens to the Düsseldorf Academy, for instance, and van de Velde became head of the Weimar Kunstgewerbeschule. But it was when the Kunstgewerbeschule was amalgamated with the Weimar School of Fine Art to create the Bauhaus, under Walter Gropius, that the new ideas were promoted most convincingly, albeit in very different ways over the years of its brief existence.

There were two distinct stages, Pevsner would come to believe, in the life of the Bauhaus. Gropius was in his early years a thinker, architect and designer of the utmost clarity and rationality, as could be seen in the Fagus factory of 1911. But by 1919 he was as susceptible as anyone else to the unsettling turmoil of the post-war years – what Pevsner described as 'that gruesome and madly stimulating atmosphere mixed of inflation and utopia'.[30] There was, unkind observers claimed, a pronounced aura of mysticism and garlic around the Weimar Bauhaus, where the ethos was that of a medieval guild and the teachers were addressed as 'Master'. Wassily Kandinsky, whose intellectual springboard was Theosophy, believed in the imminent dawn of a new epoch in which the artist's role would be to release the spiritual content of physical reality. Johannes Itten was responsible for setting up the Basic Course; head shaved and body swathed either in medieval robes or a striking purple suit, he promoted the cult of Mazdaznan, which preached spontaneity, self-fulfilment and individual expression. Gropius himself was carried away by the prevailing mood to speak in exalted terms of architecture as 'the crystallised expression of man's noblest thoughts, his human nature, his faith, his religion'. 'Let us together desire, conceive and create the new building of the future,' he wrote, 'which will combine everything – architecture, and sculpture and painting – in a *single form* which will one day rise towards the heavens from the hands of a million workers as the crystalline symbol of a new and coming faith' – a kind of 'cathedral of socialism'.[31]

However, with the move to Dessau in 1925, the school's focus appeared to shift and tighten. Now the Bauhaus began to concentrate once more on the demands of mass consumption and, more specifically, on the requirements of local manufacturers. Under the influence of

Hannes Meyer, it became more like a trade school. 'It had a different soul,' Pevsner would comment later.[32] 'In came a severer geometry.'

The Bauhaus, wrote Pevsner, was 'for more than a decade, a paramount centre of creative energy in Europe'.[33] It contained conflicts, both of personality and of ideology; it was a welding together of different theories, not a seamless homogeneous programme. The main point of its teachings, however, was oneness – the oneness of individual with society, of arts with crafts, of both of these with industry, of all arts within architecture, of all art under the rule of universal laws of form. All pupils of the Bauhaus – painters, sculptors, metalworkers, architects, cabinet-makers, industrial designers – trained together at the outset, receiving the same instruction in form, colour and the properties of materials. They would then move on to work together, ultimately looking to collaborate in '*Bau*' or 'building', in the activity that Gropius saw as the apex of all art.

Pevsner then moved to plot the course of modern architecture. He set his drama in four locations – in turn-of-the-century England, where one particular group of architects evolved a philosophy of reasonableness and clarity, which broke sharply with the historicist past; in America and France, where the technical requirements of huge office buildings and breakthroughs in engineering between them resulted in the evolution of new materials and construction processes; and in Germany, where these materials and processes were most brilliantly and consistently applied.

Undeniably, Pevsner left gaps. To be in *Pioneers*, architects had to be truly modern in spirit and intention, as well as in technical tricks – and the true spirit of the modern age included practicality and social responsibility. This, in Pevsner's view, ruled out Le Corbusier. In other writings, Pevsner acknowledged Le Corbusier's gifts – his 'creative intoxication and romanticism', which 'tell us what our age is capable of in the way of structure and of visual poetry, and what a thrilling, bracing architecture we can have if we want to'; his temperament, 'sharp as a razor blade, with a mind flashing and glittering like polished steel'; his willingness to experiment; his artistry in spatial imagination.[34] But always praise of the art was offset by reservations about the artist; 'a greater architectural creator than Gropius', Pevsner would conclude, 'but a lesser man': a chronic individualist, and, as such, outside the scope of his enquiry.*

---

*Pevsner's intellectual disapproval may have been heightened by personal dislike. Friend and pupil Ian Sutton remembered him saying, 'I met Le Corbusier once and he was very rude, as I knew he would be. I asked whether he could speak in French and I in English, because I can understand French but not speak it well. But he wouldn't. I had to ask all my questions in schoolboy French.'

In contrast, the first group of authentic 'pioneers' was characterised by simplicity, humility and integrity. In the England of 1890–1914, a Domestic Revival was under way – a reworking of native traditions that was still borrowing from the past, but borrowing with a sense of fitness and a vision of the future rather than with nostalgia. Pevsner praised figures such as Philip Webb, Norman Shaw, Voysey and Mackmurdo for 'the gradual and gentle simplification of suitable forms of the past until almost unnoticeably, fundamentals of shape and decoration were recovered'. In creating houses whose outer appearance expressed their inner requirements, Webb and Shaw used a variety of styles to match these requirements most closely, but chose those period forms that suited the twentieth century. Mackmurdo, whose social commitment was hardly in doubt, was also a creator of great originality, incorporating in his earliest houses some remarkably modern flat roofs and rows of horizontal windows. Voysey, 'as tough as a militant puritan and as gentle as a nursing sister', was a craftsman of great honesty.[35] 'Here . . . was a mind equally averse to the picturesque tricks of the Shaw school and the preciousness of Art Nouveau. From this centre bay [at Broadleys, on Lake Windermere] with its completely unmoulded mullions and transoms, from these windows cut clean and sheer into the wall, access to the architectural style of today could have been direct.'[36]

As it turned out, there was one further crucial link in the chain. Pevsner was neither the first nor the last to identify Charles Rennie Mackintosh as one of the most interesting forerunners of the Modern Movement. However, the claim was controversial even at the time, and has been contested ever since.[37] Arguably, Mackintosh was simply an original. Pevsner was, though, 'an inveterate Mackintosh worshipper', and could not resist the temptation to add his hero to the *Pioneers* canon.* His admiration was not necessarily logical, but in part at least an unreasoned aesthetic pleasure; he took from Mackintosh's work what he needed for his purposes, and either failed to recognise or chose to ignore the rest. Largely unmoved by the decorative fantasy, he preferred to focus on the juggling with space, the 'overwhelmingly full polyphony of abstract form' in buildings like the Glasgow School of Art, which in his view led naturally to elements in the work of Le Corbusier.

---

*His admiration may have derived from his close reading as a student of German art magazines of the 1920s in which Mackintosh was an extremely fashionable figure. Pevsner would write a long article on him in 1939 and a short book in 1949, and even proposed a collaboration on a longer work with Mackintosh's eventual biographer, Thomas Howarth.

After Mackintosh, however, Britain (in Pevsner's view) lost the plot of the Modern Movement:

> just about 1900. That is, at the very moment when the work of all the pioneers began to converge into one universal movement . . . The levelling tendency of the coming mass movement . . . was too much against the grain of the English character. A similar antipathy prevented the ruthless scrapping of traditions which was essential to the achievement of a style fitting our century. So at the very moment when Continental architects discovered the elements of a genuine style for the future in English building and English crafts, England herself receded into an eclectic Neo-Classicism, with hardly any bearing on present-day problems and needs.

In terms of translating modern ideas into real buildings, Pevsner had to look elsewhere. One of the most genuine pioneers was a man whom, on personal grounds, he might have preferred to leave out. Frank Lloyd Wright was an egotist of the type that he found most antipathetic. Pevsner complained of 'Mr Wright's overflowing conviction that Mr Wright is the best architect in the world'. His character was contradictory, at once tyrannical and fuzzy.[38] 'One visualises Gropius in an immaculate white laboratory overall – to Mr Wright life is all tweeds.'* But even Pevsner had to acknowledge Wright's individual genius and his undoubted influence, both structural and aesthetic, on others in the canon, including Gropius in his early years. Of the W.R. Heath House at Buffalo he wrote admiringly, 'The low spacious interiors have something irresistibly inviting'; and of the Larkin Building in the same city, 'With its sheer walls of flat bricks unrelieved by windows or niches or mouldings . . . [it] is overwhelmingly impressive, in the hard way of today.'

But these were isolated and highly idiosyncratic examples of modern building. Only Germany and the Central European countries 'responded so appreciatively to the adventurous achievements of the first pioneers that the recognised accepted style of our age could emerge from their individual experiments'. With the turbine factory that Peter Behrens built for AEG in Berlin, Germany had achieved, in Pevsner's view, 'perhaps the most beautiful industrial building ever erected up to that time', with its steel frame clearly exhibited, its side walls made of wide, perfectly spaced glass panes, its simple geometrical forms and beauty

---

*NP, 'Frank Lloyd Wright's Peaceful Penetration of Europe', *Architects' Journal*, 4/5/39.

of proportion. 'Here for the first time the imaginative possibilities of industrial architecture were visualised.'

For Pevsner it was entirely fitting that the man to extend these possibilities should have been Behrens's greatest pupil, Walter Gropius. He revelled in the 'etherealisation' of architecture that Gropius had achieved in his Fagus factory. 'For the first time a complete façade is conceived in glass . . . The usual hard separation of exterior and interior is annihilated. Light and air can pass freely through the walls so that the closed-in space is no longer different in essence from the great universe of space outside.' To an even greater extent, Gropius's 1926 building for the Dessau Bauhaus was itself a manifesto for modern principles – a pioneer work of functionalism and rationalism, 'logically transparent and virginal of lies or trivialities', in Gropius's own words, and a model of design for purpose. Here for the first time Pevsner would find the Modern Movement style incarnate.

Pioneers of the Modern Movement would ultimately become Pevsner's most contentious work, not so much because the views expressed in it were extreme, but because he offered a framework, building materials and encouragement to others who were more extreme and more narrowly ideological in their championing of modernism. He cannot entirely be blamed for the way in which his modest 'introduction' to the Modern Movement would later be turned by others into a template for modernist theory. But *Pioneers* can hardly be called dispassionate. He would later write in a review of Sigfried Giedion's *Space, Time and Architecture*, 'This changeover from telling historical truth – the whole truth – to blasting a trumpet . . . is a sin in a historian.'[39] Was he himself 'blasting a trumpet' for the Modern Movement?

The Giedion review contains another intriguing and suggestive passage:

Books in which historical and topical problems are linked up . . . are the most necessary contribution the historian can make to-day. To find in such books an exact balance of past and present is still rarer. As a rule one of the two approaches dominates, according to whether the author is primarily moved by history or by politics (in the widest sense of the word). If he is a historian first and foremost, his treatment will be to show how past ages have found their own solutions to their own problems and how consequently our age must do likewise. If on the other hand the author is above all interested in the needs of the day, he will single out those tendencies in the past which can be connected with, and preferably proved to be leading up to, the problems of the 20th century.[*]

Pevsner did think of himself as a historian and would certainly not have considered himself to be moved primarily by politics – and yet to some extent his method in *Pioneers* fitted the second description as closely as the first.

Like the *Enquiry*, *Pioneers* is essentially a descriptive framework with a good deal of doctrine embedded in it. Nevertheless, blasting a trumpet was not Pevsner's style, and *Pioneers* was not the polemic it has sometimes been made out to be. Compared with the Modern Movement's central propagandists – Gropius, Le Corbusier, Giedion, Bruno Taut – his voice was muted and his ambitions modest. The caricature, offered by critics later in his life, of a narrow doctrinaire is virtually unrecognisable. But in 1936 this did not prevent *Pioneers* being received with some mistrust, and with criticisms that would be repeated at regular intervals for the rest of Pevsner's life.

'The German people,' architect and town planner Raymond Unwin had remarked, opening the Gropius exhibition at the RIBA in 1934, 'loved working under a theory: Englishmen were not easily persuaded to a theory, were naturally suspicious of it, and afraid of ridicule should they show any great devotion to any particular theory.'[40] Pevsner, it would be implied, was somewhat mechanically wedded to 'grand theories' – functionalism, the moral responsibility of the artist, the spirit of the age – which blinkered his vision and limited his insights.

The Modern Movement in the 1930s, suggested Reyner Banham, had developed a 'Stephen Dedalus thirst for respectable father-figures'.[†] This led its advocates into focusing too closely on individuals, at the risk of producing what Geoffrey Price-Jones briskly dismissed as 'sentimental psycho-biographies'. However, in *Pioneers* these individuals were not even treated as creators in their own right, but as links in a chain – marshalled into a sequence and given scripts in which they

---

[*]In 'Judges VI, 34' in *AR*, August 1949, a review of Giedion's next work, *Mechanisation Takes Command*, Pevsner repeated the complaint: 'Dr Giedion enthrones one set of values – and very important values they are – at the expense of all other values, because they happen to be of the greatest interest to the present and future of architecture'. (Judges VI, 34 reads: 'But the spirit of the Lord came upon Gideon and he blew a trumpet.')

[†]Peter Reyner Banham (1922–88), architectural historian and commentator, a pupil, friend and admirer of Pevsner, and also one of his most cogent critics. He would become a key figure in the history of design by challenging the modernist orthodoxy to embrace technology and popular culture. See Chapters 30 and 36, and also Chapters 37, 42 and 49.

voiced neatly linked ideas or espoused the opposing sides of interesting arguments. In an argument that ran vertically rather than horizontally through a time period, they were not seen in the context even of their contemporaries, let alone set in the precise social, economic, political and technological climate in which each was working.

Even if the principle of the canon had been valid, this particular genealogy, it was objected, was hardly original. Shand had identified several of the same individuals in his 'Scenario for a Human Drama', as indeed had John Betjeman in a 1933 article on 'British Industrial Art', not to mention other commentators such as Herbert Read and Charles Marriott.[41] Pevsner, however, was looking further back and to the continent – to Gropius's own account of the origins of the Bauhaus and beyond, to the writings of Hermann Muthesius, who was really the one to have established the conventional historiography in its essentials.[42] Pevsner had already tried out his canon in embryo in his 1931 article 'Social Ideals amongst Creative Artists', and he made no claims for its originality.

However, even if he had been the first to put forward this partic-ular family tree, his critics would not have found it any more convincing. 'If you promise to throw this letter away when you have read it,' wrote Philip Johnson before the appearance of the US edition of *Pioneers*, 'I can tell you that I believe that Mr Gropius has never designed any building, whether it has appeared over his name alone or not. In other words, to say From Morris to Gropius is too much of a compliment to our estimable and excellent pedagogue, Walter Gropius.'[43] Johnson's views were shared by several disinterested witnesses.* Alfred Kurlbaum also felt that Pevsner had dedicated too much space to an over-idealised vision of Gropius – who in actuality, he argued, had given less attention to 'art for all' than the Nazis had done. Even Gropius himself would eventually object that Pevsner had perhaps over-schematised the evolution of the Bauhaus. 'They . . . believe that we always knew exactly what we were doing, and that the straight discernible line of development was always clearly visible to us, while actually so very much was done by hunch or instinct and shows only now in retrospect to have pointed steadily in the same direction.'[44]

Pevsner's portrait of C.R. Ashbee has been called 'inaccurate, unbalanced and unsympathetic', an attempt to pressgang as a 'pioneer' of the Modern Movement a man who was in fact 'no less than a

---

*It was known that Hannes Meyer had contributed much of the design of the Bauhaus buildings, which were published as 'Gropius and Meyer'.

full-blown, drastic, Romantic anti-Modernist, shaking his cultured fist at the birth of the modern world'.[45] In the correspondence they had exchanged over Pevsner's article on Ashbee and Morris, Ashbee had had an earlier chance to remonstrate with him about being depicted as a proto-modernist, but, for whatever reason, chose not to do so. Voysey, on the other hand, complained bitterly and in person at the company into which Pevsner had thrown him, as Pevsner was the first to point out.[46] A devout Christian, Voysey distrusted William Morris for his atheism, recoiled from Art Nouveau as 'unhealthy and revolting', and told Pevsner firmly, 'This new style cannot last. Our young architects have no religion. They have nothing to aspire to.'

Pevsner was lambasted equally vigorously by the champions of figures and schools he was considered to have neglected. He later defended *Pioneers* on the grounds that he had never claimed to be telling the whole story. In a letter to Philip Johnson in 1947 he admitted that there were paths he had deliberately left untravelled – the route from Art Nouveau to Expressionism, for example, or the path to the Modern Movement that started from continental neoclassicism, or indeed, 'the much weaker English NeoGeorgian which in a similarly negative way can get just as close to the modern idiom'.[47]

He himself felt that he had not done sufficient justice to artists such as Sant'Elia, Mendelsohn and Gaudí, and much later he would follow one of these other threads and create a kind of anti-canon for the outriders of irrationalism.* Ironically, his anti-heroes provoked some of his most eloquent writing. After his first visit to Gaudí's Church of the Sagrada Familia in Barcelona, Pevsner wrote breathlessly of its four towers, 'spires of a crustaceous form, details sometimes like the jazzy light fittings of 1925, sometimes like celestial cacti, sometimes like malignant growths, sometimes like the spikes of bristly dinosaurs'. The building was crazy, he concluded, but not irreligious and not vulgar. 'It is fabulous, it is miraculous, it hits you hard, it gives you no peace, it does not let go of you, and for that very reason it is proper for the Church, rousing you to prostrate yourself and to worship.' He would never, however, back down on his decision to deny the title of 'pioneer' to a man like Gaudí. Modern genius, almost certainly; but pioneer of the Modern Movement – no.

*   *   *

*See Chapter 46.

'An artist needs to be cold in our century,' Bruno Taut had written, 'as cold as steel or glass', and Pevsner agreed. 'The architect, to represent this century of ours, must be colder, cold to keep in command of mechanised production, cold to design for the satisfaction of anonymous clients.'[48] The architect who, for him, most perfectly satisfied these requirements was Gropius: 'It is the creative energy of this world in which we live and work and which we want to master, a world of science and technology, of speed and danger, of hard struggles and no personal security that is glorified in Gropius' architecture, and as long as this is the world and these are its ambitions, the style of Gropius and the other pioneers will be valid.'[49]

Pevsner was hardly alone in characterising the modern age as one of hardness, speed, scientism and social upheaval. Three years earlier John Betjeman had written: 'This generation has realised that by now there is no escape and that we must fall in with the machine, that the England of quiet lanes and elm-surrounded villages is finished, and that instead a new international civilisation has grown up in Europe of urban peoples whose church is the office, whose fields are the cinema, whose lanes are arterial roads, and whose houses are mere dormitories in a block of flats.'[50]

Betjeman could not be suspected of expressing approval of this state of affairs, merely acceptance of fact and a gloomy resignation. Pevsner at least believed that there were things men might do to mitigate this harshness, and he looked forward to more temperate times. 'What then remains for us to do, those of us who don't want to abandon what we cherish in our civilisation?' he would write some years later.[51] 'Our civilisation cannot renew itself. Twentieth century mankind is not going to turn back. It must continue on its self-chosen course. But you and I can yet work for a healthier civilisation – the parent by passing standards of ethics and if you like, aesthetics, to the child, the teacher to the pupil, and the scholar to an unknown reader.'

The art critic Eric Newton, writing in the *Manchester Guardian*, was in sympathy with the moral imperative behind *Pioneers*. In aesthetic terms, however, the practical consequences were often dreary. '[Dr Pevsner] . . . is wise when he points out that architecture is once more honestly serving the demands of humanity. But when those demands are mainly for fresh air, sanitation and no nonsense, the art they breed will inevitably be mainly an affair of plumbing and plain surfaces.'[52] Others found the implications of Pevsner's world-view more sinister than dull. 'Genius will find its own way,' he had written in this first edition, 'even in times of overpowering collective energy, even within the medium of this new style of the 20th century which, because it is a genuine style as opposed to a passing fashion, is totalitarian.' 'Totalitarian' was an unfortunate word to have chosen in 1936 to describe the spirit of the age, and much has been made of it since.*

Pevsner was offering a personal view of twentieth-century design and architecture. It was not a view he was prepared to modify as far as his own beliefs were concerned, but neither was he hell-bent on imposing it on others. What infuriated his detractors was the eager and sometimes uncritical adoption of his canon by generation after generation of students, on a very wide scale and with great persistence, to the point where *Pioneers* could be said to have skewed the teaching of art history of that particular period. Even Reyner Banham, not so much a critic as a critical admirer, wrote with some exasperation of the reverence that had come to surround the 'apostolic succession' – what Morris said (literally or figuratively) to Webb, Webb to Lethaby, Lethaby to Muthesius, Muthesius to Gropius, Gropius to Pevsner, 'and Pevsner to the whole world via umpteen editions and translations of *Pioneers*'.[†]

This popularity was far from instant. In the first five years of its life *Pioneers* sold a total of 803 copies. Even within the narrow circle of cognoscenti, it did not at that point firmly establish Pevsner as a prophet of the Modern Movement.[‡] Its 'life after death' would not begin until 1949, when the Museum of Modern Art in New York offered a republication, and relaunched the book amidst a climate of opinion that had become far more receptive to modernism.[§]

Rooted in solidly based simplification, *Pioneers* offered a clear path through the crowded and confusing field of Victorian art and architecture on to contemporary ground. It dealt with ideas that were familiar to the initiated, plus objects and buildings that were accessible to the layman, and arranged them in an interesting pattern. It treated a historical period as a whole, and dealt with architecture as part of

---

*See Chapter 48 on 'Morality and Architecture'.

[†]R. Banham, *Age of the Masters: A personal view of modern architecture* (Architectural Press, 1975). Banham was not opposed to the existence of the canon: 'There are times and places where modern architecture cannot be defined except as "what is done by modern architects".' He simply disliked the odour of sanctity that had grown up around it.

[‡]In 1948 the *Architectural Review*, with which Pevsner's links were then very close, was still giving the credit for tracing the Modern Movement's origins and establishing a canon of pioneers not to Pevsner, but to Shand.

[§]The Pelican edition of 1960, revised and partly rewritten under the new title *Pioneers of Modern Design*, accelerated the process of popularising the text.

a complex of interrelated arts. Its argument was elegant, opinionated enough to be striking, and short. It made intelligent and quite lavish use of illustrations. Above all, its language was clear, perhaps from the necessity of thinking in translation. 'Little trace remains of that murky diction in which German *Kunsthistoriker* tramp about their heavy business,' remarked Shand approvingly.*

Pevsner could be stubborn. Ready to accept factual corrections or addenda within his overall framework, he seemed unable to contemplate the notion that the methodology by which he had constructed that framework might be invalid. For the third edition, published by Pelican in 1960, he wrote a foreword acknowledging that new research on, for example, Art Nouveau, Futurism and iron architecture had necessitated additions and alterations, adding blithely: 'None, however, I am happy to say, of such a kind as to rock the structure of my argument . . . The main theses of, and the principal accents in, this book did not call for recantation or revision, which is a happy thought for an author looking back over 25 years.'†

As time went by, this refusal to recant increasingly got Pevsner into trouble. *Pioneers* was the magnet to which any discussion of the Modern Movement was constantly drawn. Pevsner was infected with guilt by association, linked to any modernist rhetoric of a particular type, and blamed for the existence of any ugly modern building with a flat roof and strip windows. 'I fear you have taken the brunt of the attack,' wrote a sympathetic scholar of modernism in 1971, 'but that is a result of your importance in setting the framework for other historians.'[53]

---

*In 'The Pre-History of the New Architecture', his review of *Pioneers* in *AR*, November 1936. Others disagreed. Geoffrey Price-Jones wrote in the *TLS* on 5/12/36, somewhat *de haut en bas*, 'Not everyone will find the author's style easy reading; though it would be ungenerous to refrain from remarking on the creditable feat of writing a book so full of information in what to him is a foreign language.'
†It is possible that the effort of radically rethinking was simply too great. Writing to Herwin Schaefer on 2/2/71, he described Schaefer's book *The Roots of Modern Design: Functional Tradition in the Nineteenth Century* (Studio Vista, 1970) as the first work profoundly to affect his own ideas on the Modern Movement. In a second Supplementary Bibliography to the second reprint of the 1960 Pelican edition, he explained that Schaefer documented the history of a more impersonal functionalism in the eighteenth and nineteenth centuries, which should really be the start of the story, and not *Pioneers*. He added, nevertheless, 'Of course, I can't alter my thesis.'

CHAPTER 18

'95% British is as far as we can go'

As his work on *Pioneers* drew to an end, Pevsner was more or less reconciled to the idea that there would be no returning in the foreseeable future to live permanently in Germany. The boundaries of the world of culture there were contracting ominously. During 1936 the modern departments of art galleries would be closed down. By the end of the year, the Reichskulturkammer or Chamber of Culture would be pronounced 'free of Jews'.

Learning to speak English like an Englishman seemed ever more imperative. He was occasionally coached by Pallister Barkas's daughter Rosalind, who had been sent over to England to attend a Quaker school in Essex. Rosalind tested him on his vocabulary and pronunciation and, sixty years later, remembered how desperately hard he was trying. 'This learning English was a part of his very existence, absolutely essential.' He was even beginning to venture into the outskirts of the English joke. Alec Clifton-Taylor's journal for 2 August 1936 records him remarking, during an all-day walk in the Surrey hills, 'Yesterday I saw in a shop-window the notice "mackintoshes for the holidays". Could that be, I wondered, just one more example of whimsical English humour?'[1]

In October 1935 Pevsner had written to Lola, 'It's time for me to come and get you.' Now in early 1936 he was looking in earnest for a family home. He had dreams of compactness, hygiene and efficiency; at one point an architect showed him plans for a small modern house – four bedrooms, a kitchen, a living room that could be divided, with a garage below – which would cost him no more than £875 plus £150 for the land, if it were to be built in London. Lola, on the other hand, did not yet really believe that she was going to have to leave Germany.

Athalie Abraham, a pupil of Miss Wilson's in Birmingham, went to Leipzig to help Lola as an au pair at around this time. She spoke good German, and she and Lola sat together in the evenings, talking and doing the family's mending. Some sixty years later, Athalie remembered vividly the day when the boys were excluded from their gym classes. With Pevsner on a regular salary from Gordon Russell, Lola could come more frequently to London now, bringing the children for occasional visits, but she was still learning no more than a bare minimum of English.

In November 1934, Pevsner had tried to reassure her that the children would have no trouble making their way in the English educational system: 'Please believe our schools are superior – the children will have an easy time here.' But Lola, taking no chances, was very strict with them, imposing great stress on herself in the process. She once hit Uta for not knowing her French verbs, forgetting that she still had a vegetable knife in her hand, and leaving a scar that lasted for months. 'She was very impulsive,' Uta remembered, 'an emotional person with quick reactions – burst into tears at least once a week.'

'You must dread the temper and hastiness of your wife,' wrote Lola. 'I often think you would be better off staying in London by yourself; then you could get on with your work, which gives you satisfaction, and your family would gain some of the glory, even at a distance . . . I wonder if I'll ever have ambition again.' By now, Pevsner had found somewhere to live: 2 Wildwood Terrace, a tall thin Victorian house on the Golders Green edge of Hampstead Heath, which he rented for ten shillings a week. At the end of March 1936, Lola and the children joined him there.

His work was in fact still disjointed. Through force of circumstance, he was producing regular articles on contemporary design in an ever-wider variety of publications. 'New Designs in Pottery and China' for *Country Life*,[2] for example, was followed by an extensive piece for *School and College Management* under the catchy title 'On the Furnishing of Girls' Schools: More Important in its Implications than You May Think'.[3] 'If a headmistress by carefully choosing colours, furniture, curtains etc. can make her pupils school-proud,' wrote Pevsner, 'she will most certainly prepare them one day to become home-proud as well, and this incorporates such fundamental qualities as tidiness, cleanliness, and a discrimination which quite often grows from matters of taste in furnishings into taste and tact in a much more general way.' Pevsner had obviously not laid down the cudgels for 'taste as an expression of inner harmony', but the educationist who provided an introduction for his piece was able to put his apparent severity into perspective, describing him revealingly as a 'tight-lipped, eye-glassed professor who would look a prim martinet were it not for his quick humorous smile'.

It was with the extracts from *Enquiry* and other articles on contemporary design that he had first breached the defences of the *Architectural Review*. He now moved on to write about design history for them, with two articles on the first uses of plywood to achieve the flush surfaces that had become so important an element in modern design.[4] And once his foot was in the door, the *Review* also took articles derived from *Pioneers* – 'Christopher Dresser, Industrial

Designer', 'C.F. Annesley Voysey: An Appreciation' and 'A Pioneer Designer – Arthur H. Mackmurdo'.[5]

These pieces on Voysey and Mackmurdo were in part at least concerned with architecture – an area where Pevsner's views already chimed closely with those of the *Review*. The opportunity to write for the magazine on architectural subjects was crucial in shaping the course of his career in England. Hitherto the history of architecture had been written primarily by architects themselves, with contributions from antiquaries and general historians; Pevsner would help to change this, and in doing so would change his own persona.

Before the founding of the *Review* in 1896, architectural publications had been for the most part technical journals, aimed at a specialist audience. The *Architectural Review*, in contrast, aimed both to serve the trade and to engage the educated middle-class layman. Architects were no longer taken at their own face value; scholars and dilettanti were employed alongside practitioners to look not simply at the styles of buildings but also at their environment and function, and to criticise rather than advertise. 'These two traditions, amateur and professional, gave birth to an architectural journalism new in literary richness and subtlety.'[6]

Throughout its first twenty-five years the magazine ranged widely in its coverage, from the Arts and Crafts through the neoclassical 'Wrenaissance' in the first decades of the new century and on to the beginnings of the International Style.[7] Its eclecticism, however, reached new heights in the hands of a man who was to become one of the most influential figures in Pevsner's life, someone he dubbed 'Golden Boy' – Hubert de Cronin Hastings. Hubert de Cronin, born in 1902 (the same year as Pevsner), had actually been christened Robert Seymour Hastings, but acquired his more distinctive names through a change of mind by his father Percival, joint proprietor of the Architectural Press, which owned the *Architectural Review*. Hubert went to work for the Architectural Press as soon as he left school at sixteen, but he had shown a great facility for drawing and in quick succession attended classes at the Slade School of Art and the Bartlett School of Architecture.* At the Bartlett, he studied under leading classical architect A.E. Richardson, but rapidly developed a distaste for neo-Georgianism. In 1927, his father asked the then-editor of the *Architectural Review*, W.G. Newton, to resign in Hubert's favour.

Pevsner later conjured up a picture of the *Review*'s unconventional

---

*Hastings illustrated two early volumes of the poetry of John Betjeman.

proprietor-cum-editor – moustached and balding, burly in his tweed suits, invariably embellished with a pink spotted handkerchief. He was a man of moods, shy and reclusive: Pevsner would recall that he had been invited to Hastings's home in Sussex only once in almost fifty years, and had met his wife only twice – once by accident. John Betjeman nicknamed him 'Obscurity', and Hugh Casson offered a range of different possible identities to match the image: 'He had a vaguely military air spiced with some rakish mystery. The land agent perhaps of a renegade duke? The proprietor of a small and exclusive fishing hotel where poaching was not unknown? A major who had retired mysteriously early from the army in order to collect butterflies or to dissect the pyramids?'* Pevsner remembered Hastings's one and only lecture, at the RIBA, delivered from beginning to end with his back to the audience.

Hastings was, however, extraordinarily creative behind the scenes. John Summerson called him 'that Diaghilev of English architecture', and in his hands the *Architectural Review* became a unique seedbed for ideas. It was Hastings's own idea to vary the choice of contributors and bring in poets, novelists and painters: Hilaire Belloc, D.H. Lawrence, Paul Nash, Osbert Sitwell, P. Morton Shand on the design of wine bottles, Evelyn Waugh on Gaudí, Robert Byron on eastern monasteries. He was, commented Osbert Lancaster, 'the first really to introduce modern journalism to trade papers', and the *Review* had for years a unique tone of voice – 'wit and irony and suave insiderism'.[8] Alongside the commentaries on architects and architecture, there were articles on films and novels, conservation and tourism. 'Every page must be a surprise,' wrote John Betjeman, an assistant editor from 1930 to 1934. 'There were colour photographs printed exotically upon silver paper, captions written like prose poems under dramatically top-lit photography and, at unexpected intervals, moderately witty spoof articles.'[9] Hastings encouraged Betjeman to use Victorian typefaces to reinforce the content of articles on nineteenth-century design, and 'extravagant pains were taken, in design, typography and illustration to produce a handsome object in its own right'.[10] 'Extravagant' was perhaps the word. The magazine's production costs were almost twice its price (2s 6d per issue); any profit depended on advertisements.[11]

When Hastings arrived as editor in 1927, the *Review* had lost the lead in coverage of the Modern Movement. By 1935, however,

*'The Elusive H. de C.', *RIBA Journal*, February 1971, p.58. Hugh Casson would join the Editorial Board of the *Review* in 1952 – see Chapter 28 below.

Hastings had made his magazine a leading forum for its discussion. He encouraged the publication of articles on the history and theory of architecture as a context for the examination of international modernism. Such political content as the magazine contained – and it never approached the radicalism of continental theorists – was attributable largely to a single figure: James Maude Richards.

Trained as an architect in the 1920s, Jim Richards had turned to journalism in the early 1930s, making his mark with an essay on industrial design and functionalism entitled 'Towards a Rational Aesthetic'. His first job was at the *Architects' Journal* and by 1935 he was an assistant editor at the *Review*, becoming increasingly important in implementing Hastings's ideas. So passionate and one-sided was the *Review* in its advocacy of modernism that Richards felt he had to develop a literary *alter ego* to write as 'James MacQuedy' in its pages, to express scepticism about some aspects of it.*

Richards had had a considerable hand in improving the English in which Pevsner's journalism was written. The *Enquiry* articles in particular needed smoothing, so Richards might have felt a trifle proprietorial about the finished version of the book. Published, at last, in 1937 by Cambridge University Press, *An Enquiry into Industrial Art in England* contained all the *Review* articles, revised and slightly cut, plus Pevsner's reflections on the data he had collected and his recommendations for the future.[12] It was dedicated to 'Carola', giving Lola her formal name, with the words, 'This book is full of thoughts of all of you'.

By the time the *Enquiry* was published, industrial art had become a hot topic and Pevsner himself was described in *DIA News*, the journal of the Design and Industry Association, as 'well known to many'. 'It is a great book,' wrote design campaigner John Gloag in the *RIBA Journal*.† 'You have done British industry and designers a

---

*One of the characters in Thomas Love Peacock's *Crotchet Castle*. 'MacQuedy' was himself supposed to be a caricature of John Ramsay McCulloch (1789–1864), the 'Liberal Snake' in Disraeli's *Vivian Grey*.

†John Gloag (1896–1981), an influential design critic, historian, founder member of the MARS Group and campaigner for the adoption of a modernist ethic in design. A brother-in-law of Jack Pritchard, he lived for some time in the 'Isokon' Lawn Road Flats. Pevsner would later commission him to write a King Penguin on *The English Tradition in Design* (1947). Gloag's *The English Tradition in Architecture* (1963) was dedicated to Pevsner, 'to celebrate 29 years of friendship'.

more profound service than you perhaps realise.' Gloag criticised the lack of an index, and the nasty typography, but added generously, 'I have one regret – that I have never written such a book myself.' 'Never has an exile to this country so promptly and so fully repaid the hospitality he has received,' wrote Herbert Read.[13]

But not all reviewers were as grateful. Christopher Cornford observed acidly in *Design*: '"Good design" is like cold rice pudding – plain, nutritious, high-minded and off-white.'[14] For many readers the lack of frivolity and the superfluity of well-meaning advice was the problem. Lancelot Edwards, writing in the *New Statesman*, saw in it a heavy-handed attempt to impose alien ideas and values on the English way. He objected to the mass-produced uniformity that he saw Pevsner as advocating, writing with more than a hint of xenophobia, 'It is time that we should see how Germanic this is and how the prospect it holds out may turn in the end to be a steam-roller threatening the existence of any private environment . . . In spite of the Totalitarian successes in Europe, it is individualists whom one may expect to do most with their lives, whether for public or personal good, in this world of uncertainties . . . Now this individualism is part of an old-fashioned thing – our national characteristic.' He sketched a portrait of 'Port Nuffield', the ideal town he saw as the logical conclusion of the *Enquiry*'s thinking:

> Here are Nos 45 and 46 with their children, 45A and B and 46A. They have just had lunch off plain china (a change of taste in the Royal Household . . . has brought this about) and are about to go out. It is a winter day, but they do not go to the cinema; that would prove them Escapists . . . At the Central Depot for Approved Designs they spend an idle hour looking at wall-papers, woven stuffs etc., and fill in a questionnaire as to their preferences . . . They buy themselves, perhaps, a plain glass sherry set and return to their plain home.[15]

'The fact that Dr Pevsner is a foreigner,' opined the *Spectator*'s critic, 'might have led him to veil his conclusions with excessive caution and tact . . . Fortunately he has realised that we are not, as a nation, averse from criticism and he has published his findings with a frankness that I have hardly ever seen surpassed in print, and which no Government report would dare to imitate.'

The nation, however, was more sensitive than the *Spectator* thought, and offence was duly taken on a number of grounds. 'There are not many more dangerous words than "taste",' wrote Geoffrey Grigson in *John O'London's Weekly*. 'It drips with self-satisfaction, superiority, and insult.' Pevsner had been rude about the Royal Academy and its 1935 exhibition of 'British Art in Industry', where the standards of taste, he claimed, were 'an easy and good-natured conservatism'. He had also cast aspersions on the nation's hygiene. At that particular moment in the 1930s it might have been better not to have drawn attention to the fact that 'Rickets, the disease mainly bred in slums, is called the English Disease in Germany'. Compounding the offence, he continued: 'Parallel with re-housing, there ought to run an equally energetic campaign for cleaner streets, cleaner and better planned suburbs and above all for cleaner children and cleaner parents, and for healthier and more modern school buildings.'

It was perhaps unsurprising that one review of the *Enquiry* was derisively titled 'Herman's a German' – but this was in fact a German whose former world was disintegrating. The invasion of the Rhineland in March 1936, the pantomime of the Berlin Olympic Games in August, the Four-Year Plan for German rearmament in September, the announcement by Mussolini of a German-Italian Fascist Axis in November were all steps towards extending and cementing the new Nazi order. There was much that, looking from England, Pevsner perhaps did not see or fully understand. 'The clearly reported happenings in Germany,' Maxwell Fry remembered with contempt, 'were misconstrued with vacuous amiability by the greater part of the country.'[16]

Certainly Pevsner seemed able to relax and enjoy himself at the farewell dinner for Gropius, who was leaving for America. Held at the Trocadero in Piccadilly on 9 March 1937, the dinner represented a roll call of the progressive design establishment and its supporters. Pevsner found himself sitting with Julian Huxley, Henry Moore, H.G. Wells, Ove Arup, Sigfried Giedion and Gordon Russell, studying a menu whose cover had been designed by László Moholy-Nagy.

Six weeks later Guernica was bombed by Hitler's Condor Legion. On 24 June, the German *Wehrmacht* was formally instructed to begin preparations for war. On 16 July, a concentration camp was opened at Buchenwald. Two days later, Hitler delivered a speech at the inauguration of the Haus der Deutschen Kunst, or Kunsthalle in Munich – the Museum of German Art, which he described as a 'symbol of the Re-energised Pure German Being'. Art, he declared, was certainly not 'produced by its time' – this was a Jewish notion. Art was the expression of the *Volk* or People, and could never date. The art of today must be the art of the German people, not modern art. The German *Volk* did not understand modern painting, with its green skies and blue grass. Art must reflect the natural, the healthy, the normal, and the *Volk* must be the judge of the normal – here Hitler was confident that he might speak for them. So-called 'modern' artists were cretins, Bolsheviks, revelling in decline and decay: the critics who extolled them were worse: and there was a need for a 'cleansing war' against them.

There was now no mistaking the drift of Nazi art policy, and Pevsner's notes on the speech, made for private reasons and not public consumption, show that he had at last acknowledged what this policy implied.[17] Hitler's speech, he wrote, was crass and philistine, violently anti-modern. Hitler sounded like the rawest art student, with no idea at all of the expressive qualities of colour or form and an embarrassingly bad writing style, crude and cliché-ridden – the style of the common man, in the worst sense. To use 'Germanness' as the sole criterion of quality, wrote Pevsner, was highly dangerous because it left too much scope for suppressing works of art as 'un-German'. He had come to this recognition very late. The following day the first exhibition of 'Degenerate Art' opened in Munich. Visitors, the official programme informed them, could see here works that destroyed any sense of the German race (Schmidt-Rottluff), portrayed cretins and paralytics as an intellectual ideal (Kokoschka), made a mockery of religion (Nolde and Klee) and revelled in prostitution as the moral programme of barbarism (Dix).

Reading Nietzsche, Pevsner was moved and disturbed by references to Naumburg, where the philosopher had gone during his last illness. 'It must, it must, it must come again,' he wrote. Lola and the children took their summer holiday in the vineyard house that year, just as they had every year since 1933, but he was thinking of the Naumburg and the holidays of the past and not the present. That August the Nazi paper *Der Stürmer* printed a cartoon depicting two girls in swimsuits at a resort, looking at a sign that read 'Prohibited for Jews', over the caption 'How nice that it's just us now!'

By mid-1937 Lola and the children were well-settled in Wildwood Terrace. The location of the house was all that he had wanted.* He

---

*Pevsner would later describe his house in the *Buildings of England* in modest terms: 'A little further N, overlooking the unkempt woodland of the Heath Extension, is the surprisingly urban Gothic Wildwood Terrace, built, with Wildwood Grove to its w would later write, 'On some critics, like this one, sunshine and greenery have a stronger effect than the very best martini', and the setting was beautiful, facing a wild part of Hampstead Heath fringed with gorse and copper beeches.[18] A two-minute walk in one direction brought one to the Heath extension and a view of the Garden Suburb, and in the other direction to a small watering place with a pond and a teahouse with a terrace; an excellent cinema was a mere quarter of an hour's walk away.

The Pevsners were able to install the remains of the Bauhaus nursery furniture which they had first bought in 1924;* but the new house was far from the convenient dwelling of their dreams. Pevsner had written happily to Lola in easier times, 'I'm sure you'll be tempted to explore the kind of cooking and housekeeping that is done here . . . Servants are very expensive, though – we'll always have to have a German au pair.' Lola was never to have the au pair (German or English) or the little house with its own little garden. In Wildwood Terrace she found a basement kitchen of striking discomfort and inconvenience, dark and dirty, with precipitously steep stairs to the dining room and, when she first arrived, no hot water. (The Pevsners did not acquire their water heater until 1939, and then it was not fitted in the kitchen.) Lola, who was extremely, even excessively house-proud, was not impressed.

Pevsner's parents, on the other hand, were still in the Hotel Kaiserhof in Leipzig. Hugo was now an invalid, and Annie nursed him devotedly. 'She might sometimes have been cutting to him,' Pevsner remarked, 'but she had a strong sense of duty.' She left the hotel rarely: 'After Hitler she didn't want to go out much. She played patience with Father . . . She did read a lot . . . She saw fewer and fewer people.' Looking back with guilt, Pevsner would suggest one possible reason for her self-imposed seclusion. 'She suffered . . . from my perverse interest in

---

. . . in 1886–7.' Wildwood was part of Eton College's Wyldes estate in Hendon and probably extended across to the northern slopes of Hampstead Heath. Wildwood Grove, near the northern border, was a terraced row begun in the 1860s. The local builder, T. Clowser, was permitted to build four houses there in 1871, and another six stood there and in Wildwood, probably Wildwood Terrace, by 1882. After a brief spell (1900–7) as a Home of Rest for Aged Poor, numbers 1 and 2 reverted to private occupation: the builder's daughter-in-law, Annie Clowser, was still living in 2 Wildwood Terrace in 1929 and it is possible that Pevsner rented directly from her. British History Online Source: Hampstead: North End, Littleworth, and Spaniard's End. *Victoria County History of the County of Middlesex: Volume IX*, T.F.T. Baker (ed.) (1989).
*The nursery furniture was designed by Bauhaus student Alma Buscher, and made on a serial pattern. It included a toy trolley/store with a seat at two-thirds height inside one end, an open-shelf unit and a puppet-theatre cupboard. The open shelf unit stood at ninety degrees to the theatre so that, with the proscenium door open, the shelves formed a third side for the 'stage'.

National Socialism, because she was interested in democracy and a part of the Leipzig business community. She no longer wanted to be seen around.'

At intervals she fell into black depression, and on more than one occasion attempted suicide. 'Those attacks came again and again,' Pevsner noted. 'Crises and remissions.' His relationship with his mother was still very complex, but by 1937 it was improving – 'after all, I was older too', and less assertive about National Socialism. 'She was very proud of me and did believe in me. Gladly typed my manuscripts until the threshold of war. She was prone to show around any report of my little successes . . . From the time when we lived further away from each other, the times when we were together were easier. Nevertheless they upset me quite a lot, there was so much that was left unsaid and unspoken.'

Among the topics that were taboo, almost certainly, was the question of leaving Germany. Money was an issue. The older Pevsners had not been at all well-off since the incident of the corrupt accountant and the takeover of the firm of Emil Barban.* 'If only,' Pevsner wrote to Lola in 1935, 'they realised that today, after the inflation, the world crisis and anti-Semitism, it is triply no shame to close shop. But will there still be enough left for them? For heaven's sake, they should use it all and not think of me – wouldn't you agree?' Finding the right blend of emotional dependence and financial independence in his relationship with his mother was a delicate business. 'We can't seem to persuade Muo that we need her. Somehow we must make her realise that we depend on her. It would be easier if she didn't have this real fear of a hand-to-mouth existence.'

Many older people in positions similar to Annie's and Hugo's were reluctant to abandon the possessions and the capital that they were no longer allowed to take out of Germany. 'If we go,' wrote Victor Klemperer, 'then we save our lives and are dependants and beggars for the rest of our lives. If we remain, then our lives are in danger but we retain the possibility of afterwards leading a life worth living.' 'I really don't want to leave Germany,' Annie had told her friend Lis Knauth firmly in 1936, 'and be a financial burden on the children – a dreadful thought.'

As a Jew in Germany in 1937, provided you were selective you could still live a fairly normal life – own your own home, use public transport, go to the cinema. Violence against Jews was not endemic,

---

*In 1934 Pevsner had been notified that one of the firm's sleeping partners had been struck off, suggesting that all those implicated in the scandal had been identified.

but remained confined to Nazi gangs; periods of violence were followed by relative calm. There had been persecution so often before, it seemed that few were able to imagine the extremes to which it might go this time. It might be possible, many thought, to coexist with non-Jews on the basis of segregation, and most Jews still had faith in the legal process as a means of defending themselves. The political opponents of the Nazi regime, who might have been able to disabuse them, had mostly been removed to concentration camps, and those who had been released were not talking. A very large number of successfully integrated Jews believed that the Nazi regime would not last.

At the end of 1937, 75 per cent of the Jewish population was still in Germany.

The expiry of Pevsner's British residence permit was looming once again. On 9 February 1938 the General Secretary of the Academic Assistance Council wrote to the Aliens Department of the Home Office asking them to end his uncertainty. 'I think it may be said that Dr Pevsner is one of the scholars who has provided a scientific equipment that has proved of benefit to this country.'[19] At the end of February the permanent permit was granted.

Meanwhile in Germany, Hitler had been made Supreme Commander of the *Wehrmacht*, ahead of the annexation of Austria in March. That month Adolf Eichmann was placed in charge of what was described as the 'Jewish Emigration' to Dachau, and all Jews were compelled to adopt the forenames of 'Israel' or 'Sarah' in addition to their own given names. In Dresden, Victor Klemperer recorded, 'A broad yellow bill with the Star of David has been stuck to every post of our fence – *Jew*.' In the space of a week in Germany, orders were given that all Jewish property must be registered and that no Aryans were to give music lessons to Jews. On 12 July it was decreed that Jews needed yellow cards in order to visit the public baths. A rhyme of the time ran '*Junge Juden, Übersee, Alte Juden, Weissensee* / Young Jews – overseas; old Jews – in Weissensee' (the main Jewish cemetery in Berlin). Around this time Lola asked Pevsner if he would register her brother Dieter with the Academic Assistance Council, with a view to helping him leave Germany.

In his work Pevsner was looking homewards in 1938. A long article entitled 'English and German Art and their interrelations' was published in *German Life and Letters* in July, perhaps in a vain attempt to remind an English public of the enduring cultural affinities that lay beneath current political antagonisms. He also contributed to a volume entitled

German Baroque Sculpture, with the main text written by Sacheverell Sitwell.*

That summer Uta, Tom and Dieter went to Leipzig for a short holiday with their Pevsner grandparents. In hindsight, it is hard to understand why Pevsner and Lola felt so little sense of danger. Restrictions on Jews were tightening all the time – identification cards would be introduced in August 1938, making it impossible for Jews to pass undetected in any sphere of life – and it was already becoming necessary for some to take shelter; Pallister Barkas had offered his house in Göttingen as a refuge to several.

It was in August that Lola's father Alfred Kurlbaum fell dangerously ill. He had already had a serious heart attack that March; now he was suffering from cirrhosis of the liver. Pevsner and Lola rushed to Leipzig, but he died on 26 August 1938, and Lola's strongest tie to Germany was gone. It was also, though he could not have guessed it, the last time that Pevsner was to see his parents.

Back in England, he had ideas for another book, on 'The Making of London', possibly elaborating on the interest in town planning that he had developed during his first visit to the city in 1930.† He would also appear to have drawn up plans for an extended programme of research on industrial design, at least partly in the hope of obtaining a fellowship at Nuffield College, Oxford, which had recently been established as a centre for postgraduate social studies. ('Naturally almost every German in the social sciences in this country is convinced that Nuffield College has been founded for his benefit,' wrote Walter Adams of the Academic Assistance Council wearily.‡) He was making headway with writing

---

*Pevsner's offering took the form of annotations on some three dozen black-and-white illustrations to the text. Moving from one work to the next, he constructed a synoptic view of German baroque sculpture as the natural outgrowth of its geographical setting and its time, the coincidence of the German national genius and the spirit of the seventeenth century. He drew a sharp contrast between the Protestant and Catholic approaches to art, rooted in the difference between their approaches to God – one a matter of direct communication, quiet and private, the other a communal experience, expressive and spectacular. German baroque sculpture, he argued, was conspicuously a product of Catholicism and of the south. The piece was not one of which he was particularly proud, although the subject was dear to him. 'It was not easy,' he remembered, 'but I was glad to get the money.' Interview with Robin Middleton in *Building Design*, 16/3/73.
†In September 1938 he took the idea to Christian Barman, former executive editor of the *Architectural Review*, then working at the London Passenger Transport Board, but Barman could not help.
‡Walter Adams/Sir William Beveridge, 22/2/38. SPSL 191/2, 122. Pevsner's proposal (SPSL, 191/2, 31–2) was ambitious, involving surveys of consumer preferences, research in factories in Holland and the United States, a regular bulletin of good design, a

articles on architecture and architectural history for a range of journals. And, on a grander scale, he devised a proposal for a topographical survey of the major monuments of Britain, county by county, in ten or so volumes, and submitted a draft outline to a number of publishers.*

Meanwhile Hitler was demanding possession of the German-speaking areas of Czechoslovakia, and British fears of German aggression were manifesting themselves in the form of cellars and basements requisitioned for air-raid shelters, trenches dug at night in public parks, barrage balloons appearing over London, and the issue of thirty-eight million gas masks.[20] In October, the same month that Germany reoccupied the Sudetenland, customs authorities in Germany and Switzerland invalidated all existing passports belonging to Jews; the reissued versions were stamped with a large red J. On 28 October, the order was given for all Polish Jews to be expelled from Germany. On 6 November, France signed a non-aggression pact with Hitler. Three days later a Polish-Jewish student named Herschel Grynszpan shot the Third Secretary at the German embassy in Paris, Ernst vom Rath, in revenge for the deportation of his parents from Germany. This was the trigger for the worst outbreak of anti-Jewish violence so far seen in Germany. Goebbels used Storm Troopers to burn synagogues and desecrate the rolls of the Torah kept in them, and to smash the windows of shops belonging to Jews, producing the sea of glass that gave the pogrom on the night of 9 November 1938 its name of 'Kristallnacht'. Ninety-one people were killed, and within weeks 35,000 men had been sent to camps at Sachsenhausen, Buchenwald and Dachau.

In Leipzig the American consul, David Buffum, witnessed the chaos, and gathered eyewitness accounts:[21]

In one of the Jewish sections an eighteen-year-old boy was hurled from a third-storey window to land with both legs broken on a street littered with burning beds and other household furniture . . . Among domestic effects thrown out of a Jewish building, a small dog descended

---

research centre on housing issues, a history of working-class housing and the formation of a reference library on 'the social aspects of art', and seems to have fallen on stony ground.
*In a long letter of 17 October 1939 addressed to Sydney Castle Roberts at Cambridge University Press, Pevsner proposed a series quite unlike the Shell Guides with 'their smart plates': it would run to some 2,400 pages – approximately sixty pages per county – and it could be done on a salary of £300 per year. The Syndics rejected the idea, having previously found it unsatisfactory to pay authors on a retainer. D. McKitterick, *History of Cambridge University Press*, Vol. 3 (2004). Routledge, on the other hand, expressed an interest which was only dampened by the outbreak of war a year later.

four flights on to a cluttered street with a broken spine . . . One apartment of exceptionally refined occupants known to this office was violently ransacked, presumably in a search for valuables which was not in vain, and one of the marauders thrust a cane through a priceless medieval painting portraying a biblical scene . . . There are reports that substantial losses have been sustained on the famous Leipzig 'Bruehl', as many of the shop windows at the time of the demolition were filled with costly furs that were seized before the windows could be boarded up . . . No attempts whatsoever were made to quench the fires, the activity of the fire brigade being confined to spraying water on adjoining buildings . . . The slightest manifestation of sympathy evoked a positive fury on the part of the perpetrators, and the crowd was powerless to do anything but turn horror-stricken eyes from the scene of abuse, or leave the vicinity.

The Brühl was, of course, the street where Hugo Pevsner had worked for the firm of Emil Barban. Annie and Hugo must have been well aware of the destruction and looting, and were almost certainly now ready to listen to pleas from Pevsner to join the family in England. For many Jews, Kristallnacht was the moment at which they were convinced that they must leave Germany and find refuge somewhere else – almost anywhere else; Stefan Zweig described a wealthy Viennese art collector seeking refuge in Haiti or San Domingo, 'atremble with the hope of going to a country which hitherto he would not have been able to find on the map'.[22]

At the same time their potential hosts, beginning to realise the scale of the problem and the magnitude of the possible influx, were imposing increasingly tight restrictions on immigration. In Britain, the number of refugees from Europe had risen from approximately 6,000 in 1933 to 70,000 in 1938. After Kristallnacht, the requirement for children to have visas was waived, but anyone over sixteen needed a passport, exit permit and visa to travel to Britain, and the issuing system was swamped. British consuls struggling to handle a flood of new applications had to check on each applicant and his or her guarantor, and the flow of approvals was far too slow to meet the increasingly frantic demand. Another wave of suicides among the Jewish population in Germany was noted in statistics. In the middle of November 1938 it was decreed that there should be no Jewish pupils in German schools. By the end of the month Jews were ordered to live only in accommodation specially designated for them. On 6 December the right to hold a driving licence was withdrawn. Two days later Jews were forbidden to attend universities.

The following week Pevsner was at the Glasgow School of Art, delivering a prestigious lecture on 'The Glasgow Revolution in Art and Design', ranging over the work of Mackmurdo, Voysey, Norman Shaw, Mackintosh and Whistler. It is inconceivable that he was not dismayed by the news from Germany. But outwardly, his life continued as normal. Lola was by his side, the children had returned safely from Leipzig, work was steadily increasing, it was possible to travel to Germany if need be. If he had views on the political situation, he kept them to himself.

In Germany itself, horrible rumours were beginning to come out of Buchenwald, the large concentration camp near Weimar. But public perceptions of the plight of German Jews were hardly acute in London, where around the end of 1938 the Central Office for Refugees issued a list of 'DOS and DON'TS for Refugees'. 'DO be as quiet and modest as possible,' they advised. 'If you do not make yourself noticeable, other people will not bother about you . . . DO be as cheerful as possible. A smiling face will make them still more your friends . . . DON'T talk German in the streets. There is nothing to show the man in the street that you are a refugee and not a Nazi.'

By the end of January 1939, Hitler had made a speech speaking of 'the extermination of the Jewish race in Europe' during a 'world war'. Pevsner's preoccupations, however, like those of the majority of people living in England, were mundane. He was in the throes of negotiating a hire-purchase agreement for a 'gas-fired wash-copper with ignition device' for his cold kitchen. He was maintaining his output of articles and reviews of books in several languages, and keeping up his varied and cosmopolitan purchasing policy for Gordon Russell, although resistance was gathering. After the German invasion of the rump of Czechoslovakia in March 1939, the Russell workforce in Broadway began to suggest that the firm should be more patriotic in its buying and selling. Of one piece of furniture they wrote, in the company magazine, *The Circular Saw*: 'the construction . . . [runs] counter to the best traditions of English cabinet-making . . . Surely the sale of these articles aggravates our own employment problem.'[23] Invited by the editor Val Freeman to respond, Pevsner argued: 'We don't bend solid beechwood as Thonet's have done for 80 years [in Austria]. Climatic conditions would not, I am told, favour such an industry . . . As long as such limitations of manufacturing and of style exist in our production . . . I am afraid 95% British is as far as we can go.' This prompted a cartoon in the next issue depicting a Russian moujik in fur hat and baggy trousers looking into the Gordon Russell showroom window at a sign reading 'Our furniture is 95% British'.[24]

Pevsner was unabashed. In June, his article 'A Plea for Contemporary Craft' compared English craftwork unfavourably with German. Germany, he wrote, had been far more successful in preserving and reviving the tradition of handicraft, partly because the introduction of large-scale industry had not done it as much damage in the first place, partly because the current government was promoting it. 'It is by no means essentially "totalitarian" encouragement,' he argued, 'and the British government might do well to emulate it'.[25]

He was, perhaps, too busy to be diplomatic, preoccupied with plans for a venture that could greatly have advanced his reputation and demonstrated his solidarity with his host country, had it come to fruition. Early in the year he had presented the *Architectural Review* with an outline proposal for a special issue of the magazine devoted to British twentieth-century architecture. A double number, it would be a survey of contemporary architectural styles in Britain covering the period 1924–39. Looking at each of the most common styles, he would trace each to its origins and indicate how it had (or had not) been affected by modernism.

The survey was to conclude with a 'classified section' that would list and illustrate twenty examples of the specifically British approach to the Modern Movement – 'practical without any modern engineering romanticism, impressive but not fussy, self-certain but not boisterous, dignified but not over-bearing – in short, British in every respect'. These would include the Comet Inn, Hatfield, 'easily the best-designed pub in Britain', and the Underground stations put up by the London Passenger Transport Board, designed by Charles Holden. In buildings like Holden's station at Arnos Grove, wrote Pevsner, 'a synthesis seems achieved between the character of our century and the inborn character of the English, a synthesis that leaves us full of hope for the future of the Modern Movement on the soil which once begot it.'[26]

The main achievement of Pevsner's special issue would have been to nip in the bud the notion that he was rigid and prescriptive in his attitudes to modern architecture. The Modern Movement, he wrote, was the only 'live' style, but the movement was not to be limited to the hard core of Gropius and Le Corbusier. It must incorporate a 'gradual evolution into national idioms', and it must respect the contributions of individuals. The special issue, however, was never to appear.*

---

*The modernist section would eventually be published under the title of 'The Modern Movement in Britain', with an introduction by Bridget Cherry, in the journal of the Twentieth Century Society, *Twentieth Century Architecture*, 8: 'British Modern', 2007. The manuscript is in GP Series II, Box 18.

Richards and Hastings had got as far as working out a possible method of presenting the material; but money was getting ever tighter, and the problems of accumulating the necessary photographs looked set to intensify as the prospect of war grew closer.

In March, Britain had publicly promised to support Poland in the event of a German attack; and in May the Military Training Act announced a six-month conscription for men of twenty and twenty-one, the first time in British history that conscription had been introduced in peacetime. Meanwhile, in Germany the women's concentration camp at Ravensbrück had opened in the same month. On 26 June 1939, Hans Posse, Pevsner's former employer at the Dresden Gemäldegalerie, had been appointed the director of the proposed new 'Führer Museum' in Linz. Posse was now charged with managing what Hitler intended to be the largest art gallery in the world. His personal duty was the purchasing of Old Masters from Belgium, the Netherlands and Italy; but he would also be responsible for doling out to provincial museums thousands of the paintings which the Nazi regime had acquired by less respectable means – plundered from churches and museums in occupied territories, or confiscated from Jewish owners.

Pevsner was far from unaware of the mounting tensions.* Francesca Wilson, ever more deeply involved through her Quaker connections in providing aid to refugees, was undoubtedly a source of information on Germany for him, and may even have recruited his help. The Scottish poet Hamish Henderson, who was also a vigorous peace campaigner, went out to Göttingen in the summer of 1939 to join a Quaker organisation that was smuggling dissidents out of Germany. At the age of eighty, he would claim that he was briefed for this mission by Pevsner, whom he met at 'a shop on Bond Street', by which he might have meant Gordon Russell Ltd.[27]

Whether or not she had involved Pevsner in her operations, Miss Wilson was certainly well informed about the political situation through a variety of contacts in or around government. The Pevsners and the Barkases were, as usual, planning family holidays in Germany that summer; Barkas himself was still living in Göttingen. In June, Miss Wilson cautioned Pevsner that he should aim to bring the children back earlier than usual. By July, she was warning both Pevsner and Barkas that 'something would happen' in August. Barkas could not bring himself

---

*It was probably no coincidence that he had chosen that spring to take practical precautions; a certificate awarded to him on 28 June 1939 by the British Red Cross Society states that 'Nicklaus [sic] Pevsner . . . having attended a course of lectures and demonstrations in First Aid to the Injured has been examined and satisfied the examiner.'

to take her seriously, and told her not to listen to her Socialist friends; if there was going to be a war, it would have broken out at the time of the invasion of the Rhineland in 1936. He badly needed to believe that he was secure in Germany: 'I'm just coming into a financially more comfortable position here . . . I think that on the whole one can judge by an objective calculation of chances of success and risks of failure.'*

Pevsner and Lola were trying all the time now to find ways of bringing Annie and Hugo over to England. Nevertheless, in August 1939 they sent all the children back to Germany to stay with Lola's sister Marianne in the Naumburg vineyard house where Pevsner had first got to know Lola, and where the children had spent so many family holidays. To have taken such a risk at this point was surely a symptom of a stubborn clinging to roots that were in danger of being torn up for good. Tom and Dieter arrived in Germany at the beginning of the month, Uta on 16 August. None had an exit visa.

---

*On 31 August 1939, Mass Observation found that only one person in five in England actually expected war to come.

PART FOUR

PEVSNER'S WAR

1939–1946

Original drawing by Berthold Wolpe
for the cover of *The Buildings of England: Essex*, 1954

CHAPTER 19

Phoney War

On 23 August 1939, the Russo-German Pact was signed. On 26 August, the German armies were mobilised; on 1 September, they invaded Poland. Two days later, Britain and France declared war on Germany.

In Leipzig, Tom and Dieter, thirteen and seven, did not need exit visas to get out of Germany. Mercifully their passports, which had been issued in England, were not stamped with the incriminating J and, if they could get to an open port, they could leave on exit permits. The man who had been Alfred Kurlbaum's confidential clerk for many years, Herr Lang, remained a loyal friend of the family and undertook to take the boys to Denmark. The little party – without Uta – set off on 1 September, the day of the invasion of Poland, and spent one night in Hamburg before crossing into Denmark, heading for Esbjerg on the west coast of the Jutland peninsula. They arrived there in the aftermath of bombing; official British policy at this early stage of the war was to hit no land targets other than dock installations, but standards of navigation were not very high, and Wellington bombers of 139 Squadron, whose real target was the main naval base at Wilhelmshafen, had dropped four bombs by mistake on Esbjerg.

Nor was their journey any safer by sea. With merchant ships scurrying for home or for neutral ports, German U-boats and British submarines had made their first sorties into the North Sea, armed with torpedoes and magnetic mines. In the first days of the war, U-boat commanders attacking merchant and other non-combatant ships were under orders to inform the enemy of their intentions; but by the second week in September, Admiral Dönitz had ordered enemy ships to be destroyed without warning. RAF Bomber Command was preparing further raids on German warships in their bases, and Royal Navy destroyers were laying mines in the approaches to them. The boys were probably mercifully oblivious of the wider threat: housed in one half of the bows of the small freighter *Frigga*, the other half being the fish store, they were prostrated with seasickness. They may have spared Pevsner these details and told him only of the boisterous party of Rhodesian Rover Scouts treating the journey as rest and recreation: he would describe their voyage later as 'a journey full of adventures which they thoroughly enjoyed', culminating in one final exploit when the ship, which they had expected to dock on the Channel coast, was forced to put them ashore in Hull. They made their way south on their own.[1]

Uta, still with her grandparents, had not even got her passport, let alone the exit visa that, as soon as she turned sixteen in March 1940, she would need in order to get away: her application had not been completed when the British consulate in Berlin started packing up, and, to her parents' acute anxiety, her papers had not yet been returned. Annie Pevsner's first instinct was to keep her in Leipzig, but Uta chose to go and stay with her aunt Marianne in Hanover. Annie and Hugo Pevsner were still staying in the Hotel Kaiserhof; Marianne and her husband Carl Walter Kockel had a family house for their children – a more practical place to shelter, among people more Uta's own age.

Annie and Hugo themselves had in any case been actively seeking to get out of Germany. Hugo, now seventy, had finally given up his business at the beginning of the year. Neither he nor Annie was prepared to deny their Jewish roots. 'I couldn't!' Lis Knauth remembered Annie crying. 'To deny my parents in their grave!' 'The older one became, the more strongly one returned to one's roots, she said. In this respect, she felt completely at one with her husband.' Pevsner and Lola had found a small flat not far from Wildwood Terrace, in Muswell Hill, but, like thousands of others, the older Pevsners had left it too late, and with the declaration of war the gates of Germany were closed. 'My parents were on the very point of joining us in London or near London,' Pevsner told Francesca Wilson. 'Now it has also to be postponed indefinitely, another highly unpleasant thought.'[2]

At the outbreak of war Germans in England, as enemy nationals, were in a position of peculiar vulnerability – and for those who were Jews, there was the added obstacle of residual anti-Semitism. 'Although I loathe anti-Semitism, I do dislike Jews,' remarked Harold Nicolson. At this point the British authorities were choosing not to make public all they knew, fearing the kind of backlash that had been produced by the propaganda excesses of the First World War. The official policy was to play down 'horror stuff'. 'Must be used very sparingly,' noted an official memo as late as 1941, 'and must deal always with treatment of indisputably innocent people. Not with violent political opponents. And not with Jews.'[3] The average Briton had not yet fully appreciated the need for sympathy; and, on the evidence of the *Jewish Chronicle* in the mid-1930s, the existing Anglo-Jewish community was hardly more welcoming: 'Anglo-Jewry had been rendered ambivalent about its own Jewishness by its desire for assimilation within a fundamentally anti-Semitic "culture".'[4]

Meanwhile, émigré populations, largely Jewish, gathered in north-west London – in Hampstead, West Hampstead, Golders Green, Finchley and Swiss Cottage. The German Refugee Hospitality Committee had its headquarters in Little Russell Street, and there were German-speaking hotels in Russell Square, German bookshops in Charlotte Street. The *Neue Londoner Zeitung* had published its first edition as early as 1932, and the Academy Cinema in Oxford Street had regular seasons of German films. But any sense of an émigré 'society' was perhaps more apparent to outsiders than real. Ernst Gombrich, who had come to England in 1936 and might have been perceived to have been part of a 'colony' of art historians centred on the Warburg Institute, would later claim, 'There was no such thing as a refugee community when we first came over – every case was different.' Some people were technically refugees, many were not, some were practising Jews, others were not, and still others were Christian converts; some had roots and existing connections in Britain, others had none.*

The Pevsners, in any case, had never sought to become part of an émigré community. While Gombrich would become a good personal friend, Pevsner would remain distanced from the Warburg circle – set apart, in Gombrich's view, not by his religious or political beliefs, but by his twentieth-century interests, his versatility as a commentator on design and architecture, and his career as an editor and journalist. He had, in any event, spent the last six years in England trying less to reproduce his former German life than to create a new one. In the autumn of 1939, certainly, his one desire was to carry on as before.

Among Pevsner's papers when he died was a newspaper cutting with a quotation from Dame Julian of Norwich:

---

*Ernst Gombrich, interview with the author, 10/6/92. Gombrich often made this point. Richard Wollheim remembered him speaking at a reception for a series of lectures celebrating 'the glory of Jewish culture'. 'There was no unitary Viennese culture, he observed, nor was there any specifically Jewish area within it. In every area there were Jews, such as Schoenberg, Freud, Schnitzler, Wittgenstein, and also non-Jews, such as Loos, Klimt . . . Kokoschka, and no discernible difference went along with this distinction; and if it had, this would have been of interest largely to the Gestapo.' Obituary of Gombrich in *ArtForum*, 2/1/2002.

He said not:
'Thou shalt not be tempested':
'Thou shalt not be travailed':
'Thou shalt not be afflicted':
But He said
'Thou shalt not be overcome'.

Pevsner's war might have been designed to demonstrate the personal relevance of Dame Julian's text. It was a time of strain, humiliation, fear and grief for him; but paradoxically it was also a time of great opportunity.

Tom and Dieter were now living for the time being in Chipping Campden, near the Gordon Russell headquarters in Broadway – evacuees like more than a million others. They had stayed briefly with one of the firm's directors, Basil Fairclough, before moving into Dovers Court, a 'Cotswold dream house' hidden away behind the village's main street, to stay with Nina Griggs and two of her four young daughters. Nina – 'a lovely, warm, affectionate woman', in Dieter's words – was the widow of the artist Frederick Landseer Griggs, who had died the previous year. He had been acclaimed as one of the finest etchers of his time; but he had originally trained as an architect, and he had designed Dovers Court himself as a twentieth-century contribution to the Arts and Crafts movement in Chipping Campden, a building conceived in harmony with its landscape and built by local labour. The house would have been very comfortable had it ever been finished; to get to their bedroom, the boys had to pass through a room marked out with studs but lacking either laths or plaster. They remembered rain dripping on to their beds through a fragmentary ceiling.

In the first weeks of the 'Phoney War' Pevsner stayed with them, cycling over to the Russell offices every day, while Dieter and Tom started the autumn term at Chipping Campden Grammar School – 'not quite our idea of what their education was to be like,' Pevsner commented ruefully to Miss Wilson. Suddenly all the progress he had made towards stability seemed to be under threat. The only real work for him at the Broadway headquarters was to wind up his department, and in November he returned to London. At the shop in Wigmore Street, there was an attempt at business as usual, with sandbags piled high outside the plate-glass window; but trading conditions were rapidly declining, and Gordon Russell himself found it hard to adapt, unwilling or unable to compromise the quality of his principal lines. Before too long, with sales plunging, he was forced by the firm's bank to resign as its managing director.

The workshops were increasingly made over to war work:

ammunition boxes, wing nosings for Mosquito aircraft and detailed models for RAF experiments. Craftsmen used to turning chair legs found themselves making retracting undercarriages in miniature and replica wind tunnels. 'Retailing is slow and dull,' Pevsner reported gloomily. 'Initiative is not required anyway. So my appointment is now part-time – 1 day out of 5½, to be exact. This does not yield the sufficient amount of coal for the home fires. Here I am therefore, going round and trying to find something. Barrows, Florence, Bodkin – the old gang. Only it is particularly difficult just now. Well, we must see. The hunt has only begun.'[5] Two weeks later, however, the government had decreed that no one could take jobs without express permission from the recently renamed Ministry of Labour and National Service, and his situation was worse. 'If things go on like this,' he told Jack Pritchard, 'I shall soon be in a position to write the Memoirs of a Job Hunting Man . . . I could accept any duration job at six quid, clerical or administrative, brain or no . . . With an extensive family such as mine and no capital whatsoever in this country, I must think of something more or less immediately.'[6]

Back in Germany, the world Pevsner had known was collapsing. In the first week of January 1940, his father died. 'He was calm and quiet as he left this life, just as he had lived it,' Annie wrote to Pevsner. 'That he was allowed to die in familiar and loved surroundings, that every single person loved him and was ready to give him all possible help . . . for this I thank the Lord.' Hugo had been very popular in the hotel – 'always so modest, sympathetic and gentlemanly' – and, unobtrusively, much loved by friends as a fair, conscientious and capable man. The synagogue was well attended for his funeral, in Siberian cold, well below freezing. (The service must have taken place at the Brodyer Synagogue on Keilstrasse, the only Leipzig synagogue to have survived Kristallnacht – spared, apparently, because 'Aryan' tenants occupied the upper floors.[7]) The mourners then moved to the Ceremonial Hall of the Neuer Israelitischer Friedhof (the New Jewish Cemetery) on Delitzscherstrasse for the burial. 'In the big hut – one can't call it anything else – there was a crowd of men,' Lis Knauth reported:

> whose conversations suddenly died when the widow entered. Her face and her bearing had quite unconscious dignity. Her flashing glance – almost arrogant – struck and blasted the unworthy surroundings. Professor Marx followed the undecorated black coffin, in the almost unbearable cold, and blessed it by throwing a handful of

dust, to send him to his last resting place, in thick snow. Nobody spoke there, not even the friends whom she had expected to do so. We were all as if paralysed . . . She said later, in tears, 'They have scratched earth over him like a dog' . . . During the drive to the hotel with Frau Dr Pollack, she said, blinking into the sun that had now come through, 'How he would have loved this – real Russian weather.'

Hugo had remained very conscious of his Russian roots. Annie treasured a little mosaic bowl that he had used for forty-five years:

It was a present on our wedding day, and stood there, most beautiful, according to old Russian custom, filled with sugar or a cake in the shape of a loaf of bread, to symbolise the wish that there should always be salt and bread in our new household . . . We never lacked salt or bread as long as the head of the household was alive . . . Later on . . . Hugo kept all his little bits and pieces in it for safety, and probably handled it every day. It went through life with him till his very last day.

He had always provided her with emotional ballast. 'His firm, quiet attitude often stiffened her own resolve,' wrote Lis. '"How can this upset you so?" he said once. "Evil returns upon the doer".' He had also, despite his poor health, managed all their personal financial affairs, as well as his business, and with his death she was swamped. 'Two business people told me separately how honest and ordered his business papers were,' Lis informed Pevsner. 'It must be dreadful to lose that kind of support.' (It was at around this time that Lola wrote to one of her father's executors, asking for payments to be made from her share of his estate to her mother-in-law, now facing the dangers of life in Nazi Germany alone.)

Shortly before his death, Hugo had been found in the middle of the night, fully dressed, on the staircase landing of the hotel, 'saying that they must go at once or else they would be fetched'.[8] This was no longer a vague and unformulated fear. Lola's uncle, Ernst Neisser, had been told to report to the SS. His wife had already committed suicide in an asylum, having become chronically depressed under the Nazi regime, and he was living with an elderly female cousin; he now killed them both with an overdose of morphine.

For Pevsner, to the pain of grief at Hugo's death was added the burden of guilt for being safe and somewhere else. 'As your parents often said, you have never caused them a moment's sorrow,' wrote a

German aunt. 'Your letter for your father's 70th birthday was his best present, and we had to read it to him over and over again.' With the best of intentions, she cruelly underlined the fact of his absence.

'Let us not envy him his rest,' Annie wrote, 'but be grateful that he has been released, and has been spared what is perhaps awaiting us.' Since the passing of the Law regarding Leases with Jews at the end of April 1939, which entitled Aryan landlords to evict Jewish tenants without redress, the municipal housing authority in Leipzig had been designating blocks of flats as *Judenwohnungen* or 'Jews' Apartments', also known as *Sammelwohnungen* or 'Collecting Houses' – a process that in other cities led eventually to the creation of fully developed ghettos. Shortly after Hugo's death, Annie was forced to leave the hotel and move to one of these houses at 2 Rosenthalgasse. Her room faced on to the river, but it was small and dark and there were no more good hotel meals – minor ills in the perspective of what was to come, but at the start of 1940 an unpleasant shock for someone who, even after leaving her own home, had been set in the ways of a comfortable bourgeois existence. Lis, who was not Jewish, brought her titbits of food, and gave her a coffee service for her birthday:

> I could not see her drinking from the ghastly restaurant cups which were regulation issue there . . . All the residents there were middle-class people, thank goodness. For the regulations gradually became harder and harder . . . No one was allowed out on the street after 9 p.m. any more. Once she took me down to the street, to the door, and said, 'How long it is since I have even seen the night sky' . . . Once towards evening she went secretly with another resident to the nearby Fürstenhof [one of Leipzig's grandest hotels] and ate chicken with rice. The waiter recognised her, but did not blink an eye, and served her most courteously. That did her good.

Annie was still a woman of considerable charm, and she made new friends in the *Judenwohnung*. She began to offer her guests cognac and drank with them, telling Lis to ask no questions about where she got it. Before too long, however, she had been moved again, to another Jews' House on Grassistrasse. A mere three streets away from her old flat and salon in Schwägrichenstrasse, this was more expensive – 100 marks a month, 'and that for a dreadfully tasteless oil painting in a "lovely gold frame",' Lis reported in disgust. 'Unfortunately she didn't win the battle to get rid of it. But the room was big and bright and looked out on the street.' She could still have visitors; Lis came to read to her in the evenings, and some of the other occupants came to listen, while Annie sewed or knitted for Uta.

Uta herself was enjoying better protective camouflage in Hanover. Carl Walter Kockel was Gentile and Marianne half-Gentile, and Uta could more easily be passed off as Aryan among their small children, who were not told that their cousin was three parts a Jew. Years later, Marianne would say that Pevsner and Lola had no real idea of the scale of the risk that she and Carl Walter were taking. C.W. had lost his university job because of his wife's half-Jewish parentage and some of his family were critical of his decision to shelter Uta. Early on, the Kockels were nearly caught out by an unexpected census; after much agonising, they entered Uta as 'visitor', and repeated this description on the police registration forms that were needed in order to draw rations. From then on, they would live in a state of continual suspense.

Five hundred miles away across a blockaded sea, Pevsner and Lola were largely oblivious. All they were officially permitted was an exchange of twenty-five-word messages, once a month, on Red Cross forms. On rare occasions – as on Hugo's death – they managed to exchange longer letters, apparently sent via relations of Lis in neutral Switzerland, but it was a risk they could not take too often, and not at all if it might draw attention to Uta.

All Pevsner could do at this point was continue his increasingly urgent search for a job. *Academies of Art* was due to be published, at last, that spring. Meanwhile he had made what was to be one of the most important contacts of his life in George Francis Troup Horne, Clerk to the Governors of Birkbeck College, who would appear to have suggested to the authorities at Birkbeck that, at a time when so many staff were being called up, Pevsner would be highly suitable as a lecturer.

Birkbeck was not a typical university college, having started life in December 1823 as London's first Mechanics' Institution, dedicated to the education of working people. By 1858 it was providing university education for people who could not afford to study full time, in a wide range of subjects besides technical and vocational skills, and thirty years later it had moved into the premises in Breams Buildings, between Fetter Lane and Chancery Lane, which it occupied in 1940. By the time Pevsner was introduced to it, Birkbeck was a school of the University of London, teaching only evening and part-time students.

The lecture he proposed to Birkbeck for February 1940 was on 'Enjoyment of Architecture', for which his manuscript notes survive.[9] It is interesting that, given free rein, he should have chosen this subject, and he wrote out the introduction in full:

There are not many among us who can say that they really enjoy architectural values, and of those who do, a good many would not know what they are, and what exactly it is they are enjoying . . . Architecture is the abstract amongst visual arts, as music is the abstract among acoustic arts. In drama your intellect is kept busy, in painting too. But in architecture and music it is left to ramble unless you can by instinct or effort keep it silent and let other spiritual faculties be on the alert . . . Satisfaction such as that which some of you may feel in entering the first court at Hampton Court, or walking up the grass slope towards Ken Wood or traversing the front colonnade of Osterley Park, will as a rule not be analysed and perhaps not even felt consciously. It is my aim . . . to put into words – very sketchily, of course – what it is we feel in looking at architecture.

What he had in mind, typically enough, was less an evocation of emotion than a practical guide to visiting buildings for pleasure. Look at architecture, he suggested, as you might listen to German *Lieder*. In a song, the text will help you, and in an opera the staging; there are similar hints in architecture, alongside the purely architectural values, which are, on the whole, the hardest to follow. Be alert for gestures that express style and mood – fantasy, as at the Tudor country house of Compton Wynyates, with its minstrels' gallery and Masonic symbols; the paradoxical combination of romance and realism in Durham Cathedral; surprise effects, like that of the dome of St Paul's Cathedral towering over narrow, winding streets below; aspiration, as at Salisbury, a 'Gothic Excelsior'.

'Almost all architectural qualities can be reduced to a very few basic components – just as in music,' he claimed. 'The architect then achieves an infinite variety of expression by their interaction' – and he proposed to supply a checklist of these components. Weight, for example: 'heavy' means that horizontal elements are dominating a façade, 'light' that vertical elements are dominant. 'Direction' means swift and uninterrupted passage of the eye upwards, forwards; 'calm' means stillness of the eye. Speed of movement, curve and symmetry can all be categories that help to unlock and illuminate the composition and character of a building. Nor should one overlook how separate features and individual buildings fit together – how the exterior of a building in a town becomes the interior of a street, for example.

The style, as well as the subject, drops strong hints of what was to come in the development of Pevsner's career in England. The prospect of addressing an intelligent but non-specialist audience at Birkbeck had prompted him to identify and demonstrate something he was good at – perhaps uniquely good. The lecture appears to have been well received, but there was no immediate response from Birkbeck to his tentative enquiries about a permanent job there, perhaps teaching a combination of art history with history or literature.* In the meantime, he turned with relief to a more familiar source of work in the *Architectural Review*, and a more reliable friend in Jim Richards.

Richards had at some point introduced Pevsner to Allen Lane, managing director of the dashing young publishing firm of Penguin Books, for whom Richards had written *An Introduction to Modern Architecture* in 1937. By 1939 Lane was looking to commission a single-volume history of European architecture for the Pelican subseries, and Richards was on the Pelican editorial board. The plans at this stage were vague, but the idea was planted. Richards's introduction was a generous one – and he supplemented it with more work for the *Review*. 'I need hardly say,' he wrote reassuringly to Pevsner, 'that [your position as an alien] does not affect us in the least. I only hope that by now you are not being made too uncomfortable by it.'[10]

In May 1940, Pevsner produced a splendidly illustrated article entitled 'Broadcasting Comes of Age: the Radio Cabinet 1919–1940', in which he returned to one of the *Enquiry*'s pet themes – the lamentable results of applying 'art' to machinery. Pevsner amused himself by compiling a pictorial record of 'radio sets through the ages', from machines with Gothic tracery on the sound panels to streamlined Bakelite objects resembling car radiators, designed to appeal to the 'engineering romanticism' of the twentieth century.

At the same time he had managed to sell a miscellany of pieces elsewhere. The *Museums Journal* took an item on 'Collections of Plaster Casts: the example of the new Royal Academy of Art at the Hague', while *Country Life* commissioned 'Style in Stamps: a century of postal design'.[11] For *The Studio* he wrote a series of short articles for a monthly series entitled 'Design Parade', which started to appear as a supplement in the magazine in April 1940.† Not surprisingly,

---

*Peter Murray claims, in *Proceedings of the British Academy*, Vol. LXX, 1984, that Pevsner put this proposal to the Master of Birkbeck, John Maud.
†SPSL 191/2, 31, 154. It seems that since 1938 Pevsner had been involved in discussions about publishing an illustrated bulletin on contemporary design. There was a scheme to launch a new arts magazine early in 1939 and he felt the bulletin might be incorporated in it. But it became clear that the magazine would only come into existence if he were prepared to edit it, and he could not combine the job with his responsibilities at Gordon Russell. He seems to have taken the idea of a bulletin to the *Studio* instead.

the articles are peppered with reminders of wartime conditions. An elegantly curved sewing chair he hoped would be used for 'the knitting of comforts', and of a selection of butter dishes he observed, 'The present size corresponds to the present ration.' Comparing a variety of curtain materials, he singled out 'a folk-weave of subdued colourings . . . very cleverly woven to obtain a black ARP-proof back . . . You can therefore simply hang these "Stranraer" curtains as they are and yet not become a thorn in the flesh of your Air Raid Warden.'

Not all his choices were utilitarian, however, and many of his old favourites featured in the parade: a fireside chair from Gordon Russell, combining strength, comfort and 'a certain as it were plump grace', and Isokon's ingenious Penguin 'donkey', to hold a single row of paperback books above a shelf for magazines. The Alvis sports saloon car that he had admired in the *Enquiry* appeared here in its new 4.3-litre version, and the wooden toys made by the Abbatts with whom he had argued about politics in 1934.* There are echoes of his regard for Charles Holden's London Underground stations in his praise for the model stations of the Trix Station Set, with its forty-five homogeneous and interchangeable units. 'Good and straightforward as the carriages of toy railways generally are in their design,' he mused, 'the stations as a rule still bristle with Victorianisms to fill with delight the hearts of Mr John Betjeman and the Betjemanites.' Toy trains, plaster casts, stamps, butter dishes – Pevsner's Phoney War seemed resolutely mundane.

---

*See Chapter 13.

CHAPTER 20

Internee 54829

Two months later, in mid-1940, Pevsner was detained as an enemy alien.

Over the previous five years he had modified his political opinions, and accepted that what was happening in Germany could not be regarded as a passing phase. On a personal level, however, he was still loyal to Wilhelm Pinder – a dangerous constancy, as Pinder was by now widely perceived to be a Nazi stalwart.

After the departure of A.E. Brinckmann (editor of the *Handbuch der Kunstwissenschaft* series) from the chair of art history in Berlin in 1935, Pinder had been happy to step into it. Although in November 1933 Pinder had signed an academics' 'Profession of Faith' to Hitler and the Nazi state, he had not always toed the party line. He had championed the work of the Bauhaus as the most recent exemplar of a true German style, and was vehement in his denunciation of the 1933 racist tract 'What is German in German art' by Nazi art historian Kurt Karl Eberlein.* 'Hysteria is not true strength,' he wrote, condemning the pamphlet as a 'hymn of hate'. 'If you translated these words into line drawings, you would have . . . the worst form of the very thing that these rampant sentences attack – bad Expressionism . . . Expressi-onanismus.'

Initially, at least, Pinder tried to help his Jewish students.† As professor in Berlin, he was not above making jokes about the Nazis and their art, and he was attacked in the SS *Black Korps* magazine in 1940. But he also made radio broadcasts for the regime, and in 1939 on the fiftieth anniversary of Hitler's birth he had delivered a speech in which he maintained that the departure of Jewish art historians from Germany had got rid of 'over-theoretical thinking'.

This made his meeting with Pevsner at an art-historical congress in London that year an uncomfortable one – and yet when *Academies*

---

*Pinder championed the Bauhaus in *Reden aus der Zeit*, 1934. Eberlein would die on the Eastern Front towards the end of the war.
†He made sure, for example, that Ernst Kitzinger had a chance to finish his doctorate in Munich in 1934 before he was forced to leave the university. Kitzinger left Germany in 1935, and worked for a time at the British Museum on the Sutton Hoo burial. He was interned in 1940 and deported to Australia. On his release in 1941 he emigrated to the US, where he became Professor of Art History at Harvard.

of Art was finally published in May 1940 by Cambridge University Press, Pevsner chose to dedicate the book to his teacher: 'To W.P. in grateful and faithful remembrance of the past'. Pevsner persisted in thinking of Pinder as nationalist rather than Nazi, and a nationalist driven by a love of German art rather than by political belief.[1] But even if he had acknowledged Pinder to be a Nazi collaborator, he might well still have felt that this dedication was something he had always planned to make, and something he owed to his former mentor.

Many scholars, both English and émigré, considered this was taking *pietas* too far, and the Pinder dedication is still held against Pevsner by some as a gesture of support for the Nazis.[*] His critics at the time were almost certainly unaware that in the eyes of the regime itself Pevsner was a clear opponent. If the articles he had written in 1934 were indeed attempts to align himself with the Nazi art establishment, they must be seen as failures; by October 1938 he had been cited in the National Socialist publication *Archiv für Buchgewerbe* as one of the proponents of a dangerous *Kunstbolschewismus* or 'art Bolshevism', for hailing the Expressionist artist Emil Nolde as 'the most important figure among today's German painters'.[2] Now, in 1940, this earned him a place in the infamous Nazi 'Black Book' or *Sonderfahndungliste G.B.* (literally, 'Special Search List, Great Britain) – the list compiled in May by Walter Schellenberg, chief of Germany's counter-espionage bureau, of 2,820 people to be taken into 'protective custody' in the event of a German invasion of Britain.

The Black Book contained a peculiar mixture of anti-Nazis, pro-Nazis and neutrals – genuine political opponents of the regime alongside people who might simply be useful hostages against seized German assets. Lady Astor and Lord Baden-Powell were on the list, with cartoonist David Low and Vera Brittain, Sigmund Freud (who had actually died the previous year), Virginia Woolf, E.M. Forster, Stephen Spender, C.P. Snow, J.B. Priestley, H.G. Wells and all the Huxleys. As Rebecca West remarked to fellow-listee Noël Coward, 'My dear, the people we should have been seen dead with.' Pevsner appeared in the list as 'Prevsner [*sic*], Nikolaus', under the heading of 'internal security dealing with cultural, artistic and scientific matters', rather than simply as a Jew – which is how the publisher Victor Gollancz appeared – or an opponent of the regime, in the

---

*One of the more moderate comments was made by Robert Goldmark of New York University in *The Art Bulletin*, 23/3, June 1941: 'That Pinder (official head of Nazi art history) should be referred to (in a footnote) as "the greatest of living German art historians" is perhaps a matter of taste.'

same category as fellow art historians Edgar Wind, Rudolf Wittkower and Fritz Saxl.

Listing by the Nazis, however, did not save him from internment by the English. He had applied for naturalisation early in 1938, as soon as he had received his unconditional residence permit. For naturalisation to be granted, the applicant had to have been in possession of this unconditional permit for at least a year. By the end of February 1939 Pevsner had satisfied that condition, but the bureaucratic process was frustratingly slow, and it had not been completed when war was declared.* For official purposes, Pevsner remained an alien.

Suspicion of foreigners had been spiralling upwards long before the formal declaration of war. Thomas Mann wrote drily of his experience at a 'remote and camouflaged' London Airport when he was trying to return to America in the summer of 1939. He was working on *Lotte in Weimar* at the time, and carrying a copy of the manuscript with him through customs. The inspecting officers were particularly suspicious of a sketch representing the seating arrangement at a dinner that Goethe had given in his house on the Frauenplan in Weimar in honour of a childhood sweetheart. It was suspected of being of strategic importance, and Mann had to deliver a short lecture on the novel in order to convince the officials that the document was blameless.

The War Office, which had started planning for internment in 1938, saw it as a military operation over which they would naturally exercise control. The Security Service, or MI5, took a similarly hard line. The émigré community, it considered, was almost certainly already seeded with spies – or, even if actual spies were few in number, the remainder of the community might easily be 'turned', or at the very least provide cover for suspect new arrivals. 'SIS have ascertained,' wrote Guy Liddell, Head of the B or Espionage Division, 'that the Gestapo are putting a "J" on the passports of agents who they want to get into this country.'[3] Internment would be far cheaper and more convenient than the constant effort to monitor and control the movements of aliens, which was an irritating distraction from serious counter-espionage. The onus would be on those detained to show why they should be released.

The Home Office took a marginally more liberal view, insisting that suspects should at least appear in front of tribunals before detention, and it was the Home Office that initially had the upper hand in the battle between departments. By the end of September 1939 tribunals

---

*On a wartime list of internees at Huyton Camp 'who have applied for a certificate of Naturalisation and whose applications are still under consideration' appears the name 'Peisner, Nicolaus [*sic*] 54829'. PRO HO 215.

had been set up to examine the credentials of every registered alien over the age of sixteen. Pevsner and Lola both appeared before the Gloucestershire Tribunal on 12 October.

Of almost 74,000 people examined, only 700 fell into the highest category of risk. Some, like the crews of captured German ships or known Nazis such as the man who had been Ribbentrop's legal adviser, were indeed very dangerous. All were interned at once. About 9,000 others, who were not refugees from the Nazi regime but, as long-term residents, could produce some evidence of loyal intent towards Britain, were not interned but were forbidden to travel or to sign on at the labour exchange. By far the largest proportion – Pevsner and his wife among them – fell into Category C; they were considered no risk to security. The Pevsners, however, were not granted the status of 'refugees from Nazi oppression'. '. . . Claims was lecturer in history of Art, Gottingen University,' reads the report, 'dismissed on account of Jewish blood, this he denies.'* Pevsner may have denied that he had Jewish blood; or he may simply have denied that this was the reason for his dismissal. Either way, to the tribunal the case was not clear-cut, and the classification was 'non-refugee' in Category C, subject to no restrictions.

With the German invasion of Denmark and Norway in April 1940, however, the Phoney War came to an end. The British Joint Intelligence Committee officially attributed the fall of Norway to the activities of 'Fifth Columnists', and unease mounted about 'the traitor within'. On 10 May, the Blitzkrieg attack launched by Germany against Holland and Belgium moved at an unprecedented pace, suggesting to many that the invaders were being helped by refugees admitted by Holland in recent months. An official memorandum on 'Operations in Holland' spoke of German parachutists helped by compatriots living there to infiltrate Dutch defences, disguised as cyclists, priests, peasants, schoolboys and nuns. Now it seemed that Britain would be the next target for invasion, and unease about aliens turned into something resembling full-scale panic. 'Nearly everyone . . . is latently somewhat anti-semitic and somewhat anti-alien,' a Mass Observation report noted. 'But ordinarily it is not the done thing to express such

---

*This information actually appears in a report on the classification of *Tom* Pevsner as a 'non-refugee' in Category C, shortly after his 16th birthday and his registration as an alien. The document, 'Regional Advisory Committee. Appeal Decision. Thomas Pevsner', PRO/HO/396/400, forms part of the 'Internees Index: Internees at Liberty in UK' kept by the Aliens Department of the Home Office. It is to be found online in the *Moving Here* database.

sentiments publicly. The news from Holland made it quite the done thing all of a sudden.'

To deal with the threat, both external and internal, the inter-departmental Home Defence (Security) Executive or Swinton Committee was set up, with wide powers over internment. The committee brought the War Office, MI5, and MI6 into action alongside the Home Office, and its establishment marked a significant toughening in policy. On 12 May, the Home Secretary John Anderson ordered the internment of all alien males in coastal areas; elsewhere, all aliens had to report daily to the police and were forbidden to use cars, lorries or bicycles. On 14 May, the Local Defence Volunteers (later renamed the Home Guard) were set up. Around this time Marylebone Borough Council sacked seventeen aliens doing ARP (Air Raid Precautions) work. 'The idea of Germans taking charge of Britons in an air raid is grotesque,' expostulated one alderman, 'particularly as it is ten chances to one that the man dropping the bomb is his cousin.'[4]

On 16 May, all Category B men were interned. Suddenly the numbers of internees had jumped from hundreds to more than 10,000, and camps began to multiply. One-fifth of these men had lived in England for more than twenty years, and one would reflect on this bitterly:

> We have been Hitler's enemies
> For years before the war.
> We knew his plans of bombing and
> Invading Britain's shore,
> We warned you of his treachery
> When you believed in peace,
> And now we are His Majesty's
> Most loyal internees.*

By 20 May, German troops had reached the Channel coast of France. Two days later the House of Commons passed an extension of the Emergency Powers Act: 'It is necessary,' explained Clement Attlee, the newly appointed Lord Privy Seal, 'that the Government should be given complete control over persons and property.' This control extended to life and death: while British citizens were already subject to the High Treason Act of 1351, non-citizens were now bound by a

---

*The verse was written by an internee who was subsequently deported to Hay Camp in Australia. Quoted in Freimut Schwarz, 'Kulturarbeit in den englischen Internierungs-camps', in H. Krug and M. Nungesser (eds), *Kunst im Exil in Großbritannien 1933–1945* (Fröhlich & Kaufmann,1986), p.283.

new Treachery Act, which prescribed the death penalty for 'any act which is designed or likely to give assistance to the naval, military or air operations of the enemy'.*

By 24 May it was clear that the British Expeditionary Force was cut off in a pocket of land around the port of Dunkirk on the Normandy coast, and on 26 May, hours before the fall of Belgium, a flotilla of small ships started arriving to take the troops off the beach. At this point the instruction was given to intern all women in Category B. Before the week was out, Sir Neville Bland, British Minister to the Dutch Government, had issued solemn words of warning on the BBC: 'Be careful at this moment how you put complete trust in any person of German or Austrian connections. If you know people of this kind who are still at large, keep your eye on them; they may be perfectly all right – but they may not.'

By 4 June the British rearguard had been withdrawn from Dunkirk, but in the weeks that followed the number of small air raids on the coast of Kent and Sussex increased. On 14 June, the Germans entered Paris. Across the Channel, roadblocks were being put up in the English countryside, road signs taken down. An invasion now seemed imminent. On 25 June all male Germans and Austrians living outside London, and all those in London who had neither refugee status nor jobs, were interned; this accounted for most of those in Category C. The remainder enjoyed two more weeks of freedom until 10 July, when the Battle of Britain started and the order was given to 'collar the lot'.

Some could not endure the prospect of incarceration. One professor of chemistry, who not long previously had spent time in a German concentration camp, took poison; an Austrian couple, fearing separation, killed themselves in Richmond Park. Pevsner faced it and was taken, though it is not clear precisely when.

On 13 July, the CID walked into Hampstead Public Library at lunchtime and asked all Germans and Austrians studying there to accompany them to the station, but by then Pevsner had been gone for almost a fortnight, probably detained at the end of June as an alien resident in London without refugee status. Lola was left without him in Wildwood Terrace.†

At the outset, the War Office was in charge of administering and

---

*Seventeen people would be executed under this act during the Second World War.
†Miriam Kochan has described the illogicality of internment policy where women were concerned. Generally speaking, only women in Category B were interned, while men in all three categories were taken. 'Women's Experience of Internment' in D. Cesarani and T. Kushner (eds), *The Internment of Aliens in Twentieth-Century Britain* (Frank Cass, 1993), pp.147–66.

guarding all internment camps, as it had wanted to be. Liaison with policy-makers in the Home Office was poor and, without any real intent to demean or deprive, conditions in the camps ranged from fair to squalid.* In many cases, the buildings themselves were to blame, as internees were crowded into spaces designed for entirely different purposes – the lion and elephant houses in the winter quarters of Bertram Mills' Circus outside Ascot; the Olympia exhibition hall in Kensington; a variety of holiday camps (a move made by an authority lacking a sense of irony); and, in Bury, a disused cotton mill standing by a stagnant canal, reeking of lubricating oil and latrines. With sixty buckets provided for 2,000 people, as Professor Paul Jacobsthal observed, 'You could see men of European reputation in an act which is normally not performed in public.'[5]

For Pevsner, the first stop was the Tote buildings at Kempton Park race course in Surrey, some fifteen miles from London. He sent Lola the non-committal standard form letter which was all that was permitted – 'I am well and will let you have my future address later. Nika Pevsner' – but commented later, 'A wide view, but gloomy dirty large rooms, bad and irregular food, nasty officers and a deep depression. The sudden shock of having become a dangerous disliked alien was hideous.' He was then moved under armed guard to Liverpool, to be one of hundreds of internees occupying three camps at Huyton on the outskirts of the city.

They were accommodated in Woolfall Heath, a newly built housing estate, and the local MP was prompted to complain that enemy aliens were going into smart new housing while British workers still lived in slums. However, the contractors' huts were still up, rubble was strewn everywhere, and Pevsner went first into a makeshift tent encampment, sharing a small canopy with three other men, 'two duds, but one . . . an upright German with blue eyes, about 55, interned in the last war, a small business man, a thoroughly good sort and the right man for a tent. Also you could lie in the grass and enjoy the sun.' The camps themselves consisted of only around seven streets of houses each, and Pevsner was fortunate to be allocated to a house quite soon. 'Providence rules one's life to an incredible extent – it's quite new to me.'

He had been luckier than he knew, as at this point he could quite easily have been deported. Even before the internment of Category C aliens, it had become obvious that the available camps would be

---

*Angus Calder points out that conditions were not always worse than they would be in many of the rest centres provided by local authorities for British citizens made homeless by the Blitz. *The People's War: Britain 1939–45* (Cape, 1969), p.189.

inadequate, and by the end of June deportations to the colonies had started; papers at the Public Record Office suggest that the original intention was to deport the great majority of internees. On 2 July, the *Arandora Star*, on her way to Canada, was sunk off the west coast of Ireland; of the 1,190 Germans, Italians and other aliens on board, more than half were drowned, many having been unable to reach the lifeboats because of the partitions of barbed wire erected on the main deck to contain them. Eight days later a large contingent of internees from Huyton were among the 2,500 passengers crammed on to the *Dunera*, sailing very much against their will from Liverpool to resettlement camps in Australia.* Pevsner was well placed to judge how easily he could have been travelling with them. As the *Dunera* was sailing, he was working in the registration and index office as a clerk, infuriated by the disorder and well aware of the element of chance in who stayed and who went.

On balance, therefore, he was grateful to be Internee 54829, of 38 Belton Road, AIC Huyton, but conditions there were far from congenial. The Commandant, it was reported, was an old colonel who organised and reorganised his guards and liked occasionally to surround a house and storm it, to keep the troops up to the mark.[6] The houses were so newly finished that they did not even have wallpaper, let alone heating or furniture. Their occupants had to stuff sacks with straw to make palliasses for beds, and there were blankets but no sheets, and no shelves or hooks; the baths were stained and full of plaster dust, and there was no hot water. Soap, razor blades and needles could be had for a price, but for weeks there were no cleaning materials or medical supplies, and lavatory paper or even newspaper was scarce. With a significant proportion of the internees over fifty or even sixty, many were in poor health; when Pevsner arrived, there had been two recent suicides.

Though a large majority of inmates were Jews, the Huyton camps housed men of all faiths and political persuasions. Some actually were rabid pro-Nazis, or men whom it was reasonable to suspect of pro-German sympathies, such as Captain Franz von Rintelen, who had been Germany's most active spy in America during the First World War. Others were people who had risked their lives in active opposition to the Nazi regime. Some were Aryan Germans who had lived in England for years but had not been naturalised, although their children were now serving in the British army. Others were orthodox Jews from

---

*Conditions on the *Dunera* were abysmal and became a scandal, which as late as 1986 prompted the film *The Dunera Boys* starring Bob Hoskins.

recently invaded countries who could speak only Yiddish or broken English. Some had already been interned in England in 1914; others, more recently, had been in Dachau and Buchenwald.

There was a disproportionate number of academics and professionals. A survey conducted by the inmates of another camp – Onchan, in the Isle of Man – revealed that of 1,491 internees, 121 were artists or writers, 113 scientists or teachers, 235 lawyers, engineers, doctors, dentists or clergymen. (Two-thirds, incidentally, had applied to join the British government service, the army or the Pioneer Corps.) The composition of the Huyton community was much the same – and, perhaps unsurprisingly, it was very soon highly organised amidst the dirt and discomfort. Each camp developed its own internal economy and labour market. Some internees earned money by letting others bathe in their houses, some collected the wood that was needed to heat this water. One man sold advice on how to get to Brazil as a refugee; another, 'a very academic fellow', built his own stove, collected herrings that had been taken from a captured German ship in Liverpool, smoked them and sold them as the German speciality *Bückling*.

Not everyone welcomed this degree of systematisation. One man interned on the Isle of Man complained that it felt like 'living again in the better periods of the Weimar Republic . . . There was an army of bureaucrats running the post office, the bank, the library, the workshops.'[7] Competition for jobs was intense, and status jealously guarded. There was some behaviour 'in the worst German tradition' – intensely political, with mock elections and debates – and a good deal of snobbishness, with intellectuals insisting on saluting each other as 'Herr Doktor' or 'Herr Professor'.

Unsurprisingly, Pevsner was irritated by this posturing. 'One should promote human kindness here,' he wrote, 'instead of all this vacuous bureaucracy and wholly unrealistic busybodying.' Nor was he comfortable in an overtly émigré society. Faith was not particularly an issue. Although it involved keeping his hat on for meals, he ate in the Kosher Eating Hut because that housed the Vegetarian Table, where he felt he got 'a little more vitamins'. He found the orthodox community unfamiliar rather than antipathetic: 'It is anthropologically really interesting, though sad. And they are quiet and not as noisy and greedy as the big marquees where most other people eat. The faithful ones are always a good sort.' It was the constant nostalgia for 'life back home' that he resisted. Some of the inmates found internment a kind of 'German holiday', 'a complete relapse, after short and imperfect acclimatisation, into former language and habits, bowing and introduction . . . The German past, which during the last years had sunk to the bottom of consciousness, came to the surface again. It was pleasant to conjure up reminiscences of childhood and later life, to talk of people and places in Berlin . . . to call up Göttingen and Marburg, Bonn and Heidelberg.'[8]

'I do not feel the massed tangle of barbed wire as a moral grievance,' wrote Pevsner, 'nor the sentries with their bayonets, just as bored as we are. What I suffer from is this "we" which I try to avoid. I do not want to be a "we" with 90% of the people here. But I will not tell you of the unpleasant ones, as there are a good many well worth knowing and being friendly with.'[9]

A few he already knew in person or by repute. One was a former customer of Gordon Russell, another the Old Harrovian nephew of a family called Regendanz, friends from London.* Ernst Gombrich's father was in Huyton, though Gombrich himself was exempt, as he had got a job monitoring German broadcasts for the BBC at the Caversham listening post. The painter Richard Ziegler – 'serious, a fine face, eccentric' – became a good friend, and the choreographer and modern dance guru Kurt Joos was an influential figure in the street.† 'An excellent man,' declared Pevsner, 'just as good at his job as in stoking the kitchen fires, milking cows (so he says) and cleaning dirty plates . . . Under Joos' fathership we get raw cabbage (excellent!), raw carrots etc.', though he could do nothing about the bromide that went into every cup of tea or coffee. 'Makes you awfully sleepy,' Pevsner complained. 'It is supposed to be necessary because of sexual desires. Maybe . . .'

He was lucky to find his first housemate supportable. Ralph Beyer was a much younger man, a sculptor and son of the Dresden art historian Oskar Beyer. He had come to England in 1937, aged sixteen, to study first with Eric Gill and then at the London Central School of Arts and Crafts. Now, at nineteen, he was married with a new baby. The British authorities who came for him had given him half an hour to pack. 'Married, untidy, poor but serious and *wertvoll* [sound],' Pevsner informed Lola, and the two of them lived quite congenially in exclusive occupancy of their semi-detached house in Belton Road. They remained on surname terms for some time, but Pevsner showed a fatherly concern for Beyer's family worries, and they had a good deal of common ground for conversation, conducted entirely in English.

---

*Wilhelm Regendanz (1882–1955) was a Berlin banker who had been associated with Ernst Röhm, commander of the *Sturm Abteilung* and vocal critic of the slow pace of the nationalist revolution under Hitler. Röhm was shot during the Night of the Long Knives in 1934 and Regendanz fled to England shortly thereafter.
†Other artist internees included John Heartfield, Martin Bloch and Samson Schames.

Although Pevsner had not met Oskar Beyer, he was aware of his work on contemporary church art and architecture, and he was an admirer of Eric Gill. 'We had endless discussions about correct English, and about sculpture, of course,' Beyer remembered. 'Talked a bit about Germany – didn't discuss politics – we were diplomatic.' The artist did some drawing and some carving in soap, the scholar a good deal of reading. They did not, perhaps, see eye to eye about cleaning – 'he was very painstaking,' Beyer remembered with just a touch of exasperation, fifty years later. 'The austere life seemed to suit Pevsner,' he observed. 'We used to go out in the back garden – he'd say "Let's go out for half a bottle of landscape."'

In Oxford alone, the trawl for internees had netted at least twelve professors with research posts in the Bodleian Library, Pitt-Rivers Museum, Warneford Hospital, Balliol, All Souls, most supported for the last five years or so by the Academic Assistance Council. After years of repression in Germany and relative obscurity in England, many were ready to lecture at the drop of a hat, and were happy to organise courses as a service to fellow-inmates. Paul Jacobsthal, a lecturer in Celtic art at Christ Church from 1937, was interned in Cowley Barracks, where he found himself surrounded by 'ghostlike professors, selling their old German stuff again after the years that they had been muzzled'. One lectured on 'his experiment on the influence of lightning on metal, illustrated by slides', while another wrote an entire history of Zionism on lavatory paper.

Pevsner was sceptical of the arrangements in Huyton. 'The "town" has organised a lecture programme,' he wrote on 1 August, 'far too big and pompous – a lot of *Leerlauf* [idling in neutral] . . . A few people *will* organise and are – I am not joking – planning a Huyton Yearbook of academic standing. It is all too surreal and ghostly' – and he preferred to set up a less formal scheme of his own. Papers in the Public Record Office in Kew refer to a 'Huyton College' being run under the direction of 'a former university administrator . . . Dr Pevsner'.[10]

With help from the new officer in charge, with whom he was 'well in' – 'a charming Oxford fellow, now chief agent to Lord Aberdare's estates' – Pevsner was moved, with Beyer, to new lodgings that he could use as a schoolhouse. 'The College', with lettering by Beyer, was, he wrote, 'the nicest house in the whole place'. 'I can sit in my window and look out and become quite still,' he continued. 'To the left, only a few yards from the corner of my house, the cornfield . . . In the distance behind the cornfield there are fields, some farm houses, a shed with a tiled roof. The lane connects my eyes with the world. Cars and

Hugo Pevsner *c*.1920:
a father ever conscious of his Russian roots.

Annie Pevsner, with Nika and his
older brother Heinz, 1902.

Nika at the age of six.

Lis Knauth: piano teacher
and lifelong family friend.

Lola's mother, Paula Neisser, *c.* 1890, middle row, second from left.

Lola's father, Alfred Kurlbaum: Supreme Court lawyer, photographed in the 1920s.

Lola (left) and her sister Marianne at the family home in Naumburg, *c.* 1916.

'Exacting freshman':
the student Nikolaus Pevsner.

Wilhelm Pinder,
Pevsner's *Doktorvater*,
controversial then as now.

Parenthood: Lola and Nikolaus Pevsner
with Uta in Leipzig, 1924.

At home in Germany:
Dresden 1925, Pevsner and
Lola playing with Uta.
Göttingen, *c*. 1930, Uta and
Pevsner on the ice.

Two of Pevsner's 'escapades':
Margot, 1924; Lise, *c*. 1930.

Doktor Pevsner, 1927.

Privatdozent:
a 'sculpture' made in
honour of *Meister* Pevsner
by one of his Göttingen
pupils, Georg O. von
Wersebe, as part of the
spoof *Festschrift* for his
thirtieth birthday in 1932.

Tom Pevsner,
German schoolboy,
c. 1934.

Passage to England:
Muriel, Enid,
Palliser and
Rosalind Barkas
in Germany in 1934.
It was through
the Barkas family
that Pevsner met
Francesca Wilson,
his passport
to a new life.

Francesca Wilson:
indomitable Quaker, friend of the refugee.

Enquirer into industrial design:
Pevsner in Miss Wilson's garden
at 35 Duchess Road, Edgbaston.

John Fletcher, Pevsner's
first host in Hampstead.

The children left behind in Germany:
Uta, Dieter and Tom, *c*. 1935.

Pevsner's mother, Annie, in 1938.
Forced, like all Jewish women in
Leipzig, to take the second name
'Sarah', she was obliged to live in a
Judenwohnung or Jews' House at
König-Johann-Strasse 30, where
she killed herself just before she
was due to be deported.

Huyton Camp, Liverpool, where in 1940 Pevsner was Internee 54829.

Wartime in Hampstead: Pevsner is third from the left, Lola beside him,
and Camilla Rodker next, in the centre.

vans pass, girls and families stare across a stile towards me. Children play. All this is happening as I write, and, later the buzz from two courses going on around me, one on phonetics, I think, and one on organised book reading.'

In the room that was his reward for organising the school, he constructed a desk – 'a blackout board on two apple boxes, quite neat' – and a chair of more boxes; he got hold of some flowers for the mantelpiece and luxuriated in the privacy. He had brought papers and notes into Huyton with him in order to continue some research into the status of the architect in the Middle Ages, but found it hard to concentrate on so specific a topic, limited perhaps by the fact that books brought or sent in for inmates tended to be confiscated (presumably for fear of coded messages) and the camp library was scanty. Soon, however, he was able to tell Lola that he was 'actually pottering about with something of wider appeal, to help in the new start' – 'wider appeal' being something of an understatement. Perhaps prompted by his introduction to Allen Lane in 1939, Pevsner was apparently considering an overview of European architecture of the kind that Lane had contemplated for the Pelican label before the war. 'He was working,' Beyer remembered later. 'He said to me that he thought there wasn't a short history in English of European architecture, so he'd do that.'

He was not tempted by the games of volleyball and football that were improvised. (The camp housed two international table-tennis champions, but no equipment.[11]) But he read novels – *Kenilworth* kept him going for some time – supplemented ordinary meals with apples and Marmite bought from the camp shop, went to the occasional play staged by inmates, and listened to music. The camps had gathered together a considerable number of musicians, both amateur and professional. 'It was moving,' remembered Paul Jacobsthal, 'when 50 unhappy men gathered in one of the narrow shabby rooms and listened to Professor Glas playing Bach, Mozart or Schubert on a worn-out piano.' Although Huyton was not as fortunate as the camp on the Isle of Man, which received two members of what was to be the Amadeus Quartet, it did have its own composer, Hans Gal, who subsequently wrote his 'Huyton Suite' for flute and two violins.* 'The everyday situation here is so gruesomely normal,' Pevsner complained. 'There is the odd good hour. What everyone suppresses, which is more tragic, is immeasurable. I hope I will not forget all this.'

In the meantime, he himself was skilful in concealing his feelings, both from his neighbours and from his wife. 'He was always cheerful,

---

*Siegmund Nissel and Peter Schidlof were interned on the Isle of Man.

I think I can say that with conviction,' Ralph Beyer recalled. 'He seemed to quite enjoy it.' 'So far I keep well and look tidy,' Pevsner reported unemotionally. 'I am sitting here at my little desk, space and stillness around me, I can see the outside world, a bit of scenery just like Germany – and it is only you and the future that haunt me.' Space, stillness, flowers on the mantelpiece, time for work and for reading novels – his intention was to reassure Lola that he was not unbearably miserable, but sensitivity was perhaps deserting him, for the life she was living in London without him was very different.

'Lola . . . is always quick to emphasise the negative rather than the positive,' Annie Pevsner remarked about her daughter-in-law in one of her letters to Pevsner that year. But the negatives were very real for Lola in the middle of 1940. Some were admittedly the product of her volatile temperament. 'I have my ups and downs as usual,' she would write later, 'ups when I look at the beautiful evening sky, downs when I look at myself.' But for the most part she presented a valiant figure – 'Lola, so respectable, so small and energetic' – in her struggles to deal with the shock of separation and the indignity of having been transformed into an enemy alien, on top of the day-to-day rigours of the Home Front.

She had always set high standards for herself, her family and her home, and she battled to preserve them, but the odds were against her. The blackout had been in force since September 1939, and all the windows in the tall, thin house on Wildwood Terrace had to be shrouded with curtains, black paint or brown paper and drawing pins. The terrace itself, always dark at night because of its position on the edge of Hampstead Heath, now had to be negotiated with extreme care in the pitch black, for fear of jutting branches, potholes or unexpected sandbags. Food rationing had been imposed in January, and Lola wrestled to make something appetising out of potatoes in the dim, cold kitchen which at the best of times had strongly resembled a cave.

Her household, too, had increased. Beside the boys, Pevsner's Aunt Sonya had turned up somewhat unexpectedly; the only space for her was a room right at the top of the house, with a roof that leaked so badly it was necessary to put up an umbrella over the bed. 'She was not intellectual nor specially intelligent,' Pevsner later recalled, 'and she had her curious traits. But we were very fond of her.' Sonya was producing knitted goods for Debenham's, and Lola delivered them; Sonya had a bad heart, so Lola carried all her meals to her room.

Lola had painful varicose veins now, which she concealed with thick stockings, and she was still prone to bouts of abdominal pain at moments of stress. These were more frequent with Pevsner away and money very tight – and her solution to the financial situation made even greater demands on her energy. She decided to take in lodgers: 'the tutor', a ginger-haired friend, someone from the *Daily Herald*. These were apparently short stays; but one was a more permanent fixture. Poet and publisher John Rodker made an improbable import to Lola's ordered, even bourgeois household, belonging, as Pevsner would write later, to 'the period of true Bohemianism, without the alloy of a private income'.*

Rodker was forty-six in 1940, the son of a Manchester corset-maker who had moved his family to the East End of London in 1900. Educated at the local Board School and the Jews' Free School, at fourteen he became a clerk, writing poetry in his free time. By 1913 he had become part of the East London group known as the 'Whitechapel Boys', alongside Mark Gertler and Isaac Rosenberg, contributing poems to *The Egoist* and A.R. Orage's *The New Age*, and had published his first volume of poetry in 1914, with a cover by David Bomberg.

Rodker was a member of the Young Socialist League and a confirmed pacifist, and at the outbreak of the First World War he became a conscientious objector and went on the run to avoid conscription or imprisonment. While in hiding at the home of the poet Robert Trevelyan, he became embroiled with writer and professional bohemian Mary Butts. Butts, born in 1890, already had a grudge against the world of convention, and more specifically against her mother, who had inherited a family home in Dorset containing a remarkable collection of drawings and watercolours by William Blake, but had seen fit to sell them both.† She left a female lover, Eleanor Rogers, for Rodker; shortly after their meeting, he was caught by the military authorities and sentenced first to imprisonment in Wandsworth, later to a period digging roads on Dartmoor. The couple married in 1918, and the following year Rodker set up a small publishing imprint known as the Ovid Press, largely underwritten by Butts's money and with her as a collaborator.

Short-lived as it was, the Ovid Press built up a remarkable list of titles: T.S. Eliot's *Ara Vos Prec* (1920), the anti-war poem *Hugh Selwyn Mauberley* by Ezra Pound (whom Rodker had succeeded as London

---

*According to his daughter Camilla Bagg, he was introduced to the Pevsners by translators Eric and Gwenda Mosbacher, who lived at 4 Wildwood Terrace.
†The Blake collection is now housed in Tate Britain.

editor of *The Little Review*, one of the most influential of all American little magazines), collections of drawings by Wyndham Lewis and Henri Gaudier-Brzeska, and a previously unpublished poem by Oscar Wilde.

In 1920 the Rodkers had a daughter, Camilla; shortly afterwards Mary left, taking the baby with her. The Ovid Press did not long survive the break, and Rodker moved to Paris. Here, in 1922, he distributed the second edition of James Joyce's *Ulysses* for Harriet Weaver's Egoist Press. Throughout the 1920s Rodker continued to publish – most notably the first English edition of Le Corbusier's *Vers une architecture* (1927)* and Pound's *Cantos 17–26* (1928) alongside his own novels, art criticism and memoirs of his wartime experiences. He had shared with Mary Butts a curiosity about sorcery and the occult, which was reflected in several of the books he edited or translated; other titles included Saikaku Ihara's *Comrade Loves of the Samurai* (1928) and his own translation of Jules Romains's *The Body's Rapture* (1933). Rodker also set up the Casanova Society to issue limited editions of classical, mostly French literature in new translations, until the Depression put paid to the prospects of expensive luxury editions. He declared bankruptcy in 1932 and temporarily abandoned publishing.

In 1940, Rodker was preoccupied with a project to publish the collected works of Sigmund Freud in the original German.† He was recently divorced from his second wife, Barbara Stanger McKenzie-Smith, and was an enigmatic figure in the household at 2 Wildwood Terrace. 'John Rodker was quiet and unassuming,' Pevsner would write years later, 'yet of great personal fascination and not without authority . . . a lady's man, with an odd, apparently irresistible, hang-dog appeal.'

He was managed by Lola, as were all members of her unwieldy ménage, through discipline and a ruthless routine. She kept her sewing box by her side, and as tea towels and shirts came out of the wash, she mended them on their way to the ironing board. Those around her were impressed and affectionate, but apprehensive for her health.

The neighbours at 3 Wildwood Terrace were some comfort. Geoffrey Grigson, who made his living less through his own verse than as a critic and inspired anthologist of others' work, had a notoriously bad temper and acerbic pen – what he described as a 'billhook' to be wielded against the pretentious, turgid or lame. Nonetheless, he was at this time a

---

*In a translation by Frederick Etchells under the title *Towards a New Architecture*.
†When Freud fled Vienna, the Nazis had burned all stocks of his published works. Rodker was working with Freud's daughter Anna to ensure that the works remained available, and set up the Imago Press for this purpose.

generous friend to the Pevsners. As he told it in his *Recollections*, he had made sure that Pevsner did not go into internment without something to read: 'When at last two hard-faced Bow Street runners arrived in the early hours of the morning to take [him] . . . I managed, clutching my pyjama trousers, to catch them up with the best parting present I could quickly think of, which was an elegant little edition, a new edition, of Shakespeare's Sonnets.' (Pevsner wrote of his first weeks in the reception centre at Kempton Park, 'Geoffrey's sonnets helped over odd hours.') Grigson continued to send book parcels from Evesham, where he was engaged in monitoring enemy broadcasts for the BBC. His first wife Frances Galt had died of tuberculosis not long before the war, and he had recently married a young Austrian girl, Bertschy Kunert. She remembered Lola as a tiny woman with dark hair, bright eyes and an enormous grin – not pretty, but full of life. Even then she had 'a rather wild air', and Bertschy, as another 'outsider', came to detect a good deal of unhappiness in Lola's situation.

Lola, she sensed, was still deeply distressed by leaving Germany, still felt intensely German, and was having great difficulty regarding herself as settled in England. As a little girl she used to say, '*Ich bin Preußin* / 'I am Prussian'; she encouraged the children to speak German at home, and she had minded desperately when Pevsner lost his German citizenship. On hearing that Bertschy was Austrian, she had said, 'I hope she is *proper* Austrian, not refugee.' She was willing to help refugees find lodgings or employment; she made great efforts at the start of the war to help the young Jewish portrait photographer Lucie Imbach, and eventually arranged for her to work for the Grigsons. But she did not identify with their plight and avoided the company of those who made much of being refugees. She also played down her Jewish roots, preferring to say that her father had 'had a preference' for Jews rather than that he had married one. (In the report of the internment tribunal which was presumably based on information supplied by Lola, she is described as Aryan.)

To Bertschy, she was a lonely and anxious figure, with her father and father-in-law not long dead, her mother-in-law in danger, and her daughter, who might have provided help and company, stranded in Germany and out of range of any but the most businesslike communication. She was worried about her sons' education, so high a priority for any German mother and a key component in successful assimilation. Tom was now almost fourteen, and his parents wanted to see him move to public school. Before the interlude at Chipping Campden Grammar School, he had been at a private prep school in St John's Wood – Arnold House – which had connections with Charterhouse. He had been accepted there, to go in the autumn term of 1940; but, on learning of Pevsner's internment, Charterhouse had withdrawn the offer. He had then applied to Sedbergh, Westminster and Highgate, and Lola was waiting anxiously to hear whether some arrangement could be made about the fees.

She toiled all day every day at labours that could have been halved at relatively little cost, washing endless quantities of sheets and towels by hand, and growing dangerously tired and overwrought. In this situation, the impression – however misleading it might have been – that Pevsner might be better off released from domestic pressures, might even be enjoying himself in a setting that sounded reminiscent of his university days, infuriated her. Not much was needed to turn ambiguity into full-blown misunderstanding, and the postal system to the camp duly obliged. In hindsight, Lola was able to diagnose what had gone wrong: 'Even the Government interferes with our most private problems because letters and the answers which are of so great importance get all old and stale.'[12]

The newly interned were not given the opportunity to write home for ten days, and in some camps were then only allowed to send two letters a week of twenty-four lines each. These were to be written on official forms, and the forms soon ran out, as they were made of a special paper that contained a hidden layer of chalk as protection against invisible ink, and the manufacturers had gone out of business when the owner and chief engineer were interned. A chronic bottleneck at the censorship office in Liverpool meant that letters from Huyton took more than two weeks to reach their destination. These first two weeks were often critical for men trying to save their businesses, keep in touch with relations threatened with deportation, make arrangements for emigration themselves or simply sustain their marriages, and the delay in their mail was destructive in the extreme. Studies of internment in Britain tend to focus on the ordeal of the internees, rather than on those they left behind them. Both sides of the Pevsners' correspondence during Pevsner's time in Huyton survive. The letters – written in English, according to the regulations – can now be read in chronological order.

The first surviving letter from Pevsner to Lola is dated 5 July 1940, and thereafter he let no more than two days go by without writing; but he could not afford to buy the supplementary forms that would have allowed him his usual long and discursive letters, and for two weeks not one of even these shorter messages reached her. By 11 July she was already beginning to sound despairing: 'I wish you would tell me all your troubles instead of hiding all your thoughts . . . I miss you terribly, I can not say more, all my thoughts go round in circles.' She promised to send him chocolate and books, informing him that she was changing from *The Times* to the *Telegraph*, to save the 6d that would be the price of one extra book: 'Of course they will always be Penguins.' 'I forwarded today critics [*sic*] from the *Listener* and the *Statesman* [most probably reviews of *Academies of Art*]. I think the censor must at least know what a famous man they have taken away from me . . . Damm it all! If I could only stop thinking of you . . .' Into the envelope she slipped a small crucifix, which her father had given her in 1915: 'Just a little remembrance.' It never reached him. A sad little letter from Tom reveals that they had still had no news a week later: 'Are you allowed to tell me all about where you are, what has been happening to you, how you are and what it is like? If so, why not (tell me, I mean) . . . We are all joining in to economise here. I have given up *Flight* and *Children's Newspaper* and swimming as far as possible. So that's 1/5d approximately a week or £3 10s a year . . . We are having our exams soon, but I don't care 2d whether I do well, or badly, or not at all.'

By 19 July, Lola must have received an early letter.* 'Your plan about my being interned sounds quite phantastic [*sic*],' she wrote. 'Fancy if they send you to Australia and me to Canada.' But he had failed to tell her any of the things she really wanted to know: 'Do you feel warm at nights? Do you take your drug? . . . Do you get vegetables? . . . Would you like to have your own knife, fork and spoon?' Nor, of course, under the eye of the censor could they discuss the anxiety uppermost in both their minds: for Annie, Uta, and their other friends and relations in enemy territory.

Lola knew Pevsner well enough to guess what he would find upsetting in his situation – 'I cannot help thinking of you being lonely under all these people you do not like' – and she promised to send cotton wool for earplugs. She was trying hard to soothe and sympathise – 'I wish you could do some of your research . . . or have they taken all your manuscripts away from you?' – but her own agitation was becoming increasingly pronounced, and her English grammar and spelling betrayed it:

Oh my dear, how long will it take till one gets used to be always procecuted . . . I am sure this time will teach me a lot, and gradually I shall no longer be frightened of writing to the Inspector of Taxes

---

*This letter, which was probably sent at the beginning of July, no longer survives; it may have been written at a point when the internment of women in Category C still seemed a possibility. The letter of 5/7/40 makes no reference to her own possible internment.

or elsewhere. But in bed I am so terrible alone. Why have they taken you away! I am reading Werther's *Leiden* [Goethe's *Sorrows of Young Werther*] again. What amount of sentiment! All beauty, every emotion makes him cry. And I can feel with him . . . I hope you get the feeling that I look properly after your children and your house . . . Live is passing by. I hardly feel alive at all. What do I live for. Just for the two boys. And to think of the future . . . I try to get used to the idea of our further home being in the slums.

By 24 July her depression had deepened to a pitch she had not experienced since 1933 'when everything broke down because of Hitler. Then I had Vati at least.' Now her father was gone, and she was struggling to cope in a house that she found ugly and uncomfortable. 'I am afraid you will never get my letters, as they are all mad and the censor might be upset. I am so sorry that I am so stupid that I seem not to be able to bear it, while you are so much better . . . Every policeman comes to fetch me.' At the bottom of the page, Lucie Imbach had added a pencilled note: 'Please don't worry about your wife. She is alright only sometimes we had to comfort her – but that is only naturally.'

Then another letter seems to have arrived in Wildwood Terrace, perhaps one of those in which Pevsner tried hard to put a brave face on his situation. He had decided that his release could only be achieved on the grounds of his academic standing. The notion incensed Lola. On 26 July, she wrote savagely:

I work for the 3 Paying guests from 7 to exactly 11 at night and spend not more than 3/6 a week, all the rest is done for *your* house and *your* children . . . I am in a state much worse than when we came over and very near suicide every night . . . The one thing I am longing for is morphium . . . The drug for the night helps me only till 5 or 6 and then I am awake in an awful state . . . And what for? For you! And you think everything is all right when you are at rest. And you even think I could enjoy myself. I know that you are always better, more clever, more charming. Everybody admires you. I am week [*sic*], nothing. Why can I not leave this world. All I suffer I have to suffer for your sake . . . I am certainly not sending Naumburg to you. That at least is mine and not yours. And for your sake I cannot be there again. Because I know that I shall not survive this war in spite of all kindnesses from all my friends here . . . Goodby and enjoy yourself being an important and most charming man in the camp.

While this missile was en route, Pevsner wrote her a letter on 1 August which makes it clear that he was totally unaware of the state she was in. He informed her that she could perhaps visit him, if she were to obtain a permit from the Chief Constable of Liverpool and the War Office, and requested that she strive for his release 'in spite of all the bother for you'. He did briefly commiserate with the stresses and strains of her life – 'I visualise you toiling away, the old ugly work, exhausting and none too satisfying, no change, no fun – oh may I be wrong!' – but he was now keeping up his pre-war habit of holding on to letters for a couple of days, to add instalments at intervals; this expression of sympathy would not reach her for more than a week, and in the meantime her sense of injury and isolation grew. 'I don't just want to feel sorry for you,' she wrote on 3 August:

> You know very well that I suffer much harder under these circumstances than other people, more than you too. And again I have my usual complexes that everybody despises me because of my temperament, and admires you because of yours . . . And no Vati to help me through these days of rage and despair. When I see a letter of yours I am absolutely shaking . . . John [Rodker] tells me that he never saw anything like it in his life before . . . Why are you always so perfect . . . Don't forget that I should be the centre of your life, not your rest . . . Schoolmaster. I wholy disapprove. It is only done for your sake. Is it for vanity's sake? Because they are so grateful? . . . Why not do your private work? . . . I am afraid that I will never get sane again.

Blissfully unaware of the depth of her bitterness and anger, Pevsner wrote her another chatty bulletin two days later. Another 500 men had arrived in the camp, and three more people had been billeted in the schoolhouse. Pevsner had, he said, been compelled to 'fight like a lion', shout and lock the door of the schoolhouse, to stop them inflicting four more on him. The camp, on the other hand, was now becoming almost too comfortable, in his view. 'It may do damage to public opinion, if people stop pitying us,' he wrote, sounding almost regretful at the loss of austerity. 'There is now a café and walks in groups outside the barbed wire (I don't do that) and a loudspeaker, and football etc.,' he blundered on, unaware that on this same day she was writing him what she called 'a very important letter from my part'.

'The last few days I have thought about you and your character,' she wrote on 5 August:

Why I am not happy with you at all and why it is possible that I want to revolt against you . . . You added the PhD to your sender's name because you felt so much the unknown soldier under a crowd which you yourself gave a name I cannot repeat . . . Now there came the change. You are now again adored, gratefully admired, important . . . You have done that without bothering for what I wish or not wish, though you easily will know what my feelings are. Have you ever been grateful to me? Have you ever thought that my life also will be hard. That what I do could be worth admiration? . . . And lately you have even added that politics are remote. 'Have you had air raids?' – exactly like 'fine day today' . . . Life for you must be in the sunshine of admiration. That is what you want from me. Why you talked incessantly of your things when I came back from a journey or you came back . . . I now realise that you are so much like your mother who suffered mainly under giving up her social work in '33. Vanity. You would never be able to think that other people might give something up for your sake. Might give up nearly everything. You have once given up when you joined Gordon Russell. But how often have I heard this. I must get freed. I can not depend so much on you mentally. That is all wrong. My life what it is now is lived only for your sake. I have lost everything which was pleasant for your sake . . . This means for me a krisis only compared with the one after Margot or Lise . . . You have always talked of duty to me. For duty's sake I have worked hard for the last years. For the children's sake to save money for their school, for your parents' sake to bring them over. For your sake because you could not find a better job I have even worked harder for the last 7 months. And you cannot give up to be important for my sake.

It was not long after this that Gertrud Bing, from the Warburg Institute, wrote to Esther Simpson, Secretary of the Academic Assistance Council, about Pevsner: 'His wife who was always a little strange seems to have lost her head completely.'[13]

On 6 August, Pevsner at last received the first indication that all was not well, when her letter of 26 July arrived. He was quick to respond: 'Was there a physical reason for that breakdown? . . . Look, Lola, honestly, believe me and talk it over with John in whose wisdom you believe – you must spend more . . . What you do now, being thoroughly dissatisfied with yourself, is in God's mind ten times more than my work here. Nobody, not I, not our friends, would have believed that you could run that house so successfully and all on your own. But please don't overdo it. It is unwise.' But he was still oblivious to the most acute and painful of her resentments, and his tone is maddeningly calm, even jovial. 'My sweet, NO – you must not think that I am happy, although I am of course trying to make the best of it,' he wrote on 9 August. 'There are these wretched attacks of libertitis – the sight of a normal motor car in the camp causing the feeling you must get in at once and be normal again . . . I had my first hot shower bath. Rather a lot of male nakedness about, but the first hot water for six weeks.' His school, he confided, was flourishing. He was offering nine English lessons a week, plus two lectures (in English) on the history of art, including 'the subject I had planned for Birkbeck College', and he had ambitions now to establish special classes for the growing number of boys in the camp; he himself would teach history, but other inmates would also offer instruction in calculus, machine design, bookkeeping and sports. He had already been allowed an escorted visit into Liverpool to buy books for this project with money sent in by the Quakers.

It was at this point that he received her devastating attack on the vanity of these projects – 'Schoolmaster. I wholly disapprove' – which angered as well as troubled him. 'More than by anything else, I am worried by your grief,' he wrote:

> To think that you are in such a state, and I stay here helpless. And even if I were with you, I know only too well your spite would go against me and neither against Hitler nor against those who have decided to intern me. That is illogical and cruel. Write what happens about my release, for God's sake . . . You answer as if letters did not take ten days. That is so wrong . . . I get that shock today – and if I answer as usual, my reply is in your hands 14–20 days after the outburst. No – I am only too careful not to let too much of these blasted depressions of mine get into letters . . . Would it help you to know that I cry all day long? Or to hear how restless and unhappy I am. My own work? I cannot concentrate – nobody can. If I make the best of it, why should I not?

More of his real feelings perhaps emerged in the melancholy little telegram he sent to Dieter to apologise for missing his eighth birthday: 'I WISH I COULD SEND YOU SOMETHING FROM HERE, BUT I CANNOT . . . IS IT NOT SILLY TO LOCK ME UP HERE.'

By this time, as a letter of 12 August reveals, Lola was becoming less frantic, but she was still irritated by his frequent instructions on how to secure his release. 'You need not give us any advice at all . . . John is my private secretary and what an enginious one . . . I really will not go to a committee and ask for money. Rather starve. Rather overwork myself.' But she ended this letter, 'Good night, love, love, love, in spite of your vanity.'

However, her 'very important' letter of 5 August had now reached Pevsner, deeply wounding him, and he was himself extremely angry. 'I am a little uneasy now as to how I should go on reporting to you what happens here,' he wrote tersely on 15 August. 'Do you realise anyway that you have not told me anything properly for some time? Your long letter was a lucid essay on my character, as expounded by one of my worst enemies, a remarkable mixture of truth and untruth. But it did not contain any details about things I had asked about more than once . . . Look, if there ever is a raid in London NW, mentioned in the papers, send wire, will you?' Lola might well have retorted that he was in more danger than she was. Although by day the Luftwaffe's bombs were concentrated on RAF airfields in the south of England, at night they were making sporadic raids on selected cities in the north, Liverpool among them.* But their shared anxiety did nothing to restore warmth.

On 21 August, Pevsner got her letter of 12 August and was finally goaded into showing his anger:

> Your last letter is more annoying than the earlier ones, because you write more calmly – and yet you say exactly the same. Why do I always have to be wise and not fall into a temper if I feel like it? . . . Your breakdown is not despair but hatred and dislike, going back at least partly to Lise . . . What can I do if you spit in every soup? . . . Take a broad view – look at the trees in front of the house and let them cure you, or listen to music, or see a good play, or go to church. But you don't want to – you're completely absorbed in your own self-pity . . . Would it be right of me to tell you about all the misery here? The censorship would not have allowed it. How could you expect me to be allowed to write if I hadn't been careful? . . . You are constantly, deliberately overworking, like a mad woman. How was I supposed to know when I wrote my first letters. I didn't even know until the Walls' first visit that you have PGs [paying guests]. Now do you think you were fair? And you dare to paint such a dreadful, malign character sketch of me? What comes out in the end is just the sort of type who is particularly odious here . . . What is the good of 'love, love, love' at the end of your letter when the contents are not despair but hatred . . . Love, love, love – can

---

*There were raids on the Liverpool docks on 3, 8 and 13 August.

that really be true? I don't believe it. And I know that in contrast to all those with whom I have contact here, the time after I return will be ugly. If only I could go back somewhere else and not be beside you there to experience those depressing first few weeks.

The following day he looked at this letter, dreadful in its bitterness, and did not relent: 'Like you, I think perhaps I shouldn't let you have all this – but as you do it to me, I shall do it to you.'

This letter contained some justification of his behaviour in Huyton. The job she so thoroughly condemned was his protection against deportation, just as his original appointment as a registration clerk had been. The 'school' was what entitled him to a room of his own, and privacy was all that was keeping him going: 'I must be able to walk up and down and suddenly lie down on my bed when I give in to despair.'

He was not overdramatising. Conditions in Huyton, though improved from the early days, were by no means as easy as he had chosen to suggest to Lola. As late as 28 August, *The Times* would carry a brief bulletin entitled 'Aliens' Sufferings in Huyton Camp: London Solicitor's Report'. Sir Waldron Smithers, MP, had sent to the Home Secretary a copy of a report he had received on the condition of aliens interned at Huyton Camp. The report opened bleakly: 'It is a long time since I can remember having spent a more miserable afternoon than I did on Tuesday at Huyton Camp.' In a covering letter Sir Waldron was quoted as saying that 'this report from a firm of solicitors of high repute made him absolutely ashamed of his country, and he asked if it was really necessary in this country to use Hitler's methods'.

In the time-lag before Pevsner's explanation reached her, Lola continued to snipe. On 23 August she wrote: 'Are you going to church? . . . Or are you feeling so much yourself again that you do not need it? . . . I am quite able to do things independently and quite clever too. You hurt me again, because you always want me to follow your plans . . . Please do *not* give any adwise. We know better here outside.'[14]

'We' now included John Rodker. A letter from Tom to his father refers to 'Uncle John' taking him to a concert at the National Gallery with the Griller Quartet. It also mentions Lola 'revelling next door till 12' with Rodker and others. Meanwhile, as the Battle of Britain reached its crisis in the last week of August, bombs fell on central London and on Liverpool, in five consecutive nights of raids. 'There are too many real tragedies about here,' Pevsner wrote, though he added drily, 'When I get your letters, I almost think I am one of them.' Gradually he and Lola stopped slashing and tearing at each other, and tried to focus on what they shared. 'It is over a year since Uta left,' Pevsner reflected. 'My desire to see and have her again grows worse. I feel so robbed of that good time in her development, don't you? . . . It is too wicked not to be with you just now . . . When shall we be together again?'

He was ashamed of the envy he felt for 'the fortunates' who were now starting to be released. 'One gets so wicked – I can hardly stand seeing them go,' he wrote on 27 August. Public opinion had been largely against mass internment by the time most Category C men were taken at the end of June, and the Academic Assistance Council helped to set up a system of appeals for the release of individual internees. Those under sixteen or over sixty, or in poor health, were the first to be freed; but among the other categories for consideration were 'persons of academic distinction with work of national import-ance'. Obviously it was here that Pevsner's best chance lay.

He certainly approached the Vice Chancellor of London University for help; and Gordon Russell later claimed 'some credit for the fact that otherwise one of our best art historians might well have found his way to Australia'.* But it seems likely that it was Frank Pick, Chief Executive of the London Passenger Transport Board and someone Pevsner had long admired, whose intervention – alongside representa-tions from the Master of Birkbeck College, Sir Frederick Kenyon of the British Museum, and Pevsner's old ally, J.A.R. Munro – was crucial in securing his release later in September.†

'I wish I were at home,' he had written sadly at the beginning of September. 'A bottle of hock and a walk with you in the Heath . . . The cornfield is now down, the sheafs still on the field. The first brown leaves appear on the trees. Sharp wind, rather bleak, and so many seagulls about. The first rabbit appeared too on the field – one year since I started marching from Campden to Broadway every day and back.' Less than two weeks later, leaving almost 20,000 other 'enemy aliens' still in captivity, he was free.

---

*Pevsner wanted to stress his potential usefulness, as a design expert, in promoting British exports, and proposed approaching other people eminent in the field of design – James Morton of Edinburgh Weavers, Josiah Wedgwood. Jack Pritchard and Kenneth Clark were also considered as sponsors.

†Pick is credited in the 'Acknowledgments' section of the *Enquiry*, as the Chairman of the Board of Trade Council for Art and Industry and guiding spirit of its 1935 and 1937 reports, one of the leading authorities on industrial design in the 1930s and, in his work at the London Passenger Transport Board, a patron of design as well as a theorist. He was also a near neighbour of the Pevsners, living round the corner at 15 Wildwood Road.

CHAPTER 21

'The year of change': 1941

At a low moment in Huyton, Pevsner had acknowledged his fears for the future, both to himself and to Lola. 'I dread it,' he had written on 1 August 1940, 'I dread the re-erecting of our wobbly building.' At least in internment he had known his place; when he came out there were no certainties, no status and no work. His marriage had been painfully jolted, his laboriously constructed livelihood had been demolished, his family was scattered – and he emerged in mid-September into the realities of the London Blitz.

On 7 September 1940, the Luftwaffe had begun day- and night-bombing. By October bombs were falling on London most nights. Large numbers of people left the city during September to take refuge in the Home Counties. The Pevsner boys went back to Chipping Campden, but Pevsner and Lola were, in Francesca Wilson's phrase, 'altogether in the thick of it', along with their paying guests.

The Grigsons had now moved out of their *pied à terre* at 3 Wildwood Terrace; returning one evening to clear some possessions, Bertschy found a tramp in the basement, and fled next door. With the sirens beginning to sound, the Pevsners, with John Rodker and another lodger, Herr Meier, were just sitting down to liver and curly salad, with apple fritters – a menu that might have been designed to the instructions of the wartime Radio Doctor, Charles Hill, who had extolled offal, not on the ration, as 'very solid organs stuffed full of food'. Within minutes the room swayed and the curtains blew in, as the first bombs fell nearby.*

On the top field of the Heath Extension above Wildwood Terrace there was a barrage balloon, a large hydrogen balloon hung with cables and anchored to a truck, to impede low-level dive-bombing attacks. Barrages could do little or nothing against high-altitude bombing, however, and the terrace was damaged that autumn by a nearby land-mine – actually a sea-mine dropped by parachute. Ceilings came down all along the terrace, and most houses lost their windows, though only the pub at the end of the road was hit directly. 'Do hope the house

---

*Herr Meier was a bookkeeper working in Costain's counting house in Dolphin Square, with a passion for modern art, which he satisfied by taking *Vogue* throughout the war.

is not too draughty,' wrote a Gordon Russell colleague to Pevsner, with British understatement.

Now Pevsner had to start the search for work again. After the brief attempt at 'business as usual', his time with Gordon Russell was effectively over: the firm had informed him that it could no longer offer him even part-time work. The *Studio* 'Design Parade' job too had collapsed, as the magazine had made alternative arrangements during his involuntary absence and told him that they would prefer to stick with the new system. 'To approach the Studio would . . . be quite hopeless,' Pevsner wrote with some bitterness to Esther Simpson at the Academic Assistance Council (now the Society for the Protection of Science and Learning). 'I started a new section for them and had right from the beginning the feeling that one of their directors did not like the idea of an outside expert being called in. He is now the very person to continue my work . . . It is all rather dirty, but I suppose an experience that many will have in some way, when they return from internment camps.'[1]

With Lola still toiling feverishly in the house and money a constant concern, he began to reassemble the fragments of his freelance career. Journalism was once more his standby. In the space of two weeks he sold to the *Spectator* a short and inconsequential review on 'The Clockmaker's Art', and a more serious piece on propaganda to *The Listener*.[2] In Robert Ziller's book *We Make History*, he argued, the British had at their disposal a potential propaganda weapon. Ziller's collection of thirty-five lithographs in a German Expressionist style depicted leading Nazis and 'types of Nazi victims amongst the German people – the workman shot while attempting to escape, his starving wife, his silent determined father, the girl whose hair was cut off and who was dragged round a town because she refused to desert her friend, a Jew'. Each picture was accompanied by a page of quotations from Nazi speeches, newspapers or pamphlets, and the overall effect was damning in the extreme. Of Ziller's caricature of Goebbels, Pevsner remarked: 'How much contempt in this mouth, how much coldness and distrust in this eye, how small the man, shrivelled up by resentment, under his oversized soldier's cap.' Any sympathy he might have shown in the 1930s for some of the Propaganda Minister's ideas on art and the people would appear to have evaporated.

To supplement his meagre income from writing, Pevsner tried to resuscitate his connection with Birkbeck. The Master, John Maud, had been sufficiently impressed by the warm reception given to Pevsner's lecture in the spring of 1940 to approach the Courtauld Institute with a proposal for a joint lectureship for him for the duration, but it would seem that the necessary funding was not forthcoming, and the college had no alternative employment to offer.[3]

'I am sorry you should have been let down by Birkbeck College,' wrote Frank Pick, who had himself continued to work hard on Pevsner's behalf after getting him out of Huyton.[4] The Ministry of Information was using significant numbers of refugees as propagandists, but the competition was very hot and strong allies were essential. Pick had been Director-General of the new ministry for a brief period, but his relationship with the new Prime Minister, Winston Churchill, was uncomfortable, and his power was declining sharply.* He could offer nothing in Information; and when Pevsner asked him for help in dealing with the Ministry of Labour, whose permission was required for aliens to have jobs, he responded, 'You will see that I have fallen out of government circles and I fear any small influence I had is now gone.'[5]

Against Lola's will, Pevsner wrote to the Society for the Protection of Science and Learning (SPSL) at the end of September, asking once more for help. He proposed finishing a book that he had begun to plan in Göttingen, on the history of the architectural profession. The book was already fully prepared in outline, with 500 pages of extracts.[†] He could also research the export value of the best British industrial products, which might be useful to the war economy as propaganda. The SPSL did not advise him to make an application on this basis – 'The Committee would much prefer Dr Pevsner to concentrate on looking for a job than on doing some interesting piece of research'[6] – but at the start of November 1940 he was offered a grant for three months at the rate of £200 per annum, which guaranteed an income of £16 13s 4d a month. He accepted, and stepped up his search for paid employment. 'It should be possible to fit me into the war machine somehow,' he wrote, but he was probably aware that it was a singularly inauspicious time for a German to be looking for a job. That autumn Sir Robert Vansittart, the Chief Diplomatic Adviser to the government, had been permitted to make a series of broadcasts on the Overseas Programme of the BBC under the title 'The Black Record: Germans Past and Present', in which he declared that Hitler was the natural product of 'a breed which from the dawn of history has been predatory and bellicose'.[‡] Given the Germans' innate predisposition

---

*Pick was subsequently sacked by Churchill, and died the following year.
†An idea of its argument is to be found in Pevsner's 1932 review of Martin S. Briggs's *The Architect in History*. 'Zur Geschichte des Architektenberufs' in *Kritische Berichte zur Kunstgeschichtlichen Literatur Jahrg.* 3/4 (1930/2), pp.97–122. But the book was never completed; the 500 pages of notes were found in his papers at his death.
‡Published in 1941 by Hamish Hamilton, Vansittart's outburst prompted angry responses

to envy, self-pity, cruelty and treachery, declared Vansittart, to differ-
entiate between Nazis and Germans, the German government and
individual Germans, would be a disaster. 'ALL GERMANS ARE GUILTY!'
shouted the Beaverbrook press, in glaring headlines – bad news for
those such as Pevsner, whose naturalisation as a British citizen was
not complete.

Paradoxically, it was German depredations that gave him his first
wartime job, clearing rubble in Kentish Town in the aftermath of the
first stages of the Blitz. The first all-out assault on London had ended
on 31 October 1940 after more than fifty consecutive nights of
bombing, although there would continue to be sporadic night raids
into the winter. The authorities had to some extent prepared for the
wrong disasters, organising too many stretcher parties for the actual
number of human casualties, but too few demolition and heavy rescue
squads to deal with the widespread damage and devastation of buildings.[7] In November Ernest Bevin made an offer of work to anyone,
English or foreign, who was unemployed and lacked a labour permit,
to help local authorities in the task of clearing up. Lowly though it
was, the job as 'rubble-shoveller' – *Schuttschipper* in German – paid
as much as the SPSL were providing, and Pevsner accepted. He also
wrote to the SPSL and politely declined to take the remaining two-
thirds of his grant. 'You will appreciate, I am sure,' he wrote to
Esther Simpson, 'that I prefer earning this sum to accepting it in
return for nothing done by me, neither research nor teaching nor
anything else.'[8]

'I admire your courage in taking the work that you have done,'
wrote Pick, when he learned of the rubble-shovelling job. 'I quite agree
with you it is not a very intelligent application of your ability in the
service of the country.'[9] But in time Pevsner himself came to see the
value of the experience. He wrote two articles about it the following
year under the pen-name of 'Ramaduri' – a Bavarian expression
meaning 'I confess'. In 'My Colleagues the Rubble-shovellers' and 'The
Psychology of the Rubble-shoveller' he explained what he had done
and why he had done it:[10]

'Why shouldn't a man like me – a creature of luxury, author, lecturer
– try to earn my money honestly and usefully, try to offer some help
to England this way, if England wasn't ready to let me help in the
way to which I was most suited? . . . Dirty work it is . . . One is

from a wide range of more liberal thinkers – e.g. Harold Laski, *The Germans – are
they human? A reply to Sir Robert Vansittart* (Victor Gollancz, 1941).

not digging the garden, after all, God's own earth, but broken tiles, decaying cement, bent and rusty pieces of iron, fragments of furniture, suits thick with filth and damp. It all has to be sorted out, until the lorries come and take it away to be burned. That's the job in its entirety. Completely without danger, of course – one shouldn't imagine oneself as standing up there on the fourth floor with a pick-axe, on the outside of the building, like an eagle. One isn't asked to do any more than dig and sort, whether one is working in a slum, where the people round about are friendly and accept you as one of them and bring you mugs of cocoa, or in the nearby tennis club, where no one gives you a glance.*

He wrote with a mixture of emotions – embarrassment, fear, distaste, pride in his own capacity to adapt to a new situation, relief at being accepted, admiration once again for the simple, the straightforward, the *Harmlose*. He was ashamed of his own reactions as an art critic, more comfortable as the social analyst he had been in the *Enquiry*:

The aesthetic pleasure one takes in the morning mist which envelops everything, or the strange patterns made by protruding beams – stern, distressing, but fascinating – or the constantly changing colours of the bricks – red as tomatoes, yellow as leather, summery pink, grey-rose, orange – it is a contrived, artificial salve for all that is unpleasant about the work. A better medicine is curiosity. What kind of people lived here? What kind of furniture did they have, what kind of pictures, what books? . . . Extraordinary how many luxury beauty products you find in the houses of poor people. Amazing to find unused linen stored under the mattress, for want of a cupboard – each man his own dryer and airer.

Pevsner's colleagues were a miscellaneous collection, some over sixty and the younger ones 'mostly C3s – one-eyed, epileptic, hard of hearing'. Many of the older ones had served in France or Italy during the First World War: 'They look at me, not without sympathy, as a curiosity, because they don't know I'm German.' He was, however, obviously a foreigner, and found himself drafted as a translator in dealing with a Czech:

---

*The digging and sorting were not without their stresses and strains. By December 1942 the Australian Mutual Provident Society was telling Pevsner that to get normal rates of insurance, he must wear a truss or have a 'radical repair operation'.

Adolf – his name is not Adolf, but that is what the English baptised him, in total ignorance of geography, when they heard he came from Prague – is one of the main sights of our group . . . To understand him, I have first to translate back into German . . . Sometimes he confuses even me, as when he wanted to know what the English greeting 'Si ja tmar' meant. It sounded so convincingly Czech, who could have seen that what he meant was 'See you tomorrow'? Or that his favourite refrain – 'Lafisool, lafisool' – was not a Bohemian folk song but Deanna Durbin's 'Love Is All'?

The best workman of all, Pevsner remarked, was fifty-nine years old. 'He used to put up and take down helter-skelters all over the country – a hale and hearty Scot, not at all averse to amorous adventures even at his age.'

An Italian restaurateur from Greenwich with a black moustache was nicknamed 'Musso' or 'Spaghetti'. Pevsner's own sobriquet was 'The Gentleman' – 'and that in my faithful old suit with the grey trousers, which had their heyday seven years ago, and the jacket covered in spots of green paint from decorating the garden fence in 1935. One said, not unkindly, that I looked like the Prince of Wales, another went so far as to assure me that in this outfit I could go straight into the Cumberland Hotel – which was, I suppose, his version of the middle-class dream of the Ritz.'

These men, his 'mates', called each other 'old cock', he noted with interest. He felt a constant mixture of respect and exasperation for the English way of doing things: 'Fear of the sack or getting your cards . . . is never far away, so one spreads the work,' he confessed:

You can do it in two ways – there's the slow motion school, and the 'Sleeping Beauty' school. I am a member of the first, although it brings on a kind of trance if one goes on with it too long . . . The 'Sleeping Beauty' method – standing absolutely motionless as soon as the foreman turns his back – I somehow couldn't manage. It is funnier to watch. The minute the foreman turns round again, everyone leaps into action, like the automata and musical boxes in the Green Vault in Dresden . . . In fact, even with this self-imposed rhythm the work is pretty strenuous, even for those who are used to this kind of thing – especially the smashing of brick walls left half standing, and the shovelling up of the rubble on to high lorries which don't seem to be able to let their sides down, God knows why. In the evenings most of these men sit at home completely inert, staring into the fire, unless they are in the shelters.

'The most improbable things are found – little crystal vases, completely untouched, amidst a labyrinth of beams where you can no longer distinguish floor from ceiling; photographs of relatives and postcards without a mark on them. One feels very intrusive' – and yet these precious finds were hardly ever reclaimed. He was horrified by the waste: 'It is, I'm afraid, the eternal English dislike of organisation.' The firm in charge of the clearing operation had no authority to sell or even give away what was found:

so we chuck each other whole piles of plates, shouting 'Catch!' and cheer when they smash. Light bulbs are thrown against the wall for the satisfying noise, and window panes are not treated with any more respect. One must realise that many of the men no longer have window panes at home – that even a cardboard box or a bread knife might be very useful. But I suppose it's all part of the typically English honesty that leaves the front door unlocked . . . 'Looting' is much rarer than I should ever have thought possible. One only takes what one has an immediate use for – a glove, perhaps, a shoe, a piece of soap, maybe a tarpaulin. Nothing is taken home, except wood for firewood. And yet the temptation is very great.

He appreciated the unexpected sensitivity and tolerance of these often uncouth crews:

One poor fellow had to give up after a few days work with us because it reminded him too much of his parents' house. When it was bombed, his father, mother and two sisters all died. He doesn't talk about it . . . Such tragedies are respected, but without comment – another example of English tact. It is a most striking quality which all my mates share, young or old, clever or dull, lazy or diligent – and it marks them out from the equivalents in any other country . . . I can't forget one scene with the lorry. A young workman, a real lad, a loud-mouth, was helping, more or less, with loading. After a while it became clear that it would go better if the lorry moved back another three metres – but the driver wasn't there, so the boy, typically, got in and started fiddling with the various levers and knobs like an old hand. That he had no idea how to drive, we didn't realise, and only twigged when he crashed, with great verve, into a lorry from the gas works parked behind him. Our horrified shouts of 'Whoa' and 'Hold'er' had no effect. The gas lorry's radiator was bent and looked awful; so did the boy, under a 'couldn't care less' exterior . . . I was waiting for the grand fortissimo finale

– when Ginger [the foreman] came up to the villain of the piece.
What a let-down – the drama was at an end. Just a few barely
audible words, not even a threat . . . What would have been the
use of a cannonade of 'Schweinhunde'? . . . O soothing, civilised
good-tempered England!

These 'Ramaduri' articles would be published in September 1941
in *Die Zeitung*, an anti-Nazi publication that was largely financed by
the Ministry of Information to produce German-language material for
an audience composed primarily of German refugees, prisoners-of-war
and interested British readers.* There is an occasional whiff of
propaganda about Pevsner's 'rubble-shovelling' articles – as when he
describes how 'Musso' organised a collection for a workmate in trouble,
'an indicator of how little the war has actually diminished the humanity
of the Englishman . . . It reassures one about the final outcome of the
war.'

In the meantime, once the rubble-clearing was over, he was out of
work again, apart from a short spell shovelling snow from the drives
of charitable acquaintances. (He performed this service, for instance,
for Dr Regendanz, now William rather than Wilhelm, with whose
nephew he had been interned in Huyton.) To the SPSL he wrote just
before Christmas 1940, 'I wish to ask you once more to keep in mind
the case of the navvy whose particulars anybody interested in
employing him can now find in the new edition of *Who is Who* [*sic*].'[11]

During the night of 11 December 1940, a German bomber returning
from a raid on Coventry ditched an unused incendiary device over the
Cotswolds. It fell in Broadway at the end of the garden attached to
the main Gordon Russell showrooms, on a thatched barn that burned
to the ground taking adjoining buildings with it. The blaze destroyed
stockpiles of furniture, including a large consignment for Sir John
Anderson, Minister for Air Raid Precautions. It also obliterated several
cases of papers that Pevsner had stored with Gordon Russell for safety.
Among them were most of his notes on Mannerism, the German
manuscript of *Academies of Art*, all his notes for *Pioneers of the
Modern Movement* and many series of lecture notes from Göttingen.
The Pevsners had also stowed some of their most precious furniture
and china there, including a set of Meissen dinner plates, which were

---

*Founded in March 1941 and based in Ludgate House, 101–11 Fleet Street, *Die
Zeitung* was staffed by a group of German refugee journalists whose aim, within their
brief from the English authorities, was to 'revive the traditions of the pre-Nazi democratic German press'. FO 371/46909.

so badly charred that Lola took wire wool and Vim to them to get them clean.

Meanwhile, in Germany that winter, the RAF had launched its first attacks on civilian targets. In Leipzig, Lis Knauth recalled that English planes overhead 'brightened the sky with innumerable "Christmas trees"'.* On Annie's floor of the Jews' house in Grassistrasse, the residents could not get to the cellar. 'The flak rolled in the air, a hellish noise, the signals were blinking. But she sat on the window sill, tense but apparently beside herself with delight. What was going on in her mind? Did she wish that somehow the end might come to her from outside? I think she did. But her suffering was not to end yet.'† Perhaps fortunately, the Pevsners in London knew none of this.

'1941,' Pevsner would write later, 'was for most of the foreign scholars or students or professional men the year of change.'[12] At its start he was still in limbo. He himself felt able to 'pass' as a local; shopping in Golders Green around this time, he was asked for directions by a Londoner, and his clear instructions met with the response, 'Thank God, you're the first Englishman I've met this morning.'‡ But in the eyes of the British government he remained indistinguishable from any other alien; and the BBC turned him down for an announcing job on the not altogether surprising grounds that his voice was 'unsuitable'.

It was, in fact, his former homeland that eventually provided him with a job again. Night-bombing showed no sign of slackening, and now a new threat had emerged, in the form of incendiary bombs. The authorities' approach to fire prevention had been slow and patchy. Many councils were ill equipped with such basics as stirrup pumps; and while most people had sandbags and buckets of water at the ready, few were prepared to sit up at night. Nor had most businesses taken any systematic precautions to protect buildings that were unoccupied out of working hours – until the night of Sunday, 29 December 1940, and the raid on the City that became known as the 'second Fire of London'. Two days later the Minister of Home Security, Herbert

* 'Christmas trees' were green flares laid to mark targets for incoming bombers.
† Lis Knauth wrote a long account of Annie Pevsner's life in Leipzig between 1939 and 1942, which she seems to have given to Pevsner several years after the war, filling in much of the detail that it was not safe to convey at the time.
‡ Ian Norrie, letter to the author, 18/6/92. The relief of this 'Londoner' at hearing what he took to be an English voice was perhaps echoed in a campaign launched in Hampstead four years later for the removal of the district's predominantly Jewish refugee population. '"A quite natural and moderate defensive feeling"? The 1945 Hampstead "anti-alien" petition', Graham D. Macklin, University of Sheffield.

Morrison, announced the start of compulsory fire-watching. Shortly afterwards, regulations were issued that could compel all men between sixteen and sixty to register for a maximum of forty-eight hours fire-watching a month, if they were not doing any on their own account.

Standing between Chancery Lane and Fetter Lane, Birkbeck College had been lucky to escape the worst of the damage in the City and it was anxious to comply with the regulations. Perhaps to make amends for the disappointment of the previous year, the college authorities now offered Pevsner employment as a firewatcher and provided modest wages for the job. 'I have received promotion,' Pevsner informed Esther Simpson at the SPSL, 'and am now fire-spotter at Birkbeck College. It is by no means the kind of return to academic surroundings that one would fancy, but it is a decided improvement.'[13]

Once again, the intermediary is likely to have been Troup Horne. 'It is now established in Birkbeck mythology,' writes Peter Murray 'that, on quiet nights, the portly figure of Trouper (the Clerk to the Governors, and himself a legendary personage) could be glimpsed on the roofs of the City engaged in activities which culminated in a note circulated to favoured members of the college: "Mr Troup Horne presents his compliments and has prepared a pigeon pie". During these activities NP would be seated on a bucket, scribbling away.'*

Whether or not the bucket was anything more than a rhetorical flourish, Pevsner was indeed writing again, working on the short history of European architecture that he had originally conceived in internment and, without knowing it, Birkbeck was providing the facilities for a new career after all. 'Something of wider appeal to help in the new start', he had called the project in Huyton. Though details do not survive, it would seem that Allen Lane had turned the tentative discussions of 1939 into a definite commission for a volume under the Pelican imprint of Penguin Books, and Pevsner had made his new beginning.

Penguin was still in its early years in 1941, an intriguing mixture of educational purpose and entrepreneurship. Its forceful and complicated founder, Allen Lane, saw a market in the 1930s in what Richard

---

*P. Murray, *Proceedings of the British Academy*, Vol. LXX, 1984, 'Nikolaus Leon Bernhard Pevsner'. Peter Murray (1920–92), a historian of the Italian Renaissance, was later Professor of the History of Art at Birkbeck. Birkbeck graduate Elizabeth Cockburn remembered Troup Horne as a gourmet with a knack for conjuring good food from such unpromising ingredients as dried egg powder; pigeon pie would presumably have been a luxury. 'Birkbeck's War Years', *Birkbeck Magazine*, 17, Spring 2005.

Hoggart has described as 'a wider social mix of people with an appetite for knowledge', and he set out to give this public books that were authoritative but readable. Allen had started out in publishing at the firm of Bodley Head, courtesy of its managing director John Lane, a distant relative. He was soon making efforts to liven up what he saw as a rather staid firm, and devised plans for a paperback line. In the teeth of opposition from the Bodley Head board, which considered soft covers rather beneath its dignity, he produced his first experimental batch of books in July 1935, a group of ten reprints priced at 6d each. This first list was a mixture of fiction and non-fiction – novels in orange and white covers, crime in green and white, biography in dark blue* – and included what one might have thought were fairly safe commercial bets, such as Hemingway's *A Farewell to Arms*, Dorothy Sayers's *The Unpleasantness at the Bellona Club*, and *Ariel*, André Maurois's life of Shelley. The Board, however, refused to take any financial responsibility for the list. Undaunted, Lane produced a second batch and got it distributed through Woolworths.

By now he was confident of the strength of his idea; he left Bodley Head to go off on his own, and on 1 January 1936 Penguin Books Ltd was formed, with Allen as managing and editorial director and his brothers Richard and John in charge of finance and sales respectively. To begin with, the Lanes rented the crypt of Holy Trinity Church; the walls were panelled with memorial slabs, and they fitted two empty tombs with metal doors to hold invoice books and petty cash. By 1937 they had risen to two small offices over a car showroom in Great Portland Street and, as business began to boom, they graduated to a full-scale office with its own warehouse in Harmondsworth.

Though its name was made at first by reprints, the firm was sufficiently focused and flexible to react to the political climate of the late 1930s by commissioning new material within its paperback format. The Penguin Specials were a series of short texts, largely political, responding to growing public concern about the international situation and the threat of war. They were well written, accessible and, above all, highly contemporary; one – Geneviève Tabouis's *Blackmail or War?* – was printed and bound within three weeks of delivery of the manuscript and sold 250,000 copies, giving Penguin its first really big sales. Pelican, too, was a series of specially commissioned studies, to be for books what the Third Programme was for radio – serious, educational,

---

*This colour coding, like the size of the books and even the bird colophon, was modelled on the German Albatross series of paperback reprints, founded in Hamburg in 1932.

but open to all, a cheap library of modern knowledge. The series was started at the instigation of W.E. Williams, the Secretary of the British Institute of Adult Education, but had the enthusiastic support of Allen Lane, who, having left school at sixteen, wanted Pelicans to be the books that people like him would have read 'if they had gone to university'.[14] The series' first title was characteristic: George Bernard Shaw's *The Intelligent Woman's Guide to Socialism, Capitalism, Sovietism and Fascism.*

On the strength of the Specials, when war broke out Penguin was given a reasonable paper quota, which helped its thin 6d volumes to stay afloat when larger, more expensive productions went under. So in encountering Allen Lane, rather than a more conventional and unwieldy publisher, once again Pevsner had been lucky with his contacts. The austere wartime format of the Pelican series, too, ultimately worked in his favour. What was required at that particular moment by a publisher working with paper rationing, a reduced budget and a desire to communicate to a wide and general audience was a bare skeleton of European architecture, an outline rather than a detailed portrait. In Huyton, away from his library, Pevsner had been forced to spend much of his time thinking about the overall shape of his account rather than the detail of its contents. With his natural capacity to analyse and synthesise, he was as ready as any scholar could have been to tackle his formidable brief.

He was clear from the outset about the limits of *An Outline of European Architecture.* If it was to fit into the Pelican format, the book could not possibly include every important building, or even every major architect: 'One building must be accepted as sufficient to illustrate one particular style or one particular point,' he wrote firmly in the foreword, and the choice of that building would be entirely personal. These buildings would not represent every single period of architecture, or even every country of Europe – and here again his criteria were subjective. For him, on this occasion, 'European' was to be largely equated with 'Western', and limited to the period from the ninth to the nineteenth centuries. This meant leaving out 'everything that is not European or – as I thus propose using the term European – Western in character. For Western civilisation is a distinct unit, a biological unit, one is tempted to say. Not for racial reasons, certainly – it is shallow materialism to assume that – but for cultural reasons.' Prehistory would be excluded, classical antiquity would be dealt with in a couple of pages, and architecture in the Eastern Mediterranean in the first thousand years AD would be ignored, as something fundamentally different from Western civilisation.

Pevsner made no pretence of even-handedness. This was a book for British readers, and therefore he chose British examples where he could. He did not include buildings where good pictures were not available, as he preferred to make illustrations do some of the work of explanation – an unusual approach at a time when few art books were highly illustrated and most relied primarily on verbal description. 'Whoever makes up his mind to write a short history of European architecture, or art, or philosophy, or drama, or agriculture,' he wrote, 'must decide in which part of Europe at any time those things happened which seem to him to express most intensely the vital will and vital feelings of Europe. It is for this reason that e.g. Germany is not mentioned for her 16th-century but for her 18th-century buildings . . . that buildings in the Netherlands are only touched upon, and Scandinavian buildings not mentioned at all.'

But for all his initial disclaimers and provisos, once he got going, in *Outline* Pevsner was writing his most impassioned and coherent defence of architecture as the supreme art form, expressing his most intense feelings and working out in print many of the theories on which he had been brought up in Germany. His argument had three basic tenets: architecture is primarily concerned with space; it is the expression in space of the spirit of its age; and it is the highest artistic expression of the human spirit because, of all the arts, architecture is most intimately connected with human life.

'A bicycle shed is a building: Lincoln Cathedral is a piece of architecture' – the book's opening statement would become famous over the years, for its pithiness and confidence as much as for any truth it might have had. It was not, after all, an original idea, drawing as it did on a distinction made by Ruskin in *The Seven Lamps of Architecture*: 'Nearly everything that encloses space on a scale sufficient for a human being to move in, is a building; the term architecture applies only to buildings designed with a view to aesthetic appeal.' Architecture, Pevsner felt, must in some way express the cultural values of its maker, and its aesthetic appeal could take three forms. (His natural fondness for lists, and for categorical statements, was well suited to the condensed 'outline' format, and he gave it full rein.) Its beauty might lie in two-dimensional effects like those of the painter – effects of ornamentation such as tracery or friezes, the relation of wall to window, the proportions of windows – or in three-dimensional effects like those of the sculptor, with the building treated as something modelled, making its impact through the use of a flat roof or a dome, or an imaginative rhythm of projections and recessions. Or it might make its statement by the three-dimensional effects it could achieve in space, and to Pevsner this form of aesthetic appeal was the most important: the effect on the senses of moving through the interior space.

'Architecture is not all a matter of walls and wall patterns,' he wrote. 'It is primarily organised space . . . To experience space it must be wandered through or at least wandered through with one's eyes.'[15] This was the idea that would shape his writing about buildings for the rest of his life, and he was scrupulous in tracing its antecedents. Writing an introduction to a bibliography of his works in 1969, he carefully acknowledged his debts. The nineteenth-century aesthetician Friedrich Theodor Vischer, writing about the viewer's empathy with a work of art, had stated: 'The vertical raises us, the horizontal widens us, the curved line moves more vividly than the straight line' and this implies 'an unconscious transfer of . . . our body . . . into the forms of the object'. This was an idea he passed to his son Robert Vischer, whose protégé August Schmarsow took it and applied it to architecture, explaining that the space enclosed by a building is experienced by the human body as an empathic feeling of height, length and breadth.* Schmarsow held the chair of art history at Leipzig, where one of his pupils at the turn of the century was Pinder; and so the theory reached Pevsner in the early 1920s, shaping the way in which he conceived of architecture, prompting him to give it primacy in his art-historical thinking, and ultimately in his life.

The architect, he argued, must have all three modes of vision – painterly, sculptural and architectural – and therefore architecture is the most comprehensive of all visual arts and has a right to claim superiority over the others.

This aesthetic superiority is, moreover, supplemented by a social superiority . . . We can avoid intercourse with what people call the Fine Arts, but we cannot escape buildings and the subtle but penetrating effects of their character, noble or mean, restrained or ostentatious, genuine or meretricious. An age without painting is conceivable, though no believer in the life-enhancing function of art would want it . . . An age without architecture is impossible as long as human beings populate this world . . . Salvation can only come from architecture as the art most closely bound up with the necessities of life, with immediate use, and functional and structural fundamentals.

*Schmarsow expressed this idea in works like *Überden Wert der drei Dimensionen im menschlichen Raumgebilde* (1893), *Das Wesen der architektonischen Schöpfung* (1894) and *Barock und Rokoko* (1897).

Here, as in his earlier writing about contemporary architecture in *Pioneers*, materials and function are key, but they are not everything. 'A style in art,' he wrote firmly, 'belongs to the world of mind, not the world of matter.' However diligently the architect seeks to fit form to function, he must also respect the demands of aesthetics. Architecture is not a purely mechanical process, it is driven by spirit – the spirit of the age – in which aesthetic components play a key role: 'Architecture is not the product of materials and purposes – nor, by the way, of social conditions – but of the changing spirits of changing ages.'

Pevsner himself made no great claims for the book. 'Presentation, I fear – not divulgation,' he said dismissively of it in 1967, ignoring the fact that what was needed and desperately desired at the time when it was written was not necessarily the revelation of new truths, but the heartfelt reaffirmation of old ones.[16] *Outline* was written with passion, a powerful piece of writing, which only slows and stutters in the theoretical, analytical and summarising passages at beginning and end. The main narrative hangs together closely, sweeping persuasively from one century to the next with superbly categorical pronouncements evoking whole architectural eras.

The 'rawness of the minds and the heaviness of the hands' of the late Anglo-Saxons is followed by the 'plainness' of the eleventh century: 'There is no wavering here – as there was none in the ruthless policy of William the Conqueror in subduing and normanising England.' In the Gothic style, however, 'motif follows motif, as branch follows branch up a tree . . . A Gothic building is never complete . . . It remains a live being influenced in its destiny by the piety of generation after generation. And as its beginning and end are not fixed in time, so they are not in space.' In the Renaissance building 'the walls appear active, enlivened by the decorative elements which in their sizes and arrangement follow laws of human reasoning. It is ultimately this humanising that makes a Renaissance building what it is.' In Britain, at least, later architecture became almost too human – the buildings of Elizabethan England, for example, 'vigorous, prolific, somewhat boastful, of a healthy and hearty soundness which, it is true, is sometimes coarse and sometimes dull – but never effeminate and never hysterical . . . The England of Queen Elizabeth . . . possessed such an overflowing vitality and was so eager to take in all that was sufficiently adventurous and picturesque and in some cases mannered that it could digest what would have caused serious trouble to a weaker age.' The subsequent failure of nerve over succeeding centuries was all the more unfortunate. 'It is the things of the spirit in which the Victorian age lacked vigour and courage,' Pevsner wrote regretfully. 'The 19th century lost the Rococo's lightness of touch and the Romantics' emotional fervour. But it stuck to variety of style, because associational values were the only values in architecture accessible to the new ruling class.'

The *Outline* is undeniably a full-blown exposition of the theory of the *Zeitgeist* and a testament to its psychological pull. As a means of condensing and freely associating a wide variety of different trends – political, social, economic, cultural – *Zeitgeist* was ideally suited to an overview, and seductive for a wartime audience that needed to make sense of its surroundings and find order in chaos by being reminded of values that remained constant. Centred in England, the book nonetheless emphasised a European unity that lay behind contemporary politics. In a display of literary ping-pong, using the extraordinary weight and breadth of reference at his command, Pevsner nipped from country to country with volleys of illuminating parallels – 'What the cathedral had been to the Middle Ages, the symphony was to the 19th century'– and occasional aces and smashes of triumphant phrasemaking. On practically every page, he risked tremendous generalisations – 'the Romantic Movement originated in England', 'the English have at no time been happy without bay windows', 'the countries of the Pyrenean Peninsula [are] possessed by a passion for overdone decoration' – and he was not afraid to rank and grade the cultural achievements of Europe with what Herbert Read would call a 'lively sense of competing values', in accordance with his own personal preferences.

At one point he quoted with great relish a remark of Inigo Jones, whom he considered to be 'the first English architect in the modern sense'. 'Outwardly every wyse man carrieth a gravity in Publicke Places,' wrote Jones, explaining his fondness for making a contrast between simple exteriors and rich interiors, 'yet inwardly hath his imaginacy set on fire, and sumtimes licenciously flying out, as nature hirself doeth often times stravagantly.' In the *Outline* Pevsner did a little of his own 'licencious flying out'. If an opportunity for a sideswipe at a bête noire presented itself, he took it; in the middle of his analysis of Sir John Soane, he found room to deplore the recent enlargement and reworking of Soane's Bank of England, 'converted by recent Governors and Directors into a podium for a piece of 20th-century commercial showiness'. The present breaks into the past again during his description of the 'spatial rapture' of Johann Balthasar Neumann's staircase at the baroque Bishop's Palace at Bruchsal, its lower levels lightened by arches in the supporting walls of the upper flights: 'one of the most deplorable of all war casualties'.

Unsurprisingly, perhaps, the German Baroque and Rococo period prompted writing that was almost rhapsodical, an unselfconscious celebration of Germanness. He delighted in tricks of spatial counterpoint that step 'beyond the bounds of what the beholder can rationally explain to himself'. At the church of St John Nepomuk in Munich, for example, 'the gallery balancing on the fingers of pirouetting termini or caryatid angels sways forward and backward, the top cornice surges up and drops down, the colour scheme is of sombre gold, browns and dark reds, glistening in sudden flashes where light falls on it . . . wildly fantastic, yet of a superb magic reality . . . sensational in a literal sense'.

At Vierzehnheiligen, Neumann's church of the Fourteen Holy Helpers, he remembered, 'The first impression on entering this vast, solitary pilgrimage church is one of bliss and elation. All is light: white, gold, pink.' This is hardly the language of an austere, or even a restrained, commentator; but Pevsner was not just wallowing in nostalgia or literary self-indulgence. He used his description of Vierzehnheiligen to demonstrate the point of the book, and the purpose of the architectural critic. The onlooker, he wrote, can easily be overwhelmed by German Rococo in all its glory, as manifested here:

> The oval central altar in the middle of the nave may well please the rustic worshippers who kneel round this gorgeous object, half a coral reef and half a fairy sedan chair. Having taken in this glory of confectionery, the layman will then look up and see on all sides glittering decoration, surf and froth and rocket, and like it immensely. But if he starts walking round, he will soon find himself in utter confusion. What he has learned and so often seen of nave and aisle and chancel seems of no value here.

To get the best out of this – 'architects' architecture as the fugue is musicians' music' – asks for 'an exact understanding, which is a job for the expert'. Pevsner's objective in the *Outline* was precisely this: to provide, as an expert, a more exact understanding of European architecture for the layman, creating in him the illusion that he already knew a good deal, and the desire to know more.

Some of the intensity and ardour of the *Outline* was perhaps injected by the circumstances in which it was conceived and written. Sketched in Huyton, the book was filled out in the midst of the Blitz. 'I remember when fire watching in the war,' wrote a fellow Birkbeck warden to Pevsner years later, 'that whatever time I called you to do your stint you were always busily writing at a shaded lamp in that gloomy common room.'* (That room, however dim, must have been busy: another Birkbeck firewatcher, E.V. Rieu, started his Penguin translation of the *Odyssey* during this period.) Though the story of the upturned bucket is more romantic, *Outline* was most probably written between common room and air-raid shelter at Birkbeck; the atmosphere on the roof was unlikely to have been conducive to peaceful reflection, as the Germans had now resumed a major bombing campaign, partly to continue the damage to Britain's war economy, but also to distract attention from the fact that they were preparing to invade Russia.

Francesca Wilson met Pevsner towards the end of April 1941. 'He was very cheerful,' she reported, 'remarkably so. He only gets about 5 hours sleep and finds himself a little exhausted, but he says that he never feels any fear. There has been a terrific amount of bombing around his district, and several bombs in the college itself. He was on the roof watching bombs showered on Thomas Wallis's, and the whole building going up in flames, on Wednesday of last week.'[17] On the night of 10 May the Luftwaffe took advantage of a brilliant 'Bombers' Moon' to attempt the complete destruction of the centre of London: 1,436 people died in a single raid, £100,000-worth of gin was obliterated in the City Road, and a quarter of a million books burned in the British Museum.[18] Most of London's major landmarks were hit – Westminster Abbey, the House of Commons, the Tower, the Mint, the Law Courts, the War Office – and at one moment fires were raging from Hammersmith to Romford. Both ends of this arc of flame were visible from Hampstead Heath, and Hampstead itself was badly hit.

'It is dust and ashes round him,' reported Miss Wilson on 14 May. Pevsner's sense of loss must have been both personal and professional as he watched historic buildings burn in the City. Asked by the *Burlington Magazine* to report on the destruction, he lamented both enemy action and the damage self-inflicted from within, drawing these two threads together in an early airing of the conservation message:[19]

Architectural losses are irreparable, but those who have seen the hideous shells of the Wren churches, of Coventry Cathedral and Chelsea Old Church, the brutal rents in the mellow red fabric of Gray's Inn, the wreckage of the Temple, and the charred walls of Holland House, will one day, I feel sure, look up to what will be

---

*G.M. Davies/NP, 1967. Terence Ingold, later Professor of Botany at Birkbeck, remembered sitting in the basement with Pevsner between shifts. 'One time I helped him select windmills photos for an *Architectural Review* article.' 'Birkbeck's war years', op. cit.

left with more respect and more love than their parents and grand-
parents who within the last fifty years allowed the demolition of
Furnival's Inn and Clifford's Inn, the Adelphi and vital parts of the
Bank of England, Lansdowne House and Chesterfield House.

He now found himself in the curious and painful position of
recording damage on both sides of the fighting. The RAF had carried
out an experimental terror raid on Mannheim in December 1940, and
the night-bombing of industrial cities in Germany, begun in May 1940,
increased through the spring of 1941. Relatively few of the bombs
reached their intended destinations – factories, stations, ammunition
dumps and the like – and by May Pevsner was drawing on other
émigrés for reports on an increasingly long list of non-military buildings lost from the towns and cities of Germany and Austria.

Dr Rosa Schapire, for instance, was a German art historian of the
previous generation, one of the first women in the field, a lecturer,
critic, reviewer, translator, dealer, patron and collector of modern art,
and founder of the *Frauenbund zur Förderung deutscher bildenden
Kunst* or Women's Association for the Promotion of New German
Art.* She was invited by Emil Nolde to become an associate member
of *Die Brücke*, and in 1924 wrote the catalogue raisonné of the works
of Karl Schmidt-Rottluff; his 1919 portrait of her is in the Tate collection. As a Jew she was forced to leave Germany, arriving in London
in August 1939 on a transit visa at the age of sixty-five.[20] With
approximately ten marks in her pocket, she was kept alive by a poorly
paid job in the contemporary collections at the Tate Gallery. Pevsner
had her combing foreign and domestic papers for details of bomb
damage to historic buildings in Germany. One of her first reports in
the spring of 1941 was of ten bombs dropped by the RAF, probably
by mistake, on the park of Sans Souci in Potsdam – the town where
Lola had been born and where Pevsner had made his preparations in
1920 for conversion to the Protestant faith.

It must have required a constant effort for Pevsner to put his past
and his family in Germany out of his mind. He was producing journalism now for both English and German audiences. Under the pen-
name of 'Peter Naumburg' – chosen presumably as a reminder of the
place that had always been a refuge – he was among the first regular

---

*Rosa Schapire (1874–1954). See S. Barron (ed.), *German Expressionism: Art and
Society 1909–23* (Thames and Hudson, 1997). She would write to John Rothenstein
in 1946: 'I was the first one who recognised the value of what the Nazis called "degenerate art". I fought for it since 1908.'

contributors to *Die Zeitung*. Reviewing the official war art at the National Gallery, he wrote: 'How very English this exhibition is. Over 200 pictures and no trace of pomposity or pathos, no aggression or melodrama, no striking of heroic attitudes, no audibly marching troops.'[21] It was the attitude that had impressed him in Birmingham in 1935, viewing George V's Silver Jubilee celebrations as an outsider, transposed to another war.

In contrast, current official art in Germany was crammed with pictures of the Führer, marching columns, predictable 'fairytale woods', the wine harvest, the 'noble neo-classicist and, up close, indecent Leda'. 'The trend towards the pompous and loud, towards kitsch, towards super-realism, towards the attention-grabbing . . . The Third Reich wallows in it now,' he lamented, in an article he entitled 'A sigh of distress over German art exhibitions'.[22] Pevsner was still prepared to defend his earlier contention that art for art's sake was pernicious, and that the modern work of art should have social meaning and relevance, but he was now able to see the consequences of pushing these views too far and allowing subject to dominate all else. 'These marching soldiers, if you really have to portray them, should be portrayed in such a way that the rhythm of their march expresses the national ideal. All we're getting here is the shallowest naturalism . . . For Heaven's sake, a picture must have something which will last for ever.'

To see art that was both aesthetically valid and capable of working to a higher purpose in the service of the state, one would now have to turn to England, he concluded. In an untitled article of around this time, he described with admiration the moves being made towards some nationalisation of the arts in a land that had famously been the home of private enterprise in this area. The war art scheme, the canteen concerts organised by ENSA (Entertainments National Service Association), the work of the British Council and the foundation of CEMA (Council for the Encouragement of Music and the Arts) – all pointed towards an assumption by the state of responsibility for culture. 'Here, very quietly, the same thing is happening as has been taking place in fascist states for years, with great display and nationalist propaganda. But while in Germany loyal Nazis form this art movement, CEMA is tolerant . . . well-informed and critical.'*

---

*CEMA was founded in 1940 on the initiative of the Pilgrim Trust, a fund for conserving the heritage of Britain. In 1942 the government assumed full financial responsibility, and Maynard Keynes was appointed chair. He was well aware of the perils of state intervention in the arts. In June 1945, when the organisation was re-created as the Arts Council, his inaugural speech echoed Pevsner's comments: 'State

It would be fascinating to know what Pevsner's German-speaking audience made of these comparisons. Meanwhile, as Jim Richards had promised, Pevsner's relationship with the *Architectural Review* had survived his internment. He now wanted to broaden the range of his writing for the magazine. Late in 1940 he had apparently approached both the *Review* and the companion *Architects' Journal* with suggestions for a series of articles on Victorian architecture, rather than design. 'There is no subject in the whole history of art that has been so neglected by serious critics as the architecture of the 19th century,' he declared boldly. Neither publication took him up on his offer; but later that summer he did at least begin to branch out beyond his 'pioneers'.

A long article entitled 'Omega', published by the *Review* in August 1941, represented Pevsner's only brush with Bloomsbury since his unsatisfactory tea party with Roger Fry in 1934. It traced the short but intriguing history of the Omega Workshops, which ran from 1913 to 1919 at 33 Fitzroy Square under Fry's proprietorship, making and selling painted furniture, printed fabrics, hand-thrown pottery and stained glass. One of Fry's aims, beyond the simple desire to promote decoration for the joy of it, was to break down the artificial barrier between 'fine' and 'decorative' arts, and he employed 'fine' artists including Duncan Grant, Nina Hamnett, Mark Gertler, Edward Wadsworth, William Roberts and Winifred Gill to make objects for daily use alongside their own work. (Often it was the income from the former that supported the latter.) Their output was supplemented by novelties which in Fry's opinion deserved a platform – puppet shows, poetry in pamphlets, children's drawings, a carefully calculated combination designed to attract a fashionable clientele. 'We should get all your disreputable and some of your aristocratic friends to come,' wrote Vanessa Bell, 'and after dinner we should repair to Fitzroy Square where would be decorated furniture, painted walls etc. Then we should all get drunk and dance and kiss. Orders would flow in and the aristocrats would feel sure they were really in the thick of things.'[23] Whether or not they danced and kissed, the clientele included Ladies Cunard, Drogheda and Ottoline Morrell, alongside George Bernard Shaw and Arnold Bennett.

Pevsner's years as a buyer of glass and textiles for Gordon Russell had left their mark and, for once, he was interested as much in the objects that the workshops produced as the way in which they worked.

---

patronage of the arts has crept in. It has happened in a very English, informal, unostentatious way . . . The task of an official body is not to teach or to censor, but to give courage, confidence and opportunity.'

Omega, he wrote, was an experiment in both art and socialism. In the spirit of the William Morris workshops and later Arts and Crafts ventures in the Cotswolds, this was a communal endeavour. Artists were kept on a small retainer, rather than being paid for individual pieces, and all products were anonymous, signed only with the mark Ω. These products, Pevsner wrote firmly, were not particularly beautiful, and they now looked 'decidedly dated', but the date that one would be tempted to attribute to them would be at least ten years later than their actual age. The pots, lampshades, rugs and footstools of Omega were interesting because they were ahead of their time in marking the emergence of Cubism and Expressionism in England.

The workshops had been given the name of the final letter of the Greek alphabet to signify that they were 'the last word' in fashion. But in the end it would turn out that modernity was not enough for Omega to survive, in the almost complete absence of any business sense. 'It is all very well to live in a quiet London square and look like an Orthopaedic Institute,' Shaw observed sharply, 'but the price you pay is that your business remains the secret of a clique.'[24] Omega could not survive what Fry described ruefully as 'the utter indifference . . . of the public', and in September 1919, after a final summer clearance sale, he cut his losses and closed it down.

Pevsner did not pretend to be entirely in sympathy with the workshops; unlike the Bauhaus, they were a shrine to individual expression, an enemy to machine production and, in his view, at least partly responsible for the *moderne*, perhaps his least favourite of all twentieth-century styles. But in the midst of the wartime gloom Pevsner's stint on the Omega trail provided some light relief. John Rodker had an Omega table and a cross-stitch chair, but the quest for other relics took Pevsner further afield. General Sir Ian Hamilton, British Commander-in-Chief at Gallipoli, invited him to see a good collection of the furniture, stained glass and mosaic floors at his London home at 1 Hyde Park Gardens. Roger Fry's sister Margery entertained him in Aylesbury to tea and oat cakes (later sending Lola the recipe).The Bloomsberries, too, had mostly moved to the country to avoid the Blitz, but E.M. Forster (the owner of an Omega curtain) received Pevsner at the Reform Club, while Vanessa Bell and Duncan Grant took him to lunch at the Café Royal. Maynard Keynes, on the other hand, evaded him: 'I am, I am sorry to say, very much occupied at the present time,' he wrote.[25] 'I do not want to be disobliging. But I should be grateful if you could excuse me from an interview. There are others who can tell you much more than I can.' ('Occupied' was something of an understatement, from a man who was then at the Treasury as personal adviser to the Chancellor of the

Exchequer, Kingsley Wood, and had recently published a book entitled 'How to Pay for the War'.)

By the time 'Omega' appeared, Pevsner had come closer to achieving his ambition of broadening his scope. Since 1935 the *Architectural Review* had been running a series devised by H. de Cronin Hastings entitled 'Criticisms'. These pieces were to be opinion rather than facts about architecture, were to focus on aesthetic rather than practical matters and were to offer some kind of challenge to architects' customary valuations of themselves. Pevsner adopted a nom de plume for his contributions – not 'Peter Naumburg' this time, but 'Peter F.R. Donner', for no discernible reason other than that *Donner* is the German word for 'thunder'. Pevsner tended to use 'P.F.R. Donner' on occasions when he wanted to be controversial, or even argue with himself in public; for example, a letter to the *Review* in September 1941 criticising the claim in the 'Omega' piece that there were no French influences on the work-shop was signed 'P.F.R. Bonner' [*sic*], and is highly likely to have been Pevsner's own afterthought. Rarely could he be described as 'thundering', though, and there is no evidence that he would have wished to deny authorship of these pieces in the long run, though he would protect the identity of 'Peter F.R. Donner' for more than twenty years.*

He was, in fact, mild in the majority of his 'Criticisms', in essays on Frank Lloyd Wright, Ledoux and Le Corbusier, and Marylebone Town Hall.† Only in September 1941 did he generate some heat by returning to the charge against what he saw as the vandalism perpe-trated in recent years against the Bank of England. Soane's original building was largely on one storey, a characteristic sequence of toplit spaces behind a windowless perimeter wall. To accommodate the Bank's increased business, the Governors commissioned Sir Herbert Baker, co-architect of New Delhi, to design a new core to the building and impose a superstructure on it. Baker set to and destroyed the Rotunda, the Lothbury Court and the Governors' Court in their entirety. He

---

*In 1967, he disagreed about pseudonyms with Reyner Banham who, as a historian, favoured revealing that 'Ivor de Wolfe' (on occasion 'de Wofle'), author of the *Architectural Review*'s controversial 'Townscape' series, was in fact the *Review*'s proprietor. Pevsner countered, 'I think that while pseudonyms can be broken orally, they should be kept sacrosanct in print until the person in question either authorises publication, or is dead.' (NP/Banham, 26/4/67. GP Series IB, Box 6.)

†'Frank Lloyd Wright, "An Organic Architecture, the Architecture of Democracy" – the Sir George Watson Lectures for 1939', *AR*, August 1941. 'Ledoux and Le Corbusier' appeared in October 1941. Claude-Nicolas Ledoux (1736–1806) was a French neoclas-sical architect: Pevsner was happy to note the alternative theory of the Modern Move-ment, which found its antecedents in neoclassicism, but he never accepted it. 'Houses by Robert Atkinson and the St Marylebone Town Hall', *AR*, November 1941.

then erected a grandiose neoclassical 'extension' that was five times the height and more than five times the volume of the existing building. It amounted, Pevsner declared, to 'an artistic tragedy', the ruination of 'one of the five or six most outstanding examples of the style of an epoch in English history'.

To extend a building of character, Pevsner believed, was problematic, but not impossible:

> Two qualities are needed in an architect to make him successful at such a job: tact and courage. A perfect balance of the two is rare nowadays . . . What actually happens almost universally . . . is that the architect shows himself possessed either by too much tact and too little courage, or by too much courage and too little tact . . . Of the second Sir Herbert Baker's Bank of England is a particularly unfortunate example . . . The new addition, though many times the volume of Soane's, looks small, Soane's work mightier than ever. Soane is taciturn (he frowns, and rightly so), Sir Herbert is polite and affable. Soane is certain of his ground; is his successor?

Neoclassicism of a far less 'affable' nature was in Pevsner's sights again in December, when he launched a scathing attack on architecture in Germany under the Nazis.[26] Was Nazi architecture great, as Hitler had claimed in January 1938? Certainly not in terms of its social purpose, given the almost complete neglect of public housing, nor in its fitness for use, since it showed a marked bias towards senselessly huge halls suited only to propaganda and mass demonstrations, and 'holiday-barracks' that were gloomy and monotonous. 'I do not hold any brief for Blackpool,' Pevsner remarked precisely, 'but I would have thought that holiday-makers had the right to expect a certain jollity.' From the point of view of aesthetics, the architecture of the Nazis was gross rather than great: 'Discrimination between bigness and greatness does not come till later. Hitler maybe has not reached that stage.' Its worst vice, however, was its excessive wallowing in synthetic emotion, its vulgarity and a sentimentality that might take the form equally of neoclassical bombast or medievalising with a 'melodramatic picture-palace quality', flashy, hollow and meretricious. The real objection to this architecture, however, was not simply its lack of taste but its 'unclean mixtures of aesthetic and associational effects'. There are no lingering vestiges of sympathy or even respect in this piece, which was to be virtually the last reference he would ever make to the Nazis in print.

* * *

In November 1941, Jim Richards decided that he wanted to tackle work more directly related to the war and approached the Ministry of Information for openings; he would spend much of the remainder of the war in Cairo.[27] At Richards's suggestion, Pevsner – as a foreign subject, in no danger of being called up – was issued with a formal invitation to become assistant editor and caretaker of the *Architectural Review*. He accepted with delight. The only other possibility of permanent employment on the horizon was the offer of a job teaching German at Charterhouse, but with *Outline* scheduled for publication, and now some kind of security at the *Review*, he had no need to clutch at this straw.* 'On his feet at last,' commented Francesca Wilson. 'After a difficult year the tide has turned.'[28]

Around him, however, the war situation was darkening, whether Pevsner looked at it as an English resident or as a German national. As far as England was concerned, 1941 had seen the fall of Tobruk in March and Rommel's advance across North Africa, followed in June by the German invasion of Crete. In November HMS *Ark Royal* had been sunk off Gibraltar; and the year would end with the entry of Japan into the war at Pearl Harbor, the loss of HMS *Repulse* and *Prince of Wales,* and the fall of Hong Kong.

Meanwhile in Germany the threats to both Uta and Annie had become incalculably more serious. The bombing of German cities was accelerating. 'The civilian population around the target areas must be made to feel the weight of the war,' Churchill had said in October 1940.[29] Six months later he declared in a broadcast to the world, 'There are less than seventy million malignant Huns – some of whom are curable and others killable.'[30] When Russia was invaded on 22 June 1941, he promised in a speech that now 'we shall bomb Germany by day as well as night in ever increasing measure, casting upon them month by month a heavier discharge of bombs, and making the German people taste and gulp each month a sharper dose of the miseries they have showered upon mankind'. The number of German cities under attack increased: Berlin, Hamburg and Stettin in September, Nuremberg in October, Cologne and Mannheim in November. The raids were rarely accurate – an official study that year estimated that fewer than one in four came within five miles of its target, and over the Ruhr this was one in ten – which scarcely detracted from the objective of creating terror among the civilian population.

For Uta and the Kockel family sheltering her in Hanover, more

---

*The opening at Charterhouse may have come through the good offices of Robert Birley, headmaster from 1935 to 1947.

intense than the fear of bombing by the British was the increasing dread of discovery by the Nazis. Under the ordinances of 1939 and 1940 Uta's citizenship had lapsed, and she was no longer a German national, at precisely the time when she was most likely to attract attention. Already seventeen, she would soon be subject to call-up for youth labour service. This would involve presenting her papers – which had of course been marked, when she first registered with the police in 1939, to show her as a 'visitor'. In an attempt to maintain the local camouflage, Marianne tried to get her into a nearby art school in Hanover. Uta started the term without apprehension (Marianne had kept from her the real danger of the situation, so that she might behave as naturally as possible), only to be confronted within a few days by a full-scale questionnaire on her origins. At this point, Carl Walter approached the school's Director, whom he trusted, and confided in him that this new pupil was not in a position to complete the form. His trust was not misplaced; the Director said he would not report Uta's presence to the authorities – but she must leave the school.

Increasingly uneasy, Carl Walter wrote to a professional colleague, Professor Weikmann, a meteorologist who was in indirect contact with Göring and had some understanding of current Nazi policies on the treatment of Jews. 'If you think there is nothing to be done, please destroy this letter,' wrote C.W. 'If we don't hear, we'll know what is what.' There was no reply. He got the same advice more directly from Wilhelm Külz, the uncle of Marianne's old school friend Margot, who had been Minister for the Interior in the Weimar government of 1926. 'You must have one thing – iron nerves,' he wrote. 'And don't try anything. Keep your heads down, make yourselves small.' The Kockels were now living in constant fear of informers, protected largely by a series of kind gestures and deliberate blind eyes. Another acquaintance, Herr Wiontzek, worked for state security. With considerable courage and generosity, he offered to use his official privilege of employing a maid and take Uta in – 'No one will look for a Jew in our house' – but the Kockels did not dare take the risk.

Make yourselves small . . . Meanwhile the first extermination camps had been established in Poland, and in July Göring had ordered Reinhardt Heydrich, chief of the Gestapo, to 'evacuate' all European Jews as a first step towards a 'final solution of the Jewish question'.

In Leipzig, Annie had been moved to a new Jews' house at König-Johann-Strasse 30, this time round the corner from Fregestrasse, where the Pevsner family had lived in 1903. Now she was in a smaller room, which she had to share with another woman, and she had little peace.

Any ring at the door could be the police, and the indignities of life were mounting.

On 1 September 1941 it became compulsory for all Jews in Germany to wear a Yellow Star – a cloth badge worn on the left breast, as big as the palm of a hand, marked with a Star of David with 'JUDE' at the centre in Hebrew-like lettering. It bred acute self-consciousness and fear, and the rate of suicides among Jews went up sharply again:

> One day there were just people on the street, and the next day, there were Jews and non-Jews . . . All of a sudden, stars were everywhere, just like Hitler had said they were . . . The badge was an obvious, visual, step back to the Middle Ages, a time before Emancipation . . . If a Jew forgot to wear their badge they could be fined or imprisoned, but often, it meant beatings or death. Jews came up with ways to remind themselves not to go out without their badge. Posters often could be found at the exit doors of apartments that warned Jews by stating: 'Remember the Badge!' 'Have you already put on the Badge?' 'The Badge!' 'Attention, the Badge!' 'Before leaving the building, put on the Badge!'[31]

Annie wore the Yellow Star – Pevsner's cousin Ellen Dreesen remembered her maid seeing her in a subway – and she complied with the ordinance that required all Jewish women without obviously Jewish names to take the middle name of 'Sarah'; but she did not do it without protest. Lis Knauth remembered, 'To one official she said, when she gave her signature, "You know, don't you, that this is a fraud? My name is not Sarah."' Annie's defiance was born of desperation. She still longed to get out of Germany; a Leipzig friend had written to Pevsner on 23 September of her 'most intense wish', and her dream that a distant relative in the Middle East might somehow be able to help.[32] She also cherished a plan to emigrate to Cuba; she had apparently received an invitation, and had gone as far as to buy a ticket for a boat that would sail on 15 November.

But time had run out. In mid-October 1941 the Nazis implemented a wholesale programme of deportation for Jews – the 'evacuation' with which Heydrich had been entrusted in July. Between 15 and 31 October almost 20,000 German Jews were sent to the Lodz ghetto in central Poland; the next group would be sent to occupied Russia, most of them to Riga or Minsk. Those picked for deportation were notified individually, sometimes with as much as a fortnight's notice, more often with only a few days. Older people – those over sixty-five – were the first to be selected, along with single mothers with children, those on public assistance, and anyone else unable to work. There was a good deal of confusion about the process. The shock of listing was quite often followed by uncertainty and deferral. 'Everything seems arbitrary,' wrote Victor Klemperer in Dresden. 'Those designated drag their suitcases to the station, drag them back, wait.' People knew what their destination might be, but few suspected what would happen to them when they got there. 'N said to me he would rather be dead and know his wife dead,' reported Klemperer, 'than see her louse-ridden and rebuilding Minsk.' Plans for the 'Final Solution' would not be formalised until 20 January 1942, at the Wannsee Conference, nor technical procedures for extermination agreed; but of the 50,000 German and Czech Jews deported to Russia in November 1941, all would in fact be dead within months. The majority of those who had been sent to Lodz in October were almost certainly among the first of the 350,000 Jews to be murdered at nearby Chelmno, the first extermination camp to become operational. Mass gassings started there in December, in sealed vans.

Annie had been sixty-five earlier in the year, and she saw friends of her own age being listed. The first hint of danger for them had come with the arrival of a questionnaire requiring the recipient to list personal effects for confiscation. This was followed shortly afterwards by directions for the journey. Each household received written instructions: take one backpack with provisions, mess kit and spoon (no knives or scissors), two blankets, sheets, warm clothing and heavy shoes – all to a maximum weight of twenty-five kilograms. Everything else would be forfeited, and all valuables and house keys had to be surrendered separately. Buildings including the Ephraim Carlebach School on Gustav-Adolph-Strasse were designated as deportation points.

Annie's former maid Anna remained loyal; but others fell away as they realised what was happening. One Gentile friend, conspicuous in her fur coat among all the black-clothed women in the Jews' House, had to pretend she was looking for a doctor on another floor. For several weeks Annie lived in limbo, as one by one the other inmates of her flat left. Lis Knauth told Annie's story: 'One day a brief note reached me: "The time has come" – signed, "A wanderer".' The questionnaire had arrived, and the destination was apparently to be Poland. Shortly afterwards Annie had a visit from two young police officers, who asked if they could come into her flat to get warm. Lis remembered her account of the meeting. '"There they sat", she said with a shadow of a smile, "behind my table, with their swastika armbands."' They had come to tell her that, after all, she was not going. 'By a miracle she had been saved and been left behind.'[33]

'The emotion with which I heard the *Leonora* overture in the Gewandhaus in those days was indescribable,' Lis remembered. 'Everything seemed all right.' For Annie, of course, relief was not so straightforward. 'The loneliness of the flat which she now shared only with the half-Jewish doctor and an old couple had shattered her nerve. "It is like a mortuary," she said . . . It was not in her generous heart to grasp at the fact that she herself was safe.'

CHAPTER 22

'Now we are scattered'

In London, Pevsner and Lola knew little of Annie's life. During 1940 they managed to exchange letters fairly frequently, but after the spring of 1941 Annie's communications tailed off; by January 1942 Pevsner had not had a word directly from her for nine months, and he was becoming desperately anxious. 'Oma [Granny] especially worries me a lot,' he confessed to Tom. 'She could write, and we write regularly. Why does she not? . . . It is a crying shame, the amount of misery Adolf has brought over everybody.'[1]

In Leipzig, Lis Knauth too was apprehensive. In December 1941, Annie had sent round a prized crystal and silver tea caddy, asking Lis to think of her at Christmas 'wherever she might be'. On Christmas Day, Lis had taken her a tree, a scrawny, shedding plant that was all she could find. 'That's just the sort of tree I need this Christmas,' Annie said, and in return gave Lis a copy of Wiekert's *Comfort of the World*, the kind of book it was customary to lend to the bereaved.

Some time in January 1942 Annie heard that she had been deferred, not exempted from transportation. 'After the great anxiety she had endured, from which she had been relieved once, it must have been too shattering for her.' Annie, it would seem, had already decided to commit suicide.* 'Everything she did now was to secure her chosen path,' wrote Lis. On 31 January – the day after Pevsner's fortieth birthday – Annie told Lis to stay away for about ten days, as there was 'danger in the air'. Their parting was 'unspeakably sad . . . Everything was already as though through a veil for her.' After more than thirty years' acquaintance, Annie now asked that they should use the familiar 'Du' form of address.

During the night of 10 February, at the age of sixty-five, she killed herself. Three days later, Lis, unknowing, went to visit her, taking an electric stove that other Jewish friends had been ordered to relinquish, and an azalea. 'I came to the front door – and had a vision of my dearly loved friend being carried out of the door. This vision was so

---

*All that year and into the next, as long as the deportations lasted, there would be a growing wave of suicides across Germany's Jewish population; a quarter of all deaths in Berlin in 1942–3 would be suicides, for example, and there were reports in the autumn of Jews paying inflated prices for the sedative Veronal. Most victims were in their sixties, and the majority were middle-class, assimilated Jews rather than members of the practising Jewish community.

clear that I went in already knowing what had happened.' She later went to view the body. 'The triple strand of her character – heart, mind and charm – lay there, with nobility, pride and grace on her dear features.' At the funeral, Lis sat on the women's side in the synagogue at the back (as a Gentile) and looked at the flowers, some sent by the florist herself. 'How often she had ridden past here, cheerful, elegant and full of life, on the train to Berlin. And yet wasn't the highest point in her life her resistance, her triumph in going under?'

Annie was buried in the Old Jewish Cemetery, not with Hugo in the new one, or with her Perlmann relations in the Südfriedhof, the largest (non-denominational) burial ground in Leipzig, where her son Heinz had been buried, in an area that she had once intended to be the Pevsner family plot.* Lis felt largely relief 'when she lay in her resting place covered with snow, saved from everything else that might have been threatening her'.

It was two months before the news of his mother's death reached Pevsner, and then only in the barest details, in a letter from Lis which, however, did not conceal the fact that Annie had taken her own life. He was profoundly shocked and tormented by guilt. 'Muo seemed to be so young and brave,' he wrote to Lis. 'How little we knew of all those worries and the horrors – what must she have gone through, and how often she must have been in despair! I reproach myself bitterly for so many things.'²

In saying they knew little of what Annie had endured, he was telling the truth. It would be seven years before Lis handed to him the last letters that Annie had written to her, and thirteen years before Lis herself wrote the memoir of Annie's final years that filled in some of the details of life in the *Judenwohnung*. At the beginning of 1942, even if Pevsner and Lola had known of the threat to Annie of deportation, they would not have known what this meant.†

Pevsner's cousin Gertrud, guessing how he would feel, tried to relieve him of the burden of self-blame. 'Don't exaggerate the weight of the

---

*Some time after Kristallnacht it was decreed that Jews were no longer to be buried in the New Jewish Cemetery – perhaps because of the devastation described by US Consul Buffum – and they had to go back to the overcrowded old one.
†Historians tend to agree that, whatever information the British government might have had, the British public knew little about the deportations and the plans for the Final Solution before the middle of 1942. See, for example, R. Breitman, *Official Secrets: What the Nazis Planned, What the British and Americans Knew* (Farrar, Straus & Giroux, 1998).

reasons that drove her to it, for you know that she didn't care too much for life, she never did. And as far as self-reproach is concerned, my dear dear Nik, you can do without it . . . You were a good, much-loved son, who made her proud. What have you left undone? They neither would nor could both come before it is too late. I am very much in the same position and dare not think any further.'[3]

Nevertheless, in a memoir completed in 1954 Pevsner was still finding it difficult to write about his mother. 'I shall never be able to speak of her objectively. My own development was, in the years of adolescence, actively in opposition to her and her values. I was unjust and cruel to her in those years – and even later, judged by the terms of infinite admiration for her wisdom and kindness in which the close friends of her last lonely years in Leipzig write and speak of her.'

Dieter, aged ten was now a chorister at Christ Church, Oxford. 'When you're in church,' Pevsner wrote to him on 26 March 1942, 'sing something really beautiful for her, and when you lie in bed at night, think of her who loved you very much – think that she is in heaven and with dear Opa [Grandpa] again.' With Tom, now sixteen, he spoke more frankly of his feelings. 'It is terrible for us – not to have been able to have been there, to tell her just once everything we had in our hearts . . . not to have been able to ask her forgiveness for this and that . . . We had relied so much on seeing her again . . . We take great joy in you, dear Thomas – the new generation. I have become the senior member of the family now, and you come next after me.' With Hugo and Annie lost to him for ever, and other relations forced out of Germany and dispersed to a variety of destinations, his invocation of 'the family' must have felt a little hollow. 'Now we are scattered,' he told his children some time later, 'and shall be even more so when Mutti and I die.'

Uta, meanwhile, seemed to be ever more distant from them. Her early letters, full of English expressions like 'super', 'thanks awfully' and 'cheerio', had been replaced by the constrained telegraphese of sporadic Red Cross forms, and he and Lola dared not enquire too closely about her, for fear of reminding the German authorities of her connections with the enemy. Still in Hanover with the Kockels, she now lived under the constant threat of conscription for youth service. In the hope of getting exemption for her, the Kockels had taken to describing her as a maid to their children, but the authorities were not convinced. Carl Walter was obliged to take her to sign up, and she was registered for munitions duty, but her call-up was not immediate.

That February, Sir Arthur Harris had become Commander-in-Chief of the RAF's Bomber Command, and set about implementing a programme of area bombing in Germany, targeting civilian areas as a means of destroying industrial morale. He would sum up the objectives of this programme the following year:

> That aim is the destruction of German cities, the killing of German workers and the disruption of civilised community life throughout Germany. It should be emphasised that the destruction of houses, public utilities, transport and lives; the creation of a refugee problem on an unprecedented scale; and the breakdown of morale both at home and at the battle fronts by fear of extended and intensified bombing are accepted and intended aims of our bombing policy, they are not by-products of attempts to hit factories.[4]

On 28 March 1942, Harris ordered a 'range-finding' attack on Lübeck, a historic Baltic town that was being used to supply the Russian Front. The purpose was to test the practicability of his strategy. 'It was not a vital target,' he admitted in his memoirs, 'but it seemed to me better to destroy an industrial town of moderate importance than to fail to destroy a large industrial city.'[5] Referring to the medieval wooden buildings that were Lübeck's principal architectural glory, he described the town as 'from the nature of its buildings easier than most cities to set on fire'. On 3 April, in retaliation, Hitler gave orders for the 'Baedeker Raids', a series of attacks on English towns and cities of little strategic significance but of noted beauty and historical importance.* On the night of 30 May, 1,096 RAF bombers flew in successive waves over Cologne, in the first mass bombing operation of the war, code-named 'Millennium'. The raid, which lasted only two and a half hours, caused destruction on an unprecedented scale: 245 hectares almost totally laid waste, 3,300 buildings destroyed, 2,500 fires started, some 500 people killed.

Why couldn't a British bomb fall on the Kockel family in Hanover, Carl Walter exclaimed at a moment of particular strain, to relieve the perpetual suspense in which they lived.† Two floors above their apartment was a family from Leipzig and he feared one of them might recognise Uta; below was an unpleasant architect named Süss whose wife, to Marianne's dismay, wished to be friends. Preferring to lie low, Marianne rebuffed her advances and the woman, offended, incited her

---

*Bath, Canterbury, Exeter, Norwich and York.
†By the end of the war Hanover would have been bombed on eighty-eight separate occasions.

husband to inform on them. They were denounced for apparently having two maids.

An SS officer came to the house, and Uta was summoned to the official bureau that dealt with the employment of domestic servants. Since she had no workbook, she had to apply for a citizen's pass. The Kockels had tried to shield her from full knowledge of the danger of her position – a considerate precaution that possibly saved her life, as she breezed confidently through her interview in ignorance of the consequences of failure. Their forethought, too, in declaring her presence as a 'visitor' in that early census in 1939 was rewarded when a hyper-vigilant official rang the police to check on her status. With her name safely confirmed as being on the police register, she was issued with the citizen's pass and workbook, which formally identified her as a maid and exempted her from more gruelling war work. But the tension of city life, with potential informers all around, was proving too much, and Marianne felt it was better to keep the family on the move. She and the children moved to the holiday home in Naumburg, leaving Carl Walter in Hanover, where he was now working for the large engineering firm of SEISMOS, making military supplies. In the country Marianne could at least supplement the meagre official food ration with home-grown potatoes, vegetables, preserves and pickles, but coal was in short supply, and the central heating could only heat one room at a time.

In England, too, the winter and spring of 1941–2 had been exceptionally cold, and life was becoming daily more restricted by the programme of austerity directed by Hugh Dalton at the Board of Trade and Lord Woolton at the Ministry of Food. The clothes ration was enough roughly for one pair of socks every four months, one pair of shoes every eight months, one shirt every twenty months, one pair of trousers and one jacket every two years, one pullover every five years and an overcoat every seven years – a restricted wardrobe that must have distressed the man who had been mortified by shabbiness, safety pins and leaking soles on his first visit to England twelve years before.[6]

Tinned fish, meat and vegetables had joined bacon, butter, sugar and fresh meat on the food ration. In February 1942 soap had gone on the list: sixteen ounces every four weeks. 'Luxuries' as defined by the government – butter knives, grape scissors, billiard tables, most jewellery – were banned altogether, as were items made of strategically important materials, such as celluloid and rubber. There was an infuriatingly short supply of dull necessities such as razor blades, coat hooks, curtain rods, prams and fireguards. Beer and tobacco – presumably on the 'bread and circuses' principle – were relatively freely available,

but Pevsner would in all probability have exchanged these two indul-
gences for the hot, deep baths that were now discouraged by the
authorities. He is unlikely to have minded the curtailing of sporting
events and the shortage of petrol for 'pleasure motoring', taking far
more delight from the fact that, somehow, during the war the fine arts
survived.

CEMA had been set up during 1940 for the purpose of helping
amateur music and drama survive the harsh conditions of wartime,
but it had also had the long-term effect of making the professional
arts available to a wider audience. Malcolm Sargent, director of the
Promenade Concerts for almost twenty years, would claim that many
people had been attracted to music for the first time during the war
'because it has been made available to them in the places they have
been in the habit of visiting in search of entertainment – theatres,
music halls, and cinemas'.[7] While they might at first have seemed a
far cry from the evenings in the box at the Leipzig Gewandhaus with
which Pevsner had grown up, Sunday-night concerts at the Orpheum,
Temple Fortune became a great source of comfort and relaxation during
1942.* 'We are making up for years of musical starvation,' Pevsner
told Tom in February. 'It is lovely to hear real music again after all
the tinned or canned music of the wireless.'

He was going to the theatre again, too, albeit in the rather idiosyncratic form of the plays put on by the Donald Wolfit Shakespeare
Company at the Strand Theatre. Wolfit, later a neighbour round the
corner at 5 Wildwood Grove, invited the Pevsners to performances of
plays such as Ben Jonson's *Volpone* – with himself, needless to say,
invariably in the lead. His flamboyant style, which effectively distracted
attention from fellow-performers, made it hard for the company to
attract supporting players of any distinction, and its scenery and
costumes, designed largely by Wolfit himself with authenticity in view,
were famously amateurish; but his energy carried the company through
the Blitz and the Battle of Britain when many other theatres closed,
and again Pevsner must have been glad of the diversion.[†]

Boarding school was an obvious way of getting the boys out of
London and away from the bombing. Dieter was settled in the Oxford
cathedral choir at Christ Church. Tom had now been two years at
Sedbergh, which had responded far more generously than Charterhouse

---

*The Orpheum became the Odeon in 1945 and ended its life in the early 1980s as
the Odeon, Golders Green. It is now Marks & Spencer.
†Wolfit was the original of 'Sir', the overpowering actor-manager figure in Ronald
Harwood's play *The Dresser*.

to Lola's appeal and had awarded him a scholarship; but as he approached his School Certificate he was toying with the idea of changing his focus from French to economics, to the disapproval of his headmaster. Pevsner's response is perhaps less revealing of Tom's attitude to work than of his own. He was anxious that Tom should not offend someone whose good report he might later need. 'You might want to get a scholarship again from school to university,' he wrote:

Even for that it is damaging if the HM regards you as a boy of no staying power. Besides – I should be a little unhappy too, if I had to think you lacking in that particular quality. It is necessary in whatever you are going to do in life. Do you think I like all the routine stuff connected with the A[rchitectural] R[eview], let alone the days and weeks of research some times without getting one inch nearer what you are after. Nor do I like the gross mistakes I am making in so new a kind of work . . . For Gord's sake [sic], don't get into the butterfly way of tasting here and tasting there and not doing the things thoroughly.

Pevsner was himself making a thorough job of tackling a new role as an ARP warden, drilling every Monday and preparing for qualifying examinations. 'The general idea of an air raid warden,' according to an official circular of 1937, 'is that he should be a responsible member of the public, chosen to be a leader and adviser of his neighbours in a small area, a street or a small group of streets, in which he is known and respected.' It was something of a testament, therefore, to the success with which the Pevsners had assimilated themselves into their Hampstead community that in the middle of the war they should both have been accepted for ARP training.

'This is on the very eve of the most momentous events,' Pevsner wrote to Tom on 11 March. 'Another quarter of an hour, and we shall have to leave to do our bit in a most realistic fire-fighting test. There will be a fire in the stables of the Bull and Bush, and what the leaflet kindly called a certain number of surprises. Imagine your mother in her chique *Windjacke*, the one that has seen many a summit of the Alps, with armlet, tin hat, gas mask, and a lot of knowledge, and your father in ditto ditto . . . A beauteous sight.' The reality, however, did not live up to the anticipation. 'The show was supposed to be good,' he reported the following day:

Evidently our wardenfolk were quite proud. I don't think it was up to much. You cannot extinguish a fire that is not there, only red

lamps and a lot of smoke. The teams did it all right, I being so
fortunate as to have to do nozzle-work. Mutti had to pump, in
another team. Then after a while the motor trailer pump of the
Manor House [Hospital] came . . . They had another go, and then
the beer party followed in the pub. No serious surprises. I had hoped
there would be a gas alarm or an odd incendiary in an unforeseen
place. No – I was not amused. But we had some wine afterwards
at home . . . Oh, I wish I had not had so much alcoholic liquor;
my tummy is busy on the most unpleasant convulsions.

John Rodker would also seem to have been training in civil defence,
but later that year he moved to Evesham to work for the BBC. His
daughter Camilla, however, now lived down the lane from the Pevsners,
within sight of 2 Wildwood Terrace, at a house called Wyldes, said to
have been the last farmhouse in London, and known to have been
visited by William Blake.* Camilla, now twenty-one, had had little in
the way of conventional parenting from either Rodker or her mother,
Mary Butts. An unflattering portrait of the couple is to be found in
the memoirs of Aleister Crowley, the self-proclaimed 'Great Beast' and
master of the occult, whom Butts took to visiting in Sicily once she
had left Rodker for the writer Cecil Maitland.†

With Maitland, Butts had embarked in the early 1920s on a five-
year debauch – or, as she preferred to call it, 'a rather beautiful
bacchanale'. Parking Camilla in London with a friend called Poppy
Vanda, she oscillated between the Left Bank in Paris and the South of
France, making a slightly self-conscious career as an epitome of the
1920s, no doubt delighted to be described by Virginia Woolf as 'part
of the underworld'. By 1925 she had left Maitland. She was writing
modernist novels, with a heightened stream-of-consciousness style,
influenced by Ronald Firbank and others whom she had helped Rodker
to publish through the Ovid Press.

She was also relying increasingly on alcohol, cocaine and even
heroin, and Rodker – to whom she was still officially married until
1927 – became increasingly uneasy about Camilla's welfare. In 1929

---

*It had also until recently been the home of one of Pevsner's heroes, Sir Raymond
Unwin, planner of Hampstead Garden Suburb.
†Crowley refers to Butts as 'a large, white, red-haired maggot' and to Rodker as a
'nauseating coleopter . . . a Whitechapel Jew who proclaimed himself a poet on the
strength of a few ungrammatical and incoherent ramblings', in J. Symonds and K.
Grant (eds), *The Confessions of Aleister Crowley, An Autohagiography* (Jonathan Cape,
1969). Cecil Maitland was a disciple of Crowley, who used him as the model for 'Peter
Pendragon' in *Diary of a Drug Fiend*.

she was brought to live with her great-aunt Ada outside Bournemouth. After her mother died, at the age of forty-seven, in 1937, Camilla remained in Bournemouth for only a couple of years before coming to look for a father whom she hardly knew, and whom she described as, at best, 'a cool customer'. It was in pursuit of him that she had ended up at Wyldes. What kept her in Hampstead, however, was a growing friendship with the Pevsners.

Lola, painfully missing her own daughter, gave Camilla

out of her generous heart . . . the nearest thing to mothering I had ever received . . . I liked the respectability of the Pevsners . . . They were just constant . . . It was my first experience of consistently affectionate friendship which endures . . . Part of the niceness of the Pevsners was that I was still Bournemouth-provincial, but they never made me feel inferior, they never stratified as British people do, you weren't instantly classified.

Pevsner himself could perhaps have done with a bit more of the 'mothering' that gave Camilla such security. During the summer of 1942 Lola spent some time out of London, staying with the Grigsons in Wiltshire. In the mid-1930s Geoffrey had bought a small and somewhat ruinous herdsman's cottage called Snowhill, outside the village of Broad Town, three miles south of Wootton Bassett. It was remote and rural, and at their invitation Lola gladly used it as a bolthole, leaving Pevsner to fend rather inadequately for himself, the lodgers, the vegetable patch and the cat.* He was, by his own confession, not at all handy – in a letter to Lola that August, he signed himself 'your stone-age Man' – and met the small practical challenges of daily life with dismay.

'I still sleep in the basement,' he wrote on 15 August:

as M [the lodger Herr Meier] has not said a word yet about moving. The plumbers in the meantime have left one evening, leaving all pipes wide open. The next morning the famous turncock came, opened the sluicegates of Metropolitan Water and out it came through the open pipes, and the floors and ceilings. So one ceiling has a yellow patch, supplying that homely touch without which an English house is not a house worth living in . . . The allotment works allright, in spite of my inferiority complex whenever I go.

---

*For the Pevsners at Snowhill, see Chapter 24.

He was suffering a little from rheumatism, 'in spite of the maté which I drink so diligently', but still managed some surprising feats in pursuit of subsistence: 'I have provided some *gratis* firewood on Sunday by sawing and breaking off dead branches of our plum tree. *Selbstversorgung*/Self-sufficiency. I tried high jumps, reached the branches and got them that way.' The house, he boasted, still stood in her absence, 'in spite of Meier's sensational accounts of bombs every night. We sleep through, provided Doormat lets us. The wretched cat, left all alone, has grown very affectionate. He licks so frantically that his mouth all dribbles. A hideous performance. I push him away, because it is so loathsome, and then feel a cad.'

In July, Pevsner received proofs of *An Outline of European Architecture* from Penguin and was hoping for publication before the end of 1942; but in the meantime he had received another offer from them – the editorship of King Penguins. One of the most attractive of all the Penguin series, the King Penguins had been designed to appeal 'to the general liking for illustrated keepsakes'.* 'At this time when so many of our galleries and museums are closed,' read an advertisement in the Penguin publicity magazine *Penguins Progress*, 'we hope [the series] will fill a useful purpose in promoting an appreciation of art and as a reminder of the pursuits of peace.' The little books represented Penguin's first use of hard covers, pictures and colour, an advance reflected in the price of one shilling as compared to the ordinary paperback price of 6d.

The original editor of the series was Elizabeth Senior, brought in on loan from a post at the British Museum. Having started with *A Book of Roses*, illustrated with Redouté prints, and *British Birds*, with illustrations taken from Gould's *Birds of Britain*, she had commissioned a volume from Pevsner on illuminated manuscripts. Familiar with the concept from the Insel-Verlag books and impressed by the Redouté volume, he had accepted; but the quality of the colour in subsequent volumes had been less good, and he had written to Senior to withdraw from the project. After she was killed in the Blitz in 1941, her correspondence, including Pevsner's letter, was passed to Allen Lane, who decided to take him up on his criticisms. 'I see you find that the King Penguins aren't good enough,' he is supposed to have written. 'Can

---

*The model for King Penguins was a German series published by the Insel-Verlag firm in Leipzig, founded by Alfred Walter Heymel, a wealthy dilettante who wanted to produce books that were art objects in themselves in terms of design, print and text.

you do better?' Prudently, Pevsner initially declined on the grounds that what the series really needed was a technical editor. Nothing daunted, Lane recruited R.B. Fishenden, a leading expert on colour printing, to solve the problems of printing small-scale reproductions. On this basis, with Fishenden as a co-editor, Pevsner was happy to accept, and would very much enjoy working with a man who he said 'combined to an exceptional degree wisdom, kindliness and tenacity'.

The King Penguin series offered its editors unlimited scope in their choice of artists and writers, given that their only brief was to identify subjects of general appeal and striking visual interest which could be tackled on a miniature scale. During its relatively short life, the series ran to seventy-six titles, emerging at a rate of roughly one every two months, on subjects from the Bayeux Tapestry to British military uniforms by way of spiders, portraits of Christ, ballooning and William Cowper's *The Diverting History of John Gilpin* with illustrations by Ronald Searle. Pevsner would entertain John Arlott to drinks, to choose the illustrations for *The Picture of Cricket*.[8] Gwen White was received in less salubrious surroundings: they met 'in the bombed-out basement of Birkbeck College and there among the dust and rubble my little book of Toys was discussed. It became No. 26.'[9]

Pevsner's natural inclination was to protect his authors and he often found himself defending the less eminent against Allen Lane's desire to economise by abandoning work that had already been commissioned and completed. However, the series was also an opportunity for him to meet celebrities; he was touchingly excited, early in 1942, to be going off to interview Max Beerbohm for his gallery of literary caricatures entitled *The Poet's Corner* (published in 1943), rather less thrilled to be rung up by James Robertson Justice in pursuit of his fee for a volume that had been dropped. Ernst Gombrich had already supplied a whole volume on *Caricature* (1940), while Sir Leonard Woolley contributed *Ur: the first phases* (1946) and Wilfrid Blunt the essay on *Tulipomania* (1950). Where he could, Pevsner also took the opportunity to involve old friends and acquaintances. Christian Barman, formerly of the London Passenger Transport Board, delivered a volume on *Early English Railways* (1950), and John Summerson produced selections from *The Microcosm of London*, with text by A.C. Pugin and illustrations by Rowlandson (1943). Pevsner's Edinburgh rival David Talbot Rice would contribute *Russian Icons* (1947) and his ally John Gloag *The English Tradition in Design* (1947).

Pevsner took on this new venture in 1942 with some trepidation. 'They are getting on slowly, the wretched K-Ps,' he wrote to Tom in

February, asking whether he might examine Tom's stamp collection with a view to a volume on stamps and art. Fishenden's virtues were not enough to deflect Lane's wrath when the quality of the colour printing did not immediately improve, and there was a gap in production of nearly two years after Elizabeth Senior's death.* But the planning and commissioning for the series were a means of entrenching Pevsner's position at Penguin. He made friends there, and came to look forward to the monthly production meetings with Fishenden, W.E. Williams and Allen Lane's dynamic assistant, Eunice Frost. 'There was a difference between meetings in the morning and meetings after lunch,' he remembered later, 'because after lunch everybody was rather gayer but rather less responsible.' The list of ideas for titles that never saw the light of day is entertaining. When the series reached its fiftieth volume in 1949, the team threw a party in the garden behind Pevsner's Gower Street office; whose idea it was to import real penguins, which kept disappearing into the bushes, history does not relate. (The penguins missed the end of the party, returning prematurely to the zoo in disgrace, after one bit a fellow-guest.)

Pevsner's own contribution to the series would be a more sober affair. Instead of the volume on illuminated manuscripts originally commissioned by Elizabeth Senior, he delivered a short essay on *The Leaves of Southwell*, the late thirteenth-century carved capitals on the columns in the Chapter House of Southwell Minster, illustrated with superb black-and-white photographs by F.L. Attenborough.[†] This was a subject that was very dear to him, and he wrote about it with passion. The Southwell leaf capitals, which he considered the most exquisite medieval foliage carving in Britain, had close similarities with the vine-leaf capitals in the cathedral at Naumburg and, like them, seemed to express all that most inspired him in the spirit of the Middle Ages.

---

*Penguin's production manager blamed the printers for failing to meet Fishenden's high standards. Bob Maynard, 'Penguin Production 1939–42', in *Miscellany 10: Twenty-One Years* (Penguin Collectors Society, 1995), p.12. But Lane's fastidiousness may have contributed: a memo of 4/10/43 laments, 'It is a pity that the plates were numbered in Arabic numerals while the references to them in the text were in Roman numerals . . . Occasionally there has been a slight mis-use of glue.' Penguin Papers, King Penguin, DM 1952/743.
†Originally a lecturer in Anglo-Saxon at Emmanuel College, Cambridge, Frederick Attenborough was in 1942 the principal of University College, Leicester. Pevsner would probably have been drawn to him as a dedicated and eminent landscape photographer; a collection of his photographs is preserved in the Centre for English Local History at Leicester University. The manuscript of *The Leaves of Southwell* would appear to have been completed in 1942, but the volume was not published until 1945.

'If these . . . were in France rather than England, they would doubt-less draw numbers of educated English pilgrims to see them,' Pevsner wrote. The Southwell Chapter House is octagonal and stone-vaulted. Inside, its walls are lined with thirty-six seats for the dean and other members of the Chapter, separated by columns supporting trefoil arches with steep gables above them. It is these columns and those of the elaborate entrance portal whose capitals are carved with a variety of animals, human faces, Green Men, but above all leaves – oak, a symbol of long life; buttercup, used on May Day to keep away evil; cinquefoil, hung around the necks of cattle as a charm against witchcraft; hawthorn, maple, vine, ivy and hop, possibly also fig, geranium and cherry, worm-wood and woody nightshade. What he loved about the leaf capitals was their perfect balance of decoration and structure – the intense naturalism, unprecedented in English carving at that time, which never obliterated their structural form. 'Leaf must remain leaf and never be reduced to abstract pattern,' he wrote, but at the same time 'stone must remain stone and not attempt to masquerade as vegetable matter'.

All *The Leaves of Southwell* had to do in order to fit into the King Penguin series was provide a selection of attractive images accompanied by a text that was sufficiently diverting to hold the reader's attention and bind the illustrations into some kind of unity. Typically, Pevsner offered far more. *The Leaves of Southwell* is nothing less than an essay on the nature of the artist in the Middle Ages – specifically, the anonymous carvers working in teams under master masons who trav-elled from place to place across Europe and brought back notebooks full of ideas to be translated into stone. Pevsner revelled in the capacity of these unnamed, uneducated craftsmen to express their faith in God in the language of their everyday experience of nature. He quoted a medieval literary expression of this idea – the credo of Wolfram von Eschenbach's Parzival, who spoke of 'keeping one's soul pledged to God without losing hold of the world' – and argued that the Chapter House at Southwell achieved the same effect without words.

'The nicest ever book about capitals,' declared A.E. Brinckmann, editor of the *Handbuch der Kunstwissenschaft*, in a letter to Pevsner after the war. *The Leaves of Southwell* is certainly one of Pevsner's most polished pieces of writing – a virtuoso display of erudition and authority, combining a huge breadth of reference with the ability to summarise. More importantly, the little book was a revelation of some of his deepest feelings – possibly the nearest he ever came to a state-ment of his own personal faith. To Ralph Beyer, who bought it in 1949, it was indeed 'almost a religious work'. Perhaps not surprisingly, when its ten pages of quotations from medieval botanical writers were set against lighter and more colourful volumes on kilts, Mexican magic and ballet, it was, in Pevsner's own words, 'a spectacularly bad seller'. One critic observed that *The Leaves of Southwell* had suffered by being part of a series 'of which the keynote is charm rather than scholarship'.[10] But it had been a luxury for Pevsner to write *Leaves* – an exercise in his own 'joy and skill' as an art historian, involving the kind of detailed research and description that he most enjoyed and now rarely had a chance to undertake.

'As so often happens,' wrote Pevsner later, 'when the lean years had come to a natural end, several things turned up at the same time.'[11] Besides the King Penguins and *The Leaves of Southwell*, 1942 also brought him an increase in his teaching. The Courtauld had continued to offer him work as an external examiner and, at intervals, as a lecturer; early in 1942 he was teaching a course there, 'trying to be polite to ladies who will answer what has not been asked, and dive off at the most unexpected points,' he told Tom in February. 'The elderly ladies keep giving the wrong answers, and I put them right gently but with a strained face. They seem to like it.' Birkbeck, too, had come to feel he should perhaps be employed inside the college as well as on the roof, and he had had a new offer of lectures – one on the decline and fall of Roman art, and another on the spirit of Roman as against Greek art. 'I am preparing as usual far too well,' he complained.[12] 'It will take ages . . . I should have known it all before. I had not polished it up in fact for twenty years.'

Other universities were cutting back on their teaching as they lost teachers as well as students to the war, and arts subjects in particular were scaled down. But Birkbeck kept operating throughout the war, merely moving lectures to weekend daylight hours to accommodate those who could not travel during the blackout. Surrounded by bombed-out buildings and empty streets, the college had a thriving, if motley, community and Pevsner was happy to join it. 'We are all freezing,' he reported, 'and people walk about in the oddest garments . . . Serious city men wear gum boots over their black trousers . . . Joad came to Birkbeck in a dark navy skiing costume, another professor I met with a balaclava.'* Like the standard of dress in the college, the

---

*Pevsner was keeping glamorous company; C.E.M. Joad, Head of Philosophy at Birkbeck, was then at the height of his popularity as a 'public intellectual' and star of the BBC's *Brains Trust*. He regularly travelled on trains without a ticket; in 1948 he was convicted, fined and sacked by the BBC.

curriculum was variegated. Every weekend, on most Sundays and some Saturdays as well, speaking at tea time in the Junior Common Room to audiences drawn from all departments of the college, Pevsner was expected to cover subjects as diverse as 'Art in Britain before the Conquest', 'The Appreciation of Sculpture', 'French Art in the Middle Ages' and 'English Architecture of the Augustan Age'. Nevertheless, he had, at last, a permanent position teaching art history in an English university, and he was happy.

His salary as a part-time lecturer was £100 a year. This did not mean that he could afford to give up the journalism that kept his name before commissioning editors. His work for the Ministry of Information in *Die Zeitung* continued in 1942 with a series of reviews of the National Gallery's 'Pictures of the Month' and a critical assessment of the Royal Academy's wartime hang. He also took the opportunity to return to the subject of the evolution of the architectural profession. This produced two articles: 'The Term "Architect" in the Middle Ages', for the journal *Speculum*, and 'Terms of Architectural Planning in the Middle Ages', which appeared in the *Journal of the Warburg and Courtauld Institutes*.[13]

Meanwhile, as assistant editor of the *Architectural Review*, he was struggling to get to grips with the technical side of his new job. In later years, Jim Richards would be adamant that Pevsner, as wartime caretaker, had not been wholly responsible for the *Review*'s content, let alone its editorial tone or political stance. His primary jobs were to round up material and oversee production, and Pevsner himself admitted that he found this challenging enough. 'I was wholly ignorant of an editor's job. I hardly knew what lower case and foredge meant,' he wrote years later.[14] Possibly aware of this, Richards kept in touch from a distance. Pevsner would call him 'the best critic with whom I have worked . . . an extremely intelligent and pleasant person', adding later, 'I gather that he strikes strangers as grim. He is not, it is just that he is exacting.'[15] By insisting on his own high standards, Richards taught his protégé a good deal about the mechanics of producing a magazine. 'He could never believe that others could be inferior to him in their capacities,' Pevsner wrote ruefully. 'If you go through these old volumes,' he added, 'you will find I think without difficulty my years, by their standard [of layout and typography] being lower than Mr Hastings' or Mr Richards'.'*

---

*NP/J. Mosley, 6/1/66. Modesty apart, he would come to take a close interest in typography. A letter of 1945 on the typeface for his *Burlington* article 'Thoughts on Henry Moore' finds him arguing the merits of Beton Luxor as opposed to Perpetua,

Hastings had promised that he too would 'keep an eye' on the newcomer, exercising more editorial control than had been his habit with Richards at the helm. Some of the most daring design decisions of these years – like the use of thin coloured papers and unorthodox typefaces – were his, as were the majority of the editorials on post-war reconstruction. Richards too would make his political views clear in the magazine's pages. An avowed socialist and internationalist, he had gone far further than Pevsner ever would towards advocating state-controlled building, pleading for the 'aesthetic virtue of regimentation' and art as an expression of the industrialisation of society. Richards was aware of Pevsner's general sympathies with modernism: 'I wouldn't have suggested anyone who I thought would radically change the policies of the paper,' he commented shortly before his death in 1992. But he never saw Pevsner as taking a leading role in political issues such as post-war planning: 'Nikolaus never would express any political opinions – as one wouldn't as a guest in somebody else's house . . . In a country he was only in the process of adopting, he wouldn't have thought himself entitled to push himself forward . . . I know how sensitive he was about it.'*

When it came to gathering material for the *Review,* however, Pevsner's contribution was more significant. Editorial influence had effectively been given to a historian at a time when the supply of new buildings had been severely restricted, and he seized the chance to focus the magazine's attention more often on the buildings of the past. He did this, doubtless to his chagrin, not from the Georgian elegance of the magazine's former headquarters in Queen Anne's Gate, now commandeered by the WRNS, but from 45 The Avenue, Cheam (telephone number VIGilant 0087). In Jim Richards's words, this was 'a large suburban villa a long way from the railway-station'.

Some people, unaware of the limited scope of his brief, were nervous about the impact that Pevsner might have on the *Architectural Review.* His sudden elevation could not have amused John Betjeman: 'I write and I write and I write under different names and in different styles, yet no one has heard of either me or my pseudonyms. I must have written the word architecture more times than there are people in England who can pronounce it properly.'[16] John Piper too had been dismayed by Pevsner's appointment, fearing that he might eradicate the quirky, folksy, anecdotal and apparently trivial from the pages of

---

and he would write a full-scale article on 'Lettering and the Festival on the South Bank' for *The Penrose Annual,* Vol. 46, 1952. GP Series IB, Box 6.
*J.M. Richards, interview with the author, 2/4/92.

the *Review*. Piper relished the accidental in art, the spontaneous design to be found in odd corners of everyday life – in cast-iron bollards and benches, on lighthouses and seaside promenades – as is obvious from a piece he submitted on the primitive art to be found in the decorative detail on swing boats and tinkers' carts, barges and ice-cream barrows. He must have been partly reassured when the article appeared in July 1943 under the title 'Cubist Folk Art', incorporating some useful supplementary information from Pevsner on the Italian origins of one particular diamond pattern.

Pevsner himself had misgivings, revealed in his remark to Tom about the 'gross mistakes' he was making in his early days. But gradually he settled into 45 The Avenue and started to stamp himself on the magazine, bringing in his acquaintances – Francesca Wilson, Geoffrey Grigson, Philip Sargant Florence – to review books, and taking the chance himself to write historical pieces on subjects that interested him. In February it was a note on the 150th anniversary of the death of Sir Joshua Reynolds. 'I have dropped a nasty brick,' he confessed to Tom, 'by writing that he painted Lady Bruce, while I should have said Lady Mary Bruce . . . Would you believe that there are fools who would write a scandalised letter because of that. And who was the fool? The librarian to Buckingham Palace. So no knighthood for me for the next few months or years.'[17]

In March it was 'The Evolution of the Easy Chair'. Anyone temperamentally less well suited to what he described as 'nonchalant sitting' it would be hard to imagine, but he managed to write a highly entertaining illustrated rundown on the progress of soft furniture, pleading for someone to design a seating equivalent of modern architecture. 'Our meals are no longer as voluminous as they were in Victorian and Edwardian days, and yet at least as nutritious in calories and vitamins. Is it not a necessary outcome of the rationalising power of 20th century civilisation that our easy chairs should also try to combine lightness and economy with comfort – just as our architecture does?'

His ideas on modernism were again on view in May 1942, in 'Nine Swallows – No Summer', in which he identified nine promising harbingers of modern architecture in Britain.* Then in August he used his

_____

*Pevsner admitted that in *Pioneers* he had not sufficiently emphasised the contributions of a few original British architects – something that had been 'pointed out' to him by 'Mr P.F.R. Donner' in a letter to the *Review*. In 'Nine Swallows' he 'perused the architectural papers of 1900 to 1914' in search of the spirit of the twentieth century – 'its new functional approach . . . new sympathy with industrially produced materials . . . new distrust of ornament'. Among the 'swallows' in which he detected these qualities were H.B. Cresswell's Queensferry factory, Lethaby's Eagle Insurance Building in position, reasonably enough, to repay his debt to an old friend and benefactor by selecting Frank Pick, who had died the previous year, as the subject of a two-part series on 'Patient Progress' in contemporary design.

From his position at the head of the London Passenger Transport Board, Pick had commissioned new work directly; and in the longer term, as an influential figure in official circles, he had raised the status of industrial design within art schools. The 'Patient Progress' article was a hymn to 'the LPTB style', which Pevsner saw as the clearest possible example of architecture in the service of the community, with the other arts in turn serving architecture. The LPTB style, devised by Pick and executed largely by Charles Holden, was a 'civilising agent', raising the visual taste of the British people and providing them with a temperate and workable environment for their most mundane and essential daily activities. Pick had engineered this environment by demanding integrated design – simple, accessible and modern – throughout the bus and underground system, not just for the buses and trains and their stops and stations, but for the numbers on the buses, the seats and kiosks on station platforms and the cantilevered roofs above them, the display panels along the walls housing posters that Pick himself had commissioned. In places, precisely because of the mundanity of the subject, Pevsner's tribute teeters on the verge of the absurd. 'The litter basket against its travertine wall,' he wrote, 'is of a perfection rarely achieved by our age when it tries to be ornamental.' A bus stop must be more than a post: 'It should at a glance appear the modest representative of an organisation promising comfort and visual pleasures.'

Pick was not a charismatic figure – Churchill (no fan) called him 'the bricklayer', and Maxwell Fry referred to him as a 'lumpy, redfaced Yorkshireman' – but he possessed strengths that Pevsner prized and qualities he shared. Highly focused himself, Pick was infuriated by lack of effort or accuracy or discipline in others. The obituary of him in the *Architectural Review* in December 1941, in all probability written by Pevsner, remarked: 'What he detested more than anything was polite inertia.' If people couldn't see 'the ethical, the vital value of these improvements [in design], they must be made to see it, gently but firmly'. The Pevsner of the *Enquiry into Industrial Art* was inclined to agree.

Birmingham and Sir R.J. Allison's Stamford Street warehouse for HM Stationery Office, London. Much of what he wrote in this article was transcribed directly from his plan for the never-published *AR* special issue of 1939.

The Pick article would be one of Pevsner's last large-scale articles on modern industrial design. More significant in indicating the direction his interests would take for the future was the series of pieces on Victorian architecture that he now began for the *Architectural Review*. This may well have been the series he had failed to persuade Richards to publish in 1941; now, sitting in Richards's editorial chair, he seized his chance.

Within the frame of *Pioneers* and the *Outline of European Architecture*, Pevsner's attitude to Victorian architecture in England had often been tinged with disapproval. In expressing the spirit of the age, and meeting the requirements of their unsophisticated patrons, these buildings were vulgar but vigorous, enterprising but frequently hideous, and his feelings towards them had seemed to veer between aesthetic horror and grudging admiration for their energy. The articles that he now ran in the *Architectural Review* between January and December 1942 hinted at a more nuanced attitude.

The 'Treasure Hunt' series appeared in the *Review* under his pseudonym of 'Peter F.R. Donner', although he allowed himself, rather coyly, to interject occasional comments and criticisms in his own persona. The pieces took the form of paper perambulations through selected areas of London, taking the readers on hunts for the architectural treasures of the nineteenth century (or, rather, what he characterised here as the 'Coburg' period, 1840-1914) in which even the most unlikely streets were rich – and these were to be, he insisted, not predominantly the churches and public and commercial buildings that might already be appreciated, but the ordinary domestic buildings that furnished people's everyday lives. Here for the first time his voice could be heard talking an audience through a built landscape, singling out for them the details that would enable them to date, place, evaluate and above all enjoy what they saw.

The introduction to the series made his purpose clear:

Ninety-nine out of a hundred people nowadays do not look at buildings at all unless by special effort . . . How many of the houses that a business man or a professional man – even an architect – passes on the way from where he lives to his tube station and from his tube station to where he works, does he take in? . . . Yet by walking so blindly he deprives himself of much that would be enjoyable – aesthetically and intellectually. Most of what lines his daily route is, of course, of the 19th century, and the 19th century is the obscurest age since 1066, so far as common knowledge of its style goes. In opening his eyes to every one of the buildings on his right and his left, the workaday passer-by would discover something of dignified proportions here, of bold treatment there, of blatant prosperity at the next corner, and of fanciful decoration further on . . . Those who care to embark on expeditions of their own will find that looking at houses can be entertainment as well as an object lesson, a family game (Date Your District) as well as a treasure hunt.

Exhorting the discerning readers of the *Architectural Review* to walk down side streets in Morden and Golders Green and appreciate the delights of the Victorian semi was a bold gesture, and the format of the series too was inventive. It worked best in the first piece, which concentrated on a single street in the City of London. Across the top of a double-page spread ran a panoramic shot taken down one side of Bishopsgate, showing the houses from number 230 to 272 – one whole block, plus a couple of interesting houses on the next corner. The text, which described these buildings from the perspective of a pedestrian standing back in the middle of the pavement on the other side of the road, ran down the centre of the page. On one side it was flanked by a 'reference column' of small photographs of similar buildings elsewhere, for comparison; down the other margin ran a string of irregular jigsaw-shaped architectural details, extracted from and carefully keyed into the panoramic view above: an Egyptianising capital or Jacobean obelisk here, an Art Nouveau frieze or Tudor gatehouse turret there.

Other areas were used instead to make points about particular architectural trends or curiosities. In February he moved from London EC to London NW to track what happened in the middle of the nineteenth century to upper-middle-class houses like those to be found in the Eton College and Belsize Estates, north of Primrose Hill. Taking three different Italianate villas, he pointed to evidence of 'the expression of extreme architectural individualism, or to put it negatively, the disintegration of the street which characterises the 19th century in its city as well as its suburban buildings'. The following month he was complaining that no one ever looked at anything in Parliament Square except Westminster Abbey and the Houses of Parliament, and was drawing attention to 'what happened to the Gothic style in the other Gothic buildings round Parliament Square and the Broad Sanctuary'. He dwelt particularly lovingly on a red marble drinking fountain – 'hefty, thick and prosperous looking' – erected to honour MPs who had supported the emancipation of slaves, but also intended to distract the thirsty from the temptation of the public house. 'This drinking-fountain movement of the 'fifties and 'sixties,' Pevsner wrote happily, 'is a signal symptom of well-meaning Mid-Victorian blindness to human nature.'*

With the leaves of Southwell doubtless still in his mind, he chose in the May 'Treasure Hunt' to pick on the 'mass-produced capitals of South Wimbledon', which proliferated in the endless streets and terraces of small suburban houses put up in the late nineteenth century to accommodate the urban overflow. The capitals were indeed based on medieval examples, 'but where the 13th century was crisp and sparing, never using more than one kind of leaf for one capital, the Victorians seem flamboyant and flabby, effusive and pedantic.'

In September he was able to play the Treasure Hunt game no more than ten minutes' walk from his own home, in the unpromising side roads running off Golders Green Road, populated with small unassuming houses that had multiplied rapidly in the area between 1910 and 1925. 'No other style is so frequently met around all the cities of England,' he pointed out. 'This is why it deserves careful analysis.' On every side, high-street builders had tried to adopt motifs introduced by architects twenty years earlier, with commendable enterprise but with a degree of clumsiness that was endearing or exasperating, depending on one's mood. Here one saw an oriel window à la Richard Norman Shaw, there a Voysey-ish corner buttress or semicircular arch, but all too often used in the wrong place or with the wrong accent, 'showing knowledge but not understanding of the idiom of contemporary architecture'. Pausing outside one example, Pevsner concluded ruefully, 'For the builders of this house Shaw, Voysey and all their contemporaries have worked in vain.'

After the reverses of the early months of 1942 – the loss of Singapore and the fall of Rangoon – public morale in Britain had been boosted by the ever-increasing ferocity of the RAF's assault on German cities. The Pevsners' feelings must have been impossibly torn by the news of each British success on German soil. Tom was happier now at Sedbergh; that summer they had all gone on a walking holiday in the Lake District with him. Dieter was enjoying a normal school life at Christ Church choir school, learning the cello, collecting stamps and hoping to play Puck in a production of *A Midsummer Night's Dream*.

Meanwhile, in Hanover, Uta felt the threat of exposure and persecution coming ever closer. That summer her small cousin Andreas was

---

*Originally constructed in Parliament Square, the Buxton Memorial Fountain, by Pevsner's bugbear, S.S. Teulon, now stands in Victoria Tower Gardens.

denounced to his next school as a part-Jew by a village schoolteacher. And then the RAF reached Hanover, and the Kockels' apartment block was phosphorus-bombed. It burned from the top, Marianne reported calmly, so Carl Walter was able to save some things from their flat on a lower floor – books, a good pair of silver candlesticks, a Barlach etching (although this was stained with blood where C.W. had cut his hand on glass shattered by the heat of the fire). He had time to lower a small sofa out of the window on a clothes line, but had to leave the much-loved bedroom furniture they had bought from the Deutsche Werkstätten; and although a woman from the flat upstairs stood guard over the increasing pile of salvaged goods in the street, the silver candlesticks were stolen by looters.

With bombing, at least the magnitude of the danger and the nature of the threat were obvious. What exposure as a Jew might have meant for Uta was not as clear, though the rumours and the fears were becoming increasingly horrible. Years after the war, Marianne recalled that in Leipzig people knew of the existence of concentration camps nearby, and suspected that what was happening there was unpleasant, from the fact that local officials maintained a no-entry zone for some distance around their perimeters. As the war progressed, they knew about the Jewish deportations. They knew that in Theresienstadt in Czechoslovakia, which had been turned into a labour camp, people were starving. They also knew about the mass killings in Russia and elsewhere in Eastern Europe, without necessarily drawing any conclusions from this about how the concentration camps might be being run, and what they were being used for.

In England by now, the picture was clearer. In September 1942 the *Manchester Guardian* had carried a remarkably detailed description of conditions in Theresienstadt – the population of 60,000 crammed into the old garrison town with no more than two square metres of living space per person, the rats, the lice, the fleas, the dozens of deaths every day from disease and starvation. In October the Russian atrocities were confirmed, with the announcement in America that the United Nations were to set up a War Crimes Commission. But in England, too, the majority of people still found it hard to conceive of the full truth and to accept these isolated horrors as part of a systematic plan for genocide, until in December 1942 the government published its White Paper on the existence of precisely such a plan. Anthony Eden made a public statement on the Nazi gas chambers, and the House of Commons stood for two minutes of appalled silence. From then on, if people did not acknowledge the reality of the Final Solution, it was because they did not want to. 'Only a voluntarily deaf and blind man could have any doubt about the fate reserved for the Jews in a German Europe,' wrote Primo Levi later in *The Periodic Table*. 'And yet, if we wanted to live, if we wished in some way to take advantage of the youth coursing through our veins, there was indeed no other resource than self-imposed blindness.'[18]

CHAPTER 23

'Contrast, surprise and irregularity'

When *An Outline of European Architecture* was published at the end of 1942, it bore the following dedication: 'This little book I dedicate to you, my three children, in East, North and West, hoping that, when you are grown up, the world will once again be safe for studying and enjoying the achievements of all nations.'* The first edition was a slim pale blue Pelican, 160 pages long on brownish wartime paper, with thirty-two darkling black-and-white plates. As the *Architects' Journal* pointed out helpfully, at 9d it was 'much less than the price of a pint of beer', and the critical reception suggested that the *Outline* represented remarkably good value for money.

Pevsner was well aware of the perils of the historical overview. A few years later, he would be ruthless in his criticism of an only slightly less ambitious project, when he wrote of A.H. Gardner's *Outline of English Architecture* (1946), 'This book has no positive point of view; it does not pull the material together in an original way. It is timid in its accents, and cannot open anybody's eyes.' These were hardly charges that anyone could have levelled at his own *Outline* – a highly personal and opinionated book whose main virtue was its vitality. Mark Girouard would later comment that it did occasionally make buildings sound rather more exciting than they were in reality – perhaps because Pevsner had not visited them; the description of Toledo Cathedral, for example, would seem to have been written from the building plan.†

Pevsner himself was conscious of the *Outline*'s flaws, and readier than anyone else to point them out. 'I tried to make space its focal point,' he wrote later, 'a very belated tribute to the Schmarsow/Pinder past – but to stress social history as well without neglecting history of style. A tall order, and one that failed in various places to varying degrees.'¹ For example, he had treated 'quite inadequately' the landscape garden – 'one of the greatest English contributions to Western architecture' – and had not done justice to any period of Spanish architecture. (Architect Roger Radford, then a student in Cambridge,

---

*Later imprints date the first edition as 1943, but some copies at least bear the date 1942.
†Pevsner had not, in fact, been to Spain when he wrote the *Outline* – almost certainly one reason for its comparative neglect in the book.

335

met Pevsner in 1947 and, as an attempted compliment, told him that a friend, touring France, claimed to have seen every building mentioned in the *Outline*. 'What a lot he must have missed,' said Pevsner.[2])

It was entirely characteristic that he should have encouraged the harshest critic to make his opinions known in the *Architectural Review*. Pevsner had not always given himself time to explore complicated themes in sufficient depth, observed art historian Geoffrey Webb, and he had perhaps put in too much about England. But other reviewers had no such reservations. 'The laymen who will buy the new Pelican book by Dr Nikolaus Pevsner – and there will be thousands of them,' wrote Herbert Read, 'will be carrying round in their pockets a miniature encyclopaedia of European architecture . . . Dr Pevsner and his publishers have between them performed a miracle in offering so much for so little.'[3]

An Outline of European Architecture would be Pevsner's best-selling book, running into seven editions in sixteen languages – Dutch, Italian, Spanish, Japanese, Hungarian, Yugoslav and Finnish among them – usually with additional material on the architecture of the countries in question.* The original edition, in line with Penguin's educational purpose, had been written primarily for their celebrated 'intelligent layman', who had not necessarily seen many buildings, and at a time when no one was able to travel widely, so Pevsner had tended to choose more familiar examples to make his points. In later editions he could cater for a more sophisticated audience with a more eclectic selection. He could also afford more illustrations. By the time of the second edition, in 1945, the number of plates had increased from thirty-two to forty-eight; six years later, the text was nearly twice as long and included sixty-four plates. When the sixth 'Jubilee' edition appeared in 1960, it would contain 600 illustrations, on the model of an edition designed by the German publishing house Prestel-Verlag, which had already produced an extended version of the book in 1958, incorporating a large number of photographs of the German baroque buildings that Pevsner so loved. By 1961 the book had sold a quarter of a million copies, and continues to sell to this day in new editions.†

The *Outline* was, in the words of John Summerson, 'a uniquely successful episode in architectural publishing'.[4] He slightly regretted

---

*In the late 1990s, *Outline* was still selling as many copies per year at Penguin as all the *Buildings of England* series combined.
†At the time of writing, the most recent edition was that from Palazzo in autumn 2009, fully illustrated in colour, with a new introduction and conclusion by Michael Forsyth.

the fact that 'as book and author grew older, they both grew in bulk'. Pevsner himself was anxious about the continuous stream of additions and insertions he was making, lest they 'gradually encrust the original thoughts'. For Summerson, it was the explosion in illustrations in later editions that disturbed the balance – 'The original text . . . now patters rather thinly through a palace of gorgeous gloss' – and he deplored the simultaneous explosion in price, to a remarkable seven guineas for the Jubilee edition.

But, carping apart, Summerson believed that the book had 'shown architectural history to the English as they have never seen it before'. The *Outline* went straight on to students' reading lists, in schools as well as universities, alongside works by Kenneth Clark, Ernst Gombrich and Bernard Berenson: it was already a set book for Higher School Certificate in 1945.* It was one of only about thirty Penguin titles to be issued in the 'Educational and Vocational Training' series, which formed part of the 'release' scheme aimed at troops leaving the armed forces, with a view to preparing them for civilian life.[5] The *Outline* was, after all, in Reyner Banham's words, 'sharp enough to slice through fatigue, mental staleness, the noise of war and transport, the hostile atmosphere of barracks and digs, to slice right through to the heart of all forms of aesthetic fuddy-duddiness'. (It was also one of about 100 titles to be included in the 'Prisoners of War Book Service', which Penguin ran from March 1943 until about February 1944 – curiously, since as a general rule the German censors banned all books by Jewish authors from entering the PoW camps, along with the works of John Buchan, most Penguin Specials, and books with 'escape' or 'tunnel' in their titles.†)

But the *Outline* also took the great buildings of Europe and the vocabulary of architecture to a wider and older audience, to people who, as Banham put it, 'were quite untouched by the *Architectural Review* and the *Burlington Magazine*', who desperately wanted some reminder of human aspirations and achievements that had outlasted the wars of the past. 'Thousands,' wrote Banham, 'must have made their discovery of Vierzehnheiligen in an air raid shelter, or the Pazzi

---

*Precursor of A-levels in the English secondary curriculum.
†'The Prisoners of War Book Service', in J. Pearson, *Penguins March On: Books for the Forces during World War II* (Penguin Collectors Society, Miscellany 11, 1996). The English censors banned the sending of all charts, tide tables and books on navigation, plus second-hand books that might contain suspect marks and messages. The German 'banned' list included Palgrave's *Golden Treasury* and Spinoza's *Ethics* (as both Palgrave and Spinoza were Jews), *Scouting for Boys* and, for some reason, the poetry of James Elroy Flecker.

Chapel in a transit camp.' To Peter Murray, it was quite simply 'one of the most important books I have ever read, a light in the darkness of those dreadful days'.[6]

And where were the children to whom the *Outline* had been dedicated, during the dark days? Tom, in Sedbergh, was the child in the North, Dieter, in Oxford, the child in the West. Uta, of course, was far further away, and no one was quite sure what her life in the East of Germany was like. Marianne would always feel that the Pevsners never realised quite how difficult and dangerous it was, assuming that being with the Kockels was a guarantee of safety for their daughter. Certainly their messages to Uta were as cheerful and commonplace as the pitiable constraints of the Red Cross form permitted – how was her harmonica practice? had her plan to go to art school come to anything? – but a very real anxiety lay beneath the surface. Pevsner quoted with concern a story he had heard at a lecture, about a letter coming from Germany that said 'We have plenty of everything, don't worry', but was annotated in the margin: 'This is rubbish – The Censor'. In the spring and summer of 1943 all the reports seemed to be of Allied success in battle – victory in North Africa, ascendancy over the U-boats in the North Atlantic, the recapture of Sicily – against a background of the ever-escalating destruction of German cities by Bomber Command. That June, Wilhelm Pinder would give a talk on German radio entitled 'The Life of Monuments'. Germany's greatest buildings, he argued defiantly, would last for ever in the consciousness of the people of the whole world, not just Germany, whatever happened. When the originals were destroyed, they left behind them an 'inner image', fainter than the reality but still accessible to anyone who had had an interior relationship with them. Realistically, this can have been scant consolation to Pevsner, reading of the obliteration of Unter den Linden, the grandest street in Berlin, where he had begun his courtship of Lola more than twenty years before, and of the ravaging of the university in Munich, where he had seen Wölfflin and taken his first steps towards a career in art history.

Unease and melancholy often became irritability. Bertschy Grigson remembered the tension and bickering at 2 Wildwood Terrace: Pevsner struggling to pull together his career of shreds and patches, Lola impatient and resentful, telling him to get his own tray when he came in from the cold: 'I've been working all day too.' Pevsner suggesting he might look for work in America, Lola retorting, 'If you go, you go alone . . . I will not live in such a *loud* country.' Lola performing miracles on a limited budget, Pevsner incensed by unnecessary mean-ness: 'Your awful preoccupation with money! Today we have eaten the last of the butter and margarine, I couldn't even have anything on my bread for supper. Today I am inviting Tomlinson for lunch even if you explode.' Even in Lola's absence there were the aggravations of an inadequate home help – 'She complains there is more work than she was expecting, makes tons of food and eats it herself' – and the ever-present lodger, Herr Meier: 'He does everything so wonderfully and so thoroughly, the ghastly nit-picker . . . He helped with the washing up on Saturday and Sunday, with the result that it took over an hour both times and there wasn't enough time to prepare the Sunday lectures and they didn't come off.'

As always in times of stress, Pevsner took refuge in work. Two of 1942's preoccupations were still in evidence in 1943. He was lecturing a good deal on English art and architecture, regularly at Birkbeck and occasionally at the Courtauld; and in his journalism he was tending to concentrate, without advertising the fact, on Victorian architecture, from the most serious to the most frivolous.

Under his own name he published an extended article on 'Model Houses for the Labouring Classes'.[7] The aim of the piece was to show how workers' housing had evolved in the latter half of the nineteenth century from upper-class philanthropy through bourgeois commercial speculation to become the acknowledged responsibility of the state. The moral purpose in such Victorian ventures as social housing undoubtedly appealed to Pevsner, but he was increasingly attracted by what he had described in 'Treasure Hunt' as the age's 'healthy and candid love of the ornamental and the fantastic'. 'The End of the Pattern Books' is both an illustrated record of the Victorian fancy for the styles of other times and other countries – an invaluable chart for Treasure Hunters set on spotting Swiss chalets, French *cottages ornées* and Pompeian villas in the suburbs – and a celebration of the extrav-agant.[8]

Pevsner also had a sober point to make. In an article on Victorian studies in America he made the claim, far more untoward then, that one should 'look at a Victorian villa in the way one approaches a Syrian church of the 6th century'.[9] In other words, the buildings of the nineteenth century were a perfectly proper object for serious study – but, he continued, not too serious. His championing of Victorian buildings would always, like many of the buildings themselves, have an element of inconsistency, spontaneity and contrariness, and stand-ards on which he insisted elsewhere were here allowed to slide. The Victorian style, he wrote firmly, 'possesses fantasy and a vernacular richness and jollity of decoration . . . Approach it strictly archaeologically and that appeal might cease to operate.'

In another area – the urban architecture of the present and future – Pevsner would find his earlier convictions challenged. After the Allied successes in the North African campaign at the end of 1942, with victory easier to imagine, the debate about the shape of post-war society had become more urgent. The Beveridge Report of December 1942 outlined the foundation of the modern welfare state by proposing a national health service and a system of social security whereby, in return for a weekly contribution, the British people would be guaranteed a minimum standard of living in times of sickness, unemployment or retirement. In 1943 the Ministry for Town and Country Planning was created out of the planning departments of the former Ministry of Works; and in December that year Lord Woolton was appointed to head a new Ministry of Reconstruction, with a seat in the Cabinet.

This, one might have thought, would be the moment for the *Architectural Review* to have seized the opportunity to press for the immediate and thoroughgoing implementation of the principles it had championed so fervently in the 1930s. With so much of Britain's urban building already destroyed or damaged, the planners might perhaps have been exhorted to continue what the bombers had begun, and then to start again from scratch, on strictly functionalist lines. Had either the *Review* or its acting assistant editor been as narrowly zealous in their modernism as some critics have suggested, this would have been the time to launch their manifesto.

Instead, at H. de Cronin Hastings's request, Pevsner and the *Review* devoted a good deal of time and space to the exploration of a theory of planning that was far more moderate, more workable and more closely rooted in English tradition. In January 1944, the *Review* had published a long and elaborate piece by its proprietor under his own name, entitled 'EXTERIOR FURNISHING or Sharawaggi: the art of making urban landscape'.* The planner of the future Britain, Hastings argued, would have an embarrassment of alternative styles from which to choose – but only one that really suited the circumstances of recent history and national character: the English Picturesque tradition. The

---

*'Sharawaggi' was a word borrowed in the eighteenth century from the Japanese (though regularly attributed to the Chinese). In the original it means 'asymmetrical'; it was used by eighteenth-century gardeners, and understood by Pevsner, to mean 'casual, asymmetrical grace' in landscape.

landscape planners of the eighteenth century had delighted in variety, contrast and irregularity. Those in charge of Britain's post-war reconstruction should take their cue from an approach to planning that had been flexible, pragmatic, sensitive to feelings as well as intellect, and essentially democratic in its respect for all tastes. 'Here lies for the urban planner the great romantic opportunity,' wrote Hastings – and it was at the same time an opportunity to make modernism psychologically acceptable to the English.

Hastings, it would seem, had published this agenda for urban planning largely on the basis of a long-established personal fondness for the picturesque landscape, which had been confirmed by his reading of Christopher Hussey's classic work *The Picturesque* some fifteen years before.[10] He had taken the precaution, however, of commissioning Pevsner to provide the historical precedent and theoretical scaffolding for his argument – to 'pick up the theory, rediscover the prophets, and apply the principles'. The *Architectural Review*, he told Pevsner, was simply applying Hussey's precepts in its day-to-day work, in looking for a way of pulling together the pieces of Britain's shattered urban landscape into a single pleasing and practical picture.

Pevsner set out to make sense of this statement with a series of articles on the nature and historical significance of the English Picturesque. He had read Hussey's book himself even before his first visit to England, and had recognised its themes everywhere on that trip – in the delightful contrast between formal buildings and informal landscape in the English countryside, and in the way towns such as Oxford had evolved organically, with formal quadrangles set next door to narrow, twisting lanes, baroque college buildings shoulder to shoulder with workmen's cottages and Victorian chapels. Now this commission from Hastings focused his ideas, and laid the foundation of an interest that would last for the rest of his working life.

Looking back on his wartime investigation for his eccentric employer, Pevsner would remember: 'As my thought in these years developed, I realised that the missing link between the Picturesque and 20th-century architecture was the picturesque theory chiefly of Uvedale Price, but also of [Richard] Payne Knight and [Humphry] Repton, and even [Joshua] Reynolds.'[11] Pevsner took from Uvedale Price his basic definition of a picturesque landscape – the kind of scene that would appeal to a painter and appear to advantage in a picture, being characterised by contrast, surprise and irregularity, rather than pattern and symmetry – and set about locating Price (1747–1829) in the context of both his immediate predecessors and his successors and critics.

Man's relationship with Nature, Pevsner argued, had shifted

dramatically during the eighteenth century. The formal garden had given way to 'nature adorned' and from then on the landscape gardener had allowed himself far greater expressiveness and more inventive use of a variety of styles and motifs. Pevsner traced the evolution of the underlying theory. First, he said, came the poets, then the men of action, and lastly the full-blown theorists. In 'The Genesis of the Picturesque', which would be published in the *Review* in November 1944, he described how the English landscape garden between 1710 and 1730 grew out of the thinking not of gardeners or architects but of philosophers and writers, and was essentially the product of an increasingly liberal political and cultural climate. Joseph Addison, for example, praised in the *Spectator* a kind of beauty that lay between the wholly artificial and the wholly wild – a humanised nature, the 'natural' as created by man. Alexander Pope described this as 'nature methodised' – arranged and elaborated with all kinds of effects, but never totally obliterated:

> But treat the goddess like a modest fair,
> Nor overdressed, nor leave her wholly bare.
> Let not each beauty everywhere be spied,
> When half the skill is decently to hide.

The practice of the new art of landscape gardening was supplied by men of action such as William Kent and Capability Brown – and they chose to aim at an impression of nature tidied rather than adorned. The effect intended was one of laissez-faire, even if a good deal of work had gone into achieving it – and Pevsner found that he had little to say about this phase, just as he would rarely have much to say about Palladian architecture. His curiosity was piqued far more thoroughly by the theorists who followed, the documenters of the true art of the Picturesque landscape gardener, and he revelled in Uvedale Price's dismissal of Capability Brown: 'Whoever views objects with a painter's eye, looks with indifference, if not with disgust, at the clump, the belts, the made water, and the eternal smoothness' of a Brown landscape.[12]

Price himself advocated a more varied and adventurous approach. The truly Picturesque might encompass incongruity, absurdity, even impropriety. Its essential qualities were intricacy (in which he included concealment and curiosity), irregularity, contrast, surprise, irritation (by which he meant stimulus and piquancy) and accident. Price, argued Pevsner, had a 'latitude of aesthetic sensibility' which raised him 'to an undated position in the history of aesthetic theory . . . We can take our problems of visual planning to Price and be certain of answers well worth pondering over.' The designers of the modern council estate, for instance, would be well advised to take his advice on using greenery to enhance buildings, as well as incorporating 'old' formal elements, like terraced or walled gardens within a new, irregular landscape.

They might perhaps also look to Price's friend and neighbour, Richard Payne Knight, another eccentric figure bursting out of the confines of his period.[13] In Pevsner's eyes, Knight's distinctive contribution was to argue that it is impossible to look at scenes and objects in a strictly aesthetic way, disregarding the subject matter. In practice, our aesthetic reactions are deflected by association of ideas; some forms delight and others disgust, not because of qualities inherent in the objects, but because of the mental processes of the beholder. It is to some extent the viewer who makes the connections and forms the pattern – and this may have been the idea that Hastings was picking up, in promoting Picturesque theory as a recipe for reconstruction. Value and meaning were to rest not in individual buildings created from an ideological blueprint to meet the demands of theory, as 1930s modernism had seemed sometimes to suggest, but in the human effort of creating a new urban landscape to please the human eye, from components jumbled by war and the passage of time.

By directing Pevsner towards the 'improvers' of the eighteenth century, Hastings unintentionally did more than anyone else to alter and soften his attitude to modern architecture and his vision for the future. Pevsner would later write to Hastings, '[My] thanks to you, without whom I would not have become one of the Picturesques and thus have acquired the saving grace of just a little bit of inconsistency.'[14]

Pevsner's interest in England's future was perhaps heightened by the awareness that there was no going back to his German past. On the afternoon of 3 December 1943, just after the curtain had risen in the Neue Theater on the first act of Wagner's *Die Walküre*, the RAF launched a massive attack on Leipzig, which continued into the next day. By the time it was finished, 1,500 people had been killed and 40,000 were homeless; 90 per cent of the publishing quarter for which the city had been famous for centuries had burned to the ground. Leipzig, wrote Pevsner, 'does not exist any longer . . . If any town has been wiped out, this one has.'[15]

He was still not confident of his position in his new homeland. Even in the editor's chair at the *Architectural Review*, he never felt secure.

'The end of the war may bring a reversion, to most of us. It might be just as well to face that,' he wrote pessimistically to Esther Simpson.[16] The only solution, it seemed, was to keep busy. '**I must work**,' his childhood hero Van Gogh had once written, 'even if it is only studies of cabbage, to get calm.' This perfectly summed up Pevsner's own attitude to mental effort as a tranquilliser.

His strategy was to hold as many options open as possible: the *Review*, the King Penguins, articles and lectures, on landscape gardening, medieval sculpture, French seventeenth-century painting, Victorian churches, German Romantic art, modern pottery. And yet, for all his versatility and willingness to diversify, his work was increasingly finding a centre of gravity. In the ten years since he had left Germany, his identity, first as a historian of Italian painting, then as an authority on British industrial design, had become an increasingly blurred silhouette. Dr Nikolaus Pevsner, it seemed, was primarily an architectural historian.

This metamorphosis was neatly encapsulated in the shift in his interest in Mannerism from paintings to buildings. In an article on 'Mannerism and Architecture' in December 1944, he suggested that there must be developments in architecture to parallel Mannerist trends in painting and sculpture. Two years later, in a long piece entitled 'The Architecture of Mannerism' (1946), he indicated what these developments might be.* Mannerist buildings must be distinguished both in their form and their emotional content from the Renaissance works that preceded and the baroque works that followed them. They cannot be confused, because they display quite clearly the forces at work in a particular epoch of history – the austerity, brutality and conflict of the Counter-Reformation, expressed in walls of excessive length without accent, the crudity of raw stone and the deliberate use of heretical detail, classical features altered or used wrongly, betraying 'a full knowledge of the law and a determination to break it'. The distinguishing features of buildings such as Michelangelo's Laurentian Library and Giulio Romano's Palazzo del Te are instability, dissonance, preciosity and unresolved ambiguity: 'In the Baroque a turbulent struggle and a triumphant end, in Mannerism an intricate and conflicting pattern and no solution anywhere.' 'This essay is a gross over-simplification,' Pevsner

---

*The piece was included by Geoffrey Grigson in the first volume of his literary periodical *The Mint*, alongside contributions by W.H. Auden, Sean O'Casey and Simone Weil. There appear to have been only two issues of *The Mint*, the second in 1948.

conceded.* Nevertheless, it was a subject he would continue to revisit, with particular reference to Elizabethan architecture as England's version of Mannerism.[17]

He had another chance that year to indulge in plotting national character and mapping it against the events of history to illustrate the character of succeeding ages. He described himself in December 1944 as having been working on a 'Chart', which seems likely to have been the curiosity that emerged five years later under the imprint of the Architectural Press, as 'English History at a glance: a CHART designed by H.A. Vetter with a historical digest by P. Dantry and E. Savage'. A slim book the size and shape of an atlas, the 'CHART' was described by its designer as a 'phasmagram' rather than a diagram, 'emphasising the imaginative and not the purely diagrammatic presentation of its contents'. The aim of the phasmagram was to present a synoptic view of English history and culture, illustrating the parallel evolution of each area of human activity by identifying the milestones in each field and plotting them all on a single map, revealing a complex web of relationships.

The chart was divided vertically into five strips of contrasting colours, representing 'the chief periods of British history' – Feudal Medieval (1066–1350), Mercantile Medieval (1350–1485), Renaissance and Reformation (1485–1600), Baroque and Rationalism (1600–1760), Romantic and Industrial (1760–1914) – with a column at the end left uncoloured, to represent modern times, dated as beginning in 1914. The chart was divided horizontally to represent the various fields of thought and activity: the land, science, economic and social history, expansion and exploration, the kings, politics and parliament, historiography, essay, criticism and satire, fiction and poetry, drama, architecture, sculpture, painting, music, philosophy and religion. Events were then represented in the appropriate cell by the names of the individuals who had most influenced them, in the form of labels coloured to correspond with the five periods.

'Chains of labels, representing names of men, run through ages . . . They form patterns, according to how strong or weak at any given moment Britain was in one particular field of human activity or thought.' The significance of these patterns was clarified in an appendix by what the editors referred to as 'annotation of the visual evidence'

---

*Pevsner's formulation of Mannerism was undermined by the publication of John Shearman's *Mannerism: Style and Civilisation* (Penguin, 1967), which, based less on intuition and more on documentary evidence, derived Mannerism from stylistic features already present in the Renaissance rather than from any historical events of the Counter-Reformation. Pevsner noted the book, but did not undertake to revise his thinking.

– and Pevsner was openly identified here as the 'annotator' for architecture, alongside Michael Tippett for music, Robert Birley for history, and so on.*

Whether or not Pevsner had a hand in designing the phasmagram – and Dieter Pevsner suspects that his father might well have been concealed behind the self-mocking pseudonym 'P. Dantry' – he will have appreciated what it set out to do. Built on the model of the *Kulturfahrplan* or 'Culture Timetable', which was a familiar German device, the 'CHART' sought to coordinate events and individuals 'according to the changing spirit of ages'. It could also have been interpreted as a graphic representation of Pinder's theory of overlapping 'generations' of individuals. Above all, the CHART was a perfect tool for identifying people working ahead of their time, Pevsner's 'pioneers'. An innovator in any field might be given a label of one colour to designate the time of his birth, but this might project into a preceding or succeeding period and appear against a background of a different colour if his ideas were out of synchronisation with his age. In the field of architecture, such Pevsnerian favourites as Voysey, Mackintosh and Charles Holden are coloured conspicuously in the hue of the following stylistic period, to show graphically that they were ahead of their time, whereas Lutyens carries the mud-brown label of the 'Romantic and Industrial' period well into modern times. And the CHART ends with a challenge that one can certainly imagine on Pevsner's lips: 'Controversial placing of names is better than no decision on placing at all.'

He might have had some difficulty in plotting his own domestic life with the same confidence. Tom, now eighteen, had joined up and was in an army training camp; both he and Dieter, still at school in Oxford, were safer away from London. That summer saw dramatic Allied advances in Europe, each time followed promptly by German strikes against the British Home Front. The fall of Monte Cassino on 18 May 1944 and the taking of Rome two weeks later were followed by the D-Day landings in Normandy on 6 June. Less than a week later London was hit by the V-1 flying bombs, the 'doodlebugs'. In July 1944 Colonel Claus von Stauffenberg led a conspiracy of general staff officers of the German army in an unsuccessful attempt on Hitler's life. On 19 August, Resistance cells in Paris rose up against the German

*This was the Robert Birley who, as headmaster of Charterhouse, had possibly offered Pevsner a job in 1941.

346

occupying garrison, and on 25 August the city was liberated by the Allies.

'It is a terrific thing, this advance now,' Pevsner wrote to Dieter on 9 September. But, as before, the advance had been followed by German retaliation. Montgomery's push with the 21st Army Group along the French coast had overrun the V-1's launch sites at the end of August, reducing the frequency of its attacks, but on the night of 8 September, London was hit for the first time by its successor. The V-2 was the first ballistic missile, a forty-seven-foot rocket carrying 2,200 pounds of explosive, which climbed to a height of sixty miles and descended at a speed of up to 2,500 mph. That night Londoners heard a new sound, a deafening crash followed by 'a noise like a faraway express train' and a sonic boom from the upper atmosphere. There was a second blast almost at once. The explosions were so loud that everyone assumed the impact had been in their own area; in fact, the first V-2s had fallen in Chiswick and Epping, as Pevsner reported to Dieter, more or less accurately: 'You hear the explosions all over London. At our house from Chiswick as well as Eltham [sic].' Nevertheless, on 17 September the blackout was replaced by the 'dim-out', which permitted an amount of light equivalent to a full moon – a great relief to those who, like the Pevsners in their tall Victorian house, had grown accustomed to wrestling with unwieldy blackout materials on high windows.

Lola had in fact been spending more and more time at the Grigsons' Wiltshire cottage, and Pevsner, stuck in London, was beginning to find the lack of communication unsettling. The social life attached to his post at the *Architectural Review* attracted him very little: 'Lunch at Prunier was chic but depressing,' he wrote on 10 September. 'I am totally unsuited to the bright lights.' Meanwhile his wife appeared to be pursuing her own life in the country, indifferent to his needs. When she failed to let him know the date when Dieter was due to have his tonsils out, making it impossible for him to visit the patient beforehand in the old Victoria Hospital in Swindon, he was furious: 'You must be living in the jungle with a loincloth made of palm leaves. Have you never heard of a European contraption called the telephone? . . . or are you too mean? I don't mind the money . . . Now don't make big child-eyes and say "I didn't know" . . . If you stay away much longer, our correspondence will become what it was in Camp . . . I am hopping mad.'

But he was aware that he was not guiltless, and often made matters worse by being brusque and unsympathetic. 'Dear Lolchen, I AM A BRUTE,' he wrote at around this time. 'It's all my fault. You are as graceful as the Three Graces put together. Why am I so beastly . . .

Of course you want the oil stove only for filling it for my benefit. It's the old story.' The old story, indeed . . . It would appear that some time in the middle of the war Pevsner had again hurt her deeply with another passing infatuation – this time with Camilla Rodker, twenty years younger (Pevsner was in his early forties, Camilla twenty-two or twenty-three) and someone whom Lola had treated almost as a daughter. Very little contemporary evidence remains, but in an undated letter, most probably written in 1943, he had declared, 'I'm through and I can promise nothing is going to happen. Why? Because the married relationship is stronger than I had thought. NO sacrifice, no charity – it is a fact. Again and again I have obstinately done wrong. You will at least no longer believe that I behave with stupid melodrama as you do. You have my promise and now let it be . . . Let's have an hour off from talking about faithfulness and sacrifice.'

In the middle of September 1944, he assured Lola, 'I really want nothing more than that you should come to like life again. And you have behaved so decently throughout the whole thing . . . Perhaps there is a way of arranging things that is more innocent and less shocking.' By most people's standards, the 'thing' had probably been innocuous enough, as with Margot and Lise, and, in Pevsner's eyes at least, it had in no way affected his feelings for Lola. With the same letter he sent her a packet of Yardley talcum powder 'as a love token. That'll banish the wicked wrinkles. My rabbit, you are so sweet with your worry. I love you terribly, you please me more than Bertschy and Camilla rolled into one.' But he knew that to someone of her temperament no infidelity was trivial and no wound was slight. After going to a recital of *Die Winterreise*, which Schubert composed in the depths of a desperate and unhappy love affair, he wrote to her: 'I couldn't help thinking of you and asking a thousand forgivenesses. I really have to take you more seriously. In my desiccation, I forget how one feels – when the whole world takes on that colour.'

He had, however, left his concern too late, and it would appear that Lola had engaged in some emotional entanglement of her own, with John Rodker. Bertschy Grigson would say later that Lola 'had an obvious crush' on Rodker, and Pevsner himself was aware of it. In October 1944, he mentioned Rodker in a note to her and burst out angrily, 'Dam' you – that'll eclipse all the rest of this letter.' After her death he would reflect: 'She had plenty of time to fall for him in my digging and fire-watching nights. The question is: did she fall for him or to him? Of course, I could never know and I shall never know, but it seems to me that she did not agree in the end, and that that fretted JR . . . I longed and urged and got nowhere, she did and had to refuse satisfaction to herself.' It was important to him to believe that Lola had not slept with Rodker, 'because that was her code of honour, and that is what discipline in the end presented . . . May I be right in this belief. May I, though I never had pity on her, when the urges pinched me.'

Lola had without doubt become very attached to Rodker. This may well have been what prompted him to move without ceremony out of Wildwood Terrace to 10 Nottingham Place, a small house in Marylebone. Camilla made a brief attempt at living with him there, which she later remembered as 'a disaster. I had a go at being a good daughter. But I detested my father. I could see what my mother hated about him.' She had then met Henry Israel (whom she subsequently married) and moved in with him, which Rodker decided to interpret as 'neglect'.*

Ever since moving into Wildwood Terrace, Rodker had spent a good deal of time with Lola, and had been a needed and valued friend. He gave her books from his press as they came out – *Soviet Anthology* in 1943 and *Love Songs of Asia* in 1944: at her death, the Russian anthology still contained dried flowers pressed between its pages. Whatever Pevsner chose to believe, Rodker probably did take Lola to bed once, for mutual consolation, and then backed hastily away from her demands for commitment. This at least is the impression one receives from a series of painful letters that Lola addressed to Rodker at around this time. 'Split personality,' wrote Lola in anguish:

> You tell me that I am one, and all the evil, the devil, comes out when I am with you . . . Why do other people not see all these bad and evil sides of me? . . . Why does nobody see in my face what a menacing human being I am? I assure you I feel kindly and tender towards you, when you are not there, when you are kind yourself. But my ways annoy you, irritate you, and you corner me, I feel caught, and so I start to bite . . . You have many friends, they all try to help you and do not irritate you because they do not make you responsible for their lives. My God, I try not to make you responsible. I tried to be an easy burden. But I wanted to penetrate more deeply . . . I am too frank. Balsac [*sic*] mentions this as a speciality of the German. Suicide should be the outcome, it would not only give me rest but mean rest to you, to Pevsner, to my children . . .

---

*Camilla Bagg, interview with the author, 26/2/92. In his will Rodker left her £100, 'as a token of affection, she being amply provided for otherwise', dividing the rest between his daughter Joan and fourth wife Marianne.

Tell me that there are some good things left, that my heart, although very sentimental, is good and strong and loving and devout, besides being possessive and imperative and bossy and tempestuous . . . I know that I am old, that I am looking old, but my heart is young and I still have enough strength to take on another big duty or responsibility.* Do you hate me for having these strengths? But I cannot help them and I have so many weaknesses . . . You are not unhappy as I am, but you are also never so happy as I can be. You do not feel that you must burst either with tears or with joy, you do not know the utter distress of the heart when '*die Sehnsucht*'/ 'yearning' overwhelms me.

It must be boaring [*sic*] to you to hear me again. It is never boaring to me to think of you. Today I remembered what a good friend you have been to your French friends. And I am sure you would have been just such a one to me if I was not of such a possessing and vehement character and if you have not taken me into your arms to go to bed with me. What a fatal thing it had been . . . Just because you felt lonely and deserted. I know it was wrong and it has been forgiven and still its shadow cannot be wiped out and I am too sentimental to get over it . . . I can understand how you must hate me. A German! It is impossible for me to behave as you want it. And still, human beings should be able to understand, to feel and love our national barriers, and you should be the first to admit this. And still I know you will call me a German, a Nazi! Yes, it is closing me in, what is left of me if I add it all up. Concentration camp, cringing, splitter, jealousy, bossy, sentimental, self-centred, asking too high a price for all the bit of work I do.

Whether or not Lola ever sent the letters is unclear: certainly, there is no reference to them in Rodker's letters to her, which are resolutely commonplace and mention Pevsner and the children often. Rodker may have received her letters and sent them back; or it may be that, like her husband, Lola stopped short of translating wish into action. The letters were found in Lola's desk after her death. Pevsner was a scrupulous historian: they were among his own papers when he died.

If Uta, now twenty, had been at home, it is possible that Lola would have been less lonely, although her relationship with her children was perhaps not a confiding one. 'I discipline them,' she wrote to Rodker, 'you may say I break their will, in order to be able to live with them

---

*She would have been little more than forty.

in community. They have to give something up, just as I give something up.' Cruelly, he seems to have told her that he was now too busy with his own family to spend so much time with her. 'How can a friendship, an intimacy, shrink into nothingness,' she protested:

> My feelings for you are like the firm sky, there are many tempestuous clouds, but the sky stays firm . . . My God, it is rather killing and I realise that I am an old infatuated woman, who takes herself much too serious. Hah, hah. I should laugh, but I am so hopelessly sentimental and selfpitying that I cannot help weeping . . . What sense has been in the last six years of my life? You want me to forget, to regret and to see myself as a funny figure of the musik hall. Well, then I cannot see any sense in living any longer, and had I not this everlasting hope that you might listen to your heart one day, I would have put an end to it all.

'I am not grateful to life,' she ended. 'I have so much. Three children, a husband and plentiful to eat. But the children are grown up and independent.* Pevsner has got a position and the work he loves more than anything else, and you – you told me: I need you. I thought I might be useful again, as I had been useful in breeding children.'

'*The work he loves more than anything else*' – Lola's old jealousy of Pevsner's work was as acute as ever, and with increasing justification. When a revised edition of *An Outline of European Architecture* appeared in 1945, Pevsner was described on the back cover as 'one of the most learned and stimulating writers on art in England'.

Cyril Connolly would later complain that the cultural renaissance during the war promoted not artists but critics:

> We are becoming a nation of culture-diffusionists. Culture-diffusion is not art. We are not making a true art. The appreciation of art is spreading everywhere, education has taken wings, we are at last getting a well-informed inquisitive public. But war-artists are not art, the Brains Trust is not art, journalism is not art, the BBC is not art . . . We are turning all our writers into commentators until one day there will be nothing left for them to comment on.[18]

---

*Tom was eighteen, Dieter only twelve, but he had been away from home at boarding school for some time.

Allowing for a considerable degree of exaggeration in this diatribe, Pevsner certainly benefited from the boom in 'commentating', and in 1945 he would find a new platform for his comments. He had first been introduced to the BBC by Geoffrey Grigson, who had worked for the Corporation since the mid-1930s. The BBC had gained immensely in power during the war from a significantly increased budget, enlarged staff and greater air time. It was therefore fertile ground for people like Pevsner, an acknowledged authority in a weighty but interesting field and blessed with both the will and the ability to communicate. He was hardly a typical BBC voice – the majority of the accents to be heard, on the 'serious' channels at any rate, were Home Counties and upper-middle-class – but as a practised lecturer, he had the great virtues of directness and a total lack of vanity or pomposity.

He made his first broadcast on 9 February 1945 – a forthright commentary on Frank Lloyd Wright and Le Corbusier, which formed part of *The Arts*, a magazine programme on the Home Service produced by Noni Wright.* For this modest contribution, the BBC thought it had to get permission from the Aliens Department of the Ministry of Labour, and duly requested Pevsner to supply them with his British Police Registration Certificate number (531502). In due course, the International Labour Branch of the Ministry responded – 'The foreigner does not require the permission of this department to fulfil the engagement' – but did query the choice of a German.

A second broadcast followed in May, entitled 'Artists and Academies'. With art education, Pevsner was still on safe ground; but on less exposed platforms than the BBC he was prepared to venture into the more precarious area of modern art, tempted there by a man who would remain one of his lifelong heroes. In February in the *Burlington Magazine* and again in November, in a short piece for the *Architectural Review* on the Shelter Sketch Book, Pevsner summarised his thoughts on Henry Moore, whom he considered the greatest living British artist. Carrying through the ideas that he had expressed twenty years before as a young art critic in Dresden, he praised Moore's shunning of pure and sterile abstraction in favour of the humanity that characterised the Shelter Sketch Book. The fastidious Pevsner, who had disliked travelling on the Underground even in its relatively comfortable peacetime state, seems to have had little sympathy with Feliks Topolski's

*Wynona 'Noni' Wright (1913–64), born in New Zealand and trained as an actress before coming to England in 1935. In 1939 she joined the Empire Section of the BBC as a talks producer.

merry, Dickensian version of the wartime Tube communities. Moore's vision of the shelterers, he wrote, was infinitely more profound and, for all its lack of colour or anecdote, more human. 'He must have spent many a night down in the rattling grottoes. He must have seen these men and women drably satisfied and these children unconcernedly at play. The greyness and the leaden weight which he saw in them are not those of war and desolation, they come of the primeval and perennial misery of inarticulate undeveloped humanity which must cry out to him just as pitifully from the crowds on the pier or at the dogs.' This view of mankind, Pevsner concluded, was a kind of 'sympathetic pessimism' – and Moore responded warmly to his assessment: 'I've found it remarkably interesting and sympathetic and I need hardly tell you how pleased I am that an article so serious and showing such a rare understanding of sculpture should have appeared on my work. I agree with a good deal of what you say, and I should like nothing better than one day soon for us to meet and talk about the thoughts you express, for many of them come very close to those that are in my own mind about my work.'[19]

Elsewhere Pevsner was reviewing in the *Spectator* for March 1945 a book by his old Birmingham rival, Thomas Bodkin, entitled *Dismembered Masterpieces: A Plea for Their Reconstruction by International Action.* He was lecturing Charterhouse schoolboys on the history and enjoyment of sculpture, and at Birkbeck was tackling the widest variety of topics so far, from the English castle to the Dutch interior, German monumental carving to painting in the age of Dryden. Meanwhile, Lola had far less to distract her from constantly nagging anxiety about Uta and the safety of the Kockel family.

The Allied advance had begun to slow in the autumn of 1944, when the British airborne landing dubbed 'Operation Market Garden' had failed at Arnhem to secure the last of the main bridges in German-occupied Holland. A surprise German offensive in the Ardennes on 16 December had driven seventy-two kilometres west towards Antwerp, creating a 'bulge' that gouged into the arc of the Allied advance and would take a month to nip off, at a cost of more than 80,000 Allied casualties. But none of this had made the prospects brighter or the conditions easier for German civilians.

Even at Naumburg, where food at least was not as scarce as in the cities, there had been a new danger. An engineer and his family were living nearby in a little cottage; during air raids Marianne had let them take shelter in the cellar of the Kurlbaum house, but the engineer's children had got bored and strayed outside to play, trampling flowers and damaging vines. When Marianne had asked them to stay inside, the engineer had taken offence. Not long afterwards, the police had come round asking questions and repeating the suggestion that Uta was a Jew. Full of fear, Marianne visited a local official, the *Bürgermeister* of Grosjena, who was also Deputy *Ortsgruppenleiter* for the area, but was nevertheless a man she knew to be sympathetic.* She told him of the police visit and showed him Uta's passport, free of the incriminating J. Thinking back on it, she was sure he knew her to be lying, but he chose to accept her evidence and intervened with the police.

His compassion was not rewarded, as he would himself be very badly treated, not by his Nazi superiors but by the Russians, in the aftermath of the Soviet offensive against East Prussia that was launched in January 1945. There was threat on every side now. Since the middle of the war, the spectre of a Russian invasion had been a constant fear in eastern Germany. Wreckage, rape and looting were known to follow in the wake of Soviet campaigns. One of Marianne's children came home crying because her teacher had told her that the way to deal with Russian invaders was to pour boiling water on them. The Kockels' house was set back from the road, so the child was afraid she would not be able to catch them before they got in.

Thousands of refugees fleeing west and south from the Russian advance were among the unknown total of those killed by the fire-bombing of Dresden on the night of 13 February 1945. Pevsner would later receive from Dr Schapire descriptions of the incineration of the place where he had begun his career. Of the Frauenkirche, 'only a cliff-like fragment of the outer wall remains,' he noted, and at the Zwinger Palace, where the Dresden Art Gallery had been housed, 'the bulbous dome is down'. The cramped lodgings opposite the Opera with room for a pram in the hall, the 'dream' flat that Lola had sketched twenty years before, the streets through which Pevsner had walked the dog Ello and cycled to his dancing classes were obliterated.

On 7 March the Americans crossed the Rhine at Remagen, and Hitler issued his 'Nero Decree', a 'scorched earth' policy that required the destruction of anything of value within Reich territory 'which could in any way be used by the enemy immediately or within the foresee-able future for the prosecution of the war'. Allied troops were advancing through scenes of increasing desolation; and now at last the full extent

---

*For the purposes of the Nazi Party, Germany was divided into major administrative regions, *Gaue*, which in turn were subdivided into *Kreise* (counties), *Ortsgruppen* (local chapters), *Zellen* (cells), and *Blocks* (blocks).

of the horror within the concentration camps became apparent, as one after the other they were liberated – in April 1945 alone, Dachau, Bergen-Belsen and Buchenwald. At some point that spring, Marianne went with Uta to the railway track near Naumburg where supplies were being distributed to a large crowd made up equally of local people and refugees from further east. Amidst the general urgency, there were some people clamouring particularly frantically. 'Everyone knew they were from Buchenwald,' Marianne remembered. She and Uta had trundled a cask of wine from Naumburg with them on a handcart; amidst a crowd of refugees struggling for gumboots, they bartered the wine for coal and oat flakes. At Christmas they had decorated their tree with streamers made from the remains of a wrecked barrage balloon; that spring the children's underclothes came from the silk of an Allied parachute salvaged from a tree.

Momentous events were telescoping into each other now: the death of Roosevelt on 12 April, the murder of Mussolini on 28 April and the German surrender in Italy the following day, Hitler's suicide on 30 April. On 4 May, German troops in Denmark, Holland and north-west Germany surrendered at Lüneberg Heath; on 7 May the German Supreme Command signed an unconditional surrender to the Allies at Reims, and the war in Europe was over.

But for Uta the greatest ordeal was still to come. In June, the Allies made official the demarcation of Germany into zones of occupation that had already been decided by the terms of the London Protocol of 12 September 1944 – and Naumburg was going to lie in the Russian zone. If Uta was going to get back to England, she was going to have to move at once. As soon as the Americans reached the town, barely ahead of the Russian advance, she went to the Public Safety Officer and explained her predicament. His solution was to hurry her to Leipzig in the hope of getting her repatriated from there; she left in a jeep, having despatched a letter to Pevsner with a desperate plea to send proof of her identity.

This was the start of a dreadful journey as a refugee, in constant fear of the pursuing Russians – Carl Walter had wished to give her Luminal to carry with her, so that she would have the means of suicide should she be caught – and of being lost in the wreckage of a shattered Germany. There had been no reply from her parents by the time she reached Leipzig, and Uta was sent on to the airport there without the all-important proof of her nationality. Reaching Liège, she spent several nights in a Displaced Persons camp surrounded by the unfamiliar accents of Polish and Russian refugees crammed forty to a room, before being moved on to Brussels. It was from here that her family began receiving her first letters, from 37 RHV Artillery Barracks on the boulevard St Michel outside the city centre, where she was cooped up 'among lots of other displaced Britishers', known as 'DPs'. 'Dearest Daddy,' she wrote in panic on 18 June 1945, 'you must help me as quickly as possible or there will be a disaster. I am absolutely despairing.' The British consul seemed unable to help her, and the Visa Section, unconvinced by her pleas that her parents were in the process of naturalisation as British citizens, were telling her she should not having risked coming to Belgium with nothing but an expired passport. She should, they said, be grateful to stay in the camp – but with no money and nowhere to go, she was terrified that she would never get away from it, that she might be sent by force back to a Germany that was not her home, that her parents would never find her.* Some people without visas were being taken back into the Russian zone; anything would be better than that. 'Do you for example know a nice Englishman who would like to marry me. I am quite serious . . . I trust you are all well and have not forgotten – your daughter Uta . . . I am so lonely.'

She had not heard from her parents for more than a year. None of their letters had got through, and in Germany the postal system had broken down. Now, for all she knew, she might be sending her appeals into a void. 'The first thing you must do is to write and tell me that you are OK and will help me,' she pleaded. 'The next thing is to send me any document that would help me to stay here until I can eventually come home, or a husband, if it comes to the worst . . . You can reach me at the address above . . . but be careful of what you write.'

Uta's letters reached Hampstead safely; whether or not they were reassuring to her anxious parents is doubtful. At the end of June she was still in the barracks in Brussels, sharing a room with five other 'displaced persons'. New people were arriving all the time, hoping to travel further west, and none was leaving, except to go back east; the barracks were increasingly crowded and uncomfortable – fourteen women, she reported, had lice – and there was nothing to do except sit in the canteen, reading, writing or worrying. 'Lots of the people here can't even speak English. They are awfully funny. There is for example a mother with 3 elderly daughters who have saved nothing during an air raid on Berlin but their two cats. They have brought them all the way in two bags which they carry around their waists.'

---

*At the end of the Second World War, twelve million people had been driven from their homes. In 1946 there would be 200,000 enquiries for children who were still lost.

Occasionally the American soldiers guarding them would escort them into the city centre to shop, but prices were terribly high and no one would change German money. 'I ought to buy a lot of things. I did not take much, because I thought I would be at home the next day.'

'I hope I shall find my room as I left it 6 years ago,' Uta wrote. 'You will probably have a shock what a terrible child I have turned out. You will have to put up with it, it is too late now.' On 4 July she heard that her visa had been granted, thanks largely to pressure applied by the Home Office at the instigation of the Society for the Protection of Science and Learning. 'What will I do when I come home? Perhaps at last work I really like.' (She was considering studying industrial art or photography.) 'How good to be able to live in a democratic country. Of course, you will be shocked when you get to know me. I love good wine, I smoke now and again, I put lipstick on when I go out and these are only the exterior signs, not the inner vices.'

Intervention had come for Uta just in time. A week later the barracks were being cleared and most of the inmates were sent back to Germany, but those with visa approval were moved to another camp, the derelict Château Lambert in the Bois de la Cambre, a large park outside Brussels. Architecturally elegant, the house was filthy, and the inmates were set to cleaning it. There was not enough water to do laundry and most of the women's clothes were falling to pieces now. The food was far less generous than in the American-run barracks on boulevard St Michel, and people began to fall ill. Uta suffered first from tonsillitis and then from painfully swollen legs; during the first week in August she was in the camp hospital. It was there that she heard the news of the atomic bombing of Hiroshima and Nagasaki, on 6 and 9 August 1945, and the collapse of resistance to the Allies in the Pacific. 'At midnight tonight,' she wrote on 11 August, 'all the boys lying downstairs started singing and cheering'; three days later, the Japanese surrendered. It would not be too long before the final bureaucratic hurdles fell and Uta could set off on the final stage of her journey home.

Meanwhile, her parents had sent her a photograph. 'I have been looking at it all yesterday and I am slowly getting used to my family. I am glad to see that mummy has not changed at all . . . The most amazing part being Tom's nose, which has grown immensely', while Dieter had come to look just like his father. It would, she thought, take her a while to get accustomed to the idea that Pevsner had now taken to smoking a pipe.

It would also take some time for old patterns of affection and behaviour to re-establish themselves. Lola in particular could not help being afraid that she had been supplanted to some extent by her sister, and Marianne, whether wittingly or not, compounded her fears by continuing to issue instructions about Uta's well-being. 'Tact has never been the strongest suit of the Kurlbaums,' wrote Pevsner to Lola on 21 August:

> and Marianne's letter hurts me, because I'm afraid it will hurt you. But always keep in mind that when in the future you are able to talk to Ma about this, she will say 'I didn't mean that'. Of course, she has had Uta for nearly six years and really thinks of her as her own child, and we thank God for that. But what she doesn't know is that you have changed so much and become so much wiser. And she also doesn't know that you have been thinking the whole time about precisely the things that she writes about.

'Anyway,' he added, 'you can set your mind at rest – I won't fall in love with *her* – pity.'

CHAPTER 24

'Pevsner in an English uniform'

'I hope I shall find my room as I left it 6 years ago' – Uta should perhaps have been less certain of finding her *country* as she had left it. On 26 July 1945 a Labour government had taken power with a landslide victory, and the way was clear for it to embark on the programme of change outlined in the Beveridge Report. In this Britain of reconstruction and reform, Pevsner found himself suddenly in demand, not so much for his new intellectual specialisms as for his earlier interest in state patronage and the application of the arts in the service of the nation. In the years immediately after the war he played an interesting role in the cultural rebuilding of Britain, while at the same time trying to define an identity for himself and find a convincing voice in which to speak to new audiences. The German academic in him would never entirely be obliterated, but would increasingly have to live alongside the English social commentator, the radio broadcaster, architectural journalist and cosmopolitan traveller.

In the immediate post-war period, great hopes were pinned on design as a force for social improvement – and Pevsner, like it or not, was still considered an influence in the field of industrial design.[1] In 1943 the government had been looking at the education of designers with a view to their usefulness in industry after the war, and had obviously found his *Enquiry into Industrial Art in England* a valuable source. 'I read just now in the Journal that the Parliamentary Under-Secretary for Planning . . . has said in an address, more use should be made of my book on industrial art,' he boasted to Lola. 'Do you remember Dieter's . . . gesture of pride with thumbs under his arms? Imagine me like that.'

He was on the steering committee for a new feature in the *Review* entitled 'Design Review'. This regular monthly bulletin of 'industrial art, new materials and manufacturing processes' had been introduced in 1944 'to put British design in order for the post-war offensive' and to keep people up to the modernist mark. (It is tempting to suppose that Pevsner might have instigated this review as a rival to the *Studio* design supplement from which he had been ignominiously removed.)

He invited the designer Sadie Speight to take responsibility for compiling the 'Design Review' features.[2] Trained as an architect, Speight had been working before the war in partnership with her husband Leslie Martin, but had since diversified into industrial design and was a leading member of the Design Research Unit chaired by Herbert Read. Her brief appears to have been actually to identify the specimens of good contemporary design to be featured in each issue, compile suitable photographs, and provide linking text. She suggested that, rather than simply presenting a miscellany, the 'Design Review' should run according to a pre-ordained programme, with distinct themes for each issue, and she had given much thought to what the themes should be.

She was working, however, to a committee, several of whom had their own ideas and their own motives for including particular products. More to the point, she was directly answerable to Pevsner. She was only four years younger than he and may well have felt that her links with the practice of design were a good deal closer and more recent than his; without a doubt she had more confidence in her own taste. She almost certainly did not expect to be told only to write on one side of the paper or to mark the photographs TOP and BOTTOM or to write her captions as a consecutive narrative in the style of a cartoon strip. Nor did she appreciate his comments on her writing style. 'There are still, if you will allow an old man to say this [he was forty-three, she was thirty-nine], a few journalistic deficiencies.'

As many of his pupils could have told Speight, this was Pevsner at his most emollient. 'Please don't think I am trying to make things difficult, or I am an arch-pedant,' he wrote. 'Excuse this carping. I only want to defend myself and warn you not to be cross, if I re-write a certain amount.' His blandishments were in vain. Speight grew more and more irritated by his direction and complained to confidant Alastair Morton: 'You probably realise from Nos. 1 and 2 how unsatisfactory it is to work with Pevsner.'* When Morton sent her samples of textiles, she responded: 'They'll all look grand in the Review (anything would in comparison with the stuff that Pevsner usually gets in).' Pevsner, for his part, was doing what he perceived to be an editor's job. It was he who had to make sure the feature ran to length and on time and in a standard format, and he did not share her opinion of her own text. 'Honestly,' he wrote, 'what I have got cannot be your or the Archi's final considered statement on scope

---

*Alastair Morton (1910–53), artist and the Artistic Director of Edinburgh Weavers, son of its founder Sir James Morton, with whom Pevsner had once discussed the possibility of employment.

and possibilities of design as applied to cloth by means of block or roller.' Livid, Speight threatened to resign: 'I must write under my own name, just as Herbert [Read], [John] Gloag and [Noel] Carrington have done, and be entirely responsible. In fact, I would be much happier doing the layout myself too.' Pevsner was taken aback, but was not afraid to meet her challenge head-on – 'You said a good many things about the Archi in general, when we paced up and down Charing Cross Road' – and travelled out to her house in Hertfordshire to discuss future plans for the magazine. He was genuinely concerned when she fell ill, which effectively ended her participation in the project, and tried to persuade her to take on further work for the *Review,* without success.*

Whether or not Pevsner had actually written much of the text of 'Design Review', it was natural that he should still be roped in as a commentator on modern design, in print and on the radio. On 26 March 1946 he vividly conveyed the urgency of the LCC's building programme for the 750,000 people in need of rehousing in London, in a broadcast entitled 'Modern Homes'. He was reviewing an exhibition staged at the Dorland Hall in Lower Regent Street by the socialist *Daily Herald*, and found much to approve in its modest practicality: a special display of 'pre-fabs', bungalows assembled from standardised prefabricated components; the best of Utility furniture; and, in particular, its 'Make Do and Mend Corner', 'showing you some cheering metamorphoses of cheese-boxes and butter-boxes, and rugs made from scraps, and toys made from cotton reels, and material home-printed by means of screw-tops, the hollow ends of keys, & so on'. Two months later he was to be found in the pages of the trade paper *Pottery and Glass*: 'Target for September: Nikolaus Pevsner Urges Manufacturers to Aim High in the Quality of Their Designs for the "Britain Can Make It" Exhibition'.

'Design Review' had anticipated that 'a more carefree and fanciful post-war world' might relax in its determination to express the contemporary spirit, and to some extent Pevsner was in sympathy with this backsliding: a period of compulsory material austerity was not the moment to insist on unrelieved intellectual asceticism. When he was approached by the Council for Visual Education to write a short pamphlet on improved design in household objects, the result – *Visual Pleasures from Everyday Things* – was a far milder document than

---

*They did, however, remain friends sufficiently for Speight and Leslie Martin to be among those congratulating Pevsner with affection on the award of the RIBA Gold Medal some twenty-five years later.

his *Enquiry* of ten years earlier.* It sought to promote better taste in cars, clocks and cutlery, furniture and fittings by directing art teachers towards the kind of examples of good design that he had gone to such trouble to accumulate in the *Enquiry*; but the objective here was enjoyment as much as improvement.

Pevsner still believed in the Ruskinian idea that it was possible to read the characters of men and nations in their art, which tended to imply that poor design was evidence of a moral flaw. Man must continually strive for beauty, he urged; but beauty was no longer to be so strictly defined. He now made no attempt to argue the hard functionalist case that beauty equals fitness for purpose: 'It is blatantly untrue in its extreme form: fitness equals beauty, and it is not even correct in the more moderate form: no beauty without fitness.' There should be more room for fancy and imagination, and designers should perhaps seek to find a modern style of ornament. 'People want ornament, for good human reasons . . . Our predominantly functional approach to design is neither the only possible approach, nor one to be specially proud of.'

To be dogmatic, Pevsner wrote, was a mistake (a significant concession in itself), but, broadly, the criteria for good design were: no sham; no jazz; and no cowardice. If workaday life was drab, then aim for a little kick, but without overdoing it, preserving the difference between 'a whisky when you feel like it and a continuous state of dipsomania'. 'For those with a fairly balanced life,' he wrote:

> the right prescription has always seemed to me this – Have at least one moving, or daring, or quaint thing about at a time. It may be a picture, the reproduction of a great man's work (but a good reproduction) which will go on speaking to you for a while and lingering in your mind like a quartet that you have heard, or it may simply be flowers. It may be a shell, or a curious stone, a mysteriously streaked piece of agate, a sampler . . . The rest of your room can then be restful, and will seem all the more satisfying for being set off by the one 'object of the month'.

This is a principle that one can imagine him putting into practice for himself; the house at Wildwood Terrace was simply decorated, to

---

*The Council for Visual Education was a conglomerate body – members included the Design and Industries Association and the Council for the Preservation of Rural England – set up in 1945 under the chairmanship of Patrick Abercrombie with a view to 'raising the uneducated taste of the majority'.

a degree that disconcerted other art historians of greater aesthetic pretensions, but among the 'restful' everyday furnishings were individual objects, carefully chosen to 'speak' and cherished throughout his life – a mixture of a few Biedermeier pieces brought from Germany, contemporary furniture (mostly Danish), and English carpets and curtains, which Lola considered the best in the world.

Since writing the *Enquiry*, Pevsner had mellowed. He had apparently become less impatient with the folly of bad taste, now that he was no longer so closely confronted with the evidence of it. He was prepared to admit that there must be a better balance between individual expressivity and the machine aesthetic than he had perhaps previously thought. In a talk for the BBC's Pacific Service on 27 January 1946, entitled 'The Function of Craft in an Industrial Age', he had no trouble in making the case for craft. 'I have the greatest respect for people who can do things with their hands – probably because I never can,' he confessed. 'They hold the world together, the people who of a Sunday settle down to repairing fuses and carburettors and grandfather clocks, and the people who for sheer fun bind books and weave scarves and graft trees and make kitchen dressers.' Skills such as these should be harnessed by industry for the good of the consumer, to provide some relief from the machine ethic in its most aggressive forms. Pevsner's intentions were good, but in these early BBC broadcasts on design the tone he adopted was uneasy, and he frequently sounded distant from his audience in a way he probably never intended. In his writing about Henry Moore's shelterers in the Underground he had used the phrases 'inarticulate undeveloped humanity', 'drably satisfied'. He would quite honestly have felt that anyone who had not had the opportunity to develop their aesthetic sense through a good upbringing and education was less fortunate than he was; too often he let this belief appear in his voice and vocabulary.

Since the Birmingham days, Pevsner had had more chance to talk to the working people whom he saw as his target audience for these broadcasts on design – most obviously to his temporary 'mates' during his days as a rubble-shoveller. But he never quite succeeded in getting on to their wavelength – literally, in the sense that he never really sounded at home on the Light Programme, which might have been described as the BBC channel for the common man. A new pattern of broadcasting was announced in the summer of 1945. The Home Service would have a middle-class mandate; the General Forces Programme would be renamed the Light Programme, and would continue to serve the popular market; and a new network, the Third

Programme, would be formed to cater for highly educated listeners. It rapidly became clear where Pevsner belonged.

In November 1946 he ventured into broadcasting for the armed forces, in the form of an item on 'Soft Furnishings in the 1940s' for Services Education on the Light Programme. 'Carpets, curtains and upholstery,' he began:

> Don't choose to startle Mrs Hookham-Flookham, don't choose out of snobbery, don't choose because you think you ought to like something . . . An orange and bright green hearthrug with a jagged pattern like an atom bomb just exploding might look fine to you at first glance – hot stuff, just as the swing you sometimes get on this very wave-length . . . But you must remember that you can turn off your wireless, but you can't turn off your carpet or your curtains.

Sinking ever deeper in the mire of unintentional condescension and assumptions about the social class and financial circumstances of his audience, Pevsner ploughed on. 'Rich women if they choose [a garment] badly can give it away and try again – even today, I'm told – but you can't.' Pevsner was not naturally ingratiating. Even his fellow rubble-shovellers had referred to him as 'The Gentleman', set apart. There is every chance, however, that his own neighbours and his professional peers would have seen him neither as a 'mate' nor as 'the gentleman'. Where precisely was Nikolaus Pevsner at home? In the summer of 1946, his identification with the cause of industrial design raised this question in more than just an abstract sense.

In July and August 1946, in the improbable guise of a British army colonel, he was sent back to Germany, at the behest of the Council of Industrial Design (CoID). By the end of the war the government was seriously concerned about British exports' ability to compete in a post-war economy. Germany, Sweden, Czechoslovakia and the United States had all made giant strides in industrial design between the wars, which had given their products an undeniable advantage. In Germany, in particular, certain industries were now to be licensed to export once more, posing a direct threat to British trade in areas such as textiles, glass, plastics, furniture, toys and light metals. The CoID, set up at the end of 1944 to 'use all practicable means to improve design in British industry', had been charged by the Board of Trade with discovering the secrets of the opposition's success by sending a mission to establish the current state of German design and explore how designers were recruited, trained and deployed.

As agreed at the Yalta Conference in February 1945, Germany had been divided at the Potsdam Conference in July–August 1945 into four zones, each under a separate military administration. Rather to his disappointment, Pevsner was headed exclusively for the British zone, which included the Ruhr and a zone in the western sector of Berlin but would not enable him to renew contacts with a group of designers and teachers in north-eastern Germany who were trying to revive the methods of the Bauhaus. He was the leader of a small team that included the CoID's Lorna Hubbard and a South African designer by the name of H.A. Niebohr, whom Pevsner described as Dutch and found 'interesting, lively, a bit of an adventurer and not very reliable'. The industries they had been allocated were light metals, light engineering and plastics; Pevsner was, he said laconically, looking at 'bakelite and hoovers'. It is likely that he was meeting various other briefs at the same time: he was also consulting on the rebuilding of historic buildings and churches in Germany, and was committed to writing articles on 'German folk art' and other subjects for the British Political Intelligence Department, with which he had been in touch since the end of 1945, lecturing on their behalf to officers at Camp 654 in Tilbury in January 1946.*

Pevsner's team was sent by train across the country to Westphalia; he then made his way back in a south-westerly direction, eventually crossing into the American zone further south. He must have been very apprehensive of what he would find. It was his first visit to Germany in eight years, during which time both his parents and Lola's father had died; on learning of the death of Georg Graf Vitzthum earlier that year he had remarked, 'all the friends over there are dead or lost to us' – lost in the sense that Leipzig and Dresden both now lay in the Russian zone. Berlin was partitioned, Prussia dissolved, cities were wrecked and the infrastructure of transport, communications and supplies was destroyed, while millions of refugees were being pushed westwards into the devastated country from the former German territories east of the Oder–Neisse line. The members of the CoID team were required to be vaccinated for typhus, typhoid and tetanus before embarkation, and were warned, 'Never leave anything of value in an unoccupied vehicle.'[3]

Pevsner would dutifully fulfil his responsibilities as an inspector. His

---

*The CoID German mission as a whole operated under the auspices of the British Intelligence Objectives Subcommittee, set up before D-Day to gather German technical information as it became available in liberated areas of Europe.

findings would be incorporated in a BIOS (British Intelligence Objectives Subcommittee) Report in 1947, in a section entitled 'Design Investigation in selected German consumer goods', which tended to suggest that design was held in greater esteem in Germany, that far more famous artists and architects worked as designers, and that both managers and engineers in many industries were better educated and culturally more sophisticated.

The conclusions of his 1937 *Enquiry* appeared to be handsomely vindicated. But, more significantly, this German expedition forced him to confront his feelings about his exile. He was trying to appear 'the well-behaved Englishman', he wrote to Dieter at the end of July 1946, in the military uniform supplied to him by the Control Commission. ('Completely unthinkable,' Marianne declared later, 'Pevsner in an English uniform.') 'I like my uniform,' he wrote, 'it is comfortable, sensible and roomy – I wouldn't mind always wearing battle dress.' Photographs show him as a tall gangling figure with thin legs ending in tight puttees, wire-rimmed spectacles glinting under his slouch beret, smiling self-consciously in his new persona. But in private he was disturbed by conflicting emotions: a blend of pity, nostalgia and guilt, with an undercurrent of anger.

23 July 1946 was the twenty-third anniversary of his marriage. It found him at Herford, an army station in the forest in Westphalia, after a long and distressing journey by train. 'It's dreadful,' he wrote to Lola:

> once you are through all the destruction, there's the good rich countryside, as always, peasants' cottages, crops, forests – and then suddenly a whole train in a station with nothing but refugees in cattle-trucks, old men, barefooted children, a mother washing clothes on the platform. Cologne and the Ruhr are fearful, ruins, ruins, ruins, uncleared rubble and unsafe walls standing everywhere, and in between less damaged houses with neat curtains, and once a room on an upper floor, inhabited but with the front wall simply missing. Had they got a rope across? – I couldn't see it. Masses of broken rolling stock by the lines, flowers growing out of goods trucks. One whole stretch of the *Reichsautobahn* a vast lorry dump . . . Germany remains a disturbing and dreadful spectacle . . . It's enough to make one weep – and believe me, at times I can hardly stop myself . . . It cuts right through you the whole time . . . I feel miserable, miserable.

Four days later, writing for Dieter's fourteenth birthday, he was scarcely better able to hide his feelings:

> Enjoy the day and enjoy the thought of the presents which you'll have before I shall be with you . . . Enjoy more than all that. Enjoy that you are not hungry . . . Potatoes – only two for supper. And chocolate? – once or twice a year, if someone gives you half a twopenny bar – etc. etc. This, dear Dieter, is how your cousins are living, the ones in the picture on the mantelpiece, and all the other children here. It's enough to make one weep, honestly . . . Well – excuse such a letter on your birthday, but I'm so full of all this sorrow. I saw Tante Marianne yesterday, and it's all so awful.

(One of Dieter's cousins, Sebastian Kockel, would die at the age of three in 1947, largely as a result of the privations the family had endured during this time.)

Marianne had travelled west on a day-pass to meet him in the village of Leichlingen outside Düsseldorf. He realised for the first time what the Kockels had been through in sheltering Uta. 'They lay awake at night trembling, in fear that they might be taken – because of us. However grateful one is, it will never be enough.' Marianne, he told Lola, had the same face as seven years ago, but her hair was rusty brown now, greying about halfway down: the side-effect of a medicine she had used to get rid of lice. He had had to sit with Marianne on the grass in a nearby park, as she was not allowed into his hotel room and there were no restaurants or cafés 'for Germans'; they shared his regulation-issue sandwiches.

He was staying in an army mess, a house that the British authorities had requisitioned from its German owners, a comfortable home full of 'quality German things'; the family now lived in the attic. They showed great dignity, he wrote, which made him feel ashamed of his own vanity and self-regard. The mother, who used to be a singer, did the cooking for the inspection party; the father, an organist, was sometimes allowed to come down and play his piano. He was playing Schubert as Pevsner wrote home on 27 July: 'I am sitting by, deliberately humble . . . all in order to show what wonderful Englishmen there are.' As this suggests, he was completely torn, veering between two sets of loyalties, between reason and instinct, dressed as an Englishman and bound to present himself as one, but incapable of feeling completely like an alien in Germany. 'Is it Huyton in reverse? Then I was on the wrong side – and today I'm on the wrong side again. At that time I could not stand the English officer types, and today I am, so to speak, one of them – and today I know that I am not really on the wrong side here. It is after all Hitler's Germany – and the boys and girls, thin but brown and strong, with not much on . . . are probably Nazis.'

'I know of course,' he wrote, '"they asked for it and they got it"' – and yet he could not help sympathising. 'It's not getting any better and I am always close to tears. One sits in the bar in the evenings and talks in English, in such a way that I would just like to get out into the forest and talk to the people.' It was, in fact, sometimes possible to meet ordinary Germans; people were unable to work late, because of the lack of coal or electricity after ten at night, and they were overwhelmingly eager to talk, about 'church, Freemasons, factory owners, party members in 1934, the persecution of the Jews, relations in England'. He was told that the worst looting had been done by the Americans as they arrived, and by the Russian women working in the occupied areas. 'The warden of a church wanted to kiss my hand – gruesome, from someone who was once a fellow citizen.' He also had to be wary: 'The German girls remain the only right ones. But I would never have the thick skin to take advantage of my store of cigarettes.'

'I comfort myself by passing on my rations from HM every day.' The eighteen-year-old daughter of the house in Leichlingen, in charge of making his sandwiches in the morning, knew what he did with them and made far more than he could possibly eat. Most found their way to the local doctor, ostensibly for his patients, but actually for his own family as well. Pevsner found a hidey-hole where he could store the sugar lumps provided for the English party to put in their tea. 'I am stealing like a magpie,' he wrote, 'biscuits, even white bread. It is a shame to let it go in the bin. I let them pour us a coffee and then "forget" to drink it . . . All this fiddling . . . but I only have to think of Franz [a young nephew] who is told at night that he can't have another slice of bread, and then says after a while, "But I have to have another one" and then I would like to go and steal a whole side of ham.' One of the inspection party – a 'vulture' – was in the habit of feeding a little dog with the hard biscuits provided for their cheese: 'They don't know how grateful a young mother of three would be for them.' 'Then when I give the mother of the girl with thin legs the biscuits I have stolen,' he wrote despairingly, 'she goes and asks for cigarettes for her husband.'

Both sides, he concluded, had been guilty, 'but one side is being punished for it, because the crude violence was more beastly here, I suppose, than the Pharisaic attitudes in England'. Thinking of the life he had temporarily left behind, he found himself overcome by waves of hostility. Lola, he wrote, might find it more satisfying to live in Germany under these harsh conditions – planting vegetables, finding wood, planning rations – than with 'all the vanity' in London. 'The answer, of course, is love,' he wrote sadly. 'One has an affection for it and doesn't want to accept the truth.'

In theory he could have returned to Germany. In September 1945, the Göttingen Conference of Rectors of Universities and Colleges of Equal Rank had adopted a resolution describing it as a 'moral obligation' for the German authorities to restore teachers to the status they had enjoyed before the Nazis had dislodged them.[4] But in practical terms Pevsner accepted that his German life was over.

With the ending of hostilities, it had, of course, become easier for his friends to help accelerate the process of his long-stalled naturalisation. His original sponsors – Sir Daniel Stevenson (Chancellor of Glasgow University), Sir James Morton (Chairman of Morton Sundour Fabrics), Frank Pick and his Oxford patron J.A.R. Munro – had all died during the war. He had rounded up another four, equally prestigious – Sir Thomas Barlow (Director-General of Civilian Clothing), John Maud (previously Master of Birkbeck, but now Permanent Secretary at the Ministry of Education), T.S.R. Boase (Director of the Courtauld Institute since 1937) and loyal ally G.F. Troup Horne – and on 4 June 1946 Pevsner had taken an oath before Miss Beryl Russell, Commissioner for Oaths, at 17 Church Row, Hampstead: 'I, Nikolai Bernhard Leon Pevsner, swear by Almighty God that I will be faithful and bear true allegiance to His Majesty King George the Sixth, His Heirs and Successors, according to law.' Registering his trade as 'editor and lecturer', he was naturalised as a British citizen under the British National and Status of Aliens Act 1914, 'entitled to all political and other rights, power and privileges and . . . subject to all obligations, duties and liabilities to which a natural-born British subject is entitled or subject'.

Pevsner was now an official Englishman, but he remained one with an accent, and his BBC producers were perhaps brave in letting him speak his mind on sensitive issues. He was, for example, outspoken on the subject of what to do with the English parish churches that had been destroyed by German bombs: he saw himself as just as much a victim of the bombing as any other Londoner, identified with the effort of clearing the damage, and in a talk entitled 'Ruins' for the BBC's Pacific Service in July 1946 he came down for the preservation of ruined churches as war memorials. 'We don't want to make the mistakes of 1914–18 again,' he argued. 'We don't want meaningless obelisks, Madame Tussaud-looking bronze soldiers in battle dress, and village crosses ordered from catalogues. And as to the other suggestions for war memorials of which you read – playing fields and health clinics, for instance – they must of course be provided. But surely it would be too cynical if hundreds in our parish had to die to get something which it is the duty of State and town councils to provide anyway.'

'Think of a church you know and care for,' he continued:

> Think of it with blossoming young trees and dark old ones around and inside, and with plenty of flowers . . . which have found their way into debris and rubble. There could be creepers to cover part of the scarred walls. Rolls of Honour might be carved into stone slabs against walls more completely preserved. And columns inside might stay as fire and bombs left them, charred and jagged, but surrounded by turf. And if there is a column missing altogether, it might be replaced by a medlar tree . . . Seats should be there too, for people who want rest – yes, and for those who want to eat their sandwiches. Why not? *Let* the living benefit from what is so true a memorial to the dead.

He also tackled a subject that was perhaps more controversial than the BBC knew. A dozen years on from his reflections on 'Art and the State' in the Nazi magazine *Der Türmer*, he prepared a talk, again for the Pacific Service, with the identical title and, it would seem, at least part of the same argument. He still argued firmly for a 'healthy relationship' between state and artist; and it was perhaps not surprising that his producer, Noni Wright, complained that his first draft was 'too theoretical and too prescriptive'. What she wanted was less historical background and rationale and more of a narrative approach, detailing recent experiments in state patronage and how they had fared. His talk would, she said, need watering down for the Dominions, where technical terms like 'Pre-Raphaelite' and 'Impressionist', and unfamiliar names like Sickert and Ford Madox Brown, would be baffling.

In the give and take with Noni Wright, Pevsner was beginning to develop a durable working relationship with the BBC. This he owed to Geoffrey Grigson, who at around this time had been responsible for another important change in the Pevsners' lives. Since 1943, when Grigson had moved his family to Keynsham to be near the BBC at Bristol, Lola and Dieter had been using the Grigsons' cottage at Snowhill in Wiltshire as a retreat. Soon after the end of the war, Grigson bought a farmhouse in the nearby village of Broad Town. He now offered to sell Pevsner and Lola the cottage and two acres of scrub-covered land for £350; they accepted at once.

The cottage lay half a mile up a rutted track from Broad Town on the lower slope of an escarpment, a few miles north of the Ridgeway, under the shadow of the Broad Town White Horse. When Grigson had bought it, it had been empty and almost derelict, and he had had to roof it and run a water pipe from the well in the garden of a neighbouring cottage to make it habitable. After a year without occupants, 'we found the cottage overgrown like the palace of the Sleeping Beauty,' Pevsner remembered later. When cleared, it had a cement front, which Lola disliked, but little had been done to modernise the interior. Water had to be pumped from the well, light came from oil lamps, ceilings were low and the beds were frequently damp, but he knew that Lola loved the simplicity of living here, as she had loved Naumburg – 'the laying of a fire, the gathering of logs for it, the picking of flowers in the woods, the closeness to beasts and their life cycles'. He himself had always been an imperfect countryman. Bertschy Grigson remembered him striving to keep his white shirt clean as he wrestled with the chemical lavatory; it offended him, she recalled, when Geoffrey had used a clean handkerchief to wipe his oily hands after some amateur car repairs. Another image that lingered was of Pevsner, 'a tall thin man in a suit', struggling with a shovel to dig a shallow grave for two cats that had had to be put down.

The relationship with Geoffrey Grigson would endure for many years, though it would more frequently be disrupted by rows after his separation from Bertschy. Developing at the same time was another friendship with an equally refractory character. Allen Lane was, in W.E. Williams's eyes, 'a yea-sayer to life', bonhomous, gossipy, a good listener who questioned everyone he met and had a passion for knowledge.[5] He could be an exhilarating employer – but to rely on him would have been a serious mistake. 'To work with him,' explained Richard Hoggart, 'one had to share his faith, accept his inspiration – and forgive him his trespasses.'[6]

Not everyone did forgive him. Lane was generous in giving extraordinary opportunities to the unknown, but he could not be trusted to keep on supporting those he had favoured; not infrequently he would promote people beyond their capabilities, and then summarily sack them. He was characterised, in Dieter Pevsner's words, by a 'cheerful ruthlessness'.* 'Gay, volatile, insecure, capricious, unreliable'

---

* 'The King Penguin', in *The Author*, Vol. XC, No. 4. Dieter Pevsner worked for Penguin Books as an editor in the first half of the 1960s, then as editorial director until 1972.

– W.E. Williams again – Lane would follow his intuition, often wrongly, and then back off, performing agile mental somersaults to get himself out of trouble.

The illustrator Richard Chopping was one victim. He had been commissioned during the war to provide the illustrations for a Penguin *Flora of the British Isles*, with text by Frances Partridge. Lane cancelled it in 1949 after the authors had been working on it for five years and, unsurprisingly, Chopping remembered him with rancour: 'Grey, well cut but never quite smart suits, as if he was too well tailored and had been poured into the mould of his clothes where there was just a little too much of him for them. Very well manicured, shaved, hair never out of place.'* Margaret Clark, who worked as assistant to Alan Glover, also vividly remembered Lane's physical presence in the Harmondsworth office. 'He worked impulsively and restlessly, walking up and down, looking out of the window, biting his nails (the only outward sign that his volatile temperament, often so injurious to others, affected him equally).'[7] 'One might be gossiping with him of this and that,' remembered Sir Robert Lusty, 'and he would be attentive and involved. Some word, some name, some project might strike a certain chord and on the instant Allen would be neither attentive nor involved. Cold little shutters would close upon the light of his eyes. Someone, something, somewhere had had it.'[8]

Pevsner was not unaware of Lane's tortuous personality, but in spite of their temperamental differences – or perhaps because of them – their relationship would always remain relatively untroubled. Lane did not like many people, according to his wife Lettice, but he found Pevsner impressive.[9] In March 1947 the oddly matched pair undertook a business trip to America together. Pevsner was to commission authors for a proposed Pelican history of art, while Lane tackled problems in the relationship between Penguin Books and Penguin USA.†

The party was travelling on the *Queen Elizabeth*, the pride of the Cunard Line. Allen and Lettice Lane were in the first-class area on C Deck, Pevsner in lesser splendour on B Deck in a cabin shared with three other people. One, Raymond Hazell, was 'a burly foul-mouthed crony of Allen's . . . very much like Eric [Graddon – his Aunt Paula's shady Irish husband], which does not make him an ideal cabin-fellow'.‡

---

*R. Chopping, 'Allen Lane: A Wrong Decision?' in *Lost Causes (Miscellany 13)* (Penguin Collectors Society, 1998). It is worth mentioning that Penguin compensated the authors generously for the cancellation of the *Flora*.

†For more on the *Pelican History of Art*, see Chapter 34.

‡Raymond Hazell was a partner of the firm Hazell, Watson & Viney, which printed many of Penguin's books.

The second was 'a Syrian with an American accent . . . [He] entertains us with stories of his embroidery business . . . Rather sordid – the Syrian wears no pyjamas, only sleeveless combinations and a white shirt, and he spits.' The final member of this ill-assorted quartet was an orthodox Jew: 'The shaving with fresh water is done from a kosher cup with Hebrew writing on it. I must not drink from it lest it be contaminated.' The confined space was oppressive, with 'no little shelves to put things' and little room to manoeuvre; on the first day he had washed his hair in salt water by mistake.

Outside the congested cabin, conditions were luxurious, if one liked that kind of thing. Pevsner clearly did not. He found the omnipresent central heating overpowering, preferring to walk on deck, though the breeze was getting ever fresher. As for the standards of interior decoration, 'the detail is often rather Waring and Gillow,' he remarked dismissively after a tour of the first-class areas, though he listed carefully every plush refinement – gymnasium, swimming pool, ballroom, smoking room – for the entertainment of Lola and Uta, left behind in the austerity of post-war London.* At the same time, he was sure they would not relish the style of life on board. He did his best to be sociable, but Allen Lane's idea of a good time on board ship was not Pevsner's. 'Forced my pace at midday and joined in with Allen and [Raymond] Hazell – wine and entrecote and brandy. I did not like it, but I could do it . . . I don't want to admit I'm not up to the bibbers, and so keep in a worse state than I might be.' He did not go so far as to dance: 'After all, Allen doesn't – he's just after the drinks.' Lettice Lane recalled them all joking in the corridor, late at night and rather drunk. 'Of course, everybody knows I'm a homosexual,' said Allen. 'I think I shall be a homosexual too-oo,' carolled Pevsner to Lettice.

'It was odd and in a way rather fun to drink whisky with Hazell in bed at midnight and play chemin de fer,' he told Lola dashingly. But for the most part he was bored and uncomfortable, longing for 'Wildwood Terrace food in Wildwood Terrace conditions' and feeling 'very much out of things and rather like a parasite'. Lettice, whom he found relaxing company, was pregnant and kept unashamedly to her bed for much of the day. As the journey progressed, this came to seem a good choice. 'One of the nicest features of the boat is the many children in groups, aged 3 to 14, wandering around aimlessly. I wish I was a bit aimless,' reflected Pevsner. Lack of purpose, however, was beyond him, and he was beginning to do a little work in the lounge.

---

*The ship's fitments were indeed by Waring & Gillow, by the 1940s a byword for respectability and value for money.

'Chocolate in the tuck shop is also free [of coupons], but don't talk to me of food,' he wrote. 'This rolling business is playing Old Harry with my head, and the quality of work may be affected by it.' By the fourth day at sea he was the only inmate of his cabin to have left his bunk. 'I am keeping up my gallant fight – but one does feel nasty . . . I felt so humiliated to be wobbly all the time and thinking constantly of my inside.' Humiliation was soon turned to vainglory when he discovered that he had been working through a 90 mph gale, 'so the sea has a reason to look as magnificent as Piz Palu, and I have a reason not to be specially attracted by duckling and roast turkey and bacon'.

Pevsner had previously tended to characterise American civilisation as a matter of streamlined cars, sports arenas, loud jazz and equally loud visual taste. 'I am in mortal terror of the Americans, chauffeurs etc,' he wrote, as they approached Manhattan Island. 'The skyline is over, magnificently barbaric and crazy. Now I'm for it.'

In the gloomy depths of the Prince George Hotel on East 28th Street, he found himself once more in a small, dark room, boiling hot.* 'It is an artificial country in many ways,' he marvelled, surrounded by people who preferred to keep the blinds down, electric light on and the heating at full blast. But out in the city he was exhilarated. 'Walking through the streets is wonderfully mad,' he wrote home on 21 March. 'The whole of this looking up business makes you giddy, and the rhythm of enormously tall and then normal is wild and bracing. The glitter of lighted windows at all heights, the wide straight avenue with its traffic, it has something oddly splendid . . . Boys all in fancy clothes and long trousers, girls of thirteen with lipstick, plenty of coloured people.'

Pevsner saw little of the Lanes while he was in New York. 'After having lived side by side on the ship, it is very different now – their chiq? [sic] apartment, parties, dinners, champagne every day . . . Allen is a celebrity . . . Very different from my life of work, a very varied existence. I wouldn't swap . . . Two bottles of iced Coca-Cola – my dream of dissipation.' He was working in the Penguin office, where he even had a secretary, rejoicing in the name of Blossom, but there was time for a visit to the famous 21 Club, with David Pleydell-Bouverie, a British architect and member of the MARS Group who had emigrated to the United States in the late 1930s. The bill, he told Lola with pleasurable horror, reached a staggering total.

As a seasoned walker in London, he had little trouble finding his

---

*A guide of 1936 lists the Prince George as 'less expensive', with 1,000 rooms at $2 upwards.

way around the streets of Manhattan, apart from the moment when he was caught jaywalking and handed a piece of paper which stated: 'You——have just been observed crossing against the traffic lights . . . During the first two months of 1947, 27 people were killed and 532 persons were injured while crossing the streets against Traffic Lights.' 'I get about by bus and underground,' he wrote. 'I go wrong a lot, but since the ticket is a flat rate it doesn't matter.' He also mastered mainline trains, having difficulty only in folding his tall frame into the sleeping compartment of a Pullman car. The novelty, he grumbled, wore off, as it might in a nudist colony.

He visited the architectural historian Henry-Russell Hitchcock, one of the two organisers of the New York Museum of Modern Art's famous 1932 show 'The International Style'. Hitchcock lived in a picturesque bargeboarded house in Connecticut. 'So now I have seen early American churches standing on their greens with white timber steeples, and the wide streets with trees and houses of 1800 or so, with no separate front gardens but trim lawns, all white weather-boarding and nice Adamish detail – all the things one has so often seen in illustrations.' He would always enjoy Hitchcock's company, even though the American was a remorseless talker; on one occasion he even started to undress for bed in mid-conversation without drawing breath. 'Russell, Russell, you really must let me say something,' remonstrated Pevsner.[10]

The bill at the 21 Club will not have come as such a shock to (and will almost certainly have been picked up by) David Pleydell-Bouverie. A grandson of the 5th Earl of Radnor, he had married Alice Astor earlier that year, and Pevsner was thrilled to be invited to visit the American aristocracy at home. 'They live up the River Hudson,' he told Lola, 'in one of the real top-notch millionaires' houses.' The mansion, Ferncliff at Rhinebeck, had belonged to Alice Astor's father, John Jacob Astor IV, who had made a fortune of well over $100 million from New York real estate. John Jacob IV went down on the *Titanic*, and part of his wealth, including Ferncliff, went to Alice. 'The house was built in 1925, neo-Georgian. But the brother's house is even grander, 1910 with an enormous iron-vaulted covered tennis court, which is also used for croquet, and a swimming pool in white marble and green mosaics, as big as the *Queen Elizabeth*.' As for his hostess, Pevsner was intrigued – 'excuse the snobbery' – both by the conspic-uous wealth and by the many marriages. She had previously been married to the former Tsarist officer and aristocrat Prince Serge Obolensky, to Raimund von Hofmannsthal (son of the poet and librett-ist Hugo von Hofmannsthal), and to British journalist Philip Harding.

'Alice Astor is thin, old, and done-up, in slacks,' reported Pevsner. 'A bit of a beard, but not grotesque. I feel sorry for her the whole time and one hopes that she has found peace with David. The towels in my bathroom were monogrammed – AO and RvonH – poor David.' (The couple divorced, and Alice Astor died in 1956.)

Pevsner visited Princeton, Vassar, Yale ('masses of Tudor and Gothic, not one decent building') and Harvard, where he spent an evening with the Gropiuses. When they met at the airport, Gropius greeted them in English; in his own home, the conversation was in German and the whole atmosphere became more relaxed.* 'Pleasant, entirely human . . . much less formidable. The house is masterly, not at all clever, nothing like Lubetkin. Nor is it cold and forbidding. By the fireplace Corb's new book with a dedication from Corb to Gropius. I should have walked off with it. Gropius does good, sound, thoughtful work and looks as handsome as ever, for all that he is over 60.' (Pevsner was now forty-five.)

In Chicago he revelled in the city's nineteenth-century public architecture: buildings such as Louis Sullivan's Carson Pirie Scott store, of which he had written in *Pioneers* 'the upper storeys exhibit the rhythm of the 20th century more uncompromisingly than any building we have met so far'. He enjoyed himself hunting for Frank Lloyd Wright houses in a refined suburb of the city – 'It's a great thrill to see them in the flesh, with their cantilevered roofs, terraces and crazy decoration, amazingly daring for 1895' – though Wright's Falling Water, in Bear Run, Pennsylvania, had failed to impress him. ('Wasn't much.')

He also visited Mies van der Rohe at the new campus he had designed for the Armour Institute where Mies had been a professor since 1938. But to reach the institute's bright, cubic simplicity Pevsner had to travel through scenes that deeply shocked him:

> Close to Mies's Institute is a vile Negro slum district, which was a really smart neighbourhood in about 1890. I was shown a block of flats, most original in plan and with marble and fountains in long glazed interior courtyards, now housing, officially, 320 Negro families but in fact 4000 people – unspeakable . . . Chicago is really a nightmare – miles and miles of misery . . . [The] pattern of desolation intrudes itself everywhere, quite close to the better quarters.

---

*Roger Radford remembered Pevsner describing this meeting for the light that it threw on Gropius, who he considered was less comfortably assimilated in the United States than younger émigrés such as Marcel Breuer. Roger Radford to the author, April 2009.

Washington erred towards the other extreme. He could not fail to be staggered by the riches he saw when he cast a professional curatorial eye over the National Gallery, but he recoiled from the pompous neoclassical environment, as he would later reveal in a BBC broadcast on 'Washington and Twentieth-Century Monumentality', dismissing the American capital as 'this place of vistas so wide and vast that one can hardly see the respective pendant buildings together. Anyway they are nearly all in the neo-Imperial-Nazi-Russian-Bank of England style with vast columns and never less than 500 feet long. One is impressed – but not favourably.'

To Lola, he described the Director's dining room at the National Gallery as 'the worst den of snobs in America', but he was mortified to find his own social sensitivities in evidence when he went to visit German friends in New York. 'Not very comfortable with them,' he admitted. 'On both occasions there were other people there – all very German-emigrant atmosphere.' He was beginning to flag now, troubled by a sore throat and a permanently upset stomach – 'perhaps the red Chianti which Serge Chermayeff gave us' – and he was shaken to hear of László Moholy-Nagy's recent demise from leukaemia. 'Strange and shameful how unarmed I feel against any approach of death.' 'I can't absorb as much as I used to,' he concluded regretfully, 'but I have seen as much of the country as I possibly could, and also the towns . . . but not much of the people, the ones I could have got to know in trains, restaurants, pubs. I don't suppose that will surprise you.'

PART FIVE

DIGGING IN

1946–1959

From Pevsner's notes, made on the move, as he travelled around, county
after county, documenting the buildings of England

CHAPTER 25

'Ballon d'essai': the beginnings of the Buildings of England

Pevsner may have felt that in daily life he lacked the common touch with ordinary people – 'the ones I could have got to know in trains, restaurants, pubs' – but on an ideological level he had no deeper wish than to share the pleasures of education with the broadest possible public. This would always be something he had in common with Allen Lane. Each subscribed in his different fashion to the notion of the 'New Jerusalem' that was to arise from the ashes of war, a happier, healthier and more egalitarian society in which universal education would create both greater practical advantages and more refined tastes, with a keener intellectual curiosity. With this shared vision in mind, since the end of the war, alongside the relationship based on the *Outline* and the King Penguins, Pevsner and Lane had been laying the foundations for their greatest collaboration.

What had been in the 1930s an increasing public appetite for serious reading became a mass hunger for cultural knowledge after the war.[1] People whose instruction had been interrupted by the war joined the growing movement for adult education. In 1946 under the Penguin imprint Homer outsold Agatha Christie, and a few years later a slim volume on the culture of the Hittites would sell 50,000 copies in two or three months, in a cultural charge led by Allen Lane.[2]

Pevsner was to join this charge by reviving the grand scheme for a topography of Britain, which had fallen on stony ground before the war.* Well before their trip to America, he and Lane had been discussing potential new directions for Penguin. In the summer of 1945, Pevsner had gone to lunch at Silverbeck, Lane's William IV house on the banks of the River Colne in Middlesex. As they strolled in the rose garden after lunch, Lane asked casually what kind of books Pevsner would publish, given a free hand. Taking the 'free hand' at face value, Pevsner took the opportunity to point out two striking gaps in English art-historical literature. There was, he remarked, no detailed survey of European art as a whole, nothing to compare with studies of individual nations – Adolfo Venturi's history of Italian art, for example, 'in 20

---

* See Chapter 18.

or 25 volumes (*orribili ma indispensabili*)' or, more significantly, Dehio's *Geschichte der deutschen Kunst*. Nor, he continued, further possessed by the spirit of enterprise, was there any English equivalent to Dehio's catalogue of significant German buildings – something that might locate English architecture in the European context and at the same time demonstrate its uniqueness.

Georg Dehio (1850–1932), one of the most influential of later nineteenth-century German art historians, had always been a fixed point in Pevsner's intellectual landscape. The young Pevsner's choice of degree course had been made against the background of the *Geschichte der deutschen Kunst*, appearing in six volumes between 1919 and 1925 to dazzle students of art history with its enthusiasm, concision and clarity. But twenty years before that, Dehio had already embarked on his *Handbuch der deutschen Kunstdenkmäler* (*Handbook of German Cultural Monuments*), a topographical survey of the most important historic buildings in Germany, whose first volume appeared in 1905.

Dehio was drawing on a tradition of inventorisation that was already well established in Germany.[3] He saw his topographical survey as a means of integrating the newly unified German nation. Every monument, he declared, was '*ein Stuck unseres nationalen Daseins*' – 'a piece of our national existence' – and his objective was to draw the pieces together into a complete picture of Germany, in the form of a guidebook for its people. 'We are in need of a means of quick orientation,' he wrote in a memorandum at the start of the series. 'I therefore move the production of a handbook which according to its name should have little bulk, be easily transported, be according to its inner organisation as clearly arranged as possible and as comfortable to use on the desk as on a journey.' This handbook appeared in five volumes between 1905 and 1912, each dedicated to a different region, setting individual buildings in their context as part of ensembles such as towns or villages, and ranking them in order of their historical and artistic importance, with churches placed first. There were no pictures, but plans of castles and churches were included.

However influential a figure Dehio had been in his German past, and however well known the *Handbuch der deutschen Kunstdenkmäler* might have been in Germany, Pevsner did not necessarily expect Allen Lane to share his enthusiasm, and it was with some stupefaction that he heard his managing director agree to both the two lofty publishing proposals. Eunice Frost, initially Lane's secretary and ultimately the first female director of Penguin, wrote years later: 'I remember them coming back to Harmondsworth – Allen rubbing his hands and smiling away at the prospect of "giving you all a lot to do" and dear Nikolaus looking *radiant*, and saying, "Yes, yes", "This we must do" and so on.'⁴

Within weeks the deal was concluded, adding two further agreements to Pevsner's contract for King Penguin. Allen Lane had, it seemed, subscribed to the survey of European art in fairly general terms, asking for 'a handbook on the History of Art and Architecture' for the Pelican label to be delivered ten years later, without detailing the number of volumes or authors. On the other project he was more specific. What he wanted from Pevsner was 'An Itinerary of England' in approximately forty volumes: descriptions and appreciations of buildings and works of art, to be accompanied by a corresponding series of picture books including 'natural beauties'.*

According to this new contract, Pevsner undertook to produce the first volume in the series before 20 July 1950, after which he would deliver a minimum of four volumes per year, as well as material for the picture books. He was not obliged to start work before 20 June 1946, after which date he would 'then devote his whole time, subject to academic engagements of which the publisher shall have particulars, to the said four undertakings: the King Penguin series, the Pelican history of art, the 'Itinerary of England' and the accompanying illustrated series. The 'Itinerary', it was predicted, would end in mid-1960. At that point, Pevsner would be granted a royalty of 10 per cent on all sales. Until then, he would receive an annual salary of £900 to cover all his work for Penguin, out of which he must pay the costs of his own secretary and a significant proportion of the travel expenses that he would incur. 'In my experience,' commented Penguin designer Hans Schmoller, 'he was quite without guile and in business matters almost naïve.'⁵ Pevsner was perhaps colluding in his own exploitation here, in his anxiety to seal the bargain. Allen Lane, he said later, 'quite unscrupulously played down what the project would entail. I probably played it down to myself too. Still, even if I had realised what it was going to mean I wouldn't have hesitated.'†

What it was eventually going to mean was a monumental series of forty-six architectural guidebooks, published between 1951 and 1974,

---

*Allen Lane was not the only person to have faith in Pevsner's abilities as a recorder of the countryside. Contemplating commissioning a radio series about Pevsner's new project, radio producer Basil Taylor wrote to another member of the BBC staff, 'He might . . . be able to produce quite an effective twentieth-century "Rural Rides", as he is a very good observer of other things beside buildings.' B. Taylor/N. Luker, 22/7/47. BBC WAC RCONT1 – Prof Nikolaus Pevsner Talks File 1A.

†In an interview with Kenneth Allsop, *Sunday Times*, 25/2/73. The magnitude of the task seems to have struck him quite quickly. A press release of 1951 launching the first *BoE* volumes quotes him as saying he expected to have outwritten Balzac by the time he had finished.

of which Pevsner would write thirty-two volumes unaided and a further ten with collaborators. He had been firmly convinced of the need for a *Buildings of England* series for almost twenty years, after searching in vain on his 1930 trip for a guidebook that could offer him any serious information about architecture. General guides were abundant, but he had found them diffuse and vague, with much of the same material duplicated in 'the happy-go-lucky English way'.[6] The writers were more given than their German counterparts to general reflections and judgements, and laid more stress on landscape and atmosphere than on hard facts.

During the 1930s increasing numbers of people had begun to tour the countryside by car. Writers such as H.V. Morton and S.P.B. Mais had catered to this revived interest in the British landscape by providing books with titles such as *Let's Get Out of Here* and *This Unknown Island*. Macmillan's *Highways and Byways* had been in existence for some time, but Batsford had been prompted to launch a new series entitled *Face of Britain* in the early 1930s; and 1936 saw the arrival of *The King's England* (Hodder & Stoughton) – 'the first census of the ancient and beautiful and curious historic possessions of England since the motor car came to make it possible'.

Researched county by county by a large team, the forty-one-volume *The King's England* was written in its entirety by the indomitable Arthur Mee (1875–1953), editor of the *Children's Newspaper* and *Children's Encyclopaedia*, who liked to style himself 'Journalist in Chief to British Youth'. An autodidact himself, he was a firm believer in self-improvement, and his approach was one of exhortation and unrelenting evocation. He celebrated what Geoffrey Grigson would later call 'the three dictatorial qualities of our guidebook trade . . . quaintness, oldness or association', paying far more attention to ambience than to architecture. *The King's England*, in the view of *Time and Tide*, was 'the sort of ecstatic inventory Macaulay loved to take', sprinkled with exclamatory capital letters and suffused with patriotic fervour. 'We have felt the touch of thousands of years of history,' Mee wrote in an introductory volume entitled *Enchanted Land*, 'and thousands of people who have made our homeland the most beautiful and the most stirring land on earth . . . It is for us to guard this Little Paradise.'

During the war guidebooks had been prohibited, which created an even sharper appetite for them once peace came. The Penguin Guides, organised by county, were followed by Paul Elek's *Vision of England*, edited by Clough and Amabel Williams-Ellis. This was a series with higher literary aspirations. It made no attempt to categorise or inventorise buildings, or even to describe them, but depended heavily on the personal reactions of notable writers to particular areas of England: artists such as Kenneth Rowntree and Barbara Jones contributed illustrations to texts by writers of the calibre of Sylvia Townsend Warner and Geoffrey Grigson. Grigson himself would later edit *About Britain*, a sequence of thirteen guides issued as part of the Festival of Britain celebrations to extol 'a European country alert, ready for the future'.

As far as purely architectural guides were concerned, Pevsner had been forced to resort in 1930 to the *Little Guides*, originally published by Methuen in the 1890s – 'indefatigably bicycle-riding', in Alec Clifton-Taylor's phrase, and thoroughly antiquarian in their attitudes. 'They seem to be more concerned to discover something old than something fine,' complained Clifton-Taylor, and all shared the Victorian assumption that the medieval parish church would inevitably be the most interesting building in a town or village.[7] They contained little information on country houses, as very few were open or accessible to the public, tended to disparage the 'pagan' architecture of the eighteenth century and rarely considered including the buildings of the Victorian age.

For London, of course, more detailed coverage was available in the form of the Survey of London, started in 1894 by C.R. Ashbee, and originally organised and carried out entirely by volunteers as a campaign for preservation.* Dating from the same period, the Victoria County History aimed eventually to create an encyclopaedic history of the counties, including some account of their buildings, based on original research – but it was proceeding at the stateliest of paces and at a level of detail that made it utterly unsuitable for the traveller, with as many as ten volumes to a county, and only a handful of counties completed.

The same criticisms could be levelled at the Royal Commission on the Historical Monuments of England, established by royal warrant in August 1908 to make an inventory of all buildings, earthworks and stone constructions in England up to 1714. By 1943 this date limit had been abolished, and the Commission was including buildings up to 1850. This extended time period made it impossible to list every single building, so that rule was now relaxed as well, and the listers described 'group monuments', areas with sample houses singled out.[8] The Commission's volumes were invaluable for their systematic coverage of medieval churches, but they were primarily intended for

---

*The Survey, brought out jointly with the London County Council from 1910, was taken over by the LCC in 1953. It later became the responsibility of the Royal Commission on the Historical Monuments of England, now merged with English Heritage.

serious research – and at the rate they were proceeding, Pevsner estimated, they would take at least 200 years to finish.

So when Pevsner and Penguin first embarked on the *Buildings of
England* (*BoE*), the main competition was perceived to be the *Shell
Guides* to the counties of Britain – and these were far from exclusively
devoted to buildings. The series had been conceived in the early 1930s
by John Betjeman while he was still at the *Architectural Review*. He
had been interested in guidebooks since the 1920s as a means of
educating public taste in accordance with his own particular enthusiasms – late Georgian and Regency architecture, for example, or the
ethos and atmosphere of Anglican churches.[9] Existing guides, he
complained, 'either give wide-angle views of Public Libraries and
Infirmaries or else they mention in detail what rent the land paid to
Hubert de Burg in 1186.'[10] Betjeman was on good terms with Jack
Beddington, Director of Publicity for Shell, and between them they
persuaded the Architectural Press's controlling director Maurice Regan
that, with subsidies from Shell, a series of county guides would be
profitable.

Betjeman started as the general editor of the series, with a proprietorial attitude to layout, letterpress and illustrations, and a clear sense
of what the books were for: 'The purchaser of the *Guides* is probably
not an intellectual in search of regional architecture of the early 19th
century but a plus-foured weekender who cannot tell a sham Tudor
roadhouse from a Cotswold manor.'[11] 'The value of the *Shell Guides*
is to tell people what places are really like now,' he would write later
to a potential author:[12]

> I have often been infuriated by reading a long entry in a *Little Guide*
> or in *Kelly* or *Pevsner* about a church, from which one would gather
> it was so full of antiquities it was like Westminster Abbey, yet when
> you get there you find the churchyard has been mown and planted
> with standard roses . . . and when you get inside you find the plaster
> has been scraped off the walls by the Victorians who also laid shiny
> new tiles on the floor, filled windows with green and pink glass and
> re-pewed everything in pitch pine with oak for the chancel, so that
> although the features described may be there, you can hardly notice
> them for modern accretions.

The keynote of each volume he wrote, should be personal opinion.
'It is the eye and the heart that are the surest guides.'

By 1939 thirteen *Shell Guides* had been published. Betjeman himself had done *Cornwall*, his favourite county. He had also roped in his friends and acquaintances. He intended that the Shell volumes should highlight the individuality of the authors as well as the counties, and *Dorset, Buckinghamshire, Wiltshire* and *Gloucestershire* had been delivered with characteristic panache by Paul Nash, John Nash, Robert Byron and Anthony West respectively.[13] Both in bulk and in style, the early volumes were light – thin and spiral-bound for ease of handling on the road and lavishly illustrated, with many design tricks inherited from Betjeman's era at the *Architectural Review*. The tone was deliberately, even self-consciously irreverent and familiar, aimed at a more sophisticated audience than *The King's England*, though (with Shell as the sponsor) still targeted at 'you, dear average motoring reader'. 'When they began,' commented Geoffrey Grigson later, 'they were a kind of "in" job . . . Hop, skip, and perhaps giggle.'[14]

Betjeman's *Cornwall* was a trial run for the format: extremely short entries on individual buildings, and an assortment of different sections with headings like 'Ferry Services', 'The Age of Saints' and 'Picnics', the tone sometimes distinctly superior, with jibes at popular culture, and stern warnings against leaving litter. When he moved on to *Devon* in 1936, he was in more whimsical mood with recurring references to ghosts and goblins, and eight lines of fairy verse on Pixies' Houses. In 1937 the series became a collaboration, when Betjeman was introduced by Jim Richards to John Piper. A keen 'church crawler', in his own phrase, who had long kept detailed topographical notebooks for pleasure, Piper was a less nostalgic and more rigorous observer than Betjeman, but he still preferred guides to be diaries, complete with prejudices and superficialities.[15] He would describe the early Shell volumes as 'larky'. Stephen Bone's study of the West Coast of Scotland, which included sections on Sea Serpents and the Northern Lights, had some of its photographs printed in purple to conjure up a backdrop of heather. *Northumberland and Durham*, written by the distinguished town planner Thomas Sharp, was far more politicised in tone – the text on one deserted pit village in County Durham read, 'Meditate a while here on man's inhumanity to man' – but still found room for the words and music to 'Blow the Wind Southerly' and a supplement on North Country Speech, while Robert Byron in *Wiltshire* included nature notes, war, sport and 'moral antiquities'.

Although in truth the *Shell Guides* too had their occasional longueurs, they would always be held up as the most readable of guidebooks. But readability was often achieved at the expense of architectural detail, which may explain why Betjeman and Piper agreed in the late 1940s to work concurrently on the *Murray's Architectural Guides*. In the nineteenth century the firm of John Murray had published one of the most celebrated series of guidebooks in the world, the *Handbooks for Travellers*, all-purpose travel companions to foreign lands as well as to every part of Great Britain. 'In their downright tone,' writes Philip Glazebrook, 'you see . . . as clear a picture of the Imperial Englishman on his travels as you see of the lands he travelled through, so that to read them is like overhearing one 19th century member of London's Travellers' Club advising another on a forthcoming journey.'

The *Handbooks* had been discontinued after the First World War; the proposal was now to revive them, taking advantage of the greater wealth of illustrative material that had become available. This was in fact to be the distinguishing feature of the *Murray's Architectural Guides*. 'The value of these guides,' wrote Betjeman, 'will be *not* that they are comprehensive but that they see the good and the character-istic with an artist's eye.'[16] The editors' three criteria for including buildings were beauty, variety and strength in the character of the particular county – which led them to exclude a large majority of modern buildings, place 'progress' pointedly in inverted commas and lapse into sentences such as 'tractors chug where once harness jingled'. The authors acknowledged in their foreword that their approach might well irritate some readers. Berkshire, for example, presented a county of mummers, cheese-rolling, watercress beds, fertility rituals and *Tom Brown's Schooldays*. But the two Betjeman–Piper collaborations on the Home Counties also celebrated the more acceptable face of 'Metro-land', the 1930s suburbs bordering the Metropolitan Line of the London Underground, and defended unfashionable Victorian stained glass and multicoloured tiles. The Gazetteers, brief but atmospheric, were little more than appendices to extended sequences of illustrations that even the *Shell Guides* must have envied, with long captions that were elegant, informative and entertaining.

The *Murray's Guides*, though chatty and highly selective, would probably, with their architectural focus, have been the closest parallels to Pevsner's series – had they survived. The outstanding photographs were probably the main factor in a cover price of eighteen shillings, which by the early 1950s had condemned the books to commercial oblivion (to the dismay of John Betjeman, who had been looking to the series for a regular income). Pevsner, in any case, was clear in his own mind when he embarked on his grand project that there was nothing in existence to compare closely with it.

What was needed was 'a workable Dehio *Handbuch* for England'.

'The Dehio is a useless book,' commented Peter Lasko, medievalist, Pevsner pupil and fourth Director of the Courtauld Institute.* 'You've got to learn the code before you use it, because everything's abbreviated eighteen times – things like "MW" for "meines Wissens", "as far as I know" – and there's no glossary. And Dehio is not readable, you couldn't sit and read it.'[17] Nor was it complete: Dehio had travelled by bicycle and had been limited by its range. 'I intended to go beyond Dehio in two ways,' wrote Pevsner, 'length and autopsy. Instead of five volumes for the whole country there should be one for each English county, and every building – exceptions excepted – should be seen by me and described and analysed on the spot.'[18]

Pevsner's objective was neither grandiose nor complicated. He simply wanted people to look at the buildings of England as they would look at any other beautiful object, not in an abstract quest for knowledge but as an everyday source of enjoyment. During his travels for the *Yorkshire: The North Riding* volume, he lingered at Sheriff Hutton Hall, home of the Ingram family. The house, remodelled in 1732, had first been built in the early seventeenth century, and he was looking for evidence of the Jacobean original. An uncentred door on the entrance side, he wrote, 'prepares the canny visitor at once for the feel that, inside, the house is still the house of Sir Arthur Ingram'. Pevsner was a lifelong 'canny visitor', and he wanted everyone to share the pleasure of being able to see beyond the first impression. Ideally, this would start at a young age. 'What I would like,' he told Birkbeck pupil Denis Evinson, 'is for every schoolboy to have his own volume of his own county in his pocket.'[19] (Pevsner, of course, had his own definition of what was portable and what size a pocket should be; when one *Buildings of England* user complained in the 1960s that the volumes could no longer be housed in a macintosh pocket, he retorted, 'In my mac they can be.'[20] Beyond the first shock of aesthetic enjoyment, he wanted people to be able to place themselves within a national tradition and feel part of an evolving culture. At the same time, it was crucial that people should be able to locate themselves and the buildings around them in a European context.

From the beginning, his analysis was largely formal. This was the discipline in which he had been brought up, and it was something he felt was lacking in England. He would write later: 'Formal analysis, what the Germans call "anonymous art history" (i.e. history not of individualities but of styles and phases) has never been as much a

---

*Peter Lasko (1924–2003) was the first Professor of Art History at East Anglia and director of the Courtauld Institute from 1974 to 1985, succeeding Sir Anthony Blunt.

universal technique in England as in Germany. Germany for a time may have overdone it, England is under-doing it.'[21] Pevsner sought to compensate – and achieved his objective largely at the expense of evocation and evaluation of what he saw.

His apparent refusal to evoke atmosphere was largely practical. Besides the obvious need to save space in a book that was intended to be portable, he was constrained by his own limitations. Geoffrey Grigson once accused him of being oblivious to the *genius loci*, but a fairer charge would have been that he felt he had no talent for expressing it. He envied and admired writers who were able to capture the feel of a place in words, but rarely attempted overtly to do it himself, because, in his view, it was not his forte. It is entertaining to compare his accounts of churches with those of John Betjeman in, say, the *Collins Guide to English Parish Churches*, where Betjeman set out his overall approach in an extended introduction.* 'There is often difficulty in opening the door,' he explained, starting at the beginning. 'If it is an old door it will invariably open inwards. So first turn the iron handle and push hard. Then if the door seems to be locked, turn the handle the other way and push hard. Then feel on the wall plate of the porch for the key. Then look under the mat. Then lift the notice board from the porch wall and look under that. Then look inside the lamp bracket outside the porch. Church keys are usually 6" or 8" long and easy to find.' Pevsner has by now dated the roof, attributed the windows and is back in the car, while Betjeman is still on the doormat savouring the ambience.

Betjeman's brand of evocation, of course, is more about church-going than about the churches themselves, and tends to turn the focus on the observer as much as the object observed. Even Pevsner's friends, however, felt that objectivity could sometimes be overdone. 'I once complained to him about a series of church descriptions,' remembered Alec Clifton-Taylor, 'that they told us everything except the one thing that we wanted to know most, which was whether the churches were any good or not.' (He probably had in mind his remark that 'Dr Pevsner . . . occasionally seems not to be able to see the church for the double-chamfered arches'.[22]) But Pevsner was unrepentant: '"You must go and look at them", he said, "and make up your own mind. I have given you the facts".'[23]

His 'facts', of course, often included some educated guesswork; and

---

*The *Collins Guide* was originally published as one volume in 1958, with the various counties covered by different people. Betjeman himself covered the churches of London, Berkshire and half of Cornwall.

the *Buildings of England*, which would frequently be accused of impersonality, are actually peppered with partialities. He admitted this openly when it came to the buildings of the nineteenth and twentieth centuries. 'Naturally, in dealing with the more recent monuments, especially those of the last hundred years, a more rigid selection had to be made than for those of the Middle Ages or the Elizabethan age. Completeness was out of the question, and so another principle had to be adopted. It is frankly my own taste.'[24]

The focus on fact was itself a partiality, a personal preference for architectural detail and stylistic detective work. Reviewing a selection of books on cathedrals for the *Architectural Review* in April 1949, he complained, 'The Salisbury book has chapter headings such as "Romance in Brass and Stone" and spends a page out of thirty-five on the life story of Thomas Seymour because his son lies buried in the cathedral. But for the relations of the architecture of Salisbury to Lincoln and Westminster and France and its peculiar qualities, for instance the curious jarring passages in the west wall-tribune-east wall design which must be deliberate breaks in the harmonious flow of the Early English design, there is not a word.'

Pevsner's principal contribution, in his own eyes, would be the same as it had been when he was writing the *Enquiry*, *Pioneers* and the *Outline*: an international outlook, and the independence of the outsider. When applied to English buildings, however, this insistence on the broader context startled and annoyed some critics, achieved as it often was at the expense of the fine detail of local history. The English antiquarian tradition aimed to set each individual building firmly and precisely in its immediate time and place. Coming from outside that tradition, Pevsner's priorities were different. 'He was actually not so interested in the historical continuity in an area,' commented John Newman, later one of his closest collaborators on the *Buildings of England*:[25]

> Being a European he hadn't got it in his bones as an English historian might have . . . He wasn't passionately interested in the county structure, the county history, and the way villages had developed . . . He was principally interested in buildings for their architectural quality and interest, and he was always putting them into patterns as he saw them, architecturally and stylistically . . . What he wanted was a proper over-view by somebody who had a sense of perspective of the whole country and would not get bogged down in tremendous enthusiasms about things which seen in the wider context were only of local interest.

Pevsner was almost certainly compelled by Penguin to exclude plans of towns or buildings for reasons of economy; but he imposed a wide range of other restrictions on himself. Buildings that were no longer standing, for instance, would rarely be commemorated. Nor would he usually tackle any more than the most significant archaeological remains. 'I know it is disgraceful,' he admitted much later, 'but I have for the whole of my life had only one day on an excavation.'[26] As the series progressed, there would be contributions on prehistory and Roman antiquities, but mostly by other people.*

Some omissions are entirely a matter of personal taste. Memorial brasses did not interest him: medieval brasses are conscientiously catalogued but with little detail, and there are few entries on later specimens.† Other exclusions were made purely to save space. 'Tracery,' he wrote sadly in *Devon*, 'often does not lend itself to brief description and is therefore rather neglected in these pages.' More puzzling is the decision to leave out bells, given their relevance to the provision and dating of towers in churches and some public buildings, but to include church plate.‡

The principal casualties, perhaps, were setting and people. Pevsner had not lost his love of walking or of scenery. But when looking at individual buildings his focus narrowed and he made himself largely oblivious of setting unless it had forced its way into the schema of the architect. It was an omission of which he was keenly aware. 'The group of church and rectory or church and vicarage is a feature in the English villagescape to which the Continent has no parallel, and its variations of style and composition are infinite. If only my volumes allowed me more space on grouping, how often would I try to draw attention to these subtle relationships, occasionally contrived but mostly the result of happy accident.'[27] He was also interested in the

---

*A prominent contributor on Roman antiquities was a young Barry Cunliffe. He and Pevsner had hoped it might eventually be possible to persuade Penguin to extract all the prehistoric and Roman material from the *BoE* and make it into separate guides, but Penguin decided instead to start a gazetteer of prehistory and Roman history from scratch.

†When a King Penguin on the subject of brasses was proposed, Pevsner wrote, 'I think that it would be a popular book, although one which would bore me.' NP/Tanya Kent (Schmoller), 29/6/48. Penguin Archive, DM 1952, Box 743.

‡Simon Bradley, current editor of the *Buildings of England*, comments that the Royal Commission on Historical Monuments was covering both plate and bells, so for the counties where RCHM volumes existed, the information on bells was there for the taking. Conversely, in areas not yet covered by the RCHM, the entries on plate required collaboration with specialists and a good deal of extra work – and in some volumes, such as *Oxfordshire* and *Cambridgeshire*, they tend to weigh down the text. Simon Bradley to the author, July 2009.

relationships between people – between patron and artist, client and architect, master and pupil. This was what had drawn him as a young man towards the theories of *Kulturgeschichte*, which set art firmly in its social context. But within the framework of the *Buildings of England*, their original occupants were largely ignored. As for their possessions, furniture and paintings were to be excluded totally unless they could be considered fixtures and fitments, and sculpture would be considered in churches, but not in houses.

Industrial architecture was given far less attention than it would now be thought to deserve – partly because Pevsner felt he knew relatively little about it, but also because he did not see it as a priority. Bridget Cherry, his successor as editor of the series, explained: 'When England was still an industrial nation, as one thought it was in the 1950s, one didn't think it was actually necessary to comment on the fact that there were factories. Now they've become historic monuments. It's a shift in perception and in research, rather than a reflection on the level of his interest.'[28]

One subject that apparently did fail to engage his curiosity was construction methods – to the extent that 'Buildings' of England almost becomes a misnomer, according to building historian Robert Thorne. The entire survey is carried out on the basis that construction is subsidiary to architecture, and there are, Thorne points out, virtually no entries in the glossary relating to construction techniques. Another Pevsnerian blind spot is his distaste for Art Deco and other manifestations of 'jazz', which led him to ignore cinemas almost completely – helping to ensure, according to his critics, that they would become an endangered species.

Otherwise, his work outside the *Buildings of England* makes it obvious that he was capable of being interested in practically anything, and that in the right place he very much enjoyed leisurely detail. An article entitled 'Wiltshire surprises', written for the *Architectural Review* in November 1962, is a good example of Pevsner at ease. His brief had been simply to explore the area around his Snowhill cottage, with photographer Eric de Maré at hand, and he luxuriated in the unaccustomed freedom. In the church at Stockton he found a tomb figure not behaving as it should:

> This lady . . . ought, of course, to lie on her back. That is what such effigies do. But then – and students as well as photographers know that to their despair – you can never see her properly, because of the arch of the recess in which she is placed. So she is turned over, but as a stone effigy, not as a body. The soles of the feet which

should have pressed gently against the pet dog don't quite do so, and the skirt and the mantle, of course, fall as if she were still lying on her back.

If the *Buildings of England* do not have the remorseless insistence of some guides on the quaint or quirky, nevertheless the odd, the imaginative, the moving and the strictly irrelevant creep in everywhere. Trees remarkable for their age, girth, height, placing or other peculiarities appear at intervals in most volumes. Informal indexes in Pevsner's notes betray an interest in animal footrests, different kinds of postboxes and holy wells, and he criticised the Royal Commission for omitting features such as signal-boxes and milestones. He had a particular fondness for funny, peculiar or affecting funerary monuments and inscriptions – here an 'excessively cross-legged knight', there a 'recumbent figure of a youth in Eton clothes on a mattress, very pathetic', or 'two cherubs, one with a cannon ball by his feet, the other carrying one on his shoulder'.*

Even if they did not appear in the text of the *Buildings of England*, curiosities rarely went completely unremarked, but were logged away as 'byproducts of work on the BoE' for use in other, less confined contexts. 'Do you know that the first bathroom was installed at St John's College, Cambridge in 1921?' he asked an Australian radio audience in 1958, trying to convey the range of his enquiry.[29] 'Do you know that underneath a Tudor hall in Hertfordshire there is a chapel . . . which is decorated with tabletops from Lyons' teashops? . . . Do you know that in the gardens of the old Crystal Palace there are life-size bronze figures of ante-diluvian animals and that once lunch was served inside the iguanodon?'

'Many thanks indeed for your long and interesting letter,' Pevsner would write politely to one correspondent towards the end of the series. 'I am certainly going to make an effort in future to include more organ cases.' He was firm in his own opinions and could sometimes be rigid in his method, but he was never under any illusion that his was the only possible way to inventorise English buildings or that the results could ever be perfect. Reflecting on topics that he had ignored, he wrote, 'Much of this another critic might have included in preference to what I have. Much also, on the other hand . . . will have been omitted simply because I did not know of its existence. Farmhouses of architectural interest especially which are not recorded

---

*The knight appears at Braunston in *Northamptonshire*, the Etonian at St Andrew's, Prestwold in *Leicestershire*, the cherubs at St Bartholomew's, Foston, *Leicestershire*.

in the literature available to me and which were by some misfortune not on any of the roads and lanes inspected, will be found to have been left out. Similarly houses of value in back streets may have been overlooked.'

The *Buildings of England* series was, in his own words, a *ballon d'essai*.* 'Trial balloons' were usually sent up to discover which way the wind was blowing; metaphorically, the phrase is usually taken to mean 'a tentative plan put forward to test opinion or reaction'. Pevsner sought reaction in the form of information. In each volume after the very first one, the initial text the reader encountered, apart from the map, would read: 'The author and publishers would be grateful to any user of this book for having any errors or omissions pointed out to them in as much detail as possible.' On Pevsner's part at least, this was a perfectly truthful statement.

Each book opened with a short foreword detailing acknowledgements and sources, and continued with an introduction briefly characterising the county and tracing its architectural history from prehistoric antiquities to the present day; later volumes would include a separate section on its geology.† The gazetteer of villages, towns and cities formed the core of the book – and from the very first volume, these entries would be supplemented with black-and-white photographs illustrating the development of the county's architectural features, from churches and their monuments to private houses and public buildings.‡ The idea of a separate series of picture books would seem to have disappeared between the signing of the contract and the publication of the first volume of the series, without trace or explanation. At the end of each book, a glossary of architectural terms, with occasional thumbnail drawings for clarification, was followed by indexes of plates, artists and places – though none of owners, patrons, styles or individual buildings.

Pevsner's reluctance to alter this layout over the years had much to do with his desire that the series should be genuinely standard in format, recognisably a single conception and, at first at least, the work of a single author. (This was one of his reasons for keeping his distance

---

*The words *ballons d'essai* appear in the introduction to *Staffordshire* (1974), the final volume in the series.
†Bridget Cherry points out that these introductions were Pevsner's own innovation: the Dehio volumes had no individual introductions.
‡In earlier volumes the photographs were grouped by type in a series of chronological sequences; in later volumes they were inserted all in one (roughly) chronological sequence.

from local historians, preferring to send them written drafts for checking at the end, rather than enlisting their help at the outset. 'He did think the whole series would be destroyed, its character would be lost, if it was put into the hands of locals,' commented Mark Girouard, an early assistant.) He would, however, let in new types of content from time to time and vary his vocabulary, embracing new epithets and sometimes whole categories of classification: John Summerson's notion of 'artisan mannerism' he liked very much and elevated to the status of capital letters, with an acknowledgement in the introduction to *Surrey*.

As for methodology, although the research for the *BoE* would become a good deal more thorough over the years, the basic principles and processes remained the same. His first step, when beginning work on a county, was to appoint one or more research assistants. Architectural historian John Harris once disparagingly described Pevsner's first research assistants as 'two dear German émigré ladies, who might just as well have been gathering information on golf courses, for all they knew about architecture'.[30] Mrs Schilling and Dr Schapire, and Miss Bondi after them, were not chosen for any specialist architectural knowledge; but they were fully qualified art historians – Gertrud Bondi was another pupil of Wilhelm Pinder – and it was the rigour of their German training that appealed to Pevsner.* Rosa Schapire in particular was rather more eminent than Harris may have realised.[†] Eccentric Dr Schapire may have been – she was rumoured once to have gone for Pevsner with a knife – and her research could at times be patchy; but she was hardly the dear incompetent old lady of Ealing comedy that Harris suggests.

The researchers worked almost entirely from secondary, not primary, sources. 'It was in the library, rather than the record office or muniment room, that the work was done,' writes Edward Hubbard, a later collaborator on the series, who has left the fullest description of the process.[31] The first task was to compile a bibliography of the works most likely to be useful as general background: biographical dictionaries of architects and sculptors, the standard works on particular periods, styles, subjects or personalities, plus books by authors Pevsner particularly admired, such as Christopher Hussey on the Picturesque, John Summerson on Georgian architecture, Howard Colvin and others on the King's Works.

---

*Under Pinder's tuition, Bondi submitted her thesis in 1932 on 'Die Kompositions-prinzipien Jacopo Bellinis und seine Rolle innerhalb der Entwicklung der venezianischen Raumsdarstellung'.
[†]See Chapter 21.

But the bulk of the relevant information, historical and topographical, was obviously specific to the county, and here it was both more necessary and more difficult to find trustworthy and comprehensive sources. The most useful single resource was the lists of buildings of historical and architectural importance prepared by the Ministry of Housing, but these Pevsner would eventually take with him on his travels, leaving the assistants to concentrate on less manageable materials. The relevant volume of Kelly's Trade Directories might be used to establish a basic topographical framework, with references to all parish churches and major public buildings. This could then be filled out with extracts from the relevant volumes of the Royal Commission and Victoria County History, and from individual county histories, though many of these were old and thin on specifically architectural information.

More detail was to be found, with some effort, in the transactions and journals of local historical and archaeological societies, usually lodged in local collections. Pevsner would soon discover that the card index of the library of the Society of Antiquaries provided the best finding aid for these – though not without cost. 'The Antiquaries is not a very happy place to work,' he would confide, five years into the series.* 'Several of my assistants find that they are not terribly popular and so one has to be careful and especially try to keep on the right side of the Librarian, Dr Deane. Also, it is advisable to keep away from the Library on Thursday afternoons, that is for the meetings of the Society, when the library is full of irritable old gentlemen.'

Periodicals were another problematic source. For individual buildings, *Country Life* was relatively easy to use; but the technical and professional architectural journals that for Pevsner's purposes were more rewarding – primarily *The Builder*, and then the *Architectural Review* and, more rarely, the *Architects' Journal* – were also far more unwieldy. 'They are the basic raw material for the study of Victorian architectural history,' Edward Hubbard would declare later, '[but] . . . their own indexing systems are highly deficient, and the trouble is that the sheer bulk of the material rendered systematic combing impossible . . . Their use for the BoE has therefore been selective, indeed arbitrary.'

For pictorial evidence, the researchers could consult the RIBA Drawings Collection, as well as the National Buildings Record for

---

*NP/ Dr Susanne (Susi) Lang, 22/10/53. Dr Lang was a researcher for the *Architectural Review*, where she worked as a research assistant and collaborator with Pevsner on several articles.

photographs.* Maps, it seems, were not systematically consulted. 'I wish I could wander round always with an old as well as a new map,' Pevsner would remark plaintively in 1957 to R.S. Schulze, research librarian and curator of the Kodak Museum. 'Once one turns to the old maps in the local library, one usually finds clues that would have been very valuable in the field.' Pevsner left clues of his own, however, from his past excursions through English towns and villages. Every research assistant inherited at the outset a box for his or her county containing miscellaneous materials that Pevsner had amassed over the years – notes, references, book reviews, cuttings, illustrations and obituaries. Some of these materials were recondite, especially in areas where he had been a pioneer, and they formed collections that it would have been impossible to replicate. He was also beginning to have a wide knowledge of students' research subjects, and could point the researchers to unpublished theses. And he continued to accumulate information on the counties himself.

Russell Burlingham was in charge of periodicals in the RIBA library in the early 1950s:[32]

I soon became aware . . . that one of my most regular readers was bent on a quite different and evidently obsessive quest. His interest . . . was directed exclusively towards the comprehensive set of THE BUILDER, whose early volumes – dusky grey and boldly gilt-lettered – bestrode the wall at the south end of the gallery . . . It was evident that my visitor was working steadily, from its earliest days (like a weevil in a tin of nourishing biscuits) through this long, long run . . . Well-pressed grey flannel trousers, brightly-polished brown Oxfords, and the kind of jacket (high-collared, tightly buttoned, and with a built-in belt, or zone, at the rear) affected by the better sort of under-graduate in the years before 1914, gave him the air of some mature revenant from those golden days . . . Only a glinting pair of professorial and faintly continental pince-nez would have perhaps (had I reflected) afforded a small clue.†

---

*Founded in 1940, the National Buildings Record – later the National Monuments Record – was a product of wartime concern for a built heritage under imminent threat.
†Geoffrey Spain would accelerate the process by taking on the task of combing *The Builder* for later volumes.

CHAPTER 26

'They've come to read the meter, Ma'

The final product of all these library labours was a set of research notes known as the 'extracts', made to Pevsner's precise prescription on half-sheets of foolscap, arranged by districts, towns and villages, with each parish on a separate sheet where possible. These, supplemented by the Ministry of Housing lists, were his ammunition and the basis of his route map when he set off round his chosen county.

Pevsner's *Buildings of England* journeys have become furred with a thick growth of anecdote. Far from spending his entire existence on the road, he was forced by the demands of university teaching to confine himself to two trips a year, rarely more than four weeks long, under constant pressure of time. To avoid the worst of the weather, he would tackle southern counties in the Easter holiday and reserve the north for the end of the summer vacation. September, he felt, was an ideal month for a trip, as there was less rain and most owners of country houses had returned from their holidays.

Each journey involved covering some 2,000 miles, criss-crossing counties on minor roads and country lanes, as well as mapping and perambulating larger towns and charting cities; but into these crowded four-week periods Pevsner had to fit not only the travelling and his actual observation of buildings, but also much of the route planning and most of the business of negotiating access. When the series began, most churches were left open during the day, so it was secular buildings that presented the problem. Making appointments in advance was not practicable for any but the largest and grandest private houses; there was no time to identify and contact owners, and constructing a detailed timetable in this way would have imposed intolerable stresses and strains on an already overloaded schedule. All he could do was turn up unannounced at house after house, hoping for the best – a trial for a man who loved order and was anything but brash.

Neil Stratford, one of his drivers in later years, remembered the Pevsnerian approach: 'I'm sorry to disturb you,' he would say, 'but I'm interested in old buildings around here – may I look at the outside of your house?' More often than not the home-owner would be intrigued and invite him in, but if this failed, he would ask to see the staircase. 'The technique is that of the confidence trickster,' Pevsner remarked apologetically.[1] 'Admittedly,' he added, 'there are occasionally defeats.'

The butler at a mansion near Barnard Castle, for instance, took a dim view of the merits of a visitor who went round the building in half an hour 'in white shorts'. A preparatory school housed in a distinguished building gave him short shrift when he arrived on the first day of term amidst hordes of small boys, parents and trunks: 'The headmaster was furious. I was barred from the house. On the spot. Rightly so, of course.' There would also be humiliations. In the early 1960s Mark Girouard and John Harris were visiting Narford Hall in Norfolk when the Pevsners, having turned up uninvited, were announced by the son of the house: 'They've come to read the meter, Ma.'*

For Pevsner, the interest of these domestic interiors was usually worth the nervous tension and occasional embarrassment. 'You can imagine that for me to enter a strange house poses riddles . . . Just one instance: a French maid, an entrance hall with Elizabethan furniture of museum quality, but buckets on the stairs to catch water from the leaking roof, and a score of Max Reger on a table and a portrait of Frederick the Great on the wall. What should one make of that?' But as a rule his particular method of analytical appreciation lent itself best to churches. During his 1930 visit to England he had described to Lola how he felt one should approach it – 'letting the interior of a church make its impact on one, stopping and receiving the impressions, holding oneself ready and quiet'.

Pevsner was reticent about his religious beliefs, and, although when he was particularly struck by the atmosphere of spirituality in a place he would say so, the impressions he was talking about here were primarily aesthetic and intellectual. Some architectural historians have lamented the tendency of church authorities to make constant and confusing alterations to their buildings for doctrinal, economic or other purely practical reasons. But for Pevsner, unravelling the tangled evidence of addition, extension, demolition, reconstruction and restoration was a perpetually absorbing challenge. 'He never tired of the archaeological puzzles presented by medieval parish churches,' writes John Newman:[2]

His practice when confronted by an unfamiliar building for the first time was invariable. He would walk round the outside first, noting every feature of interest, whether a finely designed or characteristic window or doorway or merely a tell-tale joint in the masonry which

---

*Mark Girouard, interview with the author, 23/7/97. Narford Hall was the home of the Fountaine collection of art and antiques; the owner at that time was Andrew Fountaine (1918–97), a founding member and deputy leader of the National Front.

might suggest a break in the building programme or an alteration; then he would go inside and do the same for the interior; and only after that would he get out the notes prepared for him by his research assistant, from which he would discover what had already been published by way of historical documentation or archaeological analysis. Thus by the time he read the interpretations of others he had often made up his own mind about the building's history and development. What he read might confirm his unaided deductions; if on the other hand it challenged him to justify them, a lively and argumentative text was often the result.

Pevsner's arguments were not always right. Because he had rarely had the time to conduct new historical research himself, the conclusions he defended against the interpretations of others were sometimes based largely on intuition and long-cherished beliefs. What he did do was draw attention to features that needed to be noted, examined and debated; and whether or not his own particular solutions were correct, he had opened up questions for everyone to answer.

His method of recording his observations could hardly have been more basic. At the scene he made jottings on pieces of paper small enough to hold in his hand – near-illegible scribbles full of abbreviations and minute diagrams. These he would write up later on foolscap. Down the left-hand side of the sheet he ruled one thin column, and filled it with notes in a tiny hand, putting down only the details he intended to be included in the final manuscript and leaving the rest of the page free for additions and emendations, either on the spot or back in the office. Once these had been incorporated, his basic text would be complete – and why there were not more mistakes in the finished document it is difficult to understand. It was a process demanding great physical stamina when repeated in dozens of buildings a day, whether these were scattered across a wide area or concentrated in a single busy metropolis; his legs, he complained, tended 'to get wobbly after six hours'.[3]

It also required intense concentration and a degree of single-mindedness that others sometimes found baffling and unsympathetic. He was constantly aware of the pressure of new buildings waiting to be seen, and he dreaded distraction. A single lunch invitation could spell disaster and the disruption of his timetable, and he preferred to eat sandwiches en route. He had a variety of excuses for refusing hospitality; not all of these were particularly convincing, and he was not always successful in avoiding offence, as Alec Clifton-Taylor would point out:

I remember an attractive stone-built manor house in Somerset to which I was once taken to tea. The owner was an elderly widow who loved and doted on this house in the possessive way that other people sometimes show for their children or their dogs. At the tea-table Nikolaus' name cropped up. 'Don't speak to me of Mr Pevsner', said the chatelaine: 'He came here earlier this year, and how long do you think he stayed? Twenty minutes. *Twenty minutes.* I've never been so insulted in my life. They came at half past three, so of course I asked my household to prepare tea, but by ten to four they were gone. I think he said he was writing a book about Somerset: but whatever it was, it'll be absolutely useless'.[4]

For the first fifteen years, if he had anyone with him on his travels it would be Lola. She understood what gave her husband his sense of urgency, and was more than capable of staying the pace. A typical day on the road would start at about 8.30, and rarely lasted less than eight hours; she would become expert in spotting the signs that it was over. Travel writer Geoffrey Moorhouse followed the Pevsners through two counties. 'At 5.20 p.m.,' he remembered, 'as Pevsner returned from a skirmish round the grounds of a Georgian country house, he took a cigarette from his case and Mrs Pevsner said, "That means we've finished".'* Supper would be early and usually undistinguished, in the pubs or cheap hotels that were all they could afford; Penguin paid for his petrol, but little towards the costs of accommodation, and a month away was a significant expense.

Then, after this brief interlude, it was back to work, to process the findings of the day while they were still fresh in his mind and before they were overlaid with the next day's material. Later in the series John Newman accompanied him on two journeys a week in Berkshire in 1964 and a month in Hampshire in 1965:

He'd be quite relaxed over the meal and we'd chat away . . . Hints of his past would slip out . . . In one dining-room with a particularly heavy and insistent wallpaper, he remarked, 'Oh well, when I first was over here I took a job with Gordon Russell; it's always made me work out the repeat in wallpapers' . . . Then when it was finished he'd say, 'Well, my dear, I must go upstairs and scribble, scribble,' and he'd go. He would write up the day's notes, not just in

---

*G. Moorhouse, 'A day with the Pevsners', *Guardian*, 21/4/60. Moorhouse was then the chief features writer for the *Guardian*. He wrote as a journalist until 1970, before concentrating on books. He died in 2009.

provisional form, but as the final text, as it would appear on the printed page. Naturally some amendments were made later, and gaps had to be left in the event of problems and queries, but in effect the book itself was steadily written, day by day.[5]

Meanwhile his travelling-companion-cum-driver would be preparing for tomorrow. After eight hours on the road, planning the detail of the next day's route was laborious and wearing. In towns or cities it could be difficult to locate individual buildings and chart the most illuminating course between them; in the countryside, anticipating the nature and condition of the back roads was guesswork as often as not. And then, once the programme was drawn up, Pevsner would study it, annotate it and mark the buildings he actually wanted to see, 'as distinct from those which, on the evidence of the information available, could safely be ignored'. Neil Stratford, who would drive him round Cumberland, Westmorland and Worcestershire in the 1960s, remembered him simply crossing out great clumps of notes.

There were telephone calls to make, to confirm appointments or arrange new ones for the days to come; and once the route was fixed, the appropriate extracts, maps and ministry lists had to be lined up, with any relevant correspondence or guidebooks. Geoffrey Moorhouse described the evening atmosphere: 'Mrs Pevsner squats on the bed, surrounded by maps and notes, planning tomorrow's itinerary. Pevsner sits at the table, writing steadily from his own notes, taken during the day. Occasionally a question is tossed across the room ("Lola, do you remember that Tudor brick entrance in the wall at Buckenham? Can one call them polygonal buttresses? They aren't really turrets, are they . . .") but mostly they work in silence.'[6]

Work would rarely be finished before midnight; but in cities or towns of any size, Pevsner would be up early the next morning to carry out a 'perambulation' – a tour on foot through an area past every building he considered worthy of mention, noting not just the architectural details and state of preservation of individual buildings but also their relations to each other and, where the atmosphere was particularly strong, the character of their setting. In the countryside, while they waited for breakfast's first sitting, Lola would make the sandwiches and he would sometimes complete the writing from the previous night. Then, after the most sustaining meal they could absorb, they would fill the Thermos flask from the dining-room teapot and take to the road again.

Once the trip was over, Pevsner would shut himself away for a week, in his office or down at the cottage rather than in his study at home, free from all distractions, to condense the mass of impressions into a synoptic view of the county's building history and character, which would eventually form the volume's introduction. During this period of intensive thinking he was not available to students or for work of other kinds, and was irritated by interruptions. Then, once the introduction was drafted, he would begin the long process of dealing with gaps and problems arising out of the journey – what he described as 'masses of checking letters to vicars, "occupiers", My Lord Dukes, Venerable Archdeacons, Public Librarians etc', many of them to do with buildings that had not been researched but had been noticed by chance during the travelling.[7] These letters were usually short and to the point – 'I should be grateful if you could very kindly let me know whether the wagon roofs in your church are old?'– but they ran into the hundreds, and this phase would take at least six months. As the series progressed, checking tended to run on into the printing and proofing stages, and both Pevsner and Penguin became stricter about how many alterations they could accommodate. By the 1960s the gap between the original travelling and the eventual emergence of the county volume sometimes stretched to three years, and Pevsner would send out excerpts in galley proof, to inhibit correspondents from making voluminous additions. Vicars in particular were suspect: 'If I sent them typescript,' he complained, 'they would upset the whole text to put in all their pet remarks.'[8]

The order in which Pevsner chose to confront his counties was determined by an interesting blend of practicality and whim. He felt that he should tackle the most far-flung counties earlier on, as they would present the most difficult travelling as he got older. At the same time, he wanted an even geographical spread between north and south, west and east, Home Counties and regions. He also appears to have had an eye on rival series, but in a spirit of collaboration rather than competition. 'Berkshire has not yet been prepared by any of my assistants,' he wrote to Allen Lane in July 1950, 'and I have not specially pressed for it because it is one of the two Piper and Betjeman [Murray's] guides and we had made a vague gentleman's agreement to keep away from each other's counties for the time being.'[9] And occasionally he simply gave in to the temptation of visiting a county for its landscape. 'The North Riding of Yorkshire is a wonderful county,' he wrote in the introduction to that volume in 1966. 'As work on the *Buildings of England* proceeds, such counties are getting ever rarer. When I have done Cumberland and Westmorland the best of England will be finished – the best, that is, as far as nature is concerned.'

* * *

His reason for starting the whole series where he did, however, was purely prosaic and hinged on strict post-war petrol rationing. *Middlesex* was never likely to be the most commercially attractive volume in the series, and in the event Allen Lane chose not to open with it. (It was published as BE3, in 1951.) But this was where Pevsner started his travels for the *BoE* in the summer of 1947, with the kind of modest motor expeditions that a severely restricted fuel allowance would permit. If they could get the series under way, Lane reasoned, they might be able to lever enough petrol from the authorities to embark on more ambitious trips. 'A useful point might be that such a series would be of considerable interest to the tourist trade which the government is obviously very interested in encouraging.'

'We intend to have the car thoroughly overhauled this winter,' he continued. 'The Wolseley . . . is, I consider, an extremely good job for your purpose.'[10] He was referring to a 1932 six-cylinder Wolseley Hornet, dark green with a flat-fronted radiator and illuminated radiator badge, narrow bonnet and generous running boards – but Pevsner could not have agreed with him less. 'An obstreperous vintage 1932 car' he called it in the introduction to the volume, thanking Lola and his secretary for coaxing it round the byways of the county.*

It would be fair to regard *Middlesex* as a dry run for the series. The travelling was done in fits and starts, and this is reflected in the finished product, which is both bitty and less detailed than later volumes. At the outset, Pevsner made no claim that all counties would be treated equally. Some were bound to be richer than others in architectural terms, and Middlesex, in his view, was one of the poorer ones, imposing no duty on him to be comprehensive. 'A brief survey of what is most rewarding of all periods,' he wrote, 'may in the context of this book be justified.' What is more, when Dr Bondi embarked on the extracting and compiling of the basic research, the Ministry of Housing had not yet completed its list of notable buildings in Middlesex, and Pevsner was working to a rather skimpy brief.

Throughout the text of *Middlesex* he gives every sign of having been depressed by the unregulated sprawl of what he was studying. Once London had been separated off in 1888, Middlesex, he concluded, was a torso with no head, an expanse of development with no real centre, no cathedral or 'large ecclesiastical establishment', and not much character. Its history consisted largely of the filling up with

---

*The secretary, Marjorie Stearns, would appear to have had much the same opinion of Pevsner as he had of the Wolseley; she left in 1951, having found him 'too demanding'.

suburbs of the gap between the rural area in the north and a scattering of villages and Londoners' country houses in the south, to form a dense, firmly knit, largely undifferentiated urban mesh.

Nor did the surviving monuments of earlier, better days really compensate. All in all, he concluded glumly, there was little of more than local importance until the sixteenth century. It seems to have taken Hampton Court to cheer him up, and he then actively enjoyed the traces of the Inigo Jones style that he discovered in unlikely corners of Greenford, Brentford and Ickenham. It pleased him to be able to find traces of his Victorian 'pioneers', such as the only factory ever designed by C.F.A. Voysey, a wallpaper printing works built for Sanderson's opposite their main building in Barley Mow Passage, Chiswick – 'a clean and charming design', white with bands of blue (now black) bricks.* There were later buildings, too, that he admired – some of Charles Holden's better stations for London Underground, and one or two of the LCC's new primary schools.

In contrast, he was affronted by the Art Deco Hoover works on Western Avenue, 'perhaps the most offensive of the modernistic atrocities along this road of typical by-pass factories'. Nor at this stage was he as forgiving of Victorian excess as he would later become. Ugliness was its principal crime, but he also took exception to its attitude. This he saw most vigorously exemplified at Harrow School – not just a passive blot on the landscape, but an active force sucking the life-blood out of the town and over-shadowing it with purple brick boarding houses of 'a formidably mid-Victorian character of hearty and confident gloom'. The mild scorn with which he treated Herbert Baker's handiwork at Harrow, however, was as nothing compared with the ire he reserved for the Gothic Revival architect Samuel Sanders Teulon. *Middlesex* saw the first of many outbursts, which read entertainingly today in an era when the work of Teulon is being carefully listed and restored. Sunbury had possessed a modest parish church, built in the classical style in 1752 by the Royal Clerk of the Works at Hampton Court. 'In 1856 *Teulon* descended upon this guileless building and recast it vigorously. The effects of his steamroller sensitivity are here particularly revolting.'

But Pevsner's objective was primarily to promote people's pleasure in their built environment. Even within the irritations and frustrations cramping his journeys in 1947, it is possible to detect when he was having a good day. 'The parish church of ST MARY, [Harefield],' he wrote, 'lies right in the fields, at the foot of the hill which the village

---

*Now listed Grade II.

climbs up – an irregular picturesque little building . . . The prevailing impression in the church is one of happy crowding . . . The chancel especially is as cram-full of curious objects as the rooms of the Soane Museum' – two commandment boards of frosted glass, a Georgian pulpit, pieces of armour, urns, chests, brasses, and a fine monument by Grinling Gibbons: 'The Lady [Mary Newdigate] lies in a comfortable position half sitting up: she displays a simple loose Roman robe and no emotion whatever.'

Some of Pevsner's enthusiasms seem eccentric now, particularly his singling out of workaday contemporary buildings. Because so few British architects had chosen to work in the idiom of the Modern Movement in its early days, he felt obliged to comment on every occasion when they showed signs of embracing modern principles, however unremarkable the visual results might have been. It was hardly surprising that he should have included 97 and 101 Park Avenue, Ruislip, semi-detached villas in white concrete, steel frames and plate glass by Connell, Ward and Lucas.* They stand out remarkably with their flat façades and roofs in a mock-Tudor suburban street; even Pevsner found the effect 'rather outré'. The 'pre-fabs' of Frederick Gibberd in Harrow Weald – 'palaces for the people', neat two-storeyed cabins constructed from pre-fabricated elements in plywood, iron and corrugated asbestos – also have many admirers; Pevsner extolled them as 'comely', 'an example of how aesthetically good emergency construction can be, if texture, colour, and those details which are unaffected by shortages of materials are handled with taste'. More idiosyncratic was his inclusion of the Electroflo valve factory in Park Royal: 'an example of the contemporary idiom without any embellishment whatsoever. Mr Richards calls it diagrammatic.'

Half a century later, with much new research completed, scholars have enjoyed pointing out the gaps in Pevsner's original coverage. Perhaps more culpable in *Middlesex* is his tendency to write too much on subjects that particularly intrigued him, or which he considered central to the history of taste, throwing out any balance that the volume might have had. His account of Horace Walpole's Gothic folly at Strawberry Hill, for example, is less a simple description of the house than a full-scale essay on the context and history of its building accompanied by detailed criticism of its effects – 'both amusing and awful, both Rococo and romantic' – far beyond the bounds of the terse gazetteer that the book resembles for much of its length.

---

*Though he lumps them together as a single building of 1935, whereas one was completed in 1932, the other in 1938.

Likewise, he allowed himself to write expansively on Hampstead Garden Suburb, site of his first lodging in England in the 1930s, in an attempt to analyse why, in the 'aesthetically most satisfactory . . . of all C20 garden suburbs', all of the planners' aspirations had not been realised. Somehow the middle classes had squeezed out the artisans, the single working ladies and the aged for whom Raymond Unwin and M.H. Baillie Scott had built specially designated flats, 'colleges' and quadrangles, and these comfortable citizens spent much of their time in the privacy of their own homes, rather than in communal activity. This he attributed to the fact that the Central Square, designed largely by Lutyens, contained no shops, cinemas, pubs or cafés. 'Institute education and divine worship have not proved to be as much of a permanent and non-intermittent attraction as the social reformers behind the Suburb had hoped for.'

Pevsner might have been relieved to move away from the suburbs for the next volume of the *BoE,* but many of the same practical problems awaited him in his preparations for *Cornwall.* Mrs Schilling did not have much printed material at her disposal, and made 'rather less systematic' use of the Ministry of Housing lists – while Pevsner would confess later, in the introduction to the revised edition, that he himself had not been aware of the Society of Antiquaries' index at this point, and had been forced to rely on some rather miscellaneous sources. 'We were all beginners at the job then.'

This was another county where it would be necessary to concentrate on a relatively small number of highlights. Square brackets round dozens of names reveal buildings, particularly private houses, that Pevsner had failed to reach – partly because petrol was still short, but also because he did not feel the need was so pressing. 'Cornwall possesses little of the highest aesthetic quality,' he wrote in the introduction, 'though much that is lovable and much that is moving. Nearly always, however, in analysing one's emotions, one will find that what is remembered is more the setting of architecture than architecture itself.'

One of the most vivid dreams that the young Pevsner recorded in his *Heftchen* saw him travelling with Lola in a car through precipitous country, to 'an old castle in the centre of a town. The lovers kiss.' In Cornwall in the spring of 1948 it was Lola who was at the wheel, and the car was an Austin 10; but the reality was rather less romantic and more arduous, as they struggled to start another unreliable pre-war vehicle supplied by Penguin. For the first four days, Pevsner reported frostily to Allen Lane, they had had to pay garages every morning to get the car on the road. But, once under way, these days were full of shared pleasure and interest, both expected and unexpected. In the coastal village of Tintagel it was not the so-called Arthurian ruins but the old Post Office – 'the most famous of Cornish stone cottages, low, dark, picturesque, with roofs like a cluster of hills, and of a slaty hue like elephant hide'. In the church of St Mary, Penzance, 'the altar is a spectacular affair of 1934 by Ernest Procter [an artist of the Newlyn School], with a whole prospect including the heavenly host, a corrugated silvery backcloth, jagged rays; all smacking a little of the Wurlitzer.'* Near the eastern tip of the Lizard peninsula, at St Ruan Major, they found St Rumonus, 'a deserted church among trees, with only a few farm buildings near it, so little visited that at the time of writing a white owl was nesting in the timbers of the s porch roof'.

Again and again the setting of buildings prompted Pevsner to single them out. At St Day, in the industrial settlement around Gwennap in the mid-west of the county, the church of Holy Trinity 'looks over a landscape of deserted tin mines, with their chimneys like so many monuments to the passing of human achievement, more deeply moving than the artificial picturesque mementos in c18 gardens'. Boconnoc House, at Lostwithiel, was a fine Georgian mansion with a façade by Soane, but for Pevsner 'the chief attraction is the grounds, extensive, and laid out with the generosity and the sensitivity to landscape effects which the c18 possessed and we have largely lost'.

'The same picturesque rather than strictly architectural appeal is what makes one take to the Cornish VILLAGE,' Pevsner wrote firmly. The Picturesque qualities of variety, contrast, surprise and irregularity that he appreciated so warmly in landscape gardens and in contemporary town planning were to be found on all sides in Cornwall. In Saltash, it was the juxtaposition of the high granite shafts of Brunel's Royal Albert Bridge with the fishermen's cottages at the waterside and the eighteenth-century town houses winding up the hill that excited him – 'a superb effect in the Doré sense'. At the same time he revealed himself to be resistant to some of the more conventional types of charm, taking this to the lengths of leaving out Polperro in its entirety 'because for all its prettiness, no individual buildings call for special notices. The attraction lies in the whole, not in the parts.'

It is in counties like Cornwall – counties that, in Pevsner's own phrase, have 'much to reward the picturesque traveller, the archaeologist and antiquarian' – that the contrast between the *Buildings of*

---

*This judgement had been toned down by the time of the revised edition in 1970.

England and the *Shell Guides* is most apparent, and the *Shell Guides* most obviously press their claims, with their more relaxed attitude to story-telling and their success in conveying atmosphere.

The twelfth-century church of St Enodoc, on the opposite side of the Camel estuary from Padstow, was a place that had meant a great deal to John Betjeman since his childhood holidays in Cornwall. It had been buried in the sands, only dug out and restored in 1863. It now sat on its own as Pevsner noted, 'in the middle of a golf links, in a dip, so that one can only occasionally see its little c13 spire'. Betjeman loved this effect, and wrote about it in 'Sunday Afternoon Service in St Enodoc Church, Cornwall': he would eventually choose to be buried in its churchyard, where his mother already lay. Pevsner remarks neutrally, 'the existence of a spire is unusual in Cornwall'. Not as unusual, surely, as the existence of a chapel in the middle of a golf course, and on this occasion Betjeman might have been justified in wanting to kick him.

The human side of Pevsner on the road, however, is documented in painful detail in the letters he wrote during his travels, or travails, through Nottinghamshire – and, indirectly, in the final text, which reflects his tribulations. Lola, for some reason, was unable to accompany him, and this would be the only county that he would cover entirely on his own, playing the parts of driver, leader and assistant. The volume would be dedicated 'to the driver, who gave satisfaction'; but this was something of an overstatement. Pevsner had no aptitude whatsoever as a driver. Bertschy Grigson remembered him taking and failing his test so often that the driving school was embarrassed into offering him a discount. In June 1948, writing to Allen Lane to request the loan of the Austin again, he was still under instruction. On 3 August he took his test: 'Tired, washed out, deflated, dizzy (only three whiskies), and not a bit happy,' he reported to Lola. 'I made several really awful mistakes, turning in the street with brakes on. And the examiner a woman with an Oxford accent, and known to be bitchy . . . My only reaction at the moment is intense hatred against my car.' He must actually have passed, as the end of August 1948 saw him setting out for Nottinghamshire; but he still hated the car.

It was, he conceded, all right at speed on A-roads, but backing and getting through gaps were purgatory. For the first two mornings of the trip the car failed to start, and in his frustration he broke off the crank handle. 'Not my fault, is it? – for excessive strength is not my sin with the crank.' His anxieties were not solely focused on motoring and the fact that Penguin had not applied for enough petrol. Dr

Schapire had carried out the preparatory research, and as he told Lola, 'Schapire is not as detailed as Schilling', so he was going to have to work harder, both in checking the reality of buildings against the extracts and in preparing his itineraries each evening.

'Behind the wheel I am probably awful enough, and sometimes the gears tell me so. But I stop at my corners or go slow, I overtake where necessary and try to appear less timid than I am.' To concentrate on the road, however, was to miss the detail of what he was passing, and from the start he found his multiple responsibilities exhausting. 'You should have seen me in the first days, blowing out plugs like an old hand and then lying under the car to find a lost screw. What wears me out is to think of so many things. I *do* sometimes drive with the brake on, for example. And always locking back doors, locking front door, buying bread, buying petrol, watching oil etc etc.'

He was having to arrange his own accommodation as he went along, just as on his first trip to England. He had been hoping to stay in Doncaster, but arrived to find the races in full cry and every bed occupied, which meant a long drive back to Gainsborough with an expensive hotel at the end of it. The only alternative, he wrote in tones of horror to Lola, 'was a couch in a room with a soldier, in a bungalow'. To compensate for the cost of the hotel, he bought fish and chips and smuggled them into his room to eat them out of the newspaper. 'No-one to talk to, to listen to bad temper and odd discoveries, to comfort me and keep me *bei der Stange* / up to the mark – very hard, a real horror if I think of the whole month to come.'

Over the first week, his life assumed a pattern of a kind, relieved by small diversions – listening to the Proms on hotel radios, going for a modest half-pint of Bass to relax from his labours, reading *Anna Karenina* when he finally went to bed. Food was a duty rather than a pleasure. The sandwiches he had bought in London had lasted him a week – including those with Camembert 'of which everything smells'. 'New rations bought today. I'm saving sugar and points. I'll eat raw bacon too. Good stuff. And I'm eating churches.'

By the time he reached Retford, he was suffering from neurasthenia and insomnia. 'I had a terrible turning in a sand-quarry, with someone who had to help. I've never seen such ruts in my life. I upset the car heater, and paraffin has settled on half my newly cleaned mac . . . I had to interrupt and back the car through a narrow passage. I could weep, I made such a fool of myself. And again scraped, scraped, scraped. My God – I'll never learn it, and of course it was again panicking [*sic*] with a stranger helping, and in the dark.' He cheered up somewhat back in the hotel over a beer with an affable chambermaid, who mended a seam for him: 'the hotel is friendly, humble, smells of cat'. But Retford, on the whole, was 'a horrible place, the beginning of industrial Nottinghamshire'. The A1 motor road ran past his window, and the room reeked of the paraffin on his raincoat. 'Why is life so dominated by dull practicalities?' he lamented, and *Nottinghamshire* would bear the traces of his discontent. ('EAST RETFORD: A singularly unattractive town . . . The TOWN HALL of 1867 . . . is without any of the Victorian qualities which we are to-day ready to appreciate again: a bad Mansard roof and a bad turret . . . Of the few Georgian houses in the Square and the surrounding streets not one needs special mention . . . PARISH CHURCH ST SWITHIN. Big but also unrewarding.')

The middle of September found him driving through forest and parkland in the rain, meditating on the fate of the English country house: 1938, Pevsner concluded as he surveyed the site of Clumber, was 'the date marking the end of an era in which such vast seats and estates were still usable and used. The C20 seems to have few wealthy men left with inclination or indeed means to go on with them.' At Colwick, the eighteenth-century house and the church had once formed the backdrop to a fine Stubbs painting. Now, he noted, 'church is unroofed and the Hall does catering in connexion with the racecourse'. At Rufford Abbey – a twelfth-century foundation with Tudor, Jacobean, Georgian and Victorian additions – he was shown round rooms now dirty and deserted. 'The grounds are often depressing too, with ammunition dumps. And all the deserted aerodromes and army camps. One drives through in spite of all Prohibited notices and feels in cities of the dead.'*

'Ups and downs, ups and down,' wrote Pevsner, moving on to Worksop. 'This happens to be the downest down at the moment.' It was still pouring with rain, and he could not use his mac without being overcome by paraffin fumes. The hotel was dreadful – 'fat spivish publican in braces and short sleeved shirt' – and the car was housed no better, in 'a wicked garage . . . I know I won't be able to get her out when she is cold . . . It is gloomy, especially that wicked, wicked car.' ('WORKSOP. A walk through the streets is unrewarding. The town spreads out spider fashion . . . The market place with the dull Italianate (-cum-Jacobean) CORN EXCHANGE of 1851 is not a centre. The few

---

*Rufford Abbey was purchased by Nottinghamshire County Council four years later, in 1952. Much of the early eighteenth-century north end was demolished in 1959, leaving the shell of the seventeenth-century range and the remains of the Cistercian abbey, since conserved as part of a country park, in partnership with English Heritage.

old half-timbered houses . . . are lost between much C20 imitation. The Georgian contribution is no more conspicuous.')

Although Pevsner would correct and supplement the factual information he gleaned on his travels, he did not edit out the moods in which he had seen places, and Nottinghamshire was made to pay the price of the paraffin, the scraped and dented mudguards and the spivish publican. 'Neither the architectural nor the picturesque traveller would place Nottinghamshire in his first dozen or so of English counties,' reads the opening sentence of the introduction. 'It has no ancient cathedral . . . and none of the most spectacular medieval castles or post-medieval country houses. As far as natural attractions go, there is indeed Sherwood Forest, but otherwise the countryside has little of outstanding beauty . . . In its history also, Nottinghamshire is not marked by many events of prime national importance.' 'The spires of Notts [sic],' he continues, 'are not as spectacular or frequent as those of Lincolnshire or Northamptonshire . . . For outstanding church furnishings one would hardly go to Notts . . . Notts is not rich in specially pretty villages . . . C17 and C18 monuments are disappointing in Notts.'

No passing irritations or despondencies could stop him appreciating Southwell Minster anew, and there were many small architectural pleasures. But grumbling is never far away, and some recurring Pevsnerian bêtes noires make their first appearance in *Nottinghamshire*. Like many topographical writers before him, he was a frequent critic of restoration, as opposed to preservation. 'WHATTON. St John. Architecturally almost wholly ruined by several restorations and alterations . . . Two exquisite corbels (*c.* 1300) show painfully of what the restorations have deprived us.'

Also suspect, as someone who frequently worked on decorations and fittings within these 'restored' churches, was Sir Ninian Comper. Comper was one of the busiest and most successful church architects and designers of the early twentieth century, builder of fifteen churches, decorator of many more. He had recently been at work in St Mary Magdalen, Newark – in Pevsner's view one of the two or three dozen grandest parish churches of England. 'Reredos by *Comper*, 1937,' he wrote in some annoyance, 'a shameless imitation of the late C14, all glistening with gold. It is only when one gets near it that one recognises in the figures the feeble drawing of a later follower of pre-Raphaelite traditions instead of an expected handwriting similar to that of the Wilton Diptych.' He was more charitable about Comper's efforts in Egmanton. 'ST MARY. There is no denying the fact, *Comper*'s Screen, Organ-case and Pulpit make the church. As a piece of reconstruction

413

the Screen with its rood and rood-canopy is admirable, and as pieces of a medieval revival organ-case and pulpit are admirable. But as pieces of contemporary art they are of course all valueless.'

The last sentence betrays what Pevsner considered Comper's sin to be – the arch-vice of historicism and failure to reflect the *Zeitgeist*. He was by no means the only culprit. Vincent Harris was lambasted for his conventional neoclassical Shire Hall at West Bridgford – 'recent, not yet completed, but already as dead as mutton' and Cecil Howitt fared little better with his Council House of 1927–9 in Nottingham's market place. 'Not much can be said in defence of this kind of neo-Baroque display at a date when the Stockholm Town Hall was complete and a style congenial to the C20 finally established.'

Pevsner's best defence against the charge of blandness is the amount of toning down which those in charge of later editions would feel necessary. Elizabeth Williamson was in charge of the second edition of *Nottinghamshire*, and can often be found springing to the defence of unfortunate house-owners on whom he had originally vented his spleen. 'WOLLATON HALL. Wollaton displays any amount of gaudy Netherlandish ornament,' wrote Pevsner. 'This showiness is perhaps connected with the character of the man for whom it was built. Sir Francis Willoughby is not known to us for any connexion with the cultured circles taking an interest in poetry or learning or science. He was a coal magnate; that is all that can be said, and perhaps it accounts for an odd kinship between Wollaton Hall and some Victorian imitation-Tudor *chateaux*.' 'Although an industrialist,' writes Williamson carefully, 'Sir Francis was by no means *nouveau riche*, for his aristocratic connections included the Dudleys, the Seymours, and Lady Jane Grey, his first cousin. A wish to stress this impressive lineage may have inspired some of the medievalising aspects of his house. It is extremely showy.'*

When the reviews of the first volumes of the *Buildings of England* appeared, it was clear that few critics had grasped precisely what it was that Pevsner was trying to achieve. He was regularly blamed for failing to achieve objectives he had never set himself. Otherwise,

*Elizabeth Williamson worked on the *BoE* from 1975 to 1997, first as assistant and later as Deputy Editor for the series. She revised *Buckinghamshire*, *County Durham*, *Derbyshire* and *Leicestershire and Rutland* besides *Nottinghamshire*, and would co-author the Glasgow volume of *The Buildings of Scotland*. She is now the Architectural Editor of the Victoria History of the Counties of England and a Commissioner for English Heritage.

criticisms mostly concerned his missteps on the tightrope between being dull and being inaccurate, between satisfying academics and appealing to the general reader. Alongside those who felt his approach was too narrow were those who felt that, given the constraints he had set himself, his writing was often too loose. From the very beginning there were complaints that his single-minded focus on architectural detail was too dry. At the same time, the Courtauld historian Margaret Whinney, writing in the *Burlington Magazine* in July 1952, told him off for pandering to the multitudes – 'Some space is wasted in the glossary: surely the most ignorant must know what is meant by a baluster' – at the expense of intellectual rigour: 'He is, of course, far too distinguished a scholar to believe that all sculpture in England datable before c. 1150 can justifiably be termed "barbaric"; but this is a word all too easily understood by the uninformed reader, and is, therefore, used far too often.' 'c13 for thirteenth century is surely a most tiresome inversion,' she added irritably. 'Why not 13c.?'

Others were more in sympathy with the style. 'Inventories these books are,' wrote the *Architects' Journal* reviewer, 'and wonderfully detailed ones . . . But they are much more than that. On every page one is continually made aware – sometimes by a sentence of comment, sometimes by as little as a single word, sometimes even by what isn't said – of learning, intelligence and taste of work [*sic*], placing, testing and assessing. So far as architecture is concerned, this series will relegate most other guides to the status of picture books.'

The most balanced commentary, and the shrewdest assessment of Pevsner's intentions, came – as would often be the case – from John Summerson, a writer Pevsner much admired.[11] Summerson realised that personal expression was not Pevsner's primary aim. Rather than being irritated or offended by the lack of effusiveness, as many critics seemed to be, he was amused: 'Criticism is sometimes implicit in the entries and, here and there, breaks crossly out . . . but such outbursts are rare – as rare as the very occasional tributes to some particularly striking natural setting where the author's breath has, in spite of himself, been caught.' He also clearly appreciated the need that the *Buildings of England* were designed to fulfil:

> If it is art-history you want, Pevsner is your man. And it must be admitted that it is the art-historian rather than the fabulist and antiquarian who has, till now, been the missing author in our county literature . . . These guide-books, indeed, are something more than an old kind of thing better done than it has been done before. Increasingly our whole culture is obsessed with the realism of history,

so that no work of art can satisfy us completely unless we can pin it to a juncture of events – social, economic, personal-psychological. So ardent is this passion for the time-context, that quite humble, thoughtless works – of architecture especially – become enjoyably exciting by virtue of their coincidence with an historic dot. These new guides serve the time-cult.

One other review was particularly penetrating, appearing in the *Architectural Review*, where, it was reported, Pevsner had always insisted that good reviews of his books should be accompanied by a bad one.[12] If necessary, he would write one himself; on at least one occasion he asked for the proofs of an unsigned (critical) review to go to him.[13] Even if this one was not actually written by him – it appeared over the signature of 'Ernest Savage' – it accurately pinpointed many of the reservations and misgivings that he himself had.

How does one picture the author travelling for *The Buildings of England*? He must be in a hurry all the time, a suggestion it is surely not unfair to make especially as he may well enjoy a hurry; and one that is, besides, borne out by his writing. Not, it must at once be said, by factual mistakes so much (although these also are not entirely absent) as by omissions and a certain slackness of style . . . So the principal question to ask of this series must be: Is there an alternative to Professor Pevsner's method? . . . At the rate of two counties a year Professor Pevsner will finish in 1972 – at the expense of how much in terms of energy, tenacity and those pleasures available to other mortals, one shudders to think. And also, it must be added, at the expense of much that such books might be, if they were written at leisure . . . It required courage to start this scheme and a degree of self-assurance. Professor Pevsner possesses both qualities. May we live to see him crowned the Dehio of England.

CHAPTER 27

'Truthful enthusiasm':
Birkbeck and the excursions

'This method of working of mine is really bad,' Pevsner wrote to Lola from somewhere in Nottinghamshire in 1948. 'I have lost the sense of leisure to read a book. I get absorbed all right, but my heart beats and I feel restless as if I was missing something important. As if Anna Karenina were not more important than a few measly village churches! I'm sure that the collecting of facts is all escape from thought.'

The same letter displayed a sure sign of strain: 'Crumbs, I am suddenly writing German – too bad.' During his long search for work in England, Pevsner had felt it crucially necessary to adapt and had made determined efforts to do so. Though he would continue to write his private *Heftchen* in German for some time, in August 1949 he wrote a letter officially describing his first language as English; and after this he was more and more inclined to refer to the English as 'we'.

Lola was most unlikely ever to describe the English as 'we'. Having never studied English at school, she had struggled unwillingly to learn the rudiments as a preparation for leaving Germany; more than ten years later she still spoke the language less fluently than most of their German friends, and far less accurately than Pevsner. She wrote excellent letters, long, lively, telling and personal, but with no sense of literary style, and her spelling, in his words, was 'quite improbable, even in German . . . I, wretch that I am, went on correcting her, thereby making her feel imperfect.'

She did not want to relinquish her Germanness; but even if she had, she might have found it difficult to blend into a conventional English background. Many middle-class mores of the 1950s, indeed, she despised. Back in Leipzig she had greatly sympathised with an acquaintance from a respectable bourgeois family who had wanted a baby and become pregnant with no intention of marrying the father. Now, in London, she encouraged a young friend to live with the man with whom she had fallen in love, long before there was any chance for them to get married. ('In having this feeling and admitting it,' wrote Pevsner in his memoir of her, 'she thought more directly of ourselves than I chose to.') Warm and informal, she would talk to anyone – 'most un-English', in the words of her son-in-law, Ian Hodgson – and saw little virtue in standing on one's dignity; consequently she found a good many English gatherings pompous, dull and unfriendly.

At the same time, while finding social life stiff, she was irritated by sloppiness in more practical matters. Pevsner admitted:

> She found England (and so do I, of course) untidy, unexacting and unreliable in individual workmanship and personal services . . . She did believe in discipline, imposed it on herself, but as a child had it imposed on her in a Prussian house; and Prussian and Frederick the Great were no dirty words to her. Nor were they to me . . . Lola remained German to the end, and she felt on the defensive about it: house-proud, dutiful, tidy, thrifty. Pay bills at once, never buy anything above your means, never touch hire purchase. Why should not she and I have the same bathwater, she liking it hotter than I? And why a bath a day, as is the prerequisite of the Englishman keeping clean, as she washed from face to toe every day anyway?

During the hard times of the 1920s in Germany Lola had found it difficult to spend money on trifles for herself; she found it no easier now, and would rarely even buy a cup of coffee when out on an all-day expedition. She bought few new clothes, and never threw anything away. 'Scrapping is immoral,' she declared, and tins, boxes, medicine bottles, rags and remnants were all hoarded, kept in trunks in the guest room till the opportunity to reuse them arose.

With her help, the children made all their Christmas presents for people, part of a ceremonial that meant a lot to her. Christmas was a means of keeping continuity with their former life. Both Pevsner and Lola enjoyed and valued ritual, but it had become particularly important in this new context, and Lola insisted on an unvarying sequence of events. An expedition to the National Gallery and inspection of the Christmas tree in Trafalgar Square were followed by the seasonal service for poor children in the church of St Martin-in-the-Fields and, finally, supper at Lyons Corner House on the Strand. One room in the house became the Christmas room, and people sang carols as they entered; each person had their own pile of presents on a table or stool, to be opened, according to German custom, on Christmas Eve.

'Lola did not like England really,' wrote Pevsner sadly, 'though she defended English ways to Germans . . . That made 1933 much more of a disaster for her than for me.' Although Lola and he had now been English citizens for some time, they remained continually aware of post-war life in Germany: the wreckage of buildings they had known, the deaths of friends and prominent figures (among them Wilhelm

Pinder, in 1947), and the privations being endured by those they had left behind.* Marianne and her children brought first-hand evidence of hardship when they came to visit, which stirred in him a mixture of guilt, irritation and anger on their behalf. Lola still perhaps felt traces of jealousy of the role that Marianne had played in Uta's life, but she remained extremely close to her sister and might well have returned to Germany if she had been able to decide only for herself. 'Lola always sounded like a foreigner in England,' Uta commented later, 'and I think she always felt like one.'

Pevsner, on the other hand, was now increasingly well established as a lecturer, and not just at Birkbeck and the Courtauld, but at a growing number of art schools and societies around the country. Harrow School and International Youth in Surbiton, the Unilever Club Literary Society and the Oxford Architecture Students Society, Letchworth Adult Education Institute and Winchester Circle for the Study of Art, Brighton, Southampton, Exeter, Birmingham – the circuit grew ever wider, eventually stretching as far as Sedbergh School and the Glasgow School of Art, until he made himself a rule that he would lecture no more than twice a month outside London.

On first glance it would appear that, fifteen years down the line, he had re-created the career that he had been forced to abandon when he left Göttingen. The reality, however, was different. Then he had been the archetypal young *Privatdozent*, an academic high-flyer in the conventional mould. Now he was middle-aged and a mature art historian – but perhaps no longer an academic or an orthodox scholar.

An interloper to many, he was working in an intellectual environment that remained less than wholly congenial. By the early 1950s German and British attitudes to art history had been increasingly exposed to each other for almost twenty years, but they had not really been reconciled, far less merged. 'I can understand,' wrote Erwin Panofsky, 'that from the point of view of an English gentleman the art historian is apt to look like a fellow who compares and analyses the charms of his feminine acquaintances in public instead of making love to them in private.'[1] German art history could often be biased, dogmatic, abstract and obscure. In contrast, 'when speaking or writing English, even an art historian must more or less know what he means and mean what he says, and this compulsion was exceedingly wholesome for all of us'. Nevertheless Panofsky, the most broadminded of German scholars, was

---

*Pevsner wrote an obituary for Pinder in *The Times* on 4/7/47, describing him as a man who came to see the truth about the Nazis too late, a victim rather than truly a perpetrator.

still inclined to withhold the title of 'art history' from what a great many English gentlemen did. Art history, he declared, was 'the historical analysis and interpretation of man-made objects to which we assign a more than utilitarian value', and what a large proportion of *soi-disant* 'art historians' did in England would more accurately be described as scholarly antiquarianism or connoisseurship – making love to beautiful objects and writing up their family trees. 'Broad and generalised historical studies were distrusted,' observed Reyner Banham later, 'and the wood was never examined, only the nearest tree.'*

Art history was still not established in more than a handful of universities as an independent academic degree subject with its own syllabus or faculty. 'It is evidently felt that the history of art must still twine its young shoots round the older and steadier growths of general and social history,' wrote Pevsner in 1950, and many general historians were unwilling even to allow this.[2] When Ernst Gombrich was Slade Professor in Oxford in the 1950s, he encountered historians who flatly refused to recognise art history as an academic discipline at all: 'Most of them considered the cultivation of art history the job of museum curators and collectors.'[3]

That job was, in Pevsner's eyes, a perfectly reputable one. Connoisseurship, he knew, could develop to a very high level of erudition, and had qualities that specialist scholars often lacked. 'It is as a rule presented with elegance,' he wrote, 'and that is more than one can say of much that the *Art Bulletin* publishes in America or that German learned journals used to publish. Also it has often more vitality, because it is based on a man's understanding of literature as well as art and, better still, on a man's experience in some field of practical life.' 'On the other hand,' he continued, 'the amateur is more likely to develop a bee in his bonnet because he has no solid foundation, and is likely to venture on wild theories in the absence of sufficient information of what has already been ascertained by others, especially abroad.'[4]

Rarely would these theories be assembled into anything resembling a system – an unregimented approach apparently adopted on principle at least by some connoisseurs and antiquarians. Art historian Francis Haskell, a lifelong critic of the atomism and positivism of connoisseurship, quoted the eighteenth-century French antiquarian the Comte de Caylus as an arch exponent of the creed: 'The antiquarian,' wrote

---

*Reyner Banham, 'Pelican', *AR*, November 1953. There were, of course, exceptions; Peter Ferriday points out (letter to the author 9/9/93) that works such as Summerson's *Georgian London* (1945) were doing much to raise the standard of scholarship in the field of architectural history in particular, and Howard Colvin's *Biographical Dictionary of English Architects 1660–1840* (1954) would be another landmark.

de Caylus, 'should shun every kind of system: I look upon them as an illness of the spirit.' Without going that far, archaeologist W.A. Thorpe deplored the continental fondness for pattern and synthesis at the expense of the individual object, and criticised 'the German passion for conceptual thinking in fields demanding the *ad hoc*'. 'Now that art history has crossed the Channel, and the Atlantic,' he wrote, 'it might return with advantage, from "styles" to fundamentals: materials and process, persons and places, country and reign.'

Pevsner believed strongly that while art might be the product of inspiration, there was no reason why it should not be subject to reason, rules and constructive analysis. 'Studies in the history of art are as scholarly and as disciplined a pursuit as social and constitutional history or history of thought,' he argued.[5]

Fifty years later, it would be clearer that these different strands of scholarship can peacefully coexist and even combine. In the meantime, it would not always be easy to locate Pevsner on the English art history scene. He was obviously more of a historian than a connoisseur, a narrator rather than a critic, looking at the overarching framework rather than the individual context – and yet he was not a theoriser in the grand German mode. In fact, as Will Vaughan, Emeritus Professor of History of Art at Birkbeck, has pointed out, Pevsner was not a proponent of any new methodological approach, as Panofsky was of iconology, or Gombrich of the psychology of visual perception. 'His intention . . . was more to modify and apply the methodologies he had acquired as a student, rather than challenge them as so many of his fellow émigrés were doing . . . It was his experiences as a historian working in the field that caused him to change and develop his ideas. His practice affected his theories, rather than the other way round.'[6]

Pevsner could be highly contentious in simplifying a complex picture and imposing a pattern on multiplicity, and he saw nothing wrong in subjectivity. But any battles he fought had a clear aim in view. He engaged in remarkably few academic feuds, and was less interested in intellectual debate than in the collaborative effort to extend understanding. 'The only thing I can . . . try to do,' he remarked in an early lecture, 'is to focus my search light, whatever its range may prove to be, on a junction here and a junction there, and hope that these scattered remarks of mine will give you an indication of a method which, should its usefulness convince you, you can easily adopt, and collect yourselves more detailed information from books in order to arrange it according to similar criteria.'

'He had a mind like a filing cabinet,' remembered Peter Lasko. 'He was also a workaholic, I've never known anyone work so hard.'[7] This enormous effort was not just for his own benefit, and he never allowed it to have a deadening effect. 'Where the teacher ought to endeavour to please his students,' he wrote:

is, on the one hand, by knowing his subject profoundly and not superficially and, on the other, by preserving through every hour of teaching his own enthusiasm for his subject. If you, teachers of architectural history, cannot be absorbedly interested in Anglo-Saxon church plans you cannot hope to create interest in your students. If you are unable for an hour to consider Hawksmoor churches the most fascinating thing in the world, then leave the platform to another. But if this other is fascinated but ignorant, then – perhaps – you ought to return and replace him. Fortunately the alternatives are not truthful boredom and demagogic enthusiasm. There are some who represent truthful enthusiasm.[8]

He was himself undoubtedly one of these 'truthful enthusiasts'. He had, according to one of his pupils, 'a real zest for instruction', and while he might be respected for his books, even revered for the *Buildings of England*, he was loved for his teaching.

Pevsner was absolutely convinced of the value of teaching art history.[9] He did not see it as necessarily having direct practical benefits in itself; there were very few jobs for art historians, and the Courtauld and Warburg Institutes fully satisfied the need for the requisite degrees. On the other hand, he rather resented the idea that art history could be regarded as generalised 'uplift'. He saw it primarily as a functional adjunct both to general culture – *Bildung* – and to particular subjects: modern languages, literature and history. In this he was simply continuing the train of thought he had set out in his 1933 article on 'German Art and the Secondary Schools', in which he had urged the compulsory teaching of German art history, not for its own sake – 'no, for heaven's sake, no!' – but as a crucial element in the training of future teachers of the German language, literature and history. The 'warm and knowledgeable interpretation' of a few slides, he had argued, could enhance any other subject, contributing greatly to an understanding of history.

His own 'warm and knowledgeable interpretation' took two forms: lectures and seminars. As a lecturer, he no longer had pretensions to be a specialist, even in the areas where he had once done most work. He was, he remarked in 1951, a 'General Practitioner' in this field, and some years later he refused an invitation to speak on Italian painting, once his forte: 'I am not enough of an expert to do really specialist lecturing there.'[10] Nor, however, did he choose to speak on universal themes. 'I am not a good lecturer on general topics,' he confided later.[11] 'What I can do is to deal with specific historical subjects.' What was remarkable was the variety of these subjects.

Very few of Pevsner's lectures survive in their entirety.[12] In his early days as a lecturer in London, when his English was more uncertain, he would write out large tracts of a talk in advance, with emphases indicated in red and particular phrases carefully rehearsed. But as time went on he reduced his paper preparations to no more than a fully written first paragraph, with the rest of the argument sketched out in note form, usually on a sheet of foolscap folded in half, dotted with important dates and key adjectives, and with any necessary quotations to hand on separate scraps of paper. The rest of the detail he left to be prompted by his responses to his slides. 'What he did have,' remembered Jane Fawcett, who attended his lectures in the 1960s and 1970s:

> was one or two absolutely tiny notes that he'd written down. He knew exactly when they were going to come in his lecture, and he'd be walking around on the platform, and then when he was coming to the point when he was going to have to quote, he walked back to the lectern and picked them up and read the little quote and then set off again. It wasn't ad libbing like anybody else's, it was all utterly focused, and he knew exactly which sources he'd acquired it from.[13]

Pevsner's illustrations had serious work to do; they articulated his arguments precisely and then carried the meaning further, beyond the reach of words. Armed with slides and notes, he could deliver lectures extraordinarily efficiently. He used to arrive at Birkbeck after a day's work, set up his projector and launch into his talk without the slightest hitch or hesitation. The only price to be paid was a certain inflexibility. As his working life filled up and his reputation as a speaker grew, he came to rely more and more on lectures he had already prepared. He rarely used new material and had little time to search for fresh illustrations, which limited the topics he could tackle; where he had no slides, he would turn down the invitation to speak.[14] John Newman remembered him turning up to talk in Oxford on Elizabethan country houses and lecturing on St Paul's Cathedral instead, because he had realised on the train that he had packed the wrong box of slides.

Opinions differ on the virtues of Pevsner's slide collection. He had first begun accumulating images while he was in Göttingen, and would appear to have brought many slides with him. 'He had no feeling for the quality of slides,' objected Birkbeck colleague Peter Murray. 'It was part of his puritan side . . . We used to say, "For God's sake, Nikolaus, get a proper picture of this building," and he'd say, "Oh no, that'll do, that'll do." They were taken from 19th century textbooks, rather grey colour gravure print . . . The photographs often included these awful little German clichés – you could see the border round them, and read the type underneath . . . And then they'd been fried three or four times as well.'[15] 'He dropped them in the gutter one day,' recalled Jane Fawcett, 'and half of them got cracked and they were full of mud, but he just went on using them.' (Helen Lowenthal, a member of the Victorian Society committee, once suggested to him how important it was to have good slides of Victorian buildings. 'NP said, in rather a stuffy way, "Well, I've always got on very well without, Helen," and she said, "Well, you'd have got your knighthood much sooner if you'd had colour slides."'[16])

'Pevsner's slides usually carried the murkiness of pioneer photography,' remarked David Boswell.[17] In Pevsner's defence, John Newman explained that murk was often the price to be paid for architectural and historical depth. 'If you are wanting to find a photograph of a building that really shows you what it's like, shows the detail well, shows the impression of scale and proper perspectival effect, the best things to go to are the early 20th century things that were taken on plate cameras . . . In his didactic way, he thought that those old slides actually made the point better – not about the colour, of course, but . . . the actual forms that were used.'[18]

Some ten years after having been Pevsner's pupil, Peter Lasko agreed to caretake one of his classes while he was on sabbatical. The course covered French medieval sculpture, and Lasko asked Pevsner about illustrative material.

He said, 'I've got all the slides you can possibly want. They're all in Birkbeck College, and you'll see when you open the drawers, they're arranged according to lectures.' I thought it sounded a bit odd, but I said OK, and went and looked at them, and sure enough there they were – Lecture One, Lecture Two, Lecture Three, Lecture Four, left and right, left and right, left and right, all the way through – absolutely rigid. I daresay he'd never changed it. I've never actually given two lectures on the same subject in which I've *ever* used the same slides. When I do it the second time, I don't remember what I said the first time, I'm not that organised.[19]

Lasko was not the only colleague to find this apparent fossilisation of content and technique offputting and uncreative; yet Pevsner's great gift was the ability to make his well-worn material sound fresh to a constant stream of new listeners. Having a system of this sort for lecturing, however constricting it might have been, enabled him to deliver inspiration to remarkable numbers of people over a very long period. As he saw it, his job was to open to others the fields of beauty where he himself had found such intense pleasure, by showing them where to look and how to see. He was teaching a way of thinking, not a body of thought. 'I need not say anything,' he claimed repeatedly in his lectures, 'you see it yourselves.' He worked not by challenging or dazzling his audience, but by enlisting them, building on their existing knowledge and developing their confidence, his tone almost conspiratorial. 'You know that', 'I need not tell you', he would say, referring to things that his listeners had not actually 'known', but recognised at once.

'The plot thickens' was a favourite phrase. He saw the history of art as a story, a complex narrative in which many threads were inter-woven, and he worked with constant cross-reference and allusion. 'The precisely right comparison,' he wrote, 'makes all the difference to the information becoming vivid enough to be retained in people's memory.'[20] In one lecture on the Age of Chaucer, he moved seamlessly from the 'short, stumpy people' of the Luttrell Psalter to the coming-of-age of the English language; from the timber roofs of Penshurst Place to the Peasants' Revolt; from the tracery in the choir of Lincoln Cathedral to the birth of Parliament.

Even the vestigial notes which are all that remain of some Pevsner lectures are imprinted with his personality. He rarely essayed a joke as such – in Voltaire's phrase, '*Je ne fais pas le Ha Ha!*' – but he was consistently entertaining.[21] He was not over-impressed by reputation: 'Not a beautiful picture,' he declared of Tintoretto's *Paradise*, the largest oil painting in the world. 'Not a reasonable, sound picture.' Nor did he show undue respect for the establishment. 'Have you ever tried to discover what can be the use of the Royal Academy?' he seems to have enquired in the course of a lecture on Joshua Reynolds. 'It has evidently nothing to do with the promotion of live art in England. Amongst members, hardly one or two who count. Exhibitions not taken seriously even by so staid a paper as *The Times*. School *minute*.' As for the RAF's Bomber Command, he objected, they should have taken a history of art course along with their precision-bombing briefing, which resulted in the devastation of some of the gems of German Romanesque while less valuable monuments were carefully spared.[22]

Caustic or droll, Pevsner generated a sense of extraordinary concentration and commitment. Architect and painter Robert Organ recalled an occasion on which Pevsner gestured more emphatically than usual at the slide on the screen, lost his footing and toppled off the platform; without breaking his verbal stride, he dusted himself down and climbed back up again, talking the while. Another evening he abruptly left the lecture room, bearing aloft the flaming projector cloth, which had suddenly caught fire. 'Still lecturing while he stamped it out in the corridor,' remembered Iris Omer-Cooper, 'he returned without pausing for breath or referring to the incident.'

But while Pevsner's dedication could be almost disquieting, it was never dour. 'He wasn't the right shape for an Englishman,' Lettice Lane once said, evoking a tall, formal Teutonic figure. And yet 'he would often dash up to the screen in delight,' according to Iris Omer-Cooper, 'pointing to a feature he had never noticed before, particularly in paintings.' Fred Wolsey remembered a taut figure leaning intently over the lectern, his face shiny as an apple with light reflected from the papers in front of him. Wolsey recalled roaring with laughter at a minor witticism about 'points of faith' in Pugin. 'NP looked up, beamed, said "Thank you", and continued.'

His first lectures at Birkbeck, from 1943 to 1947, were open to a general audience, but in 1948 he began to deliver lectures that were specifically aimed at supplementing other courses. For those studying English, for example, he spoke on the art-historical references in George Eliot's *Romola*. For students of modern languages he delivered a series of lectures on the art and architecture of the ages of Goethe and Schiller, Corneille, Balzac and Baudelaire. Dealing with art and architecture alongside literature and language, noting echoes and correspondences between the separate strands of cultural development, gave him the perfect opportunity to expound and evolve his ideas on the *Zeitgeist*. 'It is this spirit of the ages which I want to define,' he wrote in his notes. 'Not in the childish way of the sworn Marxist who thinks it is all just social changes, causing the others. Something much subtler, less material, less clumsy. You can call it irrational. I believe in its existence, see in it the deepest cause of evolution, and find this belief confirmed in thousands of details which once you follow the method dictated by this belief, fall into their proper places and reveal their true meaning.'

Preparing this series of vignettes on different cultures also prompted him to refine his ideas about national character – not least his thoughts on the nature of Germanness, which he could now express in a safe and neutral context. Fragmentary though they are – no more than a scattering of adjectives – his notes suggest how heartfelt these particular lectures may have been:

> Drama, violence . . . agitated, menacing . . . direct, aggressive . . . no compromise . . . Plebeian? Yes, but superb, so forceful like full blast of Wagner . . . earthy . . . shrill . . . that violence once more eternal German . . . Mysticism self-abandonment to boundless feeling. Obscure, mystic, profound. But no clarity, not reasonable . . . Over-charged . . . intricate, abstruse . . . thrill of complication . . . discordant . . . drama . . . anti-logical . . . Only in German that infuriated intensity . . . It is love of the thronging, throbbing life, not for repose and order . . . Art of night, mystery, music, not of clarity or sunlight . . . This sense of moving space, dynamic, complicated . . . Love of the extreme.

Pevsner was also appearing as a guest in Cambridge by now: 'the most popular lecturer in the University', in the view of *Varsity*, the undergraduate magazine. 'There are few lectures where the members of the audience begin collecting 20 minutes before hand, and where they gladly sit on the floor when all the seats are taken. This happens regularly at his illustrated lectures on the History of European Art and the large audience show [*sic*] no signs of diminishing throughout the term.'[23] 'There was only one other refugee art historian who lectured as well and had as large a following,' declared Peter Lasko, 'and that was [Edgar] Wind in Oxford.'[24]

To some of his students, however, Pevsner was better as a teacher than a lecturer, tailoring his observations and advice to a smaller audience and inviting more participation from them – and he was most obviously in his element at Birkbeck. His continuing allegiance there was significant. This was not a top-flight academic position. Birkbeck was an undergraduate college, but many of its students were not full-time, as the college was unique at that time in offering the opportunity of university study to working people holding down full-time jobs during the day. (Those not taking a full degree were called 'occasional students'. Pevsner once said: 'I don't mind you being an occasional student, as long as you don't just come occasionally.'[25]) Most were doing combined courses, many of which would not produce honours degrees.

In Germany the old Nikolaus Pevsner would most probably have been seeking a permanent senior post in a research establishment by now, teaching, lecturing and doing his own work, possibly even looking for a professorship. In allying himself with Birkbeck he was effectively burning those particular bridges. 'Once he'd started there and spread himself as he did,' commented Lasko, 'there wasn't really the opportunity to do enough with an academic impact for him to be given a lectureship at the Courtauld Institute or at the Warburg.'[26] To some extent he had been forced into this position by the brusque dislocation of his Göttingen career, and by the pressing need to earn money during his first years in England. He had been drawn into a wide range of jobs where teaching was just one among many activities, and he had developed a specialism – in architectural history – that led nowhere in particular in academic terms. Like other German émigré intellectuals in Britain, he was still in some contexts an outsider; unlike most of them, he was also a successful populariser, which, in some eyes at least, put a barrier between them.

But his commitment to Birkbeck grew out of more than force of circumstance. All his adult life he had believed that art existed for more than just its own sake, and that art history too had a higher purpose. It could be of immense cultural value, but not in the abstract; its function was to enrich other studies, but also to enrich life. He could not envisage many of his Birkbeck students continuing as specialist art historians (although some did). There was little scope for him to enhance his own reputation, even if that had been his aim, by creating his own circle of academic acolytes to advance his own research interests or reflect glory on him. But he could see how the lives of his students could be improved by the gift of appreciating the artefacts around them. He could sympathise keenly with the difficulties of combining private study with paid work; and while he would never be precisely a cosy man, he would be accessible to his pupils – to all his pupils, and not just the favoured few – to a degree that would have been unusual in many grander institutions. He always ate with the students, unlike other lecturers, and took an interest in their families.

His seminar teaching really started in 1948, for those students doing art history as one element in their general degree. The course stretched over three years, and covered three main areas. In the first year students would be instructed in the architecture and sculpture of the Middle Ages in France and England. In the second they would move on to Italian painting from the thirteenth to early seventeenth centuries; and for their final year they would return to architecture – this time Italy from the fifteenth to seventeenth centuries and England and France in the sixteenth and seventeenth centuries.

Pevsner preferred to amalgamate his classes into a single three-hour session on a Wednesday night, held in a room in Woburn Square from six until nine in the evening with a short break in the middle – a feat of concentration and stamina that suited his Birkbeck pupils. These were not the Courtauld debutantes of legend. Peter Murray, himself a Courtauld graduate, found the atmosphere at Birkbeck quite different. 'There was a distinct feeling that life was *ernst*, life was real', an approach to work that was necessary for people trying to fit a degree course around full-time jobs: 'You've got to want it terribly.' These students were teachers, nurses, town planners, administrators, civil servants. One, Mary Beagles, remembered, 'I could leave work as a BBC secretary at 5.30 p.m. and walk to Birkbeck College by 6 p.m., snatching a rapid meal at an Italian café in Tottenham Court Road on the way.'

Few had any previous knowledge of art history, and to Peter Murray the teaching sometimes seemed more characteristic of school than university. The British tradition of teaching the visual arts tended to be more relaxed and collaborative, a matter of talking round a table and working with photographs, an informal exchange rather than a dictating of notes. The German tradition was more hierarchical, with little pretence of democracy, and there was no question that Pevsner was the master in his classroom.

Some of his peers found this instinctive assumption of authority uncongenial. Murray felt Pevsner to be quite conscious of his own dignity: 'He knew what the answers were. It was very difficult to argue with someone as knowledgeable as he was, especially as a student. He wasn't impatient of argument, but he had quite an acid wit, he could be very short if he disliked the arguments you were producing.' To others, it was his diligence that was daunting, even oppressive, and it could make him seem unintentionally remote. 'He had no small talk,' Peter Lasko remembered:

He was a damn serious man, and his mind was usually . . . on the next thing he had to do . . . One of the memories I treasure in my mind is running into NP on Waterloo Station without him seeing me, and seeing him going straight to a seat against the wall of the station and opening his huge briefcase and getting out a pile of proofs of the Pelican History of Art and proofreading them. Five minutes on a station waiting for a train would be used for proof-reading. I don't think he ever stopped.[27]

'He did not go out of his way to charm people,' remembered Birkbeck student Ian Sutton, later one of Pevsner's editors at Thames and Hudson. 'But certainly among his students and younger colleagues he was held in real affection. Those whom he helped far outnumber those he offended.'[28] His early classes were small, sometimes no more than five or six people, who could feel a trifle exposed. 'It was rather frightening the first evening,' recalled Denis Evinson (later a regular contributor to the *Buildings of England* as an authority on Roman Catholic architecture in England). 'We began with sculpture. He lectured for a few minutes: "Now the thing we want to get out of these sculptures is to illuminate the differences, so I'm going to put some more slides up and you are going to tell me where the differences lie, and I'm going to make crushing remarks."'[29]

He was very patient with the innocent – those, for example, who did not understand building plans – but he could be distinctly short with those he thought should know better. Forty years on, a surprising number of former pupils had preserved withering comments on faulty spelling, inadequate bibliographies, confused organisation of material: 'Was this written under examination conditions, or with the help of books? In the latter case, p.1 is inexcusable', 'No-one need draw quite so badly', and so on. On occasion he was embarrassingly blunt with criticism in front of an entire class; but his more devastating reproofs were perhaps not deliberate. 'He was not always conscious of the effect he made,' explains Ian Sutton, 'and often gave the impression, I think without meaning to, that you disappointed him and that he expected better of you. I never lost this feeling.'

As the number of his students increased, to help distinguish one from another Pevsner took to jotting down terse epithets or brief descriptions for himself (to such good effect that twenty-five years later he was able to claim that early generations of students stayed 'indelibly impressed' on him).[30] Most of these notes were purely visual: 'tall, old, bosomy', 'red carnation . . . sharp nose', 'tummy'. Some were comments of a more personal nature, taking in intellect and character as well: 'silky hair, round face, not too good on S. Simeone Piccolo', 'fair, heavy, fat face, bit dumb', 'naïve – bad American style', 'short, thin, defiant', 'too chic – has not done the work – but intelligent', 'neat writing. *Fail*', 'small, Jewish, Lola likes her'. Others were openly uncharitable: 'I have not seen him at all this term – thank God.' But whatever his private thoughts he was usually tolerant, even sympathetic when his pupils needed it, turning up on examination days with bars of chocolate to keep them going and reassuring those with exam nerves. He may have had little mercy on pretension or sloppiness, but he was gentle with bores, the impoverished, the afflicted and those he knew to be lonely.

As an evening college, Birkbeck did not offer much in the way of a social life. Pevsner was one of the few teachers who tried to compensate for this by entertaining his students. None of them could possibly have missed the fact that leisure played little part in his life. The Wednesday class used to break at 7.30 for a cup of coffee in the Birkbeck refectory. Pevsner would accompany the students, but in the time it took them to drink a cup of coffee he would contrive to eat two courses, turning the break into his evening meal and departing after precisely thirteen minutes in order to be back at the slide projector for a prompt restart at 7.45. Nevertheless, at the end of the evening, before setting out on the long walk uphill to Hampstead, he would sometimes accompany his pupils to the pub or the bar of the Bonnington Hotel – 'not the Courtauld way', in the words of Will Vaughan. When he started supervising postgraduate students, he would regularly invite them to dinner as a way of introducing them to each other. Once a term, too, he would make a point of staging an evening party for all the students he was currently teaching, giving the different years a chance to mix. In this he was much more like the young *Privatdozent* he had been at Göttingen, entertaining his students to orange juice, biscuits and Beethoven on the wind-up gramophone, than the overbearing pedagogue that some took him to be.

His students were perhaps better than his peers at seeing the essential benevolence underneath. 'I remember his explaining Gothic vaulting to us,' Ian Sutton recalled:

how the ribs supported the cells and carried the stress to the buttresses and so down to the ground . . . 'One saw how this worked structurally,' he said, 'during the war, when bombing would cause the cells of the vault to drop out, leaving the rib-skeleton still standing . . . Although,' he added with some reluctance, 'honesty compels me to tell you that sometimes the opposite happened.' . . . Once he was showing pictures of the Vices and Virtues on Clermont-Ferrand Cathedral, and one girl said, 'The Vices are rather attractive, aren't they?' 'Well, Josephine,' said Pevsner, 'that's a matter of taste.'

'The first time I ever spoke to him,' recollected Denis Evinson, 'was when I asked him to autograph my *Derbyshire*. As he autographed it, he said, "I always feel like writing 'Stewart Granger'." And then he said, "I did once."'[31]

To his face at least, he was 'Dr Pevsner' to his pupils, though one of his early secretaries remembered students coming into the Penguin office and enquiring 'When's the Great Man coming in?' As she had been in Göttingen, Lola was often more at ease with Pevsner's pupils than with his colleagues. 'She was a favourite with all the students,' noted Ian Sutton, 'very small, energetic, sympathetic, a lot more under-standing of human frailty than he. In some ways, she seemed like a student herself, only a student uniquely privileged to be cheeky to the teacher.' She also came along on most of the fabled 'Pevsner guided tours'.

Pevsner's excursions, which he regarded as field trips to inspect his architectural subjects in the wild, varied in ambition. His students could expect to be invited for one whole-day excursion, one half-day and one weekend per year. Some were aimed no further afield than Lambeth Palace, Strawberry Hill or the basement of the Victoria and Albert Museum. Canterbury was a day-trip, as was Norwich, but Wells demanded a weekend (to allow for detours to Stonehenge and Longleat), as did Lincoln (which took in Grantham), and Ely and Cambridge could barely be confined within two days. For all concerned, the experience was gruelling.

The group would assemble in the early hours at the appropriate terminus to meet its leader. 'He used to dress informally in tweedy clothes,' reminisced Ian Sutton, 'such as he knew Englishmen wore at weekends. I think he even wore a hat sometimes. We were all expected to mix together and be friendly, but the party almost always included a group from the Courtauld Institute who regarded themselves as superior to the Birkbeck students, so it was not total harmony.' Arriving at their destination, the students were expected to go straight to the first appointed building – usually the cathedral – to look around on their own, without the guidebook. (Pevsner was very annoyed in Lincoln when some weaker vessels made a detour to drop off their luggage and were late.) He then quizzed them about what they had taken in, listening patiently to individual theories, pointing out what the group ought to have seen, but at the same time seizing on anything he himself had missed. 'He was avid for information and never minded where it came from. Whenever the surveyor or one of us pointed out something he had not noticed, he would respond eagerly and say "Yes, yes!"' On these occasions Lola was very much one of the group. 'She talked a lot and was sometimes scolded by NP for talking while he was trying to explain some point.'

'His knowledge of building methods and the stones was fantastic,' observed George Zarnecki.* 'We were aiming at a very detailed description of the building – masonry, chisel marks, mouldings – he was a brilliant teacher. He had an enormous knowledge. In a new situation, he could read the building step by step, unprepared.' These steps often involved leaving *terra firma*. One of the dubious rewards of accompanying Pevsner to a cathedral was to be allowed into areas normally inaccessible to the public: clerestories, vaults, lanterns, even roofs. In Canterbury Cathedral, Iris Omer-Cooper noted, 'we were required to walk along a narrow ledge quite high above the choir in order to inspect some stained glass and stonework. Heights with a sheer drop petrify me and I found myself at one point rooted to the spot, holding up the queue. NP directed the student in front of me and the one behind to hold my hand and describe the objects of the exercise if I was unable to open my eyes.'

'He would go through Lincoln Cathedral, capital by bloody capital,' complained Peter Murray:

> until about half past one, and some of them would be beginning to flag and want the loo and something to eat, and somebody would say, 'Dr Pevsner, can't we have our sandwiches' – 'Oh, well, yes, ten minutes' – and they would bolt their sandwiches and he would snap his fingers and take them round the outside . . . And then say, 'I think we've just got time for a couple of churches', and they'd get back home starving and beaten into the ground. I never dared go.

'Lola passed the master a hard-boiled egg from time to time,' recalled Ian Sutton, 'looking a bit like a small mother bird trying to feed a large chick.' 'As for loos,' in the words of Gerda Mayer, 'his face, when he was asked, would take on a helpful but vague expression. Yes, he believed they did exist (he of course had no recourse to them but he was prepared to concede that lesser mortals might) and he'd wave an uncertain hand, a hand that pointed us into the distance, a hand indicative of troubles to be surmounted, of geographically impossible locations, and the likelihood of our never returning from such an undertaking.'[32]

The evening meal would usually be taken at a café chosen to suit the purse of the poorest. While gourmets among the group sometimes found this disappointing, their leader never minded. He had, after all,

*George Zarnecki (1915–2008), an expert medievalist later commissioned to write a volume of the *Pelican History of Art* for Pevsner, was the Librarian of the Conway Library at the Courtauld Institute.

had considerable experience of the lower reaches of British cooking ever since his first visit, and had become almost fond of what some 'quick and filthies' had to offer. In Norwich, John Newman recalled, 'we ended up in some café, all pretty exhausted by then and not in the best of tempers, and on the menu were foot-long frankfurters. So NP said, "I'm going to have one of these". The frankfurter arrived and he immediately got out his tape measure; it was only 11 inches long, so this restored his humour.' 'On the return journeys from field trips,' Iris Omer-Cooper revealed, 'we had to participate in NP's beloved quiz games, e.g. "20 Questions".'

. When Lola died, one of the many past students wrote to Pevsner: 'I think she would have been pleased to know that it was on her last Birkbeck trip that Susan and I decided to get married, and that out of respect and affection for yourself and to mark those in every way enjoyable and memorable two days, we propose, when we have a son, to call him Nicholas.'[33] Without ever seeking directly to mould others in his likeness, Pevsner regularly succeeded in changing the course of other people's lives as his own had been changed by the discovery of art history. Alistair Rowan, Professor of the History of Art in University College Dublin, subsequently Principal of the Edinburgh College of Art and later Professor of a new Art History department in Cork, was the founder of the *Buildings of Ireland* series. He is unequivocal:

> It was his lectures at Queen's University in Belfast, when I was a school boy, that set me off on a career in architectural history . . . I had been taken by my art mistress, with special permission to be out late . . . I took detailed notes of practically everything he said. My teacher was amazed by my recitation of what we had been exposed to the night before. They were on English Gothic. I particularly remember his account of Peterborough, Wells and the Decorated Lady Chapel of Ely Cathedral. It was all an absolute eye opener . . . At about 15 I had certainly never experienced anything like it.

Denis Evinson, who only met him as a mature student, had the same reaction. 'He had an enormous influence on the direction in which my life has gone. He helped me to find myself, I found what I was good at, and I've got a hobby in writing that will last me into my old age.' 'I still think of you every day,' he wrote to Pevsner thirty years later, 'and thank you for pointing me in the direction of architecture.'[34]

CHAPTER 28

'A further act for the main plot': a milder modernism

Pevsner had stepped down from his position as assistant editor of the *Architectural Review* in 1945, when Jim Richards returned from the Middle East to resume the editorship. Richards was also carrying most of the editorial responsibilities for the *Architects' Journal*, and H. de Cronin Hastings set up an editorial board to support and advise him, inviting Pevsner to remain associated with the *Review* as a member of this new body, alongside cartoonist and designer Osbert Lancaster, architectural writer Ian McCallum and Hastings himself. In Pevsner's account, the editorial board was largely decorative, while the real work of the *Review* was a two-man effort.[1] 'The brilliant ideas creating what was called *AR* policy were mostly HdeC's . . . But the brilliant ideas had to be developed, had to be made viable, and the *Review* had to be brought out month in month out, and that was JMR's task . . . He was sufficiently tenacious, scrupulously reliable and masterly at detail. And all these qualities were needed to create and maintain the image HdeC had visualised.'

Not surprisingly, Richards would resent this version of history. Hastings certainly remained as forceful as ever in the post-war period. He veiled his status as the *Review*'s proprietor by the use of pseudonyms – variously 'Ivor de Wolfe' or 'de Wofle', as shorthand for 'I the Devil, the World and the Flesh'. But he was quite open in his mission to improve the human condition through architecture, impartially attacking industrial squalor and the suburban invasion of the countryside unwittingly promoted by the garden city movement. His ideas were eccentric, influential and not uncommonly presented as the thoughts of others, to give the appearance of consensus. Pevsner would later recall Hastings presenting suggestions that were obviously his own programme with the words, 'Now Jim thinks'. But Richards was never simply a mouthpiece. He was perfectly capable of resisting Hastings's more impractical notions: 'He used to trot out ideas that he hoped you would follow. If you didn't follow them, he often went in for grumpy silence for a week. I had any number of brushes with him.'[2] Richards also originated a good many proposals of his own, which he tested on the editorial board, seeing this consultative role as their main function.

All the active business of editing remained in his own hands, with practical assistance from Ian McCallum.* 'It was [Richards] who knew all the architects, who had an unparalleled knowledge of the international architectural scene, visited conferences, was the guest of governments, wrote and laid out many special numbers single-handed and was consulted by the powers-that-be much more frequently than people realised.'³ But Richards was also a campaigner with a strong ideological and crusading streak. The modernist architect Lionel Brett (later the 4th Viscount Esher) remembered him as 'rather formidably left-wing', and he must have sat incongruously on the editorial board alongside Osbert Lancaster.⁴

Since 1939 Lancaster had been a regular cartoonist for the *Daily Express*, making a speciality of lampooning the upper-middle-class pretensions of a significant slice of the *Express*'s readership through the persona of Maudie Littlehampton, his manner a curious blend of frivolity and aggression. To some extent he was attacking one set of snobberies from the perspective of another. Not born to a cultivated life of leisure, he rather aspired to it, and made much of his disdain for earnest endeavour and 'that odious prig, the knowledgeable reader', preferring the idea of effortless cultured superiority. He enjoyed moving in smart social circles, which he had entered largely through two small books: *Pillar to Post: the pocket lamp of architecture* (1938) and *Homes, Sweet Homes* (1939). In the words of Reyner Banham, these books 'made a little revolution, and architecture suddenly became part of the common currency of polite natter. This they achieved (a) by making architecture funny, and taking the mickey out of the aspects of architecture that were taken seriously in the Thirties, and (b) by making it superficially discussible by giving slick names to the rogue styles of the 19th century.'⁵

For all his affectations, Lancaster had a genuine and passionate interest in the spirit of places and in architecture as a powerful means of expressing that spirit. He was contemptuous of anything that blurred or betrayed it – it was he who coined the term 'stockbroker's Tudor' – and he included in that category a tendency to moralism in architecture that elevated concepts above feelings, 'truth' above beauty. 'The architectural merits . . . of Michel Angelo's dome,' he wrote later, 'are briskly discounted on the grounds that the whole thing is held together by a concealed chain, unstinted praise is accorded some dreary office block solely on the grounds that its supremely

---

*McCallum later became the executive editor, before leaving the *Architectural Review* to become the first Director of the American Museum at Bath.

uninteresting method of construction is clearly apparent to every casual passer-by.'⁶

Far from an admirer of modernism, Lancaster was a curious choice for the *Architectural Review* board, and it is hard to imagine how he can have got on with Pevsner – suspect not only as a former champion of the Modern Movement, but also as an intellectual and a German. Lancaster at least affected to believe that intellectuals were almost by definition foreign, and foreigners were funny or common, or both. Pevsner felt himself an honorary Englishman by now; and while he respected Lancaster's knowledge and the elegance of his writing, he was not necessarily at ease with him. In 1961, reviewing a German edition of *Here of All Places* – translated as *Häuser machen Leute* – he wrote 'How odd to meet Mr Lancaster dressed up as a foreigner. And specially odd for me. How will my ancient compatriots react? Will they not be amused?'⁷ In any event, Lancaster did not stay long at the *Review* and was replaced on the editorial board by Hugh Casson.*

For several months after VE Day the *Review* had remained in its Cheam outpost, but by the middle of 1946 it was back in the more fashionable surroundings of Queen Anne's Gate, a short street running behind Birdcage Walk at the edge of St James's Park, in an elegant rabbit warren created by throwing together five houses in a Queen Anne terrace. Pevsner went in every Wednesday for the editorial board meeting, which took place over lunch. His role was clearly defined; he was at the *Architectural Review* not as a policy-maker or even a commentator on current architectural affairs, but as a historian.

Pevsner did much to create the *Review*'s reputation for architectural history. He published a series of short essays on historical architecture of a type that had never appeared in the *Review* before (and, after his time, would never appear again). Some of these essays were among his best work; they were all highly original and in some areas sparked off research on subjects that had been completely ignored. He also wrote a multitude of reviews, and commissioned historical pieces from younger writers with whom he would work in a 'tutorial capacity', if so required. 'He never shirked any sort of work if his conscience told him he ought to volunteer,' one colleague remembered.

This was the impression Hugh Casson received at his first meeting with Pevsner:

---

*Architect, designer and artist, Sir Hugh Casson (1910–99) had been involved with the Modern Movement as partner to Christopher Nicholson. Director of Architecture for the Festival of Britain in 1951, he would later go into partnership with Neville Conder (in 1956), and serve as Provost of the Royal College of Art and President of the Royal Academy.

He looked to me that morning like a kindly postmistress – pink cheeks, gold spectacles, sweet smile, brisk, authoritative manner. Like a postmistress too he worked in a flurry of tiny bits of paper, produced from his pockets, scribbled on in his tiny script and then replaced or handed to a secretary for later action. No remark, no name, no event, no ideas passed his attention without this note-taking procedure . . . This display of discipline was impressive but at first unnerving. NP moved as quickly as a bird. He let you know he was a busy man, and he expected you to be busy too. This meant impatience with minor administrative delays, perpetually engaged telephone numbers, slack typing, inability of staff to find a reference. His criticism, like his compliments, would be quickly administered and quickly forgotten. He was always serious but never solemn.[8]

John Piper was not so sure. On the surface his relationship with Pevsner was cordial enough. They had mutual friends in Geoffrey and Bertschy Grigson and, despite Piper's misgivings, had been working together regularly at the *Review* for several years. During Pevsner's wartime interregnum he had commissioned frequent illustrations and articles from Piper.* 'We are approaching the stage when there will be no number without some JP in it,' he wrote in May 1943, and he seems to have regarded Piper as a friend. His letters to him during the early 1940s are relaxed and affable – 'We'd love to come to F[awley] B[ottom]',[†] 'Thanks for b/w illustrations and enlightening text – you won't like the layout, I had to mess it up because of unusual arrangement of the number', 'Can we all lunch together?' Bertschy Grigson gave it as her impression that Pevsner liked Piper very much, but that Piper feared and resented him, and was malicious about him behind his back with John Betjeman. Lionel Brett agreed: 'Piper was a person who had bêtes noires, and I think that for some reason Nikolaus was one of his bêtes noires . . . He actually was not far from Pevsner in his architectural opinions . . . but of course there was this absurd English prejudice against scholarship which is one of the most tiresome characteristics of the British – and a prejudice against Germans, of course.'[9]

It puzzled Pevsner that the eclecticism which enabled people like Piper to see the charm and artistic appeal of anchors, barge paintings,

---

*Pevsner would also commission a King Penguin from Piper in 1950 on the subject of Romney Marsh.
†Letters NP/John Piper, 29/7/42, 12/3/45, 31/7/45. The Pipers lived at Fawley Bottom, near Henley-on-Thames, from the mid-1930s until the 1990s.

pub signs and street lamps did not extend to cantilevers and curtain walls. 'They still feel that a liking for Blandford or the High at Oxford or indeed William Butterfield must exclude a liking for the 20th century style in architecture,' he would complain later, not understanding that these attitudes had as much to do with social ambience as with aesthetics.[10] For his part, Piper may simply have found Pevsner too *ernst* and may have shared the preconceptions of people like James Lees-Milne, who on actually meeting Pevsner was pleasantly surprised. Commissioned to write a piece on Robert Adam, he asked to talk to Pevsner and they lunched at Brooks's club. 'This man, who hitherto I have pictured as dry, pedantic and rather carping,' confessed Lees-Milne, 'proved to be friendly, eager to assist, and encouraging.'*

The *Architectural Review* at this time was not quite as it has been depicted by those who deplore the spread of modernism. They have tended to portray it as a hotbed of dour, uncompromising propaganda for international ideas, culpable at one remove for every post-war nondescript flat-roofed office block or barren housing estate. In reality, its authority was primarily confined to literary and critical circles, with very little practical reach into the building industry; and where it did exert influence over what was built in the late 1940s and 1950s, this was as part of a very much wider movement.[11]

The social role of the architect had already been a topic for debate in the 1930s following the Town and Country Planning Act of 1932, a piece of legislation enshrining a belief in the need for governmental planning. Architects as different as arch-modernist Wells Coates and Sir Giles Gilbert Scott, President of the RIBA, were agreed on the architect's responsibility to society. The architect, wrote Scott, was 'a PLANNER . . . one of the most important servants of the community, with a valuable contribution to make towards an improvement in the art of living'.[12] 'We are not so much concerned with the formal elements of "style",' agreed Coates, 'as with an architectural solution of the social and economic problems of today . . . As creative architects we are concerned with a Future which must be *planned*, rather than a Past which must be *patched up*.'[13]

This trend was accelerated by war and the urgent need – and opportunity – for widespread reconstruction, with huge numbers of buildings destroyed by the Blitz and the government in control of the building

---

*J. Lees-Milne, *Caves of Ice*, diary entry for 19/8/47. Rosemary Hill comments that Lees-Milne was 'all his life defensively un-intellectual, "ill at ease among the high-brows".' R. Hill, 'Late Worm', review of M. Bloch, *James Lees-Milne: The Life* in *London Review of Books*, 10/9/2009.

industry. 'I don't think I have ever been so miserable in my life as I am now,' lamented John Betjeman in 1944. 'We are in a slave state here and I am beginning to think I would as soon be in prison or dead. Everything one loves threatened by post-war plansters of different types.'[14]

'There was enormous pent-up energy after 1945,' writes Andrew Saint, current editor of the Survey of London:

> Six years of hostilities had reduced our cities to a mess, our towns to scruffiness and dinginess. Behind that lay the memory of pervasive depression during the 1930s and the century-old legacy of the Indus-trial Revolution: social inequalities tolerated too long, slum housing, filth in the workplace, soot in the streets and a shabby urban envir-onment without space, greenness, order or variety of scale . . . The apostles of modernism claimed that science and art could be harnessed together to offer a quality of architecture that would, impartially, transform everyone's lives. If this was to be achieved, the country would have to think big. Old cities needed to be fundamentally overhauled, complete new towns built, housing estates laid out on fresh principles, thousands of child-centred schools and dozens of universities constructed to cope with a growing population.[15]

Methods of building production were revolutionised, as those most seriously committed to the new social building programmes adopted the modernist principles advocated by Gropius and the Dessau Bauhaus. The programmes were generally in the hands of local authorities or development corporations, with direction from central government, rather than in the private sector. They were implemented by teams, largely anonymous, carrying designs over from one project to the next – an approach that worked best in buildings where standardisation was appropriate. In schools, for example, as in Hertfordshire, architects worked with educationists and industrialists to identify common needs and provide shared technical solutions, using common methods of construction and the same pre-fabricated materials, to create modular structures with standard panels on slender steel frames. However new the production method may have been, however, the buildings them-selves were not necessarily radical.

To some extent, the Heroic Age of modernism was over for the *Review*, and the editorial team were no longer determined to fight its corner without reservations. In the 1930s, remembered Hugh Casson, 'every house was a battle ground, every block of flats a fight for prin-ciple'.[16] After the war, the *Review*'s approach was more one of British compromise with the German hard line. 'We do not believe any longer in the old slogan of functional beauty,' an article of 1944 had declared, in the tones almost certainly of Hastings. 'Or rather we don't believe any more that functional beauty is the only kind of beauty.'[17]

There are hints that, for Hastings at least, this was not just an aesthetic recoil but a political change of heart as well, a prudent post-war retreat from the more totalitarian implications of modernism:

> Can democratic opinion which is by its nature diffuse be brought round to the saving grace of a Bauhaus style without the application of force? Is not the answer that the Bauhaus must accept Sharawaggi? The safety valve of inconsistency should remain open. The Picturesque approach is that safety valve. It is a democratic art. It can give satisfaction to all tastes. It is catholic and generous. It is accessible on any scale, open to a never-ending variety of expression; it encourages the amateur in his back-garden and the technician in his regional plans.

'Catholic', 'generous', 'diffuse', 'varied' – the *Review*'s philosophy was embodied in its physical surroundings, and most particularly in the Bride of Denmark pub, which Hastings had established in 1946 for its staff in the basement of the Queen Anne's Gate premises. Queen Anne was the wife of Prince George of Denmark, and her statue stood in the street outside. Inside, Hastings had put into practice the *Review*'s championing of Victorian pub values – warmth, intimacy, a series of bars, engraved mirrors, baroque mahogany counters and screens, and a ceiling cunningly faked to simulate the effects of centuries of smoking. With Ian McCallum, he collected discarded fixtures and fittings from bombed buildings – glass panels, brewers' advertisements, dark wood benches – and created a deliberately arresting collage. 'The *AR*'s mixture of hard-line Modernism, the Picturesque, love of tradition and surprise, Englishness and the exotic was conflated there,' writes Peter Davey, a former editor of the *Review*:

> A lion peered from its lair, there were cases of stuffed fish, a turtle shell, rows of dusty bottles (their contents drunk long ago by the ancestral editors), the reputed fruit of the tree of good and evil; vistas were cut short, views made longer and deflected sideways by multiple reflections full of incident, sparkle and brilliance. John Piper had painted that ceiling; H de C [Hastings] had encouraged a gang of small boys with chains to distress that wall over there.[18]

(The stuffed lion was said to have been rescued by Pevsner from a leaking stable on Lord Moyne's estate.) There was a diamond pencil for favoured guests to engrave their signatures on two mirrors flanking the original bar counter – Frank Lloyd Wright, Jacob Epstein, Bernard Miles, Alan Moorehead, Denis Compton, Walter Gropius.

Humanity was what appeared to be absent from much of what the *Review* and others had urged before the war. In an intriguing editorial entitled 'The Second Half Century' in January 1947, the editors reviewed the magazine's policy. In a crucial passage entitled 'The *Architectural Review* outlines a further act for the main plot', they acknowledged the need to negotiate with a public that had shown stubborn resistance to the Modern Movement:

> The obvious short-term objective must consist in getting back some of the scope and richness that the Act of Revolution discarded. Architecture has had for the time being deliberately to dehumanise itself, but the success of the Revolution and the subsequent consolidating period of functionalism means that it can now seek more direct contact with human aspirations without compromising any of its principles . . . Architecture must find a way of humanising itself as regards expression without in any way abandoning the principles on which the Revolution was founded.

The path to humanisation that the *Review* favoured soon became known as the 'New Empiricism', a title chosen to reflect a spirit of practical experiment that was prepared to bend modernist rules in order to suit the particular environment.[19] In too many modern houses, remarked one commentator, the average person 'felt the lack of many of the aesthetic values and the little contributions to cosiness that we human beings are so dependent upon . . . It was difficult to settle down in the new houses because the "new" human beings were not so different from the older ones.'[20] The new, more relaxed creed would be set out in a series of articles between 1947 and 1951, many pointing to Sweden, where the New Empiricism was already well established: 'The Swedish temperament is a compromise between Teuton and Anglo-Saxon. German mechanical perfectionism and love of abstractions is balanced by British individualism and earthy practicality, and now the balance, in architecture at least, is moving towards the common-sense end of the see-saw.'*

---

*Eric de Maré, 'The New Empiricism', *AR*, January 1948.

Pevsner was unquestionably in sympathy with the changed mood at the *Architectural Review*. His views on the origins and history of the Modern Movement remained the same. *Pioneers of the Modern Movement* would be republished by New York's Museum of Modern Art in 1949, with a new title – *Pioneers of Modern Design* – but an unchanged adherence to the canon of 1936, and people still looked to him as the chronicler of modernism's past. 'While there may have been many protagonists of the modern movement, none has given it such a sense of intellectual coherence as Pevsner,' wrote one grateful student.[21] Nevertheless, in accordance with his belief in the spirit of the age, he felt that the present time demanded a different architectural response – and a softer, more human one.

This tempering of mood was already obvious in his views on design, where he was no longer interested in wearing the mantle of a pioneer. In 1948, when Cambridge University Press asked him for a second edition of his *Enquiry into Industrial Art in England* he refused. The book, he said, could not simply be updated, but would need to be completely redone and his work had now moved on, so he was no longer the right person to do it. His ideas of good taste had not changed – for him the values of the Bauhaus would always remain the ideal – but he now accepted that good taste was no longer the only criterion. Design should make more allowances for human nature and the very natural desire for ornament and fantasy.

This same mellowing is apparent in his writings on architecture during the 1940s. It had been easy to sympathise with the Modern Movement in theory, when relatively few buildings had gone up, and many of them were very good. Now there was increasing evidence of what they looked like when translated by people of lesser skill and in the wrong spirit. Pevsner had sounded the first note of unease in the piece on Nazi architecture that he had written for the *Review* in 1941, in which he had been particularly disparaging of the 'holiday barracks' designed for the working man. 'There is no animation, no variety. And what strikes one as so inhuman is not only the uniformity of the building and its mad scale, but also the actual forms – forms which, I suppose, must be called of the Modern Movement. Perhaps the soundest argument against the 20th-century style in architecture is its unsympathetic treatment of legitimate human yearnings, its lack of faith in sentiment.'

He had repeated his misgivings in one of his wartime 'Treasure Hunts', a piece about recent suburban housing on the Epsom Road between Morden and Cheam, in which he had deplored the fondness of 1930s builders for adopting watered-down Modern Movement ideas.

'We know of course that this . . . stands for the better cause, the more sensible approach to housing, higher value for money, the sort of thing that is good for the people and the only honest expression of our age. We should, therefore, heartily encourage such houses. Yet sometimes I cannot help feeling that they may to a happier future look overwhelmingly bleak.'[22]

Contemporary architecture was not always at the forefront of Pevsner's mind. It was one among many interests and would concern him less as time went on. But during the years he was most closely connected with the *Architectural Review* in the mid-1940s, it was a major preoccupation. The clearest statement of his aspirations for it – one that makes it clear he was campaigning neither for uniformity nor for austerity – appeared in 1944 in a publication called *Europe*. The article, entitled 'Homes for the future', is a perfect exposition of the New Empiricist principle of adapting a rule to suit a variety of individual environments.

'Physical reconstruction is impossible on a strictly national basis,' wrote Pevsner:

> The planners will have to work . . . with a European vision. Architects will co-operate with them, and it may seem only natural to assume that the style in which they will design should be that very international style . . . Should then the buildings of new Warsaw look exactly as the buildings of new Rotterdam, new Coventry and new Genoa? My answer to this question is an emphatic NO. These pages are just as much a plea for variety of idiom as a plea for unity of style. The Gothic style of the 13th century was international, because there existed a spiritual community of European regions at that time, as there will again exist one (if a secularised one) in the 20th century. Yet Lincoln Cathedral is as English as Amiens Cathedral is French and Florence Cathedral, Italian. This is what we must again have, if we believe that a healthy European life cannot exist in uniformity and regimentation. Should international planning impose an international idiom, nearly all the visual pleasure would go out of the new buildings.

It is hard to tell how much influence individual members of the advisory board had on the *Review*'s editorial line. But given the views he already held, Pevsner was likely to be largely in tune with its overall message. His job appears to have been to set this message in a historical context and once again support editorial claims with convincing precedents. Specifically, he was required to work in parallel with

Hastings to develop the *Review*'s new creed of 'Visual Planning'. In a long editorial in June 1945 entitled 'The English Planning Tradition in the City', Hastings introduced the notion of the 'urban picturesque'. This was town design that was modern in spirit in making form serve function, yet it showed its responsibility to the past. 'The world we live in is not a private one. It was not all made in our day, and the relics of past times reach into ours and demand their share in the picture of the historic town.' London must not be reconstructed along monumental lines. The city had developed functionally, as a product of competing interests, and should not have a formal scheme artificially imposed upon it, as Haussmann had imposed order on Paris. This, wrote Hastings, was not the English way.

These were sentiments Pevsner was quick to echo after his brush with pompous academicism in Washington. In a radio talk in 1947, he described with some amusement the genesis of the American capital around 1800 in 'an absolutely patternised plan, miles across each way, with a gridiron broken up by plenty of round points with wide radiating avenues – wonderfully mad', considering that the federal staff at that time numbered about 117, and there was no reason for anyone else to live there. By the 1930s Washington was liberally adorned with oversized piles, 'as dead as so many huge doornails . . . wonders of well-meaning triteness . . . It takes your breath away all right, even if you may feel something like hit below the belt.'[23]

Far better precedents for the rebuilding of London, in Pevsner's view, were to be found further back in its own history.[24] Given a free hand, the town planners of the past might perhaps have gone for formal and axial planning – but in practice this kind of freedom is never available. Christopher Wren, for example, had originally proposed a formal scheme for the rebuilding of the City of London after the Great Fire of 1666. But for the merchants and traders working in the City, business had to be resumed as quickly as possible, and there was no one with sufficient power to override the pressure of individual interests and force through a single coordinated composition. In the same way London's famous seventeenth- and eighteenth-century squares – 'the main contribution of London to the history of European town planning' – were individually planned and not formally related. 'As you go from one square to another – say, through Bloomsbury – you have a very free and informal rhythm of large and small shapes.' All this, he concluded, shows 'a feeling for the fascination of intricacy', very different from the axial planning of Paris or the symmetry of Trajan's Forum in Rome.

The *Architectural Review* would go on to develop these ideas on urban planning into a doctrine that was the quintessence of the new empiricism: 'Townscape', the art of giving visual coherence and organisation to the jumble of buildings, streets and spaces that make up the urban environment, working with what is already there rather than attempting to start from scratch, and promoting multiple use of an area rather than striving for artificial uniformity. Hastings gave London's South Bank as an example, pointing to a photograph of Bankside teeming with different activities, 'an immense drama exhibiting the will to live in countless forms . . . The vigorous overlapping of activity in this way is anathema to text-book planners.'[25]

This 'vigorous overlapping' was given a clearer visual identity by architect and illustrator Gordon Cullen, who had arrived as the *Review*'s art editor in 1947.* In a series of articles in the 1950s he put together photographs and sketches expressing his view of the urban landscape as a series of spaces, related but not regular, packed with anecdotal detail. 'The key to our modern conception of Townscape,' he wrote, 'lies in the fact, the simple but surprising fact, that the items of the environment cannot be dissociated the one from the other. Further, the effects of juxtaposition are in themselves as exciting as the objects juxtaposed – often more so.'[26]

However much sympathy Pevsner may have had with aspects of the doctrine, he would not seem to have been closely involved in the later formulations of 'Townscape'.† He would continue to act on occasion as a mouthpiece for its theories, but confined himself largely to talking about its historical roots. 'If one now looks at Townscape in the 20th century, what I am pleading for is a happy harmony between what functionalism demands and what tradition in England endorses. That should give this country its great chance in the evolution of a 20th century townscape.'[27]

He would also appear to have been something of a bystander when it came to the fullest exemplification of 'Townscape in action', the 1951 Festival of Britain. His only comments concerned modern ornament. In an article on 'Lettering and the Festival on the South Bank', he observed that in their quest for a new kind of decoration, the Festival's architects appeared to have opted for a revival of the Picturesque virtues of variety and contrast. Although they had been urged by the Festival coordinators to select from three main types of lettering

---

*Thomas Gordon Cullen (1914–94) trained as an architect. His book *The Concise Townscape* (first published by the Architectural Press in 1961 as *Townscape*) was one of the twentieth century's most popular works on urban design.
†The *Review* produced a full-blown manifesto for Townscape in 1954, and by 1960 the magazine incorporated a regular monthly townscape feature.

– 'Egyptians, Romans or Itals' – they had managed to use them most ingeniously, sometimes employing heavy 'period' versions of these fonts to offset the lightness of glass, steel struts and aluminium latticework, sometimes selecting skeletal, almost transparent versions to sit against plain backgrounds. At every turn throughout the site, carefully worked lettering was to be found on an intriguing variety of surfaces and in unexpected places, not just on signposts and boards but on litter bins and the lintels to the public lavatories. 'We should be grateful to Heaven,' exulted Pevsner, 'that so many artists and architects and designers feel once again that the world has so many enjoyable facets.'[28]

Festival architecture, directed by Hugh Casson, had the humanity that Pevsner and others at the *Review* had been calling for, and it was gratifying to see their guiding principles turned into physical reality on the South Bank, to be copied – for a while at least – in housing projects and university campuses all over Britain. Others beyond the *Review* were equally cheered. Even the caustic John Summerson was beguiled, and mourned when the Festival was over. 'The South Bank is closed and bang goes the most life-enhancing thing in London architecture . . . We can only do this when we are, so to speak, dining the Pope . . . The same money and effort spent on permanently reconstructing the centre of some particularly frightful black town would daunt us by the sheer immorality of creating a fine thing for ourselves. It seems a pity.'[29]

The following year, Casson was knighted; and it was at this point that he was invited to join the editorial board of the *Architectural Review*. 'It was 1952. Deer-stalkered and houndstoothed the proprietor of the Architectural Press received me in his lair. (It was dimly lit and dominated by a stuffed lion.) "Would I," he asked, "be able to join the Editorial Board of the *AR*?" . . . As a practising architect, presumably I was to be lightweight contact with professional reality. NP [Pevsner] spoke for scholarship. I was honoured and delighted and said so.'[30]

CHAPTER 29

'The High Table part of the stay':
Cambridge, 1949–1954

Pevsner's detachment from the Festival of Britain was probably due to far too many other distractions. It was during the early 1950s that work first started to pile up to the point where it was a pressure even for him. By June 1952 he was complaining to Lola of 'a panic of depression'. 'When I think back [to the end of the 1940s],' he wrote, 'how lovely it was to have occasionally a couple of days alone to work, peacefully and constantly. And now? – nothing like that – which is my own fault, of course.' To his dismay, his stamina seemed sometimes to be failing him. 'Tired and slept ignominiously in Marcus' car (old man complex),' he reported gloomily. He was desperate – 'just like Muo' – for people to leave him alone, at the same time aware that professionally this would be fatal.

On top of his other commitments, he had taken on a new lecturing post – prestigious, but an eventual source of particular stress. In 1949 he had accepted the title of Slade Professor at Cambridge. This was the senior art professorship in the university, founded in 1869 alongside similar chairs in Oxford and London from a bequest of £35,000 by the collector and philanthropist Felix Slade. Previous holders had included Roger Fry and W.G. Constable, and Pevsner's immediate predecessor was Geoffrey Webb, fresh from his position as director of monuments, fine art and archives for the Control Commission in Germany.* Later holders would include Ernst Gombrich, John Pope-Hennessy, Anthony Blunt and Anita Brookner. As this list suggests, Slade professors had a wide range of interests and expertise, and were expected to cater to an equally diverse audience in Cambridge, town and gown alike.

For his inaugural lecture, Pevsner elected to speak, as a historian, about the first man to hold the post he was now taking up. The problem was that this man was Sir Matthew Digby Wyatt – Secretary

---

*Geoffrey Webb (1898–1970), an architectural historian of the English Gothic, biographer of Wren and Vanbrugh and authority on British seventeenth-century architecture. Pevsner would later ask him to write the volume on British medieval architecture for the *Pelican History of Art*.

to the Great Exhibition of 1851, surveyor for the East India Company, a Victorian eclectic of the first order and, in 1949, a highly unfashionable figure. As a writer and critic, Wyatt sympathised with Ruskin's distaste for 'shams' in architecture; but as an architect he mixed historical styles enthusiastically. He added a castellated Gothic extension with tower and spire to Brunel's Bristol Temple Meads station. He devised a grand circular mausoleum for Evelina de Rothschild at West Ham Jewish Cemetery. He gave the Roman Baths in Cambridge the classical treatment with pillars and pediment, which was preserved after the baths failed commercially and the building was let, half to the university's Pitt Club and half to Orme's Billiard Rooms. His other work included a lunatic asylum in Ealing and the Adelphi Theatre in the Strand.

The vim with which Pevsner pursued owners and proprietors for slides to illustrate his talk testified not just to his love of a bibliographic chase but also to his admiration for Wyatt's vigour, if not his nicety of taste. The results were not entirely what he had intended. To his chagrin, the audience entirely failed to take his honourable forerunner seriously and Pevsner was compelled to step down from the podium to ask them to stop laughing.

The Slade post was a visiting one, requiring only eight lectures a year, and did not bring with it residence in Cambridge. Within a year of his appointment, however, a room had been made available to him at St John's College, in Thomas Rickman's Gothic Revival New Court, for the occasions on which he wished to work in Cambridge and stay overnight.* The room was, he wrote happily, 'in the Wedding Cake, that delightful folly at the north end of the Backs, where I have a Gothic plaster ceiling of the 1820s and a polygonal bathroom with the plumbing twining over the walls like ivy.'[1] With dining rights at High Table, he began to feel that at last, after fifteen years on the outside, he was a part of the English university establishment. (He even felt secure enough to be competitive. 'Michael Jaffé was here,' he wrote to Lola in 1953, 'the one with the Fellowship at King's . . . Only a potential, not an actual menace.') He would lecture in Cambridge long after his tenure as Slade Professor – itself a record six years – had expired, and it was a source of great happiness to him almost until the end of his working life.

---

*Glyn Daniel says in his autobiography *Some Small Harvest* (Thames and Hudson, 1986), p.225, that Pevsner made the occupancy of a room in New Court a condition of becoming a Fellow of St John's. Daniel claims to have been responsible for Pevsner's election as a Fellow – a process that he suggests took fifteen years.

Part of the pleasure was simply the beauty of the surroundings. Cambridge, he wrote, was a 'miniature history of English architecture' with a roofscape of 'supreme confusion'. 'My happiness is also due to . . . the wonderful chance of being able to walk through a town for a whole mile without being hurt by the sight of a single building. That can happen in only three towns in the whole of England.'[2] The glory of his position was that he was being paid to pass on this happiness. 'It is my job at Cambridge to keep young people's eyes open, and to open them if they are still glued up – an extremely gratifying job in many ways.'

As a general lecturer, in the years after his Slade professorship had finished, he had his lectures announced in the faculties of History and of Fine Art, as well as on the overall list of university lectures, and he consistently filled one of the largest halls in Cambridge. He had no permanent position, simply lecturing by invitation, repeating the same subjects year after year because he felt there was a need as well as a demand. 'He didn't make them pretentious,' commented Ernst Gombrich, 'he just gave people what they wanted. I think that is very characteristic of Pevsner – his humility, his goodness of heart. He is a man of tremendous efficiency but he has never thrown his weight about . . . He is a craftsman, he can handle his material perfectly.'[3]

Less generous academic observers felt that, with a dearth of jobs and a glut of aspiring art historians, Pevsner should not have monopolised the opportunity to lecture on general art topics in Cambridge for so long. It was not a judgement that was shared by students. The historian Geoffrey Best (Trinity College, 1948) went regularly to his lectures for years, drawn at least partly by 'that fascinating continental intonation which was exotic to us. His lectures were Events in the lives of many of us, and phrases like "See you at Pevsner!" or "I had to miss Pevsner last Friday" were commonplace among us.' The design writer Corin Hughes-Stanton agreed:

In my experience there were only two lecturers who consistently drew capacity houses – and one of them was Pevsner. In the period just before lunch we flocked to hear him on fine art, and just before dinner (both unpopular times) we flocked to hear him on architecture.* It was at these lectures that I, as an historian, first met medical and engineering students, geographers and potential estate agents. Yet I think these lectures were probably among the least *enjoyable* I have ever attended. They were difficult to follow and, unless you

---

*In later years Pevsner lectured at 5 p.m. on Fridays, noon on Saturdays.

were in the first few rows, difficult to hear; they were so constructed that it was impossible to let one's mind wander for a moment without the risk of losing the thread of an entire lecture, or even series of lectures; they contained nothing except a string of facts; and they were accompanied by some particularly unimpressive slides. It was tough, hard work.[4]

Other listeners positively relished Pevsner's pace and concentration, in stark contrast to the style of their other lecturers. 'On the Continent,' George Mikes once wrote, 'public orators try to learn to speak fluently and smoothly: in England they take a special course in Oxonian stuttering.'[5] Michael Farr, reading English at Cambridge as a pupil of F.R. Leavis, remembered how different Pevsner seemed:*

He had a style which I had not seen in Cambridge; it was fast and intense, involving the audience with every word, gesture and slide, and yet casual too. He stood to the side of the desk with notes the size of a digital watch and apparently never took his eyes off us . . . His student audience used to roll around in helpless laughter at his slides of Keble College, the Albert Memorial and other examples of hilariously 'outrageous' Victorian design. I well remember that after a fleeting look of puzzled bewilderment he used to redden with irritation, pause for a second or two, clear his throat and then continue with dogged determination. Towards the end of his course of lectures the giggling had completely abated and his audience were silently spellbound and completely engrossed by his persuasive enthusiasm and scholarship. The pink-faced and beaming Pevsner became accustomed to acknowledging gales of genuine applause from packed attendances.

(H. de C. Hastings referred to Pevsner's Cambridge lectures as his 'revivalist meetings'.)

Students who ventured to introduce themselves to him found him approachable, just as he had been as a young teacher in Göttingen, and he made friendships that he would sustain for the rest of his life. Nicholas Taylor was invited to have tea with him before one of his Friday lectures and discovered a telling example of his ability to shut out the world in order to compose his mind: 'I expected us to meet at his college, St John's, but not a bit of it: our rendez-vous was the

---

*Shortly after leaving Cambridge, Michael Farr would work with Pevsner on a new edition of *An Enquiry into Industrial Art in Britain* – see Chapter 30.

almost deserted foyer of the Victoria Cinema in Market Hill (nowadays Marks & Spencer) – a joyless example of the Art Deco he hated, and also, as a "town" cinema, the last place anyone in Cambridge would expect to find him. We had the simplest tea and cake. And yet, facing out through storey-height windows, he was enjoying a rich panorama of King's College Chapel, the Senate House and Great St Mary's. He was in the world, and the world knew him not – and that was his choice.'

On the occasions when Pevsner stayed over after his Friday lecture, he would come to breakfast (porridge with milk) on Saturday with Geoffrey Best; in the years that followed, Best would buy postcards of buildings when he was travelling, blank out the titles, and send them to Pevsner as a test, preferably posted in different countries to add to the confusion. The architecture student Michael Murray, once qualified, used to meet him in London to reminisce about Cambridge:

> In 1976, at one of our lunches at the Bonnington Hotel, he passed me a slip of paper (which I still have) on which he had written the names GOGGAN and LEONARD DUBINSKY, and asked if I could identify them. He had been approached by art students after one of his lectures at an American University, who wanted to know where they could read more about these two interesting guys, whom he had mentioned in his talk. I was not bright enough to recognise them immediately as GAUGUIN and LEONARDO DA VINCI.

It did not take Pevsner long to become part of the Cambridge scene. He continued to champion Victorian art and architecture. 'Good luck to bad art,' he wrote bravely, alongside a piece by Ronald Bryden on 'The Art of the Bad Novel', in an article for the student magazine *Granta* in February 1953. 'Good good art' for Pevsner was the work of the sculptors of Vézelay Abbey, the paintings of Piero della Francesca, Cuyp and Constable – artists trying to be themselves and express their age in terms of form and colour. 'Bad bad art' was 'the postcard with a generously retouched photograph varnished into high gloss of a handsome young man kissing a girl with passion, a moustache and impeccable but rather dated clothes'. The intermediate categories were harder to pin down. Art with social if not aesthetic value could be either 'Bad good' or 'Good bad'. Nazi art, he argued, was possibly 'Bad good' – 'good' in the sense of having social consciousness and contact with the people, but 'bad' in the sense of being tasteful and tepid at the same time. Russian communist art, on the other hand, was more probably 'Good bad' – bad in aesthetic terms, but good in robustness. It was this vitality that made the difference for Pevsner, and explained his reluctance simply to dismiss Victorian building as many of his peers did. 'The most important thing is perhaps that [art] must be done with gusto. The maker – for instance in fairground decoration – or the designer – for instance in much Victorian architecture – must have enjoyed himself . . . Conviction can take the place of aesthetic value, that is the lesson of Good Bad.'

This same conviction was what he was looking for in contemporary architecture. The main issue in Cambridge, in the early 1950s at least, was not what individual colleges should be allowed to put up, but where the university as a whole should be allowed to expand. Cambridge was a relatively small town, and university buildings already dominated the centre, their courts and gardens stretching down to the River Cam in the long green vista of the Backs. Three different schemes had been publicly mooted by planners William Holford and Myles Wright, hired by the county council as consultants for the Cambridge Survey and Plan (1950). New colleges, or extensions to existing ones, might continue in the centre of the town; they might be concentrated on the far side of the Cam, west of the Backs; or they might be scattered haphazardly about, to minimise the impact on any one area.

Pevsner's preference was to strike out in a fresh direction and make a positive new statement rather than attempt to compromise with what was already there. In an article of May 1950 he came out in favour of the most radical of the three options – the leap across the river to extend the university west of the Backs.[6] The advantages, he wrote, were 'unobstructed sites, on which fairly high buildings can be put without spoiling the scale of anything, and sites on which modern architecture of a high aesthetic standard could at last get a chance'. Queen's Road, running parallel with the river, enclosed a substantial strip of open and undeveloped land. If that road could be closed and an alternative new one built further inland, 'the backs would then become an ideal campus, faced by the river frontages of the old colleges on one side and by the new buildings on the other. Here is a new conception of high aesthetic possibilities.'

But such new approaches to planning also required boldness in architecture, at a time when the colleges were still commissioning insipid examples of neo-Georgian and semi-modern. Pevsner put this to a live audience from his Slade chair that year, in the last of a series of lectures that he had entitled 'The Young Person's Guide to Cambridge Architecture', dealing exclusively with new buildings. The reaction was something of an anticlimax. 'No-one asked questions, no-one felt insulted, no-one defended the anaemic character of the buildings and the timidity of the colleges. No-one outdid me in insults either; no-one in fact was interested.'⁷ Perhaps he felt he had not made himself clear. Two years later he spelled out the same message quite unequivocally.⁸ The Backs, he wrote, 'are no longer backs but fronts . . . The Backs are – for better or worse – the Campus of the future.'*

For new buildings to sit well alongside the old, they would have to engage actively with them, making their own statements boldly. 'Gibbs was not afraid of King's College Chapel,' wrote Pevsner. 'Wren was not afraid of the 14th-century style of Pembroke. Why then should the Wrens and Gibbses . . . of today not be given their chance in developing the Campus of the future?' The challenge was to find architects with both nerve and sympathy. In recent years they seemed to have had one, but lacked the other. At Queens' College, the 1936 Fisher Building that closed the Backs in the south was, Pevsner complained, a 'nondescript block of flats which might stand at Edgware or Wimbledon' and no match for the 'wedding-cake' of St John's in the north. On the other hand, Sir Giles Gilbert Scott's University Library was self-assured but tactless in its curious mixture of utilitarian features with the Grand Style, a large and insensitive neighbour to anything within range.

There was one Cambridge project that seemed to have just the right combination of diplomacy and strength. On Sidgwick Avenue, over the river and behind the Backs, Hugh Casson and Neville Conder had drawn up plans for a new Faculty of Arts which looked much the kind of 'forum with a landscape centre' that Pevsner had visualised for 'the Campus of the future'. The plans, accommodating faculty buildings, institutes, museums, lecture rooms, a canteen, and space for cars and a thousand bicycles as well as a water walk, embodied Picturesque principles along the same lines as Casson's South Bank site for the Festival of Britain. Pevsner would write later that he had looked at the plans in 1952 with 'a shock of delight. Here was human scale, variety of layout, a sense of enclosure, an understanding of planting, and other landscape and townscape effects.'⁹ Casson and Conder had devised 'an intricate group of courts, as varied in size and as

---

*Pevsner was too sanguine in supposing that no one was interested in or offended by his views on new architecture in Cambridge. In Hugh Plommer he encountered an opponent who could easily outdo him in insults. See Chapter 48.

454

unexpected in visual effects as the old colleges are – the key principle of collegiate planning observed, but no details copied'.*

There was little progress on the Sidgwick Site for Pevsner to report, however, by the time the *Cambridgeshire* volume of the *Buildings of England* was published in 1954. He had been working on it at intervals all through his first years of teaching there, and the book was dedicated to 'the late Master, the Master, and the Fellows of the College of St John the Evangelist in the University of Cambridge'. The researcher was the Austrian art historian Gertrud Bondi, a Pinder pupil slightly younger than Pevsner.

The sources for the *BoE* had broadened and deepened. The author and antiquary Rupert Gunnis had published his *Dictionary of British Sculpture 1600–1851*, greatly simplifying the search for information on statues and monuments in churches and country houses, and other authorities had begun to volunteer their expertise on a wide range of topics. The pioneer industrial archaeologist Rex Wailes offered notes on the county's windmills; and Peter Thornton, then an undergraduate and unpaid assistant keeper at the Fitzwilliam Museum, undertook to research the silver collections in each college, asking only that he be given some form of official-looking identity card. 'I have found that some butlers are rightly very careful to whom they show their plate.'†
All this made it even harder for Pevsner to winnow the huge quantities of available information, and he was aware of being arbitrary. 'Church bells are not included, church chests only here and there, and moats hardly at all,' he wrote – and no portraits, but some portrait busts. 'The lack of logic here (as, no doubt, in many other matters), I have to admit.'

During his years as Slade Professor, from 1949 to 1955 – and particularly when he was working on the *Cambridgeshire* volume – Pevsner spent more time in Cambridge than he did thereafter. He wrote frequent reports to Lola. 'I enjoy the High Table part of the stay,' he confessed,

*NP, 'The Sidgwick Avenue Site' in *Cambridge Review*, 31/10/53. His admiration for the modern Picturesque character of the Sidgwick Site doubled his disappointment at Adams, Holden and Pearson's additions to the Bloomsbury precinct around Birkbeck later in the 1950s. The precinct, having the same picturesque layout, would have benefited from the same treatment, but instead they went for monumentalism and symmetry.
†P. Thornton/NP, 22/11/51. Thornton (1925–2007) would become an authority on the history of interior decoration, Secretary of the National Art Collections Fund, Keeper of the Department of Furniture at the V&A, and Curator of Sir John Soane's Museum.

but a certain amount of seclusion was also welcome. 'You always hear good music somewhere in the College . . . It really is quite a characteristic thing as one sits and works in the evenings. The gates are closed, no disturbance possible, except if students have an uproarious party with girls, which also happens.' Once the university term was over, however, the ambience was less lively and the incentive to work alone in his room was weaker. 'It is bloody quiet here and the work is an Everest. So – oh, I'm going home at 7 p.m. Don't despise me – I've got plenty of work at home as well, only it is more *gemütlich* [cosy].'

As often as not, these letters were directed to the Snowhill cottage. Lola was spending more and more time there now, and she had a life of her own in the country. But to some extent she was excluded from Pevsner's Cambridge existence as effectively as she had been excluded from his life in Huyton, and she may have resented it in the same way. She had, besides, another and more pressing reason for grievance, for Pevsner had embarked on the latest and perhaps most embarrassing of the infatuations which continued to punctuate their married life. Within a very short time of arriving in Cambridge in 1949, he had been smitten by one of his pupils, a young German girl called Lore.

Once again, this was an unrequited ardour with no consummation and, in truth, very little real substance. In Lore he seems to have seen almost exactly what he had originally seen in the fifteen-year-old Lola: an embodiment of *die Harmlose* – perceived inexperience, innocence, relative intellectual immaturity, a lack of self-consciousness, fresh looks and liveliness. These were characteristics he found both attractive in themselves and comforting in the way they made him feel: tender, protective, sympathetic, capable. The writer Isabel Quigly once asked him what he looked for in a secretary; he replied simply, 'a friendly girl'.[10] It was this uncomplicated warmth that he had missed when he first came to England on his own, and the kind of company he had longed for in his chilly lodgings in Edgbaston. Now, fifteen years after Birmingham, thirty-five years after first love in Leipzig, he may not only have been responding to the discovery of these qualities in a new *Harmlose*, but also trying to recapture an earlier self.

Pevsner may have been able to excuse this episode to himself as a romantic indulgence. Less forgiving, Bertschy Grigson had no hesitation in attributing it to the male menopause. Close to Lola during this period, Bertschy saw how much she minded, and how much Pevsner's distraction was increasing the distance between the two of them, already lengthening as he got busier. 'Why don't you allow me some freedom?' he complained, displaying some of the impatience that is not unusual in a middle-aged marriage. Lola had changed very little from the person he had courted; but there were qualities she was never going to possess, and he was at a time of life when he may have felt he might not have another chance to find what she could not give him.

Lola would never lose her energy or her interest in other people, which Pevsner regarded with a mixture of admiration and exasperation. Her willingness to engage in other people's lives dragged him in too, and her dynamism was not restful. In many ways she remained conservative. She never changed her hairstyle, or her tastes; she liked music up to Beethoven, but not much after that; and classical literature up to Tolstoy and Balzac, but little modern writing, which seemed to her to question all true values. In other regards, however, her lack of conventionality could be embarrassing. She had a tendency to speak her mind as a point of principle and a matter of course. Unsurprisingly, in constrained English circles she often felt that she was saying the wrong thing, and was more at ease with other nonconformists. She was far more physically demonstrative than Pevsner, always waiting to rush and hug him when he came in, and entirely unselfconscious in her bearing, lying flat on her stomach to read or sitting cross-legged on the floor to write letters.

Nevertheless, it was hardly a sunny and uncomplicated nature. 'She was a pessimist,' Pevsner wrote later in his memoir of her, 'always wanting to know the worst so that it should not come as a shock . . . This pessimism may have reflected a fright of life, but it was in my opinion much rather realism.' She had lost her mother early, been troubled by her father's subsequent relationships and made forlorn by his death, and had been forced to leave home and homeland to find herself in a society where she would never feel entirely comfortable. After the death of Pevsner's Aunt Sonya, who had lived with them for years, she was sometimes lonely and felt that she was no longer needed.

'The true index of a man's character,' wrote Cyril Connolly, 'is the health of his wife.' Lola was still afflicted with stomach ulcers, which provoked in Pevsner a mixture of compassion, guilt and irritation at being made to feel guilty. The straightforwardness that had once charmed him now sometimes grated. 'She was most certainly not sentimental in the sense of Jane Austen's sensibility,' he wrote. 'Her sturdy legs were standing too firmly on the ground.' Whether or not this was meant as a compliment, it is not one that would have cheered many middle-aged women, nor would Lola – never one to enjoy looking in the mirror – have been much comforted by the assurance that he found her 'fine and remarkable-looking', when she knew that the alternative attraction was young and pretty.

Lore, like Lise before her, was also part of Pevsner's academic milieu,

457

and Lola had never outgrown her feelings of intellectual inferiority. She would always be afraid that her husband had a particular fondness for clever women and that she would always fall short. 'She doubted the wisdom of schooling beyond 15 or 16,' Pevsner observed, 'and altogether of raising the respect for academic achievements above that for practical achievements' – partly in principle, but partly also, no doubt, because she had become accustomed to underrating her own academic attainments. Years later, after her death, Pevsner marked on a wedding-service sheet some lines in one of the hymns, 'Come Down, O Love Divine':

> True lowliness of heart,
> Which takes the humbler part,
> And on its own shortcomings weeps with loathing.

Lola had the uncomfortable combination of a strong personality and a capacity for self-effacement, which would sometimes result in the worst possible outcome of making a sacrifice but resenting it bitterly. From the beginning of her marriage to Pevsner she had indeed given up much for him, and was inclined to remind him of it. She often wished she had gone to university, which might have enabled her in the end to earn an independent income. As a young mother, she had been left on her own at regular intervals while he spent his summers in Italy – one of her principal complaints to her father during the difficult period after Pevsner's first passing fancy for her friend Margot. Again, during the war she had struggled with the burden of running the house – hard but essentially thankless labour – while even in the internment camp he had continued his upward climb doing the work that he loved more than anything else. Lola had an ingrained respect for authority and wanted to respect her husband; it seemed, with these undignified infatuations, as if he was doing everything he could to make respect impossible.

Divining what precisely happened with Lore is difficult. Once again, the 'affair' would seem to have been a matter of long-distance admiration, blameless interviews and telephone calls more frequent than was strictly necessary. Dieter Pevsner remembered a faintly ludicrous occasion on which his father stole out of the house in Wildwood Terrace to telephone the girl, only to dial his own home number by mistake. In later years Lore would remember the whole episode with mild enjoyment, puzzled but not offended; but at the time it would seem that Pevsner's attentions became pressing enough for her at least to mention them to her parents, who were not amused. 'And now

– as that is what you are thinking about anyway,' Pevsner wrote somewhat testily to Lola from Cambridge in an undated letter from around 1951:

there have indeed been the most extraordinary developments on the [Lore] . . . front. But please don't be worried and weep – I can tell you, they have left a very bad taste in my mouth . . . Don't make an elephant out of this before you know the details . . . Let me say once more and very seriously that this . . . experience has been a good thing. I am amused and not bothered any longer. I can grin at everybody (including the girl), being terribly helpful and obliging . . . And I can also at last see that my attitude in this whole business is not becoming. I read your letter and feel very much that this is the real thing, and not these shifty emotions of mine. Perhaps I need to be away from you to see things in their true perspective. Being with you, I get over-heated, particularly with the constant opposition. That is unhealthy.

The 'constant opposition' increasingly took the form of quarrels and raised voices. 'Our children, especially Dieter, shook their heads,' Pevsner wrote later. While at heart both seem to have acknowledged that their marriage was 'the real thing', Lola found Pevsner's involvements impossible to ignore or laugh off, and this last one damaged their relationship for several years. He was reluctant to recognise how deep the wounds might have been. She spoke of a reconciliation taking three years; he rejected this as overdramatisation. But he added, 'It is obviously not three weeks either' and wrote in a subsequent letter, 'It is a panicky business, in the end really a question of survival.' In a file that he put together when he was considering an autobiography, long after Lola's death, he accepted how unhappy he had made her. 'I never wanted another wife but Lola. I really was "strictly dishonourable" – but she couldn't understand that idea . . . She beat me, she scratched me. One night she ran out into the Heath in her night-dress to kill herself.'

'Why must everything be so violent with me?' Lola complained. In her fury with him she had fainted and hit her mouth, loosening a tooth. In situations she found desperate, hitting him was the only real recourse she had, because she could not always express what she felt, whereas Pevsner could justify, argue and consistently worst her. 'She was not a fighter with the word and . . . when I argued and nagged, she might explode. In fact, the first time ever she threw things at me or beat me with her fists was on just such an occasion . . . It was all

459

part of her being a natural phenomenon, not cowed by civilisation.'
But she never used the weapon she knew would hurt him most:

> Lola could not be vicious . . . In her worst rage over my faithless-
> ness she went just far enough to destroy some of my day-to-day
> 'little books' [work diaries], because in some cases they would mark
> engagements [with Lore], but she did not touch my work, which
> she could so easily have done. She could have thrown away, burnt,
> say, the preparations for a volume of the *Buildings of England* – for
> we were then already travelling – but this would never have occurred
> to her. She did not even – and this really borders on the super-human
> – destroy any of the *Hefte*. . . She respected, even in that state of
> fury and despair, my property.

Even when relations were at their coolest, Pevsner acknowledged how
remarkable this restraint was, given the depth of Lola's hatred for the
Heftchen, which by this time she had clearly read at least in part. 'She
insists that the reading of the Heftchen has killed something in her.'[11]

'It frightens me quite often now what bad use we make of our life
together,' he wrote sadly to her early in the 1950s. She continued to
take holidays away from him, as she had always done – she took the
children to visit Marianne in Germany in August 1950, for example –
and at this point she preferred living in the cottage in Wiltshire to
living in London. Pevsner was aware that he needed to make amends,
for her sake and for his own self-respect, but his letters home are a
mixture of penitence, shame and resentment. His aim was 'to restore
the feelings of decency in me and contentment in you that will make
a proper life together possible once more'. 'This must happen,' he
wrote, 'but it's hard to be a decent character.'

His tone is almost jocular, but with an edge of grievance. 'You said,
Don't have a good time. I'm not.' 'I have *not* bought sherry and glasses,
because of what you would think it would imply.'

> I feel like a bat or an owl, fidgety in the fine weather . . . I feel aged,
> aged, aged. Well – you'll enjoy that . . . There were Madrigals last
> night in the Backs and Monteverdi's Vespers are in King's College
> Chapel tonight. It would have been sad, but I might have gone.
> However, I know pretty certainly that the late girl friend might have
> sung in the one and might be present at the other. So I cut that out
> and read Proust instead – not a real substitute . . . The weekend is
> over and the girl has not called. So that was the last tight corner
> till the autumn.

'Don't worry about me. I stick to my private New Deal. Yours (really),' he concluded one letter. He would always be closer to Lola than to anyone else, and it was in Lola that he confided his feelings about his infatuations, despite her being the person least likely to want to hear about them. But he was still inclined to see her as partly to blame for his behaviour through her constant criticisms. He seemed rather to expect her forgiveness as a right, and was frustrated and annoyed when it took a considerable time. She was now suspicious of everyone he met, and was still not thoroughly appeased in the summer of 1952 when she would seem to have spent a short time in hospital, possibly having collapsed from over-work.*

'Tomorrow it will be 32 years since we got engaged,' he wrote to her in her hospital ward from Wildwood Terrace:

Do you remember the iron door at the entrance of Sebastian Bach Street? . . . It's not good being alone. I miss your presence, even if we quarrel more than we should . . . Can you never forget your suspicion? . . . I do feel rather desperate about this afternoon. There we are all longing to have you back, all with the warmest feelings and wishes, and you lie and weep. Weep over everything, large and small, important and trivial, sad and not a bit sad . . . Can't you forgive? I give you no reason to complain now. I am just waiting for you to be ready to accept me again, and all will be well.

In 1953 he was still writing to Lola, 'Try to like me.' Alone in Wildwood Terrace, he wrote, 'It's lonely and not *gemütlich*. But that helps in the grim mopping up of work . . . I could always do with more time than I have. I loathe myself.'

---

*Somewhat bitterly, he marked one letter of June 1953 'from Office (oh no, at the Ritz with a Windmill girl)'.

CHAPTER 30

'The grim mopping up of work'

In an interesting choice of priorities, Pevsner would appear on his passport in 1956 as 'university teacher'. Cambridge had provided imposing surroundings for his teaching, but this label was just as much a reference to his work at Birkbeck. The college had now moved from its home in Breams Buildings to a large block designed by Charles Holden between Malet Street and Woburn Square. He had no illusions about Birkbeck's lack of glamour – either intellectual or physical. The window to his room sat in a wall that could only be described as 'depressing', he wrote, and 'the interior architecture of the college, if you ask me, lacks dignity . . . The refectory is a canteen, the JCR a kind of day-room . . . and the entrance hall a lobby.'[1]

But, never one to rate aesthetic over moral values, Pevsner had great respect for Birkbeck's philosophy, and he would remain loyal to the college. Between 1952 and 1959 he offered his thoughts on an ever-widening range of topics, including Rabelais, 'the architectural setting of Jane Austen', and a scathing attack on the arrogance, parochialism, moralising, exaggeration and contradiction in the writings of Ruskin. Over at the Courtauld Institute, where he continued as an external examiner, his hand is also apparent in many of the (leading) questions faced by the candidates. 'Which do you consider to have been the more influential artist, Manet or William Morris?' 'Do you consider Art Nouveau a blind alley or a stage on the high road to the 20th century?' 'Discuss the reaction of England to the International Modern Movement style in architecture down to 1939', 'Analyse the spread of "Caravaggism" outside Italy'.

It was not unusual for him to return to the office after his Wednesday evening's teaching and a session with the students in the pub before setting off on the four-mile walk uphill to Hampstead. Even then his day might not be over, with essays to be read and papers to be marked, to the disgust of a family pet of this period, which was something of a bully. 'Doormat made me a scene when I finished 6 exam papers at 12 and would not let me sleep until 1.' Occasionally he made half-hearted efforts to cut down his workload, but these were rarely successful. He had tried, for instance, to shed the image of an authority on modern design, but found it difficult to let go completely, as Michael Farr found to his cost when he took on the task of producing a new edition of the *Enquiry into Industrial Art in England*.

Farr, besides having attended Pevsner's Cambridge lectures, had a good war record and an informed interest in modern design, and his wife Daphne was Pevsner's secretary at the *Architectural Review*. Pevsner had had no interest in revising the *Enquiry* himself. He liked and respected Farr, and at the outset happily handed over his original research, plus new material that he had accumulated in the meantime, with the intention of doing no more than 'supervising' the project. There was much new ground to cover – literally new ground, in the sense that the new survey reached far beyond the Midlands, where Pevsner's original researches had been concentrated – but also new materials, new products like refrigerators and televisions and, with the rise of the design consultant, new players in the design field. This Pevsner would have expected; but Farr also had new and different interests and priorities. Much younger, he was also much more interested in the technological side of design, and more austere in his insistence on precision and design principles – and Pevsner could not let this pass without comment. When the new work appeared, published in 1955 as *Design in British Industry: A Mid-Century Survey* (Cambridge University Press), it had not only a Pevsner foreword but also a Pevsner postscript.

In his incursions, Pevsner took the chance to argue with his former self. 'I was wrong in 1935 to think that a conspiracy of manufacturers was responsible for the garden gate with slats in the form of the rays of the rising sun . . . All these objects of fancy have their *raison d'être* . . . We have grown less stern and exacting.' He also took unfair advantage of having the last word, using the postscript not to supplement but to review what Farr had done, his tone that of a tutor marking an undergraduate essay. 'That a teapot should "represent a creative revaluation of the possibilities of the materials and techniques at the designer's disposal" takes us nowhere,' he wrote with a sideswipe at Farr's more sententious writing style and occasional lapses into jargon. Can a teapot, he queried, really make other teapots 'less relevant to contemporary artistic needs'?

Farr, however, was forgiving of the condescension. He understood that Pevsner's design tastes were unashamedly dated. Pevsner had attachments to particular shapes and styles, just as he had loyalties to theories and trains of thought, and he tended to cling to them. 'When Rover had the nerve to change their model shapes from the 1937, which was a car he liked,' Farr remembered, 'he got terribly upset and wouldn't buy it, because it had become too long. He liked a traditional Rover with a running board, that was his car.'

This forbearance was rooted in real affection. However tart Pevsner might have been in print, in Farr's experience he was invariably tolerant and kind in person. 'He was always decidedly interested in you – no matter what you were . . . You hadn't got to bone up on Chichester Cathedral in order to hold your own at the dinner table. He wouldn't catch you out . . . He loved gossip. "Oh, tell me what's going on . . . at the *Architectural Review*, or COID [Council of Industrial Design], I want to know everything".' Lola too was a close friend, and godmother to one of the Farrs' children. The Farrs lived nearby in Hampstead Garden Suburb, and Lola visited often. 'She used to buzz round the Garden Suburb with her moped, park it outside. "Daaphne!!" – and then she would come in through the door with this or that, something she'd picked up at a delicatessen, they'd talk, and she'd fly away again.'[2]

If Pevsner's interest in contemporary design was waning in the early 1950s, another enthusiasm was definitely on the rise. His increasing tolerance of 'fancy' in current popular taste ran alongside a growing fascination – part fond, part appalled – with Victorian art, architecture and design: the 'rogues' as well as the 'pioneers'. In 1951, on the centenary of the Great Exhibition of 1851, the Architectural Press had published his short monograph on *High Victorian Design*. At a time when Victorian art and design were still deeply unfashionable, this was, like *Pioneers*, a piece of writing that helped set the framework for future study.

In *High Victorian Design* Pevsner compared the courage and originality that went into the building of the Crystal Palace itself with the often regrettable vigour and ingenuity invested in the manufacture of its contents. He saw the building and the exhibits equally as products of their age, characterised like the age by energy, tenacity, technical daring, faith in commerce and industry and a thirst for information. Looking at that list of qualities – energy, tenacity, a thirst for information – it is perhaps not hard to see why Pevsner had more than a sneaking sympathy with the Victorian makers, however aesthetically lamentable the results of their endeavours might often have been. Prince Albert in particular, the Great Exhibition's champion, is a figure with whom Pevsner may have felt he had much in common. 'When Prince Albert went to open the new Grimsby Docks,' he commented, '[Henry] Cole arranged some entertainment for him in his special train. This is what it was: John Britton's *Lincoln Cathedral*, John Britton's *Peterborough Cathedral*, a plan of Lincoln, a plan of Roman Lincoln,

Sidney on Agriculture and Railways, a portfolio of Dürer woodcuts and a case of geological specimens and fossils. With all due respect to the present Royal family one cannot but assume that the choice in 1951 would have been different.' Hardly surprising then that Pevsner's 'conducted tour' of some of the exhibits in the Great Exhibition, wonderfully illuminated with illustrations from the original catalogue and contemporary journals, is itself full of vitality and enjoyment even when he is disapproving.

His explanation for the vagaries of Victorian taste was essentially the same as it had been when he wrote *Pioneers*. The 'big men with the heavy purses' were not the cultivated land-owning patrons of the past, but manufacturers, mill-owners and money-men:

> No education and no leisure, these two deficiencies explain nearly all that is aesthetically distressing about 1851. The appreciation of aesthetic values in architecture and design, of proportions, textures, harmonies of colours, requires training and time. The appreciation of the emotional values in painting and sculpture also requires a readiness to listen, to follow a lead and be captured, and this cannot be expected in one whose mind is occupied with machine and counting-house. Thus effects were bound to become louder and more obvious. A bulgy curve will be taken in more easily than a delicate one, richly glowing colours than subtle shades, and stories carved in relievo than sheer satisfying proportions.

Pevsner was of course not the first to attribute the crassness of some Victorian artefacts to the vulgarity of the people who made up their market. Some ten years earlier John Betjeman, for example, had attacked Victorian taste in his essay on 'British Industrial Art'. 'Commerce put its smelly paw on the objects of the Great Exhibition,' he wrote, though it was the 1873 and 1875 exhibitions at Alexandra Palace that were 'the high water mark of good old Victorian commercial vulgarity . . . The hideousness of the exhibits there was downright, like the dropped h of a cockney magnate.' Pevsner's essay, however, is lacking the aggression of Betjeman's. He singles out many of the faults for which High Victorian design had long been condemned – mawkishness, impracticality, slavish period imitation, and the uneasy combination of prudery and prurience – and seems to revel in them. Figurines of slumbering dogs and children, bread knives with handles in the shape of corn cobs, curtain hooks in the shape of fuchsias and anemones: all are carefully illustrated and described with a mixture of affection and pity.

As for prurience, Pevsner was openly intrigued by the Victorians' 'remarkable tendency to half-concealed impropriety'. John Bell's figurine *Dorothea* portrayed Dorothea disturbed by Don Quixote and Sancho Panza while washing her feet. 'The state of her dress gives her every reason for being embarrassed. Yet we can really see only very little more than even a Victorian bathing costume would have exposed. But what we see is given us highly realistically . . . *Dorothea* is the most convincing symbol of that bad conscience of the High Victorians which is wholly suppressed in the novels of the period but rampant in sculpture.'

The Victorian fondness for narrative was sometimes to be found in unlikely places. A papier-mâché easy chair entitled 'The Daydreamer' was 'decorated at the top with two winged thoughts – the one with birdlike pinions and crowned with roses, representing happy and joyous dreams, the other with leather bat-like wings, unpleasant and troubled ones. Behind is displayed Hope, under the figure of the rising sun . . . at the side is seen a figure of Puck.' 'There must have been a great need for the interesting story among the public to account for this,' remarked Pevsner with restraint.

Without a doubt, he was amused by individual examples of the Victorians' misplaced ingenuity, otherwise he would hardly have devoted space to 'steamship furniture convertible into a raft', or an alarm bedstead 'causing a person to arise at any given hour'. But what he had in common with Betjeman, without ever having discussed the matter with him, was a willingness to take Victorian design itself seriously as a reflection of its age. Nor were Pevsner and Betjeman lone voices by 1951. (To take just one instance, at the Victoria and Albert Museum Peter Floud was working towards an exhibition of Victorian and Edwardian decorative arts which in 1952 would do much on its own to revolutionise attitudes towards Victorian design.) But what Pevsner could do was lend the developing Victorian appreciation movement some of his newly acquired *gravitas*.

On another front he might have been perceived as receding from the vanguard as the 1950s progressed. When it came to writing about contemporary architecture, he was now quite ready to give way to younger and more passionately opinionated men.

Ian Nairn, a young journalist recently released from National Service in the RAF, had talked the *Architectural Review* into giving him a job. Brought up in the green-belt county of Surrey, he was driven by his distaste for the growth of what he labelled 'Subtopia', the lazy and hideous new development around the fringes of urban areas which simultaneously defaced both town and countryside while blurring the distinction between them. Peacetime planners were busy compounding the damage done by war. To the blight of bombed buildings, barbed wire and derelict army camps were being added concrete lamp stand-ards, superfluous roundabouts stuffed with lobelias and marigolds, intrusive advertising hoardings and a plague of signs and bollards – what Nairn called 'a bumbling chaotic dribble of objects, dumped down without thought and without love'. One entire number of the *Review* in 1955 was given over to a full-blown attack by Nairn on Subtopia entitled 'Outrage'.* 'Be cruel to dogs and children and you end up in court,' Nairn fumed. 'Be cruel to the environment, and the relevant committee will most probably commend a "valuable amenity".'³

Pevsner admired Nairn's journalistic skill, the force of his conviction and the edge that he gave to the *Review*'s sometimes genteel campaigns. A tantalising fragment of a letter refers to 'unavoidable lunch at the House of Commons with Nigel Nicolson and Harold Nicholson [*sic*], an ill-at-ease old clergyman hard to be accounted for, and . . . Ian Nairn – all à propos a debate on the Archi's "Outrage" number – a most depressing debate carried on before some twenty members at lunch time.' On the other hand, Pevsner was not always comfortable with Nairn's lack of inhibition. There was a blokeyness to him that was not Pevsner's style, as one reviewer would acidly observe: '[Nairn] is at home with the boys round the NAAFI piano – words like "dogshit" and "horse piss" spice his text – and of course in any "good cockney pub" with *real* people.'⁴

Nairn was not the only disruptive force at work within the *Archi-tectural Review*, but the other irritant to arrive in the early 1950s was a man who would be both a scourge and a fierce champion of Pevsner for the rest of his life. Reyner Banham was almost certainly introduced to the *Review* by Jim Richards, but he was already familiar to Pevsner as one of his more combative postgraduate students from the Courtauld Institute. Bearded and belligerent, Banham had served an engineering apprenticeship in the Bristol aircraft industry during the war before becoming an art journalist, and his passion was the role of technology in modern society. But Pevsner's writings had helped draw him towards the history of art. He had once missed a bus, he told Pevsner, because standing in the queue he had been wholly absorbed in reading *An Outline of European Architecture*. It is typical of both men that when

---

*The 'Outrage' articles were later gathered together and published as a book under the same title.

Banham's thesis, supervised by Pevsner, eventually emerged in 1958 (to be published two years later as *Theory and Design in the First Machine Age*), it contained a vigorous attack on Pevsner.

Though Banham was impressed by the clarity of Pevsner's exposition of the evolution of modernism – 'It was a nice, tidy propagandist's firmament, ordered by a cosmology so simple as to be almost simple-minded' – there were many points where he radically departed from the man he would eventually call his *lieber Meister*.[5] His immediate target was Pevsner's failure to appreciate the Machine Age. *Pioneers*, Banham felt, had merely paid lip service to a 'machine aesthetic', admiring machines on a superficial symbolic and stylistic level without at any stage truly appreciating them for themselves.[6] In consequence, crucial movements such as Futurism had effectively been excluded from Pevsner's history of modernism 'as if they had been madmen in the family who needed to be kept away from the gaze of the public'.[7] In addition, where Pevsner did write about technology he looked at it in terms of conventional aesthetics rather than on its own, fundamentally new terms and never managed to bring it alive or celebrate its true importance, deterred by the brashness of some of its manifestations.

Banham's great gift was to combine academic rigour with an open mind and a sharp eye for the new. 'The real force of his writing,' comments one observer, 'comes from his capacity to slide back and forth between high art and popular culture, architecture and engineering, aesthetic issues and technical concerns, scholarship and journalism . . . Pop references are inserted into the academic work and scholarly details are tossed into the journalism.'[8] He was a lifelong lover of America, and must have been profoundly irritated during this period by Pevsner's pronouncements on transatlantic philistinism. 'Overdoing is a common sin of the young and the naïve, and the Americans are both.' 'That sort of noisy show comes off in the United States where it is at least in accordance with people. It is extremely un-British, indeed un-European.'[9]

For his part, Pevsner was quite content at this stage to abet the younger man in his questioning of modernist orthodoxies. He found Banham's ideas challenging, if not always convincing, and was entertained by the exuberance and the intellectual ferocity. When they clashed in a public debate some years later, Pevsner remarked, 'This is a memorable evening from the point of view of news value. For Banham bites man has a limited news value, but man bites Banham has a lot.'[10]

Pevsner's involvement in all these different fields – Birkbeck, modern design, Victorian studies, contemporary building – had to be fitted into a schedule increasingly dislocated by travel. In the early 1950s he was travelling regularly for the *Buildings of England* – through Cambridgeshire, Hertfordshire, Derbyshire, County Durham, Essex. More and more, too, he was being invited abroad, so frequently in fact that he rationed himself to a single break from his teaching in any one term and only one major work trip per year. Refusing an invitation from the British Council to visit Bonn for a fortnight, he wrote, 'I am a hired servant – that is, an employee of Penguin Books and tied to my Penguin duties apart from my academic duties to such an extent that I cannot afford more than one such journey every year.'[11]

The single annual journeys, however, were getting more glamorous. In 1952 a 'peace-offering' trip aimed at healing the rift with Lola had taken them to South Africa, and given Pevsner his first taste of celebrity. Writing to the children from Cape Town, Lola exclaimed, 'Vati was pestered by the press and had to utter opinions about town planning and preservation of old buildings etc etc.' Broadcasts, lectures and seminars with students were interspersed with interviews, book signings and photographs. 'Does it flatter?' wrote Pevsner. 'Yes, but in my heart I am ashamed of it.' 'Even I had to give my views on Johannesburg,' added Lola, 'so you see, life is absolutely crazy . . . absolutely grand. Vati is feasted like a filmstar and his photo (and even a horrible one of mine) is in the paper every second day.'

'I behave a mixture of little grey mouse and dignified elderly lady,' she claimed; but in fact she was revelling both in the break from housework and in being publicly included in Pevsner's professional life. She carefully recorded the social whirl – visits to a gold mine and a native kraal, a somewhat improbable private showing of *Nanook of the North*, and an artist's studio where the model, stark naked, turned to Pevsner and said, 'I wonder if you knew my uncle at Trinity College.' 'We never have a normal evening,' wrote Lola happily. 'We have heard Schönberg and Bartock [*sic*], we have seen a night of Bantu singing and dancing, which gave me more pleasure than our western music, because of the slow and simple acting, and the wild and dynamic dancing. There will be a) a ladies' tea party, b) a reception, c) Anouilh's Antigone. What a life!' The political situation in the South Africa of the early 1950s, four years after the introduction of apartheid, passed virtually without comment, though Pevsner would write later, 'she saw that a man a vote in a country with so much illiteracy and so many primeval beliefs and prejudices was not an acceptable principle'. Whether this was more a reflection of his own beliefs than Lola's is unclear.

Pevsner had even fewer 'normal evenings' when he travelled without her to America in the summer of 1953, to journey from coast to coast

469

on his way to a conference on modern design in Aspen, Colorado. It was perhaps symbolic that when he landed at La Guardia airport outside New York, he was desperately trying to read P.G. Wodehouse amidst the hubbub of 'Americans talking uproariously all round'. At first he contrived to insulate himself by staying with Paul Frankl, former Professor of Art History in the Saxon town of Halle, now teaching at the Institute for Advanced Study in Princeton. Frankl, an older pupil of Heinrich Wölfflin, had produced a volume for the *Handbuch der Kunstwissenschaft* on the Romanesque style, minutely classifying its characteristics and the various stages in its evolution. Aware that Frankl wished to extend his elaborate system of categorisation to the Gothic era, six years previously Pevsner had commissioned from him a volume on Gothic architecture for the *Pelican History of Art*. He may have been hoping to discuss the progress of the work; but he was also aware that Frankl worked on a monumental scale with fanatical care, and was not to be hurried.*

After this brief period of European sanctuary, Pevsner was obliged to strike out across America to do business for Penguin in the Midwest. By the time he reached Colorado, he was hot, tired and censorious. 'You buy a local newspaper and the main headline is: Bobo Rockefeller outsmarts husband.' 'Conspicuous waste all round. Everything in cellophane, everything iced. So much to be thrown away after us. At La Guardia a machine in a cabin where you can take your own photo for 1/9. I am now longing for London and rain and Northumberland and rain. I am sitting in my room in underpants and nothing else . . . I bought *The Return of the Native* in the drug store . . . but I'm so exhausted I don't even want to read.'

Nor was the Aspen conference likely, on the face of it, to make him soften towards the American way of life. 'Weird and stimulating', he would call it later; but on first acquaintance it was the weirdness that prevailed. The conference was intended to foster enlightened business leadership by providing a forum where industrialists 'could recapture the abiding values that give our culture intellectual and spiritual substance'. That year its topic was 'Design as a Function of Management' – an investigation into the social responsibilities of design, which ought surely to have appealed to the author of the *Enquiry into Industrial Art*. But to an already weary Pevsner the festival atmosphere – 'a Babel of designers of different nationalities' – was at first simply too much, a pungent mix of earnestness and posturing, brashness and

---

*Having spent fifteen years on the writing, Frankl died in 1962, the day after receiving proofs of the illustrations, and the volume was published posthumously.

sophistication, energy and disorder. 'To lecture to such people for a week is going to be a heavy price for the scenery,' he told Lola. 'They are all such weird animals and much of it so phoney.'

The weather was sunny, but he was too inhibited to disrobe and use the hotel swimming pool, and indoors social life was a challenge. 'The evenings will be trying unless I find that one can talk shop and problems. Last night I slipped away at 10.45.' One way out was to take refuge with those who had come as spectators rather than participants:

> The women either thoroughly made up, or, thank God, the homely type with ample bosoms, and very naïve, friendly talk. And those I sit with? 'I have two grandchildren.' 'Oh, isn't that nice! I have two myself.' 'I have eight,' etc etc . . . Oh Lolchen, the evening was what they call a night club. Basement, band, and noise, noise, noise . . . Fortunately I could at the very end sit for a moment next to Perasutti [sic],* a brilliant architect but an earnest Italian, and we could speak Italian and not be understood . . . *Pericolo per la civilisazione europea . . .*'

The moment of his own lecture was approaching, and he was apprehensive. From manuscript notes that survive in his papers it would seem that he had decided to take advantage of his distance from home and experiment with a more unbuttoned style ('you guys') and ideas that he might have hesitated to air before an audience familiar with *Enquiry* and *Pioneers*.[12] 'I have no creative genius whatever,' he began. 'My main job in life is to try to teach young people to recognise and analyse values in art (mostly old art).' His mission here, however, was to tackle major fallacies in the usual discussions on industrial design. Revealingly, the seven 'fallacies' that he lists include several of his own earlier beliefs about design:

> *'Better design means better sales'*
> *'If people got the chance to see better design, they would*
>   *like it'*
> *'Nakedness is the only virtue'*
> *'Don't deny or combat national character'*
> *'Political prosperity creates great art'*
> *'Democracy is good for the future of art'*
> *'Change of heart won't come'*.

---

*Pevsner must have been referring to Enrico Peressutti (1908–75) of the Milan firm Banfi, Belgiojoso, Peressutti and Rogers.

The notes are frustratingly skeletal, and it is harder to guess what he might have said under some of these headings than others. By 'nakedness', he was referring to the lack of ornament which, as 'an old fogey of the 1930s', he personally preferred but was no longer keen to impose on others. On the subject of art and democracy, he had obviously decided to be more provocative than he might have risked being at home. 'Dictatorship can be much better – depending on the dictator,' he had scrawled, though the names of Hitler, Mussolini and Stalin were scribbled out, leaving that of Frank Pick, 'with the power but not the mentality of a dictator'.

His remaining task was to work with a class of twenty to thirty boys to prepare a public discussion:

> To make a decent show I have to prime them thoroughly. It may take hours . . . It did. I retired at 12.45 a.m. . . . I force these students to write out their statements this morning so that I can see them. They . . . want first of all to change the world. The annoying thing is that McCarthy looms large, and other students are frightened. No policy, no left-wing stuff, etc. . . . The afternoon with the students went off all right. They read their statements . . . more helpless in style and spelling than was good for them. But the audience was kind, the seven students who spoke had worked hard . . . and were in the end pleased with themselves.*

Pevsner too was pleased and touched to be treated at last as part of the Aspen community. 'They presented me in the end,' he boasted to Lola, 'with the loudest shirt they had been able to find in the town' – a reference to his animadversions on American leisurewear. (In his lecture, he had flattered American daring and energy in design as compared with Britain's lack of enterprise: 'You could not imagine English designers in wildly patterned shirts, could you?') He allowed himself occasionally to enjoy novelties rather than shying away – a fish-fry by the lake, a visit to a husky farm, a shopping expedition to find a cowgirl outfit for a small child – but a protracted absurdist 'happening' exasperated him.† 'It called itself a Spectrodrama,' he wrote crossly. 'It was a sad memory of the wild twenties, of Schwitters

---

*Joseph McCarthy, Republican Senator for Wisconsin, had started his communist witch-hunt in February 1950. When Pevsner was in the United States, McCarthy was launching regular investigations into senior figures in government, the armed forces and other agencies.
†It was staged by Alexander/Xanti Schawinski (1904–79), a Swiss Bauhaus student who had settled in America in the 1930s.

and Schlemmer, and the audience was in suppressed convulsive and hysterical laughter. It was enough to compromise the conference.' Nor was he excited by Buckminster Fuller or the geodesic dome that his disciples had erected. 'Phony,' he said tersely of the dome, and Fuller he described as 'a bit of a medicine man, with an excessively obscure literary style. I daresay it is scientific, but I can never understand it precisely.' 'Bucky Fuller last night talked for 2¾ hours with slides,' he told Lola. 'I slept in the middle.'

Charles Eames, on the other hand, he found charming, and he was fascinated by two experimental films that Eames had made with his designer wife Ray:

> One was simply the play-yard of a school they can see from their windows. It is hosed once a week, and all the film does in fifteen minutes or so is to show what the water does – drops, rills, streams, meandering, running, separating and uniting, forming drops or wavelets, and in the absence of anything to give scale looking now like the wide ocean, now like the patterns on microscope photos. Another short film (in colour) was on bread, just wandering over the surfaces of loaves and rolls, and closely watching the breaking or the slicing of bread. It had the same sense of an eye adventure. These things, I think, are extremely valuable in an age of visual atrophy.

In a more tolerant frame of mind, he was even able to weather the concluding Dance and Masquerade, which he had been dreading since the moment he arrived. 'My costume is my Smoking/dinner jacket and the shirt the students gave me. The dinner jacket is of course a joke here. Everyone I've shown it to laughs and finds it fearfully comic.'

By now, Pevsner was on the British Council's list of eminent lecturers, and under the Council's auspices he made his first visits to many buildings he had already often described to others. His visit to Greece and Turkey in 1955 required special permission from the military authorities, coinciding as it did with the continuing guerrilla campaign to drive the British out of Cyprus. Pevsner's lecture at the Polytechnic in Athens was closed to students, 'as their behaviour was unpredictable at present', and the reception for him could not be held at the British Council's offices for fear that it would be boycotted by Greek officials, but he described the visit to his host as '*ein grosses Erlebnis* [a tremendous experience] . . . we shall never cease to be grateful to you for

it.'[13] In Turkey he landed in some trouble when he baulked at incorporating – for 'diplomatic reasons' – the great sixteenth-century Turkish
architect Sinan in a lecture in Istanbul on Christopher Wren. Pevsner
was vaguely aware of Sinan's influence on Wren's pupil Hawksmoor,
but 'I am really very worried about the idea of putting Sinan into the
title of the lecture,' he protested to the British Council. 'I don't think it
would be fair on any scholar to force him to pretend (a) that he knows
about a subject he doesn't and (b) that he is going to talk about a subject
he isn't going to talk about.'[14] Nevertheless, 'Istanbul was certainly the
greatest architectural impression I have had for many years and I don't
expect another of the same intensity for many years to come.'[15]

In 1953 he went back to East Germany, at the behest of the Foreign
Office and with a Russian visa secured through diplomatic channels.
What his official mission was is unclear. But he also used the opportunity to go looking in Leipzig for traces of his family and his former
life – family graves, and the gap at 69 Brühl where the furrier's firm
and his father's office had been. It would probably be exaggerating to
describe this as an awakening of interest in his Jewish roots; but the
journey was inspired at least in part by an enquiry from John Henry
Richter, a distant relation on his mother's side. Richter, a librarian at
the University of Michigan at Ann Arbor, was bent on tracing the
descendants of Aron Neisser, and in a brief family memoir that Pevsner
wrote for his children at around this time, he made a point of drawing
their attention to their heritage.*

His own family life during these busy years sometimes seemed as
if it had been crowded out by the 'grim mopping up of work'. In a
talk on William Morris at the RIBA in 1957, he would quote some
sentences on Morris from Wilfrid Scawen Blunt, which might equally
have been applied to himself on occasion. 'I have seen him tender to
his daughter . . . and nice with her and his wife but . . . his life was
not arranged in reference to them. To the rest of the world he seemed
quite indifferent . . . The truth is he would not give up an hour of his
time to anyone, he held it to be too valuable.'

The children, of course, were no longer children. Uta, having trained
at the Architectural Association as a town planner, had left home and
in 1949 married Ian Hodgson, a young architect who would later
work with Gordon Russell's brother Dick; by 1953 they had made
Pevsner and Lola grandparents twice over, with the births of Josephine
in 1950 and Nicolas in 1953. Tom, to his father's mild disquiet, had
gone into what Pevsner described as 'the film business' and was by

---

*Aron Neisser was a nineteenth-century ancestor of Lola's mother, Paula Neisser.

now an assistant director or second unit director on films such as the classic Ealing comedy *The Ladykillers* (1955) and Stanley Donen's *Indiscreet* (1958), starring Cary Grant and Ingrid Bergman. He was, complained Pevsner, perpetually on the telephone, asleep at peculiar times of the day, or always 'out for a drink'.* The Pevsner children would always, from choice, live very close by, all three of their households eventually ending in Wildwood Terrace or the adjacent Wildwood Grove. This would be a source of enduring happiness to Pevsner; but he was at times perturbed by their more relaxed lifestyles and attitudes to child-rearing and education.

Pevsner was as disapproving of what he saw as sloppiness or disorder as he was suspicious of ostentation. Lola, with what he described as her 'Prussian heritage', had made strict housekeeping an ideology as much as a habit; and while he may have deplored her exhausting herself by insisting on boiling the sheets and scouring the basement kitchen by hand, he was comfortable in the environment she created and he respected the attitude and energy that lay behind her labours.[16] 'The fuse went, all-right, she must repair it,' he wrote in a memoir of Lola after her death:

> The stair carpet is getting bad along the edges of the treads – why should not she shift it? It means shifting yards of it? Yes, it does that. There is not much space in the house, all-right, we must fill the loft in the most economical and accessible way, and she must climb into it every time she needs certain things. A grandfather clock won't work, why should she not try and repair it? (and she did). Shopping is getting out of hand, why not buy an autocycle – and she did, when that was still almost unheard-of among women.

Michael Farr remembered Lola – and her cycle – very well from this time. 'She had a knack of being tireless and relaxed both at the same time . . . engaging in a manner I have struck in no-one else. And, unconsciously, funny too . . . funny on her autocycle . . . which popped and banged at our front gate as she unloaded a present or an invitation.' If she saw someone in need, or a job to be done, she did not hesitate. 'Old Mrs Toker [his Aunt Sonya] with her bad heart,' commented Pevsner, 'lives in a room with the rain coming through the

---

*NP/LP, 3/6/57. Over the next fifteen years Tom would be involved in films like *The Longest Day*, *Topkapi* and *The Night of the Generals*. He was assistant director to Karel Reisz for *Saturday Night and Sunday Morning*, before becoming a producer on six of the James Bond films, most noticeably executive producer for *Goldeneye*, which contains a fleeting reference, as an inside joke, to 'Pevsner Commerzbank GmbH'.

roof. We must take her into our house (and there she lived for years, and there she died). Her [Sonya's] sister Paula must economise and has nowhere to go. "I'll find her a room". She thinks it is too lower middle-class. "How much money has she really got, how much can she spend?"' For one young friend Lola found a flat, while others were helped to move house or nursed through sickness; her Christmas present list ran to more than sixty names.

These qualities of compassion and efficiency were for Pevsner vastly more important than artistic effect. 'The design of a textile or an ashtray can never be too perfect, the design of a room or a whole house can,' he wrote, and he quoted with approval Adolf Loos's story of the Poor Rich Man whose house was designed in its entirety by an architect, making it impossible to move or add anything and turning every additional family gift into a disaster.[17] 'The conflicts here are between beauty and life, or between planning and accident, or between aesthetic values and values of affection.' There was no question that in the Pevsner household the values of affection had won. Theirs was never the 'Home Beautiful' cultivated by some of their fellow art historians. They had paintings and a very few pieces of prized furniture they had brought with them from Germany, but there was little income to spend on anything but essentials. 'I am sure we are not clever with money,' Pevsner had written to Lola in the middle of 1952. 'Where does it all go?' The acute financial anxiety of the first years in England was over; but in the year that they improved the upstairs bathroom, they could not also afford a car.

Pevsner and Lola appear to have shared a small notebook entitled *'Jahr um Jahr'*, listing the addresses that would be useful from one year to the next. It has entries in both handwritings, explaining where to take cast-off clothes (the East End Jewish Scholarship Centre); how to hire 'Uncle Reg', the children's entertainer (this in Pevsner's hand); where to find a craftsman capable of repairing the seat of a rush-bottomed chair; where to write to Donald Wolfit at his country address. There are hints of glamour in bills and menus from London restaurants, a *pensione* in Venice, a small hotel in Cahors, but more evidence of a life geared to run smoothly around work, with cards for plumbers, electricians, carpet cleaners, car services and Universal Aunts.

In a turn of phrase that might have surprised some of Pevsner's professional acquaintances, Esther Simpson remembered him as 'clubbable', a genial man who enjoyed company. In a busy life, he had little patience with the kind of socialising that demanded small talk with strangers, and networking would have been an alien notion to him, but he deliberately made time to see friends. Several of the Pevsners' closest friends were old ones from Germany.

Leopold Worth, for example, Pevsner had known as a medical student in Leipzig: the Worth family often celebrated New Year's Eve at Wildwood Terrace and stayed with the Pevsners at Snowhill. (Pevsner dedicated *The Leaves of Southwell* to Worth, then serving with the British Army in Egypt and Italy, with the words 'To Major L.W., C.M.F. [Central Mediterranean Force], to remind him of the good things on our side of the Alps.')

Nevertheless, Pevsner also liked to entertain the friends he had made in England. In the years after the war when the Isobar was flourishing in the basement of the Isokon flats in Lawn Road, Hampstead, he would sometimes take small groups there for dinner – students, colleagues, neighbours and a range of other people who had little to do with his working life.*

Without necessarily being able to demonstrate it, Pevsner prized friendship very highly. This emerged in a rare public expression of emotion on the early death of Michael Ventris, the architect, Minoan scholar and decipherer of the Linear B script. Ventris, who had been brought up by his mother Dora in a flat in Highpoint 1, the iconic Modern Movement block in Highgate, had become a near neighbour in Hampstead in the early 1950s. He was killed in a car crash in 1956 at the age of thirty-four, and Pevsner paid tribute to him the following year in the course of a lecture to the Royal Institute of British Architects. 'He combined to a degree I have hardly ever found in anyone, scholarly originality with simplicity, directness and a most lovable, sometimes almost embarrassing modesty . . . Only his friends can know how intensely fond one was of him. One could not express it or show it to him, and the regret for that will remain for ever added to one's deep feeling of loss.'[18]

Ventris's deciphering of Linear B had received wide and instant publicity when he forecast it in a radio broadcast in 1952 – a significant choice of medium through which to reach an educated audience. It was a medium in which Pevsner too had been establishing himself since the late 1940s, settling in at the BBC with a recognisable radio personality. This had much to do with the fact that he preferred to speak live when he could, memorising the script for shorter talks and rehearsing in advance rather than going through the mechanics of recording, editing and cutting. His broadcasting voice was higher in pitch than his speaking voice – higher in English than in German – and his delivery rapid: 'one of the fastest

---

*The Isobar was opened in 1937. Remodelled from the block's original communal kitchen by Marcel Breuer and F.R.S. Yorke, it was run from 1939 by Philip Harben, one of the earliest television chefs.

talkers I have heard on radio,' commented the *Beckenham and Penge Advertiser* in the spring of 1954, 'yet one of the most easily followed.' His accent too found favour, at a time when BBC producers were debating the acceptability of other émigré speakers. Ernst Gombrich was difficult to use, one producer commented to another in an internal memo in March 1954, because his Viennese accent was impenetrable, and Erwin Panofsky was doubtful, but 'Pevsner and Edgar Windt [*sic*] . . . do beautifully.'[19]

Tone was another matter. Pevsner had not found it easy to strike the right note in his Forces broadcasts on the Light Programme, rather obviously taking it for granted that servicemen would need instruction in taste. Nor was he invariably comfortable in the more middle-class environment of the Home Service, as revealed by an awkward excursion on to *The Critics*.[20] The format of the programme required each of a panel of critics, chaired by playwright and theatre critic Lionel Hale, to speak for five or six minutes on their own subject – literature, film, theatre, radio, the visual arts. After each had delivered his or her review, there would be a few minutes of impromptu discussion on the same subject by the rest of the panel.

Pevsner had been invited to comment as an architectural historian on Basil Oliver's book *The Renaissance of the English Public House*, and he was eloquent to a degree that would have surprised those who did not see him as much of a reveller. Oliver, architect to Bury St Edmunds town council, had produced a manifesto for the modern pub and, rather to his own surprise, Pevsner found himself totally out of sympathy with it, returning instead to 'the splendid and, I would say as an outsider, overwhelmingly English qualities of the Victorian pub, its rich Cuban mahogany, its bevelled and diamond-cut glass, its grotesque and florid lettering, its robust posters, and its wonderfully absurd old framed prints'. '[Oliver] calls Renaissance what I'd call Decline and Fall,' complained Pevsner, and he berated:

> the many new inns of the motor roadside or the new housing estate, decent, clean places, looking for all the world like post-offices . . . All lettering in Gill Sans and Trajan Roman and no advertisements in any of the public rooms. Well, maybe these new pubs are – and here I'm quoting the Royal Commission on Licensing – 'discouraging to insobriety'. But is that quite what you want a pub to be like? . . . The Pub is a beery place, and in our climate, it must be sheltered, low, cosy – for people to stand close together . . . snugness, not smugness.

So far, so good; but off his own home ground he was far more diffident. He had little to say on the performance of Gilbert and

Sullivan that John Summerson was reviewing; and when it came to discussing an obscure play performed by an all-black cast, he fell almost totally silent, at least avoiding the embarrassing generalisations about 'Negro performers' to which some of the other panellists succumbed. A few years later, when he was asked to appear on *The Critics* again, he had no hesitation in refusing:[21] 'I have seen that I am quite unsuitable.'*

The Third Programme was a more natural home for Pevsner. From its beginnings in the autumn of 1946 its producers were looking for talks to balance the weight of music programming on the new channel. Its job was neither to cater to popular taste nor seek to change it, but to act as a centre of excellence. 'There will be few "hearing-aids" for listeners to the Third Programme,' loftily remarked its first Controller, George Barnes. Pevsner, like Allen Lane, saw no reason why the best should not be available to all, but it was on the Third Programme, with listeners numbering fewer than 5 per cent of the BBC's total audience, that he found most success in presenting ostensibly 'high-brow' topics in a natural and engaging style. His first producer there was another of Geoffrey Grigson's BBC protégés, Basil Taylor, with whom he tackled in quick succession Danish art, landscape gardening, Brueghel, the architecture of Washington and, in passing, the differences between the French, English and German approaches to art theory.[22]

By 1949 he was also working with Anna 'Niouta' Kallin, someone whose life had run along very similar channels to his own. Born in Moscow in 1896, of Russian-Jewish ancestry, she had left Russia for Berlin in 1912. After a brief period of internment in 1914, she had spent the remainder of the war years at Leipzig University, and it seems that the Pevsner family knew her during this time. She then moved to Dresden, but by the time Pevsner arrived there in 1925, she had left, travelling first to Switzerland as the mistress of Oskar Kokoschka and then, after their relationship ended, to London. She had been recruited for the Third Programme in 1946, having spent the war years monitoring Russian broadcasts for the intelligence services in Caversham. Anna Kallin was, in Michael Ignatieff's words, 'a fearless exile who seemed to unite a British conception of public service with the Russian conception of the intellectual as a moral authority'.[23] She brought to the Third Programme deep convictions of the importance of art and

---

*He was equally unsuited in some ways to television, as one of his first secretaries, Winnie Sibson, observed. Physically he was uncomfortable before the camera, and intellectually he made too few concessions to a general audience. He would also, she commented, have been driven mad by the television film-maker's practice of cutting things about. Winnie Bailey (née Sibson), interview with the author, 25/9/92.

the role of the artist in society, and had little patience with preciousness. Almost from the start there had been complaints that the Third
Programme had lost no time in becoming part of a cultural 'closed
shop'. Kallin was keen to get outside what she called 'the clique' of
regular art-critic speakers, and there was much in Pevsner's approach
to art history that appealed to her.

His very first talk for her, on 16 July 1949, was centred on art as
a radical force in society. By asking him to speak on a German topic
– German painting in the age of the Reformation – Kallin, consciously
or otherwise, tapped into some of his deepest feelings about Germany
and Germanness. In the hands of Dürer, Altdorfer, Grünewald,
Cranach, wrote Pevsner, art was a revolutionary event. The early
years of the Reformation were a time of violent religious upheaval,
characterised by the most elemental emotions – a burning concern
with sin and redemption, mystical abandonment to the passion and
mercy of Christ, fury at the conduct of the clergy. These emotions
were reflected in the ardour and directness of expression in the art
of the time – in the 'almost unbearable flogged bodies . . . and dogs
gnawing away at human bones' of a Cranach *Crucifixion*, Christ as a
'flaming apparition' against a blood-red sky in Altdorfer's *Resurrection*, and again, hideously tortured, in Grünewald's Isenheim Altar-
piece. But this intensity could not be sustained:

> once [the Reformation] had settled down, once Dürer was dead and
> once Luther had become the corpulent and competent leader of a
> national church . . . There could be no future in their frenzies. There
> is such a madly high pressure in the Isenheim Altar – it could only
> lead to explosion. It had either to burn itself out, or to collapse of
> sheer exhaustion. Art could not live at that pitch. So the art of the
> Reformation as a revolutionary event ends at the time when Dürer
> died.

Anna Kallin pursued the theme of Germanness with Pevsner in 1949
by inviting him to speak on Goethe and architecture.[24] However, their
most substantial work together was a series of four talks on Victorian
architecture. The talks were broadcast in July 1951, the year that *High
Victorian Design* was published, a sign that Victorian art and architecture were rapidly becoming a major preoccupation.

Conventional standards of judgement, he declared in his first talk,
must be waived in assessing the art and architecture of the Victorians.[25]
Granted there had been 'a very real collapse in values', but 'that architectural badness must not be explained away, but accepted and

interpreted to reach some understanding of the Victorian style'. Some illumination was perhaps to be found in the personalities and pronouncements of Pugin, Ruskin and George Gilbert Scott, one leading thinker from each era of the Victorian age. Here Pevsner aired again his antipathy for Ruskin, an inveterate moraliser in public but a 'queer character' in his private life, and moved smoothly from the particular to the general: 'These contradictions between theory and performance are fundamentally Victorian. They come from a lack of courage to take decisions.'[26]

'There is a terrible lot that was suppressed in the Victorian Age,' he continued in the third talk. 'In church architecture it remains as a rule suppressed, in secular architecture it often comes out much more rampant than the architects knew themselves. That makes the study of secular Victorian a live and in an odd way invigorating study.' His title was 'Churches and public buildings and the neglect of the common man', and his thesis was that for all the outward observances of decency and morality, the Victorians suffered from a profound lack of social conscience. Factories, workers' housing, buildings for public services were all largely neglected by the Victorian architect, whose eye was fixed firmly on the wealthy private client with a taste for display. As often as not, the buildings that resulted displayed, like their patrons, 'a certain boastfulness and a streak of megalomania'.

Equally, on the occasions where all this repressed energy did find its way into church architecture, the results were remarkable. Pevsner's love–hate relationship with individual Victorian architects was beginning to take shape. William Butterfield, architect of Oxford's Keble College, was a man of 'demonstrative originality' – neither epithet necessarily a compliment in Pevsner's frame of reference – but he was also a man of deep conviction, which for Pevsner usually justified the awkward, aggressive forms and bands of multicoloured brick. Of Butterfield's All Saints Church in Margaret Street, London, he wrote: 'It is obtrusive and graceless, but it is not timid nor dead. On the contrary, it is most violently eager to drum into you the praise of the Lord.' Where this conviction was lacking, he was less forgiving. Men like E.B. Lamb and Bassett Keeling strove like Butterfield for novelty, without possessing his formidable earnestness. 'The results are churches as original as anything Art Nouveau was to do about 1900 and singularly offensive in their clownish motifs, their ostentatious asymmetries and their wildly unprecedented details. The interior of Mr Lamb's St Martin's, Gospel Oak, must be seen to be believed.'

Pevsner used the last of his four Victorian talks, 'The Late Victorians and William Morris', to fit the final phase of the Victorian era into the frame formed by his 'pioneers'. The qualities he prized so highly in the work of William Morris – clean, unostentatious comfort and the demonstration of community ideals – he found most satisfactorily reflected in the buildings of some of his Late Victorian contemporaries. Norman Shaw's work, for example, he found a perfect antidote to High Victorianism: 'Elegance, wit, sensitivity, but none of the former robust self-assertion – work of a more sceptical, more sophisticated generation.' Bedford Park, with its Shaw church, was in his view 'the first attempt at a planned estate for the none-too-wealthy to live in civilised, attractive surroundings', an endeavour taken one step further by Cadbury's and Lever Brothers in the model villages of Bournville and Port Sunlight: 'Here at last was the principle of civilised housing applied to the working class . . . The time lag between housing for one class and for another was being overcome.'

Some listeners felt that Pevsner himself was carrying out the same kind of service in the realm of broadcasting, bridging the culture gap for the none-too-intellectual. 'Professor Pevsner has the art of presenting a mass of details – artistic, historical and sociological – in such a way that, so far from involving the wretched listener in a fog, he builds up a clear and logical picture which is extraordinarily illuminating . . . His voice, his style, and the humour with which he presents his argument turn a serious and complicated theme into a constant entertainment.'[27] The BBC, however, was not so sure. With Anna Kallin he shared seriousness of purpose and a common frame of reference. Other producers, however, sometimes found him dry, obscure and academic, and spent fruitless hours persuading him to inject a more personal tone. He greatly admired Alistair Cooke – my 'broadcasting pin-up', he wrote in 1972 – but was well aware that he could rarely achieve a similar lightness of touch. This was brought home to him most forcefully when he strayed once more into the Home Service.

Richard Keen was the producer of a series of short talks in 1952 entitled 'Englishmen's Castles'. Keen, who was thirty-one, had been at the BBC for three years.* Against his better judgement, he had been persuaded to invite Pevsner to speak alongside figures far better suited to 'Englishry', including John Betjeman and Hugh Casson, and he did his best to indicate to Pevsner what the tone of the series was intended to be. What was wanted, he wrote, was 'not . . . guide book affairs but general impressions of the houses from a personal angle, sketching in the countryside, history and curiosities of each house as well as their architecture'. Hardwick Hall or Chatsworth, Keen suggested,

---

*In the 'Talks' department, Keen would launch 'A Book at Bedtime' and invent the anthology programme 'With Great Pleasure'.

would be ideal: 'I feel it is a pity in a series like this to be too recondite in the choice of houses.'* There was little room for misunderstanding here; but Pevsner was not to be counselled. 'Bolsover is quite
a major affair . . .' he wrote, 'architecturally of great importance. I
would far prefer it to either Chatsworth or Hardwick.' His three
programmes would go out in the middle of June 1952, devoted in
turn to Lumley Castle in County Durham, Bolsover Castle in Derbyshire and Strawberry Hill in Twickenham.

With talks of this length, it was crucial to seize the audience's attention at once, as one producer politely pointed out to Pevsner: 'The only
really vital thing is to make the start a little less *elusive* for our listeners
. . . We unfortunately cannot always avoid placing the talk in the middle
of modern music and current affairs programmes where the listener's
mind is many removes [away].'[28] But Pevsner, apparently unpersuaded,
began the Bolsover broadcast by announcing bluntly, 'You had better
first of all get the Cavendishes right', and continued with several paragraphs of detail on the various marriages of Bess of Hardwick. Keen
wrote a terse internal memo when the three talks were over:

> It may be worthwhile to record some comment on the disappoint-
> ment of Pevsner's 'Englishmen's Castles' talks . . . Pevsner, as I see
> him, and as I felt when I argued against including him in this series,
> is not a descriptive writer. His speciality is the shrewd analysis and
> discussion of trends in art, and his writing is interesting largely in
> proportion as the trends he discusses are interesting . . . He has no
> talent for discursive, picturesque evocation of atmosphere . . . He
> indicated several times that he felt out of place in the series. Apart
> from anything else, he is (to my mind) unnecessarily touchy about
> his reputation as a scholar, and this inclines him to overload his
> scripts with historical detail.[29]

Fellow-producer Donald Boyd responded sharply, 'I'm afraid I do
NOT think of them as failures. Casson is Casson, Pevsner is Pevsner.
No scholarship prompts him to write badly or in sentences which
move about as well as spider crabs on land.'[30] Pevsner had support
within the BBC where it mattered. Almost certainly at the suggestion
of Anna Kallin, with a willing producer in the person of Donald Boyd,
he was to be the 1955 Reith Lecturer.

---

*Keen/NP, 7/3/52 and 21/3/52. BBC WAC RCONT1 – Prof Nikolaus Pevsner – Talks
File 1A.

CHAPTER 31

'A trifle tactless of Nikolaus':
The Englishness of English Art

The Reith Lectures had been inaugurated by the BBC in 1948 to mark
the historic contribution made to public service broadcasting by the
Corporation's first Director-General. Fifth son of a Scottish minister,
a burly man standing over six feet six inches, John Reith had, in the
words of one of his many detractors, a 'dour Calvinist mien' made
more severe by a scar on his cheek from a bullet wound suffered early
in the First World War. 'There he stalks, that wuthering height,' snapped
Winston Churchill, who blamed Reith (not without justification) for
keeping him off the air during the 1930s.

Reith had been Neville Chamberlain's Minister for Information in
1940 and Churchill's Minister for Transport, before being made Lord
Reith of Stonehaven and becoming involved in post-war reconstruction.
But it was as the BBC's Director-General in the 1930s that he had had
most impact, doing more than anyone else to define the character, ethos
and ambitions of the Corporation for half a century. Reith was adamant
that this organisation should be dedicated to 'making the nation as one
man' in cultural terms. In the 1920s a majority of adult listeners had
no formal education beyond the age of fourteen, and Reith saw a national
broadcasting channel as a powerful means of opening up to the many
what had previously been the preserve of a privileged few. He made no
attempt to disguise or soften his didactic intent; he saw the BBC, he
declared, as 'contributing consistently and cumulatively to the intellectual and moral happiness of the community'.

Unsurprisingly, then, the worthy aim of the lectures founded in
his name was 'to advance public understanding and debate about
significant issues of contemporary interest'. Each year an authority
in a different field was paid to do research and present the results
in the form of a series of weekly lectures. The series had been
launched by Bertrand Russell speaking on 'Authority and the Individual'. Since then, a feeling had grown that, with speakers such as
Robert Oppenheimer and Sir Oliver Franks, the Reith Lectures had
become rather hard work. The talks were to be heard first on the
Home Service and only later broadcast on the Third Programme, so

a highbrow approach risked missing the mark. What was more, the arts had not been touched upon.*

This may have helped to explain the selection in the winter of 1954 of Pevsner, who, in the words of *The Times*, 'has always found the way to a larger audience than his fellows'.[1] Otherwise he might not perhaps have expected such an invitation, the most prestigious that the Corporation had to offer, issued by the Director-General himself and offering a fee of 100 guineas, which for the BBC was extremely high. The letter arrived in the middle of December 1954 from Lieutenant-General Sir Ian Jacob inviting him to speak on 'some characteristics of British art and architecture, and your views of the reasons for their development in our culture'. Pevsner replied on 20 December accepting with 'the greatest pleasure – even if with some awe and misgiving'. Throughout 1955 he would be working hard with the Reith venture in view – on the seven lectures and an introduction to be published separately, and on plans for a possible book. The lectures themselves would be broadcast in October and November 1955, published almost at once in the BBC's own magazine *The Listener*, and followed at the end of November by a short television programme featuring highlights from the series. (The BBC would also make available, on request, a small selection of illustrations to accompany each broadcast.)

The Reith Lectures were originally meant to be the 'first formulation of thought stimulated by recent research or expertise'. Pevsner certainly did do extra work and more reading – drawing heavily on Francesca Wilson's new book *Strange Island: Britain through foreign eyes 1395–1840* (Longman, 1955), which he read in manuscript, writing to Eric Hobsbawm about crime and punishment in Victorian Britain and to Geoffrey Gorer about his forthcoming work on the English character. But the subject he chose was one that had been in his mind for a long time.† Many years later, reviewing Pevsner's career, John Summerson would observe: 'I can never make up my mind whether the Englishness of English art is or is not a pure invention of Pevsner's, part of some

---

*Oppenheimer, director of the Manhattan Project, had spoken on 'Science and the Common Understanding'; Franks, British Ambassador to the US, had spoken on 'Britain and the Tide of World Affairs'.

†The lectures were originally intended to be a channel for commissioning original research, but it proved too hard to persuade acknowledged authorities to take a long period of time off. In 1953 'personal experience' was added as a source of material and lecturers could speak about work already in hand rather than making fresh contributions to 'the pool of knowledge', letting Pevsner elaborate on a theme he had already explored in public.

private mythology. What is certain is that the artefacts of this pattern have become to him the kind of obsessional provocation that the world's oceans are to Sir Francis Chichester.'[2]

The idea of national character in art, of course, was neither a Pevsnerian invention nor an exclusively German notion.* But the idea was expounded most exhaustively in Germany in the nineteenth century, and Pevsner had been exposed to it by the majority, if not all, of his early teachers. Even Wölfflin had believed in a geography of art and, more specifically, in the notion of national character in art: 'after the style of the individual maker,' he wrote, 'comes the style of the particular school, the country in which the work was produced and the race amongst which the work is produced'.[3] But once again it was Wilhelm Pinder who had done most to shape Pevsner's thoughts and feelings in this area. Pinder himself was primarily concerned with the specifically German character of German art. 'In the 1930s,' writes Will Vaughan, '[Pinder] published a series of books *Vom Wesen und Werden deutscher Formen* (*Concerning the Essential Characteristics and Development of German Form*, 4 vols, 1935–53) in which he saw German art as a manifestation of the characteristics of the German race . . . He saw his own "bringing to consciousness" of German-ness in German art as part of his contribution to the Third Reich and the ultimate self realisation of the German people.'

As Pevsner was well aware, there had been far cruder formulations of cultural 'Germanness' than this in the 1930s. Theories of national character in art had begun to take on an increasingly racialist complexion in Germany as early as the latter half of the nineteenth century, woven tightly into the idea of national regeneration through art. These theories had become highly politicised in the 1930s and even more highly charged during the war. Why Pevsner did not take this more seriously when embarking on his Reith Lectures is hard to understand: a throwaway remark to the effect that 'it is bad enough that nationalism has been boosted so much in the last twenty years' was not an adequate precaution. Conceivably, looking at the study of national character in the perspective of nineteenth-century art history, he genuinely felt the most recent manifestation of the theory to be a temporary aberration – the more so because his own interest in the topic was no more political or racist than it had ever been.

As a teenager reading Dostoevsky for the first time, Pevsner had

---

*See p.111 on earlier studies of national character in art. And see also W. Vaughan, 'Behind Pevsner: Englishness as an art historical category' in D.P. Corbett (ed.), *The Geographies of Englishness* (Yale U.P., 2002), pp.347–68.

been drawn into ruminations on the Russian national character, which struck him (as indeed much struck him during those years) as *harmlos*, in Mann's term – childish, emotional, religious, instinctive. 'Silly idealism, really,' he reflected, 'to transfer his own humanity, his own ethics, on to a whole people'; but, despite these reservations, he would always find the lure of this kind of generalisation irresistible.

Very eloquent on the qualities of German art during his early years in Dresden, Pevsner became more reticent about the nature of German-ness in the 1930s, possibly out of prudence, possibly out of diminishing certainty. (He may have felt, like Victor Klemperer, that he was no longer sure what his nation's personality had become.) By that time, in any case, Pevsner had turned his attention to another country.

'He loved England!' wrote a prominent Edwardian historian of Disraeli, 'though not quite in the English way.'* It was a description that could well have been applied to Pevsner. 'Englishness of course is the purpose of my journey,' he had told Lola, embarking on his first research trip in 1930. Introducing the Reith Lectures in 1955, he would explain: 'In trying to find my bearings twenty years ago in a strange and attractive country, I could not keep the Englishness of English art separate from the Englishness of the English in other fields. I had to explore both, one as a professional, the other as an amateur.'[4]

Unsurprisingly, his first point of entry in 1930 was an architectural one. For the past seven years he had had the German Baroque before his eyes – studying the merchants' houses of Leipzig for his thesis and living among some of the era's finest buildings in Dresden – and now:

> here was the same century in England, the 18th century . . . and it was quiet and sedate, relying in architecture on proportions rather than ornament, in decoration on refinement rather than invention. The long rows of even brick fronts of Bloomsbury seemed a blessing to me, and I have never tired of their calm, of their architectural understatements, their poker face, if you like, or their stiff upper lip, their urbanity, and the secretiveness with which they hide deli-cately enriched interiors . . . That to me was England and still is England. England stands for keeping cool, for being sensible, for treating every case on its own merit – all qualities irritating to many of the hotter Germans, the intellectually more rational French, the more easily carried-away Italians.

---

*Quoted by Ian Buruma in *Playing the Game* (Jonathan Cape, 1991, p.1). The his-torian was Esmé Wingfield-Stratford (1882–1971), biographer of Churchill and author of a *History of English Patriotism* and a *History of British Civilisation*.

It was only in hindsight, under the pressure of the publicity surrounding the Reith Lectures, that Pevsner was drawn into romanticising his early relationship with England. 'As I fell in love with these English qualities, I was destined not to be a bird of passage here,' he wrote, 'and not to end in the bustle of America, as so many with a Continental upbringing did.' This was conveniently omitting the fact that in 1933 he had originally intended to settle in Italy and had been quite willing to be one of those ending in the bustle of America. But it was true that his interest in understanding Englishness had rapidly become more than purely intellectual, for when he did return to England at the end of 1933 this understanding became a crucial part first of finding a job and then of making a home.

Throughout his time in Göttingen, Pevsner had been accumulating material on nationality in art. He drew on this material in 1934, in his very first Courtauld lecture, on 'English Art: How it strikes a Foreigner', and then in the article for *Deutsche Zukunft* on 'What is English in English art'.* 'What does a German, receptive to the arts, learn when he tries to find the English character in English art?' he enquired in the article, and proposed a list of qualities that would remain his canon of 'Englishness' for the rest of his life. Humour, reserve, pragmatism, stoicism, tolerance and a spirit of compromise – all would be apparent in the genres in which he considered the English excelled. The medieval psalter, he wrote, was 'a typically English synthesis of two apparently contrasting qualities – on the one hand, an over-rich, massive decoration, executed with great technical care . . . and on the other hand the most lively sense of a quick and humorous view of the things of daily life'. Using art in this way to adorn an object for daily use was characteristic of a highly practical people. Similarly, though he was prepared to admit a capacity for escapism in such exceptions as Turner and Blake, Pevsner saw the landscapes of Constable and Bonington as more typically English, these two being 'the first to dare to observe openly and then represent, quickly and with great assurance, what they had actually seen with their own eyes. What could correspond more closely with the character of the nation which produced Roger Bacon, Duns Scotus and Francis Bacon?'

England was 'not the most talented [country] by nature for the creation and the wholehearted enjoyment of visual beauty', Pevsner concluded in 'English and German Art and their Interrelations', published in *German*

---

*See p.146.

Life and Letters in the summer of 1938.* He was aware of the hazard in this kind of sweeping generalisation – he had described himself as indulging in 'irresponsible aperçus' on the British character[5] – but it was a habit he was reluctant to break. In 1941 he was at it again, declaring in the pages of *Country Life*, no less, that 'National character is the result not only of "blood and soil", as the Nazis have it, but of blood – i.e. race – soil – i.e. geographic conditions – and history'. It was the English national character which produced ceramics that were tough and less likely to chip, glass that was sturdy, furniture that was dependable.[6]

Early in his career at Birkbeck, Pevsner sorted some of his thoughts on Englishness into a short course of lectures, and by the end of the war he had accumulated enough material to be thinking about publishing. But it was at this point, with greater access to literature in German, that he came across a book originally published in 1942 by the Viennese art historian Dagobert Frey, entitled *Englisches Wesen in der bildenden Kunst* or *The English Character as Reflected in English Art*.[†] Frey's work, wrote Pevsner, confirmed 'to an amazing and almost embarrassing degree my views, the criteria I had worked out, even the examples I had chosen to illustrate them'.

Pevsner would declare in 1955 that though Frey's book had been written during the war, 'it is absolutely free of any hostile remarks, let alone any Nazi bias – a completely objective and indeed apprecia-tive book, written with great acumen, sensitivity and a remarkably wide knowledge'.[7] Frey had, however, been a notable Nazi collabor-ator, one of three leading professors asked by the authorities to make the academic case for Poland as essentially a 'Teutonic land'. His 1941 book on Krakow denied any Slavic influence on its art or culture and his guide the following year to Lublin, one of the oldest Jewish commu-nities in Poland, mentions Jews only once.[8] Accused of involvement in the looting of art treasures from the Krakow Museum and the Royal Castle in Warsaw, he was interrogated by the Office of Strategic Serv-ices and relieved of his position in 1945.[‡] It is impossible to be sure how much of this history Pevsner knew by the time he declared

---

*Osbert Lancaster probably had this remark in mind when reviewing Pevsner's notes on *German Baroque Sculpture* (Duckworth, 1938) for the *Architectural Review* a couple of months later. 'We have always entertained a shrewd suspicion,' he retaliated, 'that . . . the visual arts were not those at which the Teuton was ever likely to shine.'
†Dagobert Frey (1883–1962), Renaissance and Baroque scholar. Initially an assistant to Max Dvořák in the Austrian Bureau of Historical Monuments, he later edited the Dehio survey of Austrian buildings.
‡He is named in the report of the US Art Looting Investigation Unit of the OSS (fore-runner of the CIA).

Englisches Wesen to be free of Nazi bias. In 1945 he may well have been ignorant of the extent of Frey's involvement with the regime; but the mere existence of so seemingly similar a book was probably enough to make him delay his own venture into print on the subject of national character in art.

Nevertheless, he was unwilling to waste the material he had been lovingly collecting for some twenty years – which may explain why, when embarking on the most widely publicised lecture series of his life, a man who never deliberately courted controversy chose this most contentious subject.

Pevsner had no political agenda. In his own eyes he was simply a historian, whose job was description, not prescription. The first 'Englishness' lecture, delivered on Sunday 16 October 1955, under the title 'The Geography of Art', spelled out the objective and purpose of his lectures – and in the process gave the clearest possible account of the kind of art historian he felt himself to be:

> Art historians differ of course in their personal preferences. The artist tends to look at the individual work for its aesthetic character and its craftsmanship regardless of its historical setting; the connoisseur for its handwriting and its genuineness regardless of its historical setting. The biographer is interested ultimately not in the individual work but in the man behind it. His question is: How did this unique individual express himself by means of his art? The historian need not underestimate the individual but he tends to neglect the individual. He is more fascinated by what men and works of one age have in common and he watches how one age develops into another. He says that the spirits of ages as he watches them are greater than the individual. He is the generaliser – and I may just as well make it clear right now that I am one of them.

The objective was not to persuade people to act in any particularly 'English' way, but to give them a better understanding of the context in which they were living – both time and place – and help them locate themselves within it. The problem was how to describe these national contexts in terms that would be clear without being crude. Pevsner was well aware of the pitfalls and he filled this introductory lecture with provisos. He had to find a way of presenting complexity within a coherent framework, and hit upon the notion of doing this by using what he called 'polarities' – presenting obvious inconsistencies as part of a plan and making contradictions the backbone of his overall structure.

In the introductory lecture he contented himself with explaining that English art might display pairs of apparently contradictory qualities, but in fact there was always a thread running between the two halves and connecting them. ('English art is the Decorated and the Perpendicular style in architecture . . . Decorated is the flowing line, Perpendicular is the straight line, but both are line and not body.') Then, having set up his theory, he indulged in a flurry of the kind of observation that would not fit into any such neat construct. (The Englishman barks 'chop' where an Italian would trill '*costoletta*'. The English use of timber vaulting in cathedrals stems from an island race's love of the sea and ships. The true Englishman insists on 'a strictly upheld inefficiency in the little business-things of every day such as the workman's job in the house'.)

Pevsner's picture of Englishness was intended to amuse, intrigue and provoke his English listeners into examining the art and architecture of their nation more closely, just as the *Enquiry* had made them face up to their woeful industrial design, just as *Pioneers* had helped them to identify the British contribution to the Modern Movement and just as the *Buildings of England* would encourage them to look harder at their built heritage. As often as not he was simply playing with ideas, bandying truisms – and then almost immediately repudiating the clichés and with them his own standing as an observer. 'I am not at all sure myself whether they are right, all of them. But then I am never a hundred per cent sure either how far I am not a foreigner and how far I am.'

At the end of this first talk Pevsner outlined the format for the rest of the series: 'I shall in every one of these lectures start from a well-known figure, fairly close to us in date, analyse a work or two of his and then see how their distinguishing qualities recur in the most unexpected periods or contexts.' The first to receive the treatment, in the second lecture, 'Hogarth and Observed Life', was England's most famous satirist, chosen to exemplify the English partiality for realism, moralism and story-telling and a national distaste for the Grand Manner. This did not mean avoiding serious themes; to Hogarth art was 'a medium for preaching'. But he chose to work not with rhetoric, religion or myth but with a documentary attention to everyday life, through illustrated cautionary tales such as *The Rake's Progress*, *Marriage à la Mode*, *The Four Stages of Cruelty* and *Gin Lane*. 'The most effective sermon,' commented Pevsner, 'is the recounting of what the observant eye sees around', without resort to symbol or allegory.

'Hogarth agreed with Dr Johnson who once said: "I had rather see the portrait of a dog I know than all the allegories you can show me." To me this is as irritating as most things the old bully said but I'm afraid it is crushingly English.'

This passion for story-telling, Pevsner continued, was not confined to painting and sculpture but overflowed into English buildings:

> England was the first country in the 18th century . . . to break the unity of interior and exterior and wrap buildings up in clothes not made for them but for buildings of other ages and purposes . . . The architect, like Hogarth as a painter, is not driven to express himself in one style and one style only . . . . He chooses a style for what you might call literary reasons.

Hogarth's choices were not to everyone's taste, as Pevsner was quick to point out when he moved on to the third Reith Lecture, 'Reynolds and Detachment', on 30 October. As the president of the Royal Academy, in his *Discourses* Reynolds exhorted his students to follow classical models and express lofty themes. The history painter, he decreed, is the painter of the highest order, for his subject is 'generally interesting' and it is his right and duty to 'deviate from vulgar and strict historical truth'. Thus, when Reynolds painted Mrs Crewe, he portrayed her as St Genevieve and tried to enlarge a particular subject into a general idea by changing her dress 'from a temporary fashion to one more permanent' and 'ennobling the character of a countenance', even if the result no longer looked much like the sitter. What Reynolds preached, however, was not always what he practised – a characteristic that Pevsner attributed to 'that familiar English ideal', compromise – and when faced with Master Crewe, he presented him dressed up as Henry VIII, a sturdy, pink-cheeked little boy standing legs wide apart in the famous pose of Holbein's portrait of the King. 'That also is parody, parody of the painter, parody of pomposity of pose, parody of the sitter – in short, the ability not to take oneself too seriously.'

The Englishman, Pevsner felt, owed his lack of self-importance to a capacity for detachment, the knack of not taking anything too greatly to heart; but detachment has its price. What detached artists gain in clarity and control they may lose in colour, warmth and resonance. 'The English portrait speaks in a lower voice, as the Englishman does today, and as indeed the muffled sound of the English language seems to demand. The English portrait conceals more than it reveals and when it reveals, it reveals with studied understatement.'

Pevsner did not see much talent for mystery in the English character. 'If you go into one of the big English parish churches of the late Middle Ages,' he remarked in the introduction to the fourth lecture, 'Perpendicular England', 'what will you find? . . . Large size, simple plan, flat chancel end, general angularity, hard separation of parts, repetitiveness, boldness of the very large openings and in the end a generally rational, surveyable, unmysterious character . . . pride and squareness and matter-of-factness.' In the flat-topped towers of these churches he saw a bluntness comparable to the clipped English monosyllable. Flat surfaces, too, were stressed with uniform, repetitious patterning: 'an English habit of rather adding part to part than of – how shall I put it? – kneading them together'. 'The English loved these long rows of blank arches [on screens], running on apparently interminably and wholly uniformly,' Pevsner continued, warming to his theme, 'the reredos . . . with row upon row of images in more or less identical niches, the close and repetitive patterns of ribs and subordinate ribs in 14th- and 15th-century vaults . . . and even, if you follow me, in the mid-nineteenth-century, its reflection in the never-ending terraces of Kensington and Bayswater.'

Against the 'horizontalism' of the serried rows of niches and arches and houses in terraces, Pevsner now set the exaggerated height and angularity which had given the Perpendicular style its name – towering naves, tall slender lights in the windows – and which was continued in the English fondness for full-length portraits, elongated figures on cathedral façades with draperies hanging in long perpendicular folds, and funerary monuments 'where husband and wife or two wives lie similarly long and stiff and motionless side by side'. Finally, these two tendencies were brought together in the conception of the grid, most obviously in the Elizabethan style. 'In the most characteristically English houses of about 1600 – at Hardwick, for instance – there is nothing but square and oblong blocks, flat roof, square-topped towers at the angles, square and oblong windows leaving little of solid wall – a rigid, rational grid . . . You can go on with this English system through the centuries after Elizabeth I and you'll find styles changing but this attitude remaining.'

At this point in the lectures Pevsner seems to have felt that it was time to offer a corrective to the somewhat subdued outline of Englishness that he had so far drawn – realism, compromise, detachment, reticence, rationality. In 'Blake and the Flaming Line' he set out to trace the progress of unreason in English art which, in accordance with his theory of 'polarities', had always run alongside the march of reason. (Blake himself preferred to speak of 'Contraries'.) For

493

some sixty years before the appearance of the Perpendicular in the mid-fourteenth century, English architecture had been characterised by a style that was in many ways its antithesis – 'capricious, wilful, unreasonable . . . illogical, unpredictable, even perverse'. The Decorated style had erupted in weird flowing tracery – 'shapes like the leaves of trees, like daggers, like kidneys, like bladders, bounded by lines like flames or like waves' – and capitals that were less like the crisp foliage of the Early English style and more like seaweed, 'bossy, knobbly and . . . undulating'.

What struck Pevsner was this apparent fascination with line at the expense of solid body. The English, he declared, 'are not a sculptural nation', sweeping aside English sculpture of the thirteenth to seventeenth centuries as generally inferior, and ascribing this weakness to a total lack of 'the Italian, the Mediterranean confidence in the body'. 'Maybe Puritanism has driven it out,' he continued, 'but Puritanism is English and its persistence in Victorian guise is English. The nude, for instance . . . has been a rarity in English painting for centuries – and is now. Just compare in your mind the Royal Academy and the Paris Salon.'

Once identified, this incorporeality coupled with a 'watchful interest in the life of line' can be found running through English art, from the spiral scrolls of Celtic decoration through the 'elegant frailty' of Gainsborough's portraits and the shallow, elongated curves of a Wedgwood vase, arriving finally and triumphantly at Blake. 'No one can fail to recognise a Blake,' declared Pevsner. 'There, whether the scene is one of bliss or terror, are his long, attenuated bodies, boneless almost, one feels, so little does he articulate the nude body . . . There are his small, strangely impersonal heads and his flowing beards, his garments also flowing gently or falling loosely and evenly in perpendicular curves . . . The curves . . . can be tense or tender, the lines flaming or flowing.'

The undulating line led Pevsner neatly to the subject of his sixth lecture: the English passion for nature and the landscape, both in painting and the Picturesque garden. 'For what are the ingredients of the landscape garden? – the winding path, not the straight avenue; the serpentine lake, not the straight canal.' For him, as for so many others, the English outdoors and all the genres of art that embraced it – landscape painting and gardening, sporting pictures, *plein-air* portraits – were inevitably conditioned by the English weather. 'Constable and the Pursuit of Nature' celebrated a new kind of atmospheric landscape painting, which moved away from self-conscious composition towards a fresh intensity of feeling and directness of expression. Constable's art, in his own phrase, was 'to be found under every hedge, and in every lane' and was characterised, in Pevsner's words, by 'the sense of breeze and never-once-arrested change'. Change and diversity were also what essentially characterised the English landscape garden. Surprise, irregularity, naturalness rather than artifice, liberty rather than coercion – the key features of the Picturesque style were also key features of the English character and a major influence on the way in which the English ordered their environment.

With little apparent effort, Pevsner had set the scene for his final lecture. In 'The Genius of the Place', broadcast on 27 November, he chose carefully from his wide range of timeless English traits in order to further a proposal that was highly specific, topical and close to his heart. Eighteenth-century landowners had a gift for consulting 'the genius of the place', treating each case on its own merit and respecting the historical, social and visual character of a site, in the Enlightenment's spirit of tolerance. Nothing could be a more important lesson for the planners of the mid-twentieth century, though for 'tolerance' one should now read 'functionalism':

> In planning and architecture today, 'each case on its own merit' is the functional approach . . . And if . . . present-day urban situations are treated functionally, taking into consideration what is practical for the walker as well as the driver, for the man in a hurry as well as the man with leisure to stand and stare, for the shopper on foot and from the car and also for those who want to enjoy the looks and the feel of where they live or work – the result would not look like Versailles, with symmetry enforced on streets and buildings. The informal . . . is at the same time the practical and the English.

To achieve modern informality by perpetuating the Picturesque tradition would of course be a kind of conservatism – very English – but the conservatism of learning from experience rather than the conservatism of inertia. By supporting the 'Townscape' proposals of the *Architectural Review* and accepting at least some new ideas from abroad, by 'humanising a rational, very intellectual style of designing buildings' in the light of native tradition, the English could reverse the current of influence and teach the continent a lesson.

Pevsner's *The Englishness of English Art* has, over the years, caused 'upsets on a national scale' (Reyner Banham's phrase). His intentions were almost certainly innocent. He was not trying to dictate what

English art should be, or to lay down a canon of 'English' characteristics that might be used to exclude or belittle or disadvantage any
individual artist, in the past, present or, most importantly, in the
future.* His best defence is a contention that could also be used as
the most serious criticism of *Englishness* – that he could not honestly
be said to be promoting any single view at all. 'It is a mark of the
perfection of the process of assimilation achieved in twenty years by
this Saxon-born *Kunsthistoriker,*' remarked Herbert Read, 'that he can
not only accept our illogicality: he can himself be as illogical as any
true-born Englishman.'⁹ Certainly Pevsner's brain was too well stocked
with exceptions for his argument ever to be completely clear-cut.

However, even if it was saved from being prescriptive by being
inconsistent, *Englishness* struck some of its audience as being both
disparaging and condescending. As Colin MacInnes would point out
in one of the most perceptive analyses of Pevsner's style, his writing
about the English and their tastes had from the beginning had the air
of 'an exploration by a curious, courteous, cultivated stranger of an
inexplicable people, half Yahoo, half Houyhnhnm'.† Michael Ignatieff
has written of Isaiah Berlin, 'If the English took to him, it was because
he offered them back their most self-approving myths . . . Isaiah more
or less accepted everything the English liked to believe about themselves:
that they were practical, untidy, eccentric, fair-minded, empirical,
common-sensical and that ubiquitous word, decent.' Pevsner's lectures
closely echoed this analysis; but he did not stop there. Listeners who
were quite happy to be characterised as level-headed, quirky and
tolerant were less delighted to be told that they were anti-aesthetic,
unprofessional and lacking in ambition.

'A trifle tactless of Nikolaus,' remarked Gombrich forty years on;
and without doubt Pevsner's reception in some quarters was made no
warmer by the fact that he was foreign. *The Times* underlined the
point in an editorial on the lectures under the heading 'The Englishness of *Kunstgeschichte'*. Pevsner acknowledged that there was an

---

*There is a detailed discussion of Pevsner's attitude to racial characterisations in art
in W. Vaughan, 'Pevsner's Art History', a paper presented at the *Fifty Years of 'The
Buildings of England'* conference at the Victoria and Albert Museum, 13–14/7/2001.
Vaughan insists Pevsner rejected the concept of *Rassenstil* (the attributing of a style to
a particular racial group). 'Rather he saw "Englishness" – as he had seen the style of
Leipzig baroque previously – as being the product of a communal culture developed
by all the peoples of Britain, no matter what their origins . . . He saw national iden-
tity as being something that changes according to situation rather than, as Pinder did,
some endemic characteristic that would constantly reassert itself in new situations.'
†C. MacInnes, 'The Englishness of Dr Pevsner', *Twentieth Century*, Vol. 22, 1960. See
Chapter 37.

issue: 'Why should I, with a never-fully-conquered foreign intonation, I who am not too certain of the difference between a centre forward and a leg volley, stand here to talk to you about the Englishness of English art?' But he suggested, as he had always done in the past, that the interloper may have a clearer view: 'In order to see clearly what's what in national character, it is perhaps a good thing at one stage to have come in from outside and then to have settled down to become part of it.'

This sense of belonging or being 'part of it' was very important to Pevsner, and after twenty years it might have seemed that he had earned it. But it seemed that he had presumed too much. Pevsner's parting words as Reith Lecturer were an appeal: 'These lectures of mine were an invitation to you to . . . consider what you have seen and read about . . . as the examples of a national art and architecture which is all your own. Or will you give me leave to say: "our" own?' The answer in some quarters was a loud and unqualified 'No'. However far he had come since 1934, the Reith Lectures had the effect for many of turning him back into an outsider again. 'I have heard it suggested,' remarked 'Pharos' in the *Spectator*, 'that Dr Pevsner's Reith lectures on "The Englishness of English Art" should properly be entitled "Die Englischheit der Englischen Kunst".'* In *The Listener*, the architect Bertram Hume saw no need to shelter behind a pseudonym. 'Determined attempts,' he wrote, 'used to be made to prove that England was Mitteleuropa: for example, the Germans exerted themselves to show that Shakespeare was a German. Now we know beyond any reasonable shadow of doubt that the opposite is the case, namely that Mitteleuropa is really England.'†

Matters were hardly improved when, in accordance with his original plan, Pevsner turned his lectures into a book, published in 1956 in both England and America. He had added some 10,000 extra words, which he used most conspicuously to lift his general conclusions out

---

Spectator, 28/10/55. Enoch Powell wrote as 'Pharos' for the publication *Scope*, but there is no evidence that he was also the *Spectator*'s 'Pharos'. He and Pevsner did correspond, on the subject of the House of Lords in the Middle Ages. Papers of Enoch Powell, Churchill Archives Centre, Cambridge. POLL 1/4/14.

†Since 'middle European' in this context is often used as a synonym for 'Jewish', Pevsner may have been mildly entertained to get a bulletin from Bournemouth two years later, after his BBC talk on 'A Pilgrim's Church in France', marked 'Popery': 'We don't want to hear anything about your French popery in England . . . You are enough to make Sir ISAAC NEWTON turn in his grave.' (Getty Papers, Series IA, Box 5.) He also kept a note sent to him by C.E. Wallis in 1970, written on the back of a Wallace's Rare Blended Scotch Whisky label, addressed to 'Professor Nicholas Pevsner, [*sic*] King's College, Cambridge', and beginning, 'I believe you hail from the Balkans.'

of the essay on 'The Genius of the Place' and elaborate them in a separate concluding chapter, which had the effect of making the whole argument more dogmatic and contentious. It is as if he were drawn against his own better judgement towards subjects over which he had skated in the lectures. 'Race is a dangerous tool.' 'The ambivalence of any conclusion drawn from race is only too familiar.' 'It is rare that in an individual artist his racial status is of use in explaining his art.' He makes all the right demurring noises – and then plunges with gusto into ethnic generalisation: 'To this day there are two distinct racial types recognisable in England, one tall with long head and long features, little facial display and little gesticulation, the other round-faced, more agile, and more active.'*

In case anyone had missed them the first time round, he repeated his animadversions on the English character. He laid into English conservatism with what appeared to be the suppressed impatience of two decades: 'One cannot be proud of . . . obsolete railway stations with unspeakably shabby and dreary waiting-rooms, nor of antediluvian dust-carts scattering more garbage than they collect.' He took a mild prod at English religion ('The Church of England demonstrates how one can be catholic without being Catholic, and occasionally protestant almost without being Protestant') and implied that the German Prince Albert had been the salvation of the Royal Family.

On his own admission, too, he had been 'carried away into a bit of propaganda' on behalf of Picturesque planning in modern architecture.† Singling out the South Bank Festival, the Casson plan for Cambridge, the new LCC housing estates and the evolving Holden and Holford plan for the City of London, he declared that such projects needed support 'against ignorance and short-sightedness and against the stupid prejudice that such newfangled ideas as would give London a modern and worthy centre must be outlandish. You see now, I hope, how thoroughly inlandish they are.' Anyone who was less than enthusiastic about recent developments in modern architecture, it seemed, was not only ignorant, short-sighted, stupid and prejudiced, but un-English in some way.

More specifically, by claiming the high ground of 'Englishness' for

---

*Simon Bradley points out that there is a strange echo of this passage in Pevsner's description of the statuary in Henry VII's Chapel in Westminster Abbey, in *London: 1. The Cities of London and Westminster*, written around the same time as *Englishness*.
†The published version of *The Englishness of English Art* was dedicated to H. de Cronin Hastings.

the Picturesque, Pevsner seemed to be implying that other twentieth-century styles were somehow wanting in this quality. Supporters of neoclassicism were quick to take exception.* A review by W.A. Eden in the *Journal of the Royal Institute of British Architects* in April 1957 spelled out the indictment most explicitly. Eden belonged to an informal group with the avowed aim of opposing Picturesque planning, and he now accused Pevsner of plundering history for propaganda: 'As an evangelist he turns to history as others of his kind often turn to the Scriptures – as a storehouse of texts that may be quoted in support of his own beliefs. His aim, it would appear, is not to understand history but to use it.'

From the rather different perspective of the *New Statesman*, John Berger, the novelist, painter and Marxist art historian, would have had Pevsner be more ambitious. He should not have baulked, declared Berger, at tackling the social, political and economic issues that explain the qualities of a society's art. In other words, he should have attempted 'an historical examination of the development of English society', tracing changes in the entire relationship between art and society throughout the centuries, as a preliminary to defining national and racial characteristics. Without this groundwork, 'the result is like a conducted tour by a very learned but inhibited guide through an endless house that has had wings added in every century since the Norman conquest. One sees innumerable pieces, but never the outside historical pattern.' Nor, in Berger's view, had Pevsner been astringent enough. 'For some reason [he] relies on being ingratiating. This book reads like a plea to an improbably highly cultured immigration officer . . . What Dr Pevsner does not seem to have realised about the English is that they love violent criticism . . . Like all flattery, [it is] finally an insult.'[10]

Pevsner may well have been hurt and taken aback by the undercurrent of acrimony. He had taken too lightly the risks of generalising to a post-war audience about racial characteristics, and he underestimated the extent of residual anti-German feeling. Certainly he seems to have lost some of his enthusiasm for the geography of art. Invited by the Pierpont Morgan Library to lecture on the topic of Englishness, he politely declined, on the grounds that 'one should not go round lecturing on a book'.

The general audience to whom he had geared his Reith Lectures, however, detected neither propaganda nor sycophancy in them. 'Here is no academician mumbling to himself on a pinnacle,' wrote the *News*

---

*Bertram Hume, scourge of *Mitteleuropa*, was a partner of Raymond Erith, principal proponent of the neoclassical tradition in the 1950s.

Chronicle, 'nor yet a diplomatist enunciating careful platitudes, but that most flattering sort of enthusiast who, coming among us, finds us fascinating.'[11] All over Britain people responded to Pevsner's closing appeal: 'Please get to know the history of English art.' The architectural historian Anthony Quiney remembered hearing the broadcasts in an RAF radar station in Scotland while on National Service. He was gripped by 'that extraordinary thin, rather amused, high-pitched voice of his, crackling away . . . It was a way of talking about art which was pretty new to me . . . As far as his thesis was concerned, the fact that later people said there wasn't much truth in it hardly mattered to me, because he was talking about things about which I knew a tiny bit and was beginning to get interested. This was a spur to go and look for myself.'[12]

CHAPTER 32

'No time to laugh'

Even if Pevsner had been disturbed by the critical reception given to *The Englishness of English Art*, he would have had little time to brood upon it. By the time of the Reith Lectures in 1955, the *Buildings of England* series was in full swing and his life had become a constant battle against the clock. He was committed to teaching and lecturing, both out of financial necessity and from a sense of vocation, and any work he did on the *BoE* project had to be fitted round the demands of the academic timetable, with research, travel and writing all squeezed into the university vacations.

As the series progressed and the volumes piled up, the pressure on Pevsner would increase, with counties constantly in preparation, in proof, in print, in revision. The early years of the *BoE*, however, were in some ways the years of his greatest contentment. The project was fresh, life was busy and varied, he had achieved a comfortable degree of recognition without being overburdened by official duties and public ceremonial. Above all, this was something he could share with Lola, a part of his work to which she could genuinely contribute. The *BoE* became during the 1950s a collaboration that did much to bridge the gap that had opened up between them during the war and the difficult years immediately afterwards.

Lola's duties were not confined to driving (and, where necessary, acting as the indicator arm) or making the sandwiches. She planned the itinerary, though not without challenge: 'I am an optimist,' Pevsner confessed, 'and there was always tug of war on the journeys for the *Buildings of England* between my conviction that we could do fifteen items and that a certain distance would be a mere three miles, and her preference for believing that it was not possible to do more than ten or eleven and that the distance was nearer six miles.' Most importantly, she was a second and often sharper pair of eyes, quick to draw his attention to features he might otherwise have missed and to restrain him from jumping to conclusions. Her contribution came most often in the form of a question: 'What's this? It doesn't seem to fit.'

Pleased to have surfed the first wave of reviews for *Middlesex*, *Nottinghamshire* and *Cornwall* (all published in 1951), Pevsner was approaching the next volumes with cautious anticipation, but with no illusions. 'I am really embarrassed with all the things people say about the BoE,' he wrote to Geoffrey Grigson.[1] 'It only shows they have not yet tried to use them.' Comprehensiveness, it was clear, was out of the question and to attempt it would almost certainly be self-defeating. 'I am only too well aware of the fact that to make such books what they really should be would require so much time that the whole series could not be done,' he told Edward French.[2] 'To get perfection would take 100 years,' he would say later in an interview. 'I shall plead, with Dr Johnson, ignorance, pure ignorance.' The only way to get to the end of the series would be to accept deficiencies of method and content with as much resilience as possible.

Devon, in Pevsner's view, exposed these deficiencies painfully. The third-largest county in England, it would eventually require two volumes, and yet he felt that too often he had not done it justice. The background materials were thin – 'The present state of research does not really justify an architectural guidebook such as this,' he observed uneasily in the Introduction to both volumes – and accumulating new detail was complicated by the distances to be covered. The driving, in narrow, winding lanes, took much longer than he had anticipated, even with Lola at the wheel of a different car, a small Standard Eight, and he found himself treating many places less thoroughly than he had intended. Luscombe Castle, for example, built by John Nash with grounds by Humphry Repton and a chapel by George Gilbert Scott, was given eight lines in the first edition of *South Devon*. 'The detailed remarks on the following pages will often be found inadequate or faulty,' Pevsner predicted.

Pressure of time might account for his occasional peevishness and weariness of tone. Church architecture in Devon, he concluded, was an affair of towers rather than spires, their Golden Age being the Perpendicular period, between 1400 and 1530. This work was 'impressive in bulk, impressive in occasional architectural details, impressive often in its furnishings, but turns out to be singularly, distressingly, standardised, when it is studied and recorded in detail'. 'Perp' arcades were 'disappointing' and of 'crushing uniformity', pulpits 'oddly coarse', fonts 'dull on the whole', late medieval sculpture 'nearly always of poor quality' and church monuments of the sixteenth and seventeenth centuries 'neither as rich as the Home Counties nor on the whole as good'. Rood screens were a bright spot – 'rightly famed', 'dazzling' – but 'Devon is not a county of brasses'. In contrast, manor houses had great variety and 'surprise of plan and detail', but were, of course, often more difficult to find and harder to get into. And where he did find beauty, it was often spoiled for him, either by the ravages of war or, conversely, by being *too* flawless.

The landscape, at least, delighted him by its generosity and variety, all 'on a large scale, as England goes, and never niggling'. But he was clear that he preferred the rougher parts to those that in his view were a touch too tailored. The fourteenth-century Dartington Hall, for example, 'has re-emerged almost too perfect from under the hands of the careful and wealthy restorers [the American heiress Dorothy Elmhirst and her English husband Leonard]. The setting and the buildings certainly combine the genuine with the comfortable and liveable to a degree which must appear even more ideal to the American than to the sloppier British.' The village of Cockington, comprehensively thatched down to the public lavatories, was 'only a little too perfectly kept to satisfy. It has become a standard afternoon trip for visitors to Torquay, and there is complete harmony between the sight-seeing townsman, the cottages ready to be admired, and the Drum Inn, by Lutyens.'

On the other hand, Exeter – a city he remembered with pleasure from his first visit to England in 1930 – had had much of its prettiness destroyed by force. 'The German bombers found Exeter primarily a medieval city, they left it primarily a Georgian and Early Victorian city . . . The Close is no longer as closed and sheltered as it used to be 150 years ago or even ten years ago. In the w the Second World War has opened out an unwelcome vista.'

Not all was negative. He revelled in the style and grace of small marine spas like Sidmouth, 'a veritable treasure house of Regency villas'. Inland, too, he found comfort in the unpretentious eighteenth-century elegance of towns like Honiton, 'all one long HIGH STREET, quite exceptionally unspoilt. There are no more than two or three buildings along its length which jar. On the other hand, there are no gems either; it is all pleasant, homely, two-storeyed Georgian . . . often with gently out-curving windows, the sort of houses John Piper likes to draw.'

Of more interest to him were the Naval Dockyard and Victualling Yard at Devonport, still largely products of the eighteenth century, but 'among the country's foremost examples of early functionalism, powerful and convincing in an undated way'. Modern architecture was relatively scarce, but there were examples of real distinction. At Dartington, for instance, between 1933 and 1936 the American modernist William Lescaze built a house for the headmaster of the Elmhirsts' progressive school, plus a row of boarding houses for the pupils, a gymnasium and some further private houses, 'of concrete plastered white, and as appropriate to Devon as they would be to California or the river Hudson, a symbol of enlightened internationalism'.* Forty years later, Peter Beacham of English Heritage remembered Pevsner's words as having helped to convince Dartington's trustees of the importance of the Lescaze buildings and the need to rescue them from neglect.

And then of course there was Exeter Cathedral, surprisingly isolated in the centre of its city, 'elephant-grey as against the warmth of the red sandstone of city walls, church walls, and monastery walls and the red brick of Georgian houses'. The interior, in his eyes, was a spatially moving ensemble of 'miraculous perfection' – wide, low, ample, individual and above all *English*. The Master of Exeter, whoever he might have been, was 'emphatically an Englishman. The proportions of his nave are utterly un-French, generously broad.' For once, Pevsner wrote, 'one would wish to be able to ascribe it to a man known by name and circumstances of life'.

As for St Mary Major (E. Ashworth, 1865–8), opposite the west front of the cathedral, it was 'major only as a disaster to the effect of the Close as a whole'. It is not impossible that the city planners had Pevsner's comment in mind when St Mary Major was demolished in 1971. At this early stage of the *BoE*, he had little sense of the impact his words might come to have and expressed his views without inhibition. Of the little Dartmoor church at Sheepstor he wrote that it was 'splendidly situated between the granite rocks on the one side and the large lake on the other', a lake that was in fact a reservoir. 'The English,' he continued conversationally, 'are much too timid about creating landscape on a large scale. A lake like this is well worth the sacrifice of an odd village or church.'

He would court controversy more frequently in the next volume in the series, which came out under the unwieldy title of *London except the Cities of London and Westminster*, known henceforth to *BoE* collectors as *London except*. Penguin had objected to the splitting of the London volume into two: Alan Glover wrote, 'I can only say that if I were walking from Charing Cross to the Bank making a rapid study of architecture I should be a bit disturbed at having to carry one fat volume in my right-hand trousers pocket and another fat volume in my left, and as you may have observed I am not over-particular about the set of my trousers.'[3] Pevsner, however, was

---

*In fact, as Bridget Cherry would later observe, they are not concrete, but plastered brick: 'Details of construction were always less significant to Pevsner than the visual effect.'

adamant. (The number of London volumes in the current edition of the *BoE* has now reached six.)

London was a controversial choice and a formidable challenge, at a point when Pevsner was still developing his methods and recruiting his assistants. Obviously the target audience would have expected England's capital city to be tackled early in the series, and sales could safely be anticipated to be good. On the other hand, for most modern buildings the timing of this volume was premature, with the post-war ban on large-scale construction still in place.

Even for Victorian buildings the evidence was thin. For Courtauld graduate Kitty Michaelson, who carried out most of the research for Pevsner between 1947 and 1951, the principal sources for the city's architectural history were the Royal Commission on Historical Monuments and the twenty-two volumes published thus far by the Survey of London.* The Royal Commission's volumes ran only until 1714 and the Survey covered little after 1800. In the circumstances, Pevsner's dedication to the volume was more than usually heartfelt: 'To the librarians of the public libraries of London without whose patient help this volume could not have been written.' (He also added in the introduction, 'By far the most valuable individual book is Mr John Summerson's admirable *Georgian London*. I owe more to it and its author than I can say.')

London except covered an area stretching from Wandsworth and Fulham in the west to Islington and Stoke Newington in the north, Poplar and Woolwich in the east, Lewisham and Lambeth in the south, leaving a void at the centre for Westminster and the City of London. Pevsner's policy, as always in the *BoE*, was to write only about what was visible, not what had been before. The bulk of London's Roman remains and its medieval buildings are to be found in Westminster and the City. Accordingly, his introduction to *London except* began in earnest with the Tudors and moved at speed through four centuries to produce a bravura potted history of London's architectural evolution in twenty-five pages.

Unfortunately, the layout of the main body of the book was nothing like as clear and illuminating as the introduction. Pevsner himself would later complain about the inadequacy of the index, which listed places and individual architects but not styles or subjects.[4] Some of the reviewers for *London except* were equally severe. In the *Times Literary Supplement*, for instance, 'M.D.W.' – almost certainly the

---

*Kitty Michaelson (1925–95), born in South Africa, studied at the Slade, graduated from the Courtauld in 1947 and later taught at the University of Edinburgh.

Courtauld art historian Margaret Whinney – was less than complimentary about unidiomatic English and lamentable illustrations. The
principal value of the book, she observed, lay in the wealth of material
on the Victorian development of London. Some of what Pevsner had
written on earlier periods was variable in its accuracy and there were
some judgements that she could only describe as 'rash'.

Pevsner would make a habit throughout the *BoE* of evolving catch-
words. For *London except* the recurring refrain would be 'Alas'. His
criticisms were often as much moral as aesthetic. He deplored unsight-
liness when it was caused by incompetence or carelessness, but he was
outraged by it when it was the product of avarice or callousness. Of
the large blocks of interwar flats on Abbey Road in Marylebone, for
example, he complained, 'Greed places them too tight, and thus the
neighbourhood will in due course be ruined.' He was equally disdainful
of the 'unshapen lumpish appearance' of Broadcasting House in Portland Place, the seat of his employment by the BBC, which 'casts a
blight on the whole delightful Georgian neighbourhood, and deprives
All Souls completely of its subtle siting value'.

Whole boroughs were cast into outer darkness. West Hampstead
'need be visited only by those in search of Victorian churches. The
houses and streets require no notice.' Lewisham 'has been singularly
unlucky in its architects'. Hammersmith was 'one of the least rewarding
boroughs of West London'. St Paul's Church (R.L. Roumieu, A.D.
Gough and J.P. Seddon, 1882) was 'not a building which it would be
easy to grow fond of', while the old St Paul's School (Waterhouse,
1881–5) was 'prim Early Gothic, terribly like a North German *Gymnasium* . . . COLET COURT, the Junior School of St Paul's, is less scho-
lastic in appearance and no more attractive.'

Pevsner was happy to be contentious. Of the 1949 *Daily Worker*
building, by Ernö Goldfinger, he wrote: 'Straightforward modern with
the concrete framework showing and pale stock brick infillings. Nothing
showy or luxurious, but a good deal of thought and sensitivity (very
different from the style a Communist newspaper would care to display
in Russia).' However, he rarely set out deliberately to insult. During
his perambulation of Whitechapel in the borough of Stepney, he noted
with disapproval two examples of the fake '*moderne*' style he had long
despised. 'At the corner of New Road, RENSOR HOUSE, a "borax"
(modernistic commercial) block, 1937, by *E. Cannell & Son*. Similar,
No. 227, CHEVIOT HOUSE, by *G.G. Winbourne*, also 1937 (was that
flashiness a special Jewish favourite?).' Pevsner was merely alluding to
the fact that Whitechapel had a large Jewish population but, as
Penguin's libel lawyer Harold Rubinstein pointed out, 'the parenthesis

following the reference to Cheviot House might be interpreted as suggesting that the architect, G. G. Winbourne, was a flashy Jew, which I am sure was not the author's intention'.*

When Pevsner did in fact give serious offence, to the point of almost landing in court, it was inadvertent. Some eight years after his long article on 'Model Houses for the Labouring Classes', he still had a genuine interest in social housing. He was affronted by what he saw as the 'insulting meanness' of much early housing for the poor. However, it was more or less as a throwaway that he remarked of one road in Camden Town, 'Arlington Street with the huge ROWTON HOUSE . . . still belongs to the slums.'

The chain of hostels known as 'Rowton Houses' were founded at the end of the nineteenth century for single working men who found themselves unable to afford decent homes in London. For sixpence a night the customer received clean sheets, a bath with hot water and somewhere to wash his clothes. Arlington House was the last of the Rowton hostels to be built and the largest, and it had been for many years an important centre for Irish labourers in London, especially construction workers. By the time Pevsner saw it, however, it was beginning a long, slow decline. The use of the word 'slum' to characterise a whole neighbourhood was controversial, Harold Rubinstein warned Penguin: 'There will always remain . . . the possibility that some touchy person affected might claim either (in the case of an architect) that his reputation has been damaged, or (in the case of an owner) that the value of his property has been depreciated.'[5] Startled, Pevsner enquired whether a complainant would really have a case. Mr Rubinstein conceded that the plaintiff would have to prove that malice had been intended, but 'unfortunately . . . there can never be any guarantee that a temperamental victim may not test a borderline case and even by gambler's luck secure a verdict through the vagaries of a Judge's digestion, or the fanaticism of a Juryman. It really comes back to a question of common sense, which, in the case of a book of this kind, usually persuades both author and publisher to run a certain amount of risk.'[6]

Author and publisher duly did run the risk – and Rowton House's

---

*H.F. Rubinstein, of Rubinstein Nash & Co., was the father of Michael Rubinstein, whom Penguin later retained in the defence of *Lady Chatterley's Lover*. It is interesting to compare earlier remarks by John Betjeman, in an essay on Jacob Epstein in a volume entitled *Twelve Jews* (ed. Hector Bolitho, Ayer Publishing, 1934): 'The word "Jewish" when used in connection with art, and particularly architecture, suggests a certain flamboyance and garishness with which we associate the interiors of cheap restaurants, an exaggeration of the mannerisms of the age in clothes, colour and decoration.'

management went forthwith to the company's solicitors for an injunction. 'The inference implicit in such a description is that these premises are in the nature of a low-class lodging house or "doss house" letting beds by the night. This is a wholly false and libellous description of the premises, which are in fact in the nature of residential chambers.'* As a public company, Rowton House could expect its shares to depreciate and its business to suffer. Had the company allowed its property to be a 'slum', it might be subject to penalties, and some of their residents might cease to be supported by public bodies. The solicitors wanted the offending passage to be deleted, the publication to be halted and damages to be paid. In the event, Rowton House contented itself with an erratum slip and an invitation to Pevsner to stay in Arlington House and modify his views.

Pevsner did not include Wildwood Terrace in *London except*. He did mention Wyldes, however, the farmhouse down the road where Camilla Rodker had stayed during the war, and he went into some detail on the interior of another building that had been particularly important to him in his own first years in London. 'All very perfect and very civilised, even if lacking in brio and small in scale,' he wrote of the semicircular staircase, stucco, inlaid doors and elaborate fireplaces at Robert Adam's Home House in Portman Square, otherwise known as the Courtauld Institute.

Gower Street, too, was there, defended at least partly on the grounds that it was despised by Ruskin, a perennial bête noire. 'Long, almost wholly unadorned brick terraces,' Pevsner wrote, 'even, soothing, dignified, and with a sense of overall planning, although certainly without much imagination'. Gower Street was, of course, now the home of the official premises of the *Buildings of England*. A single room on the top floor at number 18, on the east side at the end of the street nearest to the British Museum, was already being occupied by Penguin's accountants. The *BoE*, in the form of Pevsner and, eventually, a secretary, had taken over the room during 1946 and subsequently decamped down one floor in order to have more space. Two modest rooms were made more elegant by nameplates hand-lettered by Hans Schmoller, one of Penguin's leading designers, and a set of

---

*Rowton House solicitors to Penguin, 28/8/52. Pevsner's view was that Rowton House preferred the convenience of semi-permanent residents – such as the Irish labourers currently working on the new London airport – to itinerant users, and they were therefore anxious not to be labelled a doss house.

prints from the *Penguin Modern Painters* series hung on the walls. Pevsner was, in any event, largely oblivious to his surroundings while he was working. There was a photograph of Lola and another of his mother, and an easy chair of sorts, but, as one secretary remembered, 'it was always covered with papers, I don't remember ever seeing him sit in it'. The window at the back, too, offered little distraction, as it presented a view of the Senate House, not a building that Pevsner much admired. 'Not too bad when the trees are in leaf,' he remarked. 'I like [Charles] Holden better in those small Underground stations.'7

In any event, the Gower Street office was not a regular base for Pevsner, who came in more or less when he pleased. The *Architectural Review* offices in Queen Anne's Gate were more central for meeting colleagues, and much of his reading was done at home. It was the secretaries who spent most time in the two rooms, and it could sometimes be a solitary existence, punctuated with bouts of concentrated activity that imposed their own strains. There were certainly early holders of the position who did not last long. Of one, Pevsner wrote guiltily to Lola: 'The last scene with Miss S was painful and sad – a proper *Aussprache* [conversation] in which her complaints also came out. What were they? I am, she says, inhuman. It hit me fair and square.'*

Lola might well have sympathised with 'Miss S', but she had no objections to standing in Pevsner's shadow as long as she too had a genuine part to play. She took on a variety of secretarial tasks at intervals, but not without qualms. 'I am frightened of my job,' she wrote to him. 'Into how many copies have I to put the corrections?'8

'What he wanted,' remembered his first long-term secretary, 'was someone to make his life smoother and more amenable.' Mary Mouat joined him in September 1948, as a secretary pure and simple, with no relevant academic qualifications and little knowledge of art: for her second Christmas with him, he gave her Ernst Gombrich's *Story of Art*. 'We would brew black coffee and have a dictating session, and he might sit there and do some work on galleys and then off he'd go again, saying "Do this, do that, and pack up these . . ." A lot of the letters he'd leave to me to make the right sort of noises, simple enough. Then there were all those boring letters to these poor vicars, who didn't know the first thing about the architecture of their churches anyway.' Mary might be called upon to knock the corners off some of his more Germanic turns of phrase, or telephone potential sources with demands for abstruse information. 'You wouldn't have put him

---

*'Miss S' was probably Marjorie Stearns. See note on p.405.

in charge of a large operation,' she observed. 'He wouldn't have known where to start. He was an art historian, not an administrator.' Nor, although he sometimes seemed to know everybody, was he a networker in any deliberate way. 'He wasn't part of anything, but he seemed to infiltrate in an odd sort of way. Not consciously – he didn't set out to, he didn't want to be bothered with anything like that.' Not a man for feuds, Pevsner was never part of a coterie, and cocktail parties he considered an unwarrantable waste of time.

Mary came to be very fond of him. 'He wasn't the sort of man who needed to have a lot of friends. He didn't really socialise very much, he went to things if he had to.' Similarly, she felt he took as much interest in her as he felt like. 'He was interested in my life, he always knew what would interest Lola. It wasn't that he didn't want to know your troubles, but he didn't want to have to do anything about them, he was too busy.'

This busyness was, she believed, in part a shield – 'He didn't *want* to have a clue about practical things' – and in part even an alibi. 'He went to things if Lola had made the effort to get the tickets, but he was not one for "I must run home now and take Lola to the pictures". That didn't come into his scheme of things, and I think in the end Lola was rather a lonely lady.' But it was also partly a means of making himself feel secure. Mary was always conscious that he had no full-time job anywhere and no full-time salary ('His clothes were a bit tired') and that he felt he still needed to fight to stay abreast. 'He always said, "I haven't got time to go back" – like the men on the Kon-Tiki who couldn't go back to rescue the parrot when it fell over the side, because the raft was being carried onwards by the sea.'

Without having time for small talk, Pevsner was never cold. Anthony Quiney remembered, as one of his students, that Pevsner had in fact a readily detectable sense of humour, 'something which you had to infer from what he was saying, rather than seeing it . . . His eyes always sparkled when he was saying things seriously . . . But it didn't come naturally to be flippant . . . He'd got a light touch if he tried and thought about it, but he didn't stop for a laugh.'⁹ Mary remembered, 'he joked with his children all the time – with them he was a jokey man. You know, he could – and he was very proud of this achievement, because he wasn't a very practical man – he could pick up a complete tea service, six of everything. You had to hang the cups on his fingers. He learnt it with Gordon Russell . . . It was one of his stories.'

He also startled Mary with his patience and talent for amusing small children. He and Lola came all the way to her house in Essex. Lola had brought Mary's children chocolate money, and Pevsner dealt it out, hid it and did tricks. 'I thought, "You've surprised me".' He never failed to buy Mary a Christmas present:

> but for a man whom one would have thought knew about good taste . . . He bought me an appalling scarf one year, that particular shade of yellow-green, a real old lady's colour. Another time he came in and said, 'Mary, I couldn't think what to buy you, I hope you will find this useful.' It was a celery jug. He could do it if Lola told him what to get: if he had been told what to get and where to get it, he'd have got you the moon. But if he had to think about it . . . The presents were never wrapped up, they looked as if they had come straight from the shop.*

Mary Mouat's successor, Winnie Sibson, became his secretary in 1953. 'He didn't ride roughshod over people exactly,' she remembered, 'but because he was so intelligent, he expected a lot and tended to pile on work without realising.' By now there was regularly more than one county in preparation at a time: 'one county already in galley proof, and maybe another in page proof, and another one just coming out. It was a conveyor belt.' Wading through the mounting piles of queries and corrections, gathering in notes and diagrams from researchers, sorting and filing the material for the next county and setting it in order against the day when it would be taken on tour, Pevsner's secretaries were often lonely. 'I would have the desk all tidy and the letters ready . . . He'd breeze in and read the letters, then I'd go in and he would dictate replies or give me instructions as to what to do with them . . . He didn't stay for hours in the office – he was always tearing off somewhere.' Nor could Winnie go to his Birkbeck lectures even when he invited her, as Penguin paid so little that she was obliged to teach steno-typing in the evenings to pay her rent.

Once, in the middle of a county tour, Pevsner rang in a panic from his bed-and-breakfast and summoned her to meet him. 'I went down thinking, "Goodness, what have I done?" He couldn't find the notes to some place he wanted to visit, just one building. All that had happened was that one note had got caught in the paperclip of the

---

*When a later secretary, Wendy Martin, left to get married, he gave her trays for her electric cooker with a telegram reading: 'Warmest congratulations from the former boss PEVSNER'.

one in front of it . . . It was little things that upset him, not big things
. . . He used to take it all terribly seriously.' He was Germanic in this
way, Winnie concluded, but hardly guilty of Teutonic efficiency. He
was wholly unmathematical – 'Anything like his income tax totally
baffled him' – and often forgetful. 'He became a mad professor slightly.
He used to lose things, and they were in such obvious places. Clumsy,
too: not a sporting type – he would have been bad with a ball, I'm
sure.'

On paper at least he could be starchy (Winnie's word) – 'When he
was writing reviews, he would sniff a bit, you could tell if he was
displeased' – but with her he was rarely formal. He deplored what he
called 'chi chi' (one of his favourite terms of abuse) and was rarely
exacting in his material, as opposed to intellectual, demands. 'Most
of the time he didn't have lunch, so I used to go down to the bottom
of Store Street and just on the right was a shop which sold these
enormous pork and beef and ham sandwiches and I'd get one of each,
a great big pile, and he'd wolf his way through three. He never seemed
to get indigestion.' Winnie remembered his amusement when she gave
him a record of Peter Ustinov's unkind take-off of the worst kind of
German *lieder* singer. 'A lot of people saw only the hard-working,
obsessional German, but he was also a very kind, nice, understanding
man.'[10]

Nor was Pevsner then, or ever, the intransigent modernist crusader he
has sometimes been portrayed as being. Certainly in the very early
days of the *BoE*, when there was still relatively little modernist architecture in England, he wanted to give it as generous a coverage as he
could. Modernism was still fragile as a movement, and its supporters
felt the need to be assertive. Old buildings needed to be documented
in order to prevent their destruction, but new ones – of the right type
– had to be praised more actively, to encourage the building of more
of them. In a spirit of charity, Pevsner included every piece of modern
building where he found the Gropian virtues of precision, proportion,
transparency and frank expression of function – garages, oil refineries,
road bridges and power stations included.

But as the 1950s went on and more buildings were put up in a
modern style, he would become more selective. No longer would he
praise places on principle, and it became more obvious what he truly
admired. The deepest pleasure, intellectual, emotional and aesthetic,
always came for him when modern buildings seemed clearly to express

the spirit of their time and their social purpose. Post-war educational-
ists and politicians wanted new schools, for instance, to be reflections
of a new and better society: more open, more democratic, more flexible than the essentially Victorian structures they replaced. By 1954
Hertfordshire County Council had built more than 100 new schools
using a modular system based on standardised steel-frame units and
pre-cast concrete slabs. Each had a generous supply of light and warmth,
bright colour schemes, wide open classrooms with courtyards and
playgrounds articulating the study areas, all creating a sense of extraordinary freedom and luxury to a graduate, like Pevsner, of a turn-of-
the-century German *Gymnasium*. 'From the balancing of block against
block down to the colours of the walls, the curtain patterns, and the
door handles, everything is carefully considered and elegantly done. It
is a delightful experience to walk around and through some of these
schools.'

The same accessibility characterised the Peckham Pioneer Health
Centre in London, which had been described by no less an authority
than Gropius as an 'oasis of glass in a desert of brick'. But for Pevsner
the Centre's value lay less in its architecture than, again, in its contribution to mental and physical well-being. Built by Sir Owen Williams
in 1934–5, it was conceived as an experiment in public health by a
husband-and-wife team of doctors, George Scott Williamson and Innes
Pearse. Devoted to the cause of preventive medicine, they believed that
people's social and physical environment could decisively affect their
long-term health. They designed the Peckham centre as a combination
of clinic and club, to provide a deprived area of London with both
medical care and a social hub. Every part of the building was used,
from the swimming pool and kindergarten below the consulting rooms
to the flat roof where exercise classes were held. Internal walls were
kept to a minimum and floors were covered in cork so that children
could wander around barefoot. Pevsner loved the openness and the
idealism that was built into every detail and it was with some gloom
that he recorded, 'The architectural and functional future of the building
is in serious danger at the time of writing.' Ironically, it was the Centre's
vast expanses of glass that had led to its being closed during the war
for fear of damage from bombing, and once the continuity of the
community was broken, it never really recovered.

Pevsner approved of rigour in design. He took pleasure in the social
purpose that lay behind the work of the London County Council's
architectural office – 'a great empire in which the concrete never set',
in Jim Richards's phrase. But he responded most keenly when order,
ideals and purpose were combined with warmth and humanity. He

relished the occasional eccentricity, even irrationality, in small doses, and even in the work of architects who for him best represented the spirit of the Modern Movement in Britain. The Tecton firm, for example, had moved a fair way from scrupulous logic and reason in their undulating entrance to Dudley Zoo, and again in the Highpoint II flats that Pevsner considered to be among the best modern buildings in Britain.

His architectural ideal, nevertheless, was one of restraint and accessibility and it is no surprise that he characterised one of his favourite London buildings as 'friendly'. The Royal Festival Hall, designed by Leslie Martin and Robert Matthew and opened in 1951, was noted in *London except* for its historical significance as 'the first major public building in inner London designed in the contemporary style of architecture'. It was more personally important to Pevsner, however, as an uplifting example of the aesthetic principle that had been central to his beliefs about architecture since his student days. Architecture, he had written in *An Outline of European Architecture*, is 'primarily organised space', and the management of interior space in the Festival Hall was outstandingly successful. 'Here, chiefly in the staircases, promenades, super-imposed restaurants etc. are a freedom and intricacy of flow, in their own way as thrilling as what we see in the Baroque churches of Germany and Austria.'

Just as he was not an uncritical advocate of modernism, so he was not a remorseless foe of 'traditionalist' architecture. He is most often excoriated for wilfully neglecting, casually dismissing or even unfairly disparaging those early twentieth-century architects, usually working in a neoclassical style, who resisted what he saw as the tide of progress. This did not prevent him from having a profound respect for classical architecture, calling Greek temples 'one of the most logical direct statements of the sense of architecture ever conceived'. It was the borrowing of the trappings of antiquity that he mistrusted, the attempt by architects of later ages to endow themselves with some kind of spurious, second-hand *gravitas*. He quoted with relish Pugin's denunciation of 'the resistless torrent of Roman cement-men' in the nineteenth century: 'Every good old inn is turned into an ugly hotel with a stuccoed portico . . . and twenty per cent added to the bill . . . Every linen-draper's shop apes to be something after the palace of the Caesars.'[11]

In the twentieth century what Pevsner deplored was not so much pretension as pusillanimity. Critics have long been irritated by what they have seen as an almost perverse refusal to recognise any different motives or even any differing degrees of skill among the very many architects working with traditional styles. Pevsner, they claim, effectively wrote off men like Albert Richardson and Vincent Harris purely on principle, rather than on any objective assessment of their work. That he was well aware of the charges, perhaps even inclined to acknowledge their justice, emerges in a remark he made early in the 1960s: 'Those who look at architecture of the last fifty years detachedly will always tend to focus their interest on what is progressive rather than what is good. This is the reason why the achievements of architects not out of sympathy with tradition and of architects believing in certain classical principles, are being undervalued.'* But he was not necessarily inclined to repent, adding: 'The critic in England might be forgiven for this lack of judgment; for our Neo-Georgians have in fact been weaker and less exacting than our Moderns.'[12]

The determination to focus on what was progressive rather than what was good left some volumes of the *BoE* with virtually no twentieth-century entries at all. Of Derbyshire's modern building, for instance, Pevsner declared unambiguously: 'Nothing of note in the county.' Derbyshire was one of the two counties for which he did the travelling in 1951, the other being County Durham. There is every sign that he enjoyed the trip – the volume is dedicated 'to the memory of Monksdale', a particularly beautiful corner of the Peak District near Buxton – but he found the county an awkward one to handle in print. The variety that made it interesting to tour made it correspondingly difficult to characterise as a whole, as his method required.

Derbyshire, he felt, was weaker on churches than on domestic building, the reverse of his own tastes. It had no full-scale cathedral, or even a large abbey, and much of the richness of its architecture lay in the area least well served by his methodology. The county's great houses, such as Chatsworth and Haddon Hall, were all now open to the public and their glories were very well known. But, he observed, 'just as rewarding as these large houses are the more modest ones. There is a bewildering variety of them, and they do not fall into easily defined groups.' They required the kind of careful attention, both in the preliminary research and in the course of his travels, that he was not always able to give them. The description of Windthorpe Hall at Clay Cross is one example of this bad effect, reading simply 'small

---

*Nicholas Taylor points out that, in the cases of Richardson and Harris, Pevsner did appreciate their early work of *c.* 1910–15, when their classicism was full-bloodedly Edwardian, whereas the later work increasingly lacked conviction.

manor house, Elizabethan or somewhat later'. For the occupant in search of information, or the owner who would have liked to have been able to make more of his property's Tudor origins, this kind of description was infuriating.

He did, however, take an interest, for once, in the owner of a house. In later years he would be repeatedly criticised for his apparent indifference to the niceties of the relationships between owner and builder, patron and architect, and his neglect of family background and the kind of domestic detail that could put flesh on the bones of architectural analysis. Nine times out of ten he would probably have replied that he was a recorder of buildings, not a biographer or a social historian, and his chosen format left little space either for the occupants of houses or for their possessions, however interesting or attractive they might be. In Elizabeth, Countess of Shrewsbury (1527–1608), however, he was confronted with an owner who had, quite literally, stamped her personality on her house in ways he could not ignore, in the form of her initials – 'ES' 'ES' 'ES' 'ES' – traced four times along each of the long faces of Hardwick Hall, the last product of a towering egotism manifested in bricks and mortar.

To describe this house was to describe its owner, and with some relish Pevsner described 'Bess of Hardwick' as bullying, manipulative, grasping, scheming and on the make. The Hall was, in Pevsner's view, the ultimate status symbol, a flagrant display of luxury by a shameless arriviste. 'Her hard, able, proud character seems reflected,' he wrote, 'in its uncompromising rectangularity, its regular pattern of extremely large mullioned and transomed windows, and the somewhat coarse grandeur of the decoration inside.' Hardwick Hall was somewhat vulgar and not a little eccentric, but some of its effects, wrote Pevsner, were overwhelming. The Gallery, 166 feet long, delighted him: 'The great sensation . . . is its three bay windows, each the size of a c20 council house. On a sunny day the Gallery is as light as a factory in the modern style. Let nobody say that c20 fenestration is alien to this island.' It is hard to imagine that many other observers at that time would have noticed the Hall's resemblance to a modern factory, or appreciated it if they had, but Pevsner's delights were as idiosyncratic as his aversions and – a legacy of the *Architectural Review* – he took pleasure in surprises and incongruities.

County Durham, published in 1953, would prove to be one of the most controversial instalments in the *BoE* series, a volume of great character, highly typical of both Pevsnerian strengths and weaknesses.

Two traits stand out: passionate enthusiasm for the merits of a building, and a certain obtuseness towards some human sensitivities.

When Pevsner came to write up the entry on the city of Durham, even he was slightly startled. 'It comes to nearly 50 pages of my close writing,' he noted. 'There must be about 20,000 words at least, or 40 to 50 pages in the book. Is it worth it? . . . My brain just conks out in the end.' Not that he had any doubts about the worth of his subject. 'Durham is one of the great experiences of Europe to the eyes of those who appreciate architecture, and to the minds of those who understand architecture,' he declared. 'The group of Cathedral, Castle, and Monastery on the rock can only be compared to Avignon and Prague.' It was not just the buildings that captivated him but the rocky site itself, cut off on three sides by a tight loop of the River Wear that gives the town the feel of being on an island.

Durham exactly fitted Pevsner's conception of the ideal university town, with its steep cobbled streets and the academic buildings nested inside the castle. This, he declared, was the only one of the 128 provincial universities 'which has achieved the creation of a *milieu* that can compare with Oxbridge . . . Wandering along North and South Bailey to call on members of the university, one may well feel transported into the streets of Oxford or Cambridge. Birmingham or Manchester could never even try to achieve that.'

Inevitably, the description of the town, however affectionate, was nothing more than a preface to Pevsner's account of the cathedral, his favourite among all English cathedrals. His depiction of it is perhaps the longest sustained effort in the *BoE* to convey the sheer beauty of a building. He was never one of those writers who spent time lost in admiration of their own sensitivity. His words did not have to aim at beauty on the page, they had to act as a code or formula through which readers could reconstitute beauty for themselves; they worked through analysis rather than by association. He spoke of this volume as being 'concerned with visual affairs'.[13] His priority was to convey what one saw of a building, rather than what one felt about it, and at the same time to explain how the building had been made and how each part of the construction contributed to the whole: this for him was where beauty lay, as well as in atmosphere and aesthetic effect.

Durham Cathedral was probably the first building in Europe to have had rib-vaults, and Pevsner describes them virtually rib by rib. In his description, massiveness is awe-inspiring without being alienating, largely due to the combination of size with control:

What gives [the cathedral] supremity [*sic*] over all other Norman buildings in England or Normandy is this unexpected combination of primeval power, the power of William's conquest and of his bloody conquest of the north, with a consummate mastery of scale and proportion. All the forms used are colossal, but the effect is not cyclopic. They are composed in so noble and harmonious a way that in the end one can well forget for moments their absolute sizes.

Pevsner himself makes vastness manageable with the homely image he chooses to express the girth of the famous Durham piers, twenty-seven feet high and nearly seven feet in diameter: 'The monument to James Britton in the nave, with the deceased reclining comfortably on a mattress on which he has placed an open book, could be put inside one of the piers, and if he had a moderator lamp he could continue reading and musing in that circular cell.'*

Enjoyment radiates from every facet of Pevsner's account, marking the points at which he stopped in his perambulation before the familiar features that particularly interested, amused or excited him. The Galilee or Lady Chapel at Durham is, unusually, at the west end of the cathedral. 'The story deserves telling that [Bishop] Pudsey was so disgusted by the idea of having to admit women to the E parts of his church that he rather placed the chapel as far W as could be done. It is true anyway that a line in grey local marble in the floor of the nave just E of the main N doorway marks how far women were allowed to penetrate into the church.'

County Durham often betrays itself as an early volume of the *BoE*. There are some ungainly expressions – 'impassionate', 'supremity' – and some fine examples of the Pevsner style at its most infuriatingly reductionist. 'Hetton-le Hole. FAIRIES' CRADLE. Off Houghton Road. Supposed to be a cairn. Confirmation required,' he notes curtly, giving fairies and antiquarians equally short shrift.† However, he still found room for oddities and personal partialities that would not have found their way into many other guidebooks. The chancel screen in St Philip and St James's church in the village of Tow Law, for example, appears to have taken his fancy, unpromising though it sounds: 'Gothic forms represented by blackened fir cones, pine cones, walnuts, chestnuts, acorns, set closely together and glued on to a wooden frame. The work

---

*The moderator lamp was an oil lamp with a glass chimney, worked with a pump and spring, probably what Pevsner himself used in the cottage at Snowhill to light his own reading and musing.
†Local histories report a prehistoric burial mound. Fairy Street was built over it in the late nineteenth century.

was done in their spare time by the then Vicar, the *Rev. T.E.C. Espin, Mr W. Work* and *Mr J. Harrison*. It took fourteen months.'

Pithead baths, the blocks put up in the 1930s to provide coal miners with showers and a convenient place to wash and dry their pit clothes, delighted him. As a veteran of uncomfortable washing facilities – the shared bathrooms without locks in Italian *pensioni*, the tin bowl balanced on an upturned stool in his first English lodgings, Miss Wilson's ancient Ascot heater in Edgbaston, cracked washbasins and piercing draughts in guesthouses across England – he would have appreciated the difference that the baths made to the miners' lives, but he also saw in them some of the most obvious expressions of modern architectural ideas: 'the dominant group of chimney and water tank, boldly and squarely displayed' showing the influence of the Dutch style of W.M. Dudok, an asymmetrical massing of geometric forms that reminded him of Frank Lloyd Wright, or, in one place, a bath worthy of Erich Mendelsohn, with projecting parallel bands of brick running round curved corners.

At the other end of the sobriety scale, he recounted the excesses of Victorian ecclesiastical display with a certain grisly relish. E.B. Lamb's Christ Church, West Hartlepool, he wrote, 'certainly is something special'. Not only was the tower excessively high, at more than 100 feet, but, he observed with distaste, it had 'a roguish obelisk roof' and the crossing had 'the weeniest cupola' supported on 'cyclopic timber arches', themselves borne up by piers 'of a shape which defies description'.

Pevsner tried not to play too obviously on County Durham's reputation for industrial desolation, but he could not ignore the grating contrasts between buildings and their setting: St Paul's, Jarrow, close to the Tyneside docks, 'one of the most venerable churches in the kingdom . . . surrounded by the wasteland of years of industrial distress'; St Peter with St Cuthbert, Monkwearmouth, 'a precious relic, too precious for its sordid setting'; St Cuthbert in Darlington, thirteenth-century and 'uncommonly beautiful . . . It is a great shame that the visitor usually sees it set against the overwhelming shapes of the cooling towers of the power station further E, and that, when he approaches it nearer, he is surrounded by the uproar of the central bus station of Darlington.'

Pevsner's tone is sometimes sharp, even querulous. More dangerously, he occasionally lays himself open to the charge of sounding Southern-slanted and superior. 'Local archaeological and antiquarian work,' he wrote, 'as far as the medieval and post-medieval centuries go, has on the whole not been of a specially high order or intensity.' The *Burlington Magazine* was in the 1950s arguably the most prestigious of British art journals. Pevsner had himself been a fairly regular contributor since 1935, on good terms with two successive managing editors, Herbert Read and Tancred Borenius. But in the issue of January 1954 the *Burlington* published a review of *County Durham* that was hostile enough to become itself the subject of heated controversy. The author was Bruce Allsopp, a writer, architect and Northumbrian. Allsopp would also become the first chairman of the Society of Architectural Historians in 1955, and it may be that he took personally Pevsner's aspersions on the standards of scholarship in his county.

There were other issues on which the two men may not have seen eye-to-eye. Allsopp would later write both on the importance of individuals in the modern world and on the shortcomings of functionalism, and it could be that he was already ill-disposed towards Pevsner as a champion of modernism.[14] Whatever the source of his acrimony, acrimony there certainly was. A southerner who described Durham as 'remote' was, in Allsopp's view, likely to be doomed to failure as a chronicler of the county (particularly as compared to the author of the *Little Guide* to Durham, who lived in Darlington). 'One might hope that he would make up by sound scholarship for lack of that feeling for the county which comes from living in it,' Allsopp continued, 'but such a hope will be disappointed.' Pevsner's *County Durham* was, in his view, littered with factual errors and peculiar omissions. He did not care for the style: 'Some of the notes verge on the ludicrous.' Even more annoying, he continued, was 'the fact that Professor Pevsner sets himself the task, which he could wisely have avoided, of being an oracle of taste. He says which is the best building on the Team Valley Estate . . . He says of Scott's screen at Durham: "It should be replaced." . . . Such scraps of arrogant criticism seem quite out of place.'

This would not be the last time that Pevsner would attract the wrath of a local historian. He tended to be humble in his reception of such criticisms if he felt they were honestly offered, but they infuriated his admirers. Reyner Banham bristled: 'England is littered with librarians who are convinced that they, personally, as good as wrote the local *Buildings of England* volume themselves, and resent what they regard as shameless brain-picking and archive-robbing on Pevsner's part . . . Perhaps for the first time, [each] is faced with the classic bibliography-trauma of finding that he is not the fount and origin of all knowledge. A big fish has swum through a small pool.'[15]

Even to scholars less bellicose than Banham, Allsopp seemed unnecessarily abrasive, and a local historian rose up to defend Pevsner. In the proceedings of the Durham and Northumberland Architectural and Archaeological Society, Frank Rutherford took issue with the tone and tenor of Allsopp's review, and with another, even more unpleasant, that had appeared earlier in the *Times Literary Supplement*. 'Doubtless the area of England that Mr Pevsner knows by heart is – since man's heart is small – strictly limited, [but] . . . the TLS reviewer . . . over-reaches himself, denouncing views moderately and tentatively advanced, which have the support of some respected antiquarians, and which probably cannot be disproved. In place of some of these he offers opinions apparently just as questionable.'*

As early as 1951 Pevsner was contemplating the inexorable march of county after county with displeasure. Sitting in a café in the rue des Chats in Troyes, he wrote to Camilla Rodker, 'The wines are delicious, the sun kindly, the humour excellent,' and continued resignedly that he would see her again 'after we have eaten our way through Hert-fordshire for the wretched guides'.†

There was little solitude in Herts, he complained, with buses reaching into every corner, light industry mushrooming in all directions and an inordinate number of mental hospitals. One of these, he had to concede, was spectacular. At the time of Pevsner's visit, the Colney Hatch asylum was the main institution for the county of London, housing 3,500 inmates, served by their own farm, chapel and cemetery.‡ At either end of a florid Italianate façade 2,000 feet across, twin towers flanked a central dome, and inside patients patrolled what was said to be the longest corridor in Europe. When he tried to go inside, he was stopped by the man on the door. 'I am Professor Pevsner,' he protested. 'That's a new one,' the doorman replied.

Essex, in Pevsner's eyes, suffered even more severely than Hertford-shire from its proximity to London. Without being refreshingly rural, it was, in the absence of any significant city, something of a cultural backwater. Because he had not reckoned from his reading of the research that the county's architecture merited two volumes, he had to traverse in a single journey one of the larger English counties – and this time he and Lola were towing behind the Penguin Ford Prefect a large caravan borrowed from H. de C. Hastings.

---

*The TLS reviewer in question was Bertram Colgrave, an expert on the Venerable Bede. See p. 545 below.
†Pevsner did the travelling for *Hertfordshire* in 1951. It was published in 1953.
‡The asylum is now a block of luxury flats. The former chapel houses the gym.

'Being German,' remarked Mary Mouat, 'he did the job properly and joined the Caravan Club, in order to use their sites.' However, the weather was unkind, the roads often narrow, and the caravan was far too heavy for Lola to handle with ease. She was at the best of times an erratic, even terrifying, driver. Denis Evinson remembered Pevsner telling him that on this trip the horn sounded every time she turned right. In any event, the caravan could not provide what Pevsner required on the road. 'Here is a strange man who for some reason or other wants to sit for 3 or 4 hours in the evening and write.'[16] (At one hotel, when he insisted on having a table, the girl at the reception desk said 'What does he write – love stories?')

He made his position absolutely clear in a letter to the *Observer* in 1958, seemingly unprovoked, entitled 'The Hotel Room':

The hotel room should contain: – A BED and a BEDSIDE TABLE. Lighting is best provided for above the bed-head, but a movable bedside lamp may have other advantages. It can be put on the TABLE. A proper table is a must, as they say. It exists in nearly all hotel rooms on the Continent and yet is almost without exception lacking in England. It ought to be 3 ft. wide or 2 ft. 6 in. at least. To use it you need a SINGLE CHAIR . . . LIGHTING is a problem much connected with economy. What is needed in every room is a ceiling light with a strong bulb, a bed-side light and a basin-cum-mirror light. What else needs comment? One HOOK or preferably two against the door, and a PLUG for those who use electric shavers, an electric or gas FIRE with a 6d meter, as one usually heats with one's predecessor's shilling.

That is all, as far as we can see. You will agree that it is more a matter of common sense than of great expense. If this letter helps to convert hotel rooms in the direction outlined, I feel confident, Sir, that you will not have wasted your space.

NIKOLAUS AND CAROLA PEVSNER, Department of the History of Art, Birkbeck College.[17]

It was with feeling that the *North Yorkshire* volume was dedicated eight years later to 'those publicans and hoteliers of England who provide me with a table in my bedroom to scribble on'.

In 1952, the year of the Essex excursion, neither Pevsner was in the best of health. Lola's ulcers were giving her pain. As for Pevsner himself, according to Reyner Banham, the strain of preparing for a new county trip would usually lead to him developing some mysterious ailment a few days before setting out, and the pressures imposed by a rigid timetable did not help. While he was on the road, most often for a period of exactly four weeks, he would usually require the secretary of the day to come out from London to meet him at least twice, to bring him messages from the more impatient of his correspondents and proofs for correction or other pressing documents. Winnie Sibson remembered being embarrassed by the constant bickering that seemed to be a normal feature of life on the road for Pevsner and Lola.

There is perhaps a more than ordinary emphasis in *Essex* on the amusing, the odd and the extreme: the old windmill at Rayleigh, 'a tower mill without sails and now incongruously embattled'; the Asylum in Colchester, 'built in 1850 as a remarkably sumptuous station hotel, but not successful as such'; the pier and pavilion at Clacton-on-Sea, 'for the eye oddly mixed up with the surrounding switchback architecture'. Pevsner relished an inscription he found on the octagonal eighteenth-century font in the church of St Mary, Tollesbury: 'Good people all I pray take care, That in ye church you do not sware. As this man did.' He also spotted a notable example of architectural 'swareing' in Waltham Abbey: 'The E wall was remodelled by W. *Burges* in 1859–60 with all the robust ugliness which that architect liked. Extremely short columns with thick shaft-rings and thick crocket capitals, plenty of carved figure work and a big wheel window above – astoundingly loud after the silent severity of the nave.'

The dockland area of Silvertown, east of West Ham, provided a stark setting for another spectacular example of Victorian lack of restraint. 'Silvertown, in spite, and partly because of, its heavy war damage, has much poetry. The mixture of the vast ships in the docks, the vaster factories and mills [the Cooperative Wholesale Society, Spillers, and Tate & Lyle] . . . the small, mean, huddled and not uncomfortable houses, the scrubby vegetation of the bombed sites, and the church cannot fail to impress', particularly since the church, St Mark, was by S.S. Teulon. 'As horrid as only he can be, and yet of a pathetic self-assertion in its surroundings. No lived-in house seems anywhere near.'*

A word that occurs more than once in the volume is 'grit'. He uses it as a compliment, to suggest courage and purpose, usually in relation to buildings, however prosaic, that try to capture the spirit of a new age – the bus garage at Goldings Hill by Yorke, Rosenberg and Mardall, the railway station at Loughton by Murray Easton with its 'boldly

---

*Silvertown is now is the Borough of Newham in Greater London. St Mark's was badly damaged by fire in 1981 and subsequently deconsecrated. It opened in 2001 as the home of the Brick Lane Music Hall.

cantilevered concrete platforms', the car service station at Ilford by Cameron Kirby and, most remarkably perhaps, the oil refinery at Coryton. 'An example of how thrilling aesthetically the intricate metallic forms of industrial structures can be, when not disguised by stone, concrete or brick. The tallest of these ingenious pieces of what seems to be abstract sculpture is the Air-Lift Thermo-fin Catalytic Cracking Unit.' Pevsner can almost certainly claim to be the only architectural historian ever to have waxed lyrical about an Air-Lift Thermo-fin Catalytic Cracking Unit.*

Penguin was accustomed to printing all its volumes in large runs, and the first volumes of the *Buildings of England* (*Middlesex*, *Cornwall*, *Nottinghamshire*, *Devon* and *Derbyshire*) were all printed with runs of 25,000–30,000 each. However, none sold at anywhere near that level, and while *Derbyshire* was the first volume in the series to come out in paperback and hardback at the same time, it was also the last to be printed in such quantities. The volumes that followed would only have 20,000 copies printed, and even then they failed to cover their costs. Allen Lane was losing money on the series at the rate of around £1,000 a year. (By the end of 1956 the series would have cost him well over £5,000, with a further £11,000 invested in stock.)

None of this was due to any extravagance on Pevsner's part. (As late as the 1970s, his daily allowance to cover bed, breakfast, lunch and dinner was £7.25.) On the contrary, from the beginning he would contribute far more work on the series than he could ever realistically be paid for and often spent his own money when the travel allowance failed to stretch. Books of this length, requiring this amount of preparation and detailed research, would, it appeared, always need subsidising. (The Survey of London, for example, had had to be picked up by the London County Council.) 'I am ready to admit,' Pevsner wrote in 1954, 'that work of this kind is always a luxury – only perhaps in my case a luxury both of the author and the publisher.' There are signs that in the *BoE* Pevsner had not given Allen Lane quite what he had been expecting. 'My two volumes are emphatically not drafts,' Pevsner wrote with some hauteur in November 1949, 'but intended for setting.'[18]

In the earliest days it had amused Lane to introduce Pevsner as his

---

*Though Simon Bradley points out that this encomium is in the general tradition of Modernist admiration for spectacular industrial structures in which form palpably follows function.

'best-losing author'. Now he was not giving up on the project, but he was no longer willing to pay quite so much for the luxury. Publication ceased while Pevsner hunted for sponsors to bridge the gap. The search would take two years and bring him very close to despair. At one particularly low point in 1956, frustrated and plagued by boils, he wrote wearily to Lola, 'Oh dear, wouldn't it be better to retire?', adding later in the year, 'Anyway, I'd rather lose B of E than You. So there.'

With no experience in fundraising and little inclination for it, he was not at all clear where to look. He had no connections in government. Charitable foundations like the Pilgrim Trust were unwilling to support what was perceived as a private venture by a commercial concern. This left the private sector, and with some trepidation Pevsner approached Sir Hugh Beaver, the managing director of Arthur Guinness, Son & Co., on the principle that it was always better to apply to individuals directly. (Beaver, an engineer and industrialist, was heavily involved in post-war reconstruction as a member of the Building Industry Working Party and the Committee on New Towns.) 'As things are today in our civilisation,' Pevsner explained, 'the government cannot be expected to back a scheme which refuses to be official in tenor, and private societies and associations are too poor. So patronage has become a duty, or an unwelcome obligation or privilege, of big business.' 'In my particular case,' he added, 'the sum involved is not large per annum and the cause within the field of English art and architecture is quite big.'[19] Six months later Sir Hugh had obviously shown the right degree of interest, and there was a lunch at the Mirabelle at which Guinness agreed to cover production costs and expenses for two of the next ten volumes, if between them they could find sponsors for the other eight.

No other company appeared to have the right combination of large size and sympathetic director – 'I tried Thomas Cook, I tried Esso and I tried Shell,' Pevsner revealed later – but the business world intervened indirectly in the form of the Leverhulme Trust, set up at the wish of the soap baron and philanthropist William Hesketh Lever, 1st Lord Leverhulme.* It was in fact Sir Miles Clifford, Secretary to the grant board, who came to Pevsner's rescue.† 'It was only when I reached your office that I felt from the first moment, here is interest and appreciation,' he wrote gratefully to Clifford.[20] The Trust's support was the more valuable for being projected over a period of twelve years, starting in 1957, lifting the cloud of insecurity at least to some degree (although

---

*This was the Lord Leverhulme about whose Port Sunlight gallery (and title) Pevsner had written derisively on his first visit to England.
†Geoffrey Miles Clifford (1897–1986), Governor of the Falkland Islands 1947–54.

the grants were conditional on approval of progress every three years, which would cause problems later when Penguin failed to publish volumes on time). The sponsorship was designed to be applied to the long preparatory processes that accounted for a significant proportion of the series' costs. Research assistants, secretary, typists, specialist contributors, photographs and plans – all could be paid for out of the Leverhulme money, which was administered through Birkbeck College, as Pevsner's academic employers. This reduced the shortfall on each volume to one that Penguin could accept, and by 1956 the series had resumed on a rather steadier footing than before.

Pevsner's own salary, his office rent and his travelling expenses were not included in either the Guinness or the Leverhulme sponsorships. But by 1958 these would largely be covered by an unlikely – and, in his eyes, slightly dubious – subsidy from ABC Television. Someone had come up with the idea of making a series of short architectural programmes to accompany the channel's occasional transmissions of church services. What was called for, it was explained, was 'a highly popular approach aimed . . . at encouraging [people] to visit historical buildings [i.e. churches] during their summer holidays'.[21]

Pevsner was by no means a television habitué, but the terms ABC were offering were generous: a retainer of £1,000 per year for three years – £480 to go to Birkbeck as a contribution to his 'research fund' and £520 to Pevsner himself. He set to work happily and submitted a list of suitable churches and chapels in the area of the Midlands and the North covered by ABC, including his beloved Southwell Minster. In the end the network could not find space in the schedule. Nevertheless, they insisted on paying Pevsner, to his embarrassment. Though it was not he who had defaulted, he was uncomfortable receiving money he thought he had not earned: 'I feel a little like a cheat.'[22]

CHAPTER 33

'Poet and Pedant': Pevsner and Betjeman

Pevsner would always be his own sternest critic; but for a man who had little taste for personal confrontations and no time for professional politics, he also made some remarkably tenacious enemies. The most notorious of these was John Betjeman.

Peter Clarke made the pages of *Punch* in November 1955 with a poem headed 'A Period Piece' (a title toned-down from the sharper 'Poet and Pedant').* Its gist is clear from the second stanza:

> *A crafty Art Historian*
> *of Continental fame,*
> *I'll creep up on this Amateur*
> *and stop his little game!*

The verses chronicled what 'Astragal' in the *Architects' Journal* was already referring to as 'the celebrated imaginary feud' between Betjeman and Pevsner.† This feud was projected as a battle between amateurism and professionalism, evocation and categorisation, conservatism and modernism, emotion and intellect, Englishman and alien.

An astragal is a type of moulding commonly used to bridge gaps, and 'Astragal' was right in suggesting that the feud was imaginary, in the sense that it was almost entirely one-sided. Pevsner became well aware of Betjeman's dislike of him – he could scarcely have missed it – but he never returned it with any sustained ill-will of his own. 'Vendetta' would be a more accurate description.

In the early years of Betjeman's marriage, his wife Penelope tried to get him to see a psychiatrist to cure him of what she called 'persecution mania'. Betjeman harboured spectacular grudges and, as his biographer Bevis Hillier observes, grudges were important to him – a 'litany of slights – the snubs and rebuffs that he had hoarded, almost

---

* *Punch*, 2/11/55. Peter Clarke (1916–75) was at this point Company Secretary of *The Times*.
† 'The celebrated imaginary feud' has caught the attention of most writers on Betjeman, and forms the subject of an entire book by Timothy Mowl entitled *Stylistic Cold Wars: Betjeman versus Pevsner* (John Murray, 2000), which does neither of its protagonists any favours.

treasured, since childhood. They were his precious bane.'* He fed them by constant rehearsal, and his friends came to expect them of him. Lionel Perry, a friend from university, remarked: 'John had this great capacity for making his phobias and guilts very enjoyable conversation for a lot of other people.' Betjeman made his dislike of Pevsner a conversational leitmotif and used it, like his other vendettas, as a channel for a complex of other emotions – insecurity, disappointment, fear, envy – as well as to express some of his fundamental attitudes towards art, architecture and religious faith.

Betjeman had a great deal of charm, which he used as a weapon, a tool and a shield. He was a role-player, projecting himself in different guises all his life. His most familiar persona – tweedy guardian of the recent past – was itself misleading, more a construct placed upon him by his audience than an accurate expression of a personality that was in reality not at all cosy. As a schoolboy at Marlborough, a school dominated by classics, sport and arcane hierarchies, in none of which he displayed to advantage, he first developed the role of professional eccentric as a form of self-defence. He then took this character a good deal further as the Oxford Betjeman: aesthete at Magdalen, a college of hearties. Betjeman was High Church as a matter of taste as much as religious belief – a *bon vivant*, an adherent of the aristocracy, a snob amusedly aware that he was one.

'Camp' as a term was relatively new when Betjeman was at Oxford in the late 1920s, but the style was one that instinctively appealed to him in his role as aesthete and clown – ostentatious, affected, theatrical, ironic, allusive, frivolous, but fierce in its attack on solemnity and self-importance. It was a style he made use of with friends (homosexual or otherwise) and there is a vein of camp running through his early prose writings, if not his poetry. Susan Sontag's famous essay of 1964 describes 'camp' in terms that resonate with the young Betjeman and with certain traits of the old one: 'To perceive Camp in objects and persons is to understand Being-as-Playing-a-Role. It is the farthest extension, in sensibility, of the metaphor of life as theatre . . . Camp involves a new, more complex relation to "the serious". One can be serious about the frivolous, frivolous about the serious . . . The ultimate Camp statement: it's good because it's awful' (a statement neatly inverted in Betjeman's first post-Oxford prose publication, *Ghastly Good Taste*).

---

*Hillier, *Young Betjeman*, op. cit., p.404. Anyone writing about Betjeman is bound to draw heavily on Hillier's three-volume biography, which has a wealth of information on his family, friends, enemies, colleagues, correspondents and casual acquaintances, besides the subject himself.

Equally, in Sontag's terms, Pevsner was as un-camp, and as unsympathetic to camp, as it is possible to be. 'Camp is the consistently aesthetic experience of the world,' she wrote. 'It incarnates a victory of "style" over "content", "aesthetics" over "morality", of irony over tragedy' – that is to say, it proclaims the creed of 'Art for art's sake' that Pevsner had so consistently resisted since his student days. Again, Camp relies heavily on the private code and the inside joke. 'To camp is a mode of seduction – one which employs flamboyant mannerisms susceptible of a double interpretation; gestures full of duplicity, with a witty meaning for cognoscenti and another, more impersonal, for outsiders.' From the moment of his first arrival in England, Pevsner had been highly sensitive to the distinctions between 'insiders' and 'outsiders' – as a young academic in Birmingham striving to master ironical understatement and the English joke, visiting Oxford and trying simultaneously to penetrate the drawl and pick his way through the web of allusion and High Table vernacular. His objective was always to communicate clearly: he neither indulged in conversational freemasonry himself nor relished it in others. Nor did he find snobbery in the least lovable. He may well have been oblivious to the finer points of social gradations, as critics alleged, but when he noticed snobbery it irritated and discomfited him.

Pevsner was never the stiff pedant that Betjemanites like to depict, but equally he was not as bonhomous, as exuberant, as gregarious, as funny as their hero. Betjeman was an enthusiast who would happily agree to new projects and then not complete them; his attention span was limited, and he was easily diverted for a good lunch or a chat. In Sir Peter Parker's phrase, he had 'an infinite capacity for taking trains'. Pevsner, by comparison, was almost excessively conscientious and painstaking. John Summerson remembered: 'One always knew perfectly well that Nikolaus had something else to do, so one never detained him in the leisurely way that most people connected with the arts enjoy.'[1]

Once he was secure in his teaching career and at the helm of the *BoE*, Pevsner never made much of his academic titles. But for Betjeman, Pevsner's educational qualifications were an affront. So too was the Germanness, a trait that Betjeman had taken some care to disown in himself, his own origins having almost certainly been German in the eighteenth century. His great-great-grandfather George, who spelled his surname 'Betjemann', is thought to have been born in Bremen in 1764 before emigrating to England by the end of the century. His great-grandfather, who founded the family cabinet-making business in London, preferred to drop the second 'n'. John's father Ernest reverted to the original spelling, which appears on John's birth certificate (and, for the sake of legality, on his marriage certificate). On the other hand, John's mother – Mabel Bessie Dawson from Highbury – preferred to encourage the idea that the name was Dutch, and insisted that the second 'n' be dropped again during the First World War. This was not enough to protect John from some vicious teasing at his junior school, where two boys once danced round him in the playground shouting, 'Betjeman's a German spy – Shoot him down and let him die.' Perhaps understandably, as he grew up he preferred to go with the Dutch line. In 1927 his father wrote to him: 'I see you sign as a "one enner". Very cowardly!'[2]

Betjeman's father was a source of acute embarrassment to him – something that, like the dread of being an outsider, he had in common with Pevsner. To Betjeman, the fact that his father had been in trade was a lifelong burden. The family firm had manufactured furniture for the middle classes – when Ernest entered the business in 1899, its most successful product was 'the Betjemann patent tantalus', a device that enabled the householder to lock decanters and keep their contents safe from the servants. In 1955, almost forty years after the incident it describes, Betjeman wrote a poem entitled 'False Security' centred on the memory of a children's party in The Grove, Highgate:

Can I forget my delight at the conjuring show?
And wasn't I proud that I was the last to go?
Too overexcited and pleased with myself to know
That the words I heard my hostess's mother employ
To a guest departing, would ever diminish my joy,
I WONDER WHERE JULIA FOUND THAT STRANGE, RATHER
COMMON LITTLE BOY?

Pevsner would never be as cruel about Hugo as Betjeman was about Ernest, pillorying him in a play he wrote in Oxford as 'Mr Artsenkraft . . . a fat person with sensual lips and a hard face. His suiting is very neat and in the true business-man style. He wears a hard white collar.' Stuck with a middle-class background, Betjeman resorted to playing it up and making its 'comedy' into a virtue. He wrote to novelist G.B. Stern: 'How very kind of you to leave me your fish-knives. Of course I'll use them because I AM MIDDLE CLASS AND PROUD OF IT but I like using the language of the upper class.* This last statement is the important one. Betjeman liked how the upper classes spoke, how they looked, how they behaved, their houses, their possessions and the world they inhabited. By his own account, he was a skilful social climber, but this brought him into circles where he felt, and was encouraged to feel, inadequate. The romance of the aristocracy, dimly perceived at Marlborough, was able to flourish in Oxford. He made friends whose families inhabited great houses and he took, in his own words, his first steps in learning how to be a guest.

Ernest Betjemann had hoped, perhaps improbably, that his son would follow him into the furniture business, but, as Betjeman wrote in his verse autobiography *Summoned by Bells*: 'How could I, after Canterbury Quad, / My peers and country houses and my jokes, / Talk about samples, invoices and stock?' In the eyes of his parents-in-law, however, the peers and country houses were not 'his' by right, but merely borrowed temporarily. Betjeman had met Penelope Chetwode at the *Architectural Review*, after Hastings had refused to see her to discuss a proposed article on Indian cave temples and she had been ushered instead into Betjeman's office. She was the daughter of Philip Walhouse Chetwode, 7th Baronet of Oakley, an Old Etonian cavalry officer who by the time of his daughter's marriage had risen to become Field Marshal and Commander-in-Chief in India. Her mother Alice Stapleton-Cotton was granddaughter of a lord, daughter of a colonel. Neither approved of Penelope's choice. 'We invite people like that to our houses,' Lady Chetwode is reported to have said, 'but we don't marry them.'

Betjeman began to go bald early, and even his friends remarked on his buck teeth – 'sort of greenish', according to poet and patron Edward James, 'slightly prominent and not a good colour. He giggled a lot, so the teeth showed a lot.' Louis MacNeice, no friend, observed: 'His face was the colour of peasoup and his eyes were soupy too and his mouth was always twisting sideways in a mocking smile.' Penelope was inclined to make a joke of his features: 'You seem to have complexes about yourself and whatnot. You certainly do smell very bad & are as yellow as a quattrocentro Florentine, & you have earwigs in your nose which would revolt many people, but you must surely know by now that these defects only serve to enhance your charms in my sight.'[3]

---

*J. Betjeman/G.B. Stern, 8/6/56 (Gladys Bronwen Stern, 1890–1973, novelist and Jane Austen scholar, best known for *The Rakonitz Chronicles*). The middle-classness of fish-knives had been enshrined in Betjeman's 'How to Get On in Society', published in 1951: 'Phone for the fish-knives, Norman / As Cook is a little unnerved'.

Certainly Betjeman grew out of his worst self-consciousness about his appearance, as had Pevsner. But his insecurities, to a far greater degree than Pevsner's, extended to his work.

By the early 1960s, Betjeman had been awarded the CBE, had won the Duff Cooper Prize, seen his *Collected Poems* sell in their tens of thousands and become a national celebrity on the publication of *Summoned by Bells*. None of this was able to assure him of his own intellectual worth. 'I'm no good,' he wrote to his daughter Candida in November 1966, 'only fashionable' – and fashions are, by definition, fleeting. Eddie Mirzoeff, the producer of Betjeman's *Metroland* documentary, remembered him as having a genuine sense 'that this was a temporary phenomenon, that he was in vogue and therefore able to scratch a living, but that it wouldn't last and that he would unquestionably end in the workhouse. He used to say that regularly as a joke – but it was one of those things that you knew *wasn't* a joke.'[4] He both fiercely resented the critics of his poetry, of whom there were many, particularly in academia, and dreaded that they were right and that his work was trivial and transient.

The same was true of his writings on art and architecture. A fear of being caught out made him acutely sensitive to criticism and left him ill at ease with 'experts' – Fellows of the Society of Antiquaries (who he believed despised him as a non-scholar), academics and what he called the 'closed shop' of art historians. It particularly infuriated him that so many apparent insiders in the 'closed shop' were people who, in his view, no more 'belonged' in the English establishment than he did. He may not have invented the use of the title 'Herr-Professor-Doktor' to characterise the continental art historians who had come to Britain in the 1930s, but he certainly liked to deploy it as a term of abuse.

Betjeman might have been better able to get along with the old tradition of English antiquarianism and connoisseurship which the new art history had to some extent superseded. He had a very good eye and a talent for turning his perceptions into prose as well as poetry; he was a gifted 'natural' writer – vivid, amusing, readable. He would undoubtedly have been comfortable with the ethos of the 'gentleman amateur', favouring taste over scholarship. Whether he truly believed it or not, Betjeman often gave the impression that he felt it was better to be discerning rather than bookish, intuitive rather than diligent, a cultivated English *arbiter elegantiarum* rather than a Middle European professional student. There were large tracts of life, he considered, where professionalism simply did not belong, and the appreciation of art and architecture was one of them. 'For

Betjeman,' remembered John Summerson, 'the whole subject was one
for leisure . . . His way of talking about it was a sort of deliberate
amateurism. He never spelt out the history of a building with any
feeling of authority. He would give the dates of a building in a diffident way, as if to say "I hate this, but here they are". That was very
endearing – he didn't frighten people by his professionalism – in fact,
he didn't have any.'*

'Doctor' was Betjeman's way of characterising someone who might
be cleverer than he was – and 'Doktor' was the ultimate insult: not
just an intrusive pedant, but a foreign intrusive pedant. Betjeman
wanted to be taken seriously by other people on their terms and very
much resented it when he was not. He would write in the *Spectator*
on his fiftieth birthday: 'I started reviewing my past life, first through
a magnifying mist of self-pity – never quite made the grade, not taken
seriously by the TLS, Penguin Books, the Courtauld, the Warburg, the
Listener, the University Appointments Board, the Museums Association,
the Library Association, the Institute of Sanitary Engineers.'⁵

Betjeman bored easily and worried about money, which led him to
turn his hand to an array of different jobs and try himself out in many
roles. In consequence, he ventured into fields where he was prone to
feeling inferior to those who had inhabited them longer. What his
major 'hates' had in common was that they knew rather more than
he did in the fields where he encountered them, on their ground rather
than his own. Betjeman and Pevsner shared a greater sense of insecurity than Betjeman realised; but it remained true that Pevsner had full
academic qualifications and Betjeman did not, Pevsner worked with
academic rigour and application and Betjeman did not, Pevsner had
criteria by which he assessed serious scholarship and Betjeman would
not have met them.

Betjeman once said, only half self-mocking, that he would have
liked to have become a don 'and read English Literature to the accom-
paniment of lovely surroundings'. What happened instead at Oxford
was that he was obliged to study philology with C.S. Lewis – 'that
coarse Ulster puritan and prig' – a man who seemed to go out of his
way to create a dismal setting for himself in his North Oxford rooms.
Lewis found his pupil affected, irritating and idle. Betjeman himself
described his Oxford career as 'luncheons, luncheons all the way'.
Never likely to perform well in his Finals, he short-circuited the process

*Summerson met Betjeman through Morton Shand and was a fellow-member of the
MARS Group. He wrote articles for the *Architectural Review* under the pen-name of
'Coolmore', which Betjeman used as his nickname throughout their friendship.

by repeatedly failing the compulsory Divinity paper, getting rusticated for a term in the spring of his final year, taking a Pass degree in place of the usual Honours, electing to offer a paper for this degree in Welsh, failing the Pass examinations and being sent down for good without a degree.

He drifted into architectural journalism through his Oxford contacts, introduced by Maurice Bowra to Maurice Hastings, brother of H. de Cronin Hastings. During his stay at the *Architectural Review* as an assistant editor from 1930 to 1935 Betjeman did manage to insinuate some of his own enthusiasms: Victorian typefaces, Arts and Crafts design, the Gothic Revival. He also managed some good teases in the form of spoof letters, his own verses and unorthodox captions for serious illustrations. But in the words of Oxford friend John Edward Bowle, 'John hopelessly overdid treating the job as a joke . . . [He] expects as of right that people will look after him simply if he prattles about the place.'[6]

'"Being amusing" . . . is his great danger,' Philip Morton Shand wrote to Penelope Chetwode in 1933, shortly before she married Betjeman. 'Travel, sustained, persistent travel, is the thing he needs above all. Plus a window into another language.' Betjeman genuinely struggled with foreign languages, or at least grudged the time required to learn one well. Where Pevsner had laboured over his Toussaint-Langenscheidt parallel texts and his lists of vocabulary to make himself intelligible, first in Italian and then in English, Betjeman failed to bother. 'Language difficulties . . . make the continent of Europe so difficult for one who has had the advantage of a public school education,' he told *Vogue* in 1962.

Betjeman resigned from the *Architectural Review* in 1935, ostensibly because the pay was poor, but more probably because he had lost interest. His career over the next fifteen years, springing out of the need to supplement his income from poetry, was variegated: reviewing books and films, editing the first *Shell Guides* and writing advertising copy for Shell-Mex House, composing home hints for the *Daily Express* and editing the magazine *Decoration*, serving from 1941 to 1943 as press attaché to the British Representative in Dublin, working in Oxford as the secretary to the Oxford Preservation Trust, battling the formidable Lady Rhondda – a proprietor whom he called 'stumpy, dumpy and grumpy' – as the literary editor of her magazine *Time and Tide*. The only constant thread, besides the poems that appeared at intervals, was an ever-growing reputation as a broadcaster. Already a popular radio personality before the war, he was described in 1946 by a BBC producer as 'a speaker of great reputation and experience'.

The *Architectural Review* was his first job in journalism, and Betjeman adopted some of the protective colouring of his new habitat. He wanted to go with the flow of thinking at the *Review* and he was anxious to please Morton Shand; on occasion, he made authentic-sounding pronouncements in favour of the Modern Movement. But once he had left the magazine, he no longer needed to use its language or embrace its dogmas and could use other means to sustain the friendship with Morton Shand, whose own enthusiasm for modernism was in any case cooling. But fickle and frivolous as Betjeman may have been at the *Review*, he laid the foundations there of the contribution that he would later make – not to the history of architecture, but to its appreciation.

John Summerson made an important distinction:

> Mr Betjeman is an architectural writer . . . When he writes about buildings he does not write about them as form (and my goodness, how he despises art-historians because they do!) but as evocation . . . [Betjeman] loves to put in the names of all the architects, and the more hopelessly forgotten the names the more delighted he is with them . . . He has transferred the snobbery of the collector of old china or Japanese prints to a sphere where collecting is mercifully impossible and where its snobbery becomes on the one hand extremely funny, and on the other . . . utterly absorbing to anybody with a feeling for architecture and the oddity of mankind . . . Mr Betjeman is a serious student who can never keep an absolutely straight face, but he is a serious student.[7]

All this is true, and has its positive side, as Pevsner saw. Being a serious student, however, is not the same as being a serious scholar – and there were serious scholars who, not finding Betjeman funny, were less forgiving. Anthony Blunt, according to his brother Wilfrid, 'felt that John, who had the makings of a scholar, elected . . . to prostitute his talents by popularising what he could have directed into serious study'.[8] As for modernist architect and architectural writer Maxwell Fry, he simply found Betjeman 'a bloody nuisance . . . The key to John Betjeman's character is that he's a journalist and a Fleet Street man – and a popularist – and vain. He was the enemy to Modernism.'[9]

Pevsner, on the other hand, took Betjeman absolutely seriously as a poet. Margaret Tims, a Pevsner secretary, recalled: 'The Pevsners were quite Betjeman fans and always took his poetry on their *Buildings of England* journey', and when Pevsner was asked to contribute a favourite poem to a charity anthology, he chose Betjeman. He respected him as a topographer and writer of guidebooks: he gave Camilla Rodker a copy of the *Murray's Guide* to Berkshire, which he got Betjeman to autograph. He also appreciated Betjeman's wide acquaintance with Victorian architecture, relished his enthusiasm and admired his ability to infect other people with it. Many years later, writing an obituary for Peter Clarke, who emulated Betjeman in some respects, Pevsner made clear what he saw as Betjeman's great strengths: 'Peter Clarke was a man in the Betjeman tradition, to whom architecture was in the first place a joy . . . Good architecture of all periods aroused a personal response, which he delighted to hand on to others.' Betjeman could evoke atmosphere and personality in a manner that Pevsner could only envy. In a review of topographical books by other writers, he quoted a Betjeman couplet on a "curious" Anglo-Norman parish church in Kentish Town and added 'What church is it? I looked up my own *Buildings of England* and found it with all the poetry taken out of it. All the more blessings for Mr Betjeman.'[10]

Nevertheless, in Pevsner's eyes Betjeman was not a scholar – not even a scholar of the Victorian period, the field where his credentials were perhaps strongest.* He would almost certainly have thought it mattered that Betjeman had not got a degree. He would probably not have paid much attention to the recanting of faith in the Modern Movement, but he could not have failed to notice that Betjeman's art history lacked system and rigour. He may have admired and envied the joyous directness of Betjeman's response to buildings, but he did not care for the element of camp that sometimes crept into people's enthusiasm for Victorian detail – what he had described in the *Outline* as 'attention of the whimsical variety'. Anthony Powell remarked of Betjeman that he 'had a whim of iron'. Both whim and whimsy were foreign to Pevsner's nature, and he grew irritated with people who persisted in flippancy around serious subjects.

For his part, Betjeman believed that what he perceived as pedantry was not just dull but destructive. He was not simply battling academic art historians to preserve his *amour propre*, much though he resented condescension, but also to protect the objects of their scrutiny. 'What he did not like,' commented John Summerson, 'was the illumination of the obscure by art historians. That destroyed the bloom of

---

*In 1951, in a BBC talk on 'How to Judge Victorian Architecture', Pevsner failed to include Betjeman in his list of cognoscenti – a list that included John Summerson and himself.

obscurity. The twilight which had settled on the Victorian and Edwardian was a beautiful, tragical–comical twilight. It was not an academic problem looking for an academic answer. Hence his antagonism towards Pevsner, which for a time was obsessional. The Pevsner approach was like installing a system of floodlights in a twilight landscape.'[11]

Betjeman worked through association and allusion:

> For me . . . England stands for the Church of England, eccentric incumbents, oil-lit churches, Women's Institutes, modest village inns, arguments about cow parsley on the altar, the noise of mowing machines on Saturday afternoons, local newspapers, local auctions, the poetry of Tennyson, Crabbe, Hardy and Matthew Arnold, local talent, local concerts, a visit to the cinema, branch line trains, light railways, leaning on gates and looking across fields.[12]

He loved the process of making these associations; for him the links with people, histories, habits and rituals were what gave buildings and their contents life. How could anyone who was not English understand this cross-referenced world – and if they could not understand it, what gave them the right to analyse its buildings and its art, to dissect and flatten them? Pevsner had no roots here, no web of connections, he could not pick up all of these allusions even if he had wanted to – and in any event, within the confines of the *BoE* series he obviously had neither time nor space for associations, only for the structures themselves. His was a stripped approach and, Betjeman feared, a loveless one. In the preface to *First and Last Loves* in 1952 he launched an acid attack on Herr-Professor-Doktors 'who are writing everything down for us, sometimes throwing in a little hurried pontificating too, so we need never bother to feel or think or see again . . . Love is dead.'

Betjeman had been known, when passing a building he admired, to clap.[13] Pevsner was far more reserved: but Betjeman was wrong to suspect that he did not feel strongly about what he saw. In an interview for the Home Service in 1964 Pevsner would explain:

> Sometimes the excitement is there and very sudden. Because even if you know that there must be a, say, 13th-century parish church there, you don't know from your information whether it'll be the sort of building where the 13th-century shapes, the early Gothic forms, are particularly perfect, and so you might occasionally find a parish church that just within its own style is so perfect that it

does make you shout . . . And very occasionally you find something which is completely new to you. That happened to us the other day with what is called the transporter bridge at Middlesbrough, a most unpromising place . . . This transporter bridge is a structure of about . . . 50 years ago, which is 225 feet high, a wonderfully lacy [structure], an absolute thrill . . . We tried it out happily – and it really is an absolutely, you know, splendid monument.[14]

Within the format of the *BoE*, Pevsner was never able to write like this and people rarely had the opportunity to see him talking about the deep pleasure he took in places, but he could not conceivably have completed his formidable undertaking without it.

Even if Betjeman had had no philosophical objections to Pevsner, by the early 1950s he had some practical *casus belli*. These dated back almost twenty years, probably to the first publication of Pevsner's *Pioneers* in 1936. Betjeman himself had enjoyed 'pioneer'-spotting during his *Architectural Review* years, having more sympathy with the trailblazers than with the modernists for whom they were held to have paved the way. In his 1933 article on 'British Industrial Art' he had specifically used the term 'pioneers' and derived modern industrial design from the work of, among others, Morris, Webb, Ashbee and Voysey. He felt that, at the very least, he had staked some sort of claim on an area of taste that was now being rather efficiently invaded by outsiders.

Betjeman would seem to have felt particularly territorial about Voysey and George Walton. He too had met Voysey, but whereas Pevsner had only met him at his club, Betjeman had visited 'that little flat above Rumpelmayer's [in St James's Street] where Voysey lived in solitude'. He had had more contact with Walton, too, and ensured that his family was cared for after his death. Pevsner did not seem to be sufficiently aware or respectful of those non-German writers who had gone before him in the historiography of the Modern Movement, and Betjeman wanted to draw his attention to them.* In April 1939 he wrote Pevsner a letter that was a masterly combination of generosity, territorialism and one-upmanship.[15] 'Dear Mr Pevsner,' it began – surely in an effort to annoy, though Pevsner may well not have noticed:

---

*Some thirty-five years after the publication of *Pioneers*, Pevsner would acknowledge Betjeman as one of the first in the field to research Walton (NP, review of R. Wagner-Rieger, *Die Wiener Ringstrasse – Bild einer Epoche*, TLS, 1971), but far too late for the purpose of appeasement.

I was most interested to see your article in the RIBA Journal on Walton. I only wish you had written to me before you wrote it, as I have quite a collection of Waltoniana here including a set of glasses which Mrs Walton kindly gave to me. Where did you get that quotation from Voysey which you put on p.543? He (CFAV) wrote to me an almost similar description of GW in 1934. If you ever want more photographs of Walton's work and letters from his contemporaries about him, do let me know and I will send them to you. When I was a younger and happier man I spent a lot of time trying to discover 'pioneer' architects, but never had the time or ability to be as thorough as you are. I loved your article on Mc Murdo [sic] which was a wonderful eye-opener to me . . . I hope that one day we may meet and have conversation about these old gentlemen. Why don't you join the Art Workers' Guild? It is most ironical that in the same issue of the RIBA Journal with your Walton article given rightful prominence should appear some of Harry Redfern's work. Mrs Walton will tell you why . . . PS. I wish you had illustrated the interior of the White House and also given that portrait of GW as a Roman Emperor leaning over a pool!'

Betjeman had written one of the earliest articles on Voysey, published in the *Architectural Review* in October 1931. But when Voysey died in 1941, it was a piece by Pevsner that ran in the *Review*. Not long afterwards Pevsner joined the editorial staff – an insult to add to the injury of Betjeman's own rejection. In 1939, with a new baby and in arrears with his rent, he had asked for his *Review* job back and received an unambiguous reply from Hastings: 'The board is damned if it is going to switch everything round again to please you . . . Already you have fulfilled the prophecies of those who shall be nameless, who in their wisdom laughed and said, "In six weeks he'll be wanting to come back".'[16]

Then in 1943, with the publication of *An Outline of European Architecture*, Pevsner had some conspicuous success and, more importantly, consolidated a relationship with Allen Lane and Penguin Books which Betjeman may well have envied. Betjeman had been approached by Allen Lane in the 1930s to write a book about churches, but it never materialised: he claimed to have lost the manuscript. By September 1947, cloaked in the decent anonymity of the *Times Literary Supplement*, Betjeman's animosity was coming into view. Under the heading 'The New Pedantry', he wrote: 'The introduction of professionalism into such subjects as literature, architecture and art too often turns enjoyment to ashes', and he went on to regret that 'the vanity of prefixing "Doctor" or "Professor" to a surname and some letters after it' had 'crept from Germany and America into Britain'.

The arrival of the *Buildings of England* series was a further provo-cation. Betjeman had enjoyed his career as a writer of guidebooks: in Bevis Hillier's words, the *Shell Guides* were 'perhaps the first paid work he had undertaken – apart from writing poetry – which promised to be really congenial'.[17] Even more to the point, the *Shell* and *Murray's Guides* had represented a significant part of his income, and without a doubt he will have blamed the Penguin series for contributing to the demise of the *Murray's Guides* early in the 1950s.

An internal BBC memo of 1951 records: 'Please note that Mr Betjeman wishes never again to appear in a discussion programme with Professor Pevsner'; precisely what sin Pevsner had committed is unknown. In January 1952, reviewing L.T.C. Rolt's *The Thames from Mouth to Source* in *Time and Tide*, Betjeman praised Rolt for writing 'with an eye for landscape unimpaired by antiquarianism. He sees a building and he knows its history, but he does not isolate it from its setting and function and classify it as though for a museum, as do our Herr-Professor-Doktors of today.' He almost certainly had Pevsner in his sights, perhaps taking his cue from Morton Shand, who was wont to refer to him as 'super-Professor Nikolaus Pevsner'.* To James Lees-Milne, Betjeman complained: 'I travel third and am cut by people who count and looked down upon by the new refugee "scholars" who have killed all we like by their "research" – i.e. Nikolaus Pevsner that dull pedant from Prussia.'[18]

Behind the bitterness that Betjeman felt, there was more than a difference of opinion on how to look at buildings. He may have felt under attack from Pevsner in an even more sensitive area of his life. In 1948, the two men had clashed in the letter columns of the *Times Literary Supplement*, Pevsner in the open and Betjeman skimpily veiled under the title of 'Your reviewer'.† The review in question, a short piece entitled 'Anglicana' in March 1948, was an assault on *Stuart and Georgian Churches* by Marcus Whiffen. Again, Betjeman seems to have felt his territory had been invaded. 'Anglican churches are not country houses,' he wrote. 'Their style is less essential to an appreciation of them than is their plan; and their plan is dependent on liturgical

---

*In fact, Pevsner would not hold a personal chair until 1959: at this point he was 'Professor' only by virtue of the Cambridge Slade professorship.

†In general, Pevsner was in favour of anonymity in *TLS* reviewing, and was sorry when the practice was abandoned in the 1970s under the editorship of John Gross. He 'objected that it would make life difficult when his friends wrote bad books'. Obituary for John Gross, *Daily Telegraph*, 11/1/2011.

arrangements. A knowledge of church history is more important to a
book of this sort than an ability to analyse style.' Pevsner took issue.
'I cannot agree,' he wrote, 'that Mr Whiffen is to be blamed for talking
less of liturgical arrangements than of architecture. I for my own part
like occasionally to read a book on architecture which concentrates
on architecture. You, sir, know how rare such books are in this country.'

With little effort, Betjeman could interpret this as an attack both
on amateurism and on England, and he hit back. 'I . . . feel that this
correspondence is a little unfair on Dr Pevsner.' (Pevsner had, as usual,
omitted his title when signing his letter.) 'He is a useful and excellent
academic writer on European architecture. But when he applies cosmopolitan standards to Stuart and Georgian Anglican churches he is in
a fix. For these churches were designed . . . to give expression to the
English Book of Common Prayer.' And what, he implied, could a
foreigner know of that? A church should be judged 'by what it is like
to pray in, and how it fits the rite for which it was built or altered.
To judge on style and date alone is like passing judgement on the
chassis of a motor car without looking at the engine.'

Pevsner responded by suggesting that the form of the liturgy was
often an irrelevance; many of the churches under discussion could
quite well adapt themselves to Calvinist, Lutheran 'or for that matter,
Roman' worship.

If that was not a red rag, Betjeman certainly took it to be one, and
charged. 'If Dr Pevsner wishes to learn about English churches, I
commend to him, recently published, *The Architectural Setting of
Anglican Worship* by G.W.O. Addleshaw and Frederick Etchells FRIBA
(Faber 25s) . . . But so long as he and Mr Whiffen put style and names
of architects as a consideration before worship and the use of the eye
for beauty, we will obviously never agree about the "quality and
interest" of a church.'

Pevsner was reticent about his personal beliefs, possibly conscious
of curiosity surrounding the phenomenon of the converted Jew, more
probably because he felt religious faith to be a private matter. Neither
he nor Lola was a regular church-goer, but his faith – as far as one
can tell – was steady and quiet. When he did express it, it was with
assurance, but no solemnity. (Bridget Cherry remembers him saying,
on arriving at a church to find a service in progress, 'Really, the uses
some people put these places to . . .') He was open about his preference for austerity in worship – what he described as 'Protestant
clarity and purity'. 'My origins are in a part of Germany which is
Protestant and in this country I would certainly be called very low
church indeed,' he revealed in a radio talk in 1954. He preferred

forms of worship that needed a minimum of decoration and no intermediaries. Late in his life he would write to the vicar of an Essex parish that was then very High Church: 'I am Lutheran myself and have always found it rather painful at Thaxted to see how many objects of devotion have gradually been displayed.' Scrupulously, he was alerting the vicar to his feelings before accepting a seat on the church's Appeal Committee.[19]

Pevsner's preferences did not prevent him from appreciating how important the aesthetic component in worship could be. He stoutly defended the rococo exuberance of the Catholic churches of eighteenth-century Bavaria, which many considered histrionic and shallow, because it was the vehicle that helped the congregations of those places and that time to commune with God: 'What matters is that these churches have been the vessels of worship for innumerable simple souls, as you still see them kneel and fervently pray in them now, and that their festive character had moreover very good and perfectly legitimate reasons in the minds of those who commissioned the churches and their decoration.'[20]

His thoughts on church architecture were centred on the controversy around the new Coventry Cathedral and its architect Basil Spence. Spence was someone whom Pevsner both liked and admired, as a man as well as an artist. Some critics were disappointed by what they saw as the low key of the new cathedral and disparaged it as too 'ordinary'. For Pevsner, this was what a religious building ought to be, because worship should be a part of daily life, not a theatrical performance.

Not publicly expansive himself, Pevsner could be made uneasy by fulsomeness in others, particularly in contexts where he felt display was out of place. Betjeman was known to quote Ninian Comper's famous sentiment with approval – 'A church should bring you to your knees when first you enter it' – and it would seem that he acted upon it. Mary Mouat remarked, 'I don't think there was a feud. The only thing I heard [NP] say was, "It's really rather awful going into a church with John, he does kneel long and embarrassingly".'

Pevsner did not care for religious rank-pulling. He did not think that people were less devout because their church architecture was more flamboyant, but he rejected the notion that some people were *more* righteous or more devout because they expressed their beliefs in a more demonstrative way. In the context of Coventry Cathedral, apparently defending both Spence and himself, he wrote angrily that it did not mean that they lacked the right to build a cathedral or write about one 'because we are not as close to the spiritual content of the Church of England as, say, Sir Ninian Comper and Mr Betjeman . . .

I gather that Mr Spence does not go to church every Sunday, and I am what you would call Chapel and not Church – certainly not C of E. Can he therefore not design a cathedral, and should I keep my mouth shut about his design?'[21] The note of animus here is unusual for Pevsner and intriguing, as is the link he makes between Betjeman and Ninian Comper.

Comper's father, John Comper, was a leader of the later Anglo-Catholic phase of the Oxford Movement in Scotland, and his godfather, J.M. Neale, one of the founders of the Cambridge Camden Society.* Unsurprisingly, leading Anglo-Catholics in England gave Comper the opportunity to express his thinking as a church architect. He worked initially in a single style as one of the last promoters of the Gothic Revival, but later in a style that he described as 'Unity by Inclusion', a fusion of Gothic with classical and other elements. St Mary's Wellingborough unites a Perpendicular nave with Spanish screens and classical *baldacchino*.

His explicit aim in church design was to support the liturgy and inspire reverence in the presence of God. 'The purpose of a church is not to express the age in which it was built or the individuality of its designer,' he wrote. 'Its purpose is to move to worship, to bring a man to his knees, to refresh his soul in a weary land.'[22] 'For mankind in the mass,' Comper continued, 'the neglect of beauty spells the hardness or narrowness either of a puritan or a materialist', and his buildings glittered and glowed with burnished gilt, stained glass, jewels and luminous colouring on wood, stone, cloth, floor, ceiling.

Pevsner clearly agreed that the nature of worship must be central to the design of a church. He too would have denied that it was a church architect's job to express his individuality. However, he disagreed profoundly with Comper's assertion that 'the purpose of a church is not to express the age in which it was built'. For him, the church architect had to be able to promote worship in a manner that was appropriate to his own times, not by evoking the atmosphere of an age of faith that was gone, and certainly not through picking and mixing from the styles of different ages. A church might display the features of different eras through accretion; but when these features were deliberately juxtaposed, the result could only be affected and artificial – 'synthetic' in the worst sense. He had already made his

---

*Established in 1839, the Camden Society was a learned society founded by Cambridge undergraduates to promote a return to the church architecture of the Middle Ages. Later known as the Ecclesiological Society, it was closely associated with the doctrines of the Oxford Movement.

distaste known with his comments on Comper's work in *Nottingham-shire* – 'shameless imitation', 'feeble drawing', church furnishings that were 'valueless' as pieces of contemporary art. But it seems likely that since that time he had fallen even further out of sympathy with Comper.

Betjeman claimed in *First and Last Loves* that a church interior had been 'the first really beautiful work of man which my boyhood vividly remembers'. Though he sometimes made fun of Comper the man, it was natural that he should admire an approach to church design that was explicitly the pursuit of beauty, and his admiration was reinforced by his own undergraduate leanings towards Anglo-Catholicism. As early as 1943 he was escorting parties to the Chapel of St Sepulchre in the crypt of St Mary Magdalene, Paddington, a chantry chapel in the style of fifteenth-century Germany, in a design based on the idea of the penitent St Mary Magdalene becoming the first witness of the resurrection under a blue vault spangled with stars. Pevsner, de Cronin Hastings, John Piper, Osbert Lancaster – all were 'stupefied to silence by its magnificence', Betjeman told Comper proudly.[23] 'I am continually demolishing highbrow functionalists,' Betjeman added two years later, 'by giving them my London course of Comper which is to visit St MM Paddington and then on to St Cyprian's and then photographs of Cosham and Wellingbor-ough.'[24]

St Cyprian, Clarence Gate (1903) was another example of Comper's early style, an evocation of a fifteenth-century parish church from paintings and illustrations in medieval manuscripts, complete with the decorations and many of the ritual features that had disappeared with the Reformation. Comper wrote in 1930: 'The whole church has become a lantern and the altar is the flame within it. The high chancel and the side chancels are separated from the nave and from each other by coloured and gilded screens which, seen against the silver and jewels of the painted glass, greatly enrich the beauty of the altar but obstruct the view of it no more than a lantern hides the light it is made to contain.'

Comper himself avoided publicity and disliked exhibitions. His work was earnest and entirely without irony – functional in the sense that he could be said to work from the altar outwards, planning first the features that were directly necessary for the purposes of worship and only afterwards the structures that would surround them. Some of his patrons, however, and even more of his admirers, were blatantly attracted by the look rather than the intent of his work, and they helped to create an ethos of theatricality from which Pevsner would have shied.

When the time came for Pevsner to describe St Cyprian in *London except*, he remarked: 'If there must be medieval imitations in the 20th century it is here unquestionably done with joy and care. Beyond that appreciation can hardly go.' And here is the real crux of the antipathy that Betjeman cherished for so many years, because Pevsner added, fatally: 'There is no reason for the excesses of praise lavished on Comper's church furnishings by those who confound aesthetic with religious emotions.'

He may not have meant this to be as insulting as it sounded. He had probably not forgotten his own confusion of religious feeling and aesthetic enjoyment during the preparations for confirmation some thirty years before in Potsdam. Betjeman himself had admitted to conflating faith with sensation at the very beginning of his religious life: 'I was first, I suppose, brought to belief by my eyes and ears and nose. The smell of incense, and sight of candles, High Church services, they attracted me and I liked them.'[25]

But this was a callowness Betjeman considered he had long outgrown. He had been wounded when Evelyn Waugh had accused him of remaining in the Church of England, rather than converting to Catholicism when Penelope did, for purely aesthetic reasons: 'Really you are wrong in thinking that I regard religion as "the source of pleasurable emotions and sensation". I used to, as an undergraduate, but it has been a stern struggle for the last fourteen years.'[26] Now here was Pevsner, a man whom he already mistrusted, apparently levelling the same charge from the other end of the Christian spectrum. Betjeman's religious differences with his wife were at least partly responsible for the gradual decay of their marriage. They were acutely painful to him and were to some extent caused by his loyalty to his own brand of faith. The suggestion that this faith was in any way inauthentic – perhaps as spurious as Comper's 'medieval' church was to Pevsner – would have been deeply offensive to Betjeman, probably far more offensive than Pevsner meant it to be. The fight was on.

The savage review of *County Durham* in the *Times Literary Supplement* in July 1953 – unsigned, as was the *TLS*'s practice until 1974 – has repeatedly been attributed to Betjeman, although the *TLS* archive makes clear that it was in fact the work of Bede expert Bertram Colgrave.* Without a doubt, even if Betjeman did not write the piece, he had every sympathy with it. Alec Clifton-Taylor was one of the architectural writers whom Betjeman had invited to review for *Time*

---

*Bevis Hillier, in *Betjeman: The Bonus of Laughter* (John Murray, 2004), p.43, cites a note from Betjeman to Osbert Lancaster in June 1953 saying, 'See me on Pevs in next TLS . . . INTEGRITY & TRUTH must be safeguarded against official closed shop of ART HISTORIANS', but the original copy of the *TLS* issue in question is firmly marked up with Colgrave's name and the amount he was paid for the review.

and Tide. He now asked Betjeman if he could review *County Durham* in *Time and Tide* as a riposte to the *TLS* reviewer, who had attacked not only the volume and the *BoE* series but Pevsner's entire methodology. He was turned down with a firmness that surprised him.

'I don't blame you for disagreeing,' wrote Clifton-Taylor. 'Clearly they [the *BoE* volumes] are not for you. But I do feel grieved that you won't let me tell the readers of Time and Tide that I think there is room for both.'[27] Betjeman was adamant:

> I quite agree with you that there is room both for the personal approach and for the catalogue. But if you are writing the latter it is essential that you should be accurate. You and I know really exactly how Pevsner has compiled most of his guides. He has employed a series of *studentium* who have gone round getting things out of directories and sometimes using their own eyes, but not, I suspect, often; he has made full use often without acknowledgement of Goodhart-Rendel's card index in the RIBA [in fact he peppered his text with the acknowledgement GR]; and has visited some of the more *important* monuments in the country himself; and the result is that a thing like the guides to Notts, Durham, Devon and Cornwall are something that are neither complete as a catalogue nor distinctive as a personal approach. This I don't think is a matter of opinion but a matter of fact, and that is why I maintain that we cannot continue to praise Pevsner.*

Pevsner may or may not have learned of Betjeman's reaction from Clifton-Taylor. He may or may not have attributed the *TLS* review to Betjeman. In any event, he would appear to have been a little sharper and more pointed in his remarks thereafter. In a *TLS* review of his own he would refer to Victorian studies in Britain as 'thrown away to the flippancies of the amateur'.† And in 1958 he advised Penguin

---

*J. Betjeman/A. Clifton-Taylor, September 1953, in C. Lycett Green (ed.), *John Betjeman: Letters. Vol. II* (Methuen, 1995), p.43. Betjeman was fired from *Time and Tide* a few months later, on the grounds that the magazine needed a more European flavour.

†NP, review of H-R. Hitchcock, *Early Victorian Architecture in Britain, TLS*, 3/6/55. This was not simply a jibe at Betjeman: Pevsner included Kenneth Clark and H.S. Goodhart-Rendel in his dismissal of Victorian studies in England. 'Neither the length of Professor Hitchcock's book nor its overwhelming competence could be expected of the native. There are many reasons of national character to account for the elegance of Sir Kenneth Clark's *Gothic Revival* and the sketchiness of Mr Goodhart-Rendel's *English Architecture since the Regency* as against the massive learning and relentless descriptiveness of Professor Hitchcock.'

not to put Betjeman's *Guide to English Parish Churches* (Collins, 1958) into paperback: 'I am not in favour of our trying to do it,' wrote Pevsner:

> not only because it would certainly do damage to a certain extent to the BoE, but also for more genuinely editorial reasons. The Introduction I find superb, but the gazetteer is done in an extraordinarily uneven way. Wherever you have a paragraph of John B's own writing, it is worth reading. Otherwise you find that masses of really important churches receive a line and no more . . . The truth of the matter is of course that one cannot do a workable gazetteer for the whole country in one volume.*

And so we reach the 'Poet and Pedant' tussle portrayed by Peter Clarke:

POET:
A POET – part Victorian
part-Topographer – that's me!
(Who was it tipped you Norman Shaw
in Nineteen Thirty-three?)
Of gas-lit Halls and Old Canals
I reverently sing,
But when Big Chief I-Spy comes round
I *curse* like anything.
Oo-oh!

PEDANT:
A crafty Art Historian
of Continental fame,
I'll creep up on this Amateur
and stop his little game!
With transatlantic thoroughness
I'll note down all he's missed.
Each British Brick from Norm. to Vic.
you'll find upon my list!
(Aside: Ah – h-h!)

---

*NP/Alan Glover, 28/11/58. Penguin Papers, *BoE* General Correspondence, DM 1294/19/1. Pevsner had, however, given Betjeman permission to use his *BoE* glossary of architectural terms in the hardback edition.

POET
I tawt I taw a Gothic arch
a-peepin' out at me.
I did, I taw a Gothic arch,
and breathed a soft 'O-gee!'

PEDANT
(I analyzed it long ago upon the BBC) . . .

POET:
I thought I saw a Tennis Girl
admiring a Piscina in
a Pugin Church near Holloway –
the first I'd ever seen her in.

PEDANT:
*(He did not know she was my stooge –
a highly cultured Wienerin!)*

Contre-Danse ('Summerson's icumen in')
In abidingly lyrical   *Full of Danish empirical*
Mildly satirical   *Quite unhysterical*
                             – neo-Ruskinian

(Rah for Sir Ninian!)
                             Tecton-and-Gropius –

Strict on Subtopias –
Fine Arts Commissioners   *Bauhaus Practitioner's*
Poetry Versed.   *Knowledge I burst!*

Lost in a world that is all Norman Shavian
Wright, Le Corbusier, Nash and Basévi-an
Peristyle, Metope, Squinch, Architravian.
(*I* was the one who discovered it
FIRST.) . . .

Outside observers enjoyed and magnified the poet/pedant distinction, which became sharper still with the growth of Betjeman's reputation as a 'personality' and a populariser of great charm and skill. Shared professional interests, however, would ensure that Betjeman and Pevsner encountered each other more often, and as allies rather than antagonists. Whatever their private feelings – and Betjeman's were considerably less private than Pevsner's – they maintained a functional working relationship. It was with Betjeman's permission and, no doubt, his gratification that Pevsner lifted his description of Polperro from the *Shell Guide* when *Cornwall* was revised. Over many years they collaborated dispassionately enough in a wide range of conservation battles. As Betjeman grew older and iller, his hostility towards Pevsner gradually became a reflex action, a conversational tic to divert an audience. He continued to relegate his Pevsners to a lowly shelf in his library, but resisted the urge to throw the reviled volumes away. Winnie Sibson remembered:

It was well known that Betjeman hated Pevsner. Pevsner was hurt and bemused by this, as he was a gentle man and I never knew him to bear a grudge . . . One day I picked up the phone and a voice said: 'This is Mr Betjeman, I want to speak to Dr Pevsner's secretary.' This was so surprising that I burst out laughing, thinking it was a friend pulling my leg. He then said: 'I'm glad to hear I'm a joke in Dr Pevsner's office.' What the old rascal wanted was me to let him have two free copies of I forget which volumes of the BoE.[28]

CHAPTER 34

'Always doing'

Thomas Jefferson: 'It is wonderful how much may be done if we are always doing.'

Although Pevsner had no interest in presenting himself as a 'personality', by the mid-1950s he could not avoid being treated as one. He was no longer simply one of a group of expatriate German scholars finding a second home, but a Slade Professor, a Reith Lecturer and, by 1953, at the age of fifty-one, a Companion of the British Empire. In the Coronation Honours list he had received the CBE alongside Alastair Sim, Marie Rambert, David Lean and Osbert Lancaster.

The *Architects' Journal* for January 1956 identified him as one of its 'Men of the Year' and extracted some rare personal details: 'Retires to his Wiltshire cottage for such tasks as proof reading. If not out to see buildings on holiday, prefers them out of the way of temptation, Brittany and Dolomites in the past, Engadine holiday next year. Dislikes Dr Johnson, milk pudding, and contemporary English stained glass; likes ogee arches and spaghetti.'[1]

The short interview appeared under the title 'On Finding Oneself Out Of Date' and concluded bluntly, 'Pevsner feels he is doing too many things.' He invariably got up at 5 a.m. to work for two and a half hours before breakfast and an hour's walk across Hampstead Heath and down into Bloomsbury to arrive at the office at nine, and yet there was never enough time to relax into the comforts of sustained research – 'serious, detailed, patient work'.

The level of detail he did achieve was enough to astonish (and sometimes irritate) his correspondents. A 1958 letter to Louis Grodecki, conservator of the Musée des Plans-Reliefs in Paris, was typical: Grodecki's recent monograph on Ottonian architecture, he wrote, was admirable, but he should be aware that it was mistaken as to the proportion between height of aisle and height of nave of the cathedral at Hildesheim, 'which is 0.75:1'. However, Pevsner was spreading his effort across an extraordinarily broad spectrum,* and he never confused

---

* During one six-month stretch in 1957 the topics he tackled included the skyscraper, Jane Austen's buildings, open-air sculpture, churches in Sweden and the burial place of St Peter.

polymathy with what he felt to be true scholarship. 'In all my former specialities there are younger scholars who have comfortably out-specialised me,' he mourned: 'Denis Mahon (the specialist of specialists) on Caravaggio, Peter Floud on William Morris, John Brandon Jones on Voysey, Robert Schmutzler on Art Nouveau, Michael Farr on modern industrial design.'

He was now a Fellow of the Society of Antiquaries, a council member of the British Society of Aesthetics, a member of the preparatory committee for the eleventh Milan Triennale focusing on eclecticism and formalism in modern architecture, an adviser to the London County Council on the provision of paintings and sculpture in public places, a Commissioner for the Grandi Premi di Compasso d'Oro, Italy's leading award for industrial design. At the twenty-first anniversary of the Lawn Road Flats, it was Pevsner who gave the speech at the fondue party for past and present tenants and habitués. And in 1959 he finally became a permanent professor, with the award of a personal chair at Birkbeck, specifically designated as 'part-time', then a rare privilege at the University of London.*

Success as a lecturer was bringing invitations from countries he had never visited before: Norway, Denmark, Sweden, Spain, Australia, New Zealand. The Australian venture, on which Lola accompanied him, was a publicity trip for Penguin in 1958. He diligently visited Penguin offices, signed books, opened galleries and generally made himself visible on their behalf, but there was still time for architectural tourism, under the guidance of Joe Burke, Professor of Fine Arts at the University of Melbourne, who became a good friend. Pevsner was struck by the beauty of much Victorian architecture in Australia, and by its vulnerability. 'Sydney . . . struck me as a city in more imperative need of protective action than any I had found in England,' he remarked to the leading local paper.² There should at the very least be some system for listing buildings for conservation and preferably some kind of National Trust; Australia did not have so many historic buildings that it could afford to lose them.

This was a message he was to repeat in New Zealand. No one, it seemed, had ever come from England before to lecture on art history and, in forty lectures in a month under the auspices of the British Council, his audiences ranged from fifteen people to 300. Once again he was distressed by the lack of concern for historic buildings:

*Pevsner's successor at Birkbeck, Peter Murray, claimed Pevsner was reluctant to take a chair, which he felt should only be awarded to scholars carrying out creative research. The *BoE*, in his view, did not count.

'Preservationism is completely absent* . . . Apart from such historical monuments as Maori meeting houses, some Maori Christian churches and the early mission buildings of Bishop Selwyn, nothing is accepted as worth keeping. None of the extremely pretty farmhouses, surrounded by verandas with fretwork or cast-iron trim, is excepted.'[3] He used the publicity he was given by local papers to call for action. 'Save Auckland's old buildings,' he wrote, warning that Auckland was in danger of 'murdering its past' if it did nothing to preserve such monuments as St Mary's Church, Parnell – one of the largest wooden Gothic buildings in the world and one of the only two wooden cathedrals in the Commonwealth.

Ordinary sightseeing provided some respite. 'The thrill here,' he wrote to his secretary from Rotorua, 'is a hellish bit of scenery called the Thermal Area. The geysers are not too obliging, but the horrible thing is that right by your paths there are cracks and holes and it boils and bubbles beneath. Mud pools throwing up boiling mud are not my taste. One feels too near the foul fiend.' 'The Royal Tour goes on,' wrote Lola. 'They are terribly kind and overfeed us and we drink rather foul sherry . . . Life is crazy.' She was herself now staggering slightly under the unfamiliar burden of being a celebrity wife, 'petite Mrs Nikolaus Pevsner, London', as she was labelled in a Wellington newspaper, under the subheading 'Nomadic Life for Wife of Authority on Homes' by a journalist who was perhaps not entirely clear what Pevsner was doing in New Zealand: 'Her husband lectures on the ideal home.'

Pevsner was on his own in Canada in the following year. After expressing mild displeasure at having to go down into a basement at the Toronto Art Gallery to see two fine paintings by Joshua Reynolds which were gathering dust there, he was mortified to find a paragraph in the local paper headed 'Critic Raps Gallery: Best Works in Vaults'.

*   *   *

---

*This was an exaggeration. There was a Historic Places Trust in Wellington, whose Secretary impressed Pevsner sufficiently for him to write on his behalf to Henry Moore: 'The dream of his life is a large piece of sculpture by you to be set up in a remote valley outside Wellington which would only be reached by those who would go on a pilgrimage to it . . . He is a strange and visionary character, but a perfectly serious man and I was wondering whether in your exceeding kindness you might take the trouble of finding a photograph of the Scottish Open Air figure, sign it for him and send it to him. You would make him the happiest man in New Zealand.' NP/H. Moore, 5/8/58. Series IIB, Box 61.

Meanwhile, there was less exotic travelling to be done for the *Buildings of England*. The death of Rosa Schapire in 1954 after the publication of the first three volumes forced Pevsner to look further afield for his research assistants. Working on the *BoE*, recalled Mark Girouard, was seen by Courtauld Institute graduates as an acceptable stopgap until you could get a better job. Though Pevsner was a kindly employer, the low pay was not redeemed by any form of stimulation in the work, which consisted largely of extracting details from books in the Society of Antiquaries' library on to sheaves of file cards. Not a few of the Courtauld students whom he approached declined with thanks.

Nevertheless, there were other sources of help. Architectural historian Nicholas Taylor wrote to him while still a schoolboy at Lancing College, offering corrections and additions to several earlier volumes. 'My list,' he recalled, 'began in the Middle Ages and ended with a 1938 church and a 1956 labour exchange.' 'Your close interest is so uncommon,' wrote Pevsner, 'that I should be glad if, next time you have a chance of being in London, you would call at my office and see me.'4 Taylor duly turned up: 'And what did I see? Not the teutonic powerhouse of ruthless analysis and emphatic gesticulation I half-expected, but a tall broad-shouldered man with a gentle manner and a face like an intellectual arch-deacon: big, round spectacles with thin frames under a high brow, a narrow rippling mouth pursed in quizzical amusement and less obviously in intense concentration and a tiny, precisely enunciated voice which carries as much conviction at fifty yards as it does at fifty inches.' Taylor continued to contribute information to the series for some fifteen years, most notably on Edwardian buildings, particularly Bournemouth churches and Lutyens houses.

A less diffident approach came from an even more unexpected direction. Ian Nairn had contributed details to *Essex* and undertaken some research for *Northumberland*. Now he had a bolder proposal. 'Two suggestions which I dare not make to your face, and which I only make at all because you have said to me that the bottleneck in the guides is yourself, and that you had thought of sub-letting one of the later guides – is there any possibility of my either writing the descriptions of the less interesting buildings in each county or writing one of the Home Counties guides: say Surrey?'5 Pevsner was taken aback: 'I have so far not considered any help on the travelling and describing and still hope I might do the lot myself. The only thing that I can for the time being regard as possible would be to hand on a whole volume to someone such as [W.G.] Hoskins, who is in sympathy with our point of view and at the same time for certain counties is a much better specialist than I. That is as far as it goes for the time being.'*

Nairn's timing was off. This exchange of letters must have taken place within days of a review by him of *Hertfordshire*, *Derbyshire* and *County Durham*, which criticised both content and methodology.[6] 'The pattern of this series is now clear,' he wrote:

> and so, unhappily, is the dichotomy between inventory and guide . . . There are two distinct categories of buildings: the magna opera which have had splendidly broad and scholarly treatment . . . and the mass of less significant buildings whose descriptive text seems to have had feeling and individuality strained out to make it a comprehensive card-index . . . Could a more positive balance have been achieved? – perhaps by reducing the less interesting buildings to an index, then using the space gained in spatial and functional analysis, and continual restatement of one's feelings of the goodness and badness of buildings – which must lie beyond impartiality if it is not to become yet another refuge from having to think.

Nairn was at pains to point out that 'even with such reservations . . . the series is still more valuable than any other set of guides'. His corrections were precise, his comments interesting, and his suggestions of omissions good-humoured. (He would have included more railway stations and hotels, factories, and domestic terraces, perhaps at the expense of some second-rate churches.) His mistake was perhaps to stray on to the sacred turf of the Modern Movement:

> This policy of 'the older the more important', though here much tempered, is precisely that of 18th and 19th century guide-books, and its result is that we now have to seek diligently for 18th and 19th century architects. Professor Pevsner is going to leave future generations in the dark about many 20th century buildings. Aesthetic judgement, also, must be rigorous – if the Herts. CC schools, for example, are first-rate, then they should all receive as detailed a treatment as is given to 18th-century houses or medieval abbeys.

For the time being Pevsner decided to retain exclusive authorship.

---

*NP/I. Nairn, 16/3/54. Penguin Papers, *BoE* files, DM 1901/8/1. William George Hoskins (1908–92), well known as an expert in 'historical geography', was just about to publish his most celebrated book *The Making of the English Landscape*. Reader in Local History at Leicester, he was probably known to Pevsner through his connection with Frederick Attenborough.

The next batch of *BoE* volumes were those that had been salvaged by sponsorship. Although none was published before 1957, because of the financial crisis, Pevsner had done the travelling in 1954 and 1955 and prepared the texts in those years, which explains why they show scattered evidence of the work he had been doing at the same time to prepare for the Reith Lectures. The first, *Northumberland*, he dedicated 'to the memory of Dr Rosa Schapire, enthusiastic and indefatigable in her collaboration on "The Buildings of England" as in everything else'. He characterised the county as sturdy, masculine, rough, attractive in its provincialness, with a pronounced streak of Romanticism in later centuries, and in places he seems to be trying a little hard to match this drama in his writing. *Northumberland* certainly contains the arch example of his weakness for inverted sentences: 'Rough are the winds, rough the moors, rough the miners, rough are the castles, rough the dolerite cliffs by the Roman wall and on the coast, rough is the stone of the walls which take the place of hedges . . . and rough seems even the smoother and more precisely worked stone under the black soot of Newcastle.'*

Northumberland, he wrote, was a military county, least mountainous of the border counties and frequently overrun, and therefore unsurprisingly the county of the castle. Bamburgh Castle, to take just one example, had aesthetic ambitions above its station. The Norman original had been restored several times, most recently by Victorian arms magnate William Armstrong to make a stately home, and Pevsner could not resist quoting the Arts and Crafts garden designer Avray Tipping, who had described it as 'the acme of expenditure with a nadir of intelligent achievement'. Warkworth, on the other hand, was:

> one of the rare cases where the military engineer happened to be a great architect . . . The Warkworth Keep is a work of architecture in the sense that both its mass and its inner spaces are beautiful as well as useful. It was the Edwardian engineers of the late C13 who for the first time in England had raised castle building to an art capable of aesthetic effects as intense as those of churches.

Lola took a more prosaic view of castles and their occupants. 'There is a . . . great variety of owners,' she wrote, 'the old families who have

---

*This word order is redolent of 'Timestyle', the intricate and affected house style adopted by *Time* magazine in the 1930s (unkindly parodied by Wolcott Gibbs in the *New Yorker*: 'Backward ran sentences till reeled the mind'). But it is also not uncommon in German.

lived in the house for centuries as well as Americans, well dressed ones as well as those that look like their own gardener.'[7]

There were great houses, too, in tune with the spirit of the land: Cragside, for example, also built for William Armstrong, a gigantic essay in the Free Tudor style by Norman Shaw. 'The Northumbrian hills are not a black-and-white region,' noted Pevsner, 'but that did not worry Shaw in 1870 . . . The position chosen is one of high romantic glamour . . . The site is Wagnerian and so is here Shaw's architecture . . . One expects all the time to hear Walkyries [sic] ride through the skies over its manifold gables and chimney stacks.'

Berwick-on-Tweed provided one of the best examples of the Pevsnerian 'Perambulation' in the whole BoE series. 'Berwick,' he wrote, 'is one of the most exciting towns in England, a real town with the strongest sense of enclosure, a town of red roofs on grey houses with hardly any irritating buildings anywhere, and a town of the most intricate changes of levels.' It was this change of level that he enjoyed, and the perambulation has him toiling up and down, testimony to strong legs, occasionally breathless, but enthusiastic:

> It is enjoyable to dive down Palace Street to Palace Green . . . right into the lowest level. PALACE GREEN is a delicious oasis of old dark trees surrounded by buildings of dignity. On the E side the former GOVERNOR'S HOUSE, characteristically early C18 . . . No. 9 on the s side has a coloured bust of Wellington over the doorway. On into PALACE STREET EAST which . . . forms the Georgian Mayfair of Berwick . . . In RAVENSDOWNE nearly all houses are worth a glance. The stepped skyline of the street rising gently to the upper or Town Hall level is very pretty.

Pevsner was becoming more skilful and accommodating in his use of local experts, and was more than willing to recognise superior knowledge where it existed.* In the introduction to the next county, Somerset, he paid generous tribute to Kenneth Wickham, Eton schoolmaster, county cricketer and son of a Somerset vicar, who had written on The Churches of Somerset and had died in 1951 at the age of fifty-four: 'I would also have wished that Fate had allowed Kenneth Wickham to write his own gazetteer. His experience and his enthusiasm would

---

*In Northumberland he also made use, for the first time, of a specialist contributor, classical expert Ian Richmond, who provided notes on Hadrian's Wall and other Roman material.

have achieved something better than is within my power . . . I feel in need of an excuse for competing with his book.'

Somerset was a happy county. It was poor in contemporary architecture, but rich in many of Pevsner's other pleasures. The countryside was varied, including moors, tors and cliffs, and towns with a distinct urban character and tradition. There was a marvellous cathedral in Wells, important churches in Bristol, which gave him the chance to expand on the handling of interior space in Gothic buildings, an abiding passion. His sustained analyses of space in the Bristol choir and the Wells retrochoir, helped in each case by a carefully drawn plan of the vaults, were virtuoso examples of his ability to carry the reader spellbound through every arch and bay.

Pevsner saw the evolution and building of Bath as a prime example of Picturesque planning at its most successful, and the description of it is one of his best: lucid, coherent, illuminating on details, but focused more on the ensemble than on individual buildings. Lola, less oblivious to physical discomfort, was more conscious of the rigours of an *embarras de richesses*. 'We are still ploughing on,' she wrote to Camilla Bagg, 'a little worn and rather dirty, as the butter was melting.' Bath was 'a fearful task'. 'Still,' she continued, 'we had tea with Lord Hilton [*sic*] yesterday and shall have tea with Lady Asquith tomorrow. In between we live in a back room of the Commercial Hotel.'

Somerset eventually appeared in two volumes, one of which was dedicated to the Leverhulme Trust as co-saviour of the series. The *Shropshire* volume that followed had additional sponsorship of a more individual kind, from members of the American summer school at Attingham, near Shrewsbury. This was a summer school for the study of historic houses and their collections, designed for professional art historians with a leavening of 'financially able amateur sightseers', according to the school's American organiser, Lydia Bond Powell.[8] Attingham Park itself is a Grade I-listed Georgian house designed for Lord Berwick in 1785 by George Steuart, with a picture gallery by John Nash and a park landscaped by Humphry Repton. In 1947 it had become the first Adult Education College in Britain, under the Wardenship of Sir George Trevelyan.* Sir George is hailed now as a prototype New Age thinker for his exploration of beliefs in angels, the calming effects of crystals, the power of ley lines, communal living and organic farming. In the 1950s, however, he was best known for his work in adult education, and Helen Lowenthal, a lecturer from

---

*Sir George Trevelyan (1906–96), 4th Baronet, son of Sir Charles Trevelyan, who was a great-nephew of Macaulay and Minister for Education under Ramsay Macdonald.

the Victoria and Albert Museum, brought to him the idea of housing a summer school that would make English stately homes and their collections better known to an American audience.*

Pevsner, superficially quite different in temperament from Trevelyan, nevertheless had significant interests in common with him. Trevelyan had made personal links with Gropius and Moholy-Nagy during a six-month visit to Germany in 1928, and he had then apprenticed himself to furniture designer Peter Waals in the Cotswolds, working in the Arts and Crafts tradition of Ernest Gimson and Ernest Barnsley. Most importantly, both men were dedicated to widening educational opportunities and both believed in the value of enthusiasm. Pevsner had been one of the first five lecturers at the summer school in 1952, alongside Harold Nicolson, Anthony Blunt, Geoffrey Webb and Rudolf Wittkower, and would be a regular for decades. He served on its council for twenty years and was a patron until his death. He had rather hoped to raise $1,500 from Attingham to support the *Shropshire* volume. Less than one-third of that was eventually forthcoming, but the association with the school and with Trevelyan nevertheless helped to make the trip an 'exceptionally pleasurable' one.

'The greatest attraction of Shropshire,' Pevsner wrote, 'is that it does not attract too many . . . It is not a county of crowds.' The only blight – apart from the proliferation of imitation black-and-white timber-framed buildings, always so much bigger and more blatant than the originals – was the damage inflicted by transport and 'the smelly confusion of motor vehicles'.

At one large house in Shropshire 'the young owner himself opened the door, and when I had stammered my story, answered: "So you are here now. You have gradually been to all my relatives from Essex to Northumberland. Come in, the conducted tour can begin."' The series was already being used by estate agents as a reference point and unit of currency: some time during the 1950s Pevsner clipped and kept an advertisement for a small period house in Much Hadham as being 'listed in Pevsner'.

He was disturbed by the fact that the books seemed to be getting longer, the print runs shorter and the prices considerably higher than originally intended. *London: The Cities of London and Westminster* was the bulkiest volume so far, at 631 pages, and hardbacks could cost as much as a guinea, with paperbacks ranging from 8s 6d to

---

*Helen Lowenthal was also the moving spirit behind the foundation of NADFAS, the National Association of Decorative and Fine Art Societies, and its original vice chair.

10s 6d.* However, he recognised that the series had at least made him a permanent fixture at Penguin. Rodrigo Moynihan's 1955 painting *After the Conference* depicts all the Penguin editors at a supposed cocktail party in the Penguin board room at Harmondsworth. Pevsner stands in the middle distance alongside other series editors, who include E.V. Rieu and A.J. Ayer.†

Margaret Clark, an editorial assistant at Penguin in the 1950s, recalled Pevsner appearing to enjoy his visits to the Harmondsworth offices. The site had previously been a field of cabbages; when the Penguin building was first put up in the 1930s, long, low and single-storeyed, it stood in a zone of decaying farms and market gardens, but ribbon industrial development was under way and Heathrow was encroaching. The main offices ran along the front of the building, separated from the warehouse behind by a narrow corridor and half-glass partitions, leaving office interiors visible from both sides. It was unusual for series editors to come to Harmondsworth, but Pevsner was indifferent to hierarchy and kept clear of the office politics that Allen Lane enjoyed fostering. 'A sweet and gentle man,' Margaret Clark remembered, 'tall and thin and slightly stooping with pale face and round steel-rimmed glasses, rather like a benevolent heron . . . full of enormous enthusiasm and always very kind to the underlings. Strangely, for one so erudite, he Joined In.' 'Joining In' was rarely epicurean. Pevsner's habit was to bring a single cheese sandwich to eat in the staff canteen, and he would usually disappear early from the Penguin Christmas party, though on one occasion he disconcerted a girl from the packing department by enquiring, 'Will you drink a loving cup with me, my dear?'‡

His working relations with most of his editorial colleagues were equally cordial, though not always as relaxed. Alan Glover had been recruited as in-house Pelican editor in much the same way as Pevsner, after writing to Penguin with suggestions for improvements – though in Glover's case these were a volley of complaints and corrections which eventually persuaded Allen Lane that it would be less trouble

---

*The second London volume was dedicated 'to the memory of G.F. Troup Horne and the nights of 1941–44 at the old Birkbeck College in Bream's Buildings'.
†Each of the editors actually sat separately to Moynihan, and the backdrop was not the Penguin board room, but the Senior Common Room at the Royal College of Art, where he was Professor of Painting.
‡The Penguin party was often held on Christmas Eve, the central focus of festivities for German families, and Pevsner was needed at home to decorate the tree, exchange presents and eat a traditional dinner. Isabel Quigly, Alan Glover's editorial assistant, recalled the loving-cup incident. I. Quigly, letter to the author, 5/2/93.

to employ him. Glover was an eccentric man.[9] Born Allan McDougall, the son of a single parent, he had run away from Christ's Hospital where he was a scholarship boy, had gone to prison as a conscientious objector in the First World War, was rumoured to have been a Buddhist monk, and had definitely worked as a tattooed man in a circus – he still bore the scars where the tattoos had been erased – before turning himself into a self-taught polymath. He was a translator from French and medieval Latin, an authority on Jung, the managing editor of the *International Journal of Psychoanalysis* and had prepared editions of Byron and Shelley.

In Glover, Pevsner met his match as a master of detail. A letter from Glover about *Middlesex* in 1951 was typical:

> You will remember that you quoted a Greek inscription on a tomb in the church at Harefield. I was suspicious of this and queried it on the galleys. You crossed out my query and left it as it was. I was still suspicious of it on the page proofs and queried it again, but the query was again crossed out. Even so my suspicions were not laid to rest so I had the bad taste to ask Mr Collings to go to Harefield and look up the inscription.* As I suspected it was wrong, two letters having been left out which made all the difference between meaning and meaninglessness.[10]

He complained that in *London except* a significant number of parish churches appeared to have the wrong names, according to *Crockford's Clerical Directory*. Pevsner, abashed, acknowledged that he had relied for information on the *Little Guides*, which sometimes supplied the names that churches had had before the Reformation, after which non-scriptural saints were usually replaced with the Apostles, the Virgin Mary or All Saints. Initially suspicious and not a little resentful, he soon came to welcome Glover's zeal: confronted with a long list of emendations to an early manuscript, he wrote, 'Dear Glover, This is absolutely wonderful. You are obviously the first person looking through the typescript really in detail. My whole problem is to find people who are knowledgeable enough and will take the trouble.'[11] Before long, their relationship was positively jocular.

But his closest ally in Penguin, other than Allen Lane, was in the design department. Lane's first choice of design director was Jan

---

*Rex Collings (1925–96) served as Pevsner's editorial assistant at Penguin for some years before establishing himself as an independent publisher (the first to publish Richard Adams's *Watership Down*).

Tschichold, born in Leipzig in the same year as Pevsner and a leading advocate of modernist design in the 1920s. Hired in 1947, Tschichold produced Penguin Composition Rules a year later to standardise the design of the various series that were now included within the Penguin brand. He was succeeded in 1949 by typographer Hans Schmoller, who was responsible for the design of the *BoE* throughout the life of the series.* Pevsner was sufficiently interested in typography to have produced his article on lettering for the Festival of Britain, and he would always be concerned that the design of a book, like that of any other artefact, should serve its function well, but it was in their passion for precision that he and Schmoller were kindred spirits.

Within Penguin, Schmoller was nicknamed 'Halfpoint Schmoller', the only man who could distinguish between a Bembo full point and a Garamond full point at 200 paces.[12] 'Hans was respected by everyone,' one colleague remembered, 'but I think he'd have enjoyed being liked more. Fundamentally serious, hierarchical and "mittel European", he didn't relax easily.'[13] With Pevsner, however, there was a subcurrent of sympathy and they were good friends, working together to make each volume of the *BoE* succeed within the series' severe constraints of time and money. Faced with a mass of detail that threatened to become overwhelming, Schmoller had definite views on how to impose a standard format that would be firm but not crushing, lucid without becoming banal – small capitals for subheadings rather than blots of bold type, a strict avoidance of wide spaces between words – but he was also a pragmatist. In 1961, Pevsner asked him to make the sponsors' names more prominent in the preliminaries for *Norfolk*: 'Please do your best to reach a compromise between what is expedient and what is beautiful.'[14]

From 1955 onwards, Pevsner also had the support within Penguin of an editorial assistant for the *BoE*. An English literature graduate, Judy Perry started as a copy editor. She progressed over the years to become assistant editor and eventually co-editor, a position she held until her death in 1991. When, while working on *Surrey*, she met and married Ian Nairn, Pevsner was dismayed: 'He must have charm – people say he has: I don't feel it. She's got a strong character. We must just hope for the best, I suppose.'[15]

---

*Hans Schmoller (1916–85), born in Berlin, left Germany in 1937 to study in London, but was offered a job in Africa, where he spent the war, interned from 1940 to 1942. His parents died in Auschwitz. (He would refuse to work on a group of five books by P.G. Wodehouse that Lane wanted to publish.) Coming to Penguin in 1947 as head of typography, by 1956 he was responsible for all production, and then design director until 1976.

By the time Judy Nairn joined the *BoE*, Pevsner was more than grateful for the additional help, because his second encyclopaedic project for Penguin was under way.* After the famous meeting in the rose garden in 1945,† Allen Lane had commissioned for the Pelican label 'a handbook on the History of Art and Architecture' that would provide a survey of European art as a whole. Pevsner had had at the back of his mind the model of the German *Handbuch der Kunstwissenschaft*, a general history of Eastern and Western art, but he intended this new *Pelican History of Art* to be on a grander scale. (The topics that he and Otto Grautoff had covered between them in a single volume for the *Handbuch*, for example, would be allocated four separate volumes in the *Pelican History*.) It was the grandeur of the idea that attracted Allen Lane, and he allowed Pevsner to develop the series far beyond the original ten-year plan.

For Lane, the *Pelican History of Art* was an opportunity for up-market publishing, Penguin's most ambitious venture into hardback books, cloth-bound and, later, dignified by box slip covers. For Pevsner its primary purpose was as a teaching aid. With art history still developing as a discipline, the need for general textbooks in the English language had not yet been met. Before the war, those who possessed the knowledge to write such books were often curators or connoisseurs rather than academics. 'Few, if any, had any teaching experience and they had little idea of what was needed for a systematic treatment of the subject, having themselves learned on an apprenticeship basis.'[16] Now, with a teacher as its editor, the Pelican series could be expected to provide the systematic treatment that would be of most use to the serious student. Its volumes would not be aimed primarily at the general reader, or at the specialist academic – though Pevsner will certainly have hoped that both would use them – but at the graduate student looking to learn about an area beyond his or her particular field or at the teacher of art history preparing a survey course. The text was not to be overburdened by notes, but equally not dominated by illustrations. Pictures – some 300 of them in the typical volume – must supplement and illuminate words, not the other way round.[17]

Lane took a close interest in the logistics, but the division of the material and the choice of authors he left exclusively to Pevsner. The series was now to span a huge time period from prehistory to the present day, and it had broadened beyond the original concept of a European history to include the art of the rest of the world as well.

*Judy Nairn would also become the in-house editor for the *Pelican History of Art*.
†See Chapter 25 above.

Pevsner had to balance intellectual with practical concerns, the ambitions and ideals of his authors with Penguin's design and financial restrictions and his own desire for a standard series. A number of plans for the *Pelican History* survive – by 1953 there would be a complete plan for forty-eight-titles, to be published over twelve years – and it is possible to trace a basic shape: a broad-brush approach for pre-medieval and non-Western art, with the greatest level of detail to be found in European art of the sixteenth to eighteenth centuries, which was treated country by country and sometimes subdivided by country (as for Britain) into painting, sculpture and architecture. However, the way in which the series actually developed was also strongly influenced by Pevsner's knowledge of scholars whom he considered suitable to tackle the subject areas that had been identified.

By December 1946 he had signed contracts with John Summerson to write about architecture in Britain 1530–1830, Anthony Blunt to cover art and architecture in France 1500–1700, Rudolf Wittkower to tackle Italian baroque art and architecture 1600–1750 and Ellis Waterhouse to deliver painting in Britain 1530–1790. The choice of Henry-Russell Hitchcock for nineteenth- and twentieth-century architecture not simply in Britain, or even Europe, but throughout the world was almost certainly dictated by his sympathies with the Modern Movement. There was never any suggestion that Pevsner attempted to influence individual authors in their treatment of their subjects – George Zarnecki, commissioned to write the volume on Romanesque sculpture, recalled that he never discussed ideas with his writers, only facts – but his selection of writers inevitably reflected his own ideas on the periods under consideration.

'If I had known more about the neuroses of authors when I took on the PHA, I would never have initiated it,' Pevsner would write in 1958.[18] He pulled in leading scholars from all over the world, not simply his friends – the *Times Literary Supplement* complained that the series was 'monopolising many of our leading authorities' – but his control over his authors was light. John Summerson recalled of his volume on British architecture, 'He let me do it my own way, but when I first presented it as a whole, he objected to the order of the chapters – and he was perfectly right. I reordered the chapters, and had to alter quite a lot to make it connect. But that was the only piece of editorial persuasion that he had to inflict. I should think he thought he could have done it better himself – but he probably thought it politically wiser to have an Englishman writing on English art.' Sometimes control was gentle to the point of being casual: in several cases authors were found to have no contracts, their volumes having been commissioned purely on Pevsner's say-so and by word of mouth alone, having proceeded as a gentlemen's agreement. 'It was a most agreeable surprise to meet such a friendly person,' wrote one author to another, 'so different to the image transmitted in his extremely short letters.'[19]

Some of the authors approached, albeit experts, had never attempted to write overviews before, and some had not even written books. In many cases good intentions came to nothing – always, it seemed, to Pevsner's surprise and distress. Punctilious himself, he found it very hard to understand how people could fail to deliver what they had promised, even when their reasons might have seemed adequate to less demanding editors. Geoffrey Grigson produced nothing on *British Painting and Sculpture in the Twentieth Century*, a volume that was never recommissioned. John Pope-Hennessy agreed to write on the Italian fourteenth century, but then claimed to have lost interest and asked to do the fifteenth century instead. This had already been offered to Kenneth Clark – who subsequently asked to be excused from the task on the grounds that he was no longer a scholar.* Millard Meiss had his volume on French fourteenth-century painting removed from him. 'We don't like each other much,' Pevsner told another scholar, 'ever since I had to cancel his contract for a volume of the PHA, my reason being that he never sent me a single chapter of the volume, but, while he should have been busy on it, he wrote a completely different book in two volumes.'[20] George Zarnecki died in 2008 without finishing the manuscript on which he had been working for more than forty years. 'People were very surprised by how patient [Pevsner] was with me,' Zarnecki recalled in 1997, 'but he knew that I was struggling with earning my living.'† Pevsner was less tolerant with Rudolf Wittkower: he told Reyner Banham that on meeting Wittkower in the Warburg Library he found himself unable to exchange a civil word because the promised volume on the Italian Baroque was eighteen months late.[21]

Next to lateness, length was the most contentious issue. The original

---

*A volume on Quattrocento painting was commissioned from John Shearman, but was uncompleted on his death in 2003.
†Zarnecki in his turn was forgiving of Pevsner for a review he wrote of Zarnecki's *Polish Art* (Polish Publications Committee, 1945), in which he chastised the author for 'so strong a national prejudice that his work loses much of its value to English readers . . . The author has an axe to grind; there must nowhere appear dependence on Germany in the history of Polish art . . . Perhaps one should be prepared to excuse this kind of national self-assertion as the outcome of centuries of oppression. But it remains a pity all the same that it should mar an otherwise valuable scholarly summing-up.' 'Nationalism and Art History', 'Peter F.R. Donner' review, *Burlington*, November 1945.

specification was for each volume to be 256 pages, with a reasonably equal distribution of length between chapters – a pious hope that was disappointed more or less at once, since Summerson's volume had 348 text pages in twenty-nine chapters varying in length from five to nineteen pages. Seymour Slive and Jakob Rosenberg, contracted for 100,000 words and 200 pictures, found it impossible to deal adequately with their subject – Dutch painting 1600–1800 – in fewer than 130,000 words and 300 pictures. Pevsner made them pay the costs of the additional pictures, but was forced to accept the lengthier text. Sydney Freedberg of the Fogg Art Museum in Cambridge, Massachusetts, brought in his manuscript on sixteenth-century Italian painting at a length that would have made two volumes necessary and, when pressed to cut it, threatened to cancel his contract, with the publication date looming. 'I am furious with Freedberg about this,' fumed Pevsner to Penguin. 'It is sheer blackmail . . . All he would do is to withdraw the book and place it immediately with another publisher, leaving it to me to find a new author who will require another five years.'[22] Freedberg's volume was among the most significant and successful in the series, but Pevsner did not forgive him.

All these factors produced a series that was idiosyncratic and far from uniform. The Courtauld Institute challenged the whole approach. The Pelican series, it claimed, appeared to be based on the assumption that the groundwork in art history had all been done by the 1950s, by German art historians and others, and all that was needed now was synthesis and summary – whereas the Courtauld had devoted itself to finding new avenues of discovery and different perspectives.[23] The medievalist Peter Kidson at the Courtauld also suggested that, as the years passed, the series looked increasingly outmoded in pursuing a historical rather than a social approach. Other critics resisted the idea that broad surveys could ever have genuine academic worth, dependent as they were on generalising and synthesising from a limited number of examples with an incomplete scholarly apparatus. Too long to appeal to the general public, but too elementary for the specialist, the Pelican volumes thudded between two stools – and, some added, too many of the authors appeared to be of continental origin.

The most frequent complaint, however, was the varying allocation of space to the art of different countries. A whole volume for Belgian Baroque (written by Pevsner's lifelong friend Horst Gerson)? A single volume for European painting and sculpture 1780–1880, while the fifteenth century (one of Pevsner's particular favourites) got four volumes? Less space given to the whole of Eastern art than to medieval English painting or Central European architecture of the seventeenth and eighteenth centuries? Surely a more objective approach might have been achieved by having an advisory committee of experts rather than leaving all control in the hands of one man? Above all, critics continued to say, England was overplayed. 'It seems excessive to devote as many as seven out of the forty-eight volumes to a tributary of the main European current,' sniffed the *Burlington Magazine* in October 1953, '. . . especially since (although Doctor Pevsner could not have foreseen this) the Oxford History will be covering precisely the same ground.' (The *Oxford History of English Art* had been launched in 1949, with a roster of contributors who were exclusively English.)

More benevolent observers would make greater allowances for the fact that so huge a framework was likely to become lopsided in places, and that its individual components would vary in quality. When the *Pelican History of Art* was first launched, in 1953, Reyner Banham hailed it with enthusiasm: '[It is] as much an event in our intellectual history as was the Festival of Britain . . . a landmark in the development of English taste.'[24] Allowing for characteristic rhetoric, Banham was right to draw attention to the scale of the ambition underlying the Pelican project, which was by far the longest history of art so far produced. Writing in 1980, Creighton Gilbert, Yale Professor of Art History, observed that by the time the *Pelican History of Art* was complete it would, inevitably, be obsolete, given that art history was changing all the time. Nevertheless, he concluded, 'It will leave a large legacy of knowledge transmitted with exceptionally high standards and ingrained in extraordinary numbers of people.'[25]

CHAPTER 35

'Unbeautiful and yet of value': uncovering the Victorians

'Married life still not happy,' Pevsner confided to his *Heftchen* in December 1959. 'No violent quarrels, often cheerful harmony. But what would happen, if the children and grandchildren moved away from where we now live close together?'*

He still felt the need to document his interior life as a form of confessional and an emotional outlet, but the pressure of external events left him less time to do it. When he had first started making his records in the *Heftchen* as an introspective fourteen-year-old, one of the little blue books might last him no more than a week. By 1950 each was lasting a year; and the one he began keeping in 1953 was still not full five years later, when he lost it. (He had hidden it rather too thoroughly from a colleague.) The book he was using in 1959 was one he had started the previous year; it was red, and the entries were now in English.

Various events prompted him to make more frequent entries: the marriages of his children, their careers and those of their partners, the difficult birth of one of his grandchildren and, ludicrously, the death of the cat, which brought to the surface the temperamental differences between himself and Lola. The cat was old (fifteen) and, Pevsner confessed, 'Neither of us loved him specially. Lola was kinder to him than I who, when it was my job, gave him his food, but little else.' But as the cat went downhill and became more and more incontinent and mangy, Lola turned against him and wanted him put down at once. Pevsner was shocked: 'My argument was again *au fond* an egocentric one: if you loathe this cat in his old age and want to get rid of him, how will it be when I go dirty and disreputable?' Lola was hurt by his reaction, and they had a violent row:

> I would say this: there is a streak of hardness in her and streak of
> maudlin sentimentality in me. Out of her hardness she derives the

---

*Uta had married Ian Hodgson in 1949 and by 1959 they had three children, Josephine, Nicolas and Paul. Tom had married Inge Stadler in 1958, and Dieter had married Florence Tate in 1955.

faculty of doing necessary things for many people without hesitation and with much sacrifice. I stay inactive, yet I am hurt by the abruptness of her judgments – which are of course temperamentally more violent than mine . . . Her practical charity to man, woman and child, when it can really achieve something – preferably at once – has more value than my feelings.

His *Heftchen* were often as much a document of Lola as they were of him, and he knew she detested them. When she had read them, she had been deeply wounded. 'How could she ever have any appreciation of what a candid diary is and why it might be written?' Open to a fault herself, she did not understand the urge to record secretly thoughts that one would not publicly express. She saw that he had made entries 'critical of her, her education, even her appearance. Such is the duty of the diary writer, but it is in conflict with the human duty of the husband . . . She would have found it solace beyond words if I had sacrificed them to her as an atonement.' It was perhaps beyond him to relinquish the habit now, but it is hard to understand why he kept them in a bundle in his office marked 'For Mrs P only', since she was the person who would least have wanted to read them.

Lola's unhappiness was largely loneliness. She had never entirely replaced the close circle of friends and family that she had had to leave behind when she came to England. John Rodker had died in 1955 – a loss, however unsatisfactory the relationship might ultimately have been – and the friendship with the Grigsons had at least temporarily broken down at around the same time. Geoffrey and Bertschy Grigson had separated, and the two families appear to have had an acrimonious quarrel of the kind in which Grigson specialised.*

Her children lived nearby, but they were adults with their own lives and they protected their independence. Her frankness, and her loud voice, 'made the family feel that she wanted to interfere,' Pevsner observed, 'and so they were less appreciative of her views than she deserved. And of course she could lose her temper and storm, and then regret and cry and say "I am bad" . . . Lola still found that her children were not open enough, not honest enough to her, did not tell her where they went of an evening, did not tell of events or cares

---

*Dieter Pevsner records that 'both NP and Lola were angry and hostile on a personal level at Geoffrey's treatment of Bertschy in the separation' (email to the author, 4/8/2009). They disapproved of his relationship with Jane McIntyre, which began in the early 1950s; Jane later became Grigson's third wife, and a well-known cookery writer.

which they discussed among themselves – they probably shied from her immediately given advice as from interference.'[1]

Most painfully, she felt neglected by her husband outside the confines of the *BoE* trips. She disliked the kind of social gathering that came with success – too many people and clever talk – but rarely had the chance to go out with him alone. 'Lola still found that I had too much work and too little time for her and for human relations altogether, for the odd opera or concert or film. We hardly ever went.' In Germany she had had an identity, as daughter, sister, wife, mother, friend. 'She did become somebody here,' her son Dieter observed, 'but it took her a long time to realise it and permit herself to enjoy it a bit. Like most people, she tried always to put a brave public front on everything, and like most people she was a great deal more fragile and frantic and hysterical sometimes behind it.'

Now, towards the end of the decade, another venture was launched that would consume even more of Pevsner's time, whether or not he would have chosen it, for the rest of his life. It had been a good joke for P.G. Wodehouse to remark in 1938, 'Whatever may be said in favour of the Victorians, it is pretty generally admitted that few of them were to be trusted within reach of a trowel and a pile of bricks.'* But twenty years later, with planning schemes proposing the reconstruction of large areas of most towns and cities, Victorian buildings were prime targets for demolition.

It was the destruction of, and threats to, many choice specimens (notably Thomas Collcutt's Imperial Institute in South Kensington) that prompted the joint initiative taken by John Betjeman, already a champion of the Victorian age in the public eye, and Anne, Countess of Rosse. On 17 July 1957 Betjeman wrote to Lady Rosse, whose husband he had known at Oxford: the two men were already both founder members of the Georgian Group. Betjeman's suggestion was that now they should rally a similar band of defenders of Britain's Victorian heritage. Together they discussed a list of names.

Whatever Betjeman's private feelings may have been, Pevsner's qualifications for being included were hard to challenge. Obviously he was not alone. Christopher Hussey had been writing about Victorian country houses for *Country Life* since the early 1950s. Betjeman and Piper's *Murray's Guides*, such as they were, had provided 'as full and sympathetic a photographic survey of Victorian buildings of all kinds

---

*In *Summer Moonshine*.

as was to be found in England at that date'.[2] The *Architectural Review* had established itself as an outlet for writing about the Victorians well before Pevsner's time as assistant editor, and would continue to act as one after he stepped down.* But the amount of space that Pevsner was devoting to nineteenth-century buildings in the *Buildings of England*, unprecedented for an architectural guidebook, was perhaps the most sustained public argument for their merits. It was precisely this emphasis on Victorian buildings that, in Nicholas Taylor's view, had made *London except*, for example, so significant – 'by far the most important and most ground-breaking of all the earlier *BoE* volumes'. By including the churches of all the great names of the Victorian era and beginning the task of recording domestic architecture in the artistic enclaves of Hampstead, Chelsea and Bayswater, it provided in a single compact volume a much-needed basic primer for younger historians who wanted to begin serious research into Victorian architecture.

What is less immediately obvious is why Pevsner bothered to fight for these buildings when as often as not he liked neither how they looked nor the values they manifested in their construction. Some he did appreciate aesthetically – houses by Philip Webb, Voysey, Norman Shaw, Alexander 'Greek' Thomson, churches by Bodley, Street and Pearson. But rather more often their appearance left him reaching for adjectives such as 'distressing', 'debased', 'coarse', 'hamfisted'. In addition, Victorian design violated some of his most cherished principles. *Pioneers* incorporated a fervent onslaught on its 'profound artistic dishonesty', 'sham materials and sham techniques'; the *Outline* accused the Victorians of being 'weak in things of the spirit'. Over and over again Pevsner charged nineteenth-century architecture with being a 'fancy dress ball' of historicist styles.

Nevertheless, as John Summerson pointed out, 'Pevsner was an historian certainly before he was an aesthetician . . . However bad a building may be, the fact that a building was built is a fact of history which you can't get over. And if you find that all Victorian architecture is filth, the historian's job is not to sanctify the filth but to find out what gave rise to it.' Victorian buildings, Pevsner argued, were as much the product of their own age as Tudor or Georgian buildings were products of theirs, a source of information about that age which should

---

*Peter Ferriday – letter to the author, 5/9/93 – points out that Richards and Summerson included Victorian buildings in their catalogue of *Bombed Buildings of Britain* (Architectural Press, 1942).

not be ignored. Many of Britain's cities were Victorian monuments. 'It was that age that made them. It was in that age that they, and the whole of Britain, prospered more than in any age before or after. If we let the buildings of that age go, we destroy the visual record of the period of Britain's leadership in the civilised world.'³ 'With the disappearance of phase after phase of architecture,' he argued, 'layer after layer of historical consciousness is denuded.' To leave a whole era unexplored was to create a lacuna in architectural history.

In fact there were in Victorian architecture qualities that appealed strongly not only to Pevsner's historical sense but also to his intellect, his emotions and his sense of humour, if not his eye. The Victorian age may have been tasteless, he conceded, but taste is not everything, and it was also an age of vitality, ingenuity, confidence, gusto, an age with an edge. 'There is much in e.g. Butterfield,' he wrote, 'that is unbeautiful and yet of value, thanks to such qualities as character, intensity, bite, guts – whatever one may choose to call it . . . I have no doubt that the vast oak bookcase with bulging harpies to divide the sections from each other and with innumerable hidden pigeon-holes contrived with naïve ingenuity is better than the smooth imitation Sheraton bookcase with nothing to hate, nothing to laugh about, and nothing to like.'⁴

Reyner Banham noted Pevsner's fondness for contrariness and extremity – his fascination with 'polarities', rogue architects, anomalies:

The history in stone of English architecture, as it survives, is a manic-depressive roller-coaster ride. I often wonder if it was not this, more than anything else, that attracted Pevsner to English art in the first place. Where a tele-bromide like John Betjeman will write down some architect as a harmless, even 'colourful' eccentric, Pevsner – brought up in the Germany of Expressionism and bloodthirsty *sachlichkeit* – correctly diagnoses a dangerous nut-case, and it is on extremists that he is always at his best.⁵

There were certainly extremist architects with whom Pevsner had a love–hate relationship – E.B. Lamb, for instance. John Summerson observed, 'Pevsner . . . in the course of his peregrinations has been bowled over more than once by Lamb's churches; he picks himself up, looking rather guilty and murmurs "perverse", "mischievous".'⁶ (Pevsner called Lamb's St Martin, Gospel Oak, 'the hardest of all nuts in Hampstead . . . Unbelievably atrocious aesthetically, but the details are incredibly original . . . enormous strength of character.') With others it was simply a matter of hate. For the churches of Samuel

Sanders Teulon he could rarely muster a word of praise beyond 'impressive'; in one volume of the *BoE* alone, Teulon's work is described as sensational, crude, heavy, noisy, exceedingly insensitive, ugly, gloomy, offensive, rude and gross. But in the end there would also be a large number of Victorian buildings which he liked for no other reason than that they fell for him into the category of Good Bad art, for which he had a continuing weakness. He described one late-Victorian hospital in the North as 'a luscious villa of 1879 in which debased Jacobean mixes with Gothic and Italianate', concluding fondly, 'It is really very bad.'

Clearly, Pevsner was far from an unqualified admirer, and he would regularly upset other enthusiasts who found Victorian buildings authentically beautiful on their own terms. But he had some standing in a relatively underpopulated field of scholarship, he had a remarkable outlet in the *BoE* through which to champion the cause, he already had a public profile, influence and good connections, and he was an obvious ally to seek. Hence he found himself invited to a drinks party on 5 November 1957 at the London pied-à-terre of the Earl and Countess of Rosse to discuss the formation of a new society.

As Anne Messel, Lady Rosse had been a renowned society beauty in her youth. Her social connections were excellent, both on her own account and through her brother, stage designer Oliver Messel. She was also a formidable worker and organiser, having run a hospital for the Irish Red Cross during the war. The mother of Antony Armstrong-Jones by her first marriage to barrister Ronald Armstrong-Jones, she had become Countess of Rosse through her second marriage to Michael Parsons, the 6th Earl. The Rosses had various other establishments – a larger London house and Birr Castle, in County Offaly – but Pevsner was summoned to 18 Stafford Terrace in Kensington, which they used mostly for the hosting of parties. Part of a classical Italianate terrace on the white stucco Phillimore Estate, the house had belonged from 1874 onwards to Lady Rosse's maternal grandfather, *Punch* cartoonist Linley Sambourne, and its decoration and furnishings were in the fashionable Victorian 'Aesthetic' style, carefully preserved by the Rosses.*

Among those gathered there on 5 November with John Betjeman

---

*After the deaths of Lord and Lady Rosse, the house was turned down by the National Trust as Victorian. The Victoria and Albert Museum also declined it, and the Greater London Council bought it on condition that the Victorian Society ran it. The Society now holds it on lease and opens it to the public.

and the hosts were James Lees-Milne, the 3rd Viscount Esher, Oliver Messel, John and James Pope-Hennessy, H.S. Goodhart-Rendel, John Piper, Osbert Lancaster, Sir Hugh and Lady Casson, Belinda Norman-Butler (a descendant of both Thackeray and General Booth), Peter Ferriday, Jim Richards, Christopher Hussey, Rosamond Lehmann and Peter Clarke. Kenneth Clark had been invited, but sent apologies. Similarly, Pevsner declined this initial meeting because of 'a long-standing engagement with Guy Fawkes'. Peter Clarke celebrated the occasion in verses which noted their absence:

Oh wherefore come ye late from deserted W.8.
when rockets are bursting and bonfires burn red?
And why these quiet 'Hear-Hears!', poets, architects and peers?
and what was your plot, all ye authors well-bred?

Oh fearful was our task, for evil was the mask
of Benevolent Authority on Vandalism's face
when the Betjeman Brigade vowed to start a new Crusade
to preserve Victorian relics from Oblivion and Disgrace . . .

Supported (though by proxy) by Sir Kenneth and 'The Dok' –
See our Lion-Heart arouses us: 'The Foe is at the Gate!'
Will you let the Pass be sold? Fight as Morris fought of old
to save our priceless heritage before it's all too late! . . .'

At the first full meeting to constitute the Society formally, on 25 February 1958 at Stafford Terrace, it was Betjeman's turn to be absent, while Pevsner made his first appearance. By August 1958 the first Chair of the Society had been appointed. Viscount Esher was a patron of the arts of the old school, a collector of modern first editions, Chair of the Governors of the Old Vic theatre and keen proponent of a National Theatre.* Already the Chairman of the Society for the Protection of Ancient Buildings (SPAB), he gave the Victorian Society a generous donation towards its initial running expenses. His Vice Chairs were Betjeman and Lady Rosse, and Pevsner was a member of a Committee that included Hugh Casson, Mark Girouard and Jim Richards. The Secretary was Ian Grant, an architect and designer specialising in the restoration of Victorian interiors. His position was honorary and he found it taxing: for two and a half years, he remembered, 'I

---

*Oliver Brett (1881–1963), 3rd Viscount Esher, was the older brother of Bloomsbury painter Dorothy Brett and father of the architect Lionel Brett.

had a number of devoted friends who used to come and help me.'

The Society's first years would be spent amidst an atmosphere of continuing emergency. 'We are pioneers in a new field,' declared the Chairman. 'Vandals, profiteers and town planners – I bracket the three together – are afraid to incur the displeasure of the SPAB or the Georgian Group. But at present, no one listens to what we say.' Pevsner believed the Victorian Society should aim to become a body with the right to be consulted whenever the alteration or demolition of Victorian buildings was proposed. Its objective should be to draw up a list of buildings for preservation, and get this list accepted by the Ministry of Housing and Local Government, for incorporation in their rosters of Buildings of Architectural or Historic Interest. The list should then be made known to county, city and rural district authorities.

The Society reluctantly acknowledged that it had to be selective in what it proposed for preservation in order to maintain its credibility. Some buildings, it recognised, were entirely unsuited to modern conditions, or of secondary importance on prime sites, or prohibitively expensive to save. Among those it considered in these early years but declined to list were the old Army and Navy Club, the Chelsea and Knightsbridge Barracks and the Grand Theatre, Croydon. Greater priority was to be given to buildings of the calibre of Philip Webb's 1 Palace Green, Kensington. This had been prominently featured by Pevsner in *Pioneers*, but was under serious threat from its owners, the Crown Estate, who were converting it into flats. In the process they destroyed the interior decorations, all by Morris & Co., and inserted new windows in the north elevation.

All was not confrontation and gloom. The Victorian Society had a social side, with excursions, conducted walks, lectures and even fashion shows, the first at Drapers' Hall, later ones at Ian Grant's house in Holland Park. These events were not necessarily where Pevsner was most at home. 'He could be very disarming,' commented Ian Sutton, who would join him later on the Committee, 'but his charm was most powerful in public or semi-public situations. Within the Committee he had no circle of intimates, and he was never to be found after a meeting frittering away the rest of the evening over a drink. Time was too precious. Life was too serious. Art and ideas were too interesting.'

The Society, as the Chairman pointed out, was a broad church. Its members' reasons for joining ranged from conservationism, the scholar's desire to investigate the unexplored, and nostalgia for an age before television or the motor car, to pure curiosity and 'the wish simply to be amused'. Many were merely enthusiasts anxious to preserve and celebrate the Victorian age. Some took considerable pleasure in the links that the Society enjoyed with the aristocracy and even with royalty. Pevsner was either oblivious to, or irritated by, this element of snobbery.

But there was room in the Victorian Society both for Pevsner and for urbane Victorianophiles such as Betjeman and H.S. Goodhart-Rendel, an expert of a very different kind. With a background in Eton, Cambridge and the Grenadier Guards, Goodhart-Rendel stepped easily into the persona of the country squire when, in 1913 at the age of twenty-six, he inherited the Georgian estate of Hatchlands Park in Surrey from his grandfather, Lord Rendel.* In Maurice Wiggin's words, Goodhart-Rendel 'was a tall, spare, upright figure making his daily round in the village dressed in his grey tweed suit and soft brown trilby shouting to his dogs in a real Grenadier's voice'. He drove a Rolls-Royce Phantom II and entertained generously. A gifted composer and pianist and a skilled writer, he was also a practising architect, largely self-taught, building in an eclectic mixture of styles: Parisian classicism, neo-Georgian, an idiosyncratic Gothic revival of his own and even Art Deco, in his best-known building, St Olaf House at Hay's Wharf on the south side of the Thames. He had a particular interest in church architecture. Between the wars he had designed a significant number of Anglican buildings; after the war, as a convert, he built mostly Catholic churches, externally in an increasingly Victorian style. He once told James Lees-Milne that his 'concerns were the Roman Catholic Church, the Brigade of Guards and architecture – in that order'.

Goodhart-Rendel had held an assortment of official appointments: President of the Architectural Association, President of the RIBA, Slade Professor at Oxford, Governor of Sadler's Wells, President of the Design and Industries Association, Director of the Royal Academy of Music. He was a witty speaker on nineteenth-century architecture and architectural personalities; his lectures in the 1930s on Victorian architecture and the decorative arts (at the Victoria and Albert Museum in 1931 and as the Slade Professor in 1933–6) stood out as advertisements for a neglected period. He had known many of the older generation of architects in person and had compiled an extensive catalogue of Victorian churches. John Summerson once described him as 'the father of us all' in the appreciation of Victorian architecture.

---

*Harry Stuart Goodhart-Rendel (1887–1959) added his grandfather's name to that of his father, classics don Harry Chester Goodhart. The interior of Hatchlands Park is Robert Adam's earliest documented work in an English country house.

Pevsner admired St Olaf House, and would always acknowledge the usefulness of Goodhart-Rendel's church catalogue. He appreciated the contribution Goodhart-Rendel had made to generating interest in the Victorians – but he did not consider him to be a scholar. He publicly regretted the fact that the older man had never written the authoritative book that, with his extensive knowledge, he certainly could have done, preferring to remain an architectural essay-writer in the old English tradition. *English Architecture since the Regency*, which could have been such a book, Pevsner found not only skimpy but misguided. In it Goodhart-Rendel argued that 'art must eventually be judged by aesthetics', on whether it looks good, not whether it is original or not, or revivalist or not. This disregard for historical development and social context was anathema to Pevsner, to whom it was all-important that key individuals of this period were developing a new and original language of form. 'Mr Goodhart-Rendel blasphemes this mystery,' he wrote, in an article entitled 'Originality', 'because he lived through it and could not recognise it.'[7]

The difference of approach between the two men would be illustrated most vividly when Pevsner finally published in the *Architectural Review* in 1966 the results of an interview he had had with Goodhart-Rendel twenty years earlier. What had been meant to be a survey of the early years of the *Review* had turned into a series of reminiscences of the individual architects featured (or conspicuously not featured) in the *Review*, gossipy and personal. Notes of their conversation survive and reveal that Pevsner left out of the published article some of Goodhart-Rendel's more immoderate remarks, but what remains is hardly reverential.[8] '[Reginald] Blomfield's scholarship was all bogus – Latin quotations with false quantities.' Edwin Rickards: 'a Bohème type who could only work with exciting amatory experiences'. Halsey Ricardo: 'Typical amateur . . . spectacularly good-looking. Great theory to make buildings washable.' Guy Dawber: 'Distressing little summer houses'. Voysey: 'Not a serious architect. Everybody's maiden aunt had a little Voysey house somewhere.' Arthur Mackmurdo: 'In the same category. He did a terrible pub in Sloane Street, the sort of thing one's small daughter would design.' Charles Rennie Mackintosh: 'Much of Mackintosh was rather a fraud.' These were remarks that might have been deliberately calculated to annoy the author of *Pioneers*.

In the introduction to 'Goodhart-Rendel's Roll Call', Pevsner wrote: 'H.S. Goodhart-Rendel invented the term "rogue-architect" and used it both in the neutral sense of the rogue-elephant and in the less neutral one of the rogue pure-and-simple. He was himself a rogue-architect fully in the former sense and more than a little in the latter.' Temperamentally, the two men were worlds apart – what John Summerson described as Goodhart-Rendel's 'Englishry' would almost certainly have grated on Pevsner – and ideologically too, if Goodhart-Rendel's antipathy to architectural doctrine could itself be described as an ideology. The rift did not go unnoticed. 'By thus peopling the . . . void of the later 19th century with adequately intelligent and sensitive architects,' wrote Summerson, '[Goodhart-Rendel] goes some way to deflating what, I fancy, he most despises about contemporary architectural thought – the notion of the New Beginning and the puritan dread of eclecticism.'[9]

However, there was no need for Pevsner and Goodhart-Rendel to get on with each other in order for them to act as allies in championing Victorian architecture. When Goodhart-Rendel died in 1959, Pevsner recognised the death of an effective speaker and prominent public figure as a serious loss to the cause and to the Victorian Society as a campaigning organisation. At this point, he himself had less of a profile in Britain as a conservationist than he did abroad. His most notable excursion as a campaigner had been a largely unsuccessful effort to protect Glasgow's Ingram Street Tea Rooms, with their outstanding Mackintosh interiors. In 1949 the Tea Rooms' proprietors had made it known to Douglas Percy Bliss, Director of the Glasgow School of Art, that the Rooms would be closed within the year. Bliss informed Pevsner, and Pevsner, incensed, went public with a letter to the *Glasgow Herald*. 'Scurrying with the "Burning Cross",' muttered Bliss, who would have preferred to start manoeuvring behind the scenes.

When two months later the Glasgow Corporation had failed to take any action, Pevsner wrote again to the *Herald* in November 1949, suggesting that the tea rooms should perhaps be removed to the United States, since there appeared to be little local interest in Mackintosh's work. Four months later the Corporation bought the Tea Rooms outright for £22,000, with a view to restoring the interiors, letting some rooms for 'cultural purposes' and retaining others as a restaurant and Museum of Art Nouveau, a memorial to Charles and Margaret Mackintosh. They were swiftly discouraged by the cost of the proposal, however, and by 1955 were preparing to let the building to a jeweller and warehouseman who would keep the original features intact 'as far as practicable'.*

---

*The Tea Rooms were rented in 1957 to S. Zederbaum Ltd, a gift shop that stored its plastic bagpipes and nylon sporrans in the Billiards Room. In the 1970s the Corporation finally joined with Glasgow School of Art and the Hunterian Museum to have the interiors removed. They were stored in a lock-up in the deserted Fruitmarket, where they were vandalised, burgled and damaged by fire, until salvaged in the mid-1990s.

'That is a shocking end to a miserable story,' wrote Pevsner furiously, in a piece entitled 'No Grace for Mackintosh'.[10] 'Would Glasgow behave in the same way if the object were a series of outstanding Elizabethan interiors? . . . Or has it still not dawned on the Corporation that Mackintosh is in the same category? . . . My own hope is America. American museums collect rooms, and American scholars appreciate Mackintosh.' He would always believe that it was better ultimately to preserve a building, even if that meant dismantling it and reassembling it in a foreign country, than to allow it to decay on its native soil.* He duly wrote to all his American contacts pressing the claims of the Tea Rooms. At the same time, to cover all the angles, he suggested to the Victoria and Albert Museum that they should pre-empt any such foreign strike by taking the Tea Rooms themselves to use as their café.

Pevsner's involvement with the Victorian Society marked a more systematic engagement with campaigning and conservation. Late in 1959 he became an even greater asset when he was invited, alongside Mark Girouard and architect John Brandon-Jones, to join the official body concerned with the listing of Victorian buildings for preservation.[†] The concept of listed buildings had been introduced during the war as a way of determining which buildings should be rebuilt if they were damaged by bombing. The Town and Country Planning Act 1947 led to the compilation of the first general list of buildings of special historical or architectural importance. In theory it was possible to list and protect buildings of any date up to 1914, but in practice few post-Georgian buildings had been listed in the early years of the Act. However, in 1953 the Historic Buildings and Ancient Monuments Act created the Historic Buildings Councils. Under their aegis a countrywide survey would produce statutory lists of protected buildings over the next decades – and now Pevsner would be involved in compiling these lists, beginning by identifying the principal Victorian architects whose work was worth saving.

To be listed, buildings had to be shown to have special value within their general types, for architectural reasons, or as an illustration of social or economic history, or as involving technological innovations, or for their associations with particular individuals or events, or for their group value – as terraces, say, or in model villages. Buildings might

---

*In 1967 he wrote to John Coolidge at the Fogg Museum for an American saviour for a timber-framed house from Ipswich. Coolidge suggested the Los Angeles County Museum – 'monstrously ambitious'.
†This was a new subcommittee to the larger advisory committee on Buildings of Special or Historic Interest, chaired by city planner William Holford and reporting to the Ministry of Housing and Local Government.

be listed in Categories I, II or III. Category I could not be pulled down, while Category III would probably be allowed to go.* As for Category II, 'If the case for destruction seems conclusive and the Ministry yet finds itself reluctant to let the building go, public opinion can be brought into play and perhaps a new purpose found for the building.'

The challenge was to convince the authorities that Victorian buildings deserved to be included under these headings, and then to identify the maximum number of buildings that the Ministry could be persuaded to accept without trying their patience and risking hardening their attitude. Pevsner was under no illusions about the difficulty of the task. 'The English listing organisation still shies from Victorian and post-Victorian buildings,' he had written in March 1959, before he became part of that organisation.† Later he would describe his attempts to explain the British listing procedure to officials of the Preservation Office in Budapest. 'It seemed to the people in Hungary hilariously cumbersome. No wonder. That kind of work is more easily done in a totalitarian than in a democratic country.'

---

*The Grade III listing was abolished in 1970.
†NP, 'Time and Le Corbusier', AR, March 1959. But see Frank Kelsall, 'Not As Ugly as Stonehenge: Architecture and History in the First Lists of Historic Buildings', lecture to the Society of Architectural Historians of Great Britain, 24/11/2008, summarised in SAHGB Newsletter No. 96, Winter 2008–9, noting that early listers did have an interest in Victorian and modern buildings, but the research was lacking to support their selections. They included Peter Ferriday, H.S. Goodhart-Rendel, Stephen Dykes Bower and John Summerson, who drew up a preliminary list of buildings of interest between 1918 and 1939.

PART SIX

ESTABLISHMENT FIGURE

1960s

Roundel for the cover of the 1954
edition of *The Buildings of England: Cambridgeshire*

CHAPTER 36

'On Finding Oneself Out of Date'

The values in contemporary architecture that Pevsner prized above all others were humanity, humility and honesty, and during the 1950s – particularly the early years – he had often felt that he was seeing them embodied. Humanity, he argued, was not ruled out by high-rise building. Skyscrapers in the centre of a city could provide light, space, peace and convenient parking for office workers, he argued, in an article in the *Evening News* in 1954 (bluntly headed 'Towers in the City? I say YES'), and with a care for the skyline and for the pattern of street life, they need not destroy the character of the place.*

Residential buildings, in contrast, should not be so high. The tower settlements of Le Corbusier were for rich individuals, not for society, and even the ten-storey terraces favoured by Gropius were for Pevsner too tall. In his 1933 review of 'Rational Developments in Building', he had concluded that the best compromise might be five-storey blocks set in green space. This ideal was approached for him most nearly (though the five-storey limit was partly exceeded) on the Alton East and Alton West estates in Roehampton, completed in 1959 by the LCC Architects' Department. The Roehampton estates were international and yet English, big enough to do the job of housing large numbers and yet not inhuman, characterful without an intrusive display of ego. Twenty-five lower rectangular blocks and five taller (eleven-storey) ones, two-storey terraces and single-storey dwellings for older people were distributed in green surroundings in a manner that reflected both the English landscape tradition of the eighteenth century and the European town planning of the 1920s. 'Roehampton demonstrates the possibility of up-to-date sanity,' rejoiced Pevsner.

---

*NP, 'Towers in the City', *Evening News*, 24/11/54. He later repented of his 'YES' to tower blocks, when reminded of it by Robin Middleton. 'Did I [say that]? Serves me right. I don't know why I said that. I certainly don't say it any longer, because they are scattered around to such an extent that you don't get any vista anywhere without a high building in it. This, I think, is an awful thing – in London.' Interview in *Building Design*, 16/3/73. He was not, of course, the only one to be positive about towers and later recant. In a 1934 article entitled 'What Would Wren Have Built Today?', John Betjeman declared: 'Two dozen skyscrapers, though they would obviously dwarf St Paul's, would not take away from its beauty if they were beautiful themselves. They would alter the skyline, certainly, yet we should not sacrifice health, time, and comfort to one skyline because we have not the courage to create another.'

Alton East, in particular, was 'architecture at ease', with gently pitched roofs, pale cream brick and a Swedish feel. Alton West, completed a year later, displayed more of the influence of later Corbusier, and Pevsner showed signs of disquiet. 'Exacting,' he commented. 'The slabs are extremely interesting but unquestionably ruthless in their rhythm . . . [It] has lost some of the suppleness of movement. There is less variety in the architecture and more unité, as it were.'[1]

As for honesty in architecture, this was exemplified in Pevsner's eyes in the rebuilding of Coventry Cathedral. Basil Spence would later confess to having conceived the building in a highly emotional state, as 'a blast of praise in this materialistic age'.[2] His original plans included 'huge glass doors twenty feet high that would sink into the floor making the new Cathedral one with the old', a Chapel of Unity in the shape of a star (representing both the Star of Bethlehem and a crusader's tent, 'as unity was a modern crusade') and a great glass screen engraved with the bodies of the saints, through which anyone entering the cathedral would see the altar. 'I thought this right, because many hundreds of people had been killed in that night raid on Coventry.' He visualised the stained glass in descending bays of the nave being coloured to symbolise phases of human life: green for youth, multi-coloured for middle age, deep purple with flecks of silver for age and wisdom, gold for the afterlife. 'I feel embarrassed by these ideas now as being far too sentimental, but at the time they gave the design purpose and impetus.'

Spence had meant the plans only for the judges' eyes, but they were published in their original, highly romantic form and provoked a storm of public discussion and personal abuse. Pevsner commented later, 'The architect found himself, to his pained surprise, attacked on two fronts: for being too modern and for not being modern enough. The lay press shouted Jazz and Cinema, the experienced critics with a faith in the 20th century, called it Gothic and a compromise.'[3] He produced his own response in a radio talk entitled 'Thoughts on Coventry Cathedral'.[4] 'Can modernism be conducive to worship?' he asked. And if not, does the fault lie with modernism, or with religion? Is modernism too mundane, associated too exclusively with office, factory and housing estate? Or, on the contrary, is it *too* vital for an institution which is losing its own vitality?

Pevsner posed two questions for himself:

One: do I consider Basil Spence's design a work of genius? And two: Do I wish to see it carried out? The answer to the first is that I do not know myself. But what I feel absolutely certain of is that it is honest and that it is original, and that it possesses that rare quality: naïvety. Basil Spence's mind is full of symbolism . . . This symbolism may be sentimental, but it is the sort of thing that all kinds of minds can understand, and it will help his congregation to love the building.

Churches, Pevsner consistently argued, were not ordinary buildings, and they should not be designed simply to prompt ordinary feelings. It was right that a new cathedral, especially this new cathedral, should be executed in 'an emotional style for an emotional function'. Spence's Chapel of Gethsemane was entered through a bronze grille of thorns, 'and inside there is a plain altar, sensitively placed, and an angel with the chalice, and the disciples asleep, encrusted in *ciment fondu* with bits of glass stuck in . . . Corny? But what is corny? That which acts immediately and forcefully on the emotions of the common man. Should such a chapel, should such a cathedral, not do that?' 'Do I wish to see the building carried out?' he continued. 'Yes, most emphatically.'*

Pevsner was the first to speak out publicly in favour of the plans, and Spence was quick to express his gratitude. 'You have no idea how valuable a little encouragement is at this stage,' he wrote, after hearing the radio talk.[5] Others were less impressed by Pevsner's powers of empathy. Architectural historian Andor Gomme, for one, was disconcerted by the warmth of Pevsner's response to what was hardly a typical modernist building.† 'I felt very discouraged by yr. Piece on Coventry,' he wrote to Pevsner, 'not just that you liked it so much (such an unserious building) but that yr. Article was all in terms of uplift and emotional glows.' John Summerson felt it was too much like a continuation of the work Spence had done for the Festival of Britain, more like a Pavilion of Religious Art than a church. Banham too felt that Spence's work was behind its time, for

---

*Pevsner went with Spence to see the finished cathedral for the first time on May Day 1962. He had contributed indirectly, and in a small way, to its appearance, by introducing to Spence the young carver and sculptor Ralph Beyer. Although Spence had initially had someone else in mind for the carved inscriptions inside his cathedral, he asked to see specimens of Beyer's work and subsequently gave him the commission. (Ralph Beyer, as interviewed by Dr Louise Campbell in 1986.)
†A. Gomme/NP, 29/5/62. GP Series I, Box 2. Andor Gomme (1930–2008) would become Professor of English Literature and Architectural History at Keele, and would publish books on Francis Smith of Warwick, architecture in Glasgow and Bristol, and house-planning and design. He was also a musicologist who produced an edition of Bach's St Mark Passion. With his wife, fellow-historian Susan Koechlin, he would be a regular contributor to the *BoE*, particularly the volumes relating to the Midlands.

all its jazzy gestures – 'a real whizz! A ring-a-ding God-box!' – with no evidence of modern thinking about the role of a cathedral.[6]

Pevsner was right in diagnosing that Coventry Cathedral would become enormously popular with the public. Another project that he supported, however, would never succeed in endearing itself. This time the task was to create a suitable setting for St Paul's Cathedral by redesigning Paternoster Square, an area stretching from the cathedral churchyard to Newgate Street which had been left in ruins by the Blitz. Pevsner was delighted by the plans produced by Sir William Holford, then the most eminent town planner in Britain, largely because they were firmly in the Picturesque tradition. In a talk for the BBC in May 1956 he revelled in what he saw as the informality and lack of pretension of Holford's plan, a fine example of humility in planning. 'What it loses in monumentality, it has gained in subtlety, in intricacy, in the variety of vistas, and also in warmth.'[7] One man's informality, however, was another's inconsequence, and from the beginning Holford's cathedral precinct was resisted, for what was seen as its banality and for blocking a clear view of the Cathedral without offering any grand vistas of its own. Pevsner would continue to defend the scheme, but would later be accused of forming his impressions purely from architectural models, artist's impressions and conversations with Holford, and then failing to revise them when he saw the results – which, as translated by the Church Commissioners' architects, were significantly inferior.[8]

The brand of architecture that Pevsner favoured was, in fact, dating fast. The *Architectural Review*, which had done so much to modify and shape his views on contemporary architecture in the 1940s, had itself been under attack for some time for a failure of nerve, particularly apparent in its championing of the Picturesque, and for a betrayal of the true faith of modernism. Well before the end of the 1950s Pevsner could see that the style of contemporary building he favoured was not going to be the way ahead.

Looking back, architectural historians can now identify a host of reasons why post-war building of all kinds so often fell short of the high ideals and aspirations of the planners.[9] The building programme was too ambitious and idealistic for the economic conditions. To satisfy the urgent demand for the new houses, factories, schools and roads that were needed to reconstruct society, they built too fast and too cheaply, overestimating what new technologies and new materials could do. No one consulted the people who were to use the new buildings, and they were presented with standardised constructions, which they often found impractical and ugly.

These were conditions in which it was optimistic to expect Modern Movement principles, or buildings, to flourish or even to survive intact. Modern Movement buildings had to be constructed to strict specifications and maintained to a high standard in order to work, but these specifications and standards, difficult to fulfil even before the war, were now virtually unachievable.[10] Industry was not sufficiently mechanised, or not mechanised in the right way, to produce pre-fabricated components in the right quantity and of the right quality. Concrete rapidly streaked and discoloured and developed 'sweaty hatband stains of soot', in James Stirling's phrase. Steel oxidised, transparent materials clouded over, sharp edges crumbled, flat surfaces were uneven and troublesome to maintain. Little as Pevsner cared for much of Le Corbusier's work, he was appalled by the decrepit condition of some of his most significant buildings in France, the Villas Savoye, de Monzie and Vaucresson. 'One walks away depressed that the battle for modern architecture evidently is lost.'[11]

Many of the buildings that were going up were new without being 'modern' in the sense in which Pevsner used the word. In 1961, in a letter to H. de Cronin Hastings, he quoted William Morris's *A Dream of John Ball*: 'Men fight and lose the battle, and the thing they fought for comes about in spite of their defeat, and when it comes turns out not to be what they meant.' In the foreword to a volume on *Cambridge New Architecture* he elaborated: 'Most of what is going up points in a direction quite different from what I expected or pleaded for. The rational so-called International Modern of the Thirties abortively presented to Cambridge by Walter Gropius in his designs for Christ's never gained an *entrée*. Instead it is a much more recent irrational International Modern that spreads.'[12]

This move away from an architecture of reason had an obvious precedent. 'We are now going through a transformation of modern architecture in many ways comparable to that from Georgian to Victorian,' wrote Pevsner.[13] There were certain characteristics of the work of some Victorian architects – a predatory attitude to the styles of the past, combined with egoism and aggression – that he saw resurfacing in contemporary architecture. These phenomena dismayed him, and he had his own derogatory labels for them: 'historicism', 'expressionism' and 'brutalism', terms that he used in his own particular way.

'Historicism', in particular, he did not use in the Popperian sense, but simply to mean the borrowing of styles and motifs from an earlier historical period.* He elaborated his views in a lecture at the Royal Institute of British Architects on 10 January 1961, entitled 'Modern Architecture and the Historian, or the Return of Historicism'.† In earlier ages, recycling historical motifs was a practice that could be explained and possibly excused. In the eighteenth century one might build in the style of an earlier age in order to conform with neighbouring buildings, or to conjure up associations with, say, wisdom as expressed in a Greek temple, or in a spirit of antiquarianism, or simply for fun of the kind that Horace Walpole enjoyed in his neo-Gothic villa in Strawberry Hill. Then the nineteenth century saw a new class of patrons with no education and little taste who liked the idea of mastering the heritage by developing and displaying a certain superficial literacy in the styles of the past. But in the twentieth century, Pevsner maintained, none of these arguments was valid, for the spirit of this century was a new spirit and deserved a new style. Nevertheless, the retreat from the Modern Movement that appeared to be taking place had led, he declared, to a revival of historicism, at least among the 'weaker hearts', sometimes for reasons of extreme sensitivity or fascination with period detail, sometimes through escapism or expediency. Looking at the work of contemporary architects, one could find not only neo-Art Nouveau and its offshoots neo-Liberty and neo-Gaudí, but also neo-School of Amsterdam, neo-De Stijl and neo-German Expressionism.

In the discussion that followed his talk, Pevsner was challenged not so much on whether this borrowing had occurred as on whether it mattered. 'I find it hard to see why there should not be all these quaint eccentric departures which Professor Pevsner mentioned,'

---

*In *The Open Society and Its Enemies* (1945) and *The Poverty of Historicism* (1957), Karl Popper defines historicism as 'an approach to the social sciences which assumes that *historical prediction* is their primary aim, and which assumes that this aim is attainable by discovering the "rhythms" or the "patterns", the "laws" or the "trends" that underlie the evolution of history'. There is no evidence that Pevsner was aware of Popper's definition. He may have picked up his own use of the word from the *Architectural Review*, and Jim Richards in particular. David Watkin has pointed out (in a speech given to a conference in Milan in 1992, later published in *Apollo* as 'Sir Nikolaus Pevsner: a study in historicism') that, according to the revised *Oxford English Dictionary* (1989), the first use of the term in the Pevsnerian sense was in an unsigned editorial in the *Architectural Review* for August 1939.
†Printed in the *RIBA Journal* for April 1961 and as 'The Return of Historicism in Architecture' in *The Listener*, 16/2/61. It was this lecture which contained the slide that entertained generations of Pevsner pupils: it showed a dog peeing on a lamp post in front of the Rutherford School, London. Pevsner, focused intently on the finer points in the background, never understood why people laughed at this point.

objected John Summerson. 'Is it wrong for some young man who has read Reyner Banham to say to himself "By God, I'm a Futurist" and build something looking like a 1914 dynamo? Is it wrong for an architect to be so intoxicated by Gaudí that he goes to his drawing board swirling like a dervish? It may be silly, but it is not wrong and I do not think it is always silly.' Just having fun? – not good enough, Pevsner retorted. 'If style is the visual expression of an age, then style must matter.'[14]

Part of the problem for Pevsner was that, in borrowing from other times and other people, today's architects were often not trying modestly to disguise their own personalities but, on the contrary, to enhance and illuminate them. To a man who used 'introvert' as a term of praise,* it was alarming and slightly repellent to find new buildings seeming to show an overbearing insistence on self-expression. Not only were they ugly, in his eyes, but, if the architect's task was to reflect the spirit of the age, what did buildings like this say about the age?

One of the first symptoms of this 'expressionism' was the marked change that had taken place in the work of Le Corbusier. By the time Pevsner was mourning the fate of the Villas Savoye, de Monzie and Vaucresson, Le Corbusier himself had abandoned the strict 'Purist' canon according to which they had been built and had adopted a freer, more sculptural style. His pilgrimage chapel at Ronchamp in the Vosges Mountains had walls of elephantine thickness, pierced apparently at random with tiny windows embedded deep in the concrete, a roof whose shape was modelled on the shell of a crab, and rounded towers that evoked the ruins of Hadrian's Villa outside Rome. Pevsner acknowledged that for many people Ronchamp, standing by itself on a hillside, did serve its function of inspiring reverence and aiding worship. But other 'expressionist' buildings were indifferent alike to the claims of neighbouring buildings and to the needs of their own users. They flouted, quite deliberately, previous canons of taste and sense: uniformity, discipline, serenity and clarity of structure. 'Can one really see . . . the Sydney Opera House and Niemeyer's design for a museum at Caracas as part of the same style as the Bauhaus and the Villa Savoye, or are we watching the emergence of a mid-twentieth-century style, fantastical, anti-cubic and often anti-rational? And, if so, can Twentieth Century One and Twentieth Century Two be treated as one, without a determined caesura? I don't think they can.'†

*For example, in describing T.D. Howcroft's Salem Methodist Church, Salford, in *South Lancashire* (1969).
†NP, review of J. Joedicke, *A History of Modern Architecture*, in *AR*, February 1960.

Pevsner confessed to being disturbed by this kind of architectural overstatement, and made almost physically uncomfortable. 'Perhaps the new stretch of contrasts is too strong for me. Perhaps those who can work while two transistors in rooms adjoining left and right communicate two different programmes can take what I can't take.'[15] Random fenestration, saw-teeth, assertive materials like scarlet brick, crenellation with no purpose, giant projecting slabs left with shuttering marks – all were irritants. He was particularly aggravated by wanton and unnecessary diagonals: staircases set aslant, bridges running catty-corner, angled windows and sills sloping every which way.

Gestures for their own sake annoyed him, more particularly when they appeared to be acts of aggression against others. What he saw as brutality in building was the one development above all others which persuaded him that modern architecture was taking the wrong course. 'Brutalism' has a range of interpretations even among the people who originated it as a technical term. For Alison and Peter Smithson, who began using the word in the early 1950s, it was an allusion to *bêton brut*, raw concrete as favoured by Le Corbusier, and it entailed valuing materials and sites as found, exposing structure and leaving wood, concrete and brick bare and unfinished. Their aim was to be objective about the realities of a mass-production society 'and drag a rough poetry out of the confused and powerful forces which are at work'.[16] Materials were to be treated as fact, 'the effect of which might be inelegance and even ugliness'.

The Smithsons did not see their work as a contradiction of the first principles of the Modern Movement, but as a continuation of them, a return to conscience. 'We wish to see towns and buildings which do not make us feel ashamed, ashamed that we cannot realise the potential of the 20th century.' Reyner Banham, in *The New Brutalism: Ethic or Aesthetic?* (Architectural Press, 1966), a book which became one of the testaments of the movement, described a younger generation of architects driven to despair by what they saw as feebleness creeping into new, supposedly 'modern' buildings. The Picturesque, he wrote, 'seemed of absolutely trivial value to a younger generation to whom the given elements of the planning situation seemed to be social chaos, a world in ruins, the prospect of nuclear annihilation, and what appeared to be a complete abandonment of architectural standards on the part of their elders.' The Smithsons saw themselves as reviving the rebellious spirit of early modern architecture. Pevsner liked them personally, and very much admired individual buildings of theirs. But in other hands – those of Paul Rudolph, for instance, Kenzo Tange, or the Corbusier of the Unité and Chandigarh – 'Brutalism' seemed to him to mean bullying. 'Brutal is overpowering by sheer (brute) force – bashing, not stabbing. The bully is brutal, the hooligan is brutal . . . it seems indeed to me that the Brutalists do little to achieve what is the principal task of the architect: to create an environment conducive to a happy life. Happiness, they appear to say, is square, happiness is corny – and *je m'en fous*.'*

Pevsner undoubtedly objected as strongly to the attitudes he detected lying behind Brutalist buildings as to the aesthetic effect of the buildings themselves, and he was sceptical of the claims that Banham and others made for the motivation of the architects. Banham, who was now an assistant editor at the *Architectural Review*, had long shed the role of respectful graduate student, if indeed he had ever played it. He was interested in Pop culture and the changing role of the architect in an age of technology; he was not at all interested in 'high art' or academic respectability, and he had no compunction in pressing for a reassessment of the Modern Movement – and, by implication, the theories of its principal proponents.

The design historian Nigel Whiteley proposed five stages in the relationship between Banham and Pevsner: influence of Pevsner on Banham; disputation; rejection of Pevsner by Banham; indifference of Banham to Pevsner; defence of Pevsner by Banham.[17] 'Rejection' and 'indifference' are perhaps too strong in the context of the warmth of a relationship that lasted thirty years, but in the early 1960s their encounters could certainly be described as 'disputation'. Banham was frustrated by Pevsner's refusal to modify the text of *Pioneers* significantly for a second English edition to give more weight to the Expressionist canon: Mendelsohn, Gaudí, Sant'Elia. Pevsner found some of Banham's splenetic outbursts and rhetorical flourishes exasperating and a waste of time. In January 1962, Banham, with a mischievous misinterpretation of something Gropius had written about Kenzo Tange, succeeded in enraging the man whom Pevsner would least have wanted to offend. 'This is only *one* instance,' huffed Gropius, 'of Mr Banham's by now well-known technique of attracting attention at the cost of the level of integrity which we have come to expect of the REVIEW.' 'Dear Gropius, This is indeed an annoying thing,' responded Pevsner. 'We have had trouble of this kind with Dr Banham before and we are always trying to restrain him. He is

---

*Roughly, 'I don't give a damn.' Remarks made in a review of Banham's *New Brutalism* in the *Guardian*, November 1966.

of course an extremely intelligent man and a first-class journalist. But as soon as he is outside his scholarship strictly speaking, he tends to write too well and commit errors of tact, and sometimes even of fact, for the sake of good writing.'[18] This hardly counts as a stern rebuke to Banham, and Pevsner would always describe himself as 'happy and puzzled' to have been his teacher, while away from the fray of contemporary architecture Banham would defend Pevsner stoutly.

In 1967, during what Whiteley describes as the phase of rejection, Banham supplied the only disrespectful contribution to *Concerning Architecture*, a volume of essays compiled to mark Pevsner's sixty-fifth birthday.* The *Festschrift* is more commonly seen as an occasion to celebrate a man than to confront him, but Banham took the opportunity to accuse Pevsner of compromise, sentimentality and a betrayal of his pre-war principles.† He was not, however, saying anything to his *lieber Meister* in print that he had not already said to his face, and they remained friends. 'Dear Peter,' wrote Pevsner in 1969, 'Behind your big beard there is obviously a very sweet man.'‡ Be that as it may, about Brutalism they would never see eye to eye. Banham revelled in Brutalism's bloody-mindedness, while Pevsner hated it. Denys Lasdun diagnosed this as a temperamental response as much as an intellectual one:[19] Pevsner resisted disturbance and resented buildings that demanded an overtly emotional response.§

Pevsner would continue to be associated in the public mind with the Modern Movement. François Truffaut's 1966 film *Fahrenheit 451* focuses, like the Ray Bradbury novel, on the destruction of books in an anti-intellectual future. The first immolation scene features a batch of volumes dropped from the top of one of the slab blocks at Alton West; clearly distinguishable is the 1963 edition of Pevsner's *Outline of European Architecture* (which incidentally features his views on Alton West).[20]

Concerning Architecture, edited by John Summerson, was published under the Allen Lane imprint of Penguin the following year, in 1968.
†See p.674.
‡NP/R. Banham, 14/8/69. Pevsner always used Banham's first Christian name of Peter.
§Pevsner and Lasdun had a bumpy relationship, disjointed by a sequence of fallings-out, but held together in the end by mutual respect. NP/D. Lasdun, 6/1/67: 'Dear Denys, You are the most generous of men . . . No truce – just agreement that you are one person and I am another, both passionately believing in something worth believing in. I know, however, that I am stuck, and you must know that you can be carried away. If there is one architect in England today – and I told somebody from abroad just that last month – who should have his way even where he overshoots, it's you. So here is to 1967.'

But Pevsner himself was clear that he was no longer an advocate of the newest trends. He took his changed position seriously enough to try to resign from what he still called 'the beloved Archie'. 'One should not at 60 be one of the editors of a "modern" paper,' he wrote to Hastings in 1961.[21] 'Editors must have a coherent, consistent faith . . . in what they put in. I have not – less than you. I am an inveterate puritan and thirties-man.' He could see two ways in which he might be able to stay on, neither of which greatly appealed to him. One would be to fight the new styles and their proponents; the other would be to try and outlast them, 'to settle down to the belief that our present phase is an interlude as brief as Art Nouveau or Expressionism and that after that it will be all right again. I don't believe that – do you?'

The retreat from the Modern Movement was not just an intellectual reverse for Pevsner, the defeat of a theory; it meant the painful severing of significant links with his German past and the loss of hopes for the future which had helped sustain his new life in England.

CHAPTER 37

'Non-Stopography'

In attempting (unsuccessfully) to retire from the *Architectural Review*, Pevsner gave as one of his reasons the fact that he lacked the time to do the kind of reflecting about contemporary architecture that would help him to overcome his age. 'You,' he wrote to Hastings, 'have exactly as much leisure as you choose to have for looking at the Archie, criticising it and speculating on its future. I am too preoccupied and so I feel I am running dry. You, when you read a novel (I never do), when you go to a new play (we never do), when you see television (if you do), have automatically all the time the Archie at the back of your mind. I have the Buildings of England.'

Almost from the first, the *BoE* had been 'a tearing chase'. Now it was clear that everything about the series was developing on a larger scale than he had anticipated. 'Somebody in your department has been ingenious enough to dig out the original contract for the BoE,' Pevsner observed to a Penguin accountant in May 1960. 'According to this I would receive a royalty from the middle of this year onwards. However the contract also stated that by that time I would have finished the whole country. As I have only just reached the half-way mark I have arranged with Sir Allen that the whole contract is cancelled. The result of this will be that I have not broken a contract and that you don't owe me royalties.'[1]

He may have been conscious that the *BoE* continued to be a drain on his publisher's resources. Although the hard-won sponsorship was making some difference, Penguin was still subsidising the series hand-somely. By March 1961 the cumulative loss would be £6,763 (more than £100,000 at today's rates), with a further £16,802 (some £260,000) invested in stock. This was hardly due to any greed or extravagance on Pevsner's part; his income from the *BoE* was small and he certainly did not indulge himself on expenses. When he approached the Leverhulme Trust in 1963 with a request to renew the grant and perhaps raise it, to enable him to pay his assistants more, the administrator pointed out politely that after the first five years his economies had been so effective that there was £1,000 in hand. Pevsner was as mortified as if he had overspent. 'This is terrible, and proof of my financial and administrative negligence. As I never had a warning from Birkbeck College of over-spending or an intimation of under-spending, I just thought that if I go on being as parsimonious as possible, I should be all right. Now what can I do to get back into a respectable position? . . . My profound apologies for failing, which exercises me greatly.'²

The series had slowed partly because the other demands on Pevsner's attention limited him strictly to two journeys a year, and partly because more information was becoming available all the time. Nor, as the series and its author became better known, was it getting any easier to deal with the proprietors and custodians of the buildings he needed to inspect. 'I have to be very careful for Vicars and owners of houses not to appear funny,' he confided to Penguin's publicity department, which was in search of some 'background colour', 'or else they may be less forthcoming when I need help in churches or want to see houses. That is . . . why I have never published these aspects of the *BoE*.'³ With butlers, Pevsner had developed a degree of ruthlessness. The technique, he once told Lionel Gossman, was to engage them in conversation, insert the foot in the door and then ask if he might not see just that *one* object, visible from the doorway, and edge in.⁴ But owners were more likely to be fatally uncooperative; terse footnotes to the text flag the most frustrating rebuffs. 'I was unable to obtain permission to see this house properly.'* 'One owner of a really important house . . . proved intractable.'†

Access to churches was easier, but required diplomacy. 'One gets on very friendly terms with the vergers who can be rather savage to the casual visitor . . . The highest token of their acceptance of one in their building is when they introduce one to the secret, where the internal lavatory is.'⁵ Even more tact was required in dealing with vicars. Pevsner may rarely have named names in the *BoE*, but the gloves were off when he wrote an introduction to Alan Savidge's *The Parsonage in England*:⁶

In my travels for *The Buildings of England* I must see more parsonages than nearly anyone and meet or correspond with more parsons than most . . . The variety of parsons I come across in my architectural searches is as great as the variety of parsonages: the profoundly learned parson, foremost expert in the archaeology of his region or county or one particular aspect of it, and the blatantly ignorant and

---

*This was at Ugbrooke, Devon, home of the Lords Clifford of Chudleigh. Pevsner would doubtless have been irritated by the current website for the house, which reads: 'It is a delight and privilege to be able to share the house's history and welcoming ambience.'
†The intractable owner was the 8th Earl Poulett – see Chapter 48.

un-cooperative parson who denies the existence of a historical plaque in his church which I have seen with my own eyes and asks for a guinea when I tell him to look again on the south wall of the south chancel aisle; the parson who early on a chilly weekday morning conducts a service with glowing fervour in the presence of one little old woman, both of them unaware of me but aware of the presence of God; and the parson who could not care less, disenchanted, tired and no longer worried by the deadness of his locked church; the parson who would honestly like to keep his suburban church open but tells stories of hooligans using the vestry as a lavatory and cassocks as lavatory paper; the parson who can only be certain of his sermon after having consulted the whisky bottle in the vestry (as the sexton in the graveyard, leaning on his shovel, told me quite tolerantly).

In one church he found a puzzling 'long staff with a kind of metal clip at the top. Is it a staff for processions? "No" writes the rector, it is a mop with the actual mopping part lost.'
Before each county trip he packed with care, relying on a two-columned list:

From home: 2 food boxes; torch; 100 watt bulb; aspirin; sleeping drugs; zinc ointment; penicillin-Kodein; nail scissors; dressing gown; slippers; drip dry shirts; 4 pants; 6 socks; 8 handkerchiefs; 3 pyjamas; long pants; thick pullover; thin pullover; shoe polish; shoes; canvas jacket; mac; atlas; AA Year Book; umbrella; sun glasses; bathing trunks; Wellingtons; pocket beaker; tin opener; sharp knife; hot water bottles; magnifying glass; binoculars; pegs; coat hanger; second fountain pen; ink; second pair glasses; spare car key; measure stick; working board; lavatory paper; air cushion; clothes brush; towel. *From the office*: rubber; glue; red, blue and lead pencil; biro; ruler; rubber bands; paper clips (large); pins; foolscap paper; folders; writing paper, envelopes, stamps; cheque book; visiting cards; maps and mapping notes; town maps; road map; books on county; guidebooks; information on where to stay; correspondence; extracts; scissors; stapler; small tear-off pads; MHLG [Ministry of Housing and Local Government] lists; other volumes of BoE; list of houses open to the public.[7]

The way of writing, too, was now well settled. In its pithiness, and many of the technicalities of its format, it had been born of necessity, but gradually Pevsner had developed it into a style that was already winning admirers. 'Here was an author who was talking in a totally

new modern style,' remembered Nicholas Taylor, 'clear, precise, sometimes lyrical, often funny and with a fresh vocabulary.' The first
explicitly to draw attention to the style in public was novelist Colin
MacInnes in his 1960 article 'The Englishness of Dr Pevsner'.[8] MacInnes
was one of Pevsner's more unlikely fans – a chronicler of youth culture,
aggressively gay, habitually drunk and supremely rude.* But he was
interested in what Pevsner had to say about London; he was interested,
as both novelist and journalist, in the tailoring of language to do
particular jobs; and above all he was interested in Englishness and the
analysis of Englishness. His article on Pevsner shortly reappeared in a
collection of essays entitled *England, Half English*, published by
Penguin in 1961.

MacInnes compared Pevsner's journeys to Gulliver's travels and
Pevsner to a courteous stranger with 'the rare and enriched dual vision
of a thoroughly inside outsider'. Pevsner, he seemed to suggest, was
exploring the language of architecture in much the same way as the
buildings themselves, finding – or planting – treasures. 'Dozens, literally, of Dr Pevsner's architectural evocations are like little epigrammatic
poems,' wrote MacInnes. 'Rarely can a writer on architecture have
kidnapped so audaciously so many adjectives not usually applied to
architecture.' In *London: The Cities of London and Westminster* alone
he singled out such examples as 'lanky', 'papery', 'skinny', 'starved',
'trustworthy', 'non-committal', 'well-mannered', 'frantic', 'desperate',
'rum'. He had a particular fondness for Pevsner's adverb-adjective
combinations – 'victoriously vulgar', 'crushingly mean', 'vaguely Italianate' – and for the noun used with an adjective that no one could
have anticipated: 'soapy hardness', 'almost naughty looseness', 'confident tastelessness', 'Grecian gone gaudy'. A vocabulary like this drew
in even the non-specialist reader: 'To turn to [the glossary], from the
author's descriptive vignettes, to find exactly what he means, is an
absolutely compulsive act.'

Pevsner was taken aback by the MacInnes article – 'very curious'
– and his language was perhaps not always as consciously chosen as
MacInnes suggested. Nor were the striking adjectives necessarily the
most effective of his weapons. Sometimes the expressions that most
subtly convey his attitudes to buildings are the least quirky, as writer

---

*Colin MacInnes (1914–76) was the son of Angela Thirkell, a novelist of a very
different kind. His greatest success would be posthumous, with the filming of *Absolute
Beginners*, the second volume of a trilogy dealing with multicultural life in Notting
Hill in the 1950s and 1960s just before the race riots. He was a friend of the philosopher Richard Wollheim, who may have been a link with Pevsner. See Ed Vulliamy's
article 'Absolute MacInnes', *Observer*, 15/4/2007.

and historian Rosemary Hill has pointed out: 'Pevsner trained the most ordinary words to do what he wanted . . . Where "large" is neutral or admiring, "big", especially about something by Butterfield, is unflattering. "Not a small church" raises a large question mark over the success of W.J. Hopkins's St Eadburga's.'[9]

Where he obviously strove for effect, he occasionally stumbled – slang expressions, for example, are often self-conscious and not always right – and individual readers would develop their own particular bugbears among his favourite words. Writing from the British Embassy in Phnom Penh, diplomat Richard Hanbury-Tenison complained, 'As each volume has appeared my hopes of seeing one word drop from your vocabulary have been consistently dashed. It is "dainty", the connotations of which in this generation – whatever its 18th-century ancestry or its etymological justification – cannot be known to you.' Pevsner was in the habit of sending his descriptions of individual buildings to their owners or custodians for their comments and corrections of fact. He was invariably entertained when they altered his opinions. He had, for example, described the new buildings of the Temple in London as 'dull and monotonous'. This was corrected by the Master of the Temple to 'pleasant and dignified'.*

Very occasionally he would slip up and repeat a bon mot. Surveying the airfield at Manby in Lincolnshire, for instance, he observed, 'The water-tower looks curiously like Terza Roma, or as if it were taken out of a painting by de Chirico.'† It was a comparison that obviously pleased him and lurked in his mind, because it surfaced again two years later in *Yorkshire: The North Riding*, where Barnby Hall in Bossall is described with its three identical brick barns: 'They face the road with a high arch and a pedimental gable, and these three equal motifs look as if they were invented by de Chirico, or as if they stood in the Terza Roma.'

Peter Clarke's first meeting with Pevsner came about after he published a piece in *Punch* entitled 'Non-Stopography', which contrasted, and caricatured, the various different styles of guidebook from the *Little Guides* to Pevsner, by way of Arthur Mee and John Betjeman.[10] The *BoE* appeared as '"Dodo" Books – "Bricks of Britain" Series – (a Bauhaus-to-house search) – For Art-historians who like to

---

*Ian Sutton, 'Reminiscences', op. cit. Ian Sutton emphasises Pevsner's sense of humour – 'unexpected, understated, and (it is surely not too much to say) unmistakably English. Who else, for instance, would have added the little word in brackets to the following description of a church in Berkshire? "Also foliage capitals, a Dec REREDOS, Norfolk angels supporting the nave roof, and elephants (yes) supporting the aisle roof".'
†'Terza Roma' was Mussolini's plan for extending Rome towards Ostia and the sea.

do the thing thoroughly.' A typical entry read '*Smogge Hall.* c18. Offices of Northmet and British Restaurant. 1-2-3 hop 1-2-3 window arrangement. Characteristic double-hollow-chamfered waterspout. Not specially nice.' Pevsner thought it was funny and wrote to Clarke. He also appreciated an anonymous effort written shortly after the publication of *London except* and noted by Kitty Michaelson: 'Heartbreak House. Grade XVI. Period uncertain; largely rubble . . . Interior: ancient rusticated inhabitant with chamfered head and quint . . . OUTBUILDING to last item. Elsan period; of mean aspect; interesting graffiti; note devastated telephone directory (London A–K 1951).' One of Pevsner's own Christmas cards in later years would include a spoof *BoE* entry with a line drawing of 'The Collegiate Church of St Aldate and St Ursula, Candleford Magna' from the *Barsetshire* volume, '(now out of print)'.

If Pevsner did have any misgivings about the *BoE* – and he would continue to worry about the mistakes and omissions that were the inevitable consequence of the 'tearing chase' – he rarely communicated them to his staff. Margaret Tims, his secretary at the start of the 1960s, described her years with him as 'a punishing experience, but never dull'. He would come into the office in the morning at 9.15 expecting to start work with her at 9.30 precisely; were she to be so much as a minute late, he would be tearing open the post: 'I hope I'm not exceeding my powers?' He would dictate a stream of letters – brief replies to questions, and lapidary queries of his own, never entirely standard – in between answering the telephone, which would ring unabated through lunch, which he ate at his desk. Filing had to be meticulous, and she rarely had time to appreciate the content of the correspondence she was handling. 'I once pointed this out to him, to his great pain and surprise. It was all such a thrilling adventure to him. I doubt if any man has ever enjoyed his working life more.'

Successive secretaries would have to share the cramped Gower Street rooms with one or more research assistants, when the latter were not buried in libraries or archives. Some were volunteers, most commonly pupils. Denis Evinson would contribute material on Roman Catholic churches to the *BoE* for some twenty years. To Nikolaus Boulting, now an exhibition consultant and designer, and a former teacher at the Central School for Art and Design, fell tasks such as trawling through Horace Walpole's letters and Gertrude Jekyll's diaries for architectural references. Boulting had only just left school in the summer of 1961. His introduction to Pevsner had been brought about by his mother, who had bought Chute Lodge, a cavernous eighteenth-century house in Wiltshire, at a Home Office auction in order to transform it from its former use as a borstal and run it as a prep school. When in the course of his Wiltshire trip Pevsner made his way to Chute, Boulting's mother explained that her son would be bitterly disappointed to have missed him. The young Boulting – who had gone to the lengths of changing the spelling of his first name as a salute to Pevsner – had been a devotee of the *BoE* since his early teens, making long cycling expeditions with the appropriate volume in his pocket. He was, in fact, the model of the schoolboy that Pevsner had had in mind as the ideal consumer for the series, and Pevsner issued an invitation for him to call at the London office if he would like to talk. Boulting presented himself within days. The following year, finding himself in sudden need of a researcher, Pevsner remembered the young enthusiast, and Boulting was hired at the sum of £8 a week (before tax) to carry out general research while waiting to go to university. 'I was a child and very inexperienced, hopeless really, and it was a very reckless and generous thing to have done.'[11]

While they were working together, Boulting would sometimes walk down with Pevsner to get their lunch sandwiches in Museum Street:

> We'd walk the length of Bloomsbury Square from White's Hotel at one end to the Royal Pharmaceutical Society at the other, and he'd say 'You really ought to be able to date the buildings in this square by the railings' – a lovely idea. It *wasn't* all just in a book, and it wasn't poetic as Betjeman would do it, the patina of lichen on the brick and so on, it was a very clear-sighted way of analysing archaeological evidence without having to go to the books. You had to know what those shapes were, you'd got to know that the chunkier cast iron overtakes the elegance of wrought iron until the Edwardian age . . . There was this strange dryness about it, and yet beneath it was this wonderful analytical tool, which he was trying to get his students to use for themselves . . . The only crime would have been not to have tried.

The poet Gerda Mayer worked for Pevsner part-time in late 1963 on the preparatory work for *Bedfordshire*, extracting building references from the Victoria County History. It was uninspiring labour, and she was irritated by the 'deferential chumminess' of other research assistants, who insisted on addressing him as 'NP'. Feeling 'unfulfilled', she returned to writing poetry.[12] 'He was very resentful when I left after a few months and very prematurely,' Mayer remembered,[13] and Pevsner's letter to her bears this out. 'Dear Gerda, I don't think I ought to conceal from you that I am very shocked. You undertook a job warned by me what snags and what advantages it would have, and now you give it up for the peace of your mind, neglecting the peace of my mind. I would have thought that a commitment is a commitment, even if it turns out to be worrying.'[14] On the whole, however, Pevsner was happy with female research assistants, who he felt scored highly for patience and a meticulous eye for detail.[15] Nikolaus Boulting called them the 'Pevsner Follies', highly intelligent young women mostly from the Courtauld Institute, among them Janet Gautrey, Lesley Marlow, Helen Butterworth, Alexandra Gordon Clark and Jennifer Sherwood (the last two of whom would play a much more substantial role later in the series).

Meanwhile, Pevsner had relented in his original intention to write every word himself. He had now reached the point where he had to tackle the southern Home Counties, and he quailed. 'The reason why he was not so keen to do Surrey, Sussex or Kent,' explained John Newman, 'was that they contained a good deal of suburbia or areas where there were likely to be big houses hiding in their own grounds behind a lot of rhododendrons . . . He much preferred the open country, where things were more clearly in a historic pattern.'[16] People were less forthcoming there than in the North, Pevsner complained in a radio interview; there were more commuters and less rootedness, less tradition of living in the same house for centuries.[17] (Or to put it another way, 'he had got weary of looking for identical Norman Shaw houses with constantly changing names'.[18])

John Newman would subsequently take on the responsibility for Kent, but for his first collaboration Pevsner decided to take up the offer made to him several years before by Ian Nairn. He would do the churches of Surrey himself – but would Nairn care to cover the rhododendron-ringed houses and the other secular buildings, under his direction? (In John Piper's phrase, in Surrey Pevsner would be captain, but Nairn would be batting most of the time.)* Different though their styles were – Geoffrey Grigson, never needlessly polite, described Nairn as 'heavy, coarse and tasteless, a kind of obvious architectural oaf' – Pevsner was well aware that Nairn had vigour and an unmatched gift for evoking the *genius loci*.[19] He was genuinely delighted when *Surrey* was well received. 'Triumph of triumphs,' he responded to Alec Clifton-Taylor, who had written to congratulate him

---

*In the event, the split was largely geographical: Pevsner wrote up the north-east corner of Surrey, which became Greater London in 1965, as well as a large proportion of churches throughout the county, while Nairn covered the rest. John Piper described the arrangement in his review of *Lincolnshire*, AR, February 1965.

on the introduction to the volume. 'The whole introduction is written by Ian Nairn. That should be proof that I was not wrong in my choice.'[20] He was genuinely sorry when a second collaboration failed: invited to cover the whole of Sussex, Nairn found, in Pevsner's words, 'that when he had completed West Sussex . . . he could no longer bear to write the detailed descriptions which are essential', and he abandoned the project. 'His decision filled me with sadness,' wrote Pevsner in the foreword to the completed volume. 'He writes better than I could ever hope to write.' 'On the other hand,' he added, 'those who want something a little more cataloguey and are fervently interested in mouldings and such-like details may find my descriptions more to their liking.'

After the hiatus caused by the series' financial embarrassment in the mid-1950s, the volumes were coming out regularly now, eight in three years between 1960 and 1963. *Leicestershire* failed to rouse him to great enthusiasm. 'A modest county,' he called it, primarily agricultural, with few outstanding buildings, particularly in recent years: 'Clearly Leicestershire, Leicester, and the clients of the architects in Leicestershire have not yet understood what the new style in architecture is about.' Its period of real greatness had been in the early fourteenth century, but 'Leicestershire has suffered much from drastic restoration, and much of the aesthetic pleasure in, it may well be true to say, half her ancient churches . . . is obliterated by the zeal of the restorers'. As for new Victorian churches, with no Industrial Revolution to speak of and no steep increases in urban populations, there were relatively few, in the Church of England at least. 'Amongst Roman Catholics', on the other hand, 'a genius had appeared' in the shape of Augustus Welby Northmore Pugin. But here again there was frustration, since in Pevsner's view Pugin was 'a genius perhaps more in drawing buildings than in building them and most in rousing others' fanatic enthusiasm for the necessity of building them'. The drawings, Pevsner noted, were brilliant, rapid, unfettered, impulsive. 'All the more disappointing are most of his executed works. They are at best correct in forms and mood (Mount St Bernard), at worst of an unprecedented gloom which makes one yearn for the fantastical Gothic of the c18 or the richer forms and styles of the Victorian proper.'

The introduction to *Buckinghamshire* spells out what he disliked about the counties bordering London: 'Suburban trains run as far as Aylesbury, red buses as far as Wendover, green buses over most of the county. Londoners' houses have made of the Chalfonts and

Gerrards Cross an outer London, prosperous, snug, and devoid of visual coherence. Londoners' houses spread all along the Thames Valley and much into the Chilterns. It is a relief still to find large areas of the hills uninvaded by houses and favoured by ramblers.' In this Home County, however, the compensations were very great, and it is hard to imagine him handing over to anyone else the chance to write about the rococo decoration at Claydon, Stowe's combination of Palladian architecture with the best Picturesque garden design, the string of Victorian palaces commissioned all over the county by the Rothschild family,* the Rank laboratories at Denham by Gropius and Maxwell Fry, and Amyas Connell's 'High and Over', one of the first Modern Movement houses to be built in Britain.

He relaxed with evident enjoyment in more fleshly pleasures at West Wycombe. For once, the owner of an estate was given almost as much attention as its buildings, a fourteenth-century church 'made Georgian with great flourish' and a theatrical Italianate house built as a mid-eighteenth-century pleasure palace. Sir Francis Dashwood was less well known as the Earl of Bute's Chancellor of the Exchequer than as the founder of one of the 'Hellfire Clubs' that existed in the eighteenth century for the entertainment of upper-class rakes, with the motto, taken from Rabelais, 'Fais ce que tu voudras'. Pevsner noted with enthusiasm that the golden ball that finished the church tower, big enough to take several seats, had been described by club member John Wilkes as 'the best Globe Tavern I was ever in'. He was intrigued by the Dashwood mausoleum (John Bastard the younger of Blandford, 1764), hexagonal and open to the sky, containing the hearts of some of the club's associates. (Sir Francis and his family were buried more conventionally in a vault underneath the church.) 'A spectacular and passing strange structure of flint,' mused Pevsner, 'placed to the E of the church on the brink of the hill, and exactly in axis with the London road into High Wycombe.' He was also tempted into a detour by the caves in the hills above the house. Extended by Dashwood originally as a means of providing employment for local farm workers, they made a discreet setting for his more bacchanalian entertainments. The 11th Baronet had recently refurbished them as a tourist attraction, and Pevsner could not resist a visit. 'A surprising experience,' he remarked temperately.

Northamptonshire, 'the county of spires and squires', was the one that, period for period, Pevsner considered architecturally the richest in Britain, particularly outstanding for the seventeenth century. 'It can safely be said that the history of domestic architecture in England from

---

*Waddesdon, Halton, Mentmore, Tring and Ascott.

1560 to 1700 could be written with Northamptonshire examples alone.' With so much to see, the travels had been particularly gruelling; special tribute was paid to Lola, 'who drove with me through the county like an overworked taxi chauffeur without limited working hours or free Sundays'. In these circumstances, house owners and church guardians who saved him time by cooperating were warmly appreciated. He was lavish in his gratitude to 'all those owners of houses who put up with my visit', notably the 7th Earl Spencer and Sir Gyles Isham.* The Rev. P.P.M. Bryan, Canon of Peterborough Cathedral, received more modest thanks 'for forgiving me'.

Pevsner was later prepared to select from this wealth of buildings to list his 'Seven Wonders' for the *Northamptonshire Campaigner*. They ranged from 'the capitals of Cottingham for horizontal Knights and Ladies'† and 'the Triangular Lodge at Rushton, for reminding us of the Trinity 118 times'‡ to 'Sir Edward Spencer's monument at Great Brington for anticipating Samuel Beckett by 300 years'§ and 'the glass in the chapel at Oundle School for being modern and yet capable of fully communicating to boys, teachers, experts and anybody'. Not included in his 'Wonders' was a quasi-architectural feature to which he gave a whole page in the book: the M1 motorway, which he dubbed 'the C20 version of Watling Street'. Only fifty-five miles of the road itself had been built by the time *Northamptonshire* went to press, but Pevsner felt able to comment, with circumspection, on the existing bridges: 'The bigger ones . . . impress by a cyclopean rudeness rather than by elegance . . . Sir Owen Williams evidently wanted to impress permanence on us, and permanence is a doubtful quality in devices connected with vehicles and means of transport.' He supported his text with a photograph that is strikingly uninteresting by any standards, a decision he would later regret.

---

*The 7th Earl was grandfather of Diana, Princess of Wales. Sir Gyles Isham (1903–76) was the 12th Baronet, son of the man who had introduced garden gnomes to England. Isham had been a Hollywood actor in the 1930s, appearing as Levin in the 1935 version of *Anna Karenina* with Greta Garbo. He was also a distinguished local historian and had given Pevsner generous access to his papers.

†On the frieze round a column in the north arcade of the church of St Mary Magdalene lie four figures thought to be Mary Magdalene, the Abbot of Peterborough and the Lords of the Manor for Cottingham and Middleton.

‡Sir Thomas Tresham of Rushton was often imprisoned as a Catholic in the last years of Elizabeth's reign, and made the Triangular Lodge as a covert affirmation of his faith. On its three walls there are three windows on each of the three floors, three roof gables and a triangular chimney adorned with Tresham trefoils.

§The monument has a truncated figure emerging rather oddly out of an urn, to signify resurrection. Beckett's *Play* opens to show three urns centre stage, each with a head protruding from its mouth.

1942: Editor of the *King Penguins*, Birkbeck lecturer and Assistant Editor of the *Architectural Review*.

Hubert de Cronin Hastings, alias 'Ivor de Wolfe',
proprietor of the *Architectural Review*.

J. M. Richards: friend and protector.

Bertschy Grigson with daughter Anna.

Dieter Pevsner,
English schoolboy, *c*. 1945.

Marianne and her husband
Carl Walter Kockel, who,
at great risk, sheltered Uta
throughout the war.

Uta in England, reunited
with her parents after her
escape from Germany ahead
of the Russian advance.

Colonel Pevsner in
the Rhineland, 1946.

Penguin team:
Pevsner and Allen Lane
celebrate the fiftieth
King Penguin.
Gower Street, 1949.

Off duty at
Hampton Court.

Pevsner *à table*:
the Professor at ease
in the students' canteen.

Architecture in the wild:
cathedral excursion, 1950s.

Master at the pupils' feet: Summer School.

Truthful enthusiasm:
teaching on tour, America 1972.

The Professor in mufti: Pevsner with Lola and two of their grandchildren on holiday in the Tyrol, 1961. In *Who's Who* he listed his recreation as 'twelve-mile walks'.

'Very harmonious': married for forty years. Lola's sudden death in 1963 left Pevsner desolate.

The last of the *Buildings of England*, 1974:
Sheen Parish Church, Staffordshire.

GOM: Emeritus Professor Sir
Nikolaus Pevsner, CBE, MA, PhD,
FBA, DLitt, progenitor of forty-six
volumes of the *Buildings of England.*

c. 1930: the vineyard house
at Naumburg, beloved holiday home.

c. 1970: Pevsner revisits
old haunts, forty years
on and behind the
Iron Curtain.

With Wiltshire he had arrived at 'the county of the cottage' – the county where he and Lola spent such free time as they had at Snowhill, and the county where they would both eventually be buried. But little of a personal note is struck in the first edition. The first person rarely makes an appearance in the main text of a *BoE* volume. Only at the very end of the introduction to *Wiltshire* can one perhaps divine Pevsner's feelings:

Wiltshire would be as wonderful as it must have been in Hardy's, in Hudson's, and in Jefferies' days, if the Army, and more recently the Air Force, had not got hold of it.* . . . Meanwhile the delightful towns, not forced to expand substantially, could remain delightful, even if architecturally nibbled at by indifferent new shop fronts, fascia-boards, and council houses, if it were not for the A-road traffic roaring through them and making them intolerable. The situation is perhaps no worse in Wiltshire than anywhere else but it is felt to be more incongruous.

Wootton Bassett, the nearest town to the cottage, is dealt with briskly. Broad Town, their nearest village, rates only ten lines, three of them given to the white horse on the chalk slope above Broad Town Farm. Clyffe Pypard, slightly further away, fares better. Its manor had been largely rebuilt in the 1880s for its owner, Horatio Nelson Goddard, High Sheriff of the county. Its church, too, had been heavily restored in the 1870s by William Butterfield, but there were compensations. 'St PETER. In a lovely position below a wooded stretch of the cliff,' wrote Pevsner:

Nice wagon roof with tie-beams . . . FONT. Carved by the Rev. F. *Goddard* in 1840; and very crisply carved it is. – PULPIT. An exceptionally splendid piece, dated 1629 . . . MONUMENTS . . . Brass of a Knight, later C14, 4 ft long and very good . . . Two kneeling figures from an Elizabethan or Jacobean monument. They are all that remains, and they peep incongruously out of the rood-loft doors. – Thomas Spackman, carpenter, †1786 . . . White marble. He stands on an orange marble base, dressed in ideal clothes with a long flowing mantle and holding an eloquent pose . . . The monument displays plenty of the tools of the carpenter's trade, a gratifying sight in an age of such snobbery in monuments.

---

*W.H. Hudson (1841–1922) wrote *The Shepherd's Life: Impressions of the South Wiltshire Downs* in 1910. Richard Jefferies (1848–87) was born in Swindon; the Wiltshire countryside was the subject of most of his essays and the backdrop for his best-known book, *Bevis* (1882).

Pevsner had been nervous about Wiltshire, concerned about the challenge posed by Salisbury Cathedral – 'the purest major E.E. [Early English] building in the country' – and aware that there were an unusual number of houses in the county whose interiors deserved description. He may also have been conscious of operating under the nose and critical scrutiny of his former neighbour, Geoffrey Grigson. Grigson, who saw himself as very much an Englishman, was described by one observer as the 'premier explorer of English landscapes, litera- ture and art'.[21] Now Pevsner was, literally and metaphorically, on Grigson's turf, and he must have been aware that he had only his qualified approval.

An article entitled 'Travel with a Bookcase' in January 1963, published shortly before *Wiltshire* appeared, revealed the limits of Grigson's (at that time) rather meagre goodwill. 'Still, we have "Learned Pevsners",' he remarked:

> Learned Pevsners . . . go first into the car bookbox . . . Being so architecturally pure, they do have to be supplemented in at least two other dimensions of tourism – in archaeology, or archaeological sites, which are popular, as they should be, and which the Great Investi- gator grudgingly and unenthusiastically admits; and in associations, which he enthusiastically deplores and disregards, without mercy, as a vice of English travel aesthetics.[22]

'There is so much I know and you know which you might have made use of to my embarrassment,' Pevsner wrote to Grigson about his review of a later volume, 'quite apart from the enormous number of mistakes which every one of the volumes contains.'[23]

Whatever its defects, Pevsner knew that the series was now widely accepted as a work of reference that was likely to endure. Writing to the Leverhulme Trust to request a renewal of their grant from 1963 to 1966, he reassured them: 'I hear now and then of colleagues from other countries arranging detailed tours in England according to what counties have been published . . . I recognise from the way in which [expert critics] write that they are ready by now to accept the BoE as an institution. That is, after 11 years, more than I had hoped for.'[24]

Institutional status was also, perhaps, a provocation to others less well disposed. Pevsner realised as he wrote that he was often including material that still had question marks in the margin. In the end he simply could not check everything, and he was prepared to be picked up on every single mistake that he had made, and rebuked for every worthwhile building that he had left out. What he probably did not anticipate was a type of antagonism that had less to do with methodology or matters of fact than with character, personalities and attitudes to art.

There would always, of course, be the 'Herr-Professor-Doktor' syndrome – the accusations of pedantry and humourlessness that, it was implied, were typically German. Osbert Lancaster was a skilful practitioner of this brand of criticism. 'Fact piled on fact,' he would write of *Hampshire and the Isle of Wight*:

> all prejudice suppressed, all passion spent . . . Value-judgments occasionally slip through, but when [Pevsner] describes some communion-rails as 'enjoyable', or a housing estate as 'insipid', one feels that such forceful expressions of personal opinion must undoubtedly be due to faulty proof-reading. Only once is there a major lapse; describing Quarr Abbey he comes near to displaying enthusiasm . . . No mention is made of the . . . foundations of a small medieval chapel-of-ease . . . where the late Dr Borenius once found the fragments of a 13th century tile, a fact so supremely uninteresting that its omission seems incomprehensible.[25]

But there were also more subtle and complex antipathies at work. Reyner Banham, not one to shrink from dealing in personalities, used to refer to 'the Playboy Pansy period' of architectural writing, a time during the 1920s when 'Playboy Pleasure Principles' were preached. He had most obviously in mind the writing of Geoffrey Scott, biographer, editor and architectural historian.* Scott was briefly the lover of Maynard Keynes when both were young men, and Keynes once wrote to Lytton Strachey: 'Scott is dreadfully Oxford – a sort of aesthetic person . . . I've never seen the aesthetic point of view so close. I find I object to it on high moral grounds – though I hardly know why. It seems to trifle deliberately with sacred reality.' Banham's reaction was much the same.

Scott was neurotic, witty, an excellent raconteur and something of

---

* Geoffrey Scott (1884–1929) was the nephew of C.P. Scott, the editor of the *Manchester Guardian*. 'Marginalia', *AR*, June 1956, links Scott with the Playboy Pleasure Principles: 'The architectural classics of the Forties have a special flavour of their own – not for them the Playboy Pleasure Principles of the Twenties . . . nor the pugnacious certitude of the Thirties . . . The mark of the period is neutral, if persuasive exposition, aimed at a common reader who was, statistically at least, more common than the readers of Geoffrey Scott or Morton Shand.'

a snob.[26] He had won the Chancellor's Prize at Oxford in 1908 for an essay on 'The National Character of English Architecture', and in 1914 he published his best-known book, *The Architecture of Humanism*. He saw architecture as a fine art with its own laws, not a vehicle for moral or social values; it was to be appreciated purely with the senses, not in terms of intellectual theories or moral judgements. Accordingly, he believed that its true essence was to be found in the language of classicism – not in the Gothic Revival or the Arts and Crafts movement of the preceding fifty years, both laden with moral baggage, but in the neoclassicism which these movements had displaced. 'What the Playboy-Pansy period has done to us,' wrote Banham, 'is to narrow the English vision of architectural good to the Eighteenth Century, and at the same time to render that century's architecture absolutely and unquestionably good.'[27]

Pevsner never pretended to any particular fondness for neoclassicism in the eighteenth century, and he actively deplored its continuation in the twentieth. He had been expressing disagreement with the 'art for art's sake' argument for forty years now. He had profound sympathy for the idea that architecture should be *humane*, but his definitions of 'humane' and 'humanism' were not the same as Scott's. He was an obvious target for those critics who followed Scott in their championing of the classical tradition and the aesthetic approach to architecture, critics most typically represented by *Country Life*. Hostile observers such as Banham would always be suspicious of the narrow line that separated appreciation of the architecture of country houses from infatuation with their owners. As the architectural writer Sutherland Lyall recalled:

> We Banham disciples despised the *Country Life* lot. We knew them as, variously, the Gay Catholic National Front and the I-Dined-with-the-Earl school of architectural history. They were, we reckoned, pathetically motivated by the possibility of rubbing shoulders with their social superiors . . . They also seemed to view architectural history as an aspect of the antiques trade – all 'nose' and not too much of that boring documentary scholarship stuff.[28]

Pevsner, as a proponent of modernism, was assumed to be a socialist. He was earnest. He was Low Church, practically Nonconformist. He was perhaps 'not quite . . .', certainly 'not one of us'. The *BoE* just proved it. He showed no sympathy with the old families of England – how could he? – no interest in their good furniture and porcelain and paintings, only in their bricks and mortar. He pronounced on

'Englishness' and laid down the law about which English buildings were good and which were not, but, if the truth be told, he didn't *really* understand what it was to be English. It was a refrain that would recur until the *Buildings of England* were complete, and beyond.

CHAPTER 38

'Was it before or after 1963?'

Pevsner had known only too well from his early years in England what it was like to feel invisible. He could not help enjoying some of the increased recognition that the early 1960s brought him. Writing to John Curtis, the art editor at Penguin, about an exhibition of Penguin books in Russia, he boasted, 'I think you ought to know that the following number of books by each author were exhibited:

Shakespeare	15
Shaw	5
Pevsner	10.[1]

But this was more an expression of pleasure at successful publicity for the *Buildings of England* than personal conceit. When he noted in his *Heftchen* in 1960, 'More people on the journeys knowing who I am', it was with a mixture of gratification and regret for lost freedom of movement.

He had experienced enough odium, and was in any event sufficiently unconvinced by his own success, to find the new exposure disquieting. Even after the best part of three decades in England, he could still feel uncertain as to how securely he was seen to belong, and there was a part of him that shrank from drawing attention. When Francesca Wilson proposed featuring him in a piece she was writing about refugees now happily settled in Britain, he was horrified. 'Dear Francesca,' he wrote, in obvious distress:

> Your letter is really terribly embarrassing, and I prefer to write instead of telephoning. I do entreat you to leave me out . . . All this, you see, lies now twenty-five years and more back . . . Should one still publicly appear as the being of one particular moment? Perhaps if you are Picasso or Stravinsky. But otherwise? And is in fact 'the refugee' sufficiently a type to justify this categorisation? I have always kept my gratitude to those who helped me to settle down in England – and not least yourself. Yet I am not . . . the refugee settled successfully. My case was to a large extent one of losing a job (for whatever reasons) and deciding to go to a more promising country to start again. I went through a difficult year

or two and then got my family over complete with removal vans.'²

Pevsner was telling no more than the strict truth. He was perfectly willing to be counted publicly amongst those who had found shelter in England; the following year he would sign a letter to *The Times* asking for support for Amnesty's 'Prisoner of Conscience Appeal Fund', alongside publishers André Deutsch (Hungary) and George Weidenfeld (Austria), political cartoonist 'Vicky' (Germany), humorist George Mikes (Hungary) and military surgeon Professor J.A. Trueta (Spain): 'We who have united to sign this letter have all found asylum in Britain. We believe that there must be many more like us who have reason to express their appreciation for the hospitality which this country has shown.' But to earn the title of 'refugee', as the decision of the 1939 internment tribunal had shown, one had to have been a victim of Nazi persecution. Pevsner was not going to pose as a fervent anti-Nazi, nor did he want to position himself as Jewish alongside the majority of genuine refugees. Francesca Wilson obviously saw nothing in his past – including the remarks on National Socialism that she had been the first to report – that would inhibit him from speaking about his reasons for leaving Germany. But that was to underestimate his continuing desire to *belong*, to melt into the background. To assume the persona of a 'refugee-made-good' would be once more to mark himself out as different.

By the 1960s Pevsner was commanding a special fee as a radio personality for the BBC. The Third Programme had seemed his natural home, but since the mid-1950s it had been suffering from rising production costs – the philosopher Bernard Williams commented unkindly that it would have been cheaper to have telephoned listeners individually – and by the end of the decade the trend was towards transferring talks to the Home Service, where there would be considerably more pressure for them to be generally accessible.

Pevsner was by now working regularly with Leonie Cohn, a radio producer with particular expertise in contemporary art and architecture.* She battled to persuade him to introduce a personal note into

---

*Leonie Cohn (1917–2009) was born in East Prussia and came to England in 1938 as a Jewish refugee, granted a visa as nanny to Herbert Read's children. She joined the BBC's German Service in 1941, became a talks producer in 1952, and would later write the biography of the architect Jane Drew and work with the architectural editor Monica Pidgeon to digitise her archive of recorded conversations with architects and designers.

his talks. 'The opening at present is all history,' she complained of a programme on the Castillo de la Calahorra, a Renaissance castle in the foothills of the Sierra Nevada near Granada. 'We have always found that things like history and architectural description, being undramatic pills, have to be offered with some sugar coating – and no-one *can* do this more deliciously than you . . . It's mainly a matter of bringing yourself (or yourselves) into it.'³ But this was precisely what Pevsner was still reluctant to do, and it would seem that the Calahorra talk was never broadcast – a rare failure. Cohn tackled him again three years later about his account of Ouro Preto, a small, immaculate baroque town in the hills above Belo Horizonte in Brazil. 'A little like BoE in tone perhaps?' she queried. 'I wish you had had an adventure there: one, I mean, which would bear telling.'⁴ Pevsner was not amused. He did his best to liven up the talk with details of lunch, donkeys and brass bands, but for him the point of Ouro Preto was the thirteen baroque churches, 'all clearly of one family and yet all individually different'. 'If you still don't like it,' he wrote frostily to Cohn, 'I can't help more and, which is worse, I shall not be convinced that you are right.'⁵

Anna Kallin made similar efforts to lighten his tone. 'Don't quote too much,' she cautioned. 'This is never a good bet, the listeners like the horse's mouth, especially in your case.'⁶ He wrote the text for three lectures on the social history of the architect and sent them to her: 'Do let me know whether the whole thing is acceptable or a deep, deep disappointment.' The drafts survive in the BBC archive annotated simply: 'Cancelled – talks not interesting enough'.*

'Not interesting enough' was hardly a charge that could have been levelled at him by the editors of the *New Cambridge Modern History*, by whom he had been invited to supply the chapter on art and architecture for Volume 10, *The Zenith of European Power 1830–70*.⁷ The commission played to his greatest strength – the ability to set his ideas on Britain in their European context – and he seized the opportunity. All the leading themes of his narrative of nineteenth-century architecture were there: the moral and practical hazards inherent in the new status of the architect-artist as individual, the erratic taste of the new patrons, the importance of the English Picturesque tradition, the emergence of the Victorian forerunners of modernism. But this was also a

---

*Other talks in the early 1960s were more successful, on topics from Bloomsbury to the Bauhaus and the New York buildings of Skidmore, Owings and Merrill. Stephen Games, *Pevsner on Art and Architecture: the Radio Talks* (Methuen, 2004) has a complete list of the broadcasts. Pevsner was also broadcasting in Germany on topics such as 'Der Deutscher Geist in England', in Italy and for the BBC's Asian service.

chance to spread himself on subjects outside his usual range, in particular to write as freely about painting as he had done in his early years
as a critic and reviewer.

The chapter on the Impressionists that Pevsner had included in
Pioneers had not fared well. He had obviously not taken the criticism
to heart. Of his chapter's twenty-one pages, only seven were given to
architecture and almost as many to pen portraits of painters, mainly
French – two to Delacroix ('the highest intellect amongst all 19th-century
painters'), one and a half to Courbet ('the interesting and rare case of
a great painter with bad taste'). He traced a line from Constable to
the Barbizon School and on to the Impressionists. He studied Géricault's
Raft of the Medusa in detail. He wrote with gusto and no apparent
fear of the grand generalisation.

Pevsner was less comfortable in French than in the other languages he
spoke well; when applying to the Academic Assistance Council in
1934, he had singled out France as the one country where he would
not wish to settle. He may never quite have left behind him the anti-
French prejudices that he shared with a great many Germans who had
grown up in the years following the Treaty of Versailles and the French
invasion of the Ruhr. In 1960 he had many of his prejudices confirmed
when he was heavily involved in setting up the Council of Europe
exhibition 'Sources of the 20th Century' in Paris. Since its foundation
in 1949, the Council's publicity announced, it had been 'working to
promote awareness of a European identity based on common values'.
As an exercise in international cooperation, however, 'Sources of the
20th Century' left much to be desired, as the partners jostled each
other for space for their respective exhibits.

In architecture and design, Pevsner argued, Britain was pre-eminent
at the end of the nineteenth century, and should be given room accordingly. However, the French, as host nation, had the organisational
advantage, and the space promised to the British was progressively
whittled away until it became a challenge even to keep the exhibits
together. Pevsner was trying simultaneously to defend British turf in
Paris and pre-empt the Museum of Modern Art in New York, which
was putting together a Mackintosh room and vying for the best pieces,
and he became increasingly exasperated.

Breaking point was reached when it came to the writing-up of the
exhibition. He had held his ground and kept his calm in writing the
architecture and decorative arts sections of the exhibition catalogue;
but when it came to the permanent record, in the form of a book, he

could not contain his frustration. It was bad enough that he had had to resort to solicitors in order to be paid; now he was locked in combat with a French publisher who insisted on chopping the number of English illustrations, attaching captions that bordered on the illiterate and reversing some of the images. One, a plate of Hector Guimard's Castel Béranger, was printed on its side, despite the steps of its staircase being clearly visible heading off into space. As for the accompanying notes, in the French edition they were written 'in such a way that they contain mistakes, misjudgements and senseless statements'. Pevsner carefully rewrote them for the English edition, but – to his fury – the German edition, for which he obviously thought a higher standard would be required, duplicated the French mistakes. 'I would have to protest publicly in a German journal if they came out in their present form,' Pevsner wrote in a passion to the French publisher. 'Especially as you knew of my German background you should surely have sent me proofs . . . Don't think I am just nagging . . . There are for instance so many little remarks which are all right for a French audience but just ridiculous for a German.'[8]

He was finding there were battles to be joined on many fronts now. For the next ten years he would devote a good deal of time to providing a rationale for the teaching of art history, as the discipline came increasingly under fire. It was, of course, better established as an academic subject in universities than it had been when he first started teaching.* But Pevsner was almost more concerned with its status as part of the curriculum in schools of art and architecture, where its principal function was to provide the context within which students might develop their own practical work.

It was now more than twenty years since the publication of *Academies of Art*, but Pevsner's pronouncements on the teaching of art history were in many ways a straightforward continuation of the ideas he had expressed in that book on the social role of the artist and his training. In 1959 he had carried out for the *Architectural Review* a comparative survey of architectural teaching in fourteen countries.† This had prompted him to reflect in the *Architects' Journal*

---

*According to a survey that he carried out in 1960–1, twelve universities were now teaching it at various levels. (The survey results were published in an editorial by Ben Nicolson in the *Burlington Magazine*, May 1961.)

†The survey concluded that British architectural schools were better regulated, but their teaching was narrower in its curriculum, and they were less creative in the use of practising architects as teachers. 'These architects abroad must be less business-minded

on 'The Value of History to Students of Architecture'.[9] The architectural student's training should include architectural history for three reasons, he wrote, in a piece heavily tinged with the ideals of the Bauhaus:

1 Because any intelligent person wants to know of their antecedents.
2 Because it is enlightening and exciting to know about the behaviour of outstanding people.
3 Because it is enlightening and exciting to see events fall into place and form a comprehensible pattern. This pattern is the Zeitgeist (the spirit of the age). In visual terms it is style.

'How should architectural history be taught to students of architecture?' Pevsner concluded. 'My answer is: the hard way, and with no desire to please you in the field of selection.'

In an era of post-war reconstruction, the function of architects in society was obvious. The role of artists was less clear, which made their training a topic of increasing controversy in the 1950s and 1960s, as the system for higher education was overhauled. In the discussions among civil servants on the issue, there was an undercurrent of suspicion of artists, art students and art teachers as troublemakers, argumentative, dissident and unreliable. Why should money – often a great deal of money, as art courses were long and costly in terms of materials and facilities – be spent on people who would potentially contribute nothing to the economy?

Art students, it was proposed, might be prepared as responsible members of society in several different ways. Some should be offered the chance to take a degree, of equal academic status to any other degree. (To be more like other degrees, art courses would have to have stricter criteria for entry and for qualification, and there would need to be an academic component, easier to assess and examine.) Others would receive a training in practical vocational skills that would be significantly better than before. At a time when there was a pressing need for British exports to become more competitive, there would be greater emphasis on producing designers and other practitioners of applied arts rather than simply turning out art teachers.

The National Advisory Council on Art Education (NACAE) – more usually known as the Coldstream Committee – met for the first time

---

and satisfied with a lower income . . . This lack of educational urge or of interest in youth and the future of architecture is not flattering to the profession in Britain.'

in February 1959. It was composed of directors of education, art-school principals, artists, academics and civil servants. The chairman was William Coldstream, Slade Professor of Fine Art at University College, London, and not just a successful artist and teacher but someone who had already shown himself willing and able to take on official duties in the art world.*

Pevsner was one of six members of the committee to have been nominated by the Minister of Education, Geoffrey Lloyd. He was there as a representative of academic art education, specifically art history. No correspondence concerning his selection survives; it is probable that he was chosen in preference to other art historians largely on the basis of having written *Academies of Art*, though it may also have helped that he had shared a platform with Coldstream shortly before the formation of the committee, speaking on 'Art History and the Art School' at the Institute of Contemporary Arts (ICA).

The committee's approach was essentially a modernist one. They took a functional view of the artist rather than a romantic one; artists should be looking towards their role in society and their potential contribution to it, rather than aiming simply at individual self-expression. Artists and designers should be trained together, as they had been in the Bauhaus, to equip them with a wide range of basic technical skills and a broad cultural background. There should be more teaching by practising artists and designers. Pevsner, needless to say, was entirely comfortable with this approach, and he was quite clear on where art history fitted within it. Art students should be prepared for life after college as thinkers as well as technicians. To balance the more purely emotional training in the studio, they should undertake 'occasional purely intellectual endeavour, brain gymnastics as it were' – and this should take the form of art history. They should learn about the function of the work of art, the social status of the artist, changing attitudes to representation, the evolution of crafts and industrial design. Above all, the teaching of art history must convey the flavour and character of different ages and explain how outstanding minds had each succeeded in expressing 'a mood dominant at a certain moment'.

The Coldstream Committee's first report in 1960 recommended the creation of a new Diploma in Art and Design (DipAD) that would resemble a degree course in requiring five GCE O Levels for entry and, preferably, a year's pre-diploma course (later called a foundation

---

*William Menzies Coldstream (1908–87) was a co-founder with Graham Bell of the Euston Road School. In 1959 he was a trustee of both the National and Tate Galleries and chairman of the Art Panel of the Arts Council.

course). Students would choose one of four specialist areas: fine art, graphic design, three-dimensional design or textiles/fashion. In addition – and, from Pevsner's point of view, this was the important part – 15 per cent of the course should consist of 'non-studio' subjects: history of art and what were described as 'complementary studies'.

From their experience of previous advisory bodies, the Ministry of Education civil servants had warned the Coldstream Committee that if they wanted teachers and students to listen to them, they should not sound overly didactic. Despite the best of intentions, its members failed almost at once to avoid the trap and ran into stiff resistance as their recommendations began to be implemented. There were restrictions on the number of art colleges that were allowed to offer the new DipAD and life became harder for those colleges deemed not to be suitable. The DipAD was now the only course open to art students that would ensure their gaining a grant, and the only type of art course for which local authorities could expect direct financial support; predictably, there was felt to be serious discrimination against vocational courses. There were complaints, too, about the insistence on the teaching of art history and complementary studies, given the shortage of staff trained to do it. The bulk of the teaching was done as bread-and-butter work by artists, who had little or no interest in working as teachers.

Meanwhile in 1961 another body was set up to implement the recommendations of the Coldstream Committee. The National Council for Diplomas in Art and Design (NCDAD) was chaired by John Summerson.* Pevsner was a member of the new Council as an *ex officio* representative of the parent Coldstream Committee. The job of the NCDAD was to scrutinise all the applications from art colleges wishing to offer the new diploma, and to ensure that the new courses were both as broad and as rigorous as the first Coldstream Report had recommended. Five panels of assessors were set up, one for each of the specialist areas, plus an 'Art History and Liberal Studies' panel. As chairman of the latter, Pevsner had a potent team that included Ernst Gombrich, Leopold Ettlinger,† Norbert Lynton,‡ Michael Podro, Quentin Bell, Anita Brookner and

---

*Kenneth Clark had been top choice, much favoured by the civil servants, but he refused.

†Leopold Ettlinger (1913–89), born in Königsberg, was formerly a lecturer at the Warburg Institute. Pevsner was said to have got him a war job with the Movement for Care of Children from Germany, and Ettlinger wrote a King Penguin in 1947 on Christmas cards. By 1961 he was Professor of the History of Art at the Slade School.

‡Norbert Lynton (1927–2007) would shortly become head of Art History at the Chelsea School of Art and a *Guardian* art critic. Having arrived in England in 1938 as Norbert

Peter Murray from the field of art history, plus Gordon Russell, the philosopher Richard Wollheim and the psychiatrist Anthony Storr.

The task of the History of Art panel, in Pevsner's view, was to create standards in art colleges where there had been no past tradition of teaching art history and no staff specialising in it. Art history should provide a framework of hard facts and make it obvious why these facts were relevant. Complementary Studies should include training in the English language: a decent literary style, Pevsner insisted, was always essential, 'but particularly so in writing on art and design where journalism sins so much'. The actual subject of these studies was almost irrelevant. 'The purpose is to make the student think and argue on a subject in which his interest has been roused and which is not art . . . Psychology might be suitable, or sociology, or more factually – economics . . . What is essential is that those who teach these subjects should be in sympathy with the art student and with contemporary art and that what they teach should be coherent.'[10]

Each application to award the new diploma was considered by the panel as a whole. In addition, each college applying had to be inspected by two members in person, and the panel embarked on an elaborate programme of visits, armed with a long list of questions as to how the college proposed to teach art history. The results of their initial enquiries were not encouraging. The very first proposals for syllabuses in art history and Complementary Studies had been made without any previous experience or guidance, and it showed. There was, the panel recorded, 'a pragmatic problem' in attempting to introduce art history courses 'before the intellectual, pedagogic and supply issues could be nailed down' – i.e. before colleges knew what they were going to teach, how they were going to teach it and where on earth they were going to find people to do it.

Pevsner and his fellow-panellists were bending over backwards not to be narrowly prescriptive.* Art history absolutely should not be taught as a straightforward chronological survey, they argued. Courses should be flexible, not rigid, and a wide range of teaching styles might be suitable. Nor did the panel lay down the law as to how art history should be examined. Some (including Pevsner) felt the aim was to test both knowledge and critical faculty; others believed it was to test students' approach to personal and social situations, their power of reasoned thought and their ability to approach topics without prejudice, rather

---

Loewenstein, he had done a general degree at Birkbeck under Pevsner before taking Honours at the Courtauld Institute.
*Their attitudes are revealed in a survey that Pevsner circulated to them in mid-1964.

than to establish their mastery of any particular content. All, however, agreed that a pass in history of art should be compulsory for any student expecting to pass the DipAD as a whole, otherwise the case for teaching it would be 'fatally weakened'.

Pevsner had written with gloom about provincial art colleges thirty years before, as he traipsed around the Midlands on Philip Sargant Florence's behalf. Now once again he was often dismayed by what he found on his visits. Lecture rooms were rarely adequate – few colleges, for instance, recognised the importance of having more than one projector and screen in order to make the side-by-side comparisons that were all-revealing.* Libraries sometimes contained more coffee-table books than standard works, and teachers hardly ever exposed their students directly to works of art from the past.

He was, of course, judging by the standards of his own teaching, which continued as regularly as ever: Birkbeck on Wednesdays, Cambridge on Fridays, with extra supervisions at intervals at the Courtauld Institute. In addition, he was increasingly regarded as an authority on Victorian architecture and was called on ever more frequently to supervise postgraduate theses on the period. He had firm ideas on what postgraduate theses should be, and did not accept everyone who applied to him. 'I have always believed that theses should be rigidly matter-of-fact,' he wrote to one candidate who wished to talk to him about work that he was planning on the topic of 'Human Scale'. 'I am afraid I would not be much good at talking to you about so general a subject.' He could be finicky: the cultural commentator Stephen Bayley would write in later life to remind him that he had once offered advice 'about the promiscuous use of the exclamation mark'.[11] On Reyner Banham, he exerted pressure of a subtler kind. At the end of the first year he returned Banham's supervision fee on the grounds that 'we' had not done enough work to justify his acceptance of it. 'I learned of his profound inner sense of morality – and his good judgement of character – through a piece of deft moral blackmail that left me permanently altered,' commented Banham.[12] 'After that I worked like a Trojan – or a Pevsner.'

Pevsner had no ambitions to develop a coterie, but he did take an interest in his students and their well-being. Alan Fern was a Fulbright scholar at the Courtauld in the late 1950s. Pevsner saw him weekly, found small paying jobs for him researching articles for the *Architectural Review*, put him in touch with Ernst Gombrich,

---

*This was a tip that Pevsner may have picked up from Wölfflin, who regularly used two projectors.

made sure he was eating vegetables and was kind to his wife.[13] Alistair Rowan approached Pevsner after a lecture in Cambridge and asked for advice on his research. 'The great man came to my student digs, had a cup of tea and talked to me about the sham castles of the later 18th century that I was planning to work on. He did not think it a very good topic and always afterwards would remember that the first time we met he had advised me not to do the subject but "You made a great success of it". And his eyes would twinkle and he would smile benignly each time he said it . . . There was a kindness between us.'

What his students tended to remember was a capacity for taking pains and a willingness to use his information and influence on their behalf – not so much pulling strings as drawing on an apparently limitless web of connections and cross-references. He was 'like a benign spider' recalled Alan Crawford, who had been led by *Pioneers* to research for a B. Litt thesis on C.R. Ashbee.* Pevsner, as his supervisor, introduced him to people he knew to be working on other aspects of Ashbee's life, or those with personal memories of him, and handed over his own folder from the days in the 1950s when he had worked with Ashbee's widow on the archival material.

Pevsner had not taken from his own tutors the German habit of using pupils explicitly to further his own research.† However, where he had identified gaps in the existing state of knowledge on a subject, he was always keen to see them filled. He continued to be enthusiastic about Alan Crawford's thesis after it became obvious that Crawford's approach was going to be different from his own. Crawford very much disliked what he felt was the reductive approach of *Pioneers* to the Arts and Crafts movement. It projected Arts and Crafts simply as a step on the route to modernism, taking the Modern Movement as the starting point and working backwards rather than starting from the Arts and Crafts movement and giving it due weight as a phenomenon in its own right. To view Arts and Crafts, and C.R. Ashbee in particular, through the prism of modernism was to distort their essential

---

*Alan Crawford (1943–), historian of the decorative arts and architecture, biographer of C.R. Ashbee and C.R. Mackintosh, former chair of the Victorian Society, is currently Chairman of the Guild of Handicraft Trust.

†Working on his history of building types and preparing an article for a Dutch periodical on the development of the hotel, Pevsner wrote of doctoral student, Christopher Monkhouse, 'He has already found evidence of some hotels in England earlier than was known to me. But his *trouvailles* must remain his.' NP, 'The Genesis of the Hotel', in L. Couprie, H. van Os, E. Taverne and L. de Vries (eds), *Nederlands Kunsthistorisch Jaarboek*, 1972.

nature, which, Crawford argued, was romantic, not rationalist. These objections would be worked out at length in a full biography of Ashbee fifteen years later. At this stage, Crawford merely hinted at his disagreement. When the thesis was finished, he asked for Pevsner's comments, and still has the copy that came back with Pevsner's pencilled annotations. 'Yes!', reads one, 'Contradicting me.'*

Pevsner had inherited the German view of the relationship between *Lehrer* and *Lerner*. This was not the camaraderie which some Oxbridge dons encouraged, and it was not a partnership between equals.† Where someone was not formally a pupil, disagreement was legitimate, even stimulating. However, when a pupil, a *Lerner*, wanted to take a radically opposed tack to his own, it could be a different proposition. Andrew Saint, planning research on Norman Shaw, wanted to explore the social background to Shaw's career, an aspect he felt was of little interest to Pevsner. Saint sensed that, kind and generous with information as Pevsner undoubtedly was, he was unlikely to be swayed in his views on one of his own 'pioneers' and would look to see these views reflected in the work on Shaw. Remaining on the best of terms with Pevsner, he chose to be supervised elsewhere. Saint produced his findings as a book rather than a thesis, and received Pevsner's advice with gratitude.‡

As for the Victorian Society, in the early 1960s it was still small and not widely known, with fewer than 500 members.§ It was forged into a campaigning organisation and brought to prominence by two major campaigns – for the Euston Arch and the Coal Exchange, both in London. The Euston Arch was a huge Doric portico with four columns eight and a half feet round, linked by ornamental gates to lodges on either side. It stood in front of Euston station, a gateway

---

*Among Pevsner's papers when he died was a list, dating from the 1970s, entitled 'Good Arguments Against Me'. GP Series IIIC, Box 72.
†He did not find it hard to unbend: to one student he confessed in 1960 to being tempted to wear a poncho, 'not in Gower Street but at Cambridge, where it would no doubt enhance my popularity' – an appealing picture.
‡Andrew Saint (1946–) previously Professor of Architecture at Cambridge, is now General Editor of the Survey of London. He is the author of *Richard Norman Shaw* (1976), *The Image of the Architect* (1983), *Towards a Social Architecture: the role of school buildings in post-war England* (1987) and *Architect and Engineer: a study in sibling rivalry* (2008).
§These members were now spread across many fields, and included Evelyn Waugh, Harold Acton, Julia Trevelyan Oman, Norman St John-Stevas and illustrator Jan Pienkowski, creator of 'Meg and Mog'.

to the industries of the Midlands. It had been built to express the importance of the first trunk railway to link London with the north, and its admirers saw it as one of the outstanding monuments of the railway age. The British Transport Commission, however, in charge of overseeing nationalised railways, wanted to extend the station to make room for longer platforms, which would involve knocking down the Arch, the Great Hall and the Shareholders' Room and rebuilding the station to a stripped-classical American-inspired design. The Arch had been listed as Grade II* in 1951, but in 1960 the London County Council granted permission to demolish the station on the condition that the Arch was preserved and rebuilt elsewhere. Both Betjeman and Pevsner moved into the attack. 'If the Euston Arch were destroyed,' wrote Pevsner in a letter to the *Daily Telegraph*, 'that would be the worst loss to the Georgian style in London architecture since most of Soane's Bank of England fell shortly before the war.'[14] Soon after Pevsner's letter was published, the notice to demolish expired, and now only the Minister for Housing and Local Government could save the Arch by placing a preservation order on it. At this point, the Transport Ministry intervened. The minister was Ernest Marples, and in July 1961 he confirmed that he had approved the demolition.

The Victorian Society embarked on a campaign to raise the £180,000 estimated as the cost of moving and re-erecting the Arch, at the same time arguing that if demolition were inevitable, at the very least the stones should be numbered and stored, as had been done in the nineteenth century with Wren's Temple Bar. With only £1,000 raised, the Society joined a deputation to the Prime Minister, Harold Macmillan, on 24 October 1961. Led by the President of the Royal Academy, the deputation included both Pevsner and Betjeman, alongside Hugh Casson, Jim Richards and John Summerson. Macmillan was unmoved, and six weeks later the demolition began. There was no attempt to salvage a single stone.

'The photograph of the Euston Propylaea ought to be hung all over London as a poster to perpetuate the Cabinet's shame,' Pevsner wrote bitterly in *The Listener* in January 1962.[15] He was even more outspoken in an article in *The Lodestone*, the Birkbeck student magazine: 'Sometimes I feel like emigrating, away from the country which viciously demolished Robert Adam's Adelphi, the finest piece of London's river front, and viciously destroyed Sir John Soane's interior of the Bank of England . . . I feel it again now that the Euston Propylaea are being viciously demolished, with the hypocritical regrets of Mr Macmillan. But where should I emigrate?'* He suggested to the committee advising the minister that they should resign en bloc, but met with no response.

The Euston Arch had become a conservation cause célèbre, and its loss would in the long term make battles with the railway authorities easier to anticipate and to win. But in the short term the campaign had taken all of the Victorian Society's resources and diverted its attention from other threats that were equally serious. In *London: The Cities of London and Westminster* Pevsner had described the London Coal Exchange as 'among the twelve irreplaceable buildings of 19th-century England'. The Exchange had stood as a market floor for the trading of coal in Lower Thames Street, near Billingsgate, since 1849. It was built as a rotunda covered by a glass dome supported by iron ribs, with a curved porch and round tower. Inside, a circular court was surrounded by four tiers of offices arranged along iron galleries. The decorations, by Frederick Sang, were described as 'both appropriate and instructive, representing the various species of ferns, palms and other plants found fossilised amid strata of the coal foundation; the principal collieries and mouths of the shafts; portraits of men who have rendered service to the trade; colliers' tackle, implements &c'.[16]

The building had been damaged by bombing in the war, and had ceased to operate as an exchange in 1947 when the coal industry was nationalised. Now the Corporation of London was claiming to want the site as part of a road-widening scheme for bypassing the knot of roads that met at the Bank of England. The Victorian Society had proposed alternatives such as removing less architecturally distinguished parts of the Custom House on the opposite side of Lower Thames Street or moving the Exchange back on rollers. In February 1961, Pevsner appeared at a press conference with Betjeman and Sir Mortimer Wheeler to appeal for its preservation. But, with the campaign for the Euston Arch in full swing, it was hard to mobilise public opinion on two fronts, harder still to raise the money that might have saved the rotunda by paying for it to be dismantled and rebuilt in Melbourne, where a conservation society

---

*NP, 'A Farewell to the Euston Propylaea' in *The Lodestone*, 52, Spring 1962. He would later introduce the polemic by Peter and Alison Smithson entitled *The Euston Arch* (Thames and Hudson, 1968), though he may not have subscribed to their belief that it was an 'act of revenge of the south against the north . . . The Arch was a nag, a reminder, that what was the Empire was based on men working in the dirt up north.'

was interested.* The Coal Exchange came down at the end of 1962, but it would be ten years before the road was widened.

As the redevelopment of city centres gathered pace, an increasing number of Victorian buildings were at risk, but the Society itself was gaining strength. Viscount Esher continued as its Chairman; Ian Grant was succeeded as Secretary by Peter Fleetwood-Hesketh, who took the flat next to the SPAB committee room in Great Ormond Street so that the Society could use it as an office.† There was now a Victorian Society Listing Sub-Committee, to which Pevsner belonged. For each of the completed volumes of the *Buildings of England* he had prepared summaries of the Victorian buildings that he felt were worth fighting for, and he helped the Society to develop a network of other willing collaborators.‡

Pevsner was well aware that listing in itself did not guarantee that a building would be saved; it only made its destruction more difficult, and a low-grade listing might amount to no more than a minor delay. Too many of these lower listings might well be an irritation that would compromise the safety of buildings in a higher grade. Nor would it work to promote a suspiciously large number of buildings to Grade I: better to reserve the highest status for a handful of the least dispensable and be liberal with the more modest II* grading.

For light relief, the 'Vic Soc' staged for its members a lantern slide show through the medium of the Noakescope, a contraption found in a garage in Southend by John Betjeman and Robert Aickman.§ Eight feet high, in mahogany and brass, the Noakescope had four large protruding lenses that projected four pictures and, with some wiggling, could create the illusion of movement. The Society took itself to Alton Towers to inspect the remains of Pugin's work there, and to a number of well-preserved Victorian houses in Leicester. One member recalled, 'Two of the owners followed us round quite bemused to see people so full of admiration for the possessions that they were longing to sell.'[17]

---

*There was also a proposal that a section should be reconstructed in the Victoria and Albert Museum, and a scheme to re-erect at least the iron-framed part as a lecture or meeting room within the Barbican Estate, which was then being planned.

†Charles Peter Fleetwood-Hesketh (1905–85) was a writer, illustrator, High Sheriff of Lancashire and later the architectural correspondent of the *Daily Telegraph*. He was the author of the *Murray's Guide* to Lancashire (1955), and drew the nine-foot-long fold-out illustration for Betjeman's *Ghastly Good Taste*.

‡Andor Gomme, for example, had long been protesting about the destruction of Victorian buildings in Glasgow: Pevsner recruited him to compile lists of those he felt should be preserved.

§Robert Aickman (1914–81), a conservationist and writer, was best known as a co-founder of the Inland Waterways Association and an author of ghost stories.

By the time of the Victorian Society's *Annual Report* in 1963 there was a feeling that at last some progress was being made. 'The age of Lytton Strachey is over,' wrote Mark Girouard.[18]

> Young architects are as likely to be admirers of Butterfield as of Le Corbusier. Young dramatists litter their sets with Victorian bric à brac. A young film star has sprinted off the rugger-fields of *This Sporting Life* to buy William Burges' house in Melbury Road*. . . . Only in the more remote and savage parts of the country – in the drawing-rooms of aldermen and property tycoons, in the offices of borough engineers and cabinet ministers – has the wind of change scarcely ruffled the (Georgian-style) curtains. Unfortunately these are the people who have the greatest opportunities for pulling down Victorian buildings – opportunities which they cannot be accused of neglecting.

Pevsner was also being drawn, sometimes unwillingly, into conservation battles abroad. In 1961 he was approached by German scholars to join the fight to save the Berlin Bauakademie or architecture school, completed in 1836 by Karl Friedrich Schinkel, the leading German Neo-Classical architect of the nineteenth century. He was not convinced that concerted criticism from overseas was the most sensible approach. 'Why should the National Trust protest?' he wrote. 'I should certainly hate the idea of a protest arriving here from Russia about the pulling down of the Euston Arch' and he set his face against 'roping in Sir Anthony Blunt etc etc'.[19] His fears would seem to have been justified. To the most tactful letter he could compose he got a reply from the Director of the Architects' Department in Berlin pointing out, 'It is not us who destroyed the many historic buildings in the centre of Berlin.' The Bauakademie was demolished in 1962 to make room for the East German Ministry of Foreign Affairs.[†]

He was prepared to be more outspoken about the buildings of South Africa, confessing to being terribly disappointed to find that 'most of the old veterans had been put to sleep, a cruel thing to do . . . History seen around you in the streets is infinitely more eloquent than history which has to be searched out in libraries and museums.'[20] His bluntness may have had something to do with the second trip he had made

---

*This was Richard Harris; he sold it to rock star Jimmy Page, who outbid David Bowie.
†The new building was itself demolished in 1995 after reunification. There are current plans to reconstruct Schinkel's Bauakademie.

to South Africa in August 1961 – a visit far less comfortable than the first. He had been invited as a guest to Witwatersrand University; but his children and his young assistants very much disapproved of him going to South Africa at a time when international condemnation of the apartheid regime was at its height. The preceding year and a half had seen the killing of sixty-nine black protestors in Sharpeville, South Africa's departure from the Commonwealth, the banning of the African National Council and the move to armed resistance. Nelson Mandela had been arrested on 5 August. The history that Pevsner was seeing around him on the streets was more than architectural.

He wrote rather defensively to the High Commissioner, Sir John Maud, at the British Embassy in Pretoria, 'We found it very useful to see the other side and I was eager to meet some Nationalist politicians and ask them polite questions.'[21] It is not clear that he ever did; reports in the white press mentioned only that he appreciated their buildings. The pleasures he identified, though, were all aesthetic. The early city fathers had neglected planning, and the social consequences were poor. This was no longer an eager booming city, in Pevsner's view. He diagnosed 'a slackening of drive and will, a passivity that goes ill with Johannesburg's comparative youth', which may be the nearest he came to moving away from academic detachment towards political comment.[22]

Other foreign excursions were less controversial. In 1960 he made a whistle-stop tour of South America under the auspices of the British Council, who could well regard him as a cultural envoy, given that at least two of his books were set texts in Uruguay and Argentina. He found the pace so hectic that his back gave way: 'I was promised a Japanese bone-setter who would jump on me,' he told the British Council.[23] In Brazil he declined to give his usual talk on contemporary British architecture: 'Everything is of a so much higher pitch there, money flows so much more freely and fertility of ideas is so much more pronounced that this lecture of mine wouldn't stand a chance.'[24] He was tempted, however, when the Ministry of External Relations in Brazil invited him to study the new movement in architecture. It was only the thought of the *Buildings of England* that held him back.

'Professor Pevsner's visit came and went like a flash of lightning,' wrote Roger Hinks, representative of the British Council in France in May 1962:

He arrived on Thursday morning by the ferry and at once asked to see a building by Ledoux on the way to my house. From then on not a moment was wasted. He lectured in French (quite well, reasonably well, though of course not with his English brilliance) . . . On

Friday . . . he lectured at 11 a.m. on 'English Architecture about 1300' and at 3 p.m. on 'Sir Christopher Wren and his Churches'. In the interval he rushed round Paris and saw a quite incredible number of buildings . . . On Sunday 20th he was taken in the afternoon to the Chateau d'Écouen . . . He inspected the large housing estate at Sarcelles on the way back to Paris.* He arrived in time for a bit of dinner before hurrying off to catch his ferry train at the Gare du Nord. I found his visit most stimulating.[25]

Academics lecturing for the British Council were not always easy to handle. Pevsner was invariably willing, obliging and gregarious. On a trip to Anatolia in 1959, to visit the early Christian monastery at Alahan and the Kara Dag volcano, he had been taken about by a guide, a former shepherd called Izmail Ince. On his return to England he received a letter from Izmail asking for photographs and a story book to help him improve his English. Harking back to his own childhood fondness for animal stories Pevsner sent off *Black Beauty* and *Finn the Wolfhound*.

He had considerable social success on a later British Council trip to Hungary and Yugoslavia in 1965, recorded by his friend and fellow art historian Anna Zádor in 'The Portrait of an English Scholar'.† 'Quick, energetic motions,' she wrote, 'a professor's elegance . . . an eternally young man, who is curious to know everything, indefatigable, and who nearly doubles the available time through his corporal and spiritual freshness and quick reactions.'

Despite having his suitcase stolen between airport and hotel and a ten-hour coach journey that landed him in Zagreb at 3 a.m., Pevsner revelled in the contrasts between his expectations and the realities of life in communist Yugoslavia.‡ Contemporary architecture seemed to be International Modern rather than 'Russian architectural officialese'; the currency in hotels was the American dollar, and taxi drivers had pictures of John F. Kennedy above their mirrors. He travelled in a Chaika, 'the Russian luxury car, looking with all its

---

*Built in 1954, the Sarcelles estate was the first of Paris's 'new towns' – a high-rise settlement of rent-controlled subsidised housing developed primarily to house recent immigrants from Algeria.

†Anna Zádor (1904–95), a leading Hungarian architectural historian, was Professor at the Eötvös Loránd University in Budapest. Her article on Pevsner appeared in *Új Írás*, VI/8, 1966.

‡He published his impressions of the whole trip in an article in *New Hungarian Quarterly*, 7/21, 1966. And cf. J. Sisa, 'Nikolaus Pevsner's thoughts on Hungarian Architecture' in G. Ernyey (ed.), *Contacts in Architecture, Design, Art and Theory during the 19th and 20th Centuries* (Hungarian University of Craft and Design, 2003).

useless chromium trimmings just like an American car of a few years ago', although for the most part farm carts outnumbered cars on the roads.* 'Only once did I notice close to the road an assembly of lorries . . . As the car approached I could read what it said on them: Water Supply Department of Ghana. No comment, as prospective interviewees say.'[26]

Pevsner's son Dieter once said about his father's *Heftchen*, 'They seem to exist mainly to be the receptacles of the thoughts that are so black that they cannot be publicly expressed. All the whiter thoughts don't go there because they go into the world.' As for thoughts about his work, he tended to dismiss them – frustratingly, for the biographer – as not worth preserving, in these records at least.

The version of Pevsner in the *Heftchen* is partial, and perhaps no more 'authentic' than the version the world saw, but the self-doubt expressed there had been a feature of Pevsner's character since his adolescence and would remain a feature into his old age. 'Such a nice man to the outside world,' he wrote in 1962, 'such an un-nice man really.'[27] He was sceptical about his achievements – 'Certain honours go on, not strictly scholarly ones'[28] – and acutely conscious of the consequences of the choices he had made.

On the other hand, his life with Lola had at last become more contented, largely because she herself was more at ease. She was still shy with his colleagues and anxious to please: some found her awkward, others appreciated her lack of affectation. For Basil Spence, she cooked a whole carp, a traditional German New Year's dish; the carp can be a muddy fish and it was not a gastronomic success, but Spence was touched by the gesture. She still had reserves of pent-up energy that she could not always use, but she had got better at relaxing without feeling it was necessarily a sign of weakness. A good deal of her energy, too, could be channelled into the *Buildings of England*, and she was finally able to see that she was more than simply an appendage.

'Life with Lola on the B of E journeys very harmonious. If she dropped out, the B of E would cease,' Pevsner wrote.[29] The trip to the North Riding of Yorkshire in the summer of 1963 was a particularly companionable one. All the omens were favourable. The county was rich in the kind of scenery that gave him most pleasure and the

---

*The Chaika was in fact closely modelled on the 1955 Packard Patrician. Chaikas were only issued to top professionals, party officials, scientists, academics and other VIPs. They were also ordered in bulk by the KGB.

buildings he most enjoyed describing. Of Rievaulx Abbey, for example, he wrote, 'For the picturesque traveller it is an exquisite feast, and for the architectural historian what remains is of the highest interest.' He was comfortable with the people he met, 'so genuine, so hospitable'. This sense of ease extended here to the great landowners he was sometimes accused of indiscriminately resenting. 'At Castle Howard, Mr George Howard helped me greatly by his wide knowledge and by his Land-rover,' he wrote, and he remained on good terms with the Howards for years. Castle Howard itself delighted him; he loved the peculiarity of it, the violence of the north side and festivity of the south side, the 'virility' of the Hawksmoor Mausoleum, the wit of the work done by Vanbrugh, a man who had come into architecture 'in jest'.

'Enjoyable' is a key word in the text. Building after building in the North Riding drew him in, less as a passive observer than as a participant. St Mary's, Whitby was one of his favourite churches, and his description of it shows exactly how much he sometimes regretted the limitations that he had imposed on himself with his methodology for the *Buildings of England*. 'One should look at it,' he wrote, 'as a part of the fishing and shipping town and reach it from below, i.e. not by car but by the winding 199 steps . . . There it is then, when the exertion is over, in a splendid position, low and spreading and battlemented, a wonderful jumble of medieval and Georgian when one walks round it, but when one enters it, hard to believe and impossible not to love. It is one of the churches one is fondest of in the whole of England.' Inside, at every turn there was something to admire and enjoy: the domestic Georgian nave windows, 'no putting on of a churchy act'; the white wooden staircases, one with 'a gay and naïve Chippendale fret handrail'; the wooden interior made by ships' carpenters, with the feel of a 'tween deck; the maze of box pews from the seventeenth century, 'positively inviting Hide and Seek'. In the town of Whitby, too, everywhere one looked there was a picture: the abbey ruins high on the cliff, the cobbled alleys curling and twisting down towards the sea, the long irregular rows of houses on the busy quayside. 'Picturesque' recurs over and over again, and it is one of the counties where one most regrets that it was not his habit to take a camera on the trips.

The twentieth century also had its testaments. 'The one major monument of Middlesbrough, a European monument, one is tempted to say, is the transporter bridge of 1911, 850 ft long and 225 high and in its daring and finesse a thrill to see from anywhere.' Constructions that in other moods he might have regarded as blots on an unspoiled landscape became assets in the North Riding. 'FYLINGDALES

EARLY WARNING STATION. Built in 1961–2, and designed by the *Air Ministry Works Department*. Three perfect white globes of great size on three perfect black plinths in the grandiose undulating silence of the moor. The geometry of the space age at its most alluring and most frightening. The globes have a diameter of 140 ft and protect the tracking radar aerials. They are called rather embarrassingly Radomes.'

For once, the brackets that denoted buildings not seen in person signified real regret rather than apology. Pevsner would genuinely have liked to have gone everywhere in the North Riding. The trip had had the feel of a holiday, and Lola wrote happily about it when she got home. 'It isn't only the history which we enjoy – there are acres of marsh with waving ferns . . . Some stormy days and then hot summer, with the air filled with camomile, jasmine and lime . . . We have really enjoyed the work.'[30] It was a happy, chatty letter, enthusing about *West Side Story*, which she had just seen, detailing the merits of her various grandchildren and ending with their plans for their official holiday, a tour of the architecture of Andalucia. Then, after the holiday, 'on October 1 everyday life will start again'.

As someone who had suffered from ulcers for at least twenty years, Lola tended to be stoical about her health. She was terrified of cancer – the dread 'came up every so often in the small hours' – and would occasionally remark that she felt she would be among the first of her group to go, but from day to day she was phlegmatic. Her doctor had told her that she must get treatment for her varicose veins; but she had kept putting it off, delaying the operation until after the Spanish holiday, which itself was continually postponed. Long drives are the worst possible test for varicose veins, and on 14 September she wrote home to Camilla Bagg that, while Granada was one of the most beautiful places they had ever seen, they were perhaps trying to pack too much in and were 'stung by passing ailments'. Within a few days her legs were too painful for her to go on. The Pevsners were travelling with Leopold Worth and his wife. Dr Worth advised her to go home: he rang the German hospital in Dalston, where arrangements were made to fly her home for emergency treatment. Pevsner, Lola said, must stay on in Spain, because otherwise the Worths would have to bear the full cost of the return journey alone, and he did as she asked.

'No one expected her to die,' he wrote later, 'not our doctor, not the hospital, not certainly she herself.' When she reached London she was taken in an ambulance to hospital, but her legs were too inflamed for an immediate operation. That particular hospital did not use one measure that might have guarded against thrombosis, and she died of a pulmonary embolism on 29 September 1963, aged sixty-one. Pevsner and the rest of the party were somewhere in Spain and the hospital was unable to contact them. 'So she was alone that fateful second,' he noted briefly and with anguish.

He recorded her death in the *Heftchen* on 10 October. '∂ has died – on Sep 29.* We buried her at Clyffe Pypard on the 5 [October] . . . I found the burying not a horror, but tender and reassuring, and even her small face and small body in the hospital tender and no horror . . . The children are good to me and have taken me over. I cry, and then work, and then cry again. "My time" is over. What happens now is "after my time". *La tristesse durera toujours . . .*' However difficult their relationship had sometimes been, their lives had been tightly wound together for more than forty years and the loss was atrocious. 'Long afterwards,' recalled Ian Sutton, 'he said, trying to remember some date: "Let me see, was it before or after 1963? I date everything by when my wife died".'†

The letters that Pevsner received on Lola's death came from friends from every period and stage of their life together: from Lola's Leipzig schoolfriends, and Wolfgang Herrmann, who had seen them married; from Esther Simpson, at the Society for the Protection of Science and Learning; from Donald Wolfit, who had enlivened their war years, and Glyn Daniel, who had welcomed Pevsner to High Table in Cambridge; from the people at the *Architectural Review* – Jim Richards, Hubert de Cronin Hastings, Reyner Banham, Hugh Casson, John Piper – and the Victorian Society; from Alan Glover at Penguin and the Vice Master of Birkbeck; from the pupils and assistants who had often been friends, and the artists, architects and art historians whose company Lola had sometimes found intimidating – Philip Johnson, Ernö Goldfinger, Lionel Brett, Ernst Gombrich, John Summerson, Jane Clark for Kenneth Clark, Michael Jaffé, Denys Lasdun, Basil Spence, Anthony Blunt; from George Howard, who had so recently welcomed them on their last *Buildings of England* journey.

Some, who had known Lola longest, remembered her just for herself. Pallister Barkas, who had made the connection between her old and new lives in Göttingen and London, wrote, 'In appearance, in energy, and in enjoyment of hard work, she seemed to have aged less than any of us in over 20 years . . . So much of the gay courage of her youth greeted one on meeting her again each time one saw her.' She

---

*Pevsner always used a character resembling the Greek δ to signify Lola as part of his personal shorthand in the *Heftchen*, a form of the Gabelsberger system modified to suit his own tastes and requirements.
†A *Heftchen* entry for 30/5/64 reads: '*After* ∂: the assassination of Kennedy, the Beatles, the planting of trees in Store Street' round the corner from Gower Street.

was, wrote her friend and neighbour Ursula Bowlby, 'one of those fires at which people warm their hands'.*

Others, who had not known her, wrote only for him. Those who had known them both, as a couple, wrote most often about the working partnership that was now over. This may have been out of delicacy and a shrinking from intimacy, or from the perception that this joint work had been the most important feature of the relationship to Pevsner, or even from the fear that the work too would now stop. Geoffrey Moorhouse had travelled with them and had seen at first hand what the collaboration had been like. 'To miss such a *person*,' he wrote, 'someone rare and radiant – is hard enough. To have to continue your work without her help, when the two have been so inseparable, this, I guess, is almost not to be thought of. But from somewhere you must find the strength to carry on the *Buildings* until they are finished; it would be an irreparable blow to us all if you didn't, and she would be so disappointed.' It was a message echoed by John Betjeman, setting aside for a moment his resentment of Pevsner: 'Words aren't much help, but prayers and sympathy are one help and work is the other one. I pray you will have strength to go on with this task of yours. She will expect you to miss her of course, but she will hate you to be so unhappy that you cannot continue to work. Be sure of my prayers for you both, her in the next world and you in this.'

Unexpectedly, the most personal and most touching letters came from two of the most abrasive men of Pevsner's acquaintance, who set the work aside, spoke of the wife he had lost and sought to give him comfort. 'All the letters in the world can't help the great hole,' wrote Ian Nairn:

and anyone who ever met you together could see that this was a real marriage, something was growing and not decaying as it got older. And it hasn't stopped. It is going on now in the memories of everyone who knew Lola, but also quite literally, up there, because you both created it down here. It really will be all right in those Elysian fields – perennial renewal and perennial delight. God doesn't just stub out that kind of person and that kind of relationship.

Geoffrey Grigson agreed: 'I can't think of that vigorous energy being extinguished,' and he finished, 'Much love to you, dear wise and learned man.'

CHAPTER 39

'Mountains around': life without Lola

'You have had such a life together, quite rare,' wrote Gerhard Rosenberg. 'And now that is only an echo, *ein Nachhall*. But it will ring on a long time, until you can bear to be alone.' Pevsner would hear the echo quite clearly for years. '∂ is not forgotten,' he told the *Heftchen* in 1966. 'Nearly every day, though rarely in dreams, she is there and I think of her. Also, the carrying on in the house is to perpetuate her. The covering of her bed with the spread half of mine every night. The care for the plants.'[1] But in the weeks immediately following her death, he did everything he could to fill the void with other sounds and thoughts.

He was lucky in his family, as he was well aware. On 18 October 1963 he wrote, 'I have the children and the grandchildren – not an hour alone, if I don't want to. So far not one evening on my own. How many are really left alone.' ('Think of those poor widowers,' he would write later, 'and widows whose children, if they have any, are far away – or even only half an hour away. Think of a whole Sunday alone. What would I do? I can't make myself go to theatre, film, concert alone. Exhibitions perhaps. I pity others in my situation far more than myself.'[2]) 'Only in the narrowest family can there be relaxation . . . With people I know, I don't want to be believed to forget.'

The funeral had made him aware of how many people they knew, and how much effort Lola had put into these relationships. 'I try to take over some of the human interest in family and friends in which I have always been lacking,' he wrote two weeks after her death. 'I hope I can keep it up.' With his family he succeeded. 'You are a very good grandfather,' Uta wrote, after he had sent on to her some clothes and a tennis racquet for one of the children. 'The packages were beautifully made, with enormous quantities of corrugated cardboard.'[3] Underendowed with practical skills, he nevertheless took on some of the tasks that had seemed to come naturally to Lola and took a closer interest in his children and grandchildren's lives, with the help of careful lists of birthdays, anniversaries and past and future Christmas presents jotted in the back of his appointment diary.

Because this family circle was large, close and satisfying, he needed the company of friends less often, but valued the contacts that he had. Some were with people he had met by virtue of his professional life. Ernst Gombrich was a close and constant friend. Pevsner was on first-name terms with Agatha Christie* and Clough Williams-Ellis, lunched with Rudolf Wittkower when he was in town, and wrote regularly to Dame Veronica Wedgwood. ('It is certainly cause for pride to have asked you a question about the 17th century which you cannot answer,' he once told her. 'I feel much less depressed now about not having been able to answer it myself.'⁴) He was a friend as well as a reviewer for Benedict Nicolson, editor of the *Burlington Magazine*, who had written to him in 1961: 'I really owe you £35. When I looked down the list of horses running in the Grand National, I saw one which sounded sufficiently like you: Nicholas Silver. I backed it £2 each way. It came in first at 28 to 1.'⁵ When Maxwell Fry was ill, Pevsner was the only person to ask Jane Drew out to dinner.⁶

But some of his closest contacts were with the less well-known but longest-standing friends from his first years in England. He was still in touch with Dorothy Fletcher, his first hostess in Hampstead Garden Suburb, now old and ailing; to keep her amused he undertook to maintain a supply of lengthy volumes from the Penguin list and sent her a remarkable selection ranging from Voltaire to André Gide and D.H. Lawrence. To Lucie Imbach, the young German photographer whom he had helped to settle in London, he gave an annual subscription to *The Listener*, which he was still paying in 1972. A loyal friend, he was not always a demonstrative one. 'His Christmas card was always the first to come,' remembered Denis Evinson. 'I think he wrote them all and posted them on December 1st – they always arrived either on the 2nd or the 3rd – always a very nice card – but just "Nikolaus", not "to Denis" or "from Nikolaus" or "Cheers" or anything.'

Even with Alec Clifton-Taylor, a friend already for years, he was contained. 'I sometimes wondered whether in the fullest sense I *did* know him,' Clifton-Taylor wrote after Pevsner's death:

> whether in fact anyone did. Usually he was very reserved, even shy; one does not forget how easily he blushed . . . Nor do I ever remember seeing him convulsed with laughter. He had a ready wit and chuckled at the witticisms of others, but the base was usually cerebral . . . Only once, I think, did he open his heart to me, which was at our first meeting after the sudden death of Lola . . . It was a reunion which I was dreading, for I knew how utterly devoted they were. He told me all about it, with wonderful courage.⁷

---

*Agatha Christie (1890–1976) was probably a friend from the Isobar at the Lawn Road flats, where she lived from 1940–6.

It was a steady, uneventful, comfortable friendship enduring from the 1930s, with no element of rivalry or jealousy as Clifton-Taylor's own reputation developed.* The friendship was sustained by a stream of running jokes and mutual interests. (Between them, they amassed a fine collection of images of one or other of the Apostles wearing spectacles.†) The relationship also survived their working together, when in the 1960s Clifton-Taylor agreed to provide the geological notes to each volume of the *Buildings of England*. He was by now the author of *The Pattern of English Building* and an authority on the use of local stones, so his contribution was, and was regarded as, invaluable.‡

Home was for work or for family and, when Pevsner entertained, more often than not he took people out to dinner. The restaurants he chose were reasonably priced, and he brought his own wine. As long as it survived, he patronised the Isobar on the ground floor of the Lawn Road Flats. A later favourite was the Cresta, described in a flyer by its owner, Captain Marian Czaplicki, MBE, DSc, as 'The Polish House in Heamstead', offering 'Polish High mounteneers' design' and 'A table with candle lights'. People, continued the Captain, were welcome to linger late 'so long they enjoy the stay in my Polish house and like to listen to Polish classic music. Every Wednesday and Saturday (9–11.30). CHOPIN etc is performed at my Mini-piano by a "Chopinist", and occasionally – the Captain, le patron, is at the piano with his Polish, Russian and Austrian songs. (Music without additional charge.)' On the menu were hare, veal fried with anchovies, apple flan and a good deal of cabbage. The guest lists varied; Pevsner liked to plan these occasions, but he did not, as one story has it, compile parties by rote from an alphabetical list. One typical cast included the

---

*Pevsner did all he could to promote Clifton-Taylor's career. In 1947 he had tried to persuade Penguin to commission him for a possible Pelican volume on architectural recognition. (NP/E. Frost, 18/2/47. Penguin Papers, Eunice Frost Papers.) He was apparently responsible for introducing Clifton-Taylor to John Drummond at the BBC in the late 1960s (obituary for Drummond, *Telegraph*, 9/9/2006) which made Clifton-Taylor known to a much wider public in the 1970s through four series of television programmes on English towns.
†In October 1969 Pevsner exchanged his apostle from the Well of Moses in Dijon for Clifton-Taylor's in the Henry V chantry in Westminster Abbey.
‡It was modestly repaid. NP/A. Clifton-Taylor, 7/2/68: 'This is really abominable. I have our correspondence in front of me, and I find that in the end nothing was ever settled about money. Will you agree to accepting £10 10s per county? That is of course very little, but as you know everybody suffers for the BoE.' At the end of 1969 Clifton-Taylor suggested a pay rise might be nice. Pevsner responded, 'I would like to increase your ten guineas a piece, but as you know, nobody has yet increased my o guineas a piece.' Penguin Papers, *BoE* files, DM 1901/10/1.

Gombrichs, the Bowlbys (neighbours from beyond Wyldes Farm), the Rentons, the Franklins (who lived in the Lawn Road Flats) and Victorian specialist Priscilla Metcalf (who later edited a compilation of Pevsner's *BoE* entries on cathedrals). 'He mixed people,' remembered Nikolaus Boulting, 'and didn't think it was important to cultivate the grand.'

Too much time remained, however, in which Pevsner might think about what he had lost. After Christmas he went, as he had always done, to stay at the Lygon Arms after the New Year, for the first time without Lola. While he was there he wrote a memoir of her for the grandchildren, to match the piece on the family that he had written nine years earlier for the children. 'Even you must have felt what I had lost,' he started, 'and that you also had lost something for ever. Here is ample proof of the truth of Lola's belief in family ties, in the "clan" living so close together, and in us all helping one another.'

Pevsner was really writing for himself, trying to sum up what he had felt about Lola. Just as he had once been impatient with his mother, now he felt that he had been intolerant of Lola's shortcomings and unappreciative of her strengths, or at least not appreciative enough to refrain from hurting her. The faults that had irritated him now seemed relatively trivial: her chronic pessimism, her bluntness, the shyness that sometimes made social contacts difficult: 'Any social work, committee work, clerical work, would have been impossible for her, and she would have been impossible at it.' His treatment of her, on the other hand, was more to be condemned. This was not the place to speak about the pain he had inflicted on her with his infatuations, but he could apologise for having made her give up her lodgers. 'I was irritated by the people about the house, I thought, but really no doubt by my playing second fiddle. And in the end she gave up her lodgers, feeling deprived of what in fact, for the only time in her life, gave her a purpose independent of family . . . The lodgers were just right, personal service faithfully and cheaply rendered, and friendly, direct human relations in return. It was vicious to deprive her of that.'

The young Nika had loved Lola as one of *die Harmlose*, the 'harmless' ones, simpler, safer, happier and more attractive than he felt himself to be. He remembered now both the fourteen-year-old child she had been when they first met, and the childlike qualities that she had kept all her life. He recalled her jumping into the Saale River in flood to rescue a small dog, and doing the family's mending or writing letters sitting on the floor, or lying on her stomach to read in bed. While dressing for dinner, alone in the house, she had heard a boy breaking in; chasing and catching him, she brought him back into the house, lectured him on the error of his ways and asked for his address: 'Who but a child would believe he would give the right address?' She was easily taken in because of her own transparency, which he envied but did not try to emulate. 'Lola was profoundly, unimpeachably honest. I am not,' he wrote, excoriating himself. '"*Der Zweck heiligt die Mittel* / The end justifies the means". I am ready to use people by keeping them in the dark or telling them untrue versions of stories.' And he continued:

> I think of her so heartily laughing at any funny story, laughing also, to the detriment of literary or oratorical perfection, at her own stories before anyone else. No – she could not tell stories, because good story-telling requires a distance which she – and children – never had . . . She was at ease with low people, simple people and ill at ease with sophisticated people. It was not a matter of class, but of sophistication, of real as against artificial values. She was frightened at parties and held on to people who did not talk clever . . . She had no sense of the artificial nuances of behaviour to different people.

The pace and rhythm of his life would be different now: she followed her instincts and made decisions quickly; he delayed 'amid all the arguing of pros and cons'. The texture, too, would be less rich, because she so often saw things that he did not. When they went for walks, it was Lola who noticed the odd details, 'a nest in a tree, a cottage built of other than the current materials, crops that surely should have been harvested earlier . . . I am blind to all this and shall now be blind for the rest of my life.'

There was a little consolation to be found in the way their life together had ended. 'The very last year – it is an accident to be infinitely grateful for – was specially unworried and warm and happy.' There was comfort, too, 'that, if one must be left without the other, it should rather be me than her. Comfort that she died without anxiety or pain. And even for once that I did not sit helpless and see her in pain. Comfort finally that losing a child is more senseless than seeing that over sixty one must accept death as a natural end.' But these solaces were hardly enough.

Not long after Lola died, one of his researchers knocked at the door of his office and went in. She saw Pevsner sitting at his desk with tears running down his face, quietly left the room and made sure he remained undisturbed.[8] In the privacy of his *Heftchen* he confessed, 'I am surrounded by mountains – in future work, future initiative, future domestic life . . . Mountains around. The moment when things begin to be moved, clothes, belongings – if ever they must be. The moment to leave this house to one of the boys and move away to theirs . . . After 40 years every corner, every object, every place, every building is a memory . . . And the mountain of old age, pain, illness – to be faced alone, relatively alone.'

Work was, as ever, the refuge. 'Tears have dried,' he wrote in January 1964, 'but the pressure remains, as soon as I am not at work.' It was this pressure, perhaps, that had compelled him the previous November, barely six weeks after Lola's death, to honour the promise he had made to lecture at Yale and to speak at the opening of the new School of Art and Architecture, designed by the school's current Dean, Paul Rudolph. Yale was his favourite American university, despite his low opinion of its architecture, and they were awarding him the Howland Memorial Prize, an award given biennially to 'a citizen of any country in recognition of some achievement of marked distinction in the field of literature or fine arts or the science of government'.* Paul Rudolph, however, was a leading proponent of Brutalism, and the assembled audience did not get from Pevsner the encomium for the new building that some appear to have been expecting.

'His speech warned against the threat of form for its own sake,' one of the attendees recalled, 'and reminded everyone that the purpose of a building was to function . . . Rudolph went beet red.' Yale should perhaps not have invited a historian to speak, Pevsner suggested, because the historian works by comparisons, and in this case comparison with the original Architecture School was inevitable. Street Hall, built in 1866 by P.B. Wight, was a High Victorian brownstone in the Gothic style. To Pevsner, it represented hard individualism, a forceful reaction against the Georgian style: in his eyes, the new school was every bit as individualistic. 'Every cubic foot of this building says "Rudolph". What can a successor, maybe believing in a different routine, do with such a building? There you see, I hope, what I mean by the dangers of personality cult and the blessings of modesty, faith in service, and a certain neutrality.'†

*   *   *

---

*The terms of the award stipulate that 'the idealistic quality of the recipient's work is an important factor in his selection'.

†By 1966 Rudolph had left Yale. The building had proved uncomfortable and awkward to use, with problems of noise and temperature control, and his successor divided the interior spaces up with partitions that turned the building into a maze of small, dark, low rooms. The School has recently been restored to something more closely approaching the original conception.

Back in London, Pevsner recorded in January 1964, 'I don't cry any longer, though I would, if I went to concerts. Work goes normally, but there is not a day that I don't look at someone and think: And *you* are alive!' Six months later he was still desolate, noting 'the complete impossibility of enjoying myself alone, even of being at rest alone except under the pressure of an urgent job'. It was merciful, therefore, that at this point he was invited to become the next Chair of the Victorian Society, where urgent jobs were abundant.

Nicholas Taylor remembered: 'The invitation was initially not a formal one, and it came after a good deal of backstairs intrigue . . . On 8 October 1963, nine days after Lola, the Chairman of the Victorian Society, Viscount Esher, had died – and this came . . . at a time when the make-up of the Victorian Society committee, as the Society began to grow rapidly in membership and influence, was rapidly moving away from the Betjeman-Lady Rosse coterie towards the professional, the academic and the politically savvy (generally on the Left).'* The younger members of the Committee included Mark Girouard, Paul Thompson, Royston Lambert, Tom Pakenham and Nicholas Taylor himself. Meeting privately, they were clear on three things: 'First, Pevsner was the obvious choice as Chairman to professionalise the Society's work and give it credibility with local authorities, with which most of the decision-making on historic buildings rested; secondly, it would be disastrous if John Betjeman were drafted in by the older members, as the Society could not continue to run on sporadic gener-osity and erratic judgment from amateurs; and thirdly, in order to get away from the stigma of "lost causes", there was an urgent need to systematize casework by writing and talking appropriately to local authorities, and particularly their planners, rather than relying on "old school" camaraderie with the Tory Government (which had in any case proved fruitless).'

The reformers were in a minority; but as the weeks passed, it became clear that none of the old guard, whatever their feelings about Pevsner, was prepared to undertake the burdens of chairmanship, perhaps least of all Betjeman. Monica Dance, Secretary of the Society for the Protection of Ancient Buildings, told Ian Grant, 'John is a great one for lost causes and new societies, but when they begin to gather momentum he loses interest.'[9] So in the event, when the Committee met in the New Year, the nomination of Pevsner as Chairman was carried unanimously, and endorsed at the Society's AGM soon afterwards.

Pevsner's principal qualification was that he gave the Victorian

---

*Nicholas Taylor to the author, 7/5/2011.

Society *gravitas* and academic respectability. Lionel Brett, son of the first Chairman and himself by now the 4th Viscount Esher, considered that where the Society for the Protection of Ancient Buildings was scholarly and the Georgian Group was aristocratic, the Victorian Society had become intellectual and aggressive. Pevsner was one of the first to explain to a wider audience the point of appreciating the Victorian past. He helped to raise the Victorian Society's status above that of a club, and contributed greatly to establishing it in official eyes as a force to be consulted and to be reckoned with.

In 1964 he acquired one of his most loyal allies when Jane Fawcett succeeded Peter Fleetwood-Hesketh as Secretary. 'I was glad to be able to tell you,' he wrote to her, 'that the ill paid job for the enthusiast has gone to you.'[10] (By her account, he rejected the other shortlisted candidate, a naval commander, because he was 'too high-powered'.) Her zeal would have to support her through twelve years of unpaid overtime, delivering the Society's administration from her own home. By this point the Society's financial affairs were precarious. 'For virtually all its life, the society has been living beyond its means,' reported committee member Thomas Pakenham, 'and now the reckoning approaches.' A Pilgrim Trust grant would buy time, but fundraising would be a constant cloud on the horizon through all the years during which Pevsner and Fawcett worked together at the Society.

The crucial business forum of the Society, apart from the committee itself, was now the Cases Sub-Commmittee, which met in Pevsner's office with increasing frequency and relied on his brisk judgement and Jane Fawcett's efficiency to cope with a hugely increased workload. 'From the beginning it was clear that the normal standards would not be adequate when working with Sir Nikolaus,' Jane Fawcett recalled when she resigned in 1976. 'How could one suppose that a 9–5 commitment would suffice, when his working day ran from 5 a.m. to 9 p.m.?' Her contribution, she considered, was 'to back up his wisdom and judgment with my enthusiasm . . . Nikolaus didn't like the emotional side of any job, didn't like appealing to people's emotions, wanted things done on an intellectual level.'[11]

'Pevsner was the benevolent despot of the Victorian Society,' according to Ian Sutton, who joined the Society in 1962:

> He . . . dominated it – not always deliberately – by his phenomenal
> hard work, his reputation as a scholar, his seriousness and the force
> of his personality. Under his chairmanship the Committee was an
> energetic and devoted body, though it was not a democracy. 'If you
> want to please your chairman . . .' was how he began at least one

AGM when proposing some measure that turned out to be uncon-
stitutional. On the whole he was impatient of procedural niceties.
He liked clear-cut issues and quick decisions. In Committee he always
grasped the point faster than anyone else, proposed a solution and
passed on to something else. His contributions to discussions were
crisp, witty and practical. It was virtually impossible to make a long
speech in his presence, though many tried. Nor did he have any time
for facetiousness, one of the few English qualities that he neither
acquired nor wanted to acquire . . . To his colleagues and staff he
could be extremely kind. He was quick to provide help in case of
misfortune; and no doubt he felt many things deeply. But they did
not show . . . One could never forget that he was an exceptional
man, and someone in whose presence it was not easy to relax.[12]

'There were often jokes,' Sutton remembered, 'delivered with obvious
relish but with the same neatness and precision as all his other thoughts.'
When Pevsner heard a joke he liked, or thought of a good one, he
would jot it down and keep it. This was hardly the spontaneous
badinage of a Betjeman or a Waugh, and his style was not that of
every member of the Victorian Society. 'You wouldn't for a moment
have mistaken him for an English person, however well and fluently
and precisely he could speak,' remarked Ian Grant. 'You still would
have known after two minutes conversation that he wasn't English.'[13]
Grant found him 'relatively charmless . . . He didn't like me, I know.
I think he always saw me as a rather frivolous product of the English
upper class. Little did he know that that isn't my background at all,
I come from relatively humble origins. I think he saw me as rather
like Betjeman – useless, frivolous, tending to giggle at the wrong
moments, not taking things very seriously.' Their mutual esteem was
not deepened when, later in the 1960s, Grant was persuaded to edit
the Annual Report. It was a thankless task, involving much chasing
and harrying of contributors and, to Grant's chagrin and Pevsner's
irritation, publication dates were constantly slipping. 'He wrote me a
couple of extremely offensive letters,' Grant complained, 'as though I
was a sort of paid lackey – and since I was doing it voluntarily for
no recompense, I took that very ill indeed . . . He was absolutely
unbending – "Ian let us down". He had this very narrow vision which
allowed no kind of compromise – a moralistic vision – like his house,
terribly moralistic somehow, without a hint of luxury.'
Ian Grant's own house in Notting Hill was impeccably done up in
Victorian style with furniture and decorations from the nearby Porto-
bello Road. Pevsner was very chary of what he would describe as the

'ghastly craze' in the 1960s for collecting Victoriana, a term that he equally abominated:¹⁴ 'Please don't ever again say "Victoriana",' he wrote in the introduction to the 1966 Annual Report, 'especially as a barbaric singular.' 'There was a precious element in the Victorian Society,' Jane Fawcett observed. 'One young man turned up with a teddy bear. Nikolaus had no time for it.' Such time as he could spare for the Victorian Society – and he would increasingly worry that the Victorians were monopolising too much of his attention – he devoted to the serious business of campaigning.

The adversaries were legion: not just developers and conniving local councils moving with furtive haste, but also banks (owners of many of the more grandiose Victorian buildings), government departments, whose buildings were covered by Crown exemptions, railways, universities and, almost worst of all, the Church.*

When the Beeching axe closed many railway lines, the buildings associated with them came under threat in large numbers. Between 1964 and 1966 some 2,500 miles of line were closed, and the Victorian Society prepared a modest inventory of sixty stations worth preserving. It submitted these buildings to the Ministries of Transport and Housing, with a strong plea for their listing and a range of suggestions for the uses to which they might be put after obsolescence: museums, hostels, conference centres, even cottages.

Universities constantly astonished Pevsner by their philistinism. Oxford had a particularly virulent bout of anti-Victorian sentiment in the 1960s. Balliol 'decided to celebrate the 700th anniversary of its foundation by demolishing the building most redolent of its greatest age', Waterhouse's Brackenbury building of 1867–8. (The proposal was defeated.) Worcester College pulled out the William Burges fireplace, panelling and mantelpieces from its Hall in order to revive the incomplete eighteenth-century designs of James Wyatt. The University proposed to demolish the Indian Institute (Basil Champneys, 1886), which stood at the corner of Catte Street, facing down the Broad: the Bodleian Librarian from the Old Library buildings opposite threatened to resign in protest, and the Institute was eventually saved.

The Bishop of Southwark, Mervyn Stockwood, would say in 1965 that he did not want to be the manager of a preservation society for the rest of his life, and some of the Victorian Society's most

*Where government departments were concerned, Pevsner deplored cases like the Department of Health's demolition of 'Three Gables' in Fitzjohns Avenue, one of Norman Shaw's best surviving houses and one singled out for both description and illustration in Hermann Muthesius's *Das englische Haus*.

acrimonious exchanges would be with clergy who seemed totally blind to the aesthetic and historical worth of their assets, as well as resentful of what they regarded as intrusion from meddling laity. Having visited the Dean of Gloucester in May 1965, Pevsner reported, not without amusement, 'The Dean was very keen that we should approach representatives of the Roman Catholic Church and the non-conformist churches, since their buildings appear to be totally unprotected, but was not keen for any interference over the protection of the Church of England buildings.'[15]

The Dean's point about the vulnerability of Catholic buildings was well made. Among those under threat were Horace Walpole's villa at Strawberry Hill, which had become a Catholic teacher-training college, and Salvin's Harlaxton Manor, an extraordinary pile combining Elizabethan, Jacobean and Baroque styles, which had been being used since the war as a novitiate for the Jesuits.* However, the Church of England, in Pevsner's view, was no more conscientious, taking advantage of its position as the Established Church to seek exemption from the provisions of the Ancient Monuments Act of 1912 and the Town and Country Planning Act of 1947. 'This anomaly in planning legislation,' he wrote in a stiff letter to *The Times* in March 1965, 'is caused by an assurance given by the Archbishop of Canterbury in the House of Lords on April 30, 1912 . . . The Archbishop said that the Church could be relied on to prevent "the possible misuse of or injury to ancient monuments". No one can say that the Church of England over the years has kept this promise.'

The problem was one of liturgical reform combined with a decline in church attendance since the building boom of the Victorian period. Many vicars now wanted to remove Victorian fittings from their churches in order to bring priest and altar closer to a rather smaller congregation, in accordance with changes in the conduct of the service, for the sake of practicality, and sometimes simply because they shared the prevailing disdain for Victorian taste. Some of the finest examples of nineteenth-century reredoses, rood screens and even altars were at risk. In 1967 the Dean and Chapter of Hereford Cathedral pulled out the majestic wrought-iron choir screen by Francis Skidmore, installed as part of George Gilbert Scott's restoration of the cathedral in 1863.[†]

---

*Harlaxton had been bought before the Second World War by Violet van der Elst, a Surrey scullery maid who got rich by developing the first brushless shaving cream. The Jesuits sold Harlaxton in 1965 to Stanford University; it now belongs to the University of Evansville.
†The screen was eventually restored and displayed by the Victoria and Albert Museum in 2001.

The Victorian Society described their actions as a 'major outrage', arrogant and insensitive, and called for planning decisions at this level to be brought into the public domain. (The clergy of Salisbury Cathedral, no more sympathetic to 'Victorianising' or to Scott, had not only taken out his screen, reredoses, communion rail and chancel paving in 1960, but sold the screen and rail to Sarum Iron Works for scrap.)

'Who shall watch the very watchmen?' Pevsner asked in a *Guardian* article in 1965.* 'The watchmen in this case are the Churches, and what has to be watched is their buildings.' Take St Hilda's church in Middlesbrough, 'a dignified, quiet building' of 1838–40 by John Green of Newcastle. 'Now the Church authorities want to demolish it. They say so in no uncertain terms, calling it 1878 and by Street which does not make one's confidence soar.'† 'All the time worthwhile Victorian furnishing and fitments are being removed from churches,' he protested in *The Times* later that year. 'Semi-Italian or pretty-pretty Sunday school stuff or other kinds of *bondieuserie* go in the place of the round stone pulpit designed by Street or the transparent iron screen designed by Scott. Not that one would want everything Victorian to stay in its place. But one does want discrimination – more people who take trouble to distinguish the good Victorian from the bad, the strong from the weak, the individual from the faceless.'[16]

The Victorian Society devoted much time in 1965 – and for many years to come – to fighting the government's plans for the redevelopment of Whitehall. Pevsner, who had considerable respect for Leslie Martin, nevertheless described the Whitehall plan as 'terrifying'. To Betjeman it was 'inexcusable'. Whitehall was just one of many campaigns in which they were joined in harmony. In 1963 Pevsner had supported Betjeman in the 'battle of Bedford Park'. The first garden suburb, Bedford Park had been built at the end of the nineteenth century as an artists' village for London, with a significant number of buildings by Norman Shaw. Betjeman's aim was not simply to maintain the ambience of the area as a whole, but to get the individual buildings listed. Pevsner endorsed his ambition, and more than 300 buildings would eventually be protected in this way. This concord did not, of course, inhibit Betjeman from writing furiously to John Summerson in 1966 to enlist his support in saving St Pancras Station: 'I have been so denigrated by Karl Marx [Jim Richards] and the Professor-Doktor [Pevsner] as a lightweight wax

---

*'*Quis custodiet ipsos custodes*, Juvenal, *Satire 6*. Pevsner's piece was 'The Watchers and the Watched', *Guardian*, 29/1/65.
†St Hilda's was demolished in 1969.

fruit merchant, I will not carry the necessary guns. K [Clark] can't do it, as he is overworked, though his spirit is willing.'[17] It is not clear why Betjeman thought Summerson would be a natural ally in this campaign. Summerson had opposed him over Bedford Park, and was far less enthusiastic about St Pancras. 'Every time I look at the building,' wrote Summerson, 'I'm consumed with admiration of the cleverness of the detail, and every time I leave it I wonder why as a whole it is so nauseating . . . I really don't think one could go to a Minister and say this is a great piece of architecture, a great national monument.'[18] Pevsner, on the other hand, wrote unequivo-cally to the *Guardian* on 1 September 1966: 'St Pancras Station Must Be Saved.'*

Pevsner's position in the Victorian Society was interesting. He was a powerful weapon, but one that had to be used judiciously and one that could not always be controlled. The Society was no longer homo-geneous. New groups were established – Liverpool and Manchester in 1965, West Midlands in 1967 – and there were now more than a thousand members. John Lennon, sadly, was not one of them, although not for lack of invitation. 'From your book and otherwise,' wrote Pevsner to him on 8 March 1965, 'I have a strong feeling that you would make an ideal member of the Victorian Society.'[19] His hopes were disappointed; there was no response.

There were many points, and many occasions, on which Pevsner differed from other members, usually because he was reluctant to spring to the defence of every case that came to the Society's atten-tion.† He never wavered from his view that the Society had to be selective, or that the only criterion for its choices should be archi-tectural merit – not the picturesque value of a building or the interest of its contents, or its historical associations or its place in the land-scape. He was, for once, in entire accord with Goodhart-Rendel's pronouncement: 'I think we should deplore the treasuring of any-thing, merely to have the fun of giggling at its absurdity.' He had his own very definite predilections, in whose cause he was not above theft. Nikolaus Boulting recalled him returning from Glasgow with a guilty expression and cutlery from the Ingram Street Tea Rooms. '"I'm merely preserving it as an archivist", he said, "since the Tea Rooms are about to be demolished and all this possibly lost" . . .

---

*Gavin Stamp points out that Summerson was in the end also persuaded to argue for preservation.
†On the removal of Scott's screen from Salisbury Cathedral, for example, he wrote, 'It was a crime against the tenets of the Victorian Society, but the need of the c13 cathe-dral was indeed greater than theirs.'

It was a very beautiful spoon.'* (Dieter Pevsner remembers his father's guilt, redoubled when the immediate threat to demolish was rescinded: 'He wondered whether to make another trip to return the spoon, but decided to live with his felony.'[20]) However, some of the younger members in particular felt that Pevsner was not passionate enough about the Victorian period as a whole. Ian Sutton remembered, 'There were tensions, usually concealed. Pevsner was not as whole-hearted a Victorian as some.' He was fascinated by Goodhart-Rendel's 'rogues', but he could not love them. Temperamentally, he shrank from aggressive confidence and self-assertion, in Victorian architecture as much as in the Brutalist buildings of the 1960s.

Pevsner was readier than many to believe that a new building might in fact be an improvement on an indifferent old one, whether it be Victorian, Georgian or even earlier. In his loyalty to Picturesque theory, he was compelled to believe that new buildings could readily be absorbed into a townscape; putting a new building into old surroundings should logically be no more jarring than preserving an old building in the midst of a new estate, which was generally welcomed.† In a *Times* article entitled 'Why Not Harmonise the Old and the New?' he argued: 'Occasionally [the battle] is lost and one finds in the end that one ought to be pleased; for what has taken the place of the old is as good or better, and alive, in the sense that only the buildings of our own day can be alive.'[21]

Pevsner was not afraid of a fight when he felt it was necessary, but he did not enjoy confrontation for its own sake and, as someone who spent a good deal of time working with official bodies, he believed in the importance of remaining on good terms with civil servants. It annoyed him when the Society was, in his view, shrill, emotional or needlessly belligerent in its dealings with bureaucracy.

---

*Denis Evinson had a similar story, related to Pevsner's enthusiasm for Morris. He once effected an entry into an empty house that still wore its Morris wallpaper. Rather than simply filching some, he decided to write to the house's owner, but felt it might carry more weight if he claimed kinship, so duly wrote, 'Dear Sir, I am a relation of the late William Morris. Would you kindly allow me to take a section of that Morris paper . . . etc.' The owner turned out to be a former student, and the reply came back, 'Dear Mr Pevsner – Relation my foot!'

†Pevsner caused a stir by backing the plan for a Frank Lloyd Wright house on the Grand Canal in Venice, between the fifteenth-century Ca' Foscari and the sixteenth-century Palazzo Balbi: 'To my own mind, one of the charms of Venice is the very varied and picturesque buildings, and, probably entirely against his own will, that particular little horror of Frank Lloyd Wright's fits in perfectly with the existing variety.'

He saw conservation as a constant process of compromise, which meant not simply preventing buildings from being knocked down but sometimes just modifying the plans for new ones, or saving one building by relinquishing others. For their part, some Vic Soc members felt their Chairman was sometimes not clear or emphatic enough in pressing their case, and he could be too ready to believe, naïvely, in the good faith of their opponents. When developers assured him of their worthy intentions, he was inclined to take them at their word. This would be most apparent in the negotiations over St Katharine Docks in the 1970s, but it was a source of friction from his first years in the chair.

It was not unusual for individual Vic Soc members to offer a dissenting, often better-informed opinion on particular buildings, and Pevsner always defended their right to do so, provided they did not claim publicly to be speaking for the Society as a whole.* The problem in his case was that his view, as Chairman, was often taken as the Society's view regardless of his provisos. His opinion carried extra weight, and if it was unenthusiastic, it could have drastic consequences. Lukewarm comments in the *Buildings of England* could be turned against the Victorian Society just as readily as his more enthusiastic observations could be used to their advantage. For the Society's sake, Pevsner wrote many letters on behalf of buildings that he personally did not believe were particularly distinguished. But he did not enjoy perjuring himself even in this very mild fashion, and there were cases where, from the Society's point of view, he showed a regrettable tendency to tell the whole truth, when being economical with it would have given buildings a better chance of survival.

The Magpie and Stump, at 37 Cheyne Walk, Chelsea, was the first design by C.R. Ashbee actually to be built, in 1893–4; the house took its name from an earlier inn on the site. It was where Ashbee had his architectural office, and it became his mother's house. He had also designed and built two neighbouring houses at 38 and 39 Cheyne Walk and there was a Building Preservation Order on all three houses, but not on their contents. The Magpie and Stump's elaborate Arts and Crafts interior, complete with leather wallpaper, enamel electric-light fittings and a glazed earthenware mantelpiece, had survived until the death of the last owner in 1964. The Victorian Society originally

---

*John Brandon-Jones, for example, the Society's Deputy Chairman, was a member of the committee of the Historic Buildings Council that would advise the Department of the Environment not to call in for ministerial review the application by John Baring to demolish The Grange in Hampshire, one of the earliest Greek Revival buildings in the country.

intervened to prevent the executors from stripping it out, but then discovered that the house itself was threatened. In 1962 the Cadogan Estate had sold to the Wates property company land on the corner of Oakley Street and Cheyne Walk, which included all the buildings on Cheyne Walk between numbers 31 and 36. The company proposed to redevelop the corner site with six-storey blocks of flats. A supplementary proposal for a ten-storey block had been rejected, but Wates were appealing, in order to develop the whole site, and their plans now included 37 Cheyne Walk, the Magpie and Stump.

In February 1965, Pevsner met Norman Wates, whom he already knew, to discuss the Cheyne Walk project.* The first entries in the Victorian Society's side of the correspondence suggest that they were to talk about all three Ashbee buildings, although Wates's plans affected only the Magpie and Stump. No record of the conversation was made at the time, but when Pevsner submitted written evidence on behalf of the Victorian Society on 26 May, it was a plea for the preservation of the whole group. The public inquiry was held in June. Betjeman, knowing he was not going to be in London, had urged that someone from the Society should attend, but no one, including Pevsner, was able to do so. This was to be a disaster.

The GLC, opposing the Cheyne Walk development, argued that the *Buildings of England* spoke of numbers 37–39 as a group of architectural interest. It was at this point that Mr S.F. Crofts, representing Wates, claimed that this was no longer Pevsner's view:

> Professor Pevsner came to our offices quite voluntarily because he had heard of this matter which had arisen . . . We asked him if in his opinion no. 37 should be preserved. His answer was that it was not as good a building as no. 38 or no. 39 Cheyne Walk, although it was designed by the same architect, Ashbee, but in his opinion if the buildings we proposed were better than the existing building then No. 37 should not be preserved and that it should go. I asked him if he would be prepared to give evidence to this effect. He replied that he would prefer not to do so owing to his association with the London County Council and other bodies.[22]

---

*Norman Wates (1905–69) had helped to arrange the sponsorship of Howard Colvin's researches into the King's Works. Interested in the relationship between practical building considerations and the evolution of architectural styles, he had offered to fund the translation of medieval building accounts in order to trace this relationship. Pevsner had recommended studying the lesser-known archives of Exeter, Durham or Ely and was disappointed when Westminster Abbey was chosen, but he was grateful for Wates's role in a valuable project.

Pevsner was aghast, and responded to the inquiry by return of post:

It has been brought to my notice that Mr Cross [sic] reported on Wednesday a change of my views on No. 37 Cheyne Walk. May I say that I have not changed my views . . . What Mr Cross referred to was a private conversation between Mr Norman Wates and myself. I went to see him to plead for No's. 37 to 39, and was relieved when I heard that No's. 38 and 39 were safe. I was then asked if I would appear for Messrs. Wates on No. 37 and refused. May I now try to explain the differences between No's. 37 and 38–9. Ashbee designed No. 37 in 1894; he was 31, and still much influenced by Norman Shaw and others of that generation. When he designed No's. 38 and 39 in 1899 . . . he had found an idiom of his own, and so he produced here two of the architecturally most valuable houses of that date in England. No. 37 is not on that plane, but the group of the three is all the same very well worth preserving . . . The style to which No. 37 belongs is one which the continent and the United States avidly adopted. Good buildings representing it are getting terribly rare. This is why I would greatly regret the disappearance of No. 37.[23]

Then he added, fatally, 'If No. 37 were to be replaced by something architecturally better I might give in.' It was a view that, in this context and at this particular moment, it would have been more prudent to have kept to himself. He concluded, 'However, I have not seen what is supposed to be built, so my sympathy is all with No. 37 . . . Ashbee is an extremely rare architect, and one who was highly inventive and intelligent, and this rarity of his work is another reason why the whole group should be kept.'[24] But the damage was done. There is no question but that he considered the Magpie and Stump worth saving, but he had offered a loophole that was swiftly exploited. The Cheyne Walk corner site, including the Magpie and Stump, was cleared in 1968, the Pier House flats completed by 1974.

As part of his contribution to the process for listing nineteenth-century buildings Pevsner was involved in compiling a catalogue of the most significant architects of the period, in collaboration with Roger Dixon. This close focus on Victorian individualists may well have prompted him to reflect once again on the way in which modern architecture had evolved. He had always made it clear that in *Pioneers* he was following just one of the many possible paths from the nineteenth to the twentieth century – one that he greatly favoured, but did not consider unique. There were others, and even if he was not attracted by them, recent developments in architecture were forcing them to his attention. Now, in December 1966, in two radio broadcasts entitled 'The Anti-Pioneers', he picked up one of the alternative threads.

He began by acknowledging that his 1937 vision of the future of architecture had been wrong:

> What I thought I described was the coming of the millennium . . .
> To me what had been achieved in 1914 was *the* style of the century.
> It never occurred to me to look beyond. Here was the one and only style which fitted all those aspects which mattered, aspects of economics and sociology, of materials and function. It seemed folly to think that anybody would wish to abandon it. But human feelings are inscrutable, and what we are experiencing now is a new style completely, an anti-Pioneers style . . . a *post-modern style*, I would be tempted to call it, but the legitimate style of the nineteen-fifties and nineteen-sixties.*

'Someone ought to rewrite my book,' he urged, 'keeping its main title and saying the very reverse. I can even give that someone the recipe.' The individualism of the 'rogue' Victorians was mirrored in the originality of Art Nouveau, most obviously in the wild expressivity of Gaudí. This particular line of development was checked by the rationalism and responsibility of Muthesius and Gropius – but then this was in turn disrupted by war, which let Expressionism back in, with the visions of men such as Mendelsohn and Poelzig. From there to the architecture of the 1960s – to neo-Art Nouveau and the neo-Expressionism of the Brutalists – there was a direct line.†

He took as his case study James Stirling's Engineering Building at Leicester University:

---

*Pevsner had used the term 'post-modern' before, in his 1956 article 'On Finding Oneself Out of Date', and again in *Norfolk* (1962), where he defines it as meaning coming after 'what is now familiar as the International Style of the 1930s'.

† In 1973 Pevsner edited, with Jim Richards, a selection of essays entitled *The Anti-Rationalists*, to fill out the origins of the contemporary neo-Expressionism he so disliked. When architect and historian Dennis Sharp (1933–2010) challenged him for apparently confusing 'anti-rational' with 'irrational', Pevsner promptly arranged for Sharp to be commissioned to edit a complementary collection of articles entitled *The Rationalists* (1978), to elucidate the contentious notion of 'rationalism' in modern architecture. The two collections were published together by the Architectural Press in 2000.

To me the Leicester engineering building is Expressionism . . .
It is architecture heightened in its emotional effects by sharp
stabbing angles, an expression not of the character of the building
but of the architect . . . I want my emotions to be created in a
church by the communication with eternity, and in an opera house
by the power of music, not by the architect's mood. I do not want
to be bowled over before I have even handed in my coat at the
cloakroom.*

'The style of today is unlikely to last,' declared Pevsner. 'We cannot,
in the long run, live our day-to-day lives in the midst of explosions.'
As one correspondent observed, he was probably exaggerating the
extent of the blast, and it was a mistake to promote a situation where
neo-Expressionism was all that found its way into the history books
as *the* style of the 1950s and 1960s. There was perhaps more of a
surviving modernist cause to champion than Pevsner acknowledged.
But fighting the modernist corner in public demanded time, enthusiasm
and an up-to-date knowledge of contemporary developments, none of
which he necessarily possessed.

That he was no longer in touch or in tune with the latest trends
was brought home forcefully to him as he worked on the contemporary
entries in the *Penguin Dictionary of Architecture* during the 1960s.
The initial selection of modern architects was idiosyncratic – he deliberately left out Philip Johnson and Paul Rudolph at first and needed
prompting to include the Smithsons, Jørn Utzon, Denys Lasdun and
the partnership of Chamberlin, Powell and Bon. Some of the suggestions from other people he rejected as 'quite quite potty . . . anybody
in England who is bright and young even if their total of built buildings is negligible'.[25]

It was perhaps fortunate that he had enlisted the aid of collaborators on the *Dictionary* who could help counter the most obvious
prejudices. Pevsner had originally been persuaded to contribute only
some forty 'omnibus' entries on subjects such as 'Castle', 'Tracery' and
'Neo-Classicism'. When offered the entire project, he suggested that it
should be a joint project shared with two younger art historians

---

* Stirling retaliated (*The Listener*, 12/1/67): ' I agree with Le Corbusier – "The purpose
of construction is to make things hold together; of architecture to move us".' He added
that the 'blue brick' that Pevsner had criticised in the Engineering Building was red.
Pevsner, without backing down, was mortified: 'An abject apology to James Stirling.
My only answer to his letter is: *touché*, and I can assure him that it hurts me more
than it can possibly have hurt him.'

– Hugh Honour and John Fleming* – and that the proceeds should be divided equally between the three of them (he had originally been offered 50 per cent).

The aim was 'a useful, reasonably comprehensive, unpretentious, jargon-free dictionary for the Pelican amateur rather than for the architecture student', illustrated lightly and only with line drawings, with the emphasis on styles and their development and on the works and biographies of individual architects. More specialised entries on building and engineering were to be brief and cross-referenced to existing technical dictionaries.[26] Pevsner would write the entries on medieval, nineteenth- and twentieth-century architecture, the European and American national entries and most of the entries on style. It was an arduous task, not only for Pevsner, but also for his friends, who would receive a stream of queries. To Lord Holford, for example, he wrote urgently: 'Dear Bill, What are the dates of your advice on Canberra, of the jury on Brasilia, of the City of London Plan, and of the plan for the Precincts of St Paul's?'[27] Leslie Martin was asked simply, 'What do you think are your best buildings?' Pevsner kept finding holes in his knowledge, and contracted out topics where he knew himself to be weak: building matérials, for example, or the architecture of Mexico and Australia.

The *Penguin Dictionary* was being overseen at Penguin by the new chief editor, Tony Godwin, who had been employed by Allen Lane as fresh blood in 1960.[†] He looked on with some amusement as Pevsner struggled to align his working habits with those of his collaborators. Honour and Fleming lived in Tuscany, which involved much postal traffic as entries were batted backwards and forwards, and their approach was considerably more relaxed. Hugh Honour informed Godwin that their preference was to 'resolve the steady accumulation of an apparently anarchic mass of materials to two entries at the last moment', and Pevsner found the suspense excruciating. 'I am glad to hear that you are gingering up Honour and Glory,' he told Godwin.[28]

---

*Hugh Honour (1927–) has written on neoclassicism, Romanticism, Chinoiserie and the culture of Venice, and, with Fleming, edited encyclopaedias of world art and of the decorative arts. John Fleming (1919–2001) specialised in the cultural interchange between Italy and England in the eighteenth and nineteenth centuries. Pevsner had encouraged Fleming to write for the *Architectural Review* in the 1940s and 1950s, having been sent an article on Turkish baroque, and he encouraged both Fleming and Honour in their study of Italian Baroque sculpture and architecture. See the obituary for John Fleming by Bruce Boucher in the *Independent*, 29/5/2001.
†Anthony Godwin (1920–76), competitive, ambitious and abrasive, a champion of classless popular culture, was employed by Allen Lane first as a bookseller and then, with no publishing experience, as chief editor in 1960.

Honour and Fleming would assume increasing responsibility for updating and supplementing later editions of the *Dictionary* and would eventually take it over completely.

Pevsner's attitude to the entries on the architects of the 1960s may well be an indication of the relatively insignificant part that contemporary architecture played in his overall perspective. However, just as he continued to be cited as an authority on industrial design long after he had ceased to take an active interest in it, so now he would go on being seen in the public eye as a pundit on modern architecture, whether or not he wanted the accolade. Towards the end of 1966 he was approached by Isaiah Berlin, who had recently accepted the headship of the proposed new graduate college in Oxford, to be named after its benefactor, the businessman and philanthropist Sir Isaac Wolfson. 'May I presume on a very slight acquaintance to ask you for a very considerable favour?' Berlin started. The problem was one of selecting an architect to design buildings for the new institution:

> I am not an *Augenmensch* . . . I already have 38 colleagues, each of whom will doubtless disagree with me and also will all disagree with each other. Nothing divides men, and particularly academics, so much as aesthetic questions of this sort . . . The only prospect that I myself truly dread is that of an RIBA competition, which led to Churchill College, which does not seem to me (I only hope you agree!) a very fortunate example of contemporary British taste.

Berlin himself wanted to use a British architect, though he was very keen on Kenzo Tange and had also heard that Philip Johnson was anxious to work in Oxford. What was Pevsner's view?[29]

Berlin had inadvertently touched several nerves, and Pevsner was quick to reply:

> You say 'worthy' and I agree. You say 'Philip Johnson' and I do not agree. You say 'Kenzo Tange' and I emphatically do not agree. Philip could be guided. He has a protean character, intent on surprising his public by ever unexpected turns of style, but he is ready to accept a client's character and wishes, if they are unequivocally expressed. Kenzo Tange is much too strong to be guided, and his style would be, to my way of thinking, a disaster in Oxford.*

---

*NP/I. Berlin, 18/10/66. In a later letter, 21/11/66, Pevsner would add, 'I am not

Among English architects, Pevsner continued, being out of sympathy with recent developments, he found himself out of sympathy with both Denys Lasdun and Leslie Martin. 'Both, I may say, are personal friends, and both know where I stand.' (Be that as it may, it is hard to believe that either Lasdun or Martin would have been much impressed by his integrity or frankness, when such a significant commission was at stake. Pevsner tended to assume levels of disinterestedness in others equal to his own.) Powell and Moya were outstanding, he continued, but they had been rather overused by Oxbridge in recent years.*

'I agree with you again,' responded Berlin, 'that a sensational building in Oxford of Guggenheim Museum type . . . would be disgusting – that a college should predispose to peace, learning, and Winckelmannian virtues.'[30] So, he concluded optimistically, what about James Stirling? Pevsner contented himself with commending instead Arne Jacobsen and St Catherine's College, Oxford. 'To enter St Catherine's is to find yourself in heavenly peace, and this is the mood I think a college should convey.'[31]

Pevsner visited the proposed site for Wolfson, and Berlin visited a large number of modern buildings, but both had a shrewd suspicion which way the Fellows would jump. 'It is as you predicted,' wrote Berlin six months later, 'and you must not think too ill of us.' Powell and Moya were the favoured partnership. 'My colleagues voted: democracy occurred . . . It was the Christ Church picture gallery that did it. As you supposed.'[32]

---

surprised that Philip Johnson is keen to build an Oxford college. He is a bit of an empire builder.'
*Philip Powell (1921–2003) and Hidalgo 'Jacko' Moya (1920–94), proponents of humane modernism, had finished or were working on buildings for Brasenose and Christ Church in Oxford and St John's in Cambridge.

CHAPTER 40

'Looking at old buildings with an old man'

Pevsner had spoken in 1963 of 'mountains' to scale alone after Lola's death. Perhaps the most intimidating was the *Buildings of England*, of which she had been most closely a part. 'You must be glad,' Alan Glover had written, 'to think that her memorial is so solidly built into so much of your own life-task.' Glover was only partly right; the fact that she had been inextricably involved in the mechanics of the *BoE* made the structure all the more precarious once she was gone. Lola had handled all the practicalities of the county tours. More importantly, she had become an integral part of the process of looking at buildings.

Her support was emotional: Pevsner had once written, 'All the pleasure I have in seeing things has only been mine since I have been with you, my darling.' But she had also provided aesthetic intelligence. 'I found after many bitter experiences that she really saw more of puzzling details in churches and houses than I did,' he wrote in his memoir of her. 'Nearly always, when in the end I could in my text incorporate something not observed by anybody before, it was her eye that had seen it, not mine. So that will now cease. The BoE will lose some of their accuracy and – worse – some of their freshness.' In March 1964, with the first county trip since her death nearly upon him, he really did question whether the *Buildings of England* could continue. 'The first cathedral expedition with students without ∂,' he noted in the *Heftchen*, 'and the misery of the Berkshire journey looms larger and larger . . . Would she find it higher homage if I threw up the sponge and admitted that what we did cannot now be done by me?' 'I am more and more plagued by feelings that I may not live to finish,' he told the Leverhulme Trust.

The weeks passed, the despair began to lift, and with the gradual return of the appetite to complete the job came the realisation that he would have to devise a new system. Research assistants could not be asked to drive him around; he calculated that it would take up at least one-tenth of their time and he worried that it might affect the quality of their work. The only solution was to look for separate drivers. Dieter had offered to do at least some of the driving for the journeys that were already planned for the coming year, but he could not do it all and he certainly could not do it indefinitely. Writing to Leverhulme to explain his plight and ask for an increase in the grant in

655

order to take on these new staff, Pevsner explained that although he would do his best to convince students that this would be a good apprenticeship, worth taking for the experience alone, he might well fail to convince them and would have to offer a modest fee, in addition to paying their accommodation and travel expenses.

He was perhaps underselling himself. The first of the student drivers, John Newman, leapt at the chance. As a young classics teacher at Tonbridge School with a long-standing interest in architectural history, he had written to Pevsner in the winter of 1962 to ask when his own home county of Kent would be covered by the *Buildings of England*. Was there anything he could do to help advance the date? Pevsner had invited him to a meeting, and told him that the preliminary research for each county was normally done by a former Courtauld student. That was when Newman decided to apply to the Courtauld. He was there in the autumn of 1963 when he heard that Pevsner was looking for a driver. '"Second-year medievalist preferred". I wasn't in my second year and I wasn't a medievalist,' Newman remembered, 'but I thought "I'm not going to let this slip". So I got in touch with him, and nobody else did, so I drove him for a week in Berkshire in the spring of 1964.'*

For *Cumberland and Westmorland* the driver would be Neil Stratford.† Although he was writing his thesis at the Courtauld, it was at an evening lecture in Birkbeck that he heard Pevsner make his appeal for a driver, the only requirement being an interest in the subject and a capacity for hard labour.

Stratford remembered the whole Pevsner family anxiously seeing them off on the trip. He discovered that a little sleep in the car in the afternoon was part of Pevsner's routine, with a ritual stop on a hot day for an orange lolly. Together they covered the ground in less than three and a half weeks, despite many long drives up narrow valleys to find churches or meeting houses locked. At Bassenthwaite Lake, the rain poured as they inched up a lane and the Austin 8 settled slowly in a ford. Pevsner sat hunched, in a fishing hat, in the front of the car while Stratford crawled over the impedimenta in the back and plodded to the nearest village for help. He found a mechanic with a loud but limited vocabulary in a garage, struggling with a tractor, and persuaded him back to the car. They found Pevsner

---

*John Newman (1936–) would join the teaching staff at the Courtauld in 1967. Appointed Reader in 1987, he was the Institute's deputy director from 1989 to 1994.
†Neil Stratford (1938–) became Keeper of Medieval and Later Antiquities at the British Museum, 1975–98.

slumped despondently over the wheel, but the mechanic set to work
with a fusillade of 'fooks' and 'boogers'. As he disappeared back to
the village with the job successfully completed, Pevsner simply
commented, 'Remarkable grasp of English', and they were on their
way. Progress was sedate, but not solemn. Sheep on the roads
reminded Pevsner of a sign he had seen on a road going into Yugoslavia, translated for visiting motorists: 'Beware the sporting dog lest
he encumber your way – tootle him gently.'

Pevsner, Stratford found, was not overly reverential, but he hesitated
simply to drop in on stately homes. On the other hand, to make an
appointment often meant having to commit to spending too long in
a single place, and then there was always the risk of causing umbrage
face-to-face. Levens Hall, for example, is a Grade I-listed Elizabethan
house five miles south of Kendal with some of the oldest topiary in
the world, and a fine landscaped deer park with a great avenue of
oaks. Pevsner, however, gave offence by declining to inspect the muni-
ments room and refused even to walk to the oak avenue.* A later
driver, Michael Taylor, detailed the minute-by-minute discomfiture of
occasions like these:

> There was an itinerary to be kept and a momentum not to be lost.
> He would lower his head and, avoiding eye contact, walk slowly
> through the barrage of words whilst glancing at the proffered objects
> and praising them. Once outside he was always remorseful and
> would remain so for the rest of the day. It hurt him to have been
> abrupt but he knew that the whole success of the series depended
> not only on getting into buildings but equally on getting out of them
> too.[1]

At one grand estate Pevsner and Stratford had been invited to lunch
by the lady of the house, who then forgot that they were coming and
left for London. The owner himself, hot from hunting, was puzzled
but polite and gave them lunch, still in his riding breeches. Conversation failed to sparkle. The noble lord only took an interest twice: once
when mention was made of Harold Wilson, who had introduced a
tax on wealth – 'Damn fella!' – and again when one of them praised
the butter: 'Make it ourselves!' Pevsner, Stratford recalled, was fascinated and watched his host closely: 'Not very bright, is he?' Without

---

*Nor would he later support the appeal to stop the Barrow-in-Furness bypass slicing
across the avenue because, majestic as they might be, oaks were not *buildings*, and he
had to ration his appeals to architectural '*causes célèbres*'.

doubt, he was not as enamoured of the aristocracy as some other historians of the great country houses. On his first visit to England he had enjoyed upper-class life as theatre, but with a sharp awareness of all that he felt was undemocratic and ludicrous: 'In every corner the Middle Ages still peep out.' Thirty years on he still did not care to be patronised, and John Summerson found him 'inescapably hostile to English conservatism. One could feel him bristling under the chairmanship of people like Lord Salisbury.' But his antipathy, such as it was, tended to take the form of a general disapproval of the class system and resentment of individual grandees, not blanket disapproval of anyone with a title.*

Neil Stratford was again the driver in Worcestershire, though the arrangement caused Pevsner some initial agitation. He was tied to starting on 29 August and returning on 27 September, a later journey than usual. Stratford reassured him: 'Jenny and I are going to get married on 28th September. This fits in well with your latest return date and there is absolutely no need for me to be back earlier than the 27th as all that would happen would be that distant Aunts and Uncles would plague me with pointless questions . . . I greatly look forward to new skirmishes with sandwich making, Worcester versions of Mr Gatty and lewd hats.'†²

They stayed in Worcestershire with Freddie Charles and his wife Mary at an ancient water mill. Charles was a national authority on timber conservation, and was writing the contribution on timber-framed buildings.‡ He remembered Pevsner as a pleasant but less than voluble guest who left early in the morning, returned late for dinner, 'perhaps in time for a sherry beforehand', and talked mostly to Stratford about the day's findings, 'then disappeared till the next day. Our only contact was through a dreadful little Jack Russell terrier, called "Jack". He acquired the habit also of disappearing. Though we suspected it, we only latterly learnt that they were together, not just while Nikolaus was going through his diminutive notes but through the whole nights, through his stay. Nikolaus also took a liking to our VW caravette whose registration letters were A N P.'

---

*Amusement often replaced disapproval. Pevsner enjoyed an anecdote about Sir Edward Maufe arriving at a party and announcing himself with the words 'I'm Maufe', to which his host replied, 'Oh surely not, you've only just arrived.' Freddie Charles to the author, 29/1/92.
†Ben Jonson, *The Alchemist*: 'Thou look'st like antichrist, in that lewd hat.' Stratford coined the phrase for Pevsner's soft fisherman's hat.
‡F.W.B. Charles (1912–2002) trained as an architect and worked in the office of Maxwell Fry while Gropius was attached to it.

Pevsner typically noticed, unprompted, that two volumes of the *Pelican History of Art* were missing from their otherwise complete collection and sent them with a note: 'For Fred and Mary, from their rude visitor, Nikolaus Sept 66.'[3]

The driver for North Lancashire was Giles Clotworthy, who had attended Pevsner's lectures at Birkbeck while studying at the Courtauld in 1964.* The landlord of a bed-and-breakfast in Morecambe looked on in some surprise as the pair rearranged his living room after supper to lay out maps and papers for the evening's work. 'He went away shaking his head, to return some time later to explain, in broad Lancastrian, "Y'know, it's a funny life you're leading, lad – driving around looking at old buildings with an old man". Said within earshot of NP. I was mortified – NP was tickled pink.' Pevsner was less amused, on the other hand, when it was a case of being kept from the evening's work. A borrowed cottage on Coniston Water had a rowing skiff tied up at the bottom of the garden, and Clotworthy persuaded Pevsner, tired after a series of thirteen-hour working days, to come for an evening row on the lake. 'As I enjoyed the exercise of a vigorous pull, he fell asleep in the stern. We travelled some way before he woke and immediately demanded to be taken back to work. By then I was tired and he grew more and more impatient with the length of the return journey. Attempts to share my delight in the beauty of the natural scenery fell on extremely unappreciative ears.'[4]

Michael Taylor, the Courtauld postgraduate who drove Pevsner in Warwickshire in 1965, spent the evenings on the telephone trying to explain to owners or their butlers who Pevsner was, in order to make appointments for the following day. 'This was a nightmare for me (I dislike the phone so much that since then I have gone eleven years without one). I hated being thought a con-man or a reconnoitring burglar . . . Their reactions were sometimes hostile, sometimes bemused by our attention, occasionally flattered by it for the wrong reasons, and nearly always uninformed. No one grasped the breadth of the Professor's vision.' One owner responded with warmth, but total incomprehension: '"Want to see the chapel? Heavens. If you've gone to the bother of phoning at least I expected you'd want to see the pigs. Come, of course, but you'll have to see the pigs." It was the world of Wodehouse.'

---

*Giles Clotworthy worked for many years for the National Trust in Cornwall and was the director of Lanhydrock House. He was also the Trust's marketing manager. He now works as an independent consultant.

Worse was intruding into people's gardens to look at exteriors without permission. Lola once described herself as 'a hardened woman' after several years of trespassing, but neophytes like Taylor were still sensitive.[5] In one large moated late-medieval and Tudor manor the pair were warned away by men with staves, but the normal penalty was simply acute embarrassment:

The usual way . . . was just to drive up to the house; but this simple measure could go wrong. We had to inspect the façade of a large house which had a drive a good half-mile long, running through parkland. In front of the house the drive went round a circular lawn. Halfway down I could see four figures on the lawn. Closer, I could identify two women in pre-war bathing costumes sitting on the grass. Beside them stood a man in a blazer and a little way off a butler standing formally and holding in both hands a tray of drinks. I was horrified. There was no way out but forward, down to the house, round the lawn and the people, and back up the drive. Instinctively I speed up, wanting to diminish the ordeal. But the Professor is talking quietly both to me and to his clipboard. 'Slow down, slower my darling, three storeys, Dutch gables, central Venetian window first floor, my darling slow DOWN' (this whispered but very insistent). Meanwhile I am driving at less than walking pace, within ten feet of the group. They stare at us in silence, as stunned by our contempt-uously slow passage as by the fact that we ignore them utterly, the Professor being totally engrossed in his façade and his clipboard and his exhortations to be still slower, and I staring straight ahead, fixed of eye, like a felon passing a policeman. Their heads follow us round the lawn. Even the butler turns his head to follow our majestically slow progress, but no-one moves. The sweat is pouring off me. My face feels scarlet. Professor Pevsner is droning on about mouldings and broken pediments. Time seems to have stopped; but at last the lawn is circumnavigated and the drive lies before me. I sweated for the rest of the day.*

Whatever the drivers may have endured, the most taxing relationship of all was that of the co-writer, in the ten volumes of the *Buildings*

---

*'With Pevsner in Warwickshire', op. cit. Michael Taylor, who later became Assistant Keeper of British and Medieval Antiquities at the British Museum, did also write to Pevsner after the trip was over: 'Those five weeks were one of the great experiences of my life, and I think that I learnt more about architecture in that short time than I did in three years at university.' M. Taylor/NP, 16/8/67.

of England that were shared. When he finally reached the last volume in the series, Pevsner summed up his reasons for taking on collaborators and his views on the value of doing so. The reason was simple – 'I wanted to have the series completed in my lifetime' – but the conclusions perhaps more complicated: 'I admit that the young, with one or two exceptions, tend to write too much. Maybe they long to put in everything they know and can say, maybe a sense of proportion grows slowly. But the volumes benefit from details; also I was glad to see a generation of architectural historians entering the field who have enough all-round knowledge to deal with such books as these.'[6]

Ian Nairn had set the precedent, with *Surrey* and *Sussex*. The second collaborator, some three years later, was John Harris.* He had met Pevsner in 1953 when, with mixed feelings, he had become his editorial assistant at Penguin in Harmondsworth. Up to that point his interest in art history had been as an enthusiastic country house crawler with an informed interest in topography. He travelled in his teens in the company of his uncle Sid, an upholsterer to the upper classes in the Home Counties, who took him to country house sales and introduced him to the art of snooping in stately homes in the South of England. Large numbers of these lay abandoned and derelict after the war; most had been requisitioned by the armed forces and were either wrecked or now too expensive to maintain.[†] In the process, the literary critic John Carey has remarked unkindly, Harris 'developed aristocratic sympathies, lamenting the demise of noble dynasties – which never seems to have bothered him when he was poking around uninvited among their possessions – and remarking, with no trace of irony, on his own "extraordinary facial resemblance to the family of Harris, Earls of Malmesbury"'.[7]

Harris was not particularly well suited for his post as a Penguin editorial assistant. 'I didn't like editing, I didn't like Penguin Books, that wasn't my forte . . . I was more interested in writing.'[8] Nor was he naturally drawn to Pevsner and the *Buildings of England*. 'Even at

---

*John Harris (1931–) is an author, curator and historian of architecture, gardens and architectural drawings. He is a Fellow and Curator Emeritus of the Drawings Collection of the Royal Institute of British Architects, founding Trustee of SAVE Britain's Heritage and SAVE Europe's Heritage, and founding member and Honorary Life President of the International Confederation of Architectural Museums. He has been a non-executive director of Colnaghi art dealers and is an artistic adviser to private collectors.

†Harris's experiences would make him one of the moving spirits behind the influential V&A exhibition 'The Destruction of the Country House' in 1974, which spurred the movement to conserve British country houses.

that time I felt that NP was not an ideal topographer, not necessarily the right person. He wasn't in that great English topographical tradi-tion', and Harris considered the early volumes in the series 'parochial in their deficiencies'. Middlesex was his home county and he had found the *BoE* volume more than disappointing, annotating his copy, 'This German seems myopic and uninterested in local history.'⁹ Nevertheless, on the principle that it would be interesting to work with Pevsner, he took the job. It was short-lived. Harris says that he 'tried to explain that information-gathering needed a more professional approach'; Dr Schapire and Mrs Schilling, in his view, lacked critical judgement. On hearing this, Pevsner 'blushed and ducked into his room. I had touched upon a sensitive nerve. Not surprisingly three months later I was asked to "clear my desk".'¹⁰

However, when some six years later Harris offered his services to the *Buildings of England*, Pevsner took him on. He was not one to bear lasting grudges (defaulting *Pelican History of Art* contributors were the exception). There was a story among his students that he had once sacked someone – quite possibly this was Harris – and then a few weeks later said to his secretary, 'So-and-so was a nice boy. Why did he leave?' Harris was now working at the RIBA, cataloguing the collection of architectural drawings, and Pevsner respected his increasing knowledge and commitment. Reserving the churches of Lincolnshire for himself, and a few of the medieval secular buildings, he handed over the rest of the secular buildings to the younger man.

Harris was to do the travelling and the writing for his buildings, but he was also to do the preliminary research, and this remained a *casus belli*, at least on his part. He was never likely to enjoy the constraints under which Pevsner's research assistants worked. He claimed to have heard Pevsner say to a secretary, 'Now treat him like a servant. It'll do him good.'¹¹ 'The idea of an abstracter who humbly works away is very Germanic,' he remarked. 'The old German method . . . was that your pupils are subservient to you. Your pupils must eat humble pie, they must labour in your service, and they must get no credit.'

Another point troubling Harris was that, in his view, Pevsner required his researchers to pay too little attention to primary sources. Over the years Harris would offer a string of criticisms of Pevsner's methodology. Pevsner made no organised enquiries in County Record Offices; he did not consult the RIBA Drawings Collection; he did not seek help in any systematic way from Howard Colvin, who had published his *Dictionary of British Architects* in 1954; he did not take up Wittkow-er's offer of notes on English Palladianism; he failed to consult *Country*

Life until after the journeys; and he altogether ignored periodicals like *The Home Counties Magazine*. He added insult to injury by promulgating the idea that it took a German to show the British how it should be done. 'I said to Nikolaus that I thought it could have been set up in a different way,' remembered Harris. 'It would have been better to have devoted the first five years to having a proper abstracting programme done by a different breed of scholars . . . He didn't like this at all. I was saying, "I'm not saying that it's all wrong, but I'm thinking creatively – you have many volumes in front of you – can you improve them?" I felt he had set this whole programme up without any real consultation. He said, "I must get this thing done."'[12]

On their travels, too, Pevsner and his co-author had entirely different styles. Harris wore a bright-yellow raincoat, rode a motor scooter and affected a wide black hat. He attributed to the hat the fact that police came to speak to him several times about a variety of crimes, not only the rifling of alms boxes from churches but the murder of a night watchman. His accommodation, however, made up for these inconveniences. 'Pevsner was very much the German bourgeois Jew – a certain amount of austerity and not a lot of giggles. He totally disapproved of me,' Harris disclosed. 'When I went to Lincoln I stayed in the White Hart, he stayed in the most dreadful boarding house.* I don't believe that he had to stay in that boarding house . . . Wittkower loved comfort; it wasn't grotesquely over-indulgent, but he liked to stay in a good, comfortable hotel and go down to the bar in the early evening and have a nice drink.'[13] Pevsner's response may not have been disapproval as much as chagrin; when he had asked the Leverhulme Trust for an increased grant in order to pay his research assistants more, he specifically mentioned John Harris, who he believed had little money of his own.

'My pace was different,' Harris declared:

Pevsner would say, 'I have 23 or however many days to give to Devon, I've got to do Devon in 23 days and that is that.' He would never do it in 24. As a consequence he was forced into what I regard as an unnatural method . . . He had fixed himself into a grid and was never willing to depart from it . . . He had no curiosity. That I think is also perhaps a Germanic trait. The British have this long antiquarian tradition . . . a tradition of curiosity . . . Nikolaus would

---

*The White Hart started as a coaching inn in the fourteenth century. In the 1960s it was probably the most expensive hotel in Lincoln, in the shadow of the cathedral, opposite the castle.

only use what had been abstracted for him . . . If his abstract said, 'Here is a house, here is a lodge gate, stables, partly done by Repton,' he would incorporate that. But he would do no more than that. So unless he actually passed by the *other* lodge gate he wouldn't know it was there. He would never bother to walk down to the lake and see if there was a boathouse, or a grotto – he had no time.*

Certainly, Pevsner was pleased if he came upon treasures by accident. Geoffrey Moorhouse, travelling with the Pevsners in 1960, had recalled, '10.50 a.m. Mrs Pevsner muffs a turn and we pull up alongside a house which isn't registered in anyone's lists, with bulls-eye windows in the gables and lancets in the porch. Worth a mention. "It always pays to go the wrong way," says Pevsner, adding it to his notes.'[14] But he would not deviate on the off-chance.

Harris also felt more effort was needed in cultivating the owners. 'I kept saying to myself, "This is the way in which you are likely to create an impression which is not going to be conducive to getting a lot out of this house." When a Germanic-looking person knocks at your door with Lola standing there with this board in her hand and a pen, and Pevsner says, "I'm doing the Buildings of England, can I come in your house?" – it's not the way of doing things.' With the advantage of being English, Harris himself was more emollient. In his section of the introduction to *Lincolnshire*, he writes: 'I owe much to prating long hours with Sir Francis Hill . . . I must acknowledge all those owners who received me in their houses, particularly the Earl of Ancaster, the Earl of Yarborough, and the kindly Trollope-Bellews of Casewick.' Pevsner did not go in for prating and, with a day's worth of writing-up waiting for him when he got back to his dreadful boarding house, he did not have long hours.

The temperamental differences between the two men are reflected in their writing.† Pevsner enjoyed Lincolnshire, which was exceptionally rich in medieval churches (hence perhaps the need to delegate the county's secular buildings). Lincoln Cathedral exhibited exquisite innovations in the Early English style, and Lincolnshire was in his view the best county in England for the Decorated. On every side there were masses

---

*Harris attempted to correct this tendency in *Lincolnshire* – e.g. Gautby Great Park. 'Few places have such an air of deserted splendour. The Vyners' house, probably by *Matthew Brettingham*, has gone. The park has returned to arable. There are brick STABLES and the kitchen garden, and still the remains of the lake. On an island here stood for many years the equestrian Charles II by *Jasper Latham*. It is now at Newby in the West Riding of Yorkshire.'
†On John Harris and Pevsner, see Chapter 48.

of the kind of detail in which he revelled. 'On piers,' he wrote happily, 'a great deal will have to be said.' Tracery, towers, spires, wood carving – 'Where is one to start?' – choir stalls, misericords, screens, and several 'storehouses' of the church monuments that provided him with one of his favourite games: dating them by their style before reading their inscriptions. Nevertheless, at the back of his mind was the constant awareness that all this detail had to be contained within the standard format, and he could not afford to give his exuberance free rein in the writing.

Harris did not feel the same constraints. He allowed himself to make authorial intrusions of a type that Pevsner would never have considered: at Spilsby, 'the author was struck with lumbago by a Wild Man of the Willoughbys'.* He freely pursued his interest in social class. His writing style was elaborate, his images occasionally lurid – Louth Corn Exchange was 'wonderfully decayed . . . its façade like a rotting cadaver' – and his adjectives novel. ('Contrasty' was one that had not appeared before in the *BoE*.) His nouns had a touch of the Olde Worlde: Lincolnshire, he wrote, was a county of 'enchanting unsophisticated hostelries, with real ostlers, ironed news-papers, and an amplitude of fare' and he preferred to date one building by 'the old tongue-say that Buckingham House was its model'. Exclamation marks, which Pevsner generally eschewed, were frequent. Aswarby Park contained a pear-shaped mound 'which super-ficial examination suggests might be a barrow. It had been reported, however, that it was raised in the C19 to cover an elephant which died in a travelling circus!'

Harris's entries are vivid, detailed, articulate and entertaining, focusing less on the buildings than on the people who built them and the influence of their personalities and their circumstances on the finished structures. In dividing the volume between two authors, Pevsner was inviting comparisons. If he felt he was taking a risk, he was right. Critics of his approach and those who had had reservations about earlier volumes were now provided with ammunition.

'This series has always been "indispensable",' wrote John Piper, with inverted commas that could best be described as snide. 'It is fast becoming enjoyable too.' This he was inclined to attribute to John Harris: 'His touches of atmosphere are welcome as the flowers in May.' He was not denying what the Pevsner approach could achieve: the

---

*The Wild Man is one of the emblems of the Willoughby family, whose chapel is found in St James, Spilsby. The lumbago could, of course, have had something to do with the scooter.

description of Lincoln Cathedral, he conceded, was 'top-notch Pevsner. He gets a real grip on a subject like this and his analytic-descriptive method, relating the parts to the whole like a drawing by a fine late-Victorian architect, and then relating the whole to the rest of Europe, works beautifully.' But when the same method was applied to lesser churches, where there was often room only for the bare technical details, the results were disappointing.

'I recognise that we need straight architectural descriptions of what is *there*, the bread, in fact, before the jam (or the lemon curd, or sandwich spread) of sentimental historicising', but:

> surely these exact (but never in any case *complete*) architectural descriptions are better done by drawings or photographs? The English language boggles at them . . . Nobody could possibly know from the information here that Quadring, riding above the flat, reedy fields like a ship in full sail, has a sadly done-up interior while Gedney, ditto, ditto, is a church-crawler's paradise. Maybe I am eccentric in wanting to know these things. Opinions, judgments, feelings – I *expect* them from a book about the buildings of England – and indeed I get them in many places. 'Coningsby . . . Baptist Chapel, 1862, and without any question terrible' makes me want to go there and see it at once. It is opinions that make the wheels go round.[15]

Pevsner will have registered the praise for a variation in tone, and he had already acknowledged in his introduction to *Lincolnshire* the thoroughness of John Harris's preparations: 'His parts as against mine incorporate a good deal of first-hand research, as connoisseurs will no doubt notice.' Could the way ahead be to work with collaborators for every volume? Or even to hand over some volumes in their entirety? He still clung to his original conception: that the *Buildings of England* should be as uniform as possible, coherent, consistent and, most importantly, complete. He would not have been human if he had not wanted the *BoE* to remain his own. But he was aware of the risks of forging on alone. Reporting to the Leverhulme Trust in 1965, he estimated that, with twelve counties remaining, the series would take another six years to complete. 'I am 63 now and shall be 69 then. How I shall live up to the strain of 13-hour days, 7 days a week, for 2 months a year, to the rigours of weather, the discomforts of inferior pubs, and the crops of nettles in churchyards, remains to be seen. I have no complaints in matters of health so far, but want to be safe. An occasional volume done by another suitable person would reduce the risk.'[16]

*   *   *

Thus Pevsner worked with collaborators: Alexandra Wedgwood for *Warwickshire*, David Lloyd for *Hampshire*, Jennifer Sherwood for *Oxfordshire* and Edward Hubbard for *Cheshire*.* 'May I ask you a few personal questions?' Pevsner wrote to Hubbard in August 1965. 'Are you actually in full-time work? If so, how much do you earn? If not, would a full-time job for a year, dealing with matters close to your heart but being very badly paid, interest you?'[17] He was referring primarily to the research for *South Lancashire*, for which he wanted 'someone well versed in Victorian'. Hubbard had just founded the Victorian Society's first regional group, in Liverpool. What was more, he could drive, albeit rather cautiously, and soon found himself acting as both researcher and driver for the county.[†] He was a studious, even-tempered man, very conscientious, and Pevsner found him a soothing companion. They could enjoy some of the small jokes that Pevsner had shared with Lola, and Hubbard knew how to weather Pevsner's displeasure when a day had gone badly.[‡] When they came to work as collaborators on *Cheshire*, 'his psychological treatment of my moments of despondency [was] invaluable,' wrote Pevsner.

Edward Hubbard also brought with him what Pevsner would refer to fondly as 'the Prenton General Services Unlimited'. His parents, Jack and Ella Hubbard, lived in Prenton, a suburb of Birkenhead on Merseyside, and they welcomed Pevsner as a guest for parts of his tour of South Lancashire. Ella Hubbard did his laundry, carried out running repairs on his clothes and, for economy's sake, when Hubbard and Pevsner departed to stay in hotels in further-flung parts of the county, provided the pair with 'Perfect Packets' for their lunches – sandwiches carefully wrapped and labelled for each day, the dates decided by the keeping properties of the contents: egg, cheese, sandwich spread and paste. 'On all the occasions that NP stayed with us,' Jack Hubbard remembered, 'he placed a photo of his late wife on the mantelpiece in his bedroom.'[18]

---

*Pugin scholar Alexandra Wedgwood was from 1980 to 1998 Architectural Archivist to the Palace of Westminster. She is the Patron of the Pugin Society. David Lloyd, town planner and architectural historian, is an authority on the architecture of the South-East of England, and a consultant on conservation to the SPAB. Pevsner invited him to cover some of Hampshire, confident that he would do full justice to townscape. For Pevsner's work with Jennifer Sherwood, see Chapter 46.

†Edward Hubbard (1937–89), a Victorian specialist, would also do much of the preparatory research for *Staffordshire* as well as collaborating on *Cheshire* and later writing the whole of *Clwyd* for the *Buildings of Wales*. He died at the age of fifty-two from ankylosing spondylitis.

‡Lola might not have found so amusing the occasion on which the two found themselves in the same Bolton hotel as film star Jayne Mansfield, who electrified the dining room with her imposing bosom.

Up to this point Ian Nairn was the only one of Pevsner's collaborators to have completed more than half of a volume.* However, by 1965 Pevsner had already taken steps, informal at first, towards delegating a whole county. In 1962 he had been approached with an offer of help on the buildings of Gloucestershire from historian David Verey. Verey was well qualified. He had been working for the Historic Buildings Division of the Ministry of Housing, and had been involved in compiling the statutory list for Gloucestershire. He had written three volumes of the *Shell Guides* (for Herefordshire, Wiltshire and Mid-Wales), although it was perhaps ominous that Betjeman had been in the habit of referring to him as the Verey Light.† He was also the owner of a Grade II*-listed manor house of 1697 in the Cotswolds, and owned various other properties nearby. Pevsner made enquiries, and employed Verey part-time to work on Gloucestershire, largely on the recommendation of a trusted friend, the medieval historian Joan Evans.‡ Pencil notes of the conversation with her read: 'Honourable. M.A. – OK. A.1. . . . Good family, known to all.'

Verey would remain High Sheriff of Gloucestershire while working on the county, but he gave up his full-time job to work part-time for the *Buildings of England*, which might explain why money would be a constant issue. 'I have already warned you that there is no money in all this,' Pevsner told him at the end of January 1962. Verey was insistent that he needed an assistant, and wanted to make one of his eight cottages available to a 'lady' who could give him secretarial help, and ride his wife's horse. Would one of NP's 'old girls' like it? Or perhaps they might use a woman of his acquaintance who was now working at the Victoria and Albert?§ This scheme rapidly came to grief, but there were others over the years, and Pevsner became increasingly irritated by Verey's constant requests for money to cover the cost of his travels. Discussing it with the accountants at Birkbeck who

---

*According to Pevsner's own calculations, Nairn contributed 70 per cent of *Surrey* and 50 per cent of *Sussex*, John Harris 50 per cent of *Lincolnshire*, David Lloyd 40 per cent of *Hampshire*, Alexandra Wedgwood 20 per cent of *Warwickshire* and Edward Hubbard 20 per cent of *Cheshire*.

†Verey Lights are generally used as distress flares. Verey's volume on Mid-Wales had run into trouble when he suggested that it rained ceaselessly in Llandrindod Wells. The inhabitants protested, the story reached national television as 'local colour' and Shell were not amused.

‡Dame Joan Evans (1893–1977), an art historian, antiquary and half-sister to Arthur Evans, the excavator of Knossos, was the first woman to be elected President of the Society of Antiquaries. Her collection of more than 800 jewels is in the V&A.

§Verey proposed employing Elizabeth de Haas (d. 1999), companion to the daughter of Emery Walker, founder of the Doves Press.

disbursed the Leverhulme grant, he was adamant: 'Everybody who writes for the BoE loses. We pay assistants, but we cannot pay authors, and we have not got the Leverhulme grant for that purpose.'[19]

Pevsner was also irked by Verey's efforts to break away from the standard format of the *BoE*. By 1965 Pevsner had cause to write a little testily, 'I think that once 27 volumes are out we should not make changes unless there is a good reason.' Verey's writing on Gloucester Cathedral, for example, was beautiful, but the entry was not laid out according to Pevsner's house style, with the description of the interior separated from the monuments; the monuments themselves were not treated 'topographically' – that is to say, in the order in which the visitor would reach them; and Verey had failed to use the usual 'tele-graphese' as he had been asked to do. Pevsner finished plaintively, 'There is actually system in this madness of mine.'[20] By November 1965, Verey was asking for two volumes – and soon after that, over Penguin's protests, two volumes were a *fait accompli*. Pevsner would eventually compliment Verey generously on what he had achieved: 'You are a giant! It is perfectly obvious that I could not have done what you have done. Your work is much more evenly detailed than mine.'[21] But it had been an exceedingly long road and a hard one.

'I have just, to my great pleasure and relief, fixed up with a highly intelligent and efficient young man the writing of the Kent volumes,' Pevsner wrote to Nigel Gunnis* in 1965.[22] In John Newman, who had stepped in to do the driving when his need had been greatest, he had found someone who he felt understood exactly what he was trying to do. The county was to be treated in two halves: North-East Kent, and West Kent and the Weald. Pevsner would later, in public and in all sincerity, call these volumes 'the best in the whole series'.

---

*Brother of Rupert Gunnis, author of the *Dictionary of British Sculptors, 1650–1851* (1953), which Pevsner found invaluable.

CHAPTER 41

'More than is good for a man's work'

At the end of November 1966 Pevsner wrote to Peter Fleetwood-Hesketh, 'I have now really something like 1½–2 days a week on public affairs, and that is more than is good for a man's work.' He had been elected a Fellow of the British Academy in 1965 and appointed to the Historic Buildings Council for England the following year. On 21 October 1966, he also finally received the call from the Royal Fine Art Commission.

The RFAC's mission was 'to inquire into such questions of public amenity or of artistic importance as may be referred to [the Commissioners] from time to time by any of our Departments of State'. However, by the 1960s almost all these questions related to architecture. When Pevsner joined the RFAC, its chairman was the eminent civil servant Lord Bridges, but around half of the commissioners were architects, including Hugh Casson, Lionel Brett and Basil Spence. There were also familiar faces from the fields of architectural history and criticism: John Summerson, Jim Richards, John Piper and John Betjeman. (Piper and Betjeman had been members for some years, which, in Lionel Brett's view, may explain why Pevsner had not. 'There was always a strong anti-Pevsner party, at the centre of which were John Piper and John Betjeman. They joked about him a lot; I think they were quite fond of him in a way, but they always joked about him as a German – rather crude English jokes about Germans . . . The impression I had was that he should have been on the RFAC consistently for many years, because he was the best possible member, but he wasn't and I think it was for that reason.'*)

The RFAC spent most of its time considering proposals for new developments. It was also tasked with scrutinising alterations to protected buildings, including churches and cathedrals, and with exploring ideas 'in which the Duke of Edinburgh is interested', which for the most part concerned Victorian architecture. During Pevsner's time at the RFAC, the projects under discussion included the Regent's Park mosque, the plans for the completion of Liverpool Catholic Cathedral, the impact of the new Hoverport at Pegwell Bay near Ramsgate,

---

*Lionel Brett, interview with the author, 24/6/92. Betjeman had been a member since 1951, Piper since 1959.

the proposed remodelling of the interior of Derby Cathedral, the route of the M40 motorway across the Chilterns, the plan for Mansion House Square and the Mies van der Rohe building, and the NatWest Tower.

The Commission's brief was nationwide, but urban sprawl in the South-East was a particular preoccupation in the 1960s. Slab hotels were a recurring concern, and other high-rise buildings that might destroy skylines, restrict the sense of space in parks or set up wind-tunnels. Multi-storey car parks were coming into vogue with plan-ners: 'The parked car is just another form of urban rubbish, to be hidden as far as is possible.' But the trick was to avoid aiming at a 'spurious monumentality' for these structures, and to make sure that they were carefully sited below new developments or on the outskirts of towns.

The RFAC was a prestigious body, but not always an effective one. Its principal problem was its lack of statutory authority. It could visit, scrutinise and make recommendations: these ranged from 'acceptance with commendation' and 'active support' (for designs 'which perhaps by virtue of . . . originality, might encounter some public opposition') to 'acceptance with modifications' and 'rejection'. But it could not formally inspect and it could not enforce its recommendations. What was more, it could not always control what proposals it saw or when it saw them; where relations with the relevant authority or department were poor, the RFAC might well not be called in until working draw-ings had begun and the client was ready to place a contract.

There was also a dichotomy in the RFAC's operations between the regulation of new buildings and the conservation of old ones, as Kenneth Clark had pointed out a decade or so before: 'It is really in a completely false position; it should be split up into two bodies: one a council of preservation and the other a far larger and more authori-tative body for dealing with new buildings.'[1] As it was, the Commis-sion often ended up being unpopular both with those proposing new buildings and with those striving to protect old ones, criticised as 'supine' and 'torpid'. 'Membership of the old Royal Fine Art Commis-sion used to be akin to membership of the most exclusive club,' commented the architecture critic Martin Pawley, 'with the most courtly ritual attending the members' appraisal of one another's work.'* Even where members had no direct interest in proposals before the Commis-sion – the majority of cases – the preferred technique was usually to work behind the scenes rather than make a public commotion.

Architectural Review, c. 2000.

Pevsner was a member of the RFAC largely by virtue of his conservation work for the Victorian Society, but, as in the Vic Soc, he could not always be relied upon to turn up on the 'right' side, and it was not unusual for him to vote against the majority. The Commission as a whole, for example, would be highly critical of a proposal to build a Holiday Inn over South Kensington Station in 1970. Pevsner took issue, apparently suggesting that, though not distinguished, at least the proposed structure was not freakish. The RFAC Secretary was firm: 'Whilst I am sure that the Commission would agree with you that the banal is more acceptable than the gimmicky, this building was thought to achieve far too low a level of banality . . .'² Pevsner remained unconvinced, and recorded a dissenting vote.

'Honours converge on me now,' Pevsner wrote at the end of 1966, 'an honorary degree in July, another next June, the RIBA Gold Medal – and occasionally I think that the Sir might follow.'* His reaction to the Royal Gold Medal presented annually by the Royal Institute of British Architects was symptomatic of his mixed feelings. Without doubt, the award was among the honours that most pleased and satisfied him, a genuinely significant sign of recognition by his peers, but his acceptance speech was essentially an elaboration on the theme: 'Why me?'

The Royal Gold Medal is given to 'a person or group of people whose influence on architecture has had a truly international effect'. The RIBA panel in 1966 had wanted to honour someone other than a practising architect. 'The function of the critic is essential to us and to society,' declared Richard Sheppard, 'and never more so than today, when technology dominates every decision that faces us and issues like the location of our airports are subordinate to the till. By honouring Pevsner at a time when the Institute is in danger of becoming an unduly professional body at least we are capable of affirming the value and

---

*The honours often converged to an inconvenient degree. Between 1967 and 1969 he became an honorary Fellow of the RIBA, of St John's College, Cambridge and of the New Zealand Institute of Architects, an Associate of the Royal College of Art and an honorary member of the Accademia di Belle Arti di Venezia; he received honorary doctorates from York, Leeds, Oxford and East Anglia; he won the Society of Architectural Historians' Hitchcock Medal and the Grand Cross of Merit, the highest award given by the Federal Republic of Germany to anyone other than a foreign head of state. He may have been annoyed to find himself receiving his Oxford doctorate from the Chancellor Harold Macmillan, destroyer of the Euston Arch.

meaning of architecture instead of simply seeing it in terms of cash and cost.'*

The award to a historian was not without precedent. Within the first twenty years of its existence, the medal had been awarded in 1862 to Professor Robert Willis, an engineer, medievalist and co-author of a three-volume work on the architecture of Cambridge, and it had been won a century later by the critic and philosopher Lewis Mumford. But, as John Summerson pointed out in the ceremonial address, honouring Pevsner was a sign that architecture and architectural history were now distinct and that history deserved to be celebrated in its own right. 'This evening, architecture awards a medal to history, and I can assure you that all of those of us who play on the wicket of history are exceedingly proud to be represented by the player of your choice.'†

Pevsner was aware that John Summerson did not regard the role of the historian with undue reverence: Summerson had, he noted, 'anxiety about the universal take-over of the art historian'. He was also the most objective of critics, from whom one could expect no special favours. All the more affecting, then, to find him as the editor of *Concerning Architecture: Essays on Architectural Writers and Writing presented to Nikolaus Pevsner*, a *Festschrift* for his sixty-fifth birthday in January 1967. 'My dear Nikolaus,' read Summerson's introduction:

Here, for your birthday, is a collection of essays composed for you by some of your friends . . . The collection has something . . . of the character of the family album – the family of writers, past and present, who have been and are dedicated and industrious observers of architectural fabrics, inquiring into the how, why and when of fabrics; the art, philosophy, and craft of fabrics; and the mystery of fabrics, considered in the mesh of time. We, members of that family, salute you as a very excellent brother. We honour you for what you have achieved among us and in the world at large and wish you all happiness.

*Sir Richard Sheppard (1910–82) was a founding partner of the firm Sheppard Robson, which specialised in the design of schools and university buildings, including Churchill College, Cambridge.
†Pevsner wrote after the event (20/6/67) to Canon Bernard Mortlock (a writer on church architecture and the originator of the *Telegraph*'s 'Peterborough' column), 'John Summerson's short address was an absolute masterpiece. I admired it so much as a performance that I was quite able to forget for whole minutes on end that it was about me.'

Concerning Architecture was in large part a gift from Penguin, published by Allen Lane, designed by Hans Schmoller and presented to Pevsner at a Penguin reception, in the form of a bundle of the original manuscripts disposed in a morocco-bound box. The contributors were paid with credit notes from Berry Bros. & Rudd in St James's, and received individual letters of thanks from Pevsner.* 'Being an inveterate schoolmaster,' Pevsner told Summerson, 'I have of course in the midst of thanks drawn the attention of contributors to queries and errors.'[3]

The published volume included a pen-and-ink portrait of Pevsner by Hans Schwarz.[†] It also contained a bibliography by John Barr, Deputy Superintendent of the Reading Room at the British Museum. At Pevsner's own request, the list did not detail every single article and review from a forty-year writing career. Nevertheless, 'I have looked at it,' he wrote to Barr, 'with surprise, sometimes nostalgia, and sometimes embarrassment.'[4]

Concerning Architecture was not marked by conventional piety, either in its writing or its reception. It included 'Revenge of the Picturesque: English Architectural Polemics, 1945–65', Reyner Banham's assault on Pevsner for espousing 'the most debased English habits of compromise and sentimentality', a verbal mugging that Pevsner seems to have taken in his stride as part of a normal conversational exchange with Banham: 'It is of course thrilling for me to think of this as history, and to be told where I stood.'[5] As for its reception, architect and critic Robert Furneaux Jordan, for reasons best known to himself, saluted the occasion with a furious attack on the whole concept of the *Festschrift* as a sinister foreign conspiracy: 'Inbred . . . esoteric . . . a pyrotechnic display of erudition, profound scholarship, sheer pedantry and complete detachment from all reality . . . this book symbolises the triumph of the great Teutonic bid to make writing about art more important than art.' Pevsner did not react publicly to this outburst, with which he may have had some sympathy. *Concerning Architecture*, he wrote in his foreword to the

---

*The contributors were Reyner Banham, Hugh Casson, Basil F.L. Clarke, Alec Clifton-Taylor, Howard Colvin, Maurice Craig, Joseph Mordaunt Crook, Kerry Downes, Peter Ferriday, John Fleming, Mark Girouard, John Harris, Henry-Russell Hitchcock, Frank Jenkins, Susi Lang, Robin Middleton, John Piper, Jim Richards, Phoebe Stanton and Paul Thompson.

†Hans Schwarz (1922–2003) left Austria for England in 1938 and worked as a labourer for a year before being interned as an enemy alien. On his release he attended Birmingham School of Art. The National Portrait Gallery commissioned an oil portrait of Pevsner that was exhibited in 1969; Pevsner bought three of the sketches, one of which seems to have been borrowed for the *Festschrift*.

published volume, 'seems to me to take far too seriously the writings, often casual, of one man'.

The *Festschrift* was only one of the events to mark Pevsner's birthday, and by no means the most conspicuous one. On 26 January 1967 a full-page advertisement appeared in the *Times Literary Supplement*. A head-and-shoulders photograph featured above a large title reading:

> *Homage to Pevsner on the occasion of his*
> *sixty-fifth birthday on the 30th January 1967*
> *From His Publisher*

The text, which had cost Hans Schmoller a sleepless weekend to compose and design, ended with the words: 'Above all Pevsner has repaid a debt to the country that gave him a new home with *The Buildings of England* . . . We salute a tireless worker, a good friend, and a great scholar.' The feature was accompanied by an editorial that gave weight to the tribute by setting Pevsner's achievement in a broader professional context: 'It is thanks to the researches of a band of men and women of whom Professor Pevsner has become something of a symbol that information and understanding that were once the possession of a small group of specialists are now at hand for all who care for them.'

Not surprisingly, Pevsner was overwhelmed to the point of being uncomfortable. '1967 seems to be an annus mirabilis,' he wrote to Hans Schmoller, 'with . . . the rain of medals, medallions and distinctions. It makes me feel in need of some clobbering from someone to restore the balance.' His instinct was sound. Later attacks on his reputation stemmed at least partly from a feeling that his influence was disproportionate to the quality of what he had achieved, and this feeling might have been avoided if there had been more challenge to his work earlier. However, external clobbering was in one sense superfluous, since no critic could have been harsher with Pevsner than he was with himself. Responding to Arthur Crook, the editor of the *Times Literary Supplement*, he wrote: 'I am infinitely grateful to you for that leader. It was written so warmly and it kept in obscurity so competently what could be presented on the other side.'[6]

Pevsner had become, in his own view, a jobbing educator who had not reached any of the most prestigious positions in academic art history. He had worked in his youth to develop himself as a specialist in Italian painting, engaging at the highest level with his academic peers. Now he wrote mainly for laymen and almost never had the chance to do anything he would dignify with the title of 'research'.* He had been educated on the strictest Prussian lines, to work with focus and rigour, intolerant of error. Conflicting pressures now compelled him to live with omissions and inaccuracies on a daily basis.

The nagging feeling of spreading himself too thinly had intensified since Lola's death, as he threw himself into ever more work in ever wider fields as a means of filling the void. 'My work and my scholarship have deteriorated so much,' he wrote in July 1966.

> I feel it specially strongly when I sit on the examining board in July. The others are all genuine scholars; I am no longer. Even forgetting about the perfunctory manner in which I treat inadequacies in the Buildings of England – my writing for other [publications] is no longer above reproach. The reason is that I no longer research long enough before writing. I want to see immediate results. In fact often I write and then check if it is correct – a dangerous precedent. When I am out of the B of E and old – shall I sit again in the BM and just read? There is so much to be explored still . . . There is an even more unpleasant side to this doubt about my continued seriousness. I have put myself forward for a British Academy lecture and a year's Slade chair at Oxford. Should one do that? Is it not rock-bottom? How humiliating if in the end both my supposed patrons in their heart of hearts think: He is not good enough – and act accordingly.

This was the state of mind in which he questioned the observances of his *annus mirabilis* – 'strange festivities', as he described them in the *Heftchen*. 'That Allen Lane made it a celebration is only the gesture of a good friend – what does he find in me?† – but a Festschrift, a number of the American Journal of the Architectural Historians as another Festschrift, a leader in the TLS, and so many letters? What is it? I suppose I am an institution, for I have not broken new ground.'7

Originality was not something to which he had ever particularly aspired. He was certainly at pains to repudiate the idea that he had

---

*Pevsner wrote in his preface to *Studies in Art, Architecture and Design*, a 1968 collection of his articles, of his turning from writing for scholars to writing for laymen: 'Positively speaking it may mean a shedding of abracadabra. Negatively I need not speak; for the dangers are patent.'

†In 1968 Lane was informed by the *Observer* that he had been nominated as one of the most influential people in Britain, and he was asked for his own list of the ten people he considered had exercised most influence on the quality of life in Contemporary Britain. Pevsner appears on Lane's list alongside the Beatles, Malcolm Muggeridge and the inventor of the mini-skirt. Penguin Papers, Allen Lane Papers, DM 1819/1/2.

achieved it, pointing out at regular intervals throughout his life his indebtedness to others. As a teenager in 1918 he had described himself as an epigone, 'one who is nourished by what has gone before rather than creating something new'. Thirty-five years later, in a speech to the Aspen Summer School, he had declared firmly, 'I have no creative genius whatever.' His work on Mannerism grew directly out of studies already completed by Dvorák and Pinder, among others; the parallels between painting and the Counter-Reformation were new, but even there he was working within a tradition of *Geistesgeschichte* that was 'already ageing' when he started to write.[8] The book on *Academies of Art* pursued an interest in the social context of art that was already current in Germany. As for the *Outline*'s treatment of the history of architecture in terms of spatial theories, 'People in this country always tell me that it was I who first emphasised the importance of space in architecture, not knowing that I simply followed the existing Schmarsow etc. tradition.'[9] The theory of the Picturesque in architecture was largely Hastings's work; and even on his heroes, Gropius and Morris, he had not added to the sum of knowledge, merely brought it together in a readily digestible form.* As for the *Buildings of England*, he referred to himself in 1960 dismissively as 'a second-hand compiler of inventories'.[10]

'I have nowhere propelled my subject like the Warburg circle and like Ernst Gombrich,' wrote Pevsner.[11] This was not to say that his work had not met a need. He had, he felt, 'provided a historical foundation for something brewing among the creative people'.[12] And he had filled gaps by bringing subjects to the attention of other scholars. But his own work, according to his own standards, had 'gone thin' since the *Buildings of England* started. As he explained in the foreword to the American bibliography of his work, looking at the list of his works he could see exactly how his writings had changed over the years. They 'started with lusty generalisations and end with humble specific facts; they started with scholarship and end in what strikes me often as superficiality. The substance . . . tends to get thinner.'[13]

Pevsner had been happy with his generalisations so long as he was confident that they were rooted in very wide reading and founded on research. But now, engaged over a broader area than ever before, he could not keep pace in every field. Corresponding in May 1967 with

---

*Speaking at the RIBA on 'Architecture and William Morris' on 19 February 1957 he declared, 'Mr Brandon-Jones has managed to do in three minutes what I have not done in one hour; namely to contribute new material.' He would always credit Peter Floud with having 'revolutionised Morrisology'.

Christopher Hohler of the Courtauld Institute on a point of medieval detail, he wrote, 'I could perhaps dig into my untidy file called German Medieval Architecture. I throw into this all the references to books I ought to read, and never shall.'

There were whole topics on which he knew he had fallen behind, others where he was prepared to admit he had never known anything in the first place. 'All my ideas are thirty years old,' he told the audience at the RIBA, as he accepted their medal. 'I am a man of the 30s.'[14] 'I have been out of touch with the development of design in this country for at least the last fifteen years,' he told the cultural historian Fiona MacCarthy in 1967. 'Really, I know no more now than any reader of *Design Magazine*.' In 1968 he turned down an invitation from Karl Miller to elaborate in *The Listener* on a brief contribution he had made to a radio programme on Charles Rennie Mackintosh: 'I must have aired my views on this great man in detail four times now. There is a whole generation which has grown up . . . while I have done this. I feel sure that views different from mine are possible, and I should be the first to read them with interest.'[15] He declined to lecture on William Morris – others knew a great deal more – or English Palladianism, where he said he had nothing to contribute.[16] He apologised for failing to review a book on medieval carpentry: 'Believe me, I am a complete ignoramus on its subject . . . I find that in spite of my reading, I remain an amateur.' 'Dear George,' he wrote to Sir George Trevelyan at Attingham, 'I have never concealed my total ignorance of heraldry.'[17]

Pevsner never forgot what he had left behind him, as an academic, in Germany. He had made choices in England, and had decisions forced upon him, that had in the end opened many doors to him. But one path was closed, and it was the one he had originally chosen. There is a wistful note in a letter he wrote to Professor Heinz Ladendorf in Cologne in August 1968: 'Many thanks indeed for your long and learned paper on hands. How do you German professors do it? What with my BoE, I find that I cannot write worthwhile papers except very rarely, and then they would deal with one speciality, 19th-century architecture only. I am amazed time and again at the range over which German professors can still work and work seriously.'* To other people, Pevsner may have remained 'a German professor'. In his own eyes, that was a status that was lost for ever. 'My scholarship has been described as impeccable,' he once said in a radio broadcast, 'but I really think it is very peccable.'

---

*NP/Professor H. Ladendorf, Cologne, 27/8/68.

CHAPTER 42

'This intercalation of labours'

'This intercalation of labours . . . is no mean spiritual burden,' wrote Thomas Mann in the foreword to *Joseph and His Brothers*:

> A major work pauses for the sake of a smaller one . . . Under the pressure of the demands of the day, this too is set aside . . . And so it comes about that the author must forever carry the *totality* of his work, with all its major and minor ramifications, in his head and on his shoulders . . . Patience alone can help him – an equanimity that, if nature has not endowed him with it, must be wrested from a nervous temperament tending towards despair. Durability, steadfastness, longevity are everything, and his hope is time. 'Give me time, eternal gods,' so runs his prayer, 'and everything shall be finished'.

Patience, equanimity, durability, steadfastness: outwardly at least, Pevsner was a model of all these qualities. He need not have worried about being found unworthy of the Oxford Slade professorship, which was offered to him in 1968, although the making of appointments in art history in Oxford was undoubtedly fraught with manoeuvring and machinations. The choice of Edgar Wind as the first Professor of Art History in 1955 had itself been controversial.* Maurice Bowra had informed Hugh Trevor-Roper that Wind was 'a spellbinder, a wonderful lecturer, and . . . being a man of great resourcefulness, when he runs out of matter he invents'. Trevor-Roper concluded: 'So Professor Wind, fleeing from Smith College, arrived in Oxford, to the delight of some – the gay and the frivolous, I fear – and the chagrin of others, the grave scholars who know he is a plausible humbug. I fear he is a humbug.'[1]

Pevsner would seem to have been on the side of the 'grave scholars', characterising Wind to Lola as flashy and spurious, but it is not clear how much credence to give to rumours of a full-blown feud between them. As a popular lecturer in art history, Wind may have resented

---

*Edgar Wind (1900–71), a philosopher and art historian, studied with Adolph Goldschmidt in Berlin. An expert on Renaissance iconography, he was associated with the Warburg Institute from 1927 until after its transfer to England.

the fact that Pevsner had been chosen to be the first art historian to give the Reith Lectures. Pevsner, too, was a friend of Tom Boase, now the President of Magdalen College, who had opposed Wind's appointment.* Edgar Wind may have been the source of gossip to the effect that Pevsner was on bad terms with the Warburg Institute; but it would probably be unwarranted to detect corresponding malice in Pevsner's review of an essay by Wind explaining how Italian tyrants of the Quattrocento might espouse Platonism: 'The pages are written with a congenial enjoyment of the ways in which harmless sounding philosophy can be turned into evil plotting.'[2]

As Bowra took pleasure in pointing out, when Wind was appointed in 1955 he was a professor without a department. 'There is no school of Art-History in the University which he can lead into error by his ignorance: he will be but a professor lecturing in the void to susceptible femmes du monde.' Although by 1967 an art history department had been created in Oxford, much the same might have been said about Pevsner as Slade lecturer. He had little contact with the new department, with art history undergraduates or indeed with Fellows. His eight lectures were given on successive Friday evenings in the Oxford Playhouse, and it was only the generosity of All Souls College in giving him a room and common room rights that established some connection with the university for him and made the honour of the Slade professorship financially viable.† Pevsner's topic for the series was 'Writers on architecture in the 19th century', which enabled him to discuss the men who had documented the Gothic Revival in Britain, France and Germany.‡ The theme had long interested him, and he would later turn the lectures into a book, drawing in a good deal of extra material, although he did it without much enthusiasm.

*   *   *

---

*Boase, who had been one of Pevsner's sponsors for naturalisation in 1946, had gone to Magdalen in 1947. Pevsner remained on good terms with him despite the potential rivalry between the *Pelican History of Art* and the *Oxford History of Art*, which Boase edited, and was sure that Boase had secured him the Slade professorship.
†Felix Slade had endowed the position in 1870 at £500 p.a. and it still only paid £580 plus £100 expenses, while hotel prices had gone up more than twenty-fold since that time.
‡The lectures were entitled 'From Walpole to Rickman', 'Pugin', 'The Ecclesiologist and the Archaeologist [William Whewell and Robert Willis]', 'Ruskin', 'Viollet', 'Sir George Gilbert Scott', 'Semper' and '[James] Fergusson and [Robert] Kerr'. Alexandrina Buchanan has argued that these Slade studies were to some extent intended to complement the work he had done on his *Pioneers*, not so much to suggest a straight line of development from one set of radical writers to the next as to point up similarities of method and outlook. A. Buchanan, 'Nikolaus Pevsner and the Architectural Writers of the Nineteenth Century', in Draper, *Reassessing Nikolaus Pevsner*, op. cit.

In 1967 Pevsner stepped down as Head of the Department of Art History at Birkbeck, although he kept his personal chair, with the lecturing this entailed, and continued to supervise postgraduates. (He would finally resign the chair to become Professor Emeritus in 1969, a change that he said would mean 'little difference in work but some in income'.) If any vacuum was created by the removal of his administrative duties, it was instantly filled.

In 1968 he found himself back in Paris to oversee the British contribution to a major exhibition on 'L'Europe Gothique XIIe–XIVe siècles'. Invited by the British Council to select the exhibits, he went for illuminated manuscripts and *Opus Anglicanum*, medieval needlework in the form of several magnificent copes, filling the remainder of the allotted space with large photographs of English Gothic architecture. Once again a European project involved a maximum of bureaucracy in an atmosphere of intense ill-feeling. Exhibits were initially to be stored in the Louvre, and Pevsner was aghast at the lack of security and the dirt and chaos left by recent renovations. Masons were still at work and clouds of dust still settling. Entry was not checked and hundreds of people milled about amongst exhibits left sitting on the floor. (Pevsner was plagued with continual enquiries from the administrators of the Wallace Collection, who had lent the Dolgelly Chalice, the property of the Queen, and were understandably nervous.) Some visitors, he noted with horror, were smoking amidst piles of manuscripts and textiles.[3]

The irritations were unending. The British contribution was not given a room to itself. The French team would not disclose what they were showing, so there was an unnecessary duplication of exhibits. The French chairman demanded photographs of all exhibits on national lists. 'He wanted to keep them for a fortnight, in France,' Pevsner reported indignantly, 'but looking at the state of his coiffure, I preferred not to leave them with him.' Worst, and most predictable, the French organisers seemed determined to encroach on British territory. 'Illuminated manuscripts never have a great effect when they are shown in showcases,' he complained to the French chairman:

> Enlarged photographs of architecture you have reduced from about twelve to three. You are now reducing *Opus Anglicanum* from three to one. This means that I shall, in the end, be blamed – no doubt publicly – for producing an inadequate representation of Britain at the Paris exhibition.

In the end, Pevsner reported to the British Council, only the Italian rooms made any sense as coherent narratives; all the rest were simply assemblages of glorious objects. 'This is of course a deeply un-Gothic way of assembling things. The Gothic way . . . is the architectural way.'[4]

In 1968 Pevsner faced a new challenge: his first substantial television appearance.* He was a late starter in comparison with John Betjeman, who had already been involved with television for thirty years. By the early 1950s Betjeman was already a small-screen personality, acting as stand-in host for panel games such as *Animal, Vegetable and Mineral*, appearing with Geoffrey Grigson in a debate on the nature of the guidebook. Now Pevsner was invited, at the instigation of John Drummond, to appear in a series entitled *Contrasts* in a feature on the *Buildings of England* directed by David Cheshire. Five days of filming started in his London office, where he recounted the story of Allen Lane commissioning the *BoE* in his rose garden, and then led to Lancashire for a re-creation of the trip round the north of the county. Pevsner was not a television natural, and Edward Hubbard – brought along to play the role of driver and researcher, although he had not in fact worked in any capacity on *North Lancashire* – remembered his anxiety. Pevsner had bought a new suit and rehearsed some informalities, jotting down the key words of amusing stories that might elude him under the eye of the camera. However, lines that had been carefully learned in advance were jumbled or left out, and retakes were frequent. The only moment of spontaneity was one the director could not use: a party of German schoolboys invaded the calm of Furness Abbey near Barrow, and Pevsner quelled them with German phrases whose meaning was too patent to be broadcast.

Celebrity off the screen was easier to manage. He responded courteously to anthologists' requests for his favourite poems (Wordsworth's 'Upon Westminster Bridge' and, without prejudice, Betjeman's 'Subaltern's Love Song')[5] and was disappointed not to be able to oblige the curator of an exhibition on designers' reactions to the machine by lending choice objects from his own home: 'I wish I had such little knick-knacks as a lamp or a kettle made by the Bauhaus.'[6] The exhibition was at the University of East Anglia, which had recently founded

---

*Previous television projects – the ABC series on English churches in 1958, a potential *Monitor* series on the history of architecture, another on the palaces of Europe, and a proposed 'Levin Interview' with Bernard Levin in 1967 – had come to nothing.

a department of art history, and Pevsner had already given them his collection of museum and exhibition catalogues and colour prints, accumulated over forty years. 'I imagine it would be useful for your Institute to have a mini Witt [Library],' he told the department's new director, Peter Lasko.* 'I don't want any money for my catalogues. All I want, in my gross vanity, is a little rubber stamp made which says Ex Dono and my name.'[7]

The gift was one of several he had made since Lola's death, as part of a clearing-out process precipitated partly by a need to set his own life in order, but compounded by the practical necessity of moving out of his Birkbeck room. He disposed of a Singer sewing machine of c.1895 to the National Trust, to be placed in a Victorian property. Seven children's books from his own childhood library went to the Victoria and Albert Museum. He gave some eighty gramophone records to the BBC for distribution to 'musical old people', and offered a collection of piano music – Beethoven, Mozart, Chopin – to the principal of the Guildhall School. Many people find listening to music a comfort in bereavement; for others the release of emotion is too direct to endure, and it would seem that Pevsner had been deprived, with Lola's death, of a pleasure that he had once described as more intense than any other.

He rarely failed to respond to enquiries, however improbable. For the film director Michael Winner, what was required was urgent advice on churches that might pass as Italian.[8] *The Sentinel*, a dubious horror film, required a parched Italian backdrop for some of its scenes. At the time appointed for filming, it had been raining in Florence for weeks, while England was enduring a prolonged drought. Pevsner sent Winner to J.P. Seddon's church of St Catherine, Hoarwithy, which he called the finest Italianate church in England.† Other people's questions were an opportunity for Pevsner to think and learn as well as to inform and, in the days before electronic databases, he maintained a prodigious paper filing system for marshalling the data he needed. A typical response from his secretary to a habitual correspondent reveals the power of his memory and the depth of his patience: 'I enclose a copy

---

*Sir Robert Witt had built up a collection of around 250,000 images of works of art, which he donated to the Courtauld Institute as a reference tool.
†He was unable to help John Boorman, who wanted to meet to discuss ideas for a castle in which to set a film version of Tom Stoppard's *Rosencrantz and Guildenstern are Dead*. It must, wrote Boorman, be 'less dull and repetitive than a medieval castle and better reflecting the distorted, nightmare view of the place that Rosencrantz and Guildenstern have'. (J. Boorman/NP, 19/6/68.) Pevsner was out of London, the meeting never took place, and in the event Boorman's film was never made.

of the letter Professor Pevsner wrote to you 18 years ago about his suggestion of the architect of your house.'

Requests to support good causes now arrived every day. Pevsner became a patron equally of a Japanese garden in the Cotswolds and of the League of Friends of the German Hospital at Dalston, where Lola had died, and he obliged the National Hospital for Nervous Diseases by taking a memory test to establish what kind of information was retained most easily by the brain. ('You will see that gossip obviously sticks more than politics.') However, he could be quite sharp. His letter to the Howard League for Penal Reform was stiff to the point of rudeness after they included him without consultation in a list of possible contributors to a symposium on the death penalty.*

He was equally brisk in declining an invitation from the British Soviet Friendship Society to celebrate the fiftieth anniversary of the Soviet Union by sponsoring an illuminated address to the Soviet Ambassador: 'I have never visited Russia in my life, and so am not capable of taking sides in any way in which my opinion would be of value.' 'I decline on principle the use of my name in matters in which I have no special competence,' he added, and this principle was obviously behind his refusal, rather than any particular distaste for Soviet Friendship. Pevsner in the late 1960s was no more politically minded than he ever had been. As he put it in an article entitled 'As I See It', 'I . . . believe in a future along Socialist rather than Conservative lines', and he voted accordingly.[9] 'I have been a Labour voter for more years than I care to remember,' he told his MP in December 1969, writing to him to complain about a broken Ascot boiler and the Gas Board's failure to restore his hot water.[†] But his interest in politics was abstract and sporadic. His children could not recollect him talking about political issues except as they were relevant to any work that he may have had in hand. He found excessive wealth alien without necessarily disapproving of it: his daughter Uta remembered bemusement (and amusement) rather than hostility in his recollections of Castle Howard and its owner: 'George didn't know how many cars he had.'

---

*On occasion his name was even forged. When Richard Seifert and Partners were planning the redevelopment of the old Odhams site in Covent Garden, one particularly vitriolic letter of opposition stood out, apparently sent by Pevsner. 'Much dismay – until someone spotted the first name spelt Nicholas . . . "In fact, I have not even visited the site", Sir Nikolaus told me this morning. "The whole thing came out of the blue to me when somebody rang the Victorian Society to double check".' *Evening Standard*, 1/8/74.

†NP/Ben Whitaker MP, December 1969. He copied his letter to the chairman of the North Thames Gas Board, who apologised and ensured that the heater was repaired immediately.

In the summer of 1969 Pevsner learned that he was to be given a knighthood. As Alec Clifton-Taylor pointed out, this was offered 'without his ever having seemed to curry favour with the Establishment by anglicising the spelling of his name'.[10] It had been sixteen years since Pevsner had received the CBE and two since he had written, 'Occasionally I think that the Sir might follow.' His first reaction was strangely flat: 'Knighted. It is curious. I am conventional enough to have waited for this and wondered why it never came, just as I wonder why Buckingham Palace has for five years or so no longer invited me', though surprise may account for his stuttering English: 'And so excited must I feel about it, though I would not think so myself, that I have today typical shock effects.'* He is unlikely to have registered the fact that Bobby Charlton and Basil D'Oliveira were receiving an OBE in the same list, but surely noted both that John Betjeman was to be knighted alongside him and that the citation was different. While Betjeman was honoured as 'poet and author', Pevsner's award was 'for services to the history of art'.

Once the idea of his elevation sank in, he did not try to conceal his pleasure from his friends. 'I'm basking in the sunshine of honour,' he wrote to Edward Hubbard and his parents, 'but am at the same time snowed under letters (including Lord Snow himself whom I have met only once – and a KISS from Lady Rosse) . . . Where can I find second hand armour? Any suggestions for a coat of arms? One supporter ought to be St Pancras, but the other? Enough of flippancies. I am really very bucked.'[11] 'The title is Sir Nikolaus,' he told his old friend and former student Horst Gerson. 'Thank God it is not a life peerage, which would mean that for the sake of showing one's gratitude one would have to appear totally futilely at the House of Lords.'[12] To Eunice Frost, he revealed his underlying gratification. 'Who would have guessed in our joint King Penguin years . . .'[13]

He had indeed travelled a long way from his position as stand-in editor at Penguin, and even further from the piecemeal career of the 1930s, enduring the xenophobia of Midlands industrialists, the resentment of home-grown art historians and the patronage of Oxford High Table. Any thought that he could now be woven seamlessly

---

*Heftchen, 14/6/69. Pevsner had in fact already been considered for a knighthood 'several times', according to a letter from P.S. Milner-Barry of the Treasury seeking the opinion of Philip Hendy, Director of the National Gallery, in September 1966. Hendy's response gives a hint of why the honour had been so long in coming: 'I can't help feeling that in his case a knighthood is rather less suitable [than for the other nominee on whom he had been consulted] and am wondering whether something like the Companion of Honour would not be more in keeping with the kind of position which he occupies and the work he has done.' National Gallery Archive, NG16/226/26.

into the fabric of the British Establishment, however, would have been mistaken. He would always put art-historical principle before any consideration of social nicety, and he was perfectly willing to make waves.

He had, for example, a row of long standing with the Dean and Chapter of Westminster Abbey. In February 1967 it had come to his notice that medieval timbers from the roof of the nave and south transept of the Abbey had been destroyed. He wrote directly to *The Times*: had anyone consulted an expert on medieval timber? Had the Royal Commission on Historical Monuments been invited to conduct a survey? 'If no such survey was made, and no such expert was called in, and if the timbers were destroyed, this would not only be deeply alarming information, but it would also reveal an intolerable legal situation; for no private owner of a medieval manor house of architectural value would be allowed to do such a thing to his roof without authority from the Ministry of Housing and Local Government.'[14]

It was at this point that the Surveyor to the Fabric began to take umbrage:

> Professor Pevsner makes the mistake – not uncommon among those who do not have actual charge of buildings – of identifying restoration either with perpetuating the status quo or with exact replacement. So it quite properly may be. But to treat as inadmissible any change, whether of method, design or material, on the supposition that history is thereby falsified is unrealistic and may easily become pedantic. A myopic view is inadequate and others must judge whether the restoration of Westminster Abbey carried out over the past few years is of such an alarming nature as to create 'an intolerable legal situation'.[15]

The wording of the Surveyor's letter betrays an underlying agenda. Stephen Dykes Bower (1903–94), Surveyor since 1951, was himself an architect, a student of the Gothic Revival who specialised in the restoration of churches, a champion of Ninian Comper and, like Comper, an enthusiast for glitter and colour in church decorations. Dykes Bower had been responsible at Westminster Abbey not only for the repair of the roofs but also for the cleaning of marble and wood, the colouring and gilding of pulpit and choir stalls, the restoration and colouring of the organ case, the repainting of monuments, the adding of chandeliers and the restoration of the shrine of Edward the Confessor. He had aroused controversy with a scheme for repaving the floors to restore their original medieval appearance, since the flooring he proposed to replace was by Wren and Hawksmoor.

Sides were certainly being taken along familiar lines. Dykes Bower believed himself to be victimised by a coalition of modernists and conservationists who were united in opposing the copying of styles of the past. Pevsner, of course, would have been suspect on grounds of both modernism and conservationism. (Dykes Bower will not have forgotten the savaging in *North-East Norfolk* of his recent reconstruction of Great Yarmouth parish church as an 'opportunity lost . . . defeatist'.) Nevertheless, Pevsner's outburst had been prompted primarily by genuine concern at Westminster Abbey's apparent disregard for its history. Responding to a firm of chartered architects who had noted his letter in *The Times* and offered him timbers from the garden pavilion of Westbury Court in Gloucestershire, Pevsner explained: 'I am not indiscriminately interested in timbers, and my interest is not dendrological. What enraged me was that medieval timbers, some of them of the thirteenth century, in Westminster Abbey could be burnt without accurate drawings and photographs being made, less qua timbers than as part of a roof construction.'*

'I spend more time on the Victorian Society than, from the point of view of apportioning what time is left to me, I probably should,' Pevsner reflected in his sixty-fifth year.[16] In concentrating so hard on the Victorian era – and he realised that most of the articles he was writing were also to do with nineteenth-century architecture – he felt that he had lost some of his range. But these were the years when, at last, the defenders of Victorian buildings began to believe they were making progress.

Jane Fawcett had housed the Vic Soc office at her own address for several years, making it even harder for her to avoid working twelve-hour days. One of her principal contributions to the cause was to enable the Society to buy its own premises. She assembled a fundraising committee and deployed a wide circle of contacts to raise £100,000 and found an attractive but rundown building in Bedford Park going cheap.

The political environment for conservation was also improving. In 1967 Duncan Sandys – from the Opposition benches, but at the

---

*NP/C. Bishop of Paterson and Bishop Chartered Architects, 24/5/67. Westbury Court was acquired for the National Trust that year.

suggestion of Richard Crossman – had introduced the 1967 Civic Amenities Act as a Private Members' Bill. The Act brought in Conservation Areas, gave amenity bodies such as the Victorian Society some formal powers, and had the advantage of allowing for the consideration of integrated townscapes rather than simply dealing with individual buildings.[17] In the following year Wayland Young, the second Lord Kennet, introduced the 1968 Town and Country Planning Act.* This established the principle of listed building consent, requiring the owners of listed buildings to notify the authorities of their intention to alter or demolish them, and introduced the practice of 'spot'-listing buildings to bring them within the scope of the Act, short-circuiting a process that was often too long-drawn-out to offer endangered buildings any meaningful protection.

The immediate result of these advances was a huge increase in the number of cases coming to the attention of the Victorian Society. As Chairman, and in addition a member of the Historic Buildings Council for England, Pevsner had an increasingly influential voice, and the Pevsner letter was the ultimate weapon, which the Society wielded ever more frequently. 'He has written thousands of letters to ministers and mayors,' declared H.J. Dyos,[†] 'spent endless hours in the corridors and on the backstairs of power, suffering a hundred frustrations for one satisfying victory, constantly exercising his unique authority on our behalf wherever he could. Those who try to break the same hard ground as he's been turning over for us tell me . . . that his name carries weight even with planning officers – a sublime achievement indeed.'[18]

In his letters Pevsner employed various tactics and assumed several voices. To Sir Billy Butlin, whom he hoped to persuade to buy the Perseus Fountain from Witley Court, he wrote as one man of the world to another.[‡] With the Swindon town clerk, whom he wished to dissuade from demolishing the best part of the Railway Village built by Brunel, he was the concerned local, as the owner of a cottage in the vicinity, and his tone was one of comradeship: 'Swindon, as you, Sir, know as

---

*Wayland Hilton Young (1923–2009) was at this time a junior minister in the Ministry of Housing and Local Government. He later became Chair of the Council for the Preservation of Rural England. He succeeded to the title of the 2nd Baron Kennet in 1960.

†Harold J. Dyos, known to everyone as Jim Dyos, succeeded Pevsner as Chairman.

‡The Perseus Fountain, by W.A. Nesfield, stood in the grounds of Witley Court in Worcestershire. The house had been ruined by fire; the Vic Soc wanted the fountain sold to fund preservation of the estate. The grounds now belong to English Heritage; the house has been partly restored and the fountain is firing again.

well as I, is not rich in monuments of architecture of the past.'[19] When dealing with Scottish planning officers, he did not scruple to play on national sensitivities with a combination of flattery and threat. When Glasgow City Council signally failed to make any moves to conserve Alexander 'Greek' Thomson's Caledonian Road church – closed in 1962 and burned out by vandals in 1965 – Pevsner wrote with as much emphasis as he could muster to the City Planning Officer: 'Having specialised as a historian for the last thirty years in 19th century architecture, I ought to be believed if I say that the Caledonian Road church and the St Vincent Street church are amongst the half-dozen architecturally most valuable churches of their date anywhere in the world. I think it would be a disgrace if Glasgow allowed them to go.'*

Given the amount of time consumed by this voluminous correspondence, it is not surprising that he rarely joined in the society's leisure activities. He did, however, make his mark on Walk 53, on 24 November 1968, the occasion of the Victorian Society's tenth anniversary. The group were in a small mews examining the rear elevation of a Cubitt development when they were suddenly surrounded by police brandishing batons and blowing whistles. It was at a time of IRA terrorist activity. The Society had wandered into the back yard of a house belonging to Enoch Powell, an outspoken supporter of the Ulster Unionists, and had been identified by CID observers as a small, if unusually sedate, demonstration. Pevsner, resplendent in the 'lewd hat' of his Worcester travels, did not improve matters with a loud and facetious aside: 'Actually, we are on our way to blow up the Houses of Parliament.'

If Betjeman was the public face of the conservation of Victorian buildings, Pevsner was fast becoming the official presence whose endorsement was sought for any and every conservation battle.† 'Wherever the bulldozer threatens England's architectural history, preservationists have found a powerful champion in Professor Sir Nikolaus Pevsner,' wrote the *Hampstead and Highgate Express*. Those who appealed to him perhaps did not always realise that, because he was not moved by nostalgia but only by a strict regard for architectural quality, he would not invariably oppose the bulldozer. For Pevsner,

---

*NP/City Planning Officer, 17/2/66. Victorian Society archive at London Metropolitan Archives. LMA 4460/1/69/08. The Caledonian Road church was partly demolished and stands as a ruin, but that in St Vincent Street is still in use.
†Pevsner might have liked to have had some of Betjeman's popular appeal. He was disappointed when a radio appeal he made for the Historic Churches Preservation Trust in November 1968 raised only around £500, and was afraid the lack of success was due to his own lack of magnetism.

conservation was a complex equation. Sometimes a lesser building would have to be sacrificed, whatever its objective merits, to save a greater one, or to keep the Society's powder dry for future assaults. Sometimes the demands of the present – for more housing, or a better working environment, or a more efficient transport system – might have to take precedence over respect for the past. 'History and tradition are things you build on with pride and conviction,' according to Stephen Bayley, 'not resorts you scurry back to when you can think of nothing better to do. I believe that to deny the present is to short-change the future. These things I learnt from Nikolaus Pevsner.'[20]

Pevsner had to perform this balancing act on a grand scale and in public when he was appointed as the consultant on conservation for the development of Milton Keynes. The proposed New Town interested him as a modern version of the garden city ideal, and he was pleased to be involved in the development of the Master Plan. While other specialists advised on landscaping, traffic research, rural land use and the economic aspects of planning, Pevsner's job was to ensure that their objectives were not achieved at too high a cost to the existing towns and villages and the historical landscape of the designated area.

The Master Plan – including Pevsner's *Technical Supplement 8: Preservanda and Conservanda in Milton Keynes* – was published in 1970, but he had been invited to participate as early as 1967, and he started travelling round the area on his own, visiting noteworthy buildings (or rather revisiting them, since he had already 'done' Buckinghamshire for the *BoE*) and talking to the planners. Their terminology he did not care for – 'I am all the time busy fighting a losing battle for English English as opposed to American English, and so I am extremely sorry that you should recommend a term such as "City Structure Plan". This hanging of one noun to another has gone from German into American' – but he was happy that they were paying more attention to 'old buildings and their townscape value' than was usual in such projects.[21] Most of the individual buildings that he singled out for consideration were saved: the church of St Mary Magdalene, Willen, by Wren's assistant Robert Hooke, the windmill at New Bradwell, even the ruined church at Stantonbury ('A ruin is quite a good thing visually').

He argued strongly for keeping villages as conservation areas within the new development, even when their individual buildings were nothing special. Allowing people to go on using local churches in which worship had been uninterrupted for centuries would, he claimed, 'forge the strongest link between the new development and the soil on which it will take place'. The Development Corporation acted on his advice. 'It was the poet Cowper's country,' wrote John Betjeman to his wife, after a trip to Milton Keynes in 1980, 'which I had visited, when a Freshman at Oxford, by steam train . . . By a miracle of planning all the old villages I remembered were untouched,' he added, without realising that the miracle could be attributed at least in part to the foe.[22]

As early as 1966 Pevsner had suggested that the process for listing buildings to be preserved should be extended to include the best modern buildings of the 1930s.[23] On 6 March 1967 the subject of twentieth-century listing was raised at the listing subcommittee of the Historic Buildings Council (HBC), in all probability again by him. The Council was cautious, and the proposal was more modest: that 50–100 buildings from the years 1914–39 might be identified as worth protecting, for guidance to local authorities, if not for actual listing. Pevsner, it was agreed, might be one of the few who could judge.

He was planning to work during the summer on an article for the German magazine *Bauen und Wohnen* on the architecture of 1924–34. This would involve scrutinising all the issues of the *Architectural Review* for that period, and he offered to produce a provisional list of notable modern buildings as a by-product. Under the three headings of Categories A, B and C, he listed some forty-one secular buildings to be considered for protection on purely aesthetic or stylistic grounds. In Category A, which he considered worthy beyond doubt, he had placed twenty-three entries, ranging from the London Transport head-quarters in Victoria and Impington Village College outside Cambridge to the De La Warr Pavilion in Bexhill, Highpoint 2 and the Peter Jones store in London, as well as the Boots Pharmaceutical Factory in Beeston.

The committee deleted ten of his choices and put in some of their own; they argued, for example, with his inclusion of Patrick Gwynne's 'Homewood', built in canonical Modernist style, and put in instead the less orthodox 2 Willow Road by Ernö Goldfinger.* Category B Pevsner had marked as 'doubtful': the twelve nominations included Emberton's Royal Corinthian Yacht Club at Burnham-on-Crouch, and Goodhart-Rendel's St Olaf House and George Grey Wornum's building for the RIBA, both in London. The committee removed Battersea Power Station and included instead Chester House, the home that Giles Gilbert Scott had built for himself in Paddington, in classical

---

*Both Homewood and 2 Willow Road are now run by the National Trust.

style. They were perhaps trying to correct what Pevsner admitted was a heavy modernist bias, writing on the bottom of his document, 'This list leaves out the generation of Lutyens, GG Scott, Dawber, Newton, even Reilly. But we must watch that we don't neglect it in the end.'* Pevsner may have found the compilation of his list a slightly melancholy experience, as if he were setting a seal on the impression that these buildings, and the movement he had so much admired, were definitely now of the past. The architects themselves were going. In July 1969 he produced an obituary for Gropius, and at the end of that year wrote to Spanish architect Oriol Bohigas, 'I . . . probably represent an ideal which is fading out.'²⁴

In the area of art education, too, Pevsner was finding some of his deepest beliefs challenged. Between 1967 and 1969 the Coldstream Committee was struggling to deal with the practical difficulties involved in implementing the recommendations it had made. In the early years of the new diploma system, far more students failed their examinations. Not infrequently the cause was a poor performance in the written papers on history of art which the Committee had made compulsory. In some schools art students were simply not being taught the subject, in others they were being taught it badly, and an unfortunate minority fell victim to assessors with an unreasonably narrow view of what the curriculum should have contained. Not only the students themselves, but also their teachers and some heads of schools, objected in principle to the idea that a failure to master the history of art should prevent a student from pursuing a career as an artist. 'Coldstream represented an academic takeover of an education previously based on more intangible qualities. Romantic ideology came up against a new bureaucratic barrier.'²⁵

History of art could easily be projected as formal, elitist, conventional, a subject that put creative but ill-educated art students at an unfair disadvantage. It was identified with 'high art' at a time, in the mid-1960s, when art itself was moving to embrace the ephemeral and mundane, and it was quite out of tune with the free-thinking unorthodoxy that many art schools cherished at a moment when they either were, or hoped to be, centres for experiment and dissent.

---

*Sir Edward Guy Dawber (1861–1938) worked in late Arts and Crafts style. Ernest Newton (1856–1922) was a pupil of Norman Shaw, specialising in country houses in the English Renaissance style. Sir Charles Reilly (1874–1948) was influenced in his early years by American classicism, later a promoter of modernism.

Most art schools and colleges were resisting the move to incorporate them within the new polytechnics – institutions they saw as essentially scientific and functional. This resistance was a major factor in the wave of protest in art schools in 1968 that appeared to undermine some of the basic premises on which the Coldstream Committee was operating. The wave broke first at Hornsey College of Art, where the introduction of the new degree-level course, the DipAD, had introduced fresh tensions to a student body that was already disunited and discontented. The withholding of the student union funds that were to have paid for a sabbatical for the union president prompted a sit-in that rapidly developed into a wider questioning of the philosophies and purposes of education in art and design: where did art sit within capitalism? how were art and design feeding into consumer culture, and should they be doing so? Students who resisted the idea of becoming the servants of a supply system disliked the way in which the new DipAD appeared to entrench an ideology – Bauhaus-based – that was largely functional and left little room for the romantic ideal of individual expression.

While the sit-in continued, a range of speakers was invited to address the quasi-captive audience; among them was Pevsner, who had been an examiner at Hornsey for several years.* He was also on the official working party convened by the Coldstream Committee to respond to the student unrest, and he attended a meeting with the Hornsey students called by the Minister of Education, Shirley Williams. Those present included Jack Straw, then the President-Elect of the National Union of Students, and representatives of the colleges in which discontent had become apparent. Their main grievances, Pevsner reported to the History of Art panel, were the use of the GCE to select students for admission to art college, and the fact that vocational students had more freedom than diploma students in that they were not tied to written examinations.[26]

It was obviously necessary for both the Coldstream Committee and its sister organisation, the NCDAD, to review the programme of reforms they were trying to implement, and they launched a call for evidence from art schools, which revealed a wide range of grievances. Amidst the general criticisms of the new DipAD course (aimed primarily

---

*John Summerson and Robin Darwin also spoke, and attendees were invited to consider the proceedings of the NCDAD. Other speakers included Joan Littlewood, Richard Wollheim, Buckminster Fuller and R.D. Laing. Some critics later suggested that distinguished individuals had 'dabbled' in the protest and helped to extend it. See L. Tickner, *Hornsey 1968: The Art School Revolution* (Frances Lincoln, 2008), p.156, n.70.

at the seeming dominance of fine art at the expense of design and other vocational training) there were specific and pointed attacks on the role played in it by history of art. Authoritarian forms of knowledge, hierarchical teacher–student relationships, compulsory courses, written examinations as opposed to continuous assessment, prescription rather than flexibility – art history appeared to fail on every count. 'If an academic subject has to be introduced into the Diploma Course,' argued Rolf Brandt, from the London College of Printing, 'Mathematics would be the most beneficial to the students, Sociology could widen their horizon, Chemistry and Engineering could help them technically, but the art of the past has to be discovered by the artist himself and not rammed down his throat.'*

The Coldstream Committee and the NCDAD now set up a Joint Committee of seventeen members. Pevsner was one of four to belong to both bodies, and he was responsible for summarising the evidence on history of art and Complementary Studies for the Joint Committee. He took a firm hand with the submissions, firmly typing 'NOTHING' against more than a few statements and concluding, 'Considering the bulk of paper which we have, the results in my field proved much more meagre than I had expected.'[27]

GCEs, he conceded, should not be the only criterion for admission to art school, any more than interviews alone. Once students were admitted, more attention should be paid to their individual interests. 'The argument that too much teaching of the history of art is history of painting and sculpture is valid. The textile designer needs no Giotto (or a little will go a long way).' Teaching must be in the hands of people who were themselves interested in it. 'Lecturers in the History of Art at art colleges have been too unenthusiastic, too antiquarian, in short too dull, and that has done damage to the evaluation of the subject.'

He was not blindly committed to the concept of examinations specifically in art history: sociology, say, or the psychology of perception might be more engaging for some students. But of the need for some written examination, and some academic content in an art course, he was still in no doubt. The rationale was largely practical. 'Local authorities can't be blamed if they want to see some palpable results at the end of a period of training given to students who look so much less trustworthy than those of other institutions.' Continuous assessment could not produce these 'palpable results' because it was carried out by staff from within the art schools, who were less than objective:

*R. Brandt/NCDAD, 15/7/68. PRO 206/12 Evidence. 1968. Rolf Brandt (1906–86) was an artist, illustrator and brother of the photographer Bill Brandt.

The sad fact is that essays can't be trusted by external assessors as being the unaided work of the student. Of course unaided is relative anyway and supervision or tutorial is perfectly fair. One accepts it in universities because one takes it for granted that staff and external assessors agree on the educational nature of the essay. But in art colleges staff may well be at one with radical students who don't admit the value of the intellectual fifteen per cent [the 15 per cent of the DipAD devoted to history of art and Complementary Studies] and who may, I think I ought to say, cheat.

The need for academic content was more of a personal credo. 'Once admitted the student is to spend some of his time on using his brain . . . If he teaches, he has to communicate to children and he will be a failure if he does it dimly or stammeringly. If he is a designer he has to argue with sales directors, engineers, maybe reps, maybe members of the board, and he has to argue on their intellectual level (which is not always saying much).' Clearly, Pevsner had not forgotten what he had been told by irritated manufacturers as he trudged round the factories of the Midlands in the mid-1930s – that far too many 'artists' were too touchy and unbusinesslike to work in industry – and he must have felt there were still lessons to be learned from his *Enquiry into Industrial Art*.

The practising artists and art teachers among his colleagues may have taken exception to the implication that studio work involved no use of the brain, and that art students often had the endorsement, even encouragement, of their teachers for an attitude to the practising of their profession that was self-indulgent, ill-informed and mentally lazy. Pevsner may have felt that, outside the History of Art panel itself, he had little support within the Joint Committee. He was well aware that the history of art programme originally recommended by the Coldstream Committee was not working, and he was anxious that the Joint Committee should take action to remedy the defects that had been identified, lest history of art be dropped altogether as a result of the dissatisfaction demonstrated so vividly at Hornsey.

Pevsner drew up another paper in June 1969 in which he recommended relaxing or varying the current hard line, allowing general art history to be optional, or confined to the first year. The Joint Committee, however, failed to consider the paper until their meeting in November 1969 and then left no time to discuss it; the general feeling was that their report should include only a couple of lines on art history and leave any major decisions to the NCDAD. Pevsner was chagrined. He must have wondered what the future of his subject might be, if he could not interest a committee of artists and educators in it. He had always seen art history as a means of supporting and enriching the teaching of art, architecture, history, literature, even geography and languages. Was it now to be confined within the narrow constraints of a single-subject university degree: art history for art history's sake, an intellectual topic rather than a life-enhancing force? It was a lowering thought.

CHAPTER 43

'The only one is duty'

'Thus the engine runs down,' Pevsner had remarked gloomily in the summer of 1966, on being told that he would have to have false teeth, which he managed to postpone for eighteen months. 'My health is good for my age,' he wrote in his *Heftchen* in August 1968 when he was sixty-six:

> No illnesses so far at all, no advice to 'take it easy', still more work per day than most people. But – no physical work. Half an hour of gardening would exhaust me. Little hair, when I get aware of it at the tailor or barber. A denture which I try to keep concealed. No climbing or scrambling any longer (for the last eight years or so), i.e. giddiness and plain fright. Heavy carrying makes my heart palpitate and may hurt my spine. More and more panic at the start of a new B of England volume. Short sleep – six hours. It adds up.

He hated the disruption of moving office, after twenty-two years in Gower Street. The new rooms at 12 Bloomsbury Square were 'very plain', according to Tom Tatham, who worked on *Buildings of England* indexes with him, with no indication of their use besides a small sign outside the door saying 'Dr N. Pevsner', and little furniture other than an Isokon bookcase of which he was very proud.* The drawback was a tortuous lease that turned his occupancy into a semi-squat, pending a decision from the Ministry of Works on whether or not the British Museum might build an extension on the site.

At the same time he was threatened by the prospect of having to move out of his own house because there too the landlord wished to redevelop. In Wildwood Terrace he was closely surrounded by his children, and he was profoundly grateful to be rescued from what would have been a much more painful upheaval. His relationship with

---

*Occasionally, patients in search of a GP rang the bell. Francis Hugh 'Tom' Tatham (1917–2002) was the editor of *Whitaker's Almanack* from 1950 to 1981 and the indexer for *Wisden's Cricketers' Almanack*.

Allen Lane had been largely unclouded.* Now, learning that it would take a court case to open up the option of purchasing the freehold on the house, Lane arranged for Penguin to lend him £180 towards the costs of the case, which was successful. His relief was palpable: 'I can pay, and no breaking up of the clan.'

Pevsner's home never accorded with other people's ideas of where and how an 'arty' person should live: a Victorian house, rather than either a Georgian mews or a modernist apartment, and one devoid of either master works or Victoriana, 'a rum multi-coloured terrace house in Hampstead . . . more fierce than picturesque in spite of its setting on a gravelled lane in the woods', according to Nicholas Taylor.[1] The garden at least had become a little more ornamental in recent years with the addition of an eight-foot terracotta statue of Clio, which had adorned the Apollo pub on Tottenham Court Road along with Apollo and the other eight Muses. The building had been bought and subsequently demolished by Ambrose Heal, provoking a testy letter from Pevsner: 'As the one who a number of years ago discovered the name of the architect and the date of the building, I had hoped to get hold of one of the statues for our garden. Now I am afraid they may turn out to be too expensive. I gather you have secured them to sell them. The one most appropriate for me would of course be Clio [the muse of history].'[2] He beat Heal down from fifteen to five guineas, hired a lorry with a driver and wheedled out of the Royal Free Hospital the services of a strong porter for ten minutes. Clio was joined in 1968 by a four-foot Doulton plaque enclosing a bust of the engineering pioneer Robert Stephenson, which had graced the Birkbeck Bank in Holborn before its demolition in 1965.

The *Heftchen* make it clear that Pevsner was acutely aware of his own abiding weaknesses. One particular dream was revealing: 'Two telephones side by side. I use one, a girl without any definition [uses] the other. I am intensely in love with her, but must not proceed . . . ∂ [Lola] rushes in, jealous, but nothing of course is happening. What remains is the happiness of young love, and what the psychologist will note is the preference for not proceeding.' To the outside world, however, there was no lack of drive. He appeared a serious, unbending figure, wholly dedicated to his work.

---

*Lane had been touched by Pevsner's tribute in the *Herefordshire* foreword to 'the welcome fanaticism of Sir Allen Lane who has over all these years happily endowed . . . a series which could not possibly support itself'. 'As I think I have told you before, you are quite my favourite author and editor,' he wrote to Pevsner, who responded, 'May I retaliate to your note of 6 April by telling you . . . that you are quite my favourite publisher and sugar daddy.' (A. Lane/NP, 6/4/62. NP/A. Lane, 13/4/62.)

He was a loyal and considerate friend. The Italian engineer Mario Pancini, for example, had been the site director during the construction of the Vajont dam in northern Italy. When the Vajont gorge was inundated by a huge wave, more than 2,000 people died.* The enquiry into the disaster was protracted, blame looked like being attributed to the engineers, and Pevsner became concerned about Pancini. Shortly before the case was due to come to court, he wrote to Pancini to say that he could not be accountable for the geology of the mountain. 'Please forgive this letter, but I imagine that you would welcome a few lines from a friend in this very difficult time.'³ His reassurance was to no avail; on the eve of the case, Pancini committed suicide. When *The Times* reported his death in March 1968, Pevsner wrote a public letter to declare that he was 'the gentlest, most honest, most conscientious of men . . . If it is true that he has killed himself, the only reason can be that, after having gone through the purgatory of a five-year wait before the case was opened, he thought he knew that he could not trust the political influences acting on Italian justice.'

Pevsner, however, did not have the easy touch. 'On the telephone he could seem very abrupt,' Ian Sutton explained. 'When he had said what he had to say, he simply hung up. Chatting and being sociable was on the whole just a waste of time. More than one of his secretaries and assistants were reduced to tears without his having the least idea what he had done to upset them.' One assistant had started to come to his Birkbeck class, but had been obliged to give it up because her husband and stepson needed her at home in the evenings. When her marriage broke up and she moved out of the marital home, she told Pevsner, possibly expecting some degree of sympathy, but all he said was, 'Oh, then that means you can come back to my class.' 'He sacrificed everything to efficiency,' according to Sutton, 'and this could include the feelings of his colleagues.'

Where he understood the nature of a problem, however, and the problem was not due to any lack of effort, he was considerate. Typing his manuscripts was a chore, given his handwriting and the mass of technical vocabulary. Dorothy Dorn, his second typist, was elderly, devoted and highly conscientious; she had asked to be paid by the

---

*The Vajont dam under Monte Toc, 100 kilometres north of Venice, was one of the highest dams in the world, 262 metres high. Monte Toc's outer flanks consisted not of bedrock, as had been believed, but of an ancient landslide deposit. On 9 October 1963 heavy rains helped trigger an enormous slide, which fell into the reservoir, causing fifty million cubic metres of water to overtop the dam in a 250-metre-high wave. The dam remained intact. Ten days before the slide Pancini had asked in vain for a government surveyor to inspect the site.

number of words rather than by the hour. Gradually he became aware that she was putting in an inordinate amount of time for relatively little money and suggested a renegotiation. 'I am very glad you have raised the matter of charges,' she replied. 'Since last May it has been nagging like a sore tooth and being somewhat in awe of you I felt unable to reopen the question. Of course I am much quicker now at reading your writing . . . but that does not alter the fact that my fingers are no quicker nor will they ever be – rheumatism sees to that.' Would the budget stretch to ten shillings per thousand words? 'I enjoy working for you – you make the past come alive.'⁴ He raised her pay and asked Dieter to chase the accounts department to prevent a 'cruel delay' in paying her.

Pevsner was not a man of impulse – he did things consciously that other people might have done spontaneously – and 'casual' was a dirty word in his vocabulary. This limited the number of his acquaintances and made him more than usually reliant on a small circle around him which did not extend far beyond work and his family. Nor did he extend the field of his interests with television or the Sunday newspapers (he had given them up, with relief, after Lola's death) which left him at something of a loss when he was asked by the *Observer Colour Magazine* in 1968 to list ten people whom he considered 'to exert the most influence on the quality of contemporary life in Britain'. These names would probably be drawn from 'areas like consumer aids, design, fashion, pop, morals, education, food, and so on', they advised him kindly. 'It is . . . the quality of life and the attitude towards contemporary society we want to highlight.' His alarm was almost comical. 'This letter is in no way intended to be rude,' he assured the *Observer*'s editor. 'I have no television set, and hardly ever turn on my wireless. I go to the pictures about six times a year, and to the theatre no more often. I used to watch the development of industrial design closely, but can no longer consider myself an expert in this either. I am one of the few remaining people who use the word virtue with a straight face (not alas always applying to myself). What then should I contribute?'⁵ the *Observer* persisted, and he wrote slightly desperately, 'Don't you see I simply can't know.'

'I work nearly always,' he wrote in the *Heftchen* in the summer of 1969. 'It is always work – as an escape from philosophy, from fiercely held beliefs . . . Beliefs? The only one is duty – to fulfil what I promise or set myself to do.' The *Buildings of England* series was, of course, the stiffest challenge that he had set himself. He was now sixty-seven; he had already collected his gold watch for long service to Penguin and could have taken his pension from the company, but after the party in 1967 at which they celebrated twenty-one years of the *BoE* he chose to soldier on. Denis Evinson remembered visiting him at the Bloomsbury Square office: 'There was a framed diagram on the wall of England and Wales with the counties all marked off, coloured in red after they had been completed.' Red had now advanced across more than two-thirds of the map, but Pevsner was showing signs of fatigue. 'I sense a certain weariness in the learned and precise recitals of diagonal projections, many-shafted crossing arches, etc.,' wrote Sir Reresby Sitwell, reviewing *Cheshire* for the *Architectural Review* in July 1972.

Lancashire had perhaps taken its toll. It was a county he had feared in advance, too large to be treated in a single volume and too diverse to be easily characterised in the introduction to the main text. North Lancashire was rural and had generous compensations in the form of the Lakes, but the industrial south filled him with dread, partly because he anticipated ugliness and pollution, partly because he was acutely aware of the weight of material and the abundance of Victorian buildings in particular. The audience for Victorian architecture had been growing steadily – *South Lancashire* would be dedicated to 'all those who give so generously of their time and energy to the maintenance and development of the VICTORIAN SOCIETY' – and with it the pressure to include more than simply the very best buildings. The result was a journey round Lancashire in 1967 that took five weeks rather than the usual three and a half and left him exhausted. The driver, Tom Wesley, who had been one of the editors of *Cambridge New Architecture* in 1964, recorded: 'I drove him round the Manchester area in a never to be forgotten fifteen continuous days, Pevsner seemed not to know the concept of a week-end,' but he added that when he dropped him off in the middle of the city, Pevsner was visibly shaking.

'What have you done to Lancashire?' William Morris had asked in 1883. 'Were not the brown moors and the meadows, the clear streams and the sunny skies, wealth?' Eighty years later, for all that he had prepared himself for the destruction brought about by industrialisation, Pevsner could not avoid being depressed by the scale of it and the crassness of much of the new building that had accompanied it. His principal concern in landscape or townscape was organic unity. He cared less what the individual elements actually were than whether they had life and were combined harmoniously. He reacted against ugliness, but he disliked meanness, muddle, carelessness, compromise and selfishness even more. Lack of neighbourliness was the arch-crime.

South Lancashire, wrote Pevsner in his foreword, was 'the most difficult area I have ever had to describe'. For once his nouns are as emphatic as his adjectives – 'disgrace', 'shame', 'parasite', 'affront', 'outrage', 'defeat' – and adjectives continue to leap out: 'scandalous', 'painful', 'embarrassing', 'despicable', 'unpardonable', 'philistine', 'stupid' and, over and over again, 'mean'. His main targets were Manchester Corporation and Liverpool University, both guilty of destroying good buildings on a grand scale and of replacing them either with characterless mediocrity or with aggressive ostentation.

'To see house after house decaying, neglected, pulled down or beyond repair,' he wrote in Manchester, 'leaves one speechless with incomprehension and anger.' Hough End Hall, for example, was the home of the Mosley family in Chorlton-cum-Hardy for 400 years. 'The Corporation has not done anything to preserve it. Yet it is, or was, the best, the only major Elizabethan mansion of Manchester, red brick, on an E-plan, with mullioned and transomed windows and gables. It is an act of unpardonable callousness. At the time of writing the roof is open to the skies, and the porch has collapsed.'* In Liverpool the mighty Cotton Exchange, built in 1906 by H.A. Matear and F.W. Simon, had just lost its face, to be fronted by a dismal building for British Telecom, 'yet another act of civic vandalism'.

Almost worse than what was coming down were the new buildings that were going up: Pevsner no longer gave marks for effort. 'The historian in these evaluations turns into the critic. Users will have to accept that; they will have to take the rough with the smooth, just as I have to take the rough of Brutalism of the sixties with the smooth of the International Style of the thirties.'[6]

'New churches are springing up everywhere – especially for Catholic worship. Their hyperbolic paraboloid roofs, jabbing at you, their irregular plans, their abstract concrete patterns attack you in nearly all the new housing estates. The best, as history will perhaps confirm, are the ones which allow contemplation and concentration, i.e. which keep quiet.' Definitely noisy was the William Temple Memorial Church in Manchester's Simonsway by George Pace, built in 1964–5. 'All praise to the clients who were willing to accept so daring a design. Much praise to the architect who had the daring to submit so uncompromisingly 1960s a design. And apologies from the author of this volume who cannot appreciate for worship so aggressive a building.'

---

*The Hall has now been restored, but is completely surrounded by office blocks. Some of the unoccupied land is used by the Greater Manchester Police horse- and dog-training centre.

As for universities, which might be expected to know better, the authorities in Manchester see-sawed between timidity and gimmickry, while Liverpool University had 'rooted itself as a parasite in the finest domestic part of the city', destroying much of the best Georgian architecture and replacing it piecemeal, without any evidence of planning and with little suggestion of a coherent sense of taste. 'The whole is not a whole but a zoo, with species after species represented . . . You stand in admiration or amazement or revulsion in front of one after the other, but no sense of *universitas* results.'

Of the Arts Faculty in Abercromby Square, he wrote, 'The concrete slabs are only approximately vertical. They deviate slightly, but at different angles, and this results in a kind of seasick feeling not suited to a library.' As for the nearby Sports Centre by Denys Lasdun, it 'endeavours just as patently to be rude to the square. Nothing could be more demonstratively anti-Georgian than these concrete posts rising diagonally with equally slanting glass walls between. Rectangularity is the ground work of the Georgian century. Mr Lasdun fully realises this, and so the building must be meant as an affront.' Lasdun was furious, and wrote to the *Times Literary Supplement*:

> Pevsner is making a dead set at a particular sort of modern architecture which differs from the sort he favoured some 40 years ago. Though this suggests a dangerous rigidity in anyone who is dealing with a living art, he is entitled to his opinions on architectural aesthetics. He is not, however, entitled to impugn architects' motives by insisting that a building was '*meant*' as an affront to its neighbours.[7]

Pevsner was taken aback, but was not inclined to retract.

> Denys Lasdun's letter shows that I have hurt him. I apologise to him through you and assure him that no insult was meant. We have known each other for a good many years and have actually argued our convictions more than once, the last time inside the Royal College of Physicians, the exterior of which in relation to Nash's Terraces I would also call an affront . . . I would call an affront in the case of an architect or a building, the facing of what is already around without making an effort to come to terms with it.[8]

'If style is the visual expression of an age, then style must matter,' Pevsner had written in 1961. He did not like restlessness or disharmony in architecture because of what it said to him about the spirit of the age. 'Having grown up during a period which had the extraordinary advantage of an increasingly unified style, it does not come easy to me to see this unity breaking down.' The modernism of the 1930s had offered him the consistency and reasonableness which, rightly or wrongly, as an adolescent he had often found lacking in his mother, and a sense of order to counter the confusion and turbulence of the Weimar years. It had given him hope for a future that would be better disposed. Architecture that was, in his eyes, aggressive, self-centred and irrational took that hope away again.

The strain of pessimism in Pevsner sits oddly with the characterisation of him as an uncritical evangelist for the new. Pleased to see slums being cleared in Manchester, he was sceptical about the quality of the buildings that took their place: 'tower lumps', he called them, constructed with 'raw concrete' and 'tinny curtain walling'. He had already begun to express his unease about high-rise building in *London except*, nearly twenty years before, writing about 'the 20th century conversion of London into a city of tenements'. He could see that towers could be mass-produced, meeting the authorities' need to show speed in finding housing solutions, and he could understand why architects might like them. 'They provide the necessary vertical accents which in the 1860s would have been the church spires . . . Where, as at Eccles and Rochdale, a whole group faces the very city centre, the effect may be challenging, and in the future may well be accepted with emotional approval.' But were they what people wanted? 'Should they be accepted as living conditions by any but bachelors, spinsters, young couples without children, and old people? Will they not be the slums of fifty years hence?'

He still had the spirit to try out some new expressions – 'swagger' (the Liver Building), 'corny' (the Tower Building), 'big-boned', 'last-gasp Gothic' – alongside the old favourites: 'restless', 'ignorant', 'crisp' (a motor showroom in Bury, glass and steel painted black, 'uncommonly crisp') and 'chi-chi'.* He could still be entertained by incongruity. He relished the joviality of the setting for trying minor offences in Widnes. 'The magistrates' court is low, the walls faced with reconstructed marble and a zigzag roof, rather gay for its purpose.' However, if he found it incongruous now to be returning to Huyton, the scene of his wartime

---

*He did not intend the reader to be in any doubt about what he meant by 'chi-chi'. In the 1932 Art Deco church of St Christopher, Norris Green, 'Its new pale Wedgwood blue and cream is unpardonable. Originally it was in strong red, orange, and purple, with the stalls red and black . . . The font is star-shaped in plan and straight in elevation and all faced with mirror-glass, this also a chi-chi touch.'

internment, as observer and judge of a sort, he did not register his emotion. 'Huyton has more than one character,' he remarks, and makes a glancing mention of housing estates before passing on.

Increasingly, he accepted more help. He had the reassurance of the successful collaboration with John Newman, who was now researching and writing entire volumes in the series. 'He is doing it supremely well,' Pevsner told Allen Lane, 'and he is young. This is to tell you that if I die suddenly, I want you to approach him for the completion of the series.'⁹ On a day-to-day basis, much of the fielding of queries could be done for him now by Judy Nairn, who invoked what she called his 'Olympian letters' only when correspondents were particularly 'hornet-like'.

However, the 'Olympian' style carried its own problems. A throwaway remark by a contributor in *Hampshire* about Bournemouth's neo-Georgian Talbot Heath School for Girls – 'surprisingly acceptable, considering its architect' – brought a protest from the son of Sir Hubert Worthington, who had died a few years previously: 'Whilst I appreciate that you don't normally admire his work, the readers . . . are left wondering if he was incompetent, or a fool.'* Holy Trinity, Oare was by Teulon, and Pevsner claimed unguardedly, 'It may well be considered the ugliest church in Wiltshire.' 'This is rather sad for us,' wrote one Oare resident reproachfully, 'as the remark is so frequently quoted to us by people in the locality.'¹⁰ 'I do sympathise with you,' replied Pevsner, obviously unrepentant, and by way of compensation added, 'In Teulon's work this kind of ugliness is an asset. Take many pictures by Picasso – surely they are intended to be ugly.'

He managed something more closely resembling an apology when, in the second edition of *Essex* in 1965, he described as 'ruinous' Ramsden Crays church near Basildon, which locals had been trying hard to save. Churchwarden Miss P.M. Clark informed him, in some distress, that two of the wardens had spent their evenings and holidays for eight months restoring it. Since then it had been in constant use and the congregation was now raising money for the roof. 'Your book has both harmed and hurt us, as the church was restored with great love and hope.' Pevsner, dismayed, wrote at once to say this was 'very embarrassing'. He sent ten pounds for the roof fund.

When the Leverhulme grant expired in 1969, two counties

---

*Crispin Worthington/NP, 12/11/67. Penguin Papers, *BoE* files, DM 1901/6. Hubert Worthington (1886–1963) trained with Edwin Lutyens. He later became Professor of Architecture at the RCA, and was one of Pevsner's predecessors as Slade lecturer in Oxford.

– Oxfordshire and Staffordshire – were left uncovered. The series needed support for another year, but to his alarm Pevsner found the Trust's new Director, Lord Murray of Newhaven, less amenable than his predecessor, Miles Clifford. Murray pointed out that although the year's overrun in time represented only about 8 per cent of the total period of the *BoE* project, the overrun in Leverhulme money would be more like 20 per cent of the entire grant. Pevsner replied in something approaching panic: 'My great problem is now of course that it must be all but impossible to get another Trust to step in for just one year. That would mean that the series would, in the end, be left incomplete by two volumes. I am getting old, and this seems really a terrible perspective.'[11] Murray relented, and Leverhulme supported the *Buildings of England* to the end.

One consequence of the tightness of funds was the inexorable rise in price of the volumes. By 1970 some of the hardback editions were selling for fifty shillings (£2.50) and the paperbacks had been abandoned altogether. Pevsner, who thoroughly regretted price increases that threatened to put the books beyond the reach of the people for whom he had always intended them, received an exasperating number of letters on the subject. Another aggravation, for writer and readers alike, was the constantly shifting format of the volumes – not the layout of the text, which remained constant, but the binding of the hardback versions, which was a recurring topic for debate and experiment in the late 1960s. Pevsner was never keen on the brown binding with green label that Allen Lane favoured. On the other hand, he was the only person who really liked the white binding with bold modern lettering that was adopted for *Cumberland and Westmorland* in 1967. Impractical for fairly obvious reasons, it was ultimately replaced with a black PVC binding, which Pevsner found uninspiring.

One consolation was that the process of revision, which Pevsner had always considered crucial, was now under way. Work had been done piecemeal on individual volumes where sales were good and reprints seemed worthwhile. Enid Radcliffe was one of the first scholars to take on what Pevsner described, accurately, as an 'intricate and thankless job'. She had struggled valiantly to combine a family life with checking his constant queries and incorporating an ever-flowing stream of amendments and additions.* In 1968 Penguin had decided there

---

*Enid Radcliffe had worked on revisions for *Cornwall*, *Essex*, *Suffolk* and *Yorkshire: The West Riding*, Elizabeth Landry on *Cambridge*.

was a need for a proper system and someone to take charge of it. Pevsner's response was to write to George Zarnecki, now Deputy Director of the Courtauld Institute, and set out exactly what he needed.[12] Penguin, he explained, had agreed to appoint someone specifically to oversee a rolling programme of revisions to at least twenty of the volumes, at a full-time salary of £1,000 per annum. The job would involve a good deal of routine emendations and corrections, but there would be some discretion as to new material and the form it should take, and it was essential to find the right person. He or she must be 'very reliable', Pevsner emphasised, 'sufficiently an all-rounder to be trusted with bits of rewriting . . . a busy bee'. Without hesitation, Zarnecki recommended Bridget Cherry, a Courtauld postgraduate who was currently employed in the Institute's photographic library, working on her thesis and looking for other jobs.[13] 'She is exactly right for it,' confirmed her Courtauld contemporary Kit Galbraith, 'breadth and depth of interest and knowledge art historical (unlike most of us Courtauld products), conscientious, clever and industrious to a very impressive degree.'

Bridget Cherry's first degree had been in history, and she had gone to the Courtauld as a medievalist, but with a wide range of interests. This combination was precisely what Pevsner was looking for, as he believed that it was easier for medievalists to pick up other topics than for others to pick up medieval architecture. 'On the whole,' adds Cherry:

I think he preferred women – more methodical, practical and unassuming, not as ready to stand on their dignity about being asked to perform humble tasks. He had worked on the principle of using research assistants as a German professor would, not in the English tradition . . . I was in a very junior position at that time, and so I accepted what had to be done . . . I didn't find it particularly difficult. I suppose I began to chafe at the bit a little later on, but as things worked out, I got more and more freedom to do what I wanted . . . I wouldn't have done it for everyone. He was special.[14]

In Pevsner's lifetime, Bridget Cherry revised *Hertfordshire, London 1: The Cities of London and Westminster, Northamptonshire, Wiltshire* and *Surrey*; after his death she would revise *Devon* and produce several further volumes in a restructured account of a greatly expanded London. In 1971 she took on the role of editor for the series.*

---

*The role was initially shared with Judy Nairn.

She began work on 19 August 1968. 'The whole purpose of my existence from his point of view was that I shouldn't bother him, really.' He wrote later to Penguin, 'I cannot imagine anybody doing [the job] more competently and giving me personally so little trouble.' Their correspondence tended to be brief and to the point. 'Dear Bridget, *Northants*. 1. I am writing to Alec Clifton-Taylor to ask his advice. 2. Forget about windmills. Yours, NP.'

Pevsner was well aware of the scale of the task she was undertaking. Twenty years on, the second editions had immeasurably more material to take into account; the RIBA drawings had now been catalogued, for example, and there was the mass of information brought in by Pevsner's repeated appeals for corrections. Contact with local authorities was more systematic, and there was ever more fieldwork and more access to primary sources. He also recognised, and was grateful for, a dedication to the job that was similar to his own. She had tackled *London 1*, he told her, 'not only with competence and resourcefulness but even with enthusiasm. Considering how finnicky [*sic*] the revision had often to be, I don't know from what hidden depths this enthusiasm can have flown.'[15]

By the beginning of 1969 Cherry was being asked to take on more complicated pieces of work, such as devising the scheme for describing new college buildings for the second edition of *Cambridge*. Pevsner asked Judy Nairn to look it over for him. 'As Wittkower said in a review of Blunt's Pelican History,' she reported, 'the mathematical disposition of the material makes orientation easy, wherever one halts.'[16] By 1970 Pevsner was pressing Cherry to put herself forward more, and invited her to write a full foreword to revised volumes under her own name. 'I am very happy with the way in which you have dealt with *Surrey*, and I can only hope that users will recognise what a tremendous improvement the second edition is against the first.'[17] He was keen to delegate to her, but urged her to keep control in her own hands when dealing with contributors. Everyone wished the record of their own particular county, town, village, manor or church to be correct, understandably. They also usually wanted it to be longer and more appreciative, and often wanted it to include categories of object that he had decided twenty years ago to exclude.

Generally speaking, Pevsner enjoyed working with women, though he was never called upon to work *for* one. When A.L. Rowse made characteristically uncharitable remarks in public about Alexandra Wedgwood as the co-author of *Warwickshire*, Pevsner was quick to point out that she had worked only on Birmingham and was not guilty of the sins Rowse attributed to her. 'Please post on my apologies to the poor young lady,' replied Rowse, 'and take home the arrows, like a good St Sebastian, to your own breast.'[18] Again, in *Oxfordshire*, when Jennifer Sherwood called the early 20th-century Manor at Sibford Gower 'a riotous nightmare' and suggested that this was also the owner's view, Pevsner stood up for her against the owner's incensed husband, who demanded to know whether she had trespassed in order to inspect the house properly or had simply glanced at it from the road.*

Unwilling to take his collaborators to task for their opinions, he was even less likely to reprove them for their mistakes, given his acute awareness of his own. When a correspondent offered an explanation of the origins of the figure of Clio that graced the garden in Wildwood Terrace, Pevsner felt bound to correct him: 'The name of the architect and the date come, no doubt, from Pevsner, and Pevsner, as usual, has proved to be wrong.'[19]

For someone who was conscientious by nature, an editor insistent on punctuality and a teacher demanding of precision, it was a feat of considerable mental toughness to trudge on with the series in the knowledge of past failures and the anticipation of future ones. He was worried by the way in which his omissions could be used to condemn buildings. '"Not mentioned in Pevsner" doesn't necessarily mean I think a building is no good. Ten to one I didn't even know it existed.' In this context, accuracy was more than simply a *desiderandum*, it was a responsibility, and achieving accuracy was getting more – rather than less – difficult. It might have become easier to gain entry to stately homes, as Geoffrey Moorhouse suggested: 'Since Professor N.B.L. Pevsner became Sir Nikolaus Pevsner in 1969, he has discovered what a snobby lot we can be; you really do get better treatment in restaurants if you're a knight; and people with houses you'd like to investigate really do smarm and rub their hands and bid you welcome if you're not just another bloody academic with a slightly foreign accent.'[20] But it was harder to get into churches, which were now routinely locked against thieves and vandals; harder to drive on roads more congested with traffic; much harder to find cheap B&B or hotel rooms without booking in advance, in competition with a growing number of tourists and commercial travellers. It was all time stolen from the real task of information-gathering.

Pevsner had always been aware of the potential for the *BoE* to be

---

*D.J. Kinnish/NP, 26/1/75. The manor was in the style of a medieval castle, with a Great Hall and Minstrels' Gallery, built c.1911 by Edwardian pageant master Frank Lascelles (born Frank Stevens), son of the vicar of Sibford Gower.

a burden. When Andor Gomme expressed his intention of doing a *Buildings of Scotland* in 1959, Pevsner encouraged him, without irony, but equally without pulling any punches: 'What a splendid idea. If you are going to do this really, you will have for the rest of your life a ball and chain round your leg. You will be alternately depressed and elated and you will of course not find a publisher to pay for it . . . Scotland has 33 counties, and although there may not be much in them I feel that, if you do it single-handed, you will need 33 years.'[21]

'It is time for the Buildings of England to come to an end,' Pevsner wrote in the *Heftchen* in August 1969. '20 years back seems little, and there is no 20 years forward.'

PART SEVEN

ENDINGS

1970S

The photograph which hung on the wall of Pevsner's office. An assistant on the *Buildings of England* had given it to him: 'It's you leaving the last church in the last county.'

CHAPTER 44

'Quite enough of that now'

The weariness and pressure that Pevsner was feeling by the start of the 1970s might well have halted another man, or at least encouraged him to slow down. As Hugh Casson remembered, 'His curiosity was so tireless and his search for new knowledge so intense it seemed unhealthy. (It would certainly have earned a calming rebuke from an English nanny: "That's quite enough of that now.")'[1] Pevsner, however, had chosen this moment to embark on a major new project: a history of building types, aimed at describing how the forms of buildings reflected their functions.

What should a railway building look like? Or a bank? How would they differ from a prison or a hospital? The relationship between form and function worked partly through evocation, most obviously in the Victorian era. 'Nineteenth-century architecture is evocative architecture. Hence for instance the preference for Gothic in churches. Buildings for education were designed to evoke the Age of Pericles or the learning of the cloister. Banks and offices liked to allude to the Renaissance palazzo – i.e. to evoke Lorenzo the Magnificent. The gaol of course had to have the motifs of the medieval castle.' But function also affected plan, so that as notions of the function of a particular type of building changed – the mental institution, say, or the prison – so did the plan and thus the appearance of those buildings.

This was a subject in which Pevsner had been interested for forty years,* one that brought together his love of classification and categorisation and his fascination with Victorian architecture, and one that marked, in his own words, 'a turn from forms per se to functions and the forms, especially of plan, they created'.[2]

In 1964 he had received an invitation from the National Gallery of Art in Washington to deliver the 1967 Mellon Lectures.† He had turned

---

*Pevsner had lectured in Göttingen on nineteenth-century building types, run a seminar series in Cordoba in 1960, and another at the Courtauld in 1964. He had studied insurance offices in the wartime 'Treasure Hunt', written articles for the *Architectural Review* on universities and libraries, and looked at railway stations as part of the battle for the Euston Arch.

†The A.W. Mellon Lectures in the Fine Arts were established by the Gallery in 1949 'to bring to the people of the United States the results of the best contemporary thought and scholarship bearing upon the subject of the Fine Arts'.

it down, because it would have required him to spend six weeks in the United States and he felt unable to take that long a break from his lecturing responsibilities at home.* Once he had retired from Birkbeck, however, he was free to accept the invitation when it was repeated for 1970, and it provided him with the opportunity at last to assemble his thoughts on Victorian building types.

The New World now frightened him. He shrank from the travelling, anxious about losing his notes or other possessions, or getting mugged, or falling ill abroad. He was reluctant to leave his own library. Its 16,000 volumes had been moved to the basement of 2 Wildwood Terrace when the upper floors had started to sag, and he liked to rearrange them at intervals. But he was being offered the chance to make the case for Victorian architecture in America, and to do so before a very wide audience. The Mellon Lectures were, like the Slade Lectures, aimed less at students, postgraduates and other scholars than at a general audience. What was more, they were both prestigious – previous speakers included Jacob Bronowski, Isaiah Berlin and Stephen Spender, besides Clark, Gombrich, Blunt and others whom Pevsner would have considered his peers – and very well paid, at more than $1,000 per lecture plus $2,500 expenses for a six-week trip.

From the moment of having taken the lectures on, however, he worried about them. Looking over the materials that documented his interest in the subject, he found that they were both copious and motley. There was no systematic examination of his topic. The preparatory notes for his Göttingen lectures, where he had imposed some structure on the material, were among the papers that had been destroyed by the fire in the Gordon Russell store in 1940.

What was worse, he wanted to offer more than could be found in the existing books on individual building types, which tended to resemble technical manuals. 'Very much of value dealing with the architectural details and planning aspects of, say, hotels or banks or museums . . . is found to be hidden in letters, diaries, and novels,' he told Anna Zádor.[3] This approach, of course, demanded precisely the kind of wide reading for which he simply did not have time. Once

---

*Pevsner consistently turned down offers of extended (and very well-paid) teaching appointments in American universities, including one from Louisiana State in 1967, another from Harvard in 1971, a professorship from Colgate University in New York State, also in 1971, and a Thomas Jefferson Professorship from the University of Virginia at Charlottesville in 1975. This was in part because he knew the preparation for American teaching had to be 'pretty elaborate', and he was uncertain that he would be able any longer to reach the standard required in the time available. NP/Horst Gerson, 30/6/69.

again he had taken on a hugely ambitious task in which, by his own exacting standards, he was bound to fall short.

Pevsner became a visiting scholar in Washington for six weeks in the spring of 1970, lecturing every Sunday evening on a pair of building types, spending his days checking and filling out his references in the Library of Congress. For light relief he visited the research library at Dumbarton Oaks and took a trip round Victorian Washington with the Society of Architectural Historians, culminating in a Victorian Supper at the Village of Cross Keys (*consommé* Balmoral, *asperges* Albert, a magic-lantern show, piano selections and Brendan Gill reading 'Exuberant Victorians'). Inevitably, he became embroiled in the conservation debates current in the city, particularly the battle to save the Old Post Office, the only good example of the Richardsonian Romanesque style in the capital and, in Pevsner's words, 'the only forceful vertical' amidst a monotonous expanse of grand imitation-classical which 'stressed the horizontal'. This campaign was successful; Pevsner, however, was not impressed by the arrangements for conservation in the United States. 'The only way you can preserve a building is by buying it. When I attended some meetings of your National Trust for Historic Preservation, I asked them why Americans don't have legislation protecting historic buildings, and was told this would interfere with private enterprise.'

It was not unusual for the Mellon Lectures to be published after their delivery, but Pevsner resolved to aim higher and turn his lectures into a more extended study, resembling the book he had always wanted to write. It would still be centred on the nineteenth century, but he wanted to add examples drawn from other centuries, and he wanted to increase the number of types with which he dealt. He had originally cut down his list from around thirty types to a dozen or so for the lectures, but now he intended to reinstate them all. In the end he settled for some twenty building types ranging from the most to the least monumental, from the most ideal to the most utilitarian: national monuments, government buildings (including houses of parliament, ministries and public offices, town halls and law courts), theatres, libraries, museums, hospitals, prisons, hotels, exchanges, banks, warehouses, offices, railway stations, market halls, exhibition buildings, shops and department stores, and factories. Schools and university buildings or concert halls were not included, because they 'would have swelled the book to unmanageable proportions'. He aimed to discuss how each building type had evolved in response to social and architectural change, but also how attitudes towards function, materials and style had altered over the years.

He had no scruple in recruiting his friends to help with his unwieldy project. To Asa Briggs, for example, then Vice Chancellor of Sussex University, he wrote:

> I find that some of the best references do not come from books on architectural history . . . Thus for instance, for hospitals Florence Nightingale plays an important part, also Zola's *Au Bonheur des Dames* and its brilliant descriptions of a new department store in Paris. You can imagine that valuable references might also be in memoirs or letters. All I would like to ask you is whether you might be so good as to remember in all your reading over the next two or three years that this is the sort of thing which I want. Put a reference on a post card and send it to me and I shall be very grateful.[4]

Nevertheless, he was troubled by an unaccustomed lethargy and indecision, and had only written around one-third of the manuscript by the beginning of 1971. 'Should I just go on reading for it – for all the year,' he queried in February, 'or should I start writing here and now, prematurely, calling for lots of later additions and alteration, but proving to myself that writing still functions?' 'I can't get into that rhythm – the library rhythm of the future – easily,' he complained in March. In August he was still struggling. 'The Mellon book depresses me. The chapters are not well enough prepared. Also moving to a new one, I leave gaps in the old one, and just the heap of matters for filing is never fully cleared, because of inertia, so it will be when all chapters are written and two hundred gaps have to be filled.'

Had he had a clear run, he might have found it easier, but of course the press of his other duties had not slackened. Pevsner had a very clear conception of the role of a senior academic. It included responding to requests, however awkward or improbable they might be, and making use of his extraordinary network of connections to help younger or less well-established scholars. 'It is quite amazing,' remarked Ralph Beyer, researching the work of the Neue Kunst Fides gallery in Dresden in the 1920s and 1930s. 'You have been able to find people and their whereabouts for me who may be able to tell me about things which took place some thirty years ago.'[5]

A report Pevsner received from his secretary while he was working on the Mellon Lectures in Washington reveals exactly how miscellaneous the demands on his time, knowledge and patience could be:

An architect from Finland has written to say that he is distressed there is no volume of the PHA on Vietnam. He has just completed a thesis for the Norwegian State School of Architecture and are you interested in seeing a copy of this. What shall I say to him? A Mr Vickers from Sheffield has written to say that he has formed . . . a society for the preservation of buildings of historic or architectural interest in the area . . . Will you be President? . . . The AR have forwarded a letter and article by Dr Wolfgang Pehnt on 'Gropius the Romantic' . . . Also from the AR comes a book from Italy called 'Citta murate e sviluppo contemporaneo' for review . . . Prof Antonetto of the Associazione Culturale Italiana in Turin wants to know if you will lecture to them on a subject of your choice between December 1970 and April 1971. I presume you won't. Am I right?[6]

'Looking back over my production during the last five years or so, I think I have written more forewords than I should have done,' he told one correspondent. 'Dovecotes are not really my line.'[7] He signed up to save the original machinery of Tower Bridge, the only surviving integrated hydraulic system in the world, and recruited John Betjeman to the cause. ('It is kind of you to allow me to be associated with this idea,' responded Betjeman, apparently without irony.*) He marched down Whitehall to 10 Downing Street with Richard Wollheim, pushing a pram full of the signatures of thousands of people who had protested against the introduction of entrance fees for museums.

One of his most persistent correspondents was a destitute Singhalese scholar, Jinadasa Vijayatunga, who sat beside him in Row L of the old Reading Room at the British Museum and enlisted his help in raising money (for himself) from a range of philanthropic foundations. Without being sanguine about the outcome of these applications, Pevsner enjoyed Vijayatunga's mangling of the English language. 'I hope to see you very soon,' he wrote to C.V. Wedgwood, a friend and committee colleague, 'and I have even got a piece of agenda. This is a reference to my neighbour at the BM Library.'[8]

A woman who had recently lost her husband wrote to tell Pevsner that, to keep herself busy, she was going to visit Exeter and the cathedral. He replied at once, urging her to take a copy of *Devon* and 'correct as carefully as you can any errors or omissions you may come across. I should really be very grateful.'[9] A ten-year-old grandson was opening a new section of the Pevsner Light Railway: 'The green loco

---

*J. Betjeman/NP, 2/12/71. The bridge is now electronically powered; the original engines are preserved in the Victorian Engine Room as part of the Tower Bridge Exhibition.

is called priemier and the black is called Margaret. I am buying another black engine and do not have the faintist idea what to call it. Have you any ideas?' Another wrote to compare notes on different types of 'spagetti'.

Pevsner's working life was still, as it had always been, an English one. In 1970, however, he agreed to take part in one of the most important international exercises in post-war urban planning, as a member of the Jerusalem Committee. Plans for a 'greater Jerusalem' as Israel's capital city had been evolving for decades, to meet the urgent need for better housing and transport, commercial redevelopment and political unification. By 1970 tension had developed between the planners, who wished to stick to the Master Plan for developing the city in stages over forty years, and a government that wished to build on the hills surrounding Jerusalem as quickly as possible, to establish the unity of the city under Israeli rule. Teddy Kollek, Mayor of Jerusalem, was a liberal and a pragmatist, who had been born in Hungary and grown up in Vienna. He was keenly aware of the interest of the outside world in the future of Jerusalem, given that Israel's annexation of the east of the city was not recognised. His vision of Jerusalem was as a world spiritual centre, under Israeli sovereignty certainly, but a place where Jews, Muslims and Christians could live in harmony. He was fighting the government's proposals to expand Jerusalem's boundaries into the Occupied Territories, which, among other issues, threatened the integrity of the Master Plan. Accordingly, he now invited some thirty foreign luminaries, including Pevsner, to take part in the Town Planning subcommittee of the main Jerusalem Committee.

The Committee was a group of around 100 international experts – educators, urban planners, economists, architects, artists, writers, journalists, scientists, publishers, clergymen, lawyers – whom Kollek had assembled as an advisory body to the Mayor. There were no Muslims, who could not join without seeming to endorse Israel's claim to rule over Jerusalem. Their religious position, if not their political stance, was represented by 'orientalist' experts chosen by Kollek.

What was being proposed in the Master Plan was a new Jerusalem eight times the size of the old city; a pedestrianised Old City; a new business centre around the Damascus Gates; and a green belt around a heavily built-up centre. The advisory group chose to ignore the political implications of a Jerusalem entirely under Israeli control, but had no intention of holding back when it came to the question of architectural quality. Should one of the most important religious centres in the world be developed as an exercise in functional modernism, complete with skyscrapers, spaghetti junctions, huge housing projects and a network of highways that cut through some of Jerusalem's most sensitive sites? Did the Master Plan not threaten to destroy the character of the Old City, a place of closeness, intricacy and continual surprises? Did it seriously propose a hotel on the Mount of Olives?

Writing to Kollek afterwards, Pevsner said, 'This is to thank you privately for having given us some unforgettable days. The City, the monuments, the weather – all was happy, only our job was not quite.'[10] There was, he commented, too little fact and too much philosophy in the group's discussions. He was probably referring to Buckminster Fuller's talk of synergy and the mystery of mass phenomena, or perhaps to Louis Kahn's invocation of 'a mystical sense of theme, a pith, a life-blood not derived from an advantageous present'. But he took particular exception to the hysterical contribution from the Italian architect Bruno Zevi, who described the Master Plan as 'collective hara kiri . . . an instrument against Israel ready for use by its enemies'.* With his talk of 'the architecture of cowardice' and 'an architecture of abdication', Zevi was in Pevsner's eyes a professional provocateur. 'If he hadn't been there, escalating himself into these inflammatory speeches, tolerance would have had a better chance.' Kollek was shaken by the criticisms. In the event, the Israeli government would press ahead with its version of the Master Plan, but the Mayor would do all he could to act on his foreign advisers' wish that Jerusalem should look and feel less like a secular capital than a spiritual centre.

Pevsner's interest in urban planning dated back to the late 1920s, when he had collected a good deal of material on German new towns and the English garden city ideal. His first visit to England in 1930 had prompted the idea of a book on 'The Making of London'. This he later reformulated, under the influence of the *Architectural Review*'s theories of the modern Picturesque, as 'Visual Planning and the City of London'. He gave a paper on the subject to the Architectural Association at the end of 1945, by which time he had produced one part of a three-part draft manuscript, complete with foreword and a dedication to Hastings. In the early 1950s he would add a second part in the form of a florilegium of supporting material.† He intended to draw

---

*Bruno Zevi (1918–2000) was an Italian architect, professor, curator, author and editor.
†Bridget Cherry points out that Pevsner's interest in planning comes out very clearly in his long account of Hampstead Garden Suburb in *Middlesex*, published in 1951.

some conclusions in a final section, but the work seems to have progressed no further: in his RIBA Gold Medal speech he would refer to his 'other unwritten book'.* However, the concern for townscape never left him, and permeates the *Buildings of England* to the end.

In his eyes, the conserving of the old was as important a part of townscape as the creation of the new. He now sat on many of the official bodies responsible for conservation. Dame Jennifer Jenkins sat with him on the Historic Buildings Council for England (a body that may have suited him, as it tended to dispense with procedural minutiae). Pevsner, she remembered, had an encyclopaedic knowledge of buildings all over the country. No matter what came up on the agenda, there was always a chance that he had seen it, and he had an astonishing visual memory. When a decision had to be made as to whether Norman Shaw's Cragside should be accepted by the National Trust and supported by a substantial grant, 'he said, in effect, "Five rooms are important, and these are they . . . In the drawing room, there is *this* furniture and *those* pictures" . . . I've no reason to suppose that he'd been there at all recently.'[11]

Within the conservation movement, however, his attitudes continued to be contentious. He had no illusions about the practical difficulties, and little patience with those who were inclined to be precious about it. When a correspondent asked him what kind of career could be made in the preservation of ancient buildings, he replied: 'Why don't you come to Bene't Street [in Cambridge] one Friday at 4.30. As you know, my lecture is at 5, and I would alas need no more than five or ten minutes to answer your question.'[12] At the centre of his pragmatic approach was the belief that while there was rarely justification for simply sweeping away the old, there was also no need to resist the new as a matter of principle.

This led him into conflict with figures such as Ivor Bulmer-Thomas, a colleague on both the Historic Buildings Council and the Redundant Churches Fund, which Bulmer-Thomas had founded. A remarkable man – an MP, government minister, athlete and the author of the standard works on Greek mathematics – Bulmer-Thomas was also an outstanding controversialist. He had played a leading role in the

---

*'Visual Planning and the City of London', printed in the *Architectural Association Journal*, 61, December 1945–January 1946. The unfinished book was finally published as *Visual Planning and the Picturesque* by the Getty Research Institute in May 2010, transcribed, edited and annotated by Mathew Aitchison, with the third part filled out by excerpting Pevsner's published works. The book has an introduction by John MacArthur and Mathew Aitchison, which locates Pevsner firmly at the centre of the Townscape movement.

formation of the Historic Churches Preservation Trust and the Friends of Friendless Churches, as well as the Redundant Churches Fund, and spent much of his time in battles with the Church Commissioners. A High Church Anglo-Catholic, he vehemently opposed the idea of converting church buildings to non-religious uses in order to prolong their lives. Pevsner, on the other hand, was on record as saying, 'Personally I favour such conversions – even if a Georgian church becomes a sports centre with a swimming pool in the nave, I maintain that it is better to have a small church in the country changed to a house to live in, than not to have the church at all.'[13]

Pevsner was capable of taking a similarly brisk attitude to secular buildings, at the risk of affronting their more reverential admirers. In the late 1960s the General Director of the Bavarian National Museum in Munich appealed to him for his support in opposing the sale of Elias Holl's baroque arsenal in Augsburg to a neighbouring department store, whose proposed renovations and extension would radically have changed the building. The director was taken aback to receive a letter that began, 'Perhaps I am much more cynical than you in Germany, but . . . I am always relieved if a commercial use can be found for an old building. This is a much more satisfactory solution, at least if you think of places like Manchester and Liverpool, than letting a building remain the responsibility of the city, which very often leads to unchecked decay . . . I can only add that I hope you will not refuse to see me ever again.'*

Closer to home, Pevsner featured in *The Times* diary for testifying on the side of the developers in the battle of Russell Square.[14] The firm of Shepheard and Epstein had produced a design for a building to replace a stretch of Late Georgian houses on the south side of Russell Square which were distinguished by having been literally 'dolled up' in terracotta by the Edwardian architect Charles Fitzroy Doll. The Royal Fine Art Commission had approved the new design, but the GLC and the London Borough of Camden were resisting it on the grounds of damage to London's Georgian heritage. Pevsner – who respected Shepheard and Epstein† – had never been an admirer of Russell Square. On his first visit to England in 1930 he had described some of its Edwardian megaliths as 'the only truly nasty things I have

---

*The Zeughaus's sale to the department store was successfully blocked after public protest. Renovated in 1978–80 as an adult education and meeting centre, it now also houses a restaurant and music school.

†In the 1950s Pevsner had commissioned Peter Shepheard to produce the illustrations for two volumes in the King Penguin series – *A Book of Ducks* (1951) and *Woodland Birds* (1955).

seen so far', and he had probably had a hand in the RFAC's decision to approve. Now he appeared at the enquiry to support the developers' application. Russell Square, he declared, was already wrecked as a piece of Georgian planning: beside the looming hotels on the east side, the west side was blighted by the tower of the Senate House, and the north side was interrupted by Denys Lasdun's Institute of Education. 'Mr Lasdun has certainly not made an effort to harmonise, and I don't blame him for it. He, like myself, may well have felt that Russell Square – aesthetically – has to be given up.' The new design, on the other hand, at least tried to be accommodating. 'The façade is at once recognisable as of today, but in its scale and its absence of decoration, even mouldings, it expresses its sympathy with the Georgian past. It closes one chapter and opens another.'

In Pevsner's own working life a chapter closed in 1970, with the ending of the Coldstream enquiry into the future of art education. The Joint Committee now had to produce its report. At the beginning of February the Committee met in Hastings, where the paragraphs on art history were substantially revised; it is not clear that Pevsner was actually present. But we do know that there was, in Pevsner's view, a progressive watering-down of the language of the report. On 19 February he announced his intention to resign. Coldstream told the Committee that he had asked Pevsner to withhold his resignation until they had been able to consider his views further, but had been unable to persuade him to change his mind. At Coldstream's behest, Pevsner agreed to write a critique that could, if necessary, be used as a minority report. This critique emerged in September 1970, with the final report, as a Note of Dissent.

The Structure of Art and Design Education in the Further Educa-tion Sector, appearing ten years after the first Coldstream report, reflected a decade of changes in education and the radicalisation of students. It moved away from the integrated modernist approach of the first report by making – or rather acknowledging – a sharper distinction between art and design and giving greater weight to the separate needs of designers. 'We now would not regard the study of fine art as necessarily central to all studies,' the Joint Committee conceded.

Sections 34–41 of the third chapter of the report dealt specifically with History of Art and Complementary Studies. 'We are in no doubt that every student's course must include some serious and relevant studies in the history of art and design.' So far, so good – but the report went on: 'How these different ingredients to the course are balanced is best left to the judgement of individual colleges . . . We believe that no less than 15 per cent of the students' total time on the Diploma course should be spent on complementary studies, including the history of art and design.' In other words, the history of art was now to be merely a part of 'complementary studies', and it was for individual schools to choose how large a part.

Pevsner believed that the Joint Committee had now weakened its recommendations on art history to the point where they could be ignored, and he used his Note of Dissent to make the point. 'I find myself unable to agree with paragraphs 34–41 of Chapter 3,' he wrote:

> not so much for what they say as for what they do not say. There is a general tendency in education at present to make tasks easy or to make them appear easy. But education is not easy and cannot be . . . The college of art according to our programme reserves only fifteen per cent of the available time for strictly intellectual or, we might say, academic pursuits. I don't want them to reserve more, but I regard the fifteen per cent as a dire necessity, provided they are looked at as intellectual disciplines. It is clarity of thought and expression, it is unbiased recognition of problems, it is the capacity for discussion and it is ultimately understanding they must achieve. But to understand one must know the facts: to know the facts one must learn the facts, and to choose relevant facts one must command a surplus of facts. That is the unpalatable truth. Unpalatable to many students, unpalatable also to some of the staffs teaching studio subjects. Chapter 3 fails in my opinion by keeping silent on this truth.

Pevsner was not uniquely starchy in his insistence on the need for intellectual discipline. Gombrich had similar feelings about some degree of academic rigour in art education:

> They should acquire that chronological scaffolding which helps us all to keep some minimum order in our image of the past. As many of them have been very badly taught at school, or not at all, this minimum may well cost them those drops of sweat and tears that may be psychologically good for them . . . We must fix the line somewhere and hold it. (I may have told you how I once failed in this attempt, when I told my students at the Slade that nobody would pass who could not spell Leonardo, Raphael and Michelangelo; I could not carry out that threat without sensational slaughter.)[15]

Ultimately the Joint Committee's report was overtaken by events. The Minister of Education, Margaret Thatcher, refused to accept it *in toto*. Meanwhile the chairman of the fine arts panel of the Coldstream Committee and most of its members resigned in protest over the continuing incorporation of art schools in the new polytechnics, and the Committee was dissolved in 1971, a year after Pevsner had left.

Pevsner was deeply disappointed by what he saw as the failure of the project. At the practical level, he worried that if the history of art were not compulsory in art schools, it would not be taken seriously or taught properly. On the personal level, the Joint Committee had effectively dismissed one of his most profound convictions as a scholar and a teacher: that the study of art history could benefit not only students of other academic subjects but those preparing to go into society as artists, designers and architects.

He may also have taken the implicit questioning of the Bauhaus ideal – in the Committee's acceptance that art and design should no longer be treated so closely together – as a symptom of a more general decline of faith in modernism. His hopes of the 1940s and 1950s were receding. Meanwhile the *Architectural Review* had been having financial difficulties. H. de Cronin Hastings embarked on a grandiose project to 'redefine architecture' with a major feature entitled 'Manplan', offering photographic coverage of the ills of modern Britain accompanied by essays, mostly his own, furnishing solutions to the frustrations of contemporary life. Jim Richards, who was not convinced by the 'Manplan' project, found his editorship undermined by his proprietor.

By the end of 1970 it would be acknowledged that the 'Manplan' issues had not been a great success, and the *Review* reverted permanently to the old pattern. However, in the meantime, perhaps partly as a means of saving face, Hastings had decided to reorganise the entire editorial structure. The staff of the various different publications within the Architectural Press were now to work collectively on all of them. Each publication would continue to have its own editor, but all would work to an overall chairman of editors – and this was to be Colin Boyne, who had once been a protégé of Richards.* Richards discovered from an announcement on the *Review*'s noticeboard that he had retired as editor. He was not due to retire until 1972, and did not in the least want to go.

Pevsner gave notice at once of his intention to resign from the Advisory Board. 'I am convinced that no editor of the AR should be

---

*Colin Boyne (1921–2006) edited the *Architects' Journal* from 1949 to 1970 and chaired the editorial board of both *Journal* and *Review* from 1970 to 1974.

as old as 68,' he wrote to Hastings in July 1970. 'This time you can take it that my decision is irrevocable.' Hastings was not entirely candid in his explanation of events.[16] 'The AR has arrived at a crossroads,' he declared, 'not a very nice-looking one, that will demand new decisions all round. The trouble is we are all 68 (86 in the case of my psyche) even Jim who, as you know, has been bullying me for some time to make an honest old-age pensioner of him.'[17]

It was perhaps a sign of a guilty conscience that Hastings kept the sixty-three-year-old Richards on the staff for two years until he did actually qualify for his pension. 'It is all very odd,' Richards told Pevsner. 'I dutifully come into the office every day. There is generally a letter or two to answer. (The AR post, as instructed, is never shown to me.)'[18] Hastings wrote Pevsner a genuinely affectionate and regretful letter: 'To describe the AR's debt to you would be impossible, so would the debt we all owe you for your genuinely selfless work – gaining, as you have, nothing from the transaction beyond a boy scout's pleasure in a good deed . . . It is a pleasure, dear Sir Nikolaus, to have had so many years of friendship with you. I don't believe we've ever had a harsh word. And I trust we never shall. Yours, in admiration and *gratitude*, de Cronin.'[19]

Pevsner's resignation from the *Review* took effect on 1 January 1971, the day that Richards ceased to be its editor. He would continue to contribute reviews and articles on a freelance basis, but less often. Under a multiplicity of editors the *Review* would give more space to new buildings, in order to appeal to potential advertisers, and much less space to history. Meanwhile, Richards lived, in Pevsner's words, through 'a terrible time – truly terrible as well as disgusting', when his sixteen-year-old son was killed in a road accident in 1971. Hastings planned with Pevsner to provide distraction: 'We must rescue him if we can with efforts for a knighthood.' Jim Richards became Sir James in 1972. The following year Hastings himself retired, and the *Architectural Review* that Pevsner had known was gone.

Penguin too was changing. Pevsner had had his occasional irritations with the firm. He had very much regretted their decision to discontinue the paperback editions of the *BoE*, which went against all his idealistic hopes for putting England's architectural heritage in every schoolboy's pocket, and he was infuriated when they let individual volumes go out of print. But he had never had any serious arguments with Allen Lane, and was deeply distressed when Lane died in July 1970 after a cruelly prolonged struggle with bowel cancer.

Meanwhile Penguin pressed for two volumes a year. As the relentless flow of manuscripts continued, Pevsner advertised in *The Times* for a new typist. He got eighty replies. The applicant who had previously typed for Sir Julian Huxley recommended herself as being practised in dealing with unintelligible vocabulary, while those who had served Anna Magnani and Lionel Bart were used to transcribing notes scribbled in darkened theatres. One lady was a medical secretary from St Bartholomew's Hospital who had cut her typing teeth on doctors' handwriting; another, a subeditor on *House and Garden*, declared: 'I have been married to an illegible architect for 17 years and I am reconciled to the Englishness of his particular art, so I feel I could cope.' The Publications Secretary from the Institute of Psycho-Analysis had had experience with 'peculiar manuscripts'. And then there were the vicar's wife whose Sundays were 'a desert', the man selling automatic typewriters, the graphologist and ghost writer, and a man who owned that he could not actually type, but offered to decipher Pevsner's writing for the benefit of his secretary.

Tempted though he must have been by some of these prospects, Pevsner gave the job to Marjorie Sutherland, who had just retired from running Miss Pate's Secretarial Agency in Cambridge, where she had specialised in dons' manuscripts. She now lived on her earnings from typing, at a pound an hour. A Scot, Miss Sutherland was a woman after Pevsner's own heart, precise, level-headed and hard-working. 'I tend to be conservative in estimations [of the length of the working day],' she told him, 'preferring in practice to better a moderate promise than fall down on too high an aim.'[20] She had some practical suggestions for him: he should perhaps put unfamiliar names in capitals, make dates clearer, leave a line before a new paragraph, and watch out for his writing getting smaller at the end of a page. Even with all these improvements, she commented, she had to work in good daylight, quite often with a magnifying glass.

There may still have been half a dozen volumes waiting to be published, but in 1970 Pevsner's travels came to an end with Staffordshire. Edward Hubbard was with him as driver and assistant, having also prepared the research, and they were accompanied for the last days by Geoffrey Moorhouse, who had travelled with the Pevsners ten years before and now wanted to record the end of the epic journey. 'This time he was a bit more tense than I remember him years ago, when he was investigating Norfolk,' wrote Moorhouse.[21] 'A hand was inclined to tremble and a foot to drag – though maybe that was the result of the first and last dog in England to have bitten him.' In the Peak District they travelled 'across a valley weird with spiky hillocks' to Longnor, where Pevsner was most impressed by the building next to the market hall. '"This," he said, "will be my last gents." And went inside.'

He was very tired by the time he reached the last building of all:

> Sheen. PARSONAGE. By *Butterfield*, 1852, and if anyone wants an example of how Butterfield dealt with a parsonage of some size, here it is . . . It is all personal and forceful, but what one would dearly love to know is this: Would even the most enthusiastic young Victorian fan choose to live in this house with the same unhesitating delight with which the young of a generation before would have moved into a Georgian house of the same size?

On his office wall Pevsner had for years had a black-and-white photograph showing an old man in a grey bowler hat, with walking stick, hobbling away down a churchyard, with the church tower framed in the view behind him. An assistant had given it to him: 'It's you leaving the last church in the last county.' The *Guardian* had sent a photographer for Pevsner to re-create that pose outside the Sheen church. 'He came round the back of the building,' recorded Moorhouse:

> writing on the clipboard as he walked, then paused to examine a window before making another note. 'Does this give you great thrills of emotion?', he asked over his shoulder. 'Small ones', I said. 'Does it you?' He didn't even shake his head. 'No', was all he replied. Then he turned, putting his ball-point away, and picked up a small conker from the drive. 'My souvenir', he said, and grinned. He shoved it in his pocket, got into the car, and the saga was done. What a man. And what a performance.[22]

But the hand that trembled and the foot that dragged were signs that even Pevsner's energy was not inexhaustible. For some time he had been finding it more difficult to control his handwriting. 'Don't tell him but I swear his writing is getting smaller,' Mary Mouat wrote to Judith Tabner, as one of his secretaries to another, in April 1969. Kathleen Cox, who had typed for him seven years before, stood in again briefly and found her task much more difficult. When Pevsner retired from Birkbeck later that year, one of his presents from his students was a mechanical pencil; he confided later that he wished it had been thicker. He also now tended to choose tagliatelle when out for a meal, as it was easier to handle than spaghetti.

He summarised his ailments in the *Heftchen*: 'At 68 some functions begin to work less well. Digestion hardens, and that becomes a problem never quite forgotten. My hearing gives some trouble too. Yet all minor – no serious ailment yet, no illness.' Three months later he was not so sanguine. 'Certain signs of running down have appeared . . . Heavy carrying upsets my back. I walk more slowly too . . . Hearing worse – no good in tube or at parties.'

On Valentine's Day 1971 he recorded: 'The first knock at the door. It is Parkinson's, says the specialist. A light case. But who can say? Does it mean incapacitation? Hands – no writing, no dressing even?' Curiously, John Betjeman was suffering from the first symptoms of Parkinson's disease at much the same time. He described them vividly in a letter to James Lees-Milne: 'I have had a most interesting thing, a sort of mental disintegration, in which I lost my balance, couldn't keep my temper, telephone bell sounded like a dagger in my heart, and my lack of self-confidence was such that I couldn't write a letter, let alone an article, and felt I would never write a book or a poem again.'[23] Betjeman would later write for the Parkinson's Disease Society of the feeling of 'being unable to move your limbs at all or at least with difficulty; being unable to cross a room, let alone a street, without "freezing"; being always terrified lest you fall. These are made far worse and more terrible by the fact that whilst our bodies fail us our minds remain alert and we are aware of our deterioration.'

Parkinson's disease is incurable. The symptoms can be managed with drugs, but the side-effects can be severe, including nausea, palpitations, hair loss, anxiety and hallucinations, and after a short time Pevsner stopped taking the L-DOPA that he had been prescribed, because he could not bear the horrible dreams which the pills induced.[24] 'What remains is a steady depression such as I hardly know,' he reported. 'I have the wobbles,' he told Ernst Gombrich, meeting him at Golders Green station.

'Only now do I realise fully and every day that I am in Act Five,' he told the *Heftchen*, 'that in one's seventieth year one must look at the future as a present. The thought of disappearing makes me generally depressed . . . It's an odd thing, but this shock has suddenly made me old, i.e. I realise every day that 69 is quite a high figure, that if I die people will say: Well, after all, he was nearly seventy, that only a few years are left, that this is a race I'll lose with 100% certainty. Of course there is no reason to dread extinction, yet one does.'[25]

CHAPTER 45

'Give me time, eternal gods'

In the knowledge that his resources of energy were limited by Parkinson's disease and going to remain so, Pevsner began to husband them more carefully than before. In 1969 he had written to an admirer from Syracuse, New York, who had suggested that he might like to correspond with her mother, a widow, as she had a 'mystic intuition' that they would get on. 'Thank you for your letter,' he wrote:

> which does not only tell me about your mother, but also about yourself. If you have a very good mother, your mother has a very good daughter. Forgive me all the same if I don't do what you want me to. I am a man with far too little margin. That is a bad thing I know. But it has come that way, especially after my wife died . . . I am not lonely as I have three married children living within fifty yards of me. That is a great blessing and it enables me to devote my working time so undisturbedly to what I want to do – teaching in the universities, working on my books and joining in committees on the preservation of worthwhile buildings. All this explains, I hope, my reluctance to commit myself further.

The margin now became even narrower.

Home life was austere, but not bleak. He was not much interested in *gourmandise* – 'Grapes?' his cousin Ellen Dreesen remembered him saying, 'I buy them for Christmas' – and rarely ate out by himself. Given the choice, he preferred to eat with his children down the road, and he had always enjoyed having the company of his grandchildren in his home. 'He had a little pile of toys and books and bricks and a railway set up for them in his sitting room,' remembered Jane Fawcett. 'They could come and play there whenever they liked, even when he was working.' An American friend remembered being sent two pieces of string, carefully measured, as a guide to the purchasing of postmen's caps for them. He lent one grandchild the money (£300) to buy a car, and sent another some port and the money to buy a leather coat.

Lola's clothes were still in the cupboards. 'Proust, *Guermantes*, II 273: "It is true that people sometimes do for the dead what they would not have done for the living",' he had written in the *Heftchen*. 'A propos my little pieties for ∂ now.'[1] 'From 8 to 9 I always read,' he recorded in 1972. 'It is alarming that in doing so I always face a large mirror which shows me a man of 70 and a rather *triste* looking one. Moreover there are also Lola's photographs looking at me, and they are of a Lola nearly 10 years younger than I am.'

At home, Pevsner was surrounded by things that were important to him without being particularly valuable: a painting of the country near Naumburg, say, and a doodle by Henry Moore, which Pevsner had filched. 'Dear Henry,' wrote Pevsner:

> ... This is a minute doodle which you did sitting next to me at an Arts Council meeting in 1959. At the risk of interpreting entirely wrongly, what I should say is that you were doodling starting from the top. However, when you got near the present bottom you must suddenly have realised that what you had done was a monument, and so you quickly drew a pedestal and a bit of shadow, and then turned away from it. Am I entirely wrong?[2]

The house was no longer empty. In 1972 he advertised in most of the colleges of London University for a lodger. He was offering a room with its own bathroom and the use of cooking facilities, at a price of £1 per week to cover the electricity bill. 'Rent-free,' he wrote, 'against seven hours a week keeping the house clean and tidy. Sex and race are irrelevant.' (A Ghanaian botanist and a Chinese economist were among the students who took up the offer and provided sporadic company.)

One acquaintance said that Pevsner was punctilious at death-bed visits because he felt guilty about not being a more attentive friend in life, but there were people with whom he never fell out of touch. Lis Knauth, music teacher, Annie Pevsner's confidante and the translator of *Pioneers* into German, was still 'oldest and most faithful of friends'. She read the German edition of his collected articles for him in 1972. Alec Clifton-Taylor, living a more elegant life in a smart little house in South Kensington, was a fellow-enthusiast for the art of *looking* and a regular correspondent. Joan Evans was a friend whom he had admired both as a scholar and as a person for some forty years, and he leapt to her defence when one of his former pupils wrote a harsh review of her latest book, dismissing it as reading like a collection of file cards, badly organised and scrappy. Dame Joan was almost eighty and ill, and it is not improbable that the book may have been less than successful, but Pevsner did not see that as a reason for saying so publicly. 'That was a beastly review,' he wrote. 'You should have taken up 25% of the space and should have said that here is a book dealing for the first time with an interesting subject neglected so far . . . What worries me is that such is the passing glory of this world . . . your generation no longer connects Joan Evans with a person of her kindness, her generosity and her reasonableness.'*

Pevsner himself remained generous. To one correspondent writing a book on secret passages and underground tunnels in English country houses, he contributed the tunnel running from Ince Castle down to a Cornish smugglers' beach, and added, 'I don't know of any work on drainage over the centuries, and it would be extremely valuable if you did one.'³ He only held back if he suspected idleness or opportunism; encouraging the work of other people was one thing, doing it for them was another. An architectural student working on Butterfield sent him a questionnaire designed to 'elicit the views of modern architects and historians' and got a dusty answer: 'I do not approve of a thesis such as yours and the kind of preparation you propose . . . What you are trying to do is to get all your material served by people and, what is more, served in the terms of a questionnaire which would call forth only the most elementary answers, unless somebody like myself would write three or four pages.'

Pevsner's mood was dark as he set off with reluctance to America in the spring of 1972. He was combining lecturing on Gothic architecture at Columbia University with visits to the Avery Architectural Library in New York to check references for the *Building Types* book, then delivering a series of eight lectures as fundraisers for the Victorian Society,† before moving on to Ann Arbor, Michigan, to deliver the Raoul Wallenberg Memorial Lecture on 'Architecture as a humane art'. 'I'm a coward,' he confided to the *Heftchen* in January 1972. 'I've always been one. As a boy in jumping into the water, and later in declaring love. And now – everything – a speech, a meeting, social occasions, and seven weeks in New York, the insecurity, the hotel, the flights, the organising of myself . . . My memory is reduced to a shocking degree. People must notice it, and it's bad for official positions I have.' 'Old Age does not bother me lecturing,' he told his secretary Judith Tabner, after arriving in New York, 'but tuxedo on

---

*He had had personal experience of her generosity when on one birthday she gave him a medieval silver signet ring engraved with the Prince of Wales's feathers; he showed it to his Birkbeck students in the break between lectures, excited and moved. Emily Lane to the author, May 2009.

†His fee on the Vic Soc tour was $1,000 per lecture. The bulk of the money went to the Society, which used $6,000 to launch a major fundraising campaign.

Thursday is a mountain, starting in the Public Library is a mountain, finding my way in a railroad station is a mountain . . . To whisper the truth to you All: I'll be glad when it's over.'[4]

His apprehension had been intensified just before he left by another alarm about his health and the prospect of tests when he returned. 'Prostate – problem of old men, but also a favourite seat of cancer . . . What frightens me is pain, and I must tell the doctor to tell my children to dope me – in the end out of existence.' For the first few days in New York he was jet-lagged and depressed, suffering from nosebleeds and unhappy in the hotel near Columbia. He could not reach it without walking across the campus, which he had, ominously, been advised to avoid crossing after dark. 'The trouble is that one cannot recognise evil-doers, as the students look so thoroughly disreputable,' he complained to Judith Tabner, and he was not amused at having to take his meals in a student hostel. His room had a view 'over slums' and the campus as a whole was 'visually a total failure'. Even work could not cheer him. His first lecture on the English Gothic was not as good as it should have been, but the audience was not discerning enough to notice. One of his 'elderly fan women' had told him 'it was like drinking at the spring of Castalia to hear you lecturing'. 'Why can't one of the pretty girls who swarm around here in hundreds say so?' he grumbled.

Despite his gloomy prognostications, the audience for the second lecture reached 800, a record attendance for Columbia. He settled into the Avery Library, clocking in every day at 9 a.m. to Alcove 2. He was introduced to Alistair Cooke – 'my broadcasting pin-up' – at 19 Gramercy Park, one of New York's greatest private houses, and dined at the Harvard Club with the social historian J.H. Plumb.* Less enjoyable was the 'tuxedo' evening, the Annual General Meeting of the Pierpont Morgan Library at which he was the speaker of honour. He had forgotten his patent-leather shoes and felt dingy – shades of his first visit to England. 'I have never seen so much money together,' he told Tabner.

In Princeton, on the Victorian Society tour, his slides of 'Victorian Mansions' were stolen out of his briefcase as he dined, to be found later that night, unharmed, in a flower bed. The slides were kept in a box labelled 'Bendick's Bittermints'; Pevsner liked to picture the

---

*The host at 19 Gramercy Park was Ben Sonnenberg, a pioneer of public relations in the US. He had made the house into a salon for both public and private entertaining. Professor J.H. Plumb (1901–2001) was a British historian specialising in the eighteenth century, a gifted populariser, a generous host and *bon vivant*, famously rude and much quoted.

disappointment of the thief. His spirits sank again as he flew on to Ann Arbor. 'In the plane I feel rather sick, due to vicious onion in my food. I try to read a thesis, and I worry, because the lecture . . . is bound to be feeble. "Architecture as a humane art" – why must people invent such titles. It is bound to lead to waffling.'

Humanity was, in fact, an obligatory theme for the Raoul Wallenberg Memorial Lecture, the purpose being to honour the extraordinary efforts made by Wallenberg, an Ann Arbor architectural alumnus, to save thousands of Jews in Hungary during the war.* And, in the event, the lecture was one of Pevsner's most lucid expositions. Closed-circuit television had to be used to relay it to the dozens who had tried and failed to get into the main auditorium. 'Is architecture a humane art?' Pevsner asked. Yes, he answered, when buildings work and are seen to work for the people they are aimed at, when they make people happy and when they express human warmth. They need not be strictly rational – and here he would seem to have come round at last to Ronchamp:

> The purpose of a pilgrimage chapel is entirely spiritual. It has the purpose of being conducive to worship, and however irregular, however fantastical, this little building, I have no hesitation in believing, does just this. You arrive, it hits you hard, you are drawn into it, the windows all of crazy shapes bring in an unexpected flickering light, and everything is ready for what the faithful are looking for. So in this case the function of the building and the totally irrational way in which it is expressed are in harmony and perhaps even more than that.†

Pevsner was tiring now, in the face of what he had earlier described as 'well-meaning but tyrannical hospitality which can be quite stupefying in its warmth and insistence'. The last stop was Washington, where he returned to Dumbarton Oaks, this time as the chair of a colloquium on Picturesque gardening. 'Even the wood pigeons say the same things as two years ago,' he wrote. 'Only this time I have a suite and my

---

*The Swedish businessman Raoul Wallenberg had used his position as First Secretary of the (neutral) Swedish legation in Budapest to issue protective passes and establish safe-houses for Jews trying to avoid deportation to Auschwitz-Birkenau. He was arrested by the Russians in January 1945 and was reported to have died in prison in Moscow in 1947.
†It is tempting to suppose that Pevsner's earlier opposition to the chapel was based on photographs, his conversion on visiting it in person, but it is not possible to establish when he first went to Ronchamp.

own entrance.' His role was to guide the conversation, edit the transcript and then write a conclusion to the subsequent publication. The colloquium itself was chatty and informal, though Pevsner made himself stick to procedure. Participants, he said, must introduce themselves when speaking from the floor, 'even if you've been my friend for thirty years'. Writing up the proceedings, however, was another matter. Pevsner found himself frequently at odds with Elisabeth MacDougall, the Director of Studies in Landscape Architecture at Dumbarton Oaks. One of the first scholars to apply the principles of art history to the study of gardens, she was thorough, disciplined and, on occasion, sharp-tongued. She took him to task for inserting an account of the origins of his own interest in the Picturesque, and subedited his text with a vigour to which he was unaccustomed. His job, she pointed out, was to pull together the various threads of the discussion and present its outcome. 'The trouble, of course, is that the symposium did not really reach what you might present as a result,' he commented, with a trace of umbrage.[5]

When he got back, he had a doctor's examination which left him in acute distress. On 3 June 1972, he scrawled, almost illegibly, 'It is to be an operation, most probably cancer. Does it mean that the Mellon book can't be completed? And all the other commitments? . . . Six days waiting . . . and the pressure ahead. And the shaking hands. It seems to head for a collapse.'

Still he concealed his fears from others. During the wait for the results of his tests, he chaired a meeting of the Victorian Society and mentioned the operation, without saying what its purpose might be. Ian Sutton remembers him saying cheerfully to the committee, 'As you know, I am a scheduled ancient monument . . . No major internal alterations are permitted. I look to you to ensure my preservation.' At the end of the week, he got the results. 'After all – operation, yes, but harmless. Really no likeliness of cancer. So the above scribble is a bit ridiculous.' (His surgeon was Mr Turner Warwick and, by chance, the attending Senior Registrar was Peter Worth, son of Pevsner's old friend Leopold.)

While Pevsner was in the Middlesex Hospital convalescing, another of his committees, the Royal Fine Art Commission, was facing a barrage of criticism in the press for approving Basil Spence's designs for a commercial office block at 50 Queen Anne's Gate.* When the plans

---

*The building was originally put up as a speculative office development, but was occupied by the Home Office from 1978–2004 and now houses the Justice Department.

for the new block had first gone before the RFAC in 1959, they showed a building 240 feet high, and the Commission asked Spence to reconsider. The plans reappeared five years later, considerably scaled down to a height that was less than the existing building on the site, and the Commission stated that the design was 'on the right lines'. When the plans finally came back to the RFAC in 1968, by which time Pevsner had become a member, the Commission asked for a further slight reduction in height, but approved them. Now, four years on, the plans had been made public, provoking a furore in the architectural press – the proposed new building was just down the road from the offices of the *Architectural Review* in Queen Anne's Gate – which soon travelled to the mainstream media.

The main grounds for objection were the Brutalist bulk of the new building and its dumb-bell appearance, with heavy protrusions at top and bottom. 'I can only repeat what I have always said,' wrote Pevsner from his hospital bed to Frank Fielden at the RFAC. 'With the Watney development at the North-west end of Victoria Street and the new cliffs going up along the South side, there seems to be to me no reason whatsoever to object to Basil's new Queen Anne's Mansions. I would like you to make sure that Basil understands this. Partly because he knows quite well that his design is not my beau ideal. That however has nothing to do with it.'[6] On 10 July he wrote to *The Times*: 'Victoria Street and its environs are 1970-monumental . . . Sir Basil Spence's building makes a very convincing accent where it stands. As it happens, it adjoins also an exquisite group of 18th-century houses. These houses must of course be preserved, but development in the seventies . . . cannot be vetoed on this account.' He got a grateful response from Spence: 'Joan and I were distressed that your wonderful letter to "The Times" came from hospital . . . In times of stress like this one appreciates the action of friends.'[7]

On 12 July, Pevsner was discharged, with relief; prior to 1972 he had only ever spent a single day in hospital. 'You can imagine how sad I was when I arrived at the hospital,' he wrote to Eunice Frost, 'to realise that this was the very place where I visited Allen [Lane].'[8] Two weeks later he was impatient. 'Sigh – convalescence is slower than I had thought. It deprives me of the summer weeks of work for the Mellon book. All I can do is make lists of what is still to be done. Hundreds of bits. Depressing also is to feel one in the descendant: few teeth left, tremor makes normal writing and eating of e.g. soup impossible.'

* * *

When he was interviewed by Mavis Nicholson on Thames Television the following year, the symptoms of Parkinson's disease were more noticeable.* The shaking hand was held firmly in his lap by the good one and there were signs that shaving had become more difficult. But his glance was sharp and his speech distinct, though he stumbled over idioms. (If he had not been so single-minded in the quest to finish the *Buildings of England*, he observed, the series might have dragged on for fifty years and he would be 'growing daisies'.) He delivered a talk in French at around this time, on 'Recent Trends in Architecture', and resorted to tiny prompts in the margin for key phrases: 'du moins – at least', 'd'abord – first of all', 'd'ailleurs – by the way'. '*La qualité de mon propre français – vous ne pouvez pas imaginer,*' he confessed, acknowledging the help of Dieter and his wife Florence in polishing the text. Some Germanic word orders were creeping into his writing. 'Ellastone. CALWICH ABBEY TEMPLE. The dome is surrounded by four a little clumsy square pinnacles with ball finials.' Was he still capable of writing a book? he wondered, as he struggled with a protracted period of alterations, additions and corrections to the unwieldy manuscript of *Building Types*.

He was still in demand as a lecturer. The weekly visits to Cambridge continued virtually uninterrupted. Forty-two years after his article on 'Social Ideals amongst Creative Artists', he spoke at the National Portrait Gallery on 'Artists' Fraternities in the 19th Century'. In April 1973, he embarked on yet another lecture tour of the United States for the Victorian Society, accompanied by the Duke of Gloucester to reinforce the Society's appeal for funds.

Honours kept coming, one of the most prized an honorary degree from the Open University, which he took to be a tribute to his Birkbeck teaching, providing higher education for people with jobs. His acceptance speech was revealing: 'Your courses make Cambridge and Oxford appear a sinecure, and their class teaching methods old-fashioned,' he declared:

Here instead there is a spirit of innovation and experiment – technically and spiritually, and the intensity of training you offer is unmatched . . . The Open University attracts men and women 'without reference to age, occupation and conditions'. Some of the students seek 'material benefit', but others come because of the 'pleasure flowing from mental exercise'; for 'Knowledge is its own reward'. Knowledge is its own reward. If you want a motto, here it is.

Good Afternoon, Thames TV, 9/10/73.

Campaigns, too, continued. The days of his admiration for the M1 were long gone. 'Roads . . . do more damage than all the rest put together,' he wrote angrily. 'Roads eat up space, they make thousands of houses almost but not quite uninhabitable and, under the pretext of need, they sanction the demolition of countless buildings worth preservation or at least conservation.'[9] He fought vainly against the underground car park outside his office in Bloomsbury Square, without holding any brief whatsoever for the overground version. 'It does arouse despair and melancholy to watch so much being torn down for a very temporary vehicle,' he told Kenneth Allsop in 1973. 'In 50 years we shall have a completely different transport system. And standing everywhere will be those great slabs of concrete – tombstones for the obsolete car.'[10]

He had a personal interest in one of the cases being pursued by the Victorian Society in 1973. Dovers Court, Fred Griggs's Arts and Crafts mansion in Chipping Campden where Tom and Dieter had lived as evacuees at the outbreak of war, was under threat. When at last the house had been completed, it had been sold to the painter Frank Brangwyn, who wanted to turn it into a home for aged artists. Brangwyn, himself elderly, rarely visited his purchase and sold it again in 1943. After the war the mansion had been badly damaged by fire and left semi-derelict until 1972, when it was bought by a developer; he was now busy constructing small Cotswold-type houses in the grounds, ranged along a cul-de-sac called Griggs Close, and the Victorian Society was seriously concerned for the future of the Court itself. They urged that it should be listed and the outside restored, with as much as possible of the interior preserved, but the request was denied, on the grounds that buildings built after 1914 were still not usually eligible for formal listing.* Pevsner, perhaps remembering the first weeks of the war when he had bicycled every day from Dovers Court to the Gordon Russell offices in Broadway, had a quiet word with the relevant authorities. The mansion was listed on 4 July 1973.

His intervention was perhaps less helpful in the case of St Katharine Docks. The building firm Taylor Woodrow had been contracted by the GLC to develop the abandoned site as a mixture of homes, offices and leisure facilities. Among the surviving buildings were some fine neo-classical dock offices and a group of magnificent six-storey warehouses, of which one block – Block B, by Thomas Telford and Philip Hardwick – was listed. Taylor Woodrow planned to turn this block into a British

---

*Ironically Gordon Russell himself would seem to have been implicated in repudiating the idea of listing Dovers Court for its historical associations. Case file in the Victorian Society Archives at the London Metropolitan Archives. LMA 4460/01/13/012.

Export Centre and dispense with the rest. The Victorian Society's main objection to the proposal was that Block B formed a unified scheme with Block C, from which it was separated by the neo-classical Dock House, also by Hardwick, and that none of it should be demolished. The developers' response was that to include Block C in the new centre would be too expensive; what was needed was 'creative continuity as opposed to museum-like preservation'. In November 1973 there was a fire (for which two people were subsequently convicted) and Block B was damaged. Taylor Woodrow now argued that since it would be very expensive to restore the listed Block B to a suitable standard, they should not be compelled to keep Block C.

The Chairman and Managing Director of St Katharine by the Tower Ltd (and a director of Taylor Woodrow) was Peter Drew (1927–2007), who had restored the Dockmaster's House on the river, built by Telford, for himself and moved into it amidst all the building works. Pevsner, with fellow-Vic Soc member Trevor Russell-Cobb, accepted Peter Drew's invitation to dinner and was shown round the site in the spring of 1974.* 'Let me tell you how very much impressed I was by your plea,' Pevsner wrote to Drew afterwards. 'I shall regret the disappearance of C warehouse, but your point of gaining a complete harmony along the north side is a point worth considering . . . I know that I shall have opposition in my committee . . . It would be very much more effective if the necessary convincing is done by you and not by me.'[11]

Drew duly issued the same invitation to the rest of the Victorian Society committee, though without dinner, and Pevsner did his best to persuade them to accept it. 'He is certainly not a tycoon,' he told committee members. 'I am sure he is genuine and he is an enthusiast . . . Proof of his attitude is for instance that he has made close to his house a kind of ruin garden, i.e. a display of fragments including one high cast-iron column standing on its own. Another proof is the collection he has started of ships including the last of the Nores, i.e. light-house ships at the mouth of the Thames.' Pevsner was also influenced by the fact that Taylor Woodrow had bothered to shift a timber-framed warehouse discovered on the site and had turned it into the Dickens Inn. 'You must realise that these things cost a great deal of money which might as well have been saved.'[12]

Most of the Vic Soc members were dubious about the developers' credentials as conservationists. Peter Drew attempted to charm them, but without the conspicuous success with which he had wooed Pevsner.

*Trevor Russell-Cobb (1918–96) was a public-relations consultant, bibliophile and pioneer of industrial patronage for the arts.

The Docks scheme dragged on. In 1976 Taylor Woodrow applied to demolish all of Block B except for the façade.* When the Victorian Society objected that the restoration of Block B had been the justification given for demolishing Block C, the developers produced new reports suggesting that preservation of B was not in fact possible.

'Did Pevsner's remarkably undevious nature make him vulnerable in the struggle for conservation? Did he believe in people too much?' asked Ian Sutton later. Certainly Pevsner himself would come to suspect that he might have been taken in. 'The developers have behaved and are behaving outrageously,' he told architect and conservationist Sherban Cantacuzino in 1977.†

'I'm getting deafer,' Pevsner complained on 10 January 1974. 'Right hand shaking badly, often snoozes in the day, forgetfulness ever of the right word, upset by any changes of plan or urgent duty . . . The Mellon book [*Building Types*] in its last stages.' He was finding the stairs in Wildwood Terrace a trial now – 'You climb Everest once a week' – and devised a complex system for filing objects on the stairs to be gradually transported between floors. Long ago Geoffrey Grigson had given him a caricature of a bowed figure barely supporting himself on two sticks, which he claimed was Pevsner staggering to the end of the *Buildings of England*. It was a portrait that probably felt truer to life now than the photograph of the old man in a grey bowler making his way, relatively unimpeded, out of the last churchyard.

In the back of an address book of the mid-1970s, Pevsner made notes to help him keep his life under control: a list of birthdays (which included godchildren, secretaries and the Duke of Gloucester), the days on which his parents and Lola had died, dress sizes for reference when buying presents, accounts of his expenses when travelling (train tickets, tips in restaurants, chocolate, shoe cream, postcards, whisky), the progress of port he had laid down for a grandson in 1956. His writing, however, was now all but illegible, and some of the entries are written in other hands.

In March 1974 another, more private set of records came to an end. Half a century earlier, Lola had been shocked by the frankness of the *Heftchen* in which Pevsner had written the details of their love, and

---

*In the end, the block was completely rebuilt, but with a replica façade – except that, to the horror of conservationists, the brickwork was dark-red, instead of yellow-brown London stocks.
†NP/S.Cantacuzino, 3/8/77.

had asked him to burn them after she died. Writing the *Heftchen* was an emotional outlet on which he had come to rely, and ten years after her death he was still making entries. Now, at last, he decided that the record should stop and that part of it at least should be erased. 'I saw it come,' wrote Pevsner. 'It has gradually grown; and now today, I have been to the filing box with the *Heftchen*, have read here and there, and have thrown away all after 1921.'

He made the gesture sound more effectual than it was. It may have crossed his mind that Thomas Mann, hero and model of his early years, had destroyed his first diaries. Mann, however, had taken the precaution of burning his papers. Pevsner merely threw his away, and recorded two weeks later, in anguish:

It is not easy to destroy. Three Heftchen have been returned to me neatly addressed – 1 in German, 2 in English, 1949–51. So there is now somebody somewhere who knows my most intimate thoughts and actions. May it not be blackmail. After study I'd say Not likely. It is mostly L[ore] and all my cowardice and unhappiness . . . Now the three Heftchen are burnt, but it is nasty to think that one person with an educated handwriting knows all this of me.

He never found out who this person might have been.

Nor was the destruction complete. In the event he had thrown away only the *Heftchen* from 1923 to 1963. He kept the books he had started since Lola's death, and he decided to reprieve the *Heftchen* from 1921 to 1923. The books documenting the years of their marriage, which were revealing of her just as they were of him, were the ones he felt should be kept private. This she would undoubtedly have wanted, but it was, of course, precisely the record of their courtship and sexual initiation in 1922 and 1923 that she had originally asked him to destroy. For Pevsner, however, the forty years of a long and complicated marriage had twisted the kaleidoscope and put those three years of growing love into a different perspective:

The time up to the wedding is the best time of my life – heightened and happy. The epochs of other loves were heightened too, but unhappy . . . On rereading the *Heftchen* – how impoverished am I not to dream dreams any longer. No moments of elation – except perhaps in the mountains . . . My heart aches when I read of such love and purity . . . The reading incidentally of all these old papers has made me restless, an Abgehang [hangover] of the restlessness of being in love.

For the future historian, the destruction of the *Heftchen* was a tragedy, the loss of an irreplaceable record of the intimate thoughts and private reasoning behind a public life. For Pevsner, it was a release – or possibly an evasion. He gave his reason for destroying the *Heftchen* not as marital duty, but as shame. 'Why? Shame, yes. What else?' The shame was largely for the emotional infidelities to Lola, for which he blamed himself almost as keenly as if they had ever taken physical shape. (He described the books in which he documented his infatuations as 'morally bad'.) With the physical documents gone, he was relieved of some of the pressure to confront the truths they represented.

He had recently been asked by Robert Lusty of Hutchinson to write an autobiography, but declined without really giving his reasons. 'They would take too long to enumerate,' he wrote. 'You can be assured that I have weighed up more than once the pros and cons.'[13] He had in fact gone further. Amongst his papers, a thin folder marked 'Autobiography' contains his first scattered thoughts: notes on his parents' incompatibility, his brother's suicide and his own 'ill-fated escapades' in infatuation*. He has often woken up feeling that there is someone in the bed next to him. 'It is not Lola, as one must expect after forty years of married life, but Heinz [his brother]. Psychiatrists Please Explain!' Personal revelations are scribbled on scraps of paper alongside school reports and the other formal records of his academic life: 'Pinder – I was told years ago – called me his best pupil. It is not vanity if I kept this out of the destruction. It is just that I never knew and did not expect. I certainly did not feel myself to be anything special.' The information in 'Autobiography' is fragmentary and the reflections unpursued.

'I have made up my mind to carry on in my diverse fields as long as I can and to keep away from any emotional strain,' Pevsner wrote in 1973, six months before he destroyed the *Heftchen*.† It was taking all his energies simply to live his life; the prospect of reviewing it, with the *Heftchen* in his hands, was 'emotional strain' too intense to contemplate.

*These were the first thoughts he had actually committed to paper, though he would seem to have reflected on the subject before: a diary entry as early as August 1954 describes an autobiography of his early years as 'a tempting proposition'.
†He was declining an invitation from the International Society for Krishna Consciousness for 'an informal exchange of ideas'. NP/His Divine Grace A.C. Bhaktivedanta Swami Prabhupada, August 1973.

CHAPTER 46

'Is it in Pevsner?'

The *Buildings of England* were no respecters of illness or any other kind of weakness. The journeys were over, but the inexorable march of volumes to be compiled, edited, introduced, typed, proofread, printed, published, reviewed, revised would continue throughout the years of struggle between 1970 and 1974. Oppressed though Pevsner may occasionally have felt under the present burden, he was relieved of the greater fear of the future by the knowledge that the series would be in the safe hands of John Newman, who had agreed to see the series through to the end.[1] As for the revised editions, Bridget Cherry was in charge.* Pevsner wrote to Hans Schmoller: 'She has turned out to be a great winner and I would hate the idea of having to start with anybody else.'[2]

In the meantime the *BoE* continued to emerge. In 1970 it was *Gloucestershire* in two volumes – *The Cotswolds* and *The Vale and Forest of Dean* – written entirely by David Verey. In 1971 it was *Cheshire*, in 1972 *Dorset* (a joint effort with John Newman, who covered the secular buildings) and *Yorkshire: York and the East Riding*. *Yorkshire*, all Pevsner's own work, was dedicated simply 'for Marianne'. Since Lola's death, Pevsner had spent his holidays walking in Germany with her sister.[†]

Pevsner's tongue was perhaps loosened with the end of the series in sight, and the two final volumes contain some of his most personal pronouncements. *Oxfordshire*, documenting a county of extraordinary riches, was long overdue. His collaborator was Jennifer Sherwood, deputed to cover the county as a whole while he tackled the city of Oxford itself. She had been his senior assistant since 1965, and by 1966 he described her as 'the general handyman for all volumes'. From the outset he had been pleased with what she was doing on *Oxfordshire*: 'Very BoE'. But she had the larger proportion of the work and by far the greater share of the travelling, which she could only do at weekends, and there was a wealth of material to incorporate. The manuscript grew longer and later, and then she fell seriously ill, which

---

*In 1972, with a small child, she went part-time for a number of years. It was at this point that Penguin took on Elizabeth Williamson to share the process of revision.
[†] Marianne's husband Carl Walter Kockel had died in 1966.

delayed delivery even further. Pevsner had completed his share of the manuscript in 1969. By April 1970 he had written, 'I find it very depressing to see my Oxford slipping out of date.' However, when *Oxfordshire* was published in 1974, he found it well worth the wait. 'I don't think I have ever told you how successful I found the Intro when I read it,' he wrote to Sherwood. 'Extreme strength to your elbow.'³ *Oxfordshire* was the first Penguin hardback on a best-seller list and was reprinted almost at once.

Part of the entertainment value in what Pevsner himself wrote lies in the hint of partisanship, a whiff of a lingering prejudice against Oxford as opposed to Cambridge. He allowed some space in *Oxfordshire* for comparisons between the two. Oxford, he wrote, is industrial while Cambridge is not, and Oxford has far more serious traffic problems, but Cambridge has no such hub as Oxford's Radcliffe Camera. 'Cambridge colleges, at least a whole string of them, turn outward, Oxford colleges, many of them, turn inward.' Oxford, too, is more compact: 'There is a density of monuments here which has not the like in Europe . . . The Cambridge image is buildings in a landscape, *riant* if you are lucky, the Oxford image is a landscape made of stone, sombre at its best.' Cambridge has no skyline, Oxford 'the most telling skyline of England' although:

> dreaming spires is nonsense in every respect. Surely, in spite of St Mary, All Saints, and the cathedral, and now Nuffield, Oxford is remembered less for them than for Tom Tower, the Camera, and Magdalen tower. It is the variety of the shapes which makes the skyline. And as for 'dreaming'? Stupor say the enemies, inertia say even some of the friends, serious search for truth among the undergraduates, search for knowledge among the dons, less serious search for publicity – single out what you will, dreaming is not a figurative Oxford quality, by criteria either of the mind or the eye.

Cambridge had been on Pevsner's mind during the preparation of a second edition of *Cambridgeshire*, which eventually emerged in 1970. Since writing his foreword to *Cambridge New Architecture* in 1964, he had kept a watchful eye on developments, curious to see how far the university might have followed his advice about how it could expand. Rather than the orderly march across the Backs to create 'an ideal campus . . . of high aesthetic possibilities', he was dismayed to observe a leap made apparently at random, with little coherence or strategy that he could divine. 'Cambridge now is one of the happiest hunting grounds in Britain for specimens of the architectural style and fashions of the 1960s, large and small, elephants as well as butterflies.' There were individual successes: he would always single out the new Cripps Building at St John's College by Powell and Moya as a sensitively articulated range of buildings that managed to make a statement without interfering with its riverside neighbours, the Bridge of Sighs and Lutyens's Benson Court at Magdalene College. But the Arts Faculty by Casson and Conder, whose plans had so delighted him in 1953, had lost much of its charm by being scaled down, and one of the most recent colleges – New Hall by Chamberlin, Powell and Bon – was dismayingly historicist. ('Shades of Agra in the pool and the domed hall and shades of Byzantium in the hall itself,' he objected.)*

And then there was the History Faculty, directly across the Sidgwick Site from the Arts Faculty, in the hands of James Stirling. 'Perhaps if Sir Hugh Casson had not been so playful, James Stirling might not have been so rude,' Pevsner commented ruefully. Stirling's building, completed in 1968, was a compound of scarlet engineering brick ('hard, perfect Victorian Accrington brick redder than anything Cambridge had seen for many a decade') and aluminium glazing ('aesthetically as neutral as the glazing of a tomato-frame'). The building was roughly in the shape of an open book, with teaching offices enfolding a central library whose roof was a sharp slope of patent glazing. 'People in the last ten years have spoken about anti-art. Here . . . is anti-architecture,' wrote Pevsner. 'Here is an intelligent, resourceful architect making it his business to design a building which fulfils all the functional demands and yet is actively ugly – not ugly in the vociferous way of the brutalists, but ugly more basically by avoiding anything that might attract . . . But never mind, it hits you, the architecture hits you, and that is what the façade – and the whole building – are meant to do.' The building gave Pevsner the impression of shouting abuse at the Arts Faculty across the divide. 'Don't think, he seems to imply, you can play at architecture.' A rude building from a rude man, he concluded, a judgement borne out by Stirling's response when asked why he had designed it like this: 'To fuck Casson'.†

Architectural disappointments apart, Cambridge was a town he loved and one where he felt welcome. Oxford was a different proposition

---

*New Hall was renamed Murray Edwards College in 2008.
†Quoted in Mark Girouard, Big Jim (Chatto & Windus, 1998). Stirling was married to Mary Shand, a daughter of Philip Morton Shand. Pevsner was willing to be a co-signatory with the 'rude man' of a letter to The Times, 17/6/72, protesting against the Arts Council's refusal of an exhibition of Gropius's architectural work.

– a city rather than a town, housing a university that gave him the impression of repelling outsiders. 'In Oxford I feel more German than I do anywhere else, like an elephant in a china shop,' he had written in 1934, and almost forty years later he had not entirely overcome his sense of unease. 'I still feel that I have not that familiarity with Oxford which 25 years of weekly visits have given me at Cambridge,' he wrote. 'To an Oxford man no doubt gaffes of nomenclature and gaffes in the little snobbery concerns which one disregards at one's peril have been left in my text, apart from more serious mistakes.'

Nevertheless, he did not allow social malaise to inhibit him from voicing his opinions. Renewing the sculpted heads outside the Sheldonian Theatre would, he opined, 'completely destroy their character and worth'. (They were renewed in 1972.) The sculpture on New College tower was 'poor'; the linenfold panelling in Magdalen's hall was not original, as claimed; Somerville College was 'not very big nor very good'. In general, very pronounced Gothicism abounded (he quoted William Morris's phrase 'fakement various') because Oxford had antiquarian leanings and was resistant to radical change.

There was a certain glee, even *Schadenfreude*, in his descriptions of architectural excess. 'Sir Thomas Jackson . . . set his elephantine feet on many places in Oxford . . . Nearly always his arsenal is English. Anglo-Jackson the impudent results have been called.'* Pevsner singled out the Examination Schools, 'licentiously fabricated out of elements from the Quattrocento to the Georgian . . . What an image of examination such a building creates: the puny candidates and the moloch of the testing machinery . . . That Jackson left Oxford a grosser place than it had ever been, nobody should deny, but he left it as a place with a potential for architectural adventure, and for that one should be grateful to him.'

Pevsner managed to convey the impression that the university had somehow failed to act upon this potential for adventure and had settled complacently for the anodyne. He wrote caustically of the 'peculiar, feeble Oxford style' of the twentieth century, and favoured the university with some of his best expressions of disparagement. Sir Edward Maufe's Dolphin Building at St John's (1948) was 'retardataire'. The Rector's Lodgings at Lincoln College (Herbert Read, 1929–30) were 'well-meant neo-early-Georgian and no harm done'. Giles Gilbert Scott's addition to the north range of Magdalen in 1928–30 had been made in 'totally unrousing c17 style'. The whole of Nuffield College was a foible. Sir Herbert Baker's Rhodes House of 1929, with its neat

*By John Betjeman.

copper-roofed rotunda, mixed its motifs with a fearful gentility: 'The building is an oddity, but it has personality enough to rouse affection in some. The one whose affections were strongest,' he added, coming as near to malice as he ever did, 'was Sir Herbert Baker.'*

The university had, on the other hand, come near to redeeming itself at a stroke by commissioning one of his favourite British modern buildings. At St Catherine's College (1962), in the hands of Danish architect Arne Jacobsen, the International Modern had made its first mark in Oxford. He loved the way it looked, and believed wholeheartedly in the meaning it conveyed. 'It has . . . a clarity of structure and at the same time a serenity such as no other new college building has . . . Self-discipline is its message, expressed in terms of a geometry pervading the whole and its parts and felt wherever one moves or stops.' Pevsner was willing to admit that the smooth precision of St Catherine's, with every detail designed by Jacobsen as part of an engineered unity, could occasionally be constricting. In the Junior Common Room, for example, 'the furniture is placed with such geometrical perfection that to move a chair seems a *lèse majesté*'. But, he concluded, 'If young people don't like it, that might be an argument against them rather than against the college . . . My final verdict is that the college may have to wait until by the swing of the pendulum of history the ideal of self-permissiveness among students becomes once more the idea of self-discipline.'

As for Pevsner's own self-restraint, he stuck to his format to the end and remained within the bounds he had imposed on himself, but in the writing of *Staffordshire*, the final volume, there is an air of liberation. His criticisms are outspoken – 'Let Salisbury and Hereford be vandals and remove their Scott-Skidmore screens. Lichfield must hold out' – his pleasure in the odd and entertaining is unconfined, and by this time his acceptance of mistakes and omissions was resigned to the point of serenity. (To a letter of congratulation from an American professor, he wrote: 'You over-estimate me. The only reason why this accidentally correct statement is in my book is that my source was so much out of date as not to know about the problem.'[4])

Staffordshire was largely finished before *Oxfordshire* and could have been published in 1973, but Pevsner wanted it to be the final volume 'for reasons of my own'. These reasons remain obscure. He may have wanted the series to finish on a volume that was his own unaided

---

*This refers to Baker's autobiography *Architecture and Personalities* (1944).

work, or the county may have held particular associations for him – perhaps memories of a holiday with Lola. Certainly the volume was dedicated 'to the memory of Lola and Allen who helped as long as they lived and to whom Volumes One and Three were dedicated in 1951'.

He pulled no punches in his introduction. 'When people try to visualise Staffordshire – and few people do – it is the Black Country and the Five Towns that come up before their mental eye . . . As for the Black Country, the unbiased traveller will find it less black than he had expected: as for the Five (or to be correct Six) Towns, they could not be, urbanly speaking, much worse.' Stoke was a town he had bitterly disliked since his days on the road for Philip Sargant Florence, when he had dismissed it as a 'shapeless agglomeration' with 'an appalling atmosphere'. Now, some forty years later, he wrote:

> Here is the national seat of an industry, here is the fourteenth largest city in England, and what is it? . . . There is no centre to the whole, not even an attempt at one . . . The kilns are disappearing rapidly, which is visually a great loss; for their odd shapes were the one distinguishing feature of the Five Towns, and used to determine their character – kilns bottle-shaped, kilns conical, kilns like chimneys with swollen bases . . . The Wedgwood warehouses along the canal and the Wedgwood kilns have all been pulled down by the present owners.

The Potteries are famous for 'ceramic sanitary ware' – baths, cisterns, sinks, bidets. In Stafford, Pevsner rejoiced in the Royal Brine Baths of 1892. '"Planned and constructed by Mr W. *Blackshaw*, Borough Surveyor. The exterior was designed gratuitously by Councillor *Wormal*" (inscription *ex situ*). This explains the rampant ignorance of the tower with the big gash.' In Tean, it was the terraces of weavers' cottages in several locations: 'Specially remarkable the octagonal PRIVIES behind No. 1 and 3 New Road.' At Okeover Hall he noted, 'In the garden to the E, the NECESSARY HOUSE, i.e. a lavatory (and rather distant for such a purpose)'.

By way of contrast, Staffordshire was perhaps the richest county in England for the buildings in parks which he had always enjoyed: temples, towers, pagodas, triumphal arches, summer houses, hermits' houses. At Shugborough, home of the Earls of Lichfield, he spent happy hours pacing between the Tower of the Winds, Lantern of Demosthenes, Arch of Hadrian, Chinese House and Cat's Monument, and pored over the letters carved in a curious pattern into the base of the

Shepherd's Monument. But even Shugborough paled by comparison
with Alton Towers, where the 15th and 16th Earls of Shrewsbury had
indulged in 'a building activity on the scale of King Ludwig of Bavaria'.
The 15th Earl, Pevsner wrote, 'put in far too many buildings, in far
too many styles, far too close together. The result suits the present use
to perfection.' He enjoyed himself equally at Dudley Zoo: 'Castle Hill
and happily mixed up with the outer bailey of the castle . . . After all,
medieval castles sometimes had wild beasts in the moat. Only today
they are better housed. This is due to Messrs *Tecton* who did the
buildings for the zoo in 1936–37.' There is still real zest in his partialities, and gusto in his dislikes. 'Milton. METHODIST CHURCH. 1862
by *George B. Ford*. Really repulsive.' 'Wolverhampton. South. ST
LUKE, Upper Villiers Street. 1860–1 . . . Furiously unruly.'

The end of the *Buildings of England* was reported with interest in the
summer of 1974, not just in the architectural press but in the national
dailies and colour supplements. The series had taken almost twenty-
nine years to complete, from the proposal in the rose garden in 1945
to the publication of *Staffordshire*. The famous photograph of Pevsner
with the forty-six accumulated volumes was widely reproduced,*
though the even more staggering mountains of research material passed
unremarked to the National Monuments Record. Pevsner gave strings
of interviews on the series: on the marring of towns by high-rise buildings, indifferent shopping precincts and multi-storey car parks, on the
scarring of the countryside by motorways and on the murder of local
train routes. He was the subject of a television documentary by Will
Wyatt entitled *All the Buildings Fit to Print* and was interviewed by
Robert Robinson talking about the architecture of Cheadle.

He was also invited by the *Daily Telegraph* to select his 'favourite
buildings'. Undaunted, he chose what he described as twelve of the
best, one from each chronological period from the Anglo-Saxon to the
present day, 'best' either for their architectural value or their historical
significance as representatives of their time. The list, unsurprisingly,
was heavily weighted in favour of churches and contained three cathedrals and two Perpendicular chapels. It also included Christopher Wren
and John Loughborough Pearson, skipping lightly over the intervening
neoclassicists, and it ended triumphantly with Gropius. The complete
list, in chronological order, reads:

*As on the dust jacket of this book.

748

Bewcastle Cross (Anglo-Saxon)
Durham Cathedral (Norman)
The façade of Ripon Cathedral (Early English)
The vault of Exeter Cathedral (Decorated)
St George's Chapel, Windsor (Perpendicular)
King's College Chapel, Cambridge (Perpendicular – 'nothing prettier in the whole of England')
Astley Hall (Elizabethan/Jacobean – 'the only original British style after the Middle Ages'), or Wootton Lodge as another example of the style
St Stephen, Walbrook (Baroque)
Seaton Delaval (Baroque)
Strawberry Hill (Georgian Gothic Revival)
St Augustine, Kilburn (Victorian)
Impington Village College (Modern – 'that most overworked term "epoch-making" does indeed apply here').

The terms Pevsner used to explain his selections provide a neat précis of the qualities in buildings that gave him most pleasure: 'perfect balance', 'unified expression', 'overwhelming discipline' (that word again). One of his choices – Wootton Lodge, in Staffordshire – was 'completely and compactly English'.

The Penguin party for the end of the series had a prodigious guest list. Pevsner had been asked to invite people to whom he was most indebted – 'frequent and copious contributors' – and the roll call included specialists in windmills, indexing, church plate, Roman Catholic churches, Morris stained glass, geology, Neo-Classicism, contacts from *The Builder* and a wide range of experts on individual architects. They were joined by other people from every period of Pevsner's life in England and every phase of his career: Alec Clifton-Taylor, Gordon Russell, Jim Richards from the *Architectural Review*, Anna Kallin from the BBC, the Master and Secretary of Birkbeck, Eunice Frost from Penguin, Jane Fawcett from the Victorian Society, Ena Kendall who had written one of the most perceptive interviews of him for the *Observer*, Simon Jenkins who had often discussed the *BoE* in the *Evening Standard*, and a wide range of his peers and pupils in art history.

Penguin gave him lavish presents, chosen with care: a Staffordshire china figure of a cottage, eighty-five bottles of wine and a trip to St Petersburg, where he had never been. They also gave him royalties, which he had never previously received – an arrangement that Penguin described as 'a perhaps unparalleled self-abnegation on the part of

749

yourself and those who have helped you with the writing'. Managing
director Chris Dolley commented, 'My belief, and I may be wrong, is
that *The BoE* are now an excellent commercial proposition for us and
it is about time we exploded the myth that we lose money on them.'[5]
'Excellent' might at that time have been an overstatement, but the
account was black rather than red, and by 1974 the series was making
a perceptible profit. The offer of a royalty (to be split with co-authors
where the volumes were collaborations) was engineered by Hans
Schmoller. 'Penguin legend has it that Schmoller ensured that it was
the last item on the agenda of a long board meeting when the directors
would be too tired to argue,' commented 'Pendennis' in the *Observer.*[6]

'The future' included the *Buildings of Wales, Scotland* and *Ireland,*
which by 1974 had been in hand for some time. In his interview with
Mavis Nicholson in 1973, Pevsner had said that they were indeed
being undertaken, 'but not by me, thank God'. He had of course
played a crucial part in getting them launched. The University of Wales
helped to subsidise the Welsh series, and Dr R. Brinley Jones, Director
of the University Press, remembered, '[Pevsner] was deeply interested
in the Welsh scene . . . and partly due to his enthusiasm, his extraordinary erudition, his charm, courtesy . . . the project was launched.
I remember, with much affection, my meetings with him. There was
conviction, logic and a formidable though gentle presence.'[7]

The *Buildings of Scotland* was a project that had been long in the
making. As early as the mid-1960s Pevsner had discussed the possibility of a series with three stalwarts of the Victorian Society in
Scotland – David Walker, Colin McWilliam and Andor Gomme – but
it could not be launched until financial support was secured from the
National Trust for Scotland, for whom McWilliam had formerly
worked. In its organisation, the *Buildings of Scotland* owed a great
deal to Kitty Michaelson, Pevsner's assistant on *London except*, now
living in Edinburgh. From years of working with Pevsner, she offered
valuable advice and, initially at least, recruited and ran the research
assistants.

Colin McWilliam wrote the first volume – *Lothian except Edinburgh*
– and became the general editor. He later remembered the start of his
researches: 'For no real reason I decided to start at Dunbar. I got out
of the train and began making notes on the station. After a while the
station-master asked me what I was doing. I thought he would find
it hard to understand, so I made it very simple, and said I was compiling
an inventory of interesting buildings in Scotland with descriptions of

their history and architecture. "Oh, I see," he said. "It'll be a sort of Scottish Pevsner, then."'

The format for the new series was essentially the same, but the approach had to be different, according to Alistair Rowan, whom Pevsner invited to be general editor for the *Buildings of Ireland*, as well as the author of the first volume, *North-West Ulster: The Counties of Londonderry, Donegal, Fermanagh and Tyrone* (1979).* Two further volumes followed: *North Leinster* (1993), which Rowan co-authored with Christine Casey, and *Dublin* (2005) by Casey alone. In the 'Celtic' countries, Alistair Rowan argued, there was less richness and diversity of buildings, they were generally less well preserved and there were fewer local historians to provide source material. In consequence, it would probably be necessary to include buildings that in England might not have made the grade, and to treat buildings more as social documents than as exemplars of styles. There would also be greater emphasis on local content rather than European comparison. Rowan helped to raise the money for *North-West Ulster* – £1,000 from the Bank of Ireland – and Pevsner, he remembered, wrote to him 'not quite idiomatically, "Dear Alistair, You are the cat's pyjamas"'.† Pevsner later went on a tour round Ireland and sent Rowan two postcards. The first read simply, 'You poor man, what a terrible job.' The second, about ten days later, was longer: 'You poor, poor man, what a truly terrible job.'

The general editor for the *Buildings of Wales* was Richard Haslam, who had assisted Pevsner with his research for *Building Types*. He would also write *Powys* (1979), the first volume in the series, to be followed by *Clwyd* (1986) by Edward Hubbard, *Glamorgan* (1995) and *Gwent/Monmouthshire* (2000), by John Newman,‡ *Pembrokeshire* (2004) and *Carmarthenshire and Ceredigion* (2006) by the partnership of Thomas Lloyd, Julian Orbach and Robert Scourfield, and *Gwynedd* (2009), jointly authored by Richard Haslam, Julian Orbach and Adam Voelcker. As a veteran of the *Buildings of England*, Hubbard remarked with feeling that the 'outrider' series had 'less eyeing of the clock and the calendar'. With fewer volumes to do, appearing much less

---

*This was explained in his talk on 'The Buildings of the British Isles' at a *Buildings of England* conference in Oxford in 1993.

†Actually, even if the phrase sounded odd coming from Pevsner, it is quite idiomatic, of the same vintage and derivation as the cat's whiskers and the bee's knees.

‡Alec Clifton-Taylor had long been urging Pevsner to cover Monmouthshire within the BoE. He even put up £500 out of a charitable trust towards expenses, and was bitterly disappointed when the project was abandoned, with the formal transfer of Monmouthshire to Wales.

frequently, there was more time to do original research – although it was the authors themselves who would be doing the research, as, except in the case of the *Buildings of Scotland*, the money did not extend to providing researchers, secretaries or drivers.

Jim Richards summed up the practical importance of the *Buildings of England*. '"Is it in Pevsner?" is the first question asked about any building on which information is sought or an assessment of its significance required.'[8] 'The *Buildings of England* have had public influence on those who take decisions,' Dame Jennifer Jenkins confirmed. 'Someone like Tony Crosland, Secretary of State for the Environment, would never go on holiday without one . . . Without them, we'd have lost an infinitely larger number of buildings throughout Britain, town and country. Pevsner arrived at a crucial time.' In substantiating so many different claims to survival, Pevsner had not only saved individual buildings, he had helped to shape the kind of landscape he had advocated for so long, in which architecture of quality from every period could stand side by side in harmony.

But for Pevsner these were not the main aims of the *BoE*, merely valuable side-effects. The objective nearest to his heart was to develop in people an appetite for looking. Each volume of the *Buildings of England* was not simply a body of knowledge, but a stimulus to enquiry; it gave its readers a method of looking, and a framework of cross-references within which to locate each building they saw. 'What we see through [Pevsner],' reflected Simon Jenkins, 'is an English landscape of peculiarly intense beauty, a mosaic of tens of thousands of buildings, each one integral to the whole.'[9] For John Newman, 'The publication of each new volume of the *Buildings of England* transformed a county for its readers.'[10] Pevsner certainly believed that recognising, understanding and appreciating the buildings that surrounded one could make the world feel, at least, a better place. Grateful readers continue to justify his faith. 'Walking the two miles home,' wrote Christopher Woodward in the *Spectator* in 2005, 'the Mile End Road had become a different street; a hundred anonymous buildings had become living, friendly, complex faces. A perfect London Sunday, thanks to Pevsner.'[11]

Pevsner did not see the job as fully done. 'The series is not complete,' he wrote firmly in the introduction to the last volume. 'It is only the first round which has run its course.' He had put together the first draft, in his view, and no one was more conscious than he of its shortcomings.

It was characteristic of Pevsner that he took *Staffordshire* as an opportunity to review the defects of the series. 'The early volumes are slimmer than the later and were moreover printed in larger type. The reason for this is plain enough. I knew less, and the assistants knew less. The most valuable sources were not tapped, because we were in ignorance of them.' 'Nonconformist churches and chapels,' he continued, piling on the agony, 'being locked except for services, are severely under-represented. The same is true for even less valid reasons of schools. At first I did not take enough trouble to search for them in towns and look at them in villages. Yet they may be among the most worth-while buildings in a place.'

'At the end of the normal foreword to every volume,' he wrote:

> I have asked users to point out to me errors and omissions. This they have done faithfully, with the mortifying result that I know by now to the full how many mistakes I have made and an unsuspecting publisher has published. The next round will be revised second editions. The publisher is ready for them, an excellent reviser is busy. The more of these improved volumes I shall still see the happier I shall be. Don't be deceived, gentle reader, the first editions are only *ballons d'essai*; it is the second editions which count.

It was true that being left out of 'Pevsner', or being dismissed unfavourably, could seal the fate of a building that was under threat; he was aware of this and it bothered him. But the number of occasions when this happened pales into insignificance beside the number of buildings saved by the series. Mark Girouard, a much younger scholar than Pevsner, with different academic interests, a different writing style and many differences of opinion from him, was nevertheless quick to acknowledge this, in one of the most fair-minded assessments of the *BoE*. Now the series was finished, he wrote in *Country Life*:

> gone too will be the sport of catching Pevsner out. It is a game I have indulged in myself from time to time. I remember the ignoble pleasure I felt at discovering different façades of the same building being described on separate pages as two different buildings, or visiting a desolate site in Devon where a Victorian house demolished well before the war was blandly described as still in existence ('cheerless Gothic mansion' – but this was an early volume). All Pevsner addicts will have their own lists of crumbling follies in remote corners of parks or sumptuous cast-iron public conveniences in back squares

or Baroque ceilings in upstairs rooms not mentioned in the *Buildings of England*. It is nice to have these little moments of triumph or indignation as long as one keeps them in their place. Their place is in the shade of the one amazing achievement, the 40 counties covered in 23 years and 46 volumes, the extraordinary decision of one man in his late 40s personally to visit, list and describe all the buildings of architectural interest in England. It was a decision that a cautious man would never have made.[12]

(Pevsner agreed, and said that the series was unlikely to be replaced in a hurry: 'There won't be another madman so soon.'[13])

'Austere, proper, pedantic, diligent, serious-minded, indifferent to comfort, preferring to have a goal to strive towards.' Pevsner's description of himself as a student had in many respects remained true throughout his working life. In 1921 he had told his mother that he 'usually carries through what he plans' and quoted Goethe's introduction to *Faust*: 'He who keeps actively striving deserves the blessing of the Lord.' 'It's better not to start at all than to start and not to finish,' he had written to Lola from Birmingham. Pevsner's capacity for effort and his determination to finish were not in question. What was perhaps more remarkable in someone of his punctilious temperament was the courage to persevere with a process that inevitably resulted in flaws. He often acknowledged the intense pleasure that the *Buildings of England* had given him in letting him spend so much time studying the best of England's architecture; he tended to keep to himself the corresponding displeasure in being constantly engaged in falling short in describing it. 'I find it so miserably painful to do anything less than entirely well,' he had written in 1934, embarking on the unfamiliar field research for his *Enquiry into Industrial Art in England*. At the start of *Berkshire* he had set as a defiant epigraph '*Chi non fa, non sbaglia*' ('He who does nothing makes no mistakes'). But, as he had written to Lola a decade earlier, 'Every piece of carelessness exacts its revenge.'

'Did you ever think when you started this,' asked Mavis Nicholson, 'that your name would live for ever?' Pevsner had had no thoughts of fame in 1945 when he embarked on the series, and he replied lightly, 'For ever, of course, means fifty years', but he must have been aware that his name had taken on the status of a label that would in all probability outlive him. 'Pevsner', like 'Baedeker', had become not just a personal appellation, but a noun, as in 'Have you remembered the

Pevsner?' 'Pevsner' had also entered estate agents' vocabulary as an adjective: 'A "Pevsner" house attracts a great deal of attention when it comes on the market,' wrote one agent in 1999.[14] In some hands it even becomes a verb. Novelist Penelope Lively has written, in an article on Exmoor, 'If you are like me, you will quickly acquire a taste for "Pevsnering" – pouttering [sic] round any village, the appropriate volume in hand.'* Giving it a transitive turn, other commentators use it to mean giving an area the Pevsner treatment – that is, documenting its architectural riches.

The *New Statesman* featured him in a cartoon in 2001, nearly twenty years after his death, in their series 'Dumbing Up', which imports 'high-brow' references into popular culture – in this case, into the Australian soap drama *Prisoner: Cell Block H*. Over the caption 'Pevsner Cell Block H', a more or less recognisable figure appeared in front of a cell with a substantial woman squinting aggressively at him through the bars. His outflung arm points: 'Another interesting feature is this rather wobbly cardboard wall.'

'The style is quite easily mocked,' observed John Summerson, 'but it is a very admirable way of explaining things, and it has had a very wide appeal. You find Pevsner quoted all over the world by people who are not very deeply involved in architecture . . . quoted with sympathy in a way that I don't think anybody would ever quote Baedeker.'

Pevsner received a good deal of fan mail. 'Those who, like myself, have collected the whole of the series up to now,' wrote one reader in Liverpool, 'like to think of you as a personal friend.' The architectural historian Peter Ferriday went into a church in Gloucestershire carrying his 'Pevsner': 'My second Bible,' said the vicar.

There is dark talk of 'cliques' and 'groupies'; but affection for the Pevsners is felt well beyond his circle. Sue Limb, writing in the character of 'Dulcie Domum' in the *Weekend Guardian* in 1996, provided a good example: 'I pick up my favourite Pevsner, wander out on to the front step, and look up St Hilary's: "Inside the porch, a lively, lierne-star vault with figured bosses . . ." Aaah! That's better. Why do I always feel I've come home at last reading Pevsner, when I don't understand a word. Same with cricket.

---

*P. Lively, 'Exmoor's Rural Ways and Byways', *New York Times*, 18/9/94. Pevsner is also referred to in Lively's novel *The Road to Lichfield*. On Pevsner allusions, see Simon Bradley, 'Pevsner in Fiction, Theatre and Cinema', in *The Buildings of England; a Celebration* (Penguin Collectors Society, 2001).

Lozenge, abaci, queenposts, piscina,
silly mid-off and right-arm seamer.
Off-break, leg-break, flipper and bosie,
Strapwork and stoup, early Perp., Dec., ogee,
Cusped and sub-cusped, out of the wood,
Collapse of middle order: something
understood.'

CHAPTER 47

'Right good is rest'

When Pevsner was asked in 1964 what he intended to do when the *Buildings of England* were completed, he said simply, 'Go to sleep'.[1] Asked again in 1972, with the end in sight, he took a more realistic view. 'I don't really want to do anything. But of course I shall.' He remained the Chair of the Victorian Society. *Building Types* was still gestating. In 1974 there was the holiday in St Petersburg that Penguin had given him, though he could not be persuaded to extend this beyond twelve days in order to see Moscow. The following year he went to Monticello to collect the 1975 Thomas Jefferson Medal for architecture, with an acceptance speech composed entirely of Jefferson's own words.

In June 1975 he was invited to the launch of Camden History Society's publication on *The Streets of West Hampstead* – a magnanimous gesture on the part of the Society, given how dismissive he had been of those same streets in *London except*. 'The party was held in the front office of the then *Ham & High* [*Hampstead and Highgate Express*] premises in Perrin's Court, Hampstead,' remembered bookseller Ian Norrie. 'An open staircase with banisters on both sides, rather like one on the deck of a ship, rose to the editorial offices. When he spoke, Pevsner climbed laboriously up many steps of this, turned to the crowded gathering below and said, in his already rather quavery voice, "Now you see the ruin on the hill".'

He was in considerable pain from the inflammation of tendons in one foot, which caused his leg to swell in a way that must have frightened him, remembering the manner of Lola's death. He spent weeks on his back during the summer of 1975; for the first time he failed to go to Cambridge to lecture, and he avoided going into the office, even though Penguin offered him a hire car. Julian Orbach, now an independent architectural historian and one of the principal contributors to the *Buildings of Wales*, met him for the first time at this point, as a case worker for the Victorian Society.* Orbach was twenty-three, and for him Pevsner was:

---

*Julian Orbach (1953–) is a co-author of the three volumes on West Wales: *Pembrokeshire, Carmarthenshire and Ceredigion* and *Gwynedd*, and is currently revising *South and West Somerset* for the BoE.

something of a grandfather figure, my own grandfather having had a similar German accent after sixty years in London . . . He was by then old and charming, quite shaky . . . I remember best his childlike qualities. One day for no real reason I showed him a couple of beer mats with some architectural device on them I had picked up in a pub. His eyes gleamed and he said, 'But how did you know?', and opened a drawer in the desk full of beer mats that most improbably he had picked up around the pubs of England. It was so unexpected yet not out of character; he had an impish humour and a continued fascination with English things . . . Each committee meeting ended with him saying that he should be walking down to the tube. He didn't like spending money on taxis . . . He was parsimonious, but lived so unaware of the wider world of money that it never seemed other than delightful. One of the members would volunteer to drive him back to Golders Green. It was a small ritual . . . The business about getting him into the van with his shaky foot was always a test which he was good humoured about.

The Victorian Society had been faced with a sharp increase in its caseload after the passing of the 1968 Town and Country Planning Act. The Act threw on to amenity societies a good deal of work that had previously been done by the Ministry, by requiring local authorities to consult bodies such as the Victorian Society on every application for consent to demolish a listed building – as many as twenty cases a week, complained Pevsner, with only three weeks to comment on each application.[2] The burden was not solely administrative, for when the Society was required to send representatives to public inquiries, it had to pay their travel costs and on occasion it was also compelled to hire Counsel.

In compensation, the Society could at last begin to feel that the tide of both public and official opinion had turned in favour of intelligent conservation of the Victorian heritage. In 1972 fewer than a hundred buildings from the nineteenth and twentieth centuries had achieved listed status in the City of London; the following year there were 245 from the Covent Garden area alone. Conservation areas were proliferating. The National Trust was taking an increasing number of Victorian and Edwardian buildings under its protection – Castle Drogo, Red House, Scotney Castle, Knightshayes, Standen – at least partly in response to Pevsner's prodding.

Pevsner had overseen what was perhaps the most critical period in the Victorian Society's existence; but it was also a period during which its context was changing. As long ago as 1963, its Treasurer had pointed out that if the Society were to survive financially, it must make its administration more efficient and widen its membership. 'To invade the provinces, we must invade the professional groups . . . The Vic Soc member, at present, seems to be a Londoner with a vaguely literary (or journalistic) bent . . . We need more men with mud on their boots.' Both these adjustments had been made. Membership was now larger and more heterogeneous, and the partnership of Pevsner and Jane Fawcett had made the Society a far more effective campaigning force. But in relation to the scale of the task that now faced it, the management was small and power was concentrated in very few hands. The Committee, which included a growing number of younger members, had begun to feel that it had been reduced to rubber-stamping decisions that had already been taken. With the volume of business increasing, they suggested, this was a poor use of resources.

Financially, the Society was in a better state than it had been for some time. Its major fundraising appeal between 1972 and 1975, to which Pevsner had contributed significantly with his American tours, had been very successful. But should that money now perhaps be spent on re-forming the organisation rather than simply reinforcing the existing structure? A report was commissioned from several of the younger members who had concerns.* Its principal finding was that the burden of work could no longer reasonably be carried by a single Secretary, however dedicated, nor should decisions be made without wider consultation. There was a need for a more formal structure of committees and subcommittees, for professionalised financial management and for a larger administrative staff.

Pevsner probably saw its findings as fair criticism of his particular style of working. He was strong in defence of the work that had been done, and of decisions that had had to be made urgently, but he was also gracious in his acceptance of the fact that the Society now needed to change in ways he could not himself manage. He retired officially from the chair at the Society's Annual General Meeting on 11 June 1976 and, at Lady Rosse's suggestion, was made the Society's first President. On 1 December 1976 the Victorian Society threw a party at the Reform Club to celebrate what he and they had achieved together. One of the speeches came from Wayland Young (Lord Kennet), who

---

*The Working Party was chaired by Philip Strode; its Secretary and author of the eventual report was Alan Crawford. The other members were Peter Howell, Roderick Gradidge, Hermione Hobhouse and Andrew Saint.

had himself played a key role in instituting the system for listing buildings. Without the Victorian Society, he said, the centres of most historic towns would have disappeared. 'They've saved a hundred years.'

Pevsner's speech of farewell was poignant, more personally revealing than usual, a sign perhaps that he felt some defences could come down as he stepped back from active engagement. 'I have been fortunate throughout most of my life,' he declared, 'and I thank providence for it every day. Admittedly, I have had my grief between about 1920 and the 1940s, but even then there was much I could be grateful for.' His health, he said somewhat wistfully, had been very good into his sixties, and his family lived close round him.

Professionally also I was lucky. At the age of seventeen I knew what I wanted. It was the history of art, and I went to university lectures when I was still in the sixth form. At that time and for quite a number of years afterwards in unpaid academic jobs my parents gave the money for my studies. With immigration to England I had to rely financially on myself, and so my first job was to teach Italian to History of Art students at the Courtauld Institute. These were the early days of the Courtauld, and I was advised not to make any dates with my students while Ascot week was on . . . I am sure it did me good to have some years in the design trade [with Gordon Russell]. I am equally sure that the months of debris clearing in 1939–40 did me good.* I still remember my proud feeling on receiving my first pay packet.

'It is time for me to step down,' he concluded. 'My age is becoming an obstacle. The worst by far is the disappearing memory. In 1912 Philip Webb wrote in a letter, "I much want steadying. For example my memory fails and leads me into ugly bogs." And let me finish with another quotation. As it rhymes, who else could I have chosen but Morris? And here is the quotation:

> I am old and have seen
> Many things that have been;
> Both grief and peace
> And wane and increase.
> No tale I tell
> Of ill or well.
> But this I say:

---

*Actually 1940–1.

Night treadeth on day,
And for worst or best
Right good is rest.'*

Jane Fawcett had resigned as Secretary in August 1976. She had been
very much Pevsner's protégée and had taken on more and more of the
work of the Society as he got frailer. He acknowledged her contribution
with affection: 'If it had not been for Jane, there might have been a
Victorian Society, but its strength, its versatility and its resourcefulness
was largely Jane's.' She was replaced by Hermione Hobhouse, but the
decision-making was now in the hands of a new body, the General
Purposes Sub-Committee, 'set up to take over both the functions of the
old Finance Sub-Committee and much of the decision-making that had
formerly been carried out on an *ad hoc* basis by the Society's officers'.†

This was not, of course, the end of Pevsner's involvement with Victorian
buildings. He travelled to York in 1977 to unveil a plaque celebrating
the centenary of the railway station, which on its completion in 1877
was the largest in the world. The Victorian Society's Annual Study
Tour was in the city at the same time, and Julian Orbach remembered
meeting Pevsner before the ceremony:

> He was billeted in the Station Hotel for the night . . . Punctilious
> as ever, he decided that he would like to walk round to the other
> railway bits in York . . . to refresh his mind for his speech. We set
> out, about four or five of us in the gathering dark, through narrow
> and rather empty streets around the old station area and it became
> obvious that NP was tiring fast and would not make it back to the
> hotel. I volunteered to fetch my car – yellow GPO Morris Minor it
> was – and we decided that he should wait with the others in a small
> railway workers' pub. When I came back he was sitting at the bar
> with an almost untouched half of bitter, watching mesmerised the
> men playing darts. 'It is amazing,' he said, 'every time they throw
> one they hit just the right spot,' as if he had never seen this before.
> He had such a pure delight and was so frail, like a child at Christmas.[3]

---

*This is the poem embroidered on the bed hangings at Kelmscott Manor.
†Hugh Casson, who had been a Vice-Chair for fifteen years, decided to resign at the
same time as Pevsner.

Meanwhile, 1976 saw the publication, at last, of *A History of Building Types*, which, even if it was not the book he would once have written or would have liked to have written, was Pevsner's major work in which Victorian architecture played a leading role. 'Had he not been Pevsner, he would have retired,' Mark Girouard pointed out. 'As it is, he has merely changed his quest, and from analysing the buildings of England by counties moved on to analysing the buildings of the Western World by types. Let lesser mortals hang their heads.'[4]

Finishing *Building Types* had required an astonishing effort of will. The potential subject matter was infinite, and Pevsner lacked the time and, increasingly, the physical energy to trace sources, identify illustrations, chase the references that friends gave him from their reading, on resort hotels, college libraries, savings banks, the history of lifts, American lunatic asylums. He said more than once that he feared *Building Types* might be a posthumous publication.

That it appeared in his lifetime was largely due to Emily Lane and Ian Sutton, editors at Thames and Hudson who, at different times, had been his students and whom he knew and trusted. They had worked with him some ten years earlier on the preparation of the two-volume collection of his articles, *Studies in Art, Architecture and Design*, a task that had itself involved interminable queries, postscripts and addenda. 'Their patience knew no bounds,' Pevsner told Thomas Neurath of Thames and Hudson. 'I have never had so much help from a publisher.'[5] They would need all their patience again, to deal not only with the minutiae of the text but also with Pevsner's heightened anxieties.

Pevsner had established his reputation at least partly on his ability to generalise, but was bedevilled now by a near-obsessive concern for isolated facts. He seemed more anxious to accumulate examples of different styles of building than to explore the relationship between style and function, and he worried compulsively about specimens he might have missed, keeping lists of addenda that grew ever longer. To enjoy writing this book, he would have needed the extraordinary powers of recall he had once possessed.* But now, as he had told the Victorian Society, his memory was letting him down.

Pevsner had laid himself wide open to attack in *Building Types*, both from specialists in each of the individual building types and from those who had written their own historical overviews. The book was a reviewer's dream. Everyone could appear to advantage by pointing

---

*He once told Jane Fawcett that until he was seventy – more or less the moment when he started writing *Building Types* – he could remember the position on every printed page of every piece of information that he wanted to use.

out buildings in each category that the author had missed or misin-
terpreted. It was a familiar phenomenon for Pevsner, and he had
anticipated it to some degree. In his foreword he wrote, 'This book
appears with many faults. Had I another few years for preparation,
most of them could be corrected . . . However, at my age one is anxious
to see a book come out, better faulty than not at all.'

Faulty or not, *Building Types* earned Pevsner a Wolfson Literary
Award in 1976, a prize of £5,000 accompanied by considerable publicity.* He may have seen this more as recognition for a life's work in
architectural history than as an accolade for that particular book.
Certainly he had now reached a point where some critical observers
felt the time had come to attempt an assessment of what he had done
and the kind of man he had been.

---

*The Wolfson Literary Awards (now the Wolfson History Prizes) had been established
in 1972 by the Wolfson Foundation, with the aim of encouraging excellence in the
writing of history for the general public.

CHAPTER 48

Morality and architecture

Why did people have a problem with Pevsner?[1] For an academic who had conducted little intellectual warfare and a man who had no time for feuds, he attracted hostility that was surprisingly intense. 'Abuse in argument is always suspicious,' he observed.[2] His tone as a reviewer was always measured and devoid of animus, and he never indulged in innuendo or deliberate ambiguity. Where he gave offence, it was likely to be inadvertent, through the brusqueness of his letter-writing style, or a failure to recognise insecurity in someone junior, or a simple lack of tact.

Pevsner was not easy to shift in an argument, and certainly in later life he had a tendency to cut people short in his progress towards making his point. There were senses of humour he did not share – he was no good at all at telling funny stories, according to his family – and conversational styles with which he was ill at ease. He dismissed exaggeration, was uncomfortable with camp and resented cliquishness. 'What he didn't like was bitchiness in other people . . . backbiting,' remembered Bridget Cherry. 'He was a very straightforward person, very honest, and he didn't like politicking and intrigue. It went against his nature, and consequently he may have been a bit offhand or unforthcoming to such people.'[3]

All this would be enough to explain his distaste for Douglas Cooper – the only dislike that Winnie Sibson could remember him expressing openly during her years as his secretary. Cooper was a self-taught expert on modern art, with a private income that enabled him to build a superb collection of Cubist art. Violently hostile to the English art establishment, which he suspected (rightly) of condescending to him, he lived in the South of France and specialised in writing abusive letters in green ink to the English art press.[4] Pevsner may not have been aware that Cooper had been accused twice in the 1940s of blatant plagiarism. He was certainly conscious that Cooper was aggressively homosexual, because he was heard to remark that he did not care for all that scent. Nevertheless, his aversion did not prevent him from inviting Cooper to contribute the twentieth-century chapters to a volume of the *Pelican History of Art* on nineteenth- and twentieth-century painting and sculpture in Europe – but for reasons that are not clear, Cooper never delivered the text.*

Had Pevsner taken Cooper on as a Pelican author, he would probably have been equal to the task of dealing with his bellicosity. Since the early 1950s he had become accustomed to being under fire from a foe at least as confrontational, in the shape of Cambridge academic Hugh Plommer.† At first glance, there was little in Plommer's background – he was a classical archaeologist – to suggest grounds for violent disagreement, and Pevsner was taken aback to receive a letter early in 1953, scrawled in thick black ink and headed by a couplet from Dryden:

> For wild ambition loves to slide, not stand,
> And fortune's ice prefers to virtue's land.

'Dear Pevsner,' the letter began:

Your latest article, 'Bristol, Troyes, Gloucester', will doubtless confirm the belief of the many in the depth and scope of your erudition . . . But it seems to me, like most of your work, to build on unsubstantiated dogmas, too hastily formed, whose collapse will bring you at last into discredit. You take sidelong glances, seldom careful or accurate, at the artifacts, the buildings, sometimes the whole architectures you adduce as contrasts or analogies . . . The seeming certitude of your statements is seen to result from hurry and not from scholarly conviction. In conclusion, may I say I am horrified by the proposed arrangement of your new oecumenical art-history [the *Pelican History of Art*]? . . . You see what you compel me to think of your work. A few people remain who watch your present course with distaste and sincere regret.[5]

Pevsner's response reflected his astonishment: 'Dear Mr Plommer, It is remarkable to receive such a letter as yours, and I hope equally remarkable not to ignore it.' He dutifully thanked Plommer for drawing his attention to a building he had missed in his article on Bristol

---

*Robin Middleton suggested in his obituary for Pevsner (*Burlington*, 126/973, April 1984) that Cooper refused to write the chapters because Pevsner insisted that he include Henry Moore in his survey of the twentieth century. Middleton, now Professor Emeritus of Art History at Columbia, was one of Pevsner's first graduate students, later a lecturer in the Faculty of Architecture and Art History in Cambridge.
†Hugh Plommer (1922–83) was a Lecturer in Greek and Roman Architecture, Curator of the Museum of Classical Archaeology and a Fellow of Wolfson College, Cambridge.

Cathedral, but continued, 'Perhaps it would have been in better taste to draw my attention to this omission in a letter to the Editor, without some of your further comments. However as you choose to throw stones out of your glass-house . . .' and then he moved into the charge, pointing out an error of Plommer's own. 'It is a pity you spoil your righteous indignation by that touch . . . You also wave triumphantly at me one mistake in Nottinghamshire, one mistake in Middlesex and one omission in London. Do produce more please; others have done better than you, and well they may.'

This was, for Pevsner, a relatively testy retort, but it did not contain the makings of the kind of academic brawl that Plommer relished. Picking intellectual fights was part of his public persona as an eccentric, and he revelled in it. The Plommer files are full of letters turned down by newspaper editors as gratuitously offensive and manuscripts rejected by publishers he condemned as craven. He maintained his guerrilla campaign against Pevsner for decades. He was given to lamenting the disappearance of the English Gentleman, 'inoculated by his training and his proud position, against the sceptical excesses of Continental Europe'. Europe, it would seem, was the home of most modern errors, such as Marxism and the metric system, and he had a particular abhorrence of Germany and its scholars, especially its *Kunsthistoriker*. He denounced 'the introduction from the Continent of indefensible "modern art" and then, from Germany, of unintelligible "Art History" which purports to explain it. The very existence of such activities in Germany gave Hitler a handle against universities and Jews.'[6] There may have been an element of personal grudge in Plommer's resentment of foreign scholars. He had a reverence for the Oxbridge way of life, but he was teaching in Leeds in 1953 when he wrote the first broadside to Pevsner, who was then holder of the Cambridge Slade professorship. Pevsner lectured in the university, he was often on the radio and he wrote regularly for the *Architectural Review*. But however fashionable he might be, declared Plommer, Pevsner was a mere journalist, 'without principles or causes'.

This last comment was a marginal note pencilled into Plommer's copy of *Cambridge New Architecture*, with its foreword by Pevsner – and here lay the real root of Plommer's detestation. Pevsner had been quite wrong in supposing, back in 1952, that no one objected to the views on new buildings in Cambridge he had advanced in the last of his Slade Lectures. Plommer had objected to them then, he was affronted again in 1964 when *Cambridge New Architecture* appeared, and he campaigned for the rest of his life against modern building in Cambridge.

He particularly detested the brand of Modernism of which he took Pevsner to be the arch-prophet. Passionately devoted to the principles of the classical style, which he defined as simplicity, symmetry, politeness, consistency and centralised planning by a cultured elite, Plommer described himself as 'a lover of great ensembles'.[7] He resented the lack of attention given to Greece and Rome by Pevsner in his *Outline of European Architecture* and the general lack of sympathy for the classical style that, he felt, had enabled Pevsner to espouse its antithesis.[*] The Picturesque brand of modernism, to Plommer, was simply a licence to build anything at all, higgledy-piggledy, on the assumption that it would weather into place.[†] He bitterly opposed the Holford plans for the expansion of Cambridge University, and played a leading part in forcing the truncation of Casson and Conder's plans for the Arts Faculty.

Pevsner played the same role for Plommer as he had long done for John Betjeman, as a lightning conductor for a more general spleen and universal discontent with modern life. By the late 1970s, however, Betjeman at least was beginning to relent. His softening was barely obvious in print and in public – he used the first instalment of his *Private Eye* column, 'Nooks and Corners of the New Barbarism', to ridicule a building in Ludgate Hill on the grounds that Pevsner had praised it – but in private he could now be cordial. When he was invited to 'edit' a series of medals of lost architectural masterpieces, he wrote round his acquaintances to ask for their candidates for commemoration. The standard letter read, 'Your help in your own area will be greatly welcomed.' The letter to Pevsner had 'your own area' crossed out and the words 'your Great Britain' substituted, and it concluded, 'I hope you are much better and happy'.[‡] By 1976 Betjeman was able to write, 'I see now that anybody who is true to his own ideas is probably all right.'[8]

Certainly Pevsner felt no reticence in asking Betjeman for his advice:

---

*Pevsner might have called this a lack of confidence rather than a lack of sympathy. When asked by David Watkin (in his capacity as Secretary of the Cambridge Faculty of Architecture and History of Art) to examine a thesis entitled 'The Superstructure of the Greek Doric Temple', he refused in very short order, possibly with critics like Plommer in mind: 'I assure you I don't want to be difficult, but it is completely impossible for me to pronounce on a subject of this kind. Archaeologists are a special tribe, and Historians of Art have no training that would enable them to be competent in Greek and Roman architecture.' NP/D. Watkin, 3/9/70.

†Plommer belonged to the informal group of opponents of the Picturesque that included W.A. Eden (with whom Plommer had worked in Leeds) and Bertram Hume.

‡Pevsner's nominations for the medal series included the Bank of England, Fonthill and King Edward's School, Birmingham, and he suggested that Betjeman might also seek nominations from Andor Gomme, Nicholas Taylor and David Watkin.

'I was told the other day at West Dean that there is a connection between the house and Edward James, a collector of surrealist art. They seem to think that you are the one who knows all about that.'[9] James had financed the publication of Betjeman's first volume of poetry, *Mount Zion*, in 1931, and Betjeman responded amiably to Pevsner:

> How nice to hear from you. There is a very good ballade about West Dean by Belloc. It begins 'At Singleton in Sussex you may see / A house of flint upon a certain slope' and goes on about Mrs Willy James entertaining King Edward VII there. Somewhere in the hall there used to be a bell push which Edward VII pushed to open a cable line between England and America. Shortly before the war Mrs Willy James' son, Edward Frank Willis James, had a house in the woods designed by Dali. It was in the shape of a womb and inside it was lined with fur. There were curves in it the shape of Mae West's hips. I wonder if it is still there.*

Betjeman was still capable of rehearsing the old grudges. 'Although I have tried architectural journalism myself,' he wrote, 'art history and architectural history still seem to me to be verbiage written by uncreative people who want to make a name or a faculty for themselves with chairs and incomes attached to it ensuring dignity and a comfortable set of rooms in a college or university.'[10] However, the jibes were no longer so sharply and invariably personal, and he no longer resorted so readily to the 'Herr-Professor-Doktor' sneer.

For others, however, the preoccupation with Pevsner's Germanness lingered on, perpetuated, largely unintentionally, by Peter Clarke. Pevsner enjoyed Clarke's parodies, went to dinner at his house, and acted as a referee for him in job applications. 'Original voices like that of Peter Clarke,' he wrote, 'remind us that architecture is not just thesis material.' Clarke, for his part, had come to know Pevsner better

---

*J. Betjeman/NP, 6/9/77. Betjeman's account confirmed the link with Edward James, but otherwise may have served only to confuse. James (1907–84) inherited not only the main West Dean mansion, but also a smaller house, Monkton House, designed by Lutyens, which he decided to use as a secluded artistic retreat. He had the garden front remodelled with giant green metal columns with palm leaves; internally there were also many Surrealist flourishes. These included a pair of Dalí sofas in the shape of Mae West's lips, but the house itself was a normal shape and womb-like only in being secluded. One room had upholstered walls, but Betjeman may have transposed the fur-lined teacup of Swiss Surrealist Meret Oppenheim. The anecdote about Edward VII may have been true, as James was a godson and reputedly also a grandson.

through the Victorian Society; he greatly respected his knowledge and was aware of his sensitivities. When he was asked by *The Times,* as a staffer, to prepare an obituary of Pevsner for the stocks, he commented, '[Pevsner] hardly ever speaks of his earlier life in Germany . . . and I think he would not like this overemphasised.'[11]

However, the damage in this regard had already been done, by the verses Clarke had written in the 1950s. He was an expert mimic, especially good at a German accent. He had followed 'Poet and Pedant' in quick succession with 'Fröhliche Weihnachten von der Pevsnerreise'* – verses to be sung to the tune from the last movement of Schubert's Trout Quintet':

> From heart of Mittel-Europ
> > I make der little trip
> To show those Englische Dummkopfs
> > Some echt-Deutsch Scholarship.
> Viele Sehenswürdigkeiten
> > By others have been missed
> But now comes to enlighten
> > Der Great Categorist.
>
> Der Georgian und Viktorian
> > Ist sowieso 'getan'
> Bei Herr Professor Richardtson
> > Und Dichter Betjemann.
> While oders gifs you Stevenage,
> > Stonehenge und Gilbert Scott
> Von Pleiocene to C19
> > *I* gifs der blooming lot.
>
> Zu jeder Church in London
> > Ich schuss in froher Eil
> Und hab' schon was gefunden
> > Im echt Rundbogen-style.
> 'So beefy und hamfisted'.
> > Ich hatt' ein damgoodlook
> But soon es war gelisted
> > In meinem Penguinbook . . .

---

*'Happy Christmas from the Pevsner-Tour'.

All rest shall be resisted
Till every stone und brick
Is finally gelisted
By Herr Professor N-k.
Mit broadcast, book und lektur
roll in der £.S.D.
Der Britisch Architektur –
Ach! dat's der game for me!*

The first two verses would seem to have been published in the *Architectural Review*. The remainder were suppressed, but would be circulated over the years, with many a nudge, within the Victorian Society, usually by people who did not admire Pevsner's style. Most of the members would have found the architectural references entertaining, but not all of them appreciated the suggestion of money-grubbing or a last line that could easily have come out of the mouth of Lionel Bart's Fagin. Unable to resist a good joke, Clarke had kept the figure of Pevsner the Teuton alive and given his real detractors a weapon which was wielded with more ferocity than its creator had perhaps intended.

The disparagement of Pevsner since his death by John Harris, for example, is a curious phenomenon in which anti-Germanism is inextricably tangled with envy, wounded *amour propre* and perfectly justifiable methodological criticism. Harris himself has acknowledged that Pevsner was 'a spur and a mentor, and he knew I recognised him as such'. This was not guidance that Pevsner offered *de haut en bas*; he came genuinely to admire and respect Harris's work on the eighteenth century and promoted it where he could, in the *Architectural Review* and in the academic circles where his influence was considerable. 'Of course you can bring along the watercolour,' he told one correspondent, 'but there is no question that John Harris knows about three times as much concerning houses of that period than I do.'[12]

Harris joined Pevsner at the Lygon Arms for his sixty-fifth birthday in 1967, alongside friends and colleagues such as Hans Schmoller, Jim Richards, John Summerson and Alec Clifton-Taylor. But there were lingering resentments that he apparently never overcame. 'Sometimes I would have to come up to Gower Street, and I felt that – though I've never been particularly humble – he treated me a little bit shabbily. You felt that you were regarded as an office worker.'[13]

---

*The complete poem, which runs to eight stanzas, is to be found in Hillier, *The Bonus of Laughter*, op. cit., p.45 and n.89 on p.636. Geoffrey Best points out a convincing model for it in Charles Leland's *The Breitmann Ballads* (1871, New York).

'There was that way of working that was not entirely acceptable in England,' Harris added, getting down to what was apparently the heart of his objections to Pevsner's methodology:

Every evening he would leave the office at roughly the same time. He would walk to Goodge Street station, go down the Underground and take the train on the Northern Line. He said, 'Now, when I get on the train and sit down, I have my board, and every evening I can spend 17½ minutes writing on my board before I have to get out.' He would never think of buying a newspaper, he would never think of sitting there closing his eyes – he would have his board . . . There is something dreadfully pedantic about a man who actually recognises that he's got 17½ minutes to write on a board.

Overlooking the possibility that Pevsner might have been poking fun, with his precise timings, either at himself or at his stern interlocutor, Harris continued:

I believe it's part of his Germanic character which affected the *Buildings of England* . . . To use a military simile, Pevsner was like a German general, not Rommel but Rundstedt, shall we say, who fights a battle absolutely according to a preconceived plan – you must never deviate, you've got to do it like this, you've planned it like this and you must never deviate.* . . . If you criticise the terrible omissions in the earlier volumes, the pro-Nikolaus faction will say, 'Oh but you know, he never had the time'. This is absolute nonsense, I've demonstrated it time and time again. He never had the time because he had laid down a plan for his working life and in that plan he never deviated. The plan of his working life was the *Architectural Review*, editing the *Pelican History of Art*, editing King Penguin, editing this, editing that, the *Buildings of England*, teaching at Cambridge, teaching at Birkbeck. It was all planned like a military battle.

John Harris may have been the primary source of the idea that Pevsner disliked the upper classes on principle. 'He would never join a club,' he complained:

---

*John Harris, interview with the author, 7/4/92. Field Marshal Gerd von Rundstedt, commander of Germany's Western Offensive in 1940, was elderly and cautious, preferring conventional assault to *Blitzkrieg*. He was felt to have prevented more aggressive commanders from cutting off the British retreat before Dunkirk.

despite the fact that in actual fact it would have been very useful to him to have joined a London club where he could have entertained people. It represented something which I think was abhorrent to him . . . He was not happy with the dukes and the marquises and the earls . . . He always had that chip on his shoulder about people like Betjeman, because he saw Betjeman not only as an amateur (he never liked the amateur) but as a friend of the landed interest.

'[Pevsner] was best at describing churches and other examples of communal architecture,' declared Auberon Waugh:[14]

His socialist principles seemed to recoil from England's distinguishing glory, the domestic architecture of our manor houses, country seats and stately homes. An entry in the volume on South and West Somerset for Hinton House always gives me pleasure: 'An adequate appreciation of Hinton House is impossible, as Earl Poulett would not allow me to see the inside.' The last Lord Poulett, who died nearly 20 years ago, may have had the right idea. Somebody let Pevsner into my house at Combe Florey. 'Nice staircase of c. 1753' is his only comment about the interior. One can't very well take offence at that, but I feel my staircase has been violated whenever I reflect that his bleary socialist eyes have appraised it.

Whether or not Pevsner noticed that he had offended people, their rancour tended to be lasting and, eventually, damaging.

He was not unaccustomed to criticism. But no one had drawn the threads together into a systematic offensive, not just against Pevsner himself but against what he was thought to stand for. Plommer had perhaps come nearest, in holding Pevsner responsible for what he saw as the evils of contemporary architecture; and it was Pevsner's faith in the Modern Movement, rather than any of the other interests that had in fact consumed far more of his working life, which was eventually to bring him under sustained attack. He had achieved more prominence than he can ever have expected, or wanted, as a promoter of the Modern Movement when Modernism was in the ascendant; now he was to attract more hostility than he perhaps deserved, as an Aunt Sally for a movement under threat.

In 1977 architectural theorist Charles Jencks described anti-modernism as 'the orthodox tradition'. Pevsner was keenly aware of the growing reaction against the version of modernism to which he had been committed. People now held different views of the nature of progress. Historicism – in the Popperian sense of a belief that there is a single developmental path on which mankind is destined to walk – had been under attack since the early 1960s, from Ernst Gombrich among others. Gombrich had also fiercely challenged the notion of a single 'spirit of the age', a challenge that had then been directed specifically at Pevsner by Charles Jencks in his *Meaning in Architecture* in 1969.[15] By 1971 Stanford Anderson had produced a cogent criticism in the prestigious American *Art Bulletin* of what he called Pevsner's 'combination of notions: historical determinism, pessimism about the age, and architecture as the expression of that plight'.*

Pevsner, it was beginning to be suggested, was propounding a theory of modern architecture that led him, put crudely, systematically to overpraise buildings that were ugly and soulless and to dismiss those who championed a more humane and civilised architecture. Some of his most impassioned opponents were those who felt he had ignored a whole breed of admirable architects, and in so doing had actively damaged their reputations. The most obvious victim, they argued, was Edwin Lutyens, considered by many to be the greatest British architect of his era, but slighted by Pevsner simply because he had taken no part in the march towards modernism.

Pevsner did not, in fact, ignore Lutyens, and he struggled to be fair. Without doubt he was irritated by what he saw as a 'heavy-handed playfulness'. 'Lutyens's line was to be the perennial *enfant terrible*,' he complained. 'How much of this was spontaneous, how much methodical will always remain doubtful.' But in a full-length article in the *Architectural Review* for April 1951 entitled 'Building with Wit', and in the entry he wrote on Lutyens for the *McGraw Hill Encyclopedia of World Art* (1964), Pevsner credited him with expressing perfectly the spirit of his time, in his early years at least: '[Lutyens] shared in full the "folie de grandeur impériale" of the Edwardian period, and it made him the ideal architect of England's last crop of truly spectacular country houses.' The problem for Pevsner was that Lutyens had not changed as the times changed, and he had had what Pevsner described as a 'posthumous career' – the years during which he continued to work, completely outside the main-stream of European developments, in the style of the Edwardian period long after that period was dead. Lutyens's decision to do this

---

*Stanford Anderson (1934–) is currently Professor of History and Architecture at MIT. His remarks were made in his review of Pevsner's *Sources of Modern Architecture and Design* (1968).

might have been condoned as a prank or a *plaisanterie*, had it not also been a threat. England had been in a position to play a leading role in the Modern Movement; Lutyens's work was one of the key factors in her failure to do so. His Britannia House of 1924, for example, was in 'a style which put England back firmly from the pioneer position she had had when Lutyens was young'. 'My sympathy for [Lutyens] comes to a full stop about the year 1905,' wrote Pevsner in 1969, 'and after that I regard him as a very sinister influence.'[16]

The year of 1969 was the centenary of Lutyens's birth. Pevsner had originally accepted an invitation to join the committee in charge of running the celebrations, but on reviewing his responses to the work over the years, he thought better of it and withdrew. John Harris, the committee's chair, was put out: 'As an admirer of yours and a friend, I think you have done wrong to retire from the Lutyens committee.'[17] Others were even less forgiving of Pevsner's apparent disrespect. Roderick Gradidge, an architect, restorer, Victorian Society committee member and expert on the Arts and Crafts movement, vigorously questioned Pevsner's right to define 'Englishness' when he was apparently devoting himself to destroying the reputations of the architects who best represented the true English character.* As one of his friends pointed out, with Gradidge it was not just a matter of not suffering fools gladly, he was reluctant to suffer anyone gladly.[18] Large, loud, tattooed, kilted and pigtailed, he specialised in making scenes and was a booming and frequent critic of Pevsner. Once again, however, the attack was not systematic, and it was more likely to be made in the pub than in print. When the real assault was made, it came from a less obvious direction.

David Watkin first approached Pevsner in 1962 for advice on the choice of a topic for the short thesis that was one element in Part II of his undergraduate degree.† Pevsner steered him towards work on

---

*Roderick Gradidge (1929–2000) rejected Pevsner's line of development from Morris to Gropius by way of the Arts and Crafts movement, arguing that the logical development from Arts and Crafts was precisely the neo-Georgian and neo-Tudor architecture that Pevsner despised. Obituary for Gradidge by Alan Powers, *Guardian*, 25/1/2001. For a sympathetic portrait of an eccentric man, 'either loved or loathed', see Gavin Stamp's entry on Gradidge in the *Oxford Dictionary of National Biography* (OUP, 2004).
†David Watkin (1941–), an architectural historian, is a Fellow of Peterhouse and Professor Emeritus in the History of Architecture at the Department of Art History in Cambridge. He has also taught at the Prince of Wales's Institute of Architecture, has sat as a member of the Historic Buildings Council and is vice chairman of the Georgian

the 1866 National Gallery Competition. For a postgraduate thesis, he suggested that Watkin concentrate on the Regency collector, connoisseur, designer and arbiter of taste, Thomas Hope. There was, he warned, an existing book on Hope, in French, by the Hungarian scholar Sándor Baumgarten, but 'I would expect that a good deal can still be done about his position and influence in England and his interference with a good many things taking place during his lifetime.*

Baumgarten had had to work so hard to find unpublished material by Hope that he became convinced that Hope's family must have destroyed a good deal. Pevsner was not of much help to Watkin in bridging this gap. 'He was unable to direct me as to how to look for, or to work with, documents and archives in my research into Thomas Hope,' Watkin commented later. 'I was therefore obliged to find other scholars, notably John Harris, who could guide me in these important directions.'[19]

Watkin acknowledged that Pevsner had been of use in directing him towards John Murray when the time came to look for a publisher for the completed thesis, and in writing 'golden words' for use as propaganda on the cover.[†] Pevsner also wrote a string of references for Watkin to support his applications for research fellowships at various Cambridge colleges. 'A serious research person,' he told Trinity Hall in 1966, 'with a knack for finding out interesting information and unknown facts, and a great talent in presenting them'.[20] '[Watkin] would amply deserve a research fellowship,' he informed Jesus College later that year. 'Without much direct help from me, he has got hold of a mass of either unpublished, or uninterpreted material, and has written it up in a beautiful, elegant way.'[21] The thesis on Hope, he told both Peterhouse and Clare College in February 1967, was 'uncommonly excellent'.[22] 'You could not do better than to appoint Mr Watkin,' he suggested to the University's Faculty Board of Fine Arts when they were seeking that same month to fill the post of Librarian, a university position with tenure. 'He is very intelligent, very capable, has wide interests, and gets on well with people.'[23] Watkin took up the post in the spring of 1967.

Group. He has published widely on classical and neoclassical architecture, as well as producing two overviews of Western and English architecture, and has written monographs on Thomas Hope, John Soane, James Stuart, C.R. Cockerell and Quinlan Terry.
*NP/D. Watkin, 9/7/63. Baumgarten's book, *Le Crépuscule néo-classique. Thomas Hope*, had been published by Didier in 1958.
†Jock Murray had been a friend for some years and Pevsner offered to write personally to him with his views on Watkin's thesis and its suitability for publication. NP/D. Watkin, 6/6/67.

However, by the time his thesis was published by John Murray in 1968 as *Thomas Hope 1769–1831 and the Neo-Classical Idea*, Watkin had already formulated some of the profound objections he had to his former supervisor's ideas: not just his methods of research and his relative indifference to primary sources but his whole approach to art history. That year Watkin delivered in Cambridge a lecture entitled 'From Pugin to Pevsner', which he now claims, apparently without irony, to have regarded as a contribution to the year of revolutions in its overthrow of orthodoxy in architectural theory.[24] There is no evidence that the powers-that-be, or indeed Pevsner, noticed the lecture,* but Watkin worked it up into a short book, *Morality and Architecture*, that would be published nine years later in 1977 as a serious challenge to Pevsner's theories.

Watkin's argument was that there had been a strong and wholly misplaced strain of moralism in the way in which the history of architecture had been narrated. Architecture had been presented by writers from Pugin to Pevsner as a consequence or manifestation of some other phenomenon – religion, politics, sociology, philosophy, technology, theories of space, or the spirit of the age. It had been discussed as though it were purely an instrument of social policy, deployed to achieve supposedly 'moral' ends. For Watkin, architecture should be studied for its own sake, and this study should include consideration of style for its own sake, with the measures of success being not merely function and utility, but beauty, imagination and taste. In this he was following the line taken by Geoffrey Scott† and, like Scott (and Plommer), he championed the eternal language of classicism standing above and apart from the short-term social and political objectives of the moment. Once again, the old spectre of 'art for art's sake' had come back to haunt Pevsner.

'Moralism' had taken different forms over the years, Watkin continued. In Pugin's case, it was rooted in religion, whereas for a man like Robert Furneaux Jordan the basis was socialism. As for Pevsner, his moralism had two origins: socialist inclinations, and a devotion to the notion of *Zeitgeist*. In promoting modernism he worked from three premises. Each age had its own spirit and should build in a manner appropriate to that spirit, which in the twentieth century

---

*Pevsner wrote amicably to Watkin that autumn, 'Dear David, It suddenly occurred to me last night in bed when I turned over the pages of your book [*Thomas Hope*], that I had never written to you how delighted I am with its publication and with the way it looks. You could not have launched yourself in a more impressive way.' NP/D. Watkin, 21/11/68.
†See Chapter 37.

was one of collectivism, practicality, speed and the power of machines. The only form of architecture appropriate to this age was the architecture of the Modern Movement. To build in any other way – to satisfy individual needs or gratify individual tastes, to express individual personality rather than attempting to embody current social and political conditions – was to impede social progress, and was therefore morally wrong.

This line of thought, in Watkin's view, led Pevsner to exalt buildings of indifferent aesthetic value. 'The values of art do not lie in the sequence,' Geoffrey Scott had written, 'but in the individual terms.'[25] Pevsner only seemed to find interesting those buildings that could be placed in the sequence of the emergence of the 'modern style'. 'A building is admirable,' Watkin wrote testily, 'if an observer sees it as belonging to a date later than that when it was actually constructed.' Focusing on the sequence produced 'an art history which disregards the individual circumstances and achievements of individual artists, the alternatives they accepted or rejected, and instead manipulates actors building up to the denouement of a predetermined drama'. It was a denial of the pleasure to be found in individual genius and 'refined achievement'.

Watkin's attack on moralism, as he was at pains to point out, was not launched in a vacuum. When in 1970 he had moved to Peterhouse in Cambridge as a Research Fellow, he found there an intellectual climate which located his opposition in a wider intellectual context. The college, the oldest foundation in the university, had long been the home of conservative opposition to liberalism in general and more recently to the influence of liberal intellectuals on policy.* Watkin soon joined the circle surrounding the historian Maurice Cowling, founder of the right-wing Salisbury Group, a fierce champion of High Conservatism and a bitter opponent of 'establishment liberalism' as a rigid moralising orthodoxy. The circle, which also included historians Edward Norman and Brian Wormald and the philosopher Roger Scruton, shared, in Cowling's words, 'common prejudices against the higher liberalism and all sorts of liberal rhetoric, including ecclesiastical liberal rhetoric, and in favour of irony, geniality and malice as solvents of enthusiasm, virtue and elevation'.[26]†

---

*The Master of the college from 1955 to 1968 had been Sir Herbert Butterfield, famous as the author of *The Whig Interpretation of History*, an influential attack on 'the tendency of many historians to write on the side of Protestants and Whigs . . . to emphasise certain principles of progress in the past and to produce a story which is the ratification if not the glorification of the present'.
†Nicholas Taylor also points to the profound influence on Watkin of Monsignor Alfred Gilbey (1902–98), the University's long-serving Catholic chaplain. Gilbey, who dressed

The 'Peterhouse Right' was described by its detractors as a caucus of reaction in Cambridge, a collection of self-appointed right-wing *penseurs* with aspirational lifestyles and déclassé origins, the lifestyles – in which cultivated artistic tastes played an important part – adopted to conceal the origins.* This was the group that provided a context and a springboard for Watkin's assault on modernism, which had from its beginnings been associated in conservative minds at the very least with socialism, and at worst with Bolshevism.

In *Morality and Architecture*, published on 13 October 1977, Watkin seized with professional relish on the weaknesses in Pevsner's architectural theory – the most patent being his faith in the *Zeitgeist*. This was already the softest of targets. In Charles Jencks's words later in 1977, 'For the last 15 years or so other knights, indeed veritable battalions, have been killing off the zeitgeist.'[27] Watkin fastened on the lack of precision in Pevsner's use of the notion of *Zeitgeist* and pilloried the way in which he employed it to justify the construction of loose parallels between different spheres of life, 'guided by a theory rather than documentary evidence'. 'Knowing Michelangelo's late style as a sculptor,' he wrote scathingly, 'enables us to "prove" that it "must" have been accompanied by "a crisis of introspection" throughout the city of Rome; and we have already deduced this crisis from knowledge of the Pope's eating habits.'

It was not unreasonable to suggest that Pevsner's creed was less a developed and coherent philosophy than an assemblage of faiths. Pevsner himself had admitted in his RIBA Gold Medal speech, 'I know I am deplorably unphilosophical.' He had, after all, once described work as an *escape* from philosophy.[†] Watkin would later offer an explanation for this lack of rigour: 'He turned himself into a continuous writing machine with little time to reflect on his conceptual position.

---

in breeches, frock coat and shovel hat and excluded all women from the Fisher House chaplaincy, was opposed to all development of liberal thought since the French Revolution. In particular, he rejected egalitarianism, and adhered to the Tridentine Mass, the Mass of the Counter-Reformation.

*Giles Foden and John Mullan, 'Peterhouse blues', *Guardian*, 10/9/99. An obituary for the Harvard art historian Sydney Freedberg, the scholar with whom Pevsner had fallen out most fiercely over the *Pelican History of Art* (see Chapter 34) and a man of conservative views, provides an interesting parallel: 'What seemed to him an incongruity between his origins and the cosmopolitan world of art scholars, connoisseurs and collectors into which he quickly became absorbed no doubt prompted him to create in dress and in speech an image of fastidious refinement.' Memorial note, *Harvard University Gazette*, 23/4/98.

†Ian Sutton remembers him once asking, 'What is the attraction [of philosophy]? It can't be to find things out, because we all know that there are no answers to philosophical questions. Is it just the method, like working out a crossword?' Sutton, 'Reminiscences', op. cit.

It is difficult to trace any intellectual development in his work, he was reluctant to consider that history can be interpreted in different ways and that anyone who writes should have sufficient self-awareness to understand what ideological position he occupies.'[28]

Watkin also charged Pevsner with attempting to muster intellectual support for what were in the end simply aesthetic preferences: having found flat roofs and revealed construction pleasing, he did not explain in any detail why they were particularly expressive of contemporary needs, but set out to persuade a wider public to accept them 'as though they were the inevitable consequence of the facts of modern life and society'. Again, it is probably fair to suggest that Pevsner's commitment to modernism grew out of more than simply an objective weighing of intellectual arguments. The Modern Movement in the 1920s was for him a break with the overstuffed rooms of his mother's house, with a past that contained war, revolution, financial chaos and the suicide of his brother. Commitment to modernism was a commitment to what he *wanted* to be the spirit of the age: order, reason, restraint, straightforwardness, concern for the common good rather than selfish individualism.

But if Pevsner was writing from emotion as much as cold reason, so too was Watkin. *Morality and Architecture* is, in its tactics and techniques, a polemic. As a tract, it works through generalisation, selectivity, misrepresentation, and guilt by association, and its argument is politicised beyond anything that Pevsner ever contemplated.

Throughout the book, Watkin makes precisely the same kind of sweeping generalisation of which he accuses Pevsner. 'What we have called the historicist and *Zeitgeist*-inspired historian . . . believes in a state which is antagonistic to all groupings which come between it and the individual,' he declares, 'and which will allow no real power or autonomy to any subordinate structures, ranging from the family to the corporation.' He cites no evidence to suggest that Pevsner believed anything of the sort. As for selectivity, while Pevsner admitted to having singled out one particular thread of historical development in *Pioneers* (while explicitly drawing attention to the existence of other threads), Watkin is not as candid. He seems to base the entire edifice of his argument on a handful of sentences from works that Pevsner wrote in the 1930s, sentences that were avowedly more dogmatic and more political than anything he ever wrote again, heavily influenced by their context, and he ignores the rest.* In *Morality and Architecture*

---

*Pevsner himself pointed out, in a response to Stanford Anderson's piece in the *Art Bulletin*, that the attitude Anderson was criticising was one that appeared on the last page of *Pioneers*, but had not been expressed by Pevsner since then. More up-to-date and its follow-up *Morality and Architecture Revisited* (2001), and in articles and lectures that accompanied the sequel, Watkin has recycled these same quotations without regard to the bulk of Pevsner's work, where one can find more than enough material to rebut the suggestions that Pevsner had no concern for humanity in architecture, or for the significance of aesthetic meaning, or for the creativity of the individual architect. Even in *Pioneers* itself, in the peroration in the final chapter on which Watkin loads such emphasis, Pevsner allows that 'the great creative brain will find its own way even in times of overpowering collective energy'.*

'The artist who is representative of this century of ours must needs be cold,' wrote Pevsner in *Pioneers*, 'as he stands for a century cold as steel and glass, a century the precision of which leaves less space for self-expression than did any period before.' The new style of the twentieth century, 'because it is a genuine style as opposed to a passing fashion, is totalitarian'. 'One may regret living in such an age, but one cannot alter it,' he had written in the *Enquiry into Industrial Art in England*, arguing that the only way forward was to develop *amor fati*, a means of embracing one's destiny. He did not want the century to be cold, but he believed that it was, and that the artist who best reflected it would also be cold. Nor, in describing the century as 'totalitarian', was he approving or advocating any form of authoritarian government.† However, his choice of the word 'totalitarian' gave a hostage to fortune, which critics have used against him ever since.

'Most have been prepared to allow,' wrote Reyner Banham, 'that in 1936 it ["totalitarian"] might not have meant exactly what Allied wartime propaganda and Joe McCarthy had made it mean twenty years later.' What Pevsner meant by it is fairly clear from the word he chose to substitute for it in later editions, when it became clear

---

reflections of his attitudes were now to be found in the second edition of *Cambridgeshire* and would also be found in the forthcoming volume on *Oxfordshire*. NP/S. Anderson 8/7/71. GP Series VI, Box 135.

*Watkin could not, of course, be aware of what Pevsner had written in 1939 for the proposed special issue of the *Architectural Review* that was never published: 'Even in the most anonymous of styles it is in the end the personal genius of one man which is responsible for the one particular aesthetically most satisfactory interpretation of a common theme.' See p.241.

†See Chapter 17. Pevsner would explicitly reject the association of the Modern Movement with totalitarianism in its strictly political sense in a letter to the Austrian architectural critic Friedrich Achleitner in April 1968 – 'I think the concept . . . that the so-called Modern Movement goes with totalitarianism is a very dangerous one' – making the point that totalitarian regimes had historically favoured classicism and opposed modernist styles. NP/F. Achleitner, 23/4/68. Getty Papers, Series 1A, Box 11.

what kind of construction was being placed upon the original expression. He rewrote the sentence to read 'this new style of the 20th century which . . . is *universal*', suggesting that he may have had in mind the interpretation put upon 'totalitarian' by Thomas Mann in 1942: '"Totalitarian" in its strictly political sense is an oppressive word; we do not like it because it describes the greedy absorption of all things human by the state. But we live in fact in a totalitarian world, a world of totality, of intellectual unity and collective responsibility. It is a world of endless mutual commitment.'[29]

One of the less palatable features of *Morality and Architecture* is its attempt, using Pevsner's use of the word 'totalitarian' as a lever, to associate him with the various brands of collectivism that Watkin abhors. Watkin attributes to him an 'injunction to be "as cold as steel"', which 'cannot but remind us of the Nazi command to be "*zäh wie Leder, hart wie Stahl und schnell wie ein Windhund*"'.* Though he swiftly adds the suggestion that Pevsner would not, in fact, have wished to identify himself with National Socialism, he repeats the association when he says 'the plea for the suppression of the individual which we have noticed in Pevsner's writings was echoed by Mies van der Rohe . . . *and also by Goebbels* [my italics] who claimed that "the individual is being de-throned"'. The Nazi notion of 'suppression' was a very different one from that of Pevsner, who had only ever called for individuals to place their own individuality at the service of the collective, and to make the association between them is distasteful. Perhaps in recognition of this, Watkin once again offers a hasty disclaimer, suggesting that Pevsner might have derived his thinking on the suppression of the individual from 'the socialistic and communistic radicalism of the Weimar Republic of [his] young manhood'. In other words, he might not have been a Nazi, but a communist instead.

The allusions to communism are persistent. Watkin puts Marxist expressions – 'alienated/unalienated man', 'new Jerusalem', 'socialist industrialism' – into Pevsner's mouth. (Many of the proponents of modernism did quote Marxist sources, but Pevsner was not one of them.) 'We may define the substantive views expressed by Pevsner,' writes Watkin, 'as follows: praise of industrialism while disliking capitalism; desire for egalitarian uniformity; dislike of any avowal of aesthetic criteria; belief in "Hardness" and in "Honesty" with nothing deliberately aiming at beauty. The brutalism which underlies this

---

*This is a rough approximation of the phrase that Hitler declared to be the official motto of the Hitler Youth programme: 'tough as leather, hard as Krupps' steel and as swift as a greyhound'.

undoubtedly owes something to the Bolshevik language current in certain artistic and political circles in Europe in the early 1920s.' Again, in the Conclusion, when discussing the failure by Pevsner (who has suddenly become 'Professor Pevsner') to mention Lutyens in the final chapter of the *Outline*, entitled 'Romantic Movement, Historicism and Modern Movement', Watkin claims: 'It is like one of those Russian Communist photographs from which the presence of some politically unacceptable figure has been skilfully eliminated.'*

Fifteen years on from the publication of *Morality and Architecture*, in a lecture to a conference in Milan entitled 'Pevsner: a study in "historicism"', Watkin revealed some of what had prompted him to denounce moralism in general and Pevsner in particular.[30] 'I will say now, as I did not in 1977, that my book was in part generated by my intense dislike of the modernist architecture which I saw as doing deliberate violence to English historic towns, and which had been continuously, relentlessly, and, it must be said, successfully, promoted by Pevsner from 1936 onwards.'

Watkin's detestation of modern building seems far from purely aesthetic, and his motives in decrying Pevsner would appear to have as much to do with politics as with architecture. 'It is essential to the argument of *Pioneers of the Modern Movement* that modern design . . . is necessarily socialist,' writes Watkin. Might one not say with rather more justification that it is essential to the argument of *Morality and Architecture* that Pevsner is socialist?

Watkin would often repeat the charge that Pevsner's work was skewed by his dislike of the upper classes. He told the writer Ian Buruma in 1999 that Pevsner never understood English life. 'You see, he never met patrons, or people with money, or style, or birth.'[31] In his Milan lecture he would allege that Pevsner's decision to omit furniture, medals, tapestries, porcelain and other decorative arts from the *Pelican History of Art* was due to his distaste for connoisseurship and 'a largely un-acknowledged hostility to the concept of ownership operating as part of the power structure of a ruling class'. Pevsner's prejudice, according to Watkin, had influenced the course of art history by ensuring that the importance of patronage was not properly recognised.

---

*That these references to communism are entirely deliberate is suggested by the fact that they are continued in the sequel. In the preface to *Morality and Architecture Revisited*, Watkin quotes with disapproval Pevsner's remark in *London 1* that 'the neo-classical, neo-Georgian spectre is even now not yet laid', and adds, 'The image of laying a spectre struck me then, as now, as offensive: burying a tradition was, after all, the language of Khrushchev to Kennedy in his ugly, and false, boast, "we will bury you".'

'I think in the end the Left will be the correct path,' Pevsner had written in 1932, and he certainly remained left-leaning in the narrow sense that he saw modern architecture as an expression of a society designed to meet the needs of all equally: 'a community-based architecture, no longer hierarchical', according to John Newman. Watkin is avowedly opposed to 'the egalitarianism and cultural pluralism upheld in our age', which 'are surely intellectually and spiritually unsatisfactory at preventing the quest for the best'.[32] But Pevsner was not the best exemplar of the political beliefs that Watkin most despised. His attitudes, in Lionel Brett's view, were barely political at all, not carefully formulated dogma but simply 'unconscious left-wing attitudes – in a way, rather sentimental'.[33]

The ideas that Watkin attacks most vehemently in *Morality and Architecture* are mostly to be found in the mouths of others. It was Herbert Read who had openly advocated the existence of a classless society. It was Jim Richards, avowedly a 'progressive intellectual' and fellow-traveller in the 1930s, who had attacked 'that anti-social being, the talented amateur or connoisseur'. It was Furneaux Jordan who had constantly reiterated his loathing of 'aristocrats' and committed the ultimate crime of being vulgar. ('Vulgar' appears on nearly every page of Watkin's brisk attack on Jordan: 'vulgar sociological interpretation', 'vulgar Marxism' and the 'vulgarisation' of Pevsner's already dubious ideas on class differences as reflected in art.)

So why was so much of *Morality and Architecture* an attack on Pevsner? What attracted attention when the book was published was not so much the novelty of the argument – anticipated at various points by Scott, Popper, Gombrich, Cowling and others – as the vigour of the onslaught by a pupil on his former teacher. Of the total of some 112 pages of text, seven pages are devoted to Pugin, eight to Viollet-le-Duc, four to Lethaby, six to Furneaux Jordan, twenty-four to the other principal theorists of modernism, and forty-one – well over one-third of the book – to Pevsner.

A cautious Prefatory Note suggests that Watkin was aware of how this would look. 'As the book is not a general history of the architectural thought of the period, so it is not a comprehensive assessment of any of the individual critics concerned . . . When I criticise one aspect of their achievement it is with no wish to raise questions about the value of the whole but merely to contribute to a discussion of one theme in the history of architecture.' Sending Pevsner an advance copy, he wrote: 'I want to say how terribly sorry I am to be the cause of pain to someone who has been so consistently kind and helpful to me in my work and career. I also want to emphasise the total sincerity of the comparison I make in my Prefatory Note between the beneficent cultural influence of you and of John Ruskin.' (It is not clear whether Watkin knew how much Pevsner disliked Ruskin[34]). 'But,' Watkin continued, 'just as, whilst admiring Ruskin, we would all want to feel free to disagree with many of his ideas so I feel I must criticise your presentation of modernism. I need hardly add, of course, that there is absolutely nothing personal in these criticisms.'[36]

It is hard to take this last claim at face value. Watkin has since made public his dislike of Pevsner's style as a supervisor: Pevsner had, he claimed, no understanding of what the relationship between teacher and pupil should really be, 'especially the social life shared by students and dons'. He has confessed to 'deeply resenting' what he took to be Pevsner's 'secular moralising' about what modern architecture should be like, 'because it implied that I was immoral for disliking the architecture being promoted'.[36] He may have been equally affronted by Pevsner's pronouncements on religion, specifically on Catholicism.* *Morality and Architecture* bears the dedication 'D.O.M', which stands for *'Deo Optimo Maximo'* / 'To God the Best and Greatest', the motto of the Benedictine order. Watkin, a Roman Catholic convert, devotes considerable space at the start of his analysis of Pevsner to a critique of the early writings on Mannerism and the Counter-Reformation, disputing with some heat Pevsner's picture of the spiritual state of Italy under the Jesuits, 'where every motion of individual will must be forcibly repressed'. 'A conventional North European or Protestant idea of "Jesuitry",' snaps Watkin. Jesuit architecture, according to Pevsner in his *Mint* article on Mannerism, displayed a medieval mentality, and was emaciated, stiff, papery, insubstantial, self-conscious, dissenting, frustrated. Pevsner was also severe on the subject of Catholic forgiveness: 'Tolerance was the rule, especially where powerful people were concerned. Rather forgive too much than give a soul up for lost.' Watkin retorts, 'The language again suggests a lack of familiarity with the customs and doctrines of the Church he is writing about.' In contrast, he points to Pevsner's 'resounding panegyric on Protestantism' at the end of the *Outline*.

Pevsner's principal offence, however, may well have been his success. 'Particular attention will be paid to Professor Sir Nikolaus Pevsner,' wrote Watkin in his introduction, 'because his works are the richest

---

*Pevsner had been accused of this kind of bias before – see, for example, a letter from Colin W. Field on the subject of a remark in *Suffolk*: 'If you showed the sentence in question to any historian he would agree with me that it exhibited all the signs of an anti-Catholic mind.' C. Field/NP. Penguin Papers, Frost Papers, DM 1843/30.

in the corpus of architectural literature in recent times' – a roundabout way of saying that Pevsner had had a great deal published and his influence was disproportionate. Watkin offers particular thanks in his Prefatory Note to Professor Edward Shils, the distinguished sociologist (then at Peterhouse) known principally for his research on the role of intellectuals and their relations to power and public policy. Maurice Cowling, too, was suspicious of academics who attempted to create 'public doctrine' that might shape political decisions.[37] Pevsner, willingly or not, had reached a position, in the words of one observer, of 'an almost Mosaic authority'. *Pioneers* had been described as 'probably . . . the most widely read book on architecture published in the 20th century'.[38] Pevsner's ideas were embraced by other people with far more fervour than he had used in advancing them and, hardening into ideology, they were applied without the qualifications that he had often attached to them. 'Pevsner's very sacred cow-dom makes his highly debatable views all too acceptable to influential people,' remarked the architect Nathan Silver, 'though one sees it is not completely Pevsner's fault if his foibles are publicly valued on a scale with his virtues.'[39] Pevsner's rise had been watched with suspicion for years. Among his papers is a note from John Piper whose date might be as early as the 1950s, apologising for remarks that, Piper insisted, were not intended to hurt: 'But remember you have allies – your power increases and the young follow you.'[40] By the 1970s, according to Reyner Banham, the process might be described as 'canonisation'.

Maurice Cowling once wrote, 'Negative bloodiness is not an end in itself but is instrumental to the assertion of a conservative and national moral order which needs *active* assertion when threatened. It is a temperamental as much as an intellectual characteristic and requires a tone and posture as much as it requires an argument.'[41] If Watkin had indeed attacked a secular saint in Pevsner, *Morality and Architecture* – in many ways precisely an exercise in negative bloodiness – was nevertheless received with delight by some for its tone, posture and assertion of a 'conservative moral order'. It would become a set text for opposition to modern architecture.[42] Some new voices had joined the chorus. In the *Daily Telegraph* Paul Johnson wrote, 'All sensible and sensitive people know that modern architecture is bad and horrible, almost without exception. Mr Watkin explains why.'[43] Denys Sutton, the editor of *Apollo*, rejoiced: 'Appeasement of the Left has helped to contribute to our present unenviable position . . . The collectivists have had their way for far too long in intellectual circles; the trouncing they receive in this publication is merited.'[44] They joined some more seasoned

Pevsner-watchers. 'A brave and lonely book,' wrote John Betjeman, 'so witty, learned and unfashionable that it may be the victim of a conspiracy of silence.'[45]

Betjeman refrained from drawing attention specifically to the section on Pevsner; Osbert Lancaster had no such compunction. In a piece for the *Cambridge Review* entitled 'One in the Eye for the Zeitgeist' he gloated:

> Few characters in legend are so immediately attractive and, indeed, so admirable as the sharp-eyed lad who pointed out that the Emperor, so far from wearing new clothes, was in fact naked. In the field of architectural criticism his mantle has fallen on the author of *Morality and Architecture* . . . Convinced of their guilt by such powerful advocates of austerity as Dr Pevsner and Herr Gropius, from the 30s onwards, architects made a corner in sackcloth and ashes . . . Unfortunately . . . public reaction to the challenge of the Modern Movement remained sadly uninstructed and was indeed largely indifferent . . . Very soon this wilful and reactionary lack of enthusiastic response provoked a tougher, more militant attitude among the converted . . . Loud and heavily accented voices were raised in protest, some, such as that of Sigfried Giedion, insofar as it was possible to understand what he was saying, more in sorrow than in anger; others, notably that of Professor Pevsner himself, were tinged with surprise, annoyance and finally angry incomprehension.[46]

What Pevsner might have responded, in his 'loud and heavily accented voice', would never be revealed. In the summer of 1977 he was still working, though with increasing effort. He reported having 'difficulty with notes' after a lecture in the spring, and in July wrote to Theo Crosby, an architect and one of the founders of Pentagram, 'Your Face to Face started by amusing me and ended by frightening me. As a matter of fact, for the last three years or so I am seeing faces everywhere around. This has no consequences, but there it is. A face turns up just for one second while I am looking for something quite different, and the variety of possibilities is great.' The right word sometimes escaped him now – he wrote to one correspondent, thanking him for a book of fairy tales, 'You really are the most unexpectant person!' – and his memory continued to trouble him.[47] To the librarian at the Alexander Turnbull Library in Wellington, New Zealand, he wrote, 'Dear . . . The fact that I cannot remember your Christian name shows both how long we have been out of touch and how my memory is going the way of all senility.'* 'I am writing now,' he added, 'just to tell you how much I would like to hear from you what the last ten years or so have brought you. You can be sure I shall reply.'

It seems likely that he did not keep his promise. In August 1977 he went as usual to Germany on holiday. That summer his sister-in-law Marianne was herself ill and could not look after him as she would have liked. He went instead to a hotel, a Victorian castle near Fritzlar in northern Hesse, some thirty-two kilometres from Marburg, where Marianne was now living. Fritzlar had a medieval centre with the oldest town hall in Europe still in use and a fine Romanesque-Gothic cathedral; it was ringed by a wall studded with watchtowers. Pevsner had long been fond of it. But while there on his own he would seem to have had a small internal haemorrhage. In isolation it might have been harmless – it was of a type that sometimes heals itself – but in this case it precipitated a minor heart attack. Pevsner was taken into hospital at nearby Bad Wildungen, and his family came out to bring him home.

He spent some weeks in a private clinic in London, undergoing tests and enduring a convalescence during which he insisted on working. The letter in which he finally retired from the *Buildings of England* was dated 26 September. A week later David Watkin sent his advance copy of *Morality and Architecture*. Stefan Muthesius remembered Pevsner saying 'They are attacking me', but it is not clear how carefully he ever read the book. Ian Sutton recalled him saying in hospital that he wanted to reply to it, but could not quite muster the energy. 'I shall answer it, I suppose, but not for twelve months or so. Do you think there is any harm in delaying?'

Early in October, Pevsner tripped over the bed-table in his hospital room and broke his thigh. Pinning the bone required a major operation. The leg was put in traction, but the spasms of Parkinson's disease sprang the joint, and the operation had to be repeated. Coming so soon after the first general anaesthetic, a second one caused irreversible brain damage, reducing him to 80 per cent of his former mental capacity. Pevsner was moved to the Middlesex Hospital, which at that time led the field in geriatric rehabilitation, but his progress was slow, and he never again walked unaided. His doctors advised that anything connected with work was to be kept from him; in November enquirers were still being told that he was in no fit state to receive letters. 'Remind me to Sir Pevsner,' wrote Bunji Kobayashi, one of his *Pelican*

---

*The librarian, Janet Paul, was also a painter, publisher and art historian, created Dame Janet Paul in 1997.

History of Art authors, to Judy Nairn in January 1978. 'I am very much anxious about him.'[48]

In May 1978, Watkin sent the Pevsner family a collection of reviews of *Morality and Architecture*. He had been told by Stefan Muthesius that Pevsner himself had asked to see them, though Muthesius had added the rider that this was not necessarily a good idea. Watkin attempted to reassure Tom Pevsner: 'For those who support the book in their reviews there are as many, probably more, who attack it . . . so I do not think that if your father were to read them all he would have any sense of being without allies.'* 'I do hope that knowing about the book has not caused your father any additional pain,' Watkin added, 'and I am very upset to hear from Stefan about his continuing illness.'

Watkin had been unlucky in the timing of *Morality and Architecture*. The book would appear, from the date on its Prefatory Note, to have been completed in 1975, and it was unfortunate for Watkin that it did not appear until two years later and was then launched at a moment when Pevsner was incapacitated, down in every sense and unable to retaliate. There could be no debate with him of the kind that Watkin had probably anticipated, and an objective assessment of the book and its significance was almost impossible. Pevsner's vulnerability inflamed the feelings of friends and supporters who would in any case have been affronted by the book, and their responses were as uninhibited as those of Watkin's allies.

Reyner Banham, willing as usual to go too far, accused Watkin of 'a kind of vindictiveness of which only Christians seem capable'. Stephen Bayley would summarise it as 'an addled, sly, knowing, superior, rancorous, smarmy, sneering stinker of a book'.† Sutherland Lyall condemned a 'waspish and spiteful' text and drew attention to the preoccupation with 'reds under the beds'.[49] In a symposium convened by the *Architectural Review* to discuss the book, Charles Jencks concluded, 'It strains the evidence, it exaggerates the points so strongly that they either become unfair or false. Basically it is lacking in balance and proportion – that is in architectural virtues.'[50] Richard Wollheim, in the same symposium, declared, 'It is a reflection upon the

---

*Watkin singled out the unfavourable reviews written by Reyner Banham in the *TLS*, Richard Wollheim in the *Architectural Review*, Andrew Saint in the *New Statesman* and Lionel Brett in the *RIBA Journal*.

†*Independent*, 8/6/2001. Reviewing the revised edition, *Morality and Architecture Revisited*, Bayley wrote, 'It remains an addled, sly, etc . . .'

contemporary state of architectural aesthetics that welcome should be given to a book so negatively conceived, so abrasively written, so poorly argued, so remote from the concerns of art and artists, so full of appeals to authority, and so indifferent to countervailing considerations, as well as so sloppily produced, as *Morality and Architecture*.'*

Pevsner was discharged from hospital in June 1978. Aware of the many inconveniences of 2 Wildwood Terrace, doctors suggested a nursing home. His children preferred to arrange private nursing, with the help of money now coming in from the Holocaust Restitution Payments scheme, under which the German government made payments to victims of Nazi persecution 'for a number of reasons including loss of health, property and professional advancement'. Pevsner was doing remedial exercises and learning to walk, though he could not get up without help and would eventually have to move to the ground floor, as social services would not undertake to find volunteers to help him negotiate the steep stairs to his bedroom.

He was able to read, skimming books for their gist – mostly still non-fiction, rarely novels, though Tom Pevsner did tell Bridget Cherry of a day brightened by his having found a very early reference to the Gothic Revival in Book 1, Chapter 4 of *Tom Jones*.[51] Though he could not concentrate on any new writing, he corrected proofs of work he had done before his illness. He liked people to visit and gossip, took a keen interest in friends' lives and was forthcoming with details about his day-to-day routine, saying of one of his nurses, 'She is Scottish. Her name is Fiona. She is of a higher social class than the others, but is inclined to be tyrannical. The others will do as they are told. She won't. I don't know which is preferable.' 'I never heard him complain,' recalled Camilla Bagg. 'Still sitting at his desk, still reading a book about architecture, he once said to me, with the faintest of smiles, "Who would have thought that I would spend my last years like this?"'

Early in 1979 Trevor Russell-Cobb wrote him a long and sympathetic letter, ending, 'I hope you may be as much fortified as I have been over recent woes by Nietzsche's remarkable saying: "Why shouldn't life be intolerable?"'[52] If Pevsner ever did find life intolerable, work was, as ever, a refuge, even under the strict constraints of illness. The first volumes of the *Buildings of Scotland*, *Wales* and *Ireland* were

---

*The other participants in the symposium were Kenneth Campbell, former Housing Adviser to the LCC, who was predictably critical of *Morality and Architecture*, and Roger Scruton, who was equally predictably supportive.

coming out now, and he took a keen interest in their progress, as well as casting a proprietorial eye over the revised editions of the *Buildings of England*. The manuscript of the second edition of *Nottinghamshire* – the county travelled with so much anguish, with himself in the driver's seat, more than thirty years before – bears faint and quavery marks of his corrections, and for *Powys* he had demanded an enlarged photocopy of the proofs. Tom Pevsner wrote resignedly to its author Richard Haslam: 'I have tried unsuccessfully to persuade my father that it is unnecessary to remind you of your promise to let him have the typescript of the introduction of Powys. Professionally you know him probably better than I do, so you will not be surprised that I failed. So all I can say is that I would be grateful for all our peace of mind, if you could send it as soon as possible.'[53]

Even at this stage the honours continued to arrive: the American Institute of Architects Medal, the Karl-Friedrich-Schinkel Ring, the rank of Knight of Mark Twain.* For the conferring of his honorary doctorate from Cambridge, Pevsner had to attend in person and made the journey in an ambulance accompanied by a doctor and a nurse. Prince Philip, the Chancellor of the University, paid him a personal visit in a private room.[54] Then, in a bath chair, Pevsner joined the procession that entered the Senate House to the sound of acclamations. With the rest of the congregation he listened as the University Orator celebrated his achievements, as was customary, in Latin:

Praesento vobis Equitem Auratum . . . Nicolaum Bernardum Leonem Pevsner . . . E patria priore profugus in nostram adoptione adscitus belli terrores et incendia nobiscum subiit . . . Auctoris itinera, uxore devotissima comitante, dies longos in monumentis scrutandis, noctes in qualicumque posset deversorio scribendo consumptas, quid dicam? . . . Patriam nostram architecturam et nobis et peregrinis et posteritati aestimandam quasi filii pietate patefecit.†

---

*The citation for the AIA Medal read: 'For a half-century devoted to the recording of architecture, painting, sculpture and design, his works, never mere catalogues, are alive with his knowledge, opinion and passion; a dauntless and dedicated scholar, throughout his long career, he has been and remains a constant source of lively ideas.' The Schinkel Ring (*Deutscher Preis für Denkmalschütz*) was awarded by the German National Committee for Preservation of Monuments for achievements in conservation; Pevsner was particularly proud of it. The Twain honour was bestowed, a little promiscuously, by Cyril Clemens, a distant cousin of Mark Twain.

†'I present to you Sir . . . Nikolaus Bernhard Leon Pevsner . . . A refugee from his former country, he became one of us by adoption, and underwent with us the terrors and conflagrations of war . . . I need not dwell on the author's journeys, accompanied by his devoted wife, the long days examining the monuments, the nights spent writing

In 1982 Pevsner had his eightieth birthday. Jane Fawcett wrote, 'One of my last memories is of him sitting at his desk with, on one side, the Schinkel Ring . . . on his other side was a box of chocolates on which had been inscribed After Eighty.'[55] He was fading now and finding it harder to maintain his interest in the world outside. 'When we went to see him,' remembered Ian Sutton:

> there he was in bed, with the complete *Buildings of England* and *Pelican History of Art* arranged at the foot, as though they were the last things he wanted to see . . . It was strange to see him with time to spare, released from the consciousness that there was work waiting to be done . . . As the months went by he got weaker and deafer and more difficult to talk to. He no longer took pleasure from being visited, but sat with an unchanging expression, hardly following what we told him. When, after a while, Emily [Lane] said, 'Time we went', he just said: 'Yes, I agree'.

Alistair Rowan visited him in the spring of 1983:

> He was perfectly lucid and remembered that I was now a Professor in Dublin, but he couldn't really take in the difference between Trinity College and University College Dublin. I remember him frowning and looking at me intently when he said 'Now that I really cannot understand.' . . . I suppose it was a sad little visit, but I was glad that I had made the effort to see him. I talked a little bit with the nurse before I left and he said that Nikolaus would spend the rest of the day, and the evening, talking to him in a flood of German of which he would understand not one word.

---

them up in whatever inn was available . . . He has displayed our architectural heritage for us, for foreigners, and for posterity to appreciate, with a filial devotion.'

CONCLUSION

Roundel for the cover of the 1962
edition of *The Buildings of England: Surrey*

CHAPTER 49

'Not quite in the English way'

Pevsner died on 18 August 1983, of bronchopneumonia. He was eighty-one, and had outlived Lola by twenty years. He was buried beside her in the churchyard at Clyffe Pypard; their headstone, black granite with lettering by Will Carter of Cambridge, reads simply:*

LOLA

PEVSNER

born Kurlbaum

1902–1963

and

NIKOLAUS

her husband

1902–1983

On 6 December 1983, a memorial service brought together representatives of all his different worlds – his family, the *Architectural Review*, Birkbeck, Penguin, Cambridge, *The Buildings of England*, the Victorian Society – at the Church of Christ the King, Gordon Square, five minutes away from his Gower Street office.† Two generations of art historians were there, his peers and his students, and representatives of every major London museum and amenity group, as well as the German Ambassador and a representative of the Duke of Gloucester.

Christ the King was a church Pevsner had much admired, Gothic Revival 'on a Cathedral scale and in a Cathedral style'. The service, in contrast, was simple. The organist played familiar music:

---

*When Carter first engraved the stone for Lola in 1964, he wrote to Pevsner: 'It is one of the best things I have done . . . But I could wish it had been someone else who lay beneath.' W. Carter/NP, 4/3/64.

†A more formal memorial was established three years later with the setting up (by Bridget Cherry, John Newman, Barbara Robertson and Thomas Cocke) of the Pevsner Memorial Trust, dedicated to raising £100,000 with which to carry out a major task of restoration in his memory. The chosen task was one Pevsner himself had said was imperative, the restoration of the Clayton & Bell wall paintings at the Norman church of St Michael and All Angels, Garton-on-the-Wold, East Riding. See J. Newman and B. Cherry, 'Pevsner Commemorated', in S. Bradley and B. Cherry (eds), *The Buildings of England: A Celebration* (Penguin Collectors' Society, 2001).

the overture to Handel's Fireworks Music, 'O welche Lust!' from Beethoven's *Fidelio*, Bach's 'Wachet Auf'. Hans Schmoller read from *The Leaves of Southwell*, on which he had worked with Pevsner more than forty years before. Jim Richards read from William Morris's *The Beauty of Life*: 'I must tell you that unless you are resolved to have good and rational architecture, it is, once again, useless your thinking about art at all.' But it was Alec Clifton-Taylor, as Pevsner's oldest friend, who gave the address, a brief, affectionate outline of a long life. 'We have all come here this morning,' he said, 'to honour the memory of a great man, a good man, and a wonderful – and indeed in one respect an incomparable – friend and lover of England.'

The lesson was from Ecclesiasticus, Chapter 44: 'Let us now praise famous men.' Pevsner had indeed become famous, better known than almost any other art historian, and had helped to make art history itself known to a far wider audience. 'Ich muss werden,' he had written as a student some sixty years earlier, 'I *must* become something', and he had certainly made something of himself – but it was not what he had intended. He had aspired to be a solid German professor of art history, 'teaching, going about my business, maybe now and again writing – a German idyll'. Germany he had lost, and even his role as an art historian was not what he had meant it to be.

Pevsner once called Sir Joshua Reynolds the epitome of Englishness because he was inconsistency and compromise incarnate. 'Nor does a man always practise that which he esteems the best,' he quoted Reynolds as saying, 'but does that which he can do best . . . I have taken another course, one more suited to my abilities and to the taste of the times in which I live.' He could very easily have been speaking about himself. Always his own harshest judge, he was well aware that he had not achieved fame as a theorist in the mould of Schmarsow and Pinder; he had not taken forward the study of art history as, say, Gombrich had done; he had not advanced knowledge in any one specialist field. He was not even really a member of the English art-history establishment as it had been constituted throughout his working life – not a part of the Courtauld Institute or the Warburg Institute, or of the Christie's circle and the world of connoisseurship, or a regular part of university life. He had worked in the outside world, for Sargant Florence and for Gordon Russell. He taught, but not in academic surroundings; his base was Penguin, and when he wrote, he was writing mostly for a lay audience through the *Architectural Review* rather than for specialists through the academic journals. The politics of the art-historical world interested him very little, and changes in the study of art history itself – the growing insistence on the primacy of background documentation and archival research over stylistic analysis, and the stress on the social and economic framework for art history – largely passed him by.

Pevsner was a practitioner rather than a theorist. He did not expound an overarching methodology for his work – in fact, he made very few methodological statements at all. Reviewing the collected articles, Francis Haskell observed that Pevsner's strength lay not in the 'lusty generalisations' of his early years but in sharp insights and passing observations on an extraordinary range of topics that were loosely connected, if at all. Work for Pevsner was a constantly ongoing process, and his ideas would not always be consistent. He once quoted Walt Whitman approvingly to describe the way in which William Morris thought: 'Do I contradict myself? Very well then, I contradict myself. I am large. I contain multitudes.'

He did not try to develop a school or coterie, and did not set out to advance a particular theoretical framework. Where a theory of his did have a profound influence, it was almost by accident. For all its limitations – and Pevsner had taken pains to indicate what some of them were, even if he was oblivious to others – *Pioneers* was hugely persuasive. John Summerson once wrote that the Modern Movement demanded its own historians; a narrative was required that was clear, functional and explanatory, like the architecture it described. The Modern Movement in England was in even greater need of a chronicler: and *Pioneers* met that need: 'a book adroitly topical, starting in England and, since Gropius was then working in this country, ending in England; a book deft in its omissions, agile in its allusions, startling in its erudition, and accusing in the almost futurist stab of its last sentence. A book crystal clear and, above all, *professional.*' *Pioneers*'s strength – its simplicity – was also its weakness, because it lent itself to fossilisation. Later in his life Pevsner was heard to say that, if it were not for the royalties, he would not mind if *Pioneers of Modern Design* went out of print.[1]

His powers of persuasion certainly rankled with some critics, who considered that they gained his work more exposure than it really deserved. He himself was sometimes inclined to deplore his own accessibility. 'I am fully aware,' he wrote in the *Heftchen* in 1974, 'that in *Geschichte der Kunstgeschichte* [the history of art history] I would not exist, except as a compiler, an entrepreneur and a *vulgarisateur.*'

His tone was disparaging, just as it had been as a student in Munich in 1921: 'Am I to be no more than a lowly sweeper-up of

other men's ideas? . . . Will I become pleasant, urbane, witty, stimulating, good at engaging people's interest – and yet basically superficial and second-rate? I can imagine making a quick success and
reasonable career like that. I shall never know objectively what I am
really capable of.' Assessing himself in 1967, the year of his greatest
public success, he was inclined to believe that this was what had
happened. 'The others are all genuine scholars. I am no longer.' He
was, however, perhaps nearer the mark in declaring that he could
not judge himself objectively. 'The image that I have of myself . . .
is very vague and not at all good,' wrote the young Nika. The adult
Pevsner would be equally incapable of seeing the full worth of everything that he had achieved.

Pevsner made notes all his life, on everything he read – not just
architecture and art, but religion, economics, gardens, town planning,
English literature, church history – clarifying, collecting, classifying,
cross-referring. He made notes on envelopes and on scraps of paper
so small that he had to keep them in envelopes, on ledger paper torn
in half crossways and double pages from exercise books folded to
make little books, on the back flyleaves of books and on the reverse
of letters, both his own and other people's. In Pevsner's notes, his
different lives are interwoven: drafts of articles for the *Architectural
Review* and other journals are written on the back of Birkbeck office
memos, Gordon Russell invoices, invitation cards for a lecture on
medieval sculpture at the Courtauld Institute, proofs for the covers
of the *Buildings of England*. His article on 'Terms of Architectural
Planning in the Middle Ages' covers the back of a card from his
youthful library in Leipzig, a leaf from his diary for 30 October
1930, a letter from the potter Lucy Rie, a letter from *Die Zeitung*
about his 'Peter Naumburg' propaganda pieces, and an examination
paper discarded by one Dr Cantalamassa in the Birkbeck maths
department.

'I am large. I contain multitudes.' Pevsner's breadth of knowledge
was what made him remarkable. He arrived in England speaking
four languages and reading six, 'a young art historian', in the words
of T.S.R. Boase, 'of exceptional analytical power and range of
learning'. He added to his languages – 'It amuses me, although it
does not astonish me,' wrote Stefan Tschudi-Madsen, 'that you are
capable to struggle through some lines of Norwegian' – and continued
to widen his scope. To the subjects he had begun to master in Germany
(Saxon Baroque architecture, Italian Mannerism, the architecture of

the Modern Movement, the history of art education) and those he had developed on arriving in England (the prehistory of the Picturesque, Victorian building and design, town planning, the evolution of the architectural profession, nineteenth-century architectural writing), he could add all he had learned on industrial design during the preparation of *An Enquiry into Industrial Art*, his years with Gordon Russell and his editing of *Design Review*; all he had learned about art education, for better or worse, on the Coldstream Committee; all he had learned about conservation and the workings of the planning bureaucracy from his years with the Victorian Society and the Royal Fine Art Commission. He had edited two very different series for Penguin, requiring him not only to traverse the entire spectrum of the history of art for the *Pelican History of Art*, but also to marshal the miscellaneous in a visually engaging way for the King Penguins. 'A very big light has gone out,' wrote Alec Clifton-Taylor when Pevsner died. 'No other projected so widely, nor illumined so much.'[2]

From the range of his experience and the cast of his mind, Pevsner was as well equipped as any scholar in the world to provide the coherent overview of a broad topic, occasionally by providing fresh information, more often by making connections between the already known. 'It was a kind of athleticism,' commented John Summerson. 'He had this wonderful energy, and wanted to get things connected and tidied.' At every turn Pevsner had developed fresh contacts and identified new sources of material. From what he had amassed, he was able to construct a vast network of knowledge. What was unusual was his willingness, amounting almost to a passion, to share it.

In describing himself as an 'entrepreneur', Pevsner may have meant that he was the one who was willing to undertake the enterprise of the *Buildings of England*, with all its attendant risks and responsibilities, but he may also have had in mind the image of the intermediary, the one who makes the necessary connections between people and who matches resources to requirements. What was important to him was the furthering of knowledge, not the credit for doing it. The breadth of his own learning enabled him to identify gaps and open avenues of study for other people. 'Pevsner's omnivorousness,' wrote Robert Harbison, 'made forays into the untried tastes which were later to constitute the entire diet of specialists who went on to upbraid him for lukewarm commitment to their idées fixes.'[3]

He expected other scholars to communicate their findings and was disappointed when they preferred to keep their discoveries to themselves. For his own part, he was almost always ready to make information available to others even when he planned to use it later himself, and he invariably responded to requests for information, even if it was simply to own ignorance and refer the enquirer to an expert of his acquaintance. 'Of the sixty-odd architectural historians currently working in England,' noted Stefan Muthesius in 1990, 'there is hardly a one who did not receive advice from him.'[4] More than a few have said that they owe their careers in art history at least in part to him.

'The great professional, like the great dandy,' declared John Summerson, 'is the one who can afford to be unprofessional – to wear odd socks, to miss a trick or two if thereby something is gained in discovery or communication. This is great professionalism and this is the kind of professional that Pevsner is.'[5] Much of Pevsner's persuasiveness came from his ability to impose patterns on a confusing multiplicity of facts. Even when some of these patterns were subsequently shown to be artificial, and when some of the facts he used to construct his arguments turned out to be wrong, his mistakes were constructive in that they gave other scholars material to work with. In fields where his ideas have long been challenged, these ideas are still often points of reference and pivots around which people construct their own arguments. 'Pevsnerian' continues to have meaning as a term in discussions of the history of art, architecture and design more than half a century after the publication of his principal works.

As for *vulgarisateur*, the term simply means 'populariser'. Pevsner, however, was probably using it in full consciousness of its snobbish overtones to the English ear, aware that, in some art-historical quarters, to popularise was indeed to vulgarise and somehow to debase a currency that should ideally circulate only among the cultivated. A more generous interpretation of what he had done in the *Buildings of England*, the Reith Lectures and the *Outline of European Architecture* was offered by John Summerson, who described him as 'a bringer of riches, the entertainment, the wisdom of architectural scholarship to more people probably than any man alive'. 'I owe so much to Nik,' declared the film-maker Derek Jarman in his journal. 'Here on the top of the bus I carry in my mind an encyclopaedia of architectural detail. With this I can while away the time – ogee, architrave, crazy vault, flying buttress.'[6] 'Few days go by without my thinking how much we owe to you,' Wayland Young told Pevsner, 'and none when I have to do anything about architecture and buildings.'[7] 'He leaves two sons and a daughter,' wrote Geoffrey Moorhouse, 'but multitudes besides will be profoundly grateful that Nikolaus Pevsner has been.'*

'He has contributed immensely to the pleasure of living – and what better way is there of assessing the value of a life than that?' asked Alec Clifton-Taylor in his funeral oration. A great man and a good man, he called Pevsner, and an incomparable friend and lover of England. A great man? Pevsner was happy to use the influence that he seemed to have acquired, when it could serve a useful purpose, but he did not take his status too seriously. He wrote in some amusement to a friend: 'Clough Williams-Ellis has recently been knighted. I wrote to him to congratulate him and said he should have been knighted twenty years ago, and should now have been raised to the peerage as Lord Portmeirion. He thanked me for my letter. His answer was very nice, but it ended with the sentence, "Incidentally, I don't know who you are."'† Pevsner also once remarked that whenever he saw his name in print it was usually preceded by the word 'not', as in '19th-century plasterwork – not, as Pevsner assumed, Elizabethan'.[8]

A good man? To the students, colleagues and friends who valued his intellectual generosity, his dedication, his kindness and his integrity, that is precisely what he was. Again, Pevsner did not believe it. 'Such a nice man to the outside world, such an un-nice man really,' he had written in 1962. In the adult Pevsner, who would bite his fingernails to the end of his life, there was still much of the young Nika starting the *Heftchen* in his room in Schwägrichenstrasse and declaring, 'This is what I love in people – everything I am not.'

Pevsner was unquestionably a friend to England, and he was also a lover of England, though not exclusively and 'not quite in the English way'. He wanted to belong and be at home in England – 'Englishness of course is the purpose of my journey' – and he chose to stay there when on several occasions he was offered the opportunity to go back to Germany. When people wrote to him in German, he tended to answer them in English. But he was not English, let

---

*G. Moorhouse, 'Recorder of England', obituary for NP, *Guardian*, 19/8/83. Happily, Maxwell Fry had taken the opportunity to make this clear to Pevsner some years before, on the occasion of the RIBA Gold Medal: 'I think that the way you have devoted your scholarship and intellect to your adopted country, the way you have given your heart to it, is a compliment that we all feel. I doubt whether you really know how proud we are of you and how much you are beloved, and this, if you have not in any way guessed, is the moment to tell you.' M. Fry/NP, 3/1/67.
†NP/R. Winks, 1971. Robin Winks (1930–2003), a specialist in British imperial history and the theory and development of espionage, was then Professor of History at Yale.

alone 'more English than the English', and he never wanted to be. As a young man he had wanted desperately to be 'true' German, like Lola's family, and had felt that he had achieved it as the young Doktor Pevsner. To have lost that German identity completely would have been extraordinarily painful, and in some respects he never did. 'He did think of himself as un-English,' Ernst Gombrich considered. 'We all do, what else can we do? He knew what he was and what he was not.'

Pevsner's letters, his brief memoirs and, above all, his *Heftchen* provide the images of what he was for the first half of his life. The child aboard the imaginary horse 'Kerminsky', protected by his brother and reciting his ritual chant: 'Ubifalaralara'; the gangling adolescent on the ice of the 'turnip winter', skating uncertainly and gazing at the teenaged Lola; the earnest student in light-green knickerbockers, spreading bread and lard before pedalling into the Bavarian countryside; the young candidate for Christian conversion, walking in the gardens in Potsdam and preparing for marriage; the exile in Hampstead Garden Suburb, eating lunch from a paper bag on a foggy park bench; the German lodger in the refugee house in Edgbaston, battling with the Ascot heater and reading the Gospels in the sooty back garden; Internee 54829, eating lunch at the kosher table with his hat on; the 'gentleman' rubble-shoveller in cap, muffler and tweed suit, throwing light bulbs against the wall to hear them smash; Colonel Pevsner in English battledress in the British Zone of Occupation in the post-war Rhineland, stealing biscuits from the military ration to give to the locals and struggling to make sense of his divided loyalties. Why could he not accept the rightness of what was being done to Germany by England and its allies? 'The answer of course is love.'

All these images of the German Pevsner lie behind the picture that is most familiar now to English audiences. Pevsner the teacher, addressing packed, intent lecture rooms with the aid of black-and-white slides, face alight, oblivious to distractions. Pevsner the public figure – Reith Lecturer, BBC stalwart, committee man, patron of charities, Chairman of the Victorian Society, signer of petitions and writer of letters to *The Times*, the 'saviour of a century'. Pevsner on the road for the *Buildings of England* – wrestling with a crank handle, in a macintosh smelling of paraffin; riding the back roads in an ancient Austin with Lola at the wheel; hunched over the bedside table in innumerable cheap hotels in the evenings, writing up his notes and thinking ahead to the morning, with Lola's photograph on the mantelpiece; knocking on the doors of country houses to explain his mission for the thousandth time; training his binoculars on bosses and vaulting, tracery and glass, scaling bell towers, dating funerary monuments, seizing on telltale joints in masonry or suspect restorations; slowly leaving the Staffordshire churchyard with his conker when the job was finally done. Pevsner, the bringer of riches.

Note on Sources and Abbreviations

One of the first people I interviewed for this book began by remarking as I crossed his threshold, 'I don't know what you're going to find to say. The man did nothing but work.' After a few weeks of research, it was hard to argue. The evidence of industry was everywhere – in an extraordinary profusion of published writing, unpublished research material and professional correspondence: books, articles, reviews, lectures, letters, and the memories of friends, colleagues and students – more than enough to have occupied one man for an average lifetime.

What was hidden at the beginning was the fact that Pevsner had used writing just as assiduously to explore and document his private persona. He had kept diaries from the age of fourteen – small blue notebooks, packed into a shoebox for safe keeping, filled tightly with his own thoughts and quotations from the writings of others, with his aspirations, anxieties, antipathies, some clear, some camouflaged by a shorthand of his own devising. After his marriage he wrote at least one letter to his wife every day they were apart, some days two or three, giving her the detail of his daily working life but also discussing their marriage, their children and their future. When I was a year down the road, the Pevsner family gave me these private records, and transformed the undertaking.

An old metal trunk was labelled in Pevsner's writing: *MR THIEF. This is not locked. It contains nothing of value.* It was filled with hundreds of letters.

At intervals, more cardboard boxes arrived from the family, holding enough papers to fill two more trunks. Photographs, in an ancient brown box file so full the lid was coming off its hinges, from sepia studio portraits to colour holiday snaps, detailed every change in his appearance and his surroundings over a period of eighty years. It was the kind of archive that rarely comes the biographer's way.

The documentation for Pevsner's professional life is, of course, also invaluable – 143 boxes of business letters, manuscripts, lecture notes, transcripts, cuttings, photographs and postcards, now catalogued and carefully preserved in the Getty Research Institute in Los Angeles. They cover his years with the *Architectural Review*, his teaching career at Birkbeck and as a Slade lecturer, his life at the BBC, his profile as a committee man and public campaigner and his correspondence with many of the key figures in twentieth-century British architecture.

Kept separately, as a special collection within the archives of Penguin Books at the University of Bristol, are all the papers relating to the planning, organisation and writing of *The Buildings of England* (though the research notes for the series are archived at the National Monuments Record in Swindon). They sit alongside the forty-six volumes of the series, each with its introduction capturing the atmosphere of a county and sketching the architectural riches to come: reading the introductions alone is a lengthy business. The Penguin Archive also documents the 60-plus volumes of the *Pelican History of Art*, the *Outline of European Architecture* and the 76 King Penguins.

The Bodleian Library in Oxford holds the archives of what used to be the Society for the Protection of Science and Learning: these contain the details of Pevsner's new start in England, plus some of the false starts. The BBC Written Archives Centre at Caversham, outside Reading, holds the records of his thirty years as a broadcaster, as well as internal BBC correspondence which gives a vivid picture of how he was regarded within the Corporation, and his relationships with individual producers. The Design Council archive at the University of Brighton contains the evidence of Pevsner's post-war return to Germany in the uniform of an English colonel. The Victorian Society archives document his years as founder member, Chairman and President of the Society, as well as holding all the case files on his campaigns.

It is the accumulated richness and the interaction of the two sets of records – the private and the professional – that make up the remarkable individual that was Pevsner.

AR *Architectural Review*
GP/Getty Papers Pevsner Collection in the Getty Research Institute, Los Angeles
LP Lola Pevsner
NA The National Archives of the UK, Kew
NP Nikolaus Pevsner
Penguin Papers Penguin Archive in the Special Collections of the University of Bristol
SPSL Society for the Protection of Science and Learning Archive, Bodleian Library, University of Oxford
TLS *Times Literary Supplement*

Where no other source is indicated, documents are generally from the private papers of Nikolaus Pevsner, which are held by the Pevsner family.

Addendum to <u>*Note on Sources*</u>

In February 2012, six months after the hardback edition of the book was published, one of my sons had a week's work experience in the offices of Chatto & Windus. His first task on his first day was to open the morning post. The second letter he reached was addressed to me: an amusing coincidence. The white A4 envelope was carefully folded and stapled in half to secure a smaller envelope inside. It contained no letter, only the second envelope and two small slips of paper, unsigned, one a request to Chatto to pass the envelope unopened to me, the other a request to me to dispose of the contents as I saw fit, but with the suggestion that the Pevsner family might be interested.

The second envelope, stuck down firmly with brown paper tape and an extra layer of sellotape, contained one of Pevsner's *Heftchen*, covering the years 1953–7 – almost certainly the unfinished volume that Pevsner mislaid in 1958. There was no explanation.

The volume added little information that was wholly new; for the most part, it simply elaborated what was known from the *Heftchen* that survived and from the notes that Pevsner later made for his autobiography. The only likely explanation for its sudden appearance is that the finder saw no further need to keep its contents secret after the publication of the biography and the revelation of what the other *Heftchen* contained. His, or her, identity will remain a mystery.

Notes

CHAPTER 1

'This is how I am'

1 The main sources for Pevsner's life in these early chapters are all in his personal papers – the *Heftchen*, his 1977 notes for an autobiography (never written), and memoirs he wrote in 1942 about his mother and in 1954 about his family.
2 Stephen Games, *Pevsner: The Early Life* (Continuum, 2010), p.24.
3 On Pevsner's family background, see Heinrich Dilly, 'Sir Nikolaus in Leipzig', paper presented at a conference 'Fifty Years of The Buildings of England' at the Victoria and Albert Museum on 13–14/7/2001.
4 1954 family memoir.
5 Ibid.
6 1977 notes for autobiography.
7 Dilly, op. cit. His account is based on Leipzig's Municipal Archives, where Hugo Pevsner's file is to be found at P463.
8 See F. Ringer, *Fields of Knowledge: French Academic Culture in Comparative Perspective 1890–1920* (Cambridge, 1992), p.2.
9 M. Ignatieff, *Isaiah Berlin* (Chatto & Windus, 1998), p.25.
10 S. Zweig, *The World of Yesterday* (Cassell, 1943), pp.34, 38.

CHAPTER 2

'A talent for misery'

1 Manuscript dated 25/9/18. GP Series VI, Box 135.
2 Note of the loan on headed paper from Dr Georg Krebs, 16/5/19. GP Series VI, Box 135.
3 Fragmentary notes for 'Two Brothers' survive. GP Series VI, Box 135.

CHAPTER 3

'Castles in the air'

1 T. Mann/NP, 16/10/18. GP Series VI, Box 135.
2 M. Berghahn, *Continental Britons: German Jewish Refugees from Nazi Germany* (Berg, 1988), p.14.
3 Ibid., p.21.

CHAPTER 4

Entwicklungsroman

1 Sources for this chapter include the *Heftchen*, the 1954 family memoir, and a memoir written by Lola's sister Marianne, '1907 bis 1987: Ein Subjektiver Rückblick von Marianne Kockel' (unpublished, 1987, kindly translated for the author by Birgit Rohowsky).

CHAPTER 5

'It takes . . . diligence to make a genius'

1 E. Gombrich, 'The embattled

humanities', in *Higher Education Quarterly*, 39/3, 13/6/85.
2 NP, review of H. Wölfflin, *Renaissance and Baroque*, in *TLS*, 25/6/64.
3 Wolfgang Herrmann, interview with the author, 5/5/92.
4 Marlite Halbertsma, *Wilhelm Pinder und die deutsche Kunstgeschichte* (Wernersche Verlagsgesellschaft, 1992).

CHAPTER 7
'Germany's present ruin'

1 NP, review of H. Füssler, *Leipziger Bautradition* (Leipzig, Bibliographisches Institut, 1955) in *Architectural Review (AR)*, February 1956.
2 Dr Ute Engel, 'The Formation of Pevsner's Art History: Nikolaus Pevsner in Germany 1902–33', paper delivered at the centenary conference *Reassessing Nikolaus Pevsner*, Birkbeck College, 12–13/7/2002 and subsequently published in P. Draper (ed.), *Reassessing Nikolaus Pevsner* (Ashgate, 2004).
3 Dieter Pevsner to the author, 1993.
4 Ian Sutton, 'Reminiscences of Nikolaus Pevsner', unpublished memoir, 1992.
5 G. Craig, *Germany 1866–1946* (Oxford History of Modern Europe, OUP, 1978), p.450.
6 J. Paul, 'Nikolaus Pevsner und Dresden', *Hellerau Almanach*, 6, 2000, cites references to a letter from Pinder to the Gemäldegalerie's director, Hans Posse, supporting Pevsner's application for a voluntary post. Paul's article is cited in S. Slive, 'Nikolaus Pevsner's contribution as editor of the *Pelican History of Art* series', in Draper, op. cit.

CHAPTER 8
'Now the climb can begin'

1 Craig, op. cit., p.470.
2 Quoted in Francesca Wilson, 'A German Student and Hitlerism: the Jewish Professors', *Manchester Guardian*, June 1933.
3 Quoted from Pinder's biographer, Marlite Halbertsma, op. cit.
4 Document supplied by Ruth Rosenberg.
5 S. Zweig, op. cit.
6 'The Architecture of Mannerism', *The Mint* (Routledge, 1946).

CHAPTER 11
'Culture-politics'

1 R. Grunberger, *A Social History of the Third Reich* (Weidenfeld & Nicolson, 1971).
2 Craig, op. cit., p.639.
3 NP, review of *Le Corbusier und Jeanneret. Ihr gesamtes Werk von 1910 bis 1929* (Zurich, 1930), in *Göttingische gelehrte Anzeigen* 193, 1931. See also 'Pevsner v. Le Corbusier: article written by Pevsner in 1930 challenging Le Corbusier's thesis on the Modern Movement', article by Pevsner with comments by M. Manieri-Elia, in *Casabella*, 41/423, March 1977.
4 NP, 'Gemeinschaftsideale unter den bildenden Künstlern des 19. Jahrhunderts', in *Deutsche Vierteljahrsschrift für Literaturwissenschaft und Geistesgeschichte, Jahrg.* 9 (1931).
5 NP, review of *Rationelle Bebauungsweisen. Ergebnisse des 3 Internationalen Kongresses für Neues Bauen. Brussels, 1930* (J. Hoffman, 1931), in *Zeitschrift für Ästhetik und allgemeine Kunstwissenschaft*, 27, 1933.

6 Professor Günther Gillessen/ author, February 2002.
7 'Die deutsche Kunst und die höheren Schulen' in *Das Unterhaltungsblatt*, 3/4/33. 'Kunstgeschichte in den Lehrplänen höherer Schulen' in *Pädagogisches Zentralblatt* 4, 1933.

CHAPTER 12
'Ante-chambering'

1 Victor Klemperer, *I Shall Bear Witness* (Weidenfeld & Nicolson, 1998), p.13.

CHAPTER 13
'If a German – why this one?'

1 See, for example, Arnold Paucker, 'Speaking English with an accent', paper delivered at the conference '*Von Hitler Vertrieben: German and Austrian Exiles in Great Britain 1933–1945*', Goethe Institut, September 1993.
2 'The Architecture of Mannerism', op. cit.
3 Kenneth Clark, *Another Part of the Wood* (Coronet, 1974), p.163.
4 Ibid., p.135.
5 Lucinda Brolin, *Evening Standard*, 7/12/92.
6 'Note on Work of Dr Nikolaus Pevsner', 20/12/35 – the note Florence wrote to support Pevsner's application for a renewal of his residence permit. SPSL 191/2, 27.
7 Recorded by Florence's daughter Barbara, as noted by Games, op. cit., p.204.
8 NP, 'What is English in English Art', *Deutsche Zukunft: Wochenzeitung für Politik, Wirtschaft und Kultur*, February 1934.
9 Clark, op. cit., p.184.

10 Quoted in R. Cooper (ed.), *Refugee Scholars. Conversations with Tess Simpson* (Moorland, 1992), p.67.
11 Ernst Gombrich, interview with the author, 10/6/92.
12 Christopher Sykes, *Evelyn Waugh* (Penguin, 1975), p.83.

CHAPTER 14
'More than just an episode'

1 L. MacNeice, *The Strings Are False* (Faber, 1965), p.130.
2 *Birmingham Post* article, no date, 1934.
3 NP/LP, 8/11/33.
4 Fania Pascal in R. Rees (ed.), *Ludwig Wittgenstein: Personal Recollections* (Blackwell, 1981).
5 NP in 'The Designer in Industry: Carpets', *AR*, April 1936. The quotation from Herder comes from *Journal meiner Reise im Jahr 1769*.
6 Pauline Madge, 'An Enquiry into Pevsner's *Enquiry*', *Journal of Design History*, 1.2, 1988.
7 NP review 'The Humane Industrialist', *AR*, January 1941.
8 Berghahn, op. cit., p.70.
9 Clark, op. cit., p.158.
10 SPSL 191/2, 67.

CHAPTER 15
'*Amor fati*'

1 NP, introduction to Oskar Beyer (ed.), *Erich Mendelsohn: Letters of an architect* (Abelard-Schuman, 1967).

CHAPTER 16
'Little man, what now?'

1 R. Kralovitz, *Der gelbe Stern in Leipzig* (Walter Meckauer Kreis, 1992).
2 A. Clifton-Taylor, journal entry

recalled in his memorial address for Pevsner. *Address Given at the Memorial Service in the Church of Christ the King, Bloomsbury, for Nikolaus Pevsner*, reprinted in *Architectural History*, Vol. 28 (1985), pp.1–6.

3 SPSL 438/3, 361.
4 Zweig, op. cit., p.307.
5 Klemperer, op. cit., pp.224, 230 and 242.

CHAPTER 17

'This 1890–1900 hobby'

1 NP, Daily Report to Mr Gordon, 23/4/36. GP Series II, Box 30.
2 NP and L. Smith to Mr Gordon, 6/1/37. Ibid.
3 Ibid.
4 Caroline McGregor, 'Gribloch: The evolution of the architectural and interior design of a 1930s Scottish country house', *Architectural Heritage* 5, 1994. I am grateful to Charles O'Brien of the Pevsner Architectural Guides for alerting me to this article.
5 G Group statement, 1923.
6 Maxwell Fry, *Autobiographical Sketches* (Elek, 1975), p.148.
7 NP/Sidney K. Robinson, 5/4/72. GP, Series IA, Box 4.
8 NP, review of *Rationelle Bebauungsweisen*, op. cit.
9 *Pioneers of Modern Design: From William Morris to Walter Gropius* (Penguin, 1975), p.217. '1860–1930' in *Architectural Record*, 81, March 1937.
10 'What Can the Architectural Historian Give to the Architect?', RIBA Gold Medal Address, 20/6/67, reported in *Journal of the Royal Institute of British Architects (RIBA Journal)*, 3rd ser., 74, August 1967.
11 'From William Morris to Walter

Gropius', BBC radio talk printed in *The Listener*, 17/3/49.
12 'The Work of Walter Gropius, Royal Gold Medallist 1956', *RIBA Journal*, 3rd ser., 63, April 1956.
13 'Gropius: A moral force in architecture', NP obituary for Gropius, *Observer*, 6/7/69.
14 George Mikes (ed.), *Germany Laughs at Herself: German Cartoons since 1848* (Basserman, 1965).
15 NP's contribution, 'Le Corbusier and Frank Lloyd Wright', to BBC talk, 'The Arts', 1945. BBC Written Archives, Caversham.
16 NP/Ian J. Tod, 6/10/71.
17 See Gavin Stamp (ed.), *Britain in the Thirties*, a special issue of *Architectural Design*, Vol. 49, No. 10/11, 1979.
18 In a review of F.R.S. Yorke, *The Modern House*, in *Country Life*, 18/8/34.
19 *Britain in the Thirties*, op. cit.
20 J. Summerson, 'The MARS Group and the Thirties', in J. Bold and E. Chaney (eds), *English Architecture, Public and Private: Essays for Kerry Downes* (Hambledon Press, 1993).
21 Published in *Deutsche Vierteljahrsschrift fur Literaturwissenschaft und Geistesgeschichte* in 1936.
22 'Mr Pevsner remembers Mackmurdo', obituary in *Architects' Journal*, 16/4/42.
23 The correspondence with Mackmurdo is in GP Series II, Box 16.
24 NP, 'From William Morris to Walter Gropius', talk for the Third Programme, 6/3/49. BBC Written Archives, Caversham.

25 *Pioneers*, op. cit., p.147.
26 1908. Reprinted in A. Loos, *Trotzdem, 1900–1930* (Brenner, 1931).
27 *Ins Leere gesprochen, 1897–1900* (Brenner, 1932), p.66.
28 Ibid., p.49.
29 'Kunst und Maschine', *Dekorative Kunst*, ix, 1901–2.
30 NP, 'Any Old Bauhaus?', *The Listener*, 24/1/63.
31 W. Gropius, 'Bauhaus Manifesto and Programme', 1919.
32 NP, 'Bauhaus Comprehension', *Guardian*, 14/3/62.
33 *Pioneers*, op. cit., p.38.
34 NP, 'Le Corbusier and Frank Lloyd Wright', op. cit.
35 NP, 'From William Morris to Walter Gropius', op. cit.
36 *Pioneers*, op. cit., pp.161–2.
37 See, for example, Alan Crawford, *Charles Rennie Mackintosh* (Thames and Hudson, 1995), pp.196–7.
38 NP, 'Le Corbusier and Frank Lloyd Wright', op. cit.
39 *Burlington Magazine*, January 1943.
40 Unwin's speech, with a translation of Gropius's address, was published in the *RIBA Journal* of 19/5/34.
41 See, for example, A. Powers, 'Britain and the Bauhaus', *Apollo*, May 2006. Betjeman's article was a review of the Exhibition of British Industrial Art at Dorland Hall in *Weekend Review*, 24/6/33. Pevsner was also aware of an article by the Italian critic Persico in *L'Italia Litteraria* in June/July 1933 pointing to Josef Hoffmann, Henri van de Velde and Walter Gropius as descendants of William Morris. (NP, 'Edoardo Persico', *AR*, February 1966.)

42 G. Stamp, *Architectural Design* 49, 12, 1979, review of H. Muthesius, *The English House*.
43 P. Johnson/NP. GP Series II, Box 17.
44 W. Gropius/NP, 14/6/56. GP Series IA, Box 2.
45 Alan Crawford, *C.R. Ashbee: Architect, Designer and Romantic Socialist* (Yale University Press, 1985), p.420.
46 In 'C.F.A. Voysey: An Appreciation', *AR*, July 1937.
47 NP/P. Johnson, 3/11/47. GP Series II, Box 16.
48 *Pioneers*, op. cit., p.214.
49 Ibid., p.217.
50 J. Betjeman, reviewing M.H. Baillie Scott and E. Beresford, *Houses and Gardens* (Architecture Illustrated, 1933), in *AR*, May 1933.
51 NP, review of Lewis Mumford, *Art and Technics* (Columbia University Press, 1952), in *Magazine of Art*, December 1952, 45/8.
52 E. Newton, *Manchester Guardian*, 9/10/36.
53 I. Tod/NP, 16/9/71.

CHAPTER 18

'95% British is as far as we can go'

1 A. Clifton-Taylor, memorial address for Pevsner, op. cit.
2 *Country Life*, 13/2/37.
3 *School and College Management*, 3/7, November 1938.
4 'The First Plywood Furniture', *AR*, August 1938; and 'The History of Plywood up to 1914', *AR*, September 1939.
5 In *AR*, April 1937, July 1937 and March 1938 respectively.
6 A. Saint, *The Image of the Architect* (Yale UP, 1983), p.97.

7 See 'The First 100 Years', a special centenary issue of the *Architectural Review* in May 1996.

8 D. Dean, *The Thirties: Recalling the English Architectural Scene* (Trefoil/RIBA, 1983), p.81.

9 T. Mowl, *Stylistic Cold Wars: Betjeman versus Pevsner* (John Murray, 2000), p.33.

10 Dean, op. cit., p.81.

11 *AR* centenary issue, op. cit., p.102.

12 The typescript was read for the syndics at the Cambridge University Press by W.G. Constable and edited by Frank Kendon. D. McKitterick, *History of Cambridge University Press*, Vol. 3 (2004). Thanks to Simon Bradley of the Pevsner Architectural Guides for this information.

13 H. Read, 'An Enquiry into Public Taste', *The Listener*, 7/7/37.

14 C. Cornford, *Design*, 31/1/38.

15 L. Edwards, 'Except only Herman – and Herman's a German', *New Statesman*, 4/9/37.

16 Fry, op. cit., p.145.

17 NP, 'Hitler-Rede', 18/7/37. GP Series II, Box 22.

18 NP, 'Plein-Air Plastik in London', *Neue Zürcher Zeitung*, 19/7/57.

19 W. Adams/Mr McAlpine, Aliens Department, Home Office, 9/2/38. SPSL 438/3 HO, 361.

20 A. Calder, *The People's War: Britain 1939–45* (Jonathan Cape, 1969), p.25.

21 Nuremberg Document L–202, quoted in J. Noakes and J. Pridham, *Documents on Nazism 1919–1945* (London, 1974), pp. 473–5.

22 Zweig, op. cit., p.320.

23 Adriaan Hermsen and P.J. Wade, in the Gordon Russell company magazine, *The Circular Saw*.

24 The Gordon Russell papers are all in GP Series II, Box 30.

25 'A Plea for Contemporary Craft', *Design Industries Association News*, 3/5, June 1939.

26 '1860–1930', op. cit.

27 Interview with Hamish Henderson in *Scotsman*, 5/10/2000.

CHAPTER 19

Phoney War

1 NP/Francesca Wilson, 3/11/39. Papers kindly supplied by Fred Wolsey.

2 Ibid.

3 Ministry of Information memo, 25/7/41.

4 M. Sampson, 'Jewish Anti-semitism. The Attitudes of the Jewish Community in Britain Toward Refugees from Nazi Germany. *The Jewish Chronicle*, March 1933–September 1938' in J. Miffull (ed.), *Why Germany? National Socialism, Anti-semitism and the European Context* (Berg, Providence, RI, 1993), p.167.

5 NP/Francesca Wilson, 3/11/39.

6 NP/J. Pritchard, 16/11/39. Jack Pritchard Papers at the University of East Anglia, PP/8.

7 Andrea Lorz, 'Legacy of the Jews of Leipzig – Part 2', in *Journal of the Association of Jewish Refugees*, April 2003.

8 1954 family memoir.

9 GP Series IIIA, Box 54.

10 J.M. Richards/NP, 9/10/39. GP Series II, Box 18.

11 *Museums Journal*, January 1940. *Country Life*, 4/5/40.

CHAPTER 20

Internee 54829

1 NP, obituary for Pinder, *The Times*, 4/7/47.
2 On the occasion of Nolde's sixtieth birthday in 1927 – 'Jubi-läums-ausstellung Emil Nolde' in *Dresdener Anzeiger*.
3 N. West (ed.), *The Diaries of Guy Liddell, Vol. I. 1939–42* (Frank Cass, 2005). Entry for 24/11/39.
4 M. Kochan, *Britain's Internees in the Second World War* (Macmillan, 1983), p.21.
5 Ibid., p.99.
6 Ibid., p.69.
7 Klaus Hinrichsen, quoted by C. Benton, *A Different World: Emigré Architects in Britain 1928–58* (RIBA Heinz Gallery, 1995), p.80.
8 Paul Jacobsthal, quoted in Kochan, op. cit., p.138.
9 NP/LP, 1/8/40.
10 NA HO 215/53. August 1940 Report of Internment Camp 009: Huyton.
11 Ibid.
12 LP/NP, 5/8/40.
13 SPSL 191/2, 152.
14 LP/NP, 23/8/40.

CHAPTER 21

'The year of change'

1 NP/E. Simpson, 4/10/40. SPSL 191/2, 161.
2 NP, review of R. Symonds, *Masterpieces of English Furniture and Clocks*, in *Spectator*, 22/11/40. Review of R. Ziller, *We Make History*, in *The Listener*, 7/11/40.
3 SPSL 191/2, 154.
4 F. Pick/NP, 11/12/40. GP Series IA, Box 4.
5 Ibid.

6 E. Simpson/G. Bing, c.1/10/40. SPSL 191/2, 159.
7 Calder, op. cit., p.165.
8 NP/E. Simpson, 1/12/40. SPSL 191/2, 163.
9 F. Pick/NP, 27/11/40. GP Series IA, Box 4.
10 All quotations are from the draft German typescript for the two pieces. GP Series II, Box 22.
11 NP/E. Simpson, 20/12/40. SPSL 191/2, 170.
12 NP/E. Simpson, 21/5/43. SPSL 191/2, 184.
13 NP/E. Simpson, 11/3/41. SPSL 191/2, 177.
14 Margaret Clark, 'Getting Things Right', in *Miscellany 10: Twenty-One Years* (Penguin Collectors Society, 1995), p.41.
15 'The Architecture of Mannerism', op. cit.
16 RIBA Gold Medal Address, 1967, op. cit.
17 Francesca Wilson diary, 23/4/41. Papers supplied by Fred Wolsey.
18 Calder, op. cit., p.214.
19 NP, reviews of J. Pope-Hennessy, *History Under Fire*, with photographs by Cecil Beaton; *Britain Under Fire*, with foreword by J.B. Priestley; and E. Carter, *Grim Glory: Pictures of Britain Under Fire*, all in *Burlington Magazine*, September 1941.
20 S. Behr, 'Anatomy of the woman as collector and dealer in the Weimar period: Rosa Schapire and Johanna Eyl', in S. West and M. Meskimmon (eds), *Visions of the Neue Frau: Women and the Visual Arts in Weimar Germany* (Scolar Press, 1995).
21 *Die Zeitung*, 17/3/41.
22 Ibid., 2/8/41.
23 Quoted in Richard Shone, *Bloomsbury Portraits* – see Tate Archive: http://www.tate.org.uk/

archivejourneys/bloomsburyhtml/
art_omega_artpatron.htm

24 G.B. Shaw/Roger Fry, 22/5/14.
Quoted in Frances Spalding,
Roger Fry: Art and Life (Black
Dog, 1999), p.177.
25 Maynard Keynes/NP, 2/4/41.
GP Series II, Box 22.
26 'Criticism', *AR*, December 1941.
27 J.M. Richards, interview with the
author, 2/4/92.
28 Francesca Wilson to her mother,
10/11/41. Papers supplied by
Fred Wolsey.
29 Calder, op. cit., p.229.
30 Churchill, radio broadcast,
'Report on the War', 27/4/41.
31 http://history1900s.about.com/od/
holocaust/a/yellowstar_2.htm
32 Hedwig Kaufmann/NP, 23/9/41.
GP Series VI, Box 135.
33 Lis Knauth memoir, 'Die letzten
drei Jahre 1939–42', date
unknown.

CHAPTER 22

'Now we are scattered'

1 NP/Tom Pevsner, 1/2/42.
2 NP/L. Knauth, 26/3/42.
GP Series VI, Box 135.
3 Gertrud ?/NP, 28/3/42. GP Series
VI, Box 135.
4 25/10/43, quoted in Brereton
Greenhous et al., *The Crucible
of War, 1939–1945: History of
the Royal Canadian Air Force,
Volume III* (University of
Toronto, 1994), p.725.
5 Sir A. Harris, *Bomber Offensive*
(Greenhill Books, 1947), p.105.
6 Calder, op. cit., p.279.
7 Ibid., p.373.
8 Published in 1955.
9 G. White, letter to *The Times*,
30/8/83. *A Book of Toys* (1946)
was one of the series' best-selling
titles.
10 Eric Newton, 'The King Penguin

Books', *Penrose Annual*, XLIII
(Lund Humphries, 1949).
11 NP/Esther Simpson, 19/5/43.
SPSL 191/2, 184.
12 NP/Tom Pevsner, 18/2/42.
13 *Speculum*, Vol. 17, October
1942. *Journal of the Warburg
and Courtauld Institutes*, Vol. 5,
1942.
14 In a letter in the *RIBA Journal*
on Richards, 3/3/71.
15 NP/Professor C. Moore, Yale,
1971.
16 J. Betjeman, 'Architecture', *The
London Mercury*, November
1933.
17 NP/Tom Pevsner, 24/2/42.
18 P. Levi, *The Periodic Table*
(Everyman, 1995), p.54, 'Potas-
sium' – first published in 1975.

CHAPTER 23

'Contrast, surprise and irregularity'

1 Foreword to the bibliography
of his works by John Barr, in
W. O'Neal (ed.), *Papers of the
American Association of Architectural Bibliographers*, Vol. VII
(University Press of Virginia,
Charlottesville, 1970).
2 Roger Radford to the author,
April 2009.
3 H. Read, *Architect*, 19/3/43.
4 J. Summerson, *New Statesman*,
20/1/61, reviewing the Jubilee
edition.
5 'EVT Penguins and the
"Release" Scheme', in J. Pearson,
*Penguins March On: Books for
the Forces during World War II*
(Penguin Collectors Society,
Miscellany 11, 1996).
6 P. Murray, 'Nikolaus Bernhard
Leon Pevsner', in *Proceedings of
the British Academy*, 1984.
7 *AR*, May 1943.
8 Ibid., March 1943.

9 'American Victorian', reviews of
J. Coolidge, *Mill and Mansion:
A Study of Architecture and
Society in Lowell, Massachusetts
1820–1865*, and R. Newton,
*Town and Davis, Pioneers in
American Revivalist Architecture,
1812–1870*, in *AR*, July 1943.

10 C. Hussey, *The Picturesque:
Studies in a Point of View*
(Frank Cass, 1927).

11 NP, 'Conclusions', in *The Picturesque Garden and its Influence
outside the British Isles*
(Dumbarton Oaks, 1974), p.120.

12 'Price on Picturesque Planning', a
florilegium of Price's writings, in
AR, February 1944.

13 Pevsner gave a BBC talk on
Knight as part of the Third
Programme series 'The Visual
Arts', on 16/1/47, published in
The Listener, 30/1/47. He also
published 'Richard Payne Knight'
in *Art Bulletin*, December 1949.

14 NP/H. de C. Hastings, 19/12/61.
GP Series IB, Box 6.

15 NP note, ?1944, GP Series IB,
Box 6.

16 NP/Esther Simpson, 19/5/43.
SPSL 191/2, 184.

17 For example, in 'Double Profile:
A reconsideration of the Elizabethan Style as seen at
Wollaton', in *AR*, March 1950,
and again in a series of three
talks on 'Mannerism and Elizabethan Architecture' for the
BBC's Third Programme in
February 1964.

18 C. Connolly, 'Writers and
Society, 1940–43', in *The
Condemned Playground*
(Routledge, 1945).

19 Henry Moore/NP, 11/2/45.
GP Series IA, Box 3.

CHAPTER 24
'Pevsner in an English uniform'

1 During the war he wrote, for
Country Life, 'Style in Stamps: a
Century of Postal Design'
(4/5/40), 'English Qualities in
English Ceramics: Evolution
Rather Than Revolution'
(3/10/41) and 'English Qualities
in English Glass' (19/7/41). For
Pottery and Glass he produced
'Questionnaire: Design in the
Pottery Industry' (November
1944), and for *Harper's* 'Can
Painters Design Fabrics?'
(November 1945).

2 This description is drawn from
the much more detailed account
by Jill Seddon, 'The Architect
and the "Arch-Pedant": Sadie
Speight, Nikolaus Pevsner and
"Design Review"', in *Journal of
Design History*, 20/1, 2007.

3 The documentation of Pevsner's
mission is to be found in the
Design Council archive within
the Design Archives of Brighton
University. COID 492/1 24 1946
'Design Investigation Germany –
CID Team'.

4 NA FO 1050/1319, 'Return of
Refugee Scholars'.

5 W.E. Williams, *Allen Lane: A
Personal Portrait* (Bodley Head,
1973), p.16.

6 In an interview recorded at
Bristol University Library for the
HTV documentary *What About
a Penguin?* on 6/4/93. Published
in *The Penguin Collector*, Vol.
41, 1993.

7 'Getting Things Right' in *21
Years (Miscellany 10)*, Penguin
Collectors Society, 1995, p.37.

8 In 'Tributes to Allen Lane at a
Service of Thanksgiving for his
Life and Work 1902–1970',
privately printed, 1970.

9 Lady Lane, interview with the author, 26/7/92.

10 Ian Sutton, interview with the author, 28/9/92.

CHAPTER 25

'Ballon d'essai'

1 David Herbert, *Signal*, 70 (Children's Literature Association Quarterly, 1993), p.33.

2 O. Gurney, *The Hittites* (Penguin, 1952).

3 See, e.g., W. Wulf, 'German Inventory and Heritage – a fateful genesis from history, politics and science', *Transactions of the Ancient Monuments Society*, Vol. 41, 1997.

4 Eunice Kemp (née Frost)/Hans Schmoller, 22/9/83. Document kindly supplied by Mrs Tanya Schmoller.

5 Hans Schmoller/Stephen Games, 1984. Ibid.

6 NP, 'Recording English Monuments', review of P. Hofer, *Die Kunstdenkmäler des Kantons Bern: Die Staatsbauten der Stadt Bern*, in *TLS*, 22/5/48.

7 A. Clifton-Taylor, 'Touring with the Little Guides', in John Summerson (ed.), *Concerning Architecture: Essays on architectural writers and writing presented to Nikolaus Pevsner* (Penguin, 1968), p.245.

8 NP, review 'Cambridge to 1850', *AR*, June 1960.

9 J. Betjeman, 'A preservationist's progress', in *The Future of the Past: Attitudes to Conservation 1174–1974* (Thames and Hudson, 1976).

10 J. Betjeman/Lionel Perry, 29/3/32, in C. Lycett Green (ed.), *John Betjeman: Letters. Vol. 1, 1926–51* (Methuen, 1995), p.102.

11 Ibid., p.139.

12 J. Betjeman/Lady Juliet Smith, 5/12/63, in C. Lycett Green (ed.), *John Betjeman: Letters. Vol. 2, 1951–84* (Methuen, 1995), p.267.

13 Bevis Hillier, *John Betjeman: the biography* (John Murray, 2006), p.176. (This is the one-volume abridged version of the full three-volume biography.)

14 G. Grigson, review of a reissue of *Wiltshire*, in *AR*, March 1969.

15 Gillian Darley, 'The well-informed traveller: architectural guides 1930s–50s', paper delivered at the conference 'Pevsner's *The Buildings of England*' at the Victoria and Albert Museum, 13–14/7/2001.

16 *John Betjeman: Letters. Vol. 1*, op. cit., p.394.

17 P. Lasko, interview, loc. cit.

18 NP, introduction to 'A Select Bibliography of the Publications of Nikolaus Pevsner', in *Concerning Architecture*, op. cit.

19 Denis Evinson, interview with the author, 8/7/92.

20 NP/Dieter Pevsner, 1/7/65.

21 NP, review of H. Wölfflin, *Renaissance and Baroque*, in *TLS*, 25/6/64.

22 A. Clifton-Taylor, 'Touring with the Little Guides', op. cit., p.245.

23 A. Clifton-Taylor, obituary for Pevsner, *AR*, October 1983.

24 NP, *County Durham* (Penguin, 1953), p.41.

25 John Newman, interview with the author, 2/4/92.

26 NP/V.R. Christophers, Hammersmith and Fulham Historical Society, 2/10/71.

27 NP, introduction to A. Savidge, *The Parsonage in England* (SPCK, 1964).

28 Bridget Cherry, interview with the author, 11/3/92.

29 NP, 'Introducing the Buildings of England', radio talk for Australian Broadcasting Commission, 18/7/58.
30 Mowl, op. cit., p.112.
31 Edward Hubbard lecture, 'The preparation and research for *Buildings of England* volumes', Arlis Conference for art-history librarians, Liverpool, 1981.
32 R. Burlingham, letter to the author, 12/12/92.

CHAPTER 26

'They've come to read the meter, Ma'

1 'The Buildings of England' in *Deutsche Kunst und Denkmalpflege, Jahrgang 1977* (Deutscher Kunstverlag, 1977).
2 J. Newman, 'An Appreciation of Sir Nikolaus Pevsner', *The Best Buildings of England* (Viking, 1986).
3 NP/Edward Hubbard, 17/1/67. Penguin Papers, *BoE* files, DM 1901/2/5.
4 A. Clifton-Taylor, memorial address for Pevsner, op. cit.
5 J. Newman, interview with the author, loc. cit.
6 G. Moorhouse, 'A day with the Pevsners', *Guardian*, 21/4/60.
7 NP/Allen Lane, 8/9/48. Material kindly sent by Steve Hare ahead of its publication in *Penguin Portrait: Allen Lane and the Penguin editors, 1935–70* (Penguin, 1995). The correspondence is now in the Penguin Archive in the Special Collections of Bristol University.
8 NP/Jim Holmes, 22/3/67.
9 NP/A. Lane, July 1950. Penguin Papers, *BoE* files, DM 1901/8/1.
10 A. Lane/NP, 1947. Penguin Papers, DM 1107/BE 1.

11 J. Summerson, review of *Cornwall* and *Nottinghamshire, New Statesman*, 42, 15/9/51.
12 *AR*, December 1952.
13 Dr Susi Lang, interview with the author, 18/2/93.

CHAPTER 27

'Truthful enthusiasm'

1 E. Panofsky, 'The History of Art', in *The Cultural Migration: The European Scholar in America* (Benjamin Franklin Lectures of University of Pennsylvania, 1953).
2 NP, 'English Art History; Decorated and Perpendicular', review of Joan Evans, *English Art 1307–1461* (Clarendon Press, 1949), in *TLS*, 13/1/50.
3 E. Gombrich, 'Monuments to deception', review of Francis Haskell, *History and its Images: Art and the Interpretation of the Past* (Yale University Press, 1993), in *Financial Times*, 3/7/93.
4 NP, 'English Art History; Decorated and Perpendicular', op. cit.
5 NP, review of P. Frankl, *The Gothic* (OUP, 1961), in *TLS*, 7/4/61.
6 W. Vaughan, paper on 'Pevsner's Art History' given at 'Pevsner's *The Buildings of England*' conference, loc. cit.
7 P. Lasko, interview, loc. cit.
8 NP, 'The Value of History to Students of Architecture', *Architects' Journal*, 23/4/59.
9 See, for example, 'An Un-English Activity. 1. Reflections on Not Teaching Art History', in *The Listener*, 30/10/52.
10 NP/Martin Baldwin, Art Gallery of Toronto, 3/9/58.
11 NP/Eduard Sekler, 8/11/72. GP Series IIIB, Box 67.

12 Extensive notes for lectures,
   however, are preserved in
   GP Series III A, B and C.
13 Jane Fawcett, interview with the
   author, 14/6/93.
14 For example, NP/Alan Bowness,
   17/6/71, declining an invitation
   to speak at the Courtauld Institute on nineteenth-century
   German architecture.
15 Peter Murray, interview with the
   author, 15/2/92.
16 J. Fawcett, interview, loc. cit.
17 D. Boswell, letter to the author,
   20/5/92.
18 J. Newman, interview, loc. cit.
19 P. Lasko, interview, loc. cit.
20 NP/John Fassler, 17/12/51.
   GP Series IIIB, Box 60.
21 Thanks to Ian Sutton for the
   Voltaire note.
22 Iris Omer-Cooper, notes sent to
   the author, 16/4/92.
23 Varsity, 27/11/48.
24 P. Lasko, interview, loc. cit.
25 Emily Lane, note to the author,
   May 2009.
26 P. Lasko, interview, loc. cit.
27 Ibid.
28 I. Sutton, interview with the
   author, 23/4/92.
29 D. Evinson, interview, loc. cit.
30 NP/Ronnie Rolf, 27/8/70.
31 D. Evinson, interview, loc. cit.
32 Gerda Mayer, letter to the
   author, 17/6/92.
33 George Cusworth/NP, September
   1963.
34 D. Evinson, interview, loc. cit.

CHAPTER 28

'A further act for the main plot'

1 NP, letter to RIBA Journal,
   3/3/71.
2 J.M. Richards, interview with
   Bevis Hillier in 1982, quoted in
   Hillier, Young Betjeman, op. cit.,
   p.253.

3 NP, letter to RIBA Journal, op.
   cit.
4 Lionel Brett, Our Selves
   Unknown (Gollancz, 1985),
   p.99.
5 R. Banham, New Statesman,
   14/2/59.
6 O. Lancaster, foreword to revised
   edition of Here of All Places
   (John Murray, 1975).
7 NP, review in RIBA Journal,
   July 1961.
8 H. Casson, obituary for Pevsner,
   AR, October 1983.
9 Lionel Brett, interview with the
   author, 24/6/92.
10 NP, radio talk on 'The Picturesque and the Twentieth
   Century: modern town planning',
   31/1/54. BBC Written Archives,
   Caversham.
11 Robert Thorne, building historian, interview with the author,
   8/5/93.
12 G.G. Scott, in an introduction to
   the 1934 exhibition of International Architecture. Quoted in
   Anthony Jackson, The Politics of
   Architecture (Architectural Press,
   1970), p.63.
13 Wells Coates, Unit One: The
   Modern Movement in English
   Architecture, Painting and Sculpture (Cassell, 1934).
14 J. Betjeman/Geoffrey Taylor,
   18/8/44, in John Betjeman:
   Letters. Vol. 1, op. cit., p.347.
15 A. Saint, A Change of Heart:
   English architecture since the
   war – a policy for protection
   (Royal Commission on the
   Historical Monuments of
   England/English Heritage, 1992),
   p.5.
16 H. Casson, '100 Years of Type-
   Set Architecture', address to
   meeting of the Architectural
   Association, 26/5/48.
17 'Exterior Furnishing or

Sharawaggi: the art of making urban landscape', by 'The Editor', *AR*, January 1944.

18 P. Davey, *AR* centenary issue, op. cit.

19 J.M. Richards, 'The Next Step?', *AR*, March 1950.

20 Sven Backström, *AR*, September 1948.

21 Corin Hughes-Stanton, 'Nikolaus Pevsner: a major influence on modern design', *Design*, 1967.

22 NP, 'Treasure Hunt', *AR*, November 1942.

23 Talk printed in *The Listener*, 17/7/47 as 'Greece, Rome – and Washington: Nikolaus Pevsner on the Need for a New Style in Monumental Architecture'.

24 These views were outlined at length in 'Visual Planning and the City of London', *Architectural Association Journal*, 61, December 1945–January 1946.

25 I. De Wolfe, 'Townscape', *AR*, 105, 1949.

26 G. Cullen, 'Immediacy', *AR*, April 1953.

27 'Townscape', an 'address illustrated by lantern views' given to the Council for Visual Education in 1955. The evolution and significance of the Townscape movement, and the roles in it of both Pevsner and Hastings, are explored and reassessed in a recent thesis, 'Visual Planning and Exterior Furnishing: a critical history of the Early Townscape Movement, 1930 to 1949', by Mathew Aitchison, University of Queensland, 2008. And see also John Macarthur, 'Strange Encounters in Mid-Century British Urbanism: Townscape, Anti-Scrape and Surrealism', *Proceedings of the 24th International Conference of the Society of Architectural Historians, Australia and New Zealand*, September 2007.

28 'Lettering and the Festival on the South Bank', *The Penrose Annual*, Vol. 46, 1952.

29 J. Summerson, *New Statesman*, 6/10/51.

30 H. Casson, obituary for NP, *AR*, October 1983.

CHAPTER 29

'The High Table part of the stay'

1 NP, 'Reflections on Not Teaching Art History', *The Listener*, 30/10/52.

2 Ibid.

3 Sir Ernst Gombrich, interview with the author, 14/12/91.

4 Hughes-Stanton, op. cit.

5 G. Mikes, *How to Be an Alien* (Wingate, 1946), p.10.

6 NP, 'Visual Aspects of the Cambridge Plan', *Cambridge Review*, 13/5/50.

7 NP, foreword to Nicholas Taylor, *Cambridge New Architecture* (Trinity Hall, Cambridge, 1964).

8 NP, 'The Cambridge Campus of the Future', in *Cambridge Review*, 19/4/52.

9 NP, 'Churchill College – Some Considerations: Passions Not Aroused', *Varsity*, 17/5/58.

10 I. Quigly, letter to the author, 5/12/93.

11 *Heftchen*, 15/2/55.

CHAPTER 30

'The grim mopping up of work'

1 NP, 'The Birkbeck Memorial: Three Opinions. 3. The War Memorial', in the Birkbeck magazine *The Lodestone*, Vol. 47/2, 1956.

2 Michael Farr, interview with the author, 13/8/92.

3 I. Nairn, *Your England Revisited* (Hutchinson, 1964).

4 Peter Clarke, *AR* review 'From Uxbridge to Dagenham' of *Nairn's London* (Penguin, 1966).

5 Nigel Whiteley, paper on 'The puzzled *Lieber Meister*: Pevsner and Reyner Banham', *Reassessing Nikolaus Pevsner* conference and Ashgate publication of the conference papers, op. cit.

6 R. Banham, 'The Machine Aesthetic', *AR*, April 1955.

7 N. Whiteley, 'Banham and Otherness: Reyner Banham (1922–88) and his quest for an *architecture autre*', *Architectural History* 33, 1990.

8 Mark Wigley reviewing N. Whiteley, *Reyner Banham: Historian of the Immediate Future* (MIT Press, 2002) in *ArtForum*, December 2001.

9 NP, postscript to M. Farr, *Design in British Industry: A Mid-Century Survey* (CUP, 1955).

10 'History Repeats', discussion in the *RIBA Journal*, December 1961, of Pevsner's paper 'Modern Architecture and the Historian, or the Return of Historicism'.

11 NP/Miss D. Law, Universities Section, British Council, 3/11/54.

12 NP, lecture notes on Modern Architecture and Design, Aspen. GP Series IIIC, Box 72.

13 NP/R.P. Hinks, British Council, 22/12/55. NA BW 83/29.

14 NP/Mrs Rosemary Day, British Council, 4/11/55. NA BW 83/29.

15 NP/C. de Winton, 29/5/56. GP Series IIIB, Box 64.

16 NP/LP, 10/7/54.

17 Postscript to Farr, op. cit.

18 Pevsner made the remark in his talk 'Architecture and William Morris', read at the RIBA on 19/2/57 and published in the *RIBA Journal*, 3rd ser., 64, March 1957.

19 Leonie Cohn/Richard Walzer, 18/3/54. BBC WAC RCONT1 – Prof Nikolaus Pevsner – Talks File 1A.

20 *The Critics*, 2/11/47.

21 NP/Lorna Moore, 1/2/52. BBC Written Archives, Caversham.

22 S. Games (ed.), *Pevsner on Art and Architecture: The Radio Talks* (Methuen, 2002), p.xxxviii.

23 Ignatieff, op. cit., p.204.

24 'Aspects of Goethe – Goethe and Architecture', 19/11/49, Third Programme.

25 'How to Judge Victorian Architecture', 4/7/51, Third Programme.

26 'Victorian thought on architecture', 11/7/51, Third Programme.

27 Martin Armstrong, 'Through the Looking Glass', *The Listener*, ?September 1955.

28 Roger Cary/NP, 19/2/53. BBC Written Archives, Caversham.

29 R. Keen/E. Rowley, 25/6/52. BBC WAC RCONT1 – Prof Nikolaus Pevsner – Talks File 1A.

30 Memo, D.F. Boyd/R. Keen, 26/6/52. BBC Written Archives, Caversham.

CHAPTER 31

'A trifle tactless of Nikolaus'

1 *The Times*, 28/11/55. cf. 'Future of the Reith Lectures', *The Times*, 23/1/62.

2 J. Summerson, on Pevsner's RIBA Gold Medal award in 1967. Speech published in *AR*, August 1967.

3 Quoted by William Vaughan in his paper 'Pevsner's Art History', given at the 'Fifty Years of *The*

Buildings of England' conference at the Victoria and Albert Museum, 13–14/7/2001.

4 *Radio Times*, 14/10/55.

5 NP, 'An Exhibition of British Medieval Art', *Burlington Magazine*, 75, July 1939.

6 'English Qualities in English Ceramics: Evolution rather than Revolution', *Country Life*, 3/10/41.

7 'The Geography of Art', first Reith Lecture, 16/10/55.

8 http://www.lib.duke.edu/lilly/artlibry/dah/freyd.htm

9 H. Read, *AR*, September 1956.

10 J. Berger, *New Statesman*, 14/4/56.

11 *News Chronicle*, 21/10/55.

12 Anthony Quiney, interview with the author, 25/4/93.

CHAPTER 32

'No time to laugh'

1 NP/G. Grigson, 7/8/51.

2 NP/E. French, 26/9/51.

3 A. Glover/NP, no date. Penguin Papers, Frost Papers, DM 1843/30.

4 NP, review of C. de Tolnay, *Michelangelo: Vol. 5 – The Final Period*, in *TLS*, 27/1/61.

5 H. Rubinstein/Ms Myers, 3/12/51. Penguin Papers, *BoE* files, DM 1901/8/6.

6 H. Rubinstein/NP, 22/1/52. Ibid.

7 NP, 'On finding oneself out of date', *Architects' Journal*, 19/1/65.

8 LP/NP, 27/7/51.

9 Quiney, loc. cit.

10 Winnie Bailey, letter to the author, 25/9/92.

11 A.W. Pugin, *The True Principles of Pointed or Christian Architecture* (John Weale, 1841), pp. 56–7.

12 NP, 'Danish Puzzle', review of

H. Langkilde, *Arkitekten Kay Fisker*, in *AR*, November 1961. Fisker was a neo-Georgian before turning to the Modern Movement in the 1930s.

13 *County Durham* (Penguin, 1953), p.158.

14 B. Allsopp, *Civilisation, the Next Stage: The Importance of Individuals in the Modern World* (Oriel Press, 1969), and *Towards a Humane Architecture* (Frederick Muller, 1974).

15 R. Banham, 'England His England', review of *NE Norfolk and Norwich*, *NW and S Norfolk*, and *London: 1. The Cities of London and Westminster*, in *New Statesman*, 28/9/62.

16 NP, interview with Julian Holland, 10/1/64, Home Service. BBC Written Archives, Caversham.

17 *Observer*, 11/5/58.

18 NP/A. Lane, November 1949. Penguin Papers, *BoE* files, DM 1901/8/1.

19 NP/Beaver, 3/2/56 and 27/8/56. Penguin Papers, *BoE* files, DM 1901/4/4.

20 NP/M. Clifford, ? 1956. Penguin Papers, *BoE* files, DM 1901/4/2.

21 T. Singleton/NP, 14/3/58. Penguin Papers, *BoE* files, DM 1901/4/5.

22 NP/LP, 21/4/59.

CHAPTER 33

'Poet and Pedant'

1 Sir John Summerson, interview with the author, 3/3/92.

2 The full family history, and the saga of the two 'nns', is all in Hillier, *Young Betjeman*, op. cit., pp.2–4.

3 P. Betjeman/J. Betjeman, early 1933. Quoted in Hillier, *Young Betjeman*, op. cit., p.373.

4 Quoted in the third volume of Hillier's biography, *The Bonus of Laughter* (John Murray, 2005), p.349.

5 J. Betjeman, *Spectator*, 31/10/56.

6 J.E. Bowle, quoted in *John Betjeman: Letters. Vol. 1*, op. cit., p.434.

7 J. Summerson, *New Statesman*, 4/10/52, reviewing Betjeman's *First and Last Loves*.

8 Wilfrid Blunt, quoted in Hillier, *John Betjeman: the biography*, op. cit., p.186.

9 Maxwell Fry, quoted in Hillier, *Young Betjeman*, op. cit, p.259.

10 NP, 'The Topography of England', in *The Listener*, 11/1/62.

11 J. Summerson, in a lecture to the PEN Club, quoted in *John Betjeman: Letters. Vol. 2*, op. cit., p.140.

12 J. Betjeman, talk for the Home Service, February 1943. Quoted by Hillier, *John Betjeman: The Biography*, op. cit., p.281.

13 According to Christopher Sykes, quoted by Hillier, *Young Betjeman*, op. cit., p.174.

14 NP, interview with Julian Holland, loc. cit.

15 J. Betjeman/NP, 21/4/39. GP Series II, Box 17.

16 Quoted by Hillier, *John Betjeman: the biography*, op. cit., p.194.

17 Ibid., p.176.

18 J. Betjeman/J. Lees-Milne, 26/3/52, in *John Betjeman: Letters. Vol. 2*, op. cit., p.23.

19 NP/Rev. P.C. Elers, 21/11/74.

20 NP radio talk, 'Bavarian Rococo – or the Eloquent in Art', Home Service, 17/11/54.

21 NP, 'Thoughts on Coventry Cathedral', *The Listener*, 17/1/52.

22 N. Comper, 'Of the Atmosphere of a Church' (Sheldon, 1947). The essay is reprinted in A. Symondson, SJ, *Sir Ninian Comper: an introduction to his life and work* (Spire, 2006).

23 J. Betjeman/N. Comper, 17/10/43. Quoted by Anthony Symondson, SJ, 'An ambiguous friendship: John Betjeman, John Piper and Sir Ninian Comper', in *First and Last Loves: John Betjeman and Architecture* (Sir John Soane's Museum exhibition catalogue, 2006).

24 J. Betjeman/N. Comper, 23/12/45. Ibid.

25 Derek Stanford, *John Betjeman* (Neville Spearman, 1961), p.25.

26 J. Betjeman/E. Waugh, 26/5/47. *John Betjeman: Letters. Vol. 1*, op. cit., p.412.

27 Alec Clifton-Taylor/J. Betjeman, 18/7/1953. *John Betjeman: Letters. Vol. 2*, op. cit., p.43.

28 Winnie Bailey/Reg Read, 25/10/93.

CHAPTER 34

'Always doing'

1 'On Finding Oneself Out of Date. Men of the Year: Nikolaus Pevsner', *Architects' Journal*, 19/1/56.

2 *Observer*, Sydney, 9/8/58.

3 NP, introduction to 'The Larger Dominions', in J.M. Richards (ed.), *New Buildings in the Commonwealth* (Architectural Press, 1961).

4 NP/N. Taylor, 1/10/58.

5 I. Nairn/NP, 11/3/54. Penguin Papers, *BoE* files, DM 1901/8/1.

6 I. Nairn, *AR*, March 1954.

7 Lola Pevsner/Camilla Bagg, no date, 1953.

8 Quoted in Geoffrey Beard, *Attingham: The First Forty Years 1952 to 1991* (The Attingham Trust for the Study of the Country House in Britain, 1991).

9 For a portrait of Alan Glover (1895–1966), see S. Hare, *Penguin Portrait*, op. cit.

10 A. Glover/NP, 4/6/51. Penguin Papers, *BoE* files, DM 1901/8/1.

11 NP/A. Glover, 13/10/49. Penguin Papers, Eunice Frost Papers. DM 1843/30.

12 H. Schmoller, 'Book Design Today', *Printing Review*, Spring 1951. And see G. Cinamon (ed.), 'Hans Schmoller, his life and work', *The Monotype Recorder*, 6, April 1987.

13 Oliver Caldecott, quoted in Cinamon, op. cit.

14 Schmoller's work with Pevsner is discussed in detail in John Trevitt, 'The Buildings of England and The Pelican History of Art', in Cinamon, op. cit.

15 Ian Sutton, 'Reminiscences', op. cit.

16 Peter Murray, 'N.B.L. Pevsner', *Proceedings of the British Academy*, 1984, p.509.

17 John Trevitt, op. cit.

18 NP/Professor Turpin Bannister, University of Florida, 30/6/58. GP Series II, Box 16. Turpin Bannister (1904–82) was the first President of the Society of Architectural Historians in the US.

19 Francisco Stastny, University of San Marcos, Lima/George Kubler, Yale, 10/4/78. Penguin Papers, DM 1107/Z. Kubler (with Martin Soria) wrote *Art and Architecture in Spain and Portugal and their American Dominions* for the *Pelican History*.

20 NP/Marcia Allentuck, 3/10/73. GP Series IIIB, Box 66.

21 R. Banham, 'Out of the Air', *The Listener*, 25/8/83.

22 NP/Pamela Loveridge, Penguin, 29/8/68. Penguin Papers, DM 1107/Z.

23 http://www.courtauld.ac.uk/about/history.shtml

24 R. Banham, 'The Pelican History of Art', *AR*, November 1953.

25 'The Pelican History of Art' in *Journal of Society of Architectural Historians*, 39/2, May 1980.

CHAPTER 35

'Unbeautiful and yet of value'

1 NP, memoir of Lola, 1963–4.

2 Mark Girouard, introduction to *First and Last Loves: John Betjeman and Architecture* (Sir John Soane's Museum exhibition catalogue, 2006).

3 NP, 'As I See It', *Building Materials*, March 1967.

4 NP, 'The Preservation of the Monuments of Victorian Commerce', *The Journal of Industrial Archaeology*, 2/1, March 1965.

5 R. Banham, 'England His England', op. cit.

6 J. Summerson, *Victorian Architecture in England: Four studies in evaluation* (Columbia University Press, 1970), p.75.

7 NP, 'Originality', *AR*, June 1954.

8 NP notes on the Goodhart-Rendel conversation, GP Series II, Box 22.

9 J. Summerson, review of Goodhart-Rendel's *English Architecture Since the Regency*, *New Statesman*, 9/5/53.

10 *AR*, August 1955.

CHAPTER 36

'On Finding Oneself Out of Date'

1 NP, 'Roehampton', *AR*, July 1959.
2 In an article for the *Birmingham Post*, c.1962. And cf. his article for the *RIBA Journal*, February 1955.
3 NP, 'Faith and feasibility', in *Guardian*, 25/5/62.
4 Published in *The Listener*, 17/1/52.
5 B. Spence/NP, 14/1/52. GP Series IA, Box 4.
6 R. Banham, 'Coventry Cathedral – Strictly "Trad, Dad"', *New Statesman*, 25/5/62.
7 NP, 'A Setting for St Paul's Cathedral', printed in *The Listener*, 10/5/56.
8 Robin Simon, 'Paternoster Pevsner', *Apollo*, September 1992.
9 See, for example, A. Saint, *A Change of Heart*, op. cit.
10 P. Blake, *Form Follows Fiasco: Why Modern Architecture Hasn't Worked* (Little, Brown, 1978).
11 NP, 'Time and Le Corbusier', *AR*, March 1959.
12 NP, foreword to N. Taylor, *Cambridge New Architecture*, op. cit.
13 NP, 'Victorian Age of Building Revalued', *The Times*, 2/6/64.
14 'The Return of Historicism in Architecture', op. cit.
15 Foreword to *Cambridge New Architecture*, op. cit.
16 A. and P. Smithson, 'Thoughts in Progress', *Architectural Design*, April 1957, p.113.
17 N. Whiteley, 'The puzzled *Lieber Meister*: Pevsner and Reyner Banham', in Draper, op. cit., and *Reyner Banham: Historian of the Immediate Future* (MIT Press, 2002).

18 The Gropius/Pevsner exchange is in GP Series IB, Box 6.
19 D. Lasdun, remark made in 'Sir Nikolaus Pevsner: The Organisation Man', radio programme (presented by Stephen Games), printed in *The Listener*, 15/9/83.
20 Noticed by Andy Dunican in letter to *Building Design*, 2000 – quoted in S. Bradley and B. Cherry (eds), *The Buildings of England: a Celebration* (Penguin Collectors Society, 2001).
21 NP/H. de C. Hastings, 19/12/61. GP Series IB, Box 6.

CHAPTER 37

'Non-Stopography'

1 NP/Jack Summers, 30/5/60. Penguin Papers, *BoE* files, DM 1901/8/1.
2 NP/Miles Clifford, 6/2/63. Penguin Papers, *BoE* files, DM 1901/4/2.
3 NP/John Hitchin, Penguin publicity manager, 3/12/64.
4 Lionel Gossman, letter to the author, 19/12/2001.
5 Penguin publicity leaflet, May 1972.
6 Published by the Society for Promoting Christian Knowledge, 1964.
7 Penguin Papers, *BoE* files, DM 1901/5/5.
8 Published in *The Twentieth Century*, January 1960.
9 R. Hill, 'Positively spaced out', a review of *The Buildings of England: A Celebration*, in *London Review of Books*, 6/9/2001.
10 *Punch*, 13/10/54.
11 Nikolaus Boulting, interview with the author, 27/1/93.
12 G. Mayer, 'The flesh made word,' in *Association of Jewish Refugees Information*, January,

1993, p.2. Born in Czechoslovakia, Mayer came to England
aged eleven in 1939. She
attended Pevsner's Birkbeck
lectures before working for him.

13 Gerda Mayer, letter to the
author, 17/6/92.

14 NP/G. Mayer, 19/3/64.

15 NP/P. Lasko, University of East
Anglia, 26/10/72.

16 John Newman, interview, loc.
cit.

17 NP, interview with Julian
Holland, loc. cit.

18 Neil Stratford, interview with the
author, 25/3/93.

19 Quiney, interview, loc. cit.

20 NP/A. Clifton-Taylor, 11/1/61.

21 Jeremy Hooker, 'Geoffrey
Grigson – English Writer', in C.
Barfoot and M. Healey (eds), *My
Rebellious and Imperfect Eye:
Observing Geoffrey Grigson*
(Rodopi, 2002).

22 G. Grigson, *The Listener*,
18/1/63.

23 NP/G. Grigson, 1/7/74.

24 NP/Leverhulme, ? 1963. Penguin
Papers, *BoE* files, DM 1901/4/2.

25 O. Lancaster, *New Statesman*,
16/6/67.

26 See, e.g., Francis Morrone,
'Geoffrey Scott: "a sort of
aesthetic person"', in *New
Criterion*, June 1997.

27 R. Banham. 'Architecture of the
New Establishment', in *The
Listener*, 25/4/57.

28 Review of J. Harris, *No Voice
from the Hall: Early Memories
of a Country House Snooper*
(John Murray, 1998), in *Architects' Journal*. Sutherland Lyall,
architectural writer, critic and
former editor of *Building Design*,
was the editor, with Mary
Banham, of *A Critic Writes:
Essays by Reyner Banham*
(University of California, 1996).

CHAPTER 38

'Was it before or after 1963?'

1 NP/John Curtis, Penguin,
23/2/60. Penguin Papers, *BoE*
files, DM 1901/8/1.

2 NP/F. Wilson, 2/9/60.

3 L. Cohn/NP, 21/2/58. BBC
WAC RCONT1 – Prof Nikolaus
Pevsner – Talks File 1B.

4 L. Cohn/NP, 19/9/60. Ibid. Talks
File 2.

5 NP/L. Cohn, 25/10/60. Ibid.

6 A. Kallin/NP, 6/7/61. Ibid.

7 J.P.T. Bury (ed.), *New Cambridge
Modern History, Vol. 10* (CUP,
1960).

8 GP Series IE, Box 14.

9 *Architects' Journal*, 23/4/59.

10 NP, extracts from notes by
[History of Art] Panel Members,
NCDAD Paper, H of A Panel
6/63. NA DB 4/2.

11 S. Bayley/NP, 10/9/79. GP Series
IA, Box 1.

12 R. Banham. 'Out of the air', *The
Listener*, 25/8/83.

13 Alan Fern, conversation with the
author, 19/7/96.

14 NP, letter to *Daily Telegraph*,
19/4/60.

15 NP, 'The Topography of
England', *The Listener*,
11/1/62.

16 Peter Cunningham, *Hand-Book
of London* (John Murray, 1849).

17 Charmian Lacy, November 1959.
Victorian Society archive.

18 Thanks to Gavin Stamp for this
attribution.

19 NP/Hans Huth, Curator of
Decorative Arts, Art Institute of
Chicago, 19/1/61.

20 NP, 'Preserving Our Historic
Buildings', SABC Radio Bulletin,
23/10/61. Published in *Simon
van der Stel Foundation Bulletin*
4, April 1962.

21 NP/J. Maud, 12/10/61.

22 NP, *Johannesburg Star*, 24/8/61.
23 NP/D. Noel-Paton, 30/8/60. GP Series IIIB, Box 62.
24 NP/D. Noel-Paton, 11/7/60, 'British Council Visit to Brasilia'. GP Series IIIB, Box 62.
25 R. Hinks, 21/5/62. NA BW 83/51, 1959–61.
26 NP report. NA BW 83/121 British Council. Yugoslavia, 1965.
27 *Heftchen*, 26/6/62.
28 Ibid.
29 Ibid., 26/4/60.
30 LP to her niece Carla, 13/8/63.

CHAPTER 39
'Mountains around'

1 *Heftchen*, 23/2/66.
2 *Heftchen*, 3/1/65.
3 U. Hodgson/NP, 30/8/66.
4 NP/C.V. Wedgwood, 4/6/68.
5 Benedict Nicolson/NP, 5/4/61.
6 Doreen Craig/NP, 30/9/69.
7 A. Clifton-Taylor, obituary for NP, *AR*, October 1983.
8 Peter Ferriday, letter to the author, April 1993.
9 Quoted in Hillier, *Betjeman: The Bonus of Laughter*, op. cit., p.38.
10 NP/J. Fawcett, 23/1/64. Victorian Society archive.
11 J. Fawcett, interview with the author, 14/6/93.
12 I. Sutton, 'Pevsner in Committee', *Victorian Society Annual* 1982–3, p.5.
13 Ian Grant, interview with the author, 16/3/92.
14 NP, *Hampstead and Highgate Express*, 30/6/67.
15 NP note, 18/5/65. Victorian Society archive.
16 NP, 'Preserving Ancient Churches', *The Times*, 10/3/65.
17 J. Betjeman/J. Summerson, 14/6/66, in *John Betjeman: Letters. Vol. 2*, op. cit., p.319.

18 J. Summerson/J. Betjeman, 15/6/66. Ibid.
19 NP/J. Lennon, 8/3/65. Victorian Society archive.
20 Dieter Pevsner to the author, 26/5/2009.
21 The article appeared in a supplement entitled 'Survey of the Architecture in Britain Today', *The Times*, 3/7/61.
22 Wilkinson Howlett & Moorhouse/NP, 17/6/65. Victorian Society archive, in the London Metropolitan Archives, LMA 4460/01/55/002.
23 NP letter to the Public Inquiry, 17/6/65. Ibid.
24 NP/Wilkinson Howlett. Ibid.
25 NP/Tony Godwin, 13/12/63. GP Series II, Box 31.
26 Tony Godwin/H. Honour, 4/4/62. Ibid.
27 NP/W. Holford, 18/1/63. Ibid.
28 NP/T. Godwin, 8/7/63. Ibid.
29 Isaiah Berlin/NP, 9/9/66.
30 I. Berlin/NP, 11/11/66.
31 NP/I. Berlin, 15/11/66.
32 I. Berlin/NP, 7/6/67.

CHAPTER 40
'Looking at old buildings with an old man'

1 Michael Taylor, 'With Pevsner in Warwickshire', paper sent to the author in 1997, but also printed in Bradley and Cherry (eds), op. cit.
2 N. Stratford/NP, 1/8/66. Penguin Papers, *BoE* files, DM 1901/3/7.
3 F. Charles, letter to the author, 29/1/92.
4 G. Clotworthy, letter to the author, 30/3/93.
5 Geoffrey Moorhouse, 'A day with the Pevsners', *Guardian*, 21/4/60.
6 Introduction to *Staffordshire* (1974).

7 J. Carey, review of J. Harris, op. cit., in *Sunday Times*, 5/4/98.

8 John Harris, interview with the author, 7/4/92.

9 J. Harris, 'Nikolaus Pevsner of the *Buildings of England*: working with Pevsner', *Apollo*, December 1996.

10 Ibid.

11 Ibid.

12 John Harris, interview with the author, loc. cit.

13 Ibid.

14 G. Moorhouse, 'A day with the Pevsners', *Guardian*, 21/4/60.

15 J. Piper, 'Lincolnshire Revealed', *AR*, February 1965.

16 NP/Leverhulme, 1965. Penguin Papers, *BoE* files, DM 1901/4/2.

17 NP/E. Hubbard, August 1965. Penguin Papers, *BoE* files, DM 1901/2/5.

18 J. Hubbard, letter to the author, 16/6/92.

19 Pevsner's correspondence with Birkbeck's accountants, who were administering the Leverhulme grant, is in the Penguin Papers, *BoE* files, DM 1901/4/3.

20 Letters NP/D. Verey, 28/5/65–2/6/65. Penguin Papers, *BoE* files, DM 1901/1/5–6.

21 NP/D. Verey, 2/4/68. Ibid.

22 NP/N. Gunnis, 27/8/65.

CHAPTER 41

'More than is good for a man's work'

1 K. Clark/J. Betjeman, 20/12/51, quoted in *John Betjeman: Letters. Vol. 2*, op. cit., p.57.

2 Frank Fielden/NP, 27/10/70. GP Series ID, Box 9.

3 NP/J. Summerson, 23/3/67.

4 NP/J. Barr, 29/10/68.

5 NP/R. Banham, 23/2/67.

6 NP/Arthur Crook, 30/1/67.

7 *Heftchen*, 26/6/67.

8 NP, letter to *TLS*, 1963.

9 NP/Mrs A.M. Vogt, Zurich, 8/7/69.

10 In a review of the Royal Commission on Historical Monuments volumes on Cambridge, *AR*, June 1960.

11 *Heftchen*, 10/7/66.

12 NP, notes for his RIBA Gold Medal Speech, 1967. GP Series VI, Box 135.

13 Foreword to Barr bibliography, op. cit.

14 NP, 'What Can the Architectural Historian Give to the Architect?', op. cit.

15 NP/Karl Miller, 27/5/68.

16 NP/Reg Dodwell, Whitworth Art Gallery, Manchester, 13/6/67.

17 NP/Sir George Trevelyan, 29/6/67.

CHAPTER 42

'This intercalation of labours'

1 See Robert Oresko, 'Dear B.B', *Apollo*, November 2006, on the correspondence between Hugh Trevor-Roper and Bernard Berenson, in which Trevor-Roper set out his reservations about Wind's appointment.

2 Wind's essay was a contribution to *De Artibus Opuscula*, a *Festschrift* for Erwin Panofsky, edited by Millard Meiss (Buehler Buchdruck, 1960). Pevsner reviewed the *Festschrift* in the *TLS*.

3 NP, 'Report on the Council of Europe Meeting on February 23 and 24th, 1967', 1/3/67. GP Series IE, Box 14.

4 Ibid.

5 NP/L. Kingscote-Billinge, Devizes School, 17/7/78. GP Series IA, Box 3.

6 NP/Alistair Grieve, 23/8/68.

7 NP/P. Lasko, 26/6/67.

8 *The Times* diary, 26/8/76.

9 *Building Materials*, March 1967.

10 A. Clifton-Taylor, memorial address for NP, 6/12/83.

11 NP/Hubbards, 20/7/69.

12 NP/H. Gerson, 30/6/69.

13 NP/E. Frost, 4/8/69. Penguin Papers, Frost Papers, DM 1843/30.

14 Letters to *The Times* of 3/2/67 and 14/2/67.

15 S. Dykes-Bower to *The Times*, 18/2/67.

16 NP, 'As I See It', *Building Materials*, March 1967.

17 John Delafons, *Politics and Preservation: a policy history of the built heritage 1882–1996* (Taylor & Francis, 2007).

18 H. Dyos, on Pevsner's retirement. Victorian Society archive.

19 NP/Town Clerk, 7/2/67. Victorian Society archive, LMA 4460/01/33.

20 Stephen Bayley, in Intelligence Squared debate on 'Britain has become indifferent to beauty', 19/3/2009.

21 NP/ John de Moncheaux, 29/11/68. GP Series ID, Box 13.

22 J. Betjeman/P. Betjeman, 2/7/80, in *John Betjeman: Letters. Vol.2*, op. cit., p.563.

23 Bridget Cherry, 'Pevsner's 50: Nikolaus Pevsner and the listing of modern buildings', in *Transactions of the Ancient Monuments Society*, Vol. 46, 2002.

24 NP/O. Bohigas, 29/12/69.

25 Simon Frith and Howard Horne, *Art into Pop* (Methuen, 1987), p.42.

26 NP, 'Summary of evidence to NACAE relating to History of Art'. NACAE (SC) (69) 11. NA ED 206/19.

27 NP, 'History of Art and Complementary Studies in Colleges of Art'. NACAE (SC) (68) 9. NA ED 206/16.

CHAPTER 43

'The only one is duty'

1 Nicholas Taylor, 'The Compleat Perambulator', *Sunday Times*, 27/10/68.

2 NP/A. Heal, 22/3/61. GP Series IVC, Box 94.

3 NP/Mario Pancini, 26/2/68.

4 D. Dorn/NP. Penguin Papers, *BoE* files, DM 1901/2/2.

5 NP/Editor, John Thompson, 18/3/68.

6 NP, Introduction to *Staffordshire* (1974).

7 D. Lasdun, *TLS*, 3/2/70.

8 NP to *TLS*, 17/2/70.

9 NP/Allen Lane, 12/11/67. Penguin Papers, *BoE* files, DM 1294/17/1/7.

10 S.M. Gibbon/NP, 3/2/74. Penguin Papers, *BoE* files, DM 190/6.

11 NP/Lord Murray, 20/2/69. Penguin Papers, *BoE* files, DM 1901/4/2.

12 NP/G. Zarnecki, 21/3/68. Penguin Papers, *BoE* files, DM 1901/5/1.

13 G. Zarnecki/NP, 26/3/68. Ibid.

14 Bridget Cherry, interview with the author, 11/3/92.

15 NP/B. Cherry, 29/7/71.

16 J. Nairn/NP, 6/2/69. Penguin Papers, *BoE* files, DM 1901/5/1.

17 NP/B. Cherry, 5/2/70.

18 A.L. Rowse/NP, 23/9/74. Penguin Papers, *BoE* files, DM 1901/5/11.

19 NP/Philip May, no date. Penguin Papers, *BoE* files, DM 1901/6.

20 *Guardian*, 10/10/70.

21 NP/A. Gomme, 24/11/59. Correspondence kindly supplied by Mrs Susan Gomme.

CHAPTER 44

'Quite enough of that now'

1 H. Casson, obituary for Pevsner, *AR*, October 1983.
2 Foreword to Barr bibliography, op. cit.
3 NP/A. Zador, 20/4/70.
4 NP/A. Briggs, 22/10/70. GP Series II, Box 43.
5 R. Beyer/NP, 17/10/70.
6 J. Tabner/NP, 17/2/70. GP Series IA, Box 4.
7 NP/Ivor Bulmer-Thomas, 19/9/72. GP Series ID, Box 8.
8 NP/Dame Veronica Wedgwood, 14/12/72.
9 NP/Mrs Mary Davies, 14/1/70. Penguin Papers, *BoE* files, DM 1901/6.
10 NP/T. Kollek, 28/12/70. GP Series ID, Box 10.
11 Dame Jennifer Jenkins, interview with the author, June 1997.
12 NP/D. Thistlethwaite, 19/10/70.
13 NP, 'Is there an English Baroque?', talk on Radio 3, 9/2/73, printed in *The Listener*, 19/2/73.
14 *The Times*, 12/2/73.
15 E. Gombrich. NA ED 206/19.
16 NP/H. de C. Hastings, 3/6/70. GP Series IB, Box 6.
17 H. de C. Hastings, 16/7/70. GP Series IB, Box 6.
18 J.M. Richards/NP, 2/6/71. GP Series IB, Box 6.
19 H. de C. Hastings/NP, 16/7/70. GP Series IB, Box 6.
20 M. Sutherland/NP, 26/5/71. Penguin Papers, *BoE* files, DM 1901/3/4.
21 *Guardian*, 10/10/70.
22 G. Moorhouse, 'Recorder of England', *Guardian* obituary for NP, 19/8/83.
23 J. Betjeman/J. Lees-Milne, 29/1/70, in *John Betjeman: Letters. Vol. 2*, op. cit., p.395.
24 Information from Neil Stratford.
25 *Heftchen*, 1/3/71 and 14/3/71.

CHAPTER 45

'Give me time, eternal gods'

1 29/8/70.
2 NP/Henry Moore, 9/8/76.
3 NP/N. Newell, 4/1/72.
4 NP/J. Tabner, 14/4/72.
5 NP/E. MacDougall, 6/6/73. GP Series III, Box 66.
6 NP/F. Fielden, RFAC, 3/7/72. GP Series ID, Box 9.
7 Basil Spence/NP, 13/7/72. GP Series ID, Box 9.
8 NP/E. Frost, 1/8/72. Penguin Papers, Frost Papers, DM 1843/30.
9 *New Hungarian Quarterly*, 1971.
10 NP, interview with Kenneth Allsop, *Sunday Times*, 25/2/73.
11 NP/P. Drew, 23/5/74. Victorian Society archive in London Metropolitan Archives, LMA 4460/01/65/002.
12 NP/VicSoc Committee, 23/5/74. Ibid.
13 NP/Robert Lusty, Hutchinson & Co., 19/7/73.

CHAPTER 46

'Is it in Pevsner?'

1 NP/Dieter Pevsner, 14/10/70.
2 NP/H. Schmoller, 16/7/73.
3 NP/J. Sherwood, 15/8/73. Penguin Papers, *BoE* files, DM 1901/1/4.
4 NP/Professor R. Griffith, Maine, 16/6/71.
5 Chris Dolley, MD, Penguin/NP, 26/2/71. Penguin Papers, DM 1294/19/1.
6 Lawrence Marks, 'A prospect of Pevsner' on his eightieth birthday, 'Pendennis', *The*

Observer, 31/1/82.

7 Dr R. Brinley Jones, letter to the author, 26/2/92.

8 J.M. Richards, 'Magnificent obsession', *Observer*, 21/8/83.

9 S. Jenkins, 'Enshrined in immortal epithets', *Sunday Times*, 21/8/83.

10 Introduction to B. Cherry and J. Newman (eds), *The Best Buildings of England* (Penguin, 1986).

11 The *Spectator*, 20/8/2005.

12 Mark Girouard, 'A Monument to English Architecture: Sir Nikolaus Pevsner's Buildings of England series', *Country Life*, 30/5/74.

13 Interview with Kenneth Allsop, op. cit.

14 MD of Stacks Relocation Agency, Property page, *Sunday Times*, 18/7/99.

CHAPTER 47

'Right good is rest'

1 NP, interview with Julian Holland, loc. cit.

2 NP/Lord Sandford, Joint Parliamentary Secretary to the Ministry for Housing and Local Government under Edward Heath, 19/10/70. Victorian Society archive.

3 Julian Orbach, letter to the author, 5/3/93.

4 Mark Girouard, 'A Monument to English Architecture', op. cit.

5 NP/T. Neurath, 9/7/68. GP Series II, Box 43.

CHAPTER 48

Morality and architecture

1 See Tim Benton, 'Reassessing Nikolaus Pevsner', in *Journal of Design History*, 2006, 19(4), a review of Draper, op. cit., which

starts with the words 'Why is Pevsner a problem for British architectural historians?'

2 'Art historians of the world unite – and divide', *TLS* review, 20/8/64, of *Studies in Western Art: Acts of the Twentieth International Congress of the History of Art*, 1961 (Princeton University Press, 1963).

3 Bridget Cherry, interview with the author, 11/3/92.

4 See Richard Shone, 'Douglas Cooper: Unpublished Letters to the Editor', *Burlington Magazine*, 128, No. 1000 (July 1986).

5 H. Plommer/NP, 1953. Plommer Papers, GB 012 Ms. Add. 9367, Box 11, held in the Department of Manuscripts and University Archives, Cambridge University.

6 H. Plommer, 'The Ugciad: A History in Heroic Verse of the Corruptions in Our Higher Learning Together with a Prophecy of Its Probable End', a long poem in heroic couplets (self-published, 1979). Plommer Papers, loc. cit., Box 8.

7 Preface to Vol. 1 of the revised edition of *Simpson's History of Architectural Development* (Longmans, 1956).

8 Wilfrid De'Ath, 'The Lonely Laureate', *Illustrated London News* 262, March 1974.

9 NP/J. Betjeman, 27/7/77. GP Series IA, Box 1.

10 J. Betjeman, review in *Books and Bookmen* of David Watkin, *Morality and Architecture* (OUP, 1977).

11 P. Clarke, note in Victorian Society archives.

12 NP/Jonathan Harris, 27/11/67. GP Series IA, Box 2.

13 John Harris, interview with the author, 7/4/92.

14 Auberon Waugh, 'Way of the World', *Daily Telegraph*, 2/9/92.
15 C. Jencks, *Meaning in Architecture* (Barrie & Jenkins, 1969).
16 NP/Frederick Herrmann, 1969. GP Series IA, Box 2.
17 J. Harris/NP, 15/2/68. GP Series I, Box 2.
18 Edward Greenfield, in *Guardian* obituary, 25/1/01.
19 'Sir Nikolaus Pevsner: A study in "historicism"', *Apollo*, September 1992.
20 NP/Secretary, General Fellowships Committee, 3/3/66.
21 NP/Denys Page, 28/12/66.
22 NP/Herbert Butterfield, 3/2/67, NP/Eric Ashby, 14/2/67.
23 NP/M.E. Little, 6/2/67.
24 *Morality & Architecture Revisited* (John Murray, 2001), p.xviii.
25 G. Scott, *The Architecture of Humanism* (Constable, 1914), p.176.
26 Maurice Cowling, *Mill and Liberalism: Second Edition* (CUP, 1990), p.xxx.
27 'The Tory Interpretation of History' in the symposium 'The Edifice Crumbles' on *Morality and Architecture*, in *AR*, February 1978.
28 'Sir Nikolaus Pevsner: A study in "historicism"', op. cit.
29 Thomas Mann, speech delivered at the Library of Congress, 17/11/42.
30 The conference was held by the Facoltà di Architettura e Società at the Politecnico di Milano on 19–20/2/92.
31 I. Buruma, *Voltaire's Coconuts* (Weidenfeld & Nicolson, 1999), p.278.
32 Review of Giles Worsley, *Classical Architecture in Britain: The Heroic Age*, in *Evening Standard*, 17/7/95.
33 Lionel Brett, interview with the author, 24/6/92.
34 See Pevsner's 'The perverseness of Ruskin', a review of Kenneth Clark's *Ruskin Today* in *Guardian*, 27/11/64.
35 D. Watkin/NP, 5/10/77.
36 *Apollo* article, op. cit.
37 Kenneth Minogue, blog post for the Social Affairs Unit.
38 Clive Aslet, *Country Life*, 20/4/78.
39 Nathan Silver, *Sunday Times* series on 'Sacred Cows', 10/4/77.
40 J. Piper/NP, no date, GP Series IA, Box 4.
41 'The Sources of the New Right: Irony, Geniality & Malice', *Encounter*, November 1989, Vol. LXXIII, No. 4.
42 Bryan Appleyard, 'Building blocks: Morality and Architecture Revisited', *Literary Review*, July 2001.
43 *Daily Telegraph*, 17/12/77.
44 *Apollo*, October 1977.
45 *Sunday Times*, 4/12/77.
46 *Cambridge Review*, 3/2/78.
47 NP/G. Lambourne, 27/7/77.
48 B. Kobayashi/J. Nairn, 23/1/78. Penguin Papers, DM 1107/Z.
49 *Building Design*, 13/1/78.
50 'The Edifice Crumbles', op. cit.
51 T. Pevsner/B. Cherry, 26/12/79.
52 T. Russell-Cobb/NP, 29/1/79. GP Series VI, Box 135.
53 Tom Pevsner/Richard Haslam, 27/4/79. GP Series IA, Box 2.
54 Alec Clifton-Taylor, 'Marginalia', *AR*, August 1982.
55 J. Fawcett, obituary for NP, *AR*, October 1983.

CHAPTER 49

'Not quite in the English way'

1 Peter Ferriday, letter to the

author, 5/9/93.

2 A. Clifton-Taylor, obituary for NP, *AR*, October 1983.

3 R. Harbison, 'With Pevsner in England', *AR*, October 1984.

4 S. Muthesius, 'Nikolaus Pevsner', in H. Dilly (ed.), *Altmeister moderner Kunstgeschichte* (Dietrich Reimer Verlag, 1990).

5 J. Summerson, Gold Medal address, op. cit.

6 Journal entry, December 1989. D. Jarman, *Modern Nature: The Journals of Derek Jarman* (Overlook Press, 1994), p.206.

7 Wayland Young (Lord Kennet)/ NP, 30/1/79. GP Series IA, Box 3.

8 Michael Hall, 'Learning to look with Pevsner', *Country Life*, 16/8/2001.

Copyright Acknowledgements

Details of the author, source and publisher of all quotations are given in the Notes, and the author and publishers gratefully acknowledge the permissions that have been granted by copyright holders. Every effort has been made to contact the holders of copyright in illustrations and text quotations. Any inadvertent omissions or mistakes can be corrected in future editions.

Special acknowledgements are made to the following:

The Pevsner estate, for all quotations from Pevsner's writings, published and unpublished;

The Getty Research Institute, Los Angeles (840209), for the use of all documents lodged in the Pevsner Special Collection there;

Yale University Press and the Pevsner Architectural Guides, for excerpts from *The Buildings of England*;

Penguin Books, for administrative documents relating to the King Penguins, the *Pelican History of Art* and *The Buildings of England*. Also for the licence to reproduce excerpts from *Pioneers of Modern Design, An Outline of European Architecture* and *The Leaves of Southwell*, as well as for extracts from Susan Sontag, 'On "Camp"' and George Mikes, *How to be an Alien*;

Candida Lycett Green, for excerpts from the letters and writings of John Betjeman;

The BBC Written Archives, Caversham, for materials relating to the Reith Lectures and Pevsner's other radio broadcasts;

The British Council, for papers relating to Pevsner's overseas tours for the Council;

The Council for Assisting Refugee Academics and the Bodleian Library, University of Oxford, for material relating to Pevsner in the papers of the Society for the Protection of Science and Learning;

The Henry Moore Foundation, for an extract from a letter by Henry Moore;

The National Archives of the UK, for materials relating to Pevsner's work for the Coldstream Committee and the Royal Fine Art Commission;

The National Churches Trust, for extracts from the writings of Sir
   John Summerson;
The National Gallery Archive, for a memorandum relating to Pevsner's
   knighthood;
The Syndics of Cambridge University Library, for materials from the
   papers of Hugh Plommer;
The Victorian Society, for materials on Pevsner's case work and period
   as Chairman;

Apollo for articles relating to Edgar Wind and David Watkin;
Architectural Review for excerpts from reviews and articles by or about
   Pevsner;
Burlington Magazine for excerpts from reviews and articles by or about
   Pevsner;
News International Ltd for extracts from the *Times Literary Supple-
   ment* and *Sunday Times*;
New Statesman for excerpts from reviews of Pevsner's writing;
The *Penguin Collectors Society* for material on Allen Lane from articles
   in their publications;
The *RIBA Journal* for materials relating to Pevsner, H. de C. Hastings,
   John Summerson, Raymond Unwin and Sadie Speight;

Aitken Alexander Associates for quotations from the writings of
   Geoffrey Moorhouse;
David Higham Associates for a quotation from Penelope Lively,
   'Exmoor's Rural Ways and Byways';
Orion Books and Aufbau Verlag GmbH & Co. KG, for excerpts from
   Victor Klemperer, *I Shall Bear Witness* and *To the Bitter End*, and
   Stefan Zweig, *The World of Yesterday*;

Mrs Mary Banham and Shelley Power Literary Agency Ltd for quota-
   tions from the writings of Reyner Banham;
Stephen Bayley for the quotations from his letter and articles;
Marion Berghahn for extracts from *Continental Britons: German
   Jewish Refugees from Nazi Germany*;
Geoffrey Best for the quotation from his letters to the author;
Nikolaus Boulting for the quotations from his interview;
Christopher Burkett for quotations from Alec Clifton-Taylor's memo-
   rial address and obituary for Pevsner;
John Carey for the quotation from his review of John Harris, *No Voice
   from the Hall*;

COPYRIGHT ACKNOWLEDGEMENTS

Peter Alexander Clarke, for extracts from his father Peter Clarke's poems;

Giles Clotworthy for quotations from his letter to the author;

Alan Crawford for the quotations from his interview for Viva Voices;

Christopher Esher for quotations from the interview given by his father, Lionel Brett, 4th Viscount Esher;

Hazel Evinson for quotations from the interview given by the late Denis Evinson;

Daphne Farr for quotations from the interview given by the late Michael Farr;

Jane Fawcett for quotations from her interview;

Dr Mark Girouard for quotations from his interview and articles;

Leonie Gombrich for excerpts from the letters and writings of Ernst Gombrich;

Caroline Grigson for quotations from the letters and writings of Geoffrey Grigson;

Professor Marlite Halbertsma for quotations from Wilhelm Pinder und die deutsche Kunstgeschichte;

Richard Hanbury-Tenison for the quotation from his letter to Pevsner;

Robert Harbison for the quotation from his article;

John Harris for quotations from his interview and articles;

Rosemary Hill for the quotation from her article 'Positively spaced out';

Bevis Hillier for quotations from his biography of John Betjeman;

Ed Israel for quotations from the interview given by the late Camilla Bagg;

R. Brinley Jones for the quotation from his letter to the author;

Miriam Kochan for quotations from Britain's Internees in the Second World War;

Sue Limb, for the quotation from her 'Dulcie Domum' column;

Sutherland Lyall, for the quotations from his reviews of John Harris, No Voice from the Hall and David Watkin, Morality and Architecture;

Gerda Mayer for quotations from her letters and articles;

John Newman for quotations from his interview and writings;

Barbara Priestman for quotations from the interview given by the late Rosalind Priestman;

Alistair Rowan for the quotations from his letters;

Andrew Saint for quotations from his interview and writings;

Neil Stratford for the quotations from his interview and letters;

COPYRIGHT ACKNOWLEDGEMENTS

Michael Taylor for quotations from his article 'With Pevsner in
   Warwickshire';
William Vaughan for quotations from his paper on 'Pevsner's Art
   History';
David Walker for the quotations from his letters to the author;
Christopher Woodward for the quotation from his *Spectator* article.

Introduction to Selective Bibliography

The full bibliography of Pevsner's writings runs to more than sixty pages. It can be found online on my Pevsner website at www.pevsner. info but there was not room to include it in the hardback edition of an already very long book. Happily, in this paperback edition space has been made for a selective version.

In making the selection I have tried to represent the most important aspects of a very diverse *oeuvre*, and the various different periods of Pevsner's career – at the same time avoiding the works that are already well-documented (such as the *Buildings of England*) and focussing more on articles and reviews than on books, which are easily researched. I am obviously indebted to John R. Barr's earlier work *Sir Nikolaus Pevsner: A Bibliography* (Charlottesville: University Press of Virginia for the American Association of Architectural Bibliographers, 1970). This was incomplete only because it was published several years before the end of Pevsner's writing career, and because the *Times Literary Supplement* was still at that time preserving the anonymity of its reviewers.

The categories of writings I have chosen to list are those on Expressionism, Mannerism, design, national character in art, planning and the Picturesque, church architecture and English architecture in the twentieth century.

The pieces on Expressionism date largely from the earliest years of Pevsner's professional career, when he was writing as a young freelance critic in Dresden in the 1920s. However, the moral values underlying expressionism (with a small 'e') continued to intrigue him and he returned to the subject in the 1960s in his discussion of contemporary architecture.

The writings on Mannerism – begun in the 1920s but continuing into the 1930s and 1940s before being similarly revisited in the 1960s – are included primarily as an early contribution to a field of study that has developed considerably since Pevsner's day.

Pevsner found himself cast, not entirely willingly, as an authority on design in the 1940s and into the 1950s, and his work had a greater influence on subsequent design studies than he would have anticipated or, perhaps, desired. For this reason, I thought it worth gathering together the early writings on which this influence was founded.

Pevsner's pronouncements on national characteristics in art, linked closely with his abiding belief in the spirit of the age, became notorious in his Reith Lectures of 1955 on 'The Englishness of English Art', and are still invoked in the re-emerging debate about what it means to be English. The bibliography identifies the forerunners to 'Englishness' in Pevsner's writing, and suggests this was a theme he was reluctant to let drop.

Pevsner's researches into the Picturesque style in the eighteenth and nineteenth centuries were a key component of the *Architectural Review*'s manifesto on postwar planning in the 1950s. Pevsner's own interest in town planning, which he brought with him from Weimar Germany, can be seen from the bibliography to run virtually to the end of his writing career. An unfinished manuscript for a book on 'Visual Planning' was found in his papers after his death.

Church architecture was undoubtedly Pevsner's greatest passion, from the days of his student expeditions to the churches of Bavaria to his exit from the last church in the last county of *The Buildings of England* in the 1970s. His writings about it also illuminate his attitude to faith and religious observance.

Pevsner's attitude to modern architecture was complex. His writings on twentieth-century English architecture range far beyond promotion of the doctrines of the Modern Movement and condemnation of their apparent abandonment in the 1960s, and are included to show that his thinking was more humane and broadminded (and, occasionally, inconsistent) than is always acknowledged.

Selective Bibliography

EXPRESSIONISM

'Ludwig Meidner: Ausstellung in der Kunsthandlung Emil Richter', *Dresdner Anzeiger*, 23/3/25.

'Sturmausstellung: Neue Kunst Fides', *Dresdner Anzeiger*, 5/4/25.

'Hodler, Huf, Kirchner: Galerie Arnold', *Dresdner Anzeiger*, 4/5/25.

'Neue Kunst Fides: Jawlenski-Ausstellung', *Dresdner Anzeiger*, 13/5/25.

'Beckmann-Ausstellung', *Dresdner Anzeiger*, 30/5/25.

'Felixmüller und Böckstiegel Ausstellung bei Hugo Erfurth', *Dresdner Anzeiger*, 1/7/25.

'Pechstein-Ausstellung bei Hugo Erfurth', *Dresdner Anzeiger*, 3/11/25.

'Graphisches Kabinett Hugo Erfurth: Gotsch-Ausstellung', *Dresdner Anzeiger*, 14/12/25.

'Otto Hettner: Januar-Ausstellung der Galerie Arnold', *Dresdner Anzeiger*, 6/1/26.

'Otto Dix: Ausstellung in der Galerie Arnold', *Dresdner Anzeiger*, 6/4/26.

International Kunstausstellung, Dresden, 1926 – articles in *Dresdner Anzeiger*:

'Die ältere deutsche Malerei', 7/8/26.

'Die deutsche Malerei der Gegenwart', 19/8/26.

'Emil Nolde: Eröffnung der Jubiläumsausstellung im Städtischen Ausstellungsgebäude', *Dresdner Anzeiger*, 9/2/27, 19/2/27 and 11/3/27.

'Karl Schmidt-Rottluff: Aprilsausstellung in der Galerie Arnold', *Dresdner Anzeiger*, April 1927.

'Der Dresdner Maler Bernhard Kretzschmar: zur Gesamtausstellung im Döbelner Stadtmuseum', *Dresdner Anzeiger*, 1927.

'Edvard Munch: Galerie Arnold', *Dresdner Anzeiger*, 1927.

'Otto Dix: Ausstellung in der Neuen Kunst Fides', *Dresdner Anzeiger*, 1927.

'Finsterlin and Some Others', *Architectural Review*, 132, November 1962.

'Die Kokoschka-Ausstellung in London', *Schweizer Monatshefte*, 42, November 1962.

Review of D. Sharp, _Modern Architecture and Expressionism_ in _Architectural Review_, 141, June 1967.

MANNERISM

'Gegenreformation und Manierismus', _Repertorium für Kunstwissenschaft_, 46, 1925 (reprinted in _Studies in Art, Architecture and Design I_, 1968)

'Die Gemälde des Giovanni Battista Crespi genannt Cerano', _Jahrbuch der preussischen Kunstsammlungen_, 46, 1925.

Review of W. Weisbach, _Der Barock als Kunst der Gegenreformation_ in _Repertorium für Kunstwissenschaft_, 46, 1925.

Barockmalerei in den romanischen Ländern. Teil I: Die italienischer Malerei vom Ende der Renaissance bis zum ausgehenden Rokoko (_Handbuch der Kunstwissenschaft_ series, Akademische Verlagsgesellschaft Athenaion, Wildpark-Potsdam, 1928.

'Nachtrag zu Giovanni Battista Crespi genannt Cerano', _Jahrbuch der preussischen Kunstsammlungen_, 49, 1928.

Review of W. Arslan, _I Bassano_ in _Zeitschrift für Kunstgeschichte_, 1/2, 1932.

Review of H. Hoffmann, _Hochrenaissance, Manierismus, Frühbarock: Die italienische Kunst des 16. Jahrhunderts_ in _Burlington Magazine_, 75, September 1939.

'Mannerism and Architecture' (with particular reference to Niccolò dell'Abbate), _Architectural Review_, 96, December 1944.

'The Architecture of Mannerism', _The Mint_, 1946.

Review 'Mannerist at Work' of C. De Tolnay, _The Medici Chapel_ in _Times Literary Supplement_, 19/3/49.

Review 'Tintoretto and Mannerism' of E. Newton, _Tintoretto_ in _Architectural Review_, 111, June 1952 (with correspondence in _Architectural Review_, 112, September and November 1952).

Review of E. Wüsten, _Die Architektur des Manierismus in England_ in _Architectural Review_, 113, February 1953.

Review of F. Hartt, _Giulio Romano_ in _Journal of the Society of Architectural Historians_ (USA), ? 1959.

Review 'Gentleman from Verona' of _Michele Sanmicheli_ in _Times Literary Supplement_, 6/4/62.

Letter 'Dr Pevsner and Mannerism' in _Times Literary Supplement_, 24/5/63.

Review 'A Bent for the Eccentric' of F. Wurtenberger, _Mannerism: The European Style of the Sixteenth Century_ in _Times Literary Supplement_, 9/1/64.

Radio broadcast 'Mannerism: Elizabethan Architecture I', BBC, 21/2/64, printed in *The Listener*, 27/2/64.

Radio broadcast 'Mannerism: Elizabethan Architecture II', BBC, 27/2/64, printed in *The Listener*, 5/3/64.

Radio broadcast 'Mannerism: Elizabethan Architecture III', BBC, 6/3/64, printed in *The Listener*, 19/3/64.

Review 'Good Manners' of C. Smyth, *Mannerism and Maniera* in *Times Literary Supplement*, 19/3/64.

'L'Inghilterra e il Manierismo', *Bollettino del Centro Internazionale di Studi di Architettura Andrea Palladio*, 9, 1967.

'Palladio e il Manierismo', *Bollettino del Centro Internazionale di Studi di Architettura Andrea Palladio*, 9, 1967.

DESIGN

'A Questionnaire on Industrial Art', *Design for Today*, 3, April 1935.

'Design and the Artist Craftsman' (with Ethel Mairet), *Design for Today*, June 1935.

'Pottery: design, manufacture, marketing', *Trend in Design* (DIA Quarterly), Spring 1936.

'The Designer in Industry', *Architectural Review*, 79–80, 1936:
'Carpets', April 1936
'Furnishing fabrics', June 1936
'Gas and electric fittings – Fires', July 1936
'Gas and electric fittings – Lighting fittings', August 1936
'Architectural metalwork', September 1936
'New materials and new processes', October 1936
'The role of the architect', November 1936.

An Enquiry into Industrial Art in England (Cambridge University Press, 1937).

'New Designs in Pottery and China', *Country Life*, 13/2/37.

'Minor Masters of the 19th Century: Christopher Dresser, Industrial Designer', *Architectural Review*, 81, April 1937.

'Design for Mass Production', *DIA News*, 1/5, June 1937.

'Möbel von Gordon Russell–London', *Innen-Dekoration*, 48, August 1937.

Review 'More Shops' of M. Labò, *Architettura e Arredamento del Negozio* in *Architectural Review*, June 1938.

'The First Plywood Furniture', *Architectural Review*, 84, August 1938.

Review 'Fifty years of Arts and Crafts' of the first Arts and Crafts exhibition of 1888, (with commentary by George Bernard Shaw, first published in *The World*, 3/1/1888), *The Studio*, 116, November 1938.

'On the Furnishing of Girls' Schools: More Important in Its Implications Than You May Think', *School and College Management*, 3, November 1938.

'George Walton, his life and work', *RIBA Journal*, 3rd series, 46, 3/4/39.

'A Plea for Contemporary Crafts', *DIA News*, 3, June 1939

'The History of Plywood up to 1914', *Architectural Review*, 86, September 1939.

'Design Parade', *Studio*, 119–20, April, May, June, July 1940.

'Style in Stamps: a century of postal design', *Country Life*, 89, May 1940.

'Charles F. Annesley Voysey', *Elsevier's Maandschrift*, 50, May 1940 (revised and reprinted in *Studies in Art, Architecture and Design II*, 1968)

'Broadcasting Comes of Age – the Radio Cabinet 1919–40', *Architectural Review*, 87, May 1940.

Review of C. Townley, <u>Furnishing Your Home</u> in *Architectural Review*, 88, November 1940.

Review 'The Humane Industrialist' of R.P. Best, <u>Brass Chandelier</u> in *Architectural Review*, 89, January 1941.

'Omega', *Architectural Review*, 90, July 1941.

'The Evolution of the Easy Chair', *Architectural Review*, 91, March 1942.

'Mr. Pevsner remembers Mackmurdo', *Architects' Journal*, 16/4/42.

'Patient Progress: the Life Work of Frank Pick', *Architectural Review*, 92, August 1942 (reprinted in *Studies in Art, Architecture and Design II*, 1968)

'Questionnaire: Design in the Pottery Industry', *Pottery and Glass*, November–December 1944.

'Can Painters Design Fabrics?', *Harper's Magazine*, November 1945.

Radio broadcast 'The Future of Craft in an Industrial Age', BBC, 'Art for Everyone', 27/1/46.

Radio broadcast 'Modern Homes Exhibition', BBC, 'Art for Everyone', 26/3/46.

'Thoughts on Industrial Design', *The Highway: Journal of the Workers' Educational Association*, March 1946.

'Target for September: Nikolaus Pevsner Urges Manufacturers to Aim High in the Quality of Their Designs for the "Britain Can Make It" Exhibition', *Pottery and Glass*, May 1946.

Radio broadcast 'Britain Can Make It', BBC, 'The Visual Arts', 10/10/46.

Radio broadcast 'The House – Soft Furnishings', BBC, 'Designed for Living', 26/11/46.

'Visual Pleasures from Everyday Things: An Attempt to Establish Criteria by which the Aesthetic Qualities of Design can be Judged', (Council for Visual Education, 1946).

Review 'Design and Sales' of J. Gloag, *Industrial Art Explained* in *Architectural Review*, 101, February 1947.

'Merchandise Design and Retail Selling', *Store, Magazine of Retailing*, 11, August 1947.

Review 'Modern Design' of F. Schuster, *Der Stil unserer Zeit* in *Times Literary Supplement*, 28/8/48.

'Foreign trends in design and their effect in this country', *Architects' Journal*, 2/12/48.

'Design in relation to industry through the ages', *Journal of the Royal Society of Arts*, 97, 31/12/48 (reprinted as 'Design and Industry through the Ages' in *Studies in Art, Architecture and Design II*, 1968)

'Il Festival di Londra', *Comunità*, 12/10/51.

'COID: Progress Report. Industrial Design – 1951' (with Michael Farr, on exhibits chosen by the COID for the South Bank exhibition), *Architectural Review*, 110, December 1951.

'A Century of Industrial Design and Designers, 1851–1951' in *Designers in Britain 1851–1951: A Biennial Review of Graphic and Industrial Design. Vol.3* (Society of Industrial Artists, London, 1951).

'Art Furniture of the 1870s', *Architectural Review*, 111, January 1952.

Radio broadcast 'At Aspen in Colorado', BBC, 31/8/53.

Foreword and postscript to M. Farr, *Design in British Industry: a mid-century survey* (Cambridge University Press, 1955) – new and revised edition of *An Enquiry into Industrial Art in England*.

'Report of a Debate on the Motion that "Systems of Proportion Make Good Design Easier and Bad Design More Difficult"' (subject introduced by NP), *RIBA Journal*, 3rd series, 64, September 1957.

'Roots and Branches: the Story of Sir Gordon Russell's Development of Industrial Design', *Design*, 132, December 1959.

'Gordon Russell and twentieth-century furniture', *Architectural Review*, 132, December 1962 (reprinted as 'Patient Progress II: The Story of Gordon Russell' in *Studies in Art, Architecture and Design*, 1968)

'Philosophy of Furnishing', *Architectural Review*, 138, July 1965.

'History of the DIA [Design and Industries Association]', *DIA Yearbook*

(1965) (reprinted as 'Patient Progress III: the Design and Industries Association' in *Studies in Art, Architecture and Design II*, 1968)

NATIONAL CHARACTER IN ART

'Das Englische in der englischen Kunst: Die retrospective Ausstellung britischer Kunst in der Londoner Akademie', *Deutsche Zukunft: Wochenzeitung für Politik, Wirtschaft und Kultur* 2, 4/2/34.

'English Qualities in English Glass', *Country Life*, 19/7/41.

'English Qualities in English Ceramics: Evolution Rather Than Revolution', *Country Life*, 90, 3/10/41.

Review 'The English Eccentrics: Land of Follies in Architecture' of S. Sitwell, <u>*British Artists and Craftsmen*</u> in *Times Literary Supplement*, 14/7/51.

Review 'The Polish Style in Art' of Jerzy Zarnecki [*sic*], <u>*Polish Art*</u> in *Times Literary Supplement*, 25/8/45.

Review 'Nationalism and Art History' of G. Zarnecki, <u>*Polish Art*</u> and J. Faczynski, <u>*Studies in Polish Architecture*</u> (as 'P.F.R. Donner') in *Architectural Review*, 98, November 1945.

Radio broadcasts, the BBC Reith Lectures on 'The Englishness of English Art':

'The Geography of Art', 16/10/55, printed in *The Listener*, 20/10/55.

'Hogarth and Observed Life', 23/10/55, printed in *The Listener*, 27/10/55.

'Sir Joshua Reynolds and Detachment', 30/10/55, printed in *The Listener*, 3/11/55.

'Perpendicular England', 6/11/55, printed in *The Listener*, 10/11/55.

'Blake and the Flaming Line' 13/11/55, printed in *The Listener*, 17/11/55 (with correspondence from NP, replying to Hugh Plommer).

'Constable and the Pursuit of Nature', 20/11/55, printed in *The Listener*, 24/11/55.

'The Genius of the Place', 27/11/55, printed in *The Listener*, 1/12/55 (with correspondence from NP, replying to Douglas Cooper and other critics).

The Reith Lectures 1955 – introductory pamphlet (BBC, London, 1955).

The Englishness of English Art (Architectural Press, London, 1956).

Radio broadcast 'The National Characteristics of Art' for Asian listeners in London, BBC, February 1956.

Radio broadcast 'Some Thoughts on German Painting', BBC, 13/5/56.

Review 'Italy and the German Sense of Form' of H. Wölfflin, <u>*The Sense of Form in Art*</u> in *Times Literary Supplement*, 13/3/59.

Radio broadcast 'Deutscher Geist in England', BBC, German Service, 8/11/59.
Radio broadcast 'The Norfolkness of Norfolk Building', BBC, 23/5/60.
Ruskin and Viollet-le-Duc: Englishness and Frenchness in the Appreciation of Gothic Architecture (Thames and Hudson, 1969).

PLANNING AND THE PICTURESQUE

Planning

'Works and Planning: The New Ministry's Multiple Tasks, Research for Reconstruction, from a Correspondent', *The Times*, 18/11/42.
Review 'The First Garden City' of Bournville Village Trust, *Sixty Years of Planning* in *Architectural Review*, 92, November 1942.
'Terms of Architectural Planning in the Middle Ages', *Journal of the Warburg and Courtauld Institutes*, 5, 1942.
'Homes of the Future', *Europe*, 1944.
'Visual Planning and the City of London', *Architects' Journal*, 13/12/45 and in *Architectural Association Journal*, 61, December 1945 – January 1946.
Review of R. Tubbs, *The Englishman Builds* in *Burlington Magazine*, 88, December 1946.
Review of C. Sitte, *The Art of Building Cities* in *Architectural Review*, 100, December 1946.
Review 'Lavedan Continued' of P. Lavedan, *Histoire de l'Urbanisme: Renaissance et Temps Modernes* in *Architectural Review*, 102, September 1947.
'Visual Aspects of the Cambridge Plan' (by William Holford and Myles Wright, 1950), *Cambridge Review*, 13/3/50.
'Planning: Privacy and the Flat: Venetian Solution', *Architectural Review*, 107, May 1950.
Review 'Town-Planning' of S.E. Rasmussen, *Towns and Buildings* in *Times Literary Supplement*, 4/4/52.
'The Cambridge Campus of the Future', *Cambridge Review*, 19/4/52.
'Pioneer of the Pedestrian Network' (on a Leonardo de Vinci drawing), *Architectural Review*, 112, July 1952.
'The Sidgwick Avenue Site' (for university buildings), *Cambridge Review*, 31/10/53.
'Le Modulor: a Harmonious Measure to the Human Scale Universally Applicable to Architecture and Mechanics', *Cambridge Review*, 15/5/54.
'Towers in the City? I Say "Yes"', *Evening Standard*, 24/11/54.

Radio broadcast 'A Setting for St Paul's Cathedral', BBC, 6/5/56, printed in *The Listener*, 55, 10/5/56.
Radio broadcast 'Berlin, City of Tomorrow', BBC, 30/7/57, printed in *The Listener*, 8/8/57.
Letter 'Glass Skyscrapers' (on Ludwig Hilbersheimer), *Architectural Review*, 122, November 1957.
'Weissenhof', *Architectural Review*, 122, December 1957.
'Dr. Pevsner Broadcasts: Architecture in New Zealand, New Architecture and New Art, Towns and Traditions', *Journal of New Zealand Institute of Architects*, November 1958 (reprinted in *New Zealand Listener*, 12/12/58 and 26/12/58).
Review of H. Rosenau, *The Ideal City in its Architectural Evolution* in *Architectural Review*, 126, October 1959.
'Das neue Coventry', *Stuttgarter Zeitung*, 19/12/59.
Radio broadcast 'Bedford Park', BBC, 'Town and Country', c. 15/1/60.
Radio broadcast 'Ladbroke Estate', BBC, 'Town and Country', c. end January 1960.
Radio broadcast 'Bloomsbury', BBC, 'Town and Country', 20/3/60.
Letter 'Inner London' in *Times Literary Supplement*, 10/2/61.
Review of Band Deutscher Architekten, *Planen und Bauen im neuen Deutschland* in *Architectural Review*, 130, September 1961.
Review 'Builder of the Ideal City' of Y. Christ, *Projets et Divagations de Claude-Nicolas Ledoux, Architecte du Roi* in *Times Literary Supplement*, 12/1/62.
Letters 'The perfect suburb' (Hampstead Garden Suburb), *Times*, 17/1/62 and 30/10/62.
'Town Planning in Practice', *Architectural Review*, 134, September 1963.
'[Raymond] Unwin Centenary', *Architectural Review*, 134, September 1963.
'Cityscape: Only East Germany Rivals DC in Paralysis of Architecture', *Washington Post*, 16/1/66.
'A Master Plan' in *You Live Here: The Story of Hampstead Garden Suburb* (London, 1967).
Radio broadcast 'Jerusalem Close-Up', BBC, 14/4/71.
Review 'Building a Better Berlin' of H. Pundt, *Schinkel's Berlin* in *Times Literary Supplement*, 11/1/74.

Picturesque

'Price on Picturesque Planning' (on Sir Uvedale Price's *An Essay on the Picturesque*, 1810), *Architectural Review*, 95, February 1944 (reprinted in *Studies in Art, Architecture and Design I*, 1968)

Review of I. Wakelin Chase, _Horace Walpole: Gardenist_ (as 'P.F.R. Donner') in _Architectural Review_, 95, February 1944.

'The Genesis of the Picturesque', _Architectural Review_, 96, November 1944 (reprinted in _Studies in Art, Architecture and Design I_, 1968)

Radio broadcast 'Richard Payne Knight', BBC, 'The Visual Arts', 16/1/47, printed as 'An Eighteenth-Century Improver – Nikolaus Pevsner on Richard Payne Knight' in _The Listener_, 30/1/47.

'The Picturesque in Architecture', read at the RIBA on 25/11/47, printed in _RIBA Journal_, 3rd series, 55, December 1947.

'Reassessment IV: Three Oxford Colleges', _Architectural Review_, 106, August 1949.

'Richard Payne Knight', _The Art Bulletin_, 31/4, December 1949.

'Sir William Temple and Sharawaggi' (with Susi Lang), _Architectural Review_, 106, December 1949 (reprinted as 'A Note on Sharawaggi' in _Studies in Art, Architecture and Design I_, 1968)

Review of D. Stroud, _Capability Brown_ in _Cambridge Review_, 72, 21/4/51.

Radio broadcast 'The Picturesque and the Twentieth Century: modern town planning', BBC, 31/1/54.

'Twentieth Century Picturesque: an answer to Basil Taylor's broadcast', _Architectural Review_, 115, April 1954, with further correspondence in _Architectural Review_, 115, May 1954, and 116, July 1954.

'Roehampton: LCC Housing and the Picturesque Tradition', _Architectural Review_, 126, July 1959.

Letter 'Why Not Harmonize the Old and New?' in _The Times_, 3/7/61.

Review 'The Harmony of Old and New' of D. Dercsényi, _Historical Monuments in Hungary_ in _New Hungarian Quarterly_, 1971.

The Picturesque Garden and its Influence outside the British Isles (Dumbarton Oaks colloquium, 1972, on the History of Landscape architecture), (1974).

CHURCH ARCHITECTURE

Review of F. Crossley, _English Church Craftsmanship_ (as 'P.F.R. Donner') in _Architectural Review_, 90, December 1941.

'Englische Kathedralen', _Die Zeitung_, 15/5/42.

Letters to editor 'Stuart and Georgian Churches' on review of Marcus Whiffen, _Stuart and Georgian Churches_ in _Times Literary Supplement_, 27/3/48 and 17/4/48.

Review of G. Addleshaw and F. Etchells, _The Architectural Setting of Anglican Worship_ in _The Listener_, 28/1/48.

Review 'Cathedral Books' of W. Pantin, _Durham Cathedral_, G. Cook, _Portrait of Durham Cathedral_, J. Truby, _The Glories of Salisbury Cathedral_ and R. Mottram, _The Glories of Norwich Cathedral_ in _Architectural Review_, 105, April 1949.

'Canons of Criticism' (on the Coventry Cathedral competition), _Architectural Review_, 109, January 1951 (with related letters in _Architectural Review_, 109, March 1951).

Review of _The Cathedrals of England, English Cathedrals and Abbeys, The English Cathedrals, English Cathedrals_ in _Architectural Review_, 110, July 1951.

Radio broadcast 'Modern Architecture and the Church', BBC, 'Prospect', 6/1/52, printed as 'Thoughts on Coventry Cathedral' in _The Listener_, 17/1/52.

Radio broadcast 'Bavarian Rococo, or the Eloquent in Art', BBC, 17/1/54 (included in V & A Museum, _Rococo Art from Bavaria_, Lund Humphries, 1956).

'Design Review: German Church Furnishings', _Architectural Review_, 118, October 1955.

Review 'Swedish Church Architecture' of A. Tuulse, S. Curman and J. Roosval, _Sveriges Kyrkor Konsthistoriskt Inventarium_ in _Times Literary Supplement_, 8/3/57.

Review 'Gracious Spires' of J. Harvey, _A Portrait of English Cathedrals_ in _Times Literary Supplement_, 5/7/57.

Letter 'A Liturgical Brief' (on Rudolf Schwarz) in _Architectural Review_, 124, October 1958.

'Faith and Feasibility: Nikolaus Pevsner analyses the architecture of Coventry Cathedral', _The Guardian_, 25/5/62.

Review of B. Clarke, _The Building of the 18th-Century Church_ in _Architectural Review_, 136, September 1964.

Foreword to A. Savidge, _The Parsonage in England, Its History and Architecture_ (SPCK, London, 1964).

ENGLISH ARCHITECTURE IN THE TWENTIETH CENTURY

'The Elements of Contemporary Architecture in Britain – Historicism and Traditionalism', 1939 – draft for special issue of the _Architectural Review_ (not published).

'Criticism – Sir Herbert Baker's Extensions to the Bank of England' (as 'P.F.R. Donner'), _Architectural Review_, September 1941.

'Criticism – Houses by Robert Atkinson and the St. Marylebone Town Hall' (as 'P.F.R. Donner'), _Architectural Review_, November 1941.

'Nine Swallows, No Summer', _Architectural Review_, 91, May 1942.

Review 'The New Humanism' of A. Bertram, _The House_ in _Architectural Review_, 98, August 1945.

Radio broadcast 'The Renaissance of the English Public House', BBC, 'The Critics', 2/1/47.

Review 'Viewed from the Continent' of E. Tedeschi, _L'Architettura in Inghilterra_ and P. Meyer, _Europäische Kunstgeschichte_ in _Architectural Review_, 105, February 1949.

Radio broadcast 'Revivalisms in Architecture', BBC, 12/6/50, printed in _The Listener_, 22/6/50.

Review 'Building with Wit. The Architecture of Sir Edwin Lutyens' of A. Butler, _The Architecture of Sir Edwin Lutyens_ in _Architectural Review_, 109, April 1951.

'On Finding Oneself Out of Date. Men of the Year: Nikolaus Pevsner', _Architects' Journal_, 19/1/56.

Radio broadcast 'The New St Paul's Plan', BBC, German Service, 25/10/56.

'Welcome to Professor Martin', _Cambridge Review_, 10/11/56.

Radio broadcast 'New Trends in Architecture', BBC, German Service, 9/5/57.

'Churchill College – Some Considerations: Passions Not Aroused', _Varsity_, 17/5/58.

'Backyard Mentality' (on the Warburg Institute building), _Architectural Review_, 124, December 1958.

Radio broadcast 'Sir Basil Spence', BBC, German Service, 12/4/59.

Radio broadcast 'La Vie Artistique Contemporaine: Contemporary British Architecture', BBC, North American Service in France, 30/10/59.

'Propositions: The Editors, J.M. Richards, Nikolaus Pevsner, Hugh Casson and Hubert de Cronin Hastings, review the trend of the series ['Architecture after 1960: Propositions']', _Architectural Review_, 127, June 1960.

Obituary for Charles Holden (1875–1960), _Architectural Review_, 128, December 1960.

Radio broadcast 'The Return of Historicism in Architecture', BBC, 11/2/61, printed as 'Modern architecture and the historian, or the return of historicism' in _The Listener_, 16/2/61.

(cf. 'Moderne Architektur und der Historiker oder, die Wiederkehr des Historismus' in _Deutsche Bauzeitung_, 66, October 1961, extracted in _Historismus und bildende Kunst_, Munich, 1965).

A similar version was read to the RIBA on 10/1/61 and printed in _RIBA Journal_, 3rd series, 68, April 1961 (reprinted as 'The Return of Historicism' in _Studies in Art, Architecture and Design II_, 1968).

'Architecture in Britain Today', *South African Architectural Record*, 48, August 1963.

'Achievements in British Post-War Architecture', *Building, Lighting, Engineering* (Australia), November 1963.

Obituary of Harold Falkner (1875–1963), *Architectural Review*, 135, April 1964.

Letter 'New Scotland Yard' (on Sir Leslie Martin's plans for Whitehall) in *Architects' Journal*, 17/6/64.

'Randall Wells' (with Enid Radcliffe), *Architectural Review*, 136, November 1964 (and letter in *Architectural Review*, 137, March 1965).

Introduction to catalogue of Maxwell Fry exhibition, Eccles, 1964.

'Lutyens, Edwin Landseer' in *Encyclopedia of World Art. Volume 9* (McGraw Hill, New York, 1964).

Foreword to N. Taylor, *Cambridge New Architecture: A Guide to the Post-War Buildings* (Cambridge, 1964).

Review 'Against Novelty' of P. Collins, *Changing Ideals in Modern Architecture* in *Guardian*, 28/5/65.

'An Introduction to Modern Architecture in Britain', as part of 4 *Modern Buildings*, BBC TV for Schools, Summer Term 1966.

Radio broadcasts 'The Anti-Pioneers', BBC, 3/12/66 and 10/12/66, printed as 'Architecture in Our Time: Nikolaus Pevsner on the Anti-Pioneers' in *The Listener*, 29/12/66 and 5/1/67. (Extracts reprinted as 'The Anti-Pioneers: Extracts from Two Talks on the BBC Third Programme with a Linking Summary of Professor Pevsner's Ideas on Modern Architecture and Where It has Gone Wrong' in *Architects' Journal*, 145/5, 1/2/67).

Review 'Brutalism' of R. Banham, *The New Brutalism* in *Guardian*, 9/12/66.

'Quarr and Bellott', *Architectural Review*, 141, April 1967.

'Zehn Jahre Bauen in Grossbritannien 1924–34', *Bauen und Wohnen*, 22, December 1967.

Radio broadcast 'Looking at Modern Buildings', BBC, 'Woman's Hour', 10/10/68.

Letter 'RIBA Building' in *RIBA Journal*, September 1970.

Foreword to 3rd edition of N. Taylor and P. Booth, *Cambridge New Architecture* (Cambridge, 1970).

Index

INDEX

Buscher, Alma, 234n
Butlin, Sir Billy, 688
Butterfield, Sir Herbert, 777n
Butterfield, William, 481, 571, 605, 727
Butterworth, Helen, 601
Butts, Mary, 271–2, 319–20
Byron, Robert, 229, 387

Calahorra, Castillo de la, 612
Calder, Angus, 264n
Cambridge and University: Camden
  Society, 543; Christ's, 587; Churchill,
  653, 673n; University Library, 454;
  King's College Chapel, 749; New
  Hall/Murray Edwards, 744; NP on,
  743–4; NP on architecture, 450; NP
  made Slade Professor, 448–50, 453–4;
  NP tries to get work at, 188; NP's
  general lectures at, 450–3, 736; NP's
  enjoyment of stays there, 455–6; NP's
  guest lectures at, 427; NP's honours
  at, 672n, 790; NP's teaching at, 619;
  Peterhouse, 777–8; university's plans
  to extend, 453–5, 498; Queen's, 454;
  Roman Baths, 449; St John's, 394,
  449, 454, 654n, 672n, 744; Sidgwick
  Site, 454–5, 498, 744, 766–7; Victoria
  Cinema, 452
Cambridge University Press, 238n, 443
Camden History Society, 757
Campbell, Anne-Marie (NP's cousin –
  née Toker), 100–1
Campbell, Kenneth, 789n
Canada, 552
Canterbury, 315n; Cathedral, 433
car parks, 737; multi-storey, 671
Caracas, 589
Caravaggio, 86, 89
Carey, John, 661
Carnegie Corporation, 188, 196
cars, 179, 463
Carter, Will, 795
Casanova Society, 272
Casey, Christine, 751
Casson, Sir Hugh: background, 437n; on
  Hastings, 229; on Architectural
  Review editorial board, 437, 447; first
  impressions of NP, 437–8; on
  Review's approach to social housing,
  440; and Festival of Britain, 447; and
  Cambridge Sidgwick Site, 454–5, 744;
  radio broadcasts, 482; and Victorian
  Society, 573; and Euston Arch, 622;
  and Lola's death, 631; and RFAC,
  670; contributes to NP's Festschrift,
  674n; on NP's never-ending energy,
  713; resigns from Victorian Society,
  761n
Casson, Lady, 573

Castel Béranger, 614
Castelle, Friedrich, 165
Castle Drogo, 758
Castle Howard, 629, 684
Caylus, Comte de, 420–1
CEMA see Council for the Encourage-
  ment of Music and the Arts
Chamberlin, Powell and Bon, 651, 744
Champneys, Basil, 642
Charles, Freddie and Mary, 658–9
Charterhouse, 307, 353
Chatsworth, 101, 515
Chermayeff, Serge, 182, 208n, 209, 377
Cherry, Bridget: writes introduction to
  NP article, 241n; on lack of industrial
  architecture in BoE, 393; on BoE
  introductions, 395n; on NP and
  details of building construction, 504n;
  on NP and religion, 541; joins BoE
  team, 707–9, 742; on NP's interest
  in urban planning, 719n; on NP's
  character, 764; Tom writes to about
  NP's health, 789; sets up Pevsner
  Memorial Trust, 795n
Cheshire, David, 682
Chester, 101
Chetwode, Alice Stapleton-Cotton, Lady,
  531
Chetwode, Philip Walhouse, 531
Chicago, 376
Chipping Campden: Dovers Court, 250,
  737
Chiswick, 406
Chopping, Richard, 372
Chorlton-cum-Hardy, 702
Christie, Agatha, 381, 634
church plate, 392
churches: conservation, 642–4, 720–1;
  NP on architecture, 540–5, 584–5;
  NP on new, 702
Churchill, Winston, 285n, 307, 329, 484
CIAM (Congrès Internationaux
  d'Architecture Moderne), 209
Clacton-on-Sea, 523
Clark, Alexandra Gordon see Wedg-
  wood, Alexandra
Clark, Kenneth: lecturing style, 138–9;
  on Borenius, 140n; on Warburg, 148;
  on the art world in 1930s, 169; at the
  Ashmolean, 174; at the National
  Gallery, 175; NP considers as sponsor
  to get him out of internment, 282n;
  NP criticises, 546n; and Pelican
  History of Art, 564; and Victorian
  Society, 573; refuses to chair
  NCDAD, 617n; and Lola's death,
  631; and conservation of St Pancras,
  645; on RFAC, 671; gives Mellon
  Lectures, 714

858

Consciousness, 741n
Isermeyer, Christian Adolf, 94, 95
Isham, Sir Gyles, 604
Isle of Man: Onchan Camp, 266, 269
Israel, 718–19
Israel, Henry, 349
Italian art: Mannerism, 85–9; under
    Mussolini, 119, 128–9; NP's disser-
    tation, 77
Italy: NP's travels in, 88–9, 127–9
Itten, Johannes, 215

Jackson, Sir Thomas, 745
Jacob, Lieutenant-General Sir Ian, 485
Jacobsen, Arne, 654, 746
Jacobsthal, Professor Paul, 264, 268, 269
Jaffé, Hans, 111–12
Jaffé, Michael, 449, 631
James, Edward, 768
Jarman, Derek, 800
Jarrow, 519
Jefferies, Richard, 605
Jefferson, Thomas, 550, 757
Jekyll, Gertrude, 599
Jencks, Charles, 772, 778, 788
Jenkins, Frank, 674n
Jenkins, Gilbert, 208
Jenkins, Dame Jennifer, 720, 752
Jenkins, Simon, 749, 752
Jerusalem Committee, 718–19
Jesuits, 784
Jews: in Leipzig, 4, 5, 9, 39, 190, 253,
    310–11; problems of Russian, 6; anti-
    Semitism in and around NP, 38–40,
    43, 167, 506–7; number of German
    academic posts held by, 91n; growing
    anti-Semitism among German
    students, 92, 110, 115–16; Nazi
    moves against, 121–4, 126, 129; anti-
    Semitism among assimilated Jews,
    167; blindness of German Jews to
    what was to come, 190–1; Nuremberg
    Race Laws, 199; typical life in
    Germany in 1937, 235–6; Nazi
    measures stepped up in 1938, 236,
    237; Kristallnacht and ensuing
    emigration, 238–9; rumours of
    concentration camps start, 240; anti-
    Semitism and refugee communities in
    England, 248–9; peril for German
    Jews after outbreak of war, 252–3;
    interned as aliens in Britain, 265, 266;
    Final Solution gets under way,
    308–11; suicide among Germans, 312;
    British knowledge of Final Solution,
    313n, 333–4; German knowledge of
    Final Solution, 333; concentration
    camps liberated, 355; Wallenberg's
    attempts to save Hungarian, 733

Joad, C.E.M., 325
Johne, Lotte, 42, 65
Johnson, Paul, 785
Johnson, Philip, 221, 222, 631, 651,
    653
Johnson, Samuel, 492
Jones, Barbara, 385
Jones, Inigo, 298, 406
Jones, Dr R. Brinley, 750
Joos, Kurt, 267
Jordan, Robert Furneaux, 674, 776, 783
*Journal of the Warburg and Courtauld
    Institutes*, 326
Joyce, James, 272
Julian of Norwich, Dame, 249–50
Jungmann, Franz Emil, 17
Justice, James Robertson, 322

Kahn, Louis, 719
Kallin, Anna 'Niouta', 479–80, 482, 483,
    612, 749
Kandinsky, Wassily, 75, 113–14, 215
Kapp putsch (1920), 63–4
Kautsky, Rudolph, 68
Keeling, Bassett, 481
Keen, Richard, 482–3
Kelsall, Frank, 579n
Kempton Park race course, 264
Kendall, Ena, 749
Kent, William, 342
Kenyon, Sir Frederick, 282
Kerr, Robert, 680n
Keynes, John Maynard, 302–3n, 304–5,
    607
Kidson, Peter, 565
The King's England (guidebook), 384
Kirby, Cameron, 524
Kitzinger, Ernst, 258n
Klee, Paul, 76, 113–14, 233
Klemperer, Otto, 123
Klemperer, Victor: on dangers facing
    German academics, 122; and Heil
    Hitler! salute, 144; on Saarland
    plebiscite, 189; on membership of
    Nazi Party, 190; feels his national
    identity is destroyed, 200; on whether
    to leave Germany or not, 235; on
    Nazi Star of David measures, 236; on
    deportation of Jews to the east, 310
Knauth, Lis: teaches NP piano, 14–15;
    NP likens Francesca Wilson to, 153;
    Annie shares her worries about
    leaving Germany with, 235; Annie
    tells her she couldn't deny own
    Jewishness, 248; on Hugo's funeral,
    251–2; helps Annie after Hugo's
    death, 253; helps Pevsners correspond
    with Germany, 254; on RAF raids,
    291; account of Annie's life between

with friends, 475–7; Reith Lectures, 484–500; hunt for sponsors for *BoE*, 524–6; *BoE* expenses, 524, 594; receives CBE, 550; committee positions, 551; Victorian Society, 569–77, 621–5, 639–49, 687–90, 737–9, 759–61; involvement with listed buildings scheme, 578–9; reaction to his celebrity, 610–11; the Coldstream Committee, NCDAD, and the role of art history in art education, 116, 615–19, 692–6,722–4; conservation work abroad, 625; Lola's death, 630–2; memoir of Lola, 636–7; joins RFAC, 670–2; RIBA Gold Medal, 672–3, 678; *Festschrift*, 592, 673–5; reviews his career, 675–8; Slade Professor at Oxford, 680–1; television appearance, 682; generosity with help, 683–4, 716–17, 731; knighted, 685; Milton Keynes development, 690–2; 720–2; purchases freehold of Wildwood Terrace, 697–8; Mellon Lectures, 713–16; Jerusalem Committee, 718–19; attitude to conservation, 720–2; resigns from *Architectural Review*, 724–5; last travels for *BoE*, 725–7; Parkinson's disease, 726–7, 736; home and family life, 729; live-in housekeeper, 730; keeps up with old friends, 730–1; another trip to USA, 731–4, 736; health worries, 732, 734, 735, 739, 786–7; the end of the *Heftchen*, 740–1; declines to write autobiography, 741; finishes *BoE*, 742–50; steps down from chair of Victorian Society, 759–61; wins Wolfson Literary Award, 763; criticism in later years, 764–86, 788–9; *Morality and Architecture*, 774–86, 788–9; accident and final illness, 787–8, 789–91; death, burial and memorial service, 795–6; Memorial Trust, 795n; achievements, knowledge and qualities assessed, 796–802

WORKS: *Academies of Art Past and Present*, 176–7, 202, 254, 259, 677; adolescent writings, 27–8, 30–1, 32; *The Anti-Rationalists* (ed.), 650n; 'The Architecture of Mannerism', 344–5; 'Art of the Present and Art of the Future', 117–19; 'Artists' Fraternities in the 19th Century', 736; *Barockmalerei in den romanischen Ländern. Teil I: Die italienische Malerei vom Ende der Renaissance bis zum ausgehenden Rokoko*, 87–9; bibliography of, 674; 'Broadcasting Comes of Age:

The Radio Cabinet 1919–1940', 256; 'Building with Wit', 773; childhood writings, 11; 'The Clockmaker's Art', 284; 'Collections of Plaster Casts', 256; contribution to the 'CHART', 346; contribution to *New Cambridge Modern History*, 612–13; contribution to Sitwell's *German Baroque Sculpture*, 236–7; 'Criticisms' series, 305–6; 'Design for Mass Production', 185; *Design in British Industry*, 463; 'Design Parade' articles, 256–7, 284; 'Die Letzte Stunde', 28; Dresden reviews, 74; 'The End of the Pattern Books', 339; 'English and German Art and their Interrelations', 236, 488–9; *The Englishness of English Art*, 210, 484–500; 'Enjoyment of Architecture', 254–5; *An Enquiry into Industrial Art in England*, 177–87, 202, 230–2, 443, 462–3, 776; 'The Evolution of the Easy Chair', 328; 'A Farewell to the Euston Propylaea', 622–3; foreword to *Cambridge New Architecture*, 766; 'Frank Lloyd Wright's Peaceful Penetration of Europe', 218n; 'The Genesis of the Hotel', 620n; 'The Genesis of the Picturesque', 342; 'German Art and the Secondary Schools', 422; Giedion reviews, 219–20; 'The Glasgow Revolution in Art and Design', 240; 'Goodhart-Rendel's Roll Call', 576–7; *Heftchen* (diaries), 1, 3–4, 567–8, 628, 631n, 740–1, 802; *High Victorian Design*, 464; *A History of Building Types*, 713–16, 736, 739, 761–3; 'Homes for the Future', 444; 'Kunst-akademien und Kunstgeschichte' ('Art Schools and the History of Art'), 94; 'Kunst und Staat' ('Art and the State'), 165–6; 'Kurmusik', 27–8; *The Leaves of Southwell*, 323–5, 796; 'Lettering and the Festival on the South Bank', 327; 'The Making of London', 237; 'Model Houses for the Labouring Classes', 339; 'Modern Architecture and the Historian' ('The Return of Historicism in Architecture'), 588; 'The Modern Movement in Britain', 241n; *Morning Post* articles, 141–2; 'My Colleagues the Rubble-shovellers', 286–90; 'New Designs in Pottery and China', 227; 'Nine Swallows – No Summer', 328; 'No Grace for Mackintosh', 578; 'Omega', 303–5, 321; 'On Finding Oneself Out of Date', 650; 'On the Furnishing of Girls' Schools', 227; 'Originality', 576; *An Outline of*

www.vintage-books.co.uk